You've got access to LearningCurve!

Ways of the World + LearningCurve

Everyone's got a learning curve — what's yours?

LearningCurve, game-like online quizzing, adapts to what you already know and helps you practice what you need to learn in each chapter of your book. When you get a question wrong, feedback tells you why and links you to your book for review — with a chance to try again!

For access to LearningCurve

1. Go to **bedfordstmartins.com/strayer/LC.**
2. Click to enter your student access code. Enter it exactly as it appears on the access card that comes with this book, including any dashes, and follow the on-screen instructions.

System requirements

LearningCurve is compatible with versions of Firefox, Chrome, Internet Explorer, and Safari. Visit bedfordstmartins.com/strayer/LC for updated browser requirements. Pop-up windows should be enabled. Minimum 1024 x 768 monitor resolution required.

For technical support

- macmillanhighered.com/techsupport

Teachers: Register as an instructor at **bedfordstmartins.com/strayer/LC.**

bedfordstmartins.com/strayer/LC

Ways of the World: A Global History with Sources, Second Edition, For AP*

LearningCurve

Strayer

STUDENT ACCESS CODE

8g3-cr6-h8nd2r7b

Scratch off to reveal code. Do not peel.

6-USE CARD: This student access code is valid for six users. Each user is granted access for a time period of up to one year.

TEACHERS: To get instructor access, go to bedfordstmartins.com/strayer/LC.

For technical support:
- macmillanhighered.com/techsupport

bedfordstmartins.com/strayer/LC

Ways of the World: A Global History with Sources, Second Edition, For AP*

LearningCurve

Strayer

**RECORD THE INFORMATION YOU NEED TO ACCESS THE MEDIA.
KEEP THIS INFORMATION SECURE.**

Student's name:	Student's name:
Student's e-mail:	Student's e-mail:
Password:	Password:
Teacher's name:	Teacher's name:
Date activated:	Date activated:
Student's name:	Student's name:
Student's e-mail:	Student's e-mail:
Password:	Password:
Teacher's name:	Teacher's name:
Date activated:	Date activated:
Student's name:	Student's name:
Student's e-mail:	Student's e-mail:
Password:	Password:
Teacher's name:	Teacher's name:
Date activated:	Date activated:

*AP is a trademark registered and/or owned by the College Board, which was not involved in the production of, and does not endorse, this product.

About the cover images

The cover images, both agricultural, suggest two of the most global and transformative processes in world history. At the top, this ancient Egyptian painting from around the fifteenth century B.C.E. shows a servant measuring a field while a farmer and his wife look on. It evokes the Agricultural Revolution, which fostered population growth, required settled communities, and permitted the development of "civilizations" and all that followed from them. The bottom image, by the artist William Clark and entitled *Planting the sugar cane on Bodkins Estate Antigua* (1823), shows slaves planting sugar cane. It is illustrative of the Atlantic slave trade, which permanently linked Africa, Europe, and the Americas with revolutionary consequences for all of their peoples.

Ways of the World

A Global History
with Sources
For AP*

ROBERT W. STRAYER

The College at Brockport: State University of New York

SECOND EDITION

Bedford/St. Martin's

Boston • New York

For Saffi McNulty and her generation

For Bedford/St. Martin's

Publisher for History: Mary V. Dougherty

Executive Editor for History:
Traci M. Crowell

Director of Development for History:
Jane Knetzger

Developmental Editor: Kathryn Abbott

Production Editor: Bridget Leahy

Marketing Manager: Amy Whitaker

Assistant Production Manager: Joe Ford

Editorial Assistant: Emily DiPietro

Copy Editors: Lisa Wehrle and Steve Patterson

Indexer: Melanie Belkin

Cartography: Mapping Specialists, Ltd.

Photo Researcher: Carole Frohlich, The Visual
Connection Image Research, Inc.

Permissions Manager: Kalina K. Ingham

Senior Art Director: Anna Palchik

Text Designer: Joyce Westin

Cover Art: Top: Detail of a wall painting
in the tomb of Mennah, scribe of the
fields and estate inspector under Pharaoh
Thutmosis IV (18th Dynasty, 16th–14th
B.C.) in the cemetery of Sheikh Abd al-
Qurnah. Erich Lessing/Art Resource,
NY. Bottom: William Clark (1770–1838),
*Planting the sugar cane on Bodkins Estate
Antigua,* from *Ten Views in the Island of
Antigua, 1823.* The Art Archive at Art
Resource, NY.

Composition: Jouve

Printing and Binding: RR Donnelley and
Sons

President, Bedford/St. Martin's:
Denise B. Wydra

Presidents, Macmillan Higher Education:
Joan E. Feinberg and Tom Scotty

Director of Marketing: Karen R. Soeltz

Production Director: Susan W. Brown

Associate Production Director: Elise S. Kaiser

Managing Editor: Elizabeth M. Schaaf

Manufactured in the United States of America.

5 6   18 17 16 15

For information, write: Bedford/St. Martin's, 75 Arlington Street, Boston, MA 02116
(617-399-4000)

ISBN 978-1-4576-5404-6 (with *Launch Pad HistoryClass*)
ISBN 978-0-312-58350-7 (Student Edition)

★AP is a trademark registered and/or owned by the College Board, which was not
involved in the production of, and does not endorse, this product.

Acknowledgments

*Acknowledgments and copyrights can be found at the back of the book on pages 1207–10, which
constitute an extension of the copyright page. It is a violation of the law to reproduce these selections
by any means whatsoever without the written permission of the copyright holder.*

Preface

THE FIRST EDITION OF *WAYS OF THE WORLD* set out to present a coherent, comparative, and brief global narrative focused on the big pictures of world history. As the book's author, I have been pleased—and not a little surprised—by its commercial success and immensely gratified that it has proven useful for conveying the rich perspective of world history to so many students. The original book and the subsequent docutext version—with chapter-based sets of written and visual primary sources—have been adopted by world history instructors at some 1,000 high schools, and over 550 colleges and universities. I have been especially gratified by the response to the book from AP World History teachers. *Ways of the World* represents for me the satisfying culmination of a long involvement in world history classrooms in Ethiopia, New York, New Zealand, and California.

Feedback from instructors as well as from student readers suggests that they have appreciated the book's narrative brevity, its thematic and comparative focus, its many pedagogical features, the clarity and accessibility of its writing, and its musing or reflective tone. Perhaps most appealing has been the integrated combination of textbook and sourcebook that offers instructors such a wide range of pedagogical possibilities at a very reasonable price. For students, it has provided a "laboratory" experience, enabling them to engage directly with the evidence of documents and images—in short to "do history" even as they are reading history. It is in these aspects that many instructors have found *Ways of the World* to be remarkably congruent with the AP World History framework.

Since the publication of the first edition, technology has continued to transform teaching and learning. This edition of the text includes of a number of electronic dimensions, and I am pleased that this edition includes LearningCurve, an easy-to-assign adaptive learning tool that helps students rehearse the material in the narrative so they come to class better prepared.

What's in a Title?

The title of a book should evoke something of its character and outlook. The main title *Ways of the World* is intended to suggest at least three dimensions of the text.

The first is **diversity** or **variation**, for the "ways of the world," or the ways of being human in the world, have been many and constantly changing. This book seeks to embrace the experience of humankind in its vast diversity, while noticing the changing location of particular centers of innovation and wider influence.

Second, the title *Ways of the World* invokes major **panoramas**, **patterns**, or **pathways** in world history, as opposed to highly detailed narratives. Many world history instructors have found that students often feel overwhelmed by the sheer quantity of data that a course in global history can require of them. In the narrative sections of this book, the larger patterns or the "big pictures" of world history appear in the foreground on center stage, while the still plentiful details, data, and facts occupy the background, serving in supporting roles.

A third implication of the book's title lies in a certain **reflective** or **musing quality** of *Ways of the World*, which appears especially in the Big Picture essays that introduce each part of the book and in a Reflections section at the end of each chapter. These features of the book offer many opportunities for contemplating larger questions. The Big Picture essay for Part Six, for example, asks whether the twentieth century deserves to be considered a separate period of world history. Chapter 4 explores how historians and religious believers sometimes rub each other the wrong way. Chapter 8 probes how and why human societies change. And Chapter 22 muses about the difficulties and the usefulness of studying the unfinished stories of recent history. None of these questions have clear or easy answers, but the opportunity to contemplate them is among the great gifts that the study of history offers to us all.

The subtitle of this book, *A Global History with Sources*, refers to its docutext format. Following the narrative portion of each chapter are sets of primary written and visual sources. Each collection is organized around a particular theme, issue, or question that derives from the chapter narrative. As the title of these features suggests, they enable students to "consider the evidence" and thus begin to understand the craft of historians as well as their conclusions. All of them are thoroughly cross-referenced in the narrative, are furnished with brief headnotes that provide context for the sources, and are accompanied by a series of probing "Using the Evidence" questions appropriate for in-class discussion and writing assignments. These questions ask students to evaluate the evidence (and sometimes the lack of evidence) while considering the point of view of the author, the audience reading or viewing the sources, and the historical context in which the source was produced. Through this process, students can learn to craft historical arguments from the evidence and to hone their skills of historical interpretation and synthesis.

The Dilemma of World History: Inclusivity and Coherence

The great virtue of world history lies in its inclusiveness, for its subject matter is the human species itself. But that virtue is also the source of world history's greatest difficulty—telling a coherent story. How can we meaningfully present the planet's many and distinct peoples and their intersections with one another in the confines of a single book or a single term? What prevents that telling from bogging down in the endless detail of various civilizations or cultures, from losing the forest for the trees, from implying that history is just "one damned thing after another"?

Less Can Be More

From the beginning, *Ways of the World* set out to cope with this fundamental conundrum of world history—the tension between inclusion and coherence—in several ways. The first is the relative brevity of the narrative. This means leaving some things out or treating them more succinctly than some instructors might expect. But it also means that the textbook need not overwhelm students or dominate the course. It allows for more creativity by instructors in constructing their own world history courses, giving them the opportunity to mix and match text, sources, and other materials in distinctive ways.

The Centrality of Context: Change, Comparison, Connection

A further aid to achieving coherence amid the fragmenting possibilities of inclusion lies in maintaining the centrality of context, for in world history, nothing stands alone. Those of us who practice world history as teachers or textbook authors are seldom specialists in the particulars of what we study and teach. Rather we are "specialists of the whole," seeking to find the richest, most suggestive, and most meaningful contexts in which to embed those particulars. Our task, fundamentally, is to teach contextual thinking.

To aid in this task, *Ways of the World* repeatedly highlights three such contexts, what I call the "**three Cs**" of world history: **change**, **comparison**, and **connection**. The first "C" emphasizes large-scale **change**, both within and especially across major regions of the world. Examples include the peopling of the planet, the breakthrough to agriculture, the emergence of "civilization," the rise of universal religions, the changing shape of the Islamic world, the linking of Eastern and Western Hemispheres in the wake of Columbus's voyages, the Industrial Revolution, the rise and fall of world communism, and the acceleration of globalization during the twentieth century.

The second "C" involves frequent **comparison**, a technique of integration through juxtaposition, bringing several regions or cultures into our field of vision at the same time. It encourages reflection both on the common elements of the human experience and on its many variations. Such comparisons are pervasive throughout the book, informing both the chapter narratives and many of the docutext features. We examine the difference, for example, between the Agricultural Revolution in the Eastern and Western Hemispheres, between the beginnings of Buddhism and the early history of Christianity and Islam, between patriarchy in Athens and in Sparta, between European and Asian empires of the early modern era, between the Chinese and the Japanese response to European intrusion, between the Russian and Chinese revolutions, and many more. Many of the primary source "Considering the Evidence" features are also broadly comparative or cross-cultural. For example, the documents feature for Chapter 3 asks students to consider the nature of political authority in second-wave civilizations in Athens, Rome, China, and India. Likewise the visual sources feature for Chapter 15 uses art and architecture to examine various expression of Christianity in Reformation Europe, colonial Bolivia, seventeenth century China, and Mughal India.

The final "C" emphasizes **connection**, networks of communication and exchange that increasingly shaped the character of those societies that participated in them. For world historians, cross-cultural interaction becomes one of the major motors of historical transformation. Such connections are addressed in nearly every chapter narrative and many docutext features. Examples include the clash of the ancient Greeks and the Persians, the long-distance commercial networks that linked the Afro-Eurasian world, the numerous cross-cultural encounters spawned by the spread of Islam, the trans-hemispheric Columbian exchange of the early modern era, and the growth of a genuinely global economy.

Organizing World History: Chronology, Theme, and Region

Organizing a world history textbook or a world history course is, to put it mildly, a daunting task. How should we divide up the seamless stream of human experience into manageable and accessible pieces, while recognizing always that such divisions are artificial, arbitrary, and contested? Historians, of course, debate the issue endlessly. In structuring *Ways of the World*, I have drawn on my own sense of "what works" in the classroom, on a personal penchant for organizational clarity, and on established practice in the field. The outcome has been an effort to balance three principles of organization—chronology, theme, and region—in a flexible format that can accommodate a variety of teaching approaches and curricular strategies. Though I did not originally conceive of the book with the AP market in mind, many instructors have found *Ways of the World* to be remarkably congruent with the AP World History framework.

This book addresses the question of chronology by dividing world history into six major periods. Each of these six "parts" begins with a **Big Picture essay** that introduces the general patterns of a particular period and raises questions about the problems historians face in periodizing the human past.

Part One (to 500 B.C.E.) deals in two chapters with beginnings—of human migration and social construction from the Paleolithic era through the Agricultural Revolution and the development of the First Civilizations. Each chapter pursues important themes on a global scale, illustrating those themes with regional examples treated comparatively.

Part Two examines the millennium of second-wave civilizations (500 B.C.E. to 500 C.E.) and employs the thematic principle in exploring the major civilizations of Eurasia (Chinese, Indian, Persian, and Mediterranean), with separate chapters focusing on their empires (Chapter 3), religious and cultural traditions (Chapter 4), and social organization (Chapter 5). These Afro-Eurasian chapters are followed by a single chapter (Chapter 6) that examines regionally the second-wave era in sub-Saharan Africa and the Americas.

Part Three, embracing the thousand years between 500 and 1500 C.E., reflects a mix of thematic and regional principles. Chapter 7 focuses topically on commercial networks, while Chapters 8, 9, and 10 deal regionally with the Chinese, Islamic, and Christian worlds respectively. Chapter 11 treats pastoral societies as a broad theme and the Mongols as the most dramatic illustration of their impact on the larger stage of world history. Chapter 12, which bridges the two volumes of the book, presents an around-the-world tour in the fifteenth century, which serves both to conclude Volume 1 and to open Volume 2.

Part Four considers the early modern era (1450–1750) and treats each of its three chapters thematically. Chapter 13 compares European and Asian empires; Chapter 14 lays out the major patterns of global commerce and their consequences; and Chapter 15 focuses on cultural patterns, including the globalization of Christianity and the rise of modern science.

Part Five takes up the era of maximum European influence in the world, from 1750 to 1914. It charts the emergence of distinctively modern societies, devoting separate chapters to the Atlantic revolutions (Chapter 16) and the Industrial Revolution (Chapter 17). Chapters 18 and 19 focus on the growing impact of those European societies on the rest of humankind—on the world of formal colonies and on the still independent states of Latin America, China, the Ottoman Empire, and Japan.

Part Six, which looks at the most recent century (1914–2012), is perhaps the most problematic for world historians, given the abundance of data and the absence of time to sort out what is fundamental and what is peripheral. Its four chapters explore themes of global significance. Chapter 20 focuses on the descent of Europe into war, depression, and the Holocaust, and the global outcomes of this collapse. Chapter 21 examines global communism—its birth in revolution, its efforts to create socialist societies, its role in the cold war, and its abandonment by the end of the twentieth century. Chapter 22 turns the spotlight on the Afro-Asian-Latin American majority of the world's population, describing their exit from formal colonial rule and their emergence on the world stage as the developing countries. Chapter 23 concludes this account of the human journey by assessing the economic, environmental, and cultural dimensions of what we know as globalization.

What's New?

In preparing this second edition of *Ways of the World*, I have sought to build on the strengths of the first edition, guided by the wise counsel of many reviewers and users of the book. I am especially pleased that this second edition has grown not at all beyond the contours of the first, thus refuting an apparent law of nature that revised books increase substantially in size. To make room for new material I have made some judicious abbreviations. A revised Chapter 1, for example, incorporates both the Paleolithic and Neolithic eras, which had separate chapters in the first edition.

These and other cuts have made possible the inclusion of much that is new. Latin America and Southeast Asia have been incorporated more fully into the narrative. Gender and environmental issues are treated far more extensively and integrated throughout the narrative more smoothly than before. The discussion of early Christianity now highlights its Asian and African dimensions alongside the more familiar Roman and European aspects, while the eighteenth- and nineteenth-century Atlantic Revolutions are cast in a more global context.

An entirely new feature in *Ways of the World*, entitled "**Portraits**," provides a short biographical sketch of an individual in each chapter. Readers will meet Paneb, a notorious criminal in ancient Egypt whose life contrasts with the better-known history that celebrates the triumphs of Egyptian civilization, in Chapter 2; Cecilia Penifader, a fourteenth-century English peasant woman, whose story provides a window into the lives of ordinary rural people, in Chapter 10; Ayuba Diallo, a prominent West African Muslim who was transported into slavery in America and then traveled back to freedom and slave owning at home, in Chapter 14; and Etty Hillesum, an inspiring Dutch observer and victim of Nazi aggression and the Holocaust whose life stands as a testament to the resilience of the human spirit, in Chapter 20. These and many other portraits—some of prominent persons but most describing quite ordinary people—provide a glimpse into individual lives often obscured in the larger patterns of world history.

A number of the document and visual source features are also new in this edition. The new sources feature in Chapter 1 combines both oral tradition and visual sources to explore how scholars seek to recover history before writing. New visual source features include those of Chapter 8, focused on travel on the Silk Roads, and Chapter 12, illustrating the impact of Islam on the art of the European Renaissance. The new documents feature for Chapter 17 both celebrates and criticizes the emerging world of industrial Europe; that in Chapter 19 offers various prescriptions for changing China in the late nineteenth century; and Chapter 23's documents feature offers a range of voices from global feminism during the twentieth century.

Promoting Active Learning

As all instructors know, students can often "do the assignment" or read the required chapter and yet have nearly no understanding of it when they come to class. The problem, frequently, is passive studying—a quick once-over, perhaps some highlighting of the text—but little sustained involvement with the material. A central pedagogical problem in all teaching is how to encourage more active, engaged styles of learning. We want to enable students to manipulate the information of the book, using its ideas and data to answer questions, to make comparisons, to draw conclusions, to criticize assumptions, and to infer implications that are not explicitly disclosed in the text itself.

Ways of the World seeks to promote active learning in at least four major ways. First, the book includes access to **LearningCurve**, online adaptive quizzing that promotes engaged reading and focused review. Cross-references at the end of every major section and chapter in the text prompt students to log in and rehearse their understanding of the material they have just read. Students move at their own pace and accumulate points as they go, giving the interaction a game-like feel. Feedback for incorrect responses explains why the answer is incorrect and directs students back to the text to review before they attempt to answer the question again. The end result is a better understanding of the key elements of the text.

A second active learning element involves motivation. A **contemporary vignette** opens each chapter with a story that links the past and the present to show the continuing resonance of the past in the lives of contemporary people. Chapter 6, for example, begins by describing the inauguration in 2010 of Bolivian President Evo Morales at an impressive ceremony at Tiwanaku, the center of an ancient Andean empire and emphasizing the continuing importance of this ancient civilization in Bolivian culture. At the end of each chapter, a short **Reflections** section raises provocative, sometimes quasi-philosophical, questions about the craft of the historian and the unfolding of the human story. Hopefully, these brief essays provide an incentive for our students' own pondering and grist for the mill of vigorous class discussions.

A third technique for encouraging active learning lies in the provision of frequent contextual markers. Student readers need to know where they are going and where they have been. Thus part-opening **Big Picture essays** preview what follows in the subsequent chapters. A **chapter outline** opens each chapter, while a NEW **Map of Time** provides a chronological overview of major events and processes. In addition, a NEW **Seeking the Main Point** question helps students focus on the main theme of the chapter. Each chapter also has at least one NEW **Summing Up So Far** question that invites students to reflect on what they have learned to that point in the chapter. **Snapshots** appear in every chapter and present succinct glimpses of particular themes, regions, or time periods, adding some trees to the forest of world history. A **list of terms** at the end of each chapter invites students to check their grasp of the material. As usual with books published by Bedford/St. Martin's, a **rich illustration program** enhances the narrative. And over 100 **maps**, many enriched or redrawn for this edition, provide beautifully rendered spatial context for the unfolding of history.

Finally, active learning means approaching the text with something to look for, rather than simply dutifully completing the assignment. *Ways of the World* provides such cues in abundance. A series of **questions in the margins,** labeled "Change," "Comparison," or "Connection," allows students to read the adjacent material with a clear purpose in mind. **Big Picture Questions** at the end of each chapter deal with matters not directly addressed in the text. Instead, they provide opportunities for integration, comparison, analysis, and sometimes speculation. Questions abound as well in the **document and visual sources** features, encouraging a careful reading of both texts and images, while providing points of departure for using those sources collectively. Working with these primary sources requires students to engage actively with the text.

The AP edition of *Ways of the World: A Global History with Sources* also includes two unique active-learning features. An AP Historical Thinking Skills Primer (pp. l–lxvii) helps students read, write, and think historically. Written by Dave Neumann, Director of the History Project at California State University, Long Beach and a long-time AP teacher and exam reader, this unique primer guides students through the steps to learn and then practice the four skills emphasized by AP World History. Chapter Wrap Up review sections at the end of each chapter help students practice historical skills. Developed by AP workshop leader Deborah Smith-Johnston of the Lakeside School in Seattle, the chapter reviews walk students through a three-step process to practice and retain historical skills and content.

"It Takes a Village"

In any enterprise of significance "it takes a village," as they say. Bringing *Ways of the World* to life, it seems, has occupied the energies of several villages. Among the privileges and delights of writing and revising this book has been the opportunity to interact with my fellow villagers.

The largest of these communities consists of the people who read the first edition of the book and commented on it. I continue to be surprised at the power of this kind of collaboration, frequently finding that passages I had regarded as polished to a gleaming perfection benefited greatly from the collective wisdom and experience of these thoughtful reviewers. Many of them were commissioned by Bedford/ St. Martin's and are listed here in alphabetical order, with my great thanks: Maria S. Arbelaez, University of Nebraska–Omaha; Veronica L. Bale, Mira Costa College; Christopher Bellitto, Kean University; Monica Bond-Lamberty, Northwood High School; Edward Dandrow, University of Central Florida; Ralph Croizier, University of Victoria; Peter L. de Rosa, Bridgewater State University; Amy Forss, Metropolitan Community College; Denis Gainty, Georgia State University; Steven A. Glazer, Graceland University; Sue Gronewald, Kean University; Andrew Hamilton, Viterbo University; J. Laurence Hare, University of Arkansas; Michael Hinckley, Northern Kentucky University; Bram Hubbell, Friends Seminary; Ronald Huch, Eastern Kentucky University; Elizabeth Hyde, Kean University; Mark Lentz, University of Louisiana–Lafayette; Kate McGrath, Central Connecticut State University; C. Brid Nicholson, Kean University; Donna Patch, Westside High School; Jonathan T. Reynolds, Northern Kentucky University; James Sabathne, Hononegah High School; Christopher Sleeper, Mira Costa College; Ira Spar, Ramapo College and Metropolitan Museum of Art; Kristen Strobel, Lexington High School; Michael Vann, Sacramento State University; Peter Winn, Tufts University; and Judith Zinsser, Miami University of Ohio.

A special note of thanks to Eric Nelson of Missouri State University who has offered no end of useful suggestions while preparing much of the wonderful *Teacher's Resource Guide*. Eric also provided content for the LearningCurve adaptive quizzes and for new special features in the *Ways of the World e-Book* and provided many of the model answers for the *Annotated Teacher's Edition for Ways of the World*. I also extend a special thanks to Stanley Burstein, emeritus at California State University–Los Angeles who has been my wonderfully helpful mentor on all matters ancient. I extend special thanks also to Jay Harmon of Woodlands Christian Academy, TX, who authored the extensive annotations for the Annotated Teacher's Edition, and to Deborah Smith-Johnston who wrote the "Chapter Wrap Up" sections of the AP student edition. Contributors to the supplements also include Barbara Brun-Ozuna, Paschal High School, TX; Ryba Epstein, Rich East High School, IL; Phyllis G. Jestice, University of Southern Mississippi; James Sabathne, Hononegah High School, IL; Lisa Tran, California State University–Fullerton; Michael Vann, Sacramento State University; and Patrick Whelan, Saint Stephen's Episcopal School, FL.

The "Bedford village" has been a second community sustaining this enterprise and the one most directly responsible for the book's second edition. It would be difficult for any author to imagine a more supportive and professional publishing team. My chief point of contact with the Bedford village has been Kathryn Abbott, the development editor who also guided much of the first edition. As an experienced professor of history herself, she has masterfully summarized and analyzed numerous reviews of the manuscript and has read and reread every word, perused every map, and examined every image with great care, offering both reassurance and useful criticism. She has brought to this delicate task the sensitivity of a fine historian, the skills of an outstanding editor, and a much appreciated understanding of the author's sensibilities. Photo researcher Carole Frohlich identified and acquired the many images that grace *Ways of the World* and did so with efficiency and courtesy.

Others on the team have also exhibited that lovely combination of personal kindness and professional competence that is so characteristic of the Bedford way. Company president Denise Wydra, co-president of Macmillan Higher Education Joan Feinberg, and publisher Mary Dougherty have all kept an eye on the project amid many duties. More immediately responsible for the second edition was Traci Crowell, executive editor for history, and Jane Knetzger, director of development, who provided overall guidance as well as the necessary resources. Operating more behind the scenes in the Bedford village, a series of highly competent and always supportive people have shepherded this revised edition along its way. Associate editor Robin Soule and editorial assistant Emily DiPietro provided invaluable assistance in handling the manuscript, contacting reviewers, and keeping on top of the endless details that such an enterprise demands. Bridget Leahy has again served as production editor during the book's production and, again, did so with both grace and efficiency. Copy editor Lisa Wehrle polished the prose and sorted out my inconsistent usages with a seasoned and perceptive eye. Daniel McDonough and Janie Pierce-Bratcher have overseen the marketing process, while Bedford's history specialists John Hunger and Sean Blest and a cadre of humanities specialists and sales representatives have reintroduced the book to the academic world. Jack Cashman supervised the development of ancillary materials to support the book, and Donna Dennison ably coordinated research for the lovely covers that mark *Ways of the World*.

Yet another "village" that contributed much to *Ways of the World* consists in that group of distinguished scholars and teachers who worked with me on an earlier world history text, *The Making of the Modern World,* published by St. Martin's Press (1988, 1995). They include Sandria Freitag, Edwin Hirschmann, Donald Holsinger, James Horn, Robert Marks, Joe Moore, Lynn Parsons, and Robert Smith. That collective effort resembled participation in an extended seminar, from which I benefitted immensely. Their ideas and insights have shaped my own understanding of world history in many ways and greatly enriched *Ways of the World.*

A final and much smaller community sustained this project and its author. It is that most intimate of villages that we know as a marriage. Sharing that village with me is my wife, Suzanne Sturn. It is her work to bring ideas and people to life on stage, even as I try to do between these covers. She knows how I feel about her love and support, and no one else needs to.

To all of my fellow villagers, I offer deep thanks for an immensely rewarding experience. I am grateful beyond measure.

Robert Strayer
La Selva Beach, CA
Winter 2013

Versions and Supplements

ADOPTERS OF *Ways of the World* and their students have access to abundant resources, including documents, presentation and testing materials, volumes in the acclaimed Bedford Series in History and Culture, and much more. For more information on the offerings described below, visit the book's catalog site at **bedfordstmartins.com /highschool/strayersources/catalog**, or contact your local Bedford, Freeman, and Worth sales representative.

NEW Assign the Online, Interactive Bedford *e-Book*

With all the content of the print book—plus integrated LearningCurve, guided reading exercises, chapter video previews, and extra primary sources—the *e-Book for Ways of the World* goes well beyond the print book in both content and pedagogy. Bob Strayer narrates the short video chapter previews, and in collaboration with Eric Nelson at Southwest Missouri State, offers a guided reading exercise for each chapter based on the "Seeking the Main Point" focus question. Designed to help students read actively for key concepts and major developments, the exercise provides a tailored note-taking structure that allows them to associate relevant details and evidence with the chapter's main points as they go along. At the end of the chapter, students are prompted to answer the question in essay form. The e-Book also lets students easily search, highlight, and bookmark. Instructors can easily assign and add pages, hide and rearrange chapters, and link to quizzes and activities.

NEW Assign LearningCurve So Your Students Come to Class Prepared

As described in the Preface, students receive access to LearningCurve for *Ways of the World*, an online learning tool designed to help students rehearse content at their own pace in a non-threatening, game-like environment. The feedback for wrong answers provides instructional coaching and sends students back to the book for review. Students answer as many questions as necessary to reach a target score, with repeated chances to revisit material they haven't mastered. Assigning LearningCurve is easy for instructors, and the reporting features help instructors track overall class trends and spot topics that are giving students trouble. Like the book it serves, LearningCurve for *Ways of the World* emphasizes major concepts, comparisons, and big-picture developments.

NEW *Annotated Teacher's Edition for Ways of the World*

The Annotated Teacher's Edition provides a wealth of guidance and support for AP teachers. Annotations include model answers for questions in the book, teaching tips, Historical Thinking Skills practice, pacing guides, and exam alerts. The teacher's edition helps teachers at all levels build the most successful AP World History course they can. Author Jay Harmon, the Social Studies chair at The Woodlands Christian Academy, TX, is a former member of the AP World History test development committee and has led AP workshops in the United States, England, Germany, and Panama.

NEW *Strive for a 5: Preparing for the AP World History Examination*

This print guide provides students with narrative overviews of each historical period, chapter reviews organized around AP key concepts and themes, and AP-style practice exams, including multiple-choice and document-based questions as well as Continuity and Change Over Time and Comparison essays. Contributors include Barbara Brun-Ozuna, Paschal High School (TX), a world history consultant for the College Board and a table leader at the AP World History examination reading; Ryba Epstein, Rich East High School (IL), AP World History workshop consultant, trainer, and reader; James Sabathne, Hononegah High School (IL), an exam reader and development committee member for AP history; Lisa Tran, California State University–Fullerton; and Patrick Whelan, Saint Stephen's Episcopal School (FL), an AP teacher, workshop leader, and exam reader.

Send Students to Free Online Resources

The book's companion site at **bedfordstmartins.com/highschool/strayer** gives students a way to read, write, and study by providing plentiful quizzes and activities, study aids, and history research and writing help.

FREE **Online Study Guide.** Available at the companion site, this popular resource provides students with quizzes and activities for each chapter, including multiple-choice self-tests that focus on important concepts, flashcards that test students' knowledge of key terms, timeline activities that emphasize causal relationships, and map quizzes intended to strengthen students' geography skills. Instructors can monitor students' progress through an online Quiz Gradebook or receive email updates.

FREE **Research, Writing, and Anti-plagiarism Advice.** Available at the companion site, Bedford's **History Research and Writing Help** includes **History Research and Reference Sources**, with links to history-related databases, indexes, and journals; **More Sources and How to Format a History Paper**, with clear advice on how to integrate primary and secondary sources into research papers and how to cite and format sources correctly; **Build a Bibliography**, a simple Web-based tool known as *The Bedford Bibliographer* that generates bibliographies in four commonly used documentation styles; and **Tips on Avoiding Plagiarism**, an online tutorial that reviews the consequences of plagiarism and features exercises to help students practice integrating sources and recognize acceptable summaries.

Additional Instructor Resources

Bedford/St. Martin's has developed a rich array of supplemental teaching resources for this book and this course. They range from lecture and presentation materials and assessment tools to course management options. Most can be downloaded or ordered at **bedfordstmartins.com/highschool/strayersources/catalog**.

Teacher's Resource Guide. The *Teacher's Resource Guide* offers both experienced and first-time AP teachers tools for teaching the AP World History course. It includes information on the AP World History test format and grading standards, correlation guides that align AP World History themes and key concepts with the textbook, advice on building an AP World History syllabus, and AP-focused chapter specific resources. Contributors include Helen Grady, Springside School (PA), a former AP World History consultant to the College Board; Eric W. Nelson, Missouri State University; and Patrick Whelan, Saint Stephen's Episcopal School (FL), an AP teacher, workshop leader, and exam reader.

EXPANDED **Computerized Test Bank.** The revised and expanded test bank includes a mix of fresh, carefully crafted multiple-choice, short-answer, and essay questions for each chapter. It also contains the Big Picture, Seeking the Main Point, Margin Review, Portrait, document and visual source headnotes, and Using the Evidence questions from the textbook and model answers for each. Finally, each chapter includes a section of multiple-choice questions focused exclusively on the chapter's documents and visual sources. All questions appear in Microsoft Word format and in easy-to-use test bank software that allows instructors to add, edit, resequence, and print questions and answers. Instructors can also export questions into a variety of formats.

NEW *The Bedford Lecture Kit for Ways of the World* **Instructor's Resource CD-ROM: PowerPoint Maps, Images, Lecture Outlines, and Content for Classroom Support Systems.** This resource provides ready-made and fully customizable PowerPoint multimedia presentations that include lecture outlines with embedded maps, figures, and selected images from the textbook and extra background for instructors. Also available are maps and selected images in JPEG and

PowerPoint formats; content for classroom response systems, in Microsoft Word and PowerPoint formats; and outline maps in PDF format for quizzing or handing out. All files are suitable for copying onto transparency acetates.

NEW *Teaching Ideas for AP History: A Video Resource.* This DVD is a new professional resource for teachers of AP United States, European, and World history. In three hours of interviews with thirty AP history experts, teachers, and college professors, this video offers a wealth of advice on varied topics, including creating a syllabus, reading and writing strategies, and specific assignments to help students develop their historical thinking skills while learning historical content. The disc also includes dozens of files—from lessons plans to graphic organizers—that can be downloaded and used in class, as well as a series of downloadable discussion questions for teachers that allow the DVD to be used effectively in a formal professional development setting.

Make History—**Free Documents, Maps, Images, and Web Sites.** *Make History* combines the best Web resources with hundreds of maps and images, to make it simple to find the source material you need. Browse the collection of thousands of resources by course or by topic, date, and type. Each item has been carefully chosen and helpfully annotated to make it easy to find exactly what you need. Available at **bedfordstmartins.com/makehistory**.

Guide to Changing Editions. Designed to facilitate an instructor's transition from the previous edition of *Ways of the World* to the current edition, this guide presents an overview of major changes as well as changes in each chapter.

Videos and Multimedia. A wide assortment of videos and multimedia CD-ROMs on various topics in world history is available to qualified adopters through your Bedford, Freeman, and Worth sales representative.

Package and Save Your Students Money

Stretch your budget and package your favorite text with more! Many of the following resources can be packaged at minimal additional cost. For information on packages, discounts, and class sets, contact your local Bedford, Freeman, and Worth sales representative.

Worlds of History: A Comparative Reader. Compiled by Kevin Reilly, a widely respected world historian and community college teacher, *Worlds of History* fosters historical thinking through thematic comparisons of primary and secondary sources from around the world. Each chapter takes up a major theme—such as patriarchy, love and marriage, or globalization—as experienced by two or more cultures. "Thinking Historically" exercises build students' capacity to analyze and interpret sources one skill at a time. This flexible framework accommodates a variety of approaches to teaching world history.

The Bedford Series in History and Culture. More than 150 titles in this highly praised series combine first-rate scholarship, historical narrative, and important primary documents for undergraduate courses. Each book is brief, inexpensive, and focused on a specific topic or period. For a complete list of titles, visit **bedfordstmartins.com/history/series**.

Rand McNally Historical Atlas of the World. This collection of more than seventy full-color maps illustrates the eras and civilizations of world history from the emergence of human societies to the present.

The Bedford Glossary for World History. This handy supplement for the survey course gives students historically contextualized definitions for hundreds of terms — from *abolitionism* to *Zoroastrianism* — that they will encounter in lectures, reading, and exams.

World History Matters: A Student Guide to World History Online. Based on the popular "World History Matters" Web site produced by the Center for History and New Media, this unique resource, edited by Kristin Lehner (The Johns Hopkins University), Kelly Schrum (George Mason University), and T. Mills Kelly (George Mason University), combines reviews of 150 of the most useful and reliable world history Web sites with an introduction that guides students in locating, evaluating, and correctly citing online sources.

Trade Books. Titles published by sister companies Hill and Wang; Farrar, Straus and Giroux; Henry Holt and Company; St. Martin's Press; Picador; and Palgrave Macmillan. For more information, visit **bedfordstmartins.com/tradeup**.

A Pocket Guide to Writing in History. This portable and affordable reference tool by Mary Lynn Rampolla, now also available as a searchable e-book, provides reading, writing, and research advice useful to students in all history courses. Concise yet comprehensive advice on approaching typical history assignments, developing critical reading skills, writing effective history papers, conducting research, using and documenting sources, and avoiding plagiarism—enhanced with practical tips and examples throughout—have made this slim reference a best-seller.

A Student's Guide to History. This complete guide to success in any history course provides the practical help students need to be effective. In addition to introducing students to the nature of the discipline, author Jules Benjamin teaches a wide range of skills from preparing for exams to approaching common writing assignments, and he explains the research and documentation process with plentiful examples.

Brief Contents

Contents

Prologue: From Cosmic History to Human History   liv

The History of the Universe • The History of a Planet • The History
of the Human Species . . . in a Single Paragraph • Why World
History? • Change, Comparison, and Connection: The Three Cs
of World History

PART ONE   First Things First: Beginnings in History, to 500 B.C.E.   2

THE BIG PICTURE   Turning Points in Early World History   3

The Emergence of Humankind • The Globalization of Humankind
• The Revolution of Farming and Herding • The Turning Point of
Civilization • A Note on Dates

1.   First Peoples; First Farmers: Most of History in a Single Chapter, To 4000 B.C.E. 11

PART TWO Second-Wave Civilizations in World History, 500 B.C.E.–500 C.E. 108

---

3. State and Empire in Eurasia/North Africa, 500 B.C.E.–500 C.E. II7

4. Culture and Religion in Eurasia/North Africa, 500 B.C.E.–500 C.E.

PART THREE   An Age of Accelerating Connections, 500–1500

✓ **LearningCurve** **bedfordstmartins.com/strayer/LC**

CONSIDERING THE EVIDENCE

---

9. The Worlds of Islam: Afro-Eurasian Connections, 600–1500   411

11. Pastoral Peoples on the Global Stage: The Mongol Moment, 1200–1500   513

18. Colonial Encounters in Asia and Africa,
1750–1950   879

PART SIX   The Most Recent Century, 1914–2012

20. Collapse at the Center: World War, Depression, and the Rebalancing of Global Power, 1914–1970s

Maps

Big Picture Maps

Chapter Maps

Features

Portraits

Snapshots

Historical Thinking, Reading, and Writing Skills for AP World History

Dave Neumann

Director
The History Project at California State University–Long Beach

Students and adults alike often grumble that history is just a bunch of facts to memorize. While it's true that studying history requires data, information, and yes, facts, that's not the essence of history. History is a way of thinking about the world by looking at the past; it is a reconstruction of the past, drawing on both imagination and interpretation. In this effort, historians use a number of skills. This skills primer will help you develop the historical thinking skills you need to succeed in Advanced Placement World History and on the exam. It will also enable you to improve critical thinking, reading, and writing skills that will be useful in college or whatever endeavor you pursue after high school.

Historical Thinking Skills for World History

AP World History addresses four major skills that represent the ways historians think about the past. These skills have been described as "habits of mind." This useful phrase should remind you that a skill needs to be practiced repeatedly until it becomes second nature. Because practice is an integral part of learning to think historically, the sections that follow include exercises to help you develop these "habits of mind." Like shooting free throws, rehearsing dance moves, or playing scales, historical thinking skills need to be exercised regularly until you can use them easily and almost effortlessly.

While the skills described here are shared by all historians, world historians use them in distinctive ways. That's because world history is different from, for example, U.S. history. World history deals with a much larger region (often the entire globe) and a much longer period of time (thousands of years). Thus, world historians practice historical thinking from a very broad point of view. As we discuss each skill separately, keep in mind that these skills overlap in many ways. For example, you can't make a historical argument without also evaluating evidence. So as you develop one historical thinking skill, you will also be learning other skills.

Skill 1: Crafting Historical Arguments from Historical Evidence

The first historical thinking skill focuses our attention on using evidence to make historical arguments. The word "argument" reminds us that any attempt to explain the past requires interpretation, since our understanding of the past is limited. Arguing means making a logical—rather than an emotional—case for your interpretation of a particular historical question or controversy. To be convincing, your interpretation has to present supporting evidence. This evidence consists of both historical facts and information from primary sources.

Historical Argumentation

Historians make arguments about what life was like in the past, how or why things changed, and why those changes matter. Their arguments are informed by their deep knowledge about the subject and careful reading of primary sources. But because evidence from the past is often incomplete or difficult to understand, historians inevitably make inferences to fill the gaps in their knowledge. Not all historians make the same inferences, so there are often a variety of interpretations about most historical events.

For example, most scholars agree that the decision of some people to adopt agriculture about 11,000 years ago marked the beginning of a major world historical development. But because this development preceded writing, the only evidence scholars have comes from archeology and anthropology. Consequently, historians disagree about whether agriculture led to permanent settlement in a particular location—or vice versa. Many scholars also believe that the development of agricultural surpluses introduced disparities in status. Critics disagree, however, pointing to tomb evidence from gathering and hunting (that is, non-farming) peoples that suggests that significant differences in status already existed among some pre-agricultural peoples.

To develop this historical thinking skill, ask yourself how do historians think they know what they know about a particular event. What evidence do they provide? Does their language suggest hesitancy or uncertainty about their interpretation? Do they offer alternative explanations?

■ **EXERCISE:** On pages 26–43 of this text, how does the author explain the emergence of agriculture? What inferences does he make?

Appropriate Use of Relevant Historical Evidence

Historians make arguments about the past based on primary-source evidence. A primary source is a something produced in the era under investigation. In contrast, a secondary source is something about the era under investigation, long after the fact. It is usually the result of scholarly research of primary sources, or a distillation of such research. The narrative sections of this textbook, for example, are secondary sources. Traditionally, primary sources have consisted overwhelmingly of written sources. In fact, some historians referred to any time before writing as "prehistoric."

In the last few decades, historians have increasingly moved beyond relying exclusively on written primary sources by turning to visual sources—paintings, photographs, architecture, artifacts, etc.—and evidence from other fields of knowledge. For example, using scientific and medical information, historians have come to see the role that disease has played in history—destroying native populations in the Americas after Europeans arrived, for instance. Since no historian can be an expert in every field, historians also make use of the secondary-source scholarship of others who have studied primary sources such as ancient DNA or pottery shards in their own specialized studies.

For help with assessing primary sources, read the section, "Working with Primary Sources," on pages lxviii–lxxi of this book. Then return to this section and complete this exercise.

■ EXERCISE: Take a look at Document 2.2 in Chapter 2, "Law and Justice in Ancient Mesopotamia," on pages 95–97. Then review the chapter narrative and find the sections that provide the context for this document.

Skill 2: Chronological Reasoning

"Chronological reasoning" means thinking logically about how and why the world changes—or, sometimes, stays the same—over time. While all fields of knowledge offer arguments based on evidence or make comparisons, historians are uniquely concerned about the past and its relationship to the present. How is the world different now from how it was 50 years ago, 500 years ago, or 5,000 years ago? Why did the world change? How have some aspects of the world remained relatively the same over long periods of time? On what basis do historians simplify the long and complicated past by breaking it into smaller eras?

Historical Causation

Causation has to do with explanations about how or why changes take place in world history. Sometimes there is an obvious connection between an event and its consequence, like a cue ball striking the eight ball and making it move. And some events *are* fairly straightforward: the attack on Pearl Harbor prompted President Roosevelt to ask Congress for a declaration of war against Japan. But even this seemingly simple example is more complex. Why did Japan attack the United States? What role did the American embargo on the sale of oil have on Japan's decision? Why did the United States enact this embargo? All of these other events took place just a few years before the Pearl Harbor attack. If we go even further back, we'll gain additional insight about the larger context of the Japanese government's decision. A longer-term analysis might lead, for example, to an understanding of Japanese imperial aggression as an outgrowth of their rapid industrialization during the Meiji

Historical Causation involves:	
Multiple causes	Most events or developments, such as the Japanese attack on Pearl Harbor, occur because of a combination of factors, not just one.
Large processes	Many changes take place through major processes that are larger than any one person. Urbanization is a complex set of changes resulting from the actions of countless different individuals.
Unintended causes	Many changes take place accidentally, like the large-scale deaths of Native Americans from diseases Europeans weren't aware they were carrying.
Contingency	Events are not preordained, and history could have turned out differently. This is known as *contingency*. Because we read about major events in history already knowing their outcome, we have a tendency to think they were bound to happen, but that is not the case. The initial Spanish conquest of the Incas was very precarious, for example, and early on the Spanish might have been defeated.

Restoration of the late nineteenth century and a continuing fear of domination by Western powers.

Just as there were many factors behind the Japanese decision to bomb Pearl Harbor, most examples of historical causation involve multiple causes. Historical causation also involves large processes, unintended consequences, and contingencies, as this chart describes.

You can begin to develop the skill of determining causation by asking yourself, whenever some significant change in world history is described, what reasons explain the development. If the answer seems simple, keep digging, because there's bound to be a more complicated (and longer-term) explanation.

■ **EXERCISE:** One major controversy in world history regarding causation has to do with why Western Europe industrialized in the nineteenth century — and China didn't. How does the author explain the causes of British industrialization on pages 834–35 in Chapter 17? Which of the types of explanations from the box above does he use in his explanation?

Patterns of Continuity and Change

Historians are interested in both historical changes and persisting patterns, or "continuities." Change is easier to see: when one empire overthrows another one, that event often becomes part of the historical record. But some things stay relatively the same for long periods of time. Because continuity (such as a network of trade that remains in existence for hundreds of years) is less dramatic than change, it can be harder to spot.

What counts as continuity depends on the scale of time you're working with. The Soviet Union was continuous throughout most of the twentieth century. However, in the timeframe of Russia's history since the formation of Kievan Rus in the ninth century, the Soviet era looks more like a short-lived exception.

When historians talk about continuity, they're not implying that a particular pattern applied to everyone in the world or even in a particular region. Nor are they claiming that absolutely nothing changed in the pattern they're describing. For example, agricultural production has been continuous for thousands of years. But there are exceptions to this broad statement. On the one hand, some people have continued to be gatherer-hunters; on the other hand, methods of farming have changed substantially with technology. So the continuity of agriculture is a generalization but not a completely unchanging pattern; nor is it a pattern that applies to everyone on the planet.

To work on developing this skill, look for places in your text where an author directly indicates that a historical pattern persisted over time and explains *why* that pattern persisted. But even when an author focuses on change in world history, you can still find continuity by inference, since few things ever change completely. When the text describes a new development, ask yourself what *didn't* change. For example, while Buddhism became popular after its introduction into China, Confucianism remained an important force in Chinese culture.

> ■ **EXERCISE:** Look at the author's discussion of "The World of Islam as a New Civilization" on pages 436–41 in Chapter 9. What language does he use to convey that he is talking about patterns of continuity?

Periodization

Periodization refers to the ways that historians break the past into separate periods of time. Historians look for major turning points in history—places where the world looked very different *before* some event than it did *after*—to decide how to break the past into chunks. They then give a label to each period to convey the key characteristics and developments of that era.

Because the past is complex, particularly when talking about a subject as vast as world history, any attempt to create eras and give those eras labels can provoke disagreement. Some world historians, for example, argue for a major division at 1000 C.E., which would highlight the important role of nomadic peoples in the period between 1000 and 1450. Others prefer to maintain a single period from about 600 to 1450, since they don't think nomadic empires significantly interrupted a larger period of Afro-Eurasian contact. These disagreements often carry over into the classroom. The AP World History course used to make a break at 1914, instead of 1900; this older periodization made World War I a major turning point. Pushing the period back to the beginning of the twentieth century, as the AP World History course now does, places the war in the context of other important modern

Strayer	College Board
Part One: Beginnings in History to 500 B.C.E.	Period 1: Technological and Environmental Transformations, to c. 600 B.C.E.
Part Two: Second-Wave Civilizations in World History, 500 B.C.E.–500 C.E.	Period 2: Organization and Reorganization of Human Societies, c. 600 B.C.E. to 600 C.E.
Part Three: An Age of Accelerating Connections, 500–1500	Period 3: Regional and Transregional Interactions, c. 600 to c. 1450
Part Four: The Early Modern World, 1450–1750	Period 4: Global Interactions, c. 1450 to c. 1750
Part Five: The European Moment in World History, 1750–1914	Period 5: Industrialization and Global Integration, c. 1750 to c. 1900
Part Six: The Most Recent Century, 1914–2012	Period 6: Accelerating Global Change and Realignments, c. 1900 to Present

developments—including developments less focused on Europe, such as the rise of nationalist movements among colonial peoples.

As you develop this skill, pay regular attention to the chapter you're in, noting what major era it is described as being a part of, and thinking about what the different labels for that era say about the main "story" of that era, at least according to your teacher, your textbook, or the College Board.

■ **EXERCISE:** Compare the author's periodization in Parts One through Six to the College Board's historical periodization from the chart above. How do the author's dates and titles compare to the College Board's? What explains the similarities and the differences? Why do you suppose that periodization in world history can be so controversial?

Skill 3: Comparison and Contextualization

People don't learn things in isolation, but in relationship to other things. Historians are no different. The third category of historical thinking skills reflects the ways historians make sense of the past by placing particulars in some larger framework. For example, they understand historical events and processes by comparing them to related events and processes to see how they're similar and different. Second, historians recognize that historical evidence, including artifacts, photographs, and speeches, can only be adequately understood by knowing something about their context—that is, the time and place where they came into existence.

Comparison

Comparisons help world historians understand how a development in the past was similar to or different from another development and in this way determine what was distinctive about it. For example, through comparative study, scholars have concluded that empires that developed over the last two thousand years share key features. First, rulers have to legitimize their rule through religious or ideological traditions. Second, they have to maintain political unity by dealing with people on the peripheries of the empire. Finally, since empires develop by conquering other people groups, empires have to deal with ethnic diversity.

But while these patterns hold true for all empires, each one addresses these challenges in its own way. The Ottoman Empire justified its rule through Turkish tradition as well as Islamic belief. It rewarded loyal elites on the margins of the empire through tax breaks. And it dealt with minorities by creating the *millet* system (whereby Ottoman subjects were divided into religious communities ruled by their religious leaders). Through the tool of comparison we understand how Ottoman rulers handled common problems in unique ways.

As you develop this skill, practice comparing two nations that existed at the same time—like the Ottoman and Mughal Empires—and also compare the same government at two different points in time. For example, how was government in Song China similar to—and different from—government in Tang China? Be sure that the two things you're comparing are relatively similar, or else the comparison doesn't make much sense. For example, historians of China have pointed out that when looking at economic development in early modern China, it is better to compare that large country to developments in all of Europe rather than to tiny England only.

■ EXERCISE: Look at the author's comparison of early modern empires in the Americas, Russia, and Asia in Chapter 13. Is it fair or appropriate to compare these empires? How are these empires similar to one another? Why are they alike? What key features does he say are different? Why are they different?

Contextualization

Just as historical events make more sense when they're studied alongside similar events, historians know that any event can only be understood in "context." Context refers to the historical circumstances surrounding a particular event. World historians look for major global developments in any era to help determine context. They typically think in terms of two levels of context: an *immediate* (or short-term) context and a *broad* (or long-term) context.

The easiest way to begin thinking about context is to figure out when a particular event (or document) took place. Then brainstorm the major developments of the era. Ask yourself, "How might these larger events have shaped this event (or document)?" For example, when reading Document 20.1, on pages 1019–21, by the leader of Nazi Germany, Adolph Hitler, note that it was written in 1925–1926. What were the major *immediate* geopolitical developments of the mid-1920s? World War I had ended relatively recently when Hitler wrote *Mein Kampf*, and many Germans were unhappy with the terms of the Treaty of Versailles that had ended that conflict. Thus, you can count on the treaty and Germany's reaction to it being important to understanding Hitler's work. In the 1930s, Hitler came to power in Germany under an explicit goal of repudiating the Versailles Treaty and restoring Germany's military might. This context is crucial for understanding Germany's support for Hitler and the Nazi program.

■ **EXERCISE:** Look at "Considering the Evidence: Exchange and Status in the Early Modern World" on pages 710–17 in Chapter 14. What *immediate* developments in the seventeenth and early eighteenth centuries might have influenced the cultural patterns depicted in these illustrations? How does the *broad* context of the Columbian exchange help you understand these paintings?

Skill 4: *Historical Interpretation and Synthesis*

You first learned about how historians make arguments; now you'll practice evaluating those arguments and making your own. Since history requires making inferences about the past, it's inevitable that scholars will come to different conclusions. It can be very helpful then to study different historical interpretations about a particular event or movement over time, as interpretations often change. The final skill component, synthesis, is also related to argumentation. It is the culminating skill because it requires you to integrate all the other skills in creating your own argument.

Interpretation

Historians interpret both primary and secondary sources, evaluating points of view and considering context to create their own interpretations. Through analyzing different historical interpretations, you will see how historical interpretations change over time. We have already established that formulating a historical argument requires making inferences from evidence. The background of a particular historian (age, gender, nationality, political philosophy, time of writing, etc.) often shapes the way he or she understands or interprets the past. In many cases, knowing something about the context of a historian can help you understand his or her argument better—in the same way that understanding the context of the author of a primary source helps you understand the primary source. Sometimes, this information can help you identify the prejudices or limitations of a particular interpretation.

For example, in the early 1960s a British historian claimed that Africa had no history until Europeans took over the continent. Subsequent scholarship has shown this conclusion to be quite false, and we can assume that this historian's context as a citizen of an imperial nation writing during decolonization influenced his outlook. About the same time, an American scholar developed an influential model of modernization for "third-world countries." Later scholars have argued that this model oversimplified the world by assuming all countries would grow economically the same way the United States had.

Be careful when analyzing historical interpretations. You can't simply assume that because a scholar has *x* background he will make *y* argument. There are far too many exceptions for such a rule. Instead, begin by finding out what you can about a scholar's background and then make a hunch about how that background might shape his or her views. Then, as you read the author's argument carefully, look for evidence that he or she actually makes the kinds of arguments you anticipated. If you don't find such evidence, discard your hunch.

Synthesis

Synthesis is a culminating skill that reflects your ability to make persuasive arguments of your own from evidence. It draws on all of the other historical thinking skills—historical argumentation, appropriate use of relevant historical evidence, causation, continuity and change, periodization, comparison, contextualization, and interpretation—along with two other elements. First, you may need to draw on evidence outside the field of history. This will most likely come from the social sciences: archeology, anthropology, economics, sociology, etc. The other element is the ability to apply insights from historical evidence to a new setting. This is a creative form of comparison. Most likely, you will link some moment in the past to a contemporary problem, such as ongoing struggles for economic and political independence in the developing world in the post-colonial era, as described in Chapter 22. In so doing, you will be using the past to shed light on the present. You will have taken a major step in historical thinking, as making connections is a key part of what historians do.

Getting the Most Out of Reading World History

Active reading means reading for meaning. The big challenges of reading are length and detail. If you understand the "big picture," you can read much more quickly and effectively, because you can "see the forest for the trees." That is, you can see the main ideas and recognize how specific information is provided to illustrate those big ideas. The three stages of reading described below will help you understand the "big picture" when reading this text and others.

Pre-reading

When approaching a text such as this one, it is helpful to spend a few minutes pre-reading the material. During the pre-reading stage, you are simply getting prepared for what you will be reading. This involves two steps. First, try to determine chronology, theme(s), and region(s). Do this by looking at chapter dates, the part or unit that includes this chapter (keeping in mind that not all books are divided into parts), the chapter that came before and the one that comes next, and the chapter title. Note that the next main section of a chapter may not describe something that happened later in time; it may simply reflect a different theme about the same time and place. Second, read the "Seeking the Main Point" question that opens the chapter. The title alone should give you a clue that this is an important question for understanding the chapter. Next, try to determine the major changes, comparisons, and connections discussed in the chapter by scanning the section titles, images and captions (maps, charts, photos, etc.), and any pedagogical tools included (chronologies, key terms, document headnotes, review questions, etc.). Also, skim the introduction to the chapter—usually reading the topic sentences of this section is sufficient.

■ **EXERCISE:** Let's practice by pre-reading Part One and Chapter 1 of your textbook.

- **CHRONOLOGY:** Looking at the part title, what is the chronology of Part One? Why might there be an ending date but no starting date? Now glance at the "Map of Time" on page 13 of Chapter 1. How much time does Chapter 1 cover? Why so much?

- **THEME:** What is Part One all about? What are the big topics in this part? Take a look at the headings on pages 4 and 5, which discuss the major topics of Chapter 1 — "The Globalization of Humankind" and "The Revolution of Farming and Herding." Read the five topic sentences that begin the paragraphs in these sections. What is the first chapter going to be about? Why is the topic important? Why is it part of "Beginnings in History"? Using the contents list on page 2, what chapter comes after this one? How do they fit together? Next, look at the title and the chapter contents listed on page 11. What is the chapter about? What are the major topics of the chapter? Now flip through the images in the chapter, maps included. What else do they tell you about the chapter that you hadn't learned already?

- **REGION:** Next, take a look at "Mapping Part One" on pages 8–9. Does this part focus on particular regions or larger global processes? How do you know? Now take a look at Map 1.1 on pages 16–17 and Map 1.3 on pages 28–29 and consider the same questions about regions versus global processes.

Remember, there's no need to write this down. The point right now is just to get a clear idea of the "big picture" of the part where this chapter appears. You haven't read the chapter yet—and you haven't taken a single note. But by spending five minutes pre-reading the chapter you already have a good idea what the chapter's all about. By taking this time, you'll be able to read with a clear focus, saving yourself a lot of time later on. Now that you have a good idea of the "big picture," you're ready to begin actually reading the text.

During Reading

As you read chapters of this text, remember that reading is an active process—so stay focused. The meaning will only become clear as you work at it. The author has intentionally written an organized textbook and wants you to be able to follow along, so take advantage of the clues he's provided, especially titles and headings.

Active readers use four skills to understand texts: *questioning, clarifying, summarizing,* and *predicting.* These steps don't have to happen in a particular order. In fact, once you become comfortable with them, they'll pop up on their own in whatever order they choose, perhaps several at the same time—that's when you know that they've truly become habits of mind. Use these skills along with note-taking to get the most out of your reading.

Questioning

Historians look at the world in a particular way, and they usually organize their writing around the historical thinking skills discussed above: cause and effect, comparison, interpretation, etc. By questioning you can identify these patterns. Your textbook provides you with a series of marginal questions that help you to identify what is going on in the narrative. In addition to the "Seeking the Main Point" question that opens each chapter, each chapter also contains at least one "Summing Up So Far" question that helps you put together all that you've read to that point in the chapter. For example, take a look at the two questions on page 80. One asks you how the emergence of civilizations was revolutionary and refers to the section that you just read. The other, a "comparison" question, helps prepare you for reading the next section on Mesopotamia and Egypt.

For every section you read, you want to find out the major subject. The easiest way to do this is to ask the "reporter questions": Who? What? Where? When? Why?

1. *Who* is the section about? History texts are almost always about people. Is the focus an individual? A social group? A political entity?
2. *What* does the section say about this person or group? Texts usually describe some major event or pattern. Did they do something important? Did something happen to them?
3. *Where* did the subject being described take place? Physical location is often crucial in history. Does this location help make sense of the subject in some way?
4. *When* did the events take place? Like physical location, chronology forms part of the historical context that makes events understandable. Does the text describe something unfolding over a very short period—or a longer one? Are there crucial events that came before that make the description understandable?
5. *Why* did the event or pattern being described take place—and why does it matter? Whether talking about a dramatic development or a continuity that endured for a long period of time, historians always attempt to understand what led to it. What reasons does the text provide for the event or pattern? How is the significance of the development explained?

Clarifying

As you read, ask yourself if there are any words you don't understand. If they're crucial for making sense of the passage, can you define them using a dictionary or other outside source? If there are any sentences you don't understand, do they become clearer when you reread them or as you read further in the text?

When it comes to vocabulary, use good judgment. Is the word crucial for understanding the passage? If not, read right past it. If it *is* a crucial word, you may need to look it up in a dictionary. Before you take the time to look it up, however, check that it hasn't been defined already for you in the text.

When a longer passage throws you off, usually clearing up difficult vocabulary will help make the passage clearer. If it doesn't, simply reread the sentence slowly for a few times. If you're still unclear, back up—usually to the beginning of the paragraph—and try again. The most common way skilled readers get clarification is by rereading.

Summarizing

A summary is a brief review of the "big picture" of a particular section or chapter. After reading, briefly explain what each section is about in one sentence. Return to your questions, and be sure to look at the "Big Picture" questions in the "Second Thoughts" section at the end of the chapter narrative. They are designed to make sure that you understood the chapter.

Predicting

Based on your reading of an entire section or chapter, what do you think will come next in the text? How do you know? You may think predicting what's coming next is a waste of time, but it's a good test of how well you understand the flow of the text. If you're in a car with your family going to visit your grandmother, you probably know the route to get there. If your mother takes an unanticipated turn, it alerts you that something is different from what you were expecting—and prompts you to ask why. So if your prediction based on reading is wildly off, it may alert you to the fact that your previous idea of the "big picture" of the section was off for some reason. You may need to back up and reread a section, or at least move forward more alert to where the author is going.

Note-Taking

Of course, simply reading the text is not sufficient. You'll never remember everything that's important unless you take notes. Students experience many pitfalls when taking notes. You should only write notes *after* you understand what you have read. Actively *question, clarify, summarize,* and *predict* in your head (or out loud) as you read each chapter; then, go back through the subsections and take brief notes representing the key ideas of that section.

Brief is generally better—don't wear yourself out in the notes themselves. Find some consistent abbreviations for frequent words and use symbols. For example, an up arrow to indicate growth, a flat arrow to indicate cause/effect, and an "=" to indicate a definition, etc. Don't write everything; ask yourself if a particular point is a main idea or just an example. If you own your textbook, make annotations in the margins. If not, get a stack of sticky notes and place them in the margins for your comments.

■ **EXERCISE:** Let's practice these four skills with the introductory paragraphs to the main section, "Breakthroughs to Agriculture," on pages 26–27.

- **QUESTIONING:** What was the Agricultural Revolution? Who was involved in the Agricultural Revolution? Where did agriculture develop? When did the Agricultural Revolution take place? Why did agriculture emerge? Why do historians often consider the development of agriculture "revolutionary"?

- **CLARIFYING:** Important words like "Neolithic" and "domestication" are defined in the text itself, but are there any words that you do not understand? If there were any sentences you didn't understand, did they become clearer as you reread them or as you read on in the text?

- **SUMMARIZING:** Explain what this section is about in one sentence.

- **PREDICTING:** Based on the section you've just read, what do you think will come next in the text? How do you know?

- Now that you know what this section is about, what brief comments are worth writing down in your notes?

Post-reading

Reflecting on what you've read places information you've just learned into long-term memory. Post-reading involves the same kind of summarizing you've done section by section, but now for the entire chapter. In essence, it is a summary of your summaries. While it might seem enough to summarize the chapter verbally, writing down key ideas helps place them into long-term memory. Read through the notes that you've taken for the chapter, particularly the summary of each section. Then try to write a master summary of the entire chapter using no more than 50 words that captures the key point of each section of the chapter, as well as the chapter as a whole.

■ **EXERCISE:** Write a master summary of Chapter 1 now.

Writing about World History

This skills primer began by introducing you to the patterns of thinking you need to really understand history. The next section pointed out ways to be smart about reading your textbook. This third and final section turns to the writing skills you need to develop for the AP World History course and exam. Our focus shifts away from you *receiving* input toward you *providing* output: sharing your understanding of historical thinking skills through writing.

Most of this section will address the specific challenge of each of the three types of essays in AP World History. But first, it's important to understand two essential skills that apply to all of the essays you'll encounter. First, to successfully demonstrate what you know, you have to answer the question that has been asked. Sounds simple, but many students get in trouble on the exam by failing to address the prompt in front of them.

Every prompt contains three elements, and you need to pay attention to all of them as you plan your response to the prompt. First, there is a periodization or date range expressed in years. Obviously, you need to be sure your response addresses this era. One of the most common problems in student essays on the exam comes from providing historical information from the wrong era. Second, there is a task expressed as the main verb of the prompt: *compare, describe, explain, analyze*, etc. Pay attention to this task verb, as these tasks are not the same.

Finally, each prompt deals with a subject, expressed in two important types of nouns. A *proper noun* refers to a specific historical entity—Confucianism, the Mali empire, the Silk Road. A *common noun* typically refers to a historical concept: a key historical idea (monotheism, nationalism) or process (diffusion of culture, expansion of empire). Sometimes this process is limited in time, but often it is a pattern that occurs repeatedly in world history.

It doesn't matter how strong your content knowledge and historical skills are if you can't communicate clearly what you know. Every essay needs to have a specific, focused *thesis* that makes an argument addressing the prompt. Your thesis should be as brief as possible, while still addressing the complexity of the topic. If you explicitly respond to each of the three prompt elements clearly and accurately, you will have a strong thesis—and you'll be on your way to a persuasive essay.

Every essay needs to be organized into distinct *paragraphs*. The number of paragraphs depends on the complexity of the prompt. Typically, however, two body paragraphs won't be sufficient to address the topic thoroughly. What's most important is that you clearly announce the point you're going to make in each paragraph through a *topic sentence* that effectively covers the subject of the paragraph. Any content in the paragraph that doesn't support the topic sentence doesn't belong there.

Finally, every essay requires you to make use of *evidence* to support your claims. The type of evidence also differs depending on the type of essay. The DBQ requires you to reference each of the documents included with the question, while change-continuity and compare-contrast essays require you to draw on factual information. In every case, however, you need to both discuss relevant historical information you've learned during the course and then *explain how that information supports your claim*.

While many of these writing suggestions would apply equally to essays in other academic subjects, the essay types on the AP World History exam are all geared to the concerns of historians. Each type of essay requires the use of the historical thinking skills discussed above, often in combination with one another. For example, every essay type requires you to discuss the *historical context* of the subject you're writing about and to *appropriately use relevant evidence*.

Continuity and Change Over Time

This type of essay question tests your ability to explain change and continuity. As discussed above, historical study typically focuses on changes. In this essay type, you have to identify major changes and explain the significance of those changes—that is, why the changes matter—for the topic described in the prompt. You will also

Essay type	Visual Representation of Task
Continuity & Change	Examine one historical subject across two (or more) eras of world history. 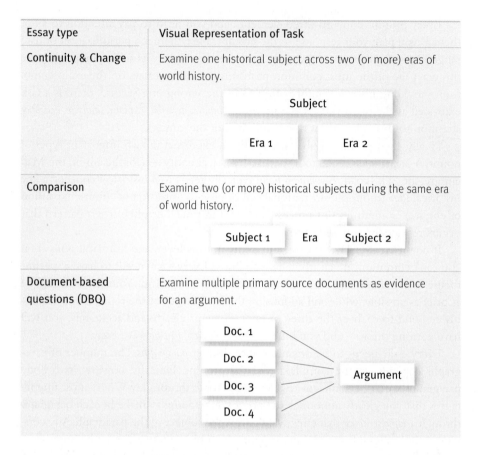
Comparison	Examine two (or more) historical subjects during the same era of world history.
Document-based questions (DBQ)	Examine multiple primary source documents as evidence for an argument.

have to analyze *why* something changed. But because some things continue largely the same for hundreds of years or more, you also have to identify continuities, explain their significance, and explain why these patterns persisted for so long.

Your essay response must clearly address both elements—continuity and change. A strong argument must do more than simply *identify* some continuities and changes. It has to *analyze* why both the continuities and changes existed and why they mattered. It's a good idea to weigh the relative value of continuities and changes. In other words, do you perceive continuities to have been more powerful than changes on the topic addressed in the prompt, or vice versa? Why do you think so? In terms of structure, avoid the temptation to organize your essay into two large paragraphs, one for continuities and one for changes. Instead, identify important topics or categories of comparison—governmental structure, trade patterns, or gender relations—and use those topics as the body paragraphs. Then, in each body paragraph, address *both* continuities *and* changes, being clear to signal your transition from one to the other.

In the same way that identifying change is an easier historical thinking skill than identifying continuity, change is also easier to write about than continuity. Historical narratives devote a lot of time to, say, reasons for the fall of the Han empire—a significant change in East Asia. So if you're writing an essay about states in that era, that information will come to mind more quickly.

After brief reflection, however, you'll realize that the Han empire endured for more than 400 years—a significant continuity. Hopefully, you'll also remember what you learned about how Han rulers governed their empire. Their techniques of government help explain why the empire lasted as long as it did. Therefore, in an essay about change and continuity in the Han empire you would want to identify a major political continuity in the era (the continued existence of the Han empire), discuss why this was significant (this large dynasty influenced a large region of East Asia), and explain why it endured (its governing techniques).

Comparison

As discussed above, comparison is one of the most basic ways historians make sense of any subject, and the AP World History exam asks you in this type of essay to write about two similar historical phenomena. You should begin your analysis by identifying broad similarities and differences. When you place two religions, two empires, or two trade patterns side by side, what do you notice? How are they similar? How are they different?

Once you move beyond the most basic level of identifying broad similarities and differences, you need to be more precise. You should begin by addressing both categories in more detail, providing specific evidence to support your broad generalizations. For example, in broad terms neither the American nor the French Revolution significantly expanded the citizenship rights of students. But a more precise statement might explain that in neither case did women get the right to vote or hold public positions. Just as with change and continuity, it's often worthwhile to indicate whether you think similarities are more significant than differences, or vice versa, and why.

You need to be careful about the structure of this essay. Many students fall into the trap of describing topic one in a body paragraph and topic two in a separate body paragraph. They assume that readers will be able to recognize the differences between the two topics this way on their own. But you'll never earn a high score that way; your comparisons need to be explicit and concrete.

Always begin each paragraph with a topic sentence that introduces the category or topic you want to compare. Be sure to use clear signal words that identify that you are shifting from similarity to difference ("Despite these similarities in ___, the two trade routes differed dramatically.") In the contrast portion of your essay be clear about the particular difference, making use of contrast words such as "conversely," "unlike," and "however" to signal your point to the reader.

In brainstorming similarities, try to step back and think in more abstract conceptual terms so you don't miss deep similarities that seem different on the surface. For example, students sometimes say that a king is different from an emperor because they focus on the different titles. But both are hereditary monarchs typically viewed as having divine authority to rule. That makes them very similar in deep ways, despite the different labels. They are much more like each other than they are to, say, a stateless society or to a democracy.

Students sometimes wonder whether they should start the paragraph with similarities or differences. One way to approach this is to deal with the less significant topic first, get it out of the way, and move on to the more significant topic. But that is really a matter of taste. What *is* important is that you provide a clear transition when you move from the compare to the contrast portion of your essay (or vice versa): "These similarities [that you've just discussed], however, were much less crucial than differences in x, y, and z." If this sounds like a repeat of your thesis statement, that's because it is. In the body of your essay, you want to echo the road map—your thesis—to help your reader know that you are making the transition that you indicated in the introductory paragraph.

Document-Based Question Essay

The document-based question, or DBQ, is a defining feature of the AP World History exam. Of all the essays, this one tends to make students the most anxious. But much of this anxiety is misplaced. Once you understand the DBQ, you will feel less worried about it—and may even come to find it your favorite essay type. Unlike the other two essay types, where you have to call on your memory to provide all the evidence, the documents in the DBQ form the basic evidence you need to use.

To do well on a DBQ, you need to go beyond the content of the documents in order to set the context, make a clear argument, and analyze the documents properly. Using documents as evidence requires the sophisticated analysis skills we discussed in the section on "Appropriate Use of Relevant Historical Evidence." That means that you have to consider the perspective or point of view of the documents. Every primary source—textual, visual, or statistical—was created for a specific purpose. That doesn't mean the author had an agenda, although sometimes that is the case. But even if the author didn't have an agenda, every document is limited and imperfect in the information it provides. Use the questions included on page lxix to interrogate each document, and then consider the limitations of each document before writing your DBQ. Then be sure to incorporate these insights about document limitations into the essay itself to make your essay more analytical—and therefore stronger.

Consider the example of a photo depicting indentured servants on a nineteenth-century sugar plantation. Students tend to view a document like that as a straightforward factual record. After all, we often hear that "pictures don't lie." But the picture was taken by someone for a particular purpose and the individuals are posed. So it's worth asking *why* someone wanted this picture taken. What purpose would this picture serve? Since it's posed, what's left out of it? How might it misrepresent—or represent in a very limited way—the realities of the indentured experience?

You also need to corroborate your documents. That means bringing the documents into "conversation" with each other. Since the documents in a DBQ don't directly refer to each other, you have to use your intuition to see connections. This relates to a distinctive task about the DBQ: you need to organize the evidence from the documents into several categories—usually at least three. The categories are sometimes stated or implied in the prompt, but you'll often have to call on your knowledge of world history and the content of the documents themselves to determine what categories (and how many) make sense. Please note that you can use the same document multiple times, so that often gives you flexibility in coming up with categories.

Finally, you have to draw on your outside knowledge. To do well, you need to position the DBQ documents within the broader context of the period, drawing on what you've learned from your textbook, from your teacher, and from any outside reading or research that you've done. Feel free to mention other sources that you may have encountered previously in your answer, especially if they offer a perspective that is missing or if the addition of outside sources helps to support your argument.

Many students feel anxious about having to write the AP World History essays. But once you become familiar with the elements of each prompt and know how to address these prompts effectively, you'll realize that there's no reason to be stressed about this. In fact, you should feel confident as you approach the writing portion of the test. Unlike the multiple-choice portion of the AP exam, the essay section gives you a lot of freedom to demonstrate what you know in an open-ended way. And if you've been thinking historically, reading the text with that lens, and sharing your ideas in class, you may begin to look forward to the opportunity to show just how developed your historical thinking skills are.

Working with Primary Sources

The task of historians might well be compared with that of Sisyphus, the ancient Greek king who, having offended the gods, was condemned to eternally roll a large rock up a mountain, only to have it ceaselessly fall back down. Like Sisyphus, historians work at a mission that can never be completely successful—to recapture the past before it is lost forever in the mists of time and fading memory. The evidence available is always partial and fragmentary. Historians themselves are limited and fallible, for they operate often at a great distance—in both time and culture—from those they are studying. And they rarely agree on important matters, divided as they are by sex, nationality, race, and values, all of which shape their understandings of the past.

Despite these challenges, scholars and students alike have long found their revisiting of the past a compelling project—intensely interesting, personally meaningful, and even fun—particularly when working with "primary" or "original" sources, which are the building blocks of all historical accounts. These sources include written documents, such as letters, diaries, law codes, official records, sacred texts, and much more, as well as visual sources, including artistic products, buildings, and artifacts—all of them generated at the time of or soon after the events that they describe or depict. Such sources are windows into the lives of our ancestors, though these windows are often smudged and foggy. Primary sources enable us to listen in on multiple conversations from the past, eavesdropping, as it were, on our ancestors, though frequently hearing only snippets. According to one witty observer, this is history as gossip.

Using primary sources effectively is no easy task. Unlike contemporary history books, which are designed explicitly for a modern audience, the sources that historians work with were produced in circumstances and with cultural assumptions that are often quite unfamiliar to twenty-first-century students. Furthermore, our ancestors' understandings of their own lives and time were subject to distortions, fabrications, misunderstandings, and ambiguity. And so working with sources requires effort—very careful reading or observation, systematic analysis, and historical imagination.

The documents and visual sources at the end of each chapter of *Ways of the World* provide an opportunity for you to practice the work of historians. It is a kind of guided "history laboratory." In working with these materials, you are "doing history," much like lab experiments in chemistry courses represent "doing science." Since each document or visual sources feature explores some theme of the chapter, the chapter narrative itself provides a broad context for analyzing these sources. The introduction to each feature and to each document or image offers more specific context or background information, while questions provide specific things to look for as you examine each document or image as well as a focus for using those sources collectively to probe larger historical issues.

Working with Written Documents

Written documents are the most common type of primary source that historians use. Analysis of documents usually begins with the basics:

- Who wrote the document?
- When and where was it written?
- What type of document is it (for example, a letter to a friend, a political decree, an exposition of a religious teaching)?

Sometimes the document itself will provide answers to these questions. On other occasions you may need to rely on the introductions.

Once these basics have been established, a historian is then likely to consider several further questions, which situate the document in its particular historical context:

- Why was the document written and for what audience? Under what circumstances was it composed?
- What point of view does it reflect? What other views or opinions is the document arguing against?

Inspiration and intention are crucial factors that shape the form and content of a source. For instance, one might examine a document differently depending on whether it was composed for a private or a public readership or whether it was intended to be read by a small elite or a wider audience.

Still another level of analysis seeks to elicit useful information from the document.

- What material in the document is believable, and what is not?
- What might historians learn from this document?
- What can the document tell us about the individual who produced it and the society from which he or she came?

Here historical imagination is essential. Informed by knowledge of the context and the content of the document, your imagination will help you to read it through the eyes of its author and its audience. How might this document have been understood at the time it was written? But in using your imagination, you must take care not to read into the documents your own assumptions and understandings. It is a delicate balance, a kind of dance that historians constantly undertake. Even documents that contain material that historians find unbelievable can be useful, for we seek not only to know what actually happened in the past but also to grasp the world as the people who lived that past understood it. Historians sometimes speak about reading documents "against the grain," looking for meanings that the author might not have intended to convey. For example, the Law Code of Hammurabi in the document feature of Chapter 2 depicts an impressive system of justice in ancient Mesopotamia, but it can also be read as an account of the numerous problems or conflicts that the society had to confront.

While each document must be read and understood individually, historians typically draw their strongest conclusions when they analyze a number of documents together. The document features in *Ways of the World* are designed to explore sets of primary sources that address a central theme of the chapter by drawing on several related texts. In the documents for Chapter 11, for example, you can reflect on the Mongol Empire by reading several accounts written by Mongols themselves and several others composed by Russian or Chinese victims of Mongol aggression. Or in Chapter 21, you will need to balance several quite positive assessments of life under Soviet dictator Joseph Stalin with others that are devastatingly critical of that communist regime during the 1930s.

Working with Visual Sources

Artifacts that derive from the material culture of the past—religious icons or paintings that add to our understanding of belief systems, a family portrait that provides insight into presentations of self in a particular time and place, a building or sculpture which reveals how power and authority were displayed in a specific empire—these kinds of evidence represent another category of primary source material that historians can use to re-create and understand the past. But such visual sources can be even more difficult to interpret than written documents. The ideas that animated the creators of particular images or artifacts are often not obvious. Nor are the understandings they conveyed to those who viewed or used them. The lovely images from the Indus River Valley civilization contained in the visual sources feature for Chapter 2, for example, remain enigmatic although still engaging to twenty-first century viewers.

Despite the difficulties of interpretation, visual sources can provide insights not offered by written documents. Various images of the Buddha shown in Chapter 4 effectively illustrate how the faith that he initiated changed as it spread beyond India to other parts of Asia. And the images deriving from World War I that are featured in the visual sources for Chapter 20 convey an immediate emotional sense about the meanings attached to that conflict that the written word can hardly match. Indeed, for pre-literate societies, such as those explored in the visual sources for Chapter 1, archeological and artistic evidence is all that remains of their history.

To use visual sources, we must try as best we can to see these pieces of evidence through the eyes of the societies that produced them and to decode the symbols and other features that imbue them with meaning. Thus, context is, if anything, even more crucial for analyzing visual evidence than it is for documents. Understanding the art of the Maya elite, featured in Chapter 6, depends heavily on some knowledge of Maya history and culture. And the images in Chapter 19 illustrating Japanese perceptions of the West in the second half of the nineteenth century require some grasp of Japan's overall historical development and its encounter with Europe and the United States.

A set of basic questions, similar to those you would ask a written document, provides a starting point for analyzing a visual source:

• When and where was the image or artifact created?

- Who made the image or artifact? Who paid for or commissioned it? For what audience(s) was it intended?
- Where was the image or artifact originally displayed or used?

Having established this basic information about the image or artifact, you may simply want to describe it, as if to someone who had never seen it before.

- If the source is an image, who or what is depicted? What activities are shown? How might you describe the positioning of figures, their clothing, hairstyles, and other visual cues?
- If the source is an object or building, how would you describe its major features?

Finally, you will want to take a stab at more interpretive issues, making use of what you know about the context in which it was created.

- What likely purpose or function did the image or artifact serve?
- What message(s) does it seek to convey?
- How could it be interpreted differently depending on who viewed or used it?
- What are the meanings of any symbols or other abstract features in the visual source?
- What can the image or artifact tell us about the society that produced it and the time period in which it was created?

Beyond analyzing particular images or objects, you will be invited to draw conclusions from sets of related visual sources that address a central theme in each chapter. What can you learn, for example, about Muslims' perceptions of their prophet Muhammad from the images contained in the visual sources feature of Chapter 9? Or what do the images in Chapter 13 show about Aztec understanding of the Spanish conquest? Moreover, you will need to assess the strengths and weaknesses of various types of visual source for answering questions posed by historians.

Primary sources—documentary and visual alike—are the foundation for all historical accounts. To read only secondary sources, such as textbooks or articles, is to miss much of the flavor and texture of history as it was actually experienced by people in the past. It is also to miss the exciting and highly controversial process by which historical narratives and analyses are constructed from scattered and fragmentary pieces of evidence. Immersing yourself in the documents and visual sources presented here allows you to catch a glimpse of the messiness, the ambiguity, the heartaches, and the achievements of history as it was lived and of the historian's craft. Enjoy!

Prologue

From Cosmic History to Human History

HISTORY BOOKS IN GENERAL, AND WORLD HISTORY TEXTBOOKS IN PARTICULAR, share something in common with those Russian nested dolls in which a series of carved figures fit inside one another. In much the same fashion, all historical accounts take place within some larger context, as stories within stories unfold. Individual biographies and histories of local communities, particularly modern ones, occur within the context of one nation or another. Nations often find a place in some more encompassing civilization, such as the Islamic world or the West, or in a regional or continental context such as Southeast Asia, Latin America, or Africa. And those civilizational or regional histories in turn take on richer meaning when they are understood within the even broader story of world history, which embraces humankind as a whole.

■ **Change**
What have been the major turning points in the pre-human phases of "big history"?

In recent decades, some world historians have begun to situate that remarkable story of the human journey in the much larger framework of both cosmic and planetary history, an approach which has come to be called "big history." It is really the "history of everything" from the big bang to the present, and it extends over the enormous, almost unimaginable time-scale of some 13.7 billion years, the current rough estimate of the age of the universe.[1]

The History of the Universe

To make this vast expanse of time even remotely comprehensible, some scholars have depicted the history of the cosmos as if it were a single calendar year (see the Snapshot). On that cosmic calendar, most of the action took place in the first few milliseconds of January 1. As astronomers, physicists, and chemists tell it, the universe that we know began in an eruption of inconceivable power and heat. Out of that explosion of creation emerged matter, energy, gravity, electromagnetism, and the "strong and "weak" forces that govern the behavior of atomic nuclei. As gravity pulled the rapidly expanding cosmic gases into increasingly dense masses, stars formed, with the first ones lighting up around 1 to 2 billion years after the big bang, or the end of January to mid-February on the cosmic calendar.

Hundreds of billions of stars followed, each with its own history, though following common patterns. They emerge, flourish for a time, and then collapse and die. In their final stages, they sometimes generate supernova, black holes, and pulsars—phenomena at least as fantastic as the most exotic of earlier creation stories. Within the stars, enormous nuclear reactions gave rise to the elements that are reflected in the periodic table known to all students of chemistry. Over eons, these stars came together

Snapshot   **The History of the Universe as a Cosmic Calendar[2]**

Big bang	January 1	13.7 billion years ago
Stars and galaxies begin to form	End of January/ mid-February	12 billion years ago
Milky Way galaxy forms	March/early April	10 billion years ago
Origin of the solar system	September 9	4.7 billion years ago
Formation of the earth	September 15	4.5 billion years ago
Earliest life on earth	Late September/ early October	4 billion years ago
Oxygen forms on earth	December 1	1.3 billion years ago
First worms	December 16	658 million years ago
First fish, first vertebrates	December 19	534 million years ago
First reptiles, first trees	December 23	370 million years ago
Age of dinosaurs	December 24–28	329–164 million years ago
First humanlike creatures	December 31 (late evening)	2.7 million years ago
First agriculture	December 31: 11:59:35	12,000 years ago
Birth of the Buddha/ Greek civilization	December 31: 11:59:55	2,500 years ago
Birth of Jesus	December 31: 11:59:56	2,000 years ago
Aztec and Inca empires	December 31: 11:59:59	500 years ago

in galaxies, such as our own Milky Way, which probably emerged in March or early April, and in even larger structures called groups, clusters, and superclusters. Adding to the strangeness of our picture of the cosmos is the recent and controversial notion that perhaps 90 percent or more of the total mass of the universe is invisible to us, consisting of a mysterious and mathematically predicted substance known to scholars only as "dark matter."

The contemplation of cosmic history has prompted profound religious or philosophical questions about the meaning of human life. For some, it has engendered a sense of great insignificance in the face of cosmic vastness. In disputing the earth-and human-centered view of the cosmos, long held by the Catholic Church, the eighteenth-century French thinker Voltaire wrote: "This little globe, nothing more than a point, rolls in space like so many other globes; we are lost in this immensity."[3]

Nonetheless, human consciousness and our awareness of the mystery of this immeasurable universe render us unique and generate for many people feelings of awe and humility that are almost religious. As tiny but knowing observers of this majestic cosmos, we have found ourselves living in a grander home than ever we knew before.

The History of a Planet

For most of us, one star, our own sun, is far more important than all the others, despite its quite ordinary standing among the billions of stars in the universe and its somewhat remote location on the outer edge of the Milky Way galaxy. Circling that star is a series of planets, formed of leftover materials from the sun's birth. One of those planets, the third from the sun and the fifth largest, is home to all of us. Human history—our history—takes place not only on the earth but also as part of the planet's history.

That history began with the emergence of the entire solar system about two-thirds of the way through cosmic history, some 4.7 billion years ago, or early September on the cosmic calendar. Geologists have learned a great deal about the history of the earth: the formation of its rocks and atmosphere; the movement of its continents; the collision of the tectonic plates that make up its crust; and the constant changes of its landscape as mountains formed, volcanoes erupted, and erosion transformed the surface of the planet. All of this has been happening for more than 4 billion years and continues still.

The most remarkable feature of the earth's history—and so far as we know unrepeated elsewhere—was the emergence of life from the chemical soup of the early planet. It happened rather quickly, only about 600 million years after the earth itself took shape, or late September on the cosmic calendar. Then for some 3 billion years, life remained at the level of microscopic single-celled organisms. According to biologists, the many species of larger multicelled creatures—all of the flowers, shrubs, and trees as well as all of the animals of land, sea, and air—have evolved in an explosive proliferation of life-forms, punctuated by massive die-offs as well, over the past 600 million years, or since mid-December on the cosmic calendar.

Each of these life forms or species has also had a history as its members struggled to find resources, cope with changing environments, and deal with competitors. The history of dinosaurs, for example, from their rise to their extinction, occupied about 165 million years, or about five days in late December on the cosmic calendar. Egocentric creatures that we are, however, human beings have usually focused their history books and history courses entirely on a single species—our own, *Homo sapiens*, humankind. On the cosmic calendar, *Homo sapiens* is an upstart primate whose entire history occurred in the last few minutes of December 31. Almost all of what we normally study in history courses—agriculture, writing, civilizations, empires, industrialization—took place in the very last minute of that cosmic year. The entire history of the United States occurred in the last second.

Yet during that very brief time, humankind has had a career more remarkable and arguably more consequential for the planet than any other species. At the heart of human uniqueness lies our amazing capacity for accumulating knowledge and skills. Other animals learn, of course, but for the most part they learn the same things over and over again. Twenty-first-century chimpanzees in the wild master the same skills as their ancestors did a million years ago. But the exceptional communication abilities provided by human language allow us to learn from one another, to express that learning in abstract symbols, and then to pass it on, cumulatively, to future generations. Thus we have moved from stone axes to lasers, from spears to nuclear weapons, from "talking drums" to the Internet, from grass huts to the pyramids of Egypt and Taj Mahal of India.

This extraordinary ability has translated into a human impact on the earth that is unprecedented among all living species.[4] Human populations have multiplied far more extensively and have come to occupy a far greater range of environments than has any other large animal. Through our ingenious technologies, we have appropriated for ourselves, according to recent calculations, some 25 to 40 percent of the solar energy that enters the food chain. We have recently gained access to the stored solar energy of coal, gas, and oil, all of which have been many millions of years in the making, and we have the capacity to deplete these resources in a few hundred or a few thousand years. Other forms of life have felt the impact of human activity, as numerous extinct or threatened species testify. Human beings have even affected the atmosphere itself as carbon dioxide and other emissions of the industrial age have warmed the climate of the planet. Thus human history has been, and remains, of great significance, not for ourselves alone, but also for the earth itself and for the many other living creatures with which we share it.

The History of the Human Species . . . in a Single Paragraph

The history of our species has occupied roughly the last 250,000 years, conventionally divided into three major phases, based on the kind of technology that was most widely practiced. The enormously long Paleolithic age, with its gathering and hunting way of life, accounts for 95 percent or more of the time that humans have occupied the planet. People utilizing a stone-age Paleolithic technology initially settled every major landmass on the earth and constructed the first human societies (see Chapter 1). Then beginning about 12,000 years ago with the first Agricultural Revolution, the domestication of plants and animals increasingly became the primary means of sustaining human life and societies. In giving rise to agricultural villages and chiefdoms, to pastoral communities depending on their herds of animals, and to state- and city-based civilizations, this agrarian way of life changed virtually everything and fundamentally reshaped human societies and their relationship to the natural order. Finally, around 1750 a quite sudden spurt in the rate of technological change, which we know as the Industrial Revolution, began to take hold. That vast increase in productivity, wealth, and human control over nature once again transformed almost every aspect of human life and gave rise to new kinds of societies that we call "modern."

Here then, in a single paragraph, is the history of humankind—the Paleolithic era, the agricultural era, and, most recently and briefly, the modern industrial era. Clearly this is a big picture perspective, based on the notion that the human species as a whole has a history that transcends any of its particular and distinctive cultures. That perspective—known variously as planetary, global, or world history—has become increasingly prominent among those who study the past. Why should this be so?

Why World History?

Not long ago—in the mid-twentieth century, for example—virtually all college-level history courses were organized in terms of particular civilizations or nations. In the United States, courses such as Western Civilization or some version of American History served to introduce students to the study of the past. Since then, however, a set of profound changes has pushed much of the historical profession in a different direction.

■ **Change**
Why has world history achieved an increasingly prominent place in American education in recent decades?

The world wars of the twentieth century, revealing as they did the horrendous consequences of unchecked nationalism, persuaded some historians that a broader view of the past might contribute to a sense of global citizenship. Economic and cultural globalization has highlighted both the interdependence of the world's peoples and their very unequal positions within that world. Moreover, we are aware as never before that our problems—whether they involve economic well-being, environmental deterioration, disease, or terrorism—respect no national boundaries. To many thoughtful people, a global present seemed to call for a global past. Furthermore, as colonial empires shrank and new nations asserted themselves on the world stage, these peoples also insisted that their histories be accorded equivalent treatment with those of Europe. An explosion of new knowledge about the histories of Asia, Africa, and pre-Columbian America erupted from the research of scholars around the world. All of this has generated a "world history movement," reflected in college and high school curricula, in numerous conferences and specialized studies, and in a proliferation of textbooks, of which this is one.

This world history movement has attempted to create a global understanding of the human past that highlights broad patterns cutting across particular civilizations and countries, while acknowledging in an inclusive fashion the distinctive histories of its many peoples. This is, to put it mildly, a tall order. How is it possible to encompass within a single book or course the separate stories of the world's various peoples? Surely it must be something more than just recounting the history of one civilization or culture after another. How can we distill a common history of humankind as a whole from the distinct trajectories of particular peoples? Because no world history book or course can cover everything, what criteria should we use for deciding what to include and what to leave out? Such questions have ensured no end of controversy among students, teachers, and scholars of world history, making it one of the most exciting fields of historical inquiry.

Change, Comparison, and Connection: The Three Cs of World History

Despite much debate and argument, one thing is reasonably clear: in world history, nothing stands alone. Every event, every historical figure, every culture, society, or civilization gains significance from its inclusion in some larger context. Most world historians would probably agree on three such contexts that define their field of study. Each of those contexts confronts a particular problem in our understanding of the past.

An initial context in which the particulars of world history can be situated is that of time and **change**. In world history, it is the "big picture" changes—those that impact large segments of humankind—that are of greatest interest. How did the transition from a gathering and hunting economy to one based on agriculture take place? How did cities, empires, and civilizations take shape in various parts of the world? What lay behind the emergence of a new balance of global power after 1500, one that featured the growing prominence of Europe on the world stage? What generated the amazing transformations of the "revolution of modernity" in recent centuries? How did the lives of women change as a result of industrialization?

A focus on change provides an antidote to a persistent tendency of human thinking that historians call "essentialism." A more common term is "stereotyping." It refers to our inclination to define particular groups of people with an unchanging or essential set of characteristics. Women are nurturing; peasants are conservative; Americans are aggressive; Hindus are religious. Serious students of history soon become aware that every significant category of people contains endless divisions and conflicts and that those human communities are constantly in flux. Peasants may often accept the status quo, except of course when they rebel, as they frequently have. Americans have experienced periods of isolationism and withdrawal from the world as well as times of aggressive engagement with it. Things change.

But some things persist, even if they also change. We should not allow an emphasis on change to blind us to the continuities of human experience. A recognizably Chinese state has operated for more than 2,000 years. Slavery and patriarchy persisted as human institutions for thousands of years until they were challenged in recent centuries, and in various forms they exist still. The teachings of Buddhism, Christianity, and Islam have endured for centuries, though with endless variations and transformations.

A second major context that operates constantly in world history books and courses is that of **comparison**. Whatever else it may be, world history is a comparative discipline, seeking to identify similarities and differences in the experience of the world's peoples. What is the difference between the development of agriculture in the Middle East and in Mesoamerica? Was the experience of women largely the same in all patriarchal societies? What did the Roman Empire and Han dynasty China have in common? Why did the Industrial Revolution and a modern way of life evolve first in Western Europe rather than somewhere else? What distinguished the French, Russian, and Chinese revolutions from one another? What different postures toward modernity emerged within the Islamic world? Describing and, if possible, explaining such similarities and differences are among the major tasks of world history. Comparison, then, is a recurring theme in this book, with expressions in every chapter.

Comparison has proven an effective tool in the struggle against Eurocentrism, the notion that Europeans or people of European descent have long been the primary movers and shakers of the historical process. That notion arose in recent centuries when Europeans were in fact the major source of innovation in the world and did for a time exercise something close to world domination. This temporary preeminence decisively shaped the way Europeans thought and wrote about their own histories and those of other people. In their own eyes, Europeans alone were progressive people, thanks to some cultural or racial superiority. Everyone else was to some degree stagnant, backward, savage, or barbarian. The unusual power of Europeans allowed them for a time to act on those beliefs and to convey such ways of thinking to much of the world. But comparative world history sets European achievements in a global and historical context, helping us to sort out what was distinctive about its development and what similarities it bore to other major regions of the world. Puncturing the pretensions of Eurocentrism has been high on the agenda of world history.

The art of comparison is a learned skill, entailing several steps. It requires, first of all, asking explicitly comparative questions and determining what particular cases will be involved. If you want to compare revolutions, for example, you would need to decide which ones you are considering—American, French, Russian, Chinese, Cuban. Defining categories of comparison is a further step. Precisely which characteristics of these revolutions will you compare—their origins, their ideologies, the social classes involved, their outcomes? Finally, how will you present your comparison? You might choose a case-by-case analysis in which you would describe, say, the American Revolution first, followed by an account of the Cuban Revolution, which makes explicit comparisons with the former. Or you might choose a thematic approach in which you would consider first the origins of both revolutions, followed by a comparison of their ideologies, and so on. You will find examples of both approaches in this book.

A third context that informs world history involves the interactions, encounters, and **connections** among different and often distant peoples. World history is often less about what happened within particular civilizations or cultures than about the processes and outcomes of their meetings with one another. Focusing on cross-cultural connections—whether those of conflict or more peaceful exchange—represents an effort to counteract a habit of thinking about particular peoples, states, or cultures as self-contained or isolated communities. Despite the historical emergence of many separate and distinct societies, none of them developed alone. Each was embedded in a network of relationships with both near and more distant peoples.

Moreover, these cross-cultural connections did not begin with Columbus. The Chinese, for example, interacted continuously with the nomadic peoples on their northern border; generated technologies that diffused across all of Eurasia; transmitted elements of their culture to Japan, Korea, and Vietnam; and assimilated a foreign religious tradition, Buddhism, which had originated in India. Though clearly distinctive, China was not a self-contained or isolated civilization.

The growing depth and significance of such cross-cultural relationships, known now as globalization, has been a distinguishing feature of the modern era. The voyages of Columbus brought the peoples of the Eastern and Western hemispheres into sustained contact for the first time with enormous global consequences. Several centuries later Europeans took advantage of their industrial power to bring much of the world temporarily under their control. The new technologies of the twentieth century have intertwined the economies, societies, and cultures of the world's peoples more tightly than ever before. During the past five centuries, the encounter with strangers, or at least with their ideas and practices, was everywhere among the most powerful motors of change in human societies. Thus world history remains always alert to the networks, webs, and cross-cultural encounters in which particular civilizations or peoples were enmeshed.

Changes, comparisons, and connections—all of them operating on a global scale—represent three contexts or frameworks that can help us bring some coherence to the multiple and complex stories of world history. They will recur repeatedly in the pages that follow.

Second Thoughts

What's the Significance?

big history, liv

cosmic calendar, liv

comparative history, lx

the three Cs, lx

Online Study Guide
bedfordstmartins.com
/highschool/strayer

Big Picture Questions

1. How do modern notions of the immense size and age of the universe affect your understanding of human history?
2. What examples of comparison, connection, and change in world history would you like to explore further as your course unfolds?
3. In what larger contexts might you place your own life history?

Next Steps: For Further Study

David Christian, *Maps of Time* (2004). A brilliant survey of "big history" by a leading world historian.

Ross Dunn, ed., *The New World History* (2000). A collection of articles dealing with the teaching of world history.

Patrick Manning, *Navigating World History* (2003). An up-to-date overview of the growth of world history, the field's achievements, and the debates within it.

For Web sites and documents related to this prologue, see **Make History** at bedfordstmartins.com /highschool/strayer.

Ways of the World

A Global History
with Sources
For AP*

PART ONE
First Things First
Beginnings in History

TO 500 B.C.E.

Contents

THE BIG PICTURE

Turning Points in Early World History

Human beings have long been inveterate storytellers. Our myths, legends, "fairy tales," oral traditions, family sagas, and more have sought to distill meaning from experience, while providing guidance for the living. Much the same might be said of modern historians, although they must operate within accepted rules of evidence. But all tellers of stories — ancient and modern alike — have to decide at what point to begin their accounts and what major turning points in those narratives to highlight. For world historians seeking to tell the story of humankind as a whole, four major "beginnings," each of them an extended historical process, have charted the initial stages of the human journey.

The Emergence of Humankind

Ever since Charles Darwin, most scholars have come to view human beginnings in the context of biological change on the planet. In considering this enormous process, we operate on a timescale quite different from the billions of years that mark the history of the universe and of the earth. According to archeologists and anthropologists, the evolutionary line of descent leading to *Homo sapiens* diverged from that leading to chimpanzees, our closest primate relatives, some 5 million to 6 million years ago, and it happened in eastern and southern Africa. There, perhaps twenty or thirty different species emerged, all of them members of the Homininae (or hominid) family of human-like creatures. What they all shared was bipedalism, the ability to walk upright on two legs. In 1976, the archeologist Mary Leakey uncovered in what is now Tanzania a series of footprints of three such hominid individuals, preserved in cooling volcanic ash about 3.5 million years ago. Two of them walked side by side, perhaps holding hands.

Over time, these hominid species changed. Their brains grew larger, as evidenced by the size of their skulls. About 2.3 million years ago, a hominid creature known as *Homo habilis* began to make and use simple stone tools. Others started to eat meat, at least occasionally. By 1 million years ago, some hominid species, especially *Homo erectus*, began to migrate out of Africa, and their remains have been found in various parts of Eurasia. This species is also associated with the first controlled use of fire.

Eventually all of these earlier hominid species died out, except one: *Homo sapiens*, ourselves. With a remarkable capacity for symbolic language that permitted the accumulation and transmission of learning, we too emerged first in Africa and quite recently, probably no more than 250,000 years ago (although specialists constantly debate these matters). For a long time, all of the small number of *Homo sapiens* lived in Africa,

Map 1.1   The Global Dispersion of Humankind (pp. 16–17)

but sometime after 100,000 years ago, they too began to migrate out of Africa onto the Eurasian landmass, then to Australia, and ultimately into the Western Hemisphere and the Pacific islands. The great experiment of human history had begun.

The Globalization of Humankind

Today, every significant landmass on earth is occupied by human beings, but it was not always so. A mere half million years ago our species did not exist, and only 100,000 years ago that species was limited to Africa and numbered, some scholars believe, fewer than 10,000 individuals. These ancient ancestors of ours, rather small in stature and not fast on foot, were armed with a very limited technology of stone tools with which to confront the multiple dangers of the natural world. But then, in perhaps the most amazing tale in all of human history, they moved from this very modest and geographically limited role in the scheme of things to a worldwide and increasingly dominant presence. What kinds of societies, technologies, and understandings of the world accompanied, and perhaps facilitated, this globalization of humankind?

The phase of human history during which these initial migrations took place is known to scholars as the Paleolithic era. The word "Paleolithic" literally means the "old stone age," but it refers more generally to a food-collecting or gathering and hunting way of life, before agriculture allowed people to grow food or raise animals deliberately. Lasting until roughly 11,000 years ago, the Paleolithic era represents over 95 percent of the time that human beings have inhabited the earth, although it accounts for only about 12 percent of the total number of people who have lived on the planet. It was during this time that *Homo sapiens* colonized the world, making themselves at home in every environmental niche, from the frigid Arctic to the rain forests of Central Africa and Brazil, in mountains, deserts, and plains. It was an amazing achievement, accomplished by no other large species. Accompanying this global migration were slow changes in the technological tool kits of early humankind as well as early attempts to impose meaning on the world through art, ritual, religion, and stories. Although often neglected by historians and history textbooks, this long period of the human experience merits greater attention and is the focus of the initial sections of Chapter 1.

The Revolution of Farming and Herding

In 2012, almost all of the world's 7 billion people lived from the food grown on farms and gardens and from domesticated animals raised for their meat, milk, or eggs. But before 11,000 years ago, no one survived in this fashion. Then, repeatedly and fairly rapidly, at least in world history terms, human communities in parts of the Middle East, Asia, Africa, and the Americas began the laborious process of domesticating animals and selecting seeds to be planted. This momentous accomplishment represents another "first" in the human story. After countless millennia of relying on the gathering of wild foods and the hunting of wild animals, why and how did human societies begin to practice farming and animal husbandry? What changes to human life did this new technology bring with it?

This food-producing revolution, also considered in Chapter 1, surely marks the single most significant and enduring transformation of the human condition. The entire period from the beginning of agriculture to the Industrial Revolution around 1750 might be considered a single phase of the human story—the age of agriculture—calculated now on a timescale of millennia or centuries rather than the more extended periods of earlier eras. Although the age of agriculture was far shorter than the immense Paleolithic era that preceded it, farming and raising animals allowed for a substantial increase in human numbers.

In the various beginnings of food production lay the foundations for some of the most enduring divisions within the larger human community. Much depended on the luck of the draw—on the climate and soils, on the various wild plants and animals that were available for domestication. Many agricultural peoples lived in small settled villages, independent of larger political structures, while drawing their food supply from their own gardens and farms. Some depended on root crops, such as potatoes in the Andes; others relied on tree crops, such as the banana; in the most favored areas, highly nutritious wild grains such as rice, wheat, or corn could be domesticated. In more arid regions where farming was difficult, some peoples, known as pastoralists, came to depend heavily on their herds of domesticated animals. Because they moved frequently and in regular patterns to search for pasturelands, they are often referred to as nomads. With regard to animal husbandry, the Americas were at a distinct disadvantage, for there were few large animals that could be tamed—no goats, sheep,

Mohenjo Daro (p. 70)

pigs, horses, camels, or cattle. In the Afro-Eurasian world, conflicts between settled agricultural peoples and more mobile pastoral peoples represented an enduring pattern of interaction across the region.

The Turning Point of Civilization

The most prominent and powerful human communities to emerge from the Agricultural Revolution were those often designated as "civilizations," more complex societies that were based in bustling cities and governed by formal states. Virtually all of the world's people now live in such societies, so that states and cities have come to seem almost natural. In world history terms, however, their appearance is a rather recent phenomenon. Not until several thousand years *after* the beginning of agriculture did the first cities and states emerge, around 3500 B.C.E. Well after 1000 C.E., substantial numbers of people still lived in communities without any state or urban structures. Nonetheless, people living in state- and city-based societies or civilizations have long constituted the most powerful and innovative human communities on the planet. They gave rise to empires of increasing size, to enduring cultural and religious traditions, to new technologies, to sharper class and gender inequalities, to new conceptions of masculinity and femininity, and to large-scale warfare.

For all of these reasons, civilizations have featured prominently in accounts of world history, sometimes crowding out the stories of other kinds of human communities. The earliest civilizations, which emerged in at least seven separate locations between 3500 and 500 B.C.E., have long fascinated professional historians and lovers of history everywhere. What was their relationship to the Agricultural Revolution? What new ways of living did they bring to the experience of humankind? These are the questions that inform Chapter 2.

A Note on Dates

Recently it has become standard in the Western world to refer to dates prior to the birth of Christ as B.C.E. (before the Common Era), replacing the earlier B.C. (before Christ) usage. This convention is an effort to become less Christian-centered and Eurocentric in our use of language, although the chronology remains linked to the birth of Jesus. Similarly, the time following the birth of Christ is referred to as C.E. (the Common Era) rather than A.D. (*Anno Domini*, Latin for "year of the Lord"). Dates in the more distant past are designated in this book as BP (before the present) or simply as so many "years ago." Of course, these conventions are only some of the many ways that human societies have reckoned time. The Chinese frequently dated important events in terms of the reign of particular emperors, while Muslims created a new calendar beginning with Year 1, marking Muhammad's forced relocation from Mecca to Medina in 622 C.E. As with so much else, the maps of time that we construct reflect the cultures in which we have been born and the historical experience of our societies.

Mapping Part One

Human entry to Americas,
30,000–15,000 BP
Chapter 1

Ishi
Chapter 1

Clovis culture
Chapter 1

Domestication of corn /
Olmec civilization
Chapters 1, 2

Domestication of potato /
Norte Chico
Chapters 1, 2

Human settlement
by 12,500 BP
Chapter 1

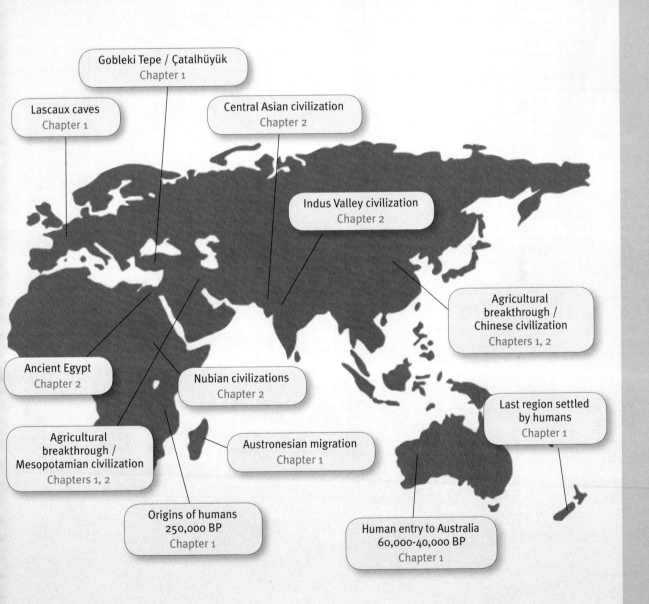

Lascaux caves
Chapter 1

Gobleki Tepe / Çatalhüyük
Chapter 1

Central Asian civilization
Chapter 2

Indus Valley civilization
Chapter 2

Agricultural
breakthrough /
Chinese civilization
Chapters 1, 2

Ancient Egypt
Chapter 2

Nubian civilizations
Chapter 2

Last region settled
by humans
Chapter 1

Agricultural
breakthrough /
Mesopotamian civilization
Chapters 1, 2

Austronesian migration
Chapter 1

Origins of humans
250,000 BP
Chapter 1

Human entry to Australia
60,000-40,000 BP
Chapter 1

First Peoples; First Farmers

Most of History in a Single Chapter

TO 4000 B.C.E.

"We do not want cattle, just wild animals to hunt and water that we can drink."[1] That was the view of Gudo Mahiya, a prominent member of the Hadza people of northern Tanzania, when he was questioned in 1997 about his interest in a settled life of farming and cattle raising. The Hadza then represented one of the very last peoples on earth to continue a way of life that was universal among humankind until 10,000 to 12,000 years ago. At the beginning of the twenty-first century, several hundred Hadza still made a living by hunting game, collecting honey, digging up roots, and gathering berries and fruit. They lived in quickly assembled grass huts located in small mobile camps averaging eighteen people and moved frequently around their remote region. Almost certainly their way of life is doomed, as farmers, governments, missionaries, and now tourists descend on them. The likely disappearance of their culture parallels the experience of many other such societies, which have been on the defensive against more numerous and powerful neighbors for 10,000 years.

NONETHELESS, THAT WAY OF LIFE SUSTAINED HUMANKIND for more than 95 percent of the time that our species has inhabited the earth. During countless centuries, human beings successfully adapted to a wide variety of environments without benefit of deliberate farming or animal husbandry. Instead, our early ancestors wrested a livelihood by gathering wild foods such as berries, nuts, roots, and grain; by scavenging dead animals; by hunting live animals; and by fishing. Known to scholars as "gathering and hunting" peoples, they were foragers

---

Paleolithic Art: The rock art of gathering and hunting peoples has been found in Africa, Europe, Australia, and elsewhere. This image from the San people of southern Africa represents aspects of their outer life in the form of wild animals and hunters with bows as well as the inner life of their shamans during a trance, reflected in the elongated figures with both human and animal features. (© De Agostini Picture Library/age fotostock) or food collectors rather than food producers. Because they used stone rather than metal tools, they also have been labeled "Paleolithic," or "Old Stone Age," peoples.

And then, around 12,000 ago years an enormous transformation began to unfold as a few human societies—in Eurasia, Africa, and the Americas alike—started to practice the deliberate cultivation of plants and the domestication of animals. This Agricultural or Neolithic (New Stone Age) Revolution marked a technological breakthrough of immense significance, with implications for every aspect of human life. This chapter, then, dealing with the long Paleolithic era and the initial transition to an agricultural way of life, represents most of human history—everything in fact before the advent of urban-based civilizations, which began around 5,500 years ago.

And yet, history courses and history books often neglect this long phase of the human journey and instead choose to begin the story with the early civilizations of Egypt, Mesopotamia, China, and elsewhere. Some historians identify "real history" with writing and so dismiss the Paleolithic and Neolithic eras as largely unknowable because their peoples did not write. Others, impressed with the rapid pace of change in human affairs in more recent times, assume that nothing much of real significance happened during the long Paleolithic era—and no change meant no history.

But does it make sense to ignore the first 200,000 years or more of human experience? Although written records are absent, scholars have learned a great deal about Paleolithic and Neolithic peoples through their material remains: stones and bones, fossilized seeds, rock paintings and engravings, and much more. Archeologists, biologists, botanists, demographers, linguists, and anthropologists have contributed much to our growing understanding of gathering and hunting peoples and early agricultural societies. (See Documents and Visual Sources: History before Writing, pp. 46–59.) Furthermore, the achievements of Paleolithic peoples—the initial settlement of the planet, the creation of the earliest human societies, the beginning of reflection on the great questions of life and death—deserve our attention. And the breakthrough to agriculture arguably represents the single most profound transformation of human life in all of history. The changes wrought by our early ancestors, though far slower than those of more recent times, were extraordinarily rapid in comparison to the transformation experienced by any other species. Those changes were almost entirely cultural or learned, rather than the product of biological evolution, and they provided the foundation on which all subsequent human history was constructed. Our grasp of the human past is incomplete—massively so—if we choose to disregard the Paleolithic and Neolithic eras.

SEEKING THE MAIN POINT

What arguments does this chapter make for paying serious attention to human history before the coming of "civilization"?

Out of Africa to the Ends of the Earth: First Migrations

The first 150,000 years or more of human experience was an exclusively African story. Around 200,000 to 250,000 years ago, in the grasslands of eastern and southern Africa, *Homo sapiens* first emerged, following in the footsteps of many other hominid

A Map of Time   (All dates BP: Before the Present)

250,000–200,000	Earliest *Homo sapiens* in Africa
100,000–60,000	Beginnings of migration out of Africa
70,000	Human entry into eastern Asia
60,000–40,000	Human entry into Australia (first use of boats)
45,000	Human entry into Europe
30,000	Extinction of large mammals in Australia
30,000–15,000	Human entry into the Americas
30,000–17,000	Cave art in Europe
25,000	Extinction of Neanderthals
16,000–10,000	End of last Ice Age (global warming)
12,000–10,000	Earliest agricultural revolutions
11,000	Extinction of large mammals in North America
After 6,000	First chiefdoms in Mesopotamia
6,000–5,000	Beginning of domestication of corn in southern Mexico
3,500–1,000	Austronesian migration to Pacific islands and Madagascar
1,000–700	Human entry into New Zealand (last major region to receive human settlers)

or human-like species before it. Time and climate have erased much of the record of these early people, and Africa has witnessed much less archeological research than have other parts of the world. Nonetheless, scholars have turned up evidence of distinctly human behavior in Africa long before its appearance elsewhere. Africa, almost certainly, was the place where the "human revolution" occurred, where "culture," defined as learned or invented ways of living, became more important than biology in shaping behavior.

What kinds of uniquely human activity show up in the early African record?[2] In the first place, human beings began to inhabit new environments within Africa—forests and deserts—where no hominids had lived before. Accompanying these movements of people were technological innovations of various kinds: stone blades and points fastened to shafts replaced the earlier hand axes; tools made from bones appeared, and so did grindstones. Evidence of hunting and fishing, not just the scavenging of dead animals, marks a new phase in human food collection. Settlements were planned around the seasonal movement of game and fish. Patterns of exchange over a distance of almost 200 miles indicate larger networks of human communication. The use of body ornaments, beads, and pigments such as ochre as well as possible planned burials suggest the kind of social and symbolic behavior that has characterized human activity ever since. The earliest evidence for this kind of human activity comes from the Blombos Cave in South Africa, where excavations in 2008 uncovered a workshop for the processing of ochre dating to around 100,000 years ago, well before such behavior surfaced elsewhere in the world.

Then, sometime between 100,000 and 60,000 years ago, human beings began their long trek out of Africa and into Eurasia, Australia, the Americas, and, much later, the islands of the Pacific (see Map 1.1). In occupying the planet, members of our species accomplished the remarkable feat of learning to live in virtually every environmental niche on earth, something that no other large animal had done; and they did it with only stone tools and a gathering and hunting technology to aid them. Furthermore, much of this long journey occurred during the difficult climatic conditions of the last Ice Age (at its peak around 20,000 years ago), when thick ice sheets covered much of the Northern Hemisphere. The Ice Age did give these outward-bound human beings one advantage, however: the amount of water frozen in northern glaciers lowered sea levels around the planet, creating land bridges among various regions that were separated after the glaciers melted. Britain was then joined to Europe; eastern Siberia was connected to Alaska; and parts of what is now Indonesia were linked to mainland Southeast Asia.

Into Eurasia

■ **Change**
What was the sequence of human migration across the planet?

Human migration out of Africa led first to the Middle East and from there westward into Europe about 45,000 years ago and eastward into Asia. Among the most carefully researched areas of early human settlement in Eurasia are those in southern France and northern Spain. Colder Ice Age climates around 20,000 years ago apparently pushed more northerly European peoples southward into warmer regions. There they altered their hunting habits, focusing on reindeer and horses, and developed new technologies such as spear throwers and perhaps the bow and arrow as well as many different kinds of stone tools. Most remarkably, they also left a record of their world in hundreds of cave paintings, depicting bulls, horses, and other animals, brilliantly portrayed in colors of red, yellow, brown, and black. Images of human beings, impressions of human hands, and various abstract designs sometimes accompanied the cave paintings (see Visual Source 1.1, p. 52).

Farther east, archeologists have uncovered still other remarkable Paleolithic adaptations to Ice Age conditions. Across the vast plains of Central Europe, Ukraine, and Russia, new technologies emerged, including bone needles, multilayered clothing, weaving, nets, storage pits, baskets, and pottery. Partially underground dwellings constructed from the bones and tusks of mammoths compensated for the absence of caves and rock shelters. All of this suggests that some of these people had lived in more permanent settlements, at least temporarily abandoning their nomadic journeys. Associated with these Eastern European peoples were numerous female figurines, the earliest of which was uncovered in 2008 in Germany and dated to at least 35,000 years ago. Carved from stone, antlers, mammoth tusks, or, occasionally, baked clay, these so-called Venus figurines depict the female form, often with exaggerated breasts, buttocks, hips, and stomachs. Similar figurines have been found all across Eurasia, raising any number of controversial questions. Does their widespread distribution suggest a network of human communication and cultural diffusion over a wide area? If so, did they move from west to east or vice versa? What do they mean in terms of women's roles and status in Paleolithic societies?

Into Australia

Early human migration to Australia, perhaps 60,000 years ago, came from Indonesia and involved another first in human affairs—the use of boats. Over time, people settled in most regions of this huge continent, though quite sparsely. Scholars estimate the population of Australia at about 300,000 in 1788, when the first Europeans arrived. Over tens of

Australian Rock Art
This Australian rock painting utilized the distinctive Aboriginal X-ray style, showing the internal bones and organs. The largest and main figure at the top is a Creation Ancestor known as Namondjok. To the right is Namarrgon, or Lightning Man, who generates the tremendous lightning storms that occur during the rainy season. The arc around his body represents the lightning, while the axes on his head, elbow, and feet are used to split the dark clouds, creating thunder and lightning. The female figure beneath Namondjok is Barrginj, the wife of Lightning Man, while the people below her, elaborately dressed, are perhaps on their way to a ceremony. (J. Marshall/Visual Connection Archive)

thousands of years, they had developed perhaps 250 languages; collected a wide variety of bulbs, tubers, roots, seeds, and cereal grasses; and hunted large and small animals, as well as birds, fish, and other marine life. A relatively simple technology, appropriate to a gathering and hunting economy, sustained Australia's Aboriginal people into modern times. When outsiders arrived in the late eighteenth century, Aboriginals still practiced that ancient way of life, despite the presence of agriculture in nearby New Guinea.

Accompanying their technological simplicity and traditionalism was the development of an elaborate and complex outlook on the world, known as the Dreamtime. Expressed in endless stories, in extended ceremonies, and in the evocative rock art of the continent's peoples, the Dreamtime recounted the beginning of things: how ancestral beings crisscrossed the land, creating its rivers, hills, rocks, and waterholes; how various peoples came to inhabit the land; and how they related to animals and to one another. In this view of the world, everything in the natural order was a vibration, an echo, a footprint of these ancient happenings, which link the current inhabitants intimately to particular places and to timeless events in the past.

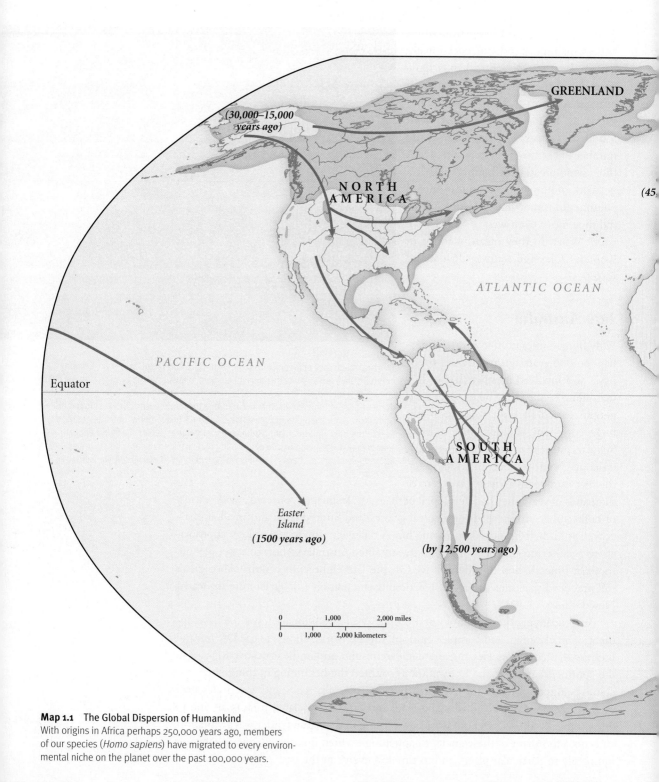

Map 1.1   The Global Dispersion of Humankind
With origins in Africa perhaps 250,000 years ago, members
of our species (*Homo sapiens*) have migrated to every environmental niche on the planet over the past 100,000 years.

The journeys of the Dreamtime's ancestral beings reflect the networks of migration, communication, and exchange that linked the continent's many Paleolithic peoples. Far from isolated groups, they had long exchanged particular stones, pigments, materials for ropes and baskets, wood for spears, feathers and shells for ornaments, and an addictive psychoactive drug known as *pituri* over distances of hundreds of miles.[3] Songs, dances, stories, and rituals likewise circulated. Precisely how far back in time these networks extend is difficult to pinpoint, but it seems clear that Paleolithic Australia, like ancient Europe, was both many separate worlds and, at the same time, one loosely connected world.

Into the Americas

The earliest settlement of the Western Hemisphere occurred much later than that of Australia, for it took some time for human beings to penetrate the frigid lands of eastern Siberia, which was the jumping-off point for the move into the Americas. Experts continue to argue about precisely when the first migrations occurred (somewhere between 30,000 and 15,000 years ago), about the route of migration (by land across the Bering Strait or by sea down the west coast of North America), about how many separate migrations took place, and about how long it took to penetrate to the tip of South America.[4] There is, however, good evidence of human activity in southern Chile by 12,500 years ago.

One of the first clearly defined and widespread cultural traditions in the Americas is associated with people who made a distinctive projectile point, known to archeologists as a Clovis point. Scattered all over North America, Clovis culture flourished briefly around 13,000 years ago. Scattered bands of Clovis people ranged over huge areas, camping along rivers, springs, and waterholes, where large animals congregated. Although they certainly hunted smaller animals and gathered many wild plants, Clovis men show up in the archeological record most dramatically as hunters of very large mammals, such as mammoths and bison. Killing a single mammoth could provide food for many weeks or, in cold weather, for much of the winter. The wide distribution of Clovis point technology suggests yet again a regional pattern of cultural diffusion and at least indirect communication over a large area.

Then, rather abruptly, all trace of the Clovis culture disappeared from the archeological record at about the same time that many species of large animals, including the mammoth and several species of horses and camels, also became extinct. Did the Clovis people hunt these animals to extinction and then vanish themselves as their source of food disappeared? Or did the drier climate that came with the end of the Ice Age cause this megafaunal extinction? Experts disagree, but what happened next was the creation of a much greater diversity of cultures as people adapted to this new situation in various ways. Hunters on the Great Plains continued to pursue bison, which largely avoided the fate of the mammoths. Others learned to live in the desert, taking advantage of seasonal plants and smaller animals, while those who lived near the sea, lakes, or streams drew on local fish and birds. Many peoples retained their gathering and hunting way of life into modern times, while others became farmers and, in a few favored regions, later developed cities and large-scale states.[5]

Into the Pacific

The last phase of the great human migration to the ends of the earth took place in the Pacific Ocean and was distinctive in many ways. In the first place, it occurred quite recently, jumping off only about 3,500 years ago from the Bismarck and Solomon Islands near New Guinea as well as from the islands of the Philippines. It was everywhere a waterborne migration, making use of oceangoing canoes and remarkable navigational skills, and it happened very quickly and over a huge area of the planet. Speaking Austronesian languages that trace back to southern China, these oceanic voyagers had settled every habitable piece of land in the Pacific basin within about 2,500 years. Other Austronesians had sailed west from Indonesia across the Indian Ocean to settle the island of Madagascar off the coast of eastern Africa. This extraordinary process of expansion made the Austronesian family of languages the most geographically widespread in the world and their trading networks, reaching some 5,000 miles from western Indonesia to the mid-Pacific, the most extensive. With the occupation of Aotearoa (New Zealand) around 1000 to 1300 C.E., the initial human settlement of the planet was finally complete (see Map 1.2).

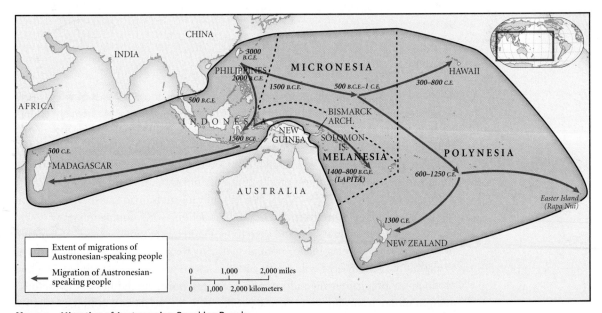

Map 1.2 Migration of Austronesian-Speaking People
People speaking Austronesian languages completed the human settlement of the earth quite recently as they settled the islands of the vast Pacific and penetrated the Indian Ocean to Madagascar, off the coast of southeast Africa.

■ Comparison
How did Austronesian migrations differ from other early patterns of human movement?

In contrast with all·of the other initial migrations, these Pacific voyages were undertaken by agricultural people who carried both domesticated plants and animals in their canoes. Both men and women made these journeys, suggesting a deliberate intention to colonize new lands. Virtually everywhere they went, two developments followed. One was the creation of highly stratified societies or chiefdoms, of which ancient Hawaiian society is a prime example. In Hawaii, an elite class of chiefs with political and military power ruled over a mass of commoners. The other development involved the quick extinction of many species of animals, especially large flightless birds such as the *moa* of New Zealand, which largely vanished within a century of human arrival. On Rapa Nui (Easter Island) between the fifteenth and seventeenth centuries C.E., deforestation accompanied famine, violent conflict, and a sharp population decline in this small island society, while the elimination of large trees ensured that no one could leave the island, for they could no longer build the canoes that had brought them there.[6]

The Ways We Were

During their long journeys across the earth, Paleolithic people created a multitude of separate and distinct societies, each with its own history, culture, language, identity, stories, and rituals, but the limitations of a gathering and hunting technology using stone tools imposed some commonalities on these ancient people. Based on the archeological record and on gathering and hunting societies that still exist in modern times, scholars have sketched out some of the common features of these early societies.

The First Human Societies

Above all else, these Paleolithic societies were small, consisting of bands of twenty-five to fifty people, in which all relationships were intensely personal and normally understood in terms of kinship. The available technology permitted only a very low population density and ensured an extremely slow rate of population growth. Some scholars speculate that this growth was dramatically interrupted around 70,000 years ago by an enormous volcanic eruption on the island of Sumatra in present-day Indonesia, resulting in a cooler and drier global climate and causing human numbers to drop to some 10,000 or less. From that point of near extinction, world population grew slowly to 500,000 by 30,000 years ago and then to 6 million by 10,000 years ago.[7] Paleolithic bands were seasonally mobile or nomadic, moving frequently and in regular patterns to exploit the resources of wild plants and animals on which they depended. The low productivity of a gathering and hunting economy normally did not allow the production of much surplus, and because people were on the move so often, transporting an accumulation of goods was out of the question.

All of this resulted in highly egalitarian societies, lacking the many inequalities of wealth and power that came later with agricultural and urban life. With no formal chiefs, kings, bureaucrats, soldiers, nobles, or priests, Paleolithic men and women were perhaps freer of tyranny and oppression than any subsequent kind of human society, even if they were more constrained by the forces of nature. Without specialists, most people possessed the same set of skills, although male and female tasks often differed sharply. The male role as hunter, especially of big game, perhaps gave rise to one of the first criteria of masculine identity: success in killing large animals.

Relationships between women and men usually were far more equal than in later societies. As the primary food gatherers, women provided the bulk of the family income. One study of the San people, a surviving gathering and hunting society in southern Africa, found that plants, normally gathered by women, provided 70 percent of the diet, while meat, hunted by men, accounted for just 30 percent. This division of labor underpinned what anthropologist Richard Lee called "relative equality between the sexes with no-one having the upper hand." Among the San, teenagers engaged quite freely in sex play, and the concept of female virginity was apparently unknown, as were rape, wife beating, and the sexual double standard. Although polygamy was permitted, most marriages were in fact monogamous because women strongly resisted sharing a husband with another wife. Frequent divorce among very young couples allowed women to leave unsatisfactory marriages easily. Lee found that longer-term marriages seemed to be generally fulfilling and stable. Both men and women expected a satisfying sexual relationship, and both occasionally took lovers, although discreetly.[8]

When the British navigator and explorer Captain James Cook first encountered the gathering and hunting peoples of Australia in 1770, he described them, perhaps a little enviously, in this way:

They live in a Tranquillity which is not disturb'd by the Inequality of Conditions: The Earth and sea of their own accord furnishes them with all things necessary for life, they covet not Magnificient houses, Household-stuff.... In short they seem'd to set no value upon any thing we gave them.... They think themselves provided with all the necessarys of Life.[9]

The Europeans who settled permanently among such people some twenty years later, however, found a society in which physical competition among men was expressed in frequent one-on-one combat and in formalized but bloody battles. It also meant recurrent, public, and quite brutal beatings of wives by their husbands.[10] And some

■ **Change**
In what ways did a gathering and hunting economy shape other aspects of Paleolithic societies?

Native Australians
A small number of Aboriginal Australians maintained their gathering and hunting way of life well into the twentieth century. Here an older woman shows two young boys how to dig for honey ants, a popular food. (Bill Bachman/Alamy)

Aboriginal myths sought to explain how men achieved power over women. Among the San, frequent arguments about the distribution of meat or the laziness or stinginess of particular people generated conflict, as did rivalries among men over women. Richard Lee identified twenty-two murders that had occurred between 1920 and 1955 and several cases in which the community came together to conduct an execution of particularly disruptive individuals. More generally, recent studies have found that in Paleolithic societies some 15 percent of deaths occurred through violence at the hands of other people, a rate far higher than in later civilizations, where violence was largely monopolized by the state.[11] Although sometimes romanticized by outsiders, the relative equality of Paleolithic societies did not always ensure a utopia of social harmony.

Like all other human cultures, Paleolithic societies had rules and structures. A gender-based division of labor usually cast men as hunters and women as gatherers. Values emphasizing reciprocal sharing of goods resulted in clearly defined rules about distributing the meat from an animal kill. Various rules about incest and adultery governed sexual behavior, while understandings about who could hunt or gather in particular territories regulated economic activity. Leaders arose as needed to organize a task such as a hunt, but without conferring permanent power on individuals. (See Document 1.1, pp. 47–50, for an insider's description of a contemporary gathering and hunting society.)

Economy and the Environment

For a long time, modern people viewed their gathering and hunting ancestors as primitive and impoverished, barely eking out a living from the land. In more recent decades, anthropologists studying contemporary Paleolithic societies—those that survived into the twentieth century—began to paint a different picture. They noted that gathering and hunting people frequently worked fewer hours to meet their material needs than did people in agricultural or industrial societies and so had more leisure time. One scholar referred to them as "the original affluent society," not because they had so much but because they wanted or needed so little.[12] Nonetheless, life expectancy was low, probably little more than thirty-five years on average. Life in the wild was surely dangerous, and dependency on the vagaries of nature rendered it insecure as well.

But Paleolithic people also acted to alter the natural environment substantially. The use of deliberately set fires to encourage the growth of particular plants certainly changed the landscape and in Australia led to the proliferation of fire-resistant eucalyptus trees at the expense of other plant species. In many parts of the world—Australia, North America, Siberia, Madagascar, Pacific islands—the extinction of various large animals followed fairly quickly after the arrival of human beings, leading scholars to suggest that Paleolithic humankind played a major role, coupled perhaps with changing climates, in the disappearance of these animals. Other hominid, or humanlike, species, such as the Neanderthals in Europe or "Flores man," discovered in 2003 in Indonesia, also perished after living side by side with *Homo sapiens* for millennia. Whether their disappearance occurred through massacre, interbreeding, or peaceful competition, they were among the casualties of the rise of humankind. Thus the biological environment inhabited by gathering and hunting peoples was not wholly natural but was shaped in part by their own hands.

The Realm of the Spirit

The religious or spiritual dimension of Paleolithic culture has been hard to pin down because bones and stones tell us little about what people thought, art is subject to many interpretations, and the experience of contemporary gathering and hunting peoples may not reflect the distant past. Clear evidence exists, however, for a rich interior life. The presence of rock art deep inside caves and far from living spaces suggests a "ceremonial space" separate from ordinary life. The extended rituals of contemporary Australian Aboriginals, which sometimes last for weeks, confirm this impression, as do numerous and elaborate burial sites found throughout the world. No full-time religious specialists or priests led these ceremonies, but part-time shamans (people believed to be especially skilled at dealing with the spirit world) emerged as the need arose. Such people often entered an altered state of consciousness or a trance while performing the ceremonies, often with the aid of psychoactive drugs.

Precisely how Paleolithic people understood the nonmaterial world is hard to reconstruct, and speculation abounds. Linguistic evidence from ancient Africa suggests a variety of understandings: some Paleolithic societies were apparently monotheistic; others saw several levels of supernatural beings, including a Creator Deity, various territorial spirits, and the spirits of dead ancestors; still others believed in an impersonal force suffused throughout the natural order that could be accessed by shamans during a trance dance.[13] The prevalence of Venus figurines and other symbols all across Europe has convinced some, but not all, scholars that Paleolithic religious thought had a strongly feminine dimension, embodied in a Great Goddess and concerned with the regeneration and renewal of life.[14] Many gathering and hunting peoples likely developed a cyclical view of time that drew on the changing phases of the moon and on the cycles of female fertility—birth, menstruation, pregnancy, new birth, and death. These understandings of the cosmos, which saw endlessly repeated patterns of regeneration and disintegration, differed from later Western views, which saw time moving in a straight line toward some predetermined goal.[15] Nor did Paleolithic people make sharp distinctions between the material and spiritual worlds, for they understood that animals, rocks, trees, mountains, and much more were animated by spirit or possessed souls of their own. Earlier scholars sometimes dubbed such views as "animistic" and regarded them as "primitive" or "simple" in comparison to later literate religions. More recent accounts generally avoid the term, preferring to focus on the specifics of particular religious traditions rather than some overall evolutionary scheme.

The Willendorf Venus
Less than four and a half inches in height and dating to about 25,000 years ago, this female figure, which was found near the town of Willendorf in Austria, has become the most famous of the many Venus figurines. Certain features—the absence of both face and feet, the coils of hair around her head, the prominence of her breasts and sexual organs—have prompted much speculation among scholars about the significance of these intriguing carvings. (Naturhistorisches Museum, Vienna, Austria/The Bridgeman Art Library)

Snapshot   **Paleolithic Era in Perspective**[16]

	Paleolithic Era (from 250,000 to 10,000 years ago)	Agricultural Era (from 10,000 to 200 years ago)	Modern Industrial Era (since 1800)
Duration of each era, as a percentage of 250,000 years	96%	4%	0.08%
Percent of people who lived, out of 80 billion total	12%	68%	20%
Percent of years lived in each era (reflects changing life expectancies)	9%	62%	29%

Settling Down: The Great Transition

■ Change

Why did some Paleolithic peoples abandon earlier, more nomadic ways and begin to live a more settled life?

Though glacially slow by contemporary standards, changes in Paleolithic cultures occurred over time as people moved into new environments, as populations grew, as climates altered, and as different human groups interacted with one another. For example, all over the Afro-Eurasian world after 25,000 years ago, a tendency toward the miniaturization of stone tools is evident, analogous perhaps to the miniaturization of electronic components in the twentieth century. Known as micro-blades, these smaller and more refined spear points, arrowheads, knives, and scrapers were carefully struck from larger cores and often mounted in antler, bone, or wooden handles.[17] Another important change in the strategies of Paleolithic people involved the collection of wild grains, which represented a major addition to the food supply beyond the use of roots, berries, and nuts. This innovation originated in northeastern Africa around 16,000 years ago.

But the most striking and significant change in the lives of Paleolithic peoples occurred as the last Ice Age came to an end between 16,000 and 10,000 years ago. What followed was a general global warming, though one with periodic fluctuations and cold snaps. Unlike the contemporary global warming, generated by human activity and especially the burning of fossil fuels, this ancient warming phase was a wholly natural phenomenon, part of a long cycle of repeated heating and cooling characteristic of the earth's climatic history. Plants and animals unable to survive in the Ice Age climate now flourished and increased their range, providing a much richer and more diverse environment for many human societies. Under these improved conditions, human populations grew, and some previously nomadic gathering and hunting communities, but not all of them, found it possible to settle down and live in more permanent settlements or villages. These societies were becoming both larger and more complex, and it was less possible to simply move away if trouble struck. Settlement also meant that households could store and accumulate goods to a greater degree than previously. Because some people were more energetic, more talented, or luckier than others, the thin edge of inequality gradually began to wear away the egalitarianism of Paleolithic communities.

Changes along these lines emerged in many places. Paleolithic societies in Japan, known as Jomon, settled down in villages by the sea, where they greatly expanded the number of animals, both land and marine, that they consumed. They also created some of the world's first pottery, along with dugout canoes, paddles, bows, bowls, and tool handles, all made from wood. A similar pattern of permanent settlement, a broader range of food sources, and specialized technologies is evident in parts of Scandinavia, Southeast Asia, North America, and the Middle East between 12,000 and 4,000 years ago. In Labrador, longhouses accommodating 100 people appear in the archeological record. Far more elaborate burial sites in many places testify to the growing complexity of human communities and the kinship systems that bound them together. Separate cemeteries for dogs suggest that humankind's best friend was also our first domesticated animal friend.

Among the most stunning and unexpected achievements of such sedentary Paleolithic people comes from the archeological complex of Göbekli Tepe (goh-BEHK-lee TEH-peh) in southeastern Turkey, under excavation since 1994. Dating to 11,600

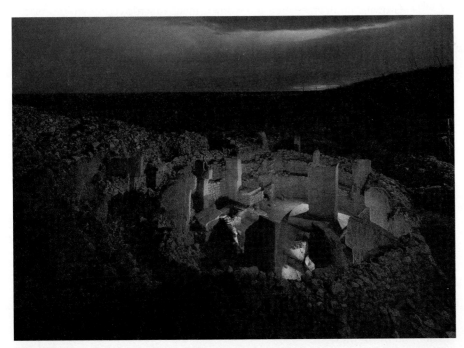

Göbekli Tepe
This monumental ceremonial site in southern Turkey, constructed by gathering and hunting people around 11,600 years ago, has surprised scholars, who have normally regarded such structures as the product of agricultural peoples. (Vincent J. Musi/National Geographic Stock)

years ago, it consists of massive limestone pillars, some weighing as much as sixteen tons, which were carved in a T shape and arranged in a set of some twenty circles or rings. Gracefully carved animals—gazelles, snakes, boars, foxes—decorate the pillars. Göbekli Tepe was probably a ceremonial site, for little evidence of human habitation has been found. Those who constructed or staffed the complex dined on animals hunted at a distance. Dubbed the "world's oldest temple," Göbekli Tepe was the product of people practicing a gathering and hunting way of life though living at least part of the year in settled villages. It represents a kind of monumental construction long associated only with agricultural societies and civilizations.[18]

Studies of more recent gathering and hunting societies, which were able to settle permanently in particular resource-rich areas, show marked differences from their more nomadic counterparts. Among the Chumash of southern California, for example, early Spanish settlers found peoples who had developed substantial and permanent structures accommodating up to seventy persons, hereditary political elites, elements of a market economy including the use of money and private ownership of some property, and the beginnings of class distinctions.

This process of settling down among gathering and hunting peoples—and the changes that followed from it—marked a major turn in human history, away from countless millennia of nomadic journeys by very small communities. It also provided the setting within which the next great transition would occur. Growing numbers of men and women, living in settled communities, placed a much greater demand on the environment than did small bands of wandering people. Therefore, it is perhaps not surprising that among the innovations that emerged in these more complex gathering and hunting societies was yet another way for increasing the food supply—agriculture.

SUMMING UP SO FAR

How do you understand the significance of the long Paleolithic era in the larger context of world history?

Breakthroughs to Agriculture

The chief feature of the long Paleolithic era—and the first human process to operate on a global scale—was the initial settlement of the earth. Then, beginning around 12,000 years ago, a second global pattern began to unfold—agriculture. The terms "Neolithic (New Stone Age) Revolution" or "Agricultural Revolution" refer to the deliberate cultivation of particular plants as well as the taming and breeding of particular animals. Thus a whole new way of life gradually replaced the earlier practices of gathering and hunting in most parts of the world. Although it took place over centuries and millennia, the coming of agriculture represented a genuinely revolutionary transformation of human life all across the planet and provided the foundation for almost everything that followed: growing populations, settled villages, animal-borne diseases, horse-drawn chariot warfare, cities, states, empires, civilizations, writing, literature, and much more.

Among the most revolutionary aspects of the age of agriculture was a new relationship between humankind and other living things, for now men and women were not simply using what they found in nature but were actively changing nature as well. They were consciously "directing" the process of evolution. The actions of farmers in the Americas, for example, transformed corn from a plant with a cob of an inch or so to one measuring about six inches by 1500. Later efforts more than doubled that length. Farmers everywhere stamped the landscape with a human imprint in the form of fields with boundaries, terraced hillsides, irrigation ditches, and canals. Animals too were transformed as selective breeding produced sheep that grew more wool, cows that gave more milk, and chickens that laid more eggs than their wild counterparts.

This was "domestication"—the taming, and the changing, of nature for the benefit of humankind—but it created a new kind of mutual dependence. Many domesticated plants and animals could no longer survive in the wild and relied on human action or protection to reproduce successfully. Similarly, human beings in the agricultural era lost the skills of their gathering and hunting ancestors, and in any event there were now too many people to live in that older fashion. As a consequence, farmers and herders became dependent on their domesticated plants and animals. From an outside point of view, it might well seem that corn and cows had tamed human beings, using people to ensure their own survival and growth as a species, as much as the other way around.

A further revolutionary aspect of the agricultural age is summed up in the term "intensification." It means getting more for less, in this case more food and resources— far more—from a much smaller area of land than was possible with a gathering and hunting technology. More food meant more people. Growing populations in turn required an even greater need for the intensive exploitation of the environment. And so was launched the continuing human effort to "subdue the earth" and to "have dominion over it," as the biblical story in Genesis recorded God's command to Adam and Eve.

Common Patterns

Perhaps the most extraordinary feature of the Neolithic or Agricultural Revolution was that it occurred, separately and independently, in many widely scattered parts of the world: the Fertile Crescent of Southwest Asia, several places in sub-Saharan Africa, China, New Guinea, Mesoamerica, the Andes, and eastern North America (see Map 1.3). Even more remarkably, all of this took place at roughly the same time (at least as measured by the 250,000-year span of human history on the planet)—between 12,000 and 4,000 years ago. These facts have generated many questions with which historians have long struggled. Why was the Agricultural Revolution so late in the history of humankind? What was unique about the period after 10,000 B.C.E. that may have triggered or facilitated this vast upheaval? In what different ways did the Agricultural Revolution take shape in its various locations? How did it spread from its several points of origin to the rest of the earth? And what impact did it have on the making of human societies?

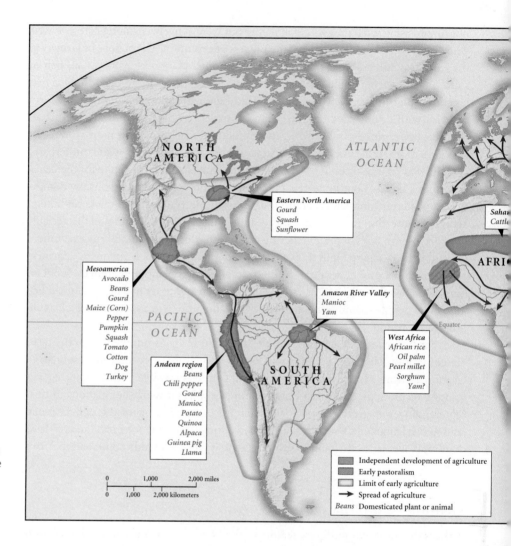

Map 1.3 The Global Spread of Agriculture and Pastoralism
From ten or more separate points of origin, agriculture spread to adjacent areas, eventually encompassing almost all of the world's peoples.

■ Change

What accounts for the emergence of agriculture after countless millennia of human life without it?

It is no accident that the Agricultural Revolution coincided with the end of the last Ice Age, a process of global warming that began some 16,000 years ago. By about 11,000 years ago, the Ice Age was over, and climatic conditions similar to those of our own time generally prevailed. This was but the latest of some twenty-five periods of glaciation and warming that have occurred over the past several million years of the earth's history and that are caused by minor periodic changes in the earth's orbit around the sun. The end of the last Ice Age, however, coincided with the migration of *Homo sapiens* across the planet and created new conditions that made agriculture more possible. Combined with active hunting by human societies, climate change in some areas helped to push into extinction various species of large mammals on which Paleolithic people had depended, thus adding to the pressure to find new food sources. The warmer, wetter, and more stable conditions, particularly in the tropical and tem-

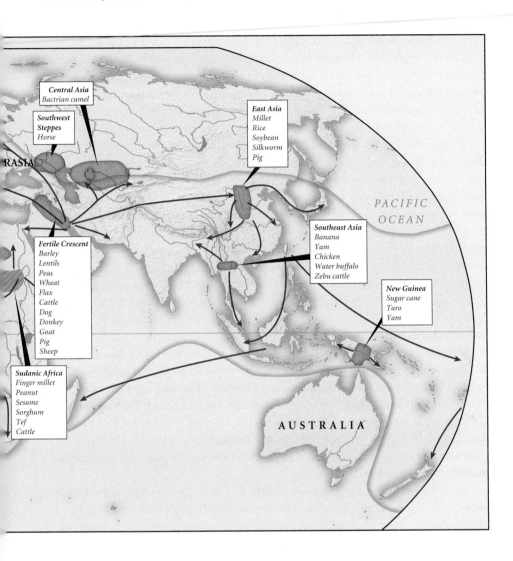

perate regions of the earth, also permitted the flourishing of more wild plants, especially cereal grasses, which were the ancestors of many domesticated crops. What climate change took away with one hand, it apparently gave back with the other.

Over their long history, gathering and hunting peoples had already developed a deep knowledge of the natural world and, in some cases, the ability to manage it actively. They had learned to make use of a large number of plants and to hunt and eat both small and large animals, creating what archeologists call a "broad-spectrum diet." In the Middle East, people had developed sickles for cutting newly available wild grain, baskets to carry it, mortars and pestles to remove the husk, and storage pits to preserve it. Peoples of the Amazon and elsewhere had learned to cut back some plants to encourage the growth of their favorites. Native Australians had built elaborate traps in which they could capture, store, and harvest large numbers of eels.

In hindsight, much of this looks like a kind of preparation for agriculture. Because women in particular had long been intimately associated with collecting wild plants, they were the likely innovators who led the way to deliberate farming, with men perhaps taking the lead in domesticating animals. Clearly the knowledge and technology necessary for agriculture were part of a longer process involving more intense human exploitation of the earth. Nowhere was agriculture an overnight invention.

Using such technologies, and benefiting from the global warming at the end of the last Ice Age, gathering and hunting peoples in various resource-rich areas were able to settle down and establish more permanent villages, abandoning their nomadic ways and more intensively exploiting the local area. In settling down, however, they soon lost some of the skills of their ancestors and found themselves now required to support growing populations. Evidence for increasing human numbers around the world during this period of global warming has persuaded some scholars that agriculture was a response to the need for additional food, perhaps even a "food crisis." Such conditions surely motivated people to experiment and to innovate in an effort to increase the food supply. Clearly, many of the breakthroughs to agriculture occurred only *after* gathering and hunting peoples had already grown substantially in numbers and had established a sedentary way of life.

Göbekli Tepe in Turkey provides a possible example of the process. Klaus Schmidt, the chief archeologist at the site, argues that the need for food to supply those who built and maintained this massive religious complex may well have stimulated the development of agriculture in the area. Certainly, some of the earliest domesticated wheat in the region has been located just twenty miles away and at roughly the same date. If this connection holds, it suggests that the human impulse to worship collectively in a village-based setting played a significant role in generating the epic transformation of the Agricultural Revolution.

These were some of the common patterns that facilitated the Agricultural Revolution. New opportunities appeared with the improved climatic conditions at the end of the Ice Age. New knowledge and technology emerged as human communities explored and exploited that changed environment. The disappearance of many large mammals, growing populations, newly settled ways of life, and fluctuations in the process of global warming—all of these represented pressures or incentives to increase food production and thus to minimize the risks of life in a new era.[19] From some combination of these opportunities and incentives emerged the profoundly transforming process of the Agricultural Revolution.

Variations

This new way of life initially operated everywhere with a simple technology—the digging stick or hoe. Plows were developed much later. But the several transitions to this hoe-based agriculture, commonly known as horticulture, varied considerably, depending on what plants and animals were available locally. For example, potatoes were found in the Andes region, but not in Africa or Asia; wheat and wild pigs existed in the Fertile Crescent, but not in the Americas. Furthermore, of the world's 200,000 plant species, only several hundred have been domesticated, and just five of these — wheat, corn, rice, barley, and sorghum — supply more than half of the calories that sustain human life. Only fourteen species of large mammals have been successfully domesticated, of which sheep, pigs, goats, cattle, and horses have been the most important. Because they are stubborn, nervous, solitary, or finicky, many animals simply cannot be readily domesticated.[20] In short, the kind of Agricultural Revolution that unfolded in particular places depended very much on what happened to be available locally, and that in turn depended on sheer luck.

Among the most favored areas — and the first to experience a full Agricultural Revolution — was the Fertile Crescent, an area sometimes known as Southwest Asia, consisting of present-day Iraq, Syria, Israel/Palestine, Jordan, and southern Turkey (see Map 1.4). In this region, an extraordinary variety of wild plants and animals

■ Comparison

In what different ways did the Agricultural Revolution take shape in various parts of the world?

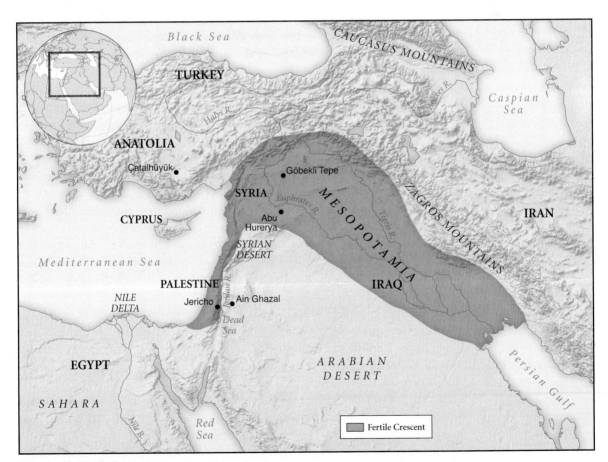

Map 1.4 The Fertile Crescent
Located in what is now called the Middle East, the Fertile Crescent was the site of many significant processes in early world history, including the first breakthrough to agriculture and later the development of some of the First Civilizations.

capable of domestication provided a rich array of species on which the now largely settled gathering and hunting people could draw. What triggered the transition to agriculture, it seems, was a cold and dry spell between 11,000 and 9500 B.C.E., a temporary interruption in the general process of global warming. Larger settled populations were now threatened with the loss of the wild plants and animals on which they had come to depend. Their solution was domestication. Figs were apparently the first cultivated crop, dating to about 9400 B.C.E. In the millennium or so that followed, wheat, barley, rye, peas, lentils, sheep, goats, pigs, and cattle all came under human control, providing the foundation for the world's first, and most productive, agricultural societies.

Archeological evidence suggests that the transition to a fully agricultural way of life in parts of this region took place quite quickly, within as few as 500 years. Signs of that transformation included large increases in the size of settlements, which now housed as many as several thousand people. In these agricultural settings, archeologists have found major innovations: the use of sun-dried mud bricks; the appearance of monuments or shrine-like buildings; displays of cattle skulls; more elaborate human burials, including the removal of the skull; and more sophisticated tools, such as sickles, polished axes, and awls.[21]

At roughly the same time, perhaps a bit later, another process of domestication was unfolding on the African continent in the eastern part of what is now the Sahara in present-day Sudan. Between 10,000 and 5,000 years ago, however, scholars tell us that there was no desert in this region, which received more rainfall than currently, had extensive grassland vegetation, and was "relatively hospitable to human life."[22] It seems likely that cattle were domesticated in this region about 1,000 years before they were separately brought under human control in the Middle East and India. At about the same time, the donkey also was domesticated in northeastern Africa near the Red Sea and spread from there into Southwest Asia, even as the practice of raising sheep and goats moved in the other direction. In terms of farming, the African pattern again was somewhat different. Unlike the Fertile Crescent, where a number of plants were domesticated in a small area, sub-Saharan Africa witnessed the emergence of several widely scattered farming practices. Sorghum, which grows well in arid conditions, was the first grain to be "tamed" in the eastern Sahara region. In the highlands of Ethiopia, teff, a tiny, highly nutritious grain, as well as enset, a relative of the banana, came under cultivation. In the forested region of West Africa, yams, oil palm trees, okra, and the kola nut (used as a flavoring for cola drinks) emerged as important crops. The scattered location of these domestications generated a less productive agriculture than in the more favored and compact Fertile Crescent, but a number of the African domesticates—sorghum, castor beans, gourds, millet, the donkey—subsequently spread to enrich the agricultural practices of Eurasian peoples.

Yet another pattern of agricultural development took shape in the Americas. Like the Agricultural Revolution in Africa, the domestication of plants in the Americas occurred separately in a number of locations—in the coastal Andean regions of western South America, in Mesoamerica, in the Mississippi River valley, and perhaps in the Amazon basin—but surely its most distinctive feature lay in the absence of animals that could be domesticated. Of the fourteen major species of large mammals that have been brought under human control, only one, the llama/alpaca, existed in the Western Hemisphere. Without goats, sheep, pigs, cattle, or horses, the peoples of the Americas lacked sources of protein, manure (for fertilizer), and power (to draw plows or pull carts, for example) that were widely available to societies in the Afro-Eurasian world. Because they could not depend on domesticated animals for meat, agricultural peoples in the Americas relied more on hunting and fishing than did peoples in the Eastern Hemisphere.

Furthermore, the Americas lacked the rich cereal grains that were widely available in Afro-Eurasia. Instead they had maize or corn, first domesticated in southern Mexico by 4000 to 3000 B.C.E. Unlike the cereal grains of the Fertile Crescent, which closely resemble their wild predecessors, the ancestor of corn, a mountain grass called teosinte (tee-uh-SIHN-tee), looks nothing like what we now know as corn or maize.

The Statues of Ain Ghazal
Among the largest of the early agricultural settlements investigated by archeologists is that of Ain Ghazal, located in the modern state of Jordan. Inhabited from about 7200 to 5000 B.C.E., in its prime it was home to some 3,000 people, who lived in multiroomed stone houses; cultivated barley, wheat, peas, beans, and lentils; and herded domesticated goats. These remarkable statues, around three feet tall and made of limestone plaster applied to a core of bundled reeds, were among the most startling finds at that site. Did they represent heroes, gods, goddesses, or ordinary people? No one really knows. (Courtesy, Department of Antiquities of Jordan [DoA]. Photo: Freer Gallery of Art and Arthur M. Sackler Gallery, Washington, DC)

Thousands of years of selective adaptation were required to develop a sufficiently large cob and number of kernels to sustain a productive agriculture, an achievement that one geneticist has called "arguably man's first, and perhaps his greatest, feat of genetic engineering."[23] Even then, corn was nutritionally poorer than the protein-rich cereals of the Fertile Crescent. To provide sufficient dietary protein, corn had to be supplemented with squash and beans, which were also domesticated in the Americas. Thus while Middle Eastern societies quite rapidly replaced their gathering and hunting economy with agriculture, that process took 3,500 years in Mesoamerica.

Another difference in the unfolding of the Agricultural Revolution lay in the north/south orientation of the Americas, which required agricultural practices to move through, and adapt to, quite distinct climatic and vegetation zones if they were to spread. The east/west axis of North Africa/Eurasia meant that agricultural innovations could spread more rapidly because they were entering roughly similar environments. Thus corn, beans, and squash, which were first domesticated in Mesoamerica, took several thousand years to travel the few hundred miles from their Mexican homeland to the southwestern United States and another thousand years or more to arrive in eastern North America. The llama, guinea pig, and potato, which were domesticated in the Andean highlands, never reached Mesoamerica.

The Globalization of Agriculture

■ **Connection**

In what ways did agriculture spread? Where and why was it sometimes resisted?

From the various places where it originated, agriculture spread gradually to much of the rest of the earth, although for a long time it coexisted with gathering and hunting ways of life. Broadly speaking, this extension of farming occurred in two ways. The first, known as diffusion, refers to the gradual spread of agricultural techniques, and perhaps of the plants and animals themselves, but without the extensive movement of agricultural people. Neighboring groups exchanged ideas and products in a down-the-line pattern of communication. A second process involved the slow colonization or migration of agricultural peoples as growing populations pushed them outward. Often this meant the conquest, absorption, or displacement of the earlier gatherers and hunters, along with the spread of the languages and cultures of the migrating farmers. In many places, both processes took place.

Triumph and Resistance

Some combination of diffusion and migration took the original agricultural package of Southwest Asia and spread it widely into Europe, Central Asia, Egypt, and North Africa between 6500 and 4000 B.C.E. Languages originating in the core region accompanied this movement of people and farming practices. Thus Indo-European languages, which originated probably in Turkey and are widely spoken even today from India to Europe, reflect this movement of culture associated with the spread of agriculture. In a similar process, the Chinese farming system moved into Southeast Asia and elsewhere, and with it a number of related language families developed. India

Bantu Migrations

received agricultural influences from the Middle East, Africa, and China alike.

Within Africa, the development of agricultural societies in the southern half of the continent is associated with the migration of peoples speaking one or another of the some 400 Bantu languages. Beginning from what is now southern Nigeria or Cameroon around 3000 B.C.E., Bantu-speaking people moved east and south over the next several millennia, taking with them their agricultural, cattle-raising, and, later, ironworking skills, as well as their languages. The Bantus generally absorbed, killed, or drove away the indigenous Paleolithic peoples or exposed them to animal-borne diseases to which they had no immunities. A similar process brought agricultural Austronesian-speaking people, who originated in southern China, to the Philippine and Indonesian islands, with similar consequences for their earlier inhabitants. Later, Austronesian speakers carried agriculture to the uninhabited islands of the Pacific and to Madagascar off the coast of southeastern Africa (see Map 1.2, p. 19).

The globalization of agriculture was a prolonged process, lasting 10,000 years or more after its first emergence in the Fertile Crescent, but it did not take hold everywhere. The Agricultural Revolution in New Guinea, for example, did not spread much beyond its core region. In particular, it did not pass to the nearby peoples of Australia, who remained steadfastly committed to gathering and hunting ways of life. The people of the west coast of North America, arctic regions, and southwestern Africa also maintained their gathering and hunting economies into the modern era. A very few, such as the Hadza, described at the beginning of this chapter, practice it still.

Some of those who resisted the swelling tide of agriculture lived in areas unsuitable to farming, such as harsh desert or arctic environments; others lived in regions of particular natural abundance, so they felt little need for agriculture. Such societies found it easier to resist agriculture if they were not in the direct line of advancing, more powerful farming people. But many of the remaining gathering and hunting peoples knew about agricultural practices from nearby neighbors, suggesting that they quite deliberately chose to resist it in favor of the freer life of their Paleolithic ancestors.

Nonetheless, by the beginning of the Common Era, the global spread of agriculture had reduced gathering and hunting peoples to a small and dwindling minority of humankind. If that process meant "progress" in certain ways, it also claimed many victims as the relentlessly expanding agricultural frontier slowly destroyed gathering and hunting societies. Whether this process occurred through the peaceful diffusion of new technologies, through intermarriage, through disease, or through the violent displacement of earlier peoples, the steady erosion of this ancient way of life has been a persistent thread of the human story over the past 10,000 years. The final chapters of

■ **Change**
What changes did the Agricultural Revolution bring in its wake?

PORTRAIT

Ishi, The Last of His People

Ishi (Courtesy of The Bancroft Library, University of California, Berkeley)

In late August of 1911, an emaciated and nearly naked man, about fifty years old, staggered into the corral of a slaughterhouse in northern California. As it turned out, he was the last member of his people, a gathering and hunting group known as the Yahi, pushed into extinction by the intrusion of more powerful farming, herding, and "civilized" societies. It was a very old story, played out for over 10,000 years since the Agricultural Revolution placed Paleolithic cultures on the defensive, inexorably eroding their presence on the earth. The tragic story of this individual allows us to put a human face on that enormous and largely unrecorded process.

Within a few days, this bedraggled and no doubt bewildered man was taken into the care of several anthropologists from the University of California, who brought him to a museum in San Francisco, where he lived until his death from tuberculosis in 1916. They called him Ishi, which means "person" in his native language, because he was unwilling to provide them with his own given name. In his culture, it was highly impolite to reveal one's name, especially to strangers.

In the mid-nineteenth century, the Yahi consisted of about 300 to 400 people living in a rugged and mountainous area of northern California. There they hunted, fished, gathered acorns, and otherwise provided for themselves in a fashion familiar to gathering and hunting peoples the world over. But the 1849 California gold rush brought a massive influx of American settlers, miners, and farmers that quickly pushed the Yahi to the edge of extinction. Yahi raiding and resistance was met by massacres at the hands of local militias and vigilantes, only too glad to "clean up the In-

---

that long story are being written in our own times. (See the Portrait of Ishi, above, for a recent example of this process.) After the Agricultural Revolution, the future, almost everywhere, lay with the farmers and herders and with the distinctive societies that they created.

The Culture of Agriculture

What did that future look like? In what ways did societies based on the domestication of plants and animals differ from those rooted in a gathering and hunting economy? In the first place, the Agricultural Revolution led to an increase in human population, as the greater productivity of agriculture was able to support much larger numbers. An early agricultural settlement uncovered near Jericho in present-day Israel probably had 2,000 people, a vast increase in the size of human communities compared to much smaller Paleolithic bands. On a global level, scholars estimate that the world's population was about 6 million around 10,000 years ago, before the Agricultural Revolution got underway, and shot up to some 50 million by 5,000 years ago and dians," killing and scalping hundreds. One such massacre in 1865 likely killed Ishi's father, while the young Ishi, his mother, and a few others escaped.

By 1870, Ishi's community had dwindled to fifteen or sixteen people, living in an even more inaccessible region of their homeland. In these desperate circumstances, traditional gender roles blurred, even as they undertook great efforts to conceal their presence. To avoid making footprints when traveling, they jumped from rock to rock; they ground acorns on smooth stones rather than on more obvious hollowed out rocks and carefully camouflaged their thatched dwellings and campfires. By 1894, this tiny Yahi community numbered only five people: Ishi, his mother, his sister or cousin, and an older man and woman.

Then in 1908, a group of American surveyors came across a naked Ishi harpooning fish in the river, and a few days later they found the tiny settlement that sheltered the remaining Yahi. Only Ishi's aged mother was present, hidden under a pile of skins and rags. They did not harm her, but they took away every moveable item—tools, food, baskets, bows and arrows—as souvenirs. Ishi returned to carry his mother away and she soon died. He never saw his sister/cousin or the others again. For some time, then,

Ishi lived absolutely alone until he stumbled into the slaughterhouse on August 29, 1911, his hair burned short in a Yahi sign of mourning.

In his new home in the museum, Ishi became something of a media sensation, willingly demonstrating his skills for visitors—fashioning tools and weapons of stone and bone, starting a fire, but refusing to make baskets, because it was women's work. Actively cooperating with anthropologists who sought to document the culture of his people, he took them on a hunt one summer, teaching them how to track and kill deer and to process the meat on the spot. All who met him remarked on his gentleness and kindness, his love of company, his delight in children, his fondness for laughing and joking. According to Alfred Kroeber, the primary anthropologist involved with Ishi: "He was the most patient man I ever knew ... without trace of self-pity or of bitterness to dull the purity of his cheerful enduringness."[24]

Questions: What accounts for the ability of Ishi's people to survive into the twentieth century? What emotional or moral posture toward Ishi's life seems most appropriate? What perspective does it lend to the larger story of the gradual erosion of gathering and hunting societies the world over?

250 million by the beginning of the Common Era. Here was the real beginning of the human dominance over other forms of life on the planet.

That dominance was reflected in major environmental transformations. In a growing number of places, forests and grasslands became cultivated fields and grazing lands. Human selection modified the genetic composition of numerous plants and animals. In parts of the Middle East within a thousand years after the beginning of settled agricultural life, some villages were abandoned when soil erosion and deforestation led to declining crop yields, which could not support mounting populations.[25] The advent of more intensive agriculture associated with city-based civilizations only heightened this human impact on the landscape.

Human life too changed dramatically in farming communities, and not necessarily for the better. Farming involved hard work and more of it than in many earlier gathering and hunting societies. The remains of early agricultural people show some deterioration in health—more tooth decay, malnutrition, and anemia, a shorter physical stature, and diminished life expectancy. Living close to animals subjected humans to new diseases—smallpox, flu, measles, chicken pox, malaria, tuberculosis, rabies—while

Nok Culture
The agricultural and iron-using Nok culture of northern Nigeria in West Africa generated a remarkable artistic tradition of terra-cotta or fired clay figures depicting animals and especially people. This one dates to somewhere between 600 B.C.E. and 600 C.E. Some scholars have dubbed this and many similar Nok sculptures as "thinkers." Does it seem more likely that this notion reflects a present-day sensibility or that it might be an insight into the mentality of the ancient artist who created the image? (Musée du Quai Branly/Scala/Art Resource, NY)

living in larger communities generated epidemics for the first time in human history. Furthermore, relying on a small number of plants or animals rendered early agricultural societies vulnerable to famine, in case of crop failure, drought, or other catastrophes. The advent of agriculture bore costs as well as benefits.

Agriculture also imposed constraints on human communities. Some Paleolithic people had settled in permanent villages, but all agricultural people did so, as farming required a settled life. A good example of an early agricultural settlement comes from northern China, one of the original independent sources of agriculture, where the domestication of rice, millet, pigs, and chickens gave rise to settled communities by about 7,000 years ago. In 1953, workers digging the foundation for a factory uncovered the remains of an ancient village, now called Banpo, near the present-day city of Xian. Millet, pigs, and dogs had been domesticated, but diets were supplemented with wild plants, animals, and fish. Some forty-five houses covered with thatch laid over wooden beams provided homes to perhaps 500 people. More than 200 storage pits permitted the accumulation of grain, and six kilns and pottery wheels enabled the production of various pots, vases, and dishes, many decorated with geometric designs and human and animal images. A large central space suggests an area for public religious or political activity, and a trench surrounding the village indicates some common effort to defend the community.

Early agricultural villages such as Banpo reveal another feature of the age of agriculture—an explosion of technological innovation. Mobile Paleolithic peoples had little use for pots, but such vessels were essential for settled societies, and their creation and elaboration accompanied agriculture everywhere. So too did the weaving of textiles, made possible by collecting the fibers of domesticated plants (cotton and flax, for example) and raising animals such as sheep. Evidence for the invention of looms of several kinds dates back to 7,000 years ago, and textiles, some elaborately decorated, show up in Peru, Switzerland, China, and Egypt. Like agriculture itself, weaving was a technology in which women were probably the primary innovators. It was a task that was compatible with child-rearing responsibilities, which virtually all human societies assigned primarily to women.[26] Another technology associated with the Agricultural Revolution was metallurgy. The working of gold and copper, then bronze, and, later, iron became part of the jewelry-, tool-, and weapon-making skill set of humankind. The long "stone age" of human technological history was coming to an end, and the age of metals was beginning.

A further set of technological changes, beginning around 4000 B.C.E., has been labeled the "secondary products revolution."[27] These technological innovations involved new uses for domesticated animals, beyond their meat and hides. Agricultural people in parts of Europe, Asia, and Africa learned to milk their animals, to harvest their wool, and to enrich the soil with their manure. Even more important, they learned to ride horses and camels and to hitch various animals to plows and carts. Because these animals did not exist in the Americas, this revolutionary new source of power and transportation was available only in the Eastern Hemisphere.

Finally the Agricultural Revolution presented to humankind the gift of wine and beer, often a blessing, sometimes a curse. As barley, wheat, rice, and grapes were domesticated, their potential for generating alcoholic beverages was soon discovered. Evidence for wine making in the mountains of present-day northwestern Iran dates to around 5400 B.C.E., though its expense rendered it an elite beverage for millennia. Chinese wine making can be traced to around 4000 B.C.E. Drunken debauchery and carousing among the aristocracy prompted an unsuccessful effort by one Chinese ruler around 1046 B.C.E. to outlaw the beverage. The precise origins of beer are unclear, but its use was already quite widespread in the Middle East by 4000 B.C.E., when a pictogram on a seal from Mesopotamia showed two figures using straws to drink beer from a large pottery jar. Regarded as a gift from the gods, beer, like bread, was understood in Mesopotamia as something that could turn a savage into a fully human and civilized person.[28]

Social Variation in the Age of Agriculture

The resources generated by the Agricultural Revolution opened up vast new possibilities for the construction of human societies, but they led to no single or common outcome. Differences in the natural environment, the encounter with strangers, and sometimes deliberate choices gave rise to several distinct kinds of societies early on in the age of agriculture, all of which have endured into modern times.

■ **Comparison**

What different kinds of societies emerged out of the Agricultural Revolution?

Pastoral Societies

One variation of great significance grew out of the difference between the domestication of plants and the domestication of animals. Many societies made use of both, but in regions where farming was difficult or impossible—arctic tundra, certain grasslands, and deserts—some people came to depend far more extensively on their animals, such as sheep, goats, cattle, horses, camels, or reindeer. Animal husbandry was a "distinct form of food-producing economy," relying on the milk, meat, and blood of animals.[29] Known as herders, pastoralists, or nomads, such people emerged in Central Asia, the Arabian Peninsula, the Sahara, and parts of eastern and southern Africa. What they had in common was mobility, for they moved seasonally as they followed the changing patterns of vegetation necessary as pasture for their animals.

The particular animals central to pastoral economies differed from region to region. The domestication of horses by 4000 B.C.E. and several thousand years later the mastery of horseback-riding skills enabled the growth of pastoral peoples all across the steppes of Central Asia by the first millennium B.C.E. Although organized primarily in kinship-based clans or tribes, these nomads periodically created powerful military confederations, which played a major role in the history of Eurasia for thousands of years. In the Inner Asian, Arabian, and Saharan deserts, domesticated camels made possible the human occupation of forbidding environments. The grasslands

The Domestication of Animals
Although farming often gets top billing in discussions of the Neolithic Revolution, the raising of animals was equally important, for they provided meat, pulling power, transportation (in the case of horses and camels), and manure. Animal husbandry also made possible pastoral societies, which were largely dependent on their domesticated animals. This rock art painting from the Sahara (now southeastern Algeria) dates to somewhere around 4000 B.C.E. and depicts an early pastoral community. (Document Henry Lhote's expedition/Visual Connection Archive)

south of the Sahara and in parts of eastern Africa supported cattle-raising pastoralists. The absence of large animals capable of domestication meant that no pastoral societies emerged in the Americas.

The relationship between nomadic herders and their farming neighbors has been one of the enduring themes of Afro-Eurasian history. Frequently, it was a relationship of conflict as pastoral peoples, unable to produce their own agricultural products, were attracted to the wealth and sophistication of agrarian societies and sought access to their richer grazing lands as well as their food crops and manufactured products. The biblical story of the deadly rivalry between two brothers—Cain, a "tiller of the ground," and Abel, a "keeper of sheep"—reflects this ancient conflict, which persisted well into modern times. But not all was conflict between pastoral and agricultural peoples. The more peaceful exchange of technologies, ideas, products, and people across the ecological frontier of pastoral and agricultural societies also served to enrich and to change both sides. In the chapters that follow, we will encounter pastoral societies repeatedly, particularly as they interact with neighboring agricultural and "civilized" peoples.

Within pastoral communities the relative equality of men and women, characteristic of most Paleolithic societies, persisted, perhaps because their work was so essential. Women were centrally involved in milking animals, in processing that milk, and in producing textiles such as felt, so widely used in Central Asia for tents, beds, rugs, and clothing. Among the Saka pastoralists in what is now Azerbaijan, women rode horses and participated in battles along with men. A number of archeological sites around the Black Sea have revealed high-status women buried with armor, swords, daggers, and arrows. In the Xinjiang region of western China, still other women were buried with the apparatus of healers and shamans, strongly suggesting an important female role in religious life.

Agricultural Village Societies

The most characteristic early agricultural societies were those of settled village-based horticultural farmers, such as those living in Banpo or Jericho. Many such societies also retained much of the social and gender equality of gathering and hunting communities, as they continued to do without kings, chiefs, bureaucrats, or aristocracies.

An example of this type of social order can be found at Çatalhüyük (cha-TAHL-hoo-YOOK), a very early agricultural village in southern Turkey. A careful excavation of the site revealed a population of several thousand people who buried their dead under their houses and then filled the houses with dirt and built new ones on top, layer upon layer. No streets divided the houses, which were constructed adjacent to one another. People moved about the village on adjoining rooftops, from which they entered their homes. Despite the presence of many specialized crafts, few signs of inherited social inequality have surfaced. Nor is there any indication of male or female dominance, although men were more closely associated with hunting wild animals and women with plants and agriculture. "Both men and women," concludes one scholar, "could carry out a series of roles and enjoy a range of positions, from making tools to grinding grain and baking to heading a household."[30] (See Visual Source 1.2, p. 54.)

In many horticultural villages, women's critical role as farmers as well as their work in the spinning and weaving of textiles no doubt contributed to a social position of relative equality with men. Some such societies traced their descent through the female line and practiced marriage patterns in which men left their homes to live with their wives' families. Archeologist Marija Gimbutas has highlighted the prevalence of female imagery in the art of early agricultural societies in Europe and Anatolia, suggesting to her a widespread cult of the Goddess, focused on "the mystery of birth, death and the renewal of life."[31] But early agriculture did not produce identical gender systems everywhere. Some practiced patrilineal descent and required a woman to live in the household of her husband. Grave sites in early eastern European farming communities reveal fewer adult females than males, indicating perhaps the practice of female infanticide. Some early written evidence from China suggests a long-term preference for male children.

In all of their diversity, many village-based agricultural societies flourished well into the modern era, usually organizing themselves in terms of kinship groups or lineages, which incorporated large numbers of people well beyond the immediate or extended family. Such a system provided the framework within which large numbers of people could make and enforce rules, maintain order, and settle disputes without going to war. In short, the lineage system performed the functions of government, but without the formal apparatus of government, and thus did not require kings or queens, chiefs, or permanent officials associated with a state organization. Despite their democratic qualities and the absence of centralized authority, village-based lineage societies sometimes developed modest social and economic inequalities. Elders could exploit the labor of junior members of the community and sought particularly to control women's reproductive powers, which were essential for the growth of the lineage. Among the Igbo of southern Nigeria well into the twentieth century, "title societies" enabled men and women of wealth and character to earn a series of increasingly prestigious "titles" that set them apart from other members of their community, although these honors could not be inherited. Lineages also sought to expand their numbers, and hence their prestige and power, by incorporating war captives or migrants in subordinate positions, sometimes as slaves.

Given the frequent oppressiveness of organized political power in human history, agricultural village societies represent an intriguing alternative to states, kingdoms, and empires, so often highlighted in the historical record. They pioneered the human settlement of vast areas; adapted to a variety of environments; maintained a substantial degree of social and gender equality; created numerous cultural, artistic, and religious traditions; and interacted continuously with their neighbors.

Chiefdoms

In other places, agricultural village societies came to be organized politically as chiefdoms, in which inherited positions of power and privilege introduced a more distinct element of inequality, but unlike later kings, chiefs could seldom use force to compel the obedience of their subjects. Instead chiefs relied on their generosity or gift giving, their ritual status, or their personal charisma to persuade their followers. The earliest such chiefdoms seem to have emerged in the Tigris-Euphrates river valley called Mesopotamia (present-day Iraq), sometime after 6000 B.C.E., when temple priests may have organized irrigation systems and controlled trade with nearby societies.

Many chiefdoms followed in all parts of the world, and the more recent ones have been much studied by anthropologists. For example, chiefdoms emerged everywhere in the Pacific islands, which had been colonized by agricultural Polynesian peoples. Chiefs usually derived from a senior lineage, tracing their descent to the first son of an imagined ancestor. With both religious and secular functions, chiefs led important rituals and ceremonies, organized the community for warfare, directed its economic life, and sought to resolve internal conflicts. They collected tribute from commoners in the form of food, manufactured goods, and raw materials. These items in turn were redistributed to warriors, craftsmen, religious specialists, and other subordinates, while chiefs kept enough to maintain their prestigious positions and imposing lifestyle.[32] In North America as well, a remarkable series of chiefdoms emerged in the eastern woodlands, where an extensive array of large earthen mounds testify to the organizational capacity of these early societies. The largest of them, known as Cahokia, flourished around 1100 C.E.

Thus the Agricultural Revolution radically transformed both the trajectory of the human journey and the evolution of life on the planet. This epic process granted to one species, *Homo sapiens*, a growing power over many other species of plants and animals and made possible an increase in human numbers far beyond what a gathering and hunting economy could support.

But if agriculture provided humankind with the power to dominate nature, it also, increasingly, enabled some people to dominate others. This was not immediately apparent, and for several thousand years, and much longer in some places, agricultural villages and pastoral communities retained much of the social equality that had characterized Paleolithic life. Slowly, though, many of the resources released by the Agricultural Revolution accumulated in the hands of a few. Rich and poor, chiefs and commoners, landowners and dependent peasants, rulers and subjects, dominant

Cahokia
Pictured here in an artist's reconstruction, Cahokia (near St. Louis, Missouri) was the center of an important agricultural chiefdom around 1100 C.E. See Chapter 6 for details. (Cahokia Mounds State Historic Site, Illinois. Painting by Lloyd K. Townsend)

men and subordinate women, slaves and free people — these distinctions, so common in the record of world history, took shape most extensively in highly productive agricultural settings, which generated a substantial economic surplus. There the endless elaboration of such differences, for better or worse, became a major feature of those distinctive agricultural societies known to us as "civilizations."

SUMMING UP SO FAR

What was revolutionary about the Agricultural Revolution?

Reflections: The Uses of the Paleolithic

Even when it is about the distant past, history is also about those who tell it in the present. We search the past, always, for our own purposes. For example, modern people have long been inclined to view their Paleolithic or gathering and hunting ancestors as primitive or superstitious, unable to exercise control over nature, and ignorant of its workings. Such a view was, of course, a kind of self-congratulation, designed to highlight the "progress" of modern humankind. It was a way of saying, "Look how far we have come."

In more recent decades, however, growing numbers of people, disillusioned with modernity, have looked to the Paleolithic era for material with which to criticize, rather than celebrate, contemporary life. Feminists have found in gathering and hunting peoples a much more gender-equal society and religious thinking that featured the divine feminine, qualities that encouragingly suggested that patriarchy was neither inevitable nor eternal. Environmentalists have sometimes identified peoples in the distant past who were uniquely in tune with the natural environment rather than seeking to dominate it. Some nutritionists have advocated a "Paleolithic diet" of wild plants and animals as well suited to our physiology. Critics of modern materialism and competitive capitalism have been delighted to discover societies in which values of sharing and equality predominated over those of accumulation and hierarchy. Still others have asked, in light of the long Paleolithic era, whether the explosive population and economic growth of recent centuries should be considered normal or natural. Perhaps they are better seen as extraordinary, possibly even pathological. All of these uses of the Paleolithic have been a way of asking, "What have we lost in the mad rush to modernity, and how can we recover it?"

Both those who look with disdain on Paleolithic "backwardness" and those who praise, often quite romantically, its simplicity and equality seek to use these ancient people for their own purposes. In our efforts to puzzle out the past, all of us—historians and students of history very much included—stand somewhere. None of us can be entirely detached when we view the past, but this is not necessarily a matter for regret. What we may lose in objectivity, we gain in passionate involvement with the historical record and the many men and women who have inhabited it. Despite its remoteness from us in time and manner of living, the Paleolithic era resonates still in the twenty-first century, reminding us of our kinship with these distant people and the significance of that kinship to finding our own way in a very different world.

Second Thoughts

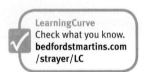

LearningCurve
Check what you know.
**bedfordstmartins.com
/strayer/LC**

Online Study Guide
bedfordstmartins.com
/highschool/strayer

What's the Significance?

Venus figurines, 14–15; 23

Dreamtime, 15

Clovis culture, 18–19

megafaunal extinction, 18–19

Austronesian migrations, 19–20

"the original affluent society," 22

shamans, 23

trance dance, 23

Paleolithic settling down, 24–26

Göbekli Tepe, 25–26; 30

Fertile Crescent, 27; 30–32

teosinte, 33–34

diffusion, 34

Bantu migration, 35

Ishi, 36–37

Banpo, 38

"secondary products revolution," 38–39

pastoral societies, 39–40

Çatalhüyük, 40–41

chiefdoms, 42–43

Big Picture Questions

1. In what ways did various Paleolithic societies differ from one another, and how did they change over time?

2. The Agricultural Revolution marked a decisive turning point in human history. What evidence might you offer to support this claim, and how might you argue against it?

3. How did early agricultural societies differ from those of the Paleolithic era?

4. Was the Agricultural Revolution inevitable? Why did it occur so late in the story of humankind?

5. "The Agricultural Revolution provides evidence for 'progress' in human affairs." How would you evaluate this statement?

Next Steps: For Further Study

Elizabeth Wayland Barber, *Women's Work: The First 20,000 Years* (1994). Explores the role of women in early technological development, particularly textile making.

Peter Bellwood, *First Farmers: The Origins of Agricultural Societies* (2005). An up-to-date account of the Agricultural Revolution, considered on a global basis.

David Christian, *This Fleeting World: A Short History of Humanity* (2008). A lovely essay by a leading world historian, which condenses parts of his earlier *Maps of Time* (2004).

Steven Mithen, *After the Ice: A Global Human History, 20,000–5000 B.C.* (2004). An imaginative tour of world archeological sites during the Agricultural Revolution.

Lauren Ristvet, *In the Beginning* (2007). A brief account of human evolution, Paleolithic life, the origins of agriculture, and the first civilizations, informed by recent archeological discoveries.

Andrew Shryock and Daniel Lord Smail, *Deep History* (2011). An interdisciplinary mapping of the human past with a focus on very long periods of time.

Fred Spier, *Big History and the Future of Humanity* (2011). An effort to place human history in the context of cosmic, geological, and biological history with a focus on the growth of complexity.

"The Agricultural Revolution," http://www.public.wsu.edu/gened/learn-modules/top_agrev/ agrev-index.html. A Web-based tutorial from Washington State University.

"Prehistoric Art," http://witcombe.sbc.edu/ARTHprehistoric.html#general. An art history Web site with a wealth of links to Paleolithic art around the world.

For Web sites and additional documents related to this chapter, see **Make History** at bedfordstmartins.com /highschool/strayer.

Documents

Considering the Evidence:
History before Writing: How Do We Know?

Written records have long been the chief source of data for historians seeking to reconstruct the past. But writing is a quite recent innovation in the long journey of humankind, emerging with the advent of the first civilizations only about 5,000 years ago. This absence of written records for earlier phases of human history is one of the reasons many world historians have neglected or avoided the Paleolithic and Neolithic eras.

And yet, all manner of techniques for probing the more distant past have evolved over the last century or so. An emerging field known as genetic anthropology uses DNA analysis to trace the movement of people across the planet. Linking genetic evidence with fossil remains, scholars have reached a general consensus that sub-Saharan Africa was the original home of our species, *Homo sapiens*. Historical linguistics, rooted in the changes that languages undergo, has also aided in tracking human movement and defining the character of particular cultures by analyzing their vocabularies. Our understanding of the widespread cultures of Indo-European- and Bantu-speaking peoples derive largely from such linguistic analysis. Archeologists have contributed much to our grasp of the unwritten past through their study of human fossil remains, tools, pottery, buildings, art, and more.

Yet another, and somewhat controversial, technique for doing history before writing lies in analogies with more recent nonliterate peoples. In the twentieth century, anthropologists and other scholars descended on the few remaining gathering and hunting peoples, studying their cultures and collecting their stories, myths, and oral traditions. For good reasons historians are often skeptical about the usefulness of such material for understanding the distant past of Paleolithic societies. Since all societies change over time, is it reasonable to think that contemporary gathering and hunting societies would resemble in any way their ancestors thousands of years ago? Furthermore, there is the problem of contamination. After all, gatherers and hunters in recent times have often mixed and mingled with agricultural societies, come under European colonial rule, or made contact with elements of modern civilization. Other scholars, and particularly teachers, have embraced these materials, even while recognizing their limitations, for they provide at least a glimpse into ways of living and thinking that have almost completely vanished from the earth. Document 1.1 allows you to make a judgment about the usefulness of this approach to history before writing.

Document 1.1

A Paleolithic Woman in the Twentieth Century

In 1971 the American anthropologist Marjorie Shostak was conducting research among the San people of the Kalahari Desert on the border of Botswana and South Africa. There she became acquainted with a fifty-year-old woman named Nisa. Although Nisa had interacted with neighboring cattle-keeping people and with Europeans, she had lived most of her life "in the bush," fully participating in the gathering and hunting culture of her ancestors. Nisa proved willing to share with Shostak the intimate details of her life, including her memories of childhood, her several marriages, the birth of her children, her relationships with various lovers, and the deaths of loved ones. Those interviews became the basis for the remarkable book from which the following excerpts derive.

■ How useful do you find Nisa's account for understanding the life of much earlier Paleolithic people? What evidence of contact with a wider world can you find in her story?

■ What does her account indicate about San attitudes toward sex and marriage? How might you compare those attitudes with those of contemporary society?

■ How does Nisa understand God, or the divine? How does she understand the purpose of the curing rituals in which she took part?

■ How would you describe Nisa's overall assessment of San life? Do you find it romanticized, realistic, or critical? What evidence from the passages supports your conclusions?

NISA

The Life and Words of an !Kung Woman
1969–1976

Life in the Bush

We are people who live in the bush, and who belong in the bush. We are not village people. I have no goats. I have no cattle. I am a person who owns nothing.

Source: Marjorie Shostak, *Nisa: The Life and Words of an !Kung Woman* (Cambridge, MA: Harvard University Press, 1981), 37, 63, 79, 80, 138–139, 140, 149, 189, 190, 203–204, 243, 267, 268, 269, 283, 284.

That's what people say I am: a poor person.... No donkey, either. I still carry things myself, in my kaross [an animal hide cloak] when I travel....

We lived and lived, and as I kept growing, I started to carry my little brother around on my shoulders. My heart was happy then; I had grown to love him and carried him everywhere. I'd play with him for a while and whenever he would start to cry, I'd take him to Mother so he could nurse. Then I'd take him back with me and we'd play together again.

That was when Kumsa was little. But once he was older and started to talk and then to run around, that's when we were mean to each other and hit and fought all the time....

We lived in the bush and my father set traps and killed steenbok and duiker and gemsbok and we lived, eating the animals and foods of the bush. We collected food, ground it in a mortar, and ate it. We also ate sweet nin berries and tsin beans. When I was growing up, there were no cows or goats.... I had never seen other peoples and didn't know anything other than life in the bush....

Whenever my father killed an animal and I saw him coming home with meat draped over a stick, balanced on one shoulder—that's what made me happy. I'd cry out, "Mommy! Daddy's coming and he's bringing *meat!*" My heart would be happy when I greeted him, "Ho, ho, Daddy! We're going to eat meat!" Or honey. Sometimes he'd go out and come home with honey. I'd be sitting around with my mother and then see something coming from way out in the bush. I'd look hard. Then, "Oooh, Daddy found a beehive! Oh, I'm going to eat honey!"... And I'd thank him and call him wonderful names....

When we were living in the bush, some people gave and others stinged. But there were always enough people around who shared, people who liked one another, who were happy living together, and who didn't fight. And even if one person did sting, the other person would just get up and yell about it, whether it was meat or anything else, "What's doing this to you, making you not give us meat?"

When I was growing up, receiving food made my heart happy. There really wasn't anything, other than stingy people, that made me unhappy. I didn't like people who wouldn't give a little of what they had....

It's the same today. Here I am, long since an adult, yet even now, if a person doesn't give something to me, I won't give anything to that person....

Marriage

...The day of the wedding, everyone was there. All of Tashay's friends were sitting around, laughing and laughing. His younger brother said, "Tashay, you're too old. Get out of the way so I can marry her. Give her to me."...They were all sitting around, talking like that. They all wanted me.

I went to my mother's hut and sat there. I was wearing lots of beads and my hair was completely covered and full with ornaments.... That night there was another dance. We danced, and some people fell asleep and others kept dancing....

The next day they started [to build the marriage hut]. There were lots of people there—Tashay's mother, my mother, and my aunt worked on the hut; everyone else sat around, talking. Late in the day, the young men went and brought Tashay to the finished hut. They set him down beside it and stayed there with him, sitting around the fire....

They came and brought me back. Then they laid me down inside the hut. I cried and cried. People told me, "A man is not something that kills you; he is someone who marries you, who becomes like your father or your older brother. He kills animals and gives you things to eat."

I listened and was quiet. Later, we went to sleep. Tashay lay down beside the opening of the hut, near the fire, and I lay down inside; he thought I might try and run away again. He covered himself with a blanket and slept....

We lived and lived, the two of us, together, and after a while I started to really like him and then, to love him. I had finally grown up and had learned how to love. I thought, "A man has sex with you. Yes, that's what a man does. I had thought that perhaps he didn't."

We lived on and I loved him and he loved me. I loved him the way a young adult knows how to love; I just *loved* him. Whenever he went away and I stayed behind, I'd miss him. I'd think, "Oh, when is my husband ever coming home? How come he's been gone so long?" I'd miss him and want him.

When he'd come back my heart would be happy, "Eh, hey! My husband left and once again has come back."

I . . . gave myself to him, gave and gave. We lay with each other and my breasts were very large. I was becoming a woman.

Loss

It was while we were visiting in the Tswana village [of cattle-keeping people] and just after Kxau was born that Tashay died. . . . I lay there and thought, "Why did this happen? The two of us gave so much to each other and lived together so happily. Now I am alone, without a husband. I am already a widow. Why did God trick me and take my husband? God is stingy! He just takes them from you. God's heart is truly far from people." . . .

Then I was without my husband and my heart was miserable. Every night I missed him and every night I cried, "I am without the man I married." I thought, "Where will I see the food that will help my children grow? Who is going to help me raise this newborn? My older brother and my younger brother are far away. Who is going to help me now?"

In your heart, your child, your mother, and your father are all equal. When any one of them dies, your heart feels pain. When your child dies, you think, "How come this little thing I held beside me and watched all that she did, today has died and left me? She was the only child I had with me. . . . This God . . . his ways are foul! Why did he give me a little one and then take her away?" . . .

The death of your parents, husband, or children—they are equal in the amount of pain you feel when you lose them. But when they all die and you have no family left, then you really feel pain. There is no one to take care of you; you are completely alone. . . .

That's the way it is. God is the one who destroys. It isn't people who do it. It is God himself.

Lovers

. . . Besa [Nisa's fourth husband] and I did argue a lot, usually about sex. . . . Every night Besa wanted me and every night he would make love to me. That Besa, something was wrong with his brain! . . . After

a while, I realized I didn't like his ways. That's when I thought, "Perhaps I will leave him. Perhaps I'll find another man and see what he is like."

I didn't leave him, not for many years. But I did have lovers and so did he. . . . Because affairs . . . is something that even people from long ago knew. Even my father's father's father's father knew. There have also always been fights where poison arrows are shot and people are killed because of that. Having affairs is one of the things God gave us. . . .

When you are a woman, you don't just sit still and do nothing—you have lovers. You don't just sit with the man of your hut, with just one man. One man can give you very little. One man gives you only one kind of food to eat. But when you have lovers, one brings you something and another brings you something else. One comes at night with meat, another with money, another with beads. Your husband also does things and gives them to you. But sitting with just one man? We don't do that. Does one man have enough thoughts for you? . . .

A Healing Ritual

. . . N/um—the power to heal—is a very good thing. This is a medicine very much like your medicine because it is strong. As your medicine helps people, our n/um helps people. But to heal with n/um means knowing how to trance. Because, it is in trance that the healing power sitting inside the healer's body—the n/um—starts to work. Both men and women learn how to cure with it, but not everyone wants to. Trance-medicine really hurts! As you begin to trance, the n/um slowly heats inside you and pulls at you. It rises until it grabs your insides and takes your thoughts away. Your mind and your senses leave and you don't think clearly. Things become strange and start to change. You can't listen to people or understand what they say. You look at them and they suddenly become very tiny. You think, "What's happening? Is God doing this?" All that is inside you is the n/um; that is all you can feel.

You touch people, laying on hands, curing those you touch. When you finish, other people hold you and blow around your head and your face. Suddenly your senses go "Phah!" and come back to you.

You think, "Eh hey, there are people here," and you see again as you usually do....

N/um is powerful, but it is also very tricky. Sometimes it helps and sometimes it doesn't, because God doesn't always want a sick person to get better.... I was a young woman when my mother and her younger sister started to teach me about drum-medicine. There is a root that helps you learn to trance, which they dug for me. My mother put it in my little leather pouch and said, "Now you will start learning this, because you are a young woman already." She had me keep it in my pouch for a few days. Then one day, she took it and pounded it along with some bulbs and some beans and cooked them together. It had a horrible taste and made my mouth feel foul. I threw some of it up. If she hadn't pounded it with the other foods, my stomach would have been much more upset and I would have thrown it

all up; then it wouldn't have done anything for me. I drank it a number of times and threw up again and again. Finally I started to tremble. People rubbed my body as I sat there, feeling the effect getting stronger and stronger. My body shook harder and I started to cry. I cried while people touched me and helped me with what was happening to me.

Eventually, I learned how to break out of myself and trance. When the drum-medicine songs sounded, that's when I would start. Others would string beads and copper rings into my hair. As I began to trance, the women would say, "She's started to trance, now, so watch her carefully. Don't let her fall." They would take care of me, touching me and helping. If another woman was also in a trance, she laid on hands and helped me. They rubbed oil on my face and I stood there—a lovely young woman, trembling—until I was finished.

Visual Sources

Considering the Evidence:
History before Writing: How Do We Know?

Physical remains provide yet another point of entry into the history of non-literate peoples. Among these, creative artistic representation has been especially useful, for it is as old as humankind itself, long preceding the emergence of urban civilizations. The most ancient of these artistic traditions are the rock paintings that Paleolithic people created all across the world. Some in Australia date to 40,000 years ago, and the tradition has continued into the twentieth-first century as artists retouched and repainted ancient images and created new ones. A contemporary Aboriginal artist explained what those paintings meant to him:

> When I look at my [dreaming] paintings it makes me feel good — happy in heart, spirit. Everything is there: all there in the caves, not lost. . . . The people keep their ceremony things and pictures — they make them new. They bring young boys for learning to the caves, telling the stories, giving the laws from grandfathers' fathers, learning to do the paintings — [the dreaming] way.[33]

Perhaps the most well-known Paleolithic rock art comes from the Lascaux caves in southern France, discovered by several teenage boys in 1940. Dating to at least 17,000 years ago, the cave walls depict various kinds of animals: numerous horses, stags, and bison; seven felines; and a single bear, rhinoceros, and bird. But no reindeer are included, although they were the main source of meat for the artists. Abstract designs consisting of dots and lines accompany many of the paintings.

Scholars have debated endlessly what insights these remarkable images might provide into the mental world of Paleolithic Europeans. Were they examples of "totemic" thinking — the belief that particular groups of men and women were associated with, or descended from, particular animals? Did they represent "hunting magic" intended to enhance the success of these early hunters? Because many of the paintings were located deep within caves, were they perhaps part of religious or ritual practices or rites of passage? Were they designed to pass on information to future generations? Were the abstract designs star charts, as one scholar has suggested? Or did these images represent

Visual Source 1.1 Lascaux Rock Art (bpk berlin/Art Resource, NY)

the visions of shamans as some have also suggested for the South African rock painting on page 10? No one really knows.

But beyond their uncertain meaning as archeological evidence for Paleolithic life, modern humans have recognized the artistic value of the Lascaux paintings, appreciating their graceful lines, use of color, and distinctive sense of perspective and sometimes movement. Tradition has it that the great twentieth-century artist Pablo Picasso remarked after viewing the caves that "we have learned nothing in 12,000 years."[34] Furthermore the art of the Lascaux caves was part of a very long artistic tradition in the region that adhered over many millennia to a set of aesthetic conventions. Thus it was a conservative tradition, linked to a long-established social order and very much unlike modern art that generally challenges contemporary society.

One of the most dramatic and perplexing images from Lascaux, shown here as Visual Source 1.1, depicts a human male figure lying in front of a wounded and enraged bison, pierced with a broken spear, and with its entrails hanging out. To the left is a rhinoceros and beneath its tail two rows of three dots.

- Based on this image as well as those on pages 10 and 15, what information about Paleolithic life might historians derive from the rock art of gathering and hunting peoples?

- No one knows for certain if the three figures in this image were painted at the same time. But if they were, it represents a very early narrative composition. How might you tell the story that the painting depicts? Is the man dead or wounded? What message would such a story convey?

- The explicit rendering of the penis indicates a male figure, but why might the artist have shown him with a bird-like face? How might he be related to the bird on a staff pictured beside him?

- What differences do you notice between the portrayal of the human figure and that of the animals?

- Do you respond to this image more as archeological evidence for Paleolithic life or from the viewpoint of cultural and artistic appreciation?

In seeking to understand the Neolithic age — occurring between the beginnings of settled agriculture and the rise of literate civilizations — historians confront much the same problem as do scholars of the preceding Paleolithic era. In the absence of writing, they must depend heavily on material remains such as art, artifacts, and architecture. In comparison with Paleolithic art, the new economy generated by agriculture gave rise to many artistic innovations. Weaving and pottery making became major industries, offering new opportunities for creative expression. While animals continued to be a focus of Neolithic art, human figures became more prominent and were more realistically depicted than in the cave paintings and Venus figurines of the Paleolithic era. But observers — both expert and amateur — continue to debate the meaning of these representations with no consensus in sight.

Among Neolithic sites, few have generated more controversy than Çatalhüyük in modern Turkey, particularly about the role of women in the religious and social life of this early agricultural village (see pp. 41–42). The first major dig at the site, undertaken by James Mellaart in the 1960s, uncovered a number of small female figurines, the most famous of which is shown here as Visual Source 1.2. It dates to about 5000 B.C.E. and is some eight inches in height. The baked-clay figure depicts a seated female whose arms are resting on two lionesses or leopards. For Mellaart, this was evidence for an ancient and powerful cult of the "mother Goddess," an idea that other scholars have dismissed. Despite the controversy, some goddess devotees have come to view Çatalhüyük as a pilgrimage site.

- Without trying to interpret this statue, how would you simply describe it?

- What features of this statue might support Mellaart's view? What alternative understandings can you imagine?

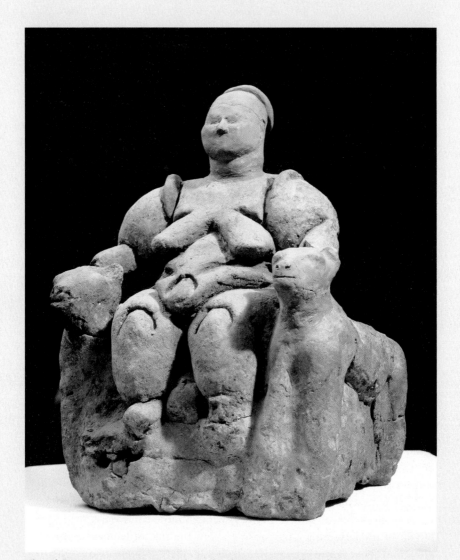

Visual Source 1.2 Women, Men, and Religion in Çatalhüyük (The Art Archive at Art Resource, NY)

■ Why might feminist scholars have been attracted to Mellaart's interpretation of this figure?

Later archeological research, ongoing since 1993 under the leadership of Ian Hodder, has called some aspects of this "mother Goddess" interpretation into question. Hodder, for example, doubts the existence of an organized cult with an attached priesthood, as Mellaart theorized. Rather, Hodder noted that the image suggests "a close connection between ritual and daily functions." He added:

I do not think that there was a separate religious elite. I think the religion was an integral part of daily life. It may be wrong to think of the Çatal art as religious or symbolic at all. It may be more that people thought that they had to paint, or make relief sculptures, in order to achieve certain practical ends (such as make the crops grow, or prevent children from dying).[35]

Furthermore, Hodder suggested that while women were certainly prominent in the symbolism of the village, there is little evidence for a "matriarchal society" in which women dominated. Rather, he wrote that "men and women had the same social status. There was a balance of power."[36]

- ■ Why do you think the life of this small Neolithic village from 7,000 or more years ago continues to provoke such passionate debate? (You might want to do a little research about the controversies surrounding Çatalhüyük.)

Beyond the artistic products of people without writing, historians have also learned much from their burial sites. Analysis of human remains often discloses something about diet, nutrition, and disease, while variations in burial materials can provide indications of social status, technology, religion, and more. Among the more famous burials of the Neolithic era was that of Otzi the Iceman, a forty-six-year-old man, about 5'5" tall, whose body was discovered in 1991 frozen in a glacier high in the Italian Alps. Properly speaking, it was not a burial at all, for Otzi, named for the region in which he was found, died far from home about 5,300 years ago in this remote mountainous area, his body left to the elements, which miraculously preserved it for over five millennia.

In his mid-forties, Otzi was an old man for his time and place, no doubt full of aches and pains. The condition of his bones and evidence of frostbite suggest that he spent much of his life in steep, cold mountainous terrain. Some fifty-seven tattoos, made by small incisions into which charcoal was rubbed, probably reflect treatments for pain relief. Traces of arsenic in his hair indicate that he was exposed to the smelting of copper. His last meals included wild goat and deer meat as well as threshed and processed wheat, perhaps in the form of bread, which suggests that he lived in an agricultural community. A gash in his hand points to hand-to-hand fighting not long before his death; a flint arrow that lodged in his back and severed an artery, as well as evidence of a blow to his head, show that Otzi did not die a natural death but was killed. His attacker appears to have then pulled out the shaft of the arrow, perhaps fearing it could identify him, for no such shaft was found among his remains. So we know how Otzi died, but not why. Even so, it is about as close as we get to a particular event in history before writing.

Materials accompanying his body fill out the picture of his life. His clothing consisted of a leather loincloth and leggings, a coat of stitched animal furs,

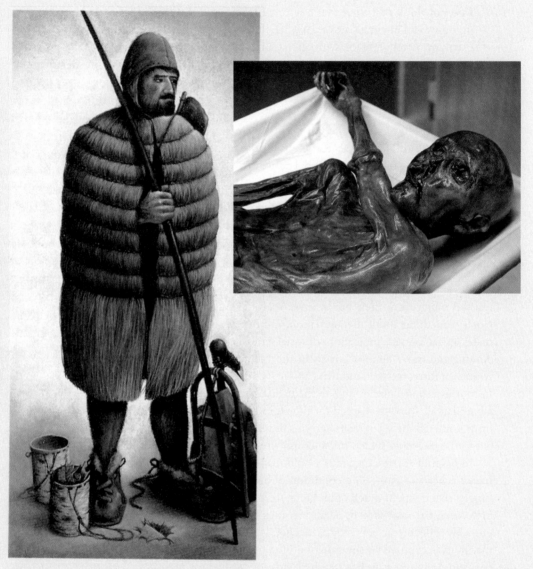

Visual Source 1.3 Otzi the Iceman (Iceman Drawing: W. Smetek/STERN/Picture Press; Skeleton: South Tyrol Museum of Archaeology, www.iceman.it)

and covering all of this, a cape of woven grass. A belt, a bearskin cap, and waterproof shoes made of bearskin and deer hide and stuffed with grass as insulation completed his outfit. An ax with a copper blade reveals that Otzi was living at the beginning of the age of metals, while stone scrappers and a flint knife indicate continued reliance on an earlier technology. He was well provisioned for a substantial journey with several small baskets, a birch bark drinking cup, several dried mushrooms, replacement materials of leather straps and sinew, a drill and a tool for sharpening flint blades, a six-foot bow and a quiver full of arrows, and a wood-framed backpack. We know that Otzi was far from his home, probably located considerably to the south of the Alpine mountain chain where he died, but no one knows why he chose to go there. Was he a shepherd herding his flock, part of an armed party involved in a skirmish with enemies, or a solitary traveler attacked by local people?

Visual Source 1.3 shows an artist's reconstruction of the Iceman and some of his accompanying materials, while the small insert shows the actual head and torso of his preserved body.

- What elements of the above description are visible in the reconstructed drawing?

- Do you think that the inferences about his life made by scholars are justified based on the evidence available?

- Create a story that takes account of what is known about Otzi, while imaginatively fleshing out something of his life and death. What additional archeological evidence would be useful in doing so?

Structures or buildings also offer insights into the life of people without writing. In the Neolithic age of agriculture, more large-scale stone structures, known as megaliths, appeared in various places, and settled farming communities required more elaborate dwellings, including some substantial stone fortifications. Among the most famous sites of the early agrarian era is Stonehenge, a series of earthworks accompanied by circles of standing stones located in southern England, where the Agricultural Revolution emerged around 4000 B.C.E. Construction of the Stonehenge site began around 3100 B.C.E. and continued intermittently for another 1,500 years.

- Have a close look at the aerial photograph of Stonehenge in Visual Source 1.4. How would you describe its major features to someone who had never seen it? What questions about the site come to mind?

Almost everything about Stonehenge has been a matter of controversy and speculation. Prominent among those debates have been the questions of motivation and function. Why was it constructed? What purposes did it serve for those early farming peoples who used it? The discovery of the cremated remains of some 240 individuals, dating to the first five centuries of its existence, has convinced some scholars that it was a burial site, perhaps for members of a single high-ranking family. It was the "domain of the dead" or an abode of the ancestors, argued one archeologist, linked ritually perhaps to a nearby village of Durrington Walls, a "land of the living" consisting of 300 to 1,000 homes.[37] Others have cast Stonehenge as an astronomical observatory, aligned with the solstices and able to predict eclipses and the movement of heavenly bodies, or perhaps a center of sun worship. Most recently, it has been

Visual Source 1.4 Stonehenge (© Skycan/Corbis)

depicted as "a place of pilgrimage for the sick and injured of the Neolithic
world," based on the number of burials in the area that show signs of serious
illness, trauma, or deformity as well as the presence of many bluestone rock
chips thought to have magical healing properties.[38]

Whatever its purposes, still other controversies surround the manner of its
construction. How were those huge slabs of rock, some as heavy as fifty tons
and others coming from a location 240 miles away, transported to Stonehenge
and put into place? Were they dragged overland or transported partway by
boat along the Avon River? Or did the movement of earlier glaciers deposit
them in the region?

■ What does a structure of the magnitude of Stonehenge suggest about the
   Neolithic societies that created it?

■ What kinds of additional evidence would be most useful to scholars
   seeking to puzzle out the mysteries of Stonehenge?

Using the Evidence:
History before Writing: How Do We Know?

1. **Comparing sources:** Which of these sources seems most useful in understanding human history before writing? Do you find Nisa's contemporary account more or less insightful than the physical remains from long ago? What are the advantages and drawbacks of each?

2. **Noticing the Great Transition:** How do these sources illustrate the transition from a Paleolithic gathering and hunting way of life (Nisa and the Lascaux rock art) to a Neolithic or agricultural society?

3. **Connecting past and present:** In what ways do these sources retain their ability to speak to people living in industrial societies of the twenty-first century? Or do they have meaning only for those who created them? Which sources do you relate to most strongly?

4. **Reflecting on speculation:** Our understanding of all of these works is highly uncertain, inviting a considerable amount of speculation, guess-work, or imagination. Why are historians willing to articulate uncertain interpretations of these ancient sources? Is this an appropriate undertaking for historians, or should scholars remain silent when the evidence does not allow them to speak with certainty and authority?

Chapter 1 Wrap Up

STEP ONE

The Word to Know: Migration

The *Oxford England Dictionary* (2012) defines *migration* as "the movement of a person or people from one country, locality, place of residence, etc., to settle in another." Use the word migration in an original sentence to explain the Bantu migrations (see p. 35).

STEP TWO

Mapping Migrations

Use the following sources, as well as the text itself and answer the questions that follow: A Map of Time, p. 13; Map 1.1 The Global Dispersion of Humankind, pp. 16–17; Map 1.2, Migration of Austronesian-Speaking People, p. 19; Map 1.3, The Global Spread of Agriculture and Pastoralism, pp. 28–29.

■ Questions

1. Explain the chronological sequence of migration across the globe.
2. Calculate approximately how far Austronesian-speaking peoples traveled by boat as they migrated to Hawaii, New Zealand, and Madagascar over the centuries from the Philippines (use the map scale). To which of the three locations did people arrive first?
3. Compare the migration of people to the spread of agriculture.
4. In your own words, explain why people migrated.
5. What were at least two effects of these migrations?

Visual Sources as Historical Evidence

This exercise will help you to understand how historians use visual images to interpret the past before written history.

1. Begin by examining the image entitled "Domestication of Animals" on p. 40.

    a. What evidence in the painting is there of pastoralism?

    b. What other observations might be drawn from this image (think about gender roles, religious rituals, and technology)?

    c. The attribution indicates this image to be from the Sahara desert, produced around 6000 years ago. Other rock art found in this same location — the Tassili Plateau — shows giraffes, savanna-like vegetation, and wells. What conclusions might you make about how the climate has changed in this area since that time?

2. Next consider these images and answer the questions that follow: Paleolithic Art, p. 10; Australian Rock Art, p. 15; Lascaux Rock Art, Visual Source 1.1, p. 52 .

    a. What can you tell about natural resources (vegetation, animals, water, sources of food, clothing, shelter) from viewing these images?

    b. What claims can you make about economics (e.g., how they made a living)?

    c. What evidence is there of each society's culture (art, religion, values)?

First Civilizations

Cities, States, and Unequal Societies

(3500 B.C.E.—500 B.C.E.)

"Where could one go if one wanted to escape civilization?" So read an inquiry from a Colorado woman on an Internet forum about "personal development" in 2007. In reply, another subscriber to the forum wrote: "Are you just tired of urban sprawl or are you fed up with people in general? I have lived 'off the land' in Kentucky, with no car, power lines, running water, phones etc. and I survived to tell the tale."[1] This ironic online conversation—using the Internet to express an interest in abandoning civilization—refers to the "back-to-the-land" movement that began in the mid-1960s as an alternative to the pervasive materialism of modern life. Growing numbers of urban dwellers, perhaps as many as a million in North America, exchanged their busy city lives for a few acres of rural land and a very different way of living.

This urge to "escape from civilization" has long been a central feature in modern life. It is a major theme in Mark Twain's famous novel *The Adventures of Huckleberry Finn*, in which the restless and rebellious Huck resists all efforts to "sivilize" him by fleeing to the freedom of life on the river. It is a large part of the "cowboy" image in American culture, and it permeates environmentalist efforts to protect the remaining wilderness areas of the country. Nor has this impulse been limited to modern societies and the Western world. The ancient Chinese teachers of Daoism likewise urged their followers to abandon the structured and demanding world of urban and civilized life and to immerse themselves in the eternal patterns of the natural order. It is a strange paradox that we count the creation of civilizations among the major achievements of humankind and yet people within

Raherka and Mersankh: Writing was among the defining features of civilizations almost everywhere. In ancient Egyptian civilization, the scribes who possessed this skill enjoyed both social prestige and political influence. This famous statue shows Raherka, an "inspector of the scribes" during Egypt's Fifth Dynasty (about 2350 B.C.E.), in an affectionate pose with his wife, Mersankh. (Réunion des Musées Nationaux/Art Resource, NY) them have often sought to escape the constraints, artificiality, hierarchies, and other discontents of civilized living.

SO WHAT EXACTLY ARE THESE CIVILIZATIONS that have generated such ambivalent responses among their inhabitants? When, where, and how did they first arise in human history? What changes did they bring to the people who lived within them? Why might some people criticize or seek to escape from them?

As historians commonly use the term, "civilization" represents a new and particular type of human society, made possible by the immense productivity of the Agricultural Revolution. Such societies encompassed far larger populations than any earlier form of human community and for the first time concentrated some of those people in sizable cities, numbering in the many tens of thousands. Both within and beyond these cities, people were organized and controlled by states whose leaders could use force to compel obedience. Profound differences in economic function, skill, wealth, and status sharply divided the people of civilizations, making them far less equal and subject to much greater oppression than had been the case in earlier Paleolithic communities, agricultural villages, pastoral societies, or chiefdoms. Pyramids, temples, palaces, elaborate sculptures, written literature, complex calendars, as well as more elaborate class and gender hierarchies, slavery, and large-scale warfare—all of these have been among the cultural products of civilization.

SEEKING THE MAIN POINT

What distinguished "civilizations" from earlier Paleolithic and Neolithic societies?

Something New: The Emergence of Civilizations

■ Change
When and where did the first civilizations emerge?

Like agriculture, civilization was a global phenomenon, showing up independently in seven major locations scattered around the world during the several millennia after 3500 B.C.E. and in a number of other smaller expressions as well (see Map 2.1). In the long run of human history, these civilizations—small breakthroughs to a new way of life—gradually absorbed, overran, or displaced people practicing other ways of living. Over the next 5,000 years, civilization, as a unique kind of human community, gradually encompassed ever-larger numbers of people and extended over ever-larger territories, even as particular civilizations rose, fell, revived, and changed.

Introducing the First Civilizations

The earliest of these civilizations emerged around 3500 B.C.E. to 3000 B.C.E. in three places. One was the "cradle" of Middle Eastern civilization, expressed in the many and competing city-states of Sumer in southern Mesopotamia (located in present-day Iraq). Much studied by archeologists and historians, Sumerian civilization likely gave rise to the world's earliest written language, which was used initially by officials to record the goods received by various temples. Almost simultaneously, the Nile River valley in northeastern Africa witnessed the emergence of Egyptian civilization, famous for its pharaohs and pyramids, as well as a separate civilization known as Nubia,

A Map of Time   (All dates B.C.E.)

3500–3000	Beginnings of Mesopotamian, Egyptian, and Norte Chico civilizations
3400–3200	Nubian kingdom of Ta-Seti
3200–2350	Period of independent Sumerian city-states
2663–2195	Old Kingdom Egypt (high point of pharaoh's power and pyramid building)
2200–2000	Beginnings of Chinese, Indus Valley, and Central Asian (Oxus) civilizations
2070–1600	Xia dynasty in China (traditionally seen as first dynasty of Chinese history)
After 2000	*Epic of Gilgamesh* compiled
1900–1500	Babylonian Empire
1792–1750	Reign of Hammurabi
1700	Abandonment of Indus Valley cities
1550–1064	New Kingdom Egypt
1200	Beginnings of Olmec civilization
760–660	Kush conquest of Egypt
586	Babylonian conquest of Judah
By 500	Egypt and Mesopotamia incorporated into Persian Empire

farther south along the Nile. Unlike the city-states of Sumer, Egyptian civilization took shape as a unified territorial state in which cities were rather less prominent. Later in this chapter, we will compare these two First Civilizations in greater detail.

Less well known and only recently investigated by scholars was a third early civilization that was developing along the central coast of Peru from roughly 3000 B.C.E. to 1800 B.C.E., at about the same time as the civilizations of Egypt and Sumer. This desert region received very little rainfall, but it was punctuated by dozens of rivers that brought the snowmelt of the adjacent Andes Mountains to the Pacific Ocean. Along a thirty-mile stretch of that coast and in the nearby interior, a series of some twenty-five urban centers emerged in an area known as Norte Chico, the largest of which was Caral, in the Supe River valley. In Norte Chico, archeologists have found monumental architecture in the form of earthen platform mounds, one of them measuring 60 feet tall and 500 feet long, as well as large public ceremonial structures, stone buildings with residential apartments, and other signs of urban life.

Norte Chico was a distinctive civilization in many ways. Its cities were smaller than those of Mesopotamia and show less evidence of economic specialization. The economy was based to an unusual degree on an extremely rich fishing industry in anchovies and sardines along the coast. These items apparently were exchanged for cotton, essential for fishing nets, as well as food crops such as squash, beans, and

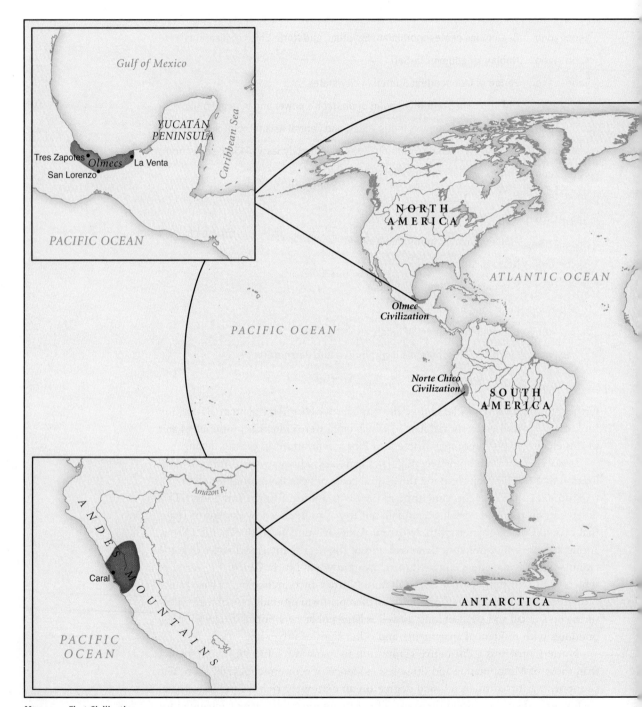

Map 2.1 First Civilizations

Seven First Civilizations emerged independently in locations scattered across the planet, all within a few thousand years, from 3500 to 1000 B.C.E.

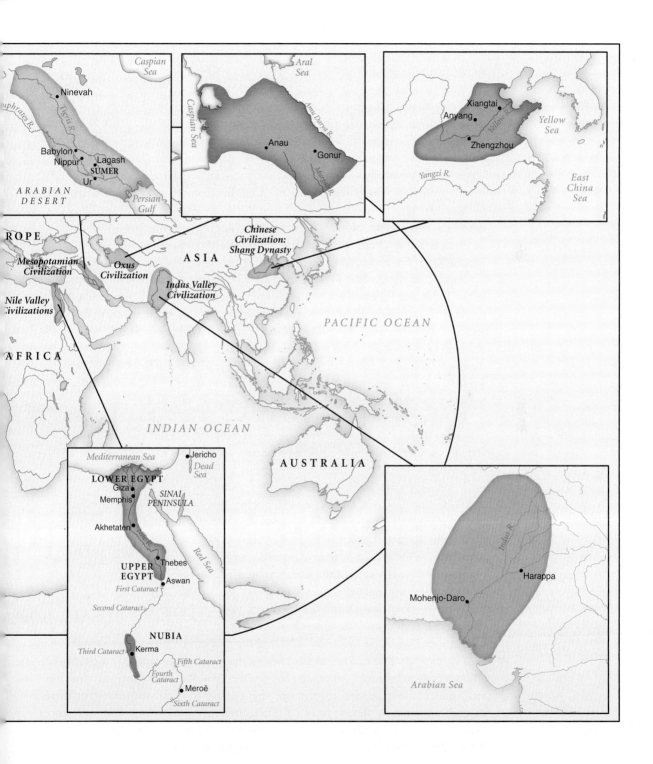

guava, all of which were grown by inland people in the river valleys using irrigation agriculture. Unlike Egyptian and Mesopotamian societies, Peruvian civilization did not rest on grain-based farming; the people of Norte Chico did not develop pottery or writing; and few sculptures, carvings, or drawings have been uncovered so far. Archeologists have, however, found a 5,000-year-old *quipu* (a series of knotted cords, later used extensively by the Inca for accounting purposes), which some scholars have suggested may have been an alternative form of writing or symbolic communication. Furthermore, the cities of Norte Chico lacked defensive walls, and archeologists have discovered little evidence of warfare, such as burned buildings and mutilated corpses. It was also an unusually self-contained civilization. The only import from the outside world evident in Norte Chico, or in Andean civilization generally, was maize (corn), which was derived ultimately from Mesoamerica, though without direct contact between the two regions. Norte Chico apparently "lighted a cultural fire" in the Andes and established a pattern for the many Andean civilizations that followed—Chavín, Moche, Wari, Tiwanaku, and, much later, Inca.[2]

Somewhat later, at least four additional First Civilizations made their appearance. In the Indus and Saraswati river valleys of what is now Pakistan, a remarkable civilization arose during the third millennium B.C.E. By 2000 B.C.E., it embraced a far larger area than Mesopotamia, Egypt, or coastal Peru and was expressed primarily in its elaborately planned cities. All across this huge area, common patterns prevailed: standardized weights, measures, architectural styles, even the size of bricks. As elsewhere, irrigated agriculture provided the economic foundation for the civilization, and a written language, thus far undeciphered, provides evidence of a literate culture.

Unlike its Middle Eastern counterparts, the Indus Valley civilization apparently generated no palaces, temples, elaborate graves, kings, or warrior classes. In short, the archeological evidence provides little indication of a political hierarchy or centralized state. This absence of evidence has sent scholars scrambling to provide an explanation for the obvious specialization, coordination, and complexity that the Indus Valley civilization exhibited. A series of small republics, rule by priests, an early form of the caste system—all of these have been suggested as alternative mechanisms of integration in this first South Asian civilization. Although no one knows for sure, the possibility that the Indus Valley may have housed a sophisticated civilization without a corresponding state has excited the imagination of scholars. (See Visual Sources: Indus Valley Civilization, pp. 103–07.)

Whatever its organization, the local environmental impact of the Indus Valley civilization, as in many others, was heavy and eventually undermined its ecological foundations. Repeated irrigation increased the amount of salt in the soil and lowered crop yields. The making of mud bricks, dried in ovens, required an enormous amount of wood for fuel, generating large-scale deforestation and soil erosion. Thus environmental degradation contributed significantly to the abandonment of these magnificent cities by about 1700 B.C.E. Thereafter, they were largely forgotten, until their rediscovery by archeologists in the twentieth century. Nonetheless, many features of this early civilization—ceremonial bathing, ritual burning, yoga positions, bulls and elephants as religious symbols, styles of clothing and jewelry — continued to nourish the later civilization of the Indian subcontinent. In fact they persist into the present.[3]

The early civilization of China, dating to perhaps 2200 B.C.E., was very different from that of the Indus Valley. The ideal — if not always the reality — of a centralized state was evident from the days of the Xia (shyah) dynasty (2070–1600 B.C.E.), whose legendary monarch Wu organized flood control projects that "mastered the waters and made them to flow in great channels." Subsequent dynasties — the Shang (1600–1046 B.C.E.) and the Zhou (JOH) (1046–771 B.C.E.) — substantially enlarged the Chinese state, erected lavish tombs for their rulers, and buried thousands of human sacrificial victims to accompany them in the next world. By the Zhou dynasty, a distinctive Chinese political ideology had emerged, featuring a ruler, known as the

Shang Dynasty Bronze
This bronze tiger, created around 1100 B.C.E., illustrates Chinese skill in working with bronze and the mythological or religious significance of the tiger as a messenger between heaven and the human world. (Asian Art & Archaeology, Inc./Corbis)

Son of Heaven. This monarch served as an intermediary between heaven and earth and ruled by the Mandate of Heaven only so long as he governed with benevolence and maintained social harmony among his people. An early form of written Chinese has been discovered on numerous oracle bones, which were intended to predict the future and to assist China's rulers in the task of governing. Chinese civilization, more than any other, has experienced an impressive cultural continuity from its earliest expression into modern times.

Central Asia was the site of yet another First Civilization. In the Oxus or Amu Darya river valley and nearby desert oases (what is now northern Afghanistan and southern Turkmenistan), a quite distinctive and separate civilization took shape very quickly after 2200 B.C.E. Within two centuries, a number of substantial fortified centers had emerged, containing residential compounds, artisan workshops, and temples, all surrounded by impressive walls and gates. Economically based on irrigation agriculture and stock raising, this Central Asian or Oxus civilization had a distinctive cultural style, expressed in its architecture, ceramics, burial techniques, seals, and more, though it did not develop a literate culture. Evidence for an aristocratic social hierarchy comes from depictions of gods and men in widely differing dress performing various functions from eating at a banquet to driving chariots to carrying heavy burdens. Visitors to this civilization would have found occasional goods from China, India, and Mesopotamia, as well as products from pastoral nomads of the steppe land and the forest dwellers of Siberia. According to a leading historian, this Central Asian civilization was the focal point of a "Eurasian-wide system of intellectual and commercial exchange."[4] Compared to Egypt or Mesopotamia, however, it had a relatively brief history, for by 1700 B.C.E., it had faded away as a civilization, at about the same time as a similar fate befell its Indus Valley counterpart. Its cities were abandoned and apparently forgotten until their resurrection by archeologists in the twentieth century. And yet its influence persisted as elements of this civilization's cultural style show up much later in Iran, India, and the eastern Mediterranean world.

A final First Civilization, known as the Olmec, took shape around 1200 B.C.E. along the coast of the Gulf of Mexico near present-day Veracruz in southern Mexico. Based on an agricultural economy of maize, beans, and squash, Olmec cities arose from a series of competing chiefdoms and became ceremonial centers filled with elaborately decorated temples, altars, pyramids, and tombs of rulers. The most famous artistic legacy of the Olmecs lay in some seventeen colossal basalt heads, weighing twenty tons or more. Recent discoveries suggest that the Olmecs may well have created the first written language in the Americas by about 900 B.C.E. Sometimes regarded as the "mother civilization" of Mesoamerica, Olmec cultural patterns—mound building, artistic styles, urban planning, a game played with a rubber ball, ritual sacrifice, and bloodletting by rulers—spread widely throughout the region and influenced subsequent civilizations, such as the Maya and Teotihuacán.

Beyond these seven First Civilizations, other, smaller civilizations also flourished. Lying south of Egypt in the Nile Valley, an early Nubian civilization known as Ta-Seti was clearly distinctive and independent of its northern neighbor, although Nubia was later involved in a long and often contentious relationship with Egypt. Likewise in China, a large city known as Sanxingdui, rich in bronze sculptures and much else, arose separately but at the same time as the more well-known Shang dynasty. As a new form of human society, civilization was beginning its long march toward encompassing almost all of humankind by the twentieth century. At the time, however, these breakthroughs to new forms of culture and society were small islands of innovation in a sea of people living in much older ways.

The Question of Origins

■ Change
What accounts for the
initial breakthroughs to
civilization?

The first question that historians ask about almost everything is "How did it get started?" Scholars of all kinds—archeologists, anthropologists, sociologists, and historians—have been arguing about the origins of civilization for a very long time, with no end in sight.[5] Amid all the controversy, one thing seems reasonably clear: civilizations had their roots in the Agricultural Revolution. That is the reason they appeared so late in the human story, for only an agricultural technology permitted human communities to produce sufficient surplus to support large populations and the specialized or elite minorities who did not themselves produce food. But not all agricultural societies or chiefdoms developed into civilizations, so something else must have been involved. It is the search for this "something else" that has provoked such great debate among scholars.

Some historians have emphasized the need to organize large-scale irrigation projects as a stimulus for the earliest civilizations, but archeologists have found that the more complex water control systems appeared long after states and civilizations had already been established. Alternatively, perhaps states responded to the human need for order as larger and more diverse populations grew up in particular localities. Others have suggested that states were useful in protecting the privileges of favored groups. Warfare and trade have figured in still other explanations for the rise of civilizations. Anthropologist Robert Carneiro combined several of these factors in a thoughtful approach to the question.[6] He argued that a growing density of population, producing more congested and competitive societies, was a fundamental motor of change, and especially in areas where rich agricultural land was limited, either by geography (oceans, deserts, mountains) or by powerful neighboring societies. Such settings provided incentives for innovations, such as irrigation or plows that could produce more food, because opportunities for territorial expansion were not readily available. But circumscribed environments with dense populations also generated intense competition among rival groups, which led to repeated warfare. A strong and highly organized state was a decided advantage in such competition. Because losers could not easily flee to new lands, they were absorbed into the winner's society as a lower class. Successful leaders of the winning side emerged as elites with an enlarged base of land, a class of subordinated workers, and a powerful state at their disposal—in short, a civilization.

Although such a process was relatively rapid by world history standards, it took many generations, centuries, or perhaps millennia to evolve. It was, of course, an unconscious undertaking in which the participants had little sense of the long-term outcome as they coped with the practical problems of survival on a day-to-day basis. What is surprising, though, is the rough similarity of the outcome in many widely separated places from about 3500 B.C.E. to the beginning of the Common Era.

However they got started (and much about this is still guesswork), the First Civilizations, once established, represented a very different kind of human society than anything that came before. All of them were based on highly productive agricultural economies. Various forms of irrigation, drainage, terracing, and flood control enabled these early civilizations to tap the food-producing potential of their regions more intensively. All across the Afro-Eurasian hemisphere, though not in the Americas, animal-drawn plows and metalworking greatly enhanced the productivity of farming. Ritual sacrifice, sometimes including people, accompanied the growth of civilization, and the new rulers normally served as high priests, their right to rule legitimated by association with the sacred.

An Urban Revolution

It was the resources from agriculture that made possible one of the most distinctive features of the First Civilizations—cities. What would an agricultural villager have made of Uruk, ancient Mesopotamia's largest city? Uruk had walls more than twenty feet tall and a population around 50,000 in the third millennium B.C.E. The city's center, visible for miles around, was a stepped pyramid, or ziggurat, topped with a temple (see the photo on p. 77). Inside the city, our village visitor would have found

■ **Change**
What was the role of cities in the early civilizations?

other temples as well, serving as centers of ritual performance and as places for the redistribution of stored food. Numerous craftspeople labored as masons, copper workers, weavers, and in many other specialties, while bureaucrats helped administer the city. It was, surely, a "vibrant, noisy, smelly, sometimes bewildering and dangerous, but also exciting place."[7] Here is how the *Epic of Gilgamesh*, Mesopotamia's ancient epic poem, describes the city:

> Come then, Enkidu, to ramparted Uruk,
> Where fellows are resplendent in holiday clothing,
> Where every day is set for celebration,
> Where harps and drums are played.
> And the harlots too, they are fairest of form,
> Rich in beauty, full of delights,
> Even the great gods are kept from sleeping at night.[8]

Equally impressive to a village visitor would have been the city of Mohenjo Daro (moe-hen-joe DAHR-oh), which flourished along the banks of the Indus River around 2000 B.C.E. With a population of perhaps 40,000, Mohenjo Daro and its sister city of Harappa featured large, richly built houses of two or three stories, complete with indoor plumbing, luxurious bathrooms, and private wells. Streets were laid out in a grid-like pattern, and beneath the streets ran a complex sewage system. Workers lived in row upon row of standardized two-room houses. Grand public buildings, including what seems to be a huge public bath, graced the city, while an enormous citadel was surrounded by a brick wall some forty-five feet high.

Mohenjo Daro
Flourishing around 2000 B.C.E., Mohenjo Daro was by far the largest city of the Indus Valley civilization, covering more than 600 acres. This photograph shows a small part of that city as it has been uncovered by archeologists during the past century. The large water-tight tank or pool, shown in the foreground, probably offered bathers an opportunity for ritual purification. (J. Mark Kenoyer/Harappa Images)

Even larger, though considerably later, was the Mesoamerican city of Teotihuacán (tay-uh-tee-wah-KAHN), located in the central valley of Mexico. It housed perhaps 200,000 people in the middle of the first millennium C.E. Broad avenues, dozens of temples, two huge pyramids, endless stone carvings and many bright frescoes, small apartments for the ordinary, palatial homes for the wealthy—all of this must have seemed another world for a new visitor from a distant village. In shopping for obsidian blades, how was she to decide among the 350 workshops in the city? In seeking relatives, how could she find her way among many different compounds, each surrounded by a wall and housing a different lineage? And what would she make of a neighborhood composed entirely of Mayan merchants from the distant coastal lowlands?

Cities, then, were central to most of the First Civilizations, though to varying degrees. They were political/administrative capitals; they functioned as centers for the production of culture, including art, architecture, literature, ritual, and ceremony; they served as marketplaces for both local and long-distance exchange; and they housed most manufacturing activity. Everywhere they generated a unique kind of society, compared to earlier agricultural villages or Paleolithic camps. Urban society was impersonal, for it was no longer possible to know everyone. Relationships of class and occupation were at least as important as those of kinship and village loyalty. Most notably, the degree of specialization and inequality far surpassed that of all preceding human communities.

The Erosion of Equality

Among the most novel features of early urban life, at least to our imaginary village visitor, was the amazing specialization of work outside of agriculture—scholars, officials, merchants, priests, and artisans of all kinds (see Document 2.5, pp. 100–01). In ancient Mesopotamia, even scribes were subdivided into many categories: junior and senior scribes, temple scribes and royal scribes, scribes for particular administrative or official functions.[9] None of these people, of course, grew their own food; they were supported by the highly productive agriculture of farmers.

Hierarchies of Class

Alongside the occupational specialization of the First Civilizations lay their vast inequalities—in wealth, status, and power. Here we confront a remarkable and persistent feature of the human journey. As ingenuity and technology created more productive economies, the greater wealth now available was everywhere piled up rather than spread out. Early signs of this erosion of equality were evident in the more settled and complex gathering and hunting societies and in agricultural chiefdoms, but the advent of urban-based civilizations multiplied and magnified these inequalities many times over, as the more egalitarian values of earlier cultures were everywhere displaced. This transition represents one of the major turning points in the social history of humankind.

As the First Civilizations took shape, inequality and hierarchy soon came to be regarded as normal and natural. Upper classes everywhere enjoyed great wealth in land or salaries, were able to avoid physical labor, had the finest of everything, and occupied the top positions in political, military, and religious life. Frequently, they were distinguished by the clothing they wore, the houses they lived in, and the manner of their burial. Early Chinese monarchs bestowed special clothing, banners, chariots, weapons, and ornaments on their regional officials, and all of these items were graded according to the officials' precise location in the hierarchy. In Mesopotamia, the punishments prescribed in the famous Code of Hammurabi (hahm-moo-RAH-bee) depended on social status (see Document 2.2, pp. 95–97). A free-born commoner who struck a person of equal rank had to pay a small fine, but if he struck "a man

■ **Change**
In what ways was social inequality expressed in early civilizations?

War and Slavery
This Mesopotamian victory monument, dating to about
2200 B.C.E., shows the Akkadian ruler Naram-Sin crushing his
enemies. Prisoners taken in such wars were a major source of
slaves in the ancient world. (Louvre, Paris/The Bridgeman Art
Library.)

who is his superior, he shall receive 60 strokes with an ox-
tail whip in public." Clearly, class had consequences.

In all of the First Civilizations, free commoners represented the vast majority of the population and included
artisans of all kinds, lower-level officials, soldiers and police,
servants, and, most numerous of all, farmers. It was their surplus production—appropriated through a variety of taxes,
rents, required labor, and tribute payments—that supported
the upper classes. At least some of these people were aware
of, and resented, these forced extractions and their position
in the social hierarchy. Most Chinese peasants, for example,
owned little land of their own and worked on plots granted
to them by royal or aristocratic landowners. An ancient poem
compared the exploiting landlords to rats and expressed the
farmers' vision of a better life:

> Large rats! Large rats!
> Do not eat our spring grain!
> Three years have we had to do with you.
> And you have not been willing to think of our toil.
> We will leave you,
> And go to those happy borders.
> Happy borders, happy borders!
> Who will there make us always to groan?[10]

At the bottom of social hierarchies everywhere were
slaves. Slavery and civilization, in fact, seem to have emerged
together. (For early references to slavery, see Document 2.2,
pp. 95–97.) Female slaves, captured in the many wars among rival Mesopotamian
cities, were put to work in large-scale semi-industrial weaving enterprises, while males
helped to maintain irrigation canals and construct ziggurats. Others worked as domestic servants in the households of their owners. In all of the First Civilizations,
slaves—derived from prisoners of war, criminals, and debtors—were available for
sale; for work in the fields, mines, homes, and shops of their owners; or on occasion
for sacrifice. From the days of the earliest civilizations until the nineteenth century, the
practice of "people owning people" was an enduring feature of state-based societies
everywhere.

The practice of slavery in ancient times varied considerably from place to place.
Egypt and the Indus Valley civilizations initially had far fewer slaves than did Mesopotamia, which was highly militarized. Later, the Greeks of Athens and the Romans
employed slaves far more extensively than did the Chinese or Indians (see Chapter 5).
Furthermore, most ancient slavery differed from the type of slavery practiced in the
Americas during recent centuries: in the early civilizations, slaves were not a primary
agricultural labor force; many children of slaves could become free people; and slavery was not associated primarily with "blackness" or with Africa.

Hierarchies of Gender

No division of human society has held greater significance for the lives of individuals than those of sex and gender. Sex describes the obvious biological differences between males and females. More important to historians, however, has been gender, which refers to the many and varied ways that cultures have assigned meaning to those sexual differences. To be gendered as masculine or feminine defines the roles and behavior considered appropriate for men and women in every human community. At least since the emergence of the First Civilizations, gender systems have been patriarchal, meaning that women have been subordinate to men in the family and in society generally. The inequalities of gender, like those of class, decisively shaped the character of the First Civilizations and those that followed.

The patriarchal ideal regarded men as superior to women and sons preferable to daughters. Men had legal and property rights unknown to most women. Public life in general was associated with masculinity, which defined men as rulers, warriors, scholars, and heads of households. Women's roles — both productive and reproductive — took place in the home, mostly within a heterosexual family, where women were defined largely by their relationship to a man: as a daughter, wife, mother, or widow. Frequently men could marry more than one woman and claim the right to regulate the social and sexual lives of the wives, daughters, and sisters in their families. Widely seen as weak but feared as potentially disruptive, women required both the protection and control of men.

But the reality of the lives of men and women did not always correspond to these ideals. Most men, of course, were far from prominent and exercised little power, except perhaps over the women and children of their own families. Gender often interacted with class to produce a more restricted but privileged life for upper-class women, who were largely limited to the home and the management of servants. By contrast, the vast majority of women always had to be out in public, working in the fields, tending livestock, buying and selling in the streets, or serving in the homes of their social superiors. A few women also operated in roles defined as masculine, acting as rulers, priests, and scholars, while others pushed against the limits and restrictions assigned to women. But most women no doubt accepted their assigned roles, unable to imagine anything approaching gender equality, even as most men genuinely believed that they were protecting and providing for their women.

The big question for historians lies in trying to explain the origins of this kind of patriarchy. Clearly it was neither natural nor of long standing. For millennia beyond measure, gathering and hunting societies had developed gender systems without the sharp restrictions and vast inequalities that characterized civilizations. Even early horticultural societies, those using a hoe or digging stick for farming, continued the relative gender equality that had characterized Paleolithic peoples. What was it, then, about civilization that seemed to generate a more explicit and restrictive patriarchy? One approach to answering this question highlights the role of a new and more intensive form of agriculture, involving the use of animal-drawn plows and the keeping and milking of large herds of animals. Unlike earlier farming practices that relied on a hoe

■ **Change**

In what ways have historians tried to explain the origins of patriarchy?

or digging stick, plow-based agriculture meant heavier work, which men were better able to perform. Taking place at a distance from the village, this new form of agriculture was perhaps less compatible with women's primary responsibility for child rearing. Furthermore, the growing population of civilizations meant that women were more often pregnant and thus more deeply involved in child care than before. Hence, in plow-based communities, men took over most of the farming work, and the status of women declined correspondingly, even though their other productive activities—weaving and food preparation, for example—continued. "As women were increasingly relegated to secondary tasks," writes archeologist Margaret Ehrenberg, "they had fewer personal resources with which to assert their status."[11]

Women have long been identified not only with the home but also with nature, for they are intimately involved in the primordial natural process of reproduction. But civilization seemed to highlight culture, or the human mastery of nature, through agriculture, monumental art and architecture, and creation of large-scale cities and states. Did this mean, as some scholars have suggested, that women were now associated with an inferior dimension of human life (nature), while men assumed responsibility for the higher order of culture?[12]

A further aspect of civilization that surely contributed to patriarchy was warfare. While earlier forms of human society certainly experienced violent conflict, large-scale military clashes with professionally led armies were a novel feature of almost all of the First Civilizations, and female prisoners of war often were the first slaves. With military service largely restricted to men, its growing prominence in the affairs of civilizations enhanced the values, power, and prestige of a male warrior class and cemented the association of masculinity with organized violence and with the protection of society and especially of its women.

Private property and commerce, central elements of the First Civilizations, may also have helped to shape early patriarchies. Without sharp restrictions on women's sexual activity, how could a father be certain that family property would be inherited by his offspring? In addition, the buying and selling associated with commerce were soon applied to male rights over women, as female slaves, concubines, and wives were exchanged among men.

Patriarchy in Practice

■ Comparison

How did Mesopotamian and Egyptian patriarchy differ from each other?

Whatever the precise origins of patriarchy, women's subordination permeated the First Civilizations, marking a gradual change from the more equal relationships of men and women within agricultural villages or Paleolithic bands. By the second millennium B.C.E. in Mesopotamia, various written laws codified and sought to enforce a patriarchal family life that offered women a measure of paternalistic protection while insisting on their submission to the unquestioned authority of men. Central to these laws was the regulation of female sexuality. A wife caught sleeping with another man might be drowned at her husband's discretion, whereas he was permitted to enjoy sexual relations with his female servants, though not with another man's wife. Divorce was far easier for the husband than for the wife. Rape was a serious offense, but the injured party was primarily the father or the husband of the victim, rather than the violated woman herself. While wealthy women might own and operate their own businesses or act on behalf of their powerful husbands, they too saw themselves as dependent. "Let all be well with [my husband]," prayed one such wife, "that I may prosper under his protection."[13]

Furthermore, women in Mesopotamian civilization were sometimes divided into two sharply distinguished categories. Under an Assyrian law code that was in effect between the fifteenth and eleventh centuries B.C.E., respectable women, those under the protection and sexual control of one man, were required to be veiled when outside the home, whereas nonrespectable women, such as slaves and prostitutes, were forbidden to wear veils and were subject to severe punishment if they presumed to cover their heads.

Finally, in some places, the powerful goddesses of earlier times were gradually relegated to the home and hearth. They were replaced in the public arena by dominant male deities, who now were credited with the power of creation and fertility and viewed as the patrons of wisdom and learning. This "demotion of the goddess," argues historian Gerda Lerner, culminated in the Hebrew Scriptures, in which a single male deity, Yahweh (YAH-way), alone undertakes the act of creation without any participation of a female counterpart. Yet this demotion did not occur always or everywhere; in Mesopotamia, for example, the prominent goddess Inanna or Istar long held her own against male gods and was regarded as a goddess of love and sexuality as well as a war deity. In a hymn to Inanna dating to around 2250 B.C.E., the poet and priestess Enheduanna declared: "It is her game to speed conflict and battle, untiring, strapping on her sandals."

Thus expressions of patriarchy varied among the first civilizations. Egypt, while clearly patriarchal, afforded its women greater opportunities than did most other First Civilizations. In Egypt, women were recognized as legal equals to men, able to own property and slaves, to administer and sell land, to make their own wills, to sign their own marriage contracts, and to initiate divorce. Moreover, married women in Egypt were not veiled as they were at times in Mesopotamia. Royal women occasionally exercised significant political power, acting as regents for their young sons or, more rarely, as queens in their own right. Clearly, though, this was seen as abnormal, for Egypt's most famous queen, Hatshepsut (r. 1472–1457 B.C.E.), was sometimes portrayed in statues as a man, dressed in male clothing and sporting the traditional false beard of the pharaoh.

The Rise of the State

What, we might reasonably ask, held ancient civilizations together despite the many tensions and complexities of urban living and the vast inequalities of civilized societies? Why did they not fly apart amid the resentments born of class and gender hierarchies? The answer, in large part, lay in yet another distinctive feature of the First

Civilizations—states. Organized around particular cities or larger territories, early states were headed almost everywhere by kings, who employed a variety of ranked officials, exercised a measure of control over society, and defended against external enemies. To modern people, the state is such a familiar reality that we find it difficult to imagine life without it. Nonetheless, it is a quite recent invention in human history, with the state replacing, or at least supplementing, kinship as the basic organizing principle of society and exercising far greater power than earlier chiefdoms. But the power of central states in the First Civilizations was limited and certainly not "totalitarian" in the modern sense of that term. The temple and the private economy rivaled and checked the power of rulers, and most authority was local rather than directed from the capital.

Coercion and Consent

■ **Change**
What were the sources of state authority in the First Civilizations?

Yet early states in Mesopotamia, Egypt, China, Mesoamerica, and elsewhere were influential, drawing their power from various sources, all of which assisted in providing cohesion for the First Civilizations. One basis of authority lay in the recognition that the complexity of life in cities or densely populated territories required some authority to coordinate and regulate the community. Someone had to organize the irrigation systems of river valley civilizations. Someone had to direct efforts to defend the city or territory against aggressive outsiders. Someone had to adjudicate conflicts among the many different peoples, unrelated to one another, who rubbed elbows in the early cities. The state, in short, solved certain widely shared problems and therefore had a measure of voluntary support among the population. For many people, it was surely useful.

The state, however, was more useful for some people than for others, for it also served to protect the privileges of the upper classes, to require farmers to give up a portion of their product to support city-dwellers, and to demand work on large public projects such as pyramids and fortifications. If necessary, state authorities had the ability, and the willingness, to use force to compel obedience. An Egyptian document described what happens to a peasant unable to pay his tax in grain:

> Now the scribe lands on the shore. He surveys the harvest. Attendants are behind him with staffs, Nubians with clubs. One says [to the peasant], "Give grain." There is none. He is beaten savagely. He is bound, thrown into a well, submerged head down. His wife is bound in his presence. His children are in fetters. His neighbors abandon them and flee.[14]

Such was the power of the state, as rulers accumulated the resources to pay for officials, soldiers, police, and attendants. This capacity for violence and coercion marked off the states of the First Civilizations from earlier chiefdoms, whose leaders had only persuasion, prestige, and gifts to back up their authority. But as states increasingly monopolized the legitimate right to use violence, rates of death from interpersonal violence declined as compared to earlier nonstate communities.[15]

Force, however, was not always necessary, for the First Civilizations soon generated ideas suggesting that state authority as well as class and gender inequalities were normal, natural, and ordained by the gods. Kingship everywhere was associated with the sacred. Ancient Chinese kings were known as the Son of Heaven, and only they or their authorized priests could perform the rituals and sacrifices necessary to keep the cosmos in balance. Mesopotamian rulers were thought to be the stewards of their city's patron gods. Their symbols of kingship—crown, throne, scepter, mace—were said to be of divine origin, sent to earth when the gods established monarchy. Egyptians, most of all, invested their pharaohs with divine qualities. Rulers claimed to embody all the major gods of Egypt, and their supernatural power ensured the regular flooding of the Nile and the defeat of the country's enemies.

A Mesopotamian Ziggurat
This massive ziggurat/temple to the Mesopotamian moon god Nanna was built around 2100 B.C.E. in the city of Ur. The solitary figure standing atop the staircase illustrates the size of this huge structure. (© Richard Ashworth/Robert Harding World Imagery/Corbis)

But if religion served most often to justify unequal power and privilege, it might also on occasion be used to restrain, or even undermine, the established order. Hammurabi claimed that his law code was inspired by Marduk, the chief god of Babylon, and was intended to "bring about the rule of righteousness in the land, to destroy the wicked and the evil-doers; so that the strong should not harm the weak."[16] Another Mesopotamian monarch, Urukagina from the city of Lagash, claimed authority from the city's patron god for reforms aimed at ending the corruption and tyranny of a previous ruler. In China during the Western Zhou dynasty (1046–771 B.C.E.), emperors ruled by the Mandate of Heaven, but their bad behavior could result in the removal of that mandate and their overthrow.

Writing and Accounting

A further support for state authority lay in the remarkable invention of writing. It was a powerful and transforming innovation, regarded almost everywhere as a gift from the gods, while people without writing often saw it as something magical or supernatural. Distinctive forms of writing emerged in most of the First Civilizations (see Snapshot, p. 79), sustaining them and their successors in many ways. Literacy defined elite status and conveyed enormous prestige to those who possessed it. (See Document 2.5, pp. 100–01, for a celebration of writing.) Because it can be learned, writing also provided a means for some commoners to join the charmed circle of the literate.

Writing as propaganda, celebrating the great deeds of the kings, was prominent, especially among the Egyptians and later among the Maya. A hymn to the pharaoh, dating to about 1850 B.C.E., extravagantly praised the ruler:

> He has come unto us . . . and has given peace to the two Riverbanks
> and has made Egypt to live; he hath banished its suffering;
> he has caused the throat of the subjects to breathe
> and has trodden down foreign countries
> he has delivered them that were robbed he has come unto us, that we may
>   [nurture up?] our children and bury our aged ones.[17]

In Mesopotamia and elsewhere, writing served an accounting function, recording who had paid their taxes, who owed what to the temple, and how much workers had earned. Thus it immensely strengthened bureaucracy. Complex calendars indicated precisely when certain rituals should be performed. Writing also gave weight and specificity to orders, regulations, and laws. Hammurabi's famous law code (see Document 2.2, pp. 95–97), while correcting certain abuses, made crystal clear that fundamental distinctions divided men and women and separated slaves, commoners, and people of higher rank.

Once it had been developed, writing, like religion, proved hard to control and operated as a wild card in human affairs. It gave rise to literature and philosophy, to astronomy and mathematics, and, in some places, to history, often recording what had long been oral traditions. On occasion, the written word proved threatening, rather than supportive, to rulers. China's so-called First Emperor, Qin Shihuangdi (r. 221–210 B.C.E.), allegedly buried alive some 460 scholars and burned their books when they challenged his brutal efforts to unify China's many warring states, or so his later critics claimed (see Chapter 3). Thus writing became a major arena for social and political conflict, and rulers always have sought to control it.

Olmec Head
This colossal statue, some six feet high and five feet wide, is one of seventeen such carvings, dating to the first millennium B.C.E., that were discovered in the territory of the ancient Olmec civilization. Thought to represent individual rulers, each of the statues has a distinct and realistically portrayed face. (© Danny Lehman/Corbis)

The Grandeur of Kings

Yet another source of state authority derived from the lavish lifestyle of elites, the impressive rituals they arranged, and the imposing structures they created. Everywhere, kings, high officials, and their families lived in luxurious palaces, dressed in splendid clothing, bedecked themselves with the loveliest jewelry, and were attended by endless servants. Their deaths triggered elaborate burials, of which the pyramids of the Egyptian pharaohs were perhaps the most ostentatious. Monumental palaces, temples, ziggurats, pyramids, and statues conveyed the imposing power of the state and its elite rulers. The Olmec civilization of Mesoamerica (1200–400 B.C.E.) erected enormous

Snapshot Writing in Ancient Civilizations

Most of the early writing systems were "logophonetic," using symbols to designate both whole words and particular sounds or syllables. Chinese characters, which indicated only words, were an exception. None of the early writing systems employed alphabets.

Location	Type	Initial Use	Example	Comment
Sumer	Cuneiform: wedge-shaped symbols on clay tablets representing objects, abstract ideas, sounds, and syllables	Records of economic transactions, such as temple payments and taxes	bird	Regarded as the world's first written language; other languages such as Babylonian and Assryian were written with Sumerian script
Egypt	Hieroglyphs ("sacred carvings"): a series of signs that denote words and consonants (but not vowels or syllables)	Business and administrative purposes; later used for religious inscriptions, stories, poetry, hymns, and mathematics	rain, dew, storm	For everyday use, less formal systems of cursive writing (known as "hieratic" and "demotic") were developed
Andes	Quipu: a complex system of knotted cords in which the color, length, type, and location of knots conveyed mostly numerical meaning	Various accounting functions; perhaps also used to express words	numerical data (possibly in codes), words, and ideas	Widely used in the Inca Empire; recent discoveries place quipus in Caral some 5,000 years ago
Indus River Valley	Some 400 pictographic symbols representing sounds and words, probably expressing a Dravidian language currently spoken in southern India	Found on thousands of clay seals and pottery; probably used to mark merchandise	6 fish	As yet undeciphered
China	Oracle bone script: pictographs (stylized drawings) with no phonetic meaning	Inscribed on turtle shells or animal bones; used for divination (predicting the future) in the royal court of Shang dynasty rulers	horse	Direct ancestor of contemporary Chinese characters
Olmec	Signs that represent sounds (syllables) and words; numbering system using bars and dots	Used to record the names and deeds of rulers and shamans, as well as battles and astronomical data	jaguar	Structurally similar to later Mayan script; Olmec calendars were highly accurate and the basis for later Mesoamerican calendars

SUMMING UP SO FAR

In what ways might the advent of "civilization" have marked a revolutionary change in the human condition? And in what ways did it carry on earlier patterns from the past?

human heads, more than ten feet tall and weighing at least twenty tons, carved from blocks of basalt and probably representing particular rulers. Somewhat later the Maya Temple of the Giant Jaguar, towering 154 feet tall, was the most impressive among many temples, pyramids, and palaces that graced the city of Tikal. All of this must have seemed overwhelming to common people in the cities and villages of the First Civilizations.

Comparing Mesopotamia and Egypt

■ **Comparison**

In what ways did Mesopotamian and Egyptian civilizations differ from each other?

A productive agricultural technology, city living, distinct class and gender inequalities, the emerging power of states—all of these were common features of First Civilizations across the world and also of those that followed. Still, these civilizations were not everywhere the same, for differences in political organization, religious beliefs and practices, the role of women, and much more gave rise to distinctive traditions. Nor were they static. Like all human communities, they changed over the centuries. Finally, these civilizations did not exist in complete isolation, for they participated in networks of interactions with near and sometimes more distant neighbors. In looking more closely at two of these First Civilizations—Mesopotamia and Egypt—we can catch a glimpse of the differences, changes, and connections that characterized early civilizations.

Environment and Culture

The civilizations of both Mesopotamia and Egypt grew up in river valleys and depended on their rivers to sustain a productive agriculture in otherwise arid lands. Those rivers, however, were radically different. At the heart of Egyptian life was the Nile, "that green gash of teeming life," which rose predictably every year to bring the soil and water that nurtured a rich Egyptian agriculture. The Tigris and Euphrates rivers, which gave life to Mesopotamian civilization, also rose annually, but "unpredictably and fitfully, breaking man's dikes and submerging his crops."[18] (See Map 2.2.) Furthermore, an open environment without serious obstacles to travel made Mesopotamia far more vulnerable to invasion than the much more protected space of Egypt, which was surrounded by deserts, mountains, seas, and cataracts. For long periods of its history, Egypt enjoyed a kind of "free security" from external attack that Mesopotamians clearly lacked.

But does the physical environment shape the human cultures that develop within it? Most historians are reluctant to endorse any kind of determinism, especially one suggesting that "geography is destiny," but in the case of Mesopotamia and Egypt, it is hard to deny some relationship between the physical setting and culture.

In at least some of its literature, the Mesopotamian outlook on life, which developed within a precarious, unpredictable, and often violent environment, viewed humankind as caught in an inherently disorderly world, subject to the whims of ca-

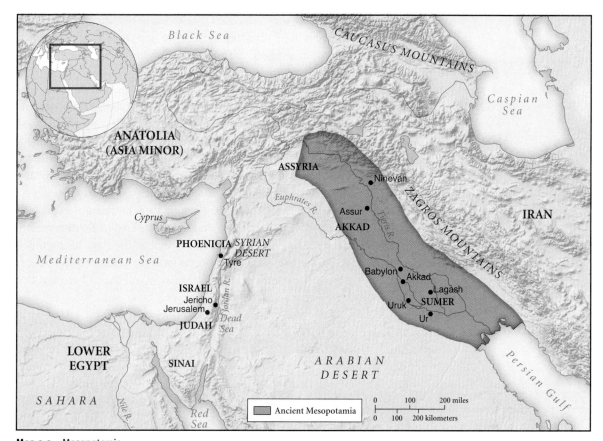

Map 2.2 Mesopotamia

After about 1,000 years of independent and competitive existence, the city-states of Sumer were incorporated into a number of larger imperial states based in Akkad, Babylon, and then Assyria.

pricious and quarreling gods, and facing death without much hope of a blessed life beyond. A Mesopotamian poet complained: "I have prayed to the gods and sacrificed, but who can understand the gods in heaven? Who knows what they plan for us? Who has ever been able to understand a god's conduct?"[19] The famous Mesopotamian *Epic of Gilgamesh* likewise depicted a rather pessimistic view of the gods and of the possibility for eternal life (see Document 2.1, pp. 92–95).

By contrast, elite literate culture in Egypt, developing in a more stable, predictable, and beneficent environment, produced a rather more cheerful and hopeful outlook on the world. The rebirth of the sun every day and of the river every year seemed to assure Egyptians that life would prevail over death. The amazing pyramids, constructed during Egypt's Old Kingdom (2663–2195 B.C.E.), reflected the firm belief that at least the pharaohs and other high-ranking people could successfully make the journey to eternal life in the Land of the West. Incantations for the dead describe an afterlife of abundance and tranquility that Gilgamesh could only have envied (see Document 2.3, p. 98). Over time, larger groups of people, beyond the pharaoh and his entourage, came to believe that they too could gain access to the afterlife if they followed proper procedures and lived a morally upright life (see Document 2.4, pp. 98–99). Thus Egyptian civilization not only affirmed the possibility of eternal life but also expanded access to it.

If the different environments of Mesopotamia and Egypt shaped their societies and cultures, those civilizations, with their mounting populations and growing demand for resources, likewise had an impact on the environment.[20] The *Epic of Gilgamesh* inscribed in mythology the deforestation of Mesopotamia. When the ruler Gilgamesh sought to make for himself "a name that endures" by building walls, ramparts, and temples, he required much timber. But to acquire it, he had first to kill Humbaba, appointed by the gods to guard the forests. The epic describes what happened next: "Then there followed confusion. . . . Now the mountains were moved and all the hills, for the guardian of the forest was killed. They attacked the cedars. . . . So they pressed on into the forest . . . and while Gilgamesh felled the first of the trees of the forest, Enkidu [the friend of Gilgamesh] cleared their roots as far as the banks of Euphrates."[21]

In Sumer (southern Mesopotamia), such deforestation and the soil erosion that followed from it sharply decreased crop yields between 2400 and 1700 B.C.E. Also contributing to this disaster was the increasing salinization of the soil, a long-term outcome of intensive irrigation. By 2000 B.C.E., there were reports that "the earth turned white" as salt accumulated in the soil. As a result, wheat was largely replaced by barley, which is far more tolerant of salty conditions. This ecological deterioration clearly weakened Sumerian city-states, facilitated their conquest by foreigners, and shifted the center of Mesopotamian civilization permanently to the north.

Egypt, by contrast, created a more sustainable agricultural system, which lasted for thousands of years and contributed to the remarkable continuity of its civilization. Whereas Sumerian irrigation involved a complex and artificial network of canals and dikes that led to the salinization of the soil, its Egyptian counterpart was much less intrusive, simply regulating the natural flow of the Nile. Such a system avoided the problem of salty soils, allowing Egyptian agriculture to emphasize wheat production, but it depended on the general regularity and relative gentleness of the Nile's annual flooding. On occasion, that pattern was interrupted, with serious consequences for Egyptian society. An extended period of low floods between 2250 and 1950 B.C.E. led to sharply reduced agricultural output, large-scale starvation, the loss of livestock, and, consequently, social upheaval and political disruption. Nonetheless, Egypt's ability to work *with* its more favorable natural environment enabled a degree of stability and continuity that proved impossible in Sumer, where human action intruded more heavily into a less benevolent natural setting.

Cities and States

Politically as well as culturally and environmentally, Mesopotamian and Egyptian civilizations differed sharply. For its first thousand years (3200–2350 B.C.E.), Mesopotamian civilization, located in the southern Tigris-Euphrates region known as Sumer, was organized in a dozen or more separate and independent city-states. Each city-state was ruled by a king, who claimed to represent the city's patron deity and who controlled the affairs of the walled city and surrounding rural area. Quite remarkably, some 80 percent of the population of Sumer lived in one or another of these city-states, making Mesopotamia the most thoroughly urbanized society of ancient times. The chief reason for this massive urbanization, however, lay in the great flaw of this system, for frequent warfare among these Sumerian city-states caused people living in rural areas to flee to the walled cities for protection. With no overarching authority, rivalry over land and water often led to violent conflict.

These conflicts, together with environmental devastation, eventually left Sumerian cities vulnerable to outside forces, and after about 2350 B.C.E., stronger peoples from northern Mesopotamia conquered Sumer's warring cities, bringing an end to the Sumerian phase of Mesopotamian civilization. First the Akkadians (2350–2000 B.C.E.) and later the Babylonians (1900–1500 B.C.E.) and the Assyrians (900–612 B.C.E.) created larger territorial states or bureaucratic empires that encompassed all or most of Mesopotamia. Periods of political unity now descended upon this First Civilization, but it was unity imposed from outside.

Egyptian civilization, by contrast, began its history around 3100 B.C.E., with the merger of several earlier states or chiefdoms into a unified territory that stretched some 1,000 miles along the Nile. For an amazing 3,000 years, Egypt maintained that unity and independence, though with occasional interruptions. A combination of wind patterns that made it easy to sail south along the Nile and a current flowing north facilitated communication, exchange, unity, and stability within the Nile Valley. Here was a record of political longevity and continuity that the Mesopotamians and many other ancient peoples could not replicate.

Cities in Egypt were less important than in Mesopotamia, although political capitals, market centers, and major burial sites gave Egypt an urban presence as well. Most people lived in agricultural villages along the river rather than in urban centers, perhaps because Egypt's greater security made it less necessary for people to gather in fortified towns. The focus of the Egyptian state resided in the pharaoh, believed to be a god in human form. He alone ensured the daily rising of the sun and the annual flooding of the Nile. All of the country's many officials served at his pleasure, and access to the afterlife lay in proximity to him and burial in or near his towering pyramids.

This image of the pharaoh and his role as an enduring symbol of Egyptian civilization persisted over the course of three millennia, but the realities of Egyptian political life did not always match the ideal, as the Portrait of Paneb so vividly illustrates (see pp. 84–85). By 2400 B.C.E., the power of the pharaoh had diminished, as local officials and nobles, who had been awarded their own land and were able to pass their positions on to their sons, assumed greater authority. When changes in the weather resulted in the Nile's repeated failure to flood properly around 2200 B.C.E., the authority of the pharaoh was severely discredited, and Egypt dissolved for several centuries into a series of local principalities.

Even when centralized rule was restored around 2000 B.C.E., the pharaohs never regained their old power and prestige. Kings were now warned that they too would

PORTRAIT

Paneb, An Egyptian Criminal

The life of Paneb (ca. thirteenth century B.C.E.) illuminates an underside of Egyptian life rather different from the images of order and harmony portrayed in much of ancient Egyptian art and literature.[22] Paneb was born into a family and a village of tomb workers—people who quarried, sculpted, and painted the final resting places of the pharaohs at a time when royal pyramids were no longer being constructed. Granted generous allowances of grain, beer, fish, vegetables, firewood, and clothing, tomb workers represented a prestigious occupation in ancient Egypt.

Paneb was apparently orphaned as a youngster and raised by another tomb-working family, that of the childless Neferhotep, a foreman of the tomb workers' crew who brought his adopted son into the profession. But Paneb quarreled violently with Neferhotep, on one occasion smashing the door to his house and threatening to kill him.

As an adult, Paneb married and sired a large family of eight or nine children. He also indulged in numerous

Paneb worshipping a coiled cobra representing the goddess Meretseger, patron deity of the burial grounds in Thebes where Paneb worked. (© The Trustees of the British Museum)

affairs with married women and was involved in at least one rape. One of his lovers was the wife of a man with whom Paneb had grown up in Neferhotep's home; the couple subsequently divorced, a frequent occurrence in ancient Egypt. In another case, Paneb seduced both a married woman and her daughter and shared the sexual favors of the daughter with his son Aapehty. It is not difficult to imagine the tensions that such behavior created in a small close-knit village.

When Paneb's adoptive father Neferhotep died—he was perhaps murdered—Paneb succeeded him as workplace foreman, thus incurring the lifelong hostility of Neferhotep's brother, Amennakht, who felt he had better claim to the job. What turned the tide in Paneb's favor was his "gift" of five servants, made to the vizier, the pharaoh's highest official, who was responsible for such appointments. To add insult to Amennakht's injury, those servants had belonged to Neferhotep himself.

have to account for their actions at the Day of Judgment. Nobles no longer sought to be buried near the pharaoh's pyramid but instead created their own more modest tombs in their own areas. Osiris, the god of the dead, became increasingly prominent, and all worthy men, not only those who had been close to the pharaoh in life, could aspire to immortality in his realm.[23]

Interaction and Exchange

■ **Connection**

In what ways were Mesopotamian and Egyptian civilizations shaped by their interactions with near and distant neighbors?

Although Mesopotamia and Egypt represented separate and distinct civilizations, they interacted frequently with each other and with both near and more distant neighbors. Even in these ancient times, the First Civilizations were embedded in larger networks of commerce, culture, and power. None of them stood alone.

While such bribes were common practice in obtaining promotions, it was Paneb's use of his position as foreman of the tomb workers' crew that got him into ever deeper trouble. He actively harassed his rival Amennakht, preventing him and his family from using the small chapel in which workers celebrated the festivals of their gods. He quarreled with the foreman of another work crew saying: "I'll attack you on the mountain and I'll kill you." Such angry outbursts led to frequent fighting and gained Paneb a reputation for brutality.

Paneb also exploited his position as foreman to his own advantage. He used—or stole—expensive tools given to the work crew for his own purposes. He ordered members of his work crew to do personal work for him—making a bed which he then sold to a high official, feeding his oxen, weaving baskets for his personal use, and preparing and decorating his own tomb, using materials pilfered from the royal tombs he was charged with constructing. On one occasion he stole the covering of a royal chariot and another time he entered a royal tomb, drank the wine intended for the pharaoh's afterlife, and in an act of enormous disrespect . . . even blasphemy . . . actually sat on the sarcophagus containing the embalmed body of the ruler.

Although rebuked from time to time by high officials, Paneb's bad behavior continued. "He could not stop his clamor," according to an official document. At some point, Paneb's son publicly denounced his father's sexual escapades. But the final straw that broke his career came from Amennakht, Paneb's long-time rival. He apparently had had enough and drew up a long list of particulars detailing Paneb's crimes. That document, from which our knowledge of Paneb largely derives, has survived. It concluded in this fashion:

> He is thus not worthy of this position. For truly, he seems well, [but] he is like a crazy person. And he kills people to prevent them from carrying out a mission of the Pharaoh. See, I wish to convey knowledge of his condition to the vizier.

The outcome of this complaint is unclear, for Paneb subsequently disappears from the historical record, and a new foreman was appointed in his place. It was not, however, Amennakht.

Questions: Since most of the evidence against Paneb comes from his archrival, how much weight should historians grant to that account? How might the story appear if written from Paneb's viewpoint? What perspectives on the Egypt of his time does Paneb's career disclose? How do those perspectives differ from more conventional and perhaps idealized understandings?

The early beginnings of Egyptian civilization illustrate the point. Its agriculture drew upon wheat and barley, which likely reached Egypt from Mesopotamia, as well as gourds, watermelon, domesticated donkeys, and cattle, which came from the Sudan to the south. The practice of "divine kingship" probably derived from the central or eastern Sudan, where small-scale agricultural communities had long viewed their rulers as sacred and buried them with various servants and officials. From this complex of influences, the Egyptians created something distinct and unique, but that civilization had roots in both Africa and Southwest Asia.[24]

Furthermore, once they were established, both Mesopotamia and Egypt carried on long-distance trade, mostly in luxury goods destined for the elite. Sumerian merchants had established seaborne contact with the Indus Valley civilization as early as 2300 B.C.E., while Indus Valley traders and their interpreters had taken up residence

Egypt and Nubia
By the fourteenth century B.C.E., Nubia was a part of an Egyptian empire. This wall painting shows Nubian princes bringing gifts or tribute, including rings and bags of gold, to Huy, the Egyptian viceroy of Nubia. The mural comes from Huy's tomb. (© The Trustees of the British Museum)

in Mesopotamia. Other trade routes connected it to Anatolia (present-day Turkey), Egypt, Iran, and Afghanistan. During Akkadian rule over Mesopotamia, a Sumerian poet described its capital of Agade:

> In those days the dwellings of Agade were filled with gold,
> its bright-shining houses were filled with silver,
> into its granaries were brought copper, tin, slabs of
> lapis lazuli [a blue gemstone], its silos bulged at the sides . . .
> its quay where the boats docked were all bustle. . . .[25]

All of this and more came from far away.

Egyptian trade likewise extended far afield. Beyond its involvement with the Mediterranean and the Middle East, Egyptian trading journeys extended deep into Africa, including Nubia, south of Egypt in the Nile Valley, and Punt, along the East African coast of Ethiopia and Somalia. One Egyptian official described his return from an expedition to Nubia: "I came down with three hundred donkeys laden with incense, ebony, . . . panther skins, elephant tusks, throw sticks, and all sorts of good products."[26] What most intrigued the very young pharaoh who sent him, however, was a dancing dwarf that accompanied the expedition back to Egypt.

Along with trade goods went cultural influence from the civilizations of Mesopotamia and Egypt. Among the smaller societies of the region to feel this influence were the Hebrews. Their sacred writings, recorded in the Old Testament, showed the influence of Mesopotamia in the "eye for an eye" principle of their legal system and in the story of a flood that destroyed the world. The Phoenicians, who were commercially active in the Mediterranean basin from their homeland in present-day Lebanon, also were influenced by Mesopotamian civilization. They venerated Asarte, a local form of the Mesopotamian fertility goddess Istar. They also adapted the Sumerian cuneiform method of writing to a much easier alphabetic system, which later became the basis for Greek and Latin writing. Various Indo-European peoples, dispersing probably from north-central Anatolia, also incorporated Sumerian deities into their own religions as well as bronze metallurgy and the wheel into their economies. When their widespread migrations carried them across much of Eurasia, they took these Sumerian cultural artifacts with them.

Egyptian cultural influence likewise spread in several directions. Nubia, located to the south of Egypt in the Nile Valley, not only traded with its more powerful neighbor but also was subject to periodic military intervention and political control from Egypt. Skilled Nubian archers were actively recruited for service as mercenaries in Egyptian armies. They often married Egyptian women and were buried in Egyptian style. All of this led to the diffusion of Egyptian culture in Nubia, expressed in building Egyptian-style pyramids, worshipping Egyptian gods and goddesses, and making use of Egyptian hieroglyphic writing. Despite this cultural borrowing, Nubia remained a distinct civilization, developing its own alphabetic script, retaining many of its own gods, developing a major ironworking industry by 500 B.C.E., and asserting its political independence whenever possible. The Nubian kingdom of Kush, in fact, invaded Egypt in 760 B.C.E. and ruled it for about 100 years. (See the Portrait of Piye, pp. 268–69.)

In the Mediterranean basin, clear Egyptian influence is visible in the art of Minoan civilization, which emerged on the island of Crete about 2500 B.C.E. More controversial has been the claim by historian Martin Bernal in a much-publicized book, *Black Athena* (1987), that ancient Greek culture—its art, religion, philosophy, and language—drew heavily upon Egyptian as well as Mesopotamian precedents. His book lit up a passionate debate among scholars. To some of his critics, Bernal seemed to undermine the originality of Greek civilization by suggesting that it had Afro-Asian origins. His supporters accused the critics of Eurocentrism. Whatever its outcome, the controversy surrounding Bernal's book served to focus attention on Egypt's relationship to black Africa and to the world of the Mediterranean basin.

Influence was not a one-way street, however, as Egypt and Mesopotamia likewise felt the impact of neighboring peoples. Pastoral peoples, speaking Indo-European languages and living in what is now southern Russia, had domesticated the horse by perhaps 4000 B.C.E. and later learned to tie that powerful animal to wheeled carts and chariots. This new technology provided a fearsome military potential that enabled various chariot-driving peoples, such as the Hittites, to threaten ancient civilizations. Based in Anatolia, the Hittites sacked the city of Babylon in 1595 B.C.E. Several centuries later, conflict between the Hittites and Egypt over control of Syria resulted in the world's first written peace treaty. But chariot technology was portable, and soon both the Egyptians and the Mesopotamians incorporated it into their own military forces. In fact, this powerful military innovation, together with the knowledge of bronze metallurgy, spread quickly and widely, reaching China by 1200 B.C.E. There it enabled the creation of a strong Chinese state ruled by the Shang dynasty. All of these developments provide evidence of at least indirect connections across parts of the Afro-Eurasian landmass in ancient times. Even then, no civilization was wholly isolated from larger patterns of interaction.

In Egypt, the centuries following 1650 B.C.E. witnessed the migration of foreigners from surrounding regions and conflict with neighboring peoples, shaking the sense of security that this Nile Valley civilization had long enjoyed. It also stimulated the normally complacent Egyptians to adopt a number of technologies pioneered earlier in Asia, including the horse-drawn chariot; new kinds of armor, bows, daggers, and swords; improved methods of spinning and weaving; new musical instruments; and olive and pomegranate trees. Absorbing these foreign innovations, Egyptians went on to create their own empire, both in Nubia and in the eastern Mediterranean regions of Syria and Palestine. By 1500 B.C.E., the previously self-contained Egypt became for several centuries an imperial state bridging Africa and Asia, ruling over substantial numbers of non-Egyptian peoples (see Map 2.3). It also became part of an international political system that included the Babylonian and later Assyrian empires of Mesopotamia as well as many other peoples of the region. Egyptian and Babylonian rulers engaged in regular diplomatic correspondence, referred to one another as "brother," exchanged gifts, and married their daughters into one another's families. Or at least

Map 2.3   An Egyptian Empire
During the New Kingdom period after 1550 B.C.E., Egypt became for several centuries an empire, extending its political control southward into Nubia and northward into Palestine.

they tried to. While Babylonian rulers were willing to send their daughters to Egypt, the Egyptians were exceedingly reluctant to return the favor, claiming that "from ancient times the daughter of the king of Egypt has not been given to anyone." To this rebuff, the disappointed Babylonian monarch replied: "You are a king and you can do as pleases you.... Send me [any] beautiful woman as if she were your daughter. Who is to say this woman is not the daughter of the king."[27]

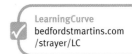

LearningCurve
bedfordstmartins.com
/strayer/LC

Reflections: "Civilization": What's in a Word?

In examining the cultures of ancient Mesopotamia and Egypt, we are worlds away from life in agricultural villages or Paleolithic camps. Much the same holds for those of the Indus Valley, Central Asia, China, Mesoamerica, and the Andes. Strangely enough, historians have been somewhat uncertain as to how to refer to these new forms of human community. Following common practice, I have called them "civilizations," but scholars have reservations about the term for two reasons. The first is its implication of superiority. In popular usage, "civilization" suggests refined behavior, a "higher" form of society, something unreservedly positive. The opposite of "civilized"—"barbarian," "savage," or "uncivilized"—is normally understood as an insult implying inferiority. That, of course, is precisely how the inhabitants of many civilizations have viewed those outside their own societies, particularly those neighboring peoples living without the alleged benefit of cities and states.

Modern assessments of the First Civilizations reveal a profound ambiguity about these new, larger, and more complex societies. On the one hand, these civilizations have given us inspiring art, profound reflections on the meaning of life, more productive technologies, increased control over nature, and the art of writing—all of which have been cause for celebration. On the other hand, as anthropologist Marvin Harris noted, "human beings learned for the first time how to bow, grovel, kneel, and kowtow."[28] Massive inequalities, state oppression, slavery, large-scale warfare, the subordination of women, and epidemic disease also accompanied the rise of civilization, generating discontent, rebellion, and sometimes the urge to escape. This ambiguity about the character of civilizations has led some historians to avoid the word, referring to early Egypt, Mesopotamia, and other regions instead as complex societies, urban-based societies, state-organized societies, or some other more neutral term.

A second reservation about using the term "civilization" derives from its implication of solidity—the idea that civilizations represent distinct and widely shared identities with clear boundaries that mark them off from other such units. It is unlikely, however, that many people living in Mesopotamia, Norte Chico, or ancient China felt themselves part of a shared culture. Local identities defined by occupation, clan affiliation, village, city, or region were surely more important for most people than those of some larger civilization. At best, members of an educated upper class who shared a common literary tradition may have felt themselves part of some more inclusive civilization, but that left out most of the population. Moreover, unlike modern nations, none of the earlier civilizations had definite borders. Any identification with that civilization surely faded as distance from its core region increased. Finally, the line between civilizations and other kinds of societies is not always clear. Just when does a village or town become a city? At what point does a chiefdom become a state? Scholars continue to argue about these distinctions.

Given these reservations, should historians discard the notion of civilization? Maybe so, but this book continues to use it both because it is so deeply embedded in our way of thinking about the world and because no alternative concept has achieved widespread acceptance for making distinctions among different kinds of human communities. When the term appears in the text, keep in mind two points. First, as used by historians, "civilization" is a purely descriptive term, designating a particular and distinctive type of human society—one with cities and states—and does not imply any judgment or assessment, any sense of superiority or inferiority. Second, it is used to define broad cultural patterns in particular geographic regions—Mesopotamia, the Peruvian coast, or China, for example—even though many people living in those regions may have been more aware of differences and conflicts than of those commonalities.

Second Thoughts

LearningCurve
Check what you know.
bedfordstmartins.com
/strayer/LC

Online Study Guide
bedfordstmartins.com
/highschool/strayer

What's the Significance?

Norte Chico/Caral, 63; 66

Indus Valley civilization, 66

Central Asian/Oxus civilization, 67–68

Olmec civilization, 68; 78

Uruk, 69–70

Mohenjo Daro/Harappa, 70

Epic of Gilgamesh, 70; 81

Code of Hammurabi, 71–72

patriarchy, 73–75

rise of the state, 75–80

Egypt: "the gift of the Nile," 80–89

Paneb, 84–85

Nubia, 86

Big Picture Questions

1. How does the use of the term "civilization" by historians differ from that of popular usage? How do you use the term?

2. "Civilizations were held together largely by force." Do you agree with this assessment, or were there other mechanisms of integration as well?

3. How did the various First Civilizations differ from one another?

4. **Looking Back:** To what extent did civilizations represent "progress" in comparison with earlier Paleolithic and Neolithic societies? And in what ways did they constitute a setback for humankind?

Next Steps: For Further Study

Cyril Aldred, *The Egyptians* (1998). A brief and up-to-date account from a widely recognized expert.

Jonathan M. Kenoyer, *Ancient Cities of the Indus Valley Civilization* (1998). A thorough and beautifully illustrated study by a leading archeologist of the area.

Samuel Noah Kramer, *History Begins at Sumer* (1981). A classic account of Sumerian civilization, filled with wonderful stories and anecdotes.

David B. O'Connor, *Ancient Nubia: Egypt's Rival in Africa* (1994). An overview of this ancient African civilization, with lovely illustrations based on a museum exhibit.

Christopher A. Pool, *Olmec Archeology and Early Mesoamerica* (2007). A scholarly and up-to-date account of the earliest civilization in Mesoamerica.

Robert Thorp, *China in the Early Bronze Age: Shang Civilization* (2006). An accessible and scholarly account of early Chinese civilization informed by recent archeological discoveries.

"The Indus Civilization," http://www.harappa.com/har/haro.html. Hundreds of vivid pictures and several brief essays on the Indus Valley civilization.

The British Museum, "Ancient Egypt," http://www.ancientegypt.co.uk/menu.html. An interactive exploration of Egyptian civilization.

For Web sites and additional documents related to this chapter, see **Make History** at bedfordstmartins.com /highschool/strayer.

Documents

Considering the Evidence:
Life and Afterlife in Mesopotamia and Egypt

The advent of writing was not only a central feature of most First Civilizations but also a great boon to later historians. Access to their early written records allows us some insight, in their own words, as to how these ancient peoples thought about their societies and their place in the larger scheme of things. Such documents, of course, tell only a small part of the story, for they most often reflect the thinking of the literate few—usually male, upper-class, powerful, and well-to-do—rather than the outlook of the vast majority who lacked such privileged positions. Nonetheless, historians have been grateful for even this limited window on the life of at least some of our ancient ancestors.

Among the First Civilizations, accessible written records are most widely available for Mesopotamia and Egypt. Those excerpted here disclose something about those peoples' understandings of life in this world—class and gender, crime and justice, occupation and kingship—as well as about what awaits in the life beyond. Such reflections about life and afterlife allow us to catch a glimpse of the social organization and cultural outlook of these First Civilizations.

Document 2.1

In Search of Eternal Life

The best known of the writings from the world of the First Civilizations is surely the *Epic of Gilgamesh*. Inscribed on clay tablets in various versions, the Gilgamesh epic has been pieced together by scholars over the past century or so. Its origins no doubt go back to stories about this legendary ruler, said to be the powerful monarch of the Sumerian city of Uruk. Compiled from earlier oral versions, the first written text of the epic dates to around 1200–600 B.C.E.

The epic poem itself recounts the adventures of Gilgamesh, said to be part human and part divine. As the story opens, he is the energetic but oppressive ruler of Uruk. The pleas of his people persuade the gods to send Enkidu, a beast-like uncivilized man from the wilderness, to counteract this oppression. But before he can confront the erring monarch, Enkidu must become civilized, a process that occurs at the hands of a seductive harlot. When the two men finally meet, they engage in a titanic wrestling match from which Gilgamesh emerges victorious. Thereafter they bond in a deep friendship and undertake a series of adventures together. In the course of these adventures, they offend the gods, who then determine that Enkidu must die. Devastated by the loss of his friend and the realization of his own mortality, Gilgamesh embarks on an extended search for eternal life. During this search, he meets a tavern owner, who is a wise goddess named Siduri, as well as Utnapishtim, the only human being ever granted immortality by the gods. In the end, however, Gilgamesh learns that eternal life is not available to mere mortals and thus his quest proves futile.

The excerpts that follow illustrate something of Mesopotamian views of kingship, of the gods, and of the possibilities of life and afterlife.

- How would you define the Mesopotamian ideal of kingship? What is the basis of the monarch's legitimacy?

- What understanding of the afterlife does the epic suggest?

- What philosophy of life comes across in the Gilgamesh story?

- How does the *Epic of Gilgamesh* portray the gods and their relationship to humankind?

The Epic of Gilgamesh
ca. 2700–2500 B.C.E.

On Kingship

[These first selections deal with the nature of kingship. They tell of the great deeds of Gilgamesh and his oppression of the people as well as recounting the instructions about kingship from Enlil, the chief Sumerian god, who is responsible for determining the destinies of humankind.]

I will proclaim to the world the deeds of Gilgamesh. This was the man to whom all things were known; this was the king who knew the countries of the world. He was wise, he saw mysteries and knew secret things, he brought us a tale of the days before the flood. He went on a long journey, was weary, worn-out with labor, returning he rested, he engraved on a stone the whole story.

When the gods created Gilgamesh they gave him a perfect body. Shamash, the glorious sun, endowed him with beauty, Adad, the god of the storm, endowed him with courage, the great gods made his beauty perfect, surpassing all others, terrifying like a great wild bull. Two-thirds they made him god and one-third man.

In Uruk he built walls, a great rampart, and the temple of blessed Eanna for the god of the firmament Anu, and for Ishtar the goddess of love.... Climb upon the wall of Uruk; walk along it, I say; regard the foundation terrace and examine the masonry: is it not burnt brick and good? The seven sages laid the foundations.

Source: *The Epic of Gilgamesh*, translated by N. K. Sanders (London: Penguin, 1972), 61–62, 70, 92–93, 101–2, 106–11.

Gilgamesh went abroad in the world, but he met with none who could withstand his arms till he came to Uruk. But the men of Uruk muttered in their houses, "Gilgamesh sounds the tocsin for his amusement, his arrogance has no bounds by day or night. No son is left with his father, for Gilgamesh takes them all, even the children; yet the king should be a shepherd to his people. His lust leaves no virgin to her lover, neither the warrior's daughter nor the wife of the noble; yet this is the shepherd of the city, wise, comely, and resolute."

Enlil of the mountain, the father of the gods, had decreed the destiny of Gilgamesh. So Gilgamesh dreamed and Enkidu said, "The meaning of the dream is this. The father of the gods has given you kingship, such is your destiny; everlasting life is not your destiny. Because of this do not be sad at heart, do not be grieved or oppressed. He has given you power to bind and to loose, to be the darkness and the light of mankind. He has given you unexampled supremacy over the people, victory in battle from which no fugitive returns, in forays and assaults from which there is no going back. But do not abuse this power, deal justly with your servants in the palace, deal justly before Shamash.

On the Search for Immortality

[As Enkidu lies dying, he tells Gilgamesh of a dream he had about the afterlife.]

"[T]his is the dream I dreamed last night. The heavens roared, and earth rumbled back an answer; between them stood I before an awful being, the somber-faced man-bird; he had directed on me his purpose. His was a vampire face, his foot was a lion's foot, his hand was an eagle's talon. He fell on me and his claws were in my hair, he held me fast and I smothered; then he transformed me so that my arms became wings covered with feathers. He turned his stare toward me, and he led me away to the palace of Irkalla, the Queen of Darkness, to the house from which none who enters ever returns, down the road from which there is no coming back.

"There is the house whose people sit in darkness; dust is their food and clay their meat. They are clothed like birds with wings for covering, they see no light, they sit in darkness. I entered the house of dust and I saw the kings of the earth, their crowns put away for ever; rulers and princes, all those who once wore kingly crowns and ruled the world in the days of old. They who had stood in the place of the gods like Anu and Enlil, stood now like servants to fetch baked meats in the house of dust, to carry cooked meat and cold water from the water-skin. In the house of dust which I entered were high priests and acolytes, priests of the incantation and of ecstasy. . . . Then I awoke like a man drained of blood who wanders alone in a waste of rushes."

[When Gilgamesh in his quest for immortality meets Siduri, the tavern keeper, he confesses to her his fear and anguish, and receives some wise counsel in return.]

"[M]y friend who was very dear to me and who endured dangers beside me, Enkidu my brother, whom I loved, the end of mortality has overtaken him. I wept for him seven days and nights till the worm fastened to him. Because of my brother I am afraid of death, because of my brother I stray through the wilderness and cannot rest. But now, young woman, maker of wine, since I have seen your face do not let me see the face of death which I dread so much."

She answered, "Gilgamesh, where are you hurrying to? You will never find that life for which you are looking. When the gods created man they allotted to him death, but life they retained in their own keeping. As for you, Gilgamesh, fill your belly with good things; day and night, night and day, dance and be merry, feast and rejoice. Let your clothes be fresh, bathe yourself in water, cherish the little child that holds your hand, and make your wife happy in your embrace; for this too is the lot of man."

[Later, when Gilgamesh reaches Utnapishtim, the only man to survive the great flood and receive eternal life from the gods, he hears a similar message.]

Utnapishtim said, "There is no permanence. Do we build a house to stand forever, do we seal a contract to hold for all time? Do brothers divide an inheritance to keep forever, does the flood-time of rivers endure? . . . From the days of old there is no permanence. The sleeping and the dead, how alike they are, they are like a painted death. What is there between the master and the servant when both have fulfilled their doom? When the Anunnaki, the judges, come together, and Mammetun the mother of destinies, together they decree the fates of men. Life and death they allot but the day of death they do not disclose."

On the Gods

[In his conversation with Utnapishtim, Gilgamesh learns something about the nature of Mesopotamian gods and the origins of the great flood, which ages ago had destroyed humankind.]

"You know the city Shurrupak, it stands on the banks of the Euphrates? That city grew old and the gods that were in it were old. . . . In those days the world teemed, the people multiplied, the world bellowed like a wild bull, and the great god was aroused by the clamor. Enlil heard the clamor and he said to the gods in council, 'The uproar of mankind is intolerable and sleep is no longer possible by reason of the babel.' So the gods agreed to exterminate mankind. . . .

"With the first light of dawn a black cloud came from the horizon; it thundered within where Adad, lord of the storm, was riding. . . . A stupor of despair went up to heaven when the god of the storm turned daylight to darkness, when he smashed the land like a cup. One whole day the tempest raged, gathering fury as it went, it poured over the people like the tides of battle; a man could not see his brother nor the people be seen from heaven. Even the gods were terrified at the flood, they fled to the highest heaven, the firmament of Anu; they crouched against the walls, cowering like curs. Then Ishtar the sweet-voiced Queen of Heaven cried out like a woman in travail: 'Alas the days of old are turned to dust because I commanded evil; why did I command this evil in the council of all the gods? I commanded wars to destroy the people, but are they not my people, for I brought them forth? Now like the spawn of fish they float in the ocean.' The great gods of heaven and of hell wept, they covered their mouths."

Document 2.2

Law and Justice in Ancient Mesopotamia

If the *Epic of Gilgamesh* affords us some insight into Mesopotamian cultural and religious thinking, the so-called Code of Hammurabi provides a glimpse of this First Civilization's social and economic life. Hammurabi (r. ca. 1795–1750 B.C.E.) was the ruler of the Babylonian Empire, which for a time gave a measure of political unity to the rival cities and kingdoms of Mesopotamia. Sometime during his reign he ordered inscribed on a large stone stele a number of laws, judgments, or decrees. They were intended, in Hammurabi's words, "to bring about the rule of righteousness in the land, to destroy the wicked and the evil-doers; so that the strong should not harm the weak . . . , to further the well-being of mankind."

■ If you knew nothing else about ancient Mesopotamia, what could you conclude from the Code of Hammurabi about the economy and society of this civilization in the eighteenth century B.C.E.? What kind of economy prevailed in the region? What distinct social groups are mentioned in the code? What rights did women enjoy and to what restrictions were they subject?

■ What can you infer from the code about the kind of social problems that afflicted ancient Mesopotamia?

■ How would you define the principles of justice that underlay Hammurabi's code? In what different ways might twenty-first-century observers and those living at the time of Hammurabi assess that system of justice?

The Law Code of Hammurabi
ca. 1800 B.C.E.

On Crime, Punishment, and Justice

2. If any one bring an accusation against a man, and the accused go to the river and leap into the river, if he sink in the river his accuser shall take possession of his house. But if the river prove that the accused is not guilty, and he escape unhurt, then he who had brought the accusation shall be put to death, while he who leaped into the river shall take possession of the house that had belonged to his accuser. . . .

3. If any one bring an accusation of any crime before the elders, and does not prove what he has charged, he shall, if it be a capital offense charged, be put to death. . . .

5. If a judge try a case, reach a decision, and present his judgment in writing; if later error shall appear in his decision, and it be through his own fault, then he shall pay twelve times the fine set by him in the case, and he shall be publicly removed from the judge's bench, and never again shall he sit there to render judgment. . . .

22. If any one is committing a robbery and is caught, then he shall be put to death. . . .

196. If a man put out the eye of another man, his eye shall be put out.

197. If he break another man's bone, his bone shall be broken. . . .

On the Economy

26. If a chieftain or a man [common soldier], who has been ordered to go upon the king's highway for war does not go, but hires a mercenary, if he withholds the compensation, then shall this officer or man be put to death, and he who represented him shall take possession of his house. . . .

30. If a chieftain or a man leave his house, garden, and field and hires it out, and some one else takes possession of his house, garden, and field and

uses it for three years: if the first owner return and claims his house, garden, and field, it shall not be given to him, but he who has taken possession of it and used it shall continue to use it. . . .

53. If any one be too lazy to keep his dam in proper condition, and does not so keep it; if then the dam break and all the fields be flooded, then shall he in whose dam the break occurred be sold for money, and the money shall replace the corn [grain] which he has caused to be ruined. . . .

104. If a merchant give an agent corn, wool, oil, or any other goods to transport, the agent shall give a receipt for the amount, and compensate the merchant therefore. Then he shall obtain a receipt from the merchant for the money that he gives the merchant. . . .

122. If any one give another silver, gold, or anything else to keep, he shall show everything to some witness, draw up a contract, and then hand it over for safe keeping. . . .

229. If a builder build a house for some one, and does not construct it properly, and the house which he built fall in and kill its owner, then that builder shall be put to death. . . .

253. If any one agree with another to tend his field, give him seed, entrust a yoke of oxen to him, and bind him to cultivate the field, if he steal the corn or plants, and take them for himself, his hands shall be hewn off. . . .

271. If any one hire oxen, cart, and driver, he shall pay one hundred and eighty ka of corn per day. . . .

On Class and Slavery

8. If any one steal cattle or sheep, or an ass, or a pig or a goat, if it belong to a god or to the court, the thief shall pay thirtyfold therefore; if they belonged to a freed man of the king he shall pay tenfold; if

the thief has nothing with which to pay, he shall be put to death. . . .

15. If any one take a male or female slave of the court, or a male or female slave of a freed man, outside the city gates, he shall be put to death. . . .

17. If any one find runaway male or female slaves in the open country and bring them to their masters, the master of the slaves shall pay him two shekels of silver. . . .

117. If any one fail to meet a claim for debt, and sell himself, his wife, his son, and daughter for money or give them away to forced labor: they shall work for three years in the house of the man who bought them, or the proprietor, and in the fourth year they shall be set free. . . .

198. If he put out the eye of a freed man, or break the bone of a freed man, he shall pay one gold mina.

199. If he put out the eye of a man's slave, or break the bone of a man's slave, he shall pay one-half of its value. . . .

202. If any one strike the body of a man higher in rank than he, he shall receive sixty blows with an ox-whip in public. . . .

215. If a physician make a large incision with an operating knife and cure it, or if he open a tumor [over the eye] with an operating knife, and saves the eye, he shall receive ten shekels in money.

216. If the patient be a freed man, he receives five shekels.

217. If he be the slave of some one, his owner shall give the physician two shekels. . . .

On Men and Women

110. If a "sister of a god" [a woman formally dedicated to the temple of a god] open a tavern, or enter a tavern to drink, then shall this woman be burned to death. . . .

128. If a man take a woman to wife, but have no intercourse with her, this woman is no wife to him.

129. If a man's wife be surprised with another man, both shall be tied and thrown into the water, but the husband may pardon his wife and the king his slaves.

130. If a man violate the wife [betrothed wife or child-wife] of another man, who has never known a man, and still lives in her father's house, and sleep with her and be surprised, this man shall be put to death, but the wife is blameless.

132. If the "finger is pointed" at a man's wife about another man, but she is not caught sleeping with the other man, she shall jump into the river for her husband. . . .

136. If any one leave his house, run away, and then his wife go to another house, if then he return, and wishes to take his wife back: because he fled from his home and ran away, the wife of this runaway shall not return to her husband.

137. If a man wish to separate from a woman who has borne him children, or from his wife who has borne him children: then he shall give that wife her dowry, and a part of the usufruct [the right to use] of field, garden, and property, so that she can rear her children. When she has brought up her children . . . she may then marry the man of her heart. . . .

142. If a woman quarrel with her husband, and say: "You are not congenial to me," the reasons for her prejudice must be presented. If she is guiltless, and there is no fault on her part, but he leaves and neglects her, then no guilt attaches to this woman, she shall take her dowry and go back to her father's house.

143. If she is not innocent, but leaves her husband, and ruins her house, neglecting her husband, this woman shall be cast into the water. . . .

148. If a man take a wife, and she be seized by disease, if he then desire to take a second wife, he shall not put away his wife who has been attacked by disease, but he shall keep her in the house which he has built and support her so long as she lives.

Source: *The Code of Hammurabi*, translated by L. W. King (New York, 1915).

Document 2.3

The Afterlife of a Pharaoh

Egyptian thinking about life, death, and afterlife bears comparison with that of Mesopotamia. In the selections that follow, we catch a glimpse of several Egyptian ways of understanding these fundamental human concerns. The first excerpt comes from a group of so-called pyramid texts, inscribed on the walls of a royal tomb as spells, incantations, or prayers to assist the pharaoh in entering the realm of eternal life among the gods in the Land of the West. This one was discovered in the tomb of the Egyptian king Teti, who ruled between roughly 2345 and 2333 B.C.E. Such texts represent the oldest religious writings in world history.

■ How is the afterlife of the pharaoh represented in this text?

■ How does it compare with depictions of the afterlife in the *Epic of Gilgamesh*?

A Pyramid Text

2333 B.C.E.

Oho! Oho! Rise up, O Teti!
Take your head, collect your bones,
Gather your limbs, shake the earth from your flesh!
Take your bread that rots not, your beer that
    sours not,
Stand at the gates that bar the common people!
The gatekeeper comes out to you, he grasps your
    hand,
Takes you into heaven, to your father Geb.
He rejoices at your coming, gives you his hands,

Kisses you, caresses you,
Sets you before the spirits, the imperishable stars. . . .
The hidden ones worship you,
The great ones surround you,
The watchers wait on you,
Barley is threshed for you,
Emmer° is reaped for you,
Your monthly feasts are made with it,
Your half-month feasts are made with it,
As ordered done for you by Geb,
your father, Rise up, O Teti, you shall not die!

Source: Miriam Lichtheim, *Ancient Egyptian Literature* (Berkeley: University of California Press, 1975), 1:41–42.

°**Emmer:** a variety of wheat.

Document 2.4

A New Basis for Egyptian Immortality

Much later, during the New Kingdom period of ancient Egyptian history (1550–1064 B.C.E.), the *Book of the Dead* was compiled, gathering together a number of magical spells designed to ensure a smooth passage to eternal life. Written on papyrus, the spells could be purchased by anyone who could afford them. The owner then inscribed his own name and title and had the document placed in his tomb. The most famous of these texts is the so-called Negative Confession, which portrays the deceased person appearing before the gods in a place of judgment to demonstrate his moral life and his fitness for a place in the Land of the West. Such practices extended to people other than just the pharaoh the possibility of magical assistance in gaining eternal life with the gods.

- What changes in Egyptian religious thinking does the Negative Confession mark?

- On what basis are the users of the Negative Confession making their claim for eternal life?

- What does the Negative Confession suggest about the sources of conflict and discord in New Kingdom Egypt? How do these compare with the social problems revealed in the Code of Hammurabi?

Book of the Dead
ca. 1550–1064 B.C.E.

When the deceased enters the hall of the goddesses of Truth, he says:

Homage to thee, O great god, thou Lord of Truth. I have come to thee, my Lord, and I have brought myself hither that I may see thy beauties. . . . I have brought Truth to thee. . . .

I have not oppressed (or wronged) [my] kinsfolk.
I have not committed evil in the place of truth.°
I have not committed acts of abomination.
I have not caused my name to appear for honors.
I have not domineered over slaves.
I have not thought scorn of the god.
I have not defrauded the poor man of his goods.
I have not caused harm to be done to the slave by his master.
I have caused no man to suffer.
I have allowed no man to go hungry.
I have made no man weep. I have slain no man.
I have not given the order for any man to be slain.
I have not caused pain to the multitude.
I have not filched the offerings in the temples.

I have not purloined the cakes of the gods.
I have not defiled myself in the pure places of the god of my city.
I have not cheated in measuring of grain.
I have not encroached upon the fields of others.
I have not added to the weight of the balance.
I have not cheated with the pointer of the scales.
I have not taken away the milk from the mouths of the babes.
I have not driven away the beasts from their pastures.
I have not netted the geese of the preserves of the gods.
I have not obstructed water when it should run.
I have not cut a cutting in a canal of rating water.
I have not extinguished a flame when it ought to burn.
I have not turned off cattle from the property of the gods.
I am pure. I am pure. I am pure. I am pure.

°**place of truth:** a temple or burial place.

Source: E. A. Wallis Budge, *Osiris, the Egyptian Religion of Resurrection* (London: P. L. Warner; New York: G. P. Putnam's Sons, 1911), 1:337–39.

Document 2.5

The Occupations of Old Egypt

Compared to small Paleolithic communities and later agricultural village societies, civilizations developed a far more complex division of labor and a much
greater sense of social hierarchy. Such features of the First Civilizations are on
display in the Egyptian text commonly known as "Be a Scribe." Dating from the
Middle Kingdom period (2066–1650 B.C.E.), it was a school text that students
training for administrative positions would copy in an effort to improve their
writing. It also conveyed to them the exalted position of a scribe in contrast to
many other occupations. One such text suggested that writing granted a kind of
immortality to the scribe: "Man decays; his corpse is dust; all his kin have perished. But a book makes him remembered through the mouth of its reciter."[29]

- What might historians learn from this text about the occupational and
  social structure of Middle Kingdom Egypt?

- What does learning to write offer to a young Egyptian? What advantages
  of a scribal position are suggested in the document?

- What timeless frustrations of a teacher are evident in this text?

Be a Scribe
ca. 2066–1650 B.C.E.

Apply yourself to [this] noble profession.... You
will find it useful.... You will be advanced by your
superiors. You will be sent on a mission.... Love
writing, shun dancing; then you become a worthy
official.... By day write with your fingers; recite by
night. Befriend the scroll, the palette. It pleases more
than wine. Writing for him who knows it is better
than all other professions. It pleases more than bread
and beer, more than clothing and ointment. It is
worth more than an inheritance in Egypt, than a
tomb in the west.

Young fellow, how conceited you are! ... But
though I beat you with every kind of stick, you do
not listen.... You are a person fit for writing, though
you have not yet known a woman. Your heart dis-
cerns, your fingers are skilled, your mouth is apt for
reciting....

But though I spend the day telling you "Write,"
it seems like a plague to you....

See for yourself with your own eye. The occupations lie before you.

The washerman's day is going up, going down.
All his limbs are weak, [from] whitening his neighbor's clothes every day, from washing their linen.

The maker of pots is smeared with soil.... [H]e
is like one who lives in the bog.

The cobbler mingles with vats. His odor is penetrating. His hands are red..., like one who is smeared
with blood....

The watchman prepares garlands and polishes
vase-stands. He spends a night of toil just as one on
whom the sun shines.

The merchants travel downstream and upstream.
They are as busy as can be, carrying goods from one
town to another. They supply him who has wants.

Source: Miriam Lichtheim, *Ancient Egyptian Literature*
(Berkeley: University of California Press, 1975), 2:168–72.

But the tax collectors carry off the gold, that most precious of metals.

The ships' crews from every house [of commerce], they receive their loads. They depart from Egypt for Syria, and each man's god is with him. [But] not one of them says: "We shall see Egypt again!"

[The] outworker who is in the fields, his is the toughest of all the jobs. He spends the day loaded with his tools, tied to his toolbox. When he returns home at night, he is loaded with the tool-box and the timbers, his drinking mug, and his whetstones. . . .

Let me also expound to you the situation of the peasant, that other tough occupation. [Comes] the inundation and soaks him . . . , he attends to his equipment. By day he cuts his farming tools; by night he twists rope. Even his midday hour he spends on farm labor. He equips himself to go to the field as if he were a warrior. . . . When he reaches his field he finds [it?] broken up. He spends time cultivating, and the snake is after him. It finishes off the seed as it is cast to the ground. He does not see a green blade. He does three plowings with borrowed grain. His wife has gone down to the merchants and found nothing for barter. . . .

If you have any sense, be a scribe. If you have learned about the peasant, you will not be able to be one. . . . Look, I instruct you to...make you become one whom the king trusts; to make you gain entrance to treasury and granary. To make you receive the shipload at the gate of the granary. To make you issue the offerings on feast days. You are dressed in fine clothes; you own horses. Your boat is on the river; you are supplied with attendants. You stride about inspecting. A mansion is built in your town. You have a powerful office, given you by the king. Male and female slaves are about you. Those who are in the fields grasp your hand, on plots that you have made. . . . Put the writings in your heart, and you will be protected from all kinds of toil. You will become a worthy official.

Do you not recall the [fate of] the unskilled man? His name is not known. He is ever burdened [like an ass carrying things] in front of the scribe who knows what he is about.

Come, [let me tell] you the woes of the soldier, and how many are his superiors: the general, the troop-commander, the officer who leads, the standard-bearer, the lieutenant, the scribe, the commander of fifty, and the garrison-captain. They go in and out in the halls of the palace, saying: "Get laborers!" He is awakened at any hour. One is after him as [after] a donkey. He toils until the Aten sets in his darkness of night. He is hungry, his belly hurts; he is dead while yet alive. When he receives the grain-ration, having been released from duty, it is not good for grinding.

He is called up for Syria. He may not rest. There are no clothes, no sandals. . . . His march is uphill through mountains. He drinks water every third day; it is smelly and tastes of salt. His body is ravaged by illness. The enemy comes, surrounds him with missiles, and life recedes from him. He is told: "Quick, forward, valiant soldier! Win for yourself a good name!" He does not know what he is about. His body is weak, his legs fail him. When victory is won, the captives are handed over to his majesty, to be taken to Egypt. . . . His wife and children are in their village; he dies and does not reach it. If he comes out alive, he is worn out from marching. . . .

Be a scribe, and be spared from soldiering! You call and one says: "Here I am." You are safe from torments. Every man seeks to raise himself up. Take note of it!

Using the Evidence: Life and Afterlife in Mesopotamia and Egypt

1. **Defining civilization:** What features of civilization, described in Chapter 2, do these documents illustrate?

2. **Making comparisons:** What similarities and differences between ancient Mesopotamian and Egyptian civilizations can you infer from these documents? How might you account for the differences?

3. **Considering past and present:** What elements of thought and practice from these early pieces of written literature resonate still in the twenty-first century? What elements remain strange or unfamiliar to modern sensibilities?

4. **Seeking further evidence:** What dimensions of these civilizations' social life and religious thinking are not addressed in these documents? What other perspectives might you want to seek out?

5. **Reading between the lines:** Historians often use documents to obtain insights or information that the authors did not intend to convey. How might these documents be used in this fashion? What are the advantages and dangers in this use of ancient texts?

Visual Sources

Considering the Evidence:
Indus Valley Civilization

In most accounts of the First Civilizations, Egypt and Mesopotamia hold center stage. And yet the civilization of the Indus River valley was much larger, and its archeological treasures have been equally impressive, though clearly distinctive. This civilization flourished around 2000 B.C.E., about a thousand years later than its better-known counterparts in the Middle East and North Africa. By 1700 B.C.E. Indus Valley civilization was in decline, as the center of Indian or South Asian civilization shifted gradually eastward to the plains of the Ganges River. In the process, all distinct memory of the earlier Indus Valley civilization vanished, to be rediscovered only in the early twentieth century as archeologists uncovered its remarkable remains. Here is yet another contrast with Egypt and Mesopotamia, where conscious memory of earlier achievements persisted long after those civilizations had passed into history.

Among the most distinctive elements of Indus Valley civilization were its cities, of which Mohenjo Daro and Harappa were the largest and are the most thoroughly investigated. Laid out systematically on a grid pattern and clearly planned, they were surrounded by substantial walls made from mud bricks of a standardized size and interrupted by imposing gateways. Inside the walls, public buildings, market areas, large and small houses, and craft workshops stood in each of the cities' various neighborhoods. Many houses had indoor latrines, while wide main streets and narrow side lanes had drains to carry away polluted water and sewage. (See p. 70 for an image of a ritual bathing pool in Mohenjo Daro.)

The images that follow are drawn from archeological investigations of the Indus Valley civilization and offer us a glimpse of its achievements and unique features. Since its written language was limited in extent and has not yet been deciphered, scholars have been highly dependent on its physical remains for understanding this First Civilization.

In many ancient and more recent societies, seals have been used for imprinting an image on a document or a product. Such seals have been among the most numerous artifacts found in the Indus Valley cities. They often carried the image of an animal—a bull, an elephant, a crocodile, a buffalo, or even a mythic creature such as a unicorn—as well as a title or inscription in a still undeciphered script. Thus the seals were accessible to an illiterate worker loading goods on organization of this civilization. Kenoyer has suggested that the great cities were likely controlled not by a single ruler, but by "a small group of elites, comprised of merchants, landowners, and ritual specialists."[31]

Visual Source 2.2, a statue seven inches tall and found in Mohenjo Daro, likely depicts one of these elite men.

- What specific features of the statue can you point out?
- What possible indication of elite status can you identify?
- What overall impression does the statue convey?

Limited archeological evidence suggests that some urban women played important social and religious roles in the Indus Valley civilization. Figurines of women or goddesses are more common than those of men. Women, apparently, were buried near their mothers and grandmothers, while men were not interred with their male relatives. The great variety of clothing, hairstyles, and decorations displayed on female figurines indicates considerable class, ethnic, and perhaps individual variation.

Visual Source 2.3 Dancing Girl (National Museum of India, New Delhi, India/Bridgeman Images.)

Among the most delightful discoveries in the Indus Valley cities is the evocative statue shown in Visual Source 2.3. It is about four inches tall and dated to around 2500 B.C.E. This young female nude is known generally as the "dancing girl." Cast in bronze using a sophisticated "lost wax" method, this statue provides evidence for a well-developed copper/bronze industry. The figure herself was portrayed in a dancer's pose, her hair gathered in a bun and her left arm covered with bangles and holding a small bowl. Both her arms and legs seem disproportionately long. She has been described variously as a queen, a high-status woman, a sacred temple dancer, and a tribal girl. Although no one really knows her precise identity, she has evoked wide admiration and appreciation. Mortimer Wheeler, a famous British archeologist, described her as "a girl perfectly, for the moment, perfectly confident of herself and the world." American archeologist Gregory Possehl, also active in the archeology of the Indus Valley civilization, commented: "We may not be certain that she was a dancer, but she was good at what she did and she knew it."[32]

- ■ What features of this statue may have provoked such observations?

- ■ How do you react to this statue? What qualities does she evoke?

- ■ What does Visual Source 2.3 suggest about views of women, images of female beauty, and attitudes about sexuality and the body?

Using the Evidence: Indus Valley Civilization

1. **Using art as evidence:** What can we learn about Indus Valley civilization from these visual sources? How does our level of understanding of this civilization differ from that of Egypt and Mesopotamia where plentiful written records are available?

2. **Considering accessibility:** Do you find the art of civilizations, such as that of the Indus Valley, more accessible to modern people than artistic products of earlier eras? Is it possible to speak of artistic "progress" or "development," or should we be content with simply noticing differences?

3. **Comparing representations of people:** Notice the various ways that human figures were portrayed in the images shown in Chapters 1 and 2, both those in the chapter narrative and in the Visual Sources section. How might you define those differences? Can you identify changes from the Paleolithic to the Neolithic eras and then to the age of First Civilizations? How are gender differences represented in these images?

4. **Seeking further evidence:** What additional kinds of archeological discoveries would be helpful in furthering our understanding of Indus Valley civilization?

Chapter 2 Wrap Up

LearningCurve
Check what you know.
**bedfordstmartins.com
/strayer/LC**

STEP ONE

The Word to Know: Civilization

The *Oxford English Dictionary* defines *civilization* as "a particular culture, society, and way of life as characteristic of a community of people; (also) a civilized society. (The state or condition of being civilized; human cultural, social, and intellectual development when considered to be advanced and progressive in nature.)" Using the word *civilization*, provide an example of a civilization discussed in Chapter 2. Describe several features that make it a complex society worthy of being named a civilization. Your answer should be two or three sentences long.

STEP TWO

First Civilizations

For two of the seven First Civilizations discussed in Chapter 2 (see Map 2.1, pp. 64–65), consider what specific factors led to the emergence of these societies. Consider geographic features, as well as the factors that lead historians to consider this society a civilization. What conclusions can you come to with respect to similarities and differences between these two societies?

Civilization	Generic cause	Specific ways this civilization emerged	→	Specific results/impact of each generic cause and the way this civilization emerged.
	Location		→	
	Role of cities		→	
	Role of social inequalities		→	
	Development of legal codes		→	
	Emergence of patriarchy		→	
	Emergence of writing		→	

Civilization	Generic cause	Specific ways this civilization emerged	→	Specific results/impact of each generic cause and the way this civilization emerged.
	Location		→	
	Role of cities		→	
	Role of social inequalities		→	
	Development of legal codes		→	
	Emergence of patriarchy		→	
	Emergence of writing		→	

STEP THREE

Writing and Social Status

This exercise will help you to understand how historians use early writing samples and artifacts to learn more about the development of distribution of labor and class as one of the criteria for early civilizations.

1. Review the Snapshot on p. 79. Why did writing emerge in most of the First Civilizations?

2. The text states: "Literacy defined elite status and conveyed enormous prestige to those who possessed it." How might writing demonstrate social status? Connect your answer to today.

3. Consider the image on p. 60 depicting a well-known Egyptian scribe, Raherka, and his wife, Mersankh. What evidence do we have that, as a scribe, he had both social prestige and political influence?

4. The textbook quotes one of the early Egyptian school texts as saying, "Man decays; his corpse is dust; all his kin have perished. But a book makes him remembered through the mouth of its reciter." How does this further support the scribe's status?

PART TWO
Second-Wave Civilizations in World History

500 B.C.E.–500 C.E.

Contents

After the First Civilizations: What Changed and What Didn't?

Studying world history has much in common with using the zoom lens of a camera. Sometimes, we pull the lens back to get a picture of the broadest possible panorama. At other times, we zoom in a bit for a middle-range shot, or even farther for a close-up of some particular feature of the historical landscape. Students of world history soon become comfortable with moving back and forth among these several perspectives.

As we bid farewell to the First Civilizations, we will take the opportunity to pull back the lens and look broadly, and briefly, at the entire age of agricultural civilizations, a period from about 3500 B.C.E., when the earliest of the First Civilizations arose, to about 1750 C.E., when the first Industrial Revolution launched a new and distinctively modern phase of world history. During these more than 5,000 years, the most prominent large-scale trend was the globalization of civilization as this new form of human community increasingly spread across the planet, encompassing more people and larger territories.

The first wave of that process, addressed in Chapter 2, was already global in scope, with expressions in Asia, Africa, and the Americas. Those First Civilizations generated the most impressive and powerful human societies created thus far, but they proved fragile and vulnerable as well. The always-quarreling city-states of ancient Mesopotamia had long ago been absorbed into the larger empires of Babylon and Assyria. By the middle of the second millennium B.C.E., the Indus Valley, Central Asian, and Norte Chico civilizations had collapsed or faded away. Egypt too fell victim to a series of foreign invaders during the first millennium B.C.E., including the forces of Nubia, Assyria, Alexander the Great, and the Roman Empire. The end of Olmec civilization around 400 B.C.E. has long puzzled historians, for it seems that the Olmecs themselves razed and then abandoned their major cities even as their civilizational style spread to neighboring peoples. About the same time, China's Zhou dynasty kingdom fragmented into a series of warring states.

Even though these First Civilizations broke down, there was no going back. Civilization as a form of human community proved durable and resilient as well as periodically fragile. Thus, in the thousand years between 500 B.C.E. and 500 C.E., new or enlarged urban-centered and state-based societies emerged to replace the First Civilizations in the Mediterranean basin, the Middle East, India, China, Mesoamerica, and the Andes. Furthermore, smaller expressions of civilization began to take shape elsewhere—in Ethiopia and West Africa, in Japan and Indonesia, in Vietnam and Cambodia. In short, the development of civilization was becoming a global process.

Many of these second-wave civilizations likewise perished, as the collapse of the Roman Empire, Han dynasty China, and the Mayan cities remind us. They were followed by yet a third wave of civilizations (roughly 500 to 1500 C.E.; see Part Three). Some of them represented the persistence or renewal of older patterns, as in the case of China, for example, while elsewhere — such as in Western Europe, Russia, Japan, and West Africa — newer civilizations emerged, all of which borrowed heavily from their more-established neighbors. The largest of these, Islamic civilization, incorporated a number of older centers of civilization, Egypt and Mesopotamia, for example, under the umbrella of a new religion. Thus, the globalization of civilization continued apace. So too did the interaction of civilizations with one another and with gathering and hunting peoples, agricultural village societies, and pastoral communities.

Continuities in Civilization

As this account of the human journey moves into the second and third waves of civilization, the question arises as to how they differed from the first ones. From a panoramic perspective, the answer is "not much." States and empires rose, expanded, and collapsed with a tiresome regularity. It is arguable, however, that little fundamental change occurred amid these constant fluctuations. Monarchs continued to rule most of the new civilizations; women remained subordinate to men in all of them; a sharp divide between the elite and everyone else persisted almost everywhere, as did the practice of slavery.[1]

Furthermore, no technological or economic breakthrough occurred to create new kinds of human societies as the Agricultural Revolution had done earlier or as the Industrial Revolution would do much later. Landowning elites had little incentive to innovate, for they benefited enormously from simply expropriating the surplus that peasant farmers produced. Nor would peasants have any reason to invest much effort in creating new forms of production when they knew full well that any gains they might generate would be seized by their social superiors. Merchants, who often were risk takers, might have spawned innovations, but they usually were dominated by powerful states and were viewed with suspicion and condescension by more prestigious social groups.

Many fluctuations, repetitive cycles, and minor changes characterize this long era of agricultural civilization, but no fundamental or revolutionary transformation of social or economic life took place. The major turning points in human history had occurred earlier with the emergence of agriculture and the birth of the First Civilizations and would occur later with the breakthrough of industrialization.

Changes in Civilization

While this panoramic perspective allows us to see the broadest outlines of the human journey, it also obscures much of great importance that took place during the second and third waves of the age of agrarian civilization. If we zoom in a bit more closely, significant changes emerge, even if they did not result in a thorough transformation of human life. Population, for example, grew more rapidly than ever before during this period, as the Snapshot illustrates. Even though the overall trend was up, important fluctuations interrupted the pattern, especially during the first millennium C.E., when no overall growth took place. Moreover, the rate of growth, though rapid in comparison with Paleolithic times, was quite slow if we measure it against the explosive expansion of recent centuries, when human numbers quadrupled in the twentieth century alone. This modest and interrupted pattern of population growth during the age of agrarian civilization reflected the absence of any fundamental economic breakthrough, which could have supported much larger numbers.

Another change lies in the growing size of the states or empires that structured civilizations. The Roman, Persian, Indian, and Chinese empires of second-wave civilizations, as well as the Arab, Mongol, and Inca empires of the third wave, all dwarfed the city-states of Mesopotamia and the Egypt of the pharaohs. Each of these empires brought together in a single political system a vast diversity of peoples. Even so, just to keep things in perspective, as late as the seventeenth century C.E., only one-third of the world's landmass was under the control of any state-based system, although these societies now encompassed a considerable majority of the world's people.

The rise and fall of these empires likewise represented very consequential changes to the people who experienced them. In the course of its growth, the Roman Empire

Snapshot   **World Population during the Age of Agricultural Civilization**[2]

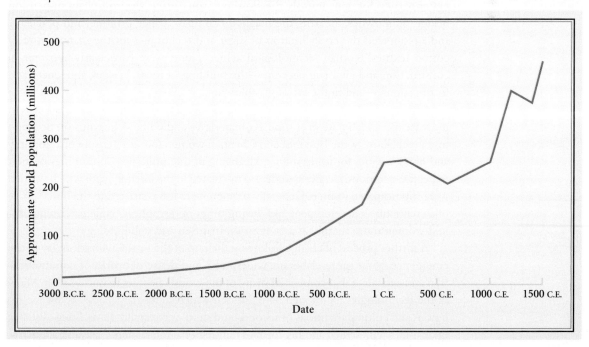

utterly destroyed the city of Carthage in North Africa, with the conquerors allegedly sowing the ground with salt so that nothing would ever grow there again. Similar bloodshed and destruction accompanied the creation of other much-celebrated states. Their collapse also had a dramatic impact on the lives of their people. Scholars have estimated that the large population of Mayan civilization shrank by some 85 percent in less than a century as that society dissolved around 840 C.E. It is difficult to imagine the sense of trauma and bewilderment associated with a collapse of this magnitude.

Second- and third-wave civilizations also generated important innovations in many spheres. Those in the cultural realm have been perhaps the most widespread and enduring. Distinctive "wisdom traditions"—the great philosophical/religious systems of Confucianism and Daoism in China; Hinduism and Buddhism in India; Greek rationalism in the Mediterranean; and Judaism, Zoroastrianism, Christianity, and Islam in the Middle East—have provided the moral and spiritual framework within which most of the world's peoples have sought to order their lives and define their relationship to the mysteries of life and death. All of these philosophical and religious systems are the product of second- and third-wave civilizations.

Although no technological breakthrough equivalent to the Agricultural or Industrial Revolution took place during this time, more modest innovations considerably enhanced human potential for manipulating the environment. China was a primary source of such technological change, though by no means the only one. "Chinese inventions and discoveries," wrote one prominent historian, "passed in a continuous flood from East to West for twenty centuries before the scientific revolution."[3] They included piston bellows, the draw-loom, silk-handling machinery, the wheelbarrow, a better harness for draft animals, the crossbow, iron casting, the iron-chain suspension bridge, gunpowder, firearms, the magnetic compass, paper, printing, and porcelain. India pioneered the crystallization of sugar and techniques for the manufacture of cotton textiles. Roman technological achievements were particularly apparent in construction and civil engineering—the building of roads, bridges, aqueducts, and fortifications—and in the art of glassblowing.

Nor were social hierarchies immune to change and challenge. India's caste system grew far more elaborate over time. Roman slaves and Chinese peasants on occasion rose in rebellion. Some Buddhist and Christian women found a measure of autonomy and opportunities for leadership and learning in the monastic communities of their respective traditions. Gender systems too fluctuated in the intensity with which women were subordinated to men. Generally women were less restricted in the initial phase of a civilization's development and during times of disruption, while patriarchy limited women more sharply as a civilization matured and stabilized.

A further process of change following the end of the First Civilizations lay in the emergence of far more elaborate, widespread, and dense networks of communication and exchange that connected many of the world's peoples to one another. Many of the technologies mentioned here diffused widely across large areas, as did the religious and cultural traditions of second- and third-wave civilizations. Long-distance trade routes represented another form of transregional interaction. Caravan trade across northern Eurasia, seaborne commerce within the Indian Ocean basin, the exchange of goods across the Sahara, river-based commerce in the eastern woodlands of North America, various trading networks radiating from Mesoamerica—all of these carried goods, and sometimes culture and religions as well. In the early centuries of the Common Era, for example, Southeast Asia attracted distant merchants and some settlers from both China and India, bringing Confucianism, Hinduism, and Buddhism to various parts of that vast region. Disease also increasingly linked distant human communities. According to the famous Greek historian Thucydides, a mysterious plague "from parts of Ethiopia above Egypt" descended on Athens in 430 B.C.E., decimating the city.[4]

In all of these ways, the world became quite different from what it had been in the age of the First Civilizations, even though fundamental economic and social patterns had not substantially changed.

The first three chapters of Part Two focus in a thematic fashion on the Eurasian/North African civilizations of the second-wave era (500 B.C.E.–500 C.E.), which hosted the vast majority of the world's population, some 80 percent or more. Chapter 3 introduces them by examining and comparing their political frameworks and especially the empires (great or terrible, depending on your point of view) that took shape in most of them. Far more enduring than their empires were the cultural or religious traditions that second-wave civilizations generated. These are examined, also comparatively, in Chapter 4. The social life of these civilizations, expressed in class, caste, slavery, and gender relationships, also varied considerably, as Chapter 5 spells out. In Chapter 6, the historical spotlight turns to inner Africa and the Americas during the second-wave era, asking whether their histories paralleled Eurasian patterns or explored alternative possibilities.

In recalling this second-wave phase of the human journey, we will have occasion to compare the experiences of its various peoples, to note their remarkable achievements, to lament the tragedies that befell them and the suffering to which they gave rise, and to ponder their continuing power to fascinate us still.

Mapping Part Two

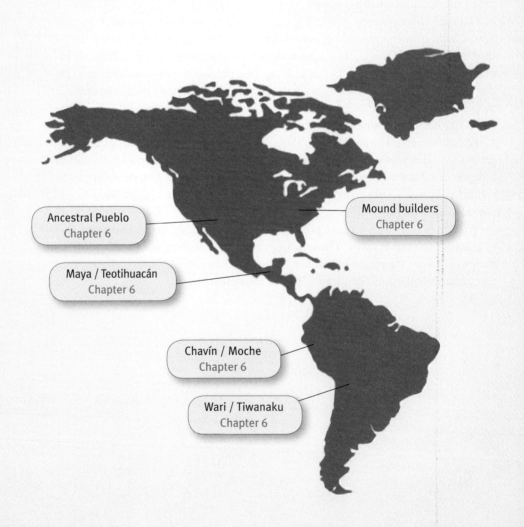

Ancestral Pueblo
Chapter 6

Mound builders
Chapter 6

Maya / Teotihuacán
Chapter 6

Chavín / Moche
Chapter 6

Wari / Tiwanaku
Chapter 6

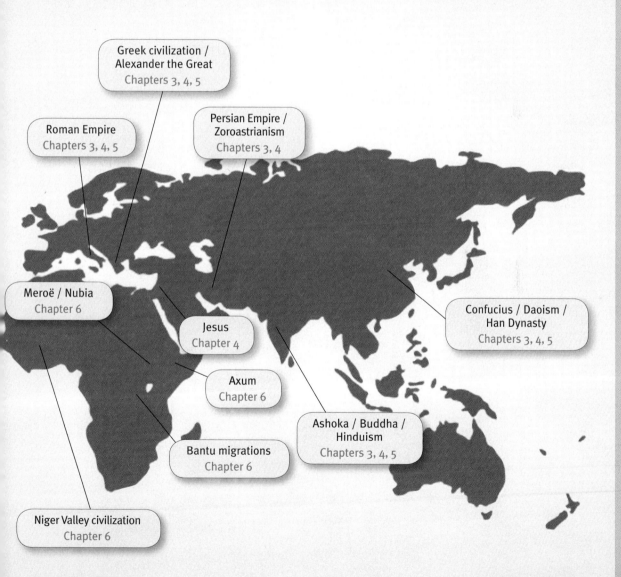

Greek civilization /
Alexander the Great
Chapters 3, 4, 5

Persian Empire /
Zoroastrianism
Chapters 3, 4

Roman Empire
Chapters 3, 4, 5

Meroë / Nubia
Chapter 6

Jesus
Chapter 4

Confucius / Daoism /
Han Dynasty
Chapters 3, 4, 5

Axum
Chapter 6

Ashoka / Buddha /
Hinduism
Chapters 3, 4, 5

Bantu migrations
Chapter 6

Niger Valley civilization
Chapter 6

State and Empire in Eurasia/North Africa

500 B.C.E.–500 C.E.

Are We Rome? It was the title of a thoughtful book, published in 2007, asking what had become a familiar question in the early twenty-first century: "Is the United States the new Roman Empire?"[1] With the collapse of the Soviet Union by 1991 and the subsequent U.S. invasions of Afghanistan and Iraq, some commentators began to make the comparison. The United States' enormous multicultural society, its technological achievements, its economically draining and over-stretched armed forces, its sense of itself as unique and endowed with a global mission, its concern about foreigners penetrating its borders, its apparent determination to maintain military superiority — all of this invited comparison with the Roman Empire. Supporters of a dominant role for the United States argued that Americans must face up to their responsibilities as "the undisputed master of the world" as the Romans did in their time. Critics warned that the Roman Empire became overextended abroad and corrupt and dictatorial at home and then collapsed, suggesting that a similar fate may await the U.S. empire. Either way, the point of reference was an empire that had passed into history some 1,500 years earlier, a continuing reminder of the significance of the distant past to our contemporary world. In fact, for at least several centuries, that empire has been a source of metaphors and "lessons" about personal morality, corruption, political life, military expansion, and much more.

Even in a world largely critical of empires, they still excite the imagination of historians and readers of history. The earliest ones show up in the era of the First Civilizations when Akkadian, Babylonian, and Assyrian empires encompassed the city-states of Mesopotamia

---

Terra-Cotta Archer: Part of the immense funerary complex constructed for the Chinese ruler Qin Shihuangdi, this kneeling archer represents the military power that reunified a divided China under the Qin dynasty in 221 B.C.E. (Asian Art & Archaeology, Inc./Corbis)

and established an enduring imperial tradition in the Middle East. Egypt became an imperial state when it temporarily ruled Nubia and the lands of the eastern Mediterranean. Following in their wake were many more empires, whose rise and fall have been central features of world history for the past 4,000 years.

BUT WHAT EXACTLY IS AN EMPIRE? At one level, empires are simply states, political systems that exercise coercive power. The term, however, is normally reserved for larger and more aggressive states, those that conquer, rule, and extract resources from other states and peoples. Thus empires have generally encompassed a considerable variety of peoples and cultures within a single political system, and they have often been associated with political or cultural oppression. Frequently, empires have given political expression to a civilization or culture, as in the Chinese and Persian empires. Civilizations have also flourished without a single all-encompassing state or empire, as in the competing city-states of Mesopotamia, Greece, and Mesoamerica or the many rival states of post-Roman Europe. In such cases, civilizations were expressed in elements of a common culture rather than in a unified political system.

The Eurasian empires of the second-wave era—those of Persia, Greece under Alexander the Great, Rome, China during the Qin (chihn) and Han dynasties, India during the Mauryan (MORE-yuhn) and Gupta dynasties—shared a set of common problems. Would they seek to impose the culture of the imperial heartland on their varied subjects? Would they rule conquered people directly or through established local authorities? How could they extract the wealth of empire in the form of taxes, tribute, and labor while maintaining order in conquered territories? And, no matter how impressive they were at their peak, they all sooner or later collapsed, providing a useful reminder to their descendants of the fleeting nature of all human creation.

Why have these and other empires been of such lasting fascination to both ancient and modern people? Perhaps in part because they were so big, creating a looming presence in their respective regions. Their armies and their tax collectors were hard to avoid. Maybe also because they were so bloody. The violence of conquest easily grabs our attention, and certainly, all of these empires were founded and sustained at a great cost in human life. The collapse of these once-powerful states is likewise intriguing, for the fall of the mighty seems somehow satisfying, perhaps even a delayed form of justice. The study of empires also sets off by contrast those times and places in which civilizations have prospered without an enduring imperial state.

But empires have also commanded attention simply because they were important. While the political values of recent times have almost universally condemned empire building, very large numbers of people—probably the majority of humankind before the twentieth century—have lived out their lives in empires, where they were often governed by rulers culturally different from themselves. These imperial states brought together people of quite different traditions and religions and so stimulated the exchange of ideas, cultures, and values. Despite their violence, exploitation, and oppression, empires also imposed substantial periods of peace

A Map of Time

750–336 B.C.E.	Era of Greek city-states
553–330 B.C.E.	Persian Achaemenid Empire
509 B.C.E.	Founding of the Roman Republic
500–221 B.C.E.	Chinese age of warring states
490–479 B.C.E.	Greco-Persian Wars
479–429 B.C.E.	Golden Age of Athens
431–404 B.C.E.	Peloponnesian War
336–323 B.C.E.	Reign of Alexander the Great
321–185 B.C.E.	India's Mauryan dynasty empire
221–206 B.C.E.	China's Qin dynasty empire
206 B.C.E.–220 C.E.	China's Han dynasty empire
200 B.C.E.–200 C.E.	High point of Roman Empire
First century B.C.E.	Transition from republic to empire in Rome
184 C.E.	Yellow Turban revolt in China
220 C.E.	Collapse of Chinese Han dynasty
320–550 C.E.	India's Gupta dynasty empire
Fifth century C.E.	Collapse of western Roman Empire

and security, which fostered economic and artistic development, commercial exchange, and cultural mixing. In many places, empire also played an important role in defining masculinity as conquest generated a warrior culture that gave particular prominence to the men who created and ruled those imperial states.

> **SEEKING THE MAIN POINT**
>
> How might you assess — both positively and negatively — the role of empires in the history of the second-wave era?

Empires and Civilizations in Collision: The Persians and the Greeks

The millennium between 500 B.C.E. and 500 C.E. in North Africa and Eurasia witnessed the flowering of second-wave civilizations in the Mediterranean world, the Middle East, India, and China. For the most part, these distant civilizations did not directly encounter one another, as each established its own political system, cultural values, and ways of organizing society. A great exception to that rule lay in the Mediterranean world and in the Middle East, where the emerging Persian Empire and Greek civilization, physically adjacent to each other, experienced a centuries-long interaction and clash. It was one of the most consequential cultural encounters of the ancient world.

Snapshot   **Distinctive Features of Second-Wave Eurasian Civilizations**

Civilization	Chinese	South Asian	Middle Eastern	Mediterranean
Political features	Unified empire under Qin and Han dynasties; "Mandate of Heaven" concept; examinations for official positions	Mauryan and Gupta empires; frequent political fragmentation	Persian Empire; royal absolutism; conquest by Alexander the Great	Greek city-states; Athenian democracy; Roman Empire; unification of Mediterranean basin
Cultural features	Confucianism/ Daoism	Hinduism/Buddhism	Zoroastrianism; Judaism; Christianity	Greek rationalism; spread of Christianity
Social features	Class hierarchy; dominance of bureaucratic and landholding elites; peasant rebellions	Caste system; purity and pollution; social position as indicator of spiritual development	Benevolent posture toward minorities in Persian Empire; Jews returned to homeland; tension between Greek and non-Greeks in Hellenistic era	Unusually prominent role of slavery in Greek and Roman society

The Persian Empire

In 500 B.C.E., the largest and most impressive of the world's empires was that of the Persians, an Indo-European people whose homeland lay on the Iranian plateau just north of the Persian Gulf. Living on the margins of the earlier Mesopotamian civilization, the Persians under the Achaemenid (ah-KEE-muh-nid) dynasty (553–330 B.C.E.) constructed an imperial system that drew on previous examples, such as the Babylonian and Assyrian empires, but far surpassed them all in size and splendor. Under the leadership of the famous monarchs Cyrus (r. 557–530 B.C.E.) and Darius (r. 522–486 B.C.E.), Persian conquests quickly reached from Egypt to India, encompassing in a single state some 35 to 50 million people, an immensely diverse realm containing dozens of peoples, states, languages, and cultural traditions (see Map 3.1).

■ **Comparison**

How did Persian and Greek civilizations differ in their political organization and values?

The Persian Empire centered on an elaborate cult of kingship in which the monarch, secluded in royal magnificence, could be approached only through an elaborate ritual. When the king died, sacred fires all across the land were extinguished, Persians were expected to shave their hair in mourning, and the manes of horses were cut short. Ruling by the will of the great Persian god Ahura Mazda (uh-HOORE-uh MAHZ-duh), kings were absolute monarchs, more than willing to crush rebellious regions or officials. Interrupted on one occasion while he was with his wife, Darius ordered the offender, a high-ranking nobleman, killed, along with his entire clan. In the eyes of many, Persian monarchs fully deserved their effusive title —"Great king, King of kings, King of countries containing all kinds of men, King in this great

Map 3.1 The Persian Empire
At its height, the Persian Empire was the largest in the world. It dominated the lands of the First Civilizations in the Middle East and was commercially connected to neighboring regions.

earth far and wide." Darius himself best expressed the authority of the Persian ruler when he observed, "what was said to them by me, night and day, it was done."[2]

But more than conquest and royal decree held the empire together. An effective administrative system placed Persian governors, called *satraps* (SAY-traps), in each of the empire's twenty-three provinces, while lower-level officials were drawn from local authorities. A system of imperial spies, known as the "eyes and ears of the King," represented a further imperial presence in the far reaches of the empire. A general policy of respect for the empire's many non-Persian cultural traditions also cemented the state's authority. Cyrus won the gratitude of the Jews when in 539 B.C.E. he allowed those exiled in Babylon to return to their homeland and rebuild their temple in Jerusalem (see Chapter 4, pp. 182–83). In Egypt and Babylon, Persian kings took care to uphold local religious cults in an effort to gain the support of their followers and officials. The Greek historian Herodotus commented that "there is no nation which so readily adopts foreign customs. They have taken the dress of the Medes and in war they wear the Egyptian breastplate. As soon as they hear of any luxury, they instantly make it their own."[3] For the next 1,000 years or more, Persian imperial bureaucracy and court life, replete with administrators, tax collectors, record keepers,

Persepolis
The largest palace in Persepolis, the Persian Empire's ancient capital, was the Audience Hall. The emperor officially greeted visiting dignitaries at this palace, which was constructed around 500 B.C.E. This relief, which shows a lion attacking a bull and Persian guards at attention, adorns a staircase leading to the Audience Hall. (© Gianni Dagli Orti/Corbis)

and translators, provided a model for all subsequent regimes in the region, including, later, those of the Islamic world.

The infrastructure of empire included a system of standardized coinage, predictable taxes levied on each province, and a newly dug canal linking the Nile with the Red Sea, which greatly expanded commerce and enriched Egypt. A "royal road," some 1,700 miles in length, facilitated communication and commerce across this vast empire. Caravans of merchants could traverse this highway in three months, but agents of the imperial courier service, using a fresh supply of horses every twenty-five to thirty miles, could carry a message from one end of the road to another in a week or two. Herodotus was impressed. "Neither snow, nor rain, nor heat, nor darkness of night," he wrote, "prevents them from accomplishing the task proposed to them with utmost speed." And an elaborate underground irrigation system sustained a rich agricultural economy in the semi-arid conditions of the Iranian plateau and spread from there throughout the Middle East and beyond.

The elaborate imperial centers, particularly Susa and Persepolis, reflected the immense wealth and power of the Persian Empire. Palaces, audience halls, quarters for the harem, monuments, and carvings made these cities into powerful symbols of imperial authority. Materials and workers alike were drawn from all corners of the empire and beyond. Inscribed in the foundation of Persepolis was Darius's commentary on what he had set in motion: "And Ahura Mazda was of such a mind, together with all the other gods, that this fortress [should] be built. And [so] I built it. And I built it secure and beautiful and adequate, just as I was intending to."[4]

The Greeks

It would be hard to imagine a sharper contrast than that between the huge and centralized Persian Empire, governed by an absolute and almost unapproachable monarch, and the small competing city-states of classical Greece, which allowed varying degrees of popular participation in political life. Like the Persians, the Greeks were an Indo-European people whose early history drew on the legacy of the First Civilizations. The classical Greece of historical fame emerged around 750 B.C.E. as a new civilization and flourished for about 400 years before it was incorporated into a succession of foreign empires. During that relatively short period, the civilization of Athens and Sparta, of Plato and Aristotle, of Zeus and Apollo took shape and collided with its giant neighbor to the east.

Calling themselves Hellenes, the Greeks created a civilization that was distinctive in many ways, particularly in comparison with the Persians. The total population of Greece and the Aegean basin was just 2 million to 3 million, a fraction of that of the Persian Empire. Furthermore, Greek civilization took shape on a small peninsula, deeply divided by steep mountains and valleys. Its geography certainly contributed to the political shape of that civilization, which found expression not in a Persian-style empire, but in hundreds of city-states or small settlements (see Map 3.2). Most were quite modest in size, with between 500 and 5,000 male citizens. But Greek civilization, like its counterparts elsewhere, also left a decisive environmental mark on the lands it encompassed. Smelting metals such as silver, lead, copper, bronze, and iron required enormous supplies of wood, leading to deforestation and soil erosion. Plato declared

Map 3.2 Classical Greece
The classical civilization of Greece was centered on a small peninsula of south-eastern Europe, but Greek settlers planted elements of that civilization along the coasts of the Mediterranean and Black seas.

that the area around Athens had become "a mere relic of the original country. . . . All the rich soil has melted away, leaving a country of skin and bone."[5]

■ Change

How did semidemocratic governments emerge in some of the Greek city-states?

Each of these city-states was fiercely independent and in frequent conflict with its neighbors, yet they had much in common, speaking the same language and worshipping the same gods. Every four years they temporarily suspended their continual conflicts to participate together in the Olympic Games, which had begun in 776 B.C.E. But this emerging sense of Greek cultural identity did little to overcome the endemic political rivalries of the larger city-states, including Athens, Sparta, Thebes, and Corinth, among many others.

Like the Persians, the Greeks were an expansive people, but their expansion took the form of settlement in distant places rather than conquest and empire. Pushed by a growing population, Greek traders in search of iron and impoverished Greek farmers in search of land stimulated a remarkable emigration. Between 750 and 500 B.C.E., the Greeks established settlements all around the Mediterranean basin and the rim of the Black Sea. Settlers brought Greek culture, language, and building styles to these new lands, even as they fought, traded, and intermarried with their non-Greek neighbors.

The most distinctive feature of Greek civilization, and the greatest contrast with Persia, lay in the extent of popular participation in political life that occurred within at least some of the city-states. It was the idea of "citizenship," of free people managing the affairs of state, of equality for all citizens before the law, that was so unique. A foreign king, observing the operation of the public assembly in Athens, was amazed that male citizens as a whole actually voted on matters of policy: "I find it astonishing," he noted, "that here wise men speak on public affairs, while fools decide them."[6] Compared to the rigid hierarchies, inequalities, and absolute monarchies of Persia and other ancient civilizations, the Athenian experiment was remarkable. This is how one modern scholar defined it:

> Among the Greeks the question of who should reign arose in a new way. Previously the most that had been asked was whether one man or another should govern and whether one alone or several together. But now the question was whether all the citizens, including the poor, might govern and whether it would be possible for them to govern as citizens, without specializing in politics. In other words, should the governed themselves actively participate in politics on a regular basis?[7]

The extent of participation and the role of "citizens" varied considerably, both over time and from city to city. Early in Greek history, only wealthy and well-born men had the rights of full citizenship, such as speaking and voting in the assembly, holding public office, and fighting in the army. Gradually, men of the lower classes, mostly small-scale farmers, also obtained these rights. At least in part, this broadening of political rights was associated with the growing number of men able to afford the armor and weapons that would allow them to serve as hoplites, or infantrymen, in the armies of the city-states. In many places, strong but benevolent rulers known as tyrants emerged for a time, usually with the support of the poorer classes, to challenge the prerogatives of the wealthy. Sparta—famous for its extreme forms of military discipline and its large population of helots, conquered people who lived in slave-like conditions—vested most political authority in its Council of Elders. The council was composed of twenty-eight men over the age of sixty, derived from the wealthier and more influential segment of society, who served for life and provided political leadership for Sparta.

It was in Athens that the Greek experiment in political participation achieved its most distinctive expression. Early steps in this direction were the product of intense class conflict, leading almost to civil war. A reforming leader named Solon emerged in 594 B.C.E. to push Athenian politics in a more democratic direction, breaking the hold of a small group of aristocratic families. Debt slavery was abolished, access to public office was opened to a wider group of men, and all citizens were allowed to take part in the Assembly. Later reformers such as Cleisthenes (KLEYE-sthuh-nees) and Pericles extended the rights of citizens even further. By 450 B.C.E., all holders of public office were chosen by lot and were paid, so that even the poorest could serve. The Assembly, where all citizens could participate, became the center of political life.

Athenian democracy, however, was different from modern democracy. It was direct, rather than representative, democracy, and it was distinctly limited. Women, slaves, and foreigners, together far more than half of the population, were wholly excluded from political participation. Nonetheless, political life in Athens was a world away from that of the Persian Empire and even from that of many other Greek cities.

Collision: The Greco-Persian Wars

In recent centuries, many writers and scholars have claimed classical Greece as the foundation of Western or European civilization. But the ancient Greeks themselves looked primarily to the East—to Egypt and the Persian Empire. In Egypt, Greek scholars found impressive mathematical and astronomical traditions on which they built. And Persia represented both an immense threat and later, under Alexander the Great, an opportunity for Greek empire building.

If ever there was an unequal conflict between civilizations, surely it was the collision of the Greeks and the Persians. The confrontation between the small and divided Greek cities and Persia, the world's largest empire, grew out of their respective patterns of expansion. A number of Greek settlements on the Anatolian seacoast, known to the Greeks as Ionia, came under Persian control as that empire extended its domination to the west. In 499 B.C.E., some of these Ionian Greek cities revolted against Persian domination and found support from Athens on the Greek mainland. Outraged by this assault from the remote and upstart Greeks, the Persians, twice in ten years (490 and 480 B.C.E.), launched major military expeditions to punish the Greeks in general and Athens in particular. Against all odds and all expectations, the Greeks held them off, defeating the Persians on both land and sea.

■ **Connection**

What were the consequences for both sides of the encounter between the Persians and the Greeks?

Though no doubt embarrassing, their defeat on the far western fringes of the empire had little effect on the Persians. However, it had a profound impact on the Greeks and especially on Athens, whose forces had led the way to victory. Beating the Persians in battle was a source of enormous pride for Greece. Years later, elderly Athenian men asked one another how old they had been when the Greeks triumphed in the momentous Battle of Marathon in 490 B.C.E. In their view, this victory was the product of Greek freedoms because those freedoms had motivated men to fight with extraordinary courage for what they valued so highly. It led to a western worldview in which Persia represented Asia and despotism, whereas Greece signified Europe and freedom. Thus was born the notion of an East/West divide, which has shaped European and North American thinking about the world into the twenty-first century.

The Greek victory also radicalized Athenian democracy, for it had been men of the poorer classes who had rowed their ships to victory and who were now in a position to insist on full citizenship. The fifty years or so after the Greco-Persian Wars were not only the high point of Athenian democracy but also the Golden Age of Greek culture. During this period, the Parthenon, that marvelous temple to the Greek goddess Athena, was built; Greek theater was born from the work of Aeschylus, Sophocles, and Euripides; and Socrates was beginning his career as a philosopher and an irritant in Athens. (See Document 3.1, pp. 146–48, in which the great Athenian statesman Pericles celebrated the uniqueness of his city.)

But Athens's Golden Age was also an era of incipient empire. In the Greco-Persian Wars, Athens had led a coalition of more than thirty Greek city-states on the basis of its naval power, but Athenian leadership in the struggle against Persian aggression had spawned an imperialism of its own. After the war, Athenian efforts to solidify Athens's dominant position among the allies led to intense resentment and finally to a bitter civil war (431–404 B.C.E.), with Sparta taking the lead in defending the traditional independence of Greek city-states. In this bloody conflict, known as the Peloponnesian War, Athens was defeated, while the Greeks exhausted themselves and magnified their distrust of one another. Thus the way was open to their eventual takeover by the growing forces of Macedonia, a frontier kingdom on the northern fringes of the Greek world. The glory days of the Greek experiment were over, but the spread of Greek culture was just beginning.

Collision: Alexander and the Hellenistic Era

■ Connection

What changes did Alexander's conquests bring in their wake?

The Macedonian takeover of Greece, led by its king, Philip II, finally accomplished by 338 B.C.E. what the Greeks themselves had been unable to achieve — the political unification of Greece, but at the cost of much of the prized independence of its various city-states. It also set in motion a second round in the collision of Greece and Persia as Philip's son, Alexander, prepared to lead a massive Greek expedition against the Persian Empire. Such a project appealed to those who sought vengeance for the earlier Persian assault on Greece, but it also served to unify the fractious Greeks in a war against their common enemy.

The story of this ten-year expedition (333–323 B.C.E.), accomplished while Alexander was still in his twenties, has become the stuff of legend (see Map 3.3). Surely it was among the greatest military feats of the ancient world in that it created a Greek empire from Egypt and Anatolia in the west to Afghanistan and India in the east. In the process, the great Persian Empire was thoroughly defeated; its capital, Persepolis (per-SEP-uh-lis), was looted and burned; and Alexander was hailed as the "king of Asia." In Egypt, Alexander, then just twenty-four years old, was celebrated as a liberator from Persian domination, was anointed as pharaoh, and was declared by Egyptian priests to be the "son of the gods." Arrian, a later Greek historian, described Alexander in this way:

> His passion was for glory only, and in that he was insatiable. . . . Noble indeed was his power of inspiring his men, of filling them with confidence, and in the moment of danger, of sweeping away their fear by the spectacle of his own fearlessness.[8]

Alexander died in 323 B.C.E., without returning to Greece, and his empire was soon divided into three kingdoms, ruled by leading Macedonian generals.

Map 3.3 Alexander's Empire and Successor States
Alexander's conquests, though enormous, did not long remain within a single empire, for his generals divided them into three successor states shortly after his death. This was the Hellenistic world within which Greek culture spread.

Alexander the Great
This mosaic of Alexander on horseback comes from the Roman city of Pompeii. It depicts the Battle of Issus (333 B.C.E.), in which Greek forces, although considerably out-numbered, defeated the Persian army, led personally by Emperor Darius III. (Erich Lessing/ Art Resource, NY)

From the viewpoint of world history, the chief significance of Alexander's amazing conquests lay in the widespread dissemination of Greek culture during what historians call the Hellenistic era (323–30 B.C.E.). Elements of that culture, generated in a small and remote Mediterranean peninsula, now penetrated the lands of the First Civilizations—Egypt, Mesopotamia, and India—resulting in one of the great cultural encounters of the ancient world.

The major avenue for the spread of Greek culture lay in the many cities that Alexander and later Hellenistic rulers established throughout the empire. Complete with Greek monuments, sculptures, theaters, markets, councils, and assemblies, these cities attracted many thousands of Greek settlers serving as state officials, soldiers, or traders. Alexandria in Egypt— the largest of these cities, with half a million people—was an enormous cosmopolitan center where Egyptians, Greeks, Jews, Babylonians, Syrians, Persians, and many others rubbed elbows. A harbor with space for 1,200 ships facilitated long-distance commerce. Greek learning flourished thanks to a library of some 700,000 volumes and the Museum, which sponsored scholars and writers of all kinds.

From cities such as these, Greek culture spread. From the Mediterranean to India, Greek became the language of power and elite culture. The Indian monarch Ashoka published some of his decrees in Greek, while an independent Greek state was established in Bactria in what is now northern Afghanistan. The attraction of many young Jews to Greek culture prompted the Pharisees to develop their own school system, as this highly conservative Jewish sect feared for the very survival of Judaism.

Cities such as Alexandria were very different from the original city-states of Greece, both in their cultural diversity and in the absence of the independence so valued by Athens and Sparta. Now they were part of large conquest states ruled by Greeks: the Ptolemaic (TOL-uh-MAY-ik) empire in Egypt and the Seleucid empire in Persia. These were imperial states, which, in their determination to preserve order, raise taxes, and maintain the authority of the monarch, resembled the much older empires of Mesopotamia, Egypt, Assyria, and Persia. Macedonians and Greeks, representing perhaps 10 percent of the population in these Hellenistic kingdoms, were clearly the elite and sought to keep themselves separate from non-Greeks. In Egypt, different legal systems for Greeks and native Egyptians maintained this separation. An Egyptian agricultural worker complained that "because I am an Egyptian," his supervisors despised him and refused to pay him.[9] Periodic rebellions expressed resentment at Greek arrogance, condescension, and exploitation.

But the separation between the Greeks and native populations was by no means complete, and a fair amount of cultural interaction and blending occurred. Alexander himself had taken several Persian princesses as his wives and actively encouraged intermarriage between his troops and Asian women. In both Egypt and Mesopotamia, Greek rulers patronized the building of temples to local gods and actively supported their priests. A growing number of native peoples were able to become Greek citizens by obtaining a Greek education, speaking the language, dressing appropriately, and assuming Greek names. In India, Greeks were assimilated into the hierarchy of the caste system as members of the Kshatriya (warrior) caste, while in Bactria a substantial number of Greeks converted to Buddhism, including one of their kings, Menander. A school of Buddhist art that emerged in the early centuries of the Common Era depicted the Buddha in human form for the first time, but in Greek-like garb with a face resembling the god Apollo (see Visual Source 4.2, p. 211). Clearly, not all was conflict between the Greeks and the peoples of the East.

In the long run, much of this Greek cultural influence faded as the Hellenistic kingdoms that had promoted it weakened and vanished by the first century B.C.E. While it lasted, however, it represented a remarkable cultural encounter, born of the collision of two empires and two second-wave civilizations. In the western part of that Hellenistic world, Greek rule was replaced by that of the Romans, whose empire, like Alexander's, also served as a vehicle for the continued spread of Greek culture and ideas.

Comparing Empires: Roman and Chinese

While the adjacent civilizations of the Greeks and the Persians collided, two other empires were taking shape—the Roman Empire on the far western side of Eurasia and China's imperial state on the far eastern end. They flourished at roughly the same time (200 B.C.E.–200 C.E.); they occupied a similar area (about 1.5 million square miles); and they encompassed populations of a similar size (50 to 60 million). They were the giant empires of their time, shaping the lives of close to half of the world's population. Unlike the Greeks and the Persians, the Romans and the Chinese were only dimly aware of each other and had almost no direct contact. Historians, however, have seen them as fascinating variations on an imperial theme and have long explored their similarities and differences.

Rome: From City-State to Empire

The rise of empires is among the perennial questions that historians tackle. Like the Persian Empire, that of the Romans took shape initially on the margins of the civilized world and was an unlikely rags-to-riches story. Rome began as a small and impoverished city-state on the western side of central Italy in the eighth century B.C.E., so weak, according to legend, that Romans were reduced to kidnapping neighboring women to maintain their city's population. In a transformation of epic proportions, Rome subsequently became the center of an enormous imperial state that encompassed the Mediterranean basin and included parts of continental Europe, Britain, North Africa, and the Middle East.

Originally ruled by a king, around 509 B.C.E. Roman aristocrats threw off the monarchy and established a republic in which the men of a wealthy class, known as patricians, dominated. Executive authority was exercised by two consuls, who were advised by a patrician assembly, the Senate. Deepening conflict with the poorer classes, called plebeians (plih–BEE–uhns), led to important changes in Roman political life. A written code of law offered plebeians some protection from abuse; a system of public assemblies provided an opportunity for lower classes to shape public policy; and a new office of tribune, who represented plebeians, allowed them to block unfavorable legislation. Romans took great pride in this political system, believing that they enjoyed greater freedom than did many of their more autocratic neighbors. The values of the republic — rule of law, the rights of citizens, the absence of pretension, upright moral behavior, keeping one's word — were later idealized as "the way of the ancestors."

With this political system and these values, the Romans launched their empire-building enterprise, a prolonged process that took more than 500 years (see Map 3.4). It began in the 490s B.C.E. with Roman control over its Latin neighbors in central Italy and over the next several hundred years encompassed most of the Italian peninsula. Between 264 and 146 B.C.E., victory in the Punic Wars with Carthage, a powerful empire with its capital in North Africa, extended Roman control over the western Mediterranean, including Spain, and made Rome a naval power. Subsequent expansion in the eastern Mediterranean brought the ancient civilizations of Greece, Egypt, and Mesopotamia under Roman domination. Rome also expanded into territories in Southern and Western Europe, including present-day France and Britain. By early in the second century C.E., the Roman Empire had reached its maximum extent. Like classical Greece, that empire has been associated with Europe. But in its own time, elites in North Africa and southwest Asia likewise claimed Roman identity, and the empire's richest provinces were in the east.

■ **Change**

How did Rome grow from a single city to the center of a huge empire?

No overall design or blueprint drove the building of empire, nor were there any precedents to guide the Romans. What they created was something wholly new — an empire that encompassed the entire Mediterranean basin and beyond. It was a piecemeal process, which the Romans invariably saw as defensive. Each addition of territory created new vulnerabilities, which could be assuaged only by more conquests. For some, the growth of empire represented opportunity. Poor soldiers hoped for land, loot, or salaries that might lift their families out of poverty. The well-to-do or well-connected gained great estates, earned promotions, and sometimes achieved public acclaim and high political office. The wealth of long-established societies in the eastern Mediterranean (Greece and Egypt, for example) beckoned, as did the

Map 3.4   The Roman Empire

At its height in the second century C.E., the Roman Empire incorporated the entire Mediterranean basin, including the lands of the Carthaginian Empire, the less-developed region of Western Europe, the heartland of Greek civilization, and the ancient civilizations of Egypt and Mesopotamia.

resources and food supplies of the less developed regions, such as Western Europe. There was no shortage of motivation for the creation of the Roman Empire.

Although Rome's central location in the Mediterranean basin provided a convenient launching pad for empire, it was the army, "well-trained, well-fed, and well-rewarded," that built the empire.[10] Drawing on the growing population of Italy, that army was often brutal in war. Carthage, for example, was utterly destroyed; the city was razed to the ground, and its inhabitants were either killed or sold into slavery. Nonetheless, Roman authorities could be generous to former enemies. Some were granted Roman citizenship; others were treated as allies and allowed to maintain

Queen Boudica

This statue in London commemorates the resistance of the Celtic people of eastern Britain against Roman rule during a revolt in 60–61 C.E., led by Queen Boudica. A later Roman historian lamented that "all this ruin was brought upon the Romans by a woman, a fact which in itself caused them the greatest shame." (Daniel Boulet, photographer)

their local rulers. As the empire grew, so too did political forces in Rome that favored its continued expansion and were willing to commit the necessary manpower and resources.

Centuries of empire building and the warfare that made it possible had an impact on Roman society and values. That vast process, for example, shaped Roman understandings of gender and the appropriate roles of men and women. Rome was becoming a warrior society in which the masculinity of upper-class male citizens was defined in part by a man's role as a soldier and a property owner. In private life this translated into absolute control over his wife, children, and slaves, including the theoretical right to kill them without interference from the state. This ability of a free man and a Roman citizen to act decisively in both public and private life lay at the heart of ideal male identity. A Roman woman could participate proudly in this warrior culture by bearing brave sons and inculcating these values in her offspring.

Strangely enough, by the early centuries of the Common Era the wealth of empire, the authority of the imperial state, and the breakdown of older Roman social patterns combined to offer women in the elite classes a less restricted life than they had known in the early centuries of the republic. Upper-class Roman women had never been as secluded in the home as were their Greek counterparts, and now the legal authority of their husbands was curtailed by the intrusion of the state into what had been private life. The head of household, or pater familias, lost his earlier power of life and death over his family. Furthermore, such women could now marry without transferring legal control to their husbands and were increasingly able to manage their own finances and take part in the growing commercial economy of the empire. According to one scholar, Roman women of the wealthier classes gained "almost complete liberty in matters of property and marriage."[11] At the other end of the social spectrum, Roman conquests brought many thousands of women as well as men into the empire as slaves, often brutally treated and subject to the whims of their masters (see Chapter 5, pp. 229–33).

The relentless expansion of empire raised yet another profound question for Rome: could republican government and values survive the acquisition of a huge empire? The wealth of empire enriched a few, enabling them to acquire large estates and many slaves, while pushing growing numbers of free farmers into the cities and poverty. Imperial riches also empowered a small group of military leaders—Marius, Sulla, Pompey, Julius Caesar—who recruited their troops directly from the ranks of the poor and whose fierce rivalries brought civil war to Rome during the first century B.C.E. Traditionalists lamented the apparent decline of republican values—simplicity, service, free farmers as the backbone of the army, the authority of the Senate—amid the self-seeking ambition of the newly rich and powerful. When the dust settled from the civil war, Rome was clearly changing, for authority was now vested primarily in an emperor, the first of whom was Octavian, later granted the title of Augustus (r. 27 B.C.E.–14 C.E.), which implied a divine status for the ruler (see Visual Source 3.4, p. 162). The republic was history; Rome had become an empire and its ruler an emperor.

But it was an empire with an uneasy conscience, for many felt that in acquiring an empire, Rome had betrayed and abandoned its republican origins. Augustus was careful to maintain the forms of the republic—the Senate, consuls, public assemblies—and referred to himself as "first man" rather than "king" or "emperor," even as he accumulated enormous personal power. And in a bow to republican values, he spoke of the empire's conquests as reflecting the "power of the Roman people" rather than of the Roman state. Despite this rhetoric, he was emperor in practice, if not in name, for he was able to exercise sole authority, backed up by his command of a professional army. Later emperors were less reluctant to flaunt their imperial prerogatives. During the first two centuries C.E., this empire in disguise provided security, grandeur, and relative prosperity for the Mediterranean world. This was the *pax Romana*, the Roman peace, the era of imperial Rome's greatest extent and greatest authority. (See Document 3.2, pp. 148–50, for a Greek celebration of the Roman Empire.)

China: From Warring States to Empire

About the same time, on the other side of Eurasia, another huge imperial state was in the making—China. Here, however, the task was understood differently. It was not a matter of creating something new, as in the case of the Roman Empire, but of restoring something old. As one of the First Civilizations, a Chinese state had emerged as early as 2200 B.C.E. and under the Xia, Shang, and Zhou dynasties had grown progressively larger. By 500 B.C.E., however, this Chinese state was in shambles. Any earlier unity vanished in an age of warring states, featuring the endless rivalries of seven competing kingdoms.

To many Chinese, this was a wholly unnatural and unacceptable condition, and rulers in various states vied to reunify China. One of them, known to history as Qin Shihuangdi (chihn shee-HUANG-dee) (i.e., Shihuangdi from the state of Qin), succeeded brilliantly. The state of Qin had already developed an effective bureaucracy, subordinated its aristocracy, equipped its army with iron weapons, and enjoyed rapidly rising agricultural output and a growing population. It also had adopted a political philosophy called Legalism, which advocated clear rules and harsh punishments as a means of enforcing the authority of the state. (See Document 3.3, pp. 150–51, for an example of Legalist thinking.) With these resources, Shihuangdi (r. 221–210 B.C.E.)

■ **Comparison**

Why was the Chinese empire able to take shape so quickly, while that of the Romans took centuries?

PORTRAIT   Trung Trac: Resisting the Chinese Empire

Empires have long faced resistance from people they conquer and never more fiercely than
in Vietnam, which was incorporated into an expanding Chinese
empire for over a thousand years
(111 B.C.E.–939 C.E.). Among the
earliest examples of Vietnamese
resistance to this occupation was
that led around 40 C.E. by Trung
Trac and her younger sister Trung
Nhi, daughters in an aristocratic,
military family. Trung Trac mar-
ried a prominent local lord Thi Sach, who was a vocal
opponent of offensive Chinese policies—high taxes, even
on the right to fish in local rivers; required payoffs to Chinese officials; and the imposition of Chinese culture on
the Vietnamese. In response to this opposition, the Chinese
governor of the region ordered Thi Sach's execution.

This personal tragedy provoked Trung Trac to take up
arms against the Chinese occupiers, quickly gaining a
substantial following among peasants and aristocrats alike.
Famously addressing some 30,000 soldiers, while dressed
in full military regalia rather than the expected mourning
clothes, she declared to the assembled crowd:

Foremost I will avenge my country.
Second I will restore the Hung lineage.
Third I will avenge the death of my husband.
Lastly I vow that these goals will be accomplished.

Within months, her forces had captured sixty-five
towns, and, for two years, they held the Chinese at bay,
while Trung Trac and Trung Nhi ruled a briefly independent state as co-queens. Chinese sources referred to Trung
Trac as a "ferocious warrior." During their rule, the sisters
eliminated the hated tribute taxes imposed by the Chi-

Trung Trac and Trung Nhi
(CPA Media)

nese and sought to restore the
authority of Vietnamese aristocrats. A large military force, said
to number some 80,000, counted
among its leaders thirty-six
female "generals," including
the Trung sisters' mother.

Soon, however, Chinese
forces overwhelmed the rebellion
and Trung Trac's support faded.
Later Vietnamese records explained the failure of the revolt
as a consequence of its female
leadership. In traditional Vietnamese accounts, the Trung
sisters committed suicide, jumping into a nearby river as
did a number of their followers.

Although the revolt failed, it lived on in stories and
legends to inspire later Vietnamese resistance to invaders—
Chinese, French, Japanese, and American alike. Men were
reminded that women had led this rebellion. "What a
pity," wrote a thirteenth-century Vietnamese historian,
"that for a thousand years after this, the men of our land
bowed their heads, folded their arms, and served the
northerners [Chinese]."[12] To this day, temples, streets, and
neighborhoods bear the name of the Trung sisters, and a
yearly celebration in their honor coincides with International Women's Day. Usually depicted riding on war elephants and wielding swords, these two women also represent the more fluid gender roles then available to some
Vietnamese women in comparison to the stricter patriarchy prevalent in China.

Question: How might you imagine the reactions to the Trung
sisters' revolt from Chinese officials, Vietnamese aristocrats,
Vietnamese peasants both male and female, and later
generations of Vietnamese men and women?

launched a military campaign to reunify China and in just ten years soundly defeated
the other warring states. Believing that he had created a universal and eternal empire, he grandly named himself Shihuangdi, which means the "first emperor." Unlike
Augustus, he showed little ambivalence about empire. Subsequent conquests extended China's boundaries far to the south into the northern part of Vietnam, to

the northeast into Korea, and to the northwest, where the Chinese pushed back the nomadic pastoral people of the steppes. (See the Portrait of Trung Trac, opposite, for an example of resistance to Chinese expansion.) Although the boundaries fluctuated over time, Shihuangdi laid the foundations for a unified Chinese state, which has endured, with periodic interruptions, to the present (Map 3.5).

Building on earlier precedents, the Chinese process of empire formation was far more compressed than the centuries-long Roman effort, but it was no less dependent on military force and no less brutal. Scholars who opposed Shihuangdi's policies were executed and their books burned. Aristocrats who might oppose his centralizing policies were moved physically to the capital. Hundreds of thousands of laborers were recruited to construct the Great Wall of China, designed to keep out northern "barbarians," and to erect a monumental mausoleum as the emperor's final resting place. (See Visual Source 3.3, p. 160.) More positively, Shihuangdi imposed a uniform system of weights, measures, and currency and standardized the length of axles for carts and the written form of the Chinese language.

Map 3.5 Classical China
The brief Qin dynasty brought unity to the heartland of Chinese civilization, and the much longer Han dynasty extended its territorial reach south toward Vietnam, east to Korea, and west into Central Asia. To the north lay the military confederacy of the nomadic Xiongnu.

As in Rome, the creation of the Chinese empire had domestic repercussions, but they were brief and superficial compared to Rome's transition from republic to empire. The speed and brutality of Shihuangdi's policies ensured that his own Qin dynasty did not last long, and it collapsed unmourned in 206 B.C.E. The Han dynasty that followed (206 B.C.E.–220 C.E.) retained the centralized features of Shihuangdi's creation, although it moderated the harshness of his policies, adopting a milder and moralistic Confucianism in place of Legalism as the governing philosophy of the states. (See Document 4.1, pp. 198–200, for a sample of Confucius's thinking.) It was Han dynasty rulers who consolidated China's imperial state and established the political patterns that lasted into the twentieth century.

Consolidating the Roman and Chinese Empires

■ **Explanation**
Why were the Roman and Chinese empires able to enjoy long periods of relative stability and prosperity?

Once established, these two huge imperial systems shared a number of common features. Both, for example, defined themselves in universal terms. The Roman writer Polybius spoke of bringing "almost the entire world" under the control of Rome, while the Chinese state was said to encompass "all under heaven." Both of them invested heavily in public works—roads, bridges, aqueducts, canals, protective walls—all designed to integrate their respective domains militarily and commercially.

Furthermore, Roman and Chinese authorities both invoked supernatural sanctions to support their rule. By the first century C.E., Romans began to regard their deceased emperors as gods and established a religious cult to bolster the authority of living rulers. It was the refusal of early Christians to take part in this cult that provoked their periodic persecution by Roman authorities.

In China, a much older tradition had long linked events on earth with the invisible realm called "heaven." In this conception, heaven was neither a place nor a supreme being, but rather an impersonal moral force that regulated the universe. Emperors were called the Son of Heaven and were said to govern by the Mandate of Heaven so long as they ruled morally and with benevolence. Peasant rebellions, "barbarian" invasions, or disastrous floods were viewed as signs that the emperor had ruled badly and thus had lost the Mandate of Heaven. Among the chief duties of the emperor was the performance of various rituals thought to maintain the appropriate relationship between heaven and earth. What moral government meant in practice was spelled out in the writings of Confucius and his followers, which became the official ideology of the empire (see Chapter 4).

Both of these second-wave civilizations also absorbed a foreign religious tradition—Christianity in the Roman world and Buddhism in China—although the process unfolded somewhat differently. In the case of Rome, Christianity was born as a small sect in a remote corner of the empire. Aided by the *pax Romana* and Roman roads, the new faith spread slowly for several centuries, particularly among the poor and lower classes. Women were prominent in the leadership of the early church, as were a number of more well-to-do individuals from urban families. After suffering intermittent persecution, Christianity in the fourth century C.E. obtained state support from emperors who hoped to shore up a tottering empire with a common religion, and thereafter the religion spread quite rapidly.

In the case of China, by contrast, Buddhism came from India, far beyond the Chinese world. It was introduced to China by Central Asian traders and received little support from Han dynasty rulers. In fact, the religion spread only modestly among Chinese until after the Han dynasty collapsed (220 C.E.), when it appealed to people who felt bewildered by the loss of a predictable and stable society. Not until the Sui (sway) dynasty emperor Wendi (r. 581–604 C.E.) reunified China did the new religion gain state support, and then only temporarily. Buddhism thus became one of several alternative cultural traditions in a complex Chinese mix, while Christianity, though divided internally, ultimately became the dominant religious tradition throughout Europe (see Chapters 8 and 10).

The Roman and Chinese empires also had a different relationship to the societies they governed. Rome's beginnings as a small city-state meant that Romans, and even Italians, were always a distinct minority within the empire. The Chinese empire, by contrast, grew out of a much larger cultural heartland, already ethnically Chinese. Furthermore, as the Chinese state expanded, especially to the south, it actively assimilated the non-Chinese or "barbarian" people. In short, they became Chinese, culturally, linguistically, and through intermarriage in physical appearance as well. Many Chinese in modern times are in fact descended from people who at one point or another were not Chinese at all.

The Roman Empire also offered a kind of assimilation to its subject peoples. Gradually and somewhat reluctantly, the empire granted Roman citizenship to various individuals, families, or whole communities for their service to the empire or in recognition of their adoption of Roman culture. In 212 C.E., Roman citizenship was bestowed on almost all free people of the empire. Citizenship offered clear advantages—the right to hold public office, to serve in the Roman military units known as legions, to wear a toga, and more—but it conveyed a legal status, rather than cultural assimilation, and certainly did not erase other identities, such as being Greek, Egyptian, or a citizen of a particular city.

Various elements of Roman culture—its public buildings, its religious rituals, its Latin language, its style of city life—were attractive, especially in Western Europe, where urban civilization was something new. In the eastern half of the empire, however, things Greek retained tremendous prestige. Many elite Romans in fact regarded Greek culture—its literature, philosophy, and art—as superior to their own and proudly sent their sons to Athens for a Greek education. To some extent, the two blended into a mixed Greco-Roman tradition, which the empire served to disseminate throughout the realm. Other non-Roman cultural traditions—such as the cult of the Persian god Mithra or the compassionate Egyptian goddess Isis, and, most extensively, the Jewish-derived religion of Christianity—also spread throughout the empire. Nothing similar occurred in Han dynasty China, except for Buddhism, which established a modest presence, largely among foreigners. Chinese culture, widely recognized as the model to which others should conform, experienced little competition from older, venerated, or foreign traditions.

Language served these two empires in important but contrasting ways. Latin, an alphabetic language depicting sounds, gave rise to various distinct languages—Spanish, Portuguese, French, Italian, Romanian—whereas Chinese did not. Chinese characters, which represented words or ideas more than sounds, were not easily transferable to other languages. Written Chinese, however, could be understood by all literate people, no matter which spoken dialect of the language they used. Thus Chinese, more than Latin, served as an instrument of elite assimilation. For all of these reasons, the various peoples of the Roman Empire were able to maintain their separate cultural identities far more than was the case in China.

Politically, both empires established effective centralized control over vast regions and huge populations, but the Chinese, far more than the Romans, developed an elaborate bureaucracy to hold the empire together. The Han emperor Wudi (r. 141– 87 B.C.E.) established an imperial academy for training officials for an emerging bureaucracy with a curriculum based on the writings of Confucius. This was the beginning of a civil service system, complete with examinations and selection by merit, which did much to integrate the Chinese empire and lasted into the early twentieth century. Roman administration was a somewhat ramshackle affair, relying more on regional aristocratic elites and the army to provide cohesion. Unlike the Chinese, however, the Romans developed an elaborate body of law, applicable equally to all people of the realm, dealing with matters of justice, property, commerce, and family life. Chinese and Roman political development thus generated different answers to the question of what made for good government. For those who inherited the Roman tradition, it was good laws, whereas for those in the Chinese tradition, it was good men.

Finally both Roman and Chinese civilizations had marked effects on the environment. The Roman poet Horace complained of the noise and smoke of the city and objected to the urban sprawl that extended into the adjacent fertile lands. Roman mining operations and the smelting of metals led to extensive deforestation and unprecedented levels of lead in the atmosphere. Large-scale Chinese ironworking during the Han dynasty contributed to substantial urban air pollution, while the growth of intensive agriculture and logging stripped the land of its grass and forest cover, causing sufficient soil erosion to turn the Hwang-ho River its characteristic yellow-brown color. What had been known simply as "the River" now became the Yellow River.

The Collapse of Empires

Empires rise, and then, with some apparent regularity, they fall, and in doing so, they provide historians with one of their most intriguing questions: what causes the collapse of these once-mighty structures? In China, the Han dynasty empire came to an end in 220 C.E.; the traditional date for the final disintegration of the Roman Empire is 476 C.E., although a process of decline had been under way for several centuries. In the Roman case, however, only the western half of the empire collapsed, while the eastern part, subsequently known as the Byzantine Empire, maintained the tradition of imperial Rome for another thousand years.

Despite these differences, a number of common factors have been associated with the end of these imperial states. At one level, they both simply got too big, too over-extended, and too expensive to be sustained by the available resources, and no fundamental technological breakthrough was available to enlarge these resources. Furthermore, the growth of large landowning families with huge estates and political clout enabled them to avoid paying taxes, turned free peasants into impoverished tenant farmers, and diminished the authority of the central government. In China, such conditions led to a major peasant revolt, known as the Yellow Turban Rebellion, in 184 C.E. (see pp. 223–24).

Rivalry among elite factions created instability in both empires and eroded imperial authority. In China, persistent tension between castrated court officials (eunuchs) loyal to the emperor and Confucian-educated scholar-bureaucrats weakened the state. In the Roman Empire between 235 and 284 C.E., some twenty-six individuals claimed the title of Roman emperor, only one of whom died of natural causes. In addition, epidemic disease ravaged both societies. The population of the Roman Empire declined by 25 percent in the two centuries following 250 C.E., a demographic disaster that meant diminished production, less revenue for the state, and fewer men available for the defense of the empire's long frontiers.

To these mounting internal problems was added a growing threat from nomadic or semi-agricultural peoples occupying the frontier regions of both empires. The Chinese had long developed various ways of dealing with the Xiongnu and other nomadic people to the north—building the Great Wall to keep them out, offering them trading opportunities at border markets, buying them off with lavish gifts, contracting marriage alliances with nomadic leaders, and conducting periodic military campaigns against them. But as the Han dynasty weakened in the second and third centuries C.E., such peoples more easily breached the frontier defenses and set up a succession of "barbarian states" in north China. Culturally, however, many of these foreign rulers gradually became Chinese, encouraging intermarriage, adopting Chinese dress, and setting up their courts in Chinese fashion.

A weakening Roman Empire likewise faced serious problems from Germanic-speaking peoples living on its northern frontier. Growing numbers of these people began to enter the empire in the fourth century C.E.—some as mercenaries in Roman armies and others as refugees fleeing the invasions of the ferocious Huns, who were penetrating Europe from Central Asia. Once inside the declining empire, various Germanic groups established their own kingdoms, at first controlling Roman emperors and then displacing them altogether by 476 C.E. Unlike the nomadic groups in China, who largely assimilated Chinese culture, Germanic kingdoms in Europe developed their own ethnic identities—Visigoths, Franks, Anglo-Saxons, and others—even as they drew on Roman law and adopted Roman Christianity. Far more than

■ **Change**
What internal and external factors contributed to the collapse of the Roman and Chinese empires?

Meeting of Attila and Pope Leo I
Among the "barbarian" invaders of the Roman Empire, none were more feared than the Huns, led by the infamous Attila. In a celebrated meeting in 452 C.E., Pope Leo I persuaded Attila to spare the city of Rome and to withdraw from Italy. This painting from about 1360 C.E. records that remarkable meeting. (National Szechenyi Library, Budapest)

in China, the fall of the Roman Empire produced a new culture, blending Latin and Germanic elements, which provided the foundation for the hybrid civilization that would arise in Western Europe.

The collapse of empire meant more than the disappearance of centralized government and endemic conflict. In post-Han China and post-Roman Europe, it also meant the decline of urban life, a contracting population, less area under cultivation, diminishing international trade, and vast insecurity for ordinary people. It must have seemed that civilization itself was unraveling.

The most significant difference between the collapse of empire in China and that in the western Roman Empire lay in what happened next. In China, after about 350 years of disunion, disorder, frequent warfare, and political chaos, a Chinese imperial state, similar to that of the Han dynasty, was reassembled under the Sui (589–618 C.E.), Tang (618–907), and Song (960–1279) dynasties. Once again, a single emperor ruled; a bureaucracy selected by examinations governed; and the ideas of Confucius informed the political system. Such a Chinese empire persisted into the early twentieth century, establishing one of the most continuous political traditions of any civilization in world history.

The story line of European history following the end of the western Roman Empire was very different indeed. No large-scale, centralized, imperial authority encompassing all of Western Europe has ever been successfully reestablished there for any length of time. The memory of Roman imperial unity certainly persisted, and many subsequently tried unsuccessfully to re-create it. But most of Western Europe dissolved into highly decentralized political systems involving nobles, knights and vassals, kings with little authority, various city-states in Italy, and small territories ruled by princes, bishops, or the pope. From this point on, Europe would be a civilization without an encompassing imperial state.

From a Chinese point of view, Western Europe's post-Roman history must seem an enormous failure. Why were Europeans unable to reconstruct something of the unity of their classical empire, while the Chinese clearly did? Surely the greater cultural homogeneity of Chinese civilization made that task easier than it was amid the vast ethnic and linguistic diversity of Europe. The absence in the Roman legacy of a strong bureaucratic tradition also contributed to European difficulties, whereas in China the bureaucracy provided some stability even as dynasties came and went. The Chinese also had in Confucianism a largely secular ideology that placed great value on political matters in the here and now. The Roman Catholic Church in Europe, however, was frequently at odds with state authorities, and its "otherworldliness" did little to support the creation of large-scale empires. Finally, Chinese agriculture was much more productive than that of Europe, and for a long time its metallurgy was more advanced.[13] These conditions gave Chinese state builders more resources to work with than were available to their European counterparts.

SUMMING UP SO FAR

In comparing the Roman and Chinese empires, which do you find more striking — their similarities or their differences?

Intermittent Empire: The Case of India

Among the second-wave civilizations of Eurasia, empire loomed large in Persian, Mediterranean, and Chinese history, but it played a rather less prominent role in Indian history. In the Indus River valley flourished the largest of the First Civilizations, embodied in exquisitely planned cities such as Harappa but with little evidence of any central political authority (see Chapter 2). The demise of this early civilization by 1500 B.C.E. was followed over the next thousand years by the creation of a new civilization based farther east, along the Ganges River on India's northern plain. That process has occasioned considerable debate, which has focused on the role of the Aryans, a pastoral Indo-European people long thought to have invaded and destroyed the Indus Valley civilization and then created the new one along the Ganges. More recent research questions this interpretation. Did the Aryans invade suddenly, or did they migrate slowly into the Indus River valley? Were they already there as a part of the Indus Valley population? Was the new civilization largely the work of Aryans, or did it evolve gradually from Indus Valley culture? Scholars have yet to reach agreement on any of these questions.[14]

■ Comparison

Why were centralized empires so much less prominent in India than in China?

However it occurred, by 600 B.C.E. what would become the second-wave civilization of South Asia had begun to take shape across northern India. Politically, that civilization emerged as a fragmented collection of towns and cities, some small republics governed by public assemblies, and a number of regional states ruled by kings. An astonishing range of ethnic, cultural, and linguistic diversity also characterized this civilization, as an endless variety of peoples migrated into India from Central Asia across the mountain passes in the northwest. These features of Indian civilization — political fragmentation and vast cultural diversity — have informed much of South Asian history throughout many centuries, offering a sharp contrast to the pattern of development in China. What gave Indian civilization a recognizable identity and character was neither an imperial tradition nor ethno-linguistic commonality, but rather a distinctive religious tradition, known later to outsiders as Hinduism, and a unique social organization, the caste system. These features of Indian life are explored further in Chapters 4 and 5.

Nonetheless, empires and emperors were not entirely unknown in India's long history. Northwestern India had been briefly ruled by the Persian Empire and then conquered by Alexander the Great. These Persian and Greek influences helped stimulate the first and largest of India's short experiments with a large-scale political system,

Arabian Sea

Bay of Bengal

Pataliputra

HIMALAYAS

Ganges R.

Indus R.

KALINGA

Maryan Empire, 250 B.C.E.

Gupta Empire, 420 C.E.

▲ Rock and pillar edicts and inscriptions of Ashoka

Map 3.6 Empire in South Asia
Large-scale empires in the Indian subcontinent were less frequent and less enduring than in China. Two of the largest efforts were those of the Mauryan and Gupta dynasties.

the Mauryan Empire (326–184 B.C.E.), which encompassed all but the southern tip of the subcontinent (see Map 3.6).

The Mauryan Empire was an impressive political structure, equivalent to the Persian, Chinese, and Roman empires, though not nearly as long-lasting. With a population of perhaps 50 million, the Mauryan Empire boasted a large military force, reported to include 600,000 infantry soldiers, 30,000 cavalry, 8,000 chariots, and 9,000 elephants. A civilian bureaucracy featured various ministries and a large contingent of spies to provide the rulers with local information. A famous treatise called the *Arthashastra* (*The Science of Worldly Wealth*) articulated a pragmatic, even amoral, political philosophy for Mauryan rulers. It was, according to one scholar, a book that showed "how the political world does work and not very often stating how it ought to work, a book that frequently discloses to a king what calculating and sometimes brutal measures he must carry out to preserve the state and the common good."[15] The state also operated many industries—spinning, weaving, mining, shipbuilding, and armaments. This complex apparatus was financed by taxes on trade, on herds of animals, and especially on land, from which the monarch claimed a quarter or more of the crop.

Mauryan India is perhaps best known for one of its emperors, Ashoka (r. 268–232 B.C.E.), who left a record of his activities and his thinking in a series of edicts carved on rocks and pillars throughout the kingdom (see Document 3.4, pp. 152–54). Ashoka's conversion to Buddhism and his moralistic approach to governance gave his reign a different tone than that of China's Shihuangdi or Greece's Alexander the Great, who, according to legend, wept because he had no more worlds to conquer. Ashoka's legacy to modern India has been that of an enlightened ruler, who sought to govern in accord with the religious values and moral teachings of Hinduism and Buddhism.

Despite their good intentions, these policies did not long preserve the empire, which broke apart soon after Ashoka's death. About 600 years later, a second brief imperial experiment, known as the Gupta Empire (320–550 C.E.) took shape. Faxian, a Chinese Buddhist traveler in India at the time, noted a generally peaceful, tolerant, and prosperous land, commenting that the ruler "governs without decapitation or corporal punishment." Free hospitals, he reported, were available to "the destitute, crippled and diseased," but he also noticed "untouchables" carrying bells to warn upper-caste people of their polluting presence.[16] Culturally, the Gupta era witnessed a flourishing of art, literature, temple building, science, mathematics, and medicine, much of it patronized by rulers. Indian trade with China also thrived, and elements of Buddhist and Hindu culture took root in Southeast Asia (see Chapter 7). Indian commerce reached as far as the Roman world. A Germanic leader named Alaric laid siege to Rome in 410 C.E., while demanding 3,000 pounds of Indian pepper to spare the city.

The Great Stupa
The Great Stupa of Sanchi, the oldest stone building in India, was commissioned by Ashoka in the third century BCE to house precious relics of the Buddha. (Sanchi, Madhya Pradesh, India / Photo © Luca Tettoni / Bridgeman Images)

Thus, India's political history resembled that of Western Europe after the collapse of the Roman Empire far more than that of China or Persia. Neither imperial nor regional states commanded the kind of loyalty or exercised the degree of influence that they did in other second-wave civilizations. India's unparalleled cultural diversity surely was one reason, as was the frequency of invasions from Central Asia, which repeatedly smashed emerging states that might have provided the nucleus for an all-India empire. Finally, India's social structure, embodied in a caste system linked to occupational groups, made for intensely local loyalties at the expense of wider identities (see Chapter 5).

Nonetheless, a frequently vibrant economy fostered a lively internal commerce and made India the focal point of an extensive network of trade in the Indian Ocean basin. In particular, its cotton textile industry long supplied cloth throughout the Afro-Eurasian world. Strong guilds of merchants and artisans provided political leadership in major towns and cities, and their wealth supported lavish temples, public buildings, and religious festivals. Great creativity in religious matters generated Hindu and Buddhist traditions that later penetrated much of Asia. Indian mathematics and science, especially astronomy, also were impressive; Indian scientists plotted the movements of stars and planets and recognized quite early that the earth was round. Clearly, the absence of consistent imperial unity did not prevent the evolution of a lasting civilization.

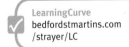
LearningCurve
bedfordstmartins.com
/strayer/LC

Reflections: Enduring Legacies of Second-Wave Empires

The second-wave empires discussed in this chapter have long ago passed into history, but their descendants have kept them alive in memory, for they have proved useful, even in the twentieth and early twenty-first centuries. Those empires have provided legitimacy for contemporary states, inspiration for new imperial ventures, and abundant warnings and cautions for those seeking to criticize more recent empires. For example, in bringing communism to China in the twentieth century, the Chinese leader Mao Zedong compared himself to Shihuangdi, the unifier of China and the brutal founder of its Qin dynasty. Reflecting on his campaign against intellectuals in general and Confucianism in particular, Mao declared to a Communist Party conference: "Emperor Qin Shihuang was not that outstanding. He only buried alive 460 Confucian scholars. We buried 460 thousand Confucian scholars. . . . To the charge of being like Emperor Qin, of being a dictator, we plead guilty."[17]

In contrast, modern-day Indians, who have sought to present their country as a model of cultural tolerance and nonviolence, have been quick to link themselves to Ashoka and his policies of inclusiveness. When the country became independent from British colonial rule in 1947, India soon placed an image of Ashoka's Pillar on the new nation's currency.

In the West, it has been the Roman Empire that has provided a template for thinking about political life. Many in Great Britain celebrated their own global empire as a modern version of the Roman Empire. If the British had been "civilized" by Roman rule, then surely Africans and Asians would benefit from falling under the control of the "superior" British. Likewise, to the Italian fascist dictator Benito Mussolini, his country's territorial expansion during the 1930s and World War II represented the creation of a new Roman Empire. Most recently, the United States' dominant role in the world has prompted the question: are the Americans the new Romans?

Historians frequently cringe as politicians and students use (and perhaps misuse) historical analogies to make their case for particular points of view in the present. But we have little else to go on except history in making our way through the complexities of contemporary life, and historians themselves seldom agree on the "lessons" of the past. Lively debate about the continuing relevance of these ancient empires shows that although the past may be gone, it surely is not dead.

Second Thoughts

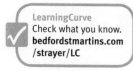
LearningCurve
Check what you know.
**bedfordstmartins.com
/strayer/LC**

Online Study Guide
bedfordstmartins.com
/highschool/strayer

What's the Significance?

Persian Empire, 120–122

Athenian democracy, 124–125

Greco-Persian Wars, 125–126

Hellenistic era, 126–129

Alexander the Great, 126–129

Augustus, 133

pax Romana, 133

Qin Shihuangdi, 133–135

Trung Trac, 134

Han dynasty, 136–138

Mauryan Empire, 141–142

Ashoka, 142

Big Picture Questions

1. What common features can you identify in the empires described in this chapter? In what ways did they differ from one another? What accounts for those differences?

2. Are you more impressed with the "greatness" of empires or with their destructive and oppressive features? Why?

3. Do you think that these second-wave empires hold "lessons" for the present, or are contemporary circumstances sufficiently unique as to render the distant past irrelevant?

4. **Looking Back:** How do these empires of the second-wave civilizations differ from the political systems of the First Civilizations?

Next Steps: For Further Study

Jane Burbank and Frederick Cooper, *Empires in World History* (2010). A fascinating account by two major scholars of the imperial theme across the world. Chapter 2 compares the Roman and Chinese empires.

Arthur Cotterell, *The First Emperor of China* (1988). A biography of Shihuangdi.

Christopher Kelley, *The Roman Empire: A Very Short Introduction* (2006). A brief, up-to-date, and accessible account of the Roman achievement.

Cullen Murphy, *Are We Rome? The Fall of an Empire and the Fate of America* (2007). A reflection on the usefulness and the dangers of comparing the Roman Empire to the present-day United States.

Sarah Pomeroy et al., *Ancient Greece* (1999). A highly readable survey of Greek history by a team of distinguished scholars.

Romila Thapar, *Ashoka and the Decline of the Mauryas* (1961). A classic study of India's early empire builder.

Illustrated History of the Roman Empire, http://www.roman-empire.net. An interactive Web site with maps, pictures, and much information about the Roman Empire.

For Web sites and additional documents related to this chapter, see **Make History** at bedfordstmartins.com /highschool/strayer.

Documents

Considering the Evidence: Political Authority in Second-Wave Civilizations

States, empires, and their rulers are surely not the whole story of the human past, although historians have sometimes treated them as though they were. But they are important because their actions shaped the lives of many millions of people. The city-states of ancient Greece, the Roman Empire, the emerging Chinese empire of the Qin dynasty, and the Indian empire of the Mauryan dynasty—these were among the impressive political structures of the second-wave era in Eurasia. Rulers seeking to establish or maintain their authority mobilized a variety of ideas to give legitimacy to their regimes. Reflection on political authority was a central issue in the discourse of educated people all across Eurasia. In the documents that follow, four contemporary observers—two rulers and two scholars—describe some of the political arrangements within Mediterranean, Chinese, and Indian civilizations. Keep in mind that each of them represents an idealized image of political authority rather than an "objective" discussion of how these political systems actually operated.

Document 3.1

In Praise of Athenian Democracy

The Greeks of Athens generated political ideas that have long been celebrated in the West, although they were exceptional even in the small world of classical Greece. (See pp. 122–25 and Map 3.2, p. 123.) The most well-known expression of praise for Athenian democracy comes from Pericles, the most prominent Athenian leader during the fifth century B.C.E. Sometimes called the "first citizen of Athens," Pericles initiated the grand building projects that still grace the Acropolis and led his city in its military struggles with archrival Sparta. To his critics, he was a populist, manipulating the masses to enhance his own power, and an Athenian imperialist whose aggressive policies ultimately ruined the city. His famous speech in praise of Athens was delivered around 431–430 B.C.E. at the end of the first year of the Peloponnesian War against Sparta. The setting was a public funeral service for Athenian citizens who had died in that conflict.

Pericles' oration was recorded by the Greek historian Thucydides (thoo-SIHD-ih-dees), who was probably present at that event.

■ How does Pericles describe Athenian democracy?

■ Does his argument for democracy derive from fundamental principles, such as human equality, or from the practical benefits that derive from such a system of government?

■ What kind of citizens does he believe democracy produces? Keep in mind that not everyone shared this idealized view of Athenian democracy. How might critics have responded to Pericles' arguments?

■ Although Pericles praised Athenian military prowess, his city lost the Peloponnesian War. In what ways does this affect your assessment of his arguments?

PERICLES

Funeral Oration

431–430 B.C.E.

Our form of government does not enter into rivalry with the institutions of others. We do not copy our neighbors, but are an example to them. It is true that we are called a democracy, for the administration is in the hands of the many and not of the few. But while the law secures equal justice to all alike in their private disputes, the claim of excellence is also recognized; and when a citizen is in any way distinguished, he is preferred to the public service, not as a matter of privilege, but as the reward of merit. Neither is poverty a bar, but a man may benefit his country whatever be the obscurity of his condition. There is no exclusiveness in our public life, and in our private intercourse we are not suspicious of one another, nor angry with our neighbor if he does what he likes.... While we are thus unconstrained in our private intercourse, a spirit of reverence pervades our public acts; we are prevented from doing wrong by respect for the authorities and for the laws....

And we have not forgotten to provide for our weary spirits many relaxations from toil; we have regular games and sacrifices throughout the year; our homes are beautiful and elegant; and the delight which we daily feel in all these things helps to banish melancholy. Because of the greatness of our city the fruits of the whole earth flow in upon us; so that we enjoy the goods of other countries as freely as of our own.

Then, again, our military training is in many respects superior to that of our adversaries. Our city is thrown open to the world, and we never expel a foreigner or prevent him from seeing or learning anything of which the secret if revealed to an enemy might profit him. We rely not upon management or trickery, but upon our own hearts and hands. And in the matter of education, whereas they from early youth are always undergoing laborious exercises which are to make them brave, we live at ease, and yet are equally ready to face the perils which they face....

For we are lovers of the beautiful, yet simple in our tastes, and we cultivate the mind without loss of manliness.... To avow poverty with us is no disgrace; the true disgrace is in doing nothing to avoid

Source: Benjamin Jowett, *Thucydides, translated into English, to which is prefixed an essay on inscriptions and a note on the geography of Thucydides*, 2nd ed. (Oxford: Clarendon Press, 1900), bk. 2, paras. 37–41.

it. An Athenian citizen does not neglect the state because he takes care of his own household; and even those of us who are engaged in business have a very fair idea of politics. We alone regard a man who takes no interest in public affairs, not as a harmless, but as a useless character; and if few of us are originators, we are all sound judges of a policy. The great impediment to action is, in our opinion, not discussion, but the want of that knowledge which is gained by discussion preparatory to action. For we have a peculiar power of thinking before we act and of acting too, whereas other men are courageous from ignorance but hesitate upon reflection. And they are surely to be esteemed the bravest spirits who, having the clearest sense both of the pains and pleasures of life, do not on that account shrink from danger. . . .

To sum up: I say that Athens is the school of Hellas, and that the individual Athenian in his own person seems to have the power of adapting himself to the most varied forms of action with the utmost versatility and grace. . . .

For we have compelled every land and every sea to open a path for our valor, and have everywhere planted eternal memorials of our friendship and of our enmity. Such is the city for whose sake these men nobly fought and died; they could not bear the thought that she might be taken from them; and every one of us who survive should gladly toil on her behalf.

Document 3.2

In Praise of the Roman Empire

By the second century C.E. the Roman Empire, now encompassing the Mediterranean basin and beyond, was in its glory days. With conquest largely completed, the *pax Romana* (Roman peace) generally prevailed and commerce flourished, as did the arts and literature. The empire enjoyed a century (96–180 C.E.) of autocratic but generally benevolent rule. In 155 C.E. a well-known scholar and orator from the city of Smyrna on the west coast of Anatolia (present-day Turkey) arrived for a visit to the imperial capital of Rome. He was Aelius Aristides (ca. 117–181 C.E.), a widely traveled Greek-speaking member of a wealthy landowning family whose members had been granted Roman citizenship several decades earlier. While in Rome, Aristides delivered to the imperial court and in front of the emperor, Antonius, a formal speech of praise and gratitude, known as a panegyric, celebrating the virtues and achievements of the Roman Empire.

- What does Aristides identify as the unique features of the Roman Empire? Which of these features in particular may have given the empire a measure of legitimacy in the eyes of its many subject peoples? What other factors, unmentioned by Aristides, may have contributed to the maintenance of Roman authority?

- What does Aristides mean by referring to the empire as a "common democracy of the world"?

- Why might Aristides, a Greek-speaking resident of a land well outside the Roman heartland, be so enamored of the empire?

- To what extent does Aristides' oration provide evidence for the development of a composite Greco-Roman culture and sensibility within the Roman Empire?

- How does this speech compare, in both style and content, with that of Pericles in Document 3.1?

AELIUS ARISTIDES

The Roman Oration

155 C.E.

A certain prose writer said about Asia that one man "rules all as far as is the course of the sun," untruly, since he excluded all Africa and Europe from the sun's rising and setting. [This refers to the Persian Empire.] But now it has turned out to be true that the course of the sun and your possessions are equal.... [N]or do you rule within fixed boundaries, nor does another prescribe the limits of your power....

About the [Mediterranean] sea the continents [Africa, Asia, and Europe] lie ... ever supplying you with products from those regions. Here is brought from every land and sea all the crops of the seasons and the produce of each land, river and lake, as well as the arts of the Greeks and barbarians.... So many merchant ships arrive here ... that the city is like a factory common to the whole earth. It is possible to see so many cargoes from India and even from [southern] Arabia.... Your farmlands are Egypt, Sicily, and all of [North] Africa which is cultivated. The arrival and departure of ships never stops....

Although your empire is so large and so great, it is much greater in its good order than in its circumference.... [Nor] are satraps° fighting against one another, as if they had no king; nor do some cities side with these and others with those.... But like the enclosure of a courtyard, cleansed of every disturbance, a circle encompasses your empire.... All everywhere are equally subjects....

You are the only ones ever to rule over free men.... [Y]ou govern throughout the whole in-

habited world as if in a single city.... You appoint governors ... for the protection and care of their subjects, not to be their masters.... And here there is a great and fair equality between weak and powerful, obscure and famous, poor and rich and noble.... To excel the barbarians in wealth and power, while surpassing the Greeks in knowledge and moderation, seems to me to be an important matter....

You have divided into two parts all the men of your empire ... and everywhere you have made citizens all those who are the more accomplished, noble, and powerful people, even if they retain their native affinities, while the remainder you have made subjects and the governed. And neither does the sea nor a great expanse of intervening land keep one from being a citizen, nor here are Asia and Europe distinguished. But all lies open to all men.... There has been established a common democracy of the world, under one man, the best ruler and director....

You have divided people into Romans [citizens] and non-Romans [subjects].... [M]any in each city are citizens of yours ... and some of them have not even seen this city.... There is no need of garrisons ..., but the most important and powerful people in each place guard their countries for you.... Yet no envy walks in your empire.... [T]here has arisen a single harmonious government which has embraced all men. [Y]ou have established a form of

---

°**satraps:** local authorities.

Source: Aelius Aristides, *The Complete Works*, vol. 2, translated by P. Charles A. Behr (Leiden: E. J. Brill, 1986), 73–97.

government such as no one else of mankind has done....Your government is like a mixture of all the constitutions [democracy, aristocracy, monarchy] without the inferior side of each....Therefore whenever one considers the power of the people and how easily they attain all their wishes and requests, he will believe that it is a democracy....But when he considers the Senate deliberating and holding office, he will believe there is no more perfect aristocracy than this. But when he has considered the overseer and president of all these [the emperor], he sees in this man the possessor of the most perfect monarchy, free of the evils of the tyrant and greater than the dignity of the king....

And the whole inhabited world, as it were attending a national festival, has laid aside ... the carrying of weapons and has turned ... to adornments and all kinds of pleasures....Everything is full of gymnasiums, fountains, gateways, temples, handicrafts, and schools ... and a boundless number of games.... Now it is possible for both Greek and barbarian ... to travel easily wherever he wishes.... [I]t is enough for his safety that he is a Roman or rather one of those under you.

Document 3.3

Governing a Chinese Empire

As the Roman Empire was taking shape in the Mediterranean basin, a powerful Chinese empire emerged in East Asia. More than in the Roman world, the political ideas and practices of imperial China drew on the past. The notion of China as a unified state ruled by a single sage/emperor who mediated between heaven and the human realm had an ancient pedigree. After a long period of political fragmentation, known as the era of warring states, such a unified Chinese state took shape once again during the short-lived Qin dynasty (221–206 B.C.E.), led by its formidable ruler Shihuangdi (see pp. 133–36). That state operated under a version of Legalism (see Chapter 4, p. 169), a political philosophy that found expression in the writings of Han Fei (280–233 B.C.E.) and that in large measure guided the practices of Shihuangdi and the Qin dynasty. Han Fei's Legalist thinking was discredited by the brutality and excesses of Shihuangdi's reign, and the Han dynasty that followed was sharply critical of his ideas, favoring instead the "government by morality" approach of Confucianism. Nonetheless, Han Fei's emphasis on the importance of laws and the need to enforce them influenced all succeeding Chinese dynasties.

■ Why is Han Fei's approach to governing China referred to as Legalism? According to him, what is required for effective government?

■ What are the "two handles"?

■ To whom does Han Fei believe his measures should apply?

■ What view of human nature underpins Han Fei's argument?

The Writings of Master Han Fei
Third Century B.C.E.

No state is forever strong or forever weak. If those who would uphold the law are strong, the state will be strong; if they are weak, the state will be weak ...

In the present age, he who can put an end to private scheming and make men uphold the public law will see his people secure and his state well-ordered; he who can block selfish pursuits and enforce the public law will see his army growing stronger and his enemies weakening. Find men who have a clear understanding of what is beneficial to the nation and a feeling for the system of laws and regulations, and place them in charge of the lesser officials; then the ruler can never be deceived by lies and falsehoods ...

A truly enlightened ruler uses the law to select men for him; he does not choose them himself. He uses the law to weigh their merits; he does not attempt to judge them for himself. Hence men of true worth will not be able to hide their talents, nor spoilers to gloss over their faults. Men cannot advance on the basis of praise alone, nor be driven from court by calumny [false charges] ...

What the law has decreed the wise man cannot dispute nor the brave man venture to contest. When faults are to be punished, the highest minister cannot escape; when good is to be rewarded, the lowest peasant must not be passed over. Hence, for correcting the faults of superiors, chastising the misdeeds of subordinates, restoring order, exposing error, checking excesses, remedying evil, and unifying the standards of the people, nothing can compare to law...If penalties are heavy, men dare not use high position to abuse the humble; if laws are clearly defined, superiors will be honored and their rights will not be invaded ...Were the ruler of men to discard law and follow his private whim, then all distinction between high and low would cease to exist.

The enlightened ruler controls his ministers by means of two handles alone. The two handles are punishment and favor. What do I mean by punishment and favor? To inflict mutilation and death on men is called punishment; to bestow honor and reward is called favor. Those who act as ministers fear the penalties and hope to profit by the rewards. Hence if the ruler wields his punishments and favors, the ministers will fear his sternness and flock to receive his benefits. But the evil ministers of the age are different. They cajole the ruler into letting them inflict punishments themselves on men they hate and bestow rewards on men they like. Now if the ruler of men does not insist on reserving to himself the right to dispense profit in the form of rewards and show his sternness in punishments, but instead hands them out on the advice of his ministers, then the people of the state will all fear the ministers and hold the ruler in contempt, will flock to the ministers and desert the ruler. This is the danger that arises when the ruler loses control of punishments and favors.

Source: Han Fei, "The Writings of Master Han Fei," in *Basic Writings of Mo Tzu, Hsun Tzu and Han Fei Tzu*, translated by Burton Watson (New York: Columbia University Press, 2003), 21, 22, 24, 28, 29.

Document 3.4

Governing an Indian Empire

Among the rulers of the classical era, Ashoka, of India's Mauryan dynasty (r. 268–232 B.C.E.), surely stands out, both for the personal transformation he experienced and for the benevolent philosophy of government that he subsequently articulated (see pp. 142–43). Ashoka's career as emperor began in a familiar fashion—ruthless consolidation of his own power and vigorous expansion of the state's frontiers. A particularly bloody battle against the state of Kalinga marked a turning point in his reign. Apparently repulsed by the destruction, Ashoka converted to Buddhism and turned his attention to more peaceful and tolerant ways of governing his huge empire. His edicts and advice, inscribed on rocks and pillars throughout his realm, outlined this distinctive approach to imperial governance.

The following document provides samples of instructions from Ashoka, who is referred to as King Piyadasi, or the Beloved of the Gods. The term "dhamma," used frequently in edicts of Ashoka, refers to the "way" or the "truth" that is embodied in religious teachings.

- How would you describe Ashoka's philosophy of state?

- How might Han Fei have responded to Ashoka's ideas?

- What specific changes did Ashoka make in state policies and practices?

- Can you think of practical reasons why he might have adopted these policies? Did he entirely abandon the use of harsher measures?

Although Ashoka's reputation as an enlightened ruler has persisted to this day, his policies ultimately were not very successful. Shortly after Ashoka's death, the Mauryan Empire broke apart into a more common Indian pattern of competing regional states that rose and fell with some regularity. Of course, Shihuangdi's much harsher Legalist policies were also unsuccessful, at least in maintaining his dynasty, which lasted a mere fifteen years.

- How might this outcome affect your assessment of Ashoka?

- What does this suggest about the relationship between political philosophies and the success or longevity of political systems?

ASHOKA

The Rock Edicts

ca. 268–232 B.C.E.

Beloved-of-the-Gods, King Piyadasi, conquered the Kalingas eight years after his coronation. One hundred and fifty thousand were deported, one hundred thousand were killed, and many more died [from other causes]. After the Kalingas had been conquered, Beloved-of-the-Gods came to feel a strong inclination towards the Dhamma, a love for the Dhamma and for instruction in Dhamma. Now Beloved-of-the-Gods feels deep remorse for having conquered the Kalingas. . . .

Now Beloved-of-the-Gods thinks that even those who do wrong should be forgiven where forgiveness is possible.

Even the forest people, who live in Beloved-of-the-Gods' domain, are entreated and reasoned with to act properly. They are told that despite his remorse Beloved-of-the-Gods has the power to punish them if necessary, so that they should be ashamed of their wrong and not be killed. Truly, Beloved-of-the-Gods desires non-injury, restraint, and impartiality to all beings, even where wrong has been done.

Now it is conquest by Dhamma that Beloved-of-the-Gods considers to be the best conquest. . . .

I have had this Dhamma edict written so that my sons and great-grandsons may not consider making new conquests, or that if military conquests are made, that they be done with forbearance and light punishment, or better still, that they consider making conquest by Dhamma only, for that bears fruit in this world and the next. May all their intense devotion be given to this which has a result in this world and the next.

1. Here (in my domain) no living beings are to be slaughtered or offered in sacrifice. . . . Formerly, in the kitchen of Beloved-of-the-Gods, King Piyadasi, hundreds of thousands of animals were killed every day to make curry. But now with the writing of this Dhamma edict only three creatures, two peacocks and a deer are killed, and the deer not always. And in time, not even these three creatures will be killed.

2. . . . [E]verywhere has Beloved-of-the-Gods . . . made provision for two types of medical treatment: medical treatment for humans and medical treatment for animals. Wherever medical herbs suitable for humans or animals are not available, I have had them imported and grown. . . . Along roads I have had wells dug and trees planted for the benefit of humans and animals.

3. Everywhere in my domain the [royal officers] shall go on inspection tours every five years for the purpose of Dhamma instruction and also to conduct other business. Respect for mother and father is good, generosity to friends, acquaintances, relatives, Brahmans and ascetics is good, not killing living beings is good, moderation in spending and moderation in saving is good.

4. In the past, for many hundreds of years, killing or harming living beings and improper behavior toward relatives, and improper behavior toward Brahmans and ascetics has increased. But now due to Beloved-of-the-Gods' Dhamma practice, the sound of the drum [for announcing the punishment of criminals] has been replaced by the sound of the Dhamma. The sighting of heavenly cars, auspicious elephants, bodies of fire, and other divine sightings has not happened for many hundreds of years. But now because Beloved-of-the-Gods, King Piyadasi, promotes restraint in the killing and harming of living beings, proper behavior towards relatives, Brahmans and ascetics, and respect for mother, father and elders, such sightings have increased.

5. In the past there were no [officers of the Dhamma] but such officers were appointed by

Source: *The Edicts of King Ashoka*, translated by Ven S. Dhammika (Kandy, Sri Lanka: Buddhist Publication Society, 1993).

me thirteen years after my coronation. Now they work among all religions for the establishment of Dhamma....They work among soldiers, chiefs, Brahmans, householders, the poor, the aged and those devoted to Dhamma—for their welfare and happiness—so that they may be free from harassment. They ... work for the proper treatment of prisoners, towards their unfettering....They are occupied everywhere....

7. Beloved-of-the-Gods, King Piyadasi, desires that all religions should reside everywhere, for all of them desire self-control and purity of heart.

8. In the past kings used to go out on pleasure tours during which there was hunting and other entertainment. But ten years after Beloved-of-the-Gods had been coronated, he went on a tour to Sambodhi° and thus instituted Dhamma tours. During these tours, the following things took place: visits and gifts to Brahmans and ascetics, visits and gifts of gold to the aged, visits to people in the countryside, instructing them in Dhamma....

12. Beloved-of-the-Gods, King Piyadasi, honors both ascetics and the householders of all religions, and he honors them with gifts and honors of various kinds....Whoever praises his own religion, due to excessive devotion, and condemns others with the thought "Let me glorify my own religion," only harms his own religion. Therefore contact [between religions] is good. One should listen to and respect the doctrines professed by others.

———————

°**Sambodhi:** the site of the Buddha's enlightenment.

Using the Evidence: Political Authority in Second-Wave Civilizations

1. **Making comparisons:** How would you describe the range of political thinking and practice expressed in these documents? What, if any, common elements do these writings share? Another approach to such a comparison is to take the ideas of one writer and ask how they might be viewed by several of the others. For example, how might Pericles, Aristides, and Han Fei have responded to Ashoka?

2. **Comparing ancient and modern politics:** What enduring issues of political life do these documents raise? What elements of political thinking and practice during the second-wave era differ most sharply from those of the modern world of the last century or two? What are the points of similarity?

3. **Distinguishing "power" and "authority":** "Power" refers to the ability of rulers to coerce their subjects into some required behavior, while "authority" denotes the ability of those rulers to persuade their subjects to obey voluntarily by convincing them that it is proper, right, or natural to do so. What appeals to "power" and "authority" can you find in these documents? How does the balance between them differ among these documents?

4. **Noticing point of view:** From what position and with what motivation did these writers compose their documents? How did this affect what they had to say?

Visual Sources

Considering the Evidence:
Representing Political Authority

In ancient times and modern alike, the exercise of power has not only been described and contested in writing but also represented visually. In societies where the vast majority of people were illiterate, the visible display of political authority—in paintings, statues, carvings, buildings, tombs—was surely more effective than the written word in generating broader public legitimacy for these regimes. The ziggurats of Mesopotamia, the pyramids and paintings of Egyptian pharaohs, the massive stone heads of Olmec rulers (see images on pp. 77, 78, and 86) illustrate visual representations of power within the First Civilizations. On an even grander scale, second-wave civilizations conveyed artistically their various conceptions of political authority. In doing so, rulers expressed their values and their self-image even as they created mythologies and rituals that endured far longer than those who generated these works of art and propaganda. Here we examine four such works deriving respectively from Persian, Greek, Chinese, and Roman civilization.

From the Persian Empire comes an impressive visual representation of political power, part of a huge multilingual inscription located on a limestone cliff some 300 feet above the ground in western Iran. Known as the Behistun Inscription, this monumental work, shown here as Visual Source 3.1, was commissioned by the Emperor Darius the Great (r. 522–486 B.C.E.) to celebrate his many victories over foreign enemies and domestic rebels alike. Those victories were accomplished, as the inscription repeatedly asserts, "by the grace of Ahuramazda," the great benevolent Deity of Zoroastrianism (see pp. 181–82). Summing up his reign, Darius declared: "On this account Ahuramazda brought me help, and all the other gods, all that there are, because I was not wicked, nor was I a liar, nor was I a despot, neither I nor any of my family. I have ruled according to righteousness. Neither to the weak nor to the powerful did I do wrong. Whosoever helped my house, him I favored; he who was hostile, him I destroyed."[18]

The central figure in the carving is Darius himself, the third from the left, holding a bow as a symbol of rulership with his foot on the chest of one of the rebels whom he had crushed. To the right stands a line of nine captives roped at the neck with their hands tied behind them, who represent other rebels or conquered peoples. To the left of Darius are two of his leading generals who have the honor of ritually carrying the monarch's bow and lance respectively. Hovering over the entire scene is the Faravahar, the ancient Near Eastern winged disk symbol, which had come to represent Ahuramazda and the Zoroastrian tradition.

- What message did Darius seek to convey in commissioning this work?

- How does it present the source of political authority in the Persian Empire?

- What role does the Faravahar play in this image?

- How might Athenian Greeks respond to this representation of political authority? Consider the possible reaction of Pericles (Document 3.1).

Very different in its style and message is Visual Source 3.2, deriving from Athens around 500 B.C.E. and shown here in a surviving Roman copy. It is a statue of two aristocratic male lovers, Harmodius and Aristogeiton, who conspired in the year 514 B.C.E. to kill the tyrant who governed Athens. At the time, the word "tyrant" did not imply a despotic or oppressive ruler, but simply someone who ruled alone and had come to power by force, often with popular

Visual Source 3.1 Behistun Inscription (age fotostock/Robert Harding)

support. The particular tyrants then in power in Athens, the brothers Hippias and Hipparchus, were in fact reasonably benevolent, but Hipparchus had made an unwelcome sexual advance to Harmodius and when rejected had publicly insulted the sister of Harmodius by questioning her virginity. Thus personal, rather than political, motives largely inspired the murder of Hipparchus and the subsequent killing of the two conspirators.

A few years later in 510 B.C.E., an invasion from Sparta finally overthrew the remaining tyrant Hippias. This opened the way to more a democratic system for Athens under the leadership of the reformer Cleisthenes, who destroyed the power of the great aristocratic families and established the central role of popular assembly, chosen by lot from among the citizens of the city. Athenian authorities then commissioned an idealized statue of the lovers, each bearing two swords, to mark the moment when freedom was restored to Athens, ignoring the sexual rivalries that triggered the killing of the tyrant. Focusing attention on the supposed purity of their intentions diminished the role of Cleisthenes, whose tactics and motives drew suspicion among some Athenians. It also diverted attention away from the role of Sparta, longtime rival of Athens, in facilitating the transition to democracy.

These were the first public statues of mere mortals, rather than gods, erected in Athens. At its base were inscribed the words of a poet: "A marvelous great light shone upon Athens when Aristogeiton and Harmodius slew Hipparchus." Drinking songs celebrated the pair who "killed the tyrants and restored equal laws to Athens," while subsequent legislation forbade slandering them and prohibited the use of their names for slaves. Later seized by the Persians during the Persian Wars, the statues were returned to a grateful Athens by Alexander the Great.

■ How does the message of these statues differ from that of Visual Source 3.1? What elements of these statues might convey the values of Athenian democracy?

■ It was common in Athenian sculpture of the time to portray males in the nude. What does their nudity add to the message of the statue?

■ What does the willingness to celebrate two male lovers suggest about the sexual attitudes of Athenians of the time?

■ How might you understand the willingness of Athenians to transform a purely personal quarrel into a political statement?

Surely the most stunning representation of political power during the second-wave era derived from China and expressed the grand conception of empire associated with Qin Shihuangdi, the so-called First Emperor (r. 221–210 B.C.E.) (see pp. 133–36). In his view, the empire he created was to be universal, even cosmic, in scope. In tours throughout his vast realm, he offered sacrifices to the various spirits, bringing them, as well as the rival kingdoms of China,

Visual Source 3.2 Harmodius and Aristogeiton (Museo Archaeologico Nazionale, Naples/The Bridgeman Art Library)

into a state of unity and harmony. One of the inscriptions he left behind suggested the scale of his reign: "He universally promulgated the shining laws, gave warp and woof to all under heaven."[19] Qin Shihuangdi saw himself in the line of ancient sage kings, who had originally given order to the world. But the empire was also to be an eternal realm. The emperor vigorously pursued personal immortality, seeking out pills, herbs, and potions believed to convey eternal life and sending expeditions to the mythical Isles of the Immortals, thought to lie off the east coast of China. All of this found expression in the vast funerary complex constructed for Qin Shihuangdi during his lifetime near the modern city of Xian.

In early 1974, some Chinese peasants digging a well stumbled across a small corner of that complex, leading to what has become perhaps the most celebrated archeological discovery of the twentieth century. In subsequent and continuing excavations, archeologists have uncovered thousands of life-size ceramic statues of soldiers of various ranks, arrayed for battle and equipped with real weapons. Other statues portrayed officials, acrobats, musicians, wrestlers, horses, bronze chariots, birds, and more—all designed to accompany Qin Shihuangdi into the afterlife.

This amazing discovery, however, was only a very small part of an immense tomb complex covering some fifty-six square kilometers and centered on the still-unexcavated burial mound of Qin Shihuangdi. Begun in 246 B.C.E. and still incomplete when Shihuangdi died in 210 B.C.E., the construction of this gigantic complex was described by the great Chinese historian Sima Qian about a century later:

> As soon as the First Emperor became king of Qin, excavations and building had been started at Mount Li, while after he won the empire, more than 700,000 conscripts from all parts of the country worked there. They dug through three subterranean streams and poured molten copper for the outer coffin, and the tomb was filled with . . . palaces, pavilions, and offices as well as fine vessels, precious stones, and rarities. Artisans were ordered to fix up crossbows so that any thief breaking in would be shot. All the country's streams, the Yellow River and the Yangtze were reproduced in quicksilver [mercury] and by some mechanical means made to flow into a miniature ocean. The heavenly constellations were above and the regions of the earth below. The candles were made of whale oil to insure the burning for the longest possible time.[20]

Buried with the First Emperor were many of the workers who had died or were killed during construction as well as sacrificed aristocrats and concubines.

This massive project was no mere monument to a deceased ruler. In a culture that believed the living and the dead formed a single community, Qin Shihuangdi's tomb complex was a parallel society, complete with walls, palaces, cemeteries, demons, spirits, soldiers, administrators, entertainers, calendars, texts, divination records, and the luxurious objects appropriate to royalty. The tomb mound itself was like a mountain, a geographic feature that in Chinese thinking was home to gods, spirits, and immortals. From this mound, Qin Shihuangdi would rule forever over his vast domain, although invisible to the living.

Visual Source 3.3 displays a part of the terra cotta army, containing some 6,000 figures, which guarded the entryway to Qin Shihuangdi's tomb, while the chapter opening picture on page 116 shows a kneeling archer, who was a part of this army. The insert image shows an exquisitely detailed bronze carriage, pulled by four horses, found some distance away, quite close to the actual burial place of the emperor. The compartment is decorated inside and out with geometric and cloud patterns, while the round roof, perhaps, represents the sun, the sky, or the heavens above. Perhaps it was intended to allow the emperor to tour his realm in the afterlife much as he had done while alive.

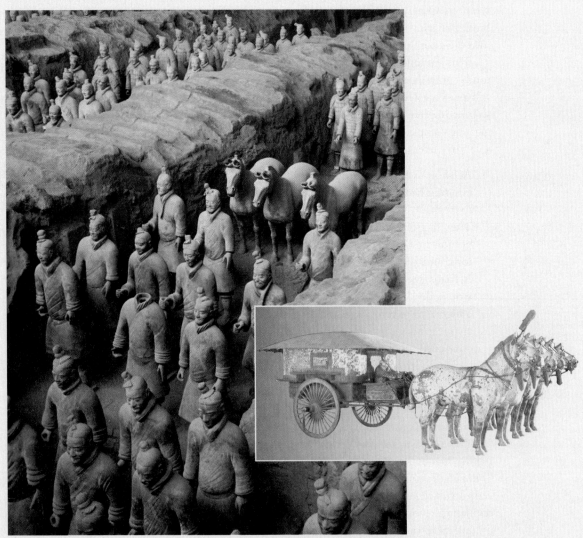

Visual Source 3.3 Qin Shihuangdi Funerary Complex (Terra Cotta Army: Dennis Cox/ChinaStock; Chariot: Private Collection/The Bridgeman Art Library)

Or did it serve a one-time purpose to transport the emperor's soul into the afterlife?

■ How do you suppose Qin Shihuangdi thought about the function of this "army" and the carriage in the larger context of his tomb complex? What might it add to his ability to exercise power and project authority?

■ How does the fact that this funerary complex was largely invisible to the general public affect your understanding of its function? How might ordinary Chinese have viewed the construction of this complex even before it was completed?

■ To what extent is the conception of political authority reflected in this funerary complex in keeping with the ideas of Han Fei in Document 3.3? How might it challenge those ideas?

■ How do you understand the religious or cosmic dimension of Chinese political thinking as reflected in this tomb complex?

Visual Source 3.4, a statue of Augustus, the first of the Roman emperors (r. 27 B.C.E.–14 C.E.) was probably created shortly after his death, though based on a somewhat earlier bronze original. It symbolized a new era of peace and abundance in Roman history, following a century of turmoil and civil war. Here Augustus is "imperator" or military commander, wearing a breastplate (see inset) and with his right arm extended as if addressing his troops. The statue was clearly intended to commemorate the victory of Augustus over the Parthian Empire, centered in Persia or Iran, in 20 B.C.E., a triumph that reversed several earlier Roman defeats. The central relief on the breastplate shows the Parthian ruler (on the right) returning to a Roman military figure the battle standard that the Parthians had seized 33 years before. "I compelled the Parthians to return the spoils and standards of three Roman armies," Augustus declared, "and humbly to beg the friendship of the Roman people."[21]

The rest of the breastplate contains various figures from Roman mythology. At the top left is the sun god Sol driving a chariot, while the top right shows the moon goddess Luna as well as Aurora, the winged goddess of dawn pouring dew from her jug. Between them Caelus, the sky god, spreads out the heavens, and at the bottom of the breastplate the earth goddess cradles two babies and holds a cornucopia overflowing with fruit. Cupid or Eros, riding a dolphin next to Augustus's right leg, evokes his mother Venus, often said to be an ancestor of Augustus. Notice that the military figure of Augustus is strangely barefoot, a portrayal usually associated with gods and heroes.

■ What does the statue suggest about the bases of Augustus's legitimacy as a ruler? What kind of future for the empire does the statue evoke?

■ Although Augustus resisted being portrayed as divine, the statue is laced with religious imagery. What does that imagery suggest about the way Augustus was coming to be viewed?

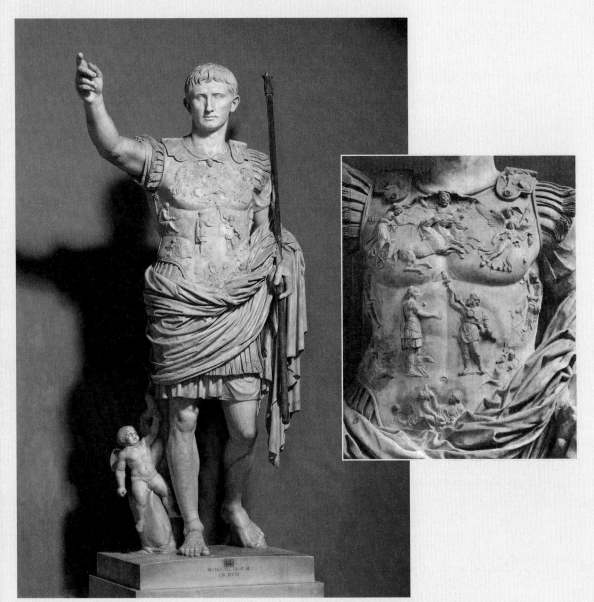

Visual Source 3.4 Augustus (Statue: Scala/Art Resource, NY; Breastplate: Alinari/Art Resource, NY)

- What elements of the statue suggest a realistic portrayal of Augustus and which show an idealized image of him? Notice particularly his face and posture. What sensibility is the artist seeking to convey?

- How might Aelius Aristides (Document 3.2, pp. 148–50) respond to this statue?

Using the Evidence:
Representing Political Authority

1. **Comparing the foundations of political authority:** Based on both the documents and visual sources, write an essay comparing the sources of political legitimacy for the states or empires of the second-wave civilizations of Eurasia.

2. **Imagining cross-cultural perceptions:** How might Augustus, Darius, or Athenian leaders respond to the funerary complex of Qin Shihuangdi and the political ideology it represented?

3. **Considering religion and political life:** To what extent and in what ways did religion underlay political authority in the civilizations of the second-wave era?

4. **Considering patriarchy and power:** What can we learn about patriarchy and its relationship to power from these sources? What role, if any, do female images play in these expressions of political power?

Chapter 3 Wrap Up

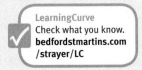

LearningCurve
Check what you know.
**bedfordstmartins.com
/strayer/LC**

STEP ONE

The Word to Know: Empire

The *Oxford English Dictionary* defines *empire* as "Supreme and extensive political dominion; *esp.* that exercised by an 'emperor'... or by a sovereign state over its dependencies." Using the word empire, explain why Persia, as discussed in Chapter 3, qualifies as an empire. Your answer should be a paragraph in length.

STEP TWO

Comparing the Rome and Han Empires

As you read pp. 129–141 in Chapter 3, take notes on each empire, using the categories listed below. Then assess how similar or different the two empires were.

	Unique characteristics of Rome	Unique characteristics of Han	Similarities between both
Growth of the empire (method of conquest, motivation for individuals within the empire)			
Method of rule (infrastructure, use of army, bureaucracy, law, resistance)			
Integration and spread of local and foreign culture (patriarchy, language, assimilation, religion)			
Reasons for decline/fall			
Legacy of empire			

Legitimacy and Political Authority

This exercise considers how both images and texts lend legitimacy to a society or empire, using the Qin Empire in China as an example. Examine the following documents and visual source: Document 3.3, "Governing a Chinese Empire, pp. 150–151; Visual Source 3.3, p. 160; and the testimonial below written by the Chinese historian Sima Qian.

Sima Qian, Grand Historian, on Qin Shihuangdi,
written during the Han Empire c. 100 B.C.E.

A new age is inaugurated by the Emperor;
Rules and measures are rectified,
The myriad things set in order,
Human affairs are made clear
And there is harmony between fathers and sons.
The Emperor in his sagacity, benevolence, and justice
Has made all laws and principles manifest.
Wherever one can go by boat or by carriage,
Men carry out their orders
And satisfy their desires;

For our Emperor in accordance with the time
Has regulated local customs,
Made waterways and divided up the land.
Caring for the common people,
He works day and night without rest;
He defines the laws, leaving nothing in doubt,
Making known what is forbidden.
The local officials have their duties,
Administration is smoothly carried out,
All is done correctly, all according to plan.
The Emperor in his wisdom
Inspects all four quarters of his realm;

■ Questions

1. In what way do these three sources demonstrate the authority of the Qin ruler?

2. What are some of the methods that it appears he used to enforce stability within the empire?

3. What accomplishments can be attributed to Shihuangdi?

4. What additional document would help you assess the merits of Qin Shihuangdi? Why would this be helpful?

Source: Yang Hsien-yi and Gladys Yang, *The Records of the Historian* (Hong Kong: Commercial Press, 1974), pp. 170–72; 177–78.

Culture and Religion in Eurasia/North Africa

500 B.C.E.–500 C.E.

In September of 2009, Kong Dejun returned to China from her home in Great Britain. The occasion was a birthday celebration for her ancient ancestor Kong Fuzi, or Confucius, born 2560 years earlier. Together with some 10,000 other people—descendants, scholars, government officials, and foreign representatives—Kong Dejun attended ceremonies at the Confucian Temple in Qufu, the hometown of China's famous sage. "I was touched to see my ancestor being revered by people from different countries and nations," she said.[1] What made this celebration remarkable was that it took place in a country still ruled by the Communist Party, which had long devoted enormous efforts to discrediting Confucius and his teachings. In the view of communist China's revolutionary leader, Mao Zedong, Confucianism was associated with class inequality, patriarchy, feudalism, superstition, and all things old and backward. But the country's ancient teacher and philosopher had apparently outlasted its revolutionary hero, for now the Communist Party claims Confucius as a national treasure and has established over 300 Confucian Institutes to study his writings. He appears in TV shows and movies, even as many anxious parents offer prayers at Confucian temples when their children are taking the national college entrance exams.

Buddhism and Daoism (DOW-i'zm) have also experienced something of a revival in China, as thousands of temples, destroyed during the heyday of communism, have been repaired and reopened. Christianity too has grown rapidly since the death of Mao in 1976. Here are reminders, in a Chinese context, of the continuing appeal of cultural traditions forged long ago. Those traditions are among the

---

China's Cultural Traditions: In this idealized painting, attributed to the Chinese artist Wang Shugu (1649–1730), the Chinese teacher Confucius presents a baby Buddha to the Daoist master Laozi. The image illustrates the assimilation of a major Indian religion into China as well as the generally peaceful coexistence of these three traditions. (The Art Archive at Art Resource, NY) most enduring legacies that second-wave civilizations have bequeathed to the modern world.

IN THE SEVERAL CENTURIES SURROUNDING 500 B.C.E., something quite remarkable happened all across Eurasia. More or less simultaneously, in China, India, the Middle East, and Greece, there emerged cultural traditions that spread widely, have persisted in various forms into the twenty-first century, and have shaped the values and outlooks of most people who have inhabited the planet over the past 2,500 years.

In China, it was the time of Confucius and Laozi (low-ZUH), whose teachings gave rise to Confucianism and Daoism, respectively. In India, a series of religious writings known as the Upanishads gave expression to the classical philosophy of Hinduism, while a religious reformer, Siddhartha Gautama (sih-DHAR-tuh GOW-tau-mah), set in motion a separate religion known later as Buddhism. In the Middle East, a distinctively monotheistic religious tradition appeared. It was expressed in Zoroastrianism, derived from the teachings of the Persian prophet Zarathustra (zar-uh-THOO-struh), and in Judaism, articulated in Israel by a number of Jewish prophets such as Amos, Jeremiah, and Isaiah. Later, this Jewish religious outlook became the basis for both Christianity and Islam. Finally, in Greece, a rational and humanistic tradition found expression in the writings of Socrates, Plato, Aristotle, and many others.

These cultural traditions differed greatly. Chinese and Greek thinkers focused more on the affairs of this world and credited human rationality with the power to understand that reality. Indian, Persian, and Jewish intellectuals, by contrast, explored the unseen realm of the divine and the relationship of God or the gods to human life. All these traditions sought an alternative to an earlier polytheism, in which the activities of various gods and spirits explained what happened in this world. These gods and spirits had generally been seen as similar to human beings, though much more powerful. Through ritual and sacrifice, men and women might placate the gods or persuade them to do human bidding. In contrast, the new cultural traditions of the second-wave era sought to define a single source of order and meaning in the universe, some moral or religious realm, sharply different from and higher than the sphere of human life. The task of humankind, according to these new ways of thinking, was personal moral or spiritual transformation—often expressed as the development of compassion—by aligning with that higher order.[2] These enormously rich and varied traditions have collectively posed the great questions of human life and society that have haunted and inspired much of humankind ever since. They also defined and legitimated the hierarchies of class and gender that distinguished the various second-wave civilizations from one another.

Why did these traditions all emerge at roughly the same time? Here we encounter an enduring issue of historical analysis: What is the relationship between ideas and the circumstances in which they arise? Are ideas generated by particular political, social, and economic conditions? Or are they the product of creative human imagination independent of the material environment? Or do they derive from some combination of the two? In the case of these cultural traditions, many historians have noted

A Map of Time

800–400 B.C.E.	Upanishads composed
8th century B.C.E.	Hebrew prophets (Amos, Hosea, Micah, Isaiah)
ca. 7th–6th centuries B.C.E.	Life of Zarathustra
600–300 B.C.E.	Emergence of Greek rationalism
6th century B.C.E.	Life of Buddha, Confucius, Laozi
586–539 B.C.E.	Jewish exile in Bablyon
558–330 B.C.E.	Achaemenid dynasty in Persia; state support for Zoroastrianism
469–399 B.C.E.	Life of Socrates
403–221 B.C.E.	Age of warring states in China
221–206 B.C.E.	Qin dynasty in China
Early 1st century C.E.	Life of Jesus
10–65 C.E.	Life of Paul
4th century C.E.	Christianity becomes state religion of Roman Empire, Armenia, Axum

the tumultuous social changes that accompanied their emergence. An iron-age technology, available since roughly 1000 B.C.E., made possible more productive economies and more deadly warfare. Growing cities, increased trade, the prominence of merchant classes, the emergence of new states and empires, new contacts among civilizations—all of these disruptions, occurring in already-literate societies, led thinkers to question older outlooks and to come up with new solutions to fundamental questions: What is the purpose of life? How should human society be ordered? What is the relationship between human life in this world and the moral or spiritual realms that lie beyond? But precisely why various societies developed their own distinctive answers to these questions remains elusive—a tribute, perhaps, to the unpredictable genius of human imagination.

SEEKING THE MAIN POINT

Fundamentally, religions are basically alike. Does the material of this chapter support or challenge this idea?

China and the Search for Order

As one of the First Civilizations, China had a tradition of state building that historians have traced back to around 2000 B.C.E. or before. When the Zhou dynasty took power in 1122 B.C.E., the notion of the Mandate of Heaven had taken root, as had the idea that the normal and appropriate condition of China was one of political unity. By the eighth century B.C.E., the authority of the Zhou dynasty and its royal court

Snapshot   **Thinkers and Philosophies of the Second-Wave Era**

Person	Date	Location	Religion/Philosophy	Key Ideas
Zoroaster	7th century B.C.E. (?)	Persia (present-day Iran)	Zoroastrianism	Single High God; cosmic conflict of good and evil
Hebrew prophets (Isaiah, Amos, Jeremiah)	9th–6th centuries B.C.E.	Eastern Mediterranean/ Palestine/Israel	Judaism	Transcendent High God; covenant with chosen people; social justice
Anonymous writers of Upanishads	800–400 B.C.E.	India	Brahmanism/ Hinduism	Brahma (the single impersonal divine reality); karma; rebirth; goal of liberation (moksha)
Confucius	6th century B.C.E.	China	Confucianism	Social harmony through moral example; secular outlook; importance of education; family as model of the state
Mahavira	6th century B.C.E.	India	Jainism	All creatures have souls; purification through nonviolence; opposed to caste
Siddhartha Gautama	6th century B.C.E.	India	Buddhism	Suffering caused by desire/ attachment; end of suffering through modest and moral living and meditation practice
Laozi, Zhuangzi	6th–3rd centuries B.C.E.	China	Daoism	Withdrawal from the world into contemplation of nature; simple living; end of striving
Socrates, Plato, Aristotle	5th–4th centuries B.C.E.	Greece	Greek rationalism	Style of persistent questioning; secular explanation of nature and human life
Jesus	early 1st century C.E.	Palestine/Israel	Christianity	Supreme importance of love based on intimate relationship with God; at odds with established authorities
Saint Paul	1st century C.E.	Palestine/Israel/ eastern Roman Empire	Christianity	Christianity as a religion for all; salvation through faith in Jesus Christ

had substantially weakened, and by 500 B.C.E. any unity that China had earlier enjoyed was long gone. What followed was a period (403–221 B.C.E.) of chaos, growing violence, and disharmony that became known as the "age of warring states" (see pp. 133–36). During these dreadful centuries of disorder and turmoil, a number of Chinese thinkers began to consider how order might be restored, how the apparent tranquility of an earlier time could be realized again. From their reflections emerged classical cultural traditions of Chinese civilization.

The Legalist Answer

One answer to the problem of disorder — though not the first to emerge — was a hardheaded and practical philosophy known as Legalism. To Legalist thinkers, the solution to China's problems lay in rules or laws, clearly spelled out and strictly enforced through a system of rewards and punishments. "If rewards are high," wrote Han Fei, one of the most prominent Legalist philosophers, "then what the ruler wants will be quickly effected; if punishments are heavy, what he does not want will be swiftly prevented."[3] (See Document 3.3, pp. 150–51, for an excerpt from the writing of Han Fei.) Legalists generally entertained a rather pessimistic view of human nature. Most people were stupid and shortsighted. Only the state and its rulers could act in their long-term interests. Doing so meant promoting farmers and soldiers, the only two groups in society who performed essential functions, while suppressing merchants, aristocrats, scholars, and other classes regarded as useless.

Legalist thinking provided inspiration and methods for the harsh reunification of China under Shihuangdi and the Qin dynasty (221–206 B.C.E.), but the brutality of that short dynasty thoroughly discredited Legalism (see pp. 133–36). Although its techniques and practices played a role in subsequent Chinese statecraft, few philosophers or rulers ever again openly advocated its ideas as the sole guide for Chinese political life. The Han and all subsequent dynasties drew instead on the teachings of China's greatest sage — Confucius.

The Confucian Answer

Born to an aristocratic family in the state of Lu in northern China, Confucius (551–479 B.C.E.) was both learned and ambitious. Believing that he had found the key to solving China's problem of disorder, he spent much of his adult life seeking a political position from which he might put his ideas into action. But no such opportunity came his way. Perhaps it was just as well, for it was as a thinker and a teacher that Confucius left a profound imprint on Chinese history and culture and also on other East Asian societies, such as Korea's and Japan's. After his death, his students collected his teachings in a short book called the *Analects*, and later scholars elaborated and commented endlessly on his ideas, creating a body of thought known as Confucianism (see Document 4.1, pp. 198–200).

■ **Comparison**
What different answers to the problem of disorder arose in classical China?

■ **Description**
Why has Confucianism been defined as a "humanistic philosophy" rather than a supernatural religion?

The Confucian answer to the problem of China's disorder was very different from that of the Legalists. Not laws and punishments, but the moral example of superiors was the Confucian key to a restored social harmony. For Confucius, human society consisted primarily of unequal relationships: the father was superior to the son; the husband to the wife; the older brother to the younger brother; and, of course, the ruler to the subject. If the superior party in each of these relationships behaved with sincerity, benevolence, and genuine concern for others, then the inferior party would be motivated to respond with deference and obedience. Harmony then would prevail. As Confucius put it, "The relation between superiors and inferiors is like that between the wind and the grass. The grass must bend when the wind blows across it." Thus, in both family life and in political life, the cultivation of *ren*—translated as human-heartedness, benevolence, goodness, nobility of heart—was the essential ingredient of a tranquil society.

But how were these humane virtues to be nurtured? Believing that people have a capacity for improvement, Confucius emphasized education as the key to moral betterment. He prescribed a broad liberal arts education emphasizing language, literature, history, philosophy, and ethics, all applied to the practical problems of government. Ritual and ceremonies were also important, for they conveyed the rules of appropriate behavior in the many and varying circumstances of life. For the "superior person," or "gentleman" in Confucian terms, this process of improvement involved serious personal reflection and a willingness to strive continuously to perfect his moral character.

Such ideas left a deep mark on Chinese culture. The discrediting of Legalism during the Qin dynasty opened the door to the adoption of Confucianism as the official ideology of the Chinese state, to such an extent that Confucianism became almost synonymous with Chinese culture. As China's bureaucracy took shape during the Han dynasty and after, Confucianism became the central element of the educational system, which prepared students for the examinations required to gain official positions. In those examinations, candidates were required to apply the principles of Confucianism to specific situations that they might encounter in office. Thus generation after generation of China's male elite was steeped in the ideas and values of Confucianism.

Family life had long been central to Chinese popular culture, expressed in the

Filial Piety
This Song dynasty painting served as an illustration of an ancient Confucian text called the "Classic of Filial Piety," originally composed sometime around the fourth century B.C.E. and subsequently reissued many times. Here, a son kneels submissively in front of his parents. The long-enduring social order that Confucius advocated began at home with unquestioning obedience and the utmost respect for parents and other senior members of the family. (National Palace Museum, Taipei, Taiwan/ The Art Archive at Art Resource, NY)

practice of ancestor veneration, including visiting the graves of the deceased, presenting them with offerings, and erecting commemorative tablets and shrines in their
honor. In Confucian thinking, the family became a model for political life, a kind of
miniature state. Filial piety, the honoring of one's ancestors and parents, was both an
end in itself and a training ground for the reverence due to the emperor and state
officials.

Confucian views of the family were rigidly patriarchal and set the tone for defining the lives of women and men alike. Those views were linked to a hierarchical
understanding of the cosmos in which an inferior and receptive Earth was in balance with the superior and creative principle of Heaven. But these were gendered
concepts with Heaven associated with things male and Earth with those female. Thus
the subordinate and deferential position of women in relation to men was rooted in
the structure of the cosmos itself. What this meant for women was spelled out by a
somewhat later woman writer, Ban Zhao (bahn jow) (45–116 C.E.) in a famous work
called *Lessons for Women*.

> Let a woman modestly yield to others.... Always let her seem to tremble and to
> fear.... Then she may be said to humble herself before others.... To guard care-
> fully her chastity ... to choose her words with care ..., to wash and scrub filth
> away ..., with whole-hearted devotion to sew and to weave, to love not gossip
> and silly laughter, in cleanliness and order to prepare the wine and food for serv-
> ing guests: [these] may be called the characteristics of womanly work.[4]

Ban Zhao called for greater attention to education for young girls, not because they
were equal to boys, but so that a young woman might be better prepared to serve
her husband. Education for boys, on the other hand, enabled them to more effectively control their wives. (See Document 5.1, pp. 244–46, for a longer selection from
Ban Zhao.)

Corresponding Confucian virtues for ideal men were contained in the paired concepts of *wen* and *wu*, both limited largely to males. The superior principle of *wen* referred to the refined qualities of rationality, scholarship, and literary and artistic abilities, while *wu* focused attention on physical and martial achievements. Thus men alone,
and superior men at that, were eligible for the civil service exams that led to political office and high prestige, while military men and merchants occupied a distinctly
lower position in male social hierarchy.[5]

Beyond defining gender expectations, Confucianism also placed great importance on history, for the ideal good society lay in the past. Confucian ideas were
reformist, perhaps even revolutionary, but they were consistently presented as an effort to restore a past golden age. Those ideas also injected a certain democratic element into Chinese elite culture, for the great sage had emphasized that "superior men"
and potential government officials were those of outstanding moral character and
intellectual achievement, not simply those of aristocratic background. Usually only
young men from wealthy families could afford the education necessary for passing
examinations, but on occasion villagers could find the resources to sponsor one of their

Chinese Landscape Paintings
Focused largely on mountains and water, Chinese landscape paintings were much influenced by the Daoist search for harmony with nature. Thus human figures and buildings were usually eclipsed by towering peaks, waterfalls, clouds, and trees. This seventeenth-century painting entitled *Temple on a Mountain Ledge* shows a Buddhist monastery in such a setting, while the poem in the upper right refers to the artist's earlier wanderings, a metaphor for the Buddhist quest for enlightenment. (Mr. and Mrs. John D. Rockefeller 3rd Collection of Asian Art/Asia Society 179.124)

bright sons, potentially propelling him into the stratosphere of the Chinese elite while bringing honor and benefit to themselves.

Confucian values clearly justified the many inequalities of Chinese society, but they also established certain expectations for the superior parties in China's social hierarchy. Thus emperors should keep taxes low, administer justice, and provide for the material needs of the people. Those who failed to govern by the moral norms of Confucian values forfeited the Mandate of Heaven and invited upheaval and their replacement by another dynasty. Likewise husbands should deal kindly with their wives and children, lest they invite conflict and disharmony in the family.

Finally, Confucianism marked Chinese elite culture by its secular, or nonreligious, character. Confucius did not deny the reality of gods and spirits. In fact, he advised people to participate in family and state rituals "as if the spirits were present," and he believed that the universe had a moral character with which human beings should align themselves. But the thrust of Confucian teaching was distinctly this-worldly and practical, concerned with human relationships, effective government, and social harmony. Asked on one occasion about his view of death and the spirits, Confucius replied that because we do not fully understand this life, we cannot possibly know anything about the life beyond. Members of the Chinese elite generally acknowledged that magic, the gods, and spirits were perhaps necessary for the lower orders of society, but educated people, they argued, would find them of little help in striving for moral improvement and in establishing a harmonious society.

The Daoist Answer

No civilization has ever painted its cultural outlook in a single color. As Confucian thinking became generally known in China, a quite different school of thought also took shape. Known as Daoism, it was associated with the legendary figure Laozi, who, according to tradition, was a sixth-century B.C.E. archivist. He is said to have penned a short poetic volume, the *Daodejing* (DOW-DAY-JIHNG) (*The Way and Its Power*), before vanishing in the wilderness to the west of China on his water buffalo. Daoist ideas were later expressed in a more explicit fashion by the philosopher Zhuangzi (369–286 B.C.E.).

In many ways, Daoist thinking ran counter to that of Confucius, who had emphasized the importance of education and earnest striving for moral improvement and good government. The Daoists ridiculed such efforts as artificial and useless, generally making things worse. In the face of China's disorder and chaos, they urged withdrawal into the world of nature and encouraged behavior that was spontaneous, individualistic, and natural. Whereas Confucius focused on the world of human relationships, the Daoists turned the spotlight on the immense realm of nature and its mysterious unfolding patterns. "Confucius roams within society," the Chinese have often said. "Laozi wanders beyond."

■ Comparison
How did the Daoist outlook differ from that of Confucianism?

The central concept of Daoist thinking is *dao*, an elusive notion that refers to the way of nature, the underlying and unchanging principle that governs all natural phenomena. According to the *Daodejing*, the dao "moves around and around, but does not on this account suffer. All life comes from it. It wraps everything with its love as in a garment, and yet it claims no honor, for it does not demand to be lord. I do not know its name and so I call it the Dao, the Way, and I rejoice in its power."[6]

Applied to human life, Daoism invited people to withdraw from the world of political and social activism, to disengage from the public life so important to Confucius, and to align themselves with the way of nature. It meant simplicity in living, small self-sufficient communities, limited government, and the abandonment of education and active efforts at self-improvement. "Give up learning," declares the *Daodejing*, "and put an end to your troubles." The flavor of the Daoist approach to life is evident in this passage from the *Daodejing*:

> A small country has few people.
> Though there are machines that can work ten to a hundred times faster
>   than man, they are not needed. . . .
> Though they have boats and carriages, no one uses them. . . .
> Men return to the knotting of ropes in place of writing.
> Their food is plain and good, their clothes fine but simple. . . .
> They are happy in their ways.
> Though they live within sight of their neighbors,
> And crowing cocks and barking dogs are heard across the way,
> Yet they leave each other in peace while they grow old and die.[7]

Like Confucianism, the Daoist perspective viewed family life as central to Chinese society, though the element of male/female hierarchy was downplayed in favor of complementarity and balance between the sexes.

Despite its various differences with the ideas of Confucianism, the Daoist perspective was widely regarded by elite Chinese as complementing rather than contradicting Confucian values (see the chapter-opening image on p. 164). Such an outlook was facilitated by the ancient Chinese concept of *yin* and *yang*, which expressed a belief in the unity of opposites (see figure).

The Yin Yang Symbol

Thus a scholar-official might pursue the Confucian project of "government by goodness" during the day, but upon returning home in the evening or following his retirement, he might well behave in a more Daoist fashion — pursuing the simple life, reading Daoist philosophy, practicing Daoist meditation and breathing exercises, or enjoying landscape paintings in which tiny human figures are dwarfed by the vast peaks and valleys of the natural world (see image on p. 172). Daoism also shaped the culture of ordinary people as it entered popular religion. This kind of Daoism sought to tap the power of the dao for practical uses and came to include magic, fortune telling, and the search for immortality. It also on occasion provided an ideology for peasant uprisings, such as the Yellow Turban Rebellion (184–204 C.E.), which imagined a utopian society without the oppression of governments and landlords (see pp. 223–24). In its many and varied forms, Daoism, like Confucianism, became an enduring element of the Chinese cultural tradition.

Cultural Traditions of Classical India

The cultural development of Indian civilization was far different from that of China. Whereas Confucianism paid little attention to the gods, spirits, and speculation about religious matters, Indian elite culture embraced the divine and all things spiritual with enthusiasm and generated elaborate philosophical visions about the nature of ultimate reality. But the Indian religious tradition — later called Hinduism — differed from other world religions as well. Unlike Buddhism, Christianity, or Islam, Hinduism had no historical founder; rather, it grew up over many centuries along with Indian civilization. Although it later spread into Southeast Asia, Hinduism was not a missionary religion seeking converts, but was, like Judaism, associated with a particular people and territory.

In fact, "Hinduism" was never a single tradition at all, and the term itself derived from outsiders — Greeks, Muslims, and later the British — who sought to reduce the infinite variety of Indian cultural patterns into a recognizable system. From the inside, however, Hinduism dissolved into a vast diversity of gods, spirits, beliefs, practices, rituals, and philosophies. This endlessly variegated Hinduism served to incorporate into Indian civilization the many diverse peoples who migrated into or invaded the South Asian peninsula over many centuries and several millennia. Its ability to accommodate this diversity gave India's cultural development a distinctive quality.

South Asian Religion: From Ritual Sacrifice to Philosophical Speculation

■ **Change**
In what ways did the religious traditions of South Asia change over the centuries?

Despite the fragmentation and variety of Indian cultural and religious patterns, an evolving set of widely recognized sacred texts provided some commonality. The earliest of these texts, known as the Vedas (VAY-duhs), were collections of poems, hymns, prayers, and rituals. Compiled by priests called Brahmins, the Vedas were for centuries transmitted orally and were reduced to writing in Sanskrit around 600 B.C.E.

In the Vedas, historians have caught fleeting glimpses of Indian civilization in its formative centuries (1500–600 B.C.E.). Those sacred writings tell of small competing chiefdoms or kingdoms, of sacred sounds and fires, of numerous gods, rising and falling in importance over the centuries. They also suggest a clearly patriarchal society, but one that afforded upper-class women somewhat greater opportunities than they later enjoyed. Vedic women participated in religious sacrifices, sometimes engaged in scholarship and religious debate, were allowed to wear the sacred thread that symbolized ritual purity in the higher castes, and could on occasion marry a man of their own choosing. The Vedas described as well the elaborate ritual sacrifices that Brahmin priests required. Performing these sacrifices and rituals with great precision enabled the Brahmins to acquire enormous power and wealth, sometimes exceeding even that of kings and warriors. But Brahmins also generated growing criticism, as ritual became mechanical and formal and as Brahmins required heavy fees to perform them.

From this dissatisfaction arose another body of sacred texts, the Upanishads (oo-PAHN-ee-shahds). Composed by largely anonymous thinkers between 800 and 400 B.C.E., these were mystical and highly philosophical works that sought to probe the inner meaning of the sacrifices prescribed in the Vedas. In the Upanishads, external ritual gave way to introspective thinking, which expressed in many and varied formulations the central concepts of philosophical Hinduism that have persisted into modern times. Chief among them was the idea of Brahman, the World Soul, the final and ultimate reality. Beyond the multiplicity of material objects and individual persons and beyond even the various gods themselves lay this primal unitary energy or divine reality infusing all things, similar in some ways to the Chinese notion of the dao. This alone was real; the immense diversity of existence that human beings perceived with their senses was but an illusion.

The fundamental assertion of philosophical Hinduism was that the individual human soul, or *atman*, was in fact a part of Brahman. Beyond the quest for pleasure, wealth, power, and social position, all of which were perfectly normal and quite legitimate, lay the effort to achieve the final goal of humankind—union with Brahman, an end to our illusory perception of a separate existence. This was *moksha* (MOHK-shuh), or liberation, compared sometimes to a bubble in a glass of water breaking through the surface and becoming one with the surrounding atmosphere.

Achieving this exalted state was held to involve many lifetimes, as the notion of *samsara*, or rebirth/reincarnation, became a central feature of Hindu thinking. Human souls migrated from body to body over many lifetimes, depending on one's actions. This was the law of *karma*. Pure actions, appropriate to one's station in life, resulted in rebirth in a higher social position or caste. Thus the caste system of distinct and ranked groups, each with its own duties, became a register of spiritual progress. Birth in a higher caste was evidence of "good karma," based on actions in a previous life, and offered a better chance to achieve moksha, which brought with it an end to the painful cycle of rebirth.

If Hinduism underpinned caste, it also legitimated and expressed India's gender system. As South Asian civilization crystalized during the second-wave era, its

Hindu Ascetics
Hinduism called for men in the final stage of life to leave ordinary ways of living and withdraw into the forests to seek spiritual liberation, or moksha. Here, in an illustration from an early thirteenth-century Indian manuscript, a holy man explores a text with three disciples in a secluded rural setting. (Réunion des Musées Nationaux/Art Resource, NY)

patriarchal features tightened. Women were increasingly seen as "unclean below the navel," forbidden to learn the Vedas, and excluded from public religious rituals. The Laws of Manu, composed probably in the early C.E. centuries, described a divinely ordained social order and articulated a gender system whose ideals endured for a millennium or more. It taught that all embryos were basically male and that only weak semen generated female babies. It advocated child marriage for girls to men far older than themselves. "A virtuous wife," the Laws proclaimed, "should constantly serve her husband like a god" and should never remarry after his death. In a famous prescription similar to that of Chinese and other patriarchal societies, the Laws declared: "In childhood a female must be subject to her father; in youth to her husband; when her lord is dead to her sons; a woman must never be independent."[8]

And yet some aspects of Hinduism served to empower women. Sexual pleasure was considered a legitimate goal for both men and women, and its techniques were detailed in the *Kamasutra*. Many Hindu deities were female, some life-giving and faithful, others like Kali fiercely destructive. Women were particularly prominent in the growing devotional cults dedicated to particular deities, where neither gender nor caste were obstacles to spiritual fulfillment.

A further feature of Hindu religious thought lay in its provision of different paths to the ultimate goal of liberation or moksha. Various ways to this final release, appropriate to people of different temperaments, were spelled out in Hindu teachings. Some might achieve moksha through knowledge or study; others by means of detached action in the world, doing one's work without regard to consequences; still others through passionate devotion to some deity or through extended meditation practice. Such ideas—carried by Brahmin priests and even more by wandering ascetics, who had withdrawn from ordinary life to pursue their spiritual development—became widely known throughout India. (See Document 4.2, pp. 200–02.)

The Buddhist Challenge

About the same time as philosophical Hinduism was emerging, another movement took shape that soon became a distinct and separate religious tradition—Buddhism. Unlike Hinduism, this new faith had a historical founder, Siddhartha Gautama

(ca. 566–ca. 486 B.C.E.), a prince from a small north Indian state. According to Buddhist tradition, the prince had enjoyed a sheltered and delightful youth but was shocked
to his core upon encountering old age, sickness, and death. Leaving family and fortune behind, he then set out on a six-year spiritual quest, finally achieving insight,
or "enlightenment," at the age of thirty-five. For the rest of his life, he taught what
he had learned and gathered a small but growing community whose members came
to see him as the Buddha, the Enlightened One, a human being who had awakened.

"I teach but one thing," the Buddha said, "suffering and the end of suffering."
To the Buddha, suffering or sorrow — experiencing life as imperfect, impermanent,
and unsatisfactory — was the central and universal feature of human life. Its cause was
desire or craving for individual fulfillment, attachment to that which inevitably changes,
particularly to the notion of a core self or ego that is uniquely and solidly "me." The

■ **Comparison**

In what ways did Bud-
dhism reflect Hindu traditions, and in what ways
did it challenge them?

cure for this "dis-ease" lay in living a modest and
moral life combined with meditation practice. Those
who followed the Buddhist path most fully could expect to achieve enlightenment, or *nirvana*, a virtually
indescribable state in which individual identity would
be "extinguished" along with all greed, hatred, and
delusion. With the pain of unnecessary suffering finally ended, the enlightened person would experience
an overwhelming serenity, even in the midst of difficulty, as well as an immense loving-kindness, or compassion, for all beings. It was a simple message, elaborated endlessly and in various forms by those who
followed him.

Much of the Buddha's teaching reflected the
Hindu traditions from which it sprang. The idea that
ordinary life is an illusion, the concepts of karma and
rebirth, the goal of overcoming the incessant demands
of the ego, the practice of meditation, the hope for
final release from the cycle of rebirth — all of these
Hindu elements found their way into Buddhist teaching. In this respect, Buddhism was a simplified and
more accessible version of Hinduism.

Other elements of Buddhist teaching, however,
sharply challenged prevailing Hindu thinking. Rejecting the religious authority of the Brahmins, the
Buddha ridiculed their rituals and sacrifices as irrelevant to the hard work of dealing with one's suffering.
Nor was he much interested in abstract speculation
about the creation of the world or the existence of
God, for such questions, he declared, "are not useful in
the quest for holiness; they do not lead to peace and

Classic Indian Buddha

This sixth-century C.E. image of the Buddha from eastern India shows
a classical representation of the great teacher. The Buddha's right hand
with palm facing the viewer indicates reassurance, or "have no fear."
The partially webbed fingers are among the *lakshanas*, or signs of a
Buddha image, that denote the Buddha's unique status. So too is the
knot on the top of his head, symbolizing enlightenment. The elongated
ear lobes reminds the viewer that earlier in his life the Buddha had
worn heavy and luxurious earrings, while his partially closed and down-
cast eyes and his bare feet indicate detachment from the world. (Image
copyright © The Metropolitan Museum of Art/Art Resource, NY)

to the direct knowledge of *nirvana*." Individuals had to take responsibility for their own spiritual development with no help from human authorities or supernatural beings. It was a religion of intense self-effort, based on personal experience. The Buddha also challenged the inequalities of a Hindu-based caste system, arguing that neither caste position nor gender was a barrier to enlightenment. The possibility of "awakening" was available to all.

But when it came to establishing a formal organization of the Buddha's most devoted followers, the prevailing patriarchy of Indian society made itself felt. Buddhist texts recount that the Buddha's foster mother, Prajapati Gotami, sought to enter the newly created order of monks but was repeatedly refused admission by the Buddha himself. Only after the intervention of the Buddha's attendant, Ananda, did he relent and allow women to join a separate order of nuns. Even then, these nuns were subjected to a series of rules that clearly subordinated them to men. Male monks, for example, could officially admonish the nuns, but the reverse was forbidden. Here is a reflection of a particular strain of Buddhist thinking that viewed women as a distracting obstacle to male enlightenment.

Nonetheless, thousands of women flocked to join the Buddhist order of nuns, where they found a degree of freedom and independence unavailable elsewhere in Indian society. Buddhist nuns delighted in the relative freedom of their order, where they largely ran their own affairs, were forbidden to do household chores, and devoted themselves wholly to the search for "awakening," which many apparently achieved. A nun named Mutta declared: "I am free from the three crooked things: mortar, pestle, and my crooked husband. I am free from birth and death and all that dragged me back."[9] (See Document 5.2, pp. 246–48, for examples of early poetry by Indian Buddhist women.)

■ Comparison
What is the difference between the Theravada and Mahayana expressions of Buddhism?

Gradually, Buddhist teachings found an audience in India. Buddhism's egalitarian message appealed especially to lower-caste groups and to women. The availability of its teaching in the local language of Pali, rather than the classical Sanskrit, made it accessible. Establishing monasteries and stupas containing relics of the Buddha on the site of neighborhood shrines to earth spirits or near a sacred tree linked the new religion to local traditions. The most dedicated followers joined monasteries, devoting their lives to religious practice and spreading the message among nearby people. State support during the reign of Ashoka (268–232 B.C.E.) (see p. 142) likewise helped the new religion gain a foothold in India as a distinct tradition separate from Hinduism.

As Buddhism spread, both within and beyond India, differences in understanding soon emerged, particularly as to how nirvana could be achieved or, in a common Buddhist metaphor, how to cross the river to the far shore of enlightenment. The Buddha had taught a rather austere doctrine of intense self-effort, undertaken most actively by monks and nuns who withdrew from society to devote themselves fully to the quest. This early version of the new religion, known as Theravada (Teaching of the Elders), portrayed the Buddha as an immensely wise teacher and model, but certainly not divine. It was more psychological than religious, a set of practices rather than a set of beliefs. The gods, though never completely denied, played little role in assisting believers in their search for enlightenment. In short, individuals were on their own in crossing the river. Clearly this was not for everyone.

By the early centuries of the Common Era, a modified form of Buddhism called Mahayana (mah-huh-YAH-nah) (Great Vehicle) had taken root in parts of India, proclaiming that help was available for the strenuous voyage. Buddhist thinkers developed the idea of *bodhisattvas* (BOH-dih-SAT-vuhs), spiritually developed people who postponed their own entry into nirvana to assist those who were still suffering. The Buddha himself became something of a god, and both earlier and future Buddhas were available to offer help. Elaborate descriptions of these supernatural beings, together with various levels of heavens and hells, transformed Buddhism into a popular religion of salvation. Furthermore, religious merit, leading to salvation, might now be earned by acts of piety and devotion, such as contributing to the support of a monastery, and that merit might be transferred to others. This was the Great Vehicle, allowing far more people to make the voyage across the river. (See the Visual Sources: Representations of the Buddha, pp. 208–15, for the evolution of Buddhism reflected in images.)

Hinduism as a Religion of Duty and Devotion

Strangely enough, Buddhism as a distinct religious practice ultimately died out in the land of its birth as it was reincorporated into a broader Hindu tradition, but it spread widely and flourished, particularly in its Mahayana form, in other parts of Asia. Buddhism declined in India perhaps in part because the mounting wealth of monasteries and the economic interests of their leading figures separated them from ordinary people. Competition from Islam after 1000 C.E. also played a role. But the most important reason for the waning of Buddhism in India was the growth during the first millennium C.E. of a new kind of popular Hinduism, which the masses found more accessible than the elaborate sacrifices of the Brahmins or the philosophical speculations of intellectuals. Expressed in the widely known epic poems known as the *Mahabharata* (mah-hah-BAH-rah-tah) and the *Ramayana*, this revived Hinduism indicated more clearly that action in the world and the detached performance of caste duties might also provide a path to liberation. It was perhaps a response to the challenge of Buddhism.

In the much-beloved Hindu text known as the Bhagavad Gita (BUH-guh-vahd GEE-tuh) (see Document 4.2, pp. 200–02), the troubled warrior-hero Arjuna is in anguish over the necessity of killing his kinsmen as a decisive battle approaches. But he is assured by his charioteer Lord Krishna, an incarnation of the god Vishnu, that performing his duty as a warrior, and doing so selflessly without regard to consequences, is an act of devotion that would lead to "release from the shackles of repeated rebirth." This was not an invitation to militarism, but rather an affirmation that ordinary people, not just Brahmins, could also find spiritual fulfillment by selflessly performing the ordinary duties of their lives: "The man who, casting off all

■ **Change**
What new emphases characterized Hinduism as it responded to the challenge of Buddhism?

threeb

nine10

nine10

eightten

nineten

nineten

desires, lives free from attachments, who is free from egoism, and from the feeling that this or that is mine, obtains tranquility." Withdrawal and asceticism were not the only ways to moksha.

Also becoming increasingly prominent was yet another religious path—the way of devotion to one or another of India's many gods and goddesses. Beginning in south India and moving northward, this *bhakti* (BAHK-tee) (worship) movement involved the intense adoration of and identification with a particular deity through songs, prayers, and rituals. By far the most popular deities were Vishnu, the protector and preserver of creation and associated with mercy and goodness, and Shiva, representing the divine in its destructive aspect, but many others also had their followers. This form of Hindu expression sometimes pushed against the rigid caste and gender hierarchies of Indian society by inviting all to an adoration of the Divine. After all, Krishna in the Bhagavad Gita had declared that "those who take shelter in Me, though they be of lower birth—women, vaishyas [merchants] and shudras [workers]—can attain the supreme destination" (see pp. 200–02).

The proliferation of gods and goddesses, and of their bhakti cults, occasioned very little friction or serious religious conflict. "Hinduism," writes a leading scholar, "is essentially tolerant, and would rather assimilate than rigidly exclude."[10] This capacity for assimilation extended to an already-declining Buddhism, which for many people had become yet another cult worshipping yet another god. The Buddha in fact was incorporated into the Hindu pantheon as the ninth incarnation of Vishnu. By 1000 C.E., Buddhism had largely disappeared as a separate religious tradition within India. Thus a constantly evolving and enormously varied South Asian religious tradition had been substantially transformed. An early emphasis on ritual sacrifice gave way to that of philosophical speculation, devotional worship, and detached action in the world. In the process, that tradition had generated Buddhism, which became the first of the great universal religions of world history, and then had absorbed that new religion back into the fold of an emerging popular Hinduism.

SUMMING UP SO FAR

How did the evolution of cultural traditions in India and China differ during the era of second-wave civilizations?

Toward Monotheism: The Search for God in the Middle East

Paralleling the evolution of Chinese and Indian cultural traditions was the movement toward a distinctive monotheistic religious tradition in the Middle East, which found expression in Persian Zoroastrianism and in Judaism. Neither of these religions themselves spread very widely, but the monotheism that they nurtured became the basis for both Christianity and Islam, which have shaped so much of world history over the past 2,000 years. Amid the proliferation of gods and spirits that had long characterized religious life throughout the ancient world, monotheism—the idea of a single supreme deity, the sole source of all life and being—was a radical cultural innovation. That conception created the possibility of a universal religion, open to all of humankind, but it could also mean an exclusive and intolerant faith.

Zoroastrianism

During the glory years of the powerful Persian Empire, a new religion arose to challenge the polytheism of earlier times. Tradition dates its Persian prophet, Zarathustra
(Zoroaster to the Greeks), to the sixth or seventh century B.C.E., although some
scholars place him hundreds of years earlier. Whenever he actually lived, his ideas
took hold in Persia and received a degree of state support during the Achaemenid
dynasty (558–330 B.C.E.). Appalled by the endemic violence of recurring cattle raids,
Zarathustra recast the traditional Persian polytheism into a vision of a single unique
god, Ahura Mazda, who ruled the world and was the source of all truth, light, and
goodness. This benevolent deity was engaged in a cosmic struggle with the forces of
evil, embodied in an equivalent supernatural figure, Angra Mainyu. Ultimately this
struggle would be decided in favor of Ahura Mazda, aided by the arrival of a final
savior who would restore the world to its earlier purity and peace. At a day of judgment, those who had aligned with Ahura Mazda would be granted new resurrected
bodies and rewarded with eternal life in Paradise. Those who had sided with evil and
the "Lie" were condemned to everlasting punishment. Zoroastrian (zohr-oh-ASS-
tree-ahn) teaching thus placed great emphasis on the free will of humankind and the
necessity for each individual to choose between good and evil.

The Zoroastrian faith achieved widespread support within the Persian heartland,
although it also found adherents in other parts of the empire, such as Egypt, Mesopotamia, and Anatolia. But it never became an active missionary religion and did not
spread widely beyond the region. Alexander the Great's invasion of the Persian Empire
and the subsequent Greek-ruled Seleucid dynasty (330–155 B.C.E.)
were disastrous for Zoroastrianism, as temples were plundered,
priests slaughtered, and sacred writings burned. But the new faith
managed to survive this onslaught and flourished again during the
Parthian (247 B.C.E.–224 C.E.) and Sassanid (224–651 C.E.) dynasties.
It was the arrival of Islam and an Arab empire that occasioned the
final decline of Zoroastrianism in Persia, although a few believers
fled to India, where they became known as Parsis ("Persians"). The
Parsis have continued their faith into present times.

Like Buddhism, the Zoroastrian faith vanished from its place of
origin, but unlike Buddhism, it did not spread beyond Persia in a
recognizable form. Some elements of the Zoroastrian belief system,
however, did become incorporated into other religious traditions.
The presence of many Jews in the Persian Empire meant that they
surely became aware of Zoroastrian ideas. Many of those ideas —
including the conflict of God and an evil counterpart (Satan); the
notion of a last judgment and resurrected bodies; and a belief in the
final defeat of evil, the arrival of a savior (Messiah), and the remaking
of the world at the end of time — found a place in an evolving Judaism. Some of these teachings, especially the concepts of heaven and

■ **Connection**

What aspects of Zoroas-
trianism and Judaism
subsequently found a
place in Christianity and
Islam?

Zoroastrian Fire Altar
Representing the energy of the Creator God Ahura
Mazda, the fire altar became an important symbol of
Zoroastrianism and was often depicted on Persian
coins in association with images of Persian rulers.
This particular coin dates from the third century C.E.
(©AAAC/Topham/The Image Works)

hell, later became prominent in those enormously influential successors to Judaism—Christianity and Islam.[11] Thus the Persian tradition of Zoroastrianism continued to echo well beyond its disappearance in the land of its birth.

Judaism

■ **Description**

What was distinctive about the Jewish religious tradition?

While Zoroastrianism emerged in the greatest empire of its time, Judaism, the Middle East's other ancient monotheistic tradition, was born among one of the region's smaller and, at the time, less significant peoples—the Hebrews. Their traditions, recorded in the Hebrew scriptures, tell of an early migration from Mesopotamia to Canaan under the leadership of Abraham. Those same traditions report that a portion of these people later fled to Egypt, where they were first enslaved and then miraculously escaped to rejoin their kinfolk in Palestine. There, around 1000 B.C.E., they established a small state, which soon split into two parts—a northern kingdom called Israel and a southern state called Judah.

In a region politically dominated by the large empires of Assyria, Babylon, and Persia, these tiny Hebrew communities lived a precarious existence. Israel was conquered by Assyria in 722 B.C.E., and many of its inhabitants were deported to distant regions, where they assimilated into the local culture. In 586 B.C.E., the kingdom of Judah likewise came under Babylonian control, and its elite class was shipped off to exile. "By the rivers of Babylon," wrote one of their poets, "there we sat down, yea, we wept, when we remembered Zion [Jerusalem]." It was in Babylonian exile that these people, now calling themselves Jews, retained and renewed their cultural identity and later a small number were able to return to their homeland. A large part of that identity lay in their unique religious ideas. It was in creating that religious tradition, rather than in building a powerful empire, that this small people cast a long shadow in world history.

Ancient Israel

From their unique historical memory of exodus from Egypt and exile in Babylon, the Hebrew people evolved over many centuries a distinctive conception of God. Unlike the peoples of Mesopotamia, India, Greece, and elsewhere—all of whom populated the invisible realm with numerous gods and goddesses—Jews found in their God, whom they called Yahweh (YAH-way), a powerful and jealous deity, who demanded their exclusive loyalty. "Thou shalt have no other gods before me"—this was the first of the Ten Commandments. It was a difficult requirement, for as the Hebrews turned from a pastoral life to agriculture, many of them were attracted by the fertility gods of neighboring peoples. Their neighbors' goddesses also were attractive, offering a kind of spiritual support that the primarily masculine Yahweh could not. Foreign deities also entered Hebrew culture through royal treaty obligations with nearby states. Thus the emerging Hebrew conception of the Divine was not quite monotheism, for the repeated demands of the Hebrew prophets to turn away from other gods show that those deities remained real for many Jews. Over time, however, the priesthood that supported the one-god theory triumphed. The Jews came to understand their relationship to Yahweh as a contract or a covenant. In return for their sole devotion and obedience to God's laws, Yahweh would consider the Jews his chosen people, favoring them in battle, causing them to grow in numbers, and bringing them prosperity and blessing.

Unlike the bickering, arbitrary, polytheistic gods of Mesopotamia or ancient Greece, which were associated with the forces of nature and behaved in quite human fashion, Yahweh was increasingly seen as a lofty, transcendent deity of utter holiness and purity, set far above the world of nature, which he had created. But unlike the impersonal conceptions of ultimate reality found in Daoism and Hinduism, Yahweh was encountered as a divine person with whom people could actively communicate. He also acted within the historical process, bringing the Jews out of Egypt or using foreign empires to punish them for their disobedience.

Furthermore, for some, Yahweh was transformed from a god of war, who ordered his people to "utterly destroy" the original inhabitants of the Promised Land, to a god of social justice and compassion for the poor and the marginalized, especially in the passionate pronouncements of Jewish prophets such as Amos and Isaiah. The prophet Isaiah describes Yahweh as rejecting the empty rituals of his chosen but sinful people: "What to me is the multitude of your sacrifices, says the Lord. . . . Wash yourselves, make yourselves clean, . . . cease to do evil, learn to do good; seek justice; correct oppression; defend the fatherless; plead for the widow."[12]

Here was a distinctive conception of the divine—singular, transcendent, personal, ruling over the natural order, engaged in history, and demanding social justice and moral righteousness above sacrifices and rituals. This set of ideas sustained a separate Jewish identity in both ancient and modern times, and it was this understanding of God that provided the foundation on which both Christianity and Islam were built.

The Cultural Tradition of Classical Greece: The Search for a Rational Order

Unlike the Jews, the Persians, or the civilization of India, Greek thinkers of the second-wave era generated no lasting religious tradition of world historical importance. The religion of these city-states brought together the unpredictable, quarreling, and lustful gods of Mount Olympus, secret fertility cults, oracles predicting the future, and the ecstatic worship of Dionysus, the god of wine. The distinctive feature of the classical Greek cultural tradition was the willingness of many Greek intellectuals to abandon this mythological framework, to affirm that the world was a physical reality governed by natural laws, and to assert that human rationality could both understand these laws and work out a system of moral and ethical life as well. In separating science and philosophy from conventional religion, the Greeks developed a way of thinking that bore some similarity to the secularism of Confucian thought in China.

Precisely why Greek thought evolved in this direction is hard to say. Perhaps the diversity and incoherence of Greek religious mythology presented its intellectuals with a challenge to bring some order to their understanding of the world. Greece's

■ **Description**
What are the distinctive features of the Greek intellectual tradition?

geographic position on the margins of the great civilizations of Mesopotamia, Egypt, and Persia certainly provided intellectual stimulation. Furthermore, the growing role of law in the political life of Athens possibly suggested that a similar regularity also underlay the natural order.

The Greek Way of Knowing

The foundations of this Greek rationalism emerged in the three centuries between 600 and 300 B.C.E., coinciding with the flourishing of Greek city-states, especially Athens, and with the growth of its artistic, literary, and theatrical traditions. The enduring significance of Greek thinking lay not so much in the answers it provided to life's great issues, for the Greeks seldom agreed with one another, but rather in its way of asking questions. Its emphasis on argument, logic, and the relentless questioning of received wisdom; its confidence in human reason; its enthusiasm for puzzling out the world without much reference to the gods — these were the defining characteristics of the Greek cultural tradition.

The great exemplar of this approach to knowledge was Socrates (469–399 B.C.E.), an Athenian philosopher who walked about the city engaging others in conversation about the good life. He wrote nothing, and his preferred manner of teaching was not the lecture or exposition of his own ideas but rather a constant questioning of the assumptions and logic of his students' thinking. Concerned always to puncture the pretentious, he challenged conventional ideas about the importance of wealth and power in living well, urging instead the pursuit of wisdom and virtue. He was critical of Athenian democracy and on occasion had positive things to say about Sparta, the great enemy of his own city. Such behavior brought him into conflict with city authorities, who accused him of corrupting the youth of Athens and sentenced him to death. At his trial, he defended himself as the "gadfly" of Athens, stinging its citizens into awareness. To any and all, he declared, "I shall question, and examine and cross-examine him, and if I find that he does not possess virtue, but says he does, I shall rebuke him for scorning the things that are most important and caring more for what is of less worth."[13] (See Document 4.3, pp. 202–04, for a more extensive excerpt from this famous speech.)

The earliest of the classical Greek thinkers, many of them living on the Ionian coast of Anatolia, applied this rational and questioning way of knowing to the world of nature. For example, Thales, drawing on Babylonian astronomy, predicted an eclipse of the sun and argued that the moon simply reflected the sun's light. He also was one of the first Greeks to ask about the fundamental nature of the universe and came up with the idea that water was the basic stuff from which all else derived, for it existed as solid, liquid, and gas. Others argued in favor of air or fire or some combination. Democritus suggested that atoms, tiny "uncuttable" particles, collided in various configurations to form visible matter. Pythagoras believed that beneath the chaos and complexity of the visible world lay a simple, unchanging mathematical order.

The Death of Socrates
Condemned to death by an Athenian jury, Socrates declined to go into exile, voluntarily drank a cup of poison hemlock, and died in 399 B.C.E. in the presence of his friends. The dramatic scene was famously described by Plato and much later was immortalized on canvas by the French painter Jacques-Louis David in 1787. (Image copyright © The Metropolitan Museum of Art/Art Resource, NY)

What these thinkers had in common was a commitment to a rational and nonreligious explanation for the material world.

Such thinking also served to explain the functioning of the human body and its diseases. Hippocrates and his followers came to believe that the body was composed of four fluids, or "humors," which caused various ailments when out of proper balance. He also traced the origins of epilepsy, known to the Greeks as "the sacred disease," to simple heredity: "it appears to me to be nowise more divine nor more sacred than other diseases, but has a natural cause . . . like other afflictions."[14] A similar approach informed Greek thinking about the ways of humankind. Herodotus, who wrote about the Greco-Persian Wars, explained his project as an effort to discover "the reason why they fought one another." This assumption that human reasons lay behind the conflict, not simply the whims of the gods, was what made Herodotus a historian in the modern sense of that word. Ethics and government also figured importantly in Greek thinking. Plato (429–348 B.C.E.) famously sketched out in *The*

Republic a design for a good society. It would be ruled by a class of highly educated "guardians" led by a "philosopher-king." Such people would be able to penetrate the many illusions of the material world and to grasp the "world of forms," in which ideas such as goodness, beauty, and justice lived a real and unchanging existence. Only such people, he argued, were fit to rule.

Aristotle (384–322 B.C.E.), a student of Plato and a teacher of Alexander the Great, represents the most complete expression of the Greek way of knowing, for he wrote or commented on practically everything. With an emphasis on empirical observation, he cataloged the constitutions of 158 Greek city-states, identified hundreds of species of animals, and wrote about logic, physics, astronomy, the weather, and much else besides. Famous for his reflections on ethics, he argued that "virtue" was a product of rational training and cultivated habit and could be learned. As to government, he urged a mixed system, combining the principles of monarchy, aristocracy, and democracy.

The Greek Legacy

The rationalism of the Greek tradition was clearly not the whole of Greek culture. The gods of Mount Olympus continued to be a reality for many people, and the ecstatic songs and dances that celebrated Dionysus, the god of wine, were anything but rational and reflective. The death of Socrates at the hands of an Athenian jury showed that philosophy could be a threat as well as an engaging pastime. Nonetheless, Greek rationalism, together with Greek art, literature, and theater, persisted long after the glory days of Athens were over. Alexander's empire and that of the Romans facilitated the spread of Greek culture within the Mediterranean basin and beyond, and not a few leading Roman figures sent their children to be educated in Athens at the Academy, which Plato had founded. An emerging Christian theology was expressed in terms of Greek philosophical concepts, especially those of Plato. Even after the western Roman Empire collapsed, classical Greek texts were preserved in the eastern half, known as the Byzantine Empire or Byzantium (see pp. 469–76 and Chapter 10).

In the West, however, direct access to Greek texts was far more difficult in the chaotic conditions of post-Roman Europe, and for centuries Greek scholarship was neglected in favor of Christian writers. Much of that legacy was subsequently rediscovered after the twelfth century C.E. as European scholars gained access to classical Greek texts. From that point on, the Greek legacy has been viewed as a central element of an emerging "Western" civilization. It played a role in formulating an updated Christian theology, in fostering Europe's Scientific Revolution, and in providing a point of departure for much of European philosophy.

Long before this European rediscovery, the Greek legacy had also entered the Islamic world. Systematic translations of Greek works of science and philosophy into Arabic, together with Indian and Persian learning, stimulated Muslim thinkers and scientists, especially in the fields of medicine, astronomy, mathematics, geography, and chemistry. It was in fact largely from Arabic translations of Greek writers that Europeans became reacquainted with the legacy of classical Greece, especially during the twelfth and thirteenth centuries. Despite the many centuries that have passed since the flourishing of ancient Greek culture, that tradition has remained, especially in the West, an inspiration for those who celebrate the powers of the human mind to probe the mysteries of the universe and to explore the equally challenging domain of human life.

The Birth of Christianity . . . with Buddhist Comparisons

About 500 years after the time of Confucius, the Buddha, Zarathustra, and Socrates, a young Jewish peasant/carpenter in the remote province of Judaea in the Roman Empire began a brief three-year career of teaching and miracle working before he got in trouble with local authorities and was executed. In one of history's most unlikely stories, the teachings of that obscure man, barely noted in the historical records of the time, became the basis of the world's second great universal religion, after that of Buddhism. This man, Jesus of Nazareth, and the religion of Christianity that grew out of his life and teaching, had a dramatic impact on world history, similar to and often compared with that of India's Siddhartha Gautama, the Buddha.

■ **Comparison**

How would you compare the lives and teachings of Jesus and the Buddha? In what different ways did the two religions evolve after the deaths of their founders?

The Lives of the Founders

The family background of the two teachers could hardly have been more different. Gautama was born to royalty and luxury, whereas Jesus was a rural or small-town worker from a distinctly lower-class family. But both became spiritual seekers, mystics in their respective traditions, who claimed to have personally experienced another and unseen level of reality. Those powerful religious experiences provided the motivation for their life's work and the personal authenticity that attracted their growing band of followers.

Both were "wisdom teachers," challenging the conventional values of their time, urging the renunciation of wealth, and emphasizing the supreme importance of love or compassion as the basis for a moral life. The Buddha had instructed his followers in the practice of *metta*, or loving-kindness: "Just as a mother would protect her only child at the risk of her own life, even so, let [my followers] cultivate a boundless heart towards all beings."[15] In a similar vein during his famous Sermon on the Mount, Jesus told his followers: "You have heard that it was said 'Love your neighbor and hate your enemy,' but I tell you 'Love your enemies and pray for those who persecute you.'"[16] (See Document 4.4, pp. 204–06, for a longer excerpt from Jesus' Sermon on the Mount.) Both Jesus and the Buddha called for the personal transformation of their followers, through "letting go" of the grasping that causes suffering, in the Buddha's teaching, or "losing one's life in order to save it," in the language of Jesus.[17]

Despite these similarities, there were also some differences in their teachings and their life stories. Jesus inherited from his Jewish tradition an intense devotion to a single personal deity with whom he was on intimate terms, referring to him as Abba ("papa" or "daddy"). According to the New Testament, the miracles he performed reflected the power of God available to him as a result of that relationship. The Buddha's original message, by contrast, largely ignored the supernatural, involved no miracles, and taught a path of intense self-effort aimed at ethical living and mindfulness as a means of ending suffering. Furthermore, Jesus' teachings had a sharper social and political edge than did those of the Buddha. Jesus spoke more clearly on behalf of the poor and the oppressed, directly criticized the hypocrisies of the powerful, and deliberately associated with lepers, adulterous women, and tax collectors, all of whom were regarded as "impure." These actions reflected his lower-class background, the Jewish tradition of social criticism, and the reality of Roman imperial rule over his people, none of which corresponded to the Buddha's experience. Finally, Jesus' public life was very brief, probably less than three years, compared to more than forty years for the Buddha. His teachings had so antagonized both Jewish and Roman authorities that he was crucified as a common criminal. The Buddha's message was apparently less threatening to the politically powerful, and he died a natural death at age eighty.

The Spread of New Religions

■ Change

In what ways was Christianity transformed in the five centuries following the death of Jesus?

Neither Jesus nor the Buddha had any intention of founding a new religion; rather, they sought to revitalize the traditions from which they had come. Nonetheless, Christianity and Buddhism soon emerged as separate religions, distinct from Judaism and Hinduism, proclaiming their messages to a much wider and more inclusive audience. In the process, both teachers were transformed by their followers into gods. According to many scholars, Jesus never claimed divine status, seeing himself as a teacher or a prophet, whose close relationship to God could be replicated by anyone.[18] The Buddha likewise viewed himself as an enlightened but fully human person, an example of what was possible for all who followed the path. But in Mahayana Buddhism, the Buddha became a supernatural being who could be worshipped and prayed to and was spiritually available to his followers. Jesus also soon became divine in the eyes of his early followers, such as Saint Paul and Saint John. According to one of the first creeds of the Church, he was "the Son of God, Very God of Very God," while his death and resurrection made possible the forgiveness of sins and the eternal salvation of those who believed.

The transformation of Christianity from a small Jewish sect to a world religion began with Saint Paul (10–65 C.E.), an early convert whose missionary journeys in the eastern Roman Empire led to the founding of small Christian communities that included non-Jews. The Good News of Jesus, Paul argued, was for everyone, and Gentile (non-Jewish) converts need not follow Jewish laws or rituals such as circumcision. In one of his many letters to these new communities, later collected as part of the New Testament, Paul wrote, "There is neither Jew nor Greek . . . neither slave nor free . . . neither male nor female, for you are all one in Christ Jesus."[19]

Despite Paul's egalitarian pronouncement, early Christianity, like Buddhism, offered a mix of opportunities and restrictions for women. Jesus himself had interacted easily with a wide range of women, and they had figured prominently among his followers. Some scholars have argued that Mary Magdalene was a part of his inner circle.[20] And women played leadership roles in the "house churches" of the first century C.E. Nonetheless, Paul counseled women to "be subject to your husbands" and declared that "it is shameful for a woman to speak in church." Men were identified with the role of Christ himself when Paul argued that "the husband is head of the wife as Christ is head of the Church."[21] It was not long before male spokesmen for the faith had fully assimilated older and highly negative views of women. As daughters of Eve, they were responsible for the introduction of sin and evil into the world and were the source of temptation for men. On the other hand, Jesus' mother Mary soon became the focus of a devotional cult; women were among the martyrs of the early church; and growing numbers of Christian women, like their Buddhist counterparts, found a more independent space in the monasteries, even as the official hierarchy of the Church became wholly male.

Nonetheless, the inclusive message of early Christianity was one of the attractions of the new faith as it spread very gradually within the Roman Empire during the several centuries after Jesus' death. The earliest converts were usually lower-stratum people—artisans, traders, and a considerable number of women—mostly from towns and cities, while a scattering of wealthier, more prominent, and better-educated people subsequently joined the ranks of Christians.[22] The spread of the faith was often accompanied by reports of miracles, healings, and the casting out of demons—all of which were impressive to people thoroughly accustomed to seeing the supernatural behind the events of ordinary life. Christian communities also attracted converts by the way their members cared for one another. In the middle of the third century C.E., the Church in Rome supported 154 priests (of whom 52 were exorcists) and some 1,500 widows, orphans, and destitute people.[23] By 300 C.E., perhaps 10 percent of the Roman Empire's population (some 5 million people) identified themselves as Christians.

Although Christians in the West often think of their faith as a European-centered religion, during the first six centuries of the Christian era, most followers of Jesus lived in the non-European regions of the Roman Empire—North Africa, Egypt, Anatolia, Syria—or outside of the empire altogether in Arabia, Persia, Ethiopia, India, and China. Saint Paul's missionary journeys had established various Christian communities in the Roman province of Asia—what is now Turkey—and also in Syria, where the earliest recorded Christian church building was located. The Syrian church also developed a unique liturgy with strong Jewish influences and a distinctive musical tradition of chants and hymns. The language of that liturgy was neither Greek nor Latin, but Syriac, a Semitic tongue closely related to Aramaic, which Jesus spoke.

From Syria, the faith spread eastward into Persia, where it attracted a substantial number of converts, many of them well educated in the sciences and medicine, by the third century C.E. Those converts also encountered periodic persecution from the Zoroastrian rulers of Persia and were sometimes suspected of political loyalty to the Roman Empire, Persia's longtime enemy and rival. To the north of Syria on the slopes of the Caucasus Mountains, the Kingdom of Armenia became the first place where rulers adopted Christianity as a state religion. In time, Christianity became — and remains to this day — a central element of Armenian national identity. A distinctive feature of Armenian Christianity involved the ritual killing of animals at the end of the worship service, probably a continuation of earlier pre-Christian practices.

Syria and Persia represented the core region of the Church of the East, distinct both theologically and organizationally from the Latin church focused on Rome and an emerging Eastern Orthodox church based in Constantinople. Its missionaries took Christianity even farther to the east. By the fourth century, and perhaps much earlier, a well-organized church had taken root in southern India, which later gained tax privileges and special rights from local rulers. In the early seventh century a Persian monk named Alopen initiated a small but remarkable Christian experiment in China, described more fully in Chapter 10. A modest Christian presence in Central Asia was also an outgrowth of this Church of the East.

In other directions as well, Christianity spread from its Palestinian place of origin. By the time Muhammad was born in 570, a number of Arabs had become Christians. One of them, in fact, was among the first to affirm Muhammad as an authentic prophet. A particularly vibrant center of Christianity developed in Egypt, where tradition holds that Jesus's family fled to escape persecution of King Herod. Egyptian priests soon translated the Bible into the Egyptian language known as Coptic, and Egyptian Christians pioneered various forms of monasticism. By 400 C.E., hundreds of monasteries, cells, and caves dotted the desert, inhabited by reclusive monks dedicated to their spiritual practices. Increasingly, the language, theology, and practice of Egyptian Christianity diverged from that of Rome and Constantinople, giving expression to Egyptian resistance against Roman or Byzantine oppression.

To the west of Egypt, a Church of North Africa furnished a number of the intellectuals of the early Church including Saint Augustine as well as many Christian martyrs to Roman persecution (see Portrait of Perpetua, pp. 192–93). Here and elsewhere the coming of Christianity not only provoked hostility from Roman political authorities but also tensions within families. The North African Carthaginian writer Tertullian (160–220 C.E.), known as the "father of Latin Christianity," described the kind of difficulties that might arise between a Christian wife and her "pagan" husband:

> She is engaged in a fast; her husband has arranged a banquet. It is her Christian duty to visit the streets and the homes of the poor; her husband insists on family business. She celebrates the Easter Vigil throughout the night; her husband expects her in his bed. . . . She who has taken a cup at Eucharist will be required to take of a cup with her husband in the tavern. She who has foresworn idolatry must inhale the smoke arising from the incense on the altars of the idols in her husband's home.[24]

Further south in Africa, Christianity became during the fourth century the state religion of Axum, an emerging kingdom in what is now Eritrea and Ethiopia (see Chapter 6). This occurred at about the same time as both Armenia and the Roman Empire officially endorsed Christianity. In Axum, a distinctively African expression of Christianity took root with open-air services, the use of drums and stringed instruments in worship, and colorful umbrellas covering priests and musicians from the elements. Linked theologically and organizationally to Coptic Christianity in Egypt, the Ethiopian church used Ge'ez, a local Semitic language and script, for its liturgy and literature.

In the Roman world, the strangest and most offensive feature of the new faith was its exclusive monotheism and its antagonism to all other supernatural powers, particularly the cult of the emperors. Christians' denial of these other gods caused them to be tagged as "atheists" and was one reason behind the empire's intermittent persecution of Christians during the first three centuries of the Common Era. All of that ended with Emperor Constantine's conversion in the early fourth century C.E. and with growing levels of state support for the new religion in the decades that followed.

Roman rulers sought to use an increasingly popular Christianity as glue to hold together a very diverse population in a weakening imperial state. Constantine and his successors thus provided Christians with newfound security and opportunities. The emperor Theodosius (r. 379–395 C.E.) enforced a ban on all polytheistic ritual

Map 4.1   The Spread of Early Christianity and Buddhism
In the five centuries after the birth of Jesus, Christianity found converts from Spain to northeast Africa, the Middle East, Central Asia, and India. In the Roman Empire, Axum, and Armenia, the new religion enjoyed state support as well. Subsequently, Christianity took root solidly in Europe and after 1000 C.E. in Russia as well. Meanwhile, Buddhism was spreading from its South Asian homeland to various parts of Asia, even as it was weakening in India itself.

Perpetua, Christian Martyr

Perpetua (Vladimir Bugarin/5d012)

"The blood of the martyrs," declared the Christian writer Tertullian, "is the seed of the church." Few of those martyrs, whose stories so inspired the persecuted converts of the early Christian centuries, could match that of Perpetua, a young woman whose prison diary provides a highly personal account of her arrest and trial.[25]

Born in 181 C.E. in the North African city of Carthage, Perpetua hailed from an upper-class Roman family and was quite well educated, literate in Latin and probably Greek, and acquainted with Roman philosophical writings. By the time she enters the historical record at age twenty-two, she had given birth to a son, had lost her husband either to death or abandonment, and had recently begun to study Christianity, one of a small but growing group of educated people who were turning toward the new faith. Coinciding with her conversion was a wave of persecutions ordered by the Roman emperor Septimus Severus,

also of North African descent and a devotee of the Egyptian cult of Isis and Osiris. Severus sought to forbid new conversions rather than punish long-established Christians. In line with this policy, in 203 C.E., the hard-line governor of the region ordered the arrest of Perpetua along with four others—two slaves, one of them a woman named Felicitas who was eight months pregnant, and two free men. Before she was taken to the prison, however, Perpetua decisively confirmed her commitment to Christianity by accepting baptism.

Once in the "dark hole" of the prison, Perpetua was terrified. It was crowded and stiflingly hot, and she was consumed with anxiety for her child. Several fellow Christians managed to bribe the prison guards to permit Perpetua to nurse her baby son. Reunited with her child, she found that "my prison had suddenly become a palace, so that I wanted to be there rather than anywhere else."

sacrifices and ordered their temples closed. Christians by contrast received patronage for their buildings, official approval for their doctrines, suppression of their rivals, prestige from imperial recognition, and, during the late fourth century, the proclamation of Christianity as the official state religion. All of this set in motion a process by which the Roman Empire, and later all of Europe, became overwhelmingly Christian. At the time, however, Christianity was expanding at least as rapidly to the east and south as it was to the west. In 500, few observers could have predicted that the future of Christianity would lie primarily in Europe rather than in Asia and Africa.

The spread of Buddhism in India was quite different from that of Christianity in the Roman Empire. Even though Ashoka's support gave Buddhism a considerable boost, it was never promoted to the exclusion of other faiths. Ashoka sought harmony among India's diverse population through religious tolerance rather than uniformity. The kind of monotheistic intolerance that Christianity exhibited in the Roman world was quite foreign to Indian patterns of religious practice. Although Buddhism subsequently died out in India as it was absorbed into a reviving Hindu-

A few days later, Perpetua's deeply distressed non-Christian father arrived for a visit, hoping to persuade his only daughter to recant her faith and save her life and the family's honor. It was a heart-breaking encounter. "Daughter," he said, "have pity on my grey head. . . . Do not abandon me to be the reproach of men. Think of your brothers, think of your mother and your aunt, think of your child, who will not be able to live once you are gone. Give up your pride! You will destroy all of us! None of us will ever be able to speak freely again if anything happens to you." Firm in her faith, Perpetua refused his entreaties and she reported that "he left me in great sorrow."

On the day of her trial, with her distraught father in attendance, the governor Hilarianus also begged Perpetua to consider her family and renounce her faith by offering a sacrifice to the emperor. Again she refused and together with her four companions was "condemned to the beasts," a humiliating form of execution normally reserved for the lower classes. Although she was now permanently separated from her child, she wrote that "we returned to the prison in high spirits." During her last days in the prison, Perpetua and the others were treated "more humanely,"

allowed to visit with family and friends, as the head of the jail was himself a Christian.

But then, on the birthday of the emperor, this small band of Christians was marched to the amphitheater, "joyfully as though they were going to heaven," according to an eyewitness account. After the prisoners strenuously and successfully resisted dressing in the robes of pagan priests, the three men were sent into the arena to contend with a boar, a bear, and a leopard. Then it was the turn of the women, Perpetua and the slave Felicitas, who had given birth only two days earlier. When a mad cow failed to kill them, a soldier was sent to finish the work. As he approached Perpetua, he apparently hesitated, but as an eyewitness account put it, "she took the trembling hand of the young gladiator and guided it to her throat." Appended to her diary was this comment from an unknown observer: "It was as though so great a woman, feared as she was by the unclean spirit, could not be dispatched unless she herself were willing."

Questions: How might you understand the actions and attitudes of Perpetua? Is her experience accessible to people living in a largely secular modern society?

---

ism, no renewal of Roman polytheism occurred, and Christianity became an enduring element of European civilization. Nonetheless, Christianity did adopt some elements of religious practice from the Roman world, including perhaps the cult of saints and the dating of the birth of Jesus to the winter solstice. In both cases, however, these new religions spread widely beyond their places of origin. Buddhism provided a network of cultural connections across much of Asia, while Christianity during its early centuries established an Afro-Eurasian presence.

Institutions, Controversies, and Divisions

As Christianity spread within the Roman Empire and beyond, it developed a hierarchical organization, with patriarchs, bishops, and priests—all men—replacing the house churches of the early years, in which women played a more prominent part. At least in some places, however, women continued to exercise leadership and even priestly roles, prompting Pope Gelasius in 494 to speak out sharply against those who encouraged women "to officiate at the sacred altars, and to take part in all matters imputed to the offices of the male sex, to which they do not belong."[26] In general, though, the exclusion of women from the priesthood established a male-dominated clergy and a patriarchal church, which has lasted into the twenty-first century.

The emerging Christian movement was, however, anything but unified. Its immense geographical reach, accompanied by inevitable differences in language, culture, and political regime, ensured that a single focus for Christian belief and practice was difficult to achieve. Doctrinal differences also tore at the unity of Christianity and embroiled church authorities in frequent controversy about the nature of Jesus (was he human, divine, or both?), his relationship to God (equal or inferior?), and the always-perplexing concept of the Trinity (God as Father, Son, and Holy Spirit). There was debate as well about what writings belonged in the Bible. A series of church councils—at Nicaea (325 C.E.), Chalcedon (451 C.E.), and Constantinople (553 C.E.), for example—sought to define an orthodox, or correct, position on these and other issues, declaring those who disagreed as *anathema* and expelling them from the Church. Thus Egyptian Christians, for example, held to the unorthodox position called Monophysite. This view, that Jesus had a single divine nature simply occupying a human body, expressed resistance to domination from Rome or Constantinople, which held that Jesus was both fully human and fully divine. Likewise the Church of the East adopted Nestorianism, another unorthodox view that emphasized the human side of Jesus' nature and distinguished its theology from the Latin and Eastern Orthodox churches.

Beyond these theological debates, political and cultural differences generated division even among the orthodox. The bishop of Rome gradually emerged as the dominant leader, or pope, of the Church in the western half of the empire, but his authority was sharply contested in the east. This division contributed to the later split between the Latin or Roman Catholic and the Greek or Eastern Orthodox branches of Christendom, a division that continues to the present (see Chapter 10). Thus the Christian world of 500 C.E. was not only geographically extensive but also politically and theologically very diverse and highly fragmented.

Buddhists too clashed over various interpretations of the Buddha's teachings, and a series of councils failed to prevent the division between Theravada, Mahayana, and other approaches. A considerable proliferation of different sects, practices, teachings, and meditation techniques subsequently emerged within the Buddhist world, but these divisions generally lacked the "clear-cut distinction between 'right' and 'wrong' ideas" that characterized conflicts within the Christian world.[27] Although Buddhist states and warrior classes (such as the famous samurai of Japan) sometimes engaged in warfare, religious differences among Buddhists seldom provided the basis for the bitterness and violence that often accompanied religious conflict within Christendom. Nor did Buddhists develop the kind of overall religious hierarchy that characterized Christianity, although communities of monks and nuns, organized in monasteries, created elaborate rules to govern their internal affairs.

LearningCurve
bedfordstmartins.com
/strayer/LC

SUMMING UP SO FAR

How might you understand the appeal of Buddhism and Christianity as opposed to the more rationalist approaches of Greek and Confucian philosophy?

⊏⊐ Reflections: Religion and Historians

To put it mildly, religion has always been a sensitive subject, and no less so for historians than for anyone else. Throughout human history the vast majority of people have simply assumed the existence of an Unseen Realm, that of the sacred or the divine, with which human beings should align themselves. More recently, as an outgrowth of the Scientific Revolution and the European Enlightenment, some have challenged that assumption, arguing that the only realities worth considering are those that can be accessed with the techniques of science. Modern secular historians, whatever their personal beliefs, feel compelled to rely on evidence available in this world. This situation has generated various tensions or misunderstandings between historians and religious practitioners.

One of these tensions involves the question of change. Most religions present themselves as timeless, partaking of eternity or at least reflecting ancient practice. In the eyes of historians, however, the religious aspect of human life changes as much as any other. The Hindu tradition changed from a religion of ritual and sacrifice to one of devotion and worship. Buddhism became more conventionally religious, with an emphasis on the supernatural, as it evolved from Theravada to Mahayana forms. A male-dominated hierarchical Christian Church, with its pope, bishops, priests, and state support, was very different from the small house churches that suffered persecution by imperial authorities in the early Christian centuries. The implication—that religions are at least in part a human phenomenon—has been troublesome to some believers.

Historians, on the other hand, have sometimes been uncomfortable in the face of claims by believers that they have actually experienced a divine reality. How could such experiences be verified, when even the biographical details of the lives of the Buddha and Jesus are difficult to prove by the standards of historians? Certainly, modern historians are in no position to validate or refute the spiritual claims of these teachers, but we need to take them seriously. Although we will never know precisely what happened to the Buddha as he sat in meditation in northern India or what transpired when Jesus spent forty days in the wilderness, clearly those experiences changed the two men and motivated their subsequent actions. Later, Muhammad likewise claimed to have received revelations from God in the caves outside Mecca. Millions of the followers of these religious leaders have also acted on the basis of what they perceived to be an encounter with the Divine or the Unseen. This interior dimension of human experience, though difficult to grasp with any precision, has been a significant mover and shaper of the historical process.

Yet a third problem arises from debates within particular religious traditions about which group most accurately represents the "real" or authentic version of the faith. Historians usually refuse to take sides in such disputes. They simply notice with interest that most human cultural traditions generate conflicting views, some of which become the basis for serious conflict in their societies.

Reconciling personal religious convictions with the perspectives of modern historical scholarship is no easy task. At the very least, all of us can appreciate the immense human effort that has gone into the making of religious traditions, and we can acknowledge the enormous significance of these traditions in the unfolding of the human story. They have shaped the meanings that billions of people over thousands of years have attached to the world they inhabit. These religious traditions have justified the vast social inequalities and oppressive states of human civilizations, but they also have enabled human beings to endure the multiple sufferings that attend human life and on occasion they have stimulated reform and rebellion. And the religions born in second-wave civilizations have guided much of humankind in our endless efforts to penetrate the mysteries of the world beyond and of the world within.

Second Thoughts

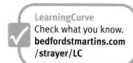

LearningCurve
Check what you know.
**bedfordstmartins.com
/strayer/LC**

Online Study Guide
bedfordstmartins.com
/highschool/strayer

What's the Significance?

Legalism, 169

Confucianism, 169–72

Ban Zhao, 171

Daoism, 172–74

Vedas, 174–75

Upanishads, 175

Siddhartha Gautama
  (the Buddha), 176–77

Theravada/Mahayana, 178–79

Bhagavad Gita, 179–80

Zoroastrianism, 181–82

Judaism, 182–83

Greek rationalism, 183

Socrates, Plato, Aristotle, 183–86

Jesus of Nazareth, 187–88

Saint Paul, 188–89

Church of the East, 190

Perpetua, 192–93

Big Picture Questions

1. Is a secular outlook on the world an essentially modern phenomenon, or does it have precedents in the second-wave era?

2. "Religion is a double-edged sword, both supporting and undermining political authority and social elites." How would you support both sides of this statement?

3. How would you define the appeal of the religious/cultural traditions discussed in this chapter? To what groups were they attractive, and why?

4. In what different ways did these religious or cultural traditions define the purposes of human life?

5. **Looking Back:** What relationships can you see between the political dimensions of second-wave civilizations described in Chapter 3 and their cultural or religious aspects discussed in this chapter?

For Web sites and additional documents related to this chapter, see **Make History** at bedfordstmartins.com /highschool/strayer.

Next Steps: For Further Study

Karen Armstrong, *The Great Transformation* (2006). A comparative and historical study of the major religions by a well-known scholar.

Robert N. Bellah, *Religion in Human Evolution: From the Paleolithic to the Axial Age* (2011). An impressive but controversial account of the origins of religion in general and those of second-wave civilizations in particular.

Peter Brown, *The Rise of Western Christendom* (2003). A history of the first 1,000 years of Christianity, cast in a global framework.

Huston Smith, *An Illustrated World's Religions* (1994). A sympathetic account of major world religions, beautifully illustrated, by a prominent scholar of comparative religion.

Arthur Waley, *Three Ways of Thought in Ancient China* (1983). A classic work, first published more than half a century ago, about the major philosophies of old China.

Jonathan S. Walters, *Finding Buddhists in Global History* (1998). A brief account that situates Buddhism in a world history framework.

BBC, "Religions," http://www.bbc.co.uk/religion/religions/. A succinct introduction to the history, beliefs, and practices of many of the world's religious traditions.

Documents

Considering the Evidence:
The Good Life in Eurasian Civilizations

What constitutes a good life for an individual person or a good society for a community of people? These are among the central questions that have occupied human beings since the beginning of conscious thought. And they certainly played a major role in the emerging cultural traditions of the second-wave civilizations all across Eurasia. The documents that follow present a sample of this thinking drawn from Confucian, Hindu, Greek, and Christian traditions.

Document 4.1

Reflections from Confucius

No one was more central to the making of Chinese civilization than Confucius (551–479 B.C.E.). In the several generations following their master's death, his disciples recalled his teachings and his conversations, recording them in a small book called the *Analects*. This text became a touchstone for all educated people in China and across much of East Asia as well. Over the centuries, extensive commentaries and interpretations of Confucius's teachings gave rise to a body of literature known generally as Confucianism, though these ideas encompassed the thinking of many others as well.

In the translation from the *Analects* that follows, the word "virtue" refers to the qualities of a complete or realized human being, sometimes referred to in Confucian literature as a "gentleman" or a "virtuous man."

- How would Confucius define such a person?

- How might one become this kind of person?

The terms "propriety" and "rites of propriety" point to an elaborate set of rituals or expectations that defined appropriate behavior in virtually every circumstance of life, depending on one's gender, age, or class.

- What role does propriety or ritual play in the making of a virtuous man?

- What understanding of "learning" or education comes through in this text?

- What is "filial piety," and why is it so important in Confucius's understanding of a good society?

- How do "virtue," "filial piety," and "learning" relate to the larger task of creating good government and a harmonious society?

- How does Confucius understand the role of the supernatural — gods, spirits, and ancestors, for example?

CONFUCIUS

The Analects

ca. 479–221 B.C.E.

The philosopher Yu said, "They are few who, being filial and fraternal, are fond of offending against their superiors. There have been none, who, not liking to offend against their superiors, have been fond of stirring up confusion. . . ."

The Master said, "To rule a country of a thousand chariots, there must be reverent attention to business, and sincerity; economy in expenditure, and love for men; and the employment of the people at the proper seasons."

The Master said, "A youth, when at home, should be filial, and, abroad, respectful to his elders. He should be earnest and truthful. He should over-flow in love to all, and cultivate the friendship of the good. When he has time and opportunity, after the performance of these things, he should employ them in polite studies."

Tsze-hsia said, "If a man withdraws his mind from the love of [beautiful women], and applies it as sincerely to the love of the virtuous; if, in serving his parents, he can exert his utmost strength; if, in serving his prince, he can devote his life; if, in his intercourse with his friends, his words are sincere: although men say that he has not learned, I will certainly say that he has."

The philosopher Tsang said, "Let there be a careful attention to perform the funeral rites to parents, and let them be followed when long gone with the

ceremonies of sacrifice; then the virtue of the people will resume its proper excellence."

The Master said, "He who exercises government by means of his virtue may be compared to the north polar star, which keeps its place and all the stars turn toward it."

The Master said, "If the people be led by laws, and uniformity sought to be given them by punishments, they will try to avoid the punishment, but have no sense of shame. If they be led by virtue, and uniformity sought to be given them by the rules of propriety, they will have the sense of shame, and moreover will become good."

The Duke Ai asked, saying, "What should be done in order to secure the submission of the people?" Confucius replied, "Advance the upright and set aside the crooked, then the people will submit. Advance the crooked and set aside the upright, then the people will not submit."

Chi K'ang asked how to cause the people to reverence their ruler, to be faithful to him, and to go on to nerve themselves to virtue. The Master said, "Let him preside over them with gravity; then they will reverence him. Let him be filial and kind to all; then they will be faithful to him. Let him advance the good and teach the incompetent; then they will eagerly seek to be virtuous."

The Master said, "If the will be set on virtue, there will be no practice of wickedness."

The Master said, "Riches and honors are what men desire. If they cannot be obtained in the proper way, they should not be held. Poverty and meanness

Source: Confucius, *The Analects*, translated by James Legge (1893).

are what men dislike. If they cannot be avoided in the proper way, they should not be avoided."

The Master said, "In serving his parents, a son may remonstrate with them, but gently; when he sees that they do not incline to follow his advice, he shows an increased degree of reverence, but does not abandon his purpose; and should they punish him, he does not allow himself to murmur."

Fan Ch'ih asked what constituted wisdom. The Master said, "To give one's self earnestly to the duties due to men, and, while respecting spiritual beings, to keep aloof from them, may be called wisdom."

The Master said, "The superior man, extensively studying all learning, and keeping himself under the restraint of the rules of propriety, may thus likewise not overstep what is right."

The Master's frequent themes of discourse were the Odes, the History, and the maintenance of the Rules of Propriety. On all these he frequently discoursed.

The Master was wishing to go and live among the nine wild tribes of the east. Some one said, "They are rude. How can you do such a thing?" The Master said, "If a superior man dwelt among them, what rudeness would there be?"

Chi Lu asked about serving the spirits of the dead. The Master said, "While you are not able to serve men, how can you serve their spirits?" Chi Lu added, "I venture to ask about death?" He was answered, "While you do not know life, how can you know about death?"

Yen Yuan asked about perfect virtue. The Master said, "To subdue one's self and return to propriety, is perfect virtue. If a man can for one day subdue himself and return to propriety, all under heaven will ascribe perfect virtue to him."

Chung-kung asked about perfect virtue. The Master said, "It is, when you go abroad, to behave to every one as if you were receiving a great guest; to employ the people as if you were assisting at a great sacrifice; not to do to others as you would not wish done to yourself; to have no murmuring against you in the country, and none in the family."

Chi K'ang asked Confucius about government. Confucius replied, "To govern means to rectify. If you lead on the people with correctness, who will dare not to be correct?"

Truly, if the ruler is not a ruler, the subject not a subject, the father not a father, the son not a son, then even if there be grain, would I get to eat it?

The Master said, "Of all people, girls and servants are the most difficult to behave to. If you are familiar with them, they lose their humility. If you maintain a reserve toward them, they are discontented."

Document 4.2

Reflections from the Hindu Scriptures

The flavor of Indian thinking about the good life and the good society is quite different from that of China. This distinctive outlook is reflected in these selections from the Bhagavad Gita (The Song of the Lord), perhaps the most treasured of Hindu writings. Its dating is highly uncertain, although most scholars put it somewhere between the fifth and second centuries B.C.E. The Bhagavad Gita itself is an episode within the *Mahabharata*, one of the huge epic poems of India's classical tradition, which describes the struggle for power between two branches of the same family. The setting of the Bhagavad Gita takes place on the eve of a great battle in which the fearless warrior Arjuna is overcome with the realization that in this battle he will be required to kill some of his own kinsmen. In his distress, he turns for advice to his charioteer, Lord Krishna, who is an incarnation of the great god Vishnu. Krishna's response to Arjuna's anguished questions, a part of which is reproduced here, conveys the essence of Hindu thinking about life and action in this world. A central question in the Bhagavad Gita is how a person can achieve spiritual fulfillment while remaining active in the world.

- What is Krishna's answer to this dilemma?

- What reasons does Krishna give for urging Arjuna to perform his duty as a warrior?

- How does Krishna describe the good society?

- What major themes of Hindu teaching can you find in this passage?

- How does this text differ from that of the *Analects*? Are they asking the same questions? What similarities in outlook, if any, can you identify in these two texts?

Bhagavad Gita
ca. Fifth to Second Century B.C.E.

The deity said, you have grieved for those who deserve no grief.... Learned men grieve not for the living nor the dead. Never did I not exist, nor you, nor these rulers of men; nor will any one of us ever hereafter cease to be. As in this body, infancy and youth and old age come to the embodied self, so does the acquisition of another body; a sensible man is not deceived about that. The contacts of the senses ... which produce cold and heat, pleasure and pain, are not permanent, they are ever coming and going. Bear them, O descendant of Bharata!

He who thinks it [a person's soul, or *atman*] to be the killer and he who thinks it to be killed, both know nothing. It kills not, [and] is not killed. It is not born, nor does it ever die, nor, having existed, does it exist no more. Unborn, everlasting, unchangeable, and primeval, it is not killed when the body is killed.... As a man, casting off old clothes, puts on others and new ones, so the embodied self, casting off old bodies, goes to others and new ones.... It is everlasting, all-pervading, stable, firm, and eternal.

It is said to be unperceived, to be unthinkable, to be unchangeable. Therefore, knowing it to be such, you ought not to grieve.... For to one that is born, death is certain; and to one that dies, birth is certain....

Having regard to your own duty also, you ought not to falter, for there is nothing better for a Kshatriya° than a righteous battle. Happy those Kshatriyas, O son of Pritha! who can find such a battle ... an open door to heaven! But if you will not fight this righteous battle, then you will have abandoned your own duty and your fame, and you will incur sin....

Your business is with action alone, not by any means with fruit. Let not the fruit of action be your motive to action. Let not your attachment be fixed on inaction. Having recourse to devotion ... perform actions, casting off all attachment, and being equable in success or ill-success; such equability is called devotion.... The wise who have obtained devotion cast off the fruit of action, and released from the shackles of repeated births, repair to that seat where there is no unhappiness....

The man who, casting off all desires, lives free from attachments, who is free from egoism and from

Source: Tashinath Trimbak Teland, trans., *The Bhagavad Gita*, in *The Sacred Books of the East*, edited by Max Mueller (Oxford: Clarendon Press, 1879–1910), 8:43–46, 48–49, 51–52, 126–28.

°**Kshatriya:** a member of the warrior/ruler caste.

the feeling that this or that is mine, obtains tranquility. This, O son of Pritha! is the Brahmic state. Attaining to this, one is never deluded, and remaining in it in one's last moments, one attains the Brahmic bliss [nirvana, or merging with the divine]. . . .

I have passed through many births, O Arjuna! and you also. I know them all, but you . . . do not know them. . . . Whensoever, O descendant of Bharata! piety languishes, and impiety is in the ascendant, I create myself. I am born age after age, for the protection of the good, for the destruction of evil-doers, and the establishment of piety. . . .

The fourfold division of castes was created by me according to the appointment of qualities and duties . . . . The duties of Brahmins, Kshatriyas, and Vaisyas, and of Sudras [SOO-druhs], too . . . are distinguished according to the qualities born of nature. Tranquillity, restraint of the senses, penance, purity, forgiveness, straightforwardness, also knowledge, experience, and belief in a future world, this is the natural duty of Brahmins. Valor, glory, courage, dexterity, not slinking away from battle, gifts, exercise of lordly power, this is the natural duty of Kshatriyas. Agriculture, tending cattle, trade, this is the natural duty of Vaisyas. And the natural duty of Sudras, too, consists in service.

Every man intent on his own respective duties obtains perfection. Listen, now, how one intent on one's own duty obtains perfection. Worshipping, by the performance of his own duty, him from whom all things proceed, and by whom all this is permeated, a man obtains perfection. One's duty, though defective, is better than another's duty well performed. Performing the duty prescribed by nature, one does not incur sin. O son of Kunti! one should not abandon a natural duty though tainted with evil; for all actions are enveloped by evil, as fire by smoke.

One who is self-restrained, whose understanding is unattached everywhere, from whom affections have departed, obtains the supreme perfection of freedom from action by renunciation. Learn from me, only in brief, O son of Kunti! how one who has obtained perfection attains the Brahman, which is the highest culmination of knowledge. A man possessed of a pure understanding, controlling his self by courage, discarding sound and other objects of sense, casting off affection and aversion, who frequents clean places, who eats little, whose speech, body, and mind are restrained, who is always intent on meditation and mental abstraction, and has recourse to unconcern, who, abandoning egoism, stubbornness, arrogance, desire, anger, and all belongings, has no thought that this or that is mine, and who is tranquil, becomes fit for assimilation with the Brahman.

Document 4.3

Reflections from Socrates

Document 4.3 comes from the tradition of Greek rationalism. The excerpt is from Socrates' famous defense of himself before a jury of 501 fellow Athenians in 399 B.C.E., as recorded by Plato, Socrates' student and disciple. Charged with impiety and corrupting the youth of the city, Socrates was narrowly condemned to death by that jury. His speech at the trial has come to be viewed as a powerful defense of intellectual freedom and the unfettered life of the mind.

■ How does Socrates respond to the charges laid against him?

■ How might Socrates define "the good life"? How does he understand "wisdom" and "virtue"? Do you think that Confucius and Socrates would agree about the nature of virtue?

■ Why does Socrates believe he has been useful to Athens?

■ What do his frequent references to God reveal about his understanding of the supernatural and its relevance to social life?

■ Why did he accept the death penalty and refuse to consider a lesser sentence? (See the photo on p. 185.)

PLATO

Apology

ca. 399 B.C.E.

I will begin at the beginning, and ask what the accusation is which has given rise to this slander of me. . . . What do the slanderers say? . . . "Socrates is an evil-doer, and a curious person, who searches into things under the earth and in heaven, and he makes the worse appear the better cause; and he teaches the aforesaid doctrines to others. . . ."

I found that the men most in repute were all but the most foolish; and that some inferior men were really wiser and better. . . .

O men of Athens, . . . God only is wise; . . . the wisdom of men is little or nothing; . . . And so I go my way, obedient to the god, and make inquisition into the wisdom of anyone, whether citizen or stranger, who appears to be wise; and if he is not wise, then . . . I show him that he is not wise; and this occupation quite absorbs me. . . .

There is another thing: young men of the richer classes, who have not much to do, come about me of their own accord; they like to hear the pretenders examined, and they often imitate me, and examine others themselves; there are plenty of persons, as they soon enough discover, who think that they know something, but really know little or nothing: and then those who are examined by them instead of being angry with themselves are angry with me: This confounded Socrates, they say; this villainous misleader of youth! . . . [T]hey repeat the ready-made charges which are used against all philosophers about teaching things up in the clouds and under the earth, and having no gods, and making the worse appear the better cause; for they do not like to confess that their pretence of knowledge has been detected. . . .

Someone will say: And are you not ashamed, Socrates, of a course of life which is likely to bring you to an untimely end? To him I may fairly answer: There you are mistaken: a man who is good for anything ought not to calculate the chance of living or dying; he ought only to consider whether in doing anything he is doing right or wrong, acting the part of a good man or of a bad. . . . Had Achilles° any thought of death and danger? For wherever a man's place is, whether the place which he has chosen or that in which he has been placed by a commander, there he ought to remain in the hour of danger; he should not think of death or of anything, but of disgrace. . . .

And therefore if you let me go now, and . . . if you say to me, Socrates, this time we will . . . let you off, but upon one condition, that you are not to inquire and speculate in this way any more, and that if you are caught doing this again you shall die; if this was the condition on which you let me go, I should reply: Men of Athens, I honor and love you; but I shall obey God rather than you, and while I have life and strength I shall never cease from the practice and teaching of philosophy, exhorting anyone whom I meet after my manner. . . . I interrogate and examine and cross-examine him, and if I think that he has no virtue, but only says that he has, I reproach him with

Source: Plato, *Apology*, translated by Benjamin Jowett (1891).

°**Achilles:** the great warrior-hero of the *Iliad*.

undervaluing the greater, and overvaluing the less.... For I do nothing but go about persuading you all, old and young alike, not to take thought for your persons and your properties, but first and chiefly to care about the greatest improvement of the soul.... Wherefore, O men of Athens, I say to you ... either acquit me or not; but whatever you do, know that I shall never alter my ways, not even if I have to die many times....

[I]f you kill such a one as I am, you will injure yourselves more than you will injure me.... For if you kill me you will not easily find another like me, who, if I may use such a ludicrous figure of speech, am a sort of gadfly, given to the state by the God; and the state is like a great and noble steed who is tardy in his motions owing to his very size, and requires to be stirred into life. I am that gadfly which God has given the state and all day long and in all places am always fastening upon you, arousing and persuading and reproaching you.... I dare say that you may feel irritated at being suddenly awakened when you are caught napping; and you may think that if you were to strike me dead ..., which you easily might,

then you would sleep on for the remainder of your lives....

[After the jury finds Socrates guilty, he accepts the sentence of death, rejecting the alternative punishments of prison or exile.]

There are many reasons why I am not grieved, O men of Athens, at the vote of condemnation. The difficulty, my friends, is not in avoiding death, but in avoiding unrighteousness....

I am not angry with my accusers, or my condemners.... Still I have a favor to ask of them. When my sons are grown up, I would ask you, O my friends, to punish them ... if they seem to care about riches, or anything, more than about virtue; or if they pretend to be something when they are really nothing, then reprove them, as I have reproved you, for not caring about that for which they ought to care, and thinking that they are something when they are really nothing. And if you do this, I and my sons will have received justice at your hands.

The hour of departure has arrived, and we go our ways—I to die, and you to live. Which is better, God only knows.

Document 4.4

Reflections from Jesus

Like Confucius, Jesus apparently never wrote anything himself. His sayings and his actions were recorded in the Gospels by his followers. The Gospel of Matthew, from which this selection is taken, was composed around 80–85 C.E. For Christian people, this passage, known as the Sermon on the Mount, has long been among the most beloved of biblical texts, regarded as a guide for effective living and the core of Jesus' ethical and moral teachings. In this selection, Jesus contrasts the "broad road" of conventional understanding and values with the "narrow road that leads to life."

- In what ways does his teaching challenge or contradict the conventional outlook of his time?

- What criticisms does he make of those referred to as hypocrites, Pharisees, and the teachers of the law?

- How would you summarize "the good life" as Jesus might have defined it?

- How might Jesus and Confucius have responded to each other's teachings?

- What is Jesus' posture toward Jewish law?

- Beyond its use as a guide for personal behavior, what are the larger social implications of the Sermon on the Mount?

The Gospel of Matthew
ca. 70–100 C.E.

Now when he [Jesus] saw the crowds, he went up on a mountainside and sat down. His disciples came to him, and he began to teach them saying:

"Blessed are the poor in spirit, for theirs is the kingdom of heaven.

"Blessed are those who mourn, for they will be comforted.

"Blessed are the meek, for they will inherit the earth.

"Blessed are those who hunger and thirst for righteousness, for they will be filled.

"Blessed are the merciful, for they will be shown mercy.

"Blessed are the pure in heart, for they will see God.

"Blessed are the peacemakers, for they will be called sons of God.

"Blessed are those who are persecuted because of righteousness, for theirs is the kingdom of heaven.

"You are the salt of the earth. But if the salt loses its saltiness, how can it be made salty again? It is no longer good for anything, except to be thrown out and trampled by men.

"You are the light of the world. A city on a hill cannot be hidden. Neither do people light a lamp and put it under a bowl. Instead they put it on its stand, and it gives light to everyone in the house. In the same way, let your light shine before men, that they may see your good deeds and praise your Father in heaven.

"Do not think that I have come to abolish the Law or the Prophets; I have not come to abolish them but to fulfill them. I tell you the truth, until heaven and earth disappear, not the smallest letter, not the least stroke of a pen, will by any means disappear from the Law until everything is accomplished. Anyone who breaks one of the least of these commandments and teaches others to do the same will be called least in the kingdom of heaven, but whoever practices and teaches these commands will be called great in the kingdom of heaven. For I tell you that unless your righteousness surpasses that of the Pharisees and the teachers of the law, you will certainly not enter the kingdom of heaven.

"You have heard that it was said to the people long ago, 'Do not murder, and anyone who murders will be subject to judgment.' But I tell you that anyone who is angry with his brother will be subject to judgment. . . .

"Therefore, if you are offering your gift at the altar and there remember that your brother has something against you, leave your gift there in front of the altar. First go and be reconciled to your brother; then come and offer your gift.

"Settle matters quickly with your adversary who is taking you to court. Do it while you are still with him on the way, or he may hand you over to the judge, and the judge may hand you over to the officer, and you may be thrown into prison. I tell you the truth, you will not get out until you have paid the last penny.

"You have heard that it was said, 'Do not commit adultery.' But I tell you that anyone who looks at a woman lustfully has already committed adultery with her in his heart. . . .

"You have heard that it was said, 'Eye for eye, and tooth for tooth.' But I tell you, Do not resist an

Source: Matthew 5–7 (New International Version).

evil person. If someone strikes you on the right cheek, turn to him the other also. And if someone wants to sue you and take your tunic, let him have your cloak as well. If someone forces you to go one mile, go with him two miles. Give to the one who asks you, and do not turn away from the one who wants to borrow from you.

"You have heard that it was said, 'Love your neighbor and hate your enemy.' But I tell you: Love your enemies and pray for those who persecute you, that you may be sons of your Father in heaven. He causes his sun to rise on the evil and the good, and sends rain on the righteous and the unrighteous. If you love those who love you, what reward will you get? Are not even the tax collectors doing that? And if you greet only your brothers, what are you doing more than others? Do not even pagans do that? Be perfect, therefore, as your heavenly Father is perfect.

"Be careful not to do your 'acts of righteousness' before men, to be seen by them. . . . So when you give to the needy, do not announce it with trumpets, as the hypocrites do in the synagogues and on the streets, to be honored by men. . . . But when you give to the needy, do not let your left hand know what your right hand is doing, so that your giving may be in secret. Then your Father, who sees what is done in secret, will reward you.

"And when you pray, do not be like the hypocrites, for they love to pray standing in the synagogues and on the street corners to be seen by men. . . . But when you pray, go into your room, close the door and pray to your Father, who is unseen. Then your Father, who sees what is done in secret, will reward you. And when you pray, do not keep on babbling like pagans, for they think they will be heard because of their many words. Do not be like them, for your Father knows what you need before you ask him. . . .

"Do not store up for yourselves treasures on earth, where moth and rust destroy, and where thieves break in and steal. But store up for yourselves treasures in heaven, where moth and rust do not destroy, and where thieves do not break in and steal. For where your treasure is, there your heart will be also. . . .

"So do not worry, saying, 'What shall we eat?' or 'What shall we drink?' or 'What shall we wear?' For the pagans run after all these things, and your heavenly Father knows that you need them. But seek first his kingdom and his righteousness, and all these things will be given to you as well. Therefore do not worry about tomorrow, for tomorrow will worry about itself. Each day has enough trouble of its own.

"Do not judge, or you too will be judged. For in the same way you judge others, you will be judged, and with the measure you use, it will be measured to you.

"Why do you look at the speck of sawdust in your brother's eye and pay no attention to the plank in your own eye? How can you say to your brother, 'Let me take the speck out of your eye,' when all the time there is a plank in your own eye? You hypocrite, first take the plank out of your own eye, and then you will see clearly to remove the speck from your brother's eye. . . .

"Ask and it will be given to you; seek and you will find; knock and the door will be opened to you. For everyone who asks receives; he who seeks finds; and to him who knocks, the door will be opened.

"Enter through the narrow gate. For wide is the gate and broad is the road that leads to destruction, and many enter through it. But small is the gate and narrow the road that leads to life, and only a few find it. . . ."

When Jesus had finished saying these things, the crowds were amazed at his teaching, because he taught as one who had authority, and not as their teachers of the law.

Using the Evidence: The Good Life in Eurasian Civilizations

1. **Making comparisons:** In describing the "good life" or the "good society," what commonalities do you see among these four documents? What differences are apparent? How might the authors of each text respond to the ideas of the others?

2. **Placing texts in context:** In what ways were these texts reacting *against* the conventional wisdom of their times? How was each shaped by the social and political circumstances in which it was composed?

3. **Relating spirituality and behavior:** What is the relationship between religion, which explores the transcendent realm of the gods or the divine, and moral behavior on earth in each of these documents? How does the "good life" relate to politics?

4. **Defining the "good person":** How do each of these texts characterize the superior person or the fully realized human being? How do they define personal virtue?

Visual Sources

Considering the Evidence:
Representations of the Buddha

Buddhism derived from a single individual, Siddhartha Gautama, born in northern India between the sixth and fourth centuries B.C.E. The son of royalty, the young Siddhartha enjoyed a splendid but sheltered upbringing encased in luxury, and his father spared no effort to protect the child from anything painful or difficult. At the age of sixteen, he was married to a beautiful cousin, Yasodhara, who bore him a son thirteen years later. Buddhist tradition tells us that while riding beyond the palace grounds, this curious and lively young man encountered human suffering in the form of an old man, a sick person, and a corpse. Shattered by these revelations of aging, illness, and death, Siddhartha determined to find the cause of such sufferings and a remedy for them. And so, at the age of twenty-nine and on the very day his son was born, the young prince left his luxurious life as well as his wife and child, shed his royal jewels, cut off his hair, and set off on a quest for enlightenment. This act of severing his ties to the attachments of ordinary life is known in Buddhist teaching as the Great Renunciation.

What followed were six years of spiritual experimentation that finally led Siddhartha to an ancient fig tree in northern India, now known as the Bodhi (enlightenment) tree. There, Buddhist sources tell us, he began a forty-nine-day period of intensive meditation that ended with an almost indescribable experience of spiritual realization. Now he was the Buddha, the man who had awakened. For the next forty years, he taught what he had learned, setting in motion the cultural tradition of Buddhism. Over many centuries, the religion evolved as it grew in numbers and intersected with various cultures throughout Asia, including those of China, Japan, Tibet, Korea, and Vietnam.

For almost five centuries after his death, which likely took place in the early fifth century B.C.E., artists represented the Buddha as an empty throne, a horse with no rider, a tree, a wheel, or in some other symbolic way, while largely shunning any depiction of him in human form. Among the most widespread of these early symbolic representations of the Buddha were images of his footprints. Found throughout Buddhist Asia, such footprints indicated the Buddha's spiritual presence and served as a focus for devotion or contemplation. They also reminded his followers that since he had passed into nirvana, he could not be physically present. One Buddhist text declared that those who looked on those footprints "shall be freed from the bonds of error, and conducted upon the Way of Enlightenment."[28]

Visual Source 4.1 shows a footprint image from northwestern India dating probably from the second century C.E. and containing a number of Buddhist symbols. In the center of each footprint is a *dharmachakra*, a wheel-like structure that had long symbolized the Buddha's teaching. Here, it surrounds a lotus flower, representing the Buddha's purity. Near the heel is a three-pronged emblem known as a *triratna*. It symbolizes the three things in which Buddhists can take refuge: the Buddha himself, his teaching, and the *sangha* (the Buddhist community). This particular footprint image also includes in the bottom corners two *yakshis*, Indian female earth spirits suggesting fertility. The position of their hands conveys a respectful greeting.

Visual Source 4.1 Footprints of the Buddha (Courtesy, John Eskenazi Ltd., London. Photo: A. C. Cooper N & P Ltd., London)

■ Why might artists have been reluctant to portray the human figure of the Buddha?

■ Why might the wheel serve as an effective symbol of the Buddha's message?

■ What does the inclusion of the *yakshis* add to the message of this image?

■ What overall religious message might this footprint convey to those who gazed on it?

By the first century C.E., the impulse to depict the Buddha in human form had surfaced, with some of the earliest examples coming from the region of South Asia known as Gandhara in what is now northern Pakistan and eastern Afghanistan (see Map 3.3, p. 127). That area had been a part of the empire of Alexander the Great and his Hellenistic successors from about 322 B.C.E. to 50 B.C.E. and had developed commercial ties to the Roman Empire as well. These early images of the Buddha reflect this Greco-Roman influence, depicting him with a face similar to that of the Greek god Apollo, dressed in a Roman-style toga, and with curly hair characteristic of the Mediterranean region.

Visual Source 4.2, from India of the second or third century C.E., depicts in Gandhara style a famous scene from the life of the Buddha—his temptation by the demon Mara and Mara's seductive daughters while meditating under the Bodhi tree.

■ How are Mara and his daughters, shown on the right, portrayed in this relief?

■ What attitude characterizes the Buddha, shown on the left and surrounded by attendants?

■ Why might Greco-Roman cultural influence have stimulated physical representations of the Buddha?

■ What larger meaning might the Buddha's followers take from this story?

By the time of India's Gupta dynasty (320–550 C.E.), the Greco-Roman influence of the Gandhara style was fading, replaced by more completely Indian images of the Buddha, which became the "classic" model, shown on page 177. Yet, as the message of the Buddha gained a mass following and spread across much of Asia, some of its early features—rigorous and time-consuming meditation practice, a focus on monks and nuns withdrawn from ordinary life, the absence of accessible supernatural figures able to provide help and comfort— proved difficult for many converts. And so the religion adapted. A new form of the faith, Mahayana Buddhism, offered greater accessibility, a spiritual path available to a much wider range of people beyond the monks and ascetics, who were the core group in early Buddhism.

Visual Source 4.2 A Gandhara Buddha (*The Temptation of Buddha by Mara and His Daughters*. India, Gandhara, 100s–200s, gray schist, 73.6 × 57.2 cm. © The Cleveland Museum of Art. Leonard C. Hanna, Jr., Fund 1997.151)

In most expressions of Mahayana Buddhism, enlightenment (or becoming a Buddha), was available to everyone; it was possible within the context of ordinary life, rather than a monastery; and it might occur within a single lifetime rather than over the course of many lives. While Buddhism had originally put a premium on spiritual wisdom, leading to liberation from rebirth and the achievement of nirvana, Mahayana expressions of the faith emphasized compassion—the ability to feel the sorrows of other people as if they were one's own. This compassionate religious ideal found expression in the notion of bodhisattvas, fully enlightened beings who postponed their own final liberation in order to assist a suffering humanity. They were spiritual beings, intermediaries between mortal humans and the Buddhas, whose countless images in sculpture or painting became objects of worship and sources of comfort and assistance to many Buddhists.

Across the world of Asian Mahayana Buddhism, the most widely popular of the many bodhisattva figures was that of Avalokitesvara, known in China as Guanyin and in Japan as Kannon. This Bodhisattva of Compassion, often portrayed as a woman or with distinctly feminine characteristics, was known as the "the one who hears the cries of the world." Calling on him or her for assistance, devotees could be rescued from all kinds of danger and distress. Women, for example, might petition for a healthy child. Moral transformation too was possible. According to the *Lotus Sutra*, a major Mahayana text, "Those who act under the impulse of hatred will, after adoring the Bodhisattva Avalokitesvara, be freed from hatred."

Among the most striking of the many representation of this bodhisattva are those that portray him or her with numerous heads, with which to hear the many cries of a suffering humanity, and with multiple arms to aid them. Visual Source 4.3 provides one illustration of such a figure, the Senju Kannon, from Japan of the eighth century C.E.

- What elements of Buddhist imagery can you identify in this statue?

- To whom might such an image appeal? And why?

- Notice the lotus flower, for centuries a rich Buddhist symbol, on which the bodhisattva is resting. With its roots in the mud, the lotus emerges on the surface of the water as a pure, beautiful, and fragrant flower. Why would the artist choose to place the bodhisattva atop such a flower?

- Some scholars have identified similarities between the Bodhisattva of Compassion and the Virgin Mary in the Christian tradition. What common elements and what differences can you identify?

Beyond numerous bodhisattvas, Mahayana Buddhism also populated the spiritual universe with various Buddhas in addition to the historical Buddha. One of these is the Maitreya Buddha or the Buddha of the future, predicted to

Visual Source 4.3 A Bodhisattva of Compassion: Kannon of 1,000 Arms (From *The Concise History of Japanese Buddhist Sculpture* (*Bijutu Shuppan-sha*). Visual Connection Archive)

appear when the teachings of the historical Buddha have been lost or forgotten. In China, this Buddha of the future was sometimes portrayed as the "laughing Buddha," a fat, smiling, contented figure, said to be modeled on a tenth-century monk named Budai, who wandered the country merrily spreading happiness and good cheer, while evoking contentment and abundance. Visual Source 4.4 illustrates this Chinese Maitreya Buddha together with some of his disciples in a carving, dating to the tenth through fourteenth centuries, in China's Feilai Feng caves.

Visual Source 4.4 The Chinese Maitreya Buddha (© Nazima Kowail/Corbis)

- How does this Buddha image differ, both physically and in its religious implications, from the other Buddhas already discussed in this feature?

- Why might this image be appealing to some Buddhists, and why might others take exception to it?

- In what ways does this figure represent an adaptation of Buddhist imagery to Chinese culture? Consider what you know about Confucian and Daoist postures to the world.

Using the Evidence:
Representations of the Buddha

1. **Tracing change:** What transformations in Buddhist belief and practice are disclosed in these images?

2. **Identifying cultural adaptation:** What evidence do these images provide about the blending of Buddhism into a variety of cultural settings?

3. **Understanding the growth of Buddhism:** What do these images suggest about the appeal of Buddhism to growing numbers of people across Asia?

4. **Considering cultural boundaries:** To what extent are these images meaningful to people outside of the Buddhist tradition? In what ways do they speak to universal human needs or desires? What is specifically Buddhist or Asian about them?

Chapter 4 Wrap Up

LearningCurve
Check what you know.
bedfordstmartins.com
/strayer/LC

STEP ONE

The Word to Know: Syncretism

The *Oxford English Dictionary* defines *syncretism* as "attempted union or reconciliation of diverse or opposite tenets or practices, esp. in philosophy or religion." Using the word syncretism, speculate how the spread of any of the religions discussed in Chapter 4 could result in syncretism of religions in different areas. For example, in Axum, Christian worship integrated African drums, instruments, and other local elements. Your answer should be a paragraph in length.

STEP TWO

Analyzing Data

Using the three timelines on page 119, 167, and 219, as well as the Snapshot on page 168, write a substantial paragraph about the rise and spread of belief systems in the second-wave era, using the questions below. Remember that contextualization refers to the ways in which historical phenomena or processes relate to broader regional, national, or global processes. How does the history of this specific region or era fit into the larger story of world history as a whole?

■ Questions

1. What was happening in the society that encouraged the development of these religious beliefs?

2. These faiths emerged in different ways in different places, all roughly simultaneously but often encountered local challenges as they became adopted. What later legacy would they have as they left their points of origin?

3. What global processes existed that led to the spread of these belief systems? For example, the spread of religious beliefs was possible due to the existence of trade networks. How did this happen?

4. Think about what is included on the Chapter 4 "A Map of Time," p. 167. Based on your understanding of this chapter, what else do you think should be included in the timeline? What more do you need to know about in order to explain the global historical context?

STEP THREE

Syncretism in Buddhist Art

This exercise will help you to understand syncretism, in particular how it influenced Buddhist art. Complete Steps 1–5 and then answer the question that follows.

1. Review Map 4.1, The Spread of Early Christianity and Buddhism, on page 191. How might the spread of both Buddhism and Christianity have influenced religious art?

2. Next, examine the image, Chinese Landscape Paintings, on page 172. How might the physical characteristics of a place have influenced Buddhist art? What religious influences are evident here?

3. How is the image on page 172 similar to or different from the painting of Confucius, baby Buddha, and Laozi on the chapter-opening page 164?

4. Next, consider the variety of Buddhist images in Chapter 4: The Classic Indian Buddha, page 177; Visual Source 4.2, A Gandhara Buddha, page 211; Visual Source 4.3, A Bodhisattva of Compassion, page 213; and Visual Source 4.4, The Chinese Maitreya Buddha, page 214. What characteristics differentiate the various Buddhist images from each other? What are the similarities among them?

5. Consider the following secondary source quote: "The artists at that time incorporated many classical Greek mythologies in their interpretation of the Buddhist legends. They tended to make Buddhist art more realistic, by giving these objects a more humanistic form."[1] In what ways does Visual Source 4.2, page 211 support this quote? Compare Visual Source 4.2 to the Classic Indian Buddha on page 177. What gives Visual Source 4.2 a more human feel?

■ Concluding Question

Based on the visual evidence in Chapter 4, what would you conclude about syncretism in South Asia from 500 B.C.E.–500 C.E.?

Society and Inequality in Eurasia/North Africa

500 B.C.E.–500 C.E.

"Caste has no impact on life today," declared Chezi K. Ganesan in 2010.[1] Certainly Mr. Ganesan's low-caste background as a Nadar, ranking just above the "untouchables," has had little impact on the career of this prosperous high-tech businessman, who shuttles between California's Silicon Valley and the city of Chennai in southern India. Yet his grandfather could not enter Hindu temples, and until the mid-nineteenth century, the women of his caste, as a sign of their low status, were forbidden to cover their breasts in the presence of Brahmin men. But if caste has proven no barrier to Mr. Ganesan, it remains significant for many others in contemporary India. Personal ads for those seeking a marriage partner in many online services often indicate an individual's caste as well as other personal data. Affirmative action programs benefiting low-caste Indians have provoked great controversy and resentment among some upper-caste groups. The brutal murder of an entire Dalit or "untouchable" family in 2006 sparked much soul searching in the India media. So while caste has changed in modern India, it has also persisted. Both the changes and the persistence have a long history.

THE MOST RECENT 250 YEARS OF WORLD HISTORY have called into question social patterns long assumed to be natural and permanent. The French, Russian, and Chinese revolutions challenged and destroyed ancient monarchies and class hierarchies; the abolitionist movement of the nineteenth century attacked slavery, largely unquestioned for millennia; the women's movement has confronted long and deeply

---

Mother and Child: Mothers and their children have been at the core of social life everywhere and a prominent theme of many artistic traditions. This lovely statue comes from the Sunga dynasty, which flourished in northeastern India from about 185–73 B.C.E. after the collapse of the Mauryan Empire. (Réunion des Musées Nationaux/Art Resource, NY) held patriarchal assumptions about the proper relationship between the sexes; and Mahatma Gandhi, during India's struggle for independence in the twentieth century, sought to raise the status of "untouchables," referring to them as Harijan, or "children of God." Nevertheless, caste, class, patriarchy, and even slavery have certainly not vanished from human society, even now. During the era of second-wave civilizations in Eurasia, these patterns of inequality found expressions and generated social tensions that endured well beyond that era.

As Chapter 3 pointed out, millions of individual men and women inhabiting the civilizations of Eurasia and North Africa lived within a political framework of states or empires. They also occupied a world of ideas, religions, and values that derived both from local folkways and from the teaching of the great religious or cultural traditions of these civilizations, as described in Chapter 4. In this chapter, we explore the social arrangements of these civilizations—relationships between rich and poor, powerful and powerless, slaves and free people, and men and women. Those relationships shaped the daily lives and the life chances of everyone and provided the foundation for political authority as well as challenges to it.

Like the First Civilizations, those of the second-wave era were sharply divided along class lines, and they too were patriarchal, with women clearly subordinated to men in most domains of life. In constructing their societies, however, these second-wave civilizations differed substantially from one another. Chinese, Indian, and Mediterranean civilizations provide numerous illustrations of the many and varied ways in which these peoples organized their social lives. The assumptions, tensions, and conflicts accompanying these social patterns provided much of the distinctive character and texture that distinguished these diverse civilizations from one another.

SEEKING THE MAIN POINT

To what extent were the massive inequalities of second-wave civilizations generally accepted, and in what ways were they resisted or challenged?

Society and the State in China

■ **Description**
How would you characterize the social hierarchy of China during the second-wave era?

Chinese society was unique in the ancient world in the extent to which it was shaped by the actions of the state. Nowhere was this more apparent than in the political power and immense social prestige of Chinese state officials, all of them male. For more than 2,000 years, these officials, bureaucrats acting in the name of the emperor both in the capital and in the provinces, represented the cultural and social elite of Chinese civilization. This class had its origins in the efforts of early Chinese rulers to find administrators loyal to the central state rather than to their own families or regions. Philosophers such as Confucius had long advocated selecting such officials on the basis of merit and personal morality rather than birth or wealth. As the Han dynasty established its authority in China around 200 B.C.E., its rulers required each province to send men of promise to the capital, where they were examined and chosen for official positions on the basis of their performance.

A Map of Time

470–400 B.C.E.	Life of Aspasia in Athens
200 B.C.E.–200 C.E.	Laws of Manu prescribing proper social behavior in India
124 B.C.E.	Imperial academy for training Chinese officials established
1st century B.C.E.	Poetry of Buddhist nuns set to writing
73 B.C.E.	Spartacus slave rebellion in Italy
Early 1st century C.E.	Reforming emperor Wang Mang in power in China
45–116 C.E.	Life of Ban Zhou in China
79 C.E.	Eruption of Mt. Vesuvius destroys Pompeii
184 C.E.	Yellow Turban Rebellion in China
After 221 C.E.	Loosening of restrictions on elite Chinese women as Han dynasty collapsed
After 500 C.E.	Slavery replaced by serfdom in Roman world
690–705 C.E.	Empress Wu reigned in China

An Elite of Officials

Over time, this system of selecting administrators evolved into the world's first professional civil service. In 124 B.C.E., Emperor Wu Di established an imperial academy where potential officials were trained as scholars and immersed in texts dealing with history, literature, art, and mathematics, with an emphasis on Confucian teachings. By the end of the Han dynasty, it enrolled some 30,000 students, who were by then subjected to a series of written examinations to select officials of various grades. Private schools in the provinces funneled still more aspiring candidates into this examination system, which persisted until the early twentieth century. In theory open to all men, this system in practice favored those whose families were wealthy enough to provide the years of education required to pass even the lower-level exams. Proximity to the capital and family connections to the imperial court also helped in gaining a position in this highest of Chinese elites. Nonetheless, village communities or a local landowner might sponsor the education of a bright young man from a commoner family, enabling him to enter the charmed circle of officialdom. One rags-to-riches story told of a pig farmer who became an adviser to the emperor himself. Thus the examination system provided a modest measure of social mobility in an otherwise quite hierarchical society.

In later dynasties, that system grew even more elaborate and became an enduring and distinguishing feature of Chinese civilization. During the Tang dynasty, the famous poet and official Po Chu-I (772–846 C.E.) wrote a poem entitled "After Passing the Examination," which shows something of the fame and fortune that awaited an accomplished student as well as the continuing loyalty to family and home that ideally marked those who succeeded:

> For ten years I never left my books,
> I went up . . . and won unmerited praise.
> My high place I do not much prize;
> The joy of my parents will first make me proud.
> Fellow students, six or seven men,
> See me off as I leave the City gate.
> My covered coach is ready to drive away;
> Flutes and strings blend their parting tune.
> Hopes achieved dull the pains of parting;
> Fumes of wine shorten the long road. . . .
> Shod with wings is the horse of him who rides
> On a Spring day the road that leads to home.[2]

Those who made it into the bureaucracy entered a realm of high privilege and great prestige. Senior officials moved about in carriages and were bedecked with robes, ribbons, seals, and headdresses appropriate to their rank. Even lower officials who served in the provinces rather than the capital were distinguished by their polished speech, their cultural sophistication, and their urban manners as well as their political authority. Proud of their learning, they were the bearers, and often the makers, of Chinese culture. "Officials are the leaders of the populace," stated an imperial edict of 144 B.C.E., "and it is right and proper that the carriages they ride in and the robes that they wear should correspond to the degrees of their dignity."[3] Some of these men, particularly in times of political turmoil, experienced tension between their official duties and their personal inclination toward a more withdrawn life of reflective scholarship. (See the Portrait of Ge Hong, pp. 222–23.)

The Landlord Class

Most officials came from wealthy families, and in China wealth meant land. When the Qin dynasty unified China by 210 B.C.E., most land was held by small-scale peasant farmers. But by the first century B.C.E., the pressures of population growth, taxation, and indebtedness had generated a class of large landowners as impoverished peasants found it necessary to sell their lands to more prosperous neighbors. This accumulation of land in sizeable estates was a persistent theme in Chinese history, and one that was frequently, though not very successfully, opposed by state authorities. Landlords of such large estates often were able to avoid paying taxes, thus decreasing state revenues and increasing the tax burden for the remaining peasants. In some cases, they could also mount their own military forces that might challenge the authority of the emperor.

One of the most dramatic state efforts to counteract the growing power of large landowners is associated with Wang Mang, a high court official of the Han dynasty who usurped the emperor's throne in 8 C.E. and immediately launched a series of startling reforms. A firm believer in Confucian good government, Wang Mang saw his reforms as re-creating a golden age of long ago in which small-scale peasant farmers represented the backbone of Chinese society. Accordingly, he ordered the great private estates to be nationalized and divided up among the landless. Government loans to peasant families, limits on the amount of land a family might own, and an end to private slavery were all part of his reform program, but these measures proved impossible to enforce. Opposition from wealthy landowners, nomadic invasions, poor harvests, floods, and famines led to the collapse of Wang Mang's reforms and his assassination in 23 C.E.

Large landowning families, therefore, remained a central feature of Chinese society, although the fate of individual families rose and fell as the wheel of fortune raised them to great prominence or plunged them into poverty and disgrace. As a class, they benefited both from the wealth that their estates generated and from the power and prestige that accompanied their education and their membership in the official elite. The term "scholar-gentry" reflected their twin sources of privilege. With homes in both urban and rural areas, members of the scholar-gentry class lived luxuriously. Multistoried houses, the finest of silk clothing, gleaming carriages, private orchestras, high-stakes gambling—all of this was part of the life of China's scholar-gentry class.

Peasants

Throughout the long course of China's civilization, the vast majority of its population consisted of peasants, living in small households representing two or three generations. Some owned enough land to support their families and perhaps even sell something

on the local market. Many others could barely survive. Nature, the state, and landlords combined to make the life of most peasants extremely vulnerable. Famines, floods, droughts, hail, and pests could wreak havoc without warning. State authorities required the payment of taxes, demanded about a month's labor every year on various public projects, and conscripted young men for military service. During the Han dynasty, growing numbers of impoverished and desperate peasants had to sell out to large landlords and work as tenants or sharecroppers on their estates, where rents could run as high as

Chinese Peasants
For many centuries, the normal activities of Chinese peasant farmers included plowing, planting, and threshing grain, as shown in this painting from China's Song dynasty (960–1279 C.E.). (Mogao Caves, Dunhuang/The Bridgeman Art Library)

Ge Hong, A Chinese Scholar in Troubled Times

Had Ge Hong lived at a different time, he might have pursued the life of a Confucian scholar and civil servant, for he was born to a well-established aristocratic family in southern China. But when he entered the world in 283 C.E., the times were clearly out of joint. The Han dynasty, which had given China four centuries of relative peace and prosperity, had fragmented into a number of competing states. Nomadic peoples invaded and ruled the northern parts of the country. Coups and rebellions were frequent. Many northern Chinese fled south to escape the chaos. The life of Ge Hong illustrates how these larger historical circumstances shaped the life of a single individual.[4]

A solitary scholar in China, such as Ge Hong sought to become. (Saint Louis Art Museum, Missouri, USA / The Bridgeman Art Library)

Ge Hong's family directly experienced the disorder when the family library was destroyed during the repeated wars of the time. Furthermore the family patriarch, Ge Hong's father, died when the young boy was only thirteen years old, an event that brought hardship and a degree of impoverishment to the family. Ge Hong reported later in his autobiography that he had to "walk long distances to borrow books" and that he cut and sold firewood to buy paper and brushes. Nonetheless, like other young men of his class, he received a solid education, reading the classic texts of Confucianism along with history and philosophy.

At about the age of fourteen or fifteen, Ge Hong began to study with the aged Daoist master Zheng Yin. He had to sweep the floor and perform other menial chores for the master while gaining access to rare and precious texts of the esoteric and alchemical arts aimed at creating the "gold elixir" that could promote longevity and transcendence. Withdrawal into an interior life, reflected in both Daoist and Buddhist thought, had a growing appeal to the elite classes of China in response to the political disturbances and disorder of public life. It was the beginning of a lifelong quest for Ge Hong.

And yet the Confucian emphasis on office holding, public service, and moral behavior in society persisted, sending Ge Hong into a series of military positions. Here too was a reflection of the disordered times of his life, for

■ Change
What class conflicts disrupted Chinese society?

one-half to two-thirds of the crop. Other peasants fled, taking to a life of begging or joining gangs of bandits in remote areas.

An eighth-century C.E. Chinese poem by Li Shen reflects poignantly on the enduring hardships of peasant life:

The cob of corn in springtime sown
In autumn yields a hundredfold.
No fields are seen that fallow lie:
And yet of hunger peasants die.
As at noontide they hoe their crops,
Sweat on the grain to earth down drops.
How many tears, how many a groan,
Each morsel on thy dish did mould![5]

in more settled circumstances, young elite men would have disdained military service, favoring a career in the civil bureaucracy. Thus in 303, at the age of twenty, he organized and led a small group of soldiers to crush a local rebellion, later reporting that he alone among military leaders prevented his troops from looting the valuables of the enemy. For his service he received the title of "wave conquering general" and 100 bolts of cloth. "I was the only one," he wrote "to distribute it among my officers, soldiers, and needy friends." At several other points in his life as well, Ge Hong accepted official appointments, some of them honorary and others more substantive.

But his heart lay elsewhere as he yearned for a more solitary and interior life. "Honor, high posts, power, and profit are like sojourning guests," he wrote in his memoir. "They are not worth all the regret and blame, worry and anxiety they cause." Thus he spent long periods of his life in relative seclusion, refusing a variety of official positions. "Unless I abandon worldly affairs," he asked, "how can I practice the tranquil Way?" To Ge Hong, withdrawal was primarily for the purpose of seeking immortality, "to live as long as heaven and earth," a quest given added urgency no doubt by the chaotic world of his own time. In his writings, he explored various techniques for enhancing qi, the vital energy that sustains all life, including breathing exercises, calisthenics, sexual practices, diet, and herbs. But

it was the search for alchemically generated elixirs, especially those containing liquid gold and cinnabar (derived from mercury), that proved most compelling to Ge Hong. Much to his regret, he lacked the resources to obtain and process these rare ingredients.

However, Ge Hong did not totally abandon the Confucian tradition and its search for social order, for he argued in his writings that the moral virtues advocated by China's ancient sage were a necessary prerequisite for attaining immortality. And he found a place in his thinking also for the rewards and punishments of Legalist thinking. Thus he sought to reconcile the three major strands of Chinese thought—Confucianism, Daoism, and Legalism—even as he acknowledged that "my practices are always ill-suited to the times."

Ge Hong spent the last years of his life on the sacred mountain of Luofu in the far south of China, continuing his immortality research until he died in 343 at the age of sixty. When his body was lifted into its coffin, contemporaries reported that it was "exceedingly light as if one were lifting empty clothing."[6] They concluded from this that Ge Hong had in fact achieved transcendence, joining the immortals in everlasting life, as he had so fervently hoped.

Question: In what ways did the larger conditions of China shape the life of Ge Hong?

Such conditions provoked periodic peasant rebellions, which have punctuated Chinese history for over 2,000 years. Toward the end of the second century C.E., wandering bands of peasants began to join together as floods along the Yellow River and resulting epidemics compounded the misery of landlessness and poverty. What emerged was a massive peasant uprising known as the Yellow Turban Rebellion because of the yellow scarves the peasants wore around their heads. (See spot map, p. 224.) That movement, which swelled to about 360,000 armed followers by 184 C.E., found leaders, organization, and a unifying ideology in a popular form of Daoism. Featuring supernatural healings, collective trances, and public confessions of sin, the Yellow Turban movement looked forward to the "Great Peace"—a golden age of equality, social harmony, and common ownership of property. Although the rebellion was suppressed by the military forces of the Han dynasty, the Yellow Turban and other peasant upheavals devastated the economy, weakened the state, and contributed to

Han Empire, c. 100 B.C.E.

Area of Yellow Turban Rebellion

Yellow Turban Rebellion

the overthrow of the dynasty a few decades later. Repeatedly in Chinese history, such peasant movements, often expressed in religious terms, registered the sharp class antagonisms of Chinese society and led to the collapse of more than one ruling dynasty.

Merchants

Peasants were oppressed in China and certainly exploited, but they were also honored and celebrated in the official ideology of the state. In the eyes of the scholar-gentry, peasants were the solid productive backbone of the country, and their hard work and endurance in the face of difficulties were worthy of praise. Merchants, however, did not enjoy such a favorable reputation in the eyes of China's cultural elite. They were widely viewed as unproductive, making a shameful profit from selling the work of others. Stereotyped as greedy, luxury-loving, and materialistic, merchants stood in contrast to the alleged frugality, altruism, and cultured tastes of the scholar-gentry. They were also seen as a social threat, as their ill-gained wealth impoverished others, deprived the state of needed revenues, and fostered resentments.

Such views lay behind periodic efforts by state authorities to rein in merchant activity and to keep them under control. Early in the Han dynasty, merchants were forbidden to wear silk clothing, ride horses, or carry arms. Nor were they permitted to sit for civil service examinations or hold public office. State monopolies on profitable industries such as salt, iron, and alcohol limited merchant opportunities. Later dynasties sometimes forced merchants to loan large sums of money to the state. Despite this active discrimination, merchants frequently became quite wealthy. Some tried to achieve a more respectable elite status by purchasing landed estates or educating their sons for the civil service examinations. Many had backdoor relationships with state officials and landlords who found them useful and were not averse to profiting from business connections with merchants, despite their unsavory reputation.

Class and Caste in India

■ **Description**

What set of ideas underlies India's caste-based society?

India's social organization shared certain broad features with that of China. In both civilizations, birth determined social status for most people; little social mobility was available for the vast majority; sharp distinctions and great inequalities characterized social life; and religious or cultural traditions defined these inequalities as natural, eternal, and ordained by the gods. Despite these similarities, the organization, flavor, and texture of ancient Indian society were distinctive compared to almost all other civilizations. These unique aspects of Indian society have long been embodied in what we now call the caste system, a term that comes from the Portuguese word *casta*, which means "race" or "purity of blood." That social organization emerged over thousands of years and in some respects has endured into modern times.

Caste as Varna

The origins of the caste system are at best hazy. An earlier idea—that caste evolved from a racially defined encounter between light-skinned Aryan invaders and the darker-hued native peoples—has been challenged in recent years, but no clear alternative theory has emerged. Perhaps the best we can say at this point is that the distinctive social system of India grew out of the interactions among South Asia's immensely varied cultures together with the development of economic and social differences among these peoples as the inequalities of "civilization" spread throughout the Ganges River valley and beyond. Notions of race, however, seem less central to the growth of the caste system than those of economic specialization and of culture.

Whatever the precise origins of the caste system, by around 500 B.C.E., the idea that society was forever divided into four ranked classes, or *varnas*, was deeply embedded in Indian thinking. Everyone was born into and remained within one of these classes for life. At the top of this hierarchical system were the Brahmins, priests whose rituals and sacrifices alone could ensure the proper functioning of the world. They were followed by the Kshatriya class, warriors and rulers charged with protecting and governing society. Next was the Vaisya class, originally commoners who cultivated the land. These three classes came to be regarded as pure Aryans and were called the "twice-born," for they experienced not only a physical birth but also formal initiation

into their respective varnas and status as people of Aryan descent. Far below these twice-born in the hierarchy of varna groups were the Sudras, native peoples incorporated into the margins of Aryan society in very subordinate positions. Regarded as servants of their social betters, they were not allowed to hear or repeat the Vedas or to take part in Aryan rituals. So little were they valued that a Brahmin who killed a Sudra was penalized as if he had killed a cat or a dog.

According to varna theory, these four classes were formed from the body of the god Purusha and were therefore eternal and changeless. Although these divisions are widely recognized in India even today, historians have noted considerable social flux in ancient Indian history. Members of the Brahmin and Kshatriya groups, for example, were frequently in conflict over which ranked highest in the

Caste in India

This 1947 photograph from *Life* magazine illustrates the "purity and pollution" thinking that has long been central to the ideology of caste. It shows a high-caste landowner carefully dropping wages wrapped in a leaf into the outstretched hands of his low-caste workers. By avoiding direct physical contact with them, he escapes the ritual pollution that would otherwise ensue. (Margaret Bourke-White/Time Life Pictures/Getty Images)

Snapshot   **Social Life and Duty in Classical India**

Much personal behavior in classical India, at least ideally, was regulated according to caste. Each caste was associated with a particular color, with a part of the body of the god Purusha, and with a set of duties.

Caste (Varna)	Color/Symbolism	Part of Purusha	Duties
Brahmin	white/spirituality	head	priests, teachers
Kshatriya	red/courage	shoulders	warriors, rulers
Vaisya	yellow/wealth	thighs	farmers, merchants, artisans
Sudra	black/ignorance	feet	labor
Untouchables (outside of the varna system; thus no color and not associated with Purusha)	—	—	polluted labor

Beyond caste, behavior was ideally defined in terms of four stages of life, at least for the first three varna groups. Each new stage was marked by a *samskara*, a ritual initiating the person into this new phase of life.

Stage of Life	Duties
Student	Boys live with a teacher (guru); learn Sanskrit, rituals, Vedas; practice obedience, respect, celibacy, nonviolence.
Householder	Marriage and family; men practice caste-based career/occupation; women serve as wives and mothers, perform household rituals and sacrifices, actively support children and elders.
Retirement	Both husband and wife withdraw to the forests following birth of grandchildren; diminished household duties; greater focus on spiritual practice; sex permitted once a month.
Wandering ascetic	Only for men (women return to household); total rejection of ordinary existence; life as wandering hermit without shelter or possessions; caste becomes irrelevant; focus on achieving moksha and avoiding future rebirth.

varna hierarchy, and only slowly did the Brahmins emerge clearly in the top position. Although theoretically purely Aryan, both groups absorbed various tribal peoples as Indian civilization expanded. Tribal medicine men or sorcerers found a place as Brahmins, while warrior groups entered the Kshatriya varna. The Vaisya varna, originally defined as cultivators, evolved into a business class with a prominent place for merchants, while the Sudra varna became the domain of peasant farmers. Finally a whole new category, ranking lower even than the Sudras, emerged in the so-called

untouchables, men and women who did the work considered most unclean and polluting, such as cremating corpses, dealing with the skins of dead animals, and serving
as executioners.

Caste as Jati

As the varna system took shape in India, another set of social distinctions also arose,
based largely on occupations. In India as elsewhere, urban-based civilization gave rise
to specialized occupations, many organized in guilds that regulated their own affairs
in a particular region. Over time, these occupationally based groups, known as *jatis*,
blended with the varna system to create India's unique caste-based society.

■ **Comparison**

What is the difference
between varna and jati
as expressions of caste?

The many thousands of jatis became the primary cell of India's social life beyond
the family or household, but each of them was associated with one of the great
classes (varnas). Thus Brahmins were divided into many separate jatis, or subcastes, as
were each of the other varnas as well as the untouchables. In a particular region or
village, each jati was ranked in a hierarchy known to all, from the highest of the
Brahmins to the lowest of the untouchables. Marriage and eating together were
permitted only within an individual's own jati. Each jati was associated with a particular set of duties, rules, and obligations, which defined its members' unique and
separate place in the larger society. Brahmins, for example, were forbidden to eat
meat, while Kshatriyas were permitted to do so. Upper-caste women covered their
breasts, while some lower-caste women were forbidden this privilege as a sign of their
subordination. "It is better to do one's own duty badly than another's well"—this
frequently quoted saying summed up the underlying idea of Indian society.

With its many separate, distinct, and hierarchically ranked social groups, Indian
society was quite different from that of China or the Greco-Roman world. It was also
unique in the set of ideas that explained and justified that social system. Foremost
among them was the notion of ritual purity and pollution applied to caste groups.
Brahmins or other high-caste people who came in contact with members of lower
castes, especially those who cleaned latrines, handled corpses, or butchered and skinned
dead animals, were in great danger of being polluted, or made ritually unclean. Thus
untouchables were forbidden to use the same wells or to enter the temples designated
for higher-caste people. Sometimes they were required to wear a wooden clapper to
warn others of their approach. A great body of Indian religious writing defined various forms of impurity and the ritual means of purification.

A further support for this idea of inherent inequality and permanent difference
derived from emerging Hindu notions of *karma*, *dharma*, and rebirth. Being born
into a particular caste was generally regarded as reflecting the good or bad deeds
(karma) of a previous life. Thus an individual's prior actions were responsible for his
or her current status. Any hope for rebirth in a higher caste rested on the faithful
and selfless performance of one's present caste duties (dharma) in this life. Doing so
contributed to spiritual progress by subduing the relentless demands of the ego.
Such teachings, like that of permanent impurity, provided powerful sanctions for the

inequalities of Indian society. So too did the threat of social ostracism because each jati had the authority to expel members who violated its rules. No greater catastrophe could befall a person than this, for it meant the end of any recognized social life and the loss of all social support.

As caste restrictions tightened, it became increasingly difficult—virtually impossible—for individuals to raise their social status during their lifetimes. However, another kind of upward mobility enabled entire jatis, over several generations, to raise their standing in the local hierarchy of caste groups. By acquiring land or wealth, by adopting the behaviors of higher-caste groups, by finding some previously overlooked "ancestor" of a higher caste, a particular jati might slowly be redefined in a higher category. India's caste system was in practice rather more fluid and changing than the theory of caste might suggest.

India's social system thus differed from that of China in several ways. It gave priority to religious status and ritual purity (the Brahmins), whereas China elevated political officials to the highest of elite positions. The caste system divided Indian society into vast numbers of distinct social groups; China had fewer, but broader, categories of society—scholar-gentry, landlords, peasants, merchants. Finally, India's caste society defined these social groups far more rigidly and with even less opportunity for social mobility than in China.

The Functions of Caste

This caste-based social structure shaped India's emerging civilization in various ways. Because caste (jati) was a very local phenomenon, rooted in particular regions or villages, it focused the loyalties of most people on a quite restricted territory and weakened the appeal or authority of larger all-Indian states. This localization is one reason that India, unlike China, seldom experienced an empire that encompassed the entire subcontinent (see Chapter 3, pp. 141–43). Caste, together with the shared culture of a diverse Hinduism, provided a substitute for the state as an integrative mechanism for Indian civilization. It offered a distinct and socially recognized place for almost everyone. In looking after widows, orphans, and the destitute, jatis provided a modest measure of social security and support. Even the lowest-ranking jatis had the right to certain payments from the social superiors whom they served.

Furthermore, caste represented a means of accommodating the many migrating or invading peoples who entered the subcontinent. The cellular, or honeycomb, structure of caste society allowed various peoples, cultures, and traditions to find a place within a larger Indian civilization while retaining something of their unique identity. The process of assimilation was quite different in China where it meant becoming Chinese ethnically, linguistically, and culturally. Finally, India's caste system facilitated the exploitation of the poor by the wealthy and powerful. The multitude of separate groups into which it divided the impoverished and oppressed majority of the population made class consciousness and organized resistance across caste lines much more difficult to achieve.

SUMMING UP SO FAR

How did India's caste system differ from China's class system?

Slavery: The Case of the Roman Empire

Beyond the inequalities of class and caste lay those of slavery, a social institution with deep roots in human history. Some have suggested that the early domestication of animals provided the model for enslaving people.[7] Certainly slave owners have everywhere compared their slaves to tamed animals. Aristotle, for example, observed that the ox is "the poor man's slave." War, patriarchy, and the notion of private property, all of which accompanied the First Civilizations, also contributed to the growth of slavery. Large-scale warfare generated numerous prisoners, and everywhere in the ancient world capture in war meant the possibility of enslavement. Early records suggest that women captives were the first slaves, usually raped and then enslaved as concubines, whereas male captives were killed. Patriarchal societies, in which men sharply controlled and perhaps even "owned" women, may have suggested the possibility of using other people, men as well as women, as slaves. The class inequalities of early civilizations, which were based on great differences in privately owned property, also made it possible to imagine people owning other people.

Slavery and Civilization

Whatever its precise origins, slavery generally meant ownership by a master, the possibility of being sold, working without pay, and the status of an "outsider" at the bottom of the social hierarchy. For most, it was a kind of "social death,"[8] for slaves usually lacked any rights or independent personal identity recognized by the larger society. By the time Hammurabi's law code casually referred to Mesopotamian slavery (around 1750 B.C.E.), it was already a long-established tradition in the region and in all of the First Civilizations. Likewise, virtually all subsequent civilizations—in the Americas, Africa, and Eurasia—practiced some form of slavery.

■ **Comparison**

How did the inequalities of slavery differ from those of caste?

Slave systems throughout history have varied considerably. In some times and places, such as ancient Greece and Rome, a fair number of slaves might be emancipated in their own lifetimes, through the generosity or religious convictions of their owners, or to avoid caring for them in old age, or by allowing slaves to purchase their freedom with their own funds. In some societies, the children of slaves inherited the status of their parents, while in others, such as the Aztec Empire, they were considered free people. Slaves likewise varied considerably in the labor they were required to do, with some working for the state in high positions, others performing domestic duties in their owner's household, and still others toiling in fields or mines in large work gangs.

The second-wave civilizations of Eurasia differed considerably in the prominence and extent of slavery in their societies. In China, it was a minor element, amounting to perhaps 1 percent of the population. Convicted criminals and their families, confiscated by the government and sometimes sold to wealthy private individuals, were among the earliest slaves in Han dynasty China. In desperate circumstances, impoverished or indebted peasants might sell their children into slavery. In southern China, teenage boys of poor families could be purchased by the wealthy, for whom they served as status symbols. Chinese slavery, however, was never very widespread and did not become a major source of labor for agriculture or manufacturing.

In India as well, people could fall into slavery as criminals, debtors, or prisoners of war and served their masters largely in domestic settings, but religious writings and secular law offered, at least in theory, some protection for slaves. Owners were required to provide adequately for their slaves and were forbidden to abandon them in old age. According to one ancient text, "a man may go short himself or stint his wife and children, but never his slave who does his dirty work for him."[9] Slaves in India could inherit and own property and earn money in their spare time. A master who raped a slave woman was required to set her free and pay compensation. The law encouraged owners to free their slaves and allowed slaves to buy their freedom. All of this suggests that Indian slavery was more restrained than that of other ancient civilizations. Nor did Indian civilization depend economically on slavery, for most work was performed by lower-caste, though free, men and women.

The Making of Roman Slavery

■ **Comparison**

How did Greco-Roman slavery differ from that of other classical civilizations?

In sharp contrast to other second-wave civilizations, slavery played an immense role in the Mediterranean, or Western, world. Although slavery was practiced in Chinese, Indian, and Persian civilizations, in the Greco-Roman world society was based on slavery. By a conservative estimate, classical Athens alone was home to perhaps 60,000 slaves, or about one-third of the total population. In Athens, ironically, the growth of democracy and status as a free person were defined and accompanied by the simultaneous growth of slavery on a mass scale. The greatest of the Greek philosophers, Aristotle, developed the notion that some people were "slaves by nature" and should be enslaved for their own good and for that of the larger society.

"The ancient Greek attitude toward slavery was simple," writes one modern scholar. "It was a terrible thing to become a slave, but a good thing to own a slave."[10] Even poor households usually had at least one or two female slaves, providing domestic work and sexual services for their owners. Although substantial numbers of Greek slaves were granted freedom by their owners, they usually did not become citizens or gain political rights. Nor could they own land or marry

Roman Slavery
This Roman mosaic from the third century C.E. shows the slave Myro serving a drink to his master, Fructus. (The Art Archive at Art Resource, NY)

citizens, and particularly in Athens they had to pay a special tax. Their status remained "halfway between slavery and freedom."[11]

Practiced on an even larger scale, slavery was a defining element of Roman society. By the time of Christ, the Italian heartland of the Roman Empire had some 2 to 3 million slaves, representing 33 to 40 percent of the population.[12] Not until the modern slave societies of the Caribbean, Brazil, and the southern United States was slavery practiced again on such an enormous scale. Wealthy Romans could own many hundreds or even thousands of slaves. (See Visual Source 5.2, p. 254.) One woman in the fifth century C.E. freed 8,000 slaves when she withdrew into a life of Christian monastic practice. Even people of modest means frequently owned two or three slaves. In doing so, they confirmed their own position as free people, demonstrated their social status, and expressed their ability to exercise power. Slaves and former slaves also might be slave owners. One freedman during the reign of Augustus owned 4,116 slaves at the time of his death.

The vast majority of Roman slaves had been prisoners captured in the many wars that accompanied the creation of the empire. In 146 B.C.E., following the destruction of the North African city of Carthage, some 55,000 people were enslaved en masse. From all over the Mediterranean basin, men and women were funneled into the major slave-owning regions of Italy and Sicily. Pirates also furnished slaves, kidnapping tens of thousands and selling them to Roman slave traders on the island of Delos. Roman merchants purchased still other slaves through networks of long-distance commerce extending to the Black Sea, the East African coast, and northwestern Europe. The supply of slaves also occurred through natural reproduction, as the children of slave mothers were regarded as slaves themselves. Such "home-born" slaves had a certain prestige and were thought to be less troublesome than those who had known freedom earlier in their lives. Finally, abandoned or exposed children could legally become the slave of anyone who rescued them.

Unlike American slavery of later times, Roman practice was not identified with a particular racial or ethnic group. Egyptians, Syrians, Jews, Greeks, Gauls, North Africans, and many other people found themselves alike enslaved. From within the empire and its adjacent regions, an enormous diversity of people were bought and sold at Roman slave markets.

Like slave owners everywhere, Romans regarded their slaves as "barbarians"—lazy, unreliable, immoral, prone to thieving—and came to think of certain peoples, such as Asiatic Greeks, Syrians, and Jews, as slaves by nature. Nor was there any serious criticism of slavery in principle, although on occasion owners were urged to treat their slaves in a more benevolent way. Even the triumph of Christianity within the Roman Empire did little to undermine slavery, for Christian teaching held that slaves should be "submissive to [their] masters with all fear, not only to the good and gentle, but also to the harsh."[13] In fact, Saint Paul used the metaphor of slavery to describe the relationship of believers to God, styling them as "slaves of Christ," while Saint Augustine (354–430 C.E.) described slavery as God's punishment for sin. Thus slavery was deeply embedded in the religious thinking and social outlook of elite Romans.

Similarly, slavery was entrenched throughout the Roman economy. No occupation was off-limits to slaves except military service, and no distinction existed between jobs for slaves and those for free people. Frequently they labored side by side. In rural areas, slaves provided much of the labor force on the huge estates, or *latifundia*, which produced grain, olive oil, and wine, mostly for export, much like the later plantations in the Americas. There they often worked chained together. In the cities, slaves worked in their owners' households, but also as skilled artisans, teachers, doctors, business agents, entertainers, and actors. In the empire's many mines and quarries, slaves and criminals labored under brutal conditions. Slaves in the service of the emperor provided manpower for the state bureaucracy, maintained temples and shrines, and kept Rome's water supply system functioning. Trained in special schools, they also served as gladiators in the violent spectacles of Roman public life. Female slaves usually served as domestic servants but were also put to work in brothels, served as actresses and entertainers, and could be used sexually by their male owners. Thus slaves were represented among the highest and most prestigious occupations and in the lowest and most degraded.

Slave owners in the Roman Empire were supposed to provide the necessities of life to their slaves. When this occurred, slaves may have had a more secure life than was available to impoverished free people, who had to fend for themselves, but the price of this security was absolute subjection to the will of the master. Beatings, sexual abuse, and sale to another owner were constant possibilities. Lacking all rights in the law, slaves could not legally marry, although many contracted unofficial unions. Slaves often accumulated money or possessions, but such property legally belonged to their masters and could be seized at any time. If a slave murdered his master, Roman law demanded the lives of all of the victim's slaves. When one Roman official was killed by a slave in 61 C.E., every one of his 400 slaves was condemned to death. For an individual slave, the quality of life depended almost entirely on the character of the master. Brutal owners made it a living hell. Benevolent owners made life tolerable and might even grant favored slaves their freedom or permit them to buy that freedom. As in Greece, manumission of slaves was a widespread practice, and in the Roman Empire, unlike Greece, freedom was accompanied by citizenship.

Resistance and Rebellion

Roman slaves, like their counterparts in other societies, responded to enslavement in many ways. Most, no doubt, did what was necessary to survive, but there are recorded cases of Roman prisoners of war who chose to commit mass suicide rather than face the horrors of slavery. Others, once enslaved, resorted to the "weapons of the weak"—small-scale theft, sabotage, pretending illness, working poorly, and placing curses on their masters. Fleeing to the anonymous crowds of the city or to remote rural areas prompted owners to post notices in public places, asking for information about their runaways. Catching runaway slaves became an organized private business. Occasional murders of slave owners made masters conscious of the dangers they faced. "Every slave we own is an enemy we harbor" ran one Roman saying.[14]

On several notable occasions, the slaves themselves rose in rebellion. The most famous uprising occurred in 73 B.C.E. when a slave gladiator named Spartacus led seventy other slaves from a school for gladiators in a desperate bid for freedom. The surprising initial success of their revolt attracted a growing following of rebellious slaves, numbering perhaps 120,000 men, women, and children at the height of the uprising. For two years, they set Italy ablaze. In a dramatic reversal of roles, they crucified some captured slave owners and set others to fighting one another in the style of gladiators. Following a series of remarkable military victories, the movement split and eventually succumbed to the vastly superior numbers of the Roman legions. A terrible vengeance followed as some 6,000 rebel slaves were nailed to crosses along the Appian Way from Rome to Capua, where the revolt had begun.

The Rebellion of Spartacus

Nothing on the scale of the Spartacus rebellion occurred again in the Western world of slavery until the Haitian Revolution of the 1790s. But Haitian rebels sought the creation of a new society free of slavery altogether. None of the Roman slave rebellions, including that of Spartacus, had any such overall plan or goal. They simply wanted to escape Roman slavery themselves. Although rebellions created a perpetual fear in the minds of slave owners, slavery itself was hardly affected.

Comparing Patriarchies

Social inequality was embedded not only in the structures of class, caste, and slavery, but also in the gender systems of second-wave civilizations, as the patriarchies of the First Civilizations (see Chapter 2, pp. 62–68) were replicated and elaborated in those that followed. Until quite recently, women's subordination in all civilizations has been so widespread and pervasive that historians have been slow to recognize that gender systems had a history, changing over time. New agricultural technologies, the rise or decline of powerful states, the incorporation of world religions, interaction with culturally different peoples — all of these developments and more generated significant change in understandings of what was appropriate masculine and feminine behavior. Most often, patriarchies were lighter and less restrictive for women in the early years of a civilization's development and during times of upheaval, when established patterns of male dominance were disrupted.

Furthermore, women were often active agents in the histories of their societies, even while largely accepting their overall subordination. As the central figures in family life, they served as repositories and transmitters of their peoples' culture. Some were able to occupy unorthodox and occasionally prominent positions outside the home as scholars, religious functionaries, managers of property and participants in commerce, and even as rulers or military leaders. In Britain, Egypt, and Vietnam, for example, women led efforts to resist their countries' incorporation into the Roman or Chinese empires. (See, for example, the Portrait of Trung Trac, p. 134 and the statue of Boudica, p. 132.) Both Buddhist and Christian nuns carved out small domains of relative freedom from male control. But these changes or challenges to male dominance occurred within a patriarchal framework, and nowhere did they evolve out of or beyond that framework. Thus a kind of "patriarchal equilibrium" ensured the long-term persistence of women's subordination despite fluctuations and notwithstanding various efforts to redefine gender roles or push against gendered expectations.[15]

Nor was patriarchy everywhere the same. Restrictions on women were far sharper in urban-based civilizations than in those pastoral or agricultural societies that lay beyond the reach of cities and empires. The degree and expression of patriarchy also varied from one civilization to another, as the discussion of Mesopotamia and Egypt in Chapter 2 illustrated. And within particular civilizations, elite women both enjoyed privileges and suffered the restrictions of seclusion in the home to a much greater extent than their lower-class counterparts whose economic circumstances required them to operate in the larger social arena. (See Documents: Patriarchy and Women's Voices, pp. 243–51, for various expressions of and reactions to patriarchy across Eurasia.) China provides a fascinating example of how patriarchy changed over time, while the contrasting patriarchies of Athens and Sparta illustrate clear variations even within the much smaller world of Greek civilization.

A Changing Patriarchy: The Case of China

■ **Change**
In what ways did the expression of Chinese patriarchy change over time, and why did it change?

As Chinese civilization took shape during the Han dynasty, elite thinking about gender issues became more explicitly patriarchal, more clearly defined, and linked to an emerging Confucian ideology (see Document 4.1, pp. 198–200). Long-established patterns of thinking in terms of pairs of opposites were now described in gendered and unequal terms. The superior principle of *yang* was viewed as masculine and related to heaven, rulers, strength, rationality, and light, whereas *yin*, the lower feminine principle, was associated with the earth, subjects, weakness, emotion, and darkness. Thus female inferiority was permanent and embedded in the workings of the universe.

What this meant more practically was spelled out repeatedly over the centuries in various Confucian texts. Two notions in particular summarized the ideal position of women, at least in the eyes of elite male writers. The adage "Men go out, women stay in" emphasized the public and political roles of men in contrast to the domestic and private domain of women. A second idea, known as the "three obediences," emphasized a woman's subordination first to her father, then to her husband, and finally to her son. "Why is it," asked one text, "that according to the rites the man takes his wife, whereas the woman leaves her house [to join her husband's family]? It is because the *yin* is lowly, and should not have the initiative; it proceeds to the *yang* in order to be completed."[16]

The Chinese woman writer and court official Ban Zhao (45–116 C.E.) (see pp. 171 and Document 5.1, p. 244–46) observed that the ancients had practiced three customs when a baby girl was born. She was placed below the bed to show that she was "lowly and weak," required always to "humble herself before others." Then she was given a piece of broken pottery to play with, signifying that "her primary duty [was] to be industrious." Finally, her birth was announced to the ancestors with an offering to indicate that she was responsible for "the continuation of [ancestor] worship in the home."[17]

Chinese Women Musicians
This tenth-century rendering by the painter Gu Hongzhong shows these upper-class women serving as musicians for a high official of a Tang dynasty emperor. It was titled *The Night Revels of Han Xizai*. The painter was apparently sent by the emperor to spy on the suspicious behavior of the minister, who in various tellings was suspected of either rebellion or undignified activity. (Werner Forman/Art Resource, NY)

Yet such notions of passivity, inferiority, and subordination were not the whole story of women's lives in ancient China. A few women, particularly the wives, concubines, or widows of emperors, were able on occasion to exercise considerable political authority. Several others led peasant rebellions. In doing so, they provoked much anti-female hostility on the part of male officials, who understood governance as a masculine task and often blamed the collapse of a dynasty or natural disasters on the "unnatural" and "disruptive" influence of women in political affairs. Others, however, praised women of virtue as wise counselors to their fathers, husbands, and rulers and depicted them positively as active agents.[18]

Within her husband's family, a young woman was clearly subordinate as a wife and daughter-in-law, but as a mother of sons, she was accorded considerable honor for her role in producing the next generation of male heirs to carry on her husband's lineage. When her sons married, she was able to exercise the significant authority of a mother-in-law. Furthermore, a woman, at least in the upper classes, often brought with her a considerable dowry, which was regarded as her own property and gave her some leverage within her marriage. Women's roles in the production of textiles, often used to pay taxes or to sell commercially, made her labor quite valuable to the family economy. And a man's wife was sharply distinguished from his concubines, for she was legally mother to all her husband's children. Furthermore, peasant women could hardly follow the Confucian ideal of seclusion in the home as their labor was required in the fields. Thus women's lives were more complex and varied than the prescriptions of Confucian orthodoxy might suggest.

Much changed in China following the collapse of the Han dynasty in the third century C.E. Centralized government vanished amid much political fragmentation

Chinese Women at Work
For a long time, the spinning and weaving of cloth were part of women's domestic work in China. So too was fishing, as illustrated by the woman at the bottom right of this Chinese painting. (Palace Museum, Beijing/Cultural Relics Press)

and conflict. Confucianism, the main ideology of Han China, was discredited, while Daoism and Buddhism attracted a growing following. Pastoral and nomadic peoples invaded northern China and ruled a number of the small states that had replaced the Han government. These new conditions resulted in some loosening of the strict patriarchy of Han dynasty China over the next five or six centuries.

The cultural influence of nomadic peoples, whose women were far less restricted than those of China, was noticed, and criticized, by more Confucian-minded male observers. One of them lamented the sad deterioration of gender roles under the influence of nomadic peoples:

> In the north of the Yellow river it is usually the wife who runs the household. She will not dispense with good clothing or expensive jewelry. The husband has to settle for old horses and sickly servants. The traditional niceties between husband and wife are seldom observed, and from time to time he even has to put up with her insults.[19]

Others criticized the adoption of nomadic styles of dress, makeup, and music. By the time of the Tang dynasty (618–907), writers and artists depicted elite women as capable of handling legal and business affairs on their own and on occasion riding horses and playing polo, bareheaded and wearing men's clothing. Tang legal codes even recognized a married daughter's right to inherit property from her family of birth. Such images of women were quite different from those of Han dynasty China.

A further sign of a weakening patriarchy and the cause of great distress to advocates of Confucian orthodoxy lay in the unusual reign of Empress Wu (r. 690–705 C.E.), a former high-ranking concubine in the imperial court, who came to power amid much palace intrigue and was the only woman ever to rule China with the title of emperor. With the support of China's growing Buddhist establishment, Empress Wu governed despotically, but she also consolidated China's civil service examination system for the selection of public officials and actively patronized scholarship and the arts. Some of her actions seem deliberately designed to elevate the position of women. She commissioned the biographies of famous women, decreed that the mourning period for mothers be made equal to that for fathers, and ordered the creation of a Chinese character for "human being" that suggested the process of birth flowing from one woman without a prominent male role. Her reign was brief and unrepeated.

The growing popularity of Daoism provided new images of the feminine and new roles for women. Daoist texts referred to the *dao* as "mother" and urged the traditionally feminine virtues of yielding and passive acceptance rather than the male-oriented striving of Confucianism. Daoist sects often featured women as priests, nuns, or reclusive meditators, able to receive cosmic truth and to use it for the benefit of others. A variety of female deities from Daoist or Buddhist traditions found a place in Chinese village religion,[20] while growing numbers of women found an alternative to family life in Buddhist monasteries. None of this meant an end to patriarchy, but it does suggest some change in the tone and expression of that patriarchy. However, during the Song dynasty that followed, a more restrictive patriarchy reemerged. (See Chapter 8.)

Contrasting Patriarchies: Athens and Sparta

The patriarchies of second-wave civilizations not only fluctuated over time but also varied considerably from place to place. Nowhere is this variation more apparent than in the contrasting cases of Athens and Sparta, two of the leading city-states of Greek civilization (see Map 3.2, p. 123). Even within this small area, the opportunities available to women and the restrictions imposed on them differed substantially. Although Athens has been celebrated as a major expression of democracy and rationalism, its posture toward women was far more restrictive than that of the highly militaristic and much less democratic Sparta.

■ Comparison

How did the patriarchies of Athens and Sparta differ from each other?

In the several centuries between about 700 and 400 B.C.E., as the free male citizens of Athens moved toward unprecedented participation in political life, the city's women experienced growing limitations. They had no role whatsoever in the assembly, the councils, or the juries of Athens, which were increasingly the focus of life for free men. In legal matters, women had to be represented by a guardian, and court proceedings did not even refer to them by name, but only as someone's wife or mother.

Greek thinkers, especially Aristotle, provided a set of ideas that justified women's exclusion from public life and their general subordination to men. According to Aristotle, "a woman is, as it were, an infertile male. She is female in fact on account of a kind of inadequacy." That inadequacy lay in her inability to generate sperm, which contained the "form" or the "soul" of a new human being. Her role in the reproductive process was passive, providing a receptacle for the vital male contribution. Compared often to children or domesticated animals, women were associated with instinct and passion and lacked the rationality to take part in public life. "It is the best for all tame animals to be ruled by human beings," wrote Aristotle. "In the same way, the relationship between the male and the female is by nature such that the male is higher, the female lower, that the male rules and the female is ruled."[21]

As in China, elite Athenian women were expected to remain inside the home, except perhaps for religious festivals or funerals. Even within the home, women's space was quite separate from that of men. Although poorer women, courtesans, and prostitutes had to leave their homes to earn money, collect water, or shop, ideal behavior for upper-class women assigned these tasks to slaves or to men and involved a radical segregation of male and female space. "What causes women a bad reputation," wrote

A Woman of Athens

This grave stele from about 400 B.C.E. marked the final resting place of Hegeso, a wealthy Athenian woman, shown in the women's quarter of a Greek home examining her jewelry, perhaps for the last time, while attended by her slave. The domestic setting of this grave marker contrasts with that common for men, which usually showed them as warriors in a public space. (Marie Mauzy/Art Resource, NY)

the Greek playwright Euripides in *The Trojan Women*, "is not remaining inside."

Within the domestic realm, Athenian women were generally married in their mid-teens to men ten to fifteen years older than themselves. Their main function was the management of domestic affairs and the production of sons who would become active citizens. These sons were expected to acquire a literate education, while their sisters were normally limited to learning spinning, weaving, and other household tasks. The Greek writer Menander exclaimed: "Teaching a woman to read and write? What a terrible thing to do! Like feeding a vile snake on more poison." Nor did women have much economic power. Although they could own personal property obtained through dowry, gifts, or inheritance, land was usually passed through male heirs. By law, women were forbidden to buy or sell land and could negotiate contracts only if the sum involved was valued at less than a bushel of barley.

There were exceptions, although rare, to the restricted lives of upper-class Athenian women, the most notable of which was Aspasia (ca. 470–400 B.C.E.). She was born in the Greek city of Miletus, on the western coast of Anatolia, to a wealthy family that believed in educating its daughters. As a young woman, Aspasia found her way to Athens, where her foreign birth gave her somewhat more freedom than was normally available to the women of that city. She soon attracted the attention of Pericles, Athens's leading political figure. The two lived together as husband and wife until Pericles' death in 429 B.C.E., although they were not officially married. Treated as an equal partner by Pericles, Aspasia proved to be a learned and witty conversationalist who moved freely in the cultured circles of Athens. Her foreign birth and her apparent influence on Pericles provoked critics to suggest that she was a *hetaera*, a professional, educated, high-class entertainer and sexual companion, similar to a Japanese geisha. Although little is known about Aspasia, a number of major Athenian writers commented about her, both positively and negatively. She was, by all accounts, a rare and remarkable woman in a city that offered little opportunity for individuality or achievement to its female population.

The evolution of Sparta differed in many ways from that of Athens. Early on, Sparta solved the problem of feeding a growing population not by creating overseas colonies as did many Greek city-states, but by conquering their immediate neighbors and reducing them to a status of permanent servitude, not far removed from slavery. Called helots, these dependents far outnumbered the free citizens of Sparta and represented a permanent threat of rebellion. Solving this problem shaped Spartan society decisively. Sparta's answer was a militaristic regime, constantly ready for war to keep the helots in their place. To maintain such a system, all boys were removed from their families at the age of seven to be trained by the state in military camps, where they learned the ways of war. There they remained until the age of thirty. The ideal Spartan male was a warrior, skilled in battle, able to endure hardship, and willing to die for his city. Mothers are said to have told their sons departing for battle to "come back with your shield . . . or on it." Although economic equality for men was the ideal, it was never completely realized in practice. And unlike Athens, political power was exercised primarily by a small group of wealthy men.

This militaristic and far-from-democratic system had implications for women that, strangely enough, offered them greater freedoms and fewer restrictions. As in many warrior societies, their central task was reproduction—bearing warrior sons for Sparta. To strengthen their bodies for childbearing, girls were encouraged to take part in sporting events—running, wrestling, throwing the discus and javelin, even driving chariots. At times, women and men alike competed in the nude before mixed audiences. Their education, like that of boys, was prescribed by the state, which also insisted that newly married women cut their hair short, unlike adult Greek women elsewhere. Thus Spartan women were not secluded or segregated, as were their Athenian counterparts.

Furthermore, Spartan young women, unlike those of Athens, usually married men of their own age, about eighteen years old, thus putting the new couple on a more equal basis. Marriage often began with a trial period to make sure the new couple could produce children, with divorce and remarriage readily available if they could not. Because men were so often away at war or preparing for it, women exercised much more authority in the household than was the case in Athens.

It is little wonder that the freedom of Spartan women appalled other Greeks, who believed that it undermined good order and state authority. Aristotle complained that the more egalitarian inheritance practices of Spartans led to their women controlling some 40 percent of landed estates. In Sparta, he declared, women "live in every sort of intemperance and luxury" and "the [male] rulers are ruled by women." Plutarch, a Greek writer during the heyday of the Roman Empire, observed critically that "the men of Sparta always obeyed their wives." The clothing worn by Spartan women to give them greater freedom of movement seemed immodest to other Greeks.

Nonetheless, in another way, Sparta may have been more restrictive than Athens and other Greek city-states, particularly in its apparent prohibition of homosexuality. At least this was the assertion of the

A Girl of Sparta
This figurine portrays a young female Spartan athlete or runner. Compare her clothing with that worn by Hegeso on page 238. (British Museum, London/The Bridgeman Art Library)

Athenian writer Xenophon (427–355 B.C.E.), who stated that Sparta's legendary founder Lycurgus "caused lovers to abstain from sexual intercourse with boys."[22] Elsewhere, however, homoerotic relationships were culturally approved and fairly common for both men and women, although this did not prevent their participants from entering heterosexual marriages as well. The ideal homosexual relationship — between an older man and a young adolescent boy — was viewed as limited in time, for it was supposed to end when the boy's beard began to grow. Unlike contemporary Western societies where sexuality is largely seen as an identity, the ancient Greeks viewed sexual choice more casually and as a matter of taste.

Sparta clearly was a patriarchy, with women serving as breeding machines for its military system and lacking any formal role in public life, but it was a lighter patriarchy than that of Athens. The joint efforts of men and women seemed necessary to maintain a huge class of helots in permanent subjugation. Death in childbirth was considered the equivalent of death in battle, for both contributed to the defense of Sparta, and both were honored alike. In Athens, on the other hand, growing freedom and democracy were associated with the strengthening of the male-dominated, property-owning household, and within that household, the cornerstone of Athenian society, men were expected to exercise authority. Doing so required increasingly severe limitations and restrictions on the lives of women. Together, the cases of Athens and Sparta illustrate how the historical record appears in a different light when viewed through the lens of gender. Athens, so celebrated for its democracy and philosophical rationalism, offered little to its women, whereas Sparta, often condemned for its militarism and virtual enslavement of the helots, provided a somewhat wider scope for the free women of the city.

LearningCurve
bedfordstmartins.com
/strayer/LC

Reflections: Arguing with Solomon and the Buddha

"What has been will be again . . . there is nothing new under the sun." Recorded in the Old Testament book of Ecclesiastes and generally attributed to King Solomon, this was a despairing view about the essential changelessness and futility of human life. In contrast, central to Buddhist teachings has been the concept of "impermanence" — the notion that "everything changes; nothing remains without change." These observations were intended to point to other levels of reality that lay beyond the dreary constancy or the endless changeability of this world. For students of history, however, these comments from Solomon and the Buddha serve to focus attention on issues of change and continuity in the historical record of second-wave Eurasian civilizations. What is more impressive — the innovations and changes or the enduring patterns and lasting features of these civilizations?

Clearly there were some new things under the sun, even if they had roots in earlier times. The Greek conquest of the Persian Empire under the leadership of Alexander the Great was both novel and unexpected. The Roman Empire encompassed the entire Mediterranean basin in a single political system for the first time. Buddhism and Christianity emerged as new, distinct, and universal religious traditions, although both bore the marks of their origin in Hindu and Jewish religious thinking respectively. The collapse of dynasties, empires, and civilizations long thought to be solidly entrenched—the Chinese and Roman, for example—must surely have seemed to people of the time as something new. Historians therefore might take issue with Solomon's dictum, should we seek to apply it to the history of the second-wave era.

Students of the past might also argue a little with the Buddha and his insistence on the "impermanence" of everything. Much that was created in the second-wave era—particularly its social and cultural patterns—has demonstrated an impressive continuity over many centuries, even if it also changed in particular ways over time. China's scholar-gentry class retained its prominence throughout the ups and downs of changing dynasties into the twentieth century. India's caste-based social structure still endures as a way of thinking and behaving for hundreds of millions of men and women on the South Asian peninsula. Although slavery gave way to serfdom in the post-Roman world, it was massively revived in Europe's American colonies after 1500 and remained an important and largely unquestioned feature of all civilizations until the nineteenth century. Patriarchy, with its assumptions of male superiority and dominance, has surely been the most fundamental, long-lasting, and taken-for-granted feature of all civilizations. Not until recent centuries were those assumptions effectively challenged, but even then patriarchy has continued to shape the lives and the thinking of the vast majority of humankind. And many hundreds of millions of people in the twenty-first century still honor or practice religious and cultural traditions begun during the second-wave era.

Neither the insight of Solomon nor that of the Buddha, taken alone, offers an effective guide to the study of history, for continuity and change alike have long provided the inextricable warp and woof of historical analysis. Untangling their elusive relationship has figured prominently in the task of historians and has contributed much to the enduring fascination of historical study.

Second Thoughts

What's the Significance?

China's scholar-gentry class, 220–21
Wang Mang, 221
Ge Hong, 222–23
Yellow Turban Rebellion, 223–24
caste as varna and jati, 225–28
"ritual purity" in Indian social practice, 228
Greek and Roman slavery, 229–33

Spartacus, 233
the "three obediences," 234–35
patriarchy, 234–40
Empress Wu, 236
Aspasia and Pericles, 238
Helots, 238–39

LearningCurve
Check what you know.
bedfordstmartins.com
/strayer/LC

Online Study Guide
bedfordstmartins.com
/highschool/strayer

Big Picture Questions

1. What is the difference between class and caste?
2. Why was slavery so much more prominent in Greco-Roman civilization than in India or China?
3. What philosophical, religious, or cultural ideas served to legitimate the class and gender inequalities of second-wave civilizations?
4. What changes in the patterns of social life in second-wave civilizations can you identify? What accounts for these changes?
5. **Looking Back:** Cultural and social patterns of civilizations seem to endure longer than the political framework of states and empires. What evidence from Chapters 3, 4, and 5 might support this statement? How might you account for this phenomenon? Is there evidence that could support a contrary position?

For Web sites and additional documents related to this chapter, see **Make History** at bedfordstmartins.com /highschool/strayer.

Next Steps: For Further Study

Jeannine Auboyer, *Daily Life in Ancient India* (2002). A social history of ancient India, with a focus on caste, ritual, religion, and art.

Sue Blundell, *Women in Ancient Greece* (1999). A well-written academic study, with occasional humorous stories and anecdotes.

Keith Bradley, *Slavery and Society at Rome* (1994). A scholarly but very readable account of slavery in the Roman Empire.

Michael Lowe, *Everyday Life in Early Imperial China* (1968). A vivid description of social life during the Han dynasty.

Merry Weisner-Hanks, *Gender in History* (2001). A thoughtful overview by a leading scholar in both women's history and world history.

"Women in World History," http://chnm.gmu.edu/wwh/index.html. Documents, reviews, and lesson plans for learning and teaching about women's history in a global context.

Documents

Considering the Evidence:
Patriarchy and Women's Voices

In American colleges and universities, courses in world history as well as those in women's history and gender history entered the curriculum at about the same time, both of them growing rapidly in the last decades of the twentieth century. During that time, world historians have increasingly sought to address on a global level the issues about gender raised by other historians within a national or local setting:

- How did patriarchy emerge and change over time? How was it expressed and experienced?

- What mix of opportunities and limitations did women encounter in various societies and at various times?

- To what extent were women able to act in the arena of public life and in domestic settings?

- How did different cultural traditions define appropriate gender roles and gender identities, both feminine and masculine?

In exploring such questions, historians face a major problem: the scarcity of sources written by women themselves, especially in the premodern era. Furthermore, most of the female-authored sources we do have derive from elite women. As a result, scholars must sometimes make careful use of documents written by men, often "reading between the lines" to discern the perspectives of women. The documents that follow explore various expressions of patriarchy and the women's voices that emerged within them in several of the second-wave civilizations.

Document 5.1

A Chinese Woman's Instructions to Her Daughters

Confucius himself apparently said little about women, perhaps reflecting his assumptions about their limited importance in Chinese society. Nonetheless, Confucianism as a social philosophy, formulated by the sage's later followers, had profound implications for the lives of women. Those sentiments found expression in the work of Ban Zhao (45–116 C.E.), a remarkable woman born into an elite family with connections to the imperial court. Although she received a fine literary education, she was married at the age of fourteen, gave birth to several children, and was widowed early in life. In keeping with Chinese tradition, Ban Zhou never remarried, but she had a significant career as a court historian and as an adviser to the empress-dowager (the widow of a deceased emperor). Her most famous work, *Lessons for Women*, was an effort to apply the principles of Confucianism to the lives and behavior of women.

- Why do you think Ban Zhao began her work in such a self-deprecating manner?

- In what ways does *Lessons for Women* reflect Confucian attitudes (see Document 4.1, pp. 198–200)?

- How would Ban Zhao define an ideal woman? An ideal man? An ideal marriage?

- In what ways is she critical of existing attitudes and practices regarding women?

- How does she understand the purposes of education for boys and for girls?

BAN ZHAO

Lessons for Women
Late First Century C.E.

I, the unworthy writer, am unsophisticated, unenlightened, and by nature unintelligent, but I am fortunate both to have received not a little favor from my scholarly Father, and to have had a cultured mother and instructresses upon whom to rely for a literary education as well as for training in good manners. More than forty years have passed since at the age of fourteen I took up the dustpan and the broom in the Cao family [the family into which she married]. During this time with trembling heart I feared constantly that I might disgrace my parents, and that I might multiply difficulties for both the women and the men of my husband's family. Day and night I was distressed in heart, but I labored without confessing weariness. Now and

Source: Nancy Lee Swann, trans., *Pan Chao: Foremost Woman Scholar of China* (New York: Century, 1932), 82–90.

hereafter, however, I know how to escape from such fears.

Being careless, and by nature stupid, I taught and trained my children without system. . . . I do grieve that you, my daughters, just now at the age for marriage, have not . . . learned the proper customs for married women. I fear that by failure in good manners in other families you will humiliate both your ancestors and your clan. . . . At hours of leisure I have composed . . . these instructions under the title, *Lessons for Women*.

Humility

On the third day after the birth of a girl the ancients observed three customs: first to place the baby below the bed; second to give her a potsherd° with which to play; and third to announce her birth to her ancestors by an offering. Now to lay the baby below the bed plainly indicated that she is lowly and weak, and should regard it as her primary duty to humble herself before others. To give her potsherds with which to play indubitably signified that she should practice labor and consider it her primary duty to be industrious. To announce her birth before her ancestors clearly meant that she ought to esteem as her primary duty the continuation of the observance of worship in the home.

These three ancient customs epitomize woman's ordinary way of life and the teachings of the traditional ceremonial rites and regulations. Let a woman modestly yield to others; let her respect others; let her put others first, herself last. . . . Always let her seem to tremble and to fear. When a woman follows such maxims as these then she may be said to humble herself before others. . . .

Let a woman retire late to bed, but rise early to duties; let her nor dread tasks by day or by night. . . . When a woman follows such rules as these, then she may be said to be industrious.

Let a woman be correct in manner and upright in character in order to serve her husband. . . . Let her love not gossip and silly laughter. Let her cleanse and purify and arrange in order the wine and the food for the offerings to the ancestors. When a

---

°**potsherd:** a piece of a broken pot.

woman observes such principles as these, then she may be said to continue ancestral worship.

Husband and Wife

The Way of husband and wife is intimately connected with Yin and Yang and relates the individual to gods and ancestors. Truly it is the great principle of Heaven and Earth, and the great basis of human relationships. . . .

If a husband be unworthy, then he possesses nothing by which to control his wife. If a wife be unworthy, then she possesses nothing with which to serve her husband. If a husband does not control his wife, then the rules of conduct manifesting his authority are abandoned and broken. If a wife does not serve her husband, then the proper relationship between men and women and the natural order of things are neglected and destroyed. As a matter of fact the purpose of these two is the same.

Now examine the gentlemen of the present age. They only know that wives must be controlled, and that the husband's rules of conduct manifesting his authority must be established. They therefore teach their boys to read books and study histories. But they do not in the least understand that husbands and masters must also be served, and that the proper relationship and the rites should be maintained. Yet only to teach men and not to teach women—is that not ignoring the essential relation between them? According to the "Rites" [a classic text], it is the rule to begin to teach children to read at the age of eight years, and by the age of fifteen years they ought then to be ready for cultural training. Only why should it not be that girls' education as well as boys' be according to this principle?

Respect and Caution

As Yin and Yang are not of the same nature, so man and woman have different characteristics. The distinctive quality of the Yang is rigidity; the function of the Yin is yielding. Man is honored for strength; a woman is beautiful on account of her gentleness. Hence there arose the common saying: "A man though born like a wolf may, it is feared, become a weak monstrosity; a woman though born like a mouse may, it is feared, become a tiger."

Now for self-culture nothing equals respect for others. . . . Consequently it can be said that the Way of respect and acquiescence is woman's most important principle of conduct. . . . Those who are steadfast in devotion know that they should stay in their proper places. . . .

If husband and wife have the habit of staying together, never leaving one another, and following each other around within the limited space of their own rooms, then they will lust after and take liberties with one another. From such action improper language will arise between the two. This kind of discussion may lead to licentiousness. But of licentiousness will be born a heart of disrespect to the husband. Such a result comes from not knowing that one should stay in one's proper place. . . .

If wives suppress not contempt for husbands, then it follows that such wives rebuke and scold their husbands. If husbands stop not short of anger, then they are certain to beat their wives. The correct relationship between husband and wife is based upon harmony and intimacy, and conjugal love is grounded in proper union. Should actual blows be dealt, how could matrimonial relationship be preserved? Should sharp words be spoken, how could conjugal love exist? If love and proper relationship both be destroyed, then husband and wife are divided.

Womanly Qualifications

A woman ought to have four qualifications: (1) womanly virtue; (2) womanly words; (3) womanly bearing; and (4) womanly work. Now what is called womanly virtue need not be brilliant ability, exceptionally different from others. Womanly words need be neither clever in debate nor keen in conversation. Womanly appearance requires neither a pretty nor a perfect face and form. Womanly work need not be work done more skillfully than that of others.

To guard carefully her chastity; to control circumspectly her behavior; in every motion to exhibit modesty; and to model each act on the best usage, this is womanly virtue.

To choose her words with care; to avoid vulgar language; to speak at appropriate times; and nor to weary others with much conversation, may be called the characteristics of womanly words.

To wash and scrub filth away; to keep clothes and ornaments fresh and clean; to wash the head and bathe the body regularly, and to keep the person free from disgraceful filth, may be called the characteristics of womanly bearing.

With whole-hearted devotion to sew and to weave; to love not gossip and silly laughter; in cleanliness and order to prepare the wine and food for serving guests, may be called the characteristics of womanly work. . . .

Implicit Obedience

Whenever the mother-in-law says, "Do not do that," and if what she says is right, unquestionably the daughter-in-law obeys. Whenever the mother-in-law says, "Do that," even if what she says is wrong, still the daughter-in-law submits unfailingly to the command. Let a woman not act contrary to the wishes and the opinions of parents-in-law about right and wrong; let her not dispute with them what is straight and what is crooked. Such docility may be called obedience which sacrifices personal opinion. Therefore the ancient book, *A Pattern for Women*, says: "If a daughter-in-law who follows the wishes of her parents-in-law is like an echo and shadow, how could she not be praised?"

Document 5.2

An Alternative to Patriarchy in India

About the same time that Ban Zhao was applying the principles of Confucianism to women in China, *The Laws of Manu* was being compiled in India. A core text of ancient Indian civilization, those laws defined and sharply circumscribed the behavioral expectations appropriate for women. According to one passage,

"In childhood a female must be subject to her father, in youth to her husband, when her lord is dead to her sons; a woman must never be independent."

One path of release for women from such conditions of Indian patriarchy lay in becoming a Buddhist nun and entering a monastery where women were relatively less restricted and could exercise more authority than in ordinary life. Known as *bikkhunis*, such women composed hundreds of poems in the early centuries of Indian Buddhism. They were long recited and transmitted in an oral form and brought together in a collection known as the *Psalms of the Sisters*, which was set to writing probably during the first century B.C.E. These poems became part of the officially recognized Buddhist scriptures, known as the Pali Canon. As such, they represent the only early text in any of the world's major religions that was written by women and about the religious experience of women. A selection of those poems follows here.

- What kinds of women were attracted to Buddhist monastic life? What aspects of life as a *bikkhuni* appealed to them?

- What views of the world, of sensuality, and of human fulfillment are apparent in these poems?

- In what ways might these poems represent a criticism of Hindu patriarchy?

- What criticism of these women would you anticipate? How might advocates of Hindu patriarchy view the renunciation that these nuns practiced?

- How do these poems reflect core Buddhist teachings?

Psalms of the Sisters
First Century B.C.E.

Sumangala's Mother

O woman well set free! how free am I,
How throughly free from kitchen drudgery!
Me stained and squalid 'mong my cooking-pots
My brutal husband ranked as even less
Than the sunshades he sits and weaves alway.
Purged now of all my former lust and hate,
I dwell, musing at ease beneath the shade
Of spreading boughs — O, but 'tis well with me!

Source: *Psalms of the Sisters*, vol. 1 in *Psalms of the Early Buddhists*, translated by Mrs. Rhys Davids (London: Henry Frowde, Oxford University Press Warehouse, Amen Corner, E.C., 1909), poems 21, 39, 49, 54, 70.

A Former Courtesan

How was I once puff'd up, incens'd with the
  bloom of my beauty,
Vain of my perfect form, my fame and success
  'midst the people,
Fill'd with the pride of my youth, unknowing the
  Truth and unheeding!
Lo! I made my body, bravely arrayed, deftly
  painted,
Speak for me to the lads, whilst I at the door of
  the harlot
Stood, like a crafty hunter, weaving his snares, ever
  watchful.
Yea, I bared without shame my body and wealth
  of adorning;

Manifold wiles I wrought, devouring the virtue
   of many.
To-day with shaven head, wrapt in my robe,
I go forth on my daily round for food; . . .
Now all the evil bonds that fetter gods
And men are wholly rent and cut away. . . .
Calm and content I know Nibbana's Peace.

The Daughter of a Poor Brahmin

Fallen on evil days was I of yore.
No husband had I, nor no child, no friends
Or kin—whence could I food or raiment find?
   As beggars go, I took my bowl and staff,
And sought me alms, begging from house to
   house,
Sunburnt, frost-bitten, seven weary years.
Then came I where a woman Mendicant
Shared with me food, and drink, and welcomed me,
And said: "Come forth into our homeless life!" . . .
I heard her and I marked, and did her will.

The Daughter of a Wealthy Treasurer

Daughter of Treas'rer Majjha's famous house,
Rich, beautiful and prosperous, I was born
To vast possessions and to lofty rank.
Nor lacked I suitors—many came and wooed;
The sons of Kings and merchant princes came
With costly gifts, all eager for my hand. . . .

But I had seen th' Enlightened, Chief o' the
   World, The One Supreme. [the Buddha]
And [I] knew this world should see me ne'er
   return.
Then cutting off the glory of my hair,
I entered on the homeless ways of life.
'Tis now the seventh night since first all sense
Of craving drièd up within my heart.

The Goldsmith's Daughter

A maiden I, all clad in white, once heard
The Norm,° and hearkened eager, earnestly,
So in me rose discernment of the Truths.
Thereat all worldly pleasures irked me sore,
For I could see the perils that beset
This reborn compound, 'personality,'
And to renounce it was my sole desire.
So I forsook my world—my kinsfolk all,
My slaves, my hirelings, and my villages,
And the rich fields and meadows spread around,
Things fair and making for the joy of life—
All these I left, and sought the Sisterhood,
Turning my back upon no mean estate. . . .
See now this Subhā, standing on the Norm,
Child of a craftsman in the art of gold!
Behold! she hath attained to utter calm. . . .

—————————

°**Norm:** Buddhist teaching.

Document 5.3

Roman Women in Protest

On occasion women not only wrote but also acted in the public arena. A particularly well-known example of such action took place in Rome in the wake of the Second Punic War with Carthage in North Africa. In 218 B.C.E. the Carthaginian commander Hannibal had invaded the Italian peninsula and threatened Rome itself. In those desperate circumstances Roman authorities passed the Oppian Laws (215 B.C.E.), which restricted women's use of luxury goods so as to preserve resources for the war effort. Twenty years later (195 B.C.E.), with Rome now secure and prosperous, Roman women demanded the repeal of those laws and in the process triggered a major debate among Roman officials. That debate and the women's protest that accompanied it were chronicled early in the first century C.E. by Livy, a famous Roman historian.

- How did Roman women make their views known? Do you think the protesters represented all Roman women or those of a particular class?

- How might you summarize the arguments favoring the retention of the law (Cato) and those favoring its repeal (Lucius Valerius)? To what extent did the two men actually differ in their views of women?

- How might one of the Roman women involved in the protest have made her own case?

- What can we learn from Livy's account about the social position of Roman women and the attitudes of Roman men?

- This document was written by a male historian several hundred years after the events he describes, and it records the speeches of two other male officials. How might this affect the ability of historians to use it for understanding Roman women?

LIVY

History of Rome
Early First Century C.E.

The law said that no woman might own more than half an ounce of gold nor wear a multi-colored dress nor ride in a carriage in the city or in a town within a mile of it, unless there was a religious festival. . . . [A] crowd of men, both supporters and opponents [of repeal], filled the Capitoline Hill. The matrons, whom neither counsel nor shame nor their husbands' orders could keep at home, blockaded every street in the city and every entrance to the Forum. As the men came down to the Forum, the matrons besought them to let them, too, have back the luxuries they had enjoyed before, giving as their reason that the republic was thriving and that everyone's private wealth was increasing with every day. This crowd of women was growing daily, for now they were even gathering from the towns and villages. Before long they dared go up and solicit the consuls, praetors, and other magistrates; but one of

the consuls could not be moved in the least, Marcus Porcius Cato, who spoke in favor of the law:

"If each man of us, fellow citizens, had established that the right and authority of the husband should be held over the mother of his own family, we should have less difficulty with women in general; now, at home our freedom is conquered by female fury, here in the Forum it is bruised and trampled upon, and, because we have not contained the individuals, we fear the lot. . . .

"Indeed, I blushed when, a short while ago, I walked through the midst of a band of women. Had not respect for the dignity and modesty of certain ones (not them all!) restrained me. . . . I should have said, 'What kind of behavior is this? Running around in public, blocking streets, and speaking to other women's husbands! Could you not have asked your own husbands the same thing at home? Are you more charming in public with others' husbands than at home with your own? And yet, it is not fitting even at home . . . for you to concern yourselves with what laws are passed or repealed here.' Our ancestors did not want women to conduct any—not even

Source: Livy, "History of Rome" in *Women's Life in Greece and Rome*, 2nd ed., edited by Mary R. Lefkowitz and translated by Maureen B. Fant (Baltimore: Johns Hopkins Press, 1982), 143–47.

private—business without a guardian; they wanted them to be under the authority of parents, brothers, or husbands; we (the gods help us!) even now let them snatch at the government and meddle in the Forum and our assemblies. What are they doing now on the streets and crossroads, if they are not persuading the tribunes to vote for repeal? Give the reins to their unbridled nature and this unmastered creature. . . . They want freedom, nay license . . . in all things. If they are victorious now, what will they not attempt? . . . As soon as they begin to be your equals, they will have become your superiors. . . .

"What honest excuse is offered, pray, for this womanish rebellion? 'That we might shine with gold and purple,' says one of them, 'that we might ride through the city in coaches on holidays and working-days.' . . .

"The woman who can spend her own money will do so; the one who cannot will ask her husband. Pity that husband—the one who gives in and the one who stands firm! What he refuses, he will see given by another man. Now they publicly solicit other women's husbands, and, what is worse, they ask for a law and votes, and certain men give them what they want. . . . Fellow citizens, do not imagine that the state which existed before the law was passed will return . . . , as when wild animals are first chafed by their chains and then released."

After this . . . Lucius Valerius spoke on behalf of the motion [to repeal the law]. . . .

"[Cato] . . . has called this assemblage 'secession' and sometimes 'womanish rebellion,' because the matrons have publicly asked you, in peacetime when the state is happy and prosperous, to repeal a law passed against them during the straits of war. . . .

'What, may I ask, are the women doing that is new, having gathered and come forth publicly in a case which concerns them directly? Have they never appeared in public before this? . . . Listen to how often they have done so—always for the public good. From the very beginning—the reign of Romulus—when the Capitoline had been taken by the Sabines and there was fighting in the middle of the Forum, was not the battle halted by the women's intervention between the two lines? . . . When Rome was in the hands of the Gauls, who ransomed it? Indeed the

matrons agreed unanimously to turn their gold over to the public need. . . . Indeed, as no one is amazed that they acted in situations affecting men and women alike, why should we wonder that they have taken action in a case which concerns themselves? . . . We have proud ears indeed, if, while masters do not scorn the appeals of slaves, we are angry when honorable women ask something of us. . . .

"Who then does not know that this is a recent law, passed twenty years ago? Since our matrons lived for so long by the highest standards of behavior without any law, what risk is there that, once it is repealed, they will yield to luxury? . . .

"Shall it be our wives alone to whom the fruits of peace and tranquility of the state do not come? . . . Shall we forbid only women to wear purple? When you, a man, may use purple on your clothes, will you not allow the mother of your family to have a purple cloak, and will your horse be more beautifully saddled than your wife is garbed? . . .

"[Cato] has said that, if none of them had anything, there would be no rivalry among individual women. By Hercules! All are unhappy and indignant when they see the finery denied them permitted to the wives of the Latin allies, when they see them adorned with gold and purple, when those other women ride through the city and they follow on foot, as though the power belonged to the other women's cities, not to their own. This could wound the spirits of men; what do you think it could do to the spirits of women, whom even little things disturb? They cannot partake of magistracies, priesthoods, triumphs, badges of office, gifts, or spoils of war; elegance, finery, and beautiful clothes are women's badges, in these they find joy and take pride, this our forebears called the women's world. When they are in mourning, what, other than purple and gold, do they take off? What do they put on again when they have completed the period of mourning? What do they add for public prayer and thanksgiving other than still greater ornament? Of course, if you repeal the Oppian law, you will not have the power to prohibit that which the law now forbids; daughters, wives, even some men's sisters will be less under your authority—never, while her men are well, is a woman's slavery cast off; and even they hate the freedom created by widowhood and orphanage. They prefer their adornment to be subject to your judgment, not the law's; and you ought to hold them in marital power and guardianship, not slavery; you should prefer to be called fathers and husbands to masters. The consul just now used odious terms when he said 'womanish rebellion' and 'secession'. For there is danger — he would have us believe — that they will seize the Sacred Hill as once the angry plebeians did. . . . It is for the weaker sex to submit to whatever you advise. The more power you possess, all the more moderately should you exercise your authority."

When these speeches for and against the law had been made, a considerably larger crowd of women poured forth in public the next day; as a single body they besieged the doors of the Brutuses, who were vetoing their colleagues' motion, and they did not stop until the tribunes took back their veto. . . . Twenty years after it was passed, the law was repealed.

Using the Evidence:
Patriarchy and Women's Voices

1. **Comparing gender systems:** Based on these documents, how might you compare the gender systems of China, India, and the Roman Empire? What common features of patriarchy did they share? In what ways did they differ?

2. **Evaluating the possibilities of action for women:** In what ways were women able to challenge at least some elements of their societies? Do these documents exhibit anything similar to the feminist thinking or action of our own times?

3. **Internalizing social values:** To what extent did women in these civilizations internalize or accept the patriarchal values of their societies? Why might they have done so?

4. **Making judgments:** If you were a woman living during these times, which of these civilizations would you prefer to live in and why? Do you think this kind of question — judging the past by the standards of the present — is a valid approach to historical inquiry?

Visual Sources

Considering the Evidence: Pompeii as a Window on the Roman World

You could hear the shrieks of women, the wailing of infants, and the shouting of men; some were calling their parents, others their children or their wives, trying to recognize them by their voices. People bewailed their own fate or that of their relatives, and there were some who prayed for death in their terror of dying. Many besought the aid of the gods, but still more imagined there were no gods left, and that the universe was plunged into eternal darkness for evermore.[23]

Written by a prominent Roman known as Pliny the Younger, this eyewitness account details reactions to the volcanic eruption of Mount Vesuvius, located on the southwestern side of the Italian peninsula, on August 24, 79 C.E. That eruption buried the nearby city of Pompeii, located about 150 miles south of Rome, but it also preserved the city, frozen in time, until archaeologists began to uncover it in the mid-eighteenth century (see Map 3.4, p. 131). Now substantially excavated, Pompeii is an archaeological and historical treasure, offering a unique window into life of a Roman city during the first century C.E.

As this city of perhaps 20,000 people emerged from layers of ash, it stood revealed as a small but prosperous center of commerce and agriculture, serving as a point of entry for goods coming to southern Italy by sea. Pompeii also hosted numerous vineyards, production facilities for wine and olive oil, and a fisheries industry. In addition, the city was a tourist destination for well-to-do Romans. The houses of the wealthy were elegant structures, often built around a central courtyard, and decorated with lovely murals displaying still-life images, landscapes, and scenes from Greek and Roman mythology. An inscription found on the threshold of one house expressed the entrepreneurial spirit of the town: "Gain is pure joy."[24]

Laid out in a grid pattern with straight streets, the city's numerous public facilities included a central bathing/swimming pool, some twenty-five street fountains, various public bathhouses, and a large food market as well as many bars and small restaurants. More than thirty brothels, often featuring explicit erotic art, offered sexual services at relatively inexpensive prices. One inscription, apparently aimed at local tourists, declared: "If anyone is looking for some

Visual Source 5.1 Terentius Neo and His Wife (Scala/Art Resource, NY)

they compete for her attention. In the third image, two men playing dice are arguing.

- Why do you think a tavern owner might have such paintings in his place of business?

- What might we learn about tavern life from these images?

- What roles did women play in the tavern?

- What differences do you notice between these paintings and those depicting the lives of the upper classes?

The excavated ruins of Pompeii have much to tell us about the religious as well as the social life of the Roman world in the first century C.E., before Christianity had spread widely. Based on ritual observance rather than doctrine or theology, Roman religious practice sought to obtain the favor of the gods as a way of promoting success, prosperity, and good fortune. A core expression of the diverse and eclectic world of Roman religion was the imperial cult. In Pompeii, a number of temples were dedicated to one or another of the deified emperors, employing together a large cadre of priests and priestesses. Linked to the imperial cult were temples devoted to the traditional Greco-Roman gods such as Apollo, Venus, and Jupiter.

Probably more important to ordinary people were their *lararia* (household shrines), often a niche in the wall that housed paintings or sculptures of *lares* (guardian spirits or deities believed to provide protection within the home). Families offered gifts of fruit, cakes, and wine to these spirits, and the lararia were the focal point for various sacrifices and rituals associated with birth, marriage, and death. Visual Source 5.4 shows one of these shrines, uncovered in the home of two wealthy brothers, former slaves both named Vettius. Protecting the family from external danger were two lares, standing on either side of the lararium and holding their drinking horns. In the center was the *genius*, the spirit of the male head of household. Dressed in a toga and offering a sacrifice, this spirit embodied the character of the man, especially his procreative powers, and so guaranteed many children for the household. The snake at the bottom represented still other benevolent guardian spirits of the family in a fashion very different from Christian symbolism of the snake.

- Why might such a shrine and the spirits it accommodated be more meaningful for many people than the state-approved cults?

- What significance might you find in the temple-like shape of the lararium?

In addition to the official cults and the worship of household gods, by the first century C.E. a number of newer traditions, often called "mystery religions," were spreading widely in the Roman Empire. Deriving from the eastern realm of the empire and beyond (Greece, Egypt, and Persia, for example), these mys-

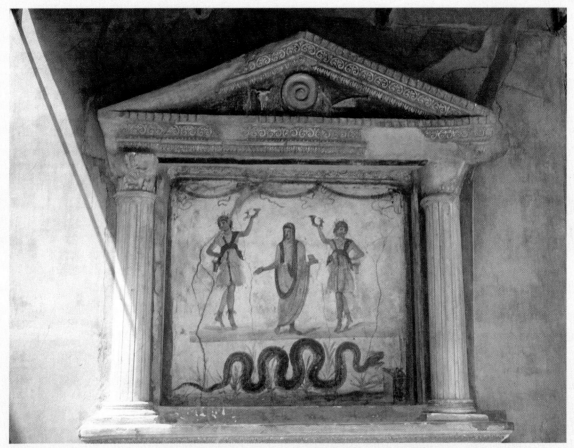

Visual Source 5.4 A Domestic Shrine (Alinari/Art Resource, NY)

tery religions illustrate the kinds of cultural exchange that took place within the Empire. They offered an alternative to the official cults, for they were more personal, emotional, and intimate, usually featuring a ritual initiation into sacred mysteries, codes of moral behavior, and the promise of an afterlife. Among the most popular of these mystery cults in Pompeii was that of Isis, an Egyptian goddess who restored her husband/brother, Osiris, to life and was worshipped as a compassionate protector of the downtrodden.

Another mystery cult, this one of Greek origin, was associated with Dionysus, a god of wine, ecstasy, and poetic inspiration and especially popular with women. Often associated with drunkenness, trance states, wild dancing, and unrestrained sexuality, the cult of Dionysus encouraged at least the temporary abandonment of conventional inhibitions and social restrictions as initiates sought union with Dionysus. A series of wall paintings on a Pompeii building known as the Villa of Mysteries depicts the process of initiation into the cult of Dionysus, perhaps in preparation for marriage. Visual Source 5.5

Visual Source 5.5　Mystery Religions: The Cult of Dionysus (© Werner Forman/Corbis)

shows a particularly dramatic phase of that initiation in which a woman is ritually whipped, while a naked devotee dances ecstatically with a pair of cymbals above her head and a companion holds a rod of phallic symbolism sacred to Dionysus. In any such process of religious initiation, the initiate undergoes a series of trials or purifications in which he or she "dies" symbolically, achieves mystical union with the god, and is "reborn" into the new community of the cult.

- What aspects of the initiation process are visible in this image?

- How might you understand the role of whipping in the initiation process? How would you interpret the relationship of the initiate and the woman on whose lap she is resting her head?

- In what way is sexual union, symbolized by the rod, significant in the initiation?

- Why do you think Roman authorities took action against these mystery religions, even as they did against Christianity?

- What did the mystery cults of Isis or Dionysus provide that neither the state cults nor household gods might offer?

Using the Evidence:
Pompeii as a Window on the Roman World

1. **Characterizing Pompeii:** What does the art of Pompeii, as reflected in these visual sources, tell us about the social and religious life of this small Roman city in the first century C.E.?

2. **Noticing class differences:** What class or social distinctions are apparent in these visual sources?

3. **Identifying gender roles:** What do these visual sources suggest about the varied lives and social roles of women and men in Pompeii?

Chapter 5 Wrap Up

STEP ONE

The Word to Know: Class

The *Oxford English Dictionary* defines *class* as "a division or stratum of society consisting of people at the same economic level or having the same social status. A system of ordering society whereby people are divided into strata of this type; the pattern of social division created by such a system; a person's position in society as defined by this." In a paragraph, compare caste in India to slavery in Rome. How did these practices of social division allow for a small number of elites to remain in power?

STEP TWO

Contextualization

Review Chapters 3–5 and answer the following questions to try to place the events of the three thematic chapters into the larger context of the era.

1. How do the individual changes that happened at this time in Eurasia and Northern Africa reflect larger global patterns? Think about the slavery in Rome and the existence of slavery elsewhere at the same time. Why has this labor system persisted to the present day?

2. How did religious beliefs as well as local practice help to reinforce the patriarchy that emerged across the Eurasian continent?

Women in Second-Wave Civilizations

Consider Document 5.1, "A Chinese Woman's Instructions to Her Daughters" and Document 5.2, "Psalms of the Sisters" (pp. 244–48), as well as the information in the text, and describe how women learned their place in society in China, India, Athens, and Sparta. Was it through informal education at home, through religious traditions, through society in general, or some combination of all three?

CHAPTER SIX

Commonalities and Variations

Africa and the Americas

500 B.C.E.—1200 C.E.

In early 2010, Bolivian President Evo Morales was inaugurated for his second term in office, the only person from the country's Native American population ever elected to that post since independence from Spain in 1825. The day before the official ceremony in the capital of La Paz, Morales traveled to Tiwanaku (tee-wah-NAH-coo), the center of an impressive empire that had flourished in the Andean highlands between 400 and 1000 C.E., long before either the Inca or the Spanish ruled the area. There he sought to link himself and his administration to this ancient culture, a symbol of Bolivian nationalism and indigenous pride. On his arrival, Morales was ritually cleansed with holy water and herbs and dressed in a llama wool robe. After offerings were made to Pachamama, an Andean earth goddess and to Tata Inti, the Inca sun god, Morales was invested with symbols of both kingship and spiritual leadership, thus joining political and religious sources of authority. Proclaiming a new multinational state, Morales declared: "Gone forever is the colonial state, which allowed the looting of our natural resources, and gone also is the discriminatory [against native peoples] colonial state."[1] This recent ceremony provides a reminder that memories of American second-wave civilizations remained alive and were available for mobilizing political support and legitimating political authority in the very different circumstances of the early twenty-first century.

FOR MANY PEOPLE, THE SECOND-WAVE ERA EVOKES most vividly the civilizations of Eurasia—the Greeks and the Romans, the Persians and the Chinese, and the Indians of South Asia—yet those were not the only civilizations of that era. During this period, the Mesoamerican

---

The Maya Temple of the Great Jaguar in Tikal: Located in the Maya city of Tikal in present-day Guatemala, this temple was constructed in the eighth century C.E. and excavated by archeologists in the late nineteenth century. It served as the tomb of the Tikal ruler Jasaw Chan K'awiil I (682–734). Some 144 feet tall, it was topped by a three-room temple complex and a huge roofcomb showing the ruler on his throne. Carved on a wooden beam inside the temple is an image of the ruler protected by a huge jaguar along with illustrations of his military victories. (Peter M. Wilson/Alamy)

Maya and the Andean Tiwanaku thrived, as did several civilizations in sub-Saharan Africa, including Meroë (MER-oh-ee), Axum (AHK-soom), and the Niger River valley. Furthermore, those peoples who did not organize themselves around cities or states likewise had histories of note and alternative ways of constructing their societies, although they are often neglected in favor of civilizations. This chapter explores the histories of the varied peoples of Africa and the Americas during this phase of world history. On occasion, those histories will extend some centuries beyond the chronological boundaries of the second-wave era in Eurasia because patterns of historical development around the world did not always coincide precisely.

SEEKING THE MAIN POINT

To what extent did the histories of Africa and the Americas parallel those of Eurasia? In what ways did they forge new or different paths?

Continental Comparisons

■ Comparison
What similarities and differences are noticeable among the three major continents of the world?

At the broadest level human cultures evolved in quite similar fashion around the world. All, of course, were part of that grand process of human migration that initially peopled the planet. Beginning in Africa, that vast movement of humankind subsequently encompassed Eurasia, Australia, the Americas, and Pacific Oceania. Almost everywhere, gathering and hunting long remained the sole basis for sustaining life and society. Then, on the three supercontinents—Eurasia, Africa, and the Americas—the momentous turn of the Agricultural Revolution took place independently and in several distinct areas of each landmass (see Chapter 1). That revolutionary transformation of human life subsequently generated, in particularly rich agricultural environments of all three regions, those more complex societies that we know as civilizations, featuring cities, states, monumental architecture, and great social inequality (see Chapter 2). In these ways, the historical trajectory of the human journey has a certain unity and similarity across quite distinct continental regions. This commonality provides the foundation for a genuinely global history of humankind. At the beginning of the Common Era, that trajectory had generated a total world population of about 250 million people, substantially less than the current population of the United States alone. By contemporary standards, it was still a sparsely populated planet.

The world's human population was then distributed very unevenly across the three giant continents, as the Snapshot on page 264 indicates. If these estimates are even reasonably accurate, then during the second-wave era Eurasia was home to more than 80 percent of the world's people, Africa about 11 percent, and the Americas between 5 and 7 percent. That unevenness in population distribution is part of the reason why world historians focus more attention on Eurasia than on Africa or the Americas. Here lies one of the major differences among the continents.

There were others as well. The absence of most animals capable of domestication meant that no pastoral societies developed in the Americas, and apart from llamas and alpacas in the Andes, no draft animals were available to pull plows or carts or to carry heavy loads for long distances. Africa too lacked wild sheep, goats, chickens,

A Map of Time

750–200 B.C.E.	Chavín religious movement in Peruvian Andes
730 B.C.E.	Nubian conquest of Egypt
300 B.C.E.–100 C.E.	Kingdom of Meroë in upper Nile valley
300 B.C.E.–900 C.E.	Niger Valley civilization in West Africa
200 B.C.E.–400 C.E.	Hopewell "mound-building" culture in U.S. eastern woodlands
1st to 7th century C.E.	Flourishing of Axum (East Africa) and Moche (coastal Peru) civilizations; spread of Bantu-speaking people in eastern and southern Africa
250–900 C.E.	Classical Maya civilization
300–600 C.E.	Flourishing of Teotihuacán
4th century C.E.	Introduction of Christianity to Axum
400–1000 C.E.	Tiwanaku and Wari in the Andes
860–1130 C.E.	Chaco culture in U.S. Southwest
900–1250 C.E.	Cahokia

horses, and camels, but its proximity to Eurasia meant that these animals, once domesticated, became widely available to African peoples. Metallurgy in the Americas was likewise far less developed than in Eurasia and Africa, where iron tools and weapons played such an important role in economic and military life. In the Americas, writing was limited to the Mesoamerican region and was most highly developed among the Maya, whereas in Africa it was confined to the northern and northeastern parts of the continent. In Eurasia, by contrast, writing emerged elaborately in many regions. Furthermore, civilizations in Africa and the Americas were fewer in number and generally smaller than those of Eurasia, and larger numbers of their people lived in communities that did not feature cities and states.

A final continental comparison distinguishes the history of Africa from that of the Americas. Geography placed Africa adjacent to Eurasia, while it separated the Americas from both Africa and Eurasia. This has meant that parts of Africa frequently interacted with Eurasian civilizations. In fact, Mediterranean North Africa was long part of a larger zone of Afro-Eurasian interaction. Ancient Egyptian civilization was certainly in contact with Crete, Syria, and Mesopotamia and provided inspiration for the Greeks. The entire North African coastal region was incorporated into the Roman Empire and used to produce wheat and olives on large estates with slave labor. Christianity spread widely across North Africa, giving rise to some of the early Church's most famous martyrs and theologians. The Christian faith found an even more permanent foothold in the lands now known as Ethiopia.

Snapshot   Continental Population in the Second-Wave Era[2]

(Note: Population figures for such early times are merely estimates and are often controversial among scholars. Percentages do not always total 100 percent due to rounding.)

	Eurasia	Africa	North America	Central/South America	Australia/ Oceania	Total World
Area (in square miles and as percentage of world total)						
	21,049,000 (41%)	11,608,000 (22%)	9,365,000 (18%)	6,880,000 (13%)	2,968,000 (6%)	51,870,000
Population (in millions and as percentage of world total)						
400 B.C.E.	127 (83%)	17 (11%)	1 (0.7%)	7 (5%)	1 (0.7%)	153
10 C.E.	213 (85%)	26 (10%)	2 (0.8%)	10 (4%)	1 (0.4%)	252
200 C.E.	215 (84%)	30 (12%)	2 (0.8%)	9 (4%)	1 (0.4%)	257
600 C.E.	167 (80%)	24 (12%)	2 (1%)	14 (7%)	1 (0.5%)	208
1000 C.E.	195 (77%)	39 (15%)	2 (0.8%)	16 (6%)	1 (0.4%)	253

Arabia was another point of contact with Eurasia for African peoples. The arrival of the domesticated camel, probably from Arabia, generated a nomadic pastoral way of life among some of the Berber peoples of the western Sahara during the first three centuries C.E. A little later, camels also made possible trans-Saharan commerce, which linked interior West Africa to the world of Mediterranean civilization. Over many centuries, the East African coast was a port of call for Egyptian, Roman, and Arab merchants, and that region subsequently became an integral part of Indian Ocean trading networks. The transoceanic voyages of Austronesian-speaking sailors from Southeast Asia brought various food crops of that region, bananas for example, to Madagascar and from there to the East African mainland. The Americas, by contrast, developed almost wholly apart from this Afro-Eurasian network until that separation was breeched by the voyages of Columbus in 1492.

To illustrate the historical developments of the second-wave era beyond Eurasia/ North Africa, this chapter examines first the civilizations that emerged in sub-Saharan Africa and the Americas. Then our historical spotlight turns to several regions on both continents that remained outside the zone of civilization, reminding us that the histories of many peoples took shape without the cities, states, and empires that were so prominent within that zone.

Civilizations of Africa

When historians refer to Africa in premodern times, they are speaking generally of a geographic concept, a continental landmass, and not a cultural identity. Certainly few, if any, people living on the continent at that time thought of themselves as Africans. Like Eurasia or the Americas, Africa hosted numerous separate societies, cultures, and civilizations with vast differences among them as well as some interaction between them.

Many of these differences grew out of the continent's environmental variations. Small regions of Mediterranean climate in the northern and southern extremes, large deserts (the Sahara and the Kalahari), even larger regions of savanna grasslands, tropical rain forest in the continent's center, highlands and mountains in eastern Africa — all of these features, combined with the continent's enormous size, ensured endless variation among Africa's many peoples. Africa did, however, have one distinctive environmental feature: bisected by the equator, it was the most tropical of the world's three supercontinents. Persistent warm temperatures caused the rapid decomposition of vegetable matter called humus, resulting in poorer and less fertile soils and a less productive agriculture than in the more temperate Eurasia. Those climatic conditions also spawned numerous disease-carrying insects and parasites, which have long created serious health problems in many parts of the continent. It was within these environmental constraints that African peoples made their histories. In several distinct regions of the continent — the upper Nile valley, northern Ethiopia/Eritrea, and the Niger River valley — small civilizations flourished during the second-wave era, while others followed later.

Meroë: Continuing a Nile Valley Civilization

In the Nile Valley south of Egypt lay the lands of Nubian civilization, almost as old as Egypt itself. Over many centuries, Nubians both traded and fought with Egypt, and on one occasion the Nubian Kingdom of Kush conquered Egypt and ruled it for a century (see Portrait of Piye, pp. 268–69). While borrowing heavily from Egypt, Nubia remained a distinct and separate civilization (see Chapter 2). As Egypt fell increasingly under foreign control, Nubian civilization came to center on the southern city of Meroë (MER-oh-ee), where it flourished between 300 B.C.E. and 100 C.E. (see Map 6.1).

Politically, the Kingdom of Meroë was governed by an all-powerful and sacred monarch, a position held on at least ten occasions by women, governing alone or as co-rulers with a male monarch. Unlike the female pharaoh Hatshepsut in Egypt, who was portrayed in male clothing, Meroë queens appeared in sculptures as women and with a prominence and power equivalent to their male counterparts. In accordance with ancient traditions, such rulers were buried along with a number of human sacrificial victims. The city of Meroë and other urban centers housed a wide variety of economic specialties — merchants, weavers, potters, and masons, as well as servants,

■ **Connection**

How did the history of Meroë and Axum reflect interaction with neighboring civilizations?

Map 6.1   Africa in the Second-Wave Era
During the second-wave era, older African civilizations such as Egypt and Nubia persisted and changed, while new civilizations emerged in Axum and the Niger River valley. South of the equator, Bantu-speaking peoples spread slowly, creating many new societies and identities.

laborers, and slaves. The smelting of iron and the manufacture of iron tools and weapons were especially prominent industries. The rural areas surrounding Meroë were populated by peoples who practiced some combination of herding and farm-ing and paid periodic tribute to the ruler. Rainfall–based agriculture was possible in Meroë, and consequently farmers were less dependent on irrigation. This meant that the rural population did not need to concentrate so heavily near the Nile and was less directly controlled from the capital than was the case in Egypt, where state authorities were required to supervise an irrigation system serving a dense population along the river.

The wealth and military power of Meroë derived in part from extensive long-distance trading connections, to the north via the Nile and to the east and west by means of camel caravans. Its iron weapons and cotton cloth, as well as its access to gold, ivory, tortoiseshells, and ostrich feathers, gave Meroë a reputation for great riches in the world of northeastern Africa and the Mediterranean. The discovery in Meroë of a statue of the Roman emperor Augustus, probably seized during a raid on Roman Egypt, testifies to contact with the Mediterranean world. Culturally, Meroë seemed to move away from the heavy Egyptian influence of earlier times. A local lion god, Apedemek,

A Bracelet from Meroë

This gold bracelet, dating to about 100 B.C.E., illustrates the skill of Meroë's craftsmen as well as the kingdom's reputation as one of the wealthiest states of the ancient world. (Nubian, Meroitic Period, 100 B.C. Object Place: Sudan, Nubia, Gebel Barkal, Pyramid 8. Gold, enamel. Height x length: 1.8 x 12.5 cm (11/16 x 4 15/16 in.). Museum of Fine Arts, Boston. Harvard University — Boston Museum of Fine Arts Expedition. 20.333. Photograph © 2014 Museum of Fine Arts, Boston.)

grew more prominent than Egyptian deities such as Isis and Osiris, while the use of Egyptian-style writing declined as a new and still undeciphered Meroitic script took its place.

In the centuries following 100 C.E., the Kingdom of Meroë declined, in part because of deforestation caused by the need for wood to make charcoal for smelting iron. Furthermore as Egyptian trade with the African interior switched from the Nile Valley route to the Red Sea, the resources available to Meroë's rulers diminished and the state weakened. The effective end of the Meroë phase of Nubian civilization came with the kingdom's conquest in the 340s C.E. by the neighboring and rising state of Axum. In the centuries that followed, three separate Nubian states emerged, and Coptic (Egyptian) Christianity penetrated the region. For almost a thousand years, Nubia was a Christian civilization, using Greek as a liturgical language and constructing churches in Coptic or Byzantine fashion. After 1300 or so, political division, Arab immigration, and the penetration of Islam eroded this Christian civilization, and Nubia became part of the growing world of Islam (see Chapter 10).

Axum: The Making of a Christian Kingdom

If Meroë represented the continuation of an old African/Nubian civilization, Axum marked the emergence of a new one. (For various accounts about or from Axum, see Documents: Axum and the World, pp. 292–98.) Axum lay in the Horn of Africa, in what is now Eritrea and northern Ethiopia (see Map 6.1). Its economic foundation was a highly productive agriculture that used a plow-based farming system, unlike most of the rest of Africa, which relied on the hoe or digging stick. Axum's agriculture

PORTRAIT

Piye, Kushite Conqueror of Egypt

During the eighth century B.C.E., a remarkable reversal took place in northeastern Africa. The ancient Kingdom of Kush in the southern Nile Valley, long under the control of Egypt, conquered its former ruler and governed it for a century. The primary agent of that turnabout was Piye,

Piye in front of the seated god Amun while to his right and below, defeated rulers prostrate before him. (From James Henry Breasted, The Piankhi Stela, Ancient Records of Egypt *(Chicago, 1906), Part IV, 816ff.)*

a Kushite ruler (r. 752–721 B.C.E.), who recorded his great victory in a magnificent inscription that provides some hints about his own personality and outlook on the world.[3]

The very beginning of the inscription discloses Piye's self-image, for he declares himself a "divine emanation, living image of Atum," the Egyptian creator-god closely connected to kingship. Like most of the Kushite elite, Piye had thoroughly assimilated much of Egyptian culture and religion, becoming perhaps "more Egyptian than the Egyptians."[4] Even the inscription was written in hieroglyphic Egyptian and in the style of earlier pharaohs. Who better then to revive an Egypt that, over the past several centuries, had become hopelessly fragmented and

that also had neglected the worship of Amun? Thus Piye's conquest reflected the territorial ambitions of Kush's "Egyptianized" rulers, a sense of divinely inspired mission to set things right in Egypt, and the opportunity presented by the sorry state of Egyptian politics.

If we are to believe the inscription, Piye went to war reluctantly and only in response to requests from various Egyptian "princes, counts, and generals." Furthermore he was careful to pay respect to the gods all along the way. After celebrating the new year in 730 B.C.E., Piye departed from his capital of Napata and made an initial stop in Thebes, a southern Egyptian city already controlled by Kushite forces. There he took part in the annual Opet Festival, honoring Amun, his wife Mut (Egypt's mother goddess), and their offspring Khonsu, associated with the moon. Moving north, Piye then laid siege to Hermopolis, located in middle Egypt. From a high tower, archers poured arrows into the city and "slingers" hurled stones, "slaying people among them

generated substantial amounts of wheat, barley, millet, and teff, a highly nutritious grain unique to that region. By 50 C.E. or so, a substantial state had emerged, stimulated by its participation in the rapidly increasing Red Sea and Indian Ocean commerce, which was itself a product of growing Roman demand for Indian pearls, textiles, and especially pepper. At Adulis, then the largest port on the East African coast, a wide range of merchants sought the products of the African interior — animal hides, rhinoceros horn, ivory, obsidian, tortoiseshells, and slaves. Taxes on this trade provided a major source of revenue for the Axumite state and the complex society that grew up within it. Thus the decline of Meroë and the rise of Axum were both connected to changing patterns of long-distance commerce.[5]

The interior capital city, also known as Axum, was a center of monumental building and royal patronage for the arts. The most famous buildings were huge stone obelisks, which most likely marked royal graves. Some of them were more than 100 feet tall and at the time were the largest structures in the world hewn from a single piece of rock. The language used at court, in the towns, and for commerce was Geez, daily," according to the inscription. Soon the city had become "foul to the nose," and its ruler, Prince Namlot, prepared for surrender. He sent his wife and daughter, lying on their bellies, to plead with the women in Piye's entourage, begging them to intercede with Piye, which they did. Grandly entering the city, Piye went first to the temple of the chief god, where he offered sacrifices of "bulls, calves and fowl." To establish his authority, he then "entered every chamber of [Namlot's] house, his treasury and his magazines." Piye pointedly ignored the women of Namlot's harem when they greeted him "in the manner of women." Yet in the stable, he was moved by the suffering of the horses. He seized Namlot's possessions for his treasury and assigned his enemy's grain to the temple of Amun.

And so it went as Piye moved northward. Many cities capitulated without resistance, offering their treasure to the Kushites. Presenting himself as a just and generous conqueror, Piye declared that "not a single one has been slain therein, except the enemies who blasphemed against the god, who were dispatched as rebels." However, it was a different story when he arrived outside of the major north Egyptian city of Memphis, then ruled by the Libyan chieftain Tefnakht. There "a multitude of people were slain" before Tefnakht was induced to surrender, sending an envoy to Piye to deliver an abject and humiliating speech: "Be thou appeased! I have not beheld thy face for shame; I cannot stand before thy flame, I tremble at thy might." The city was ritually cleansed; proper respect was paid to the gods, who confirmed Piye's kingship; and tribute was collected. Soon all resistance collapsed, and Piye, once ruler of a small Kushite kingdom, found himself master of all Egypt.

And then, surprisingly, he departed, leaving his underlings in charge and his sister as the High Priestess and wife of Amun in Thebes. His ships "were laden with silver, gold, copper, clothing, and everything of the Northland, every product of Syria, and all sweet woods of God's Land [Egypt]. His majesty sailed up-stream, with glad heart." Never again did Piye set foot in Egypt, preferring to live out his days in his native country, where he was buried in an Egyptian-style pyramid. But he had laid the foundation for a century of Kushite rule in Egypt, reunifying that ancient country, reinvigorating the cult of Amun, and giving expression to the vitality of an important African civilization.

Questions: How did Piye understand himself and his actions in Egypt? How might modern historians view his conquests?

written in a script derived from South Arabia. The Axumite state exercised a measure of control over the mostly Agaw-speaking people of the country through a loose administrative structure focusing on the collection of tribute payments. To the Romans, Axum was the third major empire within the world they knew, following their own and the Persian Empire.

Through its connections to Red Sea trade and the Roman world, particularly Egypt, Axum was introduced to Christianity in the fourth century C.E. Its monarch at the time, King Ezana, adopted the new religion about the same time as Constantine did in the Roman Empire. Early in his reign, the kingdom's coins featured images of gods derived from southern Arabia, while by the end, they were inscribed with the Christian cross. Supported by royal authority, Christianity took root in Axum, linking that kingdom religiously to Egypt, where a distinctive Christian church known as Coptic was already well established. (See Chapter 4, pp. 190–91, and Chapter 10, pp. 467–69.) Although Egypt subsequently became largely Islamic, reducing its Christian community to a small minority, Christianity maintained a dominant position in

The Columns of Axum
Dating to the time when Axum first encountered Christianity (300–500 C.E.), this column, measuring some seventy-nine feet tall, probably served as a funeral monument for the kingdom's ancient rulers. (McPHOTO/ZAD/age fotostock)

the mountainous terrain of highland Ethiopia and in the early twenty-first century still represents the faith of perhaps 60 percent of the country's population.

During the fourth through the sixth century C.E., Axum mounted a campaign of imperial expansion that took its forces into the Kingdom of Meroë and across the Red Sea into Yemen in South Arabia. By 571, the traditional date for the birth of Muhammad, an Axumite army, including a number of African war elephants, had reached the gates of Mecca, but it was a fairly short-lived imperial venture. The next several centuries were ones of decline for the Axumite state, owing partly to environmental changes, such as soil exhaustion, erosion, and deforestation, brought about by intensive farming. Equally important was the rise of Islam, which altered trade routes and diminished the revenue available to the Axumite state. Its last coins were struck in the early seventh century. When the state revived several centuries later, it was centered farther south on the Ethiopian plateau. In this new location, there emerged the Christian church and the state that present-day Ethiopia has inherited, but the link to ancient Axum was long remembered and revered.

With their long-distance trading connections, urban centers, centralized states, complex societies, monumental architecture, written languages, and imperial ambitions, both Meroë and Axum paralleled on a smaller scale the major features of the second-wave civilizations of Eurasia. Furthermore, both were in direct contact with the world of Mediterranean civilizations. Across the continent in West Africa, a rather different civilization took shape.

Along the Niger River: Cities without States

■ **Description**
How does the experience of the Niger Valley challenge conventional notions of "civilization"?

The middle stretches of the Niger River in West Africa witnessed the emergence of a remarkable urbanization (see Map 6.1, p. 266). A prolonged dry period during the five centuries after 500 B.C.E. brought growing numbers of people from the southern Sahara into the fertile floodplain of the middle Niger in search of more reliable access to water. Accompanying them were their domesticated cattle, sheep, and goats, their agricultural skills, and their ironworking technology. Over many centuries (roughly 300 B.C.E.–900 C.E.), the peoples of this region created a distinctive city-based civilization. The most fully studied of the urban clusters that grew up along the middle Niger was the city of Jenne-jeno (jihn-AY jihn-OH), which at its high point probably housed more than 40,000 people.

Among the most distinctive features of the Niger Valley civilization was the apparent absence of a corresponding state structure. Unlike the cities of Egypt, China, the Roman Empire, or Axum, these middle Niger urban centers were not encompassed within some larger imperial system. Nor were they like the city-states of ancient Mesopotamia, in which each city had its own centralized political structure, embodied in a monarch and his accompanying bureaucracy. According to a leading historian of the region, they were "cities without citadels," complex urban centers that apparently operated without the coercive authority of a state, for archeologists have found in their remains few signs of despotic power, widespread warfare, or deep social inequalities.[6] In this respect, these urban centers resemble the early cities of the Indus Valley civilization, where likewise little archeological evidence of centralized state structures has been found (see Chapter 2).

In place of such hierarchical organization, Jenne-jeno and other cities of the region emerged as clusters of economically specialized settlements surrounding a larger central town. The earliest and most prestigious of these specialized occupations was iron smithing. Working with fire and earth (ore) to produce this highly useful metal, the smiths of the Niger Valley were both feared and revered. Archeologist Roderick McIntosh, a leading figure in the excavation of Jenne-jeno, argued that "their knowledge of the transforming arts—earth to metal, insubstantial fire to the mass of iron—was the key to a secret, occult realm of immense power and immense danger."[7]

Other specializations followed. Villages of cotton weavers, potters, leather workers, and griots (praise-singers who preserved and recited the oral traditions of their societies) grew up around the central towns. Gradually these urban artisan communities became occupational castes, whose members passed their jobs and skills to their children and could marry only within their own group. In the surrounding rural areas, as in all urban-based civilizations, farmers tilled the soil and raised their animals, but specialization also occurred in food production as various ethnic groups focused on fishing, rice cultivation, or some other agricultural pursuit. At least for a time, these middle Niger cities represented an African alternative to an oppressive state, which in many parts of the world accompanied an increasingly complex urban economy and society. A series of distinct and specialized economic groups shared authority and voluntarily used the services of one another, while maintaining their own identities through physical separation.

Terra-cotta Statue from Jenne-jeno
The artistic tradition of Niger Valley civilization includes a number of terra-cotta couples, reflecting perhaps the emphasis on the separate but complementary roles of men and women in much of African thought. This statue and others like it date to sometime after the twelfth century and may express the resistance of an indigenous tradition to the growing penetration of Islam. (Werner Forman/Art Resource, NY)

Accompanying this unique urbanization, and no doubt stimulating it, was a growing network of indigenous West African commerce. The middle Niger flood-plain supported a rich agriculture and contained clay for pottery, but it lacked stone, iron ore, salt, and fuel. This scarcity of resources was the basis for a long-distance commerce that operated by boat along the Niger River and overland by donkey to the north and south. Iron ore from more than 50 miles away, copper from mines 200 miles distant, gold from even more distant sources, stones and salt from the Sahara — all of these items have been found in Jenne-jeno, exchanged no doubt for grain, fish, smoked meats, iron implements, and other staples. Jenne-jeno itself was an impor-tant transshipment point in this commerce, in which goods were transferred from boat to donkey or vice versa. By the 500s C.E., there is evidence of an even wider commerce and at least indirect contact, from Mauritania in the west to present-day Mali and Burkina-Faso in the east.

In the second millennium C.E., new historical patterns developed in West Africa (see Chapter 7). A number of large-scale states or empires emerged in the region — Ghana, Mali, and Songhay, among the most well known. At least partially responsible for this development was the flourishing of a camel-borne trans-Saharan commerce, previously but a trickle across the great desert. As West Africa became more firmly connected to North Africa and the Mediterranean, Islam penetrated the region, mark-ing a gradual but major cultural transformation. All of this awaited West Africa in later centuries, submerging, but not completely eliminating, the decentralized city life of the Niger Valley.

Civilizations of Mesoamerica

Westward across the Atlantic Ocean lay the altogether separate world of the Ameri-cas. Although geography encouraged some interaction between African and Eur-asian peoples, the Atlantic and Pacific oceans ensured that the cultures and societies of the Western Hemisphere operated in a world apart from their Afro-Eurasian counterparts. Nor were the cultures of the Americas stimulated by the kind of fruit-ful interaction among their own peoples that played such an important role in the Eastern Hemisphere. Nothing similar to the contact between Egypt and Mesopota-mia, or Persia and the Greeks, or the extensive communication along the Silk Road trading network enriched the two major centers of civilization in the Americas — Mesoamerica and the Andes — which had little if any direct contact with each other. Furthermore, the remarkable achievements of early American civilizations and cul-tures occurred without the large domesticated animals or ironworking technologies that were so important throughout the Eastern Hemisphere.

Accounts of pre-Columbian American societies often focus primarily on the Az-tec and Inca empires (see Chapter 12), yet these impressive creations, flourishing in the fifteenth and early sixteenth centuries, were but the latest in a long line of civili-zations that preceded them in Mesoamerica and the Andes respectively. These two regions housed the vast majority of the population of the Americas. Here the historical spotlight focuses on the long period following the First Civilizations of the Olmecs and Norte Chico but preceding the Aztecs and Incas, roughly 500 B.C.E.–1300 C.E.

Stretching from central Mexico to northern Central America, the area known as Mesoamerica was, geographically speaking, one of "extraordinary diversity compressed into a relatively small space."[8] That environment ranged from steamy lowland rain forests to cold and windy highland plateaus, cut by numerous mountains and valleys and generating many microclimates. Such conditions contributed to substantial linguistic and ethnic diversity and to many distinct and competing cities, chiefdoms, and states.

Despite this diversity, Mesoamerica was also a distinct region, bound together by elements of a common culture. Its many peoples shared an intensive agricultural technology devoted to raising maize, beans, chili peppers, and squash. They prepared maize in a distinctive and highly nutritious fashion and based their economies on market exchange. They practiced religions featuring a similar pantheon of male and female deities, understood time as a cosmic cycle of creation and destruction, practiced human sacrifice, and constructed monumental ceremonial centers. Furthermore they employed a common ritual calendar of 260 days and hieroglyphic writing, and they interacted frequently among themselves. During the first millennium B.C.E., for example, the various small states and chiefdoms of the region, particularly the Olmec, exchanged a number of luxury goods used to display social status and for ritual purposes—jade, serpentine, obsidian tools, ceramic pottery, shell ornaments, stingray spines, and turtle shells. As a result, aspects of Olmec culture, such as artistic styles, temple pyramids, the calendar system, and rituals involving human sacrifice, spread widely throughout Mesoamerica and influenced many of the civilizations that followed.

The Maya: Writing and Warfare

Among Mesoamerican civilizations, none has attracted more attention than that of the Maya. Scholars have traced the beginnings of the Maya people to ceremonial centers constructed as early as 2000 B.C.E. in present-day Guatemala and the Yucatán region of Mexico (see Map 6.2). During the first millennium B.C.E., a number of substantial urban centers with concentrated populations and monumental architecture had emerged in the region. In northern Guatemala, for example, the archeological site of El Mirador was home to tens of thousands of people, a pyramid/temple said by some to be the largest in the world, and a stone-carved frieze depicting the Maya creation story known as the Popul Vuh.

But it was during a later phase of Maya civilization, between 250 and 900 C.E., that their most well-known

Map 6.2 Civilizations of Mesoamerica
During the second-wave era, Maya civilization and the large city of Teotihuacán represented the most prominent features of Meso-american civilization.

cultural achievements emerged. Intellectuals, probably priests, developed a mathematical system that included the concept of zero and place notation and was capable of complex calculations. They combined this mathematical ability with careful observation of the night skies to plot the cycles of planets, to predict eclipses of the sun and the moon, to construct elaborate calendars, and to calculate accurately the length of the solar year. The distinctive art of the Maya elite was likewise impressive to later observers (see Visual Sources: Art and the Maya Elite, pp. 299–305).

■ **Comparison**

With what Eurasian civilizations might the Maya be compared?

Accompanying these intellectual and artistic achievements was the creation of the most elaborate writing system in the Americas, which used both pictographs and phonetic or syllabic elements. Carved on stone and written on bark paper or deerskin books, Mayan writing recorded historical events, masses of astronomical data, and religious or mythological texts. Temples, pyramids, palaces, and public plazas abounded, graced with painted murals and endless stone carving. It is not surprising that early scholars viewed Maya civilization as a peaceful society led by gentle stargazing priest-kings devoted to temple building and intellectual pursuits.

The economic foundations for these cultural achievements were embedded in an "almost totally engineered landscape."[9] The Maya drained swamps, terraced hillsides, flattened ridgetops, and constructed an elaborate water management system. Much of this underpinned a flourishing agriculture, which supported a very rapidly growing and dense population by 750 C.E. This agriculture sustained substantial elite classes of nobles, priests, merchants, architects, and sculptors, as well as specialized artisans producing pottery, tools, and cotton textiles. And it was sufficiently productive to free a large labor force for work on the many public structures that continue to amaze contemporary visitors.

These many achievements took place within a highly fragmented political system of city-states, local lords, and regional kingdoms with no central authority, with frequent warfare, and with the extensive capture and sacrifice of prisoners (see Visual Source 6.2, p. 302). The larger political units of Maya civilization were densely populated urban and ceremonial centers, ruled by powerful kings and on a few occasions queens. They were divine rulers or "state shamans" able to mediate between humankind and the supernatural. One of these cities, Tikal (tee-KAHL), contained perhaps 50,000 people, with another 50,000 or so in the surrounding countryside, by 750 C.E.[10] (See the chapter-opening photo, p. 260, of a temple from Tikal.) Some of these city-states were clearly imperialistic, but none succeeded in creating a unified Maya empire. Various centers of Maya civilization rose and fell; fluctuating alliances among them alternated with periods of sporadic warfare; ruling families intermarried; the elite classes sought luxury goods from far away—jade, gold, shells, feathers from exotic birds, cacao—to bolster their authority and status. In its political dimensions, Maya civilization more closely resembled the competing city-states of ancient Mesopotamia or classical Greece than the imperial structures of Rome, Persia, or China.

But large parts of that imposing civilization collapsed with a completeness and finality rare in world history. Clearly this was not a single or uniform phenomenon, as flourishing centers of Maya civilization persisted in the northern Yucatàn, and many Maya survived to fight the Spanish in the sixteenth century. But in the southern regions where the collapse was most complete, its outcomes were devastating. In less than a century following the onset of a long-term drought in 840, the population of the low-lying southern heartland of the Maya dropped by 85 percent or more as famine, epidemic, and fratricidal warfare reaped a horrific toll. It was a catastrophe from which there was no recovery. Elements of Maya culture survived in scattered settlements, but the great cities were deserted, and large-scale construction and artistic work ceased. The last date inscribed in stone corresponds to 909 C.E. As a complex civilization, the Maya had passed into history.

Explaining this remarkable demise has long kept scholars guessing, with recent accounts focusing on ecological and political factors.[11] Rapid population growth after 600 C.E. pushed total Maya numbers to perhaps 5 million or more and soon outstripped available resources, resulting in deforestation and the erosion of hillsides. Under such conditions, climate change in the form of prolonged droughts in the 800s may well have placed unbearable pressures on Maya society. Political disunity and endemic rivalries, long a prominent feature of Maya civilization, prevented a coordinated and effective response to the emerging catastrophe. Warfare in fact became more frequent as competition for increasingly scarce land for cultivation became sharper. Rulers dependent on ritual splendor for their legitimacy competed to mount ever more elaborate temples, palaces, and pageants, requiring more labor and taxes from their subjects and tribute from their enemies. Whatever the precise explanation, the Maya collapse, like that of the Romans and others, illustrates the fragility of civilizations, whether they are embodied in large empires or organized in a more decentralized fashion.

Teotihuacán: The Americas' Greatest City

At roughly the same time as the Maya flourished in the southern regions of Mesoamerica, the giant city of Teotihuacán (tay-uh-tee-wah-KAHN), was also thriving further north in the Valley of Mexico. Begun around 150 B.C.E. and apparently built to a plan rather than evolving haphazardly, the city came to occupy about eight square miles and by 550 C.E. had a population variously estimated between 100,000 and 200,000. It was by far the largest urban complex in the Americas at the time and one of the six largest in the world. Beyond this, much about Teotihuacán is unknown, such as its original name, the language of its people, the kind of government that ordered its life, and the precise function of its many deities.

Physically, the city was enormously impressive, replete with broad avenues, spacious plazas, huge marketplaces, temples, palaces, apartment complexes, slums, waterways, reservoirs, drainage systems, and colorful murals. Along the main north/south boulevard, now known as the Street of the Dead, were the grand homes of the elite, the headquarters of state authorities, many temples, and two giant pyramids. One of them, the Pyramid of the Sun, had been constructed over an ancient tunnel leading

■ **Connection**

In what ways did Teotihuacán shape the history of Mesoamerica?

Teotihuacán
Taken from the summit of the Pyramid of the Moon, this photograph looks down the famous Avenue of the Dead to the Pyramid of the Sun in the upper left. (Alison Wright/Photo Researchers)

to a cave and may well have been regarded as the site of creation itself, the birthplace of the sun and the moon. At the Temple of the Feathered Serpent, archeologists have found the remains of some 200 people, their hands and arms tied behind them; they were the apparently unwilling sacrificial victims meant to accompany the high-ranking persons buried there into the afterlife.

Off the main avenues in a grid-like pattern of streets lay thousands of residential apartment compounds, home to the city's commoners, each with its own kitchen area, sleeping quarters, courtyards, and shrines. In these compounds, perhaps in groups of related families or lineages, lived many of the farmers who tilled the lands outside the city. Thousands of Maya specialists—masons, leather workers, potters, construction laborers, merchants, civil servants—also made their homes in these apartments. So too did skilled makers of obsidian blades, who plied their trade in hundreds of separate workshops, generating products that were in great demand throughout Mesoamerica. At least two small sections of the city were reserved exclusively for foreigners.

Buildings, both public and private, were decorated with mural paintings, sculptures, and carvings. Many of these works of art display abstract geometric and stylized images. Others depict gods and goddesses, arrayed in various forms—feathered serpents, starfish, jaguars, flowers, and warriors. One set of murals shows happy people cavorting in a paradise of irrigated fields, playing games, singing, and chasing butterflies, which were thought to represent the souls of the dead. Another portrays dancing warriors carrying elaborate curved knives, to which were attached bleeding human hearts.

The art of Teotihuacán, unlike that of the Maya, has revealed few images of self-glorifying rulers or individuals. Nor did the city have a tradition of written public inscriptions as the Maya did, although a number of glyphs or characters indicate at least a limited form of writing. One scholar has suggested that "the rulers of Teotihuacán might have intentionally avoided the personality cult of the dynastic art and writing" so characteristic of the Maya.[12] Perhaps those rulers constituted an oligarchy or council of high-ranking elites rather than a single monarch.

However it was governed, Teotihuacán cast a huge shadow over Mesoamerica, particularly from 300 to 600 C.E. A core region of perhaps 10,000 square miles was administered directly from the city itself, while tribute was no doubt exacted from other areas within its broader sphere of influence. At a greater distance, the power of Teotihuacán's armies gave it a presence in the Maya heartland more than 600 miles to the east. At least one Maya city, Kaminalijuyu in the southern highlands, was completely taken over by the Teotihuacán military and organized as a colony. In Tikal, a major lowland Maya city, in the year 378 C.E., agents of Teotihuacán apparently engineered a coup that placed a collaborator on the throne and turned the city for a time into an ally or a satellite. Elsewhere — in the Zapotec capital of Monte Alban, for example — murals show unarmed persons from Teotihuacán engaged in what seems to be more equal diplomatic relationships.

At least some of this political and military activity was no doubt designed to obtain, either by trade or by tribute, valued commodities from afar — food products, cacao beans, tropical bird feathers, honey, salt, medicinal herbs. The presence in Teotihuacán of foreigners, perhaps merchants, from the Gulf Coast and Maya lowlands, as well as much pottery from those regions, provides further evidence of long-distance trade. Moreover, the sheer size and prestige of Teotihuacán surely persuaded many, all across Mesoamerica, to imitate the architectural and artistic styles of the city. Thus, according to a leading scholar, "Teotihuacán meant something of surpassing importance far beyond its core area."[13] Almost a thousand years after its still-mysterious collapse around 650 C.E., the peoples of the Aztec Empire dubbed the great metropolis as Teotihuacán, the "city of the gods."

Civilizations of the Andes

Yet another and quite separate center of civilization in the Americas lay in the dramatic landscape of the Andes. Bleak deserts along the coast supported human habitation only because they were cut by dozens of rivers flowing down from the mountains, offering the possibility of irrigation and cultivation. The offshore waters of the Pacific Ocean also provided an enormously rich marine environment with an endless supply of seabirds and fish. The Andes themselves, a towering mountain chain

Map 6.3 Civilizations of the Andes
No single civilization dominated the Andes region during the second-wave era. Rather a number of religious movements, states, and empires rose and fell before the entire region was encompassed by the Inca Empire in the fifteenth century.

with many highland valleys, afforded numerous distinct ecological niches, depending on altitude. Andean societies generally sought access to the resources of these various environments through colonization, conquest, or trade — seafood from the coastal regions; maize and cotton from lower-altitude valleys; potatoes, quinoa, and pasture land for their llamas in the high plains; tropical fruits and cocoa leaf from the moist eastern slope of the Andes.

The most well-known of the civilizations to take shape in this environment was that of the Incas, which encompassed practically the entire region, some 2,500 miles in length, in the fifteenth century. Yet the Incas represented only the most recent and the largest in a long history of civilizations in the area.

The coastal region of central Peru had in fact generated one of the world's First Civilizations, known as Norte Chico, dating back to around 3000 B.C.E. (see Chapter 2). During the two millennia between roughly 1000 B.C.E. to 1000 C.E., a number of Andean civilizations rose and passed away. Because none of them had developed writing, historians are largely dependent on archeology for an understanding of these civilizations.

Chavín: A Pan-Andean Religious Movement

■ Connection

What kind of influence did Chavín exert in the Andes region?

In both the coastal and highland regions of Peru, archeologists have uncovered numerous local ceremonial centers or temple complexes, dating to between 2000 and 1000 B.C.E. Then around 900 B.C.E., one of them, situated in the Andean highlands at a village called Chavín (cha-BEEN) de Huántar, became the focus of a religious movement that soon swept through both coastal and highland Peru, aided by its strategic location on trade routes to both the coastal region to the west and the Amazon rain forest to the east.

By perhaps 750 B.C.E., this small center had become a town of 2,000 to 3,000 people, with clear distinctions between an elite class, who lived in stone houses, and ordinary people, with adobe dwellings. An elaborate temple complex included numerous galleries, hidden passageways, staircases, ventilation shafts, drainage canals, and distinctive carvings. Chavín artwork suggests influences from both the desert coastal region and the rain forests. Major deities were represented as jaguars, crocodiles, and snakes, all of them native to the Amazon basin. Shamans or priests likely made use of the San Pedro cactus, native to the Andes Mountains, employing its hallucinogenic properties to penetrate the supernatural world. Some of the fantastic artwork of this civilization—its jaguar-human images, for example—may well reflect the visions of these religious leaders.

Over the next several centuries, this blended religious movement proved attractive across much of Peru and beyond, as Chavín-style temple architecture, sculpture, pottery, religious images, and painted textiles were widely imitated within the region. Chavín itself became a pilgrimage site and perhaps a training center for initiates.[14] Although some evidence suggests violence and warfare, no Chavín "empire" emerged. Instead, a widespread religious cult, erected on the back of a trading network, provided for the first time and for several centuries a measure of economic and cultural integration to much of the Peruvian Andes.

Moche: A Civilization of the Coast

By 200 B.C.E., the pan-Andes Chavín cult had faded, replaced by a number of regional civilizations. Among them, Moche (MOH-chee) civilization clearly stands out. Dominating a 250-mile stretch of Peru's northern coast and incorporating thirteen river valleys, the Moche people flourished between about 100 and 800 C.E. Their economy was rooted in a complex irrigation system, requiring constant maintenance, which funneled runoff from the Andes into fields of maize, beans, and squash and acres of cotton, all fertilized by rich bird droppings called guano. Moche fishermen also harvested millions of anchovies from the bountiful Pacific.

■ **Description**

What features of Moche life characterize it as a civilization?

Politically, Moche was governed by warrior-priests, some of whom lived atop huge pyramids, the largest of which was constructed from 143 million sun-dried bricks. There shaman-rulers, often under the influence of hallucinogenic drugs, conducted ancient rituals that mediated between the world of humankind and that of the gods. They also presided over the ritual sacrifice of human victims, drawn from their many prisoners of war, which became central to the politico-religious life of the Moche. Images on Moche pottery show a ruler attired in a magnificent feather headdress and seated on a pyramid, while a parade of naked prisoners marches past him. Other scenes of decapitation and dismemberment indicate the fate that awaited those destined for sacrifice. For these rulers, the Moche world was apparently one of war, ceremony, and diplomacy.

The immense wealth of this warrior-priest elite and the exquisite artistry of Moche craftsmen are reflected in the elaborate burials accorded the rulers. At one site near the town of Sipan, Peruvian archeologists uncovered the final resting place of three such individuals, one of whom they named the Lord of Sipan. Laid in adobe burial chambers, one above the other, each was decked out in his ceremonial regalia—elaborate gold masks, necklaces, and headdresses; turquoise and gold bead bracelets; cotton tunics covered with copper plates; a gold rattle showing a Moche warrior smashing a prisoner with his war club; and a copper knife. In 2005, in another remarkable discovery dating to about 450 C.E., archeologists found the burial place of a high-status woman, who was in her late twenties and heavily tattooed. She had been

The Lord of Sipan
The Moche ruler in the center of the grave, dating to about 290 C.E., was about forty years old when he died and, at five feet five inches, was quite tall for the time. Except for early signs of arthritis, he was in good health and seems to have performed little physical labor during his life. Accompanying him in death were the four individuals shown here, plus three young women, a priest, a guard, a dog, and considerable food and drink. (© Kevin Schafer/Corbis)

laid to rest with hundreds of funeral objects, including gold sewing needles; weaving tools; much gold, silver, and copper jewelry; and a female sacrificial victim lying beside her. Even more suggestive were two elaborate war clubs and twenty-three spear throwers. Was she perhaps a warrior, a priest, or a ruler?

The most accessible aspect of Moche life and much of what scholars know about the Moche world derive from the superb skill of their craftspeople, such as metal workers, potters, weavers, and painters. Face masks, figures of animals, small earrings, and other jewelry items, many plated in gold, display amazing technical abilities and a striking artistic sensibility. Decorating their ceramic pottery are naturalistic portraits of noble lords and rulers and images from the life of common people, including the blind and the sick. Battle scenes show warriors confronting their enemies with raised clubs. Erotic encounters between men and women and gods making love to humans likewise represent common themes, as do grotesque images of their many gods and goddesses. Much of this, of course, reflects the culture of the Moche elite. We know much less about the daily life of the farmers, fishermen, weavers, traders, construction workers, and servants whose labor made that elite culture possible.

These cultural achievements, however, rested on fragile environmental foundations, for the region was subject to drought, earthquakes, and occasional torrential rains associated with El Niño episodes (dramatic changes in weather patterns caused by periodic warming of Pacific Ocean currents). During the sixth century C.E., some combination of these forces caused extended ecological disruption, which seriously undermined Moche civilization. In these circumstances, the Moche were vulnerable to aggressive neighbors and possibly to internal social tensions as well. By the end of the eighth century C.E., that civilization had passed into history.[15]

Wari and Tiwanaku: Empires of the Interior

Far more than the Moche and other coastal civilizations, the interior empires of Wari (wah-ree) and Tiwanaku provided a measure of political integration and cultural commonality for the entire Andean region. Growing out of ancient settlements, these two states flourished between 400 and 1000 C.E., Wari in the northern highlands and Tiwanaku to the south. Both were centered in large urban capitals, marked by monumental architecture and stratified populations numbering in the tens of thousands. Both governments collected surplus food in warehouses as an insurance against times of drought and famine.

But neither state controlled a continuous band of territory. Adapting to their vertical environment, both empires established colonies at lower elevations on the eastern and western slopes of the Andes as well as throughout the highlands, seeking access to resources such as seafood, maize, chili peppers, cocoa, hallucinogenic plants, obsidian, and feathers from tropical birds. Caravans of llamas linked distant centers, allowing the exchange and redistribution of goods, while the religious prestige and ceremonial power of the capital city provided further integration. Cultural influences from the center, such as styles of pottery and textiles, spread well beyond the regions of direct political control. Similar religious symbols and images prevailed in both places, including the ancient Andean Staff God, a deity portrayed with a staff in each hand.

But Wari and Tiwanaku were hardly carbon copies of one another. Wari's agriculture employed an elaborate system of hillside terracing and irrigation, using snow melt from the Andes. A seventeenth-century Jesuit missionary thought the hillsides of the Wari region "were covered with flights of stairs." Tiwanaku's highly productive farming economy, by contrast, utilized a "raised field" system in which artificially elevated planting surfaces in swampy areas were separated by small irrigation canals. Tiwanaku, furthermore, has become famous for its elaborately fitted stone walls and buildings, while Wari's tombs and temples were built of field stone set in mud mortar and covered with smooth plaster. Cities in the Wari region seemed built to a common plan and linked to the capital by a network of highways, which suggests a political system more tightly controlled from the center than in Tiwanaku.[16]

■ **Description**
What was the significance of Wari and Tiwanaku in the history of Andean civilization?

Despite these differences and a 300 mile common border, little overt conflict or warfare occurred between Wari and Tikanaku. In areas where the two peoples lived near one another, they apparently did not mingle much. They each spoke their own language, wore different clothing, furnished their homes with distinctive goods, and looked to their respective capital cities for inspiration.[17]

In the several centuries following 1000 C.E., both civilizations collapsed, their impressive cities permanently abandoned. What followed was a series of smaller kingdoms, one of which evolved into the Inca Empire that gave to Andean civilization a final and spectacular expression before all of the Americas was swallowed up in European empires from across the sea. The Inca themselves clearly drew on the legacy of Wari and Tiwanaku, adopting aspects of their imperial models and systems of statecraft, building on the Wari highway system, and utilizing similar styles of dress and artistic expression. Such was the prestige of Tiwanaku centuries after its collapse that the Inca claimed it as their place of origin.

SUMMING UP SO FAR

What features common to all civilizations can you identify in the civilizations of Africa and the Americas? What distinguishing features give them a distinctive identity?

Alternatives to Civilization: Bantu Africa

World historians are frequently occupied, sometimes almost exclusively, with civilizations, and understandably so, since those urban and state-based communities were clearly the most powerful, expansive, and innovative societies, later embracing almost the entire population of the planet. And yet, it is useful to remind ourselves that other ways of organizing human communities evolved alongside civilizations, and they too made history. Two such regions were Africa south of the equator and North America. They shared environments that featured plenty of land and relatively few people compared to the greater population densities and pressure on the land that characterized many civilizations.

In the vast region of Africa south of the equator, the most significant development during the second-wave era involved the accelerating movement of Bantu-speaking peoples into the enormous subcontinent. It was a process that had begun many centuries earlier, probably around 3000 B.C.E., from a homeland region in what are now southeastern Nigeria and the Cameroons. In the long run, that movement of peoples generated some 400 distinct but closely related languages, known collectively as Bantu. By the first century C.E., agricultural peoples speaking Bantu languages and now bearing an ironworking technology had largely occupied the forest regions of equatorial Africa, and at least a few of them had probably reached the East African coast. In the several centuries that followed, they established themselves quite rapidly in most of eastern and southern Africa (see Map 6.1, p. 266), introducing immense economic and cultural changes to a huge region of the continent.

Bantu expansion was not a conquest or invasion such as that of Alexander the Great; nor was it a massive and self-conscious migration like that of Europeans to the Americas in more recent times. Rather, it was a slow movement of peoples, perhaps a few extended families at a time, but taken as a whole, it brought to Africa south of the equator a measure of cultural and linguistic commonality, marking it as a distinct region of the continent.

Cultural Encounters

That movement of peoples also generated numerous cross-cultural encounters, as the Bantu-speaking newcomers interacted with already established societies, changing both of them in the process. Among those encounters, none was more significant than that between the agricultural Bantu and the gathering and hunting peoples who earlier occupied this region of Africa. Their interaction was part of a long-term global phenomenon in which farmers largely replaced foragers as the dominant people on the planet (see Chapter 1).

■ **Connection**

In what ways did the arrival of Bantu-speaking peoples stimulate cross-cultural interaction?

In these encounters, Bantu-speaking farmers had various advantages. One was numerical, as agriculture generated a more productive economy, enabling larger numbers to live in a smaller area than was possible with a gathering and hunting way of life. Another advantage was disease, for the farmers brought with them both parasitic and infectious diseases — malaria, for example — to which foraging people had little immunity. A third advantage was iron, so useful for tools and weapons, which Bantu migrants brought to many of their interactions with peoples still operating with stone-age technology. Thus, gathering and hunting peoples were displaced, absorbed, or largely eliminated in most parts of Africa south of the equator — but not everywhere.

In the rain forest region of Central Africa, the foraging Batwa (BAH-twah) (Pygmy) people, at least some of them, became "forest specialists" who produced honey, wild game, elephant products, animal skins, and medicinal barks and plants, all of which entered regional trading networks in exchange for the agricultural products of their Bantu neighbors. They also adopted Bantu languages, while maintaining a nonagricultural lifestyle and a separate identity. For their part, the Bantu farmers regarded their Batwa neighbors as first-comers to the region and therefore closest to the ancestral and territorial spirits that determined the fertility of the land and people. Thus, as forest-dwelling and Bantu-speaking farmers grew in numbers and created chiefdoms, those chiefs appropriated the Batwa title of "owners of the land" for themselves, claimed Batwa ancestry, and portrayed the Batwa as the original "civilizers" of the earth.[18]

In other ways as well, Bantu cultures changed as they encountered different peoples. In the drier environment of East Africa, the yam-based agriculture of the West African Bantu homeland was unable to support their growing numbers, so Bantu farmers increasingly adopted grains as well as domesticated sheep and cattle from the already established people of the region. Their agriculture also was enriched by acquiring a variety of food crops from Southeast Asia — coconuts, sugarcane, and especially bananas — which were brought to East Africa by Indonesian sailors and immigrants early in the first millennium C.E. Bantu farmers then spread this agricultural package and their acquired ironworking technology throughout the vast area of eastern and southern Africa, probably reaching present-day South Africa by 400 C.E. They also brought a common set of cultural and social practices, which diffused widely across Bantu Africa. One prominent historian described these practices as encompassing,

> in religion, the centrality of ancestor observances; in philosophy, the problem of evil understood as the consequence of individual malice or of the failure to honor one's ancestors; in music, an emphasis on polyrhythmic performance with drums as the key instrument; in dance, a new form of expression in which a variety of prescribed body movements took preference over footwork; and in agriculture, the pre-eminence of women as the workers and innovators.[19]

All of this became part of the common culture of Bantu-speaking Africa.

Society and Religion

In the thousand years or so (500–1500 C.E.) that followed their initial colonization of Africa south of the equator, agricultural Bantu-speaking peoples also created a wide variety of quite distinct societies and cultures. Some—in present-day Kenya, for example—organized themselves without any formal political specialists at all. Instead they made decisions, resolved conflicts, and maintained order by using kinship structures or lineage principles supplemented by age grades, which joined men of a particular generation together across various lineages. Elsewhere, lineage heads who acquired a measure of personal wealth or who proved skillful at mediating between the local spirits and the people might evolve into chiefs with a modest political authority. In several areas, such as the region around Lake Victoria or present-day Zimbabwe, larger and more substantial kingdoms evolved. Along the East African coast after 1000 C.E., dozens of rival city-states linked the African interior with the commerce of the Indian Ocean basin (see Chapter 7, pp. 324–28).

Many societies in the Bantu-speaking world developed gender systems that were markedly less patriarchal than those of established urban-based civilizations. Male ironworkers in the Congo River basin, for example, sought to appropriate the power and prestige of female reproductive capacity by decorating their furnaces with clay breasts and speaking of their bellows as impregnating the furnaces. Among the Luba people of Central Africa, male rulers operated in alliance with powerful women, particularly spirit mediums, who were thought to contain the spirit of the king. Only a woman's body was considered sufficiently strong to acquire this potent and dangerous presence. Luba art represented female ancestors as "keepers of secret royal knowledge." And across a wide area of south-central Africa, a system of "gender parallelism" associated female roles with village life (child care, farming, food preparation, making pots, baskets, and mats), while masculine identity revolved around hunting and forest life (fishing, trapping, collecting building materials and medicinal plants). It was a "separate but equal" definition of gender roles.[20]

In terms of religion, Bantu practice in general placed less emphasis on a High or Creator God, who was viewed as remote and largely uninvolved in ordinary life, and focused instead on ancestral or nature spirits. The power of dead ancestors might be accessed through rituals of sacrifice, especially of cattle. Supernatural power deriving from ancient heroes, ancestors, or nature spirits also resided in charms, which could be activated by proper rituals and used to control the rains, defend the village, achieve success in hunting, or identify witches. Belief in witches was widespread, reflecting the idea that evil or misfortune was the work of malicious people. Diviners, skilled in penetrating the world of the supernatural, used dreams, visions, charms, or trances to identify the source of misfortune and to prescribe remedies. Was a particular illness the product of broken taboos, a dishonored ancestor, an unhappy nature spirit, or a witch? Was a remedy to be found in a cleansing ceremony, a sacrifice to an ancestor, the activation of a charm, or the elimination of a witch?[21]

Unlike the major monotheistic religions, with their "once and for all" revelations from God through the Christian Bible or the Muslim Quran, Bantu religious practice was predicated on the notion of "continuous revelation"—the possibility of constantly receiving new messages from the world beyond. Moreover, unlike Buddhism, Christianity, or Islam, Bantu religions were geographically confined, intended to explain, predict, and control local affairs, with no missionary impulse or inclination toward universality.

A Female Luba Ancestral Statue
Representations of powerful women, often ancestral figures, were frequent in the wood carvings of the Bantu-speaking Luba people of Central Africa. Many of them showed women touching their breasts, a gesture signifying devotion, respect, and the holding of secret knowledge. (Musee du Quai Branly/ Scala/Art Resource, NY)

Alternatives to Civilization: North America

The peoples of the Americas in the pre-Columbian era might be divided into three large groupings (see Map 12.5, p. 581). The most prominent and well known are those of the Mesoamerican and Andean regions, where cities, states, and dense populations created civilizations recognizably similar to those of Afro-Eurasia. Elsewhere, gathering and hunting peoples carried on the most ancient of human adaptations to the environment. Arctic and subarctic cultures, the bison hunters of the Great Plains, the complex and settled communities of the Pacific coast of North America, nomadic bands living in the arid regions of southern South America—all of these represent the persistence of gathering and hunting ways of living in substantial regions of the Americas.

Even larger areas—the eastern woodlands of the United States, Central America, the Amazon basin, the Caribbean islands—were populated by peoples sometimes defined as "semi-sedentary."[22] These were agricultural societies, although less intensive and productive than those of Mesoamerica or the Andes and supporting usually much smaller populations. Nor did they generate large urban centers or inclusive empires (Map 6.4).

These peoples who lived beyond the direct reach of the major civilizations also made their own histories, changing in response to their unique environments, their interactions with outsiders, and their own visions of the world. The Anasazi of the southwestern United States, now called the Ancestral Pueblo, and the mound-building cultures of the eastern woodlands provide two illustrations from North America.

The Ancestral Pueblo: Pit Houses and Great Houses

■ Comparison

In what ways were the histories of the Ancestral Pueblo and the Mound Builders similar to each other, and how did they differ?

The southwestern region of North America, an arid land cut by mountain ranges and large basins, first acquired maize from its place of origin in Mesoamerica during the second millennium B.C.E., but it took roughly 2,000 years for that crop, later supplemented by beans and squash, to become the basis of a settled agricultural way of living. In a desert region, farming was risky, and maize had to be gradually adapted to the local environment. Not until around 600 to 800 C.E. did permanent village life take hold widely. People then lived in pit houses with floors sunk several feet below ground level. Some settlements had only a few such homes, whereas others contained twenty-five or more. By 900 C.E., many of these villages also included kivas, much larger pit structures used for ceremonial purposes, which symbolized the widespread belief that humankind emerged into this world from another world below. Individual settlements were linked to one another in local trading networks and sometimes in wider webs of exchange that brought them buffalo hides, copper, turquoise, seashells, macaw feathers, and coiled baskets from quite distant locations.

These processes of change—growing dependence on agriculture, increasing population, more intensive patterns of exchange—gave rise to larger settlements and adjacent aboveground structures known as pueblos. The most spectacular of these took shape in Chaco canyon in what is now northwestern New Mexico. There, between 860 and 1130 C.E., five major pueblos emerged. This Chaco Phenomenon encompassed 25,000 square miles and linked some seventy outlying settlements to

Map 6.4   North America in the Second-Wave Era
A sparsely populated North America hosted a number of semi-sedentary agricultural societies as well as various gathering and hunting peoples rather than the "civilizations" characteristic of Mesoamerica and the Andes.

Legend:
- Mound-building cultures
- Ancestral Pueblo cultures

Map labels: ROCKY MTS., CALIFORNIA, Missouri R., Mesa Verde, Chaco Canyon, Casa Grande, Rio Grande, Adena (Hopewell culture), Cahokia, Ohio R., Mississippi R., APPALACHIAN MTS.

Pueblo Bonito
Called Pueblo Bonito ("pretty village") by the Spanish, this great house of the Ancestral Pueblo people was at its high point in the eleventh century C.E. The circular structures, known as kivas, were probably ceremonial sites. Their prominence, and the absence of major trash collections, have persuaded some scholars that Pueblo Bonito was more of a ritual center than a residential town. (Courtesy, Chaco Canyon National Historic Park)

the main centers. The population was not large, perhaps as few as 5,000 people, although experts continue to debate the issue. The largest of these towns, or "great houses," Pueblo Bonito, stood five stories high and contained more than 600 rooms and many kivas. Hundreds of miles of roads, up to forty feet wide, radiated out from Chaco, likewise prompting much debate among scholars. Without wheeled carts or large domesticated animals, such an elaborate road system seems unnecessary for ordinary trade or travel. Did the roads represent, as some scholars speculate, a "sacred landscape which gave order to the world," joining its outlying communities to a "Middle Place," an entrance perhaps to the underworld?[23]

Among the Chaco elite were highly skilled astronomers who constructed an observatory of three large rock slabs situated so as to throw a beam of light across a spiral rock carving behind it at the summer solstice. By the eleventh century, Chaco also had become a dominant center for the production of turquoise ornaments, which became a major item of regional commerce, extending as far south as Mesoamerica. Not all was sweetness and light, however. Warfare, internal conflict, and occasional cannibalism (a matter of much controversy among scholars) apparently increased in frequency as an extended period of drought in the half century following 1130 brought this flourishing culture to a rather abrupt end. By 1200, the great houses had been abandoned and their inhabitants scattered in small communities that later became the Pueblo peoples of more recent times.

Peoples of the Eastern Woodlands: The Mound Builders

Unlike the Chaco region in the southwest, the eastern woodlands of North America and especially the Mississippi River valley hosted an independent Agricultural Revolution. By 2000 B.C.E., many of its peoples had domesticated local plant species, including sunflowers, sumpweed, goosefoot, some gourds and squashes, and a form of artichoke. These few plants, however, were not sufficient to support a fully settled agricultural village life; rather they supplemented diets derived from gathering and hunting without fundamentally changing that ancient way of life. Such peoples created societies distinguished by arrays of large earthen mounds, found all over the United States east of the Mississippi, prompting archeologists to dub them the Mound Builders.[24] The earliest of them date to around 2000 B.C.E., but the most elaborate and widespread took shape between 200 B.C.E. and 400 C.E., commonly called the Hopewell culture, after an archeological site in Ohio.

Several features of the Hopewell culture have intrigued archeologists. Particularly significant are the striking burial mounds and geometric earthworks, sometimes covering areas equivalent to several city blocks, and the wide variety of artifacts found within them—smoking pipes, human figurines, mica mirrors, flint blades, fabrics, and jewelry of all kinds. The mounds themselves were no doubt the focus of elaborate burial rituals, but some of them were aligned with the moon with such precision as to allow the prediction of lunar eclipses. Developed most elaborately in the Ohio River valley, Hopewell-style earthworks, artifacts, and ceremonial pottery have also been found throughout the eastern woodlands region of North America. Hopewell centers in Ohio contained mica from the Appalachian Mountains, volcanic glass from Yellowstone, conch shells and sharks' teeth from the Gulf of Mexico, and copper from the Great Lakes. All of this suggests a large "Hopewell Interaction Sphere," linking this entire region in a loose network of exchange, as well as a measure of cultural borrowing of religious ideas and practices.[25]

The next and most spectacular phase in the history of these mound-building peoples took shape as corn-based agriculture, derived ultimately but indirectly from Mexico, gained ground in the Mississippi valley after 800 C.E., allowing larger populations and more complex societies to emerge. The dominant center was Cahokia, near present-day St. Louis, Missouri, which flourished from about 900 to 1250 C.E. Its central mound, a terraced pyramid of four levels, measured 1,000 feet long by 700 feet wide, rose more than 100 feet above the ground, and occupied fifteen acres. It was the largest structure north of Mexico, the focal point of a community numbering 10,000 or more people, and the center of a widespread trading network (see an artist's reconstruction of Cahokia on p. 43).

Cahokia emerged and flourished at about the same time as did the great houses of Chaco canyon, but its settlements were far larger than those of its southwestern counterpart. Both were made possible by the arrival of corn-based agriculture, originating in Mesoamerica, though direct contact with Mexico is much more apparent in Chaco. Finally, Cahokia emerged as the climax of a long history of mound-building cultures in the eastern woodlands, whereas Chaco was more of a "start-up" culture, developing quite quickly "with a relatively shallow history."[26]

Evidence from burials and from later Spanish observers suggests that Cahokia and other centers of this Mississippi culture were stratified societies with a clear elite and with rulers able to mobilize the labor required to build such enormous structures. One high-status male was buried on a platform of 20,000 shell beads, accompanied by 800 arrowheads, sheets of copper and mica, and a number of sacrificed men and women nearby.[27] Well after Cahokia had declined and was abandoned, sixteenth-century Spanish and French explorers encountered another such chiefdom among the Natchez people, located in southwestern Mississippi. Paramount chiefs, known as Great Suns, dressed in knee-length fur coats and lived luxuriously in deerskin-covered homes. An elite class of "principal men" or "honored peoples" clearly occupied a different status from commoners, sometimes referred to as "stinkards." These sharp class distinctions were blunted by the requirement that upper-class people, including the Great Suns, had to marry "stinkards."

The military capacity of these Mississippi chiefdoms greatly impressed European observers, as this Spanish account indicates:

> The next day the cacique [paramount chief] arrived with 200 canoes filled with men, having weapons . . . the warriors standing erect from bow to stern, holding bows and arrows. . . . [F]rom under the canopy where the chief man was, the course was directed and orders issued to the rest. . . . [W]hat with the awnings, the plumes, the shields, the pennons, and the number of people in the fleet, it appeared like a famous armada of galleys.[28]

Here then in the eastern woodlands of North America were peoples who independently generated a modest Agricultural Revolution, assimilated corn and beans from distant sources, developed increasingly complex societies, and created monumental structures, new technologies, and artistic traditions. In doing so, they gave rise to a regional cultural complex that enveloped much of the United States east of the Mississippi in a network of ceremonial, economic, and cultural exchange. But given the presence of two unrelated language families, Algonquin and Iroquoian, the peoples of the eastern woodlands lacked the kind of linguistic commonality that provided the Bantu region of Africa with a measure of cultural unity.

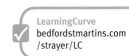

LearningCurve
bedfordstmartins.com
/strayer/LC

Reflections: Deciding What's Important: Balance in World History

Among the perennial problems that teachers and writers of world history confront is sorting through the vast record of times past and choosing what to include and what to leave out. A related issue involves the extent to which particular peoples or civilizations will be treated. Should the Persians get as much space as the Greeks? Does Africa merit equal treatment with Eurasia? Where do the Americas fit in the larger human story? What, in short, are the criteria for deciding what is important in recalling the history of the human venture?

One standard might be duration. Should ways of living that have endured for longer periods of time receive greater attention than those of lesser length? If historians followed only this criterion, then the Paleolithic era of gathering and hunting should occupy 90 percent or more of any world history text. On the other hand, perhaps change is more important than continuity. If so, then something new merits more space than something old. Thus we pay attention to both agriculture and civilizations because they represent significant turning points in human experience. Population provides yet another principle for determining inclusion. That, of course, is the reason that Eurasia/North Africa, with over 80 percent of the world's population, is addressed in three chapters of this section, whereas inner Africa and the Americas together receive just one chapter. There is also the related issue of influence. Buddhism, Christianity, and Islam spread more widely and shaped the lives of more people than did the religions of the Maya or the Bantu-speaking peoples of Africa. Do they therefore deserve more extended treatment? Still another factor involves the availability of evidence. In this respect, Eurasia generated far more written records than either Africa or the Americas did, and therefore its history has been investigated far more thoroughly.

A final possible criterion involves the location of the historian and his or her audience. The recent development of world history as a field of study has sought vigorously to counteract a Eurocentric telling of the human story. Still, is there anything inherently wrong with an account of world history that is centered on one's own people? When I taught history in an Ethiopian high school in the mid-1960s, I was guided by an Afrocentric curriculum, which focused first on Ethiopian history, then on Africa as a whole, and finally on the larger world. Might a world historian from the Middle East, for example, legitimately strike a somewhat different balance in the treatment of various civilizations than someone writing for a largely Western audience or for Chinese readers?

Any account of the world's past will mix and match these criteria in various and contested ways. Among historians, there exists neither a consensus about this question nor any formula to ensure a "proper" balance. You may want to consider whether the balance struck in this chapter, this section, and the book as a whole is appropriate or somehow out of line.

Second Thoughts

What's the Significance?

LearningCurve
Check what you know.
bedfordstmartins.com
/strayer/LC

Online Study Guide
bedfordstmartins.com
/highschool/strayer

Big Picture Questions

1. "The particular cultures and societies of Africa and of the Americas discussed in this chapter developed largely in isolation." What evidence would support this statement, and what might challenge it?
2. How do you understand areas of the world, such as Bantu Africa and North America, that did not generate "civilizations"? Do you see them as "backward," as moving slowly toward civilization, or as simply different?
3. How did African proximity to Eurasia shape its history? And how did American separation from the Eastern Hemisphere affect its development?
4. **Looking Back:** "The histories of Africa and the Americas during the second-wave era largely resemble those of Eurasia." Do you agree with this statement? Explain why or why not.

Next Steps: For Further Study

For Web sites and additional documents related to this chapter, see **Make History** at bedfordstmartins.com /highschool/strayer.

Richard E. W. Adams, *Ancient Civilizations of the New World* (1997). A broad survey based on current scholarship of the Americas before Columbus.

Christopher Ehret, *The Civilizations of Africa* (2002). A recent overview of African history before 1800 by a prominent scholar.

Brian M. Fagan, *Ancient North America* (2005). A prominent archeologist's account of North American history.

Eric Gilbert and Jonathan T. Reynolds, *Africa in World History* (2004). An accessible account of African history set in a global context.

Guy Gugliotta, "The Maya: Glory and Ruin," *National Geographic* (August 2007). A beautifully illustrated account of the rise and fall of Maya civilization.

Charles Mann, *1491* (2005). A journalist's thoughtful account, delightfully written, of the controversies surrounding the history of the Americas before 1492.

Ancient Africa's Black Kingdoms, http://www.homestead.com/wysinger/ancientafrica.html. A Web site exploring the history of Nubia.

Maya Adventure, http://www.smm.org/sln/ma. A collection of text and pictures about the Maya, past and present.

Documents

Considering the Evidence:
Axum and the World

In the world of ancient African history, Axum has occupied a unique position in several ways. (See Map 6.1, p. 266, and pp. 267–70.) It is one of the few places in Africa, outside of Egypt, for which considerable documentary evidence exists. Some of the written sources—royal inscriptions and coins, for example—derive from within Axum itself, while others come from Greco-Roman and Christian visitors. Furthermore, after the rise of Islam, Axum—and its Ethiopian successor state—was the major surviving outpost of a Christian tradition, which had earlier spread widely across northern and northeastern Africa. Finally, Axum has demonstrated an impressive cultural and religious continuity. Even after the decline of the Axumite Empire by the eighth century C.E., the city of Axum remained a major pilgrimage site for Christians, while Ethiopian kings into the twentieth century were crowned there.[29] The documents that follow offer a series of windows on this African kingdom.

Document 6.1

A Guidebook to the World of Indian Ocean Commerce

The earliest documentary reference to Axum was composed during the first century C.E. in an anonymous text known as *The Periplus of the Erythraean Sea*. Likely written by a sea captain from Roman-controlled Egypt, the *Periplus* offers a guide to the places and conditions that merchants might encounter as they traversed the Red Sea and the East African coast while on their way to India.

■ According to this text, why is the Axumite port of Adulis significant?

■ What evidence does the *Periplus* provide about Axum's cultural and economic ties to the larger world?

■ Based on the list of imports and exports, how would you describe Axum's role in the international commerce of the first century C.E.?

■ How might Axum's participation in long-distance trade have stimulated and sustained its growth as an empire?

The Periplus of the Erythraean Sea
First Century C.E.

Below Ptolemais of the Hunts°... there is Adulis, a port established by law.... Before the harbor lies the so-called Mountain Island, about two hundred stadia° sea-ward from the very head of the bay, with the shores of the mainland close to it on both sides. Ships bound for this port now anchor here because of attacks from the land.... Opposite Mountain Island, on the mainland twenty stadia from shore, lies Adulis, a fair-sized village, from which there is a three-days' journey to Coloe, an inland town and the first market for ivory. From that place to the city of the people called Axumites there is a five days' journey more; to that place all the ivory is brought from the country beyond the Nile ... and thence to Adulis. Practically the whole number of elephants and rhinoceros that are killed live in the places inland, although at rare intervals they are hunted on the seacoast even near Adulis. Before the harbor of that market-town, out at sea on the right hand, there lie a great many little sandy islands called Alalaei, yielding tortoise-shell, which is brought to market there by the Fish-Eaters.

And about eight hundred stadia beyond there is another very deep bay, with a great mound of sand piled up at the right of the entrance; at the bottom of which the opsian° stone is found, and this is the only place where it is produced. These places ... are governed by Zoscales,° who is miserly in his ways and always striving for more, but otherwise upright, and acquainted with Greek literature.

There are imported into these places undressed cloth made in Egypt for the Berbers; robes from Arsinoe; cloaks of poor quality dyed in colors; double-fringed linen mantles; many articles of flint glass, and others of murrhine, made in Diospolis;° and brass, which is used for ornament and in cut pieces instead of coin; sheets of soft copper, used for cooking utensils and cut up for bracelets and anklets for the women; iron, which is made into spears used against the elephants and other wild beasts, and in their wars. Besides these, small axes are imported, and adzes and swords; copper drinking-cups, round and large; a little coin° for those coming to the market [probably foreign merchants living in Adulis]; wine of Laodicea and Italy, not much; olive oil, not much; for the king, gold and silver plate made after the fashion of the country, and for clothing, military cloaks, and thin coats of skin, of no great value. Likewise from the district of Ariaca° across this sea, there are imported Indian iron, and steel, and Indian cotton cloth;... and girdles, and coats of skin and mallow-colored cloth, and a few muslins, and colored lac.° There are exported from these places ivory, and tortoise-shell and rhinoceros-horn. The most from Egypt is brought to this market from the month of January....

°**Ptolemais of the Hunts:** near modern Port Sudan on the Red Sea.

°**stadia:** 1 stadium = ⅛ mile.

°**opsian:** obsidian.

°**Zoscales:** an Axumite ruler.

Source: Wilfred H. Schoff, *The Periplus of the Erythraean Sea* (New York: Longman, Green, 1912), secs. 4–6.

°**Diospolis:** Thebes.

°**coin:** Roman money.

°**Ariaca:** an area in western India.

°**lac:** a resinous secretion of an insect, used in the form of shellac.

Document 6.2

The Making of an Axumite Empire

At its high point in the mid-fourth century C.E., Axum ruled an empire stretching from Meroë in the upper Nile Valley, across much of what is now Eritrea and Ethiopia, and incorporating parts of southern Arabia on the opposite side of the Red Sea. Document 6.2 comes from an Axumite inscription written in Greek on a stone throne adorned with figures of the Greek gods Hercules and Mercury. Commissioned by an unknown Axumite monarch, the inscription dates probably from the second or third century C.E. It was copied and then published in the sixth century by Cosmas, a Greek merchant born in Alexandria, Egypt, who had become a monk. This text describes some of the conquests that generated the Axumite Empire.

■ What internal evidence from the document itself dates it prior to Axum's acceptance of Christianity?

■ How would you describe the point of view from which the document was written?

■ What techniques of imperial control does the document reveal?

■ How might you account for the obvious Greek influence that is apparent in the inscription?

■ How would you describe the religious or ideological underpinnings of this empire? Why might the Axumite ruler who commissioned this inscription single out Ares, Zeus, and Poseidon for special attention?

Inscription on a Stone Throne
Second or Third Century C.E.

Having after this with a strong hand compelled the nations bordering on my kingdom to live in peace, I made war upon the following nations, and by force of arms reduced them to subjection. I warred first with the nation of Gaze [Axum, probably in an internal struggle for power], then with Agame and Sigye, and having conquered them, I exacted the half of all that they possessed. . . . [*There follows a long list of other peoples that this ruler conquered.*]

I proceeded next against the Tangaltae, who adjoin the borders of Egypt; and having reduced them I made a footpath giving access by land into Egypt from that part of my dominions. Next I reduced Annine and Metine—tribes inhabiting precipitous mountains. My arms were next directed against the Sesea nation. These had retired to a high mountain difficult of access; but I blockaded the mountain on every side, and compelled them to come down and surrender. I then selected for myself the best of their young men and their women, with their sons and daughters and all besides that they possessed. The tribes of Rhausi I next brought to submission: a bar-

Source: J. W. McCrindle, trans. and ed., *The Christian Topography of Cosmas, an Egyptian Monk* (London: Hakluyt Society, 1897), 59–66.

barous race spread over wide waterless plains in the interior of the frankincense country. [Advancing thence toward the sea,] I encountered the Solate, whom I subdued, and left with instructions to guard the coast.

All these nations, protected though they were by mountains all but impregnable, I conquered, after engagements in which I was myself present. Upon their submission I restored their territories to them, subject to the payment of tribute. Many other tribes besides these submitted of their own accord, and became likewise tributary. And I sent a fleet and land forces against the Arabitae and Cinaedocolpitae who dwelt on the other side of the Red Sea [southern Arabia], and having reduced the sovereigns of both, I imposed on them a land tribute and charged them to make traveling safe both by sea and by land. . . .

I first and alone of the kings of my race made these conquests. For this success I now offer my thanks to my mighty god, Ares,° who begat me, and by whose aid I reduced all the nations bordering on my own country. . . . Of these expeditions, some were conducted by myself in person, and ended in victory, and the others I entrusted to my officers. Having thus brought all the world under my authority to peace, I came down to Adulis and offered sacrifice to Zeus,° and to Ares, and to Poseidon,° whom I entreated to befriend all who go down to the sea in ships.° Here also I reunited all my forces, and setting down this Chair [throne] in this place, I consecrated it to Ares in the twenty-seventh year of my reign.

°**Ares:** the Greek god of warfare and slaughter.

°**Zeus:** the chief god of the Greek pantheon.

°**Poseidon:** the Greek god of the sea.

°Note that many Axumite deities derived from southern Arabia but came to be identified with the gods of the Greek pantheon.

Document 6.3

The Coming of Christianity to Axum

The introduction of Christianity in the mid-fourth century C.E. represented a major change in the cultural history of Axum. It meant that Axum would be more closely aligned to Christian Egypt and Byzantium than to South Arabia, from which many of its earlier cultural traditions had derived. Document 6.3 relates the story of the coming of Christianity to Axum. It was written by Rufinus (345–410 C.E.), a Christian monk and writer who was born in Italy but spent much of his life in Jerusalem, where he heard this story from those who had taken part in it. Note that Greco-Roman writers of this time used "India" to refer vaguely to East Africa and southern Arabia as well as the South Asian peninsula.

- According to this document, by what means was Christianity introduced to Axum? What do you think was the relative importance of Frumentius and Aedesius, as opposed to Roman merchants living in Axum?

- Why do you think the Axumite royal family was so receptive to this foreign religion? How might the story differ if told from the ruling family's perspective?

- How does the fact that this document was written by outsiders shape the emphasis of the story?

RUFINUS

On the Evangelization of Abyssinia
Late Fourth Century C.E.

One Metrodorus, a philosopher, is said to have penetrated to further India [the Red Sea area including Axum] in order to view places and see the world. Inspired by his example, one Meropius, a philosopher [and a Christian merchant] of Tyre,° wished to visit India with a similar object, taking with him two small boys who were related to him and whom he was educating in humane studies. The younger of these was called Aedesius, the other Frumentius. When, having seen and taken note of what his soul fed upon, the philosopher had begun to return, the ship on which he traveled put in for water or some other necessary at a certain port. It is the custom of the barbarians of these parts that, if ever the neighboring tribes report that their treaty with the Romans is broken, all Romans found among them should be massacred. The philosopher's ship was boarded; all with himself were put to the sword.

The boys were found studying under a tree and preparing their lessons, and, preserved by the mercy of the barbarians, were taken to the king [of Axum]. He made one of them, Aedesius, his cup-bearer. Frumentius, whom he had perceived to be sagacious and prudent, he made his treasurer and secretary. Thereafter they were held in great honor and affection by the king. The king died, leaving his wife with an infant son [Ezana] as heir of the bereaved kingdom. He gave the young men liberty to do what they pleased but the queen besought them with tears, since she had no more faithful subjects in the whole kingdom, to share with her the cares of governing the kingdom until her son should grow up, especially Frumentius, whose ability was equal to guiding the kingdom, for the other, though loyal and honest of heart, was simple.

While they lived there and Frumentius held the reins of government in his hands, God stirred up his heart and he began to search out with care those of the Roman merchants who were Christians and to give them great influence and to urge them to establish in various places conventicles to which they might resort for prayer in the Roman manner. He himself, moreover, did the same and so encouraged the others, attracting them with his favor and his benefits, providing them with whatever was needed, supplying sites for buildings and other necessaries, and in every way promoting the growth of the seed of Christianity in the country. When the prince [Ezana] for whom they exercised the regency had grown up, they completed and faithfully delivered over their trust, and, though the queen and her son sought greatly to detain them and begged them to remain, returned to the Roman Empire.

Aedesius hastened to Tyre to revisit his parents and relatives. Frumentius went to Alexandria, saying that it was not right to hide the work of God. He laid the whole affair before the bishop and urged him to look for some worthy man to send as bishop over the many Christians already congregated and the churches built on barbarian soil. Then Athanasius (for he had recently assumed the episcopate), having carefully weighed and considered Frumentius' words and deeds, declared in a council of the priests: "What other man shall we find in whom the Spirit of God is as in thee, who can accomplish these things?" And he consecrated him and bade him return in the grace of God whence he had come. And when he had arrived in India [Axum] as bishop, such grace is said to have been given to him by God that apostolic miracles were wrought by him and a countless number of barbarians were converted by him to the faith. From which time Christian peoples and churches have been created in the parts of India, and the priesthood has begun. These facts I know not from vulgar report but from the mouth of Aedesius himself, who had been Frumentius' companion and was later made a priest in Tyre.

Source: Quoted in A. H. M. Jones and Elizabeth Monroe, *A History of Abyssinia* (Oxford: Oxford University Press, 1935), 26–27.

°**Tyre:** a city in Lebanon.

Document 6.4

Axum and the Gold Trade

The foundations of the Axumite state lay not only in its military conquests and its adoption of a new religion but also in its economic ties to the larger world. Among these ties was its reputation as a major source of gold for the Roman Empire. Document 6.4 describes the distinctive fashion in which Axumite traders obtained the gold from the African peoples living on the margins of the Axumite state. The author, Cosmas (see Document 6.2, pp. 294–95), was involved in this trade.

- How would you define the pattern of exchange described in this document? Was it state-directed trade, private enterprise, or both? To what problems of cross-cultural interaction was it a response?

- Who, if anyone, had the upper hand in this trade? Was it conducted between politically equal parties?

- What purposes did this trade serve for the people who mined and "sold" the gold?

- Beyond the peaceful trade for gold described here, what other purposes did this region serve for Axum?

COSMAS

The Christian Topography
Sixth Century C.E.

The country known as that of Sasu is itself near the ocean, just as the ocean is near the frankincense country,° in which there are many gold mines. The King of the Axumites accordingly, every other year, through the governor of Agau, sends thither special agents to bargain for the gold, and these are accompanied by many other traders—upwards, say, of five hundred—bound on the same errand as themselves. They take along with them to the mining district oxen, lumps of salt, and iron, and when they reach its neighborhood, they make a halt at a certain spot and form an encampment, which they fence round with a great hedge of thorns. Within this they live, and having slaughtered the oxen, cut them in pieces, and lay the pieces on the top of the thorns, along with the lumps of salt and the iron. Then come the natives bringing gold in nuggets like peas, and lay one or two or more of these upon what pleases them—the pieces of flesh or the salt or the iron, and then they retire to some distance off. Then the owner of the meat approaches, and if he is satisfied he takes the gold away, and upon seeing this, its owner comes and takes the flesh or the salt or the iron. If, however, he is not satisfied, he leaves the gold, when the native, seeing that he has not taken it, comes and either puts down more gold, or takes up what he had laid down, and goes away. Such is the mode in

Source: J. W. McCrindle, trans. and ed., *The Christian Topography of Cosmas, an Egyptian Monk* (London: Hakluyt Society, 1897), 52–54, 67.

°**frankincense country:** probably what is now Somalia.

which business is transacted with the people of that country, because their language is different and interpreters are hardly to be found.

The time they stay in that country is five days more or less, according as the natives, more or less readily coming forward, buy up all their wares. On the journey homeward they all agree to travel well-armed, since some of the tribes through whose country they must pass might threaten to attack them from a desire to rob them of their gold. The space of six months is taken up with this trading expedition, including both the going and the returning. In going they march very slowly, chiefly because of the cattle, but in returning they quicken their pace lest on the way they should be overtaken by winter and its rains. For the sources of the river Nile lie somewhere in these parts, and in winter, on account of the heavy rains, the numerous rivers which they generate obstruct the path of the traveler. The people there have their winter at the time we have our summer . . . and during the three months the rain falls in torrents, and makes a multitude of rivers all of which flow into the Nile.

The facts which I have just recorded fell partly under my own observation and partly were told me by traders who had been to those parts. . . .

For most of the slaves which are now found in the hands of merchants who resort to these parts are taken from the tribes of which we speak. As for the Semenai, where . . . there are snows and ice, it is to that country the King of the Axumites expatriates anyone whom he has sentenced to be banished.

Using the Evidence: Axum and the World

1. **Assessing sources:** How does each of these documents reflect the distinctive perspective of its author? What different perspectives can you notice between those documents written from within Axum and those written by outsiders? How did the particular social role that each author represents (missionary, monarch, merchant) affect his view of Axum?

2. **Considering external influences:** Based on these documents, how would you describe Axum's various relationships with the world beyond its borders? How did its geographical location shape those relationships? (See Map 6.1, p. 266.) In what ways did those external connections influence Axum's historical development? From another perspective, how did Axum actively assimilate foreign influences or deliberately take advantage of opportunities that came from outside?

3. **Explaining the rise and significance of Axum:** How might you account for the flourishing of Axum? What was the religious and military significance of Axum within the region?

4. **Comparing civilizations:** In what ways might Axum be viewed as a smaller-scale version of the second-wave civilizations of Eurasia? In what ways did it differ from them?

5. **Seeking further evidence:** What else would you like to know about Axum? If you could uncover one additional document, what would you want it to reveal?

Visual Sources

Considering the Evidence:
Art and the Maya Elite

"The ancient Maya world," writes a major scholar of the region, "was a world of Maya art."[30] In magnificent architecture, carvings, pottery, ceramic figures, wall paintings, and illustrated books, Maya culture was suffused by a distinctive style of artistic expression, more complex, subtle, extensive, and innovative than any other in the Americas. Commissioned by Maya rulers, that art centered on life at court, depicting kings, nobles, warriors, and wealthy merchants together with the women, musicians, and artists who served them. The many deities who populated the Maya universe also appeared frequently in Maya art, which represents a major source for historians studying that civilization. While the Maya had writing, their literature was less extensive than that of Eurasian cultures, and much of it was tragically destroyed during the early decades of Spanish rule. The images that follow provide a window into the life of the Maya elite during its classical era (see the map on p. 273).

Visual Source 6.1 shows a royal couple from the Maya city of Yaxchilan in the year 724 C.E. with the king, Shield Jaguar, on the left, and his primary wife, Lady Xok, on the right. In helping him dress for a war-related ceremony or sacrifice, Lady Xok offers her husband his helmet, the head of a jaguar, an animal that was widely associated with strength, bravery, aggression, warfare, and high social status. The T-shaped frame at the center top, which contains a number of Maya glyphs (written symbols), indicates a doorway and thus sets the action in an interior space. The king is wearing cotton body armor and carrying a knife, while his wife is clad in a *huipil*, a blouse similar to those still worn by Maya women in southern Mexico.

- What elements of their dress and decoration serve to mark their high status?

- What aspects of the physical appearance of this couple might represent ideal male and female characteristics in Maya culture? Pay attention to their hair, foreheads, and noses, as well as to the attitude suggested by their faces.

- What might you infer about the relationship of Shield Jaguar and Lady Xok from this carving? Notice the relatively equal size of the two figures and the gesture that Shield Jaguar makes with his left hand. Keep in mind that the carving comes from a temple in Yaxchilan dedicated to Lady Xok.

Visual Source 6.1 Shield Jaguar and Lady Xok: A Royal Couple of Yaxchilan (Enrique Franco Torillos)

Warfare was frequent among Maya cities and thus a common theme in court art. Fought with spear throwers, lances, clubs, axes, swords, and shields, Maya wars were depicted as chaotic affairs aimed at the capture of individual prisoners, who were destined for sacrifice or slavery. Those prisoners were often named in the glyphs that accompanied the portrayal of battles along with the inscription "He is seized/roped."

Visual Source 6.2, a reconstructed image, comes from a Maya archeological site in southern Mexico called Bonampak (BOHN-uhm-PAHK), well known for its vivid murals. Depicting events that took place in 792 C.E., this mural shows King Chan Muwan of Bonampak (in the center) holding a staff and receiving nine prisoners of war from his victorious noble warriors. To the right of the king in this painting are two allies from the nearby city of Yaxchilan, followed by the king's wife, his mother, and a servant-musician playing a conch. To the king's left are six more high-ranking warriors from Bonampak, while lower-level warriors guard each side of the door at the bottom.

The prisoners hold center stage in the mural. Notice in particular the dead captive sprawling below the king's staff as a severed head lies on a bed of leaves below him. The four small images at the top indicate constellations, showing the favorable configuration of the sky for this occasion. The turtle on the far right, for example, depicts the constellation Gemini, while the three stars on its back represent what we know as Orion's belt.

- What can you infer about Maya warfare and court practice from this mural?

- What do the various postures of the captives suggest?

- Notice that a number of the captives have blood dripping from their fingers. What does this indicate? What might be happening to the prisoner at the far left of the painting?

- What status distinctions can you observe among the figures in the mural? Notice the jaguar skins worn by the king and three other warriors.

- What meaning might you attach to the presence of the king's wife and mother at this event?

The bleeding and ultimately the sacrifice of the captives in Visual Source 6.2 was part of a more pervasive practice of bloodletting that permeated Maya religious and court life. Significant occasions—such as birth, marriage, death, planting crops, and dedicating buildings—were sanctified with human blood, the most valued and holy substance in the world. Behind this practice lay the Maya belief in the mutual relationship of humans and their gods. Two of the major scholars in this field explain: "The earth and its creatures were created through a sacrificial act of the gods, and human beings, in turn, were required to strengthen and nourish the gods."[31] The means of doing so was blood. The massive loss of blood often triggered a trancelike state that the Maya experienced

Visual Source 6.2 The Presentation of Captives (Peabody Museum, Harvard University, Cambridge, MA, USA/The Bridgeman Art Library)

as mystical union with their gods or ancestors. The lancets used to draw blood— usually from the tongue in women and often from the penis in men—were invested with sacred power.

Kings and their wives were central to this bloodletting ritual, as Visual Source 6.3 so vividly shows. Here we meet again Shield Jaguar and Lady Xok, depicted also in Visual Source 6.1. The date of this carving is October 28, 709 C.E. The king is holding a large torch, suggesting that the ritual occurs at night, while his kneeling wife draws a thorn-studded rope through her perforated tongue. The rope falls into a basket of bloody paper, which will be burned with the

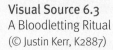

Visual Source 6.3
A Bloodletting Ritual
(© Justin Kerr, K2887)

resulting smoke nourishing the gods. Shield Jaguar too will soon let his own blood flow, for the glyphs accompanying this carving declare that "he is letting blood" and "she is letting blood."

■ What details can you notice in the exquisitely carved work?

■ What significance might you attribute to the fact that the couple is performing this ritual together?

■ Why do you think Lady Xok is kneeling?

■ Notice the shrunken head in Shield Jaguar's headdress. How would you assess its significance? How might it enhance his status?

■ To what extent is this pervasive bloodletting a uniquely Mesoamerican religious practice? What roles do blood and sacrifice play in other religious traditions?

Among the most well-known and intriguing features of Maya life was a ball game in which teams of players, often two on a side, sought to control a rubber ball, using only their thighs, torsos, and upper arms to make it hit a marker or ring. Deeply rooted in Maya mythology, the game had long been popular throughout the Maya territory and elsewhere in Mesoamerica. On one level, it was sport, often played simply for entertainment and recreation. But the game also reflected and symbolized the prevalence of warfare among Maya cities. As one recent account put it: "The game re-enacted the paradigms for war and sacrifice, where the skillful and blessed triumph and the weak and undeserving are vanquished."[32] The ball game was yet another occasion for the shedding of blood, as losing players, often war captives, were killed, sometimes bound in ball-like fashion and rolled down the steps of the court to their death. Thus the larger mythic context of the ball game was the eternal struggle of life and death, so central to Maya religious thinking.

Visual Source 6.4, a rollout of a vase dating from the seventh or eighth century C.E., depicts the ball game in action. The two players on each side echo the Hero Twins of Maya mythology, famous ball players who triumphed over the lords of the underworld in an extended game and who were later transformed triumphantly into the sun and moon. The glyphs accompanying this image named two kings of adjacent cities, suggesting that the game may have been played on occasion as a substitute for warfare between rival cities.

- What might the elaborate dress of the players suggest about the function of the game and the status of its players?

- Notice the deer headdress on the player at the far left and the vulture image on the corresponding player at the far right. What do the headdresses suggest about the larger mythic context in which the game was understood?

Visual Source 6.4 The Ball Game (© Justin Kerr, K2803)

■ Notice the heavy protective padding around the waist as well as the wrappings around one knee, foot, and upper arm of the two lead players. What was the purpose of such padding? Keep in mind that the rubber ball, shown here in an exaggerated form, was roughly the size of a modern volleyball but weighed perhaps seven or eight pounds.

■ How might you compare this ancient Maya ball game to contemporary athletic contests? Consider the larger social meaning of the game as well as its more obvious features.

Using the Evidence:
Art and the Maya Elite

1. **Considering art as evidence:** What can you learn from these visual sources about the values, preoccupations, and outlook of the Maya elite? What are the strengths and limitations of art as a source of evidence? What other kinds of evidence would you want to discover to further your understanding of the Maya elite?

2. **Assessing gender roles:** In what ways are women and men depicted in these visual sources? What might this suggest about their respective roles in the elite circles of Maya society?

3. **Making comparisons:** How might you compare the life of the Maya elite depicted in these visual sources with that of the Roman elite of Pompeii shown in the Visual Sources section of Chapter 5 (pp. 252–59)? For a second comparison, consider the similarities and differences of Maya and Axumite civilizations.

4. **Considering the values of the historian:** What feelings or judgments do these visual sources evoke in you? Which of your values might get in the way of a sympathetic understanding of the Maya elite?

Chapter 6 Wrap Up

LearningCurve
Check what you know.
bedfordstmartins.com
/strayer/LC

STEP ONE

The Word to Know: Eurocentrism

The *Oxford English Dictionary* defines *eurocentrism* as "having or regarding Europe as its center; focusing on Europe to the exclusion of the rest of the world; implicitly regarding Europeans or European culture as pre-eminent." Read the Reflections section on pp. 289–290 and consider it in light of the definition above. Write a brief paragraph addressing these questions: Does this chapter sufficiently address the imbalance considering that three out of four chapters in Part Two largely focus on Asia, Europe, and North Africa? Do Africa and the Americas belong together in one chapter?

STEP TWO

Mapping Africa and the Americas

1. Using a blank map of the world, write labels for the following locations in Africa: Ghana, Egypt, Nubia, Axum, and San. Shade in the area in which the Bantu people originated and where they spread. For the Americas, shade in and label the area of the Maya civilization, the Moche, the Chimu (Chavín), the Wari and the Tiwanaku civilizations, as well as the ancestral Pueblo cultures and mound-building cultures of North America.

2. Consider Map 6.1, "Africa in the Second-Wave Era" (p. 266) in combination with the text. Which of the places labeled on the map represent civilizations, which are cities without states, and which are civilizations without cities or states? Describe a way this could be denoted differently on the map.

3. Using both the text and the map, describe the connections within Africa at this time period (trade, cultural, migration, and technology).

4. Looking at the map, as well as the text in Chapter 6 and those parts of North Africa addressed in Chapters 3 and 4, describe the ways in which Africa was connected with the larger Afro-Eurasian world. How did this differ from the Americas at this time?

Understanding Demographics

Demography is the study of characteristics and statistics of human population. It can provide insights into the cause and effect of disease, technology, migration, and new interactions on a given population. Examine the following charts and then answer the questions below: Snapshot: Paleolithic Era in Perspective (p. 24); Snapshot: World Population during the Age of Agricultural Civilization (p. 111); and Snapshot: Continental Population in the Second-Wave Era (p. 264).

1. Looking at the Snapshot on page 24, which era had the longest duration? Which era had the greatest percentage of humans? What assumption can be made about the shift in numbers showing the percent of years lived in each era?

2. Next, consider the Snapshot on page 111. What factors might account for the occasional dips in population?

3. Finally, evaluate the Snapshot on page 264. In the era from 400 B.C.E. to 1000 C.E., which two regions had the most consistent numbers and percentages of population? Which region consistently had the largest percentage of the global population? Which two regions doubled in population?

PART THREE

An Age of Accelerating Connections

500–1500

Contents

THE BIG PICTURE

Defining a Millennium

History seldom turns sharp corners, and historians often have difficulty deciding just when one phase of the human story ends and another begins. Between roughly 200 and 850 C.E., many of the second-wave states and civilizations (Han dynasty China, the Roman Empire, Gupta India, Meroë, Axum, Maya, Teotihuacán, Moche) experienced severe disruption, decline, or collapse. For many historians, this has marked the end of an era and the start of a new period of world history. Furthermore, almost everyone agrees that the transatlantic voyages of Columbus beginning in 1492 represent yet another new departure in world history. This coupling of the Eastern and Western hemispheres set in motion historical processes that transformed most of the world and signaled the beginning of the modern era.

But how are we to understand the thousand years (roughly 500 to 1500) between the end of the second-wave era and the beginning of modern world history? Historians, frankly, have had some difficulty defining a distinct identity for this millennium, a problem reflected in the vague terms used to describe it: a postclassical era, a medieval or "middle" period between the ancient and modern, or, as in this book, an age of third-wave civilizations. At best, these terms indicate where this period falls in the larger time frame of world history, but none of them are very descriptive.

Third-Wave Civilizations: Something New, Something Old, Something Blended

A large part of the problem lies in the rather different trajectories of various regions of the world during this millennium. It is not easy to identify clearly defined features that encompass all major civilizations or human communities during this period and distinguish them from what went before. We can, however, point to several distinct patterns during this third-wave era.

In some areas, for example, wholly new but smaller civilizations arose where none had existed before. Along the East African coast, Swahili civilization emerged in a string of thirty or more city-states, very much engaged in the commercial life of the Indian Ocean basin. The kingdoms of Ghana, Mali, and Songhay, stimulated and sustained by long-distance trade across the Sahara, represented a new West African civilization. In the area now encompassed by Ukraine and western Russia, another new civilization, known as Kievan Rus, likewise took shape with a good deal of cultural borrowing from Mediterranean civilization. East and Southeast Asia also witnessed new centers of civilization. Those in Japan, Korea, and Vietnam were strongly influenced by China, while Srivijaya on the Indonesian island of Sumatra and later the Angkor kingdom, centered in present-day Cambodia, drew on the Hindu and Buddhist traditions of India.

All of these represent a continuation of a well-established pattern in world history—the globalization of civilization. Each of the new third-wave civilizations was, of course, culturally unique, but like their predecessors of the first and second waves, they too featured states, cities, specialized economic roles, sharp class and gender inequalities, and other elements of "civilized" life. As newcomers to the growing number of civilizations, all of them borrowed heavily from larger or more established centers.

The largest, most expansive, and most widely influential of the new third-wave civilizations was surely that of Islam. It began in Arabia in the seventh century C.E., projecting the Arab peoples into a prominent role as builders of an enormous empire while offering a new, vigorous, and attractive religion. Viewed as a new civilization defined by its religion, the world of Islam came to encompass many other centers of civilization—Egypt, Mesopotamia, Persia, India, the interior of West Africa and the coast of East Africa, Spain, southeastern Europe, and more. Here was a uniquely cosmopolitan or "umbrella" civilization that "came closer than any had ever come to uniting all mankind under its ideals."[1]

Yet another, and quite different, historical pattern during the third-wave millennium involved those older civilizations that persisted or were reconstructed. The Byzantine Empire, embracing the eastern half of the old Roman Empire, continued the patterns of Mediterranean Christian civilization and persisted until 1453, when it was overrun by the Ottoman Turks. In China, following almost four centuries of fragmentation, the Sui, Tang, and Song dynasties (589–1279) restored China's imperial unity and reasserted its Confucian tradition. Indian civilization retained its ancient patterns of caste and Hinduism amid vast cultural diversity, even as parts of India fell under the control of Muslim rulers.

Variations on this theme of continuing or renewing older traditions took shape in the Western Hemisphere, where two centers of civilization—in Mesoamerica and in the Andes—had been long established. In Mesoamerica, the collapse of classical Maya civilization and of the great city-state of Teotihuacán by about 900 C.E. opened the way for other peoples to give new shape to this ancient civilization. The most well-known of these efforts was associated with the Mexica or Aztec people, who created a powerful and impressive state in the fifteenth century. About the same time, on the western rim of South America, a Quechua-speaking people, now known as the Inca, incorporated various centers of Andean civilization into a huge bureaucratic empire. Both the Aztecs and the Incas gave a new political expression to much older patterns of civilized life.

Yet another pattern took shape in Western Europe following the collapse of the Roman Empire. There would-be kings and church leaders alike sought to maintain links with the older Greco-Roman-Christian traditions of classical Mediterranean civilization. In the absence of empire, however, new and far more decentralized societies emerged, led now by Germanic peoples and centered in Northern and West-

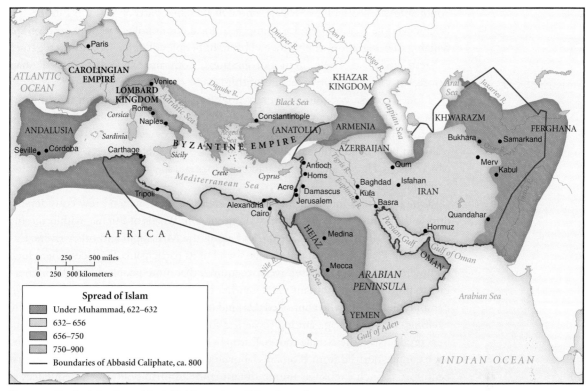

Map 9.2   The Arab Empire and the Initial Expansion of Islam (p. 420)

ern Europe, considerably removed from the older centers of Rome and Athens. It was a hybrid civilization, combining old and new, Greco-Roman and Germanic elements, in a distinctive blending. For five centuries or more, this region was a relative backwater, compared to the more vibrant, prosperous, and powerful civilizations of Byzantium, the Islamic world, and China. During the centuries after 1000 C.E., however, Western European civilization emerged as a rapidly growing and expansive set of competitive states, willing, like other new civilizations, to borrow extensively from their more developed neighbors.

The Ties That Bind: Transregional Interaction in the Third-Wave Era

These quite different patterns of development within particular civilizations have made it difficult to define the Third Wave era in a single, all-encompassing fashion. In another way, though, a common theme emerges, for during this time, the world's various regions, cultures, and peoples interacted with one another far more extensively. More than before, change in human societies was the product of contact with strangers, or at least with their ideas, armies, goods, or diseases. In a variety of places—island

Southeast Asia, coastal East Africa, Central Asian cities, parts of Western Europe, the Islamic Middle East, and the Inca Empire—local cosmopolitan regions emerged in which trade, migration, or empire had brought peoples of different cultures together in a restricted space. These "mini-globalizations," both larger and more common than before, became a distinctive feature of third-wave civilizations.

None of these civilizations were wholly isolated or separate from their neighbors, although the range and intensity of cross-cultural interaction certainly varied over time. In limited ways, that had been true for earlier civilizations as well. But the scale and pace of such interaction accelerated considerably between 500 and 1500. Much of Part Three highlights these intersections and spells out their many and varied consequences.

One pattern of interaction lay in long-distance trade, which grew considerably during the third-wave millennium—along the Silk Roads of Eurasia, within the Indian Ocean basin, across the Sahara, and along the Mississippi and other rivers. Everywhere it acted as an agent of change for all of its participants. In places where such commerce was practiced extensively, it required that more people devote their energies to producing for a distant market rather than for the consumption of their own communities. Those who controlled this kind of trade often became extremely wealthy, exciting envy or outrage among those less fortunate. Many societies learned about new products via these trade routes. Europe's knowledge of pepper and other spices, for example, derived from Roman seaborne trade with India beginning in the first century C.E. Such exchange among distant lands also had political consequences as many new states or empires were constructed on the basis of resources derived from long-distance commerce. Furthermore, religious ideas, technologies, and diseases also made their ways along those paths of commerce, disrupting older ways of living and offering new opportunities as well.

Yet another mechanism of cross-cultural interaction lay in large empires. Not only did they incorporate many distinct cultures within a single political system, but their size and stability also provided the security that encouraged travelers and traders to journey long distances from their homelands. Empires, of course, were nothing new in world history, but many of those associated with third-wave civilizations were distinctive. In the first place, they were larger. The Arab Empire, which accompanied the initial spread of Islam, stretched from Spain to India. Even more extensive was the Mongol Empire of the thirteenth and fourteenth centuries. In the Western Hemisphere, the Inca Empire encompassed dozens of distinct peoples in a huge state that ran some 2,500 miles along the spine of the Andes Mountains.

Furthermore, the largest of these empires were the creation of nomadic or pastoral peoples. Earlier empires in the Mediterranean basin, China, India, and Persia had been the work of settled farming societies. But now, in the thousand years between 500 and 1500, peoples with a recent history of a nomadic or herding way of life entered the stage of world history as empire builders—Arabs, Berbers, Turks, Mongols, Aztecs— ruling over agricultural peoples and established civilizations.

Together, large-scale empires and long-distance trade facilitated the spread of ideas, technologies, food crops, and germs far beyond their points of origin. Buddhism spread from India to much of Asia; Christianity encompassed Europe and took root in distant Russia, even as it contracted in the Middle East and North Africa. Hinduism attracted followers in Southeast Asia; and more than any other religion, Islam became an Afro-Eurasian phenomenon with an enormous reach. Beyond the connections born of commerce and conquest, those of culture and religion generated lasting ties among many peoples of the Eastern Hemisphere.

Technologies, too, were diffused widely. Until the sixth century C.E., China maintained a monopoly on the manufacture of raw silk. Then this technology spread beyond East Asia, allowing the development of a silk industry in the eastern Mediterranean and later in Italy. India too contributed much to the larger world—crystallized sugar, a system of numerals and the concept of zero, techniques for making cotton textiles, and many food crops. In the Americas, corn gradually diffused from Mesoamerica, where it was initially domesticated, to North America, where it stimulated population growth and the development of more complex societies. Disease also linked distant communities. The plague, or Black Death, decimated many parts of Eurasia and North Africa as it made its deadly way from east to west in the fourteenth century.

A focus on these accelerating connections across cultural boundaries puts the historical spotlight on merchants, travelers, missionaries, migrants, soldiers, and administrators—people who traveled abroad rather than those who stayed at home. This cross-cultural emphasis in world history raises provocative questions about what happens when cultures interact or when strangers meet. How did external stimuli operate to produce change within particular societies? How did individuals or societies decide what to accept and what to reject when confronted with new ideas or practices? In what ways did they alter foreign customs or traditions to better meet their own needs and correspond to their own values?

Much of the readily visible "action" in third-wave civilizations, as in all earlier civilizations, featured male actors. The vast majority of rulers, traders, soldiers, religious officials, and long-distance travelers were men, as were most heads of households and families. The building of states and empires, so prominent in the third-wave era, meant war and conquest, fostering distinctly masculine warrior values and reinforcing the dominant position of men. Much of what follows in Part Three is, frankly, men's history.

But it is useful to remember that behind all of this lay a vast realm of women's activity, long invisible to historians or simply assumed. Women sustained the family life that was the foundation of all human community; they were the repositories of language, religious ritual, group knowledge, and local history; their labor generated many of the products that entered long-distance trade routes as well those that fed and clothed their communities. The changing roles and relationships of men and women and their understandings of gender also figure in the chapters that follow.

Mapping Part Three

Complex gathering and hunting cultures
Chapter 12

Ancestral Pueblo
Chapter 7

Aztec Empire
Chapters 7, 12

Maya cities
Chapter 7

Inca Empire
Chapters 7, 12

Iroquois Confederacy
Chapters 7, 12

Eastern woodlands
Chapters 7, 12

Amazon River trade
Chapter 12

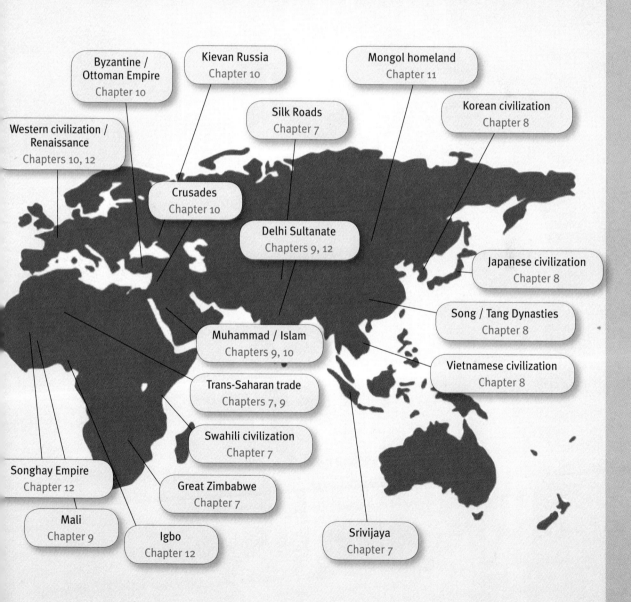

Western civilization /
Renaissance
Chapters 10, 12

Byzantine /
Ottoman Empire
Chapter 10

Kievan Russia
Chapter 10

Mongol homeland
Chapter 11

Silk Roads
Chapter 7

Korean civilization
Chapter 8

Crusades
Chapter 10

Delhi Sultanate
Chapters 9, 12

Japanese civilization
Chapter 8

Song / Tang Dynasties
Chapter 8

Muhammad / Islam
Chapters 9, 10

Vietnamese civilization
Chapter 8

Trans-Saharan trade
Chapters 7, 9

Swahili civilization
Chapter 7

Songhay Empire
Chapter 12

Great Zimbabwe
Chapter 7

Mali
Chapter 9

Igbo
Chapter 12

Srivijaya
Chapter 7

Commerce and Culture

500–1500

"In the spring of 2004 I was looking for an appropriate college graduation present for my son Ateesh and decided on an Apple iPod music player. . . . I placed my order online. . . . I was astonished by what followed. I received a confirmation e-mail within minutes . . . [and learned that] the product was being shipped not from California but from Shanghai, China. . . . Ateesh's personalized iPod landed on our New Haven [Connecticut] doorstep barely 40 hours after I had clicked "Buy."[1] To Nayan Chanda, a fifty-eight-year-old journalist, born and educated in India and at the time working at Yale University, this was an astonishing transaction. Probably it was less surprising to his son. But both of them, no doubt, understood this kind of commercial exchange as something quite recent in human history.

And in the speed of the transaction, it surely was. But from the perspective of world history, exchange among distant peoples is not altogether new and the roots of economic globalization lie deep in the past. In fact, just three years after purchasing his son's iPod, Nayan Chanda wrote a well-received book titled *Bound Together*, describing how traders, preachers, adventurers, and warriors had long created links among peoples living in widely separated cultures and civilizations. Those early transregional interactions and their capacity for transforming human societies, for better and for worse, played an increasingly significant role in this era of third-wave civilizations, a millennium of accelerating connections.

THE EXCHANGE OF GOODS AMONG COMMUNITIES occupying different ecological zones has long been a prominent feature of human history.

Travels on the Silk Road: This Chinese ceramic figurine from the Tang dynasty (618–907 C.E.) shows a group of musicians riding on a camel along the famous Silk Road commercial network that long linked the civilizations of western and eastern Eurasia. The bearded figures represent Central Asian merchants, while the others depict Chinese. (©Asian Art & Archaeology, Inc./Corbis)

Coastlands and highlands, steppes and farmlands, islands and mainlands, valleys and mountains, deserts and forests—each generates different products. Furthermore, some societies have been able to monopolize, at least temporarily, the production of particular products—such as silk in China, certain spices in Southeast Asia, and incense in southern Arabia—which others have found valuable. This uneven distribution of goods and resources, whether natural or resulting from human activity, has long motivated exchange, not only within particular civilizations or regions but among them as well. In the world of 500–1500, long-distance trade became more important than ever before in linking and shaping distant societies and peoples. For the most part, it was indirect, a chain of separate transactions in which goods traveled farther than individual merchants. Nonetheless, a network of exchange and communication extending all across the Afro-Eurasian world, and separately in parts of the Americas as well, slowly came into being.

Why was trade important? How did it generate change within the societies that it connected? Economically speaking, commerce often altered consumption and shaped daily life. West Africans, for example, imported scarce salt, necessary for human diets and useful for seasoning and preserving food, from distant mines in the Sahara in exchange for the gold of their region. Over several millennia, incense such as frankincense and myrrh, grown in southern Arabia and the adjacent region of northern Somalia, found eager consumers in ancient Egypt and Babylon, India and China, Greece and Rome. Used for medicinal purposes, religious ceremonies, and as an antidote to the odors of unsanitary cities, incense also bore the "aroma of eros." "I have perfumed my bed with myrrh, aloes, and cinnamon," declared a harlot featured in the Old Testament Book of Proverbs. "Come, let us take our fill of love till morning."[2] Trade also affected the working lives of many people, encouraging them to specialize in producing particular products for sale in distant markets rather than for use in their own communities. Trade, in short, diminished the economic self-sufficiency of local societies, even as it altered the structure of those societies as well. Merchants often became a distinct social group, viewed with suspicion by others because of their impulse to accumulate wealth without actually producing anything themselves. In some societies, trade became a means of social mobility, as Chinese merchants, for example, were able to purchase landed estates and establish themselves within the gentry class. Long-distance trade also enabled elite groups in society to distinguish themselves from commoners by acquiring prestigious goods from a distance—silk, tortoiseshell, jade, rhinoceros horn, or particular feathers. The association with faraway or powerful societies, signaled by the possession of their luxury goods, often conveyed status in communities more remote from major civilizations.

Trade also had the capacity to transform political life. The wealth available from controlling and taxing trade motivated the creation of states in various parts of the world and sustained those states once they had been constructed. Furthermore, commerce posed a set of problems to governments everywhere. Should trade be left in private hands, as in the Aztec Empire, or should it be controlled by the state, as in the

A Map of Time

3rd millennium B.C.E.	Beginnings of silk industry in China
200 B.C.E.–200 C.E.	Initial flourishing of Silk Road commerce
By 1st century B.C.E.	Spread of Buddhism to Central Asian cities and northern China
430 B.C.E.	Trade-borne disease enters Greece from Egypt
Early centuries C.E.	Knowledge of monsoons enables expansion of Indian Ocean commerce
300–400 C.E.	Beginning of trans-Saharan trade
350	All-water route opened between India and China
6th century	Chinese monopoly on silk production broken
7th century	Rise of Islam
670–1025	Srivijaya kingdom
800–1300	Khmer kingdom of Angkor
1000–1500	Swahili civilization along East African coast
13th and 14th centuries	Mongol Empire revitalizes Silk Road commerce
1250–1350	Kingdom of Zimbabwe in southeastern Africa
1275–1292	Marco Polo in China
1346–1350	Black Death enters Europe via transcontinental trade routes
1354	Ibn Battuta visits West Africa
15th century	Aztec and Inca empires facilitate commercial exchange in the Americas

Inca Empire? How should state authorities deal with men of commerce, who were both economically useful and potentially disruptive?

Moreover, the saddlebags of camel caravans or the cargo holds of merchant vessels carried more than goods. Trade became the vehicle for the spread of religious ideas, technological innovations, disease-bearing germs, and plants and animals to regions far from their places of origin. In just this fashion, Buddhism made its way from India to Central and East Asia, and Islam crossed the Sahara into West Africa. So did the pathogens that devastated much of Eurasia during the Black Death. These immense cultural and biological transformations were among the most significant outcomes of the increasingly dense network of long-distance commerce during the era of third-wave civilizations.

SEEKING THE MAIN POINT

In what ways did long-distance commerce act as a motor of change in premodern world history?

Silk Roads: Exchange across Eurasia

The Eurasian landmass has long been home to the majority of humankind as well as to the world's most productive agriculture, largest civilizations, and greatest concentration of pastoral peoples. Beyond its many separate societies and cultures, Eurasia also gave rise to one of the world's most extensive and sustained networks of exchange among its diverse peoples. Known as the Silk Roads, a reference to their most famous product, these land-based trade routes linked pastoral and agricultural peoples as well as the large civilizations on the continent's outer rim (see Map 7.1). None of its numerous participants knew the full extent of this network's reach, for it was largely a "relay trade" in which goods were passed down the line, changing hands many times before reaching their final destination. Nonetheless, the Silk Roads provide a certain unity and coherence to Eurasian history alongside the distinct stories of its separate civilizations and peoples.

The Growth of the Silk Roads

■ Change

What lay behind the emergence of Silk Road commerce, and what kept it going for so many centuries?

The beginnings of the Silk Roads lay in both geography and history. As a geographic unit, Eurasia is often divided into inner and outer zones that represent quite different environments. Outer Eurasia consists of relatively warm, well-watered areas, suitable for agriculture, which provided the setting for the great civilizations of China, India, the Middle East, and the Mediterranean. Inner Eurasia—the lands of eastern Russia and Central Asia—lies farther north and has a harsher and drier climate, much of it not conducive to agriculture. Herding their animals from horseback, the pastoral people of this region had for centuries traded with and raided their agricultural neighbors to the south. Products of the forest and of semi-arid northern grasslands known as the steppes—such as hides, furs, livestock, wool, and amber—were exchanged for the agricultural products and manufactured goods of adjacent civilizations. The movement of pastoral peoples for thousands of years also served to diffuse Indo-European languages, bronze metallurgy, horse-based technologies, and more all across Eurasia.

The construction of the second-wave civilizations and their imperial states during the last five centuries B.C.E. added another element to these earlier Eurasian connections. From the south, the Persian Empire invaded the territory of pastoral peoples in present-day Turkmenistan and Uzbekistan. From the west, Alexander the Great's empire stretched well into Central Asia. From the east, China's Han dynasty extended its authority westward, seeking to control the nomadic Xiongnu and to gain access to the powerful "heavenly horses" that were so important to Chinese military forces. By the early centuries of the Common Era, indirect trading connections, often brokered by pastoral peoples, linked these Eurasian civilizations in a network of transcontinental exchange.

Silk Road trading networks prospered most when large and powerful states provided security for merchants and travelers. Such conditions prevailed during the second-wave era when the Roman and Chinese empires anchored long-distance

Map 7.1 The Silk Roads
For 2,000 years, goods, ideas, technologies, and diseases made their way across Eurasia on the several routes of the Silk Roads.

commerce at the western and eastern ends of Eurasia. Silk Road trade flourished again during the seventh and eighth centuries C.E. as the Byzantine Empire, the Muslim Abbasid (ah-BAH-sihd) dynasty, and Tang dynasty China created an almost continuous belt of strong states across Eurasia. In the thirteenth and fourteenth centuries, the Mongol Empire briefly encompassed almost the entire route of the Silk Roads in a single state, giving a renewed vitality to long-distance trade. Over many centuries, various technological innovations, such as yokes, saddles, and stirrups, made the use of camels, horses, and oxen more effective means of transportation across the vast distances of the Silk Roads.

Goods in Transit

During prosperous times especially, a vast array of goods (detailed in the Snapshot on p. 320) made its way across the Silk Roads, often carried in large camel caravans that traversed the harsh and dangerous steppes, deserts, and oases of Central Asia. In high demand and hard to find, most of these goods were luxury products, destined for an elite and wealthy market, rather than staple goods, for only readily moved commodities of great value could compensate for the high costs of transportation across such long and forbidding distances.

Of all these luxury goods, it was silk that came to symbolize this Eurasian network of exchange. From its origin in China during the fourth millennium B.C.E., that civilization long held a monopoly on silk production, even as that precious fabric

Snapshot   **Economic Exchange along the Silk Roads**

Region	Products Contributed to Silk Road Commerce
China	silk, bamboo, mirrors, gunpowder, paper, rhubarb, ginger, lacquerware, chrysanthemums
Forest lands of Siberia and grasslands of Central Asia	furs, walrus tusks, amber, livestock, horses, falcons, hides, copper vessels, tents, saddles, slaves
India	cotton textiles, herbal medicine, precious stones, spices
Middle East	dates, nuts, almonds, dried fruit, dyes, lapis lazuli, swords
Mediterranean basin	gold coins, glassware, glazes, grapevines, jewelry, artworks, perfume, wool and linen textiles, olive oil

increasingly found a growing market all across the linked commercial network of the Afro-Eurasian world after 300 B.C.E. or so. Although the silk trade itself was largely in the hands of men, women figured hugely in the process both in terms of supply and demand. For many centuries, Chinese women, mostly in the rural areas, were responsible for every step of the ingenious and laborious enterprise of silk production. They tended the mulberry trees on whose leaves silk worms fed; they unwound the cocoons in very hot water to extract the long silk fibers; they turned these fibers into thread and wove them into textiles. Thus Chinese homes became the primary site of textile production with rural women as its main labor force. By the time of the Tang dynasty (618–907 C.E.), women were making a large contribution to the household economy, to technological innovation in the silk industry, and to the state, which depended heavily on peasant taxes, often paid in cloth. Despite these contributions, many rural families persisted in poverty as the thirteenth-century writer Wen-hsiang indicated:

> The silkworms have finished their third sleep and are famished. The family is poor, without cash to buy the mulberry leaves to feed them. What can they do? Hungry silkworms do not produce silk. . . . The daughter is twenty but does not have wedding clothes. Those the government sends to collect taxes are like tigers. If they have no clothes to dress their daughter, they can put the [wedding] off. If they have no silk to turn over to the government, they will go bankrupt.[3]

■ **Significance**

What made silk such a highly desired commodity across Eurasia?

Elite Chinese women, and their men as well, also furnished part of the demand for these luxurious fabrics, which marked their high status. So too did Chinese officials, who required huge quantities of silk to exchange for much needed horses and to buy off "barbarian" invaders from the north. Beyond China, women in many cultures ardently sought Chinese silk for its comfort and its value as a fashion statement. The demand for silk, as well as for cotton textiles from India, was so great in the Roman Empire that various Roman writers were appalled at the drain of resources that it represented. They also were outraged at the moral impact of wearing revealing silk garments. "I can see clothes of silk," lamented Seneca the Younger in the first century C.E., "if materials that do not hide the body, nor even one's decency, can be called clothes. . . . Wretched flocks of maids labour so that the adulteress may be visible through her thin dress, so that her husband has no more acquaintance than any outsider or foreigner with his wife's body."[4]

By the sixth century C.E., the knowledge and technology for producing raw silk had spread beyond China. An old Chinese story attributes it to a Chinese princess who smuggled out silkworms in her turban when she was married off to a Central Asian ruler. In a European version of the tale, Christian monks living in China did the deed by hiding some silkworms in a bamboo cane, an act of industrial espionage that allowed an independent silk-producing and silk-weaving industry to take hold in the Byzantine Empire. However it happened, Koreans, Japanese, Indians, and Persians likewise learned how to produce this precious fabric.

As the supply of silk increased, its many varieties circulated even more extensively across Afro-Eurasian trade routes. In Central Asia, silk was used as currency and as a means of accumulating wealth. In both China and the Byzantine Empire, silk became a symbol of high status, and governments passed laws that restricted silk clothing to members of the elite. Furthermore, silk became associated with the sacred in the expanding world religions of Buddhism and Christianity. Chinese Buddhist pilgrims who made their way to India seeking religious texts and relics took with them large quantities of silk as gifts to the monasteries they visited. Buddhist monks in China received purple silk robes from Tang dynasty emperors as a sign of high honor. In the world of Christendom, silk wall hangings, altar covers, and vestments became highly prestigious signs of devotion and piety. Because no independent silk industry developed in Western Europe until the twelfth century C.E., a considerable market developed for silks imported from the Islamic world. Ironically, the splendor of Christian churches depended in part on Islamic trading networks and on silks manufactured in the Muslim world. Some of those silks were even inscribed with passages in Arabic from the Quran, unbeknownst to their European buyers.[5] By the twelfth century, the West African king of Ghana was wearing silk, and that fabric circulated in Egypt, Ethiopia, and along the East African coast as well.

Compared to contemporary global commerce, the volume of trade on the Silk Roads was modest, and its focus on luxury goods limited its direct impact on most people. Nonetheless, it had important economic and social consequences. Peasants in the Yangzi River delta of southern China sometimes gave up the cultivation of food crops, choosing to focus instead on producing silk, paper, porcelain, lacquer-ware, or iron tools, much of which was destined for the markets of the Silk Roads. In this way, the impact of long-distance trade trickled down to affect the lives of ordinary farmers. Furthermore, favorably placed individuals could benefit immensely from long-distance trade. The twelfth-century Persian merchant Ramisht made a personal fortune from his long-distance trading business and with his profits purchased an enormously expensive silk covering for the Kaaba, the central shrine of Islam in Mecca.[6]

■ **Connection**

What were the major economic, social, and cultural consequences of Silk Road commerce?

Cultures in Transit

■ **Change**

What accounted for the spread of Buddhism along the Silk Roads?

More important even than the economic impact of the Silk Roads was their role as a conduit of culture. Buddhism in particular, a cultural product of Indian civilization, spread widely throughout Central and East Asia, owing much to the activities of merchants along the Silk Roads. From its beginnings in India during the sixth century B.C.E., Buddhism had appealed to merchants, who preferred its universal message to that of a Brahmin-dominated Hinduism that privileged the higher castes. Indian traders and Buddhist monks, sometimes supported by rulers such as Ashoka, brought the new religion to the trans-Eurasian trade routes. To the west, Persian Zoroastrianism largely blocked the spread of Buddhism, but in the oasis cities of Central Asia, such as Merv, Samarkand, Khotan, and Dunhuang, Buddhism quickly took hold. By the first century B.C.E., many of the inhabitants of these towns had converted to Buddhism, and foreign merchant communities soon introduced it to northern China as well.[7]

Conversion to Buddhism in the oasis cities was a voluntary process, without the pressure of conquest or foreign rule. Dependent on long-distance trade, the inhabitants and rulers of those sophisticated and prosperous cities found in Buddhism a link to the larger, wealthy, and prestigious civilization of India. Well-to-do Buddhist merchants could earn religious merit by building monasteries and supporting monks. The monasteries in turn provided convenient and culturally familiar places of rest and resupply for merchants making the long and arduous trek across Central Asia. Many of these cities became cosmopolitan centers of learning and commerce. Scholars have found thousands of Buddhist texts in the city of Dunhuang, where several branches of the Silk Roads joined to enter western China, together with hundreds of cave temples, lavishly decorated with murals and statues.

Outside of the oasis communities, Buddhism progressed only slowly among pastoral peoples of Central Asia. The absence of a written language was an obstacle to the penetration of a highly literate religion, and their nomadic ways made the founding of monasteries, so important to Buddhism, quite difficult. But as pastoralists became involved in long-distance trade or came to rule settled agricultural peoples, Buddhism seemed more attractive. The nomadic Jie people, who controlled much of northern China after the collapse of the Han dynasty, are a case in point. Their ruler in the early fourth century C.E., Shi Le, became acquainted with a Buddhist monk called Fotudeng, who had traveled

Dunhuang
Located in western China at a critical junction of the Silk Roads trading network, Dunhuang was also a center of Buddhist learning, painting, and sculpture as that religion made its way from India to China and beyond. In some 492 caves, a remarkable gallery of Buddhist art has been preserved. These images of Buddhist deities and heavenly beings date from the sixth century C.E. (© Benoy K. Behl)

widely on the Silk Roads. The monk's reputation as a miracle worker, a rainmaker, and a fortune-teller and his skills as a military strategist cemented a personal relationship with Shi Le and led to the conversions of thousands and the construction of hundreds of Buddhist temples. In China itself, Buddhism remained for many centuries a religion of foreign merchants or foreign rulers. Only slowly did it become popular among the Chinese themselves, a process examined more closely in Chapter 8.

As Buddhism spread across the Silk Roads from India to Central Asia, China, and beyond, it also changed. The original faith had shunned the material world, but Buddhist monasteries in the rich oasis towns of the Silk Roads found themselves very much involved in secular affairs. Some of them became quite wealthy, receiving gifts from well-to-do merchants, artisans, and local rulers. The begging bowls of the monks became a symbol rather than a daily activity. Sculptures and murals in the monasteries depicted musicians and acrobats, women applying makeup, and even drinking parties.[8]

Doctrines changed as well. It was the more devotional Mahayana form of Buddhism (see Chapter 4)—featuring the Buddha as a deity, numerous bodhisattvas, an emphasis on compassion, and the possibility of earning merit—that flourished on the Silk Roads, rather than the more austere psychological teachings of the original Buddha. Moreover, Buddhism picked up elements of other cultures while in transit on the Silk Roads. In the area northwest of India that had been influenced by the invasions of Alexander the Great, statues of the Buddha reveal distinctly Greek influences. The Greco-Roman mythological figure of Herakles, the son of Zeus and associated with great strength, courage, masculinity, and sexual prowess, was used to represent Vajrapani, one of the divine protectors of the Buddha. In a similar way, the gods of many peoples along the Silk Roads were incorporated into Buddhist practice as bodhisattvas. (See Visual Sources 4.2, 4.4 and 7.4, pp. 211, 214, and 360.)

Disease in Transit

Beyond goods and cultures, diseases too traveled the trade routes of Eurasia, and with devastating consequences.[9] Each of the major population centers of the Afro-Eurasian world had developed characteristic disease patterns, mechanisms for dealing with them, and in some cases immunity to them. But when contact among human communities occurred, people were exposed to unfamiliar diseases for which they had little immunity or few effective methods of coping. An early example involved the Greek city-state of Athens, which in 430–429 B.C.E. was suddenly afflicted by a new and still unidentified infectious disease that had entered Greece via seaborne trade from Egypt, killing perhaps 25 percent of its army and permanently weakening the city-state.

Even more widespread diseases affected the Roman Empire and Han dynasty China as the Silk Roads promoted contact all across Eurasia. Smallpox and measles devastated the populations of both empires, contributing to their political collapse. Paradoxically, these disasters may well have strengthened the appeal of Christianity in Europe and Buddhism in China, for both of them offered compassion in the face of immense suffering.

■ **Connection**

What was the impact of disease along the Silk Roads?

Again in the period between 534 and 750 C.E., intermittent outbreaks of bubonic plague ravaged the coastal areas of the Mediterranean Sea as the black rats that carried the disease arrived via the seaborne trade with India, where they originally lived. What followed was catastrophic. Constantinople, the capital city of the Byzantine Empire, lost thousands of people per day during a forty-day period in 534 C.E., according to a contemporary historian. Disease played an important role in preventing Byzantium from reintegrating Italy into its version of a renewed Roman Empire encompassing the Mediterranean basin. The repeated recurrence of the disease over the next several centuries also weakened the ability of Christendom to resist Muslim armies from Arabia in the seventh century C.E.

The most well-known dissemination of disease was associated with the Mongol Empire, which briefly unified much of the Eurasian landmass during the thirteenth and fourteenth centuries C.E. (see Chapter 11). That era of intensified interaction facilitated the spread of the Black Death — identified variously with the bubonic plague, anthrax, or a package of epidemic diseases — from China to Europe. Its consequences were enormous. Between 1346 and 1348 up to half of the population of Europe perished from the plague. "A dead man," wrote the Italian writer Boccaccio, "was then of no more account than a dead goat."[10] Despite the terrible human toll, some among the living benefited. Tenant farmers and urban workers, now in short supply, could demand higher wages or better terms. Some landowning nobles, on the other hand, were badly hurt as the price of their grains dropped and the demands of their dependents grew.

A similar death toll afflicted China and parts of the Islamic world. The Central Asian steppes, home to many nomadic peoples including the Mongols, also suffered terribly, undermining Mongol rule and permanently altering the balance between pastoral and agricultural peoples to the advantage of settled farmers. In these and many other ways, disease carried by long-distance trade shaped the lives of millions and altered their historical development.

In the long run of world history, the exchange of diseases gave Europeans a certain advantage when they confronted the peoples of the Western Hemisphere after 1500. Exposure over time had provided them with some degree of immunity to Eurasian diseases. In the Americas, however, the absence of domesticated animals, the less intense interaction among major centers of population, and isolation from the Eastern Hemisphere ensured that native peoples had little defense against the diseases of Europe and Africa. Thus, when their societies were suddenly confronted by Europeans and Africans from across the Atlantic, they perished in appalling numbers. Such was the long-term outcome of the very different histories of the two hemispheres.

Sea Roads: Exchange across the Indian Ocean

If the Silk Roads linked Eurasian societies by land, sea-based trade routes likewise connected distant peoples all across the Eastern Hemisphere. For example, since the days of the Phoenicians, Greeks, and Romans, the Mediterranean Sea had been an avenue of maritime commerce throughout the region, a pattern that continued during the third-wave era. The Italian city of Venice emerged by 1000 C.E. as a major center of that commercial network, with its ships and merchants active in the Mediterranean and Black seas as well as on the Atlantic coast. Much of its wealth derived from control of expensive and profitable imported goods from Asia, many of which came up the Red Sea through the Egyptian port of Alexandria. There Venetian merchants picked up those goods and resold them throughout the Mediterranean basin. This type of trans-regional exchange linked the maritime commerce of the Mediterranean Sea to the much larger and more extensive network of seaborne trade in the Indian Ocean basin.

Until the creation of a genuinely global oceanic system of trade after 1500, the Indian Ocean represented the world's largest sea-based system of communication and exchange, stretching from southern China to eastern Africa (see Map 7.2). Like the Silk Roads, this trans-oceanic trade—the Sea Roads—also grew out of the vast environmental and cultural diversities of the region. The desire for various goods not available at home—such as porcelain from China, spices from the islands of Southeast Asia, cotton goods and pepper from India, ivory and gold from the East African coast—provided incentives for Indian Ocean commerce. Transportation costs were lower on the Sea Roads than on the Silk Roads because ships could accommodate larger and heavier cargoes than camels. This meant that the Sea Roads could eventually

Map 7.2 The Sea Roads
Paralleling the Silk Road trading network, a sea-based commerce in the Indian Ocean basin connected the many peoples between China and East Africa.

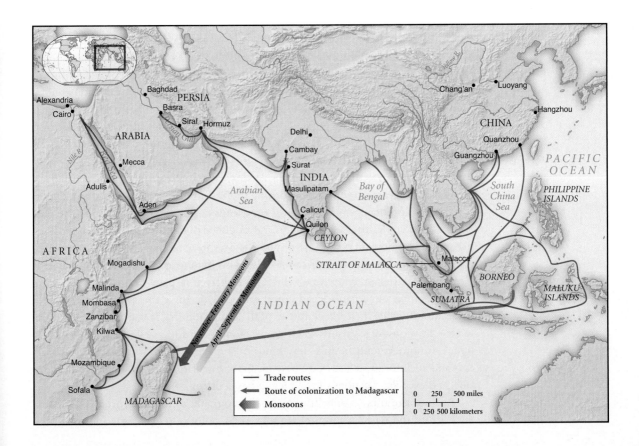

carry more bulk goods and products destined for a mass market—textiles, pepper, timber, rice, sugar, wheat—whereas the Silk Roads were limited largely to luxury goods for the few.

What made Indian Ocean commerce possible were the monsoons, alternating wind currents that blew predictably eastward during the summer months and westward during the winter (see Map 7.2, p. 325). An understanding of monsoons and a gradually accumulating technology of shipbuilding and oceanic navigation drew on the ingenuity of many peoples—Chinese, Malays, Indians, Arabs, Swahilis, and others. Collectively they made "an interlocked human world joined by the common highway of the Indian Ocean."[11]

But this world of Indian Ocean commerce did not occur between entire regions and certainly not between "countries," even though historians sometimes write about India, Indonesia, Southeast Asia, or East Africa as a matter of shorthand or convenience. It operated rather across an "archipelago of towns" whose merchants often had more in common with one another than with the people of their own hinterlands.[12] These urban centers, strung out around the entire Indian Ocean basin, provided the nodes of this widespread commercial network.

Weaving the Web of an Indian Ocean World

The world of Indian Ocean commerce was long in the making, dating back to the time of the First Civilizations. Seaborne trade via the Persian Gulf between ancient Mesopotamia and the Indus Valley civilization is reflected in archeological finds in both places. Perhaps the still-undeciphered Indian writing system was stimulated by Sumerian cuneiform. The ancient Egyptians, and later the Phoenicians, likewise traded down the Red Sea, exchanging their manufactured goods for gold, ivory, frankincense, and slaves from the coasts of Ethiopia, Somalia, and southern Arabia. These ventures mostly hugged the coast and took place over short distances. Malay sailors, however, were an exception to this rule. Speaking Austronesian languages, they jumped off from the islands of present-day Indonesia during the first millennium B.C.E. and made their way in double-outrigger canoes across thousands of miles of open ocean to the East African island of Madagascar. There they introduced their language and their crops—bananas, coconuts, and cocoyams—which soon spread to the mainland, where they greatly enriched the diets of African peoples. Also finding its way to the continent was a Malayo-Polynesian xylophone, which is still played in parts of Africa today.

The tempo of Indian Ocean commerce picked up in the era of second-wave civilizations during the early centuries of the Common Era, as mariners learned how to ride the monsoons. Various technological innovations also facilitated Indian Ocean trade—improvements in sails, new kinds of ships called junks with sternpost rudders and keels for greater stability, new means of calculating latitude such as the astrolabe, and evolving versions of the magnetic needle or compass.

Around the time of Christ, the Greek geographer Strabo reported that "great fleets [from the Roman Empire] are sent as far as India, whence the most valuable

Snapshot   **Economic Exchange in the Indian Ocean Basin**

Region	Products Contributed to Indian Ocean Commerce
Mediterranean basin	ceramics, glassware, wine, gold, olive oil
East Africa	ivory, gold, iron goods, slaves, tortoiseshells, quartz, leopard skins
Arabia	frankincense, myrrh, perfumes
India	grain, ivory, precious stones, cotton textiles, spices, timber, tortoiseshells
Southeast Asia	tin, sandlewood, cloves, nutmeg, mace
China	silks, porcelain, tea

cargoes are brought back to Egypt and thence exported again to other places."[13] Merchants from the Roman world, mostly Greeks, Syrians, and Jews, established settlements in southern India and along the East African coast. The introduction of Christianity into both Axum and Kerala (in southern India) testifies to the long-term cultural impact of that trade. In the eastern Indian Ocean and the South China Sea, Chinese and Southeast Asian merchants likewise generated a growing commerce, and by 100 C.E. Chinese traders had reached India.

The fulcrum of this growing commercial network lay in India itself. Its ports bulged with goods from both west and east, as illustrated in the Snapshot above. Its merchants were in touch with Southeast Asia by the first century C.E., and settled communities of Indian traders appeared throughout the Indian Ocean basin and as far away as Alexandria in Egypt. Indian cultural practices, such as Hinduism and Buddhism, as well as South Asian political ideas began to take root in Southeast Asia.

In the era of third-wave civilizations between 500 and 1500, two major processes changed the landscape of the Afro-Eurasian world and wove the web of Indian Ocean exchange even more densely than before. One was the economic and political revival of China, some four centuries after the collapse of the Han dynasty. Especially during the Tang and Song dynasties (618–1279), China reestablished an effective and unified state, which actively encouraged maritime trade. Furthermore, the impressive growth of the Chinese economy sent Chinese products pouring into the circuits of Indian Ocean commerce, while providing a vast and attractive market for Indian and Southeast Asian goods. Chinese technological innovations, such as larger ships and the magnetic compass, likewise added to the momentum of commercial growth.

A second transformation in the world of Indian Ocean commerce involved the sudden rise of Islam in the seventh century C.E. and its subsequent spread across much of the Afro-Eurasian world (see Chapter 9). Unlike Confucian culture, which was quite suspicious of merchants, Islam was friendly to commercial life; the Prophet Muhammad himself had been a trader. The creation of an Arab Empire, stretching from the Atlantic Ocean through the Mediterranean basin and all the way to India,

■ **Change**
What lay behind the flourishing of Indian Ocean commerce in the postclassical millennium?

brought together in a single political system an immense range of economies and cultural traditions and provided a vast arena for the energies of Muslim traders.

Those energies greatly intensified commercial activity in the Indian Ocean basin. Middle Eastern gold and silver flowed into southern India to purchase pepper, pearls, textiles, and gemstones. Muslim merchants and sailors, as well as Jews and Christians living within the Islamic world, established communities of traders from East Africa to the south China coast. Efforts to reclaim wasteland in Mesopotamia to produce sugar and dates for export stimulated a slave trade from East Africa, which landed thousands of Africans in southern Iraq to work on plantations and in salt mines under horrendous conditions. A massive fifteen-year revolt (868–883) among these slaves badly disrupted the Islamic Abbasid Empire before that rebellion was brutally crushed.[14]

Beyond these specific outcomes, the expansion of Islam gave rise to an international maritime culture by 1000, shared by individuals living in the widely separated port cities around the Indian Ocean. The immense prestige, power, and prosperity of the Islamic world stimulated widespread conversion, which in turn facilitated commercial transactions. Even those who did not convert to Islam, such as Buddhist rulers in Burma, nonetheless regarded it as commercially useful to assume Muslim names.[15] Thus was created "a maritime Silk Road ... a commercial and informational network of unparalleled proportions."[16] After 1000, the culture of this network was increasingly Islamic.

Sea Roads as a Catalyst for Change: Southeast Asia

■ Connection

In what ways did Indian influence register in Southeast Asia?

Oceanic commerce transformed all of its participants in one way or another, but nowhere more so than in Southeast Asia and East Africa, at opposite ends of the Indian Ocean network. In both regions, trade stimulated political change as ambitious or aspiring rulers used the wealth derived from commerce to construct larger and more centrally governed states or cities. Both areas likewise experienced cultural change as local people were attracted to foreign religious ideas from Confucian, Hindu, Buddhist, or Islamic sources. As on the Silk Roads, trade was a conduit for culture.

Located between the major civilizations of China and India, Southeast Asia was situated by geography to play an important role in the evolving world of Indian Ocean commerce. During the third-wave era, a series of cities and states or kingdoms emerged on both the islands and mainland of Southeast Asia, representing new civilizations in this vast region (Map 7.3). That process paralleled a similar development of new civilizations in East and West Africa, Japan, Russia, and Western Europe in what was an Afro-Eurasian phenomenon. In Southeast Asia, many of those new societies were stimulated and decisively shaped by their interaction with the sea-based trade of Indian Ocean.[17]

The case of Srivijaya (SREE-vih-juh-yuh) illustrates the connection between commerce and state building. When Malay sailors, long active in the waters around Southeast Asia, opened an all-sea route between India and China through the Straits of Malacca around 350 C.E., the many small ports along the Malay Peninsula and the coast of Sumatra began to compete intensely to attract the growing number of traders and travelers making their way through the straits. From this competition emerged the Malay kingdom of Srivijaya, which dominated this critical choke point of Indian Ocean trade from 670 to 1025. A number of factors—Srivijaya's plentiful supply of gold; its access to the source of highly sought-after spices, such as cloves, nutmeg, and mace; and the taxes levied on passing ships—provided resources to attract supporters, to fund an embryonic bureaucracy, and to create the military and naval forces that brought some security to the area.

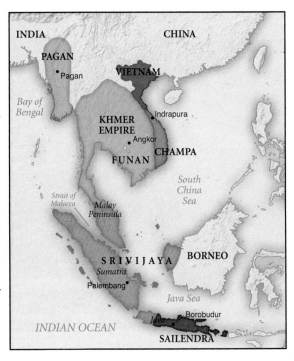

The inland states on the mainland of Southeast Asia, whose economies were based more on domestically produced rice than international trade, nonetheless participated in commerce of the region. The state of Funan, which flourished during the first six centuries of the Common Era in what is now southern Vietnam and eastern Cambodia, hosted merchants from both India and China. Archeologists have found Roman coins as well as trade goods from Persia, Central Asia, and Arabia in the ruins of its ancient cities. The Khmer kingdom of Angkor (flourished 800–1300) exported exotic forest products, receiving in return Chinese and Indian handicrafts, while welcoming a considerable community of Chinese merchants. Traders from Champa in what is now central and southern Vietnam operated in China, Java, and elsewhere, practicing piracy when trade dried up. Champa's effort to control the trade between China and Southeast Asia provoked warfare with its commercial rivals.

Map 7.3 Southeast Asia ca. 1200 C.E.
Both mainland and island Southeast Asia were centrally involved in the commerce of the Indian Ocean basin, and both were transformed by that experience.

Beyond the exchange of goods, commercial connections served to spread elements of Indian culture across much of Southeast Asia, even as Vietnam was incorporated into the Chinese sphere of influence. (See Chapter 8 for more on Chinese influence in Vietnam.) Indian alphabets such as Sanskrit and Pallava were used to write a number of Southeast Asian languages. Indian artistic forms provided models for Southeast Asian sculpture and architecture, while the Indian epic *Ramayana* became widely popular across the region.

Politically, Southeast Asian rulers and elites found attractive the Indian belief that leaders were god-kings, perhaps reincarnations of a Buddha or the Hindu deity Shiva, while the idea of karma conveyed legitimacy to the rich and powerful based on their moral behavior in earlier lives. Srivijaya monarchs, for example, employed Indians as advisers, clerks, or officials and assigned Sanskrit titles to their subordinates. The capital city of Palembang was a cosmopolitan place, where even the parrots were said to speak four languages. While these rulers drew on indigenous beliefs that chiefs possessed magical powers and were responsible for the prosperity of their people, they also

Borobudur
This huge Buddhist monument, constructed probably in the ninth century c.e., was subsequently abandoned and covered with layers of volcanic ash and vegetation as Java came under Islamic influence. It was rediscovered by British colonial authorities in the early nineteenth century and has undergone several restorations over the past two centuries. Although Indonesia is a largely Muslim country, its small Buddhist minority still celebrates the Buddha's birthday at Borobudur. (Robert Harding World Imagery/Alamy)

made use of imported Indian political ideas and Buddhist religious concepts, which provided a "higher level of magic" for rulers as well as the prestige of association with Indian civilization.[18] They also sponsored the creation of images of the Buddha and various bodhisattvas whose faces resembled those of deceased kings and were inscribed with traditional curses against anyone who would destroy them. Srivijaya grew into a major center of Buddhist observance and teaching, attracting thousands of monks and students from throughout the Buddhist world. The seventh-century Chinese monk Yi Jing was so impressed that he advised Buddhist monks headed for India to study first in Srivijaya for several years.

Elsewhere as well, elements of Indian culture took hold in Southeast Asia. The Sailendra kingdom in central Java, an agriculturally rich region closely allied with Srivijaya, mounted a massive building program between the eighth and tenth centuries featuring Hindu temples and Buddhist monuments. The most famous, known as Borobudur, is an enormous mountain-shaped structure of ten levels, with a three-mile walkway and elaborate carvings illustrating the spiritual journey from ignorance and illusion to full enlightenment. The largest Buddhist monument anywhere in the world, it is nonetheless a distinctly Javanese creation, whose carved figures have Javanese features and whose scenes are clearly set in Java, not India. Its shape resonated with an ancient Southeast Asian veneration of mountains as sacred places and the abode of ancestral spirits. Borobudur represents the process of Buddhism becoming culturally grounded in a new place.

Hinduism too, though not an explicitly missionary religion, found a place in Southeast Asia. It was well rooted in the Champa kingdom, for example, where Shiva was worshipped, cows were honored, and phallic imagery was prominent. But it was in the prosperous and powerful Angkor kingdom of the twelfth century C.E. that Hinduism found its most stunning architectural expression in the temple complex known as Angkor Wat. The largest religious structure in the premodern world, it sought to express a Hindu understanding of the cosmos, centered on a mythical Mt. Meru, the home of the gods in Hindu tradition. Later, it was used by Buddhists as well, with little sense of contradiction. To the west of Angkor, the state of Pagan likewise devoted enormous resources to shrines, temples, and libraries inspired by both Hindu and Buddhist faiths.

This extensive Indian influence in Southeast Asia has led some scholars to speak of the "Indianization" of the region, similar perhaps to the earlier spread of Greek

Angkor Wat
Constructed in the early twelfth century, the Angkor Wat complex was designed as a state temple, dedicated to the Hindu god Vishnu and lavishly decorated with carved bas-reliefs depicting scenes from Hindu mythology. By the late thirteenth century, it was in use by Buddhists as it is to this day. This photo shows a small section of the temple and three Buddhist monks in their saffron robes. (© Jose Fuste Raga/Corbis)

culture within the empires of Alexander the Great and Rome. In the case of Southeast Asia, however, no imperial control accompanied Indian cultural influence. It was a matter of voluntary borrowing by independent societies that found Indian traditions and practices useful and were free to adapt those ideas to their own needs and cultures. Traditional religious practices mixed with the imported faiths or existed alongside them with little conflict. And much that was distinctively Southeast Asian persisted despite influences from afar. In family life, for example, most Southeast Asian societies traced an individual's ancestry from both the mother's and father's line in contrast to India and China where patrilineal descent was practiced. Furthermore, women had fewer restrictions and a greater role in public life than in the more patriarchal civilizations of both East and South Asia. They were generally able to own property together with their husbands and to initiate divorce. According to a Chinese visitor to Angkor, "it is the women who are concerned with commerce." Women in Angkor also served as gladiators, warriors, members of the palace staff, and as poets, artists, and religious teachers. Almost 1800 realistically carved images of women decorate the temple complex of Angkor Wat. In neighboring Pagan, a thirteenth-century Queen Pwa Saw exercised extensive political and religious influence for some forty years amid internal intrigue and external threats, while donating some of her lands and property to a Buddhist temple. Somewhat later, but also via Indian Ocean commerce, Islam too began to penetrate Southeast Asia, as the world of seaborne trade brought yet another cultural tradition to the region.

Sea Roads as a Catalyst for Change: East Africa

■ Connection

What was the role of Swahili civilization in the world of Indian Ocean commerce?

On the other side of the Indian Ocean, the transformative processes of long-distance trade were likewise at work, giving rise to an East African civilization known as Swahili. Emerging in the eighth century C.E., this civilization took shape as a set of commercial city-states stretching all along the East African coast, from present-day Somalia to Mozambique.

The earlier ancestors of the Swahili lived in small farming and fishing communities, spoke Bantu languages, and traded with the Arabian, Greek, and Roman merchants who occasionally visited the coast during the second-wave era. But what stimulated the growth of Swahili cities was the far more extensive commercial life of the western Indian Ocean following the rise of Islam. As in Southeast Asia, local people and aspiring rulers found opportunity for wealth and power in the growing demand for East African products associated with an expanding Indian Ocean commerce. Gold, ivory, quartz, leopard skins, and sometimes slaves acquired from interior societies, as well as iron and processed timber manufactured along the coast, found a ready market in Arabia, Persia, India, and beyond. At least one East Africa giraffe found its way to Bengal in northeastern India, and from there was sent on to China. In response to such commercial opportunities, an African merchant class developed, villages turned into sizable towns, and clan chiefs became kings. A new civilization was in the making.

Between 1000 and 1500, that civilization flourished along the coast, and it was a very different kind of society than the farming and pastoral cultures of the East African interior. It was thoroughly urban, centered in cities of 15,000 to 18,000 people, such as Lamu, Mombasa, Kilwa, Sofala, and many others. Like the city-states of ancient Greece, each Swahili city was politically independent, generally governed by its own king, and in sharp competition with other cities. No imperial system or larger territorial states unified the world of Swahili civilization. Nor did any of them control a critical choke point of trade, as Srivijaya did for the Straits of Malacca. Swahili cities were commercial centers that accumulated goods from the interior and exchanged them for the products of distant civilizations, such as Chinese porcelain and silk, Persian rugs, and Indian cottons. While the transoceanic journeys occurred largely in Arab vessels, Swahili craft navigated the coastal waterways, concentrating goods for shipment abroad. Swahili cities were class-stratified societies with sharp distinctions between a mercantile elite and commoners.

The Swahili Coast of East Africa

Culturally as well as economically, Swahili civilization participated in the larger Indian Ocean world. Arab, Indian, and Persian merchants were welcome visitors, and some settled permanently. Many ruling families of Swahili cities claimed Arab or Persian origins as a way of bolstering their prestige, even while they dined from Chinese porcelain and dressed in Indian cottons. The Swahili language, widely spoken in East Africa today, was grammatically an African tongue within the larger Bantu family of languages, but it was written in Arabic script and contained a number of Arabic loan words. A small bronze lion found in the Swahili city of Shanga and dating to about 1100 illustrates the distinctly cosmopolitan character of Swahili culture. It depicted a clearly African lion, but it was created in a distinctly Indian artistic style and was made from melted-down Chinese copper coins.[19]

Furthermore, Swahili civilization rapidly became Islamic. Introduced by Arab traders, Islam was voluntarily and widely adopted within the Swahili world. Like Buddhism in Southeast Asia, Islam linked Swahili cities to the larger Indian Ocean world, and these East African cities were soon dotted with substantial mosques. When Ibn Battuta (IH-buhn ba-TOO-tuh), a widely traveled Arab scholar, merchant, and public official, visited the Swahili coast in the early fourteenth century, he found altogether Muslim societies in which religious leaders often spoke Arabic, and all were eager to welcome a learned Islamic visitor. But these were African Muslims, not colonies of transplanted Arabs. "The rulers, scholars, officials, and big merchants as well as the port workers, farmers, craftsmen, and slaves, were dark-skinned people speaking African tongues in everyday life."[20]

Islam sharply divided the Swahili cities from their African neighbors to the west, for neither the new religion nor Swahili culture penetrated much beyond the coast until the nineteenth century. Economically, however, the coastal cities acted as intermediaries between the interior producers of valued goods and the Arab merchants who carried them to distant markets. Particularly in the southern reaches of the Swahili world, this relationship extended the impact of Indian Ocean trade well into the African interior. Hundreds of miles inland, between the Zambezi and Limpopo rivers, lay rich sources of gold, much in demand on the Swahili coast. The emergence of a powerful state, known as Great Zimbabwe, seems clearly connected to the growing trade in gold to the coast as well as to the wealth embodied in its large herds of cattle.

At its peak between 1250 and 1350, Great Zimbabwe had the resources and the labor power to construct huge stone enclosures entirely without mortar, with walls sixteen feet thick and thirty-two feet tall. "[It] must have been an astonishing sight," writes a recent historian, "for the subordinate chiefs and kings who would have come there to seek favors at court."[21] Here in the interior of southeastern Africa lay yet another example of the reach and transforming power of Indian Ocean commerce.

SUMMING UP SO FAR

To what extent did the Silk Roads and the Sea Roads operate in a similar fashion? How did they differ?

Sand Roads: Exchange across the Sahara

In addition to the Silk Roads and the Sea Roads, another important pattern of long-distance trade—this one across the vast reaches of the Sahara—linked North Africa and the Mediterranean world with the land and peoples of interior West Africa. Like the others, these Sand Road commercial networks had a transforming impact, stimulating and enriching West African civilization and connecting it to larger patterns of world history during the third-wave era.

Commercial Beginnings in West Africa

Trans-African trade, like the commerce of the Silk Roads and the Sea Roads, was rooted in environmental variation. The North African coastal regions, long part of Roman or later Arab empires, generated cloth, glassware, weapons, books, and other manufactured goods. The great Sahara held deposits of copper and especially salt, while its oases produced sweet and nutritious dates. While the sparse populations of the desert were largely pastoral and nomadic, farther south lived agricultural peoples who grew a variety of crops, produced their own textiles and metal products, and mined a considerable amount of gold. The agricultural regions of sub-Saharan Africa are normally divided into two ecological zones: the savanna grasslands immediately south of the Sahara, which produced grain crops such as millet and sorghum; and the forest areas farther south, where root and tree crops such as yams and kola nuts predominated. These quite varied environments provided the economic incentive for the exchange of goods.

The earliest long-distance trade within this huge region was not across the Sahara at all, but largely among the agricultural peoples themselves in the area later known to Arabs as the Sudan, or "the land of black people." During the first millennium B.C.E., the peoples of Sudanic West Africa began to exchange metal goods, cotton textiles, gold, and various food products across considerable distances using boats along the

Niger River and donkeys overland. On the basis of this trade, a number of independent urban clusters emerged by the early centuries of the Common Era. The most well known was Jenne-jeno, which was located at a crucial point on the Niger River where goods were transshipped from boat to donkey or vice versa.[22] This was the Niger Valley civilization, described in Chapter 6.

Gold, Salt, and Slaves: Trade and Empire in West Africa

A major turning point in African commercial life occurred with the introduction of the camel to North Africa and the Sahara in the early centuries of the Common Era. This remarkable animal, which could go for ten days without water, finally made possible the long trek across the Sahara. It was camel-owning dwellers of desert oases who initiated regular trans-Saharan commerce by 300 to 400 C.E. Several centuries later, North African Arabs, now bearing the new religion of Islam, also organized caravans across the desert.

■ **Connection**
What changes did trans-Saharan trade bring to West Africa?

What they sought, above all else, was gold, which was found in some abundance in the border areas straddling the grasslands and the forests of West Africa. From its source, it was transported by donkey to transshipment points on the southern edge of the Sahara and then transferred to camels for the long journey north across the desert. African ivory, kola nuts, and slaves were likewise in considerable demand in the desert, the Mediterranean basin, and beyond. In return, the peoples of the Sudan received horses, cloth, dates, various manufactured goods, and especially salt from the rich deposits in the Sahara.

Thus the Sahara was no longer simply a barrier to commerce and cross-cultural interaction; it quickly became a major international trade route that fostered new relationships among distant peoples. The caravans that made the desert crossing could be huge, with as many as 5,000 camels and hundreds of people. Traveling mostly at night to avoid the daytime heat, the journey might take up to seventy days, covering fifteen to twenty-five miles per day. For well over 1,000 years, such caravans traversed the desert, linking the interior of West Africa with lands and people far to the north.

As in Southeast Asia and East Africa, this long-distance trade across the Sahara provided both incentives and resources for the construction of new and larger political structures. It was the peoples of the western and central Sudan, living between the forests and the desert, who were in the best position to take advantage of these new opportunities. Between roughly 500 and 1600, they constructed a series of states, empires, and city-states that reached from the Atlantic coast to Lake Chad, including Ghana, Mali, Songhay, Kanem, and the city-states of the Hausa people (see Map 7.4). All of them were monarchies with elaborate court life and varying degrees of administrative complexity and military forces at their disposal. All drew on the wealth of trans-Saharan trade, taxing the merchants who conducted it. In the wider world, these states soon acquired a reputation for great riches. An Arab traveler in the tenth century C.E. described the ruler of Ghana as "the wealthiest king on the face of the earth because of his treasures and stocks of gold."[23] At its high point in the fourteenth

Map 7.4 The Sand Roads

For a thousand years or more, the Sahara was an ocean of sand that linked the interior of West Africa with the world of North Africa and the Mediterranean but separated them as well.

century, Mali's rulers monopolized the import of strategic goods such as horses and metals; levied duties on salt, copper, and other merchandise; and reserved large nuggets of gold for themselves while permitting the free export of gold dust.

This growing integration with the world of international commerce generated the social complexity and hierarchy characteristic of all civilizations. Royal families and elite classes, mercantile and artisan groups, military and religious officials, free peasants and slaves—all of these were represented in this emerging West African civilization. So too were gender hierarchies, although without the rigidity of more established Eurasian civilizations. Rulers, merchants, and public officials were almost always male, and by 1200 earlier matrilineal descent patterns had been largely replaced by those tracing descent through the male line. Male bards, the repositories for their communities' history, often viewed powerful women as dangerous, not to be trusted, and a seductive distraction for men. But ordinary women were central to agricultural production and weaving; royal women played important political roles in many places; and oral traditions and mythologies frequently portrayed a complementary rather than hierarchal relationship between the sexes. According to a recent scholar:

> Men [in West African civilization] derive their power and authority by releasing and accumulating *nyama* [a pervasive vital power] through acts of transforming one thing into another—making a living animal dead in hunting, making a lump of metal into a fine bracelet at the smithy. Women derive their power from similar acts of transformation—turning clay into pots or turning the bodily fluids of sex into a baby.[24]

Certainly the famous Muslim traveler, Ibn Battuta, visiting Mali in the fourteenth century, was surprised, and appalled, at the casual intimacy of unmarried men and women. (See Document 7.3, pp. 350–53.)

As in all civilizations, slavery found a place in West Africa. Early on, most slaves had been women, working as domestic servants and concubines. As West African civilization crystallized, however, male slaves were put to work as state officials, porters, craftsmen, miners harvesting salt from desert deposits, and especially agricultural laborers producing for the royal granaries on large estates or plantations. Most came from non-Islamic and stateless societies farther south, which were raided during the dry season by cavalry-based forces of West African states, though some white slave women from the eastern Mediterranean also made an appearance in Mali. A song in honor of one eleventh-century ruler of Kanem boasted of his slave-raiding achievements.

> The best you took (and sent home) as the first fruits of battle. The children crying on their mothers you snatched away from their mothers. You took the slave wife from a slave, and set them in lands far removed from one another.[25]

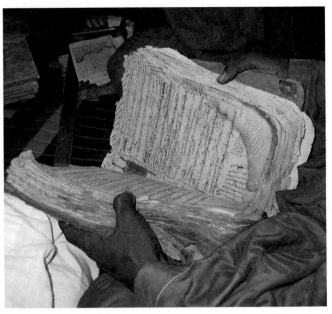

Manuscripts of Timbuktu
The West African city of Timbuktu, a terminus of the Sand Roads commercial network, became an intellectual center of Islamic learning — both scientific and religious. Its libraries were stocked with books and manuscripts, often transported across the Sahara from the heartland of Islam. Many of these have been preserved, as this recent photograph shows, and are now being studied once again. (Photo 2000: Alida Jay Boye, Timbuktu Manuscripts Project, University of Oslo)

Most of these slaves were used within this emerging West African civilization, but a trade in slaves also developed across the Sahara. Between 1100 and 1400, perhaps 5,500 slaves per year made the perilous trek across the desert, where most were put to work in the homes of the wealthy in Islamic North Africa.

These states of Sudanic Africa developed substantial urban and commercial centers — such as Koumbi-Saleh, Jenne, Timbuktu, Gao, Gobir, and Kano — where traders congregated and goods were exchanged. Some of these cities also became centers of manufacturing, creating finely wrought beads, iron tools, or cotton textiles, some of which entered the circuits of commerce. Visitors described them as cosmopolitan places where court officials, artisans, scholars, students, and local and foreign merchants all rubbed elbows. As in East Africa, Islam accompanied trade and became an important element in the urban culture of West Africa. (See Document 7.3, pp. 350–53, and Chapter 9.) The growth of long-distance trade had stimulated the development of an African civilization, which was linked to the wider networks of exchange in the Eastern Hemisphere.

An American Network: Commerce and Connection in the Western Hemisphere

Before the voyages of Columbus, the world of the Americas developed quite separately from that of Afro-Eurasia. Intriguing hints of occasional contacts with Polynesia and other distant lands have been proposed, but the only clearly demonstrated connection was that occasioned by the brief Viking voyages to North America around

PORTRAIT

Thorfinn Karlsfeni, Viking Voyager

A Viking ship similar to that used by Thorfinn Karlsfeni and other Viking explorers.
(Yvette Cardozo/Alamy)

While the peoples of eastern and western hemispheres remained almost completely isolated from one another before Columbus, the Viking journeys to North America, part of a larger age of Viking expansion, represent an exception to that generalization. Between 800 and 1050, Scandinavian Vikings had raided, traded, and sometimes settled across much of Europe, generating a fearful reputation. They also colonized Iceland and Greenland, and from that base sought yet more land in North America. Yet their trans-Atlantic voyages, although impressive feats of oceanic exploration, represented a historical dead-end, for they bore no long-term consequences. Their significance lies in their role as a prelude to Columbus rather than in any immediate outcomes.

Among those voyagers was Thorfinn Karlsefni, who set off from southern Greenland in the spring of 1007 bound for what he called Vinland, what we know as North America. A well-born, wealthy merchant and seaman of Norwegian Viking background, he had come the previous summer from his home in Iceland to the small Viking community in Greenland on a trading mission. There he found winter accommodations with Eric the Red, a pioneer of Nordic settlement in Greenland. He also found a wife, Gudrid, the widow of one of Eric's sons. Two of Eric's sons, including Leif Ericsson, had previously made the journey to Vinland. And so, during that long winter, talk turned to another voyage, for that land was reputed to be rich in furs, timber, and other valuable resources. Thus, Thorfinn came to lead 160 people, including his new wife and other women, on three ships heading to a virtually unknown land. The story of that voyage comes to us from two Icelandic sagas, based on oral traditions and committed to writing several hundred years after the events they describe.[26]

Arriving along the coast of what is now Newfoundland, Thorfinn and his people first looked for pasture land for the cattle that had accompanied them. With food in short supply, the first winter was very difficult and provoked a religious controversy. The Christians among the group "made prayers to God for food," but Thorhall, a large, soli-

the year 1000. (See Portrait.) Certainly, no sustained interaction between the peoples of the two hemispheres took place. But if the Silk, Sea, and Sand Roads linked the diverse peoples of the Eastern Hemisphere, did a similar network of interaction join and transform the various societies of the Western Hemisphere?

■ Comparison

In what ways did networks of interaction in the Western Hemisphere differ from those in the Eastern Hemisphere?

Clearly, direct connections among the various civilizations and cultures of the Americas were less densely woven than in the Afro-Eurasian region. The llama and the potato, both domesticated in the Andes, never reached Mesoamerica; nor did the writing system of the Maya diffuse to Andean civilizations. The Aztecs and the Incas, contemporary civilizations in the fifteenth century, had little if any direct contact with each other. The limits of these interactions owed something to the absence of horses, donkeys, camels, wheeled vehicles, and large oceangoing vessels, all of which facilitated long-distance trade and travel in Afro-Eurasia.

Geographic or environmental differences added further obstacles. The narrow bottleneck of Panama, largely covered by dense rain forests, surely inhibited contact tary, and "foul-mouthed" hunter, declared: "Has it not been that the Redbeard [Thor, the Norse god of thunder] has proved a better friend than your Christ?"

The following spring, the small Viking community had its first encounter with native peoples when dozens of canoes described in the sagas as "black, and ill favoured" appeared offshore. What followed was a kind of mutual inspection, as the natives "stayed a while in astonishment" and then rowed away. They returned the following year, this time to barter. The Vikings offered red cloth and milk porridge in exchange for furs and skins. But what began as a peaceful encounter ended badly when a bull from the Norsemen's herd erupted out of the forest bellowing loudly. The surprised and frightened locals quickly departed, and, when they returned three weeks later, violence erupted. Considerably outnumbered and attacked with catapults and a "great shower of missiles," Thorfinn and his company reacted with "great terror."

This encounter and the "fear of hostilities" that it provoked persuaded the Vikings "to depart and return to their own country." As they made their way north along the coast, they came upon a group of five natives sleeping near the sea. Perhaps in revenge, the Vikings simply killed them. In another incident before departing for home, they captured two boys, baptized them as Christians, and taught

them the Viking language. After three difficult years in this remote land, Thorfinn and Gudrid returned home, with a son named Snorri, the first European born in the Western Hemisphere.

Although intermittent Viking voyages to North America probably occurred over the next several centuries, they established no permanent presence. Their numbers were small, and they lacked the support of a strong state, such as Columbus and the Spanish conquistadores later enjoyed. For some time, many doubted that those voyages had occurred at all. But in the 1960s, archeological work on the northern tip of the island of Newfoundland uncovered the remains of a Norse settlement dating to the time of Thorfinn's visit. Eight sod dwellings, evidence of iron-working and boat repair, household items such as needles and spindles confirmed the existence of a Viking settlement, consisting of both men and women. The interaction of Thorfinn and the other Vikings with native peoples of North America raised, but did not answer, the question of how the epic encounter of these two continents would turn out. The later voyages of Columbus and other West Europeans provided that answer.

Question: How might these interactions have appeared if they were derived from the sagas of the native peoples?

between South and North America. Furthermore, the north/south orientation of the Americas—which required agricultural practices to move through, and adapt to, quite distinct climatic and vegetation zones—slowed the spread of agricultural products. By contrast, the east/west axis of Eurasia meant that agricultural innovations could diffuse more rapidly because they were entering roughly similar environments. Thus nothing equivalent to the long-distance trade of the Silk, Sea, or Sand Roads of the Eastern Hemisphere arose in the Americas, even though local and regional commerce flourished in many places. Nor did distinct cultural traditions such as Buddhism, Christianity, and Islam spread so widely to integrate distant peoples.

Nonetheless, scholars have discerned "a loosely interactive web stretching from the North American Great Lakes and upper Mississippi south to the Andes."[27] (See Map 7.5, p. 340.) Partly, it was a matter of slowly spreading cultural elements, such as the gradual diffusion of maize from its Mesoamerican place of origin to the southwestern United States and then on to eastern North America as well as to much of South

Map 7.5

The American Web

Transcontinental interactions within the American web were more modest than those of the Afro-Eurasian hemisphere. The most intense areas of exchange and communication occurred within the Mississippi valley, Mesoamerican, and Andean regions.

America in the other direction. A game played with rubber balls on an outdoor court has left traces in the Caribbean, Mexico, and northern South America. Construction in the Tantoc region of northeastern Mexico resembled the earlier building styles of Cahokia, indicating the possibility of some interaction between the two regions.[28] The spread of particular pottery styles and architectural conventions likewise suggests at least indirect contact over wide distances.

Commerce too played an important role in the making of this "American web." A major North American chiefdom at Cahokia, near present-day St. Louis, flourished from about 900 to 1250 at the confluence of the Mississippi, Illinois, and Missouri rivers (see pp. 288–89). Cahokia lay at the center of a widespread trading network that brought it shells from the Atlantic coast, copper from the Lake Superior region, buffalo hides from the Great Plains, obsidian from the Rocky Mountains, and mica from the southern Appalachian Mountains. Sturdy dugout canoes plied the rivers of the eastern woodlands, loosely connecting their diverse societies. Early European explorers and travelers along the Amazon and Orinoco rivers of South America reported active networks of exchange that may well have operated for many centuries. Caribbean peoples using large oceangoing canoes had long conducted an inter-island trade, and the Chincha people undertook ocean-based exchange in copper, beads, and shells along the Pacific coasts of Peru and Ecuador in large seagoing rafts.[29] Another regional commercial network, centered in Mesoamerica, extended north to what is now the southwestern United States and south to Ecuador and Colombia. Many items from Mesoamerica — copper bells, macaw feathers, tons of shells — have been found in the Chaco region of New Mexico. Residents of Chaco also drank liquid chocolate, using jars of Mayan origin and cacao beans imported from Mesoamerica, where the practice began.[30] Turquoise, mined and worked among the Ancestral Pueblo (see pp. 286–88) flowed in the other direction.

But the most active and dense networks of communication and exchange in the Americas lay within, rather than between, the regions that housed the two great civilizations of the Western Hemisphere — Mesoamerica and the Andes. During the flourishing of Mesoamerican civilization (200–900 C.E.), both the Maya cities in the Yucatán area of Mexico and Guatemala and the huge city-state of Teotihuacán in central Mexico maintained commercial relationships with one another and throughout the region. In addition to this land-based trade, the Maya conducted a seaborne commerce, using large dugout canoes holding forty to fifty people, along both the Atlantic and Pacific coasts.[31]

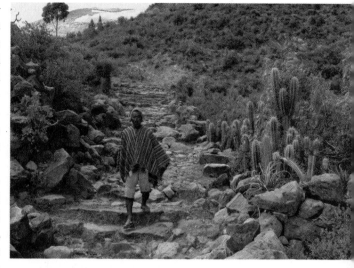

Although most of this trade was in luxury goods rather than basic necessities, it was critical to upholding the position and privileges of royal and noble families. Items such as cotton clothing, precious jewels, and feathers from particular birds marked the status of elite groups and served to attract followers. Controlling access to such high-prestige goods was an important motive for war among Mesoamerican states.[32] Among the Aztecs of the fifteenth century, professional merchants known as pochteca (pohch-TEH-cah) undertook large-scale trading expeditions both within and well beyond the borders of their empire, sometimes as agents for the state or for members of the nobility, but more often acting on their own as private businessmen.

Inca Roads

Used for transporting goods by pack animal or sending messages by foot, the Inca road network included some 2,000 inns where travelers might find food and shelter. Messengers, operating in relay, could cover as many as 150 miles a day. Here a modern-day citizen of Peru walks along an old Inca trail road. (Loren McIntyre/lorenmcintyre.com)

Unlike the Aztec Empire, in which private traders largely handled the distribution of goods, economic exchange in the Andean Inca Empire during the fifteenth century was a state-run operation, and no merchant group similar to the Aztec pochteca emerged there. Instead, great state storehouses bulged with immense quantities of food, clothing, military supplies, blankets, construction materials, and more, all carefully recorded on *quipus* (knotted cords used to record numerical data) by a highly trained class of accountants. From these state centers, goods were transported as needed by caravans of human porters and llamas across the numerous roads and bridges of the empire. Totaling some 20,000 miles, Inca roads traversed the coastal plain and the high Andes in a north/south direction, while lateral roads linked these diverse environments and extended into the eastern rain forests and plains as well. Despite the general absence of private trade, local exchange took place at highland fairs and along the borders of the empire with groups outside the Inca state.

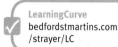

LearningCurve
bedfordstmartins.com
/strayer/LC

Reflections: Economic Globalization — Ancient and Modern

The densely connected world of the modern era, linked by ties of commerce and culture around the planet, certainly has roots in much earlier patterns. Particularly in the era of third-wave civilizations from 500 to 1500, the Silk, Sea, and Sand Roads of the Afro-Eurasian world and the looser networks of the American web linked distant peoples both economically and culturally, prompted the emergence of new states, and sustained elite privileges in many ancient civilizations. In those ways, they resembled the globalized world of modern times.

In other respects, though, the networks and webs of the premodern millennium differed sharply from those of more recent centuries. Most people still produced primarily for their own consumption rather than for the market, and a much smaller range of goods was exchanged in the marketplaces of the world. Far fewer people then were required to sell their own labor for wages, an almost universal practice in modern economies. Because of transportation costs and technological limitations, most trade was in luxury goods rather than in necessities. In addition, the circuits of commerce were rather more limited than the truly global patterns of exchange that emerged after 1500.

Furthermore, the world economy of the modern era increasingly had a single center—industrialized Western European countries—which came to dominate much of the world both economically and politically during the nineteenth century. Though never completely equal, the economic relationships of earlier times occurred among much more equivalent units. For example, no one region dominated the complex pattern of Indian Ocean exchange, although India and China generally offered manufactured goods, while Southeast Asia and East Africa mostly contributed agricultural products or raw materials. And with the exception of the brief Mongol control of the Silk Roads and the Inca domination of the Andes for a century, no single power exercised political control over the other major networks of world commerce.

Economic relationships among third-wave civilizations, in short, were more balanced and multicentered than those of the modern era. Although massive inequalities occurred within particular regions or societies, interaction among the major civilizations operated on a rather more equal basis than in the globalized world of the past several centuries. With the rise of China, India, Turkey, and Brazil, as major players in the world economy of the twenty-first century, are we perhaps witnessing a return to that earlier pattern?

Second Thoughts

LearningCurve
Check what you know.
**bedfordstmartins.com
/strayer/LC**

Online Study Guide
bedfordstmartins.com
/highschool/strayer

What's the Significance?

Silk Roads, 318–24

Black Death, 323–24

Indian Ocean trading network, 324–34

Srivijaya, 328–30

Borobudur, 330–31

Angkor Wat, 331

Swahili civilization, 333–34

Great Zimbabwe, 334

Sand Roads, 334–37

Ghana, Mali, Songhay, 335–37

trans-Saharan slave trade, 335–37

American web, 337–41

Thorfinn Karlsfeni, 338–39

pochteca, 341

Big Picture Questions

1. What motivated and sustained the long-distance commerce of the Silk Roads, Sea Roads, and Sand Roads?

2. Why did the peoples of the Eastern Hemisphere develop long-distance trade more extensively than did those of the Western Hemisphere?

3. "Cultural change derived often from commercial exchange in the third-wave era." What evidence from this chapter supports this observation?

4. In what ways was Afro-Eurasia a single interacting zone, and in what respects was it a vast region of separate cultures and civilizations?

5. **Looking Back:** Compared to the cross-cultural interactions of earlier times, what was different about those of the third-wave era?

Next Steps: For Further Study

Jerry Bentley, *Old World Encounters* (1993). A wonderfully succinct and engaging history of cross-cultural interaction all across Afro-Eurasia before 1500.

William J. Bernstein, *A Splendid Exchange* (2008). A global account of "how trade shaped the world."

E. W. Bovill, *The Golden Trade of the Moors* (1970). A classic account of the trans-Saharan trade.

Nayan Chanda, *Bound Together* (2007). Places contemporary globalization in a rich world historical context.

K. N. Chaudhuri, *Trade and Civilization in the Indian Ocean* (1985). A well-regarded study that treats the Indian Ocean basin as a single region linked by both commerce and culture during the third-wave era.

Philip Curtin, *Cross-Cultural Trade in World History* (1984). Explores long-distance trade as a generator of social change on a global level.

Xinru Liu, *The Silk Road in World History* (2010). A brief, accessible, and up-to-date account by a leading scholar.

Silk Road Seattle, http://depts.washington.edu/silkroad/. A wonderful Web site about the Silk Road with many artistic images and maps as well as extensive narrative description of vast network of exchange.

For Web sites and additional documents related to this chapter, see **Make History** at bedfordstmartins.com /highschool/strayer.

Documents

Considering the Evidence:
Travelers' Tales and Observations

During the third-wave millennium, as long-distance trade flourished and large transregional empires grew, opportunities increased for individuals to travel far beyond their homelands. Their accounts have provided historians with invaluable information about particular regions and cultures, as well as about interactions among disparate peoples. The authors of these accounts, perhaps inadvertently, also reveal much about themselves and about the perceptions and misperceptions generated by cross-cultural encounters. The selections that follow provide three examples of intrepid long-distance travelers and their impressions of the societies they encountered on their arduous journeys.

Document 7.1

A Chinese Buddhist in India

In 629, Xuanzang (SCHWEN-ZAHNG) (600–664 C.E.), a highly educated Buddhist monk from China, made a long and difficult journey to India through some of the world's most daunting deserts and mountain ranges, returning home in 645 C.E. after sixteen years abroad. His motives, like those of many other Buddhist travelers to India, were essentially religious. "I regretted that the teachings of [Buddhism] were not complete and the scriptures deficient in my own country," he wrote. "I have doubts and have puzzled in my mind, but I could find no one to solve them. That was why I decided to travel to the West."[33] In India, the homeland of Buddhism, he hoped to find the teachers and the sacred texts that would answer his questions, enrich Buddhist practice in China, and resolve the many disputes that had created serious divisions within the Buddhist community of his own country.

During a ten-year stay in India, Xuanzang visited many of the holy sites associated with the Buddha's life and studied with leading Buddhist teachers, particularly those at Nalanda University, a huge monastic complex dedicated to Buddhist scholarship (see Map 7.1, p. 319). He traveled widely within India and established a personal relationship with Harsha, the ruler of the state that then encompassed much of northern India. On his return journey to China, he carried hundreds of manuscripts, at least seven statues of the Buddha, and even some relics. Warmly greeted by the Chinese emperor, Xuanzang spent the last two decades of his life translating the texts he had collected into Chinese. He also wrote an account of his travels, known as the *Record of the Western Regions*, and shared his recollections with a fellow monk and translator named Huili, who subsequently wrote a biography of Xuanzang.[34] The selections that follow derive from these two accounts and convey something of Xuanzang's impressions of Indian civilization in the seventh century C.E.

■   What surprised or impressed Xuanzang on his visit to India? What features of Indian life might seem most strange to a Chinese visitor?

■   How might these selections serve to illustrate or to contradict the descriptions of Indian civilization found in Chapters 3–5?

■   What can this document contribute to our understanding of Buddhist practice in India?

HUILI
A Biography of the Tripitaka Master
Seventh Century C.E.

[Certainly the emotional highlight of Xuanzang's travels in India was his visit to the site of the Buddha's enlightenment under the famous Bodhi tree. The great traveler's biographer, Huili, recorded his Master's response.]

Upon his arrival there, the Master worshipped the Bodhi tree and the image of the Buddha attaining enlightenment made by Maitreya Bodhisattva. After having looked at the image with deep sincerity, he prostrated himself before it and deplored sadly, saying with self-reproach, "I do not know where I was born in the course of transmigration at the time when the Buddha attained enlightenment. I could only come here at this time. . . . It makes me think that my karmic hindrances must have been very heavy!" While he was saying so, his eyes brimmed

with sorrowful tears. As that was the time when the monks dismissed the summer retreat, several thousand people forgathered from far and near. Those who saw the Master were choked by sobs in sympathy with him.

[The great Buddhist monastery/university at Nalanda was likewise a major destination of Xuanzang's journey. It must have been a place of wonder and delight to the Chinese monk, as he described it to Huili.]

Ten thousand monks always lived there, both hosts and guests. They studied Mahayana teachings and the doctrines of the eighteen schools, as well as worldly books such as the Vedas. They also learned about works on logic, grammar, medicine, and divination. . . . Lectures were given at more than a hundred places in the monastery every day, and the students studied diligently without wasting a single moment. As all the monks who lived there were men of virtue, the atmosphere in the monastery was naturally solemn and dignified. For more than seven hundred years since its establishment, none

Source: Li Rongxi, trans., *A Biography of the Tripitaka Master of the Great Ci'en Monastery of the Great Tang Dynasty* (Berkeley, CA: Numata Center for Buddhist Translation, 1995), 89–90, 94–95.

of the monks had committed any offence. Out of respect for them, the king gave more than a hundred villages for their sustenance. Each village had two hundred families, who daily provided several hundred *shi* of polished nonglutinous rice, butter, and milk. Thus the students could enjoy sufficient supplies of the four requisites without the trouble of going to beg for them. It was because of this effort of their supporters that the scholars could gain achievements in learning.

XUANZANG

Record of the Western Region
Seventh Century C.E.

[Selections from Xuanzang's more general description of Indian civilization follow here drawn from his own account.]

On Towns and Villages

The towns and villages have inner gates; the walls are wide and high; the streets and lanes are tortuous, and the roads winding. The thoroughfares are dirty and the stalls arranged on both sides of the road with appropriate signs. Butchers, fishers, dancers, executioners, and scavengers, and so on [untouchables], have their abodes without [outside] the city. In coming and going these persons are bound to keep on the left side of the road till they arrive at their homes. Their houses are surrounded by low walls and form the suburbs. The earth being soft and muddy, the walls of the towns are mostly built of brick or tiles. . . .

On Buddhist Studies

The different schools are constantly at variance, and their contending utterances rise like the angry waves of the sea. The different sects have their separate masters. . . . There are eighteen schools, each claiming pre-eminence. The partisans of the Great and Little Vehicle are content to dwell apart. There are some who give themselves up to quiet contemplation, and devote themselves, whether walking or standing still or sitting down, to the acquirement of wisdom and insight; others, on the contrary, differ from these in raising noisy contentions about their faith. According to their fraternity, they are governed by distinctive rules and regulations. . . .

The *Vinaya* discourses [rules governing monastic life] are equally Buddhist books. He who can entirely explain one class of these books is exempted from the control of the *karmadâna*.° If he can explain two classes, he receives in addition the equipments of an upper seat (*room*); he who can explain three classes has allotted to him different servants to attend to and obey him; he who can explain four classes has "pure men" allotted to him as attendants; he who can explain five classes of books is then allowed an elephant carriage; he who can explain six classes of books is allowed a surrounding escort. When a man's renown has reached to a high distinction, then at different times he convokes an assembly for discussion. He judges of the superior or inferior talent of those who take part in it; he distinguishes their good or bad points; he praises the clever and reproves the faulty; if one of the assembly distinguishes himself by refined language, subtle investigation, deep penetration, and severe logic, then he is mounted on an elephant covered with precious ornaments, and conducted by a numerous suite to the gates of the convent.

If, on the contrary, one of the members breaks down in his argument, or uses poor and inelegant phrases, or if he violates a rule in logic and adapts his words accordingly, they proceed to disfigure his face with red and white, and cover his body with dirt and dust, and then carry him off to some deserted spot or leave him in a ditch. Thus they distinguish between the meritorious and the worthless, between the wise and the foolish.

Source: Samuel Beal, trans., *Su-Yu-Ki: Buddhist Records of the Western World* (London: K. Paul, Trench, Trubner, 1906), vol. 1, bk. 2, 73–74, 77, 79–84.

°*karmadâna*: a high monastic official.

On Caste and Marriage

With respect to the division of families, there are four classifications. The first is called the Brâhman, men of pure conduct. They guard themselves in religion, live purely, and observe the most correct principles. The second is called Kshattriya, the royal caste. For ages they have been the governing class: they apply themselves to virtue and kindness. The third is called Vaiśyas, the merchant class: they engage in commercial exchange, and they follow profit at home and abroad. The fourth is called Sûdra, the agricultural class: they labor in plowing and tillage. In these four classes purity or impurity of caste assigns to every one his place. When they marry they rise or fall in position according to their new relationship. They do not allow promiscuous marriages between relations. A woman once married can never take another husband. Besides these there are other classes of many kinds that intermarry according to their several callings.

On Manners and Justice

With respect to the ordinary people, although they are naturally light-minded, yet they are upright and honorable. In money matters they are without craft, and in administering justice they are considerate. They dread the retribution of another state of existence, and make light of the things of the present world. They are not deceitful or treacherous in their conduct, and are faithful to their oaths and promises. In their rules of government there is remarkable rectitude, whilst in their behavior there is much gentleness and sweetness. With respect to criminals or rebels, these are few in number, and only occasionally troublesome. When the laws are broken or the power of the ruler violated, then the matter is clearly sifted and the offenders imprisoned. There is no infliction of corporal punishment; they are simply left to live or die, and are not counted among men. When the rules of propriety or justice are violated, or when a man fails in fidelity or filial piety, then they cut his nose or his ears off, or his hands and feet, or expel him from the country or drive him out into the desert wilds. For other faults, except these, a small payment of money will redeem the punishment. In the investigation of criminal cases there is no use of rod or staff to obtain proofs (*of guilt*).

Document 7.2

A European Christian in China

Of all the travelers along the Silk Road network, the best known and most celebrated, at least in the West, was Marco Polo (1254–1324). Born and raised in the prosperous commercial city-state of Venice in northern Italy, Marco Polo was a member of a family prominent in the long-distance trade of the Mediterranean and Black sea regions. At the age of seventeen, Marco accompanied his father and an uncle on an immense journey across Eurasia that, by 1275, brought the Polos to China, recently conquered by the Mongols. It was, in fact, the relative peace that the Mongols had created in their huge transcontinental empire that facilitated the Polos' journey (see Map 11.1, p. 522). For the next seventeen years, they lived in China, where they were employed in minor administrative positions by Khublai Khan, the country's Mongol ruler. During these years, Marco Polo apparently traveled widely within China where he gathered material for the book about his travels, which he dictated to a friend after returning home in 1295.

Marco Polo's journey and the book that described it, generally known as *The Travels of Marco Polo*, were important elements of the larger process by which an emerging West European civilization reached out to and became aware of the older civilizations of the East. Christopher Columbus carried a marked-up copy of the book on his transatlantic journeys, believing that he was seeking by sea the places Marco Polo had visited by land. Some modern scholars are skeptical about parts of Marco Polo's report, and a few even question whether he ever got to China at all, largely because he omitted any mention of certain prominent features of Chinese life, for example, foot binding, the Great Wall, and tea drinking. Most historians, however, accept the basic outlines of Marco Polo's account, even as they notice exaggerations as well as an inflated perception of his own role within China. The selection that follows conveys Marco Polo's description of the city of Hangzhou, which he referred to as Kinsay. At the time of Marco Polo's visit, it was among the largest cities in the world.

- How would you describe Marco Polo's impressions of the city? What did he notice? What surprised him?

- Why did Marco Polo describe the city as "the finest and the noblest in the world"?

- What marks his account of the city as that of a foreigner and a Christian?

- What evidence of China's engagement with a wider world does this account offer?

MARCO POLO
The Travels of Marco Polo
1299

The city is beyond dispute the finest and the noblest in the world. In this we shall speak according to the written statement which the Queen of this Realm sent to Bayan, the [Mongol] conqueror of the country for transmission to the Great Kaan, in order that he might be aware of the surpassing grandeur of the city and might be moved to save it from destruction or injury. I will tell you all the truth as it was set down in that document. For truth it was, as the said Messer Marco Polo at a later date was able to witness with his own eyes. . . .

First and foremost, then, the document stated the city of Kinsay to be so great that it hath an hundred miles of compass. And there are in it 12,000 bridges of stone. . . . [Most scholars consider these figures a considerable exaggeration.] And though the bridges be so high, the approaches are so well contrived that carts and horses do cross them.

The document aforesaid also went on to state that there were in this city twelve guilds of the different crafts, and that each guild had 12,000 houses in the occupation of its workmen. Each of these houses contains at least twelve men, whilst some contain twenty and some forty. . . . And yet all these craftsmen had full occupation, for many other cities of the kingdom are supplied from this city with what they require.

Source: *The Book of Sir Marco Polo the Venetian Concerning the Kingdoms and Marvels of the East*, 3rd ed., translated and edited by Henry Yule, revised by Henri Cordier (London: John Murray, 1903), 2:185–206.

The document aforesaid also stated that the number and wealth of the merchants, and the amount of goods that passed through their hands, were so enormous that no man could form a just estimate thereof. And I should have told you with regard to those masters of the different crafts who are at the head of such houses as I have mentioned, that neither they nor their wives ever touch a piece of work with their own hands, but live as nicely and delicately as if they were kings and queens. The wives indeed are most dainty and angelical creatures! Moreover it was an ordinance laid down by the King that every man should follow his father's business and no other, no matter if he possessed 100,000 bezants.°

Inside the city there is a Lake . . . and all round it are erected beautiful palaces and mansions, of the richest and most exquisite structure that you can imagine, belonging to the nobles of the city. There are also on its shores many abbeys and churches of the Idolaters [Buddhists]. In the middle of the Lake are two Islands, on each of which stands a rich, beautiful, and spacious edifice, furnished in such style as to seem fit for the palace of an Emperor. And when any one of the citizens desired to hold a marriage feast, or to give any other entertainment, it used to be done at one of these palaces. And everything would be found there ready to order, such as silver plate, trenchers, and dishes, napkins and table-cloths, and whatever else was needful. . . . Sometimes there would be at these palaces an hundred different parties; some holding a banquet, others celebrating a wedding . . . in so well-ordered a manner that one party was never in the way of another. . . .

Both men and women are fair and comely, and for the most part clothe themselves in silk, so vast is the supply of that material, both from the whole district of Kinsay, and from the imports by traders from other provinces. And you must know they eat every kind of flesh, even that of dogs and other unclean beasts, which nothing would induce a Christian to eat. . . .

You must know also that the city of Kinsay has some 3,000 baths, the water of which is supplied by springs. They are hot baths, and the people take great delight in them, frequenting them several times a month, for they are very cleanly in their persons. They are the finest and largest baths in the world. . . .

And the Ocean Sea comes within twenty-five miles of the city at a place called Ganfu, where there is a town and an excellent haven, with a vast amount of shipping which is engaged in the traffic to and from India and other foreign parts, exporting and importing many kinds of wares, by which the city benefits. . . .

I repeat that everything appertaining to this city is on so vast a scale, and the Great Kaan's yearly revenues therefrom are so immense, that it is not easy even to put it in writing. . . .

In this part are the ten principal markets, though besides these there are a vast number of others in the different parts of the town. . . . [T]oward the [market] squares are built great houses of stone, in which the merchants from India and other foreign parts store their wares, to be handy for the markets. In each of the squares is held a market three days in the week, frequented by 40,000 or 50,000 persons, who bring thither for sale every possible necessary of life, so that there is always an ample supply of every kind of meat and game. . . .

Those markets make a daily display of every kind of vegetables and fruits. . . . [V]ery good raisins are brought from abroad, and wine likewise. . . . From the Ocean Sea also come daily supplies of fish in great quantity, brought twenty-five miles up the river. . . . All the ten market places are encompassed by lofty houses, and below these are shops where all sorts of crafts are carried on, and all sorts of wares are on sale, including spices and jewels and pearls. Some of these shops are entirely devoted to the sale of wine made from rice and spices, which is constantly made fresh, and is sold very cheap. Certain of the streets are occupied by the women of the town, who are in such a number that I dare not say what it is. They are found not only in the vicinity of the market places, where usually a quarter is assigned to them, but all over the city. They exhibit themselves splendidly attired and abundantly perfumed, in finely garnished houses, with trains of waiting-women. These women are extremely accomplished in all the arts of allurement, and readily adapt their conversation to all

---

°**bezant:** a Byzantine gold coin.

sorts of persons, insomuch that strangers who have once tasted their attractions seem to get bewitched, and are so taken with their blandishments and their fascinating ways that they never can get these out of their heads. . . .

Other streets are occupied by the Physicians, and by the Astrologers, who are also teachers of reading and writing; and an infinity of other professions have their places round about those squares. In each of the squares there are two great palaces facing one another, in which are established the officers appointed by the King to decide differences arising between merchants, or other inhabitants of the quarter. . . .

The crowd of people that you meet here at all hours . . . is so vast that no one would believe it possible that victuals enough could be provided for their consumption, unless they should see how, on every market-day, all those squares are thronged and crammed with purchasers, and with the traders who have brought in stores of provisions by land or water; and everything they bring in is disposed of. . . .

The natives of the city are men of peaceful character, both from education and from the example of their kings, whose disposition was the same. They know nothing of handling arms, and keep none in their houses. You hear of no feuds or noisy quarrels or dissensions of any kind among them. Both in their commercial dealings and in their manufactures they are thoroughly honest and truthful, and there is such a degree of good will and neighborly attachment among both men and women that you would take the people who live in the same street to be all one family.

And this familiar intimacy is free from all jealousy or suspicion of the conduct of their women. These they treat with the greatest respect, and a man who should presume to make loose proposals to a married woman would be regarded as an infamous rascal. They also treat the foreigners who visit them for the sake of trade with great cordiality and entertain them in the most winning manner, affording them every help and advice on their business. But on the other hand they hate to see soldiers, and not least those of the Great Kaan's garrisons, regarding them as the cause of their having lost their native kings and lords.

Document 7.3

An Arab Muslim in West Africa

For most of the third-wave millennium, the world of Islam was far more extensive than that of Christendom. Nothing more effectively conveys both the extent and the cultural unity of the Islamic world than the travels of Ibn Battuta (1304–1368). Born in Morocco, this learned Arab scholar traversed nearly 75,000 miles during his extraordinary journeys, which took him to Spain, Anatolia, West and East Africa, Arabia, Iraq, Persia, Central and Southeast Asia, India, and China. He traveled at various times as a pilgrim, as a religious seeker, as a legal scholar, and frequently in the company of Muslim merchants. Remarkably, almost all of his extensive travels occurred within the realm of Islam, where he moved among people who shared his faith and often his Arabic language. Marco Polo, by contrast, had felt himself constantly an outsider, "a stranger in a strange land," for he was traveling almost everywhere beyond the borders of Christendom. But as a visitor from a more-established Islamic society, Ibn Battuta was often highly critical of the quality of Islamic observance in the frontier regions of the faith.

One such frontier region was West Africa, where a new civilization was taking shape, characterized by large empires such as Mali, a deep involvement in trans-Saharan commerce, and the gradual assimilation of Islam (see Map 7.4, p. 336, and pp. 334–37 and 432–33). The new faith had been introduced by North African Muslim traders and had found a growing acceptance, particularly in the urban centers, merchant communities, and ruling classes of West African kingdoms. On the last of his many journeys, Ibn Battuta crossed the Sahara Desert with a traders' caravan to visit Mali in 1352. Upon returning home the following year, he dictated his recollections and experiences to a scribe, producing a valuable account of this West African civilization in the fourteenth century.

- How would you describe Ibn Battuta's impression of Mali? What surprised or shocked him? What did he appreciate?

- What does Ibn Battuta's description of his visit to Mali reveal about his own attitudes and his image of himself?

- What might historians learn from this document about the nature and extent of Islam's penetration in this West African empire? What elements of older and continuing West African cultural traditions are evident in the document?

- What specifically does Ibn Battuta find shocking about the women he encounters on his travels in West Africa?

- What indications of Mali's economic involvement with a wider world are evident in the document?

IBN BATTUTA
Travels in Asia and Africa
1354

Thus we reached the town of Iwalatan° after a journey from Sijilmasa of two months to a day. Iwalatan is the northernmost province of the blacks. . . . The garments of its inhabitants, most of whom belong to the Massufa tribe, are of fine Egyptian fabrics.

Their women are of surpassing beauty, and are shown more respect than the men. The state of affairs amongst these people is indeed extraordinary. Their men show no signs of jealousy whatever; no one claims descent from his father, but on the contrary from his mother's brother. A person's heirs are his sister's sons, not his own sons. This is a thing which I have seen nowhere in the world except among the Indians of Malabar. But those are heathens; these people are Muslims, punctilious in observing the hours of prayer, studying books of law, and memorizing the Koran. Yet their women show no bashfulness before men and do not veil themselves, though they are assiduous in attending the prayers.

°**Iwalatan:** Walata.

Source: Ibn Battuta, *Travels in Asia and Africa 1325–1354*, translated and edited by H. A. R. Gibb (London: Broadway House, 1929), 319–34.

The women there have "friends" and "companions" amongst the men outside their own families, and the men in the same way have "companions" amongst the women of other families. A man may go into his house and find his wife entertaining her "companion," but he takes no objection to it. One day at Iwalatan I went into the qadi's° house, after asking his permission to enter, and found with him a young woman of remarkable beauty. When I saw her I was shocked and turned to go out, but she laughed at me, instead of being overcome by shame, and the qadi said to me "Why are you going out? She is my companion." I was amazed at their conduct, for he was a theologian and a pilgrim [to Mecca] to boot. . . .

When I decided to make the journey to Malli,° which is reached in twenty-four days from Iwalatan if the traveler pushes on rapidly, I hired a guide from the Massufa—for there is no necessity to travel in a company on account of the safety of that road—and set out with three of my companions. . . .

A traveler in this country carries no provisions, whether plain food or seasonings, and neither gold nor silver. He takes nothing but pieces of salt and glass ornaments, which the people call beads, and some aromatic goods. When he comes to a village the womenfolk of the blacks bring out millet, milk, chickens, pulped lotus fruit, rice, "funi" (a grain resembling mustard seed, from which "kuskusu"° and gruel are made), and pounded haricot beans. . . .

Thus I reached the city of Malli, the capital of the king of the blacks. I stopped at the cemetery and went to the quarter occupied by the whites, where I asked for Muhammad ibn al-Faqih. I found that he had hired a house for me and went there. . . . I met the qadi of Malli, 'Abd ar-Rahman, who came to see me; he is a black, a pilgrim [to Mecca], and a man of fine character. I met also the interpreter Dugha, who is one of the principal men among the blacks. All these persons sent me hospitality gifts of food and treated me with the utmost generosity. . . .

The sultan° of Malli is Mansa Sulayman. . . . He is a miserly king, not a man from whom one might hope for a rich present. It happened that I spent these two months without seeing him, on account of my illness. Later on he held a banquet . . . to which the commanders, doctors, qadis, and preachers were invited, and I went along with them. Reading-desks were brought in, and the Koran was read through, then they prayed for our master Abu'l-Hasan° and also for Mansa Sulayman.

When the ceremony was over I went forward and saluted Mansa Sulayman. . . . When I withdrew, the [sultan's] hospitality gift was sent to me. . . . I stood up thinking . . . that it consisted of robes of honor and money, and lo!, it was three cakes of bread, and a piece of beef fried in native oil, and a calabash of sour curds. When I saw this I burst out laughing, and thought it a most amazing thing that they could be so foolish and make so much of such a paltry matter.

On certain days the sultan holds audiences in the palace yard, where there is a platform under a tree, with three steps; this they call the "pempi." It is carpeted with silk and has cushions placed on it. [Over it] is raised the umbrella, which is a sort of pavilion made of silk, surmounted by a bird in gold, about the size of a falcon. The sultan comes out of a door in a corner of the palace, carrying a bow in his hand and a quiver on his back. On his head he has a golden skullcap, bound with a gold band which has narrow ends shaped like knives, more than a span in length. His usual dress is a velvety red tunic, made of the European fabrics called "mutanfas." The sultan is preceded by his musicians, who carry gold and silver guimbris,° and behind him come three hundred armed slaves. He walks in a leisurely fashion, affecting a very slow movement, and even stops from time to time. On reaching the pempi he stops and looks round the assembly, then ascends it in the sedate manner of a preacher ascending a mosque-pulpit. As he takes his seat the drums, trumpets, and bugles are sounded. Three slaves go out at a run to summon

---

°**qadi:** judge.

°**Malli:** the city of Mali.

°**kuskusu:** couscous.

°**sultan:** ruler.

°**Abu'l-Hasan:** the sultan of Morocco.

°**guimbris:** two-stringed guitars.

the sovereign's deputy and the military commanders, who enter and sit down. Two saddled and bridled horses are brought, along with two goats, which they hold to serve as a protection against the evil eye....

The blacks are of all people the most submissive to their king and the most abject in their behavior before him.... If he summons any of them while he is holding an audience in his pavilion, the person summoned takes off his clothes and puts on worn garments, removes his turban and dons a dirty skull-cap, and enters with his garments and trousers raised knee-high. He goes forward in an attitude of humility and dejection and knocks the ground hard with his elbows, then stands with bowed head and bent back listening to what he says. If anyone addresses the king and receives a reply from him, he uncovers his back and throws dust over his head and back, for all the world like a bather splashing himself with water....

On feast-days ..., the poets come in. Each of them is inside a figure resembling a thrush, made of feathers, and provided with a wooden head with a red beak, to look like a thrush's head. They stand in front of the sultan in this ridiculous makeup and recite their poems. I was told that their poetry is a kind of sermonizing in which they say to the sultan: "This pempi which you occupy was that whereon sat this king and that king, and such and such were this one's noble actions and such and such the other's. So do you too do good deeds whose memory will outlive you." ... I was told that this practice is a very old custom amongst them, prior to the introduction of Islam, and that they have kept it up.

The blacks possess some admirable qualities. They are seldom unjust, and have a greater abhorrence of injustice than any other people. Their sultan shows no mercy to anyone who is guilty of the least act of it. There is complete security in their country. Neither traveler nor inhabitant in it has anything to fear from robbers or men of violence. They do not confiscate the property of any white man who dies in their country, even if it be uncounted wealth. On the contrary, they give it into the charge of some trustworthy person among the whites, until the rightful heir takes possession of it. They are careful to observe the hours of prayer, and assiduous in attending them in congregations, and in bringing up their children to them.

On Fridays, if a man does not go early to the mosque, he cannot find a corner to pray in, on account of the crowd. It is a custom of theirs to send each man his boy [to the mosque] with his prayer-mat; the boy spreads it out for his master in a place befitting him [and remains on it] until he comes to the mosque....

Another of their good qualities is their habit of wearing clean white garments on Fridays. Even if a man has nothing but an old worn shirt, he washes it and cleans it, and wears it to the Friday service. Yet another is their zeal for learning the Koran by heart.... I visited the qadi in his house on the day of the festival. His children were chained up, so I said to him, "Will you not let them loose?" He replied, "I shall not do so until they learn the Koran by heart."

Among their bad qualities are the following. The women servants, slave-girls, and young girls go about in front of everyone naked, without a stitch of clothing on them. Women go into the sultan's presence naked and without coverings, and his daughters also go about naked. Then there is their custom of putting dust and ashes on their heads, as a mark of respect, and the grotesque ceremonies we have described when the poets recite their verses. Another reprehensible practice among many of them is the eating of carrion, dogs, and asses.

I went on ... to Gawgaw,° which is a large city on the Nile,° and one of the finest towns in the land of the blacks. It is also one of their biggest and best-provisioned towns, with rice in plenty, milk, and fish.... The buying and selling of its inhabitants is done with cowry shells, and the same is the case at Malli. I stayed there about a month.

°**Gawgaw:** Gogo.

°**Nile:** Niger. The Niger River was long regarded by outsiders as a tributary of the Nile.

Using the Evidence: Travelers' Tales and Observations

1. **Describing a foreign culture:** Each of these documents was written by an outsider to the people or society he is describing. What different postures toward these foreign cultures are evident in the sources? How did the travelers' various religions shape their perception of places they visited? How did they view the women of their host societies? Were these travelers more impressed by the similarities or by the differences between their home cultures and the ones they visited?

2. **Defining the self-perception of authors:** What can we learn from these documents about the men who wrote them? What motivated them to travel so far from home? How did they define themselves in relationship to the societies they observed?

3. **Assessing the credibility of sources:** What information in these sources would be most valuable for historians seeking to understand India, China, and West Africa in the third-wave era? What statements in these sources might be viewed with the most skepticism? You will want to consider the authors' purposes and their intended audiences in evaluating their writings.

4. **Considering outsiders' accounts:** What are the advantages and limitations for historians in drawing on the writings of foreign observers?

Visual Sources

Considering the Evidence: Traveling the Silk Roads

Merchants, mercenaries, monks, and missionaries were among the prominent sojourners who traversed the Silk Roads from China to Europe, traveling much of the time in Central or Inner Asia (see Map 7.1, p. 319). Hailing from an immense variety of cultures, both travelers and the people living permanently along the Silk Roads turned this vast region into a vital Eurasian arena of exchange. Perhaps most obviously, it was a commercial crossroads that featured trade in numerous goods, originating from the agricultural civilizations, pastoral societies, and gathering and hunting cultures of the region. (See Snapshot 1, p. 320.) It was also a realm of cultural and religious encounters. Buddhism, Judaism, Christianity, Islam, Manichaeism (man-ih-KEE-iz'm), elements of Greek and Chinese culture—all of these traditions spread via the Silk Roads network, finding new expressions far from their places of origin. Finally, the territory encompassing the Silk Roads was an imperial crossroads, for there the empires or military federations periodically established by pastoral societies clashed with the established civilizations and states of China, India, the Middle East, and Europe to the south and west.

Over the past century or so, scholars have learned much about life along the Silk Roads. Ancient manuscripts in many languages have brought to light Manichean prayers, commercial contracts, lawsuits, medical prescriptions, erotic tales, and a letter from a merchant stranded far from home because of war. Stopping places on the trade routes, known as caravanserai, have been uncovered in oases or ancient market cities, and long-sealed caves have disclosed amazing treasures of Buddhist art.[35] The images that follow show something of life and travel on the Silk Roads and the cultural exchanges that ensued.

Among the first things that impressed travelers on the Silk Roads were the dangers from nature and man alike. Much of the route passed through harrowing terrain. Traveling from China to India in the seventh century, Xuangzang (see Document 7.1, p. 344) encountered mountains "so dangerously steep and tall that they seem to touch the sky." Marco Polo traversed a desert that appeared endless, where water was scarce and "birds and beasts there are none," and where sandstorms and hallucinations were a peril to travelers. Furthermore when armies clashed or political authority broke down, human threats were added to those of nature.

Visual Source 7.1 shows such an occasion. An eighth-century painting, it was discovered in the Magao Caves near Dunhuang, a major stop on the Silk Roads and a center of Buddhist art and learning. It depicts a group of Tibetan and Central Asian merchants (on the right) who have encountered bandits or avaricious border guards (on the left). Required to unload their goods, they await their fate—an extortionate payment, robbery of their goods, or maybe death. But in the Buddhist culture that pervaded much of the Silk Road network, legend had it that a wealthy merchant had gained safety during his travels by invoking the assistance of the bodhisattva Guanyin. (See Visual Source 4.3, p. 213, for a Japanese image of this bodhisattva of compassion.) The panel above the merchants reads in part: "If you all call upon his name, then from the malicious bandits you shall contrive to be delivered. . . . Men, by the mere calling upon his name, they shall forthwith gain deliverance."[36]

Visual Source 7.1 Silk Road Merchants Encounter Bandits (CPA Media)

- What message did this painting seek to convey?

- What else might you learn about the Silk Roads from this image?

- What might have been the possible outcomes to the story that this scene describes?

If travelers faced peril on the Silk Roads, they also found places of rest and refreshment. The caravanserai provided lodging for merchants and their servants, warehouses for their goods, shelter and food for their animals in an open courtyard, and opportunities for trade in the bazaars. Visual Source 7.2, a sixth-century painting also from the Magao Caves, shows a caravan finding accommodations in such a place. Providing these services, including wells and bridges, was one way for wealthy Buddhist patrons to gain merit.

- What specific activities can you identify in the painting?

- Which of those activities might be thought capable of generating religious merit? Notice for example, the several figures at the bottom left of the image.

- What additional information about the Silk Roads is apparent in this image compared to what derives from Visual Source 7.1?

- Why might merchants in particular find Buddhism an appealing faith?

In addition to merchants, the Silk Roads also hosted numerous Buddhist monks, some of them headed for India in search of holy texts and sacred relics. Others traveled from town to town teaching the message of the Buddha. Thus, at least until the rise of Islam, Buddhism was a common feature in the experience of many participants in the Silk Roads network and a point of contact

Visual Source 7.2 A Stop at a Caravanserai (CPA Media)

between Central Asian peoples and the civilizations of India and China. Visual
Source 7.3, a tenth-century Chinese painting also from the Magao Caves,
shows a traveling monk on the Silk Road. Notice that the monk is leading a
tiger, long a symbol of protection and courage and a messenger between heaven
and the human world (see the photo on p. 322). It also recalls a much-told story
of the Buddha, in an earlier life, compassionately offering his blood and body
to feed some starving tiger cubs and their mother.

- What function does the small Buddha sitting on a cloud at the upper left
  play in this painting?

- On his back the monk is carrying a heavy load of Buddhist texts, or
  sutras. Why do you think Buddhist monks were so eager to acquire and
  to disseminate such texts? (See also Document 7.1, pp. 344–47.)

- At the end of the monk's staff hangs what is probably a container for relics,
  perhaps a bone or a tuft of hair from the Buddha himself. Why might such
  relics have had such an appeal for the faithful? Can you identify a similar
  veneration of relics in other religious traditions?

Travelers on the Silk Roads would surely have noticed the sheer cultural
variety of the people they encountered. In the bazaars of market town and cara-
vanserais, many languages could be heard. Caravans might include merchants
from various places, as the chapter-opening image on page 314 shows. And the
more observant of such travelers might also become aware of the mixing and
blending of these cultural traditions, as reflected in the art objects and religious
practices of the region.

The Kushans, a pastoral nomadic people originally from the area around
Dunhuang at the far western edge of China, provide an example of this process. In the early centuries B.C.E., they had migrated to the region that now
makes up northwestern India, Pakistan, Afghanistan, and Tajikistan, where they
established a sizable and prosperous empire linked to the Silk Road trading network. It was a remarkably cosmopolitan place, and it flourished until the third
or fourth century C.E. That empire, according to one recent account, "created
stable conditions at the heart of Central Asia, allowing for the great flowering
of trans-Eurasian mercantile and cultural exchange that occurred along the
Silk Roads."[37]

Since parts of this empire had earlier been ruled by Alexander the Great
and his Greek successors (see pp. 126–29), classical Mediterranean culture was
a prominent element of Kushan culture. The Kushans used the Greek alphabet to write their official language, which was derived from India. The greatest of the Kushan rulers, Kanishka (ruled ca. 127–153 C.E.), styled himself
"Great King, King of Kings, Son of God," a title that had both Persian and
Chinese precedents. Hindu devotional cults as well as Buddhism flourished,
and the Kushan Empire became a launching pad for the spread of Buddhism

Visual Source 7.3 A Buddhist Monk on the Silk Road (© Benoy K. Behl)

Visual Source 7.4 Greek Culture, Buddhism, and the Kushans
(© Victoria and Albert Museum, London)

into Central Asia and ultimately into China and Japan. It was here that the earliest human representations of the Buddha were sculpted, and often with distinctly Greek features. (See Visual Source 4.2, p. 211.) Despite these outside influences, Kushan artists depicted their rulers in typical steppe nomadic style: on horseback, wearing loose trousers, heavy boots, and knee-length robes.

Visual Source 7.4, a Kushan pendant dating to the fourth century C.E., illustrates this cultural blending. It features Hariti, originally a fearsome Hindu goddess who abducted and killed children, feeding their flesh to her own offspring. But in an encounter with the Buddha, Hariti repented and was transformed into a compassionate protector of children. Here she is depicted holding in her right hand a lotus blossom, a prominent Buddhist symbol; her left hand holds another lotus flower supporting a flask or cornucopia overflowing with pomegranates (symbolizing food and abundance). According to local mythology, the Buddha had offered Hariti pomegranates (often said to resemble human flesh) as a substitute for the children she was devouring.

While the content of this pendant is thoroughly Indian and Buddhist, scholars believe that this representation of Hariti was probably modeled after the Greek goddess Tyche (TEE-chee), also portrayed holding a cornucopia. Furthermore, her short tunic worn with a belt was likewise of Greek or Hellenistic origin. A further cultural influence is found in the decorations that surround the image, for the border of pearls and stylized flowers derives from Persia.

- Why do you think the Kushan artist who created this pendant chose to weave together so many distinct cultural strands?

- What does the story of Hariti's transformation tell us about the impact of Buddhism in the region?

- Why might the Greek goddess Tyche have been used as a model for Hariti? (Hint: you might want to do a little research on Tyche before answering this question.)

Among the Central Asian peoples of Silk Roads, none had a longer-lasting impact on world history than the Turks, a term that refers to a variety of groups speaking related Turkic languages. Originating as pastoral nomads in what is now Mongolia, Turkic peoples gradually migrated westward, occupying much of Central Asia, sometimes creating sizeable empires and settling down as farmers. But the greatest transformation of Turkic culture was a product of conversion to Islam. That process took place between the tenth and fourteenth centuries, as Muslim armies penetrated Central Asia and Muslim merchants became prominent traders on the Silk Roads.

Also very important in the Turks' conversion to Islam were Muslim holy men known as dervishes. Operating within the Sufi tradition of Islam, dervishes were spiritual seekers who sought a direct personal experience of the Divine Reality and developed reputations for good works, personal kindness, and sometimes magical or religious powers. A Turkic tale from the fourteenth century tells the story of one such holy man, Baba Tukles, sent by God to convert a ruler named Ozbek Khan. To overcome the opposition of the khan's traditional shamans, Baba Tukles invited one of the shamans to enter a fiery-hot oven pit with him. The shaman was instantly incinerated, while the Muslim holy man emerged unscathed from that test of religious power.[38] Such tales of the supernatural and the conversion of rulers contributed to the attractiveness of Islam among Turkic peoples and have been a common feature in the spread of all of the major world religions.

Visual Source 7.5, a painting dating from the sixteenth century, shows a number of Turkish dervishes performing the turning or whirling dance associated with the Sufi religious order established in the thirteenth century by the great mystical poet Rumi.

Intended to bring participants into direct contact with the Divine, the whirling dance itself drew on the ideas and practices of ancient Central Asian religious life in which practitioners, known as shamans, entered into an ecstatic state of consciousness and connection to the spirit world. "Especially in Central Asia, the Caucasus and Anatolia," writes one scholar, "the mystical ecstasy [of the whirling dance] was understood in the spirit of the shamanic tradition."[39] This blending of two religious traditions—mystical or Sufi Islam and shamanism—represents yet another example of the cultural interactions that washed across the Silk Roads during the third-wave millennium.

- What image of these dervishes was the artist trying to convey?

- Why might such holy men have been effective carriers of Islam in Central Asia?

- Notice the musical instruments that accompany the turning dance—sticks on the left, a flutelike instrument known as a ney in the center, and drums on the right. What do you think this music and dance contributed to the religious experience of the participants?

Visual Source 7.5 Islam, Shamanism, and the Turks (The Art Archive at Art Resource, NY)

Using the Evidence: Traveling the Silk Roads

1. **Considering cross-cultural interactions:** The pastoral peoples of the Silk Roads region and the settled agricultural civilizations adjacent to them did not live in closed or separate worlds. What evidence contained in these visual sources supports or challenges this assertion?

2. **Defining motives:** What needs or desires inspired the economic and cultural interactions of the Silk Roads?

3. **Explaining religious change:** What do these visual sources suggest about the appeal of Buddhism and later Islam to the peoples of the Silk Roads?

4. **Evaluating the usefulness of visual sources:** What do these visual sources add to the narrative account of the Silk Roads on pages 344–54? In what ways are they limited as evidence for historical inquiry?

Chapter 7 Wrap Up

LearningCurve
Check what you know.
bedfordstmartins.com
/strayer/LC

STEP ONE

The Word to Know: Globalization

The *Oxford English Dictionary* defines *globalization* as "the action, process, or fact of making global; *esp.* (in later use) the process by which businesses or other organizations develop international influence or start operating on an international scale, widely considered to be at the expense of national identity." While some would argue that globalization is a twenty-first century phenomenon, the evidence in the chapter makes the case that globalization was in place in the eastern hemisphere between 500 C.E. and 1500 C.E. Write a brief paragraph detailing this evidence.

STEP TWO

Mapping Globalization

Refer to the text and the following maps from Chapter 7: Map 7.1, "The Silk Roads," p. 319; Map 7.2, "The Sea Roads," p. 325; Map 7.3, "Southeast Asia ca. 1200 C.E.," p. 329; "The Swahili Coast of East Africa," p. 333; Map 7.4, "The Sand Roads," p. 336; and Map 7.5, "The American Web, p. 340.

   Using either a *single* outline map of the world, or a hand-drawn world map, complete the following:

1. Draw the Silk Roads, the Sea Roads, the Sand Roads, and the American trade connections, as color coded arrows on the map (for example, blue for the Sea Roads, red for the Sand Roads, etc.—include a key).

2. Label specific goods that were transported in both directions on all four routes. Pay particular attention to the Snapshots on pages 320 and 327, but remember to also get information from the text.

3. What moved along these trade routes besides trade goods? Label this information on the map next to the arrows themselves. Be as specific as possible (not just "religion", but *which* faith for example.)

4. Include the following cities on your map: Antioch, Chang'an, Venice, Kilwa, Calicut, Guangzhou, Palembang, Timbuktu, Cuzco, and Cahokia. Why are these cities significant? In order to demonstrate their cosmopolitan nature, and their role in the global economy, add one brief phrase as "annotation" to your map.

Exploring Point of View (POV) in Travelers' Narratives

For each of documents in the Considering the Evidence section of Chapter 7 (pp. 344–54), consider the author's background and think about how his point of view is revealed within the text.

1. Xuanzang (Document 7.1): What evidence confirms that Xuanzeng is not only a foreigner in India but also a devoted Buddhist from a Confucian society?

2. Marco Polo (Document 7.2): What evidence from Marco Polo's account makes it apparent he sees the world from both the perspective of a merchant and a Christian who had traveled beyond his own culture?

3. Ibn Battuta (Document 7.3): As a Muslim traveler in Muslim lands, what values does Ibn Battuta convey that he cares most about? How might this connect back to the various jobs he held as he traveled?

4. Write a half-page reflection comparing how the author's tone in each of these passages conveys additional information about their own backgrounds (their religious beliefs, cosmopolitanism, and birthplaces) and about what they reported.

智多星吳用

東溪村の人にて字を吳學究道号を加亮流先生とふ陣添八孔明太公望よ不劣陰謀詭智蠡ふも勝たり梁山泊乃軍師なり

China and the World

East Asian Connections

500–1300

"China will be the next superpower."[1] That was the frank assertion of an article in the British newspaper the *Guardian* in June 2006. Nor was it alone in that assessment. As the new millennium dawned, headlines with this message appeared with increasing frequency in public lectures, in newspaper and magazine articles, and in book titles all across the world. China's huge population, its booming economy, its massive trade surplus with the United States, its entry into world oil markets, its military potential, and its growing presence in global political affairs — all of this suggested that China was headed for a major role, perhaps even a dominant role, in the world of the twenty-first century. Few of these authors, however, paused to recall that China's prominence on the world stage was hardly something new or that its nineteenth- and twentieth-century position as a "backward," weak, or dependent country was distinctly at odds with its long history. Is China perhaps poised to resume in the twenty-first century a much older and more powerful role in world affairs?

IN THE WORLD OF THIRD-WAVE CIVILIZATIONS, even more than in earlier times, China cast a long shadow. Its massive and powerful civilization, widely imitated by adjacent peoples, gave rise to a China-centered "world order" encompassing most of eastern Asia.[2] China extended its borders deep into Central Asia, while its wealthy and cosmopolitan culture attracted visitors from all over Eurasia. None of its many neighbors — whether nomadic peoples to the north and west or smaller peripheral states such as Tibet, Korea, Japan, and Vietnam — could escape its gravitational pull. All of them had to deal

Chinese Astronomy: The impressive achievements of Chinese astronomy included the observation of sunspots, supernovae, and solar and lunar eclipses as well as the construction of elaborate star maps and astronomical devices such as those shown here. The print itself is of Japanese origin and shows a figure wearing the dragon robes of a Chinese official. It illustrates the immense cultural influence of China on its smaller Japanese neighbor. (© The Trustees of the British Museum) with China. Far beyond these near neighbors, China's booming economy and many technological innovations had ripple effects all across the Afro-Eurasia world.

Even as China so often influenced the world, it too was changed by its many interactions with non-Chinese peoples. Northern nomads—"barbarians" to the Chinese—frequently posed a military threat and on occasion even conquered and ruled parts of China. The country's growing involvement in international trade stimulated important social, cultural, and economic changes within China itself. Buddhism, a religion of Indian origin, took root in China, and, to a lesser extent, so did Christianity and Islam. In short, China's engagement with the wider world became a very significant element in a global era of accelerating connections.

SEEKING THE MAIN POINT

Chinese history has often been viewed in the West as impressive perhaps, but largely static or changeless and self-contained or isolated. In what ways might the material in this chapter counteract such impressions?

Together Again: The Reemergence of a Unified China

The collapse of the Han dynasty around 220 C.E. ushered in more than three centuries of political fragmentation in China and signaled the rise of powerful and locally entrenched aristocratic families. It also meant the incursion of northern nomads, many of whom learned Chinese, dressed like Chinese, married into Chinese families, and governed northern regions of the country in a Chinese fashion. Such conditions of disunity, unnatural in the eyes of many thoughtful Chinese, discredited Confucianism and opened the door to a greater acceptance of Buddhism and Daoism among the elite. (See Portrait of Ge Hong in Chapter 5, pp. 222–23.)

Those centuries also witnessed substantial Chinese migration southward toward the Yangzi River valley, a movement of people that gave southern China some 60 percent of the country's population by 1000. That movement of Chinese people, accompanied by their intensive agriculture, set in motion a vast environmental transformation, marked by the destruction of the old-growth forests that once covered much of the country and the retreat of the elephants that had inhabited those lands. Around 800 C.E., the Chinese official and writer Liu Zongyuan lamented what was happening.

> A tumbled confusion of lumber as flames on the hillside crackle
> Not even the last remaining shrubs are safeguarded from destruction
> Where once mountain torrents leapt—nothing but rutted gullies.[3]

A "Golden Age" of Chinese Achievement

■ **Change**
Why are the centuries of the Tang and Song dynasties in China sometimes referred to as a "golden age"?

Unlike the fall of the western Roman Empire, where political fragmentation proved to be a permanent condition, China regained its unity under the Sui dynasty (589–618). Its emperors solidified that unity by a vast extension of the country's canal system, stretching some 1,200 miles in length and described by one scholar as "an engineering feat without parallel in the world of its time."[4] Those canals linked northern and

A Map of Time

39	Trung sisters rebellion against China in Vietnam
4th–6th centuries	Early state building in Korea
300–800	Buddhism takes root in China
589–618	Sui dynasty and the reunification of China
604	Seventeen Article Constitution in Japan
618–907	Tang dynasty in China
688	Withdrawal of Chinese military forces from Korea
794–1192	Heian period in Japanese history
845	Suppression of Buddhism in China
868	First printed book in China
939	Vietnam establishes independence from China
960–1279	Song dynasty in China
ca. 1000	Invention of gunpowder in China; beginning of foot binding
1000	*Tale of Genji* (Japan)
1279–1369	Mongol rule in China

southern China economically and contributed much to the prosperity that followed. But the ruthlessness of Sui emperors and a futile military campaign to conquer Korea exhausted the state's resources, alienated many people, and prompted the overthrow of the dynasty.

This dynastic collapse, however, witnessed no prolonged disintegration of the Chinese state. The two dynasties that followed—the Tang (618–907) and the Song (960–1279)—built on the Sui foundations of renewed unity (see Map 8.1, p. 368). Together they established patterns of Chinese life that endured into the twentieth century, despite a fifty-year period of disunity between the two dynasties. Culturally, this era has long been regarded as a "golden age" of arts and literature, setting standards of excellence in poetry, landscape painting, and ceramics. (See Visual Sources: The Leisure Life of China's Elites, pp. 404–09.) Particularly during the Song dynasty, an explosion of scholarship gave rise to Neo-Confucianism, an effort to revive Confucian thinking while incorporating into it some of the insights of Buddhism and Daoism.

Politically, the Tang and Song dynasties built a state structure that endured for a thousand years. Six major ministries—personnel, finance, rites, army, justice, and public works—were accompanied by the Censorate, an agency that exercised surveillance over the rest of the government, checking on the character and competence of public officials. To staff this bureaucracy, the examination system was revived and made

Map 8.1   Tang and Song Dynasty China

During the third-wave millennium, China interacted extensively with its neighbors. The Tang dynasty extended Chinese control deep into Central Asia, while the Song dynasty witnessed incursions by the nomadic Jurchen people, who created the Jin Empire, which ruled parts of northern China.

more elaborate, facilitated by the ability to print books for the first time in world history. Efforts to prevent cheating on the exams included searching candidates entering the examination hall and placing numbers rather than names on their papers. Schools and colleges proliferated to prepare candidates for the rigorous exams, which became a central feature of upper-class life. A leading world historian has described Tang dynasty China as "the best ordered state in the world."[5]

Selecting officials on the basis of merit represented a challenge to established aristocratic families' hold on public office. Still, a substantial percentage of official positions went to the sons of the privileged, even if they had not passed the exams. Moreover, because education and the examination system grew far more rapidly than the number of official positions, many who passed lower-level exams could not be accommodated with a bureaucratic appointment. Often, however, they were able to combine landowning and success in the examination system to maintain an immense cultural prestige and prominence in their local areas. Despite the state's periodic efforts to redistribute land in favor of the peasantry, the great families of large landowners continued to encroach on peasant plots, a recurring pattern in rural China from ancient times to the present.

Underlying these cultural and political achievements was an "economic revolution" that made Song dynasty China "by far the richest, most skilled, and most populous country on earth."[6] The most obvious sign of China's prosperity was its rapid growth in population, which jumped from about 50 million or 60 million during the Tang dynasty to 120 million by 1200. Behind this doubling of the population were remarkable achievements in agricultural production, particularly the adoption of a fast-ripening and drought-resistant strain of rice from Vietnam.

Many people found their way to the cities, making China the most urbanized country in the world. Dozens of Chinese cities numbered over 100,000, while the Song dynasty capital of Hangzhou was home to more than a million people. A Chinese observer in 1235 provided a vivid description of that city.[7] Specialized markets abounded for meat, herbs, vegetables, books, rice, and much more, with troupes of actors performing for the crowds. Restaurants advertised their unique offerings — sweet bean soup, pickled dates, juicy lungs, meat pies, pigs' feet — and some offered vegetarian fare for religious banquets. Inns of various kinds appealed to different groups. Those that served only wine, a practice known as "hitting the cup," were regarded as "unfit for polite company." "Luxuriant inns," marked by red lanterns, featured prostitutes and "wine chambers equipped with beds." Specialized agencies managed elaborate dinner parties for the wealthy, complete with a Perfume and Medicine Office to "help sober up the guests." Schools for musicians offered thirteen different courses. Numerous clubs provided companionship for poets, fishermen, Buddhists, physical fitness enthusiasts, antiques collectors, horse lovers, and many other groups. No wonder the Italian visitor Marco Polo described Hangzhou later in the thirteenth century as "beyond dispute the finest and noblest [city] in the world."[8] (See Document 7.2, pp. 347–50, for a fuller description of Marco Polo's impressions of Hangzhou.)

Supplying these cities with food was made possible by an immense network of internal waterways — canals, rivers, and lakes — stretching perhaps 30,000 miles. They provided a cheap transportation system that bound the country together economically and created the "world's most populous trading area."[9]

Industrial production likewise soared. In both large-scale enterprises employing hundreds of workers and in smaller backyard furnaces, China's iron industry increased

Kaifeng
This detail comes from a huge watercolor scroll, titled *Upper River during Qing Ming Festival*, originally painted during the Song dynasty. It illustrates the urban sophistication of Kaifeng and other Chinese cities at that time and has been frequently imitated and copied since then. (Palace Museum, Beijing/Cultural Relics Press)

its output dramatically. By the eleventh century, it was providing the government with 32,000 suits of armor and 16 million iron arrowheads annually, in addition to supplying metal for coins, tools, construction, and bells in Buddhist monasteries. Technological innovation in other fields also flourished. Inventions in printing, both woodblock and movable type, generated the world's first printed books, and by 1000 relatively cheap books on religious, agricultural, mathematical, and medical topics became widely available in China. Its navigational and shipbuilding technologies led the world. The Chinese invention of gunpowder created within a few centuries a revolution in military affairs that had global dimensions. (See Snapshot, p. 320.)

Most remarkably, perhaps, all of this occurred within the world's most highly commercialized society, in which producing for the market, rather than for local consumption, became a very widespread phenomenon. Cheap transportation allowed peasants to grow specialized crops for sale, while they purchased rice or other staples on the market. In addition, government demands for taxes paid in cash rather than in kind required peasants to sell something—their products or their labor—in order to meet their obligations. The growing use of paper money as well as financial instruments such as letters of credit and promissory notes further contributed to the commercialization of Chinese society. Two prominent scholars have described the outcome: "Output increased, population grew, skills multiplied, and a burst of inventiveness made Song China far wealthier than ever before—or than any of its contemporaries."[10]

Women in the Song Dynasty

The "golden age" of Song dynasty China was perhaps less than "golden" for many of its women, for that era marked yet another turning point in the history of Chinese patriarchy. Under the influence of steppe nomads, whose women led less restricted lives, elite Chinese women of the Tang dynasty era, at least in the north, had participated in social life with greater freedom than in earlier times. Paintings and statues show aristocratic women riding horses, while the Queen Mother of the West, a Daoist deity, was widely worshipped by female Daoist priests and practitioners (see p. 406 and Visual Sources 8.2 and 8.4, pp. 406 and 408). By the Song dynasty, however, a reviving Confucianism and rapid economic growth seemed to tighten patriarchal restrictions on women and to restore some of the earlier Han dynasty notions of female submission and passivity.

■ **Change**
In what ways did women's lives change during the Tang and Song dynasties?

Once again Confucian writers highlighted the subordination of women to men and the need to keep males and females separate in every domain of life. The Song dynasty historian and scholar Sima Guang (1019–1086) summed up the prevailing view: "The boy leads the girl, the girl follows the boy; the duty of husbands to be resolute and wives to be docile begins with this."[11] For men, masculinity came to be defined less in terms of horseback riding, athleticism, and the warrior values of northern nomads and more in terms of the refined pursuits of calligraphy, scholarship, painting, and poetry. Corresponding views of feminine qualities emphasized women's weakness, reticence, and delicacy. Women were also frequently viewed as a distraction to men's pursuit of a contemplative and introspective life. The remarriage of widows, though legally permissible, was increasingly condemned, for "to walk through two courtyards is a source of shame for a woman."[12]

The most compelling expression of a tightening patriarchy lay in foot binding. Apparently beginning among dancers and courtesans in the tenth or eleventh century C.E., this practice involved the tight wrapping of young girls' feet, usually breaking the bones of the foot and causing intense pain. During and after the Song dynasty, foot binding spread widely among elite families and later became even more widespread in Chinese society. It was associated with new images of female beauty and eroticism that emphasized small size, frailty, and deference and served to keep women restricted to the "inner quarters," where Confucian tradition asserted that they belonged. Many mothers imposed this painful procedure on their daughters, perhaps to enhance their marriage prospects and to assist them in competing with concubines for the attention of their husbands.[13] For many women it became a rite of passage and source of some pride in their tiny feet and the beautiful slippers that encased them, even the occasion for poetry for some literate women. Foot binding also served to

Foot Binding
While the practice of foot binding painfully deformed the feet of young girls and women, it was also associated esthetically with feminine beauty, particularly in the delicate and elaborately decorated shoes that encased their bound feet. (Foot: Jodi Cobb/National Geographic Stock; Shoe: ClassicStock/Masterfile)

distinguish Chinese women from their "barbarian" counterparts and elite women from commoners and peasants.

Furthermore, a rapidly commercializing economy undermined the position of women in the textile industry. Urban workshops and state factories, run by men, increasingly took over the skilled tasks of weaving textiles, especially silk, which had previously been the work of rural women in their homes. Although these women continued to tend silk worms and spin silk thread, they had lost the more lucrative income-generating work of weaving silk fabrics. But as their economic role in textile production declined, other opportunities beckoned in an increasingly prosperous Song China. In the cities, women operated restaurants, sold fish and vegetables, and worked as maids, cooks, and dressmakers. The growing prosperity of elite families funneled increasing numbers of women into roles as concubines, entertainers, courtesans, and prostitutes. Their ready availability surely reduced the ability of wives to negotiate as equals with their husbands, setting women against one another and creating endless household jealousies.

In other ways, the Song dynasty witnessed more positive trends in the lives of women. Their property rights expanded, in terms of controlling their own dowries and inheriting property from their families. "Neither in earlier nor in later periods," writes one scholar, "did as much property pass through women's hands" as during the Song dynasty.[14] Furthermore, lower-ranking but ambitious officials strongly urged the education of women, so that they might more effectively raise their sons and increase the family's fortune. Song dynasty China, in short, offered a mixture of tightening restrictions and new opportunities to its women.

China and the Northern Nomads: A Chinese World Order in the Making

From early times to the nineteenth century, China's many interactions with a larger Eurasian world shaped both China's own development and that of world history more generally. The country's most enduring and intense interaction with foreigners lay to the north, involving the many nomadic pastoral or semi-agricultural peoples of the steppes. Living in areas unable to sustain Chinese-style farming, the northern nomads had long focused their economies around the raising of livestock (sheep, cattle, goats) and the mastery of horse riding. Organized locally in small, mobile, kinship-based groups, sometimes called tribes, these peoples also periodically created much larger and powerful states or confederations that could draw on the impressive horsemanship and military skills of virtually the entire male population of their societies. Such specialized pastoral societies needed grain and other agricultural products from China, and their leaders developed a taste for Chinese manufactured and luxury goods — wine and silk, for example — with which they could attract and reward followers. Thus the nomads were drawn like a magnet toward China, trading, raiding, and extorting to obtain the resources so vital to their way of life. For 2,000 years or more, pressure from the steppes and the intrusion of nomadic peoples were constant factors in China's historical development.

From the nomads' point of view, the threat often came from the Chinese, who periodically directed their own military forces deep into the steppes, built the Great Wall to keep the nomads out, and often proved unwilling to allow pastoral peoples easy access to trading opportunities within China.[15] And yet the Chinese needed the nomads. Their lands were the source of horses, so essential for the Chinese military. Other products of the steppes and the forests beyond, such as skins, furs, hides, and amber, were also of value in China. Furthermore, pastoral nomads controlled much of the Silk Road trading network, which funneled goods from the West into China. The continuing interaction between China and the northern nomads brought together peoples occupying different environments, practicing different economies, governing themselves with different institutions, and thinking about the world in quite different ways.

■ **Connection**

How did the Chinese and their nomadic neighbors to the north view each other?

The Tribute System in Theory

An enduring outcome of this cross-cultural encounter was a particular view the Chinese held of themselves and of their neighbors, fully articulated by the time of the Han dynasty (200 B.C.E.–200 C.E.) and lasting for more than two millennia. That understanding cast China as the "middle kingdom," the center of the world, infinitely superior to the "barbarian" peoples beyond its borders. With its long history, great cities, refined tastes, sophisticated intellectual and artistic achievements, bureaucratic state, literate elite, and prosperous economy, China represented "civilization." All of this, in Chinese thinking, was in sharp contrast to the rude cultures and primitive life of the northern nomads, who continually moved about "like beasts and birds," lived in tents,

■ **Connection**

What assumptions underlay the tribute system?

ate mostly meat and milk, and practically lived on their horses, while making war on everyone within reach. Educated Chinese saw their own society as self-sufficient, requiring little from the outside world, while barbarians, quite understandably, sought access to China's wealth and wisdom. Furthermore, China was willing to permit that access under controlled conditions, for its sense of superiority did not preclude the possibility that barbarians could become civilized Chinese. China was a "radiating civilization," graciously shedding its light most fully to nearby barbarians and with diminished intensity to those farther away.[16]

Such was the general understanding of literate Chinese about their own civilization in relation to northern nomads and other non-Chinese peoples. That worldview also took shape as a practical system for managing China's relationship with these people. Known as the "tribute system," it was a set of practices that required non-Chinese authorities to acknowledge Chinese superiority and their own subordinate place in a Chinese-centered world order. Foreigners seeking access to China had to send a delegation to the Chinese court, where they would perform the kowtow, a series of ritual bowings and prostrations, and present their tribute—produce of value from their countries—to the Chinese emperor. In return for these expressions of submission, he would grant permission for foreigners to trade in China's rich markets and would provide them with gifts or "bestowals," often worth far more than the tribute they had offered. This was the mechanism by which successive Chinese dynasties attempted to regulate their relationships with northern nomads; with neighboring states such as Korea, Vietnam, Tibet, and Japan; and, after 1500, with those European barbarians from across the sea.

Often, this system seemed to work. Over the centuries, countless foreign delegations proved willing to present their tribute, say the required words, and perform the necessary rituals required to gain access to the material goods of China. Aspiring non-Chinese rulers also gained prestige as they basked in the reflected glory of even this subordinate association with the great Chinese civilization. The official titles, seals of office, and ceremonial robes they received from China proved useful in their local struggles for power.

The Tribute System in Practice

■ **Connection**

How did the tribute system in practice differ from the ideal Chinese understanding of its operation?

But the tribute system also disguised some realities that contradicted its assumptions. On occasion, China was confronting not separate and small-scale barbarian societies, but large and powerful nomadic empires able to deal with China on at least equal terms. An early nomadic confederacy was that of the Xiongnu, established about the same time as the Han dynasty and eventually reaching from Manchuria to Central Asia (see Map 3.5, p. 135). Devastating Xiongnu raids into northern China persuaded the Chinese emperor to negotiate an arrangement that recognized the nomadic state as a political equal, promised its leader a princess in marriage, and, most important, agreed to supply him annually with large quantities of grain, wine, and silk. Although

The Tribute System
This Qing dynasty painting shows an idealized Chinese version of the tribute system. The Chinese emperor receives barbarian envoys, who perform rituals of subordination and present tribute in the form of a horse. (Réunion des Musées Nationaux/Art Resource, NY)

these goods were officially termed "gifts," granted in accord with the tribute system, they were in fact tribute in reverse or even protection money. In return for these goods, so critical for the functioning of the nomadic state, the Xiongnu agreed to refrain from military incursions into China. The basic realities of the situation were summed up in this warning to the Han dynasty in the first century B.C.E.:

> Just make sure that the silks and grain stuffs you bring the Xiongnu are the right measure and quality, that's all. What's the need for talking? If the goods you deliver are up to measure and good quality, all right. But if there is any deficiency or the quality is no good, then when the autumn harvest comes, we will take our horses and trample all over your crops.[17]

Something similar occurred during the Tang dynasty as a series of Turkic empires arose in Mongolia. Like the Xiongnu, they too extorted large "gifts" from the Chinese. One of these peoples, the Uighurs, actually rescued the Tang dynasty from a serious internal revolt in the 750s. In return, the Uighur leader gained one of the Chinese emperor's daughters as a wife and arranged a highly favorable exchange of poor-quality horses for high-quality silk that brought half a million rolls of the precious fabric annually into the Uighur lands. Despite the rhetoric of the tribute system, the Chinese were not always able to dictate the terms of their relationship with the northern nomads.

Steppe nomads were generally not much interested in actually conquering and ruling China. It was easier and more profitable to extort goods from a functioning Chinese state. On occasion, though, that state broke down, and various nomadic groups moved in to "pick up the pieces," conquering and governing parts of China. Such a process took place following the fall of the Han dynasty and again after the collapse of the Tang dynasty, when the Khitan (kee-THAN) (907–1125) and then the Jin or Jurchen (JER-chihn) (1115–1234) peoples established states that encompassed parts of northern China as well as major areas of the steppes to the north. Both of them required the Chinese Song dynasty, located farther south, to deliver annually huge quantities of silk, silver, and tea, some of which found its way into the Silk Road trading network. The practice of "bestowing gifts on barbarians," long a part of the tribute system, allowed the proud Chinese to imagine that they were still in control of the situation even as they were paying heavily for protection from nomadic incursion. Those gifts, in turn, provided vital economic resources to nomadic states.

Cultural Influence across an Ecological Frontier

■ **Connection**

In what ways did China and the nomads influence each other?

When nomadic peoples actually ruled parts of China, some of them adopted Chinese ways, employing Chinese advisers, governing according to Chinese practice, and, at least for the elite, immersing themselves in Chinese culture and learning. This process of "becoming Chinese" went furthest among the Jurchen, many of whom lived in northern China and learned to speak Chinese, wore Chinese clothing, married Chinese husbands and wives, and practiced Buddhism or Daoism. On the whole, however, Chinese culture had only a modest impact on the nomadic people of the northern steppes. Unlike the native peoples of southern China, who were gradually absorbed into Chinese culture, the pastoral societies north of the Great Wall generally retained their own cultural patterns. Few of them were incorporated, at least not for long, within a Chinese state, and most lived in areas where Chinese-style agriculture was simply impossible. Under these conditions, there were few incentives for adopting Chinese culture wholesale. But various modes of interaction—peaceful trade, military conflict, political negotiations, economic extortion, some cultural influence— continued across the ecological frontier that divided two quite distinct and separate ways of life. Each was necessary for the other.

On the Chinese side, elements of steppe culture had some influence in those parts of northern China that were periodically conquered and ruled by nomadic peoples. The founders of the Sui and Tang dynasties were in fact of mixed nomad and Chinese ancestry and came from the borderland region where a blended Chinese/Turkic culture had evolved. High-ranking members of the imperial family personally led their troops in battle in the style of Turkic warriors. Furthermore, Tang dynasty China was awash with foreign visitors from all over Asia—delegations bearing tribute, merchants carrying exotic goods, bands of clerics or religious pilgrims bringing new religions such as Christianity, Islam, Buddhism, and Manichaeism. For a time in the Tang dynasty, almost anything associated with "western barbarians"—Central Asians, Persians, Indians, Arabs—had great appeal among northern Chinese elites. Their music, dancing, clothing, foods, games, and artistic styles found favor among the upper classes. The more traditional southern Chinese, feeling themselves heir to the legacy of the Han dynasty, were sharply critical of their northern counterparts for allowing women too much freedom, for drinking yogurt rather than tea, for listening to "western" music, all of which they attributed to barbarian influence. Around 800 C.E., the poet Yuan Chen gave voice to a growing backlash against this too easy acceptance of things "Western":

Ever since the Western horsemen began raising smut and dust,
Fur and fleece, rank and rancid, have filled Hsien and Lo [two Chinese cities].
Women make themselves Western matrons by the study of Western makeup.
Entertainers present Western tunes, in their devotion to Western music.[18]

Coping with China: Comparing Korea, Vietnam, and Japan

Also involved in tributary relationships with China were the newly emerging states and civilizations of Korea, Vietnam, and Japan. Unlike the northern nomads, these societies were thoroughly agricultural and sedentary. During the first millennium C.E., they were part of a larger process—the globalization of civilization—which produced new city- and state-based societies in various parts of the world. Proximity to their giant Chinese neighbor decisively shaped the histories of these new East Asian civilizations, for all of them borrowed major elements of Chinese culture. But unlike the native peoples of southern China, who largely became Chinese, the peoples of Korea, Vietnam, and Japan did not. They retained distinctive identities, which have lasted into modern times. While resisting Chinese political domination, they also appreciated Chinese culture and sought the source of Chinese wealth and power. In such ways, these smaller East Asian civilizations resembled the "developing" Afro-Asian societies of the twentieth century, which embraced "modernity" and elements of Western culture, while trying to maintain their political and cultural independence from the European and American centers of that modern way of life. Korea, Vietnam, and Japan, however, encountered China and responded to it in quite different ways.

■ **Connection**

In what ways did China have an influence in Korea, Vietnam, and Japan? In what ways was that influence resisted?

Korea and China

Immediately adjacent to northeastern China, the Korean peninsula and its people have long lived in the shadow of their imposing neighbor (see Map 8.2). Temporary Chinese conquest of northern Korea during the Han dynasty and some colonization by Chinese settlers provided an initial channel for Chinese cultural influence, particularly in the form of Buddhism. Early Korean states, which emerged in the fourth through seventh centuries C.E., all referred to their rulers with the Chinese term *wang* (king). Bitter rivals with one another, these states strenuously resisted Chinese political control, except when they found it advantageous to join with China against a local enemy. In the seventh century, one of these states—the Silla (SHEE-lah) kingdom—allied with Tang dynasty China to bring some political unity to the peninsula for the first time. But Chinese efforts to set up puppet regimes and to assimilate Koreans to Chinese culture provoked sharp military resistance, persuading the Chinese to withdraw their military forces in 688 and to establish a tributary relationship with a largely independent Korea.

Under a succession of dynasties—the Silla (688–900), Koryo (918–1392), and Yi (1392–1910)—Korea generally maintained its political independence while participating in China's tribute system. Its leaders actively embraced the connection with

Independence for Vietnam
In 938, Vietnamese forces under the leadership of General Ngo Quyen defeated the Chinese in the Battle of Bach Dang River, thus ending a thousand years of direct Chinese rule. This image is one of many that celebrate that victory. (CPA Media)

Thus Chinese-style irrigated agriculture was introduced; Vietnamese elites were brought into the local bureaucracy and educated in Confucian-based schools; Chinese replaced the local language in official business; Chinese clothing and hairstyles became mandatory; and large numbers of Chinese, some fleeing internal conflicts at home, flooded into the relative security of what they referred to as "the pacified south," while often despising the local people.[20] The heavy pressure of the Chinese presence generated not only a Vietnamese elite thoroughly schooled in Chinese culture but also periodic rebellions, on several occasions led by women. (See the portrait of Trung Trac, p. 134.)

The weakening of the Tang dynasty in the early tenth century C.E. finally enabled a particularly large rebellion to establish Vietnam as a separate state, though one that carefully maintained its tributary role, sending repeated missions to do homage at the Chinese court. Nonetheless, successive Vietnamese dynasties found the Chinese approach to government useful, styling their rulers as emperors, claiming the Mandate of Heaven, and making use of Chinese court rituals, while expanding their state steadily southward. More so than in Korea, a Chinese-based examination system in Vietnam functioned to undermine an established aristocracy, to provide some measure of social mobility for commoners, and to create a merit-based scholar-gentry class to staff the bureaucracy. Furthermore, the Vietnamese elite class remained deeply committed to Chinese culture, viewing their own country less as a separate nation than as a southern extension of a universal civilization, the only one they knew.[21]

Beyond the elite, however, there remained much that was uniquely Vietnamese, such as a distinctive language, a fondness for cockfighting, and the habit of chewing betel nuts. More importantly, Vietnam long retained a greater role for women in social and economic life, despite heavy Chinese influence. In the third century C.E., a woman leader of an anti-Chinese resistance movement declared: "I want to drive away the enemy to save our people. I will not resign myself to the usual lot of women who bow their heads and become concubines." Female nature deities and a "female Buddha" continued to be part of Vietnamese popular religion, even as Confucian-based ideas took root among the elite. In the centuries following independence from China as Vietnam expanded to the south, northern officials tried in vain to impose more orthodox Confucian gender practices in place of local customs that allowed women to choose their own husbands and married men to live in the households of their wives. So persistent were these practices that a seventeenth-century Chinese visitor opined, with disgust, that Vietnamese preferred the birth of a girl to that of a boy. These features of Vietnamese life reflected larger patterns of Southeast Asian culture that distinguished it from China. And like Korea, the Vietnamese developed a variation of Chinese writing called *chu nom* ("southern script"), which provided the basis for an independent national literature and a vehicle for the writing of most educated women.[22]

Japan and China

Unlike Korea and Vietnam, the Japanese islands were physically separated from China by 100 miles or more of ocean and were never successfully invaded or conquered by their giant mainland neighbor (see Map 8.4). Thus Japan's very extensive borrowing from Chinese civilization was wholly voluntary, rather than occurring under conditions of direct military threat or outright occupation. The high point of that borrowing took place during the seventh to the ninth centuries C.E., as the first more or less unified Japanese state began to emerge from dozens of small clan-based aristocratic chiefdoms. That state found much that was useful in Tang dynasty China and set out, deliberately and systematically, to transform Japan into a centralized bureaucratic state on the Chinese model. (See Documents: The Making of Japanese Civilization, pp. 395–403.)

The initial leader of this effort was Shotoku Taishi (572–622), a prominent aristocrat from one of the major clans. He launched a series of large-scale missions to China, which took hundreds of Japanese monks, scholars, artists, and students to the mainland, and when they returned, they put into practice what they had learned. He issued the Seventeen Article Constitution, proclaiming the Japanese ruler as a Chinese-style emperor and encouraging both Buddhism and Confucianism. In good Confucian fashion, that document emphasized the moral quality of rulers as a foundation for social harmony (see Document 8.1, pp. 395–97). In the decades that followed, Japanese authorities adopted Chinese-style court rituals and a system of court rankings for officials as well as the Chinese calendar. Subsequently, they likewise established Chinese-based taxation systems, law codes, government ministries, and provincial administration, at least on paper. Two capital cities, first Nara and then Heian (Kyoto), arose, both modeled on the Chinese capital of Chang'an.

Map 8.4 Japan
Japan's distance from China enabled it to maintain its political independence and to draw selectively from Chinese culture.

The Samurai of Japan
This late nineteenth-century image shows a samurai warrior on horseback clad in armor and a horned helmet while carrying a sword as well as a bow and arrows. The prominence of martial values in Japanese culture was one of the ways in which Japan differed from its Chinese neighbor, despite much borrowing. (Library of Congress, ID # pd 01046)

Chinese culture, no less than its political practices, also found favor in Japan. Various schools of Chinese Buddhism took root, first among the educated and literate classes and later more broadly in Japanese society, deeply affecting much of Japanese life. Art, architecture, education, medicine, views of the afterlife, attitudes toward suffering and the impermanence of life — all of this and more reflected the influence of Buddhist culture in Japan.[23] The Chinese writing system — and with it an interest in historical writing, calligraphy, and poetry — likewise proved attractive among the elite.

The absence of any compelling threat from China made it possible for the Japanese to be selective in their borrowing. By the tenth century, deliberate efforts to absorb additional elements of Chinese culture diminished, and formal tribute missions to China stopped, although private traders and Buddhist monks continued to make the difficult journey to the mainland. Over many centuries, the Japanese combined what they had assimilated from China with elements of their own tradition into a distinctive Japanese civilization, which differed from Chinese culture in many ways.

In the political realm, for example, the Japanese never succeeded in creating an effective centralized and bureaucratic state to match that of China. Although the court and the emperor retained an important ceremonial and cultural role, their real political authority over the country gradually diminished in favor of competing aristocratic families, both at court and in the provinces. A Chinese-style university trained officials, but rather than serving as a mechanism for recruiting talented commoners into the political elite, it enrolled students who were largely the sons of court aristocrats.

As political power became increasingly decentralized, local authorities developed their own military forces, the famous *samurai* warrior class of Japanese society. Bearing their exquisite curved swords, the samurai developed a distinctive set of values featuring great skill in martial arts, bravery, loyalty, endurance, honor, and a preference for death over surrender. This was *bushido* (boo-shee-doh), the way of the warrior. (See Document 8.4, pp. 401–03.) Japan's celebration of the samurai and of military virtues contrasted sharply with China's emphasis on intellectual achievements and political office holding, which were accorded higher prestige than bearing arms. "The educated men of the land," wrote a Chinese minister in the eleventh century, "regard the carrying of arms as a disgrace."[24] The Japanese, clearly, did not agree.

Religiously as well, Japan remained distinctive. Although Buddhism in many forms took hold in the country, it never completely replaced the native beliefs and practices, which focused attention on numerous *kami*, sacred spirits associated with human ancestors and various natural phenomena. Much later referred to as Shinto, this tradition provided legitimacy to the imperial family, based on claims of descent from the sun goddess. (See Document 8.2, pp. 397–99.) Because veneration of the kami lacked an elaborate philosophy or ritual, it conflicted very little with Buddhism. In fact, numerous kami were assimilated into Japanese Buddhism as local expressions of Buddhist deities or principles.

Japanese literary and artistic culture likewise evolved in distinctive ways, despite much borrowing from China. As in Korea and Vietnam, there emerged a unique writing system that combined Chinese characters with a series of phonetic symbols. A highly stylized Japanese poetic form, known as tanka, developed early and has remained a favored means of expression ever since. (See portrait of Izumi Shikibu, pp. 384–85, for the life of Japan's best-known female tanka poet.) Particularly during the Heian period of Japanese history (794–1192), a highly refined esthetic culture found expression at the imperial court, even as the court's real political authority melted away. Court aristocrats and their ladies lived in splendor, composed poems, arranged flowers, and conducted their love affairs. "What counted," wrote one scholar, "was the proper costume, the right ceremonial act, the successful turn of phrase in a poem, and the appropriate expression of refined taste."[25] Much of our knowledge of this courtly culture comes from the work of women writers, who composed their diaries and novels in the vernacular Japanese script, rather than in the classical Chinese used by elite men. *The Tale of Genji*, a Japanese novel written by the woman author Murasaki Shikibu around 1000, provides an intimate picture of the intrigues and romances of court life. (So too does Sei Shonagon's *Pillow Book*, excerpted in Document 8.3, pp. 399–400.)

At this level of society, Japan's women, unlike those in Korea, largely escaped the more oppressive features of Chinese Confucian culture, such as the prohibition of remarriage for widows, seclusion within the home, and foot binding. Perhaps this is because the most powerful Chinese influence on Japan occurred during the Tang dynasty, when Chinese elite women enjoyed considerable freedom. Japanese women continued to inherit property; Japanese married couples often lived apart or with the wife's family; and marriages were made and broken easily. None of this corresponded to Confucian values. When Japanese women did begin to lose status in the twelfth century and later, it had less to do with Confucian pressures than with the rise of a warrior culture. As the personal relationships of samurai warriors to their lords replaced marriage alliances as a political strategy, the influence of women in political life was reduced, but this was an internal Japanese phenomenon, not a reflection of Chinese influence.

Japan's ability to borrow extensively from China while developing its own distinctive civilization perhaps provided a model for its encounter with the West in the nineteenth century. Then, as before, Japan borrowed selectively from a foreign culture without losing either its political independence or its cultural uniqueness.

■ **Comparison**

In what different ways did Japanese and Korean women experience the pressures of Confucian orthodoxy?

SUMMING UP SO FAR

In what different ways did Korea, Vietnam, Japan, and northern nomads experience and respond to Chinese influence?

Izumi Shikibu, Japanese Poet and Lover

Nowhere in world history has poetry played a more central role than in the imperial court of Japan, located in the capital city of Heian-kyo (now Kyoto) between the ninth and twelfth centuries. There amid the political posturing and the love affairs of aristocratic women and men, almost every event, public or private, called for a poem—the first sighting of spring blossoms or a new moon; births, deaths, and marriages; various official rituals; the morning after a romantic encounter. "It is poetry," wrote one famous Japanese author in the early tenth century, "which . . . awakens the world of invisible spirits . . . , softens the relationship between men and women, and consoles the hearts of fierce warriors."[26] Izumi Shikibu, Japan's most illustrious female poet, was a master of this art, particularly in the lyric five-line, thirty-one-syllable form known as tanka. In her exquisite poetry, we can catch a glimpse of her erotic intensity, expressed in many scandalous love affairs, as well as her engagement in more spiritual pursuits.

Izumi Shikibu
(Courtesy National Diet Library (http://
dl.ndl.go.jp/info:ndljp/pid/1313149/1))

Born around 975 as the daughter of a midlevel official, Izumi grew up in the imperial court where a literary education was essential for girls of her status, for at least in matters of poetry and the arts, women and men operated on an equal basis. At about the age of 20, Izumi married a provincial governor, but she soon began an affair with Prince Tametaka, son of the emperor, shocking court society partly because of the sharp difference in their social positions. Tametaka's death in 1002, widely credited to his sexual excess with Izumi, only deepened the scandal and led to Izumi's divorce from her husband and estrangement from her family. Addressing her parents and sisters in a poem, she declared: "One of you / I was, but am no more."[27]

Less than a year later, she ignited another scandal by taking up with Tametaka's brother, Prince Atsumichi. The first year of this affair became the subject of Izumi's famous *Diary*. When the Prince sent her a sprig of orange blossoms, she responded with a poem: "Rather than recall / in these flowers / the fragrance of the past, / I would like to hear

China and the Eurasian World Economy

Beyond China's central role in East Asia was its economic interaction with the wider world of Eurasia generally. On the one hand, China's remarkable economic growth, taking place during the Tang and Song dynasties, could hardly be contained within China's borders and clearly had a major impact throughout Eurasia. On the other hand, China was recipient as well as donor in the economic interactions of the third-wave era, and its own economic achievements owed something to the stimulus of contact with the larger world.

Spillovers: China's Impact on Eurasia

One of the outcomes of China's economic revolution lay in the diffusion of its many technological innovations to peoples and places far from East Asia as the movements of traders, soldiers, slaves, and pilgrims conveyed Chinese achievements abroad. (See the this nightingale's voice, / to know if his song is as sweet." What followed was a year of nocturnal visits, frequent absences, rumors and gossip, doubts and longings, and the endless exchange of poems. Finally Izumi took up residence in the Prince's compound, much to the distress of his principal wife. Atsumichi's death in 1007 prompted an outpouring of poetry mourning the loss of her great love. "I long for the sound / of your voice. / The face / I see so clearly / doesn't say a word."[28]

Despite Izumi's behavior, she was subsequently appointed as a lady-in-waiting for the Empress Akiko, for her literary reputation added splendor to the court. But the scandal of her personal life continued to shadow her. A rival literary figure at the court, the renowned Lady Murasaki, author of *The Tale of Genji*, commented: "How interestingly Izumi Shikibu writes. Yet what a disgraceful person she is."[29] A subsequent marriage to a much older provincial governor took Izumi away from the court for the rest of her life. But her affairs continued. "I do not feel in the least disposed to sleep alone," she wrote.[30]

Her poetry gave frequent expression to erotic love and to the anguished yearning that accompanied it. "Lying alone, / my black hair tangled, / uncombed / I long for the one / who touched it first." To a monk who left his fan behind after a visit, she wrote, "I think / you may have briefly forgotten / this fan, / but everyone must know / how it came to be dropped."

Izumi's experiences of love within her social circle gave her an acute sense of the ephemerality of all things. "Come quickly—as soon as / these blossoms open, / they fall. / This world exists / as a sheen of dew on flowers." Her understanding of impermanence was reinforced by her Buddhist faith with its emphasis on the transience of human life. From time to time, she felt the desire to withdraw into a monastery, and she did take periodic retreats in mountain temples. Even there, however, Izumi experienced the pull of the world. "Although I try / to hold the single thought / of Buddha's teaching in my heart, / I cannot help but hear / the many crickets' voices calling as well."[31]

Perhaps Izumi's best-known poem was composed when she was still in her teens, though it has sometimes been viewed as a prayer on her deathbed. Written to a Buddhist cleric, it reveals her early and continuing desire for spiritual enlightenment, symbolized here as the light of the moon. "From utter darkness / I must embark upon an / even darker road / O distant moon, cast your light / from the rim of the mountains."[32]

Question: How do you understand Izumi's involvement in multiple love relationships and her religious sensibilities?

Snapshot, p. 386, for a wider view of Chinese technological achievements.) Chinese techniques for producing salt by solar evaporation spread to the Islamic world and later to Christian Europe. Papermaking, known in China since the Han dynasty, spread to Korea and Vietnam by the fourth century C.E., to Japan and India by the seventh, to the Islamic world by the eighth, to Muslim Spain by 1150, to France and Germany in the 1300s, and to England in the 1490s. Printing, likewise a Chinese invention, rapidly reached Korea, where movable type became a highly developed technique, and Japan as well. Both technologies were heavily influenced by Buddhism, which accorded religious merit to the reproduction of sacred texts. The Islamic world, however, highly valued handwritten calligraphy and generally resisted printing as impious until the nineteenth century. The adoption of printing in Europe was likewise delayed because of the absence of paper until the fourteenth century. Then movable type was reinvented by Johannes Gutenberg in the fifteenth century, although it is unclear whether he was aware of Chinese and Korean precedents. With implications for mass literacy, bureaucracy, scholarship, the spread of religion, and the exchange of information,

■ **Connection**

In what ways did China participate in the world of Eurasian commerce and exchange, and with what outcomes?

$\mathcal{S}$napshot   **Chinese Technological Achievements**[33]

Before the technological explosion of the European Industrial Revolution during the eighteenth and nineteenth centuries, China had long been the major center of global technological innovation. Many of those inventions spread to other civilizations where they stimulated imitation or modification. Since Europe was located at the opposite end of the Eurasian continent from China, it often took considerable time for those innovations to give rise to something similar in the West. That lag is also a measure of the relative technological development of the two civilizations in premodern times.

Innovation	First Used in China (approximate)	Adoption/Recognition in the West: Time lag in years (approximate)
Iron plow	6th–4th century B.C.E.	2000+
Cast iron	4th century B.C.E.	1000–1200
Efficient horse collar	3rd–1st century B.C.E.	1000
Paper	2nd century B.C.E.	1000
Wheelbarrow	1st century B.C.E.	900–1000
Rudder for steering ships	1st century C.E.	1100
Iron chain suspension bridge	1st century C.E.	1000–1300
Porcelain	3rd century C.E.	1500
Magnetic compass for navigation	9th–11th century C.E.	400
Gunpowder	9th century C.E.	400
Chain drive for transmission of power	976 C.E.	800
Moveable type printing	1045 C.E.	400

papermaking and printing were Chinese innovations of revolutionary and global dimensions.

Chinese technologies were seldom simply transferred from one place to another. More often a particular Chinese technique or product stimulated innovations in more distant lands in accordance with local needs.[34] For example, as the Chinese formula for gunpowder, invented around 1000, became available in Europe, together with some early and simple firearms, these innovations triggered the development of cannons in the early fourteenth century. Soon cannons appeared in the Islamic world and by 1356 in China itself, which first used cast iron rather than bronze in their construction. But the highly competitive European state system drove the "gunpowder revolution" much further and more rapidly than in China's imperial state. Chinese textile, metallurgical, and naval technologies likewise stimulated imitation and innovation all across

Eurasia. An example is the magnetic compass, a Chinese invention eagerly embraced by mariners of many cultural backgrounds as they traversed the Indian Ocean.

In addition to its technological influence, China's prosperity during the Song dynasty greatly stimulated commercial life and market-based behavior all across the Afro-Eurasian trading world. China's products—silk, porcelain, lacquerware—found eager buyers from Japan to East Africa, and everywhere in between. The immense size and wealth of China's domestic economy also provided a ready market for hundreds of commodities from afar. For example, the lives of many thousands of people in the spice-producing islands of what is now Indonesia were transformed as they came to depend on Chinese consumers' demand for their products. "[O]ne hundred million [Chinese] people," wrote historian William McNeill, "increasingly caught up within a commercial network, buying and selling to supplement every day's livelihood, made a significant difference to the way other human beings made their livings throughout a large part of the civilized world."[35] Such was the ripple effect of China's economic revolution.

On the Receiving End: China as Economic Beneficiary

If Chinese economic growth and technological achievements significantly shaped the Eurasian world of the third-wave era, that pattern of interaction was surely not a one-way street, for China too was changed by its engagement with a wider world. During this period, for example, China had learned about the cultivation and processing of both cotton and sugar from India. From Vietnam, around 1000, China gained access to the new, fast-ripening, and drought-resistant strains of rice that made a highly productive rice-based agriculture possible in the drier and more rugged regions of southern China. This marked a major turning point in Chinese history as the frontier region south of the Yangzi River grew rapidly in population, overtaking the traditional centers of Chinese civilization in the north.

Technologically as well, China's extraordinary burst of creativity owed something to the stimulus of cross-cultural contact. Awareness of Persian windmills, for example, spurred the development of a distinct but related device in China. Printing arose from China's growing involvement with the world of Buddhism, which put a spiritual premium on the reproduction of the Buddha's image and of short religious texts that were carried as charms. It was in Buddhist monasteries during the Tang dynasty that the long-established practice of printing with seals was elaborated by Chinese monks into woodblock printing. The first printed book, in 868 C.E., was a famous Buddhist text, the *Diamond Sutra*. Gunpowder too seems to have had an Indian and Buddhist connection. An Indian Buddhist monk traveling in China in 644 C.E. identified soils that contained saltpeter and showed that they produced a purple flame when put into a fire. This was the beginning of Chinese experiments, which finally led to a reliable recipe for gunpowder.

A further transforming impact of China's involvement with a wider world derived from its growing participation in Indian Ocean trade. By the Tang dynasty, thousands of ships annually visited the ports of southern China, and settled communities of foreign merchants—Arabs, Persians, Indians, Southeast Asians—turned some of these cities into cosmopolitan centers. Buddhist temples, Muslim mosques and cemeteries, and Hindu phallic sculptures graced the skyline of Quanzhou, a coastal city in southern China. Occasionally the tensions of cultural diversity erupted in violence, such as the massacre of tens of thousands of foreigners in Canton during the 870s when Chinese rebel forces sacked the city. Indian Ocean commerce also contributed much to the transformation of southern China from a subsistence economy to one more heavily based on producing for export. In the process, merchants achieved a degree of social acceptance not known before, including their frequent appointment to high-ranking bureaucratic positions. Finally, much-beloved stories of the monkey god, widely popular even in contemporary China, derived from Indian sources transmitted by Indian Ocean commerce.[36]

China and Buddhism

By far the most important gift that China received from India was neither cotton, nor sugar, nor the knowledge of saltpeter, but a religion, Buddhism. The gradual assimilation of this South Asian religious tradition into Chinese culture illustrates the process of cultural encounter and adaptation and invites comparison with the spread of Christianity into Europe. Until the adoption of Marxism in the twentieth century, Buddhism was the only large-scale cultural borrowing in Chinese history. It also made China into a launching pad for Buddhism's dispersion to Korea and from there to Japan as well. Thus, as Buddhism faded in the land of its birth, it became solidly rooted in much of East Asia, providing an element of cultural commonality for a vast region (see Map 8.5).

Making Buddhism Chinese

■ **Change**

What facilitated the rooting of Buddhism within China?

Buddhism initially entered China via the Silk Road trading network during the first and second centuries C.E. The stability and prosperity of the Han dynasty, then at its height, ensured that the new "barbarian" religion held little appeal for native Chinese. Furthermore, the Indian culture from which Buddhism sprang was at odds with Chinese understandings of the world in many ways. Buddhism's commitment to a secluded and monastic life for monks and nuns seemed to dishonor Chinese family values, and its concern for individual salvation or enlightenment appeared selfish, contradicting the social orientation of Confucian thinking. Its abstract philosophy ran counter to the more concrete, "this-worldly" concerns of Chinese thinkers; and the Buddhist concept of infinite eons of time, endlessly repeating themselves, was quite a stretch for the Chinese, who normally thought in terms of finite family generations or dynastic cycles. No wonder that for the first several centuries C.E., Buddhism was largely the preserve of foreign merchants and monks living in China.

Map 8.5 The World of Asian Buddhism
Born in India, Buddhism later spread widely throughout much of Asia to provide a measure of cultural or religious commonality across this vast region.

In the half millennium between roughly 300 and 800 C.E., however, Buddhism took solid root in China within both elite and popular culture, becoming a permanent, though fluctuating, presence in Chinese life. How did this remarkable transformation unfold? It began, arguably, with the collapse of the Han dynasty around 200 C.E. The chaotic, violent, and politically fragmented centuries that followed seriously discredited Confucianism and opened the door to alternative understandings of the world. Nomadic rulers, now governing much of northern China, found Buddhism useful in part because it was foreign. "We were born out of the marches," declared one of them, "and though we are unworthy, we have complied with our appointed destiny and govern the Chinese as their prince. . . . Buddha being a barbarian god is the very one we should worship."[37] Rulers and elite families provided patronage for Buddhist monasteries, temples, and works of art. In southern China, where many northern aristocrats had fled following the disastrous decline of the Han dynasty, Buddhism provided some comfort in the face of a collapsing society. Its emphasis on ritual, morality, and contemplation represented an intellectually and esthetically satisfying response to times that were so clearly out of joint.

Meanwhile, Buddhist monasteries increasingly provided an array of social services for ordinary people. In them, travelers found accommodation; those fleeing from China's many upheavals discovered a place of refuge; desperate people received charity; farmers borrowed seed for the next planting; the sick were treated; children learned to read. And for many, Buddhism was associated with access to magical powers as reports of miracles abounded. Battles were won, rain descended on drought-ridden areas, diseases were cured, and guilt was relieved—all through the magical ministrations of charismatic monks.

Accompanying all of this was a serious effort by monks, scholars, and translators to present this Indian religion in terms that Chinese could more readily grasp. Thus the Buddhist term *dharma*, referring to the Buddha's teaching, was translated as *dao*, or "the way," a notion long familiar in both Daoist and Confucian thinking (see Chapter 4). The Buddhist notion of "morality" was translated with the Confucian term that referred to "filial submission and obedience." Some Indian concepts were modified in the process of translation. For example, the idea that "husband supports wife," which reflected a considerable respect for women and mothers in early Indian Buddhism, became in translation "husband controls wife."[38]

As Buddhism took hold in China, it was primarily in its broader Mahayana form—complete with numerous deities, the veneration of relics, many heavens and hells, and bodhisattvas to aid the believer—rather than the more psychological and individualistic Theravada Buddhism (see Chapter 4). One of the most popular forms of Buddhism in China was the Pure Land School, in which faithfully repeating the name of an earlier Buddha, the Amitabha, was sufficient to ensure rebirth in a beautifully described heavenly realm, the Pure Land. In its emphasis on salvation by faith, without arduous study or intensive meditation, Pure Land Buddhism became a highly popular and authentically Chinese version of the Indian faith.

China's reunification under the Sui and early Tang dynasties witnessed growing state support for Buddhism. The Sui emperor Wendi (ruled 581–604 C.E.) had monasteries constructed at the base of China's five sacred mountains, further identifying the imported religion with traditional Chinese culture. He even used Buddhism to justify his military campaigns. "With a hundred victories in a hundred battles," he declared, "we promote the practice of the ten Buddhist virtues."[39] With state support and growing popular acceptance, monasteries became centers of great wealth, largely exempt from taxation, owning large estates; running businesses such as oil presses, water mills, and pawn shops; collecting gems, gold, and lavish works of art; and even employing slaves. But Buddhism, while solidly entrenched in Chinese life by the early Tang dynasty, never achieved the independence from state authorities that the Christian church acquired in Europe. The examinations for becoming a monk were supervised by the state, and education in the monasteries included the required study of the Confucian classics. In the mid-ninth century, the state showed quite dramatically just how much control it could exercise over the Buddhist establishment.

Losing State Support: The Crisis of Chinese Buddhism

The impressive growth of Chinese Buddhism was accompanied by a persistent undercurrent of resistance and criticism. Some saw the Buddhist establishment, at least potentially, as a "state within a state" and a challenge to imperial authority. More important was a deepening resentment of its enormous wealth. One fifth-century critic, referring to monks, put the issue squarely: "Why is it that their ideals are noble and far-reaching and their activities still are base and common? [They] become merchants and engage in barter, wrangling with the masses for profit."[40] When state treasuries were short of funds, government officials cast a covetous eye on wealthy and tax-exempt monasteries. Furthermore, Buddhism was clearly of foreign origin and offensive for that reason to some Confucian and Daoist thinkers. The celibacy of the monks and their withdrawal from society, the critics argued, undermined the Confucian-based family system of Chinese tradition.

■ **Change**
What were the major sources of opposition to Buddhism within China?

Such criticisms took on new meaning in the changed environment of China after about 800 C.E. Following centuries of considerable foreign influence in China, a growing resentment against foreign culture, particularly among the literate classes, increasingly took hold. The turning point may well have been the An Lushan rebellion (755–763), in which a general of foreign origin led a major revolt against the Tang dynasty. Whatever its origin, an increasingly xenophobic reaction set in among the upper classes, reflected in a desire to return to an imagined "purity" of earlier times.[41] In this setting, the old criticisms of Buddhism became more sharply focused. In 819, Han Yu, a leading figure in the Confucian counterattack on Buddhism, wrote a scathing memorial to the emperor, criticizing his willingness to honor a relic of the Buddha's finger.

> Now the Buddha was of barbarian origin. His language differed from Chinese speech; his clothes were of a different cut; his mouth did not pronounce the prescribed words of the Former Kings. . . . He did not recognize the relationship between prince and subject, nor the sentiments of father and son. . . . I pray that Your Majesty will turn this bone over to the officials that it may be cast into water or fire.[42]

Several decades later, the Chinese state took direct action against the Buddhist establishment as well as against other foreign religions. A series of imperial decrees between 841 and 845 ordered some 260,000 monks and nuns to return to normal life as tax-paying citizens. Thousands of monasteries, temples, and shrines were either destroyed or turned to public use, while the state confiscated the lands, money, metals, and serfs belonging to monasteries. Buddhists were now forbidden to use gold, silver, copper, iron, and gems in constructing their images. These actions dealt a serious blow to Chinese Buddhism. Its scholars and monks were scattered, its creativity diminished, and its institutions came even more firmly under state control.

Despite this persecution, Buddhism did not vanish from China. At the level of elite culture, its philosophical ideas played a role in the reformulation of Confucian thinking that took place during the Song dynasty. At the village level, Buddhism became one element of Chinese popular religion, which also included the veneration of ancestors, the honoring of Confucius, and Daoist shrines and rituals. Temples frequently included statues of Confucius, Laozi, and the Buddha, with little sense of any incompatibility among them. "Every black-haired son of Han," the Chinese have long said, "wears a Confucian thinking cap, a Daoist robe, and Buddhist sandals." (See photo, p. 164.) Unlike Europe, where an immigrant religion triumphed over and excluded all other faiths, Buddhism in China became assimilated into Chinese culture alongside its other traditions.

LearningCurve
bedfordstmartins.com
/strayer/LC

⊥⌐ Reflections: Why Do Things Change?

The rapidity of change in modern societies is among the most distinctive features of recent history, but change and transformation, though at various rates, have been constants in the human story since the very beginning. Explaining how and why human societies change is perhaps the central issue that historians confront, no matter which societies or periods of time they study. Those who specialize in the history of some particular culture or civilization often emphasize sources of change operating within those societies, although there is intense disagreement as to which are most significant. The ideas of great thinkers, the policies of leaders, struggles for power, the conflict of classes, the invention of new technologies, the growth or decline in population, variations in local climate or weather—all of these and more have their advocates as the primary motor of historical transformation.

Of course, it is not necessary to choose among them. The history of China illustrates the range of internal factors that have driven change in that civilization. The political conflicts of the "era of warring states" provided the setting and the motivation for the emergence of Confucianism and Daoism, which in turn have certainly shaped the character and texture of Chinese civilization over many centuries. The personal qualities and brutal policies of Shihuangdi surely played a role in China's unification and in the brief duration of the Qin dynasty. The subsequent creation of a widespread network of canals and waterways as well as the country's technological achievements served to maintain that unity over very long periods of time. But the massive inequalities of Chinese society generated the peasant upheavals, which periodically shattered that unity and led to new ruling dynasties. Sometimes natural events, such as droughts and floods, triggered those rebellions.

World historians, more than those who study particular civilizations or nations, have been inclined to find the primary source of change in contact with strangers, in external connections and interactions, whether direct or indirect. The history of China and East Asia provide plenty of examples for this point of view as well. Conceptions of China as the "middle kingdom," infinitely superior to all surrounding societies, grew out of centuries of involvement with its neighbors. Some of those neighbors became Chinese as China's imperial reach grew, especially to the south. Even those that did not, such as Korea, Vietnam, and Japan, were decisively transformed by proximity to the "radiating civilization" of China. China's own cuisine, so distinctive in recent centuries, may well be a quite recent invention, drawing heavily on Indian and Southeast Asian cooking. Buddhism, of course, is an obvious borrowing from abroad, although its incorporation into Chinese civilization and its ups and downs within China owed much to internal cultural and political realities.

In the end, clear distinctions between internal and external sources of change in China's history—or that of any other society—are perhaps misleading. The boundary between "inside" and "outside" is itself a constantly changing line. Should the borderlands of northern China, where Chinese and Turkic peoples met and mingled, be regarded as internal or external to China itself? And, as the histories of Chinese Buddhism and of Japanese culture so clearly indicate, what comes from beyond is always transformed by what it encounters within.

Second Thoughts

What's the Significance?

Sui dynasty, 366–67

Tang dynasty, 367–68

Song dynasty, 367–72

Hangzhou, 369

economic revolution, 369–71

foot binding, 371–72

tribute system, 373–76

Xiongnu, 374–75

Khitan/Jurchen people, 375–76

Silla dynasty (Korea), 377–79

hangul, 379

chu nom, 381

Shotoku Taishi, 381

bushido, 382

Izumi Shikibu, 384–85

Chinese Buddhism, 388–92

Emperor Wendi, 390

LearningCurve
Check what you know.
**bedfordstmartins.com
/strayer/LC**

Online Study Guide
bedfordstmartins.com
/highschool/strayer

Big Picture Questions

1. How can you explain the changing fortunes of Buddhism in China?

2. How did China influence the world of the third-wave era? How was China itself transformed by its encounters with a wider world?

3. How might China's posture in the world during the Tang and Song dynasty era compare to its emerging role in global affairs in the twenty-first century?

4. **Looking Back:** In what ways did Tang and Song dynasty China resemble the earlier Han dynasty period, and in what ways had China changed?

For Web sites and additional documents related to this chapter, see **Make History** at bedfordstmartins.com /highschool/strayer.

Next Steps: For Further Study

Samuel Adshead, *Tang China: The Rise of the East in World History* (2004). Explores the role of China within the larger world.

Patricia Ebrey, *The Inner Quarters* (1993). A balanced account of the gains and losses experienced by Chinese women during the changes of the Song dynasty.

Mark Elvin, *The Pattern of the Chinese Past* (1973). A classic account of the Chinese economic revolution.

James L. Huffman, *Japan in World History* (2010). The first three chapters of this recent work place Japan's early history in the framework of world history.

Paul S. Ropp, *China in World History* (2010). An up-to-date telling of China's historical development, cast in a global context.

Arthur F. Wright, *Buddhism in Chinese History* (1959). An older account filled with wonderful stories and anecdotes.

Upper River during the Qing Ming Festival, http://www.ibiblio.org/ulysses/gec/painting/qingming/ full.htm. A scrolling reproduction of a huge Chinese painting, showing in detail the Song dynasty city of Kaifeng.

Documents

Considering the Evidence:
The Making of Japanese Civilization

Japan was among the new third-wave civilizations that took shape between 500 and 1500. Each of them was distinctive in particular ways, but all of them followed the general patterns of earlier civilizations in the creation of cities, states, stratified societies, patriarchies, written languages, and more. Furthermore, many of them borrowed extensively from nearby and older civilizations. In the case of Japan, that borrowing was primarily from China, its towering neighbor to the west. The documents that follow provide glimpses of a distinctive Japanese civilization in the making, even as that civilization selectively incorporated elements of Chinese thinking and practice.

Document 8.1

Japanese Political Ideals

As an early Japanese state gradually took shape in the sixth and seventh centuries, it was confronted by serious internal divisions of clan, faction, and religion. Externally, Japanese forces had been expelled from their footholds in Korea, while Japan also faced the immense power and attractiveness of a reunified China under the Sui and Tang dynasties. In these circumstances, Japanese authorities sought to strengthen their own emerging state by adopting a range of Chinese political values and practices. This Chinese influence in Japanese political thinking was particularly apparent in the so-called Seventeen Article Constitution issued by Shotoku, which was a set of general guidelines for court officials.

- What elements of Buddhist, Confucian, or Legalist thinking are reflected in this document? (Review pp. 169–72 and 176–79 and Documents 3.3, pp. 150–51, and 4.1, pp. 198–200.)

- What can you infer about the internal problems that Japanese rulers faced?

- How might Shotoku define an ideal Japanese state?

■ Why do you think Shotoku omitted any mention of traditional Japanese gods or spirits or the Japanese claim that their emperor was descended from the sun goddess Amaterasu?

Despite this apparent embrace of all things Chinese, Shotoku's attitude toward China itself is less clear. In various letters that he sent to the Chinese Sui dynasty ruler, Shotoku inscribed them as follows: "The Son of Heaven of the Land of the Rising Sun to the Son of Heaven of the Land of the Setting Sun." Another read: "The Eastern Emperor Greets the Western Emperor."[43] Considering their country as the Middle Kingdom, greatly superior to all its neighbors, Chinese court officials were incensed at these apparent assertions of equality. It is not clear whether Shotoku was deliberately claiming equivalence with China or if he was simply unaware of how such language might be viewed in China.

SHOTOKU

The Seventeen Article Constitution

604

1. Harmony is to be valued, and an avoidance of wanton opposition to be honored. All men are influenced by class feelings, and there are few who are intelligent. Hence there are some who disobey their lords and fathers, or who maintain feuds with the neighboring villages. But when those above are harmonious and those below are friendly, and there is concord in the discussion of business, right views of things spontaneously gain acceptance....

2. Sincerely reverence the three treasures ... the Buddha, the Law [teachings], and the Priesthood [community of monks]....

3. When you receive the Imperial commands, fail not scrupulously to obey them. The lord is Heaven, the vassal is Earth. Heaven overspreads, and Earth upbears....[W]hen the superior acts, the inferior yields compliance.

4. The Ministers and functionaries should make decorous behavior their leading principle.... If the superiors do not behave with decorum, the inferiors are disorderly....

5. Ceasing from gluttony and abandoning covetous desires, deal impartially with the [legal] suits which are submitted to you....

6. Chastise that which is evil and encourage that which is good. This was the excellent rule of antiquity....

7. Let every man have his own charge, and let not the spheres of duty be confused. When wise men are entrusted with office, the sound of praise arises. If unprincipled men hold office, disasters and tumults are multiplied. In this world, few are born with knowledge: wisdom is the product of earnest meditation. In all things, whether great or small, find the right man, and they will surely be well managed....

10. Let us cease from wrath, and refrain from angry looks. Nor let us be resentful when others differ from us. For all men have hearts, and each heart has its own leanings.... [All] of us are simply ordinary men....

11. Give clear appreciation to merit and demerit, and deal out to each its sure reward or punishment. In these days, reward does not attend upon merit, nor punishment upon crime. You high functionaries, who have charge of public affairs, let it be your task to make clear rewards and punishments....

Source: W. G. Aston, trans., *Nihongi: Chronicles of Japan from the Earliest Times to A.D. 697* (London: Paul, Trench, Truebner, 1896), 2:129–33.

12. Let not the provincial authorities or the [local nobles] levy exactions on the people. In a country, there are not two lords. . . . The sovereign is the master of the people of the whole country. . . .

15. To turn away from that which is private, and to set our faces toward that which is public — this is the path of a Minister. . . .

16. Let the people be employed [in forced labor] at seasonable times. This is an ancient and excellent rule. Let them be employed, therefore, in the winter months, when they are at leisure. But from spring to autumn, when they are engaged in agriculture or with the mulberry trees, the people should not be so employed. For if they do not attend to agriculture, what will they have to eat? If they do not attend the mulberry trees, what will they do for clothing?

17. Decisions on important matters should not be made by one person alone. They should be discussed with many.

Document 8.2

The Uniqueness of Japan

Despite Japan's extensive cultural borrowing from abroad, or perhaps because of it, Japanese writers often stressed the unique and superior features of their own country. Nowhere is this theme echoed more clearly than in *The Chronicle of the Direct Descent of Gods and Sovereigns*, written by Kitabatake Chikafusa (1293–1354). A longtime court official and member of one branch of Japan's imperial family, Kitabatake wrote at a time of declining imperial authority in Japan, when two court centers competed in an extended "war of the courts." As an advocate for the southern court, Kitabatake sought to prove that the emperor he served was legitimate because he had descended in unbroken line from the Age of the Gods. In making this argument, he was also a spokesman for the revival of Japan's earlier religious tradition of numerous gods and spirits, known later as Shintoism.

■ In Kitabatake's view, what was distinctive about Japan in comparison to China and India?

■ How might the use of Japan's indigenous religious tradition, especially the Sun Goddess, serve to legitimize the imperial rule of Kitabatake's family?

■ How did Kitabatake understand the place of Confucianism and Buddhism in Japan and their relationship to Shinto beliefs?

KITABATAKE CHIKAFUSA

The Chronicle of the Direct Descent of Gods and Sovereigns

1339

Japan is the divine country. The heavenly ancestor it was who first laid its foundations, and the Sun Goddess left her descendants to reign over it forever and ever. This is true only of our country, and nothing similar may be found in foreign lands. That is why it is called the divine country.

In the age of the gods, Japan was known as the "ever-fruitful land of reed-covered plains and luxuriant ricefields." This name has existed since the creation of heaven and earth.... [I]t may thus be considered the prime name of Japan. It is also called the country of the great eight islands. This name was given because eight islands were produced when the Male Deity and the Female Deity begot Japan.... Japan is the land of the Sun Goddess [Amaterasu]. Or it may have thus been called because it is near the place where the sun rises....Thus, since Japan is a separate continent, distinct from both India and China and lying in a great ocean, it is the country where the divine illustrious imperial line has been transmitted.

The creation of heaven and earth must everywhere have been the same, for it occurred within the same universe, but the Indian, Chinese, and Japanese traditions are each different....

In China, nothing positive is stated concerning the creation of the world, even though China is a country which accords special importance to the keeping of records....

The beginnings of Japan in some ways resemble the Indian descriptions, telling as it does of the world's creation from the seed of the heavenly gods. However, whereas in our country the succession to the throne has followed a single undeviating line since the first divine ancestor, nothing of the kind has ex-

isted in India. After their first ruler, King People's Lord, had been chosen and raised to power by the populace, his dynasty succeeded, but in later times most of his descendants perished, and men of inferior genealogy who had powerful forces became the rulers, some of them even controlling the whole of India. China is also a country of notorious disorders. Even in ancient times, when life was simple and conduct was proper, the throne was offered to wise men, and no single lineage was established. Later, in times of disorder, men fought for control of the country. Thus some of the rulers rose from the ranks of the plebians, and there were even some of barbarian origin who usurped power. Or some families after generations of service as ministers surpassed their princes and eventually supplanted them. There have already been thirty-six changes of dynasty since Fuxi, and unspeakable disorders have occurred.

Only in our country has the succession remained inviolate from the beginning of heaven and earth to the present. It has been maintained within a single lineage, and even when, as inevitably has happened, the succession has been transmitted collaterally, it has returned to the true line. This is due to the ever-renewed Divine Oath and makes Japan unlike all other countries....

Then the Great Sun Goddess ... sent her grandchild to the world below.... [The Sun Goddess] uttered these words of command: "Thou, my illustrious grandchild, proceed thither and govern the land. Go, and may prosperity attend thy dynasty, and may it, like Heaven and Earth, endure forever."...

Because our Great Goddess is the spirit of the sun, she illuminates with a bright virtue which is incomprehensible in all its aspects but dependable alike in the realm of the visible and invisible. All sovereigns and ministers have inherited the bright seeds of the divine light, or they are descendants of the deities who received personal instruction from the Great Goddess. Who would not stand in reverence before

Source: William Theodore de Bary et al., *Sources of Japanese Tradition* (New York: Columbia University Press, 2001), 1:358–63.

this fact? The highest object of all teachings, Buddhist and Confucian included, consists in realizing this fact and obeying in perfect consonance its principles. It has been the power of the dissemination of the Buddhist and Confucian texts which has spread these principles. . . . Since the reign of the Emperor Ōjin, the Confucian writings have been disseminated, and since Prince Shōtoku's time Buddhism has flourished in Japan. Both these men were sages incarnate, and it must have been their intention to spread a knowledge of the way of our country, in accordance with the wishes of the Great Sun Goddess.

Document 8.3

Social Life at Court

For many centuries, high culture in Japan—art, music, poetry, and literature—found a home in the imperial court, where men and women of the royal family and nobility, together with various attendants, mixed and mingled. That aristocratic culture reached its high point between the ninth and twelfth centuries, but, according to one prominent scholar, it "has shaped the aesthetic and emotional life of the entire Japanese people for a millennium."[44] Women played a prominent role in that culture, both creating it and describing it. Among them was Sei Shonagon (966–1017), a lady-in-waiting to the Empress Sadako. In her *Pillow Book*, a series of brief and often witty observations, Sei Shonagon described court life as well as her own likes and dislikes.

- What impression does Sei Shonagon convey about the relationship of men and women at court?

- How would you describe her posture toward men, toward women, and toward ordinary people? What insight can you gain about class differences from her writing?

- In what ways does court life, as Sei Shonagon describes it, reflect Buddhist and Confucian influences, and in what ways does it depart from, and even challenge, those traditions?

SEI SHONAGON

Pillow Book

ca. 1000

That parents should bring up some beloved son of theirs to be a priest is really distressing. No doubt it is an auspicious thing to do; but unfortunately most people are convinced that a priest is as unimportant as a piece of wood, and they treat him accordingly. A priest lives poorly on meager food, and cannot even sleep without being criticized. While he is young, it is only natural that he should be curious about all sorts of things, and, if there are women about, he will probably peep in their

Source: Ivan Morris, trans. and ed., *The Pillow Book of Sei Shonagon* (New York: Columbia University Press, 1991), 25–26, 39, 44–45, 47, 49–50, 53, 254–55.

direction (though, to be sure, with a look of aversion on his face). What is wrong about that? Yet people immediately find fault with him for even so small a lapse....

A preacher ought to be good-looking. For, if we are properly to understand his worthy sentiments, we must keep our eyes on him while he speaks; should we look away, we may forget to listen. Accordingly an ugly preacher may well be the source of sin....

When I make myself imagine what it is like to be one of those women who live at home, faithfully serving their husbands—women who have not a single exciting prospect in life yet who believe that they are perfectly happy—I am filled with scorn....

I cannot bear men who believe that women serving in the Palace are bound to be frivolous and wicked. Yet I suppose their prejudice is understandable. After all, women at Court do not spend their time hiding modestly behind fans and screens, but walk about, looking openly at people they chance to meet. Yes, they see everyone face to face, not only ladies-in-waiting like themselves, but even Their Imperial Majesties (whose august names I hardly dare mention), High Court Nobles, senior courtiers, and other gentlemen of high rank. In the presence of such exalted personages the women in the Palace are all equally brazen, whether they be the maids of ladies-in-waiting, or the relations of Court ladies who have come to visit them, or housekeepers, or latrine-cleaners, or women who are of no more value than a roof-tile or a pebble. Small wonder that the young men regard them as immodest! Yet are the gentlemen themselves any less so? They are not exactly bashful when it comes to looking at the great people in the Palace. No, everyone at Court is much the same in this respect....

Hateful Things

...A man who has nothing in particular to recommend him discusses all sorts of subjects at random as though he knew everything....

An admirer has come on a clandestine visit, but a dog catches sight of him and starts barking. One feels like killing the beast.

One has been foolish enough to invite a man to spend the night in an unsuitable place—and then he starts snoring.

A gentleman has visited one secretly. Though he is wearing a tall, lacquered hat, he nevertheless wants no one to see him. He is so flurried, in fact, that upon leaving he bangs into something with his hat. Most hateful!...

A man with whom one is having an affair keeps singing the praises of some woman he used to know. Even if it is a thing of the past, this can be very annoying. How much more so if he is still seeing the woman!...

A good lover will behave as elegantly at dawn as at any other time. He drags himself out of bed with a look of dismay on his face. The lady urges him on: "Come, my friend, it's getting light. You don't want anyone to find you here." He gives a deep sigh, as if to say that the night has not been nearly long enough and that it is agony to leave. Once up, he does not instantly pull on his trousers. Instead he comes close to the lady and whispers whatever was left unsaid during the night. Even when he is dressed, he still lingers, vaguely pretending to be fastening his sash....

Indeed, one's attachment to a man depends largely on the elegance of his leave-taking. When he jumps out of bed, scurries about the room, tightly fastens his trouser-sash, rolls up the sleeves of his Court cloak, over-robe, or hunting costume, stuffs his belongings into the breast of his robe and then briskly secures the outer sash—one really begins to hate him....

It is very annoying, when one has visited Hase Temple and has retired into one's enclosure, to be disturbed by a herd of common people who come and sit outside in a row, crowded so close together that the tails of their robes fall over each other in utter disarray. I remember that once I was overcome by a great desire to go on a pilgrimage. Having made my way up the log steps, deafened by the fearful roar of the river, I hurried into my enclosure, longing to gaze upon the sacred countenance of Buddha. To my dismay I found that a throng of commoners had settled themselves directly in front of me, where they were incessantly standing up, prostrating themselves, and squatting down again. They looked like so many basket-worms as they crowded together in their hideous clothes, leaving hardly an inch of space between themselves and me. I really felt like pushing them all over sideways.

Document 8.4

The Way of the Warrior

As the Japanese imperial court gradually lost power to military authorities in the countryside, a further distinctive feature of Japanese civilization emerged in the celebration of martial virtues and the warrior class—the samurai—that embodied those values. From the twelfth through the mid-nineteenth century, public life and government in Japan was dominated by the samurai, while their culture and values, known as bushido, expressed the highest ideals of political leadership and of personal conduct. At least in the West, the samurai are perhaps best known for preferring death over dishonor, a posture expressed in *seppuku* (ritual suicide). But there was much more to bushido, for the samurai served not only as warriors but also as bureaucrats—magistrates, land managers, and provincial governors—acting on behalf of their lords (*daimyo*) or in service to military rulers, the *shoguns*. Furthermore, although bushido remained a distinctively Japanese cultural expression, it absorbed both Confucian and Buddhist values as well as those of the indigenous Shinto tradition.

The two selections that follow reflect major themes of an emerging bushido culture, the way of the warrior. The first excerpt comes from the writings of Shiba Yoshimasa (1349–1410), a feudal lord, general, and administrator as well as a noted poet, who wrote a manual of advice for the young warriors of his own lineage. Probably the man who most closely approximated in his own life the emerging ideal of a cultivated warrior was Imagawa Ryoshun (1325–1420), famous as a poet, a military commander, and a devout Buddhist. The second excerpt contains passages from a famous and highly critical letter Imagawa wrote to his adopted son (who was also his younger brother). The letter was published and republished hundreds of times and used for centuries as a primer or school text for the instruction of young samurai.

■ Based on these accounts, how would you define the ideal samurai?

■ What elements of Confucian, Buddhist, or Shinto thinking can you find in these selections? How do these writers reconcile the peaceful emphasis of Confucian and Buddhist teachings with the military dimension of bushido?

■ What does the Imagawa letter suggest about the problems facing the military rulers of Japan in the fourteenth century?

SHIBA YOSHIMASA

Advice to Young Samurai

ca. 1400

Wielders of bow and arrow should behave in a manner considerate not only of their own honor, of course, but also of the honor of their descendants. They should not bring on eternal disgrace by solicitude for their limited lives.

That being said, nevertheless to regard your one and only life as like dust or ashes and die when you shouldn't is to acquire a worthless reputation. A genuine motive would be, for example, to give up your life for the sake of the sole sovereign, or serving under the commander of the military in a time of need; these would convey an exalted name to children and descendants. Something like a strategy of the moment, whether good or bad, cannot raise the family reputation much.

Warriors should never be thoughtless or absent-minded but handle all things with fore-thought. . . .

It is said that good warriors and good Buddhists are similarly circumspect. Whatever the matter, it is vexing for the mind not to be calm. Putting others' minds at ease too is something found only in the considerate. . . .

When you begin to think of yourself, you'll get irritated at your parents' concern and defy their instructions. Even if your parents may be stupid, if you obey their instructions, at least you won't be violating the principle of nature. What is more, eighty to ninety percent of the time what parents say makes sense for their children. It builds up in oneself to become obvious. The words of our parents we defied in irritation long ago are all essential. You should emulate even a bad parent rather than a good stranger; that's how a family culture is transmitted and comes to be known as a person's legacy. . . .

Even if one doesn't perform any religious exercises and never makes a visit to a shrine, neither deities nor buddhas will disregard a person whose mind is honest and compassionate. In particular, the Great Goddess of Ise,° the great bodhisattva Hachiman,° and the deity of Kitano° will dwell in the heads of people whose minds are honest, clean, and good.

°**Great Goddess of Ise:** Amaterasu, the sun goddess.

°**Hachiman:** a Japanese deity who came to be seen as a Buddhist bodhisattva.

°**Kitano:** patron god of learning.

Source: Thomas Cleary, trans. and ed., *Training the Samurai Mind* (Boston: Shambhala, 2008), 18–20.

IMAGAWA RYOSHUN

The Imagawa Letter

1412

As you do not understand the Arts of Peace° your skill in the Arts of War° will not, in the end, achieve victory.

You like to roam about, hawking and cormorant fishing, relishing the purposelessness of taking life.

You live in luxury by fleecing the people and plundering the shrines.

To build your own dwelling you razed the pagoda and other buildings of the memorial temple of our ancestors.

°**Arts of Peace:** literary skills including poetry, history, philosophy, and ritual.

°**Arts of War:** horsemanship, archery, swordsmanship.

Source: From Carl Steenstrup, trans., "The Imagawa Letter," *Monumenta Nipponica* 28, no. 3 (1973), 295–316.

You do not distinguish between good and bad behavior of your retainers, but reward or punish them without justice.

You permit yourself to forget the kindness that our lord and father showed us; thus you destroy the principles of loyalty and filial piety.

You do not understand the difference in status between yourself and others; sometimes you make too much of other people, sometimes too little.

You disregard other people's viewpoints; you bully them and rely on force.

You excel at drinking bouts, amusements, and gambling, but you forget the business of our clan.

You provide yourself lavishly with clothes and weapons, but your retainers are poorly equipped.

You ought to show utmost respect to Buddhist monks and priests and carry out ceremonies properly.

You impede the flow of travelers by erecting barriers everywhere in your territory.

Whether you are in charge of anything—such as a province or a district—or not, it will be difficult to put your abilities to any use if you have not won the sympathy and respect of ordinary people.

Just as the Buddhist scriptures tell us that the Buddha incessantly strives to save mankind, in the same way you should exert your mind to the utmost in all your activities, be they civil or military, and never fall into negligence.

It should be regarded as dangerous if the ruler of the people in a province is deficient even in a single [one] of the cardinal virtues of human-heartedness, righteousness, propriety, wisdom, and good faith.

You were born to be a warrior, but you mismanage your territory, do not maintain the army, and are not ashamed although people laugh at you. It is, indeed, a mortifying situation for you and our whole clan.

Using the Evidence: The Making of Japanese Civilization

1. **Considering cultural borrowing and assimilation:** What evidence of cultural borrowing can you identify in these documents? To what extent did those borrowed elements come to be regarded as Japanese?

2. **Looking for continuities:** What older patterns of Japanese thought and practice persisted despite much cultural borrowing from China?

3. **Noticing inconsistencies and change:** No national culture develops as a single set of ideas and practices. What inconsistencies, tensions, or differences in emphasis can you identify in these documents? What changes over time can you find in these selections?

4. **Considering Confucian reactions:** How might Confucian scholars respond to each of these documents? (See Document 4.1, pp. 198–200.)

Visual Sources

Considering the Evidence:
The Leisure Life of China's Elites

From the earliest centuries of Chinese civilization, that country's artists have painted—on pottery, paper, wood, and silk; in tombs, on coffins, and on walls; in albums and on scrolls. Relying largely on ink rather than oils, their brushes depicted human figures, landscapes, religious themes, and images of ordinary life. While Chinese painting evolved over many centuries, both in terms of subject matter and technique, by most accounts it reached a high point of artistic brilliance during the Tang and Song dynasties.

Here, however, we are less interested in the aesthetic achievements of Chinese painting than in what those works can show us about the life of China's elite class—those men who had passed the highest-level examinations and held high office in the state bureaucracy and those women who lived within the circles of the imperial court. While they represented only a tiny fraction of China's huge population, such elite groups established the tone and set the standards of behavior for Chinese civilization. For such people, leisure was a positive value, a time for nurturing relationships and cultivating one's character in good Confucian or Daoist fashion. According to the Tang dynasty writer and scholar Duan Chengshi,

> Leisure is good.
> Dusty affairs don't entangle the mind.
> I sit facing the tree outside the window
> And watch its shadow change direction three times.[45]

Action and work, in the Chinese view of things, need to be balanced by self-reflection and leisure. In the visual sources that follow, we can catch a glimpse of how the Chinese elite lived and interacted with one another, particularly in their leisure time.

Leading court officials and scholar-bureaucrats must have been greatly honored to be invited to an elegant banquet, hosted by the emperor himself, such as that shown in Visual Source 8.1. Usually attributed to the emperor Huizong (1082–1135)—who was himself a noted painter, poet, calligrapher, and collector—the painting shows a refined dinner gathering of high officials drinking tea and wine with the emperor presiding at the left.[46] This emperor's great attention to the arts rather than to affairs of state gained him a reputation as a negligent and dissolute ruler. His reign ended in disgrace as China suffered a humiliating defeat at the hands of northern nomadic Jin people, who took the emperor captive.

- What features of this painting contribute to the impression of imperial elegance?

- What mood does this painting evoke?

- What social distinction among the figures in the painting can you discern?

- How is the emperor depicted in this painting in comparison to that on page 375? How would you explain the difference?

- How might you imagine the conversation around this table?

Visual Source 8.1 A Banquet with the Emperor (National Palace Museum, Taipei, Taiwan/bpk Berlin/ The Art Archive at Art Resource, NY)

Elite women of the court likewise gathered to eat, drink, and talk, as illustrated in Visual Source 8.2, an anonymous Tang dynasty painting on silk. Hosting the event is the empress, shown seated upright in the middle of the left side of the table, holding a fan and wearing a distinctive headdress. Her guests and paid professional musicians sit around the table.

■ How does this gathering of elite women differ from that of the men in Visual Source 8.1? How might their conversation differ from that of the men?

■ To what extent are the emperor and empress in Visual Sources 8.1 and 8.2 distinguished from their guests? How do you think the emperor and empress viewed their roles at these functions? Were they acting as private persons among friends or in an official capacity?

■ What differences in status among these women can you identify?

■ What view of these women does the artist seek to convey?

■ What does the posture of the women suggest about the event?

Visual Source 8.2 At Table with the Empress (National Palace Museum, Taipei, Taiwan/Werner Forman/Art Resource, NY)

Confucian cultural ideals gave great prominence to literature, poetry, and scholarly pursuits as leisure activities appropriate for "gentlemen." Confucius himself had declared that "gentlemen make friends through literature, and through friendship increase their benevolence." Thus literary gatherings of scholars and officials, often in garden settings, were common themes in Tang and Song dynasty paintings. Visual Source 8.3, by the tenth-century painter Zhou Wenju, provides an illustration of such a gathering.

- What marks these figures as cultivated men of literary or scholarly inclination?

- What meaning might you attribute to the outdoor garden setting of this image and that of Visual Source 8.1?

- Notice the various gazes of the four figures. What do they suggest about the character of this gathering and the interpersonal relationships among its participants? Are they interacting or engaged in solitary pursuits?

- Do you think the artist was seeking to convey an idealized image of what a gathering of "gentlemen" ought to be or a realistic portrayal of an actual event? What elements of the painting support your answer?

Visual Source 8.3 A Literary Gathering (Palace Museum, Beijing/Cultural Relics Press)

Not all was poetry and contemplation of nature in the leisure-time activities of China's elite. Nor were men and women always so strictly segregated as the preceding visual sources may suggest. Visual Source 8.4 illustrates another side of Chinese elite life. These images are part of a long tenth-century scroll painting entitled *The Night Revels of Han Xizai*. Apparently, the Tang dynasty emperor Li Yu became suspicious that one of his ministers, Han Xizai, was overindulging in suspicious night-long parties in his own home. He therefore commissioned the artist Gu Hongzhong to attend these parties secretly and to record the events in a painting, which he hoped would shame his wayward but talented official into more appropriate and dignified behavior. The entire scroll shows men and women together, sometimes in flirtatious situations, while open sleeping areas suggest sexual activity.

- What kinds of entertainment were featured at this gathering?

- What aspects of these parties shown in the scroll paintings might have caused the emperor some concern? Refer back to the female musicians

Visual Source 8.4 An Elite Night Party (Palace Museum, Beijing/Cultural Relics Press)

shown on page 406, which derives from the same painting. In what respects
might these kinds of gatherings run counter to Confucian values?

■ How are women portrayed in these images? In what ways are they
relating to the men in the paintings?

Using the Evidence: The Leisure Life of China's Elites

1. **Describing elite society:** Based on these visual sources, write a brief
   description of the social life of Chinese elites during the Tang and Song
   dynasties.

2. **Defining the self-image of an elite:** What do these visual sources
   suggest about how members of the elite ideally viewed themselves? In
   what ways do those self-portraits draw upon Confucian, Daoist, or
   Buddhist teachings?

3. **Noticing differences in the depiction of women:** In what different
   ways are women represented in these paintings? Keep in mind that all
   of the artists were men. How might this affect the way women were
   depicted? How might female artists have portrayed them differently?

4. **Using images to illustrate change:** Reread the sections on Chinese
   women (pp. 371–72 and 406–09). How might these images be used to
   illustrate the changes in women's lives that are described in those pages?

5. **Seeking additional sources:** What other kinds of visual sources might
   provide further insight into the lives of Chinese elites?

Chapter 8 Wrap Up

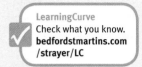

LearningCurve
Check what you know.
**bedfordstmartins.com
/strayer/LC**

STEP ONE

The Word to Know: Tribute

The *Oxford English Dictionary* defines *tribute* as "a tax or impost paid by one prince or state to another in acknowledgement of submission or as the price of peace, security, and protection; rent or homage paid in money or an equivalent by a subject to his sovereign or a vassal to his lord." Describe the Chinese tribute system in theory and in practice. Based on what happened with nomadic raiders, should this be called tribute something else, perhaps appeasement? Write a brief paragraph addressing these questions.

STEP TWO

The Achievements of Tang and Song China

Use the chart below to identify the achievements of the Chinese during the Tang and Song dynasties. In some cases, the text refers to the joint accomplishments of the two, and in other cases attributes it to one dynasty in particular.

	Tang (618–907)	Song (960–1279)	Both Tang and Song
Political			
Cultural			
Economic			
Technological			

Continuity in Japanese Culture

The documents for Chapter 8 (pp. 395–403) contain evidence of continuity in Japan, even as Japan "borrowed" certain elements from China. Write a brief essay citing the evidence in these documents that demonstrate continuity in Japanese culture. Then explain why, even in the face of change, people in authority would want to emphasize stability. Supplement your answers with information from the text where possible.

وَكَادَ يَنْزِعُ الجِمَالَ الشُّمَّ وَاشْتَدَّ

مَا الحَجُّ سَيْرَكَ تَأْوِيبًا وَإِدْلَاجَا وَلَا الْعِيَابَمْ أَحْمَالًا وَإِحْدَاجَا

الحَجُّ أَنْ تَقْصِدَ البَيْتَ الحَرَامَ عَلَى تَحْرِيكَ لِلْحَجِّ لَا تَبْغِي بِهِ حَاجَا

وَأَنْ تُعَطِّي كَأَهْلِ الْإِنْصَافِ مُنْتَخِذًا رَدْعَ الهَوَى هَادِيًا وَالْحَقَّ مِنْهَاجَا

The Worlds of Islam

Afro-Eurasian Connections

600–1500

"There were tens of thousands of pilgrims, from all over the world. They were of all colors, from blue-eyed blondes to black-skinned Africans. But we were all participating in the same ritual, displaying a spirit of unity and brotherhood that my experiences in America had led me to believe never could exist between the white and non-white. . . . I have never before seen sincere and true brotherhood practiced by all colors together, irrespective of their color."[1] So said Malcolm X, the American black radical leader and convert to Islam, following his participation in the hajj, the Muslim pilgrimage to Mecca, in 1964. That experience persuaded him to abandon his earlier commitment to militant black separatism, for he was now convinced that racial barriers could indeed be overcome within the context of Islam.

As the twenty-first century dawned, Islam had acquired a noticeable presence in the United States, with more than 1,200 mosques and an estimated 8 million Muslims. Here was but one sign of the growing international significance of the Islamic world. Independence from colonial rule, the Iranian Revolution of 1979, repeated wars between Israel and its Arab neighbors, the rising price of oil — all of this focused global attention on the Islamic world in the second half of the twentieth century. Then in the new millennium, the 2001 attacks on the United States, American military action in Afghanistan and Iraq, and in 2011 the popular uprisings in the Middle East known as the Arab Spring as well as the killing of Osama bin Laden likewise signaled the growing role of Islamic civilization in world affairs.

The Hajj: The pilgrimage to Mecca, known as the hajj, has long been a central religious ritual in Islamic practice. It also embodies the cosmopolitan character of Islam as pilgrims from all over the vast Islamic realm assemble in the city where the faith was born. This painting shows a group of joyful pilgrims, led by a band, on their way to Mecca. (Bibliothèque nationale de France)

AS IN CHINA, MUSLIM SOCIETIES OVER MUCH OF THE PAST CENTURY have been seeking to overcome several hundred years of humiliating European intrusion and to find their place in the modern world. In doing so, many Muslims have found inspiration and encouragement in the early history of their civilization and their faith. For a thousand years (roughly 600–1600), peoples claiming allegiance to Islam represented a highly successful, prosperous, and expansive civilization, encompassing parts of Africa, Europe, the Middle East, and Asia. While Chinese culture and Buddhism provided the cultural anchor for East Asia during the third-wave millennium and Christianity did the same for Europe, the realm of Islam touched on both of them and decisively shaped the history of the entire Afro-Eurasian world.

The significance of a burgeoning Islamic world during the third-wave era was enormous. It thrust the previously marginal and largely nomadic Arabs into a central role in world history, for it was among them and in their language that the newest of the world's major religions was born. The sudden emergence and rapid spread of that religion in the seventh century C.E. was accompanied by the creation of a huge empire that stretched from Spain to India. Both within that empire and beyond it, a new and innovative civilization took shape, drawing on Arab, Persian, Turkish, Greco-Roman, South Asian, and African cultures. It was clearly the largest and most influential of the new third-wave civilizations. Finally, the broad reach of Islam generated many of the great cultural encounters of this age of accelerating connections, as Islamic civilization challenged and provoked Christendom, penetrated and was transformed by African cultures, and also took root in India, Central Asia, and Southeast Asia. The spread of Islam continued in the modern era so that by the beginning of the twenty-first century, some 1.2 billion people, or 22 percent of the world's population, identified as Muslims. It was second only to Christianity as the world's most widely practiced religion, and it extended far beyond the Arab lands where it had originated.

SEEKING THE MAIN POINT

In what ways did the civilization of Islam draw on other civilizations in the Afro-Eurasian world? And in what respects did it shape or transform those civilizations?

The Birth of a New Religion

Most of the major religious or cultural traditions of the second-wave era had emerged from the core of established civilizations—Confucianism and Daoism from China, Hinduism and Buddhism from India, Greek philosophy from the Mediterranean world, and Zoroastrianism from Persia. Christianity and Islam, by contrast, emerged more from the margins of Mediterranean and Middle Eastern civilizations. Christianity, of course, appeared among a small Middle Eastern people, the Jews, in a remote province of the Roman Empire, while Islam took hold in the cities and deserts of the Arabian Peninsula.

The Homeland of Islam

The central region of the Arabian Peninsula had long been inhabited by nomadic Arabs, known as Bedouins, who herded their sheep and camels in seasonal migrations. These peoples lived in fiercely independent clans and tribes, which often engaged

A Map of Time

570–632	Life of Muhammad
632–661	Era of Rightly Guided Caliphs
633–644	Muslim conquest of Persia
650s	Quran compiled
656–661; 680–692	Civil war; emergence of Sunni/Shi'a split
661–750	Umayyad caliphate
750–900	High point of Abbasid caliphate
711–718	Conquest of Spain
751	Battle of Talas River
756	Baghdad established as capital of Abbasid Caliphate
800–1000	Emergence of Sufism
1099	Crusaders seize Jerusalem
1206	Delhi sultanate established in India
1258	Mongols sack Baghdad; formal end of Abbasid caliphate
1324	Mansa Musa pilgrimage to Mecca
1453	Ottoman Empire conquers Constantinople; end of Byzantine Empire
1492	Christian reconquest of Spain complete; end of Muslim Spain
1526	Mughal Empire established in India

in bitter blood feuds with one another. They recognized a variety of gods, ancestors, and nature spirits; valued personal bravery, group loyalty, and hospitality; and greatly treasured their highly expressive oral poetry. But there was more to Arabia than camel-herding nomads. In scattered oases, the highlands of Yemen, and interior mountain communities, sedentary village-based agriculture was practiced, and in the northern and southern regions of Arabia, small kingdoms had flourished in earlier times. Arabia also sat astride increasingly important trade routes that connected the Indian Ocean world with that of the Mediterranean Sea, a location that gave rise to cosmopolitan commercial cities, whose values and practices were often in conflict with those of traditional Arab tribes (see Map 9.1, p. 414).

One of those cities, Mecca, came to occupy a distinctive role in Arabia. Though somewhat off the major long-distance trade routes, Mecca was the site of the Kaaba, the most prominent religious shrine in Arabia, which housed representations of some 360 deities and was the destination for many pilgrims. Mecca's dominant tribe, the Quraysh (koor-EYE'SH), had come to control access to the Kaaba and grew wealthy by taxing the local trade that accompanied the annual pilgrimage season. By the sixth century, Mecca was home to people from various tribes and clans as well as

■ **Description**

In what ways did the early history of Islam reflect its Arabian origins?

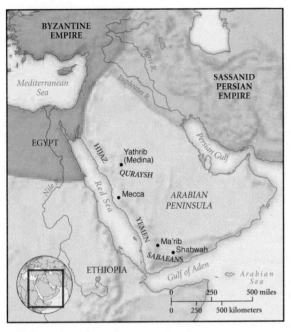

Map 9.1 Arabia at the Time of Muhammad
Located adjacent to the Byzantine and Persian empires, the eastern coast of Arabia was the site of a major trade route between the Indian Ocean and the Mediterranean Sea.

■ **Description**
What did the Quran expect from those who followed its teachings?

an assortment of individual outlaws, exiles, refugees, and foreign merchants, but much of its growing wealth was concentrated in the hands of a few ruling Quraysh families.

Furthermore, Arabia was located on the periphery of two established and rival civilizations of that time — the Byzantine Empire, heir to the Roman world, and the Sassanid Empire, heir to the imperial traditions of Persia. This location, coupled with long-distance trade, ensured some familiarity with the larger world, particularly in the cities and settled farming regions of the peninsula. Many Jews and Christians as well as some Zoroastrians lived among the Arabs, and their monotheistic ideas became widely known. By the time of Muhammad, most of the settled Arabs had acknowledged the preeminent position of Allah, the supreme god of the Arab pantheon, although they usually found the lesser gods, including the three daughters of Allah, far more accessible. Moreover, they increasingly identified Allah with Yahweh, the Jewish High God, and regarded themselves too as "children of Abraham." A few Arabs were beginning to explore the possibility that Allah/Yahweh was the only God and that the many others, residing in the Kaaba and in shrines across the peninsula, were nothing more than "helpless and harmless idols."[2]

To an outside observer around 600, it might well have seemed that Arabs were moving toward Judaism religiously or that Christianity, the most rapidly growing religion in western Asia, would encompass Arabia as well. Any such expectations, however, were thoroughly confounded by the dramatic events of the seventh century.

The Messenger and the Message

The catalyst for those events and for the birth of this new religion was a single individual, Muhammad Ibn Abdullah (570–632 C.E.), who was born in Mecca to a Quraysh family. As a young boy, Muhammad lost his parents, came under the care of an uncle, and worked as a shepherd to pay his keep. Later he became a trader and traveled as far north as Syria. At the age of twenty-five, he married a wealthy widow, Khadija, herself a prosperous merchant, with whom he fathered six children. A highly reflective man deeply troubled by the religious corruption and social inequalities of Mecca, he often undertook periods of withdrawal and meditation in the arid mountains outside the city. There, like the Buddha and Jesus, Muhammad had a powerful, overwhelming religious experience that left him convinced, albeit reluctantly, that he was Allah's messenger to the Arabs, commissioned to bring to them a scripture in their own language. (See Visual Sources: The Life of the Prophet, pp. 454–61, for images from the life of Muhammad.)

According to Muslim tradition, the revelations began in 610 and continued periodically over the next twenty-two years. Those revelations, recorded in the Quran, became the sacred scriptures of Islam, which to this day most Muslims regard as the very words of God and the core of their faith. Intended to be recited rather than simply read for information, the Quran, Muslims claim, when heard in its original Arabic, conveys nothing less than the very presence of the Divine. Its unmatched poetic beauty, miraculous to Muslims, convinced many that it was indeed a revelation from God. One of the earliest converts testified to its power: "When I heard the Quran, my heart was softened and I wept and Islam entered into me."[3] (See Document 9.1, pp. 445–46, for selections from the Quran.)

Muslims, Jews, and Christians
The close relationship of three Middle Eastern monotheistic traditions is illustrated in this fifteenth-century Persian painting, which portrays Muhammad leading Moses, Abraham, and Jesus in prayer. The fire surrounding the Prophet's head represents his religious fervor. The painting reflects the Islamic belief that the revelations granted to Muhammad built on and completed those given earlier to Jews and Christians. (Bibliothèque nationale de France)

In its Arabian setting, the Quran's message, delivered through Muhammad, was revolutionary. Religiously, it was radically monotheistic, presenting Allah as the only God, the all-powerful Creator, good, just, and merciful. Allah was the "Lord sustainer of the worlds, the Compassionate, the Caring, master of the day of reckoning" and known to human beings "on the farthest horizon and within their own selves."[4] Here was an exalted conception of Deity that drew heavily on traditions of Jewish and Christian monotheism. As "the Messenger of God," Muhammad presented himself in the line of earlier prophets — Abraham, Moses, Jesus, and many others. He was the last, "the seal of the prophets," bearing God's final revelation to humankind. It was not so much a call to a new faith as an invitation to return to the old and pure religion of Abraham from which Jews, Christians, and Arabs alike had deviated. Jews had wrongly conceived of themselves as a uniquely "chosen people"; Christians had made their prophet into a god; and Arabs had become wildly polytheistic. To all of this, the message of the Quran was a corrective.

Submission to Allah ("Muslim" means "one who submits") was the primary obligation of believers and the means of achieving a God-conscious life in this world and a place in paradise after death. According to the Quran, however, submission was not merely an individual or a spiritual act, for it involved the creation of a whole new society. Over and again, the Quran denounced the prevailing social practices of an increasingly prosperous Mecca: the hoarding of wealth, the exploitation of the poor, the charging of high rates of interest on loans, corrupt business deals, the abuse of women, and the neglect of widows and orphans. Like the Jewish prophets of the Old Testament, the Quran demanded social justice and laid out a prescription for its implementation. It sought a return to the older values of Arab tribal life — solidarity, equality, concern for the poor — which had been undermined, particularly in Mecca, by growing wealth and commercialism.

The message of the Quran challenged not only the ancient polytheism of Arab religion and the social injustices of Mecca but also the entire tribal and clan structure of Arab society, which was so prone to war, feuding, and violence. The just and moral society of Islam was the *umma* (UMH-mah), the community of all believers, replacing tribal, ethnic, or racial identities. Such a society would be a "witness over the nations," for according to the Quran, "You are the best community evolved for mankind, enjoining what is right and forbidding what is wrong."[5] In this community, women too had an honored and spiritually equal place. "The believers, men and women, are protectors of one another," declared the Quran.[6] The umma, then, was to be a new and just community, bound by a common belief rather than by territory, language, or tribe.

The core message of the Quran — the remembrance of God — was effectively summarized as a set of five requirements for believers, known as the Pillars of Islam. The first pillar expressed the heart of the Islamic message: "There is no god but Allah, and Muhammad is the messenger of God." The second pillar was ritual prayer, performed five times a day. Accompanying practices, including cleansing, bowing, kneeling, and prostration, expressed believers' submission to Allah and provided a frequent reminder, amid the busyness of daily life, that they were living in the presence of God. The third pillar, almsgiving, reflected the Quran's repeated demands for social justice by requiring believers to give generously to support the poor and needy of the community. The fourth pillar established a month of fasting during Ramadan, which meant abstaining from food, drink, and sexual relations from the first light of dawn to sundown. It provided an occasion for self-purification and a reminder of the needs of the hungry. The fifth pillar encouraged a pilgrimage to Mecca, known as the hajj (HAHJ), during which believers from all over the Islamic world assembled once a year and put on identical simple white clothing as they reenacted key events in Islamic history. For at least the few days of the hajj, the many worlds of Islam must surely have seemed a single realm.

A further requirement for believers, sometimes called the sixth pillar, was "struggle," or *jihad* in Arabic. Its more general meaning, which Muhammad referred to as the "greater jihad," was an interior personal effort of each believer against greed and selfishness, a spiritual striving toward living a God-conscious life. In its "lesser" form, the "jihad of the sword," the Quran authorized armed struggle against the forces of unbelief and evil as a means of establishing Muslim rule and of defending the umma from the threats of infidel aggressors. The understanding and use of the jihad concept has varied widely over the many centuries of Islamic history and remains a matter of much controversy among Muslims in the twenty-first century.

The Transformation of Arabia

As the revelations granted to Muhammad became known in Mecca, they attracted a small following of some close relatives, a few prominent Meccan leaders, and an assortment of lower-class dependents, freed slaves, and members of poorer clans. Those teachings also soon attracted the vociferous opposition of Mecca's elite families, par-ticularly those of Muhammad's own tribe, the Quraysh. Muhammad's claim to be a "messenger of Allah," his unyielding monotheism, his call for social reform, his con-demnation of Mecca's business practices, and his apparent disloyalty to his own tribe enraged the wealthy and ruling families of Mecca. So great had this opposition be-come that in 622 Muhammad and his small band of followers emigrated to the more welcoming town of Yathrib, soon to be called Medina, the city of the Prophet. This agricultural settlement of mixed Arab and Jewish population had invited Muhammad to serve as an arbitrator of their intractable conflicts. The emigration to Yathrib, known in Arabic as the *hijra* (HIHJ-ruh) (the journey), was a momentous turning point in the early history of Islam and thereafter marked the beginning of a new Islamic calendar.

■ **Change**
How was Arabia trans-formed by the rise of Islam?

The new community, or umma, that took shape in Medina was a kind of "super-tribe," but very different from the traditional tribes of Arab society. Membership was a matter of belief rather than birth, allowing the community to expand rapidly. Fur-thermore, all authority, both political and religious, was concentrated in the hands of Muhammad, who proceeded to introduce radical changes. Usury was outlawed, tax-free marketplaces were established, and a mandatory payment to support the poor was imposed.

In Medina, Muhammad not only began to create a new society but also declared his movement's independence from its earlier affiliation with Judaism. In the early years, he had anticipated a warm response from Jews and Christians, based on a com-mon monotheism and prophetic tradition, and had directed his followers to pray fac-ing Jerusalem. But when some Jewish groups allied with his enemies, Muhammad acted harshly to suppress them, exiling some and enslaving or killing others. This was not, however, a general suppression of Jews since others among them remained loyal to Muhammad's new state. But the Prophet now redirected his followers' prayer toward Mecca, essentially declaring Islam an Arab religion, though one with a uni-versal message.

From its base in Medina, the Islamic community rapidly extended its reach through-out Arabia. Early military successes against Muhammad's Meccan opponents con-vinced other Arab tribes that the Muslims and their God were on the rise, and they sought to negotiate alliances with the new power. Growing numbers converted. The religious appeal of the new faith, its promise of material gain, the end of incessant warfare among feuding tribes, periodic military actions skillfully led by Muhammad, and the Prophet's willingness to enter into marriage alliances with leading tribes — all of this contributed to the consolidation of Islamic control throughout Arabia. In 630, Muhammad triumphantly and peacefully entered Mecca itself, purging the Kaaba of its idols and declaring it a shrine to the one God, Allah. By the time Muhammad died in 632, most of Arabia had come under the control of this new Islamic state, and many had embraced the new faith.

Thus the birth of Islam differed sharply from that of Christianity. Jesus' teaching about "giving to Caesar what is Caesar's and to God what is God's" reflected the mi-nority and subordinate status of the Jews within the Roman Empire. Early Christians found themselves periodically persecuted by Roman authorities for more than three centuries, requiring them to work out some means of dealing with an often hostile state. The answer lay in the development of a separate church hierarchy and the concept of two coexisting authorities, one religious and one political, an arrangement that persisted even after the state became Christian.

The young Islamic community, by contrast, found itself constituted as a state, and soon a huge empire, at the very beginning of its history. Muhammad was not only a religious figure but also, unlike Jesus or the Buddha, a political and military leader able to implement his vision of an ideal Islamic society. Nor did Islam give rise to a separate religious organization, although tension between religious and political goals frequently generated conflict. No professional clergy mediating between God and humankind emerged within Islam. Teachers, religious scholars, prayer leaders, and judges within an Islamic legal system did not have the religious role that priests held within Christianity. No distinction between religious law and civil law, so important in the Christian world, existed within the realm of Islam. One law, known as the *sharia* (shah-REE-ah), regulated every aspect of life. The sharia (literally, "a path to water," which is the source of life) evolved over the several centuries following the birth of this new religion and found expression in a number of separate schools of Islamic legal practice.

In little more than twenty years (610–632), a profound transformation had occurred in the Arabian Peninsula. What would subsequently become a new religion had been born, though it was one with roots in earlier Jewish, Christian, and Zoroastrian traditions. A new and vigorous state had emerged, bringing peace to the warring tribes of Arabia. Within that state, a distinctive society had begun to take shape, one that served ever after as a model for Islamic communities everywhere. In his farewell sermon, Muhammad described the outlines of this community:

> All mankind is from Adam and Eve, an Arab has no superiority over a non-Arab nor a non-Arab has any superiority over an Arab; also a white has no superiority over a black nor a black has any superiority over a white — except by piety and good action. Learn that every Muslim is a brother to every Muslim and that the Muslims constitute one brotherhood.[7]

The Making of an Arab Empire

It did not take long for the immense transformations occurring in Arabia to have an impact beyond the peninsula. In the centuries that followed, the energies born of those vast changes profoundly transformed much of the Afro-Eurasian world. The new Arab state became a huge empire, encompassing all or part of Egyptian, Roman/ Byzantine, Persian, Mesopotamian, and Indian civilizations. The Islamic faith spread widely within and outside that empire. So too did the culture and language of Arabia, as many Arabs migrated far beyond their original homeland and many others found it advantageous to learn Arabic. From the mixing and blending of these many peoples emerged the new and distinctive third-wave civilization of Islam, bound by the ties of a common faith but divided by differences of culture, class, politics, gender, and religious understanding. These enormously consequential processes—the making of a new religion, a new empire, and a new civilization—were central to world history during the third-wave millennium.

War, Conquest, and Tolerance

Within a few years of Muhammad's death in 632, Arab armies engaged the Byzantine and Persian Sassanid empires, the great powers of the region. It was the beginning of a process that rapidly gave rise to an Arab empire that stretched from Spain to India, penetrating both Europe and China and governing most of the lands between them (see Map 9.2). In creating that empire, Arabs were continuing a long pattern of tribal raids into surrounding civilizations, but now these Arabs were newly organized in a state of their own with a central command able to mobilize the military potential of the entire population. The Byzantine and Persian empires, weakened by decades of war with each other and by internal revolts, continued to view the Arabs as a mere nuisance rather than a serious threat. But by 644 the Sassanid Empire had been defeated by Arab forces, while Byzantium, the remaining eastern regions of the old Roman Empire, soon lost the southern half of its territories. Beyond these victories, Muslim forces, operating on both land and sea, swept westward across North Africa, conquered Spain in the early 700s, and attacked southern France. To the east, Arab armies reached the Indus River and seized some of the major oases towns of Central Asia. In 751, they inflicted a crushing defeat on Chinese forces in the Battle of Talas River, which had lasting consequences for the cultural evolution of Asia, for it checked the further expansion of China to the west and made possible the conversion to Islam of Central Asia's Turkic-speaking people. Most of the violence of conquest involved imperial armies, though on occasion civilians too were caught up in the fighting and suffered terribly. In 634, for example, a battle between Byzantine and Arab forces in Palestine resulted in the death of some 4,000 villagers.

> ■ **Change**
> Why were Arabs able to construct such a huge empire so quickly?

The motives driving the creation of the Arab Empire were broadly similar to those of other empires. The merchant leaders of the new Islamic community wanted to capture profitable trade routes and wealthy agricultural regions. Individual Arabs found in military expansion a route to wealth and social promotion. The need to harness the immense energies of the Arabian transformation was also important. The fragile unity of the umma threatened to come apart after Muhammad's death, and external expansion provided a common task for the community.

While many among the new conquerors viewed the mission of empire in terms of jihad, bringing righteous government to the peoples they conquered, this did not mean imposing a new religion. In fact for the better part of a century after Muhammad's death, his followers usually referred to themselves as "believers," a term that appears in the Quran far more often than "Muslims" and one that included pious Jews and Christians as well as newly monotheistic Arabs. Such a posture eased the acceptance of the new political order, for many people recently incorporated in the emerging Arab

Map 9.2 The Arab Empire and the Initial Expansion of Islam, 622–900 C.E.
Far more so than with Buddhism or Christianity, the initial spread of Islam was both rapid and extensive. And unlike the other two world religions, Islam quickly gave rise to a huge empire, ruled by Muslim Arabs, which encompassed many of the older civilizations of the region.

Empire were already monotheists and familiar with the core ideas and practices of the Believers' Movement—prayer, fasting, pilgrimage, revelation, and prophets. Furthermore, the new rulers were remarkably tolerant of established Jewish and Christian faiths. The first governor of Arab-ruled Jerusalem was a Jew. Many old Christian churches continued to operate and new ones were constructed. A Nestorian Christian patriarch in Iraq wrote to one of his bishops around 647 C.E. observing that the new rulers "not only do not fight Christianity, they even commend our religion, show honor to the priests and monasteries and saints of the Lord, and make gifts to the monasteries and churches."[8] Formal agreements or treaties recognized Jews, Christians, and Zoroastrians as "people of the book," giving them the status of *dhimmis* (dihm-mees), protected but second-class subjects. Such people were permitted to freely practice their own religion, so long as they paid a special tax known as the *jizya*. Theoretically the tax was a substitute for military service, supposedly forbidden to non-Muslims. In practice, many dhimmis served in the highest offices within Muslim kingdoms and in their armies as well.

In other ways too, the Arab rulers of an expanding empire sought to limit the disruptive impact of conquest. To prevent indiscriminate destruction and exploitation of conquered peoples, occupying Arab armies were restricted to garrison towns, segregated from the native population. Local elites and bureaucratic structures were incorporated into the new Arab Empire. Nonetheless, the empire worked many changes on its subjects, the most enduring of which was the mass conversion of Middle Eastern peoples to what became by the eighth century the new and separate religion of Islam.

Conversion

For some people, no doubt, converting to Islam was or subsequently became a matter of profound spiritual or psychological transformation, but far more often, at least initially, it was "social conversion," defined as "movement from one religiously defined social community to another."[9] It happened at various rates and in different ways, but in the four centuries or so after the death of Muhammad, millions of individuals and many whole societies within the Arab Empire found their cultural identity bound up with a belief in Allah and the message of his prophet. They had become Muslims. How had this immense cultural change occurred?

In some ways, perhaps, the change was not so dramatic, as major elements of Islam—monotheism; ritual prayer and cleansing ceremonies; fasting; divine revelation; the ideas of heaven, hell, and final judgment—were quite familiar to Jews, Christians, and Zoroastrians. Furthermore, Islam was from the beginning associated with the sponsorship of a powerful state, quite unlike the experience of early Buddhism or Christianity. Conquest called into question the power of old gods, while the growing prestige of the Arab Empire attracted many to Allah. Although deliberately forced conversion was rare, living in an Islamic-governed state provided a variety of incentives for claiming Muslim identity.[10] Slaves and prisoners of war were among the early converts, particularly in Persia. Converts could also avoid the jizya, the tax imposed on non-Muslims. In Islam, merchants found a religion friendly to commerce, and in the Arab Empire they enjoyed a huge and secure arena for trade. People aspiring to official positions found conversion to Islam an aid to social mobility.

Conversion was not an automatic or easy process. Vigorous resistance delayed conversion for centuries among the Berbers of North Africa; a small group of zealous Spanish Christians in the ninth century provoked their own martyrdom by publicly insulting the Prophet; and some Persian Zoroastrians fled to avoid Muslim rule. More generally, though, a remarkable and lasting religious transformation occurred throughout the Arab Empire.

In Persia, for example, between 750 and 900, about 80 percent of the population had made the transition to a Muslim religious identity. But they did so in a manner quite distinct from the people of Iraq, Syria, Egypt, and North Africa. In these regions, converts to Islam gradually abandoned their native languages, adopted Arabic, and

■ **Explanation**
What accounts for the widespread conversion to Islam?

came to see themselves as Arabs. In Iran or Persia, by contrast, Arab conquest did not involve cultural Arabization, despite some initial efforts to impose the Arabic language. By the tenth century, the vast majority of Persians had become Muslims, but the Persian language, Farsi (still spoken in modern Iran), flourished, enriched now by a number of Arabic loan words and written in an Arabic script. In 1010, that language received its classic literary expression when the Persian poet Ferdowsi completed his epic work, the *Shahnama* (*The Book of Kings*). A huge text of some 60,000 rhyming couplets, it recorded the mythical and pre-Islamic history of Iran and gave an enduring expression to a distinctly Persian cultural identity. Thus, in places where large-scale Arab migration had occurred, such as Egypt, North Africa, and Iraq, Arabic culture and language, as well as the religion of Islam, took hold. Such areas are today both Muslim and Arab, while the peoples of Iran, Turkey, and Pakistan, for example, have "Islamized" without "Arabizing."

The preservation of Persian language and culture had enormous implications for the world of Islam. Many religious ideas of Persian Zoroastrianism—an evil satanic power, final judgment, heaven and hell, paradise—found their way into Islam, often indirectly via Jewish or Christian precedents. In Iran, Central Asia, India, and later in the Ottoman Empire, Islam was accompanied by pervasive Persian influences. Persian administrative and bureaucratic techniques; Persian court practices with their palaces, gardens, and splendid garments; Persian architecture, poetry, music, and painting—all of this decisively shaped the high culture of these eastern Islamic lands. One of the Abbasid caliphs, himself an Arab, observed: "The Persians ruled for a thousand years and did not need us Arabs even for a day. We have been ruling them for one or two centuries and cannot do without them for an hour."[11]

Divisions and Controversies

The ideal of a unified Muslim community, so important to Muhammad, proved difficult to realize as conquest and conversion vastly enlarged the Islamic umma. A central problem was that of leadership and authority in the absence of Muhammad's towering presence. Who should hold the role of caliph (KAY-lihf), the successor to Muhammad as the political leader of the umma, the protector and defender of the faith? That issue crystallized a variety of emerging conflicts within the Islamic world—between early and later converts, among various Arab tribes and factions, between Arabs and non-Arabs, between privileged and wealthy rulers and their far less fortunate subjects. Many of these political and social conflicts found expression in religious terms as various understandings of the Quran and of Muhammad's life and teachings took shape within the growing Islamic community.

■ **Comparison**

What is the difference between Sunni and Shia Islam?

The first four caliphs, known among most Muslims as the Rightly Guided Caliphs (632–661), were close "companions of the Prophet," selected by the Muslim elders of Medina. Division surfaced almost immediately as a series of Arab tribal rebellions and new "prophets" persuaded the first caliph, Abu Bakr, to suppress them forcibly. The third and fourth caliphs, Uthman and Ali, were both assassinated, and by 656, less than twenty-five years after Muhammad's death, civil war pitted Muslim against Muslim.

Out of that conflict emerged one of the deepest and most enduring rifts within the Islamic world. On one side were the Sunni Muslims (SOON-nee), who held that the caliphs were rightful political and military leaders, selected by the Islamic community. On the other side of this sharp divide was the Shia (SHEE-ah) (an Arabic word meaning "party" or "faction") branch of Islam. Its adherents felt strongly that leadership in the Islamic world should derive from the line of Ali and his son Husayn, blood relatives of Muhammad, both of whom died at the hands of their political or religious enemies.

In the beginning, therefore, this divide was simply a political conflict without serious theological or religious mean-

The Kaaba
Located in Mecca, this stone structure covered with a black cloth and known as the Kaaba, was originally home to the numerous deities of pre-Islamic Arabia. Cleansed by Muhammad, it became the sacred shrine of Islam and the destination of countless pilgrims undertaking the hajj. Part of that ritual involves circling the Kaaba seven times, as shown here in a photograph from 2004. (Dan Mohiuddin/Visual Connection Archive)

ing, but over time the Sunni/Shia split acquired deeper significance. For Sunni Muslims, religious authority in general emerged from the larger community, particularly from the religious scholars known as *ulama* (oo-leh-MAH). Shia Muslims, on the other hand, invested their leaders, known as *imams*, with a religious authority that the caliphs lacked, allowing them to infallibly interpret divine revelation and law. For much of early Islamic history, Shia Muslims saw themselves as the minority opposition within Islam. They felt that history had taken a wrong turn and that they were "the defenders of the oppressed, the critics and opponents of privilege and power," while the Sunnis were the advocates of the established order.[12] Various armed revolts by Shias over the centuries, most of which failed, led to a distinctive conception of martyrdom and to the expectation that their defeated leaders were merely in hiding and not really dead and that they would return in the fullness of time. Thus a messianic element entered Shia Islam. The Sunni/Shia schism became a lasting division in the Islamic world, reflected in conflicts among various Islamic states, and was exacerbated by further splits among the Shia. Those divisions echo still in the twenty-first century.

As the Arab Empire grew, its caliphs were transformed from modest Arab chiefs into absolute monarchs of the Byzantine or Persian variety, complete with elaborate court rituals, a complex bureaucracy, a standing army, and centralized systems of taxation and coinage. They were also subject to the dynastic rivalries and succession disputes common to other empires. The first dynasty, following the era of the Rightly Guided Caliphs, came from the Umayyad (oo-MEYE-ahd) family (ruled 661–750).

Under its leadership, the Arab Empire expanded greatly, caliphs became hereditary rulers, and the capital moved from Medina to the cosmopolitan Roman/Byzantine city of Damascus in Syria. Its ruling class was an Arab military aristocracy, drawn from various tribes. But Umayyad rule provoked growing criticism and unrest. The Shia viewed the Umayyad caliphs as illegitimate usurpers, and non-Arab Muslims resented their second-class citizenship in the empire. Many Arabs protested the luxurious living and impiety of their rulers. The Umayyads, they charged, "made God's servants slaves, God's property something to be taken by turns among the rich, and God's religion a cause of corruption."[13]

Such grievances lay behind the overthrow of the Umayyads in 750 and their replacement by a new Arab dynasty, the Abbasids. With a splendid new capital in Baghdad, the Abbasid caliphs presided over a flourishing and prosperous Islamic civilization in which non-Arabs, especially Persians, now played a prominent role. But the political unity of the Abbasid Empire did not last long. Beginning in the mid-ninth century, many local governors or military commanders effectively asserted the autonomy of their regions, while still giving formal allegiance to the caliph in Baghdad. Long before Mongol conquest put an official end to the Abbasid Empire in 1258, the Islamic world had fractured politically into a series of "sultanates," many ruled by Persian or Turkish military dynasties.

A further tension within the world of Islam, though one that seldom produced violent conflict, lay in different answers to the central question: What does it mean to be a Muslim, to submit wholly to Allah? That question took on added urgency as the expanding Arab Empire incorporated various peoples and cultures that had been unknown during Muhammad's lifetime. One answer lay in the development of the sharia (see Document 9.3, pp. 448–50), the body of Islamic law developed by religious scholars, the ulama, primarily in the eighth and ninth centuries.

Based on the Quran, the life and teachings of Muhammad, deductive reasoning, and the consensus of scholars, the emerging sharia addressed in great detail practically every aspect of life. It was a blueprint for an authentic Islamic society, providing detailed guidance for prayer and ritual cleansing; marriage, divorce, and inheritance; business and commercial relationships; the treatment of slaves; political life; and much more. Debates among the ulama led to the creation of four schools of law among Sunni Muslims and still others in the lands of Shia Islam. To the ulama and their followers, living as a Muslim meant following the sharia and thus participating in the creation of an Islamic society.

A second and quite different understanding of the faith emerged among those who saw the worldly success of Islamic civilization as a distraction and deviation from the purer spirituality of Muhammad's time. Known as Sufis (SOO-fees), they represented Islam's mystical dimension, in that they sought a direct and personal experience of the Divine. Through renunciation of the material world, meditation on the words of the Quran, chanting the names of God, the use of music and dance, the veneration of Muhammad and various "saints," Sufis pursued an interior life, seek-

■ **Comparison**

In what ways were Sufi Muslims critical of mainstream Islam?

ing to tame the ego and achieve spiritual union with Allah. To describe that inexpressible experience, they often resorted to metaphors of drunkenness or the embrace of lovers. "Stain your prayer rug with wine," urged the famous Sufi poet Hafiz, referring to the intoxication of the believer with the divine presence. (See Document 9.4, pp. 451–52, for another expression of Sufi religious sensibility from the thirteenth-century poet Rumi.)

This mystical tendency in Islamic practice, which became widely popular by the ninth and tenth centuries, was sharply critical of the more scholarly and legalistic practitioners of the sharia. To Sufis, establishment teachings about the law and correct behavior, while useful for daily living, did little to bring the believer into the presence of God. For some, even the Quran had its limits. Why spend time reading a love letter (the Quran), asked one Sufi master, when one might be in the very presence of the Beloved who wrote it?[14] Furthermore, they felt that many of the ulama had been compromised by their association with worldly and corrupt governments. Sufis therefore often charted their own course to God, implicitly challenging the religious authority of the ulama. For these orthodox religious scholars, Sufi ideas and practice verged on heresy, as Sufis on occasion claimed unity with God, received new revelations, or incorporated novel religious practices from outside the Islamic world.

Sufis and Worldly Power This early seventeenth-century painting from India illustrates the tension between Sufis and worldly authorities. Here the Muslim Mughal Emperor Jahangir gives his attention to the white-bearded Sufi holy man rather than to the kings and artists shown in the bottom left. (Freer Gallery of Art, Smithsonian Institution, Washington, D.C. Purchase, F1942.15a)

Despite their differences, the legalistic emphasis of the ulama and Sufi spirituality never became irreconcilable versions of Islam. A major Islamic thinker, al-Ghazali (1058–1111), himself both a legal scholar and a Sufi practitioner, in fact worked out an intellectual accommodation among different strands of Islamic thought. Rational philosophy alone could never enable believers to know Allah, he argued. Nor were revelation and the law sufficient, for Muslims must know God in their hearts, through direct personal encounter with Allah. Thus Sufism entered mainstream Islamic thinking, and Sufi spiritual practices long served as an element of popular Islam. Nonetheless, differences in emphasis remained an element of tension and sometimes discord within the world of Islam.

Women and Men in Early Islam

What did the rise of Islam and the making of the Arab Empire mean for the daily lives of women and their relationship with men? Virtually every aspect of this question has been and remains highly controversial. The debates begin with the Quran itself. Did its teachings release women from earlier restrictions, or did they impose new limitations? At the level of spiritual life, the Quran was quite clear and explicit: men and women were equal.

■ **Change**

How did the rise of Islam change the lives of women?

Men and Women at Worship

This sixteenth-century Persian painting of a mosque service shows older men with beards toward the front, younger men behind them, and veiled women and children in a separate area. (Bodleian Library, University of Oxford, Ms. Ouseley. Add 24, fol. 55v)

Those who surrender themselves to Allah and accept the true faith; who are devout, sincere, patient, humble, charitable, and chaste; who fast and are ever mindful of Allah — on these, both men and women, Allah will bestow forgiveness and rich reward.[15]

But in social terms, and especially within marriage, the Quran, like the written texts of almost all civilizations, viewed women as inferior and subordinate: "Men have authority over women because Allah has made the one superior to the other, and because they spend their wealth to maintain them. Good women are obedient."[16] More specifically, the Quran provided a mix of rights, restrictions, and protections for women. Female infanticide, for example, widely practiced in many cultures as a means of gender selection, was now forbidden for Muslims. Women were given control over their own property, particularly their dowries, and were granted rights of inheritance, but at half the rate of their male counterparts. Marriage was considered a contract between consenting parties, thus making marriage by capture illegitimate. Divorce was possible for both parties, although it was far more readily available for men. The practice of taking multiple husbands, which operated in some pre-Islamic Arab tribes, was prohibited, while polygyny (the practice of having multiple wives) was permitted, though more clearly regulated than before. Men were limited to four wives and required to treat each of them equally. The difficulty of doing so has been interpreted by some as virtually requiring monogamy. Men were, however, permitted to have sexual relations with female slaves, but any children born of those unions were free, as was the mother once her owner died. Furthermore, men were strongly encouraged to marry orphans, widows, and slaves.

Such Quranic prescriptions were but one factor shaping the lives of women and men. At least as important were the long-established practices of the societies into which Islam spread and the growing sophistication, prosperity, and urbanization of Islamic civilization. As had been the case in Athens and China during their "golden ages," Muslim women, particularly in the upper classes, experienced growing restrictions as Islamic civilization flourished culturally and economically in the Abbasid era. In early Islamic times, a number of women played visible public roles, particularly Muhammad's youngest wife, Aisha. Women prayed in the mosques, although separately, standing beside the men. Nor were women generally veiled or secluded. As the Arab empire grew in size and splendor, however, the position of women became more limited. The second caliph, Umar, asked women to offer prayers at home. Now veiling and the seclusion of women became standard practice among the upper and ruling classes, removing them from public life. Separate quarters within the homes of the wealthy were the domain of women, from which they could emerge only completely veiled. The caliph Mansur (ruled 754–775) carried this separation of the sexes even further when he ordered a separate bridge for women to be built over the Euphrates River in the new capital of Baghdad. Such seclusion was less possible for lower-class women, who lacked the servants of the rich and had to leave the home for shopping or work.

Such practices derived far more from established traditions of Middle Eastern cultures than from the Quran itself, but they soon gained an Islamic rationale in the writings of Muslim thinkers. The famous philosopher and religious scholar al-Ghazali clearly saw a relationship between Muslim piety and the separation of the sexes:

> It is not permissible for a stranger to hear the sound of a pestle being pounded by a woman he does not know. If he knocks at the door, it is not proper for the woman to answer him softly and easily because men's hearts can be drawn to [women] for the most trifling [reason]. . . . However, if the woman has to answer the knock, she should stick her finger in her mouth so that her voice sounds like that of an old woman.[17]

Other signs of a tightening patriarchy—such as "honor killing" of women by their male relatives for violating sexual taboos and, in some places, clitorectomy (female genital cutting)—likewise derived from local cultures, with no sanction in the Quran or Islamic law. Where they were practiced, such customs often came to be seen as Islamic, but they were certainly not limited to the Islamic world. In many cultures, concern with family honor linked to women's sexuality dictated harsh punishments for women who violated sexual taboos.

Negative views of women, presenting them variously as weak, deficient, and a sexually charged threat to men and social stability, emerged in the *hadiths* (hah-DEETHS), traditions about the sayings or actions of Muhammad, which became an important source of Islamic law. (See Document 9.2, pp. 447–48, for examples of hadiths.) A changing interpretation of the Adam and Eve story illustrates the point. The Quran attaches equal blame to both Adam and Eve for yielding to the temptation of Satan, and both alike ask for and receive God's forgiveness. Nothing suggests that Eve tempted or seduced Adam into sin. In later centuries, however, several hadiths and other writings took up Judeo-Christian versions of the story that blamed Eve, and thus women in general, for Adam's sin and for the punishment that followed, including expulsion from the garden and pain in childbirth.[18]

Even as women faced growing restrictions in society generally, Islam, like Buddhism and Christianity, also offered new outlets for them in religious life. The Sufi practice of mystical union with Allah allowed a greater role for women than did mainstream Islam. Some Sufi orders had parallel groups for women, and a few welcomed women as equal members. Among the earliest of well-known Sufi practitioners was Rabia, an eighth-century woman from Basra, who renounced numerous proposals of marriage and engaged, apparently successfully, in repeated religious debates with men. The greatest of the Sufi scholars, Ibn al-Arabi (1165–1240), sang the praises of divine beauty in an explicitly feminine form. The spiritual equality that the Quran accorded to male and female alike allowed women also to aspire to union with God. But for some male Sufi scholars, such as the twelfth-century mystical poet Attar, doing so meant that "she is a man and one cannot any more call her a woman."[19]

Beyond Sufi practice, within the world of Shia Islam, women teachers of the faith were called mullahs, the same as their male counterparts. Islamic education, either in the home or in Quranic schools, allowed some to become literate and a few to achieve higher levels of learning. Visits to the tombs of major Islamic figures as well as the ritual of the public bath likewise provided some opportunity for women to interact with other women beyond their own family circle.

Islam and Cultural Encounter: A Four-Way Comparison

In its earliest centuries, the rapid spread of Islam had been accompanied by the creation of an immense Arab Empire, very much in the tradition of earlier Mediterranean and Middle Eastern empires. By the tenth century, however, little political unity remained, and in 1258 even the powerless symbol of that earlier unity vanished as Mongol forces sacked Baghdad and killed the last Abbasid caliph. But even as the empire disintegrated, the civilization that was born within it grew and flourished. Perhaps the most significant sign of a flourishing Islamic civilization was the continued spread of the religion both within and beyond the boundaries of a vanishing Arab Empire (see Map 9.3), although that process differed considerably from place to place. The examples of India, Anatolia, West Africa, and Spain illustrate the various ways that Islam penetrated these societies as well as the rather different outcomes of these epic cultural encounters.

The Case of India

■ **Comparison**

What similarities and differences can you identify in the spread of Islam to India, Anatolia, West Africa, and Spain?

In South Asia, Islam found a permanent place in a long-established civilization as invasions by Turkic-speaking warrior groups from Central Asia, recently converted to Islam, brought the faith to northern India. Thus the Turks became the third major carrier of Islam, after the Arabs and Persians, as their conquests initiated an enduring encounter between Islam and a Hindu-based Indian civilization. Beginning around 1000, those conquests gave rise to a series of Turkic and Muslim regimes that governed much of India until the British takeover in the eighteenth and nineteenth centuries. The early centuries of this encounter were violent indeed, as the invaders smashed Hindu and Buddhist temples and carried off vast quantities of Indian treasure. With the establishment of the Sultanate of Delhi in 1206 (see Map 9.4), Turkic rule became more systematic, although their small numbers and internal conflicts allowed only a very modest penetration of Indian society.

In the centuries that followed, substantial Muslim communities emerged in India, particularly in regions less tightly integrated into the dominant Hindu culture. Disillusioned Buddhists as well as low-caste Hindus and untouchables found the more egalitarian Islam attractive. So did peoples just beginning to make the transition to

Map 9.3 The Growing World of Islam, 900–1500
Islam as a religion, a civilization, and an arena of commerce continued to grow even as the Arab Empire fragmented.

settled agriculture. Others benefited from converting to Islam by avoiding the tax imposed on non-Muslims. Sufis were particularly important in facilitating conversion, for India had always valued "god-filled men" who were detached from worldly affairs. Sufi holy men, willing to accommodate local gods and religious festivals, helped to develop a "popular Islam" that was not always so sharply distinguished from the more devotional forms of Hinduism.

Unlike the earlier experience of Islam in the Middle East, North Africa, and Persia, where Islam rapidly became the dominant faith, in India it was never able to claim more than 20 to 25 percent of the total population. Furthermore, Muslim communities were especially concentrated in the Punjab and Sind regions of northwestern India and in Bengal to the east. The core regions of Hindu culture in the northern Indian plain were not seriously challenged by the new faith, despite centuries of Muslim rule. One reason perhaps lay in the sharpness of the cultural divide between Islam and Hinduism. Islam was the most radically monotheistic of the world's religions, forbidding any representation of Allah, while Hinduism was surely among the most prolifically polytheistic, generating endless statues and images of the Divine in many forms. The Muslim notion

Map 9.4 The Sultanate of Delhi
Between 1206 and 1526 a number of Muslim dynasties ruled northern India as the Delhi sultanate, while an explicitly Hindu kingdom of Vijayanagar arose in the south after 1340. It drew on north Indian Muslim architectural features and made use of Muslim mercenaries for its military forces.

of the equality of all believers contrasted sharply with the hierarchical assumptions of the caste system. The sexual modesty of Muslims was deeply offended by the open eroticism of some Hindu religious art.

Although such differences may have limited the appeal of Islam in India, they also may have prevented it from being absorbed into the tolerant and inclusive embrace of Hinduism as had so many other religious ideas, practices, and communities. The religious exclusivity of Islam, born of its firm monotheistic belief and the idea of a unique revelation, set a boundary that the great sponge of Hinduism could not completely absorb.

Certainly not all was conflict across that boundary. Many prominent Hindus willingly served in the political and military structures of a Muslim-ruled India. Mystical seekers after the divine blurred the distinction between Hindu and Muslim, suggesting that God was to be found "neither in temple nor in mosque." "Look within your heart," wrote the great fifteenth-century mystic poet Kabir, "for there you will find both [Allah] and Ram [a famous Hindu deity]."[20] During the early sixteenth century, a new and distinct religious tradition emerged in India, known as Sikhism (SIHK-iz'm), which blended elements of Islam, such as devotion to one universal God, with Hindu concepts, such as karma and rebirth. "There is no Hindu and no Muslim. All are children of God," declared Guru Nanak (1469–1539), the founder of Sikhism.

Nonetheless, Muslims usually lived quite separately, remaining a distinctive minority within an ancient Indian civilization, which they now largely governed but which they proved unable to completely transform.

The Case of Anatolia

■ **Change**

In what ways was Anatolia changed by its incorporation into the Islamic world?

At the same time as India was being subjected to Turkic invasion, so too was Anatolia (now modern Turkey), where the largely Christian and Greek-speaking population was then governed by the Byzantine Empire (see Map 9.2, p. 420, and Map 9.5). Here, as in India, the invaders initially wreaked havoc as Byzantine authority melted away in the eleventh century. Sufi practitioners likewise played a major role in the process of conversion. The outcome, however, was a far more profound cultural transformation than in India. By 1500, the population was 90 percent Muslim and largely Turkic-speaking, and Anatolia was the heartland of the powerful Turkish Ottoman Empire that had overrun Christian Byzantium. Why did the Turkic intrusion into Anatolia generate a much more thorough Islamization than in India?

One factor clearly lies in a very different demographic balance. The population of Anatolia—perhaps 8 million—was far smaller than India's roughly 48 million people, but far more Turkic-speaking peoples settled in Anatolia, giving them a much greater cultural weight than the smaller colonizing force in India. Furthermore, the disruption of Anatolian society was much more extensive. Massacres, enslavement, famine, and flight led to a sharp drop in the native population. The Byzantine state had been fatally weakened. Church properties were confiscated, and monasteries were destroyed or deserted. Priests and bishops were sometimes unable to serve their congregations. Christians, though seldom forced to convert, suffered many discriminations. They had to wear special clothing and pay special taxes, and they were forbidden to ride saddled horses or carry swords. Not a few Christians came to believe that these disasters represented proof that Islam was the true religion.[21] Thus Byzantine civilization in Anatolia, previously focused on the centralized institutions of church and state, was rendered leaderless and dispirited, whereas India's decentralized civilization, lacking a unified political or religious establishment, was better able to absorb the shock of external invasion while retaining its core values and identity.

The Turkish rulers of Anatolia built a new society that welcomed converts and granted them material rewards and opportunity for high office. Moreover, the cultural barriers to conversion were arguably less severe than in India. The common monotheism of Islam and Christianity, and Muslim respect for Jesus and the Christian scriptures, made conversion easier than crossing the great gulf between Islam and Hinduism. Such similarities lent support to the suggestion of some Sufi teachers that the two religions were but different versions of the same faith. Sufis also established schools, mills, orchards, hospices, and rest places for travelers and thus replaced the destroyed or decaying institutions of Christian Anatolia.[22] All of this contributed to the thorough religious transformation of Anatolia and laid a foundation for the Ottoman Empire, which by 1500 became the most impressive and powerful state within the Islamic world.

But the Islamization of Anatolia occurred within a distinctly Turkish context. A Turkish language, not Arabic, predominated. Some Sufi religious practices, such as ecstatic turning dances, derived from Central Asian Turkic shamanism (see Visual Source 7.5, p. 362). And Turkic

Map 9.5 The Ottoman Empire by the Mid-fifteenth Century
As Turkic-speaking migrants bearing the religion of Islam penetrated Anatolia, the Ottoman Empire took shape, reaching into southeastern Europe and finally displacing the Christian Byzantine Empire. Subsequently, it came to control much of the Middle East and North Africa as well.

traditions offering a freer, more gender-equal life for women, common among pastoral people, persisted well after conversion to Islam, much to the distress of the Arab Moroccan visitor Ibn Battuta during his travels among them in the fourteenth century: "A remarkable thing that I saw . . . was the respect shown to women by the Turks, for they hold a more dignified position than the men. . . . The windows of the tent are open and her face is visible, for the Turkish women do not veil themselves."[23] He was not pleased.

The Case of West Africa

Still another pattern of Islamic expansion prevailed in West Africa. Here Islam accompanied Muslim traders across the Sahara rather than being brought by invading Arab or Turkic armies. Its gradual acceptance in the emerging civilization of West African states in the centuries after 1000 was largely peaceful and voluntary, lacking the incentives associated elsewhere with foreign conquest. Introduced by Muslim merchants from an already Islamized North Africa, the new faith was accepted primarily in the urban centers of the West African empires—Ghana, Mali, Songhay, Kanem-Bornu, and others (see Map 9.6 and the portrait of Mansa Musa, pp. 434–35). For African merchant communities, Islam provided an important link to Muslim trading partners, much as Buddhism had done in Southeast Asia. For the monarchs and their courts, it offered a source of literate officials to assist in state administration as well as religious legiti-

Map 9.6 West Africa and the World of Islam Both trans-Saharan commerce and Islam linked the civilization of West Africa to the larger Muslim world.

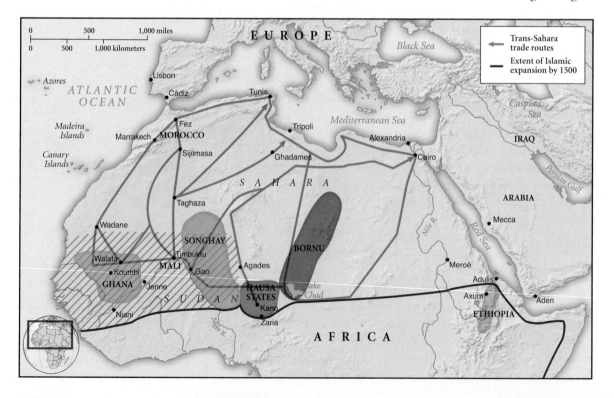

macy, particularly for those who gained the prestige conferred by a pilgrimage to Mecca. Islam was a world religion with a single Creator-God, able to comfort and protect people whose political and economic horizons had expanded well beyond the local realm where ancestral spirits and traditional deities might be effective. It had a religious appeal for societies that were now participating in a wider world.

By the sixteenth century, a number of West African cities had become major centers of Islamic religious and intellectual life, attracting scholars from through-

The Great Mosque at Jenne
This mosque in the city of Jenne, initially constructed in the thirteenth century, illustrates the assimilation of Islam into West African civilization. (Antonello Lanzelloto/age fotostock)

out the Muslim world. Timbuktu boasted more than 150 lower-level Quranic schools and several major centers of higher education with thousands of students from all over West Africa and beyond. Libraries held tens of thousands of books and scholarly manuscripts (see the image on p. 439). Monarchs subsidized the construction of mosques as West Africa became an integral part of a larger Islamic world. Arabic became an important language of religion, education, administration, and trade, but it did not become the dominant language of daily life. Nor did West Africa experience the massive migration of Arab peoples that had promoted the Arabization of North Africa and the Middle East. Moreover, in contrast to India and Anatolia, Sufi holy men played a far more modest role until at least the eighteenth century. Scholars, merchants, and rulers, rather than mystic preachers, initially established Islam in West Africa.

Islam remained the culture of urban elites and spread little into the rural areas of West Africa until the nineteenth century. No thorough religious transformation occurred in West Africa as it had in Anatolia. Although many rulers adopted Islam, they governed people who steadfastly practiced African religions and whose sensibilities they had to respect if social peace were to prevail. Thus they made few efforts to impose the new religion on their rural subjects or to govern in strict accordance with Islamic law. The fourteenth-century Arab visitor Ibn Battuta was appalled that practicing Muslims in Mali permitted their women to appear in public almost naked and to mingle freely with unrelated men. "The association of women with men is agreeable to us," he was told, "and a part of good conduct to which no suspicion attaches. They are not like the women of your country."[24] Ibn Battuta also noted with disapproval a "dance of the masks" on the occasion of an Islamic festival and the traditional practice of sprinkling dust on their heads as a sign of respect for the king. (See Document 7.3, pp. 350–53, for a fuller account of Ibn Battuta's travels in West Africa.) Sonni Ali, a fifteenth-century ruler of Songhay, observed Ramadan and built mosques, but he also consulted traditional diviners and performed customary sacrifices. In such ways, Islam became Africanized even as parts of West Africa became Islamized.

PORTRAIT

Mansa Musa, West African Monarch and Muslim Pilgrim

In 1324, Mansa Musa, the ruler or *mansa* of the Kingdom of Mali, set out on an arduous journey from his West African homeland to the holy city of Mecca. His kingdom stretched from the Atlantic coast a thousand miles or more to the fabled inland city of Timbuktu and beyond, even as his pilgrimage to Mecca reflected the growing penetration of Islam in this emerging West African civilization. Mansa Musa was a pious Muslim, fluent in Arabic, inclined on occasion to free a few slaves, and an avid builder of mosques.

Mansa Musa (Bibliothèque nationale de France)

In the fourteenth century, Mali was an expanding empire. According to Musa, one of his immediate predecessors had launched a substantial maritime expedition "to discover the furthest limits of the Atlantic Ocean."[25] The voyagers never returned, and no other record of it exists, but it is intriguing to consider that Africans and Europeans alike may have been exploring the Atlantic at roughly the same time. Mansa Musa, however, was more inclined to expand on land as he sought access to the gold fields to the south and the trans-Saharan trade network to the north.

Control of this lucrative commercial complex enriched Mansa Musa's empire, enabled a major building program of mosques and palaces, and turned the city of Timbuktu into a thriving center of trade, religion, and intellectual life. Merchants and scholars from across West and North Africa flocked to the city.

Mansa Musa's journey to Mecca has fascinated observers then and now. Such a pilgrimage has long been one of the duties—and privileges—of all Muslims. It also added the prestigious title of *hajji* to their names. For rulers in particular it conveyed a spiritual power known as *baraka*, which helped legitimate their rule.

When Mansa Musa began his journey in 1324, he was accompanied by an enormous entourage, with thousands of fellow pilgrims, some 500 slaves, his wife and other women, hundreds of camels, and a huge quantity of gold. It was the gold that attracted the most attention, as he distributed it lavishly along his journey. Egyptian sources reported that the value of gold in their country was depressed for years after his visit. On his return trip, Mansa

The Case of Spain

The chief site of Islamic encounter with Christian Europe occurred in Spain, called al-Andalus by Muslims, which was conquered by Arab and Berber forces in the early eighth century during the first wave of Islamic expansion. By the tenth century, Muslim Spain was a vibrant civilization, often portrayed as a place of harmony and tolerance between its Muslim rulers and its Christian and Jewish subjects.

Certainly Spain's agricultural economy was the most prosperous in Europe during this time and its capital of Córdoba was among the largest and most splendid cities in the world. Muslims, Christians, and Jews alike contributed to a brilliant high culture in which astronomy, medicine, the arts, architecture, and literature flourished. Furthermore, social relationships among upper-class members of different faiths were easy and frequent. By 1000, perhaps 75 percent of the population had converted to Islam. Many of the remaining Christians learned Arabic, veiled their women, stopped eating pork, appreciated Arabic music and poetry, and sometimes married Muslims. One Chris-

Musa apparently had exhausted his supply and had to borrow money from Egyptian merchants at high interest rates. Those merchants also made a killing on Musa's pilgrims, who, unsophisticated in big-city shopping, were made to pay far more than their purchases were worth. Europeans too now became aware of Mansa Musa, featuring him holding a large nugget of gold in a famous map from 1375 with a caption reading: "This Negro lord is called Musa Mali. . . . So abundant is the gold found in his country that he is the richest and most noble king in all the land."[26]

In Cairo, Mansa Musa displayed both his pride and his ignorance of Islamic law. Invited to see the sultan of Egypt, he was initially reluctant because of a protocol requirement to kiss the ground and the sultan's hand. He consented only when he was persuaded that he was really prostrating before God, not the sultan. And in conversation with learned clerics, Mansa Musa was surprised to learn that Muslim rulers were not allowed to take the beautiful unmarried women of their realm as concubines. "By God, I did not know that," he replied. "I hereby leave it and abandon it utterly."[27]

In Mecca, Mansa Musa completed the requirements of the hajj, dressing in the common garb of all pilgrims, repeatedly circling the Kaaba, performing ritual prayers, and visiting various sites associated with Muhammad's life, including a side trip to the Prophet's tomb in Medina. He also sought to recruit a number of sharifs, prestigious descendants of Muhammad's family, to add Islamic luster to his kingdom. After considerable difficulty and expense, he found four men who were willing to return with him to what Arabs understood to be the remote frontier of the Islamic world. Some reports suggested that they were simply freed slaves, hoping for better lives.

In the end, perhaps Mansa Musa's goals for the pilgrimage were achieved. On a personal level, one source reported that he was so moved by the pilgrimage that he actually considered abandoning his throne altogether and returning to Mecca where he might live as "a dweller near the sanctuary [the Kaaba]."[28] His visit certainly elevated Mali's status in the Islamic world. Some 200 years after that visit, one account of his pilgrimage placed the Sultan of Mali as one of four major rulers in the Islamic world, equal to those of Baghdad and Egypt. Mansa Musa would have been pleased.

Question: What significance did Mansa Musa likely attach to his pilgrimage? How might Egyptians, Arabians, and Europeans have viewed it?

tian bishop complained that Spanish Christians knew the rules of Arabic grammar better than those of Latin. During the reign of Abd al-Rahman III (ruled 912–961), freedom of worship was declared as well as the opportunity for all to rise in the bureaucracy of the state.

But this so-called golden age of Muslim Spain was both limited and brief. Even assimilated or Arabized Christians remained religious infidels and second-class citizens in the eyes of their Muslim counterparts, and by the late tenth century toleration began to erode. The Córdoba-based regime fragmented into numerous rival states. Warfare with the remaining Christian kingdoms in northern Spain picked up in the tenth and eleventh centuries, and more puritanical and rigid forms of Islam entered Spain from North Africa. Under the rule of al-Mansur (ruled 981–1002), an official policy of tolerance turned to one of overt persecution against Christians, which now included the plundering of churches and the seizure of their wealth, although he employed many Christian mercenaries in his armies. Social life also changed. Devout Muslims avoided contact with Christians; Christian homes had to be built lower than those of Muslims; priests were forbidden to carry a cross or a Bible, lest they offend Muslim sensibilities; and Arabized Christians were permitted to live only in particular places. Thus, writes one scholar, "the era of harmonious interaction between Muslim and Christian in Spain came to an end, replaced by intolerance, prejudice, and mutual suspicion."[29]

That intolerance intensified as the Christian reconquest of Spain gained ground after 1200. The end came in 1492, when Ferdinand and Isabella, the Catholic monarchs of a unified Spain, took Granada, the last Muslim stronghold on the Iberian Peninsula. To Christopher Columbus, who witnessed the event before leaving on his first trans-Atlantic voyage, it was a grand Christian triumph. "I saw the royal banners of your Highnesses planted by force of arms upon the towers of the Alhambra," he wrote. To Muslims, it was a catastrophe. Tradition has it that Boabdil, the final ruler of Muslim Granada, wept as he left his beloved city for the last time. Observing his grief, Boabdil's mother famously said to him: "Thou dost weep like a woman for what thou couldst not defend as a man."

After the conquest, many Muslims were forced to emigrate, replaced by Christian settlers. While those who remained under Christian rule were legally guaranteed freedom of worship, they were forbidden to make converts, to give the call to prayer, or to go on pilgrimage. And all Jews, some 200,000 of them, were expelled from the country. In the early seventeenth century, even Muslim converts to Christianity were likewise banished from Spain. And yet cultural interchange persisted for a time. The translation of Arab texts into Latin continued under Christian rule, while Christian churches and palaces were constructed on the sites of older mosques and incorporated Islamic artistic and architectural features.

Thus Spain, unlike most other regions incorporated into the Islamic world, experienced a religious reversal as Christian rule was reestablished and Islam painfully eradicated from the Iberian Peninsula. In world historical terms, perhaps the chief significance of Muslim Spain was its role in making the rich heritage of Islamic learning available to Christian Europe. As a cross-cultural encounter, it was largely a one-way street. European scholars wanted the secular knowledge — Greek as well as Arab — that had accumulated in the Islamic world, and they flocked to Spain to acquire it. That knowledge of philosophy, mathematics, medicine, optics, astronomy, botany, and more played a major role in the making of a new European civilization in the thirteenth century and beyond. Muslim Spain remained only as a memory.

SUMMING UP SO FAR

"Islam had a revolutionary impact on every society that it touched." What evidence might support this statement, and what might challenge it?

The World of Islam as a New Civilization

As the religion spread and the Abbasid dynasty declined, the civilization of Islam, unlike that of China but similar to Western Christendom, operated without a dominant political center, bound more by a shared religious culture than by a shared state. Twice that civilization was threatened from outside. The most serious intrusion came during the thirteenth century from the Mongols, whose conquest of Central Asia and Persia proved devastating while incorporating many Muslims within the huge Mongol domains (see Chapter 11). Less serious but more well known, at least in the West, were the Christian crusaders who established in the twelfth and thirteenth centuries several small and temporary outposts along the eastern Mediterranean (see Chapter 10).

Despite these external threats and its various internal conflicts, Islamic civilization flourished and often prospered, embracing at least parts of virtually every other civilization in the Afro-Eurasian hemisphere. It was in that sense "history's first truly global civilization," although the Americas, of course, were not involved.[30] What held the Islamic world together? What enabled many people to feel themselves part of a single civilization despite its political fragmentation, religious controversies, and cultural and regional diversity?

Networks of Faith

At the core of that vast civilization was a common commitment to Islam. No group was more important in the transmission of those beliefs and practices than the ulama. These learned scholars were not "priests" in the Christian sense, for in Islam, at least theoretically, no person could stand between the believer and Allah. Rather they served as judges, interpreters, administrators, prayer leaders, and reciters of the Quran, but especially as preservers and teachers of the sharia. Supported mostly by their local communities, some also received the patronage of sultans, or rulers, and were therefore subject to criticism for corruption and undue submission to state authority. In their homes, mosques, shrines, and Quranic schools, the ulama passed on the core teachings of the faith. Beginning in the eleventh century, formal colleges called *madrassas* offered more advanced instruction in the Quran and the sayings of Muhammad; grammar and rhetoric; sometimes philosophy, theology, mathematics, and medicine; and, above all else, law. Teaching was informal, mostly oral, and involved much memorization of texts. It was also largely conservative, seeking to preserve an established body of Islamic learning.

The ulama were an "international elite," and the system of education they created served to bind together an immense and diverse civilization. Common texts were shared widely across the world of Islam. Students and teachers alike traveled great distances in search of the most learned scholars. From Indonesia to West Africa, educated Muslims inhabited a "shared world of debate and reference."[31]

Paralleling the educational network of the ulama were the emerging religious orders of the Sufis. By the tenth century, particular Sufi *shaykhs* (shakes), or teachers, began to attract groups of disciples who were eager to learn their unique devotional practices and techniques of personal transformation. The disciples usually swore allegiance to their teacher and valued highly the chain of transmission by which those teachings and practices had come down from earlier masters. In the twelfth and thirteenth centuries, Sufis began to organize in a variety of larger associations, some limited to particular regions and others with chapters throughout the Islamic world. The

■ **Description**

What makes it possible to speak of the Islamic world as a distinct and coherent civilization?

Qadiriya order, for example, began in Baghdad but spread widely throughout the Arab world and into sub-Saharan Africa.

Sufi orders were especially significant in the frontier regions of Islam because they followed conquering armies or traders into Central and Southeast Asia, India, Anatolia, parts of Africa, and elsewhere. Their devotional teachings, modest ways of living, and reputation for supernatural powers gained a hearing for the new faith. Their emphasis on personal experience of the Divine, rather than on the law, allowed the Sufis to accommodate elements of local belief and practice and encouraged the growth of a popular or blended Islam. The veneration of deceased Sufi "saints," or "friends of God," particularly at their tombs, created sacred spaces that enabled Islam to take root in many places despite its foreign origins. But that flexibility also often earned Sufi practitioners the enmity of the ulama, who were sharply critical of any deviations from the sharia.

Like the madrassas and the sharia, Sufi religious ideas and institutions spanned the Islamic world and were yet another thread in the cosmopolitan web of Islamic civilization. Particular devotional teachings and practices spread widely, as did the writings of such famous Sufi poets as Hafiz and Rumi. (For the poetry of Rumi, see Document 9.4, pp. 451–52.) Devotees made pilgrimages to the distant tombs of famous teachers, who, they often believed, might intercede with God on their behalf. Wandering Sufis, in search of the wisdom of renowned shaykhs, found fellow seekers and welcome shelter in the compounds of these religious orders.

In addition to the networks of the Sufis and the ulama, many thousands of people, from kings to peasants, made the grand pilgrimage to Mecca—the hajj—no doubt gaining some sense of the umma. There men and women together, hailing from all over the Islamic world, joined as one people to rehearse the central elements of their faith. The claims of local identities based on family, clan, tribe, ethnicity, or state never disappeared, but now overarching them all was the inclusive unity of the Muslim community.

Networks of Exchange

■ **Connection**

In what ways was the world of Islam a "cosmopolitan civilization"?

The world of Islamic civilization cohered not only as a network of faith but also as an immense arena of exchange in which goods, technologies, food products, and ideas circulated widely. It rapidly became a vast trading zone of hemispheric dimensions. In part, this was due to its central location in the Afro-Eurasian world and the breaking down of earlier political barriers between the Byzantine and Persian empires. Furthermore, commerce was valued positively within Islamic teaching, for Muhammad himself had been a trader. The pilgrimage to Mecca, as well as the urbanization that accompanied the growth of Islamic civilization, likewise fostered commerce. Baghdad, established in 756 as the capital of the Abbasid Empire, soon grew into a magnificent city of half a million people. The appetite of urban elites for luxury goods stimulated both craft production and the desire for foreign products.

Thus Muslim merchants, Arabs and Persians in particular, quickly became prominent and sometimes dominant players in all of the major Afro-Eurasian trade routes of the third-wave era—in the Mediterranean Sea, along the revived Silk Roads, across the Sahara, and throughout the Indian Ocean basin (see Chapter 7). By the eighth century, Arab and Persian traders had established a commercial colony in Canton in southern China, thus linking the Islamic heartland with Asia's other giant and flourishing economy. Various forms of banking, partnerships, business contracts, and instruments for granting credit facilitated these long-distance economic relationships and generated a prosperous, sophisticated, and highly commercialized economy that spanned the Old World.[32]

The vast expanses of Islamic civilization also contributed to ecological change as agricultural products and practices spread from one region to another, a process already under way in the earlier Roman and Persian empires. The Muslim conquest of northwestern India opened the Middle East to a veritable treasure trove of crops that had been domesticated long before in South and Southeast Asia, including rice, sugarcane, new strains of sorghum, hard wheat, bananas, lemons, limes, watermelons, coconut palms, spinach, artichokes, and cotton. Some of these subsequently found their way into the Middle East and Africa and by the thirteenth century to Europe as well.[33] Both cotton and sugarcane, associated with complex production processes and slave labor, came to play central roles in the formation of the modern global system after 1500. These new crops, together with the diffusion of Middle Eastern and Indian irrigation systems, contributed to an "Islamic Green Revolution" of increased food production as well as to population growth, urbanization, and industrial development across the Islamic world.

A Muslim Astronomical Observatory
Drawing initially on Greek, Indian, and Persian astronomy, the Islamic world after 1000 developed its own distinctive tradition of astronomical observation and prediction, reflected in this Turkish observatory constructed in 1557. Muslim astronomy subsequently exercised considerable influence in both China and Europe. (University Library, Istanbul, Turkey/The Bridgeman Art Library)

Technology too diffused widely within the realm of Islam. Ancient Persian techniques for obtaining water by drilling into the sides of hills now spread across North Africa as far west as Morocco. Muslim technicians made improvements on rockets, first developed in China, by developing one that carried a small warhead and another used to attack ships.[34] Papermaking techniques entered the Abbasid Empire from China in the eighth century, with paper mills soon operating in Persia, Iraq, and Egypt. This revolutionary technology, which everywhere served to strengthen bureaucratic governments, passed from the Middle East into India and Europe over the following centuries.

Ideas likewise circulated across the Islamic world. The religion itself drew heavily and quite openly on Jewish and Christian precedents. Persia also contributed much in the way of bureaucratic practice, court ritual, and poetry, with Persian becoming a major literary language in elite circles. Scientific, medical, and philosophical texts, especially from ancient Greece, the Hellenistic world, and India, were systematically

Snapshot   **Key Achievements in Islamic Science and Scholarship**

Person/Dates	Achievement
al-Khwarazim (790–840)	Mathematician; spread use of Arabic numerals in Islamic world; wrote first book on algebra
al-Razi (865–925)	Discovered sulfuric acid; wrote a vast encyclopedia of medicine drawing on Greek, Syrian, Indian, and Persian work and his own clinical observation
al-Biruni (973–1048)	Mathematician, astronomer, cartographer; calculated the radius of the earth with great accuracy; worked out numerous mathematical innovations; developed a technique for displaying a hemisphere on a plane
Ibn Sina (Avicenna) (980–1037)	Prolific writer in almost all fields of science and philosophy; especially known for *Canon of Medicine*, a fourteen-volume work that set standards for medical practice in Islamic and Christian worlds for centuries
Omar Khayyam (1048–1131)	Mathematician; critic of Euclid's geometry; measured the solar year with great accuracy; Sufi poet; author of *The Rubaiyat*
Ibn Rushd (Averroës) (1126–1198)	Translated and commented widely on Aristotle; rationalist philosopher; made major contributions in law, mathematics, and medicine
Nasir al-Din Tusi (1201–1274)	Founder of the famous Maragha observatory in Persia (data from Maragha probably influenced Copernicus); mapped the motion of stars and planets
Ibn Khaldun (1332–1406)	Greatest Arab historian; identified trends and structures in world history over long periods of time

translated into Arabic, for several centuries providing an enormous boost to Islamic scholarship and science. In 830, the Abbasid caliph al-Mamun, himself a poet and scholar with a passion for foreign learning, established the House of Wisdom in Baghdad as an academic center for this research and translation. Stimulated by Greek texts, a school of Islamic thinkers known as Mutazalites ("those who stand apart") argued that reason, rather than revelation, was the "surest way to truth."[35] In the long run, however, the philosophers' emphasis on logic, rationality, and the laws of nature was subject to increasing criticism by those who held that only the Quran, the sayings of the Prophet, or mystical experience represented a genuine path to God.

But the realm of Islam was much more than a museum of ancient achievements from the civilizations that it encompassed. Those traditions mixed and blended to generate a distinctive Islamic civilization with many new contributions to the world of learning.[36] (See the Snapshot on p. 440.) Using Indian numerical notation, for example, Arab scholars developed algebra as a novel mathematical discipline. They also undertook much original work in astronomy and optics. They built on earlier Greek and Indian practice to create a remarkable tradition in medicine and pharmacology. Arab physicians such as al-Razi and Ibn Sina accurately diagnosed many diseases, such as hay fever, measles, smallpox, diphtheria, rabies, and diabetes. In addition, treatments such as using a mercury ointment for scabies, cataract and hernia operations, and filling teeth with gold emerged from Arab doctors. The first hospitals, traveling clinics, and examinations for physicians and pharmacologists also were developed within the Islamic world. In the eleventh and twelfth centuries, this enormous body of Arab medical scholarship entered Europe via Spain, and it remained at the core of European medical practice for many centuries.[37]

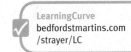

LearningCurve
bedfordstmartins.com
/strayer/LC

Reflections: Past and Present: Choosing Our History

Prominent among the many uses of history is the perspective it provides on the present. Although historians sometimes worry that an excessive "present-mindedness" may distort our perception of the past, all of us look to history, almost instinctively, to comprehend the world we now inhabit. Given the obvious importance of the Islamic world in the international arena of the twenty-first century, how might some grasp of the early development of Islamic civilization assist us in understanding our present circumstances?

Certainly that history reminds us of the central role that Islam played in the Afro-Eurasian world for a thousand years or more. From 600 to 1600 or later, it was a proud, cosmopolitan, often prosperous, and frequently powerful civilization that spanned Africa, Europe, the Middle East, and Asia. What followed were several centuries of European or Western imperialism that many Muslims found humiliating, even if some were attracted by elements of modern Western culture. In their recent efforts to overcome those centuries of subordination and exploitation, Muslims have found encouragement and inspiration in reflecting on the more distant and perhaps more glorious past. But they have not all chosen to emphasize the same past. Those labeled as "fundamentalists" have often viewed the early Islamic community associated with Medina, Mecca, and Muhammad as a model for Islamic renewal in the present. Others, often known as Islamic modernizers, have looked to the somewhat later achievements of Islamic science and scholarship as a foundation for a more open engagement with the West and the modern world.

The history of Islam also reveals to us a world of great diversity and debate. Sharp religious differences between Sunni and Shia understandings of the faith; differences in emphasis between advocates of the sharia and of Sufi spirituality; political conflicts among various groups and regions within the larger Islamic world; different postures toward women in Arab lands and in West Africa—all of this and more divided the umma and divide it still. Recalling that diversity is a useful reminder for any who would tag all Muslims with a single label.

A further dimension of that diversity lies in the many cultural encounters that the spread of Islam has spawned. Sometimes great conflict and violence have accompanied those encounters as in the Crusades and in Turkic invasions of India and Anatolia. At other times and places, Muslims and non-Muslims have lived together in relative tranquility and tolerance—in Spain, in West Africa, in India, and in the Ottoman Empire. Some commentaries on the current interaction of Islam and the West seem to assume an eternal hostility or an inevitable clash of civilizations. The record of the past, however, shows considerable variation in the interaction of Muslims and others. While the past certainly shapes and conditions what happens next, the future, as always, remains open. Within limits, we can choose the history on which we seek to build.

Second Thoughts

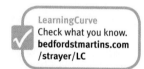

LearningCurve
Check what you know.
**bedfordstmartins.com
/strayer/LC**

Online Study Guide
bedfordstmartins.com
/highschool/strayer

What's the Significance?

Quran, 415–16

umma, 416

Pillars of Islam, 416

hijra, 417

sharia, 418

jizya, 420

ulama, 423, 437

Umayyad caliphate, 423–24

Abbasid caliphate, 424

Sufism, 424–25

al-Ghazali, 425

Sikhism, 430

Ibn Battuta, 432–33

Timbuktu, 433

Mansa Musa, 434–35

al-Andalus, 434–36

madrassas, 437

House of Wisdom, 440

Ibn Sina, 440–41

Big Picture Questions

1. How might you account for the immense religious and political/military success of Islam in its early centuries?

2. In what ways might Islamic civilization be described as cosmopolitan, international, or global?

3. "Islam was simultaneously a single world of shared meaning and interaction and a series of separate, distinct, and conflicting communities." What evidence could you provide to support both sides of this argument?

4. What changes did Islamic expansion generate in those societies that encountered it, and how was Islam itself transformed by those encounters?

5. **Looking Back:** What distinguished the early centuries of Islamic history from a similar phase in the history of Christianity and Buddhism?

Next Steps: For Further Study

Reza Aslan, *No God but God* (2005). A well-written and popular history of Islam by an Iranian immigrant to the United States.

Fred M. Donner, *Muhammad and the Believers* (2010). An innovative account of the first century of Islam by a leading scholar of that era.

Richard Eaton, *Islamic History as Global History* (1990). A short account by a major scholar that examines Islam in a global framework.

John Esposito, ed., *The Oxford History of Islam* (1999). Up-to-date essays on various periods and themes in Islamic history. Beautifully illustrated.

Francis Robinson, ed., *Cambridge Illustrated History of the Islamic World* (1996). A series of essays by major scholars, with lovely pictures and maps.

Judith Tucker, *Gender and Islamic History* (1994). A brief overview of the changing lives of Islamic women.

"The Travels of Ibn Battuta: A Virtual Tour with the Fourteenth Century Traveler," http://fms-sfusd-ca .schoolloop.com/Battuta. A beautifully illustrated journey across the Islamic world in the early 1300s.

For Web sites and additional documents related to this chapter, see **Make History** at bedfordstmartins.com /highschool/strayer.

Documents

Considering the Evidence: Voices of Islam

Like all great religious traditions, Islam found expression in various forms. Its primary text, the Quran, claimed to represent the voice of the Divine, God's final revelation to humankind. Other early Islamic writings, known as hadith, recorded the sayings and deeds of the Prophet Muhammad. Still others reflected the growing body of Islamic law, the sharia, which sought to construct a social order aligned with basic religious teachings. Devotional practices and expressions of adoration for Allah represented yet another body of Islamic literature. All of this gave rise to differing interpretations and contending views, generating for Islam a rich and complex literary tradition that has been the source of inspiration and debate for almost 1,400 years. From this immense body of work, we present just a few samples of the voices of Islam.

Document 9.1

The Voice of Allah

To Muslims, the Quran contains the very words of God. The Arabic term *quran* itself means "recitation," and the faithful believe that the angel Gabriel spoke God's words to Muhammad, who then recited them. Often called "noble" or "glorious," the Quran, compiled into an established text within thirty years of the Prophet's death, was regarded as a book without equal, written in the most sublime Arabic. Copying it was an act of piety, memorizing it was the starting point for Muslim education, and reciting it was both an art form and a high honor. Organized in 114 Surahs (chapters), the Quran was revealed to Muhammad over a period of some twenty-two years. Often the revelations came in response to particular problems that the young Islamic community and the Prophet were facing. The selections that follow convey something of the Quran's understanding of God, of humankind, of the social life prescribed for believers, of relations with non-Muslims, and much more.

■ How does the Quran's understanding of Allah resemble Jewish and Christian ideas about God, and how does it differ from them?

- What specific prescriptions for social life do these selections contain? Notice in particular those directed toward the weakest members of society. How would you describe the Quran's view of a good society?

- What attitudes toward non-Muslims do these passages suggest?

- What circumstances surrounding the birth of Islam might help to explain the references in the Quran to fighting and warfare?

- The sacred texts of all religious traditions provide ample room for conflicting understandings and interpretations. What debates or controversies might arise from these passages?

The Quran
Seventh Century C.E.

On God/Allah

In the name of God, the infinitely compassionate and infinitely merciful. Praise be to God, Lord of all the worlds; the compassionate, the merciful; Ruler on the Day of Reckoning. You alone do we worship, and You alone do we ask for help. Guide us on the straight path, the path of those who have received your grace, not the path of those who have brought down wrath, nor of those who wander astray. (1)

In the name of Allah, the beneficient, the merciful. Say: He is Allah, the One. He is Allah, the eternal, who was never born nor ever gave birth. The One beyond compare. (112)

Wherever you turn, there is the face of God. (2:115)

Now verily, it is We who have created man, and We know what his innermost self whispers within him: for We are closer to him than his neck-vein. (50:16)

We will show them Our signs on the farthest horizons, and within their own selves, until it becomes manifest to them that this is the Truth. (41:53)

On Jesus

Behold! the angels said, 'Oh Mary! God gives you glad tidings of a Word from Him. His name will be Christ Jesus, the son of Mary, held in honour in this world and the Hereafter, and in (the company of) those nearest to God. He shall speak to the people in childhood and in maturity. He shall be (in the company) of the righteous. . . . And God will teach him the Book and Wisdom, the Law and the Gospel.' (3:45–48)

On Society

And thus have We willed you to be a community of the middle way, so that [with your lives] you might bear witness to the truth before all mankind. . . . (2:143)

Behold, those who sinfully devour the possessions of orphans but fill their bellies with fire: for [in the life to come] they will have to endure a blazing flame! (4:10)

You shall do good unto your parents and kinsfolk, and the orphans, and the poor; and you shall speak unto all people in a kindly way; and you shall be constant in prayer; and you shall spend in charity. (2:83)

And if any of those whom you rightfully possess [slaves] desire [to obtain] a deed of freedom, write it out for them if you are aware of any good in them: and give them [their] share of the wealth of God

Source: Muhammad Asad, *The Message of the Qur'ān* (Bristol: Book Foundation, 2003).

which He has given you. And do not, in order to gain some of the fleeting pleasures of this worldly life, coerce your [slave] maidens into whoredom if they happen to be desirous of marriage.... (24:33)

On Men and Women

Verily, for all men and women who have surrendered themselves unto God ..., and all men and women who give in charity, and all self-denying men and self-denying women, and all men and women who are mindful of their chastity, and all men and women who remember God unceasingly: for [all of] them has God readied forgiveness of sins and a mighty reward. (33:35)

Men are the protectors and maintainers of women, because God has given the one more (strength) than the other, and because they support them from their means. Therefore the righteous women are devoutly obedient, and guard in (the husband's) absence what God would have them guard. As to those women on whose part ye fear disloyalty and ill-conduct, admonish them (first), (Next), refuse to share their beds, (And last) beat them (lightly); but if they return to obedience, seek not against them Means (of annoyance): For God is Most High, great (above you all). (4:34)

O you who believe. You are forbidden to inherit women against their will. Nor should you treat them with harshness.... On the contrary, live with them on a footing of kindness and equity. (4:19)

On War and Jihad

There shall be no coercion in matters of faith. (2:256)

And fight in God's cause against those who wage war against you, but do not commit aggression, for, verily, God does not love aggressors. And slay them wherever you may come upon them, and drive them away from wherever they drove you away, for oppression is even worse than killing. And fight not against them near the Inviolable House of Worship unless they fight against you there first, but if they fight against you, slay them: such shall be the recompense of those who deny the truth. (2:190–92)

Now when you meet [in war] those who are bent on denying the truth, smite their necks until you overcome them fully, and then tighten their bonds; but thereafter [set them free,] either by an act of grace or against ransom, so that the burden of war may be lifted.... And as for those who are slain in God's cause, never will He let their deeds go to waste. (47:4)

On Tolerance

And tell My servants that they should speak in the most kindly manner [unto those who do not share their beliefs]: verily, Satan is always ready to stir up discord between men.... (17:53)

Unto every community have We appointed [different] ways of worship, which they ought to observe. (22:67)

Unto every one of you have We appointed a [different] law and way of life. And if God had so willed, He could surely have made you all one single community: but [He willed it otherwise] in order to test you....Vie, then, with one another in doing good works! (5:48)

All believers are but brethren. Hence, [whenever they are at odds,] make peace between your two brethren, and remain conscious of God, so that you might be graced with His mercy. (49:10)

Make no distinction between any of God's messengers; for they all say, "We have heard and we pay heed." Grant us your forgiveness, O our Sustainer, for it is with You that all journeys end. (2:285)

Document 9.2

The Voice of the Prophet Muhammad

As an expression of Islam, the sayings and deeds of Muhammad, known as the hadiths, are second in importance only to the Quran. In various collections of hadiths, Muslims hear the voice and witness the actions of their prophet. While they do not have the authority of divine revelation, these statements have served to guide and inspire Muslims to this day.

In the several centuries following his death, an enormous number of stories about Muhammad circulated within the Islamic community. Scholars gradually developed methods of authentication designed to discover which of these stories most reliably represented the Prophet's words and actions. Considerable controversy accompanied this process, and no single collection of hadiths has ever achieved universal acceptance. One of the earliest and most highly respected of these collections was the work the Persian scholar al-Bukhari (810–870). Traveling extensively throughout the Islamic world, al-Bukhari is said to have collected some 600,000 stories, memorized 200,000 of them, and finally authenticated and published 7,275. The selections that follow suggest something of the range and variety of the hadiths, particularly as they relate to social life.

- What portrait of Muhammad emerges from this record of his sayings and actions?

- How do these hadiths reflect or build on the teaching of the Quran in Document 9.1?

- What religious and social values do these hadiths highlight?

- In what ways do these hadiths reflect common themes in many of the world's "wisdom traditions," and in what respects are they distinctly Islamic?

The Hadith
Eighth and Ninth Centuries

If a slave serves honestly his [earthly] master and worships earnestly his [heavenly] Lord, he will have a double recompense.

He who shows concern for the widows and the unfortunate [ranks as high] as one who goes on Jihād

in the way of Allah, or one who fasts by day and who rises at night [for prayer].

In this world be as a stranger, or as one who is just passing along the road.

To look at a woman is forbidden, even if it is a look without desire, so how much the more is touching her.

Said he—upon whom be Allah's blessing and peace—"Avoid seven pernicious things." [His

Source: Arthur Jeffery, ed. and trans., *A Reader on Islam* (The Hague: Mouton, 1962), 81–86.

Companions] said: "And what are they, O Apostle of Allah?" He answered: "Associating anything with Allah, sorcery, depriving anyone of life where Allah has forbidden that save for just cause, taking usury, devouring the property of orphans, turning the back on the day of battle, and slandering chaste believing women even though they may be acting carelessly."

To be stationed on the frontier for one day during Holy War is better than (to possess) this world and all that is on it. A place in Paradise the size of one of your whip-lashes is better than this world and all that is on it....

If a man sees something in [the conduct of] his ruler which he dislikes let him put up with it patiently, for there is no one who separates himself even a span from the community and dies [in that separation], but dies a pagan death....

Said the Prophet ... : "I had a look into Paradise and I saw that the poor made up most of its inhabitants, and I had a look into Hell and saw that most of its inhabitants were women...."

Treat women-folk kindly, for woman was created of a rib.

Said the Apostle of Allah ... : "O band of youths, let him among you who is able to make a home get married, and let him who is not able betake himself to fasting for he will find in that a quencher [of his passions]."

The worst of foods is that of a feast to which the rich have been invited and the poor overlooked....

Said the Apostle of Allah ... : "Do not wear silks and satins, and do not drink from gold and silver vessels nor eat from dishes made thereof, for these things are theirs in this world but ours in the world to come." ...

Said the Prophet ... : "He who drinks wine in this world and repents not of it will be forbidden it in the world to come." ...

Al-Aqra said: "I have ten sons but never have I kissed any one of them." The Apostle of Allah ... looked at him, and then said: "He who does not show tenderness will not have tenderness shown him."

Document 9.3

The Voice of the Law

While Christian scholarship emphasized theology and correct belief, learned Muslims gave more attention to law and correct behavior. That law was known as the sharia, an Arabic term that referred to a path toward water, which is the source of life. To many Muslims, that was the role of law—to construct the good society within which an authentic religious life could find expression.

The sharia emerged as the early Islamic community confronted the practical problems of an expanding empire with a very diverse population. But no single legal framework developed. Rather, four major schools of Islamic law crystallized, agreeing on fundamentals but differing in emphasis. How much weight should be given to the hadiths and which of them were most reliably authentic? What scope should reason and judgment have in applying religious principles to particular circumstances? Despite disagreement on such questions, each of the four approaches to legal interpretation sought to be all-embracing, providing highly detailed guidance on ritual performance, personal behavior, marriage and family matters, crime and punishment, economic transactions, and political action. The selections that follow, drawn from various legal traditions, illustrate this comprehensive nature of Islamic law and its centrality in an evolving Islamic civilization.

■ What do you find most striking about the legal prescriptions in these passages?

■ In what ways do these selections draw on and apply the teachings of the Quran and the hadiths?

■ How does the role of law in early Islamic civilization differ from that of modern Western society?

■ Why do you think the role of law was so central, so highly detailed, and so comprehensive in Islamic civilization?

■ What do this document and Document 9.2 suggest about the problems that the early Islamic community confronted?

The Sharia
Ninth Century

On Prayer

The five prayers are obligatory for every Muslim who has reached the age of puberty and has the use of reason, except for women who are menstruating or recovering from childbirth.

If Muslims deny the necessity of prayer through ignorance, one must instruct them; if they deny it willfully, they have apostatized. . . .

On *Zakat*°

The obligation pertains only to a free Muslim who has complete ownership of the property on which it is due. . . . *Zakat* is due only on animals, agricultural products, precious metals, objects intended for sale, the products of mines, and treasure troves.

Whoever has the obligation to pay *zakat* and is able must pay it; if not, they commit a fault for which they must answer. If anyone refuses to pay it and denies its obligatory character, they have committed apostasy and may be put to death. If they refuse it from avarice, they shall have the amount taken from them and be given a sentence at the judge's discretion.

_____

°*Zakat:* alms for the poor.

Source: John Alden Williams, trans. and ed., *The Word of Islam* (Austin: University of Texas Press, 1994), 71, 80–82, 88–89, 94–95, 98–101, 104–5.

On Marriage

[Marriage] is contracted by means of declaration and consent. When both parties are Muslims, it must be contracted in the presence of two male or one male and two female Muslim witnesses who are free, sane, and adult. . . .

It is not lawful for a man to marry two women who are sisters or to cohabit with two sisters who are his slaves. . . .

A man may not marry his slave-girl unless he sets her free first, and a woman may not marry her slave, since marriage has as its object that the children belong equally to both parents, and ownership and slavery are not equal states.

Similarly, marriage with an idolatress is forbidden, until she accepts Islam or a religion of the Book.

It is not lawful for a man already married to a free woman to marry a slave. . . . However, a man may lawfully marry a free woman after a slave.

A free man may marry four women, free or slave, but no more. It is unlawful for a slave to marry more than two women. . . .

On Government

There are ten things a Caliph° must do in public affairs:

_____

°**Caliph:** successor to Muhammad as political leader of the Islamic community.

1) Maintain religion according to its established principles.
2) Apply legal judgments for litigants so that equity reigns without aiding the oppressor or weakening the oppressed.
3) Protect the flock . . . so that people may gain their living and move from place to place securely.
4) Apply the *hudud*, or punishments of the Law, so as to secure God's prohibitions from violation.
5) Fortify the marches so that the enemy will not appear due to neglect, shedding the blood of any Muslim or protected person.
6) Wage *jihad* against those who reject Islam so that they become either Muslims or protected people.
7) Collect the *zakat* and taxes on conquered territory . . . without fear or oppression.
8) Administer treasury expenditures.
9) Delegate loyal and trustworthy people.
10) Directly oversee matters and not delegate his authority seeking to occupy himself with either pleasure or devotion. . . .

It is necessary therefore to cause the masses to act in accord with divine laws in all the affairs, both in this world and in the world to come. The authority to do so was possessed by the prophets and after them by their successors.

On Men and Women

It is not permitted to men or women to eat or drink or keep unguents° in vessels of gold or silver. . . .

It is not permitted for a man to wear silk, but it is permitted for a woman. . . .

It is not permitted for a man to wear gold or silver, except for silver on a ring, or on a weapon.

°**unguents:** ointments.

It is not permitted for a man to look at a strange woman.° . . . A woman frequently needs to bare her hands and face in transactions with men. Abu Hanifa said it was also permitted to look at her feet and Abu Yusuf said it was permitted to look at her forearms as well. . . . However, if a man is not secure from feeling lust, he should not look needlessly even at the face or hands, to avoid sin. He is not allowed to touch her face or hands even if he is free from lust, whether he be young or old.

On the Economy

It is disliked to corner the market in food for humans or animals if it occurs in a town where this may prove harmful to the people. It is disliked to sell weapons in a time of trouble.

There is no harm in selling fruit juice to someone who will make wine of it, since the transgression is not in the juice but in the wine after it has been changed. . . .

Earning a living by changing money is a great danger to the religion of the one who practices it. . . . It is the duty of the *muhtasib*° to search out the money changers' places of business and spy on them, and if he finds one of them practicing usury or doing something illegal . . . he must punish that person. . . .

Owners of ships and boats must be prevented from loading their vessels above the usual load, for fear of sinking. . . . If they carry women on the same boat with men, there must be a partition between them.

Sellers of [pottery] are not to overlay any that are pierced or cracked with gypsum . . . and then sell them as sound.

°**strange woman:** a woman from outside one's immediate family.

°**muhtasib:** an inspector of the markets.

Document 9.4

The Voice of the Sufis

Alongside the law, there ran a very different current of Islamic thinking and expression known as Sufism. The Sufis, sometimes called the "friends of God," were the mystics of Islam, those for whom the direct, personal, and intoxicating experience of Divine Presence was of far greater importance than the laws, regulations, and judgments of the sharia (see pp. 448–50). Organized in hundreds of separate orders, or "brotherhoods," the Sufis constituted one of the transregional networks that linked the far-flung domains of the Islamic world. Often they were the missionaries of Islam, introducing the faith to Anatolia, India, Central Asia, and elsewhere.

Among the most prominent exemplars of Sufi sensibility was Rumi (1207–1273), born in what is now Afghanistan and raised in a Persian cultural tradition. Rumi's family later migrated to Anatolia, and Rumi lived most of his adult life in the city of Konya, where he is buried. There he wrote extensively, including a six-volume work of rhymed couplets known as the *Mathnawi*. Following Rumi's death, his son established the Mevlevi Sufi order, based on Rumi's teachings and known in the West as the "whirling dervishes," on account of the turning dances that became a part of their practice.

Rumi's poetry has remained a sublime expression of the mystical dimension of Islamic spiritual seeking and has provided inspiration and direction for millions, both within and beyond the Islamic world. In the early twenty-first century, Rumi was the best-selling poet in the United States. The selections that follow provide a brief sample of the Sufi approach to religious life.

■ How would you define the religious sensibility of Rumi's poetry?

■ How does it differ from the approach to Islam reflected in the sharia?

■ What criticisms might the orthodox legal scholars (ulama) have made regarding the Sufi understanding of Islam?

Inscription in Rumi's Tomb
Thirteenth Century

Come, come, whoever you are,
Wanderer, worshipper, lover of leaving.
It doesn't matter.
Ours is not a caravan of despair.

Come, even if you have broken your vow a
    thousand times,
Come, yet again, come, come.

Source: A frequently quoted inscription hanging inside the tomb of Rumi and generally, though not universally, attributed to him; translator unknown.

RUMI

Poem
Thirteenth Century

I searched for God among the Christians and on the Cross and therein I found Him not.
I went into the ancient temples of idolatry; no trace of Him was there.

I entered the mountain cave of Hira and then went as far as Qandhar but God I found not....
Then I directed my search to the Kaaba, the resort of old and young; God was not there even.
Turning to philosophy I inquired about him from ibn Sina but found Him not within his range....
Finally, I looked into my own heart and there I saw Him; He was nowhere else.

Source: M. M. Sharif, *A History of Muslim Philosophy* (Wiesbaden: Harrassowitz, 1966), 2:838.

RUMI

Mathnawi
Thirteenth Century

Whether one moves slowly or with speed
the one who is a seeker will be a finder.
Always seek with your whole self,
for the search is an excellent guide on the way.
Though you are lame and limping,
though your figure is bent and clumsy,

always creep towards the One. Make that One your quest.
By speech and by silence and by fragrance,
catch the scent of the king everywhere.

Listen, open a window to God
and begin to delight yourself
by gazing upon Him through the opening.
The business of love is to make that window in the heart ...
Gaze incessantly on the face of the Beloved!
Listen, this is in your power, my friend.

Source: Camille and Kabir Helminski, trans., *Jewels of Remembrance* (Boston: Threshold Books, 1996), 8, 172.

Using the Evidence:
Voices of Islam

1. **Defining differences within Islam:** In what different ways do the various voices of Islam represented in these documents understand and express the common religious tradition of which they are all a part? What grounds for debate or controversy can you identify within or among them?

2. **Comparing religious traditions:** How would you compare Islamic religious ideas and practices with those of other traditions such as Hinduism, Buddhism, and Christianity?

3. **Considering gender and Islam:** How do these documents represent the roles of men and women in Islamic society? Pay particular attention to differences in emphasis.

4. **Seeking additional sources:** Notice that all of these documents derive from literate elites, and each of them suggests or prescribes appropriate behavior. What additional documents would you need if you were to assess the impact of these prescriptions on the lives of ordinary people? What specific questions might you want to pose to such documents?

Visual Sources

Considering the Evidence: The Life of the Prophet

In addition to the teachings of the Quran, Muslims have long revered their Prophet as the most complete expression of God-conscious humanity and an example for all who would follow the path of Islam. In the several centuries after his death, Muslim scholars collected every detail of his life and sought to draw lessons about behavior based on his moral qualities and actions: his utter devotion to Allah; his bravery and decisiveness in battle; his honesty in business affairs; his flexibility, compassion, and willingness to forgive in dealing with enemies; his habit of consulting with companions before making a decision; his generosity and kindness to the poor and enslaved. Early biographies of Muhammad also made much of his sexual virility and attraction to women, which combined with his tenderness toward them to create a new model of Islamic masculinity.[38] The images that follow illustrate four major events in the life of Muhammad, long familiar to Muslims everywhere.

These images derive from the tradition of Persian or Turkish miniature painting—small, colorful, and exquisitely detailed works often used to illustrate books or manuscripts. One art historian described them as "little festivals of color in images separated from each other by pages of text."[39] Scenes from the life of the Prophet Muhammad appeared occasionally in this art form, which flourished especially from the thirteenth through the sixteenth centuries. They provide a window into the ways Muslims have understood their prophet and sought to learn from his example.

Representation of the Prophet Muhammad has long been controversial within Islamic societies. While not prohibited in the Quran, visual depictions of the Prophet have often been discouraged or even forbidden to prevent idolatry. Nonetheless, Muhammad was on occasion portrayed in Persian and Turkish miniature painting, sometimes in full face, but often with his face obscured. Such depictions, however, were limited to illustrations of particular events in books of history or poetry. They were never used to decorate mosques or the Quran. Nor were they employed as a teaching tool or for devotional purposes as was frequently the case in Christian religious art.

According to all Muslims, the central and defining experience in Muhammad's life occurred in the year 610 C.E. in his initial encounter with an angel, usually identified as Gabriel, an event that marked the beginning of his revelations.[40] For some time before this dramatic event, Muhammad had been in the habit of withdrawing to a cave outside Mecca for prayer and meditation. On this occasion, however, a towering and overpowering presence of the angel appeared to him, filling the entire horizon, squeezing the very breath from his body, and commanding him to "recite" or to "read." After repeated protests that "I am not a reciter/reader," Muhammad found himself speaking what became the first revelation of the Quran.

When the vision passed, Muhammad fled in terror to his wife Khadija, fearing that he might be mad or possessed of some demonic spirit. Seeking to comfort him, Khadija took her husband to her learned cousin Waraqa, a Christian, who assured Muhammad that "he is the prophet of his people" and the recipient of revelation from the same God who had earlier granted similar messages to Abraham, Moses, and Jesus, among others. Further revelations followed over the next twenty-two years until Muhammad's death in 632, after which they were compiled into the Quran.

Visual Source 9.1, an early fourteenth-century Persian miniature painting, depicts this encounter between Muhammad and Gabriel.

- What impression of this encounter does the artist seek to convey by the posture of the two figures?

- What religious meaning might Muslims derive from the idea that the revelation to Muhammad came through an angelic messenger rather than directly from Allah?

- Traditional accounts of Muhammad's encounter with the angel stress the mysterious and overpowering "otherness" of the Divine Presence, which accounts for Muhammad's initial fear and terror. What is the religious significance of such a depiction of the Divine? To what extent does this image convey that impression?

- Muslims have traditionally stressed that their prophet was illiterate, based in part on his response to the angel: "I am not a reader." Why might it be important to Muslims to believe that Muhammad was illiterate?

By far the most frequently portrayed event in the life of Muhammad was the *miraj*, the Prophet's Night Journey, said to have taken place in 619 or 620. The Quran refers briefly to God taking the Prophet "from the sacred place of worship to the far distant place of worship." This passage became the basis for a story, much embellished over the centuries, of rich and deep meaning for Muslims. In this religious narrative, Muhammad was led one night by the angel Gabriel from Mecca to Jerusalem. For the journey he was given a *buraq*, a mythical winged creature with the body of a mule or donkey and the face of a woman. Upon arriving in Jerusalem, Muhammad led prayers for an assembly of earlier prophets including Abraham, Moses, and Jesus. (See p. 415 for a

■ What meaning might the artist seek to convey by the image of the world below and slightly to the right of the buraq?

■ What is the significance of Muhammad's encounter with earlier prophets such as Abraham, Moses, and Jesus? Note the Quranic reference to Jesus in Document 9.1.

■ Review the discussion of the Sufi tradition of Islam on pages 424–25. How might Sufis have understood the Night Journey? How does this Muslim metaphor for the spiritual quest compare with that of the Byzantine icon shown in Visual Source 10.3, page 511?

The circumstances of Muhammad's life required that he act as a political leader at the same time as he was seeking to convey a new religious message. By 622, intense hostility to that revolutionary message had forced him out of Mecca to a new base in Medina, where he became a lawgiver, creating a social and political framework for his small band of followers. Violent opposition from various quarters and the absence of any overall political authority in the Arabian Peninsula made it necessary for Muhammad to become also a military strategist to protect his fledgling community. In these ways his task was very different from that of the Buddha or Jesus.

Among the leading adversaries of the embryonic community of "believers" in Medina were the forces of Muhammad's own Quarysh clan in Mecca. An important turning point in that struggle occurred in 624 at the Battle of Badr in western Arabia. Despite being outnumbered more than three to one (about 1,000 Meccans but only around 300 "believers" from Medina), Muhammad's forces emerged victorious. While the Meccans fought in traditional Arab style with much individual bravado and no unified command, Muhammad's men were carefully drilled, well organized, and effectively led. To Muslims, however, it was not human ingenuity but divine intervention that occasioned this unlikely triumph. The Quran reported that Allah had sent some 3,000 angels to assist Muhammad's forces and reminded the believers that "it was not you that slew the enemy, but it was God that slew them."

This battle established the new Muslim community as a force to be reckoned with in Arabia and was enormously encouraging to the "believers." It was also the occasion for a series of revelations to Muhammad about the treatment of prisoners. They should not be abused in any way, but released, offered for ransom, or allowed to earn enough money to purchase their freedom. According to a traditional saying (hadith) of the Prophet, Muhammad asked his followers to treat captives as members of their own families. "You must feed them as you feed yourselves and clothe them as you clothe yourselves."

Visual Source 9.3, a sixteenth-century Turkish miniature painting, shows the preparation for the battle at Badr. Muhammad, shown in green dress with his face obscured, is sending waves of horsemen into the struggle. While others of his followers watch from behind, two of his close associates appear at the bottom right, and an angel hovers over the scene.

Visual Source 9.3 The Battle at Badr (Louvre, Paris/© Christian Larrieu/The Bridgeman Art Library)

- What elements of this image might suggest a natural or human understanding of the Muslim victory at Badr? And what might indicate divine intervention as an explanation?

- Documentary sources report only two horses and seventy camels on the side of the "believers" at this battle and suggest a more rag-tag group of

Visual Source 9.4 The Destruction of the Idols (Bibliothèque nationale de France)

fighters than the image portrays. Why do you think the artist presented a rather more impressive picture?

■ What religious meanings did Muhammad and Muslims in general extract from the battle at Badr?

In 630, just six years after the battle at Badr, Muhammad and some 10,000 soldiers triumphantly entered Mecca, almost completely without violence, and in a posture of reconciliation rather than revenge. In sharp contrast to traditional Arab practice, Muhammad issued a general amnesty for those who had opposed him. Then he turned his attention to the religious rationale of his entire movement. Riding his favorite camel, Muhammad circled the Kaaba seven times, shouting "Allahu Akbar" (God is greater), thus declaring the triumph of the "believer's movement." Refusing to enter the Kaaba until it had been purified from its idolatry, Muhammad ordered its 360 idols and paintings removed. He then smashed each one, reciting the Quranic verse: "The truth has come and falsehood has vanished away." Thus the Kaaba was cleansed and, in Muslim thinking, restored to its original purpose as a focal point for the worship of Allah alone.

Visual Source 9.4, an eleventh-century Persian miniature painting, portrays this dramatic event, showing Muhammad, enveloped in holy fire, seated on a white horse, while his followers look on. The intact idols ring the top and left sides of the image, while a few of the destroyed statues appear in the upper left.

- What view of pre-Islamic Arab religion do the images of the idols suggest?

- What fundamental religious teachings or spiritual truths does this painting seek to convey? How might you understand the Muslim concern with idolatry?

- Some traditions suggest that Muhammad ordered pictures of Mary and Jesus within the Kaaba to be left intact. What purpose might this tradition serve?

Using the Evidence: The Life of the Prophet

1. **Noticing point of view:** Consider these four visual sources together with the other images within the chapter. What general impression of the Islamic world emerges? What point of view, if any, is reflected in this selection of visual sources? Do they convey a positive, negative, or neutral impression of Islamic civilization? Explain your answer with specific references to the various images.

2. **Considering Muhammad:** Based on these images, how might you describe the understanding of Muhammad that they present? In what ways is Muhammad an exemplar for Muslims of a fully realized human being? Do such images have any usefulness for knowing "what really happened" as opposed to grasping Muslim views of their prophet?

3. **Comparing Muslim and Christian religious art:** What differences can you notice between the religious art of Islam, shown here, and that of Byzantine Christianity as reflected in the Visual Sources for Chapter 10?

4. **Reflecting on religious history:** What do these images reveal about Muslim understandings of their relationship to earlier religious practices? What did they accept from the past and what did they reject? How does that understanding compare with Buddhist and Christian views of their place in religious history?

5. **Comparing documentary and visual sources:** What do these images add to your understanding of Islam compared to what you derived from the documents?

Chapter 9 Wrap Up

LearningCurve
Check what you know.
**bedfordstmartins.com
/strayer/LC**

STEP ONE

The Word to Know: Cosmopolitan

The *Oxford English Dictionary* defines *cosmopolitan* as "having the characteristics which arise from, or are suited to, a range over many different countries; free from national limitations or attachments." Write a brief paragraph answering this question: How and why was the Islamic world of the tenth through fourteenth centuries cosmopolitan? Within your response be sure to provide specific evidence to support your argument.

STEP TWO

Comparison: Islam & Cultural Encounters

Review the section, "Islam and Cultural Encounter: A Four-Way Comparison (pp. 428–436). As Then fill in the chart below on how Islam spread to each of these four regions.

	India	Anatolia	West Africa	Spain
Role of migration				
Role of trade				
Role of cultural exchange				
Methods of conversion				
Unique cultural developments				

STEP THREE

Documenting Egalitarianism in Islam

In terms of race and class, what textual evidence exists in Documents 9.1, 9.2, and 9.3 that supports Malcolm X's claim on p. 411 that Islam supports an egalitarian world? What textual evidence contradicts Malcolm X's contention?

The Worlds of Christendom

Contraction, Expansion, and Division

500–1300

Yao Hong, a Chinese woman, was about twenty years of age, when, distraught at discovering that her husband was having an affair, she became a Christian sometime around 1990. As a migrant from a rural village to Shanghai, Yao Hong found support and a sense of family in a Christian community. Interviewed in 2010, she observed, "Whether they know you or not, they treat you as a brother or sister. If you have troubles, they help out with money or material assistance or spiritual aid." Nor did she find the Christian faith alien to her Chinese culture. To the contrary, she felt conversion to Christianity as a patriotic act, even a way of becoming more fully modern. "God is rising here in China," she declared. "If you look at the United States or England, their gospel is very advanced. Their churches are rich, because God blesses them. So I pray for China."[1]

YAO HONG IS BUT ONE OF MANY MILLIONS who have made Christianity a very rapidly growing faith in China over the past thirty years or so. Other Asian countries — South Korea, Taiwan, Singapore, the Philippines, Vietnam, and parts of India — also host substantial Christian communities. Even more impressively, the non–Muslim regions of Africa have witnessed an explosive advance of Christianity during the twentieth century, while Latin America, long a primarily Catholic region, has experienced a spectacular growth of Pentecostal Protestant Christianity since the 1970s. In the early twenty-first century, over 60 percent of the world's Christians lived in Asia, Africa, or Latin America. Thus Europe and North America, long regarded as the centers of the Christian world, have been increasingly outnumbered in the census of global Christianity.

Charlemagne: This fifteenth-century manuscript painting depicts Charlemagne, King of the Franks, who was crowned Emperor by the pope in 800 C.E. His reign illustrates the close and sometimes conflicted relationship of political and religious authorities in an emerging European civilization. It also represents the futile desire of many in Western Europe to revive the old Roman Empire, even as a substantially new civilization was taking shape in the aftermath of the Roman collapse several centuries earlier. (Victoria & Albert Museum, London, UK/The Bridgeman Art Library)

Interestingly enough, the sixth- and seventh-century world of Christendom revealed a broadly similar pattern. Christianity then enjoyed an Afro-Eurasian reach with flourishing communities in Arabia, Egypt, North Africa, Ethiopia, Nubia, Syria, Armenia, Persia, India, and China, as well as Europe. (See Chapter 4, pp. 188–93.) But during the next thousand years, radical changes reshaped that Christian world. Its African and Asian outposts largely vanished, declined, or were marginalized as Christianity became primarily a European phenomenon for the next thousand years or more.

During this millennium, Christianity came to provide a measure of cultural commonality for the diverse peoples of western Eurasia, much as Chinese civilization and Buddhism did for those of East Asia and Islam did for the Middle East and beyond. By 1300, almost all of these societies—from Ireland and England in the west to Russia in the east—had embraced in some form the teachings of the Jewish carpenter called Jesus. At the same time, that part of the Christian world became deeply divided. Its eastern half, known as the Byzantine Empire or Byzantium (bihz-ANN-tee-uhm), encompassed much of the eastern Mediterranean basin while continuing the traditions of the Greco-Roman world, though on a smaller scale, until its conquest by the Muslim Ottoman Empire in 1453. Centered on the magnificent city of Constantinople, Byzantium gradually evolved a particular form of Christianity known as Eastern Orthodoxy within a distinctive third-wave civilization.

In Western or Latin Christendom, encompassing what we now know as Western Europe, the setting was far different. There the Roman imperial order had largely vanished by 500 C.E., accompanied by the weakening of many features of Roman civilization. Roads fell into disrepair, cities decayed, and long-distance trade shriveled. What replaced the old Roman order was a highly localized society—fragmented, decentralized, and competitive—in sharp contrast to the unified state of Byzantium. Like Byzantium, the Latin West ultimately became thoroughly Christian, but it was a gradual process lasting centuries, and its Roman Catholic version of the faith, increasingly centered on the pope, had an independence from political authorities that the Eastern Orthodox Church did not. Moreover, the Western church in particular and its society in general were far more rural than Byzantium and certainly had nothing to compare to the splendor of Constantinople. However, slowly at first and then with increasing speed after 1000, Western Europe emerged as an especially dynamic, expansive, and innovative third-wave civilization, combining elements of its Greco-Roman past with the culture of Germanic and Celtic peoples to produce a distinctive hybrid, or blended, civilization.

Thus the story of global Christendom in the era of third-wave civilizations is one of contractions and expansions. As a religion, Christianity contracted sharply in Asia and Africa even as it expanded in Western Europe and Russia. As a civilization, Christian Byzantium flourished for a time, then gradually contracted and finally disappeared. The trajectory of civilization in the West traced an opposite path, at first contracting as the Roman Empire collapsed and later expanding as a new and blended civilization took hold in Western Europe.

SEEKING THE MAIN POINT

In what different ways did the history of Christianity unfold in various parts of the Afro-Eurasian world during the third-wave era?

A Map of Time

4th century	Christianity becomes state religion of Armenia, Axum, and Roman Empire
5th–6th centuries	Introduction of Christianity into Nubia
476	Collapse of western Roman Empire
527–565	Justinian rules Byzantine Empire
7th century	Introduction of Christianity into China; initial spread of Islam
726–843	Iconoclasm in Byzantium
800	Charlemagne crowned as new "Roman Emperor"
988	Conversion of Kievan Rus to Christianity
1054	Mutual excommunication of pope and patriarch
1095–1291	Crusaders in the Islamic world
12th–13th centuries	Translations of Greek and Arab works available in Europe
1346–1350	Black Death in Europe
1453	Turks capture Constantinople; end of Byzantine Empire
1492	Christian reconquest of Spain completed; Columbus's first voyage

Christian Contraction in Asia and Africa

How had Christianity become by 1500 a largely European faith, with its earlier and promising Asian and African communities diminished, defeated, or disappeared? The answer, in large measure, was Islam. The wholly unforeseen birth of yet another monotheistic faith in the Middle East, its rapid spread across much of the Afro-Eurasian world, the simultaneous creation of a large and powerful Arab Empire, the emergence of a cosmopolitan and transcontinental Islamic civilization—these were the conditions, described more fully in Chapter 9, that led to the contraction of Christendom in Asia and Africa, leaving Europe as the principal center of the Christian faith.[2]

■ **Comparison**

What variations in the experience of African and Asian Christian communities can you identify?

Asian Christianity

It was in Arabia, the homeland of Islam, that the decimation of earlier Christian communities occurred most completely and most quickly, for within a century or so of Muhammad's death in 632, only a few Christian groups remained. During the eighth century, triumphant Muslims marked the replacement of the old religion by using pillars of a demolished Christian cathedral to construct the Grand Mosque of Sana'a in southern Arabia.

The Dome of the Rock, Jerusalem
To Muslims, the Dome of the Rock was constructed on the site from which Muhammad ascended into the presence of Allah during his Night Journey. It was the first large-scale building in the Islamic world and drew heavily on Roman, Byzantine, and Persian precedents. Its location in Jerusalem marked the arrival of a competing faith to Jews and Christians who had long considered the city sacred. (© Aaron Horowitz/Corbis)

Elsewhere in the Middle East, other Jewish and Christian communities soon felt the impact of Islam. When expanding Muslim forces took control of Jerusalem in 638 and subsequently constructed the Muslim shrine known as the Dome of the Rock (687–691), that precise location had long been regarded as sacred. To Jews, it contained the stone on which Abraham prepared to offer his son Isaac as a sacrifice to God, and it was the site of the first two Jewish temples. To Christians, it was a place that Jesus had visited as a youngster to converse with learned teachers and later to drive out the moneychangers. Thus, when the Umayyad caliph (successor to the prophet) Abd al-Malik ordered a new construction on that site, he was appropriating for Islam both Jewish and Christian legacies. But he was also demonstrating the victorious arrival of a new faith and announcing to Christians and Jews that "the Islamic state was here to stay."[3]

In Syria and Persia with more concentrated populations of Christians, accommodating policies generally prevailed. Certainly Arab conquest of these adjacent areas involved warfare, largely against the military forces of existing Byzantine and Persian authorities, but not to enforce conversion. In both areas, however, the majority of people turned to Islam voluntarily, attracted perhaps by its aura of success. A number of Christian leaders in Syria, Jerusalem, Armenia, and elsewhere negotiated agreements with Muslim authorities whereby remaining Christian communities were guaranteed the right to practice their religion, largely in private, in return for payment of a special tax.

Much depended on the attitudes of local Muslim rulers. On occasion churches were destroyed, villages plundered, fields burned, and Christians forced to wear distinctive clothing. By contrast, a wave of church building took place in Syria under Muslim rule, and Christians were recruited into the administration, schools, translation services, and even the armed forces of the Arab Empire. In 649, only 15 years after Damascus had been conquered by Arab forces, a Nestorian Bishop wrote: "These Arabs fight not against our Christian religion; nay rather they defend our faith, they revere our priests and Saints, and they make gifts to our churches and monasteries."[4]

Thus the Nestorian Christian communities of Syria, Iraq, and Persia, sometimes called the Church of the East, survived the assault of Islam, but they did so as shrinking communities of second-class subjects regulated minorities forbidden from propagating their message to Muslims. They also abandoned their religious paintings and sculptures, fearing to offend Muslims, who generally objected to any artistic representation of the Divine.

But further east, a small and highly creative Nestorian church, initiated in 635 by a Persian missionary monk, had taken root in China with the approval of the country's Tang dynasty rulers. Both its art and literature articulated the Christian message using Buddhist and Daoist concepts. The written texts themselves, known as the Jesus Sutras, refer to Christianity as the "Religion of Light from the West" or the "Luminous Religion." They describe God as the "Cool Wind," sin as "bad karma," and a good life as one of "no desire" and "no action." "People can live only by dwelling in the living breath of God," the Jesus Sutras declare. "All the Buddhas are moved by this wind, which blows everywhere in the world."[5] The contraction of this remarkable experiment owed little to Islam, but derived rather from the vagaries of Chinese politics. In the mid-ninth century the Chinese state turned against all religions of foreign origin, Islam and Buddhism as well as Christianity (see Chapter 8). Wholly dependent on the goodwill of Chinese authorities, this small outpost of Christianity withered.

Later the Mongol conquest of China in the thirteenth century offered a brief opportunity for Christianity's renewal, as the religiously tolerant Mongols welcomed Nestorian Christians as well as various other faiths. A number of prominent Mongols became Christians, including one of the wives of Chinggis Khan. Considering Jesus as a powerful shaman, Mongols also appreciated that Christians, unlike Buddhists, could eat meat and unlike Muslims, could drink alcohol, even including it in their worship.[6] But Mongol rule was short, ending in 1368, and the small number of Chinese Christians ensured that the faith almost completely vanished with the advent of the vigorously Confucian Ming dynasty.

Nestorian Stele

The Nestorian Stele is a large limestone block inscribed with a text detailing the early history of Christianity in China. At the top a Christian cross arising out of a white cloud (a characteristic Daoist symbol) and a lotus flower (an enduring Buddhist image) illustrate the blended character of this Christian experiment in China. (Photographer: Dr Hugh Houghton, © The University of Birmingham, UK. Reproduced with permission)

African Christianity

The churches of Africa, like those of the Middle East, also found themselves on the defensive and declining in the face of an expanding Islam. Across coastal North Africa, widespread conversion to Islam over several centuries reduced to virtual extinction Christian communities that had earlier provided many of the martyrs and intellectuals of the early Church.

In Egypt, however, Christianity had become the religion of the majority by the time of the Muslim conquest around 640, and for the next 500 years or so, large numbers continued to speak Coptic and practice their religion as *dhimmis*, legally inferior but protected people paying a special tax, under relatively tolerant Muslim rulers. Many found Arab government less oppressive than that of their former Byzantine overlords, who considered Egyptian Christians heretics. By the thirteenth century, things changed dramatically as Christian crusaders from Europe and Mongol invaders from the east threatened Egypt. In these circumstances, the country's Muslim rulers came to suspect the political loyalty of their Christian subjects. The mid-fourteenth century witnessed violent anti-Christian pogroms, destruction of churches, and the forced removal of Christians from the best land. Many felt like "exiles in their own country." As a result, most rural Egyptians converted to Islam and moved toward the use of Arabic rather than Coptic, which largely died out. Although Egypt was becoming an Arab and Muslim country, a substantial Christian minority persisted among the literate in urban areas and in monasteries located in remote regions. In the early twenty-first century, Egyptian Christians still numbered about 10 percent of the population.

Even as Egyptian Christianity was contracting, a new center of African Christianity was taking shape during the fifth and sixth centuries in the several kingdoms of Nubia to the south of Egypt, where the faith had been introduced by Egyptian traders and missionaries. Parts of the Bible were translated into the Nubian language, while other writings appeared in Greek, Arabic, and the Ethiopian language of Ge'ez. A great cathedral in the Nubian city of Faras was decorated with magnificent murals, and the earlier practice of burying servants to provide for rulers in the afterlife stopped abruptly. At times, kings served as priests, and Christian bishops held state offices. By the mid-seventh century, both the ruling class and many commoners had become Christian. At the same time, Nubian armies twice defeated Arab incursions, following which an agreement with Muslim Egypt protected this outpost of Christianity for some 600 years. But pressures mounted in the 1200s and 1300s as Egypt adopted a more hostile stance toward Christians, while Islamized tribes from the desert and Arab migrants pushed against Nubia. By 1500 Nubian Christianity, like its counterparts in coastal North Africa, had largely disappeared.

An important exception to these various contractions of Asian and African Christianity lay in Ethiopia. There the rulers of Axum had adopted Christianity in the fourth century, and it subsequently took root among the general population as well. (See Chapter 4, p. 191, and Chapter 6, pp. 267–70.) Over the centuries of Islamic expansion, Ethiopia became a Christian island in a Muslim sea, protected by its mountainous geography and its distance from major centers of Islamic power. Many Muslims also remembered gratefully that Christian Ethiopia had sheltered some of the beleaguered and persecuted followers of Muhammad in Islam's early years. Nonetheless, the spread of Islam largely cut Ethiopia off from other parts of Christendom and rendered its position in northeast Africa precarious.

In its isolated location, Ethiopian Christianity developed some of its most distinctive features. One of these was a fascination with Judaism and Jerusalem, reflected in a much-told story about the visit of an Ethiopian Queen of Sheba to King Solomon. The story includes an episode in which Solomon seduces the Queen, producing a child who becomes the founding monarch of the Ethiopian state. Since

Solomon figures in the line of descent to Jesus, it meant that Ethiopia's Christian rulers could legitimate their position by tracing their ancestry to Jesus himself. Furthermore, Ethiopian monks long maintained a presence in Jerusalem's Church of the Holy Sepulcher, said to mark the site where Jesus was crucified and buried. Then, in the twelfth century, the rulers of a new Ethiopian dynasty constructed a remarkable series of twelve linked underground churches, apparently attempting to create a New Jerusalem on Christian Ethiopian soil, as the original city lay under Muslim control. Those churches are in use to this day in modern Ethiopia, where over 60 percent of the country's population retain their affiliation with this ancient Christian church.

The Church of St. George, Lalibela, Ethiopia
Excavated from solid rock in the twelfth century, the churches of Lalibela were distinctive Christian structures, invisible from a distance and apparent only when looking down on them from ground level. Local legend has it that their construction was aided by angels. This one in the shape of a cross is named for St. George, the patron saint of Ethiopia. (© Heltler/Robert Harding World/Corbis)

Byzantine Christendom: Building on the Roman Past

The contraction of the Christian faith and Christian societies in Asia and Africa left Europe and Anatolia, largely by default, as the centers of Christendom. The initial expansion of Islam and the Arab Empire had quickly stripped away what had been the Middle Eastern and North African provinces of the Roman Empire and had brought Spain under Muslim control. But after the Mediterranean frontier between the Islamic and Christian worlds stabilized somewhat in the early eighth century, the immediate threat of Muslim incursions into the heartland of Christendom lifted, although border conflicts persisted. It was within this space of relative security, unavailable to most African and Asian Christian communities, that the diverging histories of the Byzantine Empire and Western Europe took shape.

Unlike most empires, Byzantium has no clear starting point. Its own leaders, as well as its neighbors and enemies, viewed it as simply a continuation of the Roman Empire. Some historians date its beginning to 330 C.E., when the Roman emperor Constantine, who began to favor Christianity during his reign, established a new capital, Constantinople, on the site of an ancient Greek city called Byzantium. At the end of that century, the Roman Empire was formally divided into eastern and western halves, thus launching a division of Christendom that has lasted into the twenty-first century.

Although the western Roman Empire collapsed during the fifth century, the eastern half persisted for another thousand years. Housing the ancient civilizations of Egypt, Greece, Syria, and Anatolia, the eastern Roman Empire (Byzantium) was far wealthier, more urbanized, and more cosmopolitan than its western counterpart; it possessed a much more defensible capital in the heavily walled city of Constantinople; and it had a shorter frontier to guard. Byzantium also enjoyed access to the Black Sea and command of the eastern Mediterranean. With a stronger army, navy, and merchant marine as well as clever diplomacy, its leaders were able to deflect the Germanic and Hun invaders who had overwhelmed the western Roman Empire.

■ Continuity
and Change
In what respects did
Byzantium continue the
patterns of the classical
Roman Empire? In what
ways did it diverge from
those patterns?

Much that was late Roman — its roads, taxation system, military structures, centralized administration, imperial court, laws, Christian church — persisted in the east for many centuries. Like Tang dynasty China seeking to restore the glory of the Han era, Byzantium consciously sought to preserve the legacy of classical Greco-Roman civilization. Constantinople was to be a "New Rome," and people referred to themselves as "Romans." Fearing contamination by "barbarian" customs, emperors forbade the residents of Constantinople from wearing boots, trousers, clothing made from animal skins, and long hairstyles, all of which were associated with Germanic peoples, and insisted instead on Roman-style robes and sandals. But much changed as well over the centuries, marking the Byzantine Empire as the home of a distinctive civilization.

The Byzantine State

Perhaps the most obvious change was one of scale, as the Byzantine Empire never approximated the size of its Roman predecessor (see Map 10.1). The western Roman Empire was permanently lost to Byzantium, despite Emperor Justinian's (r. 527–565) impressive but short-lived attempt to reconquer the Mediterranean basin. The rapid Arab/Islamic expansion in the seventh century resulted in the loss of Syria/Palestine, Egypt, and North Africa. Nonetheless, until roughly 1200, a more compact Byzantine Empire remained a major force in the eastern Mediterranean, controlling Greece, much of the Balkans (southeastern Europe), and Anatolia. A reformed administrative system gave appointed generals civil authority in the empire's provinces and allowed them to raise armies from the landowning peasants of the region. From that territorial base, the empire's naval and merchant vessels were active in both the Mediterranean and Black seas.

In its heyday, the Byzantine state was an impressive creation. Political authority remained tightly centralized in Constantinople, where the emperor claimed to govern all creation as God's worldly representative, styling himself the "peer of the Apostles" and the "sole ruler of the world." The imperial court tried to imitate the awesome grandeur of what they thought was God's heavenly court, but in fact it resembled ancient Persian imperial splendor. Aristocrats trained in Greek rhetoric and literature occupied high positions in the administration, participating in court ceremonies that maintained their elite status. Parades of these silk-clad officials added splendor to the imperial court, which also included mechanical lions that roared, birds that sang, and an immense throne that quickly elevated the emperor high above his presumably awestruck visitors. Nonetheless, this centralized state touched only lightly on the lives of most people, as it focused primarily on collecting taxes, main-

Map 10.1 The Byzantine Empire

The Byzantine Empire reached its greatest extent under Emperor Justinian in the mid-sixth century C.E. It subsequently lost considerable territory to various Christian European powers as well as to Muslim Arab and Turkic invaders.

taining order, and suppressing revolts. "Personal freedom in the provinces was constrained more by neighbors and rival households," concluded one historian, "than by the imperial government."[7]

After 1085, Byzantine territory shrank, owing to incursions by aggressive Western European powers, by Catholic Crusaders, and by Turkic Muslim invaders. The end came in 1453 when the Turkic Ottoman Empire, then known as the "sword of Islam," finally took Constantinople. One eyewitness to the event wrote a moving lament to his fallen city:

> And the entire city was to be seen in the tents of the [Turkish] camp, the city deserted, lying lifeless, naked, soundless, without either form or beauty. O city, head of all cities, center of the four corners of the world, pride of the Romans, civilizer of the barbarians. . . . Where is your beauty, O paradise . . . ? Where are the bodies of the Apostle of my Lord . . . ? Where are the relics of the saints, those of the martyrs? Where are the remains of Constantine the Great and the other emperors? . . . Oh, what a loss![8]

The Byzantine Church and Christian Divergence

■ Comparison

How did Eastern Orthodox Christianity differ from Roman Catholicism?

Intimately tied to the state was the Church, a relationship that became known as caesaropapism. Unlike Western Europe, where the Roman Catholic Church maintained some degree of independence from political authorities, in Byzantium the emperor assumed something of the role of both "Caesar," as head of state, and the pope, as head of the Church. Thus he appointed the patriarch, or leader, of the Orthodox Church; sometimes made decisions about doctrine; called church councils into session; and generally treated the Church as a government department. "The [Empire] and the church have a great unity and community," declared a twelfth-century patriarch. "Indeed they cannot be separated."[9] A dense network of bishops and priests brought the message of the Church to every corner of the empire, while numerous monasteries accommodated holy men, whose piety, self-denial, and good works made them highly influential among both elite and ordinary people.

Eastern Orthodox Christianity had a pervasive influence on every aspect of Byzantine life. It legitimated the supreme and absolute rule of the emperor, for he was a God-anointed ruler, a reflection of the glory of God on earth. It also provided a cultural identity for the empire's subjects. Even more than being "Roman," they were orthodox, or "right-thinking," Christians for whom the empire and the Church were equally essential to achieving eternal salvation. Constantinople was filled with churches and the relics of numerous saints. And the churches were filled with icons—religious paintings of Jesus, Mary, and numerous saints—some of them artistic masterpieces, that many believed conveyed Divine Presence to believers. (For more on icons, see Visual Sources: Reading Byzantine Icons, pp. 507–11.) Complex theological issues about the Trinity and especially about the relationship of God and Jesus engaged the attention of ordinary people. One fourth-century bishop complained: "I wish to know the price of bread; one answers 'The Father is greater than the Son.' I inquire whether my bath is ready; one answers 'The Son has been made out of nothing.'"[10] Partisans of competing chariot-racing teams, known as the Greens and the Blues, vigorously debated theological issues as well as the merits of their favorite drivers.

In its early centuries and beyond, the Christian movement was rent by theological controversy and political division. Followers of Arius, an Egyptian priest, held that Jesus had been created by God the Father rather than living eternally with Him. Nestorius, the fifth-century bishop of Constantinople, argued that Mary had given birth only to the human Jesus, who then became the "temple" of God. This view, defined as heretical in the Western Christian world, predominated in a separate Persian church, which spread its views to India, China, and Arabia.

But the most lasting and deepest division within the Christian world occurred as Eastern Orthodoxy came to define itself against an emerging Latin Christianity centered on papal Rome. Both had derived, of course, from the growth of Christianity in the Roman Empire and therefore had much in common—the teachings of Jesus; the Bible; the sacraments; a church hierarchy of patriarchs, bishops, and priests; a missionary impulse; and intolerance toward other religions. Despite these shared features, any sense of a single widespread Christian community was increasingly replaced by an awareness of difference, competition, and outright hostility that even a common fear of Islam could not overcome. In part, this growing religious divergence reflected the political separation and rivalry between the Byzantine Empire and the emerging kingdoms of Western Europe. As the growth of Islam in the seventh century (described more fully in Chapter 9) submerged earlier centers of Christianity in the Middle East and North Africa, Constantinople and Rome alone remained as alternative hubs of the Church. But they were now in different states that competed with each other for territory and for the right to claim the legacy of imperial Rome.

Beyond such political differences were those of language and culture. Although Latin remained the language of the Church and of elite communication in the West, it was abandoned in the Byzantine Empire in favor of Greek, which remained the basis for Byzantine education. More than in the West, Byzantine thinkers sought to formulate Christian doctrine in terms of Greek philosophical concepts.

Differences in theology and church practice likewise widened the gulf between Orthodoxy and Catholicism, despite agreement on fundamental doctrines. Disagreements about the nature of the Trinity, the source of the Holy Spirit, original sin, and the relative importance of faith and reason gave rise to much controversy. So too, for a time, did the Byzantine efforts to prohibit the use of icons, popular paintings of saints and biblical scenes, usually painted on small wooden panels. (See Visual Sources: Reading Byzantine Icons, pp. 507–11.) Other more modest differences also occasioned mutual misunderstanding and disdain. Priests in the West shaved and, after 1050 or so, were supposed to remain celibate, while those in Byzantium allowed their beards to grow long and were permitted to marry. Orthodox ritual called for using bread leavened with yeast in the Communion, but Catholics used unleavened bread. Far more significant was the question of authority. Eastern Orthodox leaders sharply rejected the growing claims of Roman popes to be the sole and final authority for all Christians everywhere.

The rift in the world of Christendom grew gradually from the seventh century on, punctuated by various efforts to bridge the mounting divide between the western

St. Mark's Basilica
Consecrated in 1094, this ornate cathedral, although located in Venice, Italy, is a classic example of Byzantine architecture. Such churches represented perhaps the greatest achievement of Byzantine art and were certainly the most monumental expressions of Byzantine culture. (Erich Lessing/Art Resource, NY)

and eastern branches of the Church. A sign of this continuing deterioration occurred in 1054 when representatives of both churches mutually excommunicated each other, declaring in effect that those in the opposing tradition were not true Christians. The Crusades, launched in 1095 by the Catholic pope against the forces of Islam, made things worse. Western Crusaders, passing through the Byzantine Empire on their way to the Middle East, engaged in frequent conflict with local people and thus deepened the distrust between them. From the western viewpoint, Orthodox practices were "blasphemous, even heretical." One western observer of the Second Crusade noted that the Greeks "were judged not to be Christians and the Franks [French] considered killing them a matter of no importance."[11] During the Fourth Crusade in 1204, western forces seized and looted Constantinople and ruled Byzantium for the next half century. Their brutality only confirmed Byzantine views of their Roman Catholic despoilers as nothing more than barbarians. According to one Byzantine account, "they sacked the sacred places and trampled on divine things . . . they tore children from their mothers . . . and they defiled virgins in the holy chapels, fearing neither God's anger nor man's vengeance."[12] After this, the rupture in the world of Christendom proved irreparable.

Byzantium and the World

■ **Connection**

In what ways was the Byzantine Empire linked to a wider world?

Beyond its tense relationship with Western Europe, the Byzantine Empire, located astride Europe and Asia, also interacted intensively with its other neighbors. On a political and military level, Byzantium continued the long-term Roman struggle with the Persian Empire. That persisting conflict weakened both of them and was one factor in the remarkable success of Arab armies as they poured out of Arabia in the seventh century. Although Persia quickly became part of the Islamic world, Byzantium held out, even as it lost considerable territory to the Arabs. A Byzantine military innovation, known as "Greek fire"—a potent and flammable combination of oil, sulfur, and lime that was launched from bronze tubes—helped to hold off the Arabs. It operated something like a flamethrower and subsequently passed into Arab and Chinese arsenals as well. Byzantium's ability to defend its core regions delayed for many centuries the Islamic advance into southeastern Europe, which finally occurred at the hands of the Turkish Ottoman Empire in the fifteenth and sixteenth centuries.

Economically, the Byzantine Empire was a central player in the long-distance trade of Eurasia, with commercial links to Western Europe, Russia, Central Asia, the Islamic world, and China. Its gold coin, the bezant, was a widely used currency in the Mediterranean basin for more than 500 years, and wearing such coins as pendants was a high-status symbol in the less developed kingdoms of Western Europe.[13] The luxurious products of Byzantine craftspeople—jewelry, gemstones, silver and gold work, linen and woolen textiles, purple dyes—were much in demand. Its silk industry, based on Chinese technology, supplied much of the Mediterranean basin with this precious fabric.

The cultural influence of Byzantium was likewise significant. Preserving much of ancient Greek learning, the Byzantine Empire transmitted this classical heritage to the Islamic world as well as to the Christian West. In both places, it had an immensely stimulating impact among scientists, philosophers, theologians, and other intellectuals. Some saw it as an aid to faith and to an understanding of the world, while others feared it as impious and distracting. (See "Reason and Faith" later in this chapter.)

Byzantine religious culture also spread widely among Slavic-speaking peoples in the Balkans and Russia. As lands to the south and the east were overtaken by Islam, Byzantium looked to the north. By the early eleventh century, steady military pressure had brought many of the Balkan Slavic peoples, especially the Bulgars, under Byzantine control. Christianity and literacy accompanied this Byzantine offensive. Already in the ninth century, two Byzantine missionaries, Cyril and Methodius, had developed an alphabet, based on Greek letters, with which Slavic languages could be written. This Cyrillic script made it possible to translate the Bible and other religious literature into these languages and greatly aided the process of conversion.

The Conversion of Russia

The most significant expansion of Orthodox Christianity occurred among the Slavic peoples of what is now Ukraine and western Russia. In this culturally diverse region, which also included Finnic and Baltic peoples as well as Viking traders, a modest state known as Kievan Rus (KEE-yehv-ihn ROOS)—named after the most prominent city, Kiev—emerged in the ninth century. Like many of the new third-wave civilizations, the development of Rus was stimulated by trade, in this case along the Dnieper River, linking Scandinavia and Byzantium. Loosely led by various princes, especially the prince of Kiev, Rus was a society of slaves and freemen, privileged people and commoners, dominant men and subordinate women. This stratification marked it as a third-wave civilization in the making (see Map 10.3, p. 481).

Religion reflected the region's cultural diversity, with the gods and practices of many peoples much in evidence. Ancestral spirits, household deities, and various gods related to the forces of nature were in evidence with Perun, the god of thunder, perhaps the most prominent. Small numbers of Christians, Muslims, and Jews were likewise part of the mix. Then, in the late tenth century, a decisive turning point occurred. The growing interaction of Rus with the larger world prompted Prince Vladimir of Kiev to affiliate with one of the major religions of the area. He was searching for a faith that would unify the diverse peoples of his region, while linking Rus into wider networks of communication and exchange. According to ancient chronicles, he actively considered Judaism, Islam, and Roman Catholicism, before finally deciding on Eastern Orthodoxy, the religion of Byzantium. He rejected Islam, the chronicles tell us, because it prohibited alcoholic drink and "drinking is the joy of the Russes." The splendor of Constantinople's Orthodox churches apparently captured the imagination of Rus's envoys, for there, they reported, "We knew not whether we were in heaven or on earth."[14] Political and commercial considerations no doubt also played a role in Vladimir's decision, and he acquired a sister of the Byzantine emperor as his bride, along with numerous Byzantine priests and advisers. Whatever the precise process, it was a freely made decision. Eastern Orthodox Christianity thus came to Rus without

■ **Connection**

How did links to Byzantium transform the new civilization of Kievan Rus?

the pressure of foreign military defeat or occupation. Eventually, it took deep root among the Russian people.

It was a fateful choice with long-term implications for Russian history, for it brought this fledgling civilization firmly into the world of Orthodox Christianity, separating it from both the realm of Islam and the Roman Catholic West. Like many new civilizations, Rus borrowed extensively from its older and more sophisticated neighbor. Among these borrowings were Byzantine architectural styles, the Cyrillic alphabet, the extensive use of icons, a monastic tradition stressing prayer and service, and political ideals of imperial control of the Church, all of which became part of a transformed Rus. Orthodoxy also provided a more unified identity for this emerging civilization and religious legitimacy for its rulers. Centuries later, when Byzantium had fallen to the Turks, a few Russian church leaders proclaimed the doctrine of a "third Rome." The original Rome had abandoned the true faith, and the second Rome, Constantinople, had succumbed to Muslim infidels. Moscow was now the third Rome, the final protector and defender of Orthodox Christianity. Though not widely proclaimed in Russia itself, such a notion reflected the "Russification" of Eastern Orthodoxy and its growing role as an element of Russian national identity. It was also a reminder of the enduring legacy of a thousand years of Byzantine history, long after the empire itself had vanished.

Western Christendom: Rebuilding in the Wake of Roman Collapse

The western half of the European Christian world followed a rather different path than that of the Byzantine Empire. For much of the third-wave millennium, it was distinctly on the margins of world history, partly because of its geographic location at the far western end of the Eurasian landmass. Thus it was at a distance from the growing routes of world trade—by sea in the Indian Ocean and by land across the Silk Roads to China and the Sand Roads to West Africa. Not until the Eastern and Western hemispheres were joined after 1500 did Western Europe occupy a geographically central position in the global network. Internally, Europe's geography made political unity difficult. It was a region in which population centers were divided by mountain ranges and dense forests as well as by five major peninsulas and two large islands (Britain and Ireland). However, its extensive coastlines and interior river systems facilitated exchange within Europe, while a moderate climate, plentiful rainfall, and fertile soils enabled a productive agriculture that could support a growing population.

Political Life in Western Europe

■ **Change**

What replaced the Roman order in Western Europe?

In the early centuries of this era, history must have seemed more significant than geography, for the Roman Empire, long a fixture of the western Mediterranean region, was gone. The traditional date marking the collapse of the empire is 476, when the German general Odoacer overthrew the last Roman emperor in the West. In itself not very important, this event has come to symbolize a major turning point in the West, for much that had characterized Roman civilization also weakened, declined, or disappeared in the several centuries before and after 476. Any semblance of large-scale centralized rule vanished. Disease and warfare reduced Western Europe's population by more than 25 percent. Land under cultivation contracted, while forests, marshland, and wasteland expanded. Urban life too diminished sharply, as Europe reverted to a largely rural existence. Rome at its height was a city of 1 million people, but by the tenth century it numbered perhaps 10,000. Public buildings crumbled from lack of care. Outside Italy, long-distance trade dried up as Roman roads deteriorated, and money exchange gave way to barter in many places. Literacy lost ground as well. Germanic peoples, whom the Romans had viewed as barbarians—Goths, Visigoths, Franks, Lombards, Angles, Saxons—now emerged as the dominant peoples of Western Europe. In the process, Europe's center of gravity moved away from the Mediterranean toward the north and west.

Yet much that was classical or Roman persisted, even as a new order emerged in Europe. On the political front, a series of regional kingdoms—led by Visigoths in Spain, Franks in France, Lombards in Italy, and Angles and Saxons in England—arose to replace Roman authority. But many of these Germanic peoples, originally organized in small kinship-based tribes with strong warrior values, had already been substantially Romanized. Contact with the Roman Empire in the first several centuries C.E. had generated more distinct ethnic identities among them, militarized their societies, and gave greater prominence to Woden, their god of war. As Germanic peoples migrated into or invaded Roman lands, many were deeply influenced by Roman culture, especially if they served in the Roman army. On the funeral monument of one such person was the telling inscription: "I am a Frank by nationality, but a Roman soldier under arms."[15]

The prestige of things Roman remained high, even after the empire itself had collapsed. Now as leaders of their own kingdoms, the Germanic rulers actively embraced written Roman law, using fines and penalties to provide order and justice in their new states in place of feuds and vendettas. One Visigoth ruler named Athaulf (r. 410–415), who had married a Roman noblewoman, gave voice to the continuing attraction of Roman culture and its empire.

> At first I wanted to erase the Roman name and convert all Roman territory into a Gothic empire.... But long experience has taught me that ... without law a state is not a state. Therefore I have more prudently chosen the different glory of reviving the Roman name with Gothic vigour, and I hope to be acknowledged by posterity as the initiator of a Roman restoration.[16]

Several of the larger, though relatively short-lived, Germanic kingdoms also had aspirations to re-create something of the unity of the Roman Empire. Charlemagne (SHAHR-leh-mane) (r. 768–814), ruler of the Carolingian Empire, occupying what is now France, Belgium, the Netherlands, and parts of Germany and Italy, erected an embryonic imperial bureaucracy, standardized weights and measures, and began

Map 10.2   Western Europe in the Ninth Century
Charlemagne's Carolingian Empire brought a temporary political unity to parts of Western Europe, but it was subsequently divided among his three sons, who waged war on one another.

to act like an imperial ruler (see Document 10.3, pp. 502–04). On Christmas Day of the year 800, he was crowned as a new Roman emperor by the pope, although his realm splintered shortly after his death (see Map 10.2). Later Otto I of Saxony (r. 936–973) gathered much of Germany under his control, saw himself as renewing Roman rule, and was likewise invested with the title of emperor by the pope. Otto's realm, subsequently known as the Holy Roman Empire, was largely limited to Germany and soon proved little more than a collection of quarreling principalities. Though unsuccessful in reviving anything approaching Roman imperial authority, these efforts testify to the continuing appeal of the classical world, even as a new political system of rival kingdoms blended Roman and Germanic elements.

Society and the Church

Within these new kingdoms, a highly fragmented and decentralized society widely known as feudalism emerged with great local variation. In thousands of independent, self-sufficient, and largely isolated landed estates or manors, power—political, economic, and social—was exercised by a warrior elite of landowning lords. In the constant competition of these centuries, lesser lords and knights swore allegiance to greater lords or kings and thus became their vassals, frequently receiving lands and plunder in return for military service.

Such reciprocal ties between superior and subordinate were also apparent at the bottom of the social hierarchy, as Roman-style slavery gradually gave way to serfdom. Unlike slaves, serfs were not the personal property of their masters, could not be arbitrarily thrown off their land, and were allowed to live in families. However, they were bound to their masters' estates as peasant laborers and owed various payments and services to the lord of the manor. One family on a manor near Paris in the ninth century owed four silver coins, wine, wood, three hens, and fifteen eggs per year. Women generally were required to weave cloth and make clothing for the lord, while men labored in the lord's fields. In return, the serf family received a small farm and such protection as the lord could provide. In a violent and insecure world adjusting to the absence of Roman authority, the only security available to many individuals or families lay in these communities, where the ties to kin, manor, and lord constituted the primary human loyalties. It was a world apart from the stability of life in imperial Rome or its continuation in Byzantium.

Also filling the vacuum left by the collapse of empire was the Church, later known as Roman Catholic, yet another link to the now defunct Roman world. Its hierarchical organization of popes, bishops, priests, and monasteries was modeled on that of the Roman Empire and took over some of its political, administrative, educational, and welfare functions. Latin continued as the language of the Church even as it gave way to various vernacular languages in common speech. In fact, literacy in the classical languages of Greek and Latin remained the hallmark of educated people in the West well into the twentieth century.

Like the Buddhist establishment in China, the Church subsequently became quite wealthy, with reformers often accusing it of forgetting its central spiritual mission. It also provided a springboard for the conversion of Europe's many "pagan" peoples. Numerous missionaries, commissioned by the pope, monasteries, or already converted rulers, fanned out across Europe, generally pursuing a "top-down" strategy. Frequently it worked, as local kings and warlords found status and legitimacy in association with a literate and "civilized" religion that still bore something of the grandeur of Rome. With "the wealth and protection of the powerful," ordinary people followed their rulers into the fold of the Church.[17]

This process was similar to Buddhism's appeal for the nomadic rulers of northern and western China following the collapse of the Han dynasty. Christianity, like Buddhism, also bore the promise of superior supernatural powers, and its spread was frequently associated with reported miracles of healing, rainfall, fertility, and victory in battle.

But it was not an easy sell. Outright coercion was sometimes part of the process. (See Document 10.3, pp. 502–04.) More often, however, softer methods prevailed. The Church proved willing to accommodate a considerable range of earlier cultural practices, absorbing them into an emerging Christian tradition. For example, amulets and charms to ward off evil became medals with the image of Jesus or the Virgin Mary; traditionally sacred wells and springs became the sites of churches; and festivals honoring ancient gods became Christian holy days. December 25 was selected as the birthday of Jesus, for it was associated with the winter solstice, the coming of more light, and the birth or rebirth of various deities in pre-Christian European traditions. By 1100, most of Europe had embraced Christianity. Even so, for centuries priests and bishops had to warn their congregations against the worship of rivers, trees, and mountains, and for many people, ancient gods, monsters, trolls, and spirits still inhabited the land. The spreading Christian faith, like the new political framework of European civilization, was a blend of many elements. (For more on the rooting of Christianity in Western Europe, see Documents: The Making of Christian Europe, pp. 499–506.)

Church authorities and the nobles/warriors who exercised political influence reinforced each other. Rulers provided protection for the papacy and strong encouragement for the faith. In return, the Church offered religious legitimacy for the powerful and the prosperous. "It is the will of the Creator," declared the teaching of the Church, "that the higher shall always rule over the lower. Each individual and class should stay in its place [and] perform its tasks."[18] But Church and nobility competed as well as cooperated, for they were rival centers of power in post-Roman Europe. Particularly controversial was the right to appoint bishops and the pope himself; this issue, known as the investiture conflict, was especially prominent in the eleventh and twelfth centuries. Was the right to make such appointments the responsibility of the Church alone, or did kings and emperors also have a role? In the compromise that ended the conflict, the Church won the right to appoint its own officials, while secular rulers retained an informal and symbolic role in the process.

Accelerating Change in the West

The pace of change in this emerging civilization picked up considerably in the several centuries after 1000. For the preceding 300 years, Europe had been subject to repeated invasions from every direction. Muslim armies had conquered Spain and threatened the rest of Europe. Magyar (Hungarian) invasions from the east and Viking incursions from the north likewise disrupted and threatened post-Roman Europe (see Map 10.3). But by the year 1000, these invasions had been checked and the invaders absorbed into settled society. The greater security and stability that came with relative peace arguably opened the way to an accelerating tempo of change. The climate also seemed to cooperate. A generally warming trend after 750 reached its peak in the eleventh and twelfth centuries, enhancing agricultural production.

■ **Change**

In what ways was European civilization changing after 1000?

Whatever may have launched this new phase of European civilization, commonly called the High Middle Ages (1000–1300), the signs of expansion and growth were widely evident. The population of Europe grew from perhaps 35 million in 1000 to about 80 million in 1340. With more people, many new lands were opened for cultivation in a process paralleling that of China's expansion to the south at the same time. Great lords, bishops, and religious orders organized new villages on what had recently been forest or wasteland. Marshes were drained; land was reclaimed from the sea in the Netherlands; everywhere trees were felled. By 1300, the forest cover of Europe had been reduced to about 20 percent of the land area. "I believe that the forest . . . covers the land to no purpose," declared a German abbot, "and hold this to be an unbearable harm."[19]

The increased production associated with this agricultural expansion stimulated a considerable growth in long-distance trade, much of which had dried up in the aftermath of the Roman collapse. One center of commercial activity lay in Northern Europe from England to the Baltic coast and involved the exchange of wood, beeswax, furs, rye, wheat, salt, cloth, and wine. The other major trading network centered on northern Italian towns such as Florence, Genoa, and Venice. Their trading part-

Map 10.3 Europe in the High Middle Ages
By the eleventh century, the national monarchies that would organize European political life — France, Spain, England, Poland, and Germany — had begun to take shape. The earlier external attacks on Europe from Vikings, Magyars, and Muslims had largely ceased, although it was clear that European civilization was developing in the shadow of the Islamic world.

ners were the more established civilizations of Islam and Byzantium, and the primary objects of trade included the silks, drugs, precious stones, and spices from Asia. At great trading fairs, particularly those in the Champagne area of France near Paris, merchants from Northern and Southern Europe met to exchange the products of their respective areas, such as northern woolens for Mediterranean spices. Thus the self-sufficient communities of earlier centuries increasingly forged commercial bonds among themselves and with more distant peoples.

The population of towns and cities likewise grew on the sites of older Roman towns, at trading crossroads and fortifications, and around cathedrals all over Europe. Some towns had only a few hundred people, but others became much larger. In the early 1300s, London had about 40,000 people, Paris had approximately 80,000, and Venice by the end of the fourteenth century could boast perhaps 150,000. To keep these figures in perspective, Constantinople housed some 400,000 people in 1000, Córdoba in Muslim Spain about 500,000, the Song dynasty capital of Hangzhou more than 1 million in the thirteenth century, and the Aztec capital of Tenochtitlán perhaps 200,000 by 1500. Nonetheless, urbanization was proceeding apace in Europe, though never hosting more than 10 percent of the population. These towns gave rise to and attracted new groups of people, particularly merchants, bankers, artisans, and university-trained professionals such as lawyers, doctors, and scholars. Many of these groups, including university professors and students, organized themselves into guilds (associations of people pursuing the same line of work) to regulate their respective professions. Thus from the rural social order of lord and peasant, a new more productive and complex division of labor took shape in European society.

A further sign of accelerating change in the West lay in the growth of territorial states with more effective institutions of government commanding the loyalty, or at least the obedience, of their subjects. Since the disintegration of the Roman Empire, Europeans' loyalties had focused on the family, the manor, or the religious community, but seldom on the state. Great lords may have been recognized as kings, but their authority was extremely limited and was exercised through a complex and decentralized network of feudal relationships with earls, counts, barons, and knights, who often felt little obligation to do the king's bidding. But in the eleventh through the thirteenth century, the nominal monarchs of Europe gradually and painfully began to consolidate their authority, and the outlines of French, English, Spanish, Scandinavian, and other states began to appear, each with its own distinct language and culture (see Map 10.3, p. 481). Royal courts and embryonic bureaucracies were established, and groups of professional administrators appeared. Such territorial kingdoms were not universal, however. In Italy, city-states flourished as urban areas grew wealthy and powerful, whereas the Germans remained divided among a large number of small principalities within the Holy Roman Empire.

These changes, which together represented the making of a new civilization, had implications for the lives of countless women and men. (See the portrait of Cecilia Penifader, pp. 484–85, for an account of a rural unmarried woman's life in England during this time.) Economic growth and urbanization initially offered European women substantial new opportunities. Women were active in a number of urban professions, such as weaving, brewing, milling grain, midwifery, small-scale retailing, laundering, spinning, and prostitution. In twelfth-century Paris, for example, a list of 100 occupations identified 86 as involving women workers, of which 6 were exclusively female. In England, women worked as silk weavers, hatmakers, tailors, brewers, and leather processors and were entitled to train female apprentices in some of these trades. In Frankfurt, about one-third of the crafts and trades were entirely female, another 40 percent were dominated by men, and the rest were open to both. Widows of great merchants sometimes continued their husbands' businesses, and one of them, Rose Burford, lent a large sum of money to the king of England to finance a war against Scotland in 1318.

Much as economic and technological change in China had eroded female silk production, by the fifteenth century, artisan opportunities were declining for European women as well. Most women's guilds were gone, and women were restricted or banned from many others. Even brothels were run by men. In England, guild regulations now outlawed women's participation in manufacturing particular fabrics and forbade their being trained on new and larger weaving machines. Women might still spin thread, but the more lucrative and skilled task of weaving fell increasingly to men. Technological progress may have been one reason for this change. Water- and animal-powered grain mills replaced the hand-grinding previously undertaken by women, and larger looms making heavier cloth replaced the lighter looms that women had worked. Men increasingly took over these professions and trained their sons as apprentices, making it more difficult for women to remain active in these fields.

The Church had long offered some women an alternative to home, marriage, family, and rural life. As in Buddhist lands, substantial numbers of women, particularly from aristocratic families, were attracted to the secluded monastic life of poverty, chastity, and obedience within a convent, in part for the relative freedom from male control that it offered. Here was one of the few places where women might exercise authority as abbesses of their orders and obtain a measure of education. The twelfth-century Abbess Hildegard of Bingen, for example, won wide acclaim for her writings on theology, medicine, botany, and music.

But by 1300, much of the independence that such abbesses and their nuns had enjoyed was curtailed and male control tightened, even as veneration of the Virgin Mary swept across Western Christendom. Restrictions on women hearing confessions, preaching, and chanting the Gospel were now more strictly enforced. The educational activities of monastic centers, where men and women could both participate, now gave way to the new universities where only ordained men could study and teach. Furthermore, older ideas of women's intellectual inferiority, the impurity of menstruation, and her role as a sexual temptress were mobilized to explain why women could never be priests and must operate under male control.

Another religious opportunity for women, operating outside of monastic life and the institutional church, was that of the Beguines. These were groups of laywomen, often from poorer families in Northern Europe, who lived together, practiced celibacy, and devoted themselves to weaving and to working with the sick, the old, and the poor. Though widely respected for their piety and service, their independence from the church hierarchy prompted considerable opposition from both religious and secular authorities suspicious of women operating outside of male control, and the movement gradually faded away. More acceptable to male authorities was the role of in Newfoundland in North America, and more durably in Greenland and Iceland. (See Portrait of Thorfinn Karlsfeni in Chapter 7, pp. 338–39.) As Western economies grew, merchants, travelers, diplomats, and missionaries brought European society into more intensive contact with more distant peoples and with Eurasian commercial networks. By the thirteenth and fourteenth centuries, Europeans had direct, though limited, contact with India, China, and Mongolia. Europe clearly was outward bound.

Nothing more dramatically revealed European expansiveness and the religious passions that informed it than the Crusades, a series of "holy wars" that captured the imagination of Western Christendom for several centuries, beginning in 1095. In European thinking and practice, the Crusades were wars undertaken at God's command and authorized by the pope as the Vicar of Christ on earth. They required participants to swear a vow and in return offered an indulgence, which removed the penalties for any confessed sins, as well as various material benefits, such as immunity from lawsuits and a moratorium on the repayment of debts. Any number of political, economic, and social motives underlay the Crusades, but at their core they were religious wars. Within Europe, the amazing support for the Crusades reflected an understanding of them "as providing security against mortal enemies threatening the spiritual health of all Christendom and all Christians."[23] Crusading drew on both Christian piety and the warrior values of the elite, with little sense of contradiction between these impulses.

The most famous Crusades were those aimed at wresting Jerusalem and the holy places associated with the life of Jesus from Islamic control and returning them to Christendom (see Map 10.4). Beginning in 1095, wave after wave of Crusaders from all walks of life and many countries flocked to the eastern Mediterranean, where they temporarily carved out four small Christian states, the last of which was recaptured by Muslim forces in 1291. Led or supported by an assortment of kings, popes, bishops, monks, lords, nobles, and merchants, the Crusades demonstrated a growing European capacity for organization, finance, transportation, and recruitment, made all the more impressive by the absence of any centralized direction for the project. They also demonstrated considerable cruelty. The seizure of Jerusalem in 1099 was accompanied by the slaughter of many Muslims and Jews as the Crusaders made their way, according to perhaps exaggerated reports, through streets littered with corpses and ankle deep in blood to the tomb of Christ.

Crusading was not limited to targets in the Islamic Middle East, however. Those Christians who waged war for centuries to reclaim the Iberian Peninsula from Muslim hands were likewise declared "crusaders," with a similar set of spiritual and material benefits. So too were Scandinavian and German warriors who took part in wars to conquer, settle, and convert lands along the Baltic Sea. The Byzantine Empire and Russia, both of which followed Eastern Orthodox Christianity, were also on the receiving end of Western crusading, as were Christian heretics and various enemies of the pope in Europe itself. Crusading, in short, was a pervasive feature of European expansion, which persisted as Europeans began their oceanic voyages in the fifteenth century and beyond.

Map 10.4 The Crusades

Western Europe's crusading tradition reflected the expansive energy and religious impulses of an emerging civilization. It was directed against Muslims in the Middle East, Sicily, and Spain as well as the Eastern Orthodox Christians of the Byzantine Empire. The Crusades also involved attacks on Jewish communities, probably the first organized mass pogroms against Jews in Europe's history.

Surprisingly perhaps, the Crusades had little lasting impact, either politically or religiously, in the Middle East. European power was not sufficiently strong or long-lasting to induce much conversion, and the small European footholds there had come under Muslim control by 1300. The penetration of Turkic-speaking peoples from Central Asia and the devastating Mongol invasions of the thirteenth century were far more significant in Islamic history than were the temporary incursions of European Christians. In fact, Muslims largely forgot about the Crusades until the late nineteenth and early twentieth centuries, when their memory was revived in the context of a growing struggle against European imperialism.

In Europe, however, crusading in general and interaction with the Islamic world in particular had very significant long-term consequences. Spain, Sicily, and the Baltic region were brought permanently into the world of Western Christendom, while a declining Byzantium was further weakened by the Crusader sacking of Constantinople in 1204 and left even more vulnerable to Muslim Turkish conquest. In Europe

The Crusades
This fourteenth-century painting illustrates the Christian seizure of Jerusalem during the First Crusade in 1099. The crowned figure in the center is Godefroi de Bouillon, a French knight and nobleman who played a prominent role in the attack and was briefly known as the king of Jerusalem. (Snark/Art Resource, NY)

itself, popes strengthened their position, at least for a time, in their continuing struggles with secular authorities. Tens of thousands of Europeans came into personal contact with the Islamic world, from which they picked up a taste for the many luxury goods available there, stimulating a demand for Asian goods. They also learned techniques for producing sugar on large plantations using slave labor, a process that had incalculable consequences in later centuries as Europeans transferred the plantation system to the Americas. Muslim scholarship, together with the Greek learning that it incorporated, also flowed into Europe, largely through Spain and Sicily.

If the cross-cultural contacts born of crusading opened channels of trade, technology transfer, and intellectual exchange, they also hardened cultural barriers between peoples. The rift between Eastern Orthodoxy and Roman Catholicism deepened further and remains to this day a fundamental divide in the Christian world. Christian anti-Semitism was both expressed and exacerbated as Crusaders on their way to Jerusalem found time to massacre Jews, regarded as "Christ-killers," in a number of European cities, particularly in Germany. Such pogroms, however, were not sanctioned by the Church. A leading figure in the second crusade, Bernard of Clairvaux, declared that "it is good that you march against the Muslims, but anyone who touches a Jew to take his life, is as touching Jesus himself."[24] European empire building, especially in the Americas, continued the crusading notion that "God wills it." And more recently, over the past two centuries, as the world of the Christian West and that of Islam collided, both sides found many occasions in which images of the Crusades, however distorted, proved politically popular or ideologically useful.[25]

SUMMING UP SO FAR

How did the historical development of the European West differ from that of Byzantium in the third-wave era?

The West in Comparative Perspective

At one level, the making of Western civilization was unremarkable. Civilizations had risen, fallen, renewed themselves, and evolved at many times and in many places. The European case has received extraordinary scrutiny, not so much because of its special significance at the time, but because of its later role as a globally dominant region. However we might explain Europe's subsequent rise to prominence on the world stage, its development in the several centuries after 1000 made only modest ripples beyond its own region. In some respects, Europe was surely distinctive, but it was not yet a major player in the global arena. Comparisons, particularly with China and the Islamic world, help to place these European developments in a world history context.

Catching Up

As the civilization of the West evolved, it was clearly less developed in comparison to Byzantium, China, India, and the Islamic world. Europe's cities were smaller, its political authorities weaker, its economy less commercialized, and its technology inferior to the more established civilizations. Muslim observers who encountered Europeans saw them as barbarians. An Arab geographer of the tenth century commented on Europeans: "Their bodies are large, their manners harsh, their understanding dull, and their tongues heavy ... Those of them who are farthest to the north are the most subject to stupidity, grossness and brutishness."[26] Muslim travelers over the next several centuries saw more to be praised in West African kingdoms, where Islam was practiced and gold was plentiful.

Furthermore, thoughtful Europeans who directly encountered other peoples often acknowledged their own comparative backwardness. "In our time," wrote a twelfth-century European scholar, "it is in Toledo [a Spanish city long under Muslim rule] that the teaching of the Arabs ... is offered to the crowds. I hastened there to listen to the teaching of the wisest philosophers of this world."[27] The Italian traveler Marco Polo in the thirteenth century proclaimed Hangzhou in China "the finest and noblest [city] in the world" (see Document 7.2, pp. 347–50, for more about Marco Polo's travels to China). In the early sixteenth century, Spanish invaders of Mexico were stunned at the size and wealth of the Aztec capital, especially its huge market, claiming that "we had never seen such a thing before."[28]

Curious about the rest of the world, Europeans proved quite willing to engage with and borrow from the more advanced civilizations to the east. Growing European economies, especially in the northwest, reconnected with the Eurasian trading system, with which they had lost contact after the fall of Rome. Now European elites eagerly sought spices, silks, porcelain, and sugar from afar even as they assimilated various technological, intellectual, and cultural innovations, as the Snapshot demonstrates. When the road to China opened in the thirteenth and fourteenth centuries, many Europeans, including the merchant-traveler Marco Polo, were more than willing to make the long and difficult journey, returning with amazing tales of splendor and abundance far beyond what was available in Europe. When Europeans took to the oceans in the fifteenth and sixteenth centuries, they were seeking out the sources of African and Asian wealth. Thus the accelerating growth of European civilization was accompanied by its reintegration into the larger Afro-Eurasian networks of exchange and communication.

In this willingness to borrow, Europe resembled several other third-wave civilizations of the time. Japan, for example, took much from China; West Africa drew heavily on Islamic civilization; and Russia actively imitated Byzantium. All of them were then

■ **Change**

In what ways did borrowing from abroad shape European civilization after 1000?

$\mathcal{S}$napshot   **European Borrowing**

Like people in other emerging civilizations of the third-wave era, Europeans borrowed extensively from their near and more distant counterparts. They adapted these imports, both technological and cultural, to their own circumstances and generated distinctive innovations as well.

Borrowing	Source	Significance
Horse collar	China/Central Asia via Tunisia	Enabled heavy plowing and contributed to European agricultural development
Stirrup	India/Afghanistan	Revolutionized warfare by enhancing cavalry forces
Gunpowder	China	Enhanced the destructiveness of warfare
Paper	China	Enabled bureaucracy; fostered literacy; prerequisite for printing
Spinning wheel	India	Sped up production of yarn, usually by women at home
Wheelbarrow	China	Labor saving device for farm and construction work
Aristotle	Byzantium/Islamic Spain	Recovery of classical Greek thought
Medical knowledge/treatments	Islamic world	Sedatives, antiseptics, knowledge of contagious diseases, surgical techniques, optics enriched European medicine
Christian mysticism	Muslim Spain	Mutual influence of Sufi, Jewish, and Christian mysticism
Music/poetry	Muslim Spain	Contributed to tradition of troubadour poetry about chivalry and courtly love
Mathematics	India/Islamic world	Foundation for European algebra
Chess	India/Persia	A game of prestige associated with European nobility

developing civilizations, in a position analogous perhaps to the developing countries of the twentieth century.

Technological borrowing required adaptation to the unique conditions of Europe and was accompanied by considerable independent invention as well. Together these processes generated a significant tradition of technological innovation that allowed Europe by 1500 to catch up with, and in some areas perhaps to surpass, China and the Islamic world. That achievement bears comparison with the economic revolution of Tang and Song dynasty China, although Europe began at a lower level and depended more on borrowing than did its Chinese counterpart (see Chapter 8). But in the several centuries surrounding 1000 at both ends of Eurasia, major processes of technological innovation were under way.

In Europe, technological breakthroughs first became apparent in agriculture as Europeans adapted to the very different environmental conditions north of the Alps in the several centuries following 500 C.E. They developed a heavy wheeled plow that could handle the dense soils of Northern Europe far better than the light or "scratch" plow used in Mediterranean agriculture. To pull the plow, Europeans began to rely increasingly on horses rather than oxen and to use iron horseshoes and a more efficient collar, which probably originated in China or Central Asia and could support much heavier loads. In addition, Europeans developed a new three-field system of crop rotation, which allowed considerably more land to be planted at any one time. These were the technological foundations for a more productive agriculture that could support the growing population of European civilization, and especially its urban centers, far more securely than before.

Beyond agriculture, Europeans began to tap non-animal sources of energy in a major way, particularly after 1000. A new type of windmill, very different from an earlier Persian version, was widely used in Europe by the twelfth and thirteenth centuries. The water-driven mill was even more important. The Romans had used such mills largely to grind grain, but their development was limited, since few streams flowed all year and many slaves were available to do the work. By the ninth century, however, water mills were rapidly becoming more evident in Europe. In the early

European Technology
Europeans' fascination with technology and their religious motivation for investigating the world are apparent in this thirteenth-century portrayal of God as a divine engineer, laying out the world with a huge compass. (Erich Lessing/Art Resource, NY)

fourteenth century, a concentration of sixty-eight mills dotted a one-mile stretch of the Seine River near Paris. In addition to grinding grain, these mills provided power for sieving flour, tanning hides, making beer, sawing wood, manufacturing iron, and making paper. Devices such as cranks, flywheels, camshafts, and complex gearing mechanisms, when combined with water or wind power, enabled Europeans of the High Middle Ages to revolutionize production in a number of industries and to break with the ancient tradition of depending almost wholly on animal or human muscle as sources of energy. So intense was the interest of European artisans and engineers in tapping mechanical sources of energy that a number of them experimented with perpetual-motion machines, an idea borrowed from Indian philosophers.

Technological borrowing also was evident in the arts of war. Gunpowder was invented in China, but Europeans were probably the first to use it in cannons, in the early fourteenth century, and by 1500 they had the most advanced arsenals in the world. In 1517, one Chinese official, on first encountering European ships and weapons, remarked with surprise,

"The westerns are extremely dangerous because of their artillery. No weapon ever made since memorable antiquity is superior to their cannon."[29] Advances in ship-building and navigational techniques—including the magnetic compass and sternpost rudder from China and adaptations of the Mediterranean or Arab lateen sail, which enabled vessels to sail against the wind—provided the foundation for European mastery of the seas.

Europe's passion for technology was reflected in its culture and ideas as well as in its machines. About 1260, the English scholar and Franciscan friar Roger Bacon wrote of the possibilities he foresaw, and in doing so, he expressed the confident spirit of the age:

> Machines of navigation can be constructed, without rowers . . . which are borne under the guidance of one man at a greater speed than if they were full of men. Also a chariot can be constructed, that will move with incalculable speed without any draught animal. . . . Also flying machines may be constructed so that a man may sit in the midst of the machine turning a certain instrument by means of which wings artificially constructed would beat the air after the manner of a bird flying . . . and there are countless other things that can be constructed.[30]

Pluralism in Politics

■ Comparison

Why was Europe unable to achieve the kind of political unity that China experienced? What impact did this have on the subsequent history of Europe?

Unlike the large centralized states of Byzantium, the Islamic world, and China, this third-wave European civilization never regained the earlier unity it had under Roman rule. Rather, political life gradually crystallized into a system of competing states (France, Spain, England, Sweden, Prussia, the Netherlands, and Poland, among others) that has persisted into the twenty-first century and that the European Union still confronts. Geographic barriers, ethnic and linguistic diversity, and the shifting balances of power among its many states prevented the emergence of a single European empire, despite periodic efforts to re-create something resembling the still-remembered unity of the Roman Empire.

This multicentered political system shaped the emerging civilization of the West in many ways. It gave rise to frequent wars, enhanced the role and status of military men, and drove the "gunpowder revolution." Thus European society and values were militarized far more than in China, which gave greater prominence to scholars and bureaucrats. Intense interstate rivalry, combined with a willingness to borrow, also stimulated European technological development. By 1500, Europeans had gone a long way toward catching up with their more advanced Asian counterparts in agriculture, industry, war, and sailing.

Thus endemic warfare did not halt European economic growth. Capital, labor, and goods found their way around political barriers, while the common assumptions of Christian culture and the use of Latin and later French by the literate elite fostered communication across political borders. Europe's multistate system thus provided enough competition to be stimulating but also sufficient order and unity to allow economic endeavors to prosper.

The states within this emerging European civilization also differed from those to the east. Their rulers generally were weaker and had to contend with competing sources of power. Unlike the Orthodox Church in Byzantium, with its practice of caesaropapism, the Roman Catholic Church in the West maintained a degree of independence from state authority that served to check the power of kings and lords. European vassals had certain rights in return for loyalty to their lords and kings. By the thirteenth century, this meant that high-ranking nobles, acting through formal councils, had the right to advise their rulers and to approve new taxes.

This three-way struggle for power among kings, warrior aristocrats, and church leaders, all of them from the nobility, enabled urban-based merchants in Europe to achieve an unusual independence from political authority. Many cities, where wealthy merchants exercised local power, won the right to make and enforce their own laws and appoint their own officials. Some of them—Venice, Genoa, Pisa, and Milan, for example—became almost completely independent city-states. Elsewhere, kings granted charters that allowed cities to have their own courts, laws, and governments, while paying their own kind of taxes to the king instead of feudal dues. Powerful, independent cities were a distinctive feature of European life after 1100 or so. By contrast, Chinese cities, which were far larger than those of Europe, were simply part of the empire and enjoyed few special privileges. Although commerce was far more extensive in China than in an emerging European civilization, the powerful Chinese state favored the landowners over merchants, monopolized the salt and iron industries, and actively controlled and limited merchant activity far more than the new and weaker royal authorities of Europe were able to do.

The relative weakness of Europe's rulers allowed urban merchants more leeway and, according to some historians, paved the way to a more thorough development of capitalism in later centuries. It also led to the development of representative institutions or parliaments through which the views and interests of these contending forces could be expressed and accommodated. Intended to strengthen royal authority by consulting with major social groups, these embryonic parliaments did not represent the "people" or the "nation" but instead embodied the three great "estates of the realm"—the clergy (the first estate), the landowning nobility (the second estate), and urban merchants (the third estate).

Reason and Faith

A further feature of this emerging European civilization was a distinctive intellectual tension between the claims of human reason and those of faith. Christianity had developed in a world suffused with Greek rationalism. Some early Christian thinkers sought to maintain a clear separation between the new religion and the ideas of Plato and Aristotle. "What indeed has Athens to do with Jerusalem?" asked Tertullian (150–225 C.E.), an early church leader from North Africa. More common, however, was the notion that Greek philosophy could serve as a "handmaiden" to faith, more fully disclosing the truths of Christianity. In the reduced circumstances of Western Europe after the collapse of the Roman Empire, the Church had little direct access

■ **Comparison**

In what different ways did classical Greek philosophy and science have an impact in the West, in Byzantium, and in the Islamic world?

to the writings of the Greeks, although some Latin translations and commentaries provided a continuing link to the world of classical thought.

But intellectual life in Europe changed dramatically in the several centuries after 1000, amid a rising population, a quickening commercial life, emerging towns and cities, and the Church's growing independence from royal or noble authorities. Moreover, the West was developing a legal system that provided a measure of independence for a variety of institutions—towns and cities, guilds, professional associations, and especially universities. An outgrowth of earlier cathedral schools, these European universities—in Paris, Bologna, Oxford, Cambridge, Salamanca—became "zones of intellectual autonomy" in which scholars could pursue their studies with some freedom from the dictates of religious or political authorities, although that freedom was never complete and was frequently contested.[31]

This was the setting in which European Christian thinkers, a small group of literate churchmen, began to emphasize, quite self-consciously, the ability of human reason to penetrate divine mysteries and to grasp the operation of the natural order. An early indication of this new emphasis occurred in the late eleventh century when students in a monastic school in France asked their teacher, Anselm, to provide them a proof for the existence of God based solely on reason, without using the Bible or other sources of divine revelation.

The new interest in rational thought was applied first and foremost to theology, the "queen of the sciences" to European thinkers. Here was an effort to provide a rational foundation for faith, not to replace faith or to rebel against it. Logic, philosophy, and rationality would operate in service to Christ. Of course, some opposed this new emphasis on human reason. Bernard of Clairvaux, a twelfth-century French abbot, declared, "Faith believes. It does not dispute."[32] His contemporary and intellectual opponent, the French scholar William of Conches, lashed out: "You poor fools. God can make a cow out of a tree, but has he ever done so? Therefore show some reason why a thing is so or cease to hold that it is so."[33]

European intellectuals also applied their newly discovered confidence in human reason to law, medicine, and the world of nature, exploring optics, magnetism, astronomy, and alchemy. Slowly and never completely, the scientific study of nature, known as "natural philosophy," began to separate itself from theology. In European universities, natural philosophy

European University Life in the Middle Ages
This fourteenth-century manuscript painting shows a classroom scene from the University of Bologna in Italy. Note the sleeping and disruptive students. Some things apparently never change. (bpk, Berlin/Kupferstichkabinett, Staatliche Museen, Berlin, Germany/Joerg P. Anders/ Art Resource, NY)

was studied in the faculty of arts, which was separate from the faculty of theology, although many scholars contributed to both fields.

This mounting enthusiasm for rational inquiry stimulated European scholars to seek out original Greek texts, particularly those of Aristotle. They found them in the Greek-speaking world of Byzantium and in the Islamic world, where they had long ago been translated into Arabic. In the twelfth and thirteenth centuries, an explosion of translations from Greek and Arabic into Latin, much of it undertaken in Spain, gave European scholars direct access to the works of ancient Greeks and to the remarkable results of Arab scholarship in astronomy, optics, medicine, pharmacology, and more. Much of this Arab science was now translated into Latin and provided a boost to Europe's changing intellectual life, centered in the new universities. One of these translators, Adelard of Bath (1080–1142), remarked that he had learned, "under the guidance of reason from Arabic teachers," not to trust established authority.[34]

It was the works of the prolific Aristotle, with his logical approach and "scientific temperament," that made the deepest impression. His writings became the basis for university education and largely dominated the thought of Western Europe in the five centuries after 1200. In the work of the thirteenth-century theologian Thomas Aquinas, Aristotle's ideas were thoroughly integrated into a logical and systematic presentation of Christian doctrine. In this growing emphasis on human rationality, at least partially separate from divine revelation, lay one of the foundations of the later Scientific Revolution and the secularization of European intellectual life.

Surprisingly, nothing comparable occurred in the Byzantine Empire, where knowledge of the Greek language was widespread and access to Greek texts was easy. Although Byzantine scholars kept the classical tradition alive, their primary interest lay in the humanities (literature, philosophy, history) and theology rather than in the natural sciences or medicine. Furthermore, both state and church had serious reservations about Greek learning. In 529, the emperor Justinian closed Plato's Academy in Athens, claiming that it was an outpost of paganism. Its scholars dispersed into lands that soon became Islamic, carrying Greek learning into the Islamic world. Church authorities as well were suspicious of Greek thought, sometimes persecuting scholars who were too enamored with the ancients. Even those who did study the Greek writers did so in a conservative spirit, concerned to preserve and transmit the classical heritage rather than using it as a springboard for creating new knowledge. "The great men of the past," declared the fourteenth-century Byzantine scholar and statesman Theodore Metochites, "have said everything so perfectly that they have left nothing for us to say."[35]

In the Islamic world, Greek thought was embraced "with far more enthusiasm and creativity" than in Byzantium.[36] A massive translation project in the ninth and tenth centuries made Aristotle and many other Greek writers available in Arabic. That work contributed to a flowering of Arab scholarship, especially in the sciences and natural philosophy, between roughly 800 and 1200 (see Chapter 9), but it also stimulated a debate about faith and reason among Muslim thinkers, many of whom greatly admired

Greek philosophical, scientific, and medical texts. As in the Christian world, the issue was whether secular Greek thought was an aid or a threat to the faith. Western European church authorities after the thirteenth century had come to regard natural philosophy as a wholly legitimate enterprise and had thoroughly incorporated Aristotle into university education, but learned opinion in the Islamic world swung the other way. Though never completely disappearing from Islamic scholarship, the ideas of Plato and Aristotle receded after the thirteenth century in favor of teachings that drew more directly from the Quran or from mystical experience. Nor was natural philosophy a central concern of Islamic higher education as it was in the West. The integration of political and religious life in the Islamic world, as in Byzantium, contrasted with their separation in the West, where there was more space for the independent pursuit of scientific subjects.

LearningCurve
bedfordstmartins.com
/strayer/LC

Reflections: Remembering and Forgetting: Continuity and Surprise in the Worlds of Christendom

Many of the characteristic features of Christendom, which emerged during the era of third-wave civilizations, have had a long life, extending well into the modern era. The crusading element of European expansion was prominent among the motives of Spanish and Portuguese explorers. Europe's grudging freedom for merchant activity and its eagerness to borrow foreign technology arguably contributed to the growth of capitalism and industrialization in later centuries. The endemic military conflicts of European states, unable to recover the unity of the Roman Empire, found terrible expression in the world wars of the twentieth century. The controversy about reason and faith resonates still, at least in the United States, in debates about the authority of the Bible in secular and scientific matters. The rift between Eastern Orthodoxy and Roman Catholicism remains one of the major divides in the Christian world. Modern universities and the separation of religious and political authority likewise have their origins in the European Middle Ages. Such a perspective, linking the past with what came later, represents one of the great contributions that the study of history makes to human understanding. We are limited and shaped by our histories.

Yet that very strength of historical study can be misleading, particularly if it suggests a kind of inevitability, in which the past determines the future. Knowing the outcome of the stories we tell can be a serious disadvantage, for it may rob the people we study of the freedom and uncertainty that they surely experienced. In 500, few people would have predicted that Europe would become the primary center of Christianity, while the African and Asian expressions of that faith withered away. As late as 1000, the startling reversal of roles between the Eastern and Western wings of Christendom, which the next several centuries witnessed, was hardly on the horizon. At that time, the many small, rural, unsophisticated, and endlessly quarreling warrior-based societies of Western Europe would hardly have borne comparison with the powerful Byzantine Empire and its magnificent capital of Constantinople. Even in 1500, when Europe had begun to catch up with China and the Islamic world in various ways, there was little to predict its remarkable transformation over the next several centuries and the dramatic change in the global balance of power that this transformation produced.

Usually students of history are asked to remember. But forgetting can also be an aid to historical understanding. To recapture the unexpectedness of the historical process and to allow ourselves to be surprised, it may be useful on occasion to forget what we know about what happened next and to see the world as contemporaries viewed it.

Second Thoughts

LearningCurve
Check what you know.
**bedfordstmartins.com
/strayer/LC**

What's the Significance?

Nubian Christianity, 464; 468

Jesus sutras, 467

Ethiopian Christianity, 468–69

Byzantine Empire, 469–76

Constantinople, 470

Justinian, 470

caesaropapism, 472

Eastern Orthodox Christianity, 472–74

icons, 473

Prince Vladimir of Kiev, 475

Kievan Rus, 475–76

Charlemagne, 477–78

Holy Roman Empire, 478; 481

Roman Catholic Church, 478–80

Western Christendom, 480–85

Cecilia Penifader, 484–85

Crusades, 485–88

Online Study Guide
bedfordstmartins.com
/highschool/strayer

Big Picture Questions

1. What accounts for the different historical trajectories of the Byzantine and West European expressions of Christendom?

2. How did Byzantium and Western Europe interact with each other and with the larger world of the third-wave era?

3. In what respects was the civilization of the Latin West distinctive and unique, and in what ways was it broadly comparable to other third-wave civilizations?

4. **Looking Back:** How does the evolution of the Christian world in the third-wave era compare with that of Tang and Song dynasty China and of the Islamic world?

Next Steps: For Further Study

Bonnie S. Anderson and Judith P. Zinsser, *A History of Their Own* (2000). An overview of European women's history by two prominent scholars.

Edward Grant, *Science and Religion from Aristotle to Copernicus* (2004). Demonstrates the impact of Greek philosophy and science in Europe, with comparisons to Byzantium and the Islamic world.

Barbara A. Hanawalt, *The Middle Ages: An Illustrated History* (1999). A brief and beautifully illustrated introduction to the Middle Ages in European history.

For Web sites and additional documents related to this chapter, see **Make History** at bedfordstmartins.com /highschool/strayer.

Rowena Loverance, *Byzantium* (2004). A lavishly illustrated history of the Byzantine Empire, drawing on the rich collection of artifacts in the British Museum.

Diarmaid MacCulloch, *Christianity: The First Three Thousand Years* (2010). A recent and much-praised overview of the history of Christendom.

Christopher Tyerman, *Fighting for Christendom: Holy Wars and the Crusades* (2005). A very well-written, up-to-date history of the Crusades designed for nonspecialists.

"Middle Ages," http://www.learner.org/exhibits/middleages. An interactive Web site with text and images relating to life in Europe after the collapse of the Roman Empire.

Documents

Considering the Evidence:
The Making of Christian Europe

Like Buddhism and Islam, Christianity had become a universal religion, taking root well beyond its place of origin. In its early centuries, this new faith, born in a Jewish context in Roman Palestine, spread throughout the Roman Empire, where it received state support during the fourth century C.E. In the centuries that followed the collapse of the western Roman Empire, Christianity also took hold among the peoples of Western Europe in what are now England, France, Germany, and Scandinavia. While we often think about this region as solidly Christian, Western Europe in the period between 500 and 1000 C.E. was very much on the frontier of the Christian world. During those centuries, a number of emerging monarchs of post-Roman Europe found the Christian faith and the Church useful in consolidating their new and fragile states by linking them to the legacy of the Roman Empire. But the making of Christian Europe was a prolonged and tentative process, filled with setbacks, resistance, and struggles among variant versions of the faith as well as growing acceptance and cultural compromise. The documents that follow illustrate that process.

Document 10.1

The Conversion of Clovis

Among the Germanic peoples of post-Roman Western Europe, none were of greater significance than the Franks, occupying the region of present-day France (see Map 10.1, p. 471). By the early sixth century, a loosely unified Frankish kingdom had emerged under the leadership of Clovis (r. 485–511), whose Merovingian dynasty ruled the area until 751. Clovis's conversion to Christianity was described about a century later by a well-known bishop and writer, Gregory of Tours (538–594). It was an important step in the triumph of Christianity over Frankish "paganism." It also marked the victory of what would later become Roman Catholicism, based on the idea of the Trinity, over a rival form of the Christian faith, known as Arianism, which held that Jesus was a created divine being subordinate to God the Father.

- According to Gregory, what led to the conversion of Clovis?

- What issues are evident in the religious discussions of Clovis and his wife, Clotilda?

- Notice how Gregory modeled his picture of Clovis on that of Constantine, the famous Roman emperor whose conversion to Christianity in the fourth century gave official legitimacy and state support to the faith (see Chapter 4). What message did Gregory seek to convey in making this implied comparison?

- How might a modern secular historian use this document to help explain the spread of Christianity among the Franks?

GREGORY OF TOURS
History of the Franks
Late Sixth Century

[Clovis] had a first-born son by queen Clotilda, and as his wife wished to consecrate him in baptism, she tried unceasingly to persuade her husband, saying: "The gods you worship are nothing, and they will be unable to help themselves or any one else. For they are graven out of stone or wood or some metal.... They are endowed rather with the magic arts than with the power of the divine name. But he [God] ought rather to be worshipped who created by his word heaven and earth, the sea and all that in them is out of a state of nothingness ... [and] by whose hand mankind was created...."

But though the queen said this, the spirit of the king was by no means moved to belief, and he said: "It was at the command of our gods that all things were created and came forth, and it is plain that your God has no power and, what is more, he is proven not to belong to the family of the gods." Meantime the faithful queen made her son ready for baptism; she gave command to adorn the church with hang-

ings and curtains, in order that he who could not moved by persuasion might be urged to belief by this mystery. The boy, whom they named Ingomer, died after being baptized, still wearing the white garments in which he became regenerate. At this the king was violently angry, and reproached the queen harshly, saying: "If the boy had been dedicated in the name of my gods he would certainly have lived; but as it is, since he was baptized in the name of your God, he could not live at all." To this the queen said: "I give thanks to the omnipotent God, creator of all, who has judged me not wholly unworthy, that he should deign to take to his kingdom one born from my womb. My soul is not stricken with grief for his sake, because I know that, summoned from this world as he was in his baptismal garments, he will be fed by the vision of God...."

The queen did not cease to urge him to recognize the true God and cease worshipping idols. But he could not be influenced in any way to this belief, until at last a war arose with the Alamanni,° in which he was driven by necessity to confess what before he had of his free will denied. It came about

Source: Gregory Bishop of Tours, *History of the Franks*, translated by Ernest Brehaut (New York: Columbia University Press, 1916; copyright renewed 1944), bk. 2, selections from secs. 27, 29, 30, 31, 36–41.

°**Alamanni:** a Germanic people.

that as the two armies were fighting fiercely, there was much slaughter, and Clovis's army began to be in danger of destruction. He saw it and raised his eyes to heaven, and with remorse in his heart he burst into tears and cried: "Jesus Christ, whom Clotilda asserts to be the son of the living God . . . , I beseech the glory of thy aid, with the vow that if thou wilt grant me victory over these enemies . . . , I will believe in thee and be baptized in thy name. For I have invoked my own gods but, as I find, they have withdrawn from aiding me; and therefore I believe that they possess no power, since they do not help those who obey them. . . ." And when he said thus, the Alamanni turned their backs, and

began to disperse in flight. And when they saw that their king was killed, they submitted to the dominion of Clovis, saying: "Let not the people perish further, we pray; we are yours now." And he stopped the fighting, and after encouraging his men, retired in peace and told the queen how he had had merit to win the victory by calling on the name of Christ. This happened in the fifteenth year of his reign. . . .

And so the king confessed all-powerful God in the Trinity, and was baptized in the name of the Father, Son and Holy Spirit, and was anointed with the holy ointment with the sign of the cross of Christ. And of his army more than 3,000 were baptized.

Document 10.2

Advice on Dealing with "Pagans"

In their dealings with the "pagan" or non-Christian peoples and kings of Western Europe, church authorities such as missionaries, bishops, and the pope himself sometimes advocated compromise with existing cultural traditions rather than overt hostility to them. Here Pope Gregory (r. 590–604) urges the bishop of England to adopt a strategy of accommodation with the prevailing religious practices of the Anglo-Saxon peoples of the island. It was contained in a famous work about the early Christian history of England, composed by a Benedictine monk known as The Venerable Bede and completed about 731.

- What can we learn about the religious practices of the Anglo-Saxons from Bede's account?

- In what specific ways did the pope urge toleration? And why did he advocate accommodation or compromise with existing religious practices? Keep in mind that the political authorities in England at the time had not yet become thoroughly Christian.

- What implication might Gregory's policies have for the beliefs and practices of English converts?

POPE GREGORY

Advice to the English Church

601

[T]he temples of the idols in that nation [England] ought not to be destroyed; but let the idols that are in them be destroyed; let holy water be made and sprinkled in the said temples, let altars be erected, and relics placed. For if those temples are well built, it is requisite that they be converted from the worship of devils to the service of the true God; that the nation, seeing that their temples are not destroyed, may remove error from their hearts, and knowing and adoring the true God, may the more familiarly resort to the places to which they have been accustomed.

And because they have been used to slaughter many oxen in the sacrifices to devils, some solemnity must be exchanged for them on this account, as that on the day of the dedication, or the nativities of the holy martyrs, whose relics are there deposited, they may build themselves huts of the boughs of trees, about those churches which have been turned to that

use from temples, and celebrate the solemnity with religious feasting, and no more offer beasts to the Devil, but kill cattle to the praise of God in their eating, and return thanks to the Giver of all things for their sustenance; to the end that, while some gratifications are outwardly permitted them, they may the more easily consent to the inward consolations of the grace of God. For there is no doubt that it is impossible to efface everything at once from their obdurate minds; because he who endeavors to ascend to the highest place, rises by degrees or steps, and not by leaps.

Thus the Lord made Himself known to the people of Israel in Egypt; and yet He allowed them the use of the sacrifices which they were wont to offer to the Devil, in his own worship; so as to command them in his sacrifice to kill beasts, to the end that, changing their hearts, they might lay aside one part of the sacrifice, while they retained another; that while they offered the same beasts which they were wont to offer, they should offer them to God, and not to idols; and thus they would no longer be the same sacrifices.

Source: The Venerable Bede, *The Ecclesiastical History of the English Nation*, edited by Ernest Rhys (London: J. M. Dent and Sons; New York: E. P. Dutton, 1910), 52–53.

Document 10.3

Charlemagne and the Saxons

The policies of peaceful conversion and accommodation described in Document 10.2 did not prevail everywhere, as Charlemagne's dealings with the Saxons reveals. During late eighth and early ninth centuries C.E., Charlemagne (r. 768–814) was the powerful king of the Franks. He turned his Frankish kingdom into a Christian empire that briefly incorporated much of continental Europe, and he was crowned as a renewed Roman emperor by the pope. In the course of almost constant wars of expansion, Charlemagne struggled for over thirty years (772–804) to subdue the Saxons, a "pagan" Germanic people who inhabited a region on the northeastern frontier of Charlemagne's growing empire (see Map 10.2, p. 478). The document known as the *Capitulary on Saxony* outlines a series of laws, regulations, and punishments (known collectively as a capitulary) regarding religious practice of the Saxons. This document reveals both the coercive policies of Charlemagne and the vigorous resistance of the Saxons to their forcible incorporation into his Christian domain.

■ What does this document reveal about the kind of resistance that the Saxons mounted against their enforced conversion?

■ How did Charlemagne seek to counteract that resistance?

■ What does this document suggest about Charlemagne's views of his duties as ruler?

CHARLEMAGNE

Capitulary on Saxony

785

1. It was pleasing to all that the churches of Christ, which are now being built in Saxony and consecrated to God, should not have less, but greater and more illustrious honor, than the fanes° of the idols had had. . . .

3. If any one shall have entered a church by violence and shall have carried off anything in it by force or theft, or shall have burned the church itself, let him be punished by death.

4. If any one, out of contempt for Christianity, shall have despised the holy Lenten fast and shall have eaten flesh, let him be punished by death. But, nevertheless, let it be taken into consideration by a priest, lest perchance any one from necessity has been led to eat flesh.

5. If any one shall have killed a bishop or priest or deacon, let him likewise be punished capitally.

6. If any one deceived by the devil shall have believed, after the manner of the pagans, that any man or woman is a witch and eats men, and on this account shall have burned the person, or shall have given the person's flesh to others to eat, or shall have eaten it himself, let him be punished by a capital sentence.

7. If any one, in accordance with pagan rites, shall have caused the body of a dead man to be

burned and shall have reduced his bones to ashes, let him be punished capitally. . . .

9. If any one shall have sacrificed a man to the devil, and after the manner of the pagans shall have presented him as a victim to the demons, let him be punished by death.

10. If any one shall have formed a conspiracy with the pagans against the Christians, or shall have wished to join with them in opposition to the Christians, let him be punished by death; and whoever shall have consented to this same fraudulently against the king and the Christian people, let him be punished by death. . . .

17. Likewise, in accordance with the mandate of God, we command that all shall give a tithe of their property and labor to the churches and priests;

18. That on the Lord's day no meetings and public judicial assemblages shall be held, unless perchance in a case of great necessity or when war compels it, but all shall go to the church to hear the word of God, and shall be free for prayers or good works. Likewise, also, on the especial festivals they shall devote themselves to God and to the services of the church, and shall refrain from secular assemblies.

°**fanes:** temples.

Source: D. C. Munro, trans., *Translations and Reprints from the Original Sources of European History*, vol. 6, no. 5, *Selections from the Laws of Charles the Great* (Philadelphia: University of Pennsylvania Press, 1900), 2–4.

19. Likewise,... all infants shall be baptized within a year....

21. If any one shall have made a vow at springs or trees or groves, or shall have made any offerings after the manner of the heathen and shall have partaken of a repast in honor of the demons, if he shall be a noble, [he must pay a fine of] 60 solidi,° if a freeman 30, if a litus° 15.

_____

°**solidi:** gold coins.

°**litus:** neither a slave nor a free person.

Documents 10.4 and 10.5

The Persistence of Tradition

Conversion to Christianity in Western Europe was neither easy nor simple. Peoples thought to have been solidly converted to the new faith continued to engage in earlier practices. Others blended older traditions with Christian rituals. The two documents that follow illustrate both patterns. Document 10.4 describes the encounter between Saint Boniface (672–754), a leading missionary to the Germans, and the Hessians during the eighth century. It was written by one of Boniface's devoted followers, Willibald, who subsequently composed a biography of the missionary. Document 10.5 comes from a tenth-century Anglo-Saxon manuscript known as the *Leechbook*, a medical text that describes cures for various problems caused by "elves and nightgoers."

- What practices of the Hessians conflicted with Boniface's understanding of Christianity? How did he confront the persistence of these practices?

- What do these documents reveal about the process of conversion to Christianity?

- How might Pope Gregory (Document 10.2), Charlemagne (Document 10.3), and Boniface (Document 10.4) have responded to the cures and preventions described in the *Leechbook*?

WILLIBALD

Life of Boniface
ca. 760 C.E.

Now many of the Hessians who at that time had acknowledged the Catholic faith were confirmed by the grace of the Holy Spirit and received the laying-on of hands. But others, not yet strong in the spirit, refused to accept the pure teachings of the church in their entirety. Moreover, some continued secretly, others openly, to offer sacrifices to trees and springs, to inspect the entrails of victims; some practiced divination, legerdemain, and incantations; some turned their attention to auguries, auspices, and other sacrificial rites; while others, of a more reasonable character, forsook all the profane

_____

Source: Willibald, "Life of Boniface," in *The Anglo-Saxon Missionaries in Germany*, translated by C. H. Talbot (London: Sheed and Ward, 1954), 45–46.

practices of the [heathens] and committed none of these crimes.

With the counsel and advice of the latter persons, Boniface in their presence attempted to cut down . . . a certain oak of extraordinary size, called in the old tongue of the pagans the Oak of Jupiter. Taking his courage in his hands (for a great crowd of pagans stood by watching and bitterly cursing in their hearts the enemy of the gods), he cut the first notch. But when he had made a superficial cut, suddenly, the oak's vast bulk, shaken by a mighty blast of wind from above crashed to the ground shivering its topmost branches into fragments in its fall. As if by the express will of God (for the brethren present had done nothing to cause it) the oak burst asunder into four parts, each part having a trunk of equal length.

At the sight of this extraordinary spectacle the heathens who had been cursing ceased to revile and began, on the contrary, to believe and bless the Lord. Thereupon the holy bishop took counsel with the brethren, built an oratory° from the timber of the oak and dedicated it to Saint Peter the Apostle. He then set out on a journey to Thuringia. . . . Arrived there, he addressed the elders and the chiefs of the people, calling on them to put aside their blind ignorance and to return to the Christian religion that they had formerly embraced.

———————————

°**oratory:** a place of prayer.

The Leechbook
Tenth Century

Work a salve against elfkind and nightgoers, . . . and the people with whom the Devil has intercourse. Take eowohumelan, wormwood, bishopwort, lupin, ashthroat, henbane, harewort, haransprecel, heathberry plants, cropleek, garlic, hedgerife grains, githrife, fennel. Put these herbs into one cup, set under the altar, sing over them nine masses; boil in butter and in sheep's grease, add much holy salt, strain through a cloth; throw the herbs in running water. If any evil temptation, or an elf or nightgoers, happen to a man, smear his forehead with this salve, and put on his eyes, and where his body is sore, and cense him [with incense], and sign [the cross] often. His condition will soon be better.

. . . Against elf disease . . . Take bishopwort, fennel, lupin, the lower part of *ælfthone*, and lichen from the holy sign of Christ [cross], and incense; a handful of each. Bind all the herbs in a cloth, dip in hallowed font water thrice. Let three masses be sung over it, one "Omnibus sanctis [For all the saints]," a second "Contra tribulationem [Against tribulation]," a third "Pro infirmis [For the sick]." Put then coals in a coal pan, and lay the herbs on it. Smoke the man with the herbs before . . . [9 A.M.] and at night; and sing a litany, the Creed [Nicene], and the Pater noster [Our Father]; and write on him Christ's mark on each limb. And take a little handful of the same kind of herbs, similarly sanctified, and boil in milk; drip holy water in it thrice. And let him sip it before his meal. It will soon be well with him.

Against the Devil and against madness, . . . a strong drink. Put in ale hassock, lupin roots, fennel, ontre, betony, hind heolothe, marche, rue, wormwood, nepeta (catmint), helenium, *ælfthone*, wolfs comb. Sing twelve masses over the drink; and let him drink. It will soon be well with him.

A drink against the Devil's temptations: thefanthorn, cropleek, lupin, ontre, bishopwort, fennel, has-sock, betony. Sanctify these herbs; put into ale holy water. And let the drink be there in where the sick man is. And continually before he drinks sing thrice over the drink, . . . "God, in your name make me whole (save me)."

———————————

Source: Karen Louise Jolly, *Popular Religion in Late Saxon England: Elf Charms in Context* (Chapel Hill: University of North Carolina Press, 1996), 159–67.

Using the Evidence: The Making of Christian Europe

1. **Describing cultural encounters:** Consider the spread of Christianity in Europe from the viewpoint of those seeking to introduce the new religion. What obstacles did they encounter? What strategies did they employ? What successes and failures did they experience?

2. **Describing cultural encounters . . . from another point of view:** Consider the same process from the viewpoint of new adherents to Christianity. What were the motives for or the advantages of conversion for both political elites and ordinary people? To what extent was it possible to combine prevailing practices and beliefs with the teachings of the new religion?

3. **Defining a concept:** The notion of "conversion" often suggests a quite rapid and complete transformation of religious commitments based on sincere inner conviction. In what ways do these documents support or challenge this understanding of religious change?

4. **Noticing point of view and assessing credibility:** From what point of view is each of the documents written? Which statements in each document might historians find unreliable and which would they find most useful?

Visual Sources

Considering the Evidence:
Reading Byzantine Icons

Within the world of Byzantine or Eastern Orthodox Christianity, the icon—a Greek word meaning image, likeness, or picture—came to have a prominent role in both public worship and private devotion. Since Christianity had emerged in a Roman world filled with images—statues of the emperor, busts of ancestors and famous authors, frescoes, and murals—it is hardly surprising that Christians felt a need to represent their faith in some concrete fashion. Icons fulfilled that need.

The creation of icons took off in earnest as Christianity became the official religion of the Roman Empire in the fourth century C.E. Usually painted by monks, icons depicted Jesus, the Virgin Mary, saints, scenes from biblical stories, church feasts, and more. To Byzantine believers, such images were "windows on heaven," an aid to worship that conveyed the very presence of God, bestowing divine grace on the world. They were also frequently associated with miracles, and on occasion people scraped paint off an icon, mixing it with water to produce a "holy medicine" that could remedy a variety of ailments. Icons also served a teaching function for a largely illiterate audience. As Pope Gregory II in the eighth century explained:

> What books are to those who can read, that is a picture to the ignorant who look at it; . . . Hence, for Barbarians especially a picture takes the place of a book.[37]

Icons were deliberately created—or "written"—as flat, two-dimensional images, lacking the perspective of depth. This nonrepresentational, nonrealistic portrayal of human figures was intended to suggest another world and to evoke the mysteries of faith that believers would encounter as they knelt before the image, crossed themselves, and kissed it. The images themselves were full of religious symbolism. The posture of the body, the position of the hand, and the fold of the clothing were all rich with meaning: a saint touching his hand to his cheek conveyed sorrow; a halo surrounding the head of a human figure reflected divinity or sacredness. Likewise, colors were symbolic: red stood for either love or the blood of martyrs; blue suggested faith, humility, or heaven; and purple indicated royalty. Those who painted icons were bound by strict traditions derived from the distant past. Lacking what we might consider "artistic freedom," they sought to faithfully replicate earlier models.

In Judaism, Christianity, and Islam alike, the artistic representation of God occasioned heated debates. After all, the Ten Commandments declared, "You shall not make for yourselves a graven image or any likeness of anything that is in heaven above." Almost since the beginning of Christian art, an undercurrent of opposition had criticized efforts to represent the Divine in artistic form. Between 726 and 843, Byzantine emperors took the offensive against the use of icons in worship, arguing that they too easily became "idols," distracting believers from the adoration of God himself. Some scholars suggest that this effort, known as iconoclasm (icon breaking), also reflected a concern of religious and political authorities in Byzantium about the growing power of monks, who both created icons and ardently supported their use in worship. It may also have owed something to a desire to avoid offending a rapidly expanding Islamic world, which itself largely prohibited the representation of the human form.[38] Icons were collected from both homes and churches and burned in public square. Thousands of monks fled, and active supporters of icon use were subject to severe punishment. Some critics accused the emperor of sympathy with Islam. But by 843 this controversy was resolved in favor of icon use, an event still commemorated every year in Orthodox churches as the Triumph of Orthodoxy. Thereafter, the creation and use of icons flourished in the Byzantine Empire and subsequently in Russia, where Eastern Christianity began to take root in the late tenth century.

The three icons reproduced here provide an opportunity to "read" these visual sources and to imagine what religious meaning they may have conveyed to the faithful of Byzantine Christianity.

Visual Source 10.1, among the oldest icons in existence, dates from the sixth century and survived the destruction of icons during the century of iconoclasm. In contrast to many images of the suffering Jesus on the cross, this icon belongs to a tradition of icon painting that depicts Jesus as Christ Pantokrator, a Greek term translated as "Almighty," "Ruler of All," or "Sustainer of the World." Wearing a dark purple robe and surrounded by a halo of light, Jesus holds a copy of the gospels in his left hand. Notice that Jesus' right hand is raised in blessing with the three fingers together representing the trinity and the two remaining fingers symbolizing the dual nature of Christ, both human and divine. Many observers have suggested that this important theological statement of Christ's divine and human nature is also conveyed in the asymmetrical character of the image.

■ What differences can you notice in the two sides of Christ's face? (Pay attention to the eyebrows, the irises and pupils, the hair, the mustache, and the cheeks. Notice also the difference in color between the face and the hands.)

Visual Source 10.1 Christ Pantokrator
(Ancient Art & Architecture Collection, Ltd.)

■ How does this image portray Jesus as an all-powerful ruler?

■ How does this depiction of Jesus differ from others you may have seen?

■ Which features of this image suggest Christ's humanity and which might portray his divinity?

Icons frequently portrayed important stories from the Bible, none of which was more significant than that of the nativity. Visual Source 10.2, from fifteenth-century Russia, graphically depicts the story of Jesus' birth for the faithful. The central person in the image is not Jesus but his mother, Mary, who in Orthodox theology was known as the God-bearer.

■ Why do you think Mary is pictured as facing outward toward the viewer rather than focusing on her child?

■ Notice the three rays from heaven, symbolizing the trinity — God the Father, the Son, and the Holy Spirit — represented by the three figures at the top. What other elements of the biblical story of Jesus' birth can you identify in the image?

■ The figure in the bottom left is that of a contemplative and perhaps troubled Joseph, Mary's husband-to-be. What do you imagine that Joseph is thinking? Why might he be troubled?

■ Facing Joseph is an elderly person, said by some to represent Satan and by others to be a shepherd comforting Joseph. What thinking might lie behind each of these interpretations?

Visual Source 10.3 is a twelfth-century Byzantine painting intended to illustrate an instructional book for monks, written in the sixth century by Saint John Climacus. Both the book and the icon are known as the *Ladder of Divine Ascent*. Written by an ascetic monk with a reputation for great piety and wisdom, the book advised monks to renounce the world with its many temptations and vices and to ascend step by step toward union with God. The

Visual Source 10.2 The Nativity (Private Collection/The Bridgeman Art Library)

Visual Source 10.3 Ladder of Divine Ascent
(© Roger Wood/Corbis)

icon served as a visual illustration of that process. The monks are climbing the ladder of the spiritual journey toward God but are beset by winged demons representing various sins—lust, anger, and pride, for example—which are described in Climacus's book. Some have fallen off the ladder into the mouth of a dragon, which represents hell.

- How does this icon portray the spiritual journey?

- What sources of help are available for the monks on the ladder? Notice the figures in the upper left and lower right.

- What message might beginning monks have taken from this image?

Using the Evidence: Reading Byzantine Icons

1. **Viewing icons from opposing perspectives:** How might supporters and opponents of icons have responded to these visual sources?

2. **Identifying religious ideas in art:** What elements of religious thought or practice can you identify in these icons? In what ways were these religious ideas represented artistically?

3. **Comparing images of Jesus:** In what different ways is Jesus portrayed in the three icons? What similarities can you identify?

4. **Comparing religious art cross-culturally:** How might you compare these icons to the Buddha images in Chapter 4? Consider their purposes, their religious content, and their modes of artistic representation.

Chapter 10 Wrap Up

LearningCurve
Check what you know.
**bedfordstmartins.com
/strayer/LC**

STEP ONE

The Word to Know: Feudalism

The *Oxford English Dictionary* defines *feudalism* (or the feudal system) as "the system of polity which prevailed in Europe during the Middle Ages and which was based on the relation of superior and vassal arising out of the holding of lands in feud." Based on your reading of Chapter 10, write a brief paragraph explaining how feudalism worked in Western Europe (Christendom) in the third-wave era. Consider especially feudalism's emphasis on social hierarchy in your answer.

STEP TWO

Religion and Its Impact in Third-Wave Civilizations

In this exercise, consider the impact of religion on third-wave societies. Using the chart below, fill in the first column with the factors that spurred religious change (the "impetus"), then use the second column to detail the effects of that change. Finally, use the last column to note the continuities in each civilization.

Third-Wave Civilization	Impetus for change	Effects of change	What stayed the same
Middle East (Syria, Persia)			
China Nestorians			
Egypt or Nubia (choose one)			
Ethiopia			
Byzantium			
Rus			
Western Christendom			

STEP THREE

Analyzing Religious Icons

As described in the text, religious icons fulfilled a variety of purposes including education of illiterate worshippers, mystical symbolism, and as portable objects of faith. Continue to practice reading images in this exercise as you consider the role icons played in both Eastern Orthodox and Russian religious practice.

1. According to Lauren Cross of the Museum of Russian Icons, "The Orthodox Church teaches that an icon is a two-way door of communication that not only shows us a person or an event but makes it present." Use Visual Source 10.2 to explain how the icon might help to bring the church "closer" to a believer.

2. Visual sources, like all historical documents, are subject to differing interpretations. Choose either Visual Source 10.1 or 10.3 and analyze that image from two different points of view (e.g., Christian and Islam or Byzantine and Western Christian).

3. Use the Internet to find an image of a Russian icon from the same era (500–1300). What are the symbols and meanings in the image you found? How are they similar to or different from the visual sources in Chapter 10?

Pastoral Peoples on the Global Stage

The Mongol Moment

1200–1500

In 1937, the great Mongol warrior Chinggis Khan (CHEEN-gihs kahn) lost his soul, some seven centuries after his death. According to Mongol tradition, a warrior's soul was contained in his spirit banner, consisting of strands of hair from his best horses attached to a spear. For many centuries, Chinggis Khan's spirit banner had been housed in a Buddhist monastery in central Mongolia, where lamas (religious teachers) had tended it.[1] But in the 1930s, Mongolia, then under communist control and heavily dominated by Stalin's Soviet Union, launched a brutal anti-religious campaign that destroyed many monasteries and executed some 2,000 monks. In the confusion that ensued, Chinggis Khan's spirit banner, and thus his soul, disappeared.

By the end of the twentieth century, as communism faded away, the memory of Chinggis Khan, if not his spirit banner, made a remarkable comeback in the land of his birth. Vodka, cigarettes, a chocolate bar, two brands of beer, the country's best rock band, and the central square of the capital city all bore his name, while his picture appeared on Mongolia's stamps and money. Rural young people on horseback sang songs in his honor, and their counterparts in urban Internet cafés constructed Web sites to celebrate his achievements. The country organized elaborate celebrations in 2006 to mark the 800th anniversary of his founding of the Mongol Empire.

ALL OF THIS IS A REMINDER OF THE ENORMOUS AND SURPRISING role that the Mongols played in the Eurasian world of the thirteenth and fourteenth centuries and of the continuing echoes of that long-vanished empire. More generally, the story of the Mongols serves as a useful corrective to the almost exclusive focus that historians often

---

Chinggis Khan at Prayer: This sixteenth-century Indian painting shows Chinggis Khan at prayer in the midst of battle. He is perhaps praying to Tengri, the great sky god, on whom the Mongol conqueror based his power. (Werner Forman/Art Resource, NY)

devote to agricultural peoples and their civilizations, for the Mongols, and many other such peoples, were pastoral nomads who disdained farming while centering their economic lives around their herds of animals. Normally they did not construct elaborate cities, enduring empires, or monumental works of art, architecture, and written literature. Nonetheless, they left an indelible mark on the historical development of the entire Afro-Eurasian hemisphere, and particularly on the agricultural civilizations with which they so often interacted.

SEEKING THE MAIN POINT

What has been the role in world history of pastoral peoples in general and the Mongols in particular?

Looking Back and Looking Around: The Long History of Pastoral Nomads

The "revolution of domestication," beginning around 11,500 years ago, involved both plants and animals. People living in more favored environments were able to combine farming with animal husbandry and on this economic foundation generated powerful and impressive civilizations with substantial populations. But on the arid margins of agricultural lands, where productive farming was difficult or impossible, an alternative kind of food-producing economy emerged around 4000 B.C.E., focused on the raising of livestock. Peoples practicing such an economy learned to use the milk, blood, wool, hides, and meat of their animals to occupy lands that could not support agricultural societies. Some of those animals also provided new baggage and transportation possibilities. Horses, camels, goats, sheep, cattle, yaks, and reindeer were the primary animals that separately, or in some combination, enabled the construction of pastoral or herding societies. Such societies took shape in the vast grasslands of inner Eurasia and sub-Saharan Africa, in the Arabian and Saharan deserts, in the subarctic regions of the Northern Hemisphere, and in the high plateau of Tibet. Pastoralism emerged only in the Afro-Eurasian world, for in the Americas the absence of large animals that could be domesticated precluded a herding economy. But where such animals existed, their domestication shaped unique societies adapted to diverse environments.

The World of Pastoral Societies

■ **Comparison**

In what ways did pastoral societies differ from their agricultural counterparts?

Despite their many differences, pastoral societies shared several important features that distinguished them from settled agricultural communities and civilizations. Pastoral societies' generally less productive economies and their need for large grazing areas meant that they supported far smaller populations than did agricultural societies. People generally lived in small and widely scattered encampments of related kinfolk rather than in the villages, towns, and cities characteristic of agrarian civilizations. Beyond the family unit, pastoral peoples organized themselves in kinship-based groups or clans that claimed a common ancestry, usually through the male line. Related clans might on occasion come together as a tribe, which could also absorb unrelated people into the community. Although their values stressed equality and individual achievement, in some pastoral societies clans were ranked as noble or commoner, and con-

A Map of Time

ca. 4000 B.C.E.	Beginning of pastoral economies
ca. 1000 B.C.E.	Beginning of horseback riding
ca. 200 B.C.E.–200 C.E.	Xiongnu Empire
6th–10th centuries	Various Turkic empires
7th–10th centuries	Arab Empire
10th–14th centuries	Conversion of Turkic peoples to Islam
11th–12th centuries	Almoravid Empire
1162–1227	Life of Temujin (Chinggis Khan)
1209–1368	Mongol rule in China
1237–1480	Mongol rule in Russia
1241–1242	Mongol attacks on Eastern Europe
1258	Mongol seizure of Baghdad
1274, 1281	Failed Mongol attacks on Japan
1295	Mongol ruler of Persia converts to Islam
1348–1350	High point of Black Death in Europe

siderable differences emerged between wealthy aristocrats owning large flocks of animals and poor herders. Many pastoral societies held slaves as well.

Furthermore, nomadic societies generally offered women a higher status, fewer restrictions, and a greater role in public life than their counterparts in agricultural civilizations. Everywhere women were involved in productive labor as well as having domestic responsibility for food and children. The care of smaller animals such as sheep and goats usually fell to women, although only rarely did women own or control their own livestock. Among the Mongols, the remarriage of widows carried none of the negative connotations that it did among the Chinese, and women could initiate divorce. Mongol women frequently served as political advisers and were active in military affairs as well. (See Portrait of Khutulun, pp. 530–31.) A thirteenth-century European visitor, the Franciscan friar Giovanni DiPlano Carpini, recorded his impressions of Mongol women:

> Girls and women ride and gallop as skillfully as men. We even saw them carrying quivers and bows, and the women can ride horses for as long as the men; they have shorter stirrups, handle horses very well, and mind all the property. [Mongol] women make everything: skin clothes, shoes, leggings, and everything made of leather. They drive carts and repair them, they load camels, and are quick and vigorous in all their tasks. They all wear trousers, and some of them shoot just like men.[2]

Snapshot   **Varieties of Pastoral Societies**[3]

Region and Peoples	Primary Animals	Features
Inner Eurasian steppes (Xiongnu, Yuezhi, Turks, Uighurs, Mongols, Huns, Kipchaks)	Horses; also sheep, goats, cattle, Bactrian (two-humped) camel	Domestication of horse by 4000 B.C.E.; horseback riding by 1000 B.C.E.; site of largest nomadic empires
Southwestern and Central Asia (Seljuks, Ghaznavids, Mongol Il-khans, Uzbeks, Ottomans)	Sheep and goats; used horses, camels, and donkeys for transport	Close economic relationship with neighboring towns; provided meat, wool, milk products, and hides in exchange for grain and manufactured goods
Arabian and Saharan deserts (Bedouin Arabs, Berbers, Tuareg)	Dromedary (one-humped) camel; sometimes sheep	Camel caravans made possible long-distance trade; camel-mounted warriors central to early Arab/Islamic expansion
Grasslands of sub-Saharan Africa (Fulbe, Nuer, Turkana, Masai)	Cattle; also sheep and goats	Cattle were a chief form of wealth and central to ritual life; little interaction with wider world until nineteenth century
Subarctic Scandinavia, Russia (Sami, Nenets)	Reindeer	Reindeer domesticated only since 1500 C.E.; many also fished
Tibetan plateau (Tibetans)	Yaks; also sheep, cashmere goats, some cattle	Tibetans supplied yaks as baggage animal for overland caravan trade; exchanged wool, skins, and milk with valley villagers and received barley in return

■ **Connection**

In what ways did pastoral societies interact with their agricultural neighbors?

Certainly literate observers from adjacent civilizations noticed and clearly disapproved of the freedom granted to pastoral women. Ancient Greek writers thought that the pastoralists with whom they were familiar were "women governed." To Han Kuan, a Chinese Confucian scholar in the first century B.C.E., China's northern nomadic neighbors "[made] no distinction between men and women."[4]

The most characteristic feature of pastoral societies was their mobility. As people frequently on the move, they are often referred to as nomads because they shifted their herds in regular patterns to systematically follow the seasonal changes in vegetation and water supply. It was a life largely dictated by local environmental conditions and based on turning grass, which people cannot eat, into usable food and energy. Nor were nomads homeless; they took their homes, often elaborate felt tents, with them. According to a prominent scholar of pastoral life, "They know where they are going and why."[5]

Although nomadic pastoralists represented an alternative to the agricultural way of life that they disdained, they were almost always deeply connected to, and often dependent on, their agricultural neighbors. Few nomadic peoples could live solely from the products of their animals, and most of them actively sought access to the foodstuffs, manufactured goods, and luxury items available from the urban workshops and farming communities of nearby civilizations. Particularly among the nomadic peoples of inner Eurasia, this desire for the fruits of

The Scythians

An ancient horse-riding nomadic people during the second-wave era, the Scythians occupied a region in present-day Kazakhstan and southern Russia. Their pastoral way of life is apparent in this detail from an exquisite gold necklace from the fourth century B.C.E. (Private Collection/Photo Boltin Picture Library/The Bridgeman Art Library)

civilization periodically stimulated the creation of tribal confederations or nomadic states that could more effectively deal with the powerful agricultural societies on their borders. The Mongol Empire of the thirteenth century was but the most recent and largest in a long line of such efforts, dating back to the first millennium B.C.E.

Constructing a large state among nomadic pastoralists was no easy task. Such societies generally lacked the surplus wealth needed to pay for the professional armies and bureaucracies that everywhere sustained the states and empires of agricultural civilizations. And the fierce independence of widely dispersed pastoral clans and tribes as well as their internal rivalries made any enduring political unity difficult to achieve. Nonetheless, charismatic leaders, such as Chinggis Khan, were periodically able to weld together a series of tribal alliances that for a time became powerful states. In doing so, they often employed the device of "fictive kinship," designating allies as blood relatives and treating them with a corresponding respect.

Despite their limited populations, such states had certain military advantages in confronting larger and more densely populated civilizations. They could draw on the horseback riding and hunting skills of virtually the entire male population and some women as well. Easily transferred to the role of warrior, these skills, which were practiced from early childhood, were an integral part of pastoral life. But what sustained nomadic states was their ability to extract wealth, through raiding, trading, or extortion, from agricultural civilizations such as China, Persia, and Byzantium. As long as that wealth flowed into pastoral states, rulers could maintain the fragile alliances among fractious clans and tribes. When it was interrupted, however, those states often fragmented.

Pastoral nomads interacted with their agricultural neighbors not only economically and militarily but also culturally as they "became acquainted with and tried on for size all the world and universal religions."[6] At one time or another, Judaism, Buddhism, Islam, and several forms of Christianity all found a home somewhere among the nomadic peoples of inner Eurasia. So did Manichaeism, a religious tradition born in third-century Persia and combining elements of Zoroastrian, Christian, and Buddhist practice. Usually conversion was a top-down process as nomadic elites and rulers adopted a foreign religion for political purposes, sometimes changing religious allegiance as circumstances altered. Nomadic peoples, in short, did not inhabit a world totally apart from their agricultural and civilized neighbors.

Surely the most fundamental contribution of pastoralists to the larger human story was their mastery of environments unsuitable for agriculture. Through the creative use of their animals, they brought a version of the food-producing revolution and a substantial human presence to the arid grasslands and desert regions of Afro-Eurasia. As the pastoral peoples of the Inner Asian steppes learned the art of horseback riding, by roughly 1000 B.C.E., their societies changed dramatically. Now they could accumulate and tend larger herds of horses, sheep, and goats and move more rapidly over a much wider territory. New technologies, invented or adapted by pastoral societies, added to the mastery of their environment and spread widely across the Eurasian steppes, creating something of a common culture in this vast region. These innovations included complex horse harnesses, saddles with iron stirrups, a small compound bow that could be fired from horseback, various forms of armor, and new kinds of swords. Agricultural peoples were amazed at the centrality of the horse in pastoral life. As a Roman historian noted about the Huns, "From their horses, by day and night every one of that nation buys and sells, eats and drinks, and bowed over the narrow neck of the animal relaxes in a sleep so deep as to be accompanied by many dreams."[7]

Before the Mongols: Pastoralists in History

What enabled pastoral peoples to make their most visible entry onto the stage of world history was the military potential of horseback riding, and of camel riding somewhat later. Their mastery of mounted warfare made possible a long but intermittent series of nomadic empires across the steppes of inner Eurasia and parts of Africa. For 2,000 years, those states played a major role in Afro-Eurasian history and represented a standing challenge to and influence upon the agrarian civilizations on their borders.

The Xiongnu Confederacy

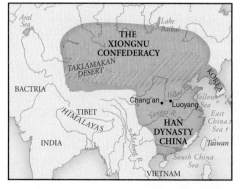

One early large-scale nomadic empire was associated with the people known as the Xiongnu, who lived in the Mongolian steppes north of China (see Chapter 8). Provoked by Chinese penetration of their territory, the Xiongnu in the third and second centuries B.C.E. created a huge military confederacy that stretched from Manchuria deep into Central Asia. Under the charismatic leadership of Modun (r. 210–174 B.C.E.), the Xiongnu Empire effected a revolution in nomadic life. Earlier fragmented and egalitarian societies were now transformed into a far more centralized and hierarchical political system in which power was concentrated in a divinely sanctioned ruler and differences between "junior" and "senior" clans became more prominent. "All the people who draw the bow have now become one family," declared Modun. Tribute, exacted from other nomadic peoples and from China itself, sustained the Xiongnu Empire and forced the Han dynasty emperor Wen to acknowledge, unhappily, the equality of people he regarded as barbarians. "Our two great nations," he declared, no doubt reluctantly, "the Han and the Xiongnu, stand side by side."[8]

Although it subsequently disintegrated under sustained Chinese counterattacks, the Xiongnu Empire created a model that later Turkic and Mongol empires emulated. Even without a powerful state, various nomadic or semi-nomadic peoples played a role in the collapse of the already weakened Chinese and Roman empires and in the subsequent rebuilding of those civilizations (see Chapter 3).

It was during the era of third-wave civilizations (500–1500) that nomadic peoples made their most significant mark on the larger canvas of world history. Arabs, Berbers, Turks, and Mongols—all of them of nomadic origin—created the largest and most influential empires of that millennium. The most expansive religious tradition of the era, Islam, derived from a largely nomadic people, the Arabs, and was carried to new regions by another nomadic people, the Turks. In that millennium, most of the great civilizations of outer Eurasia—Byzantium, Persia, India, and China—had come under the control of previously nomadic people, at least for a time. But as pastoral nomads entered and shaped the arena of world history, they too were transformed by the experience.

The first and most dramatic of these nomadic incursions came from Arabs. In the Arabian Peninsula, the development of a reliable camel saddle somewhere between 500 and 100 B.C.E. enabled nomadic Bedouin (desert-dwelling) Arabs to fight effectively from atop their enormous beasts. With this new military advantage, they came to control the rich trade routes in incense running through Arabia. Even more important, these camel nomads served as the shock troops of Islamic expansion, providing many of the new religion's earliest followers and much of the military force that carved out the Arab Empire. Although intellectual and political leadership came from urban merchants and settled farming communities, the Arab Empire was in some respects a nomadic creation that subsequently became the foundation of a new and distinctive civilization.

Even as the pastoral Arabs encroached on the world of Eurasian civilizations from the south, Turkic-speaking nomads were making inroads from the north. Never a single people, various Turkic-speaking clans and tribes migrated from their homeland in Mongolia and southern Siberia generally westward and entered the historical record as creators of a series of nomadic empires between 552 and 965 C.E., most of them lasting little more than a century. Like the Xiongnu Empire, they were fragile alliances of various tribes headed by a supreme ruler known as a *kaghan*, who was supported by a faithful corps of soldiers called "wolves," for the wolf was the mythical ancestor of Turkic peoples. From their base in the steppes, these Turkic states confronted the great civilizations to their south—China, Persia, Byzantium—alternately raiding

■ Significance

In what ways did the Xiongnu, Arabs, Turks, and Berbers make an impact on world history?

Seljuk Tiles
Among the artistic achievements of Turkic Muslims were lovely ceramic tiles used to decorate mosques, minarets, palaces, and other public spaces. They contained intricate geometric designs, images of trees and birds, and inscriptions from the Quran. This one, dating from the thirteenth century, was used in a Seljuk palace, built as a summer residence for the Sultan in the city of Konya in what is now central Turkey. (© Zater Kizilkaya/Images and Stories)

them, allying with them against common enemies, trading with them, and extorting tribute payments from them. Turkic language and culture spread widely over much of Inner Asia, and elements of that culture entered the agrarian civilizations. In the courts of northern China, for example, yogurt thinned with water, a drink derived from the Turks, replaced for a time the traditional beverage of tea, and at least one Chinese poet wrote joyfully about the delights of snowy evenings in a felt tent.[9]

A major turning point in the history of the Turks occurred with their conversion to Islam between the tenth and fourteenth centuries. This extended process represented a major expansion of the faith and launched the Turks into a new role as the third major carrier of Islam, following the Arabs and the Persians. It also brought the Turks into an increasingly important position within the heartland of an established Islamic civilization as they migrated southward into the Middle East. There they served first as slave soldiers within the Abbasid caliphate, and then, as the caliphate declined, they increasingly took political and military power themselves. In the Seljuk Turkic Empire of the eleventh and twelfth centuries, centered in Persia and present-day Iraq, Turkic rulers began to claim the Muslim title of *sultan* (ruler) rather than the Turkic *kaghan*. Although the Abbasid caliph remained the formal ruler, real power was exercised by Turkic sultans.

Not only did Turkic peoples become Muslims themselves, but they carried Islam to new areas as well. Their invasions of northern India solidly planted Islam in that ancient civilization. In Anatolia, formerly ruled by Christian Byzantium, they brought both Islam and a massive infusion of Turkic culture, language, and people, even as they created the Ottoman Empire, which by 1500 became one of the great powers of Eurasia (see pp. 576–78). In both places, Turkic dynasties governed and would continue to do so well into the modern era. Thus Turkic people, many of them at least, had transformed themselves from pastoral nomads to sedentary farmers, from creators of steppe empires to rulers of agrarian civilizations, and from polytheistic worshippers of their ancestors and various gods to followers and carriers of a monotheistic Islam.

Broadly similar patterns prevailed in Africa as well. All across northern Africa and the Sahara, the introduction of the camel, probably during the first millennium B.C.E., gave rise to pastoral nomadic societies. Much like the Turkic-speaking pastoralists of

Central Asia, many of these peoples later adopted Islam, but at least initially had little formal instruction in the religion. In the eleventh century C.E., a reform movement arose among the Sanhaja Berber pastoralists, living in the western Sahara, only recently converted to Islam, and practicing it rather superficially. It was sparked by a scholar, Ibn Yasin, who returned from a pilgrimage to Mecca around 1039 seeking to purify the practice of the faith among his own people in line with orthodox principles. That religious movement soon became an expansive state, the Almoravid Empire, which incorporated a large part of northwestern Africa and in 1086 crossed into southern Spain, where it offered vigorous opposition to Christian efforts to conquer the region.

The Almoravid Empire

For a time, the Almoravid state enjoyed considerable prosperity, based on its control of much of the West African gold trade and the grain-producing Atlantic plains of Morocco. The Almoravids also brought to Morocco the sophisticated Islamic culture of southern Spain, still visible in the splendid architecture of the city of Marrakesh, for a time the capital of the Almoravid Empire. By the mid-twelfth century, that empire had been overrun by its long-time enemies, Berber farming people from the Atlas Mountains. But for roughly a century, the Almoravid movement represented an African pastoral people, who had converted to Islam, came into conflict with their agricultural neighbors, built a short-lived empire, and had a considerable impact on neighboring civilizations in both North Africa and Europe.

Breakout: The Mongol Empire

Of all the pastoral peoples who took a turn on the stage of world history, the Mongols made the most stunning entry. Their thirteenth-century breakout from Mongolia gave rise to the largest land-based empire in all of human history, stretching from the Pacific coast of Asia to Eastern Europe (see Map 11.1). This empire joined the nomadic peoples of the inner Eurasian steppes with the settled agricultural civilizations of outer Eurasia more extensively and more intimately than ever before. It also brought the major civilizations of Eurasia — Europe, China, and the Islamic world — into far more direct contact than in earlier times. Both the enormous destructiveness of the process and the networks of exchange and communication that it spawned were the work of the Mongols, numbering only about 700,000 people. It was another of history's unlikely twists.

For all of its size and fearsome reputation, the Mongol Empire left a surprisingly modest cultural imprint on the world it had briefly governed. Unlike the Arabs, the Mongols bequeathed to the world no new language, religion, or civilization. Whereas Islam offered a common religious home for all converts — conquerors and conquered alike — the Mongols never tried to spread their own faith among subject peoples. Their religion centered on rituals invoking the ancestors, which were performed around the family hearth. Rulers sometimes consulted religious specialists, known as shamans,

Map 11.1

The Mongol Empire

Encompassing much of Eurasia, the Mongol Empire was divided into four khanates after the death of Chinggis Khan.

who might predict the future, offer sacrifices, and communicate with the spirit world, and particularly with Tengri, the supreme sky god of the Mongols. There was little in this tradition to attract outsiders, and in any event the Mongols proved uninterested in religious imperialism.

The Mongols offered the majority of those they conquered little more than the status of defeated, subordinate, and exploited people, although people with skills were put to work in ways useful to Mongol authorities. Unlike the Turks, whose languages and culture flourish today in many places far from the Turkic homeland, Mongol culture remains confined largely to Mongolia. Furthermore, the Mongol Empire, following in the tradition of Xiongnu and Turkic state building, proved to be "the last, spectacular bloom of pastoral power in Inner Eurasia."[10] Some Mongols themselves became absorbed into the settled societies they conquered. After the decline and disintegration of the Mongol Empire, the tide turned against the pastoralists of inner

Eurasia, who were increasingly swallowed up in the expanding Russian or Chinese empires. Nonetheless, while it lasted and for a few centuries thereafter, the Mongol Empire exercised an enormous impact throughout the entire Eurasian world.

From Temujin to Chinggis Khan: The Rise of the Mongol Empire

World historians are prone to focus attention on large-scale and long-term processes of change in explaining "what happened in history," but in understanding the rise of the Mongol Empire, most scholars have found themselves forced to look closely at the role of a single individual—Temujin (TEM-oo-chin) (1162–1227), later known as Chinggis Khan (universal ruler). The twelfth-century world into which he was born found the Mongols an unstable and fractious collection of tribes and clans, much reduced from a somewhat earlier and more powerful position in the shifting nomadic alliances in what is now Mongolia. "Everyone was feuding," declared a leading Mongol shaman. "Rather than sleep, they robbed each other of their possessions. . . . There was no respite, only battle. There was no affection, only mutual slaughter."[11]

■ **Description**
Identify the major steps in the rise of the Mongol Empire.

The early life of Temujin showed few signs of a prominent future. The boy's father had been a minor chieftain of a noble clan, but he was murdered by tribal rivals before Temujin turned ten, and the family was soon deserted by other members of the clan. As social outcasts, Temujin's small family, headed by his resourceful mother, was forced to live by hunting, fishing, and gathering wild foods. Without livestock, they had fallen to the lowest level of nomadic life. In these desperate circumstances, Temujin's remarkable character came into play. His personal magnetism and courage and his inclination to rely on trusted friends rather than ties of kinship allowed him to build up a small following and to ally with a more powerful tribal leader. This alliance received a boost from Chinese patrons, who were always eager to keep the nomads divided. Military victory over a rival tribe resulted in Temujin's recognition as a chief in his own right with a growing band of followers.

Temujin's rise to power amid the complex tribal politics of Mongolia was a surprise to everyone. It took place among shifting alliances and betrayals, a mounting string of military victories, the indecisiveness of his enemies, a reputation as a leader generous to friends and ruthless to enemies, and the incorporation of warriors from defeated tribes into his own forces. In 1206, a Mongol tribal assembly recognized Temujin as Chinggis Khan, supreme leader of a now unified Great Mongol Nation (see Document 11.1, pp. 542–44). It was a remarkable achievement, but one little noticed beyond the highland steppes of Mongolia. That would soon change.

The unification of the Mongol tribes raised an obvious question: What was Chinggis Khan to do with the powerful army he had assembled? Without a common task, the new and fragile unity of the Mongols would surely dissolve into quarrels and chaos; and without external resources to reward his followers, Chinggis Khan would be hard-pressed to maintain his supreme position. Both considerations pointed in a single direction — expansion, particularly toward China, long a source of great wealth for nomadic peoples.[12]

In 1209, the first major attack on the settled agricultural societies south of Mongolia set in motion half a century of a Mongol world war, a series of military campaigns, massive killing, and empire building without precedent in world history. In the process, Chinggis Khan, followed by his sons and grandsons (Ogodei, Mongke, and Khubilai), constructed an empire that contained China, Korea, Central Asia, Russia, much of the Islamic Middle East, and parts of Eastern Europe (see Map 11.1, p. 522). "In a flash," wrote a recent scholar, "the Mongol warriors would defeat every army, capture every fort, and bring down the walls of every city they encountered. Christians, Muslims, Buddhists, and Hindus would soon kneel before the dusty boots of illiterate young Mongol horsemen."[13]

Various setbacks marked the outer limits of the Mongol Empire — the Mongols' withdrawal from Eastern Europe (1242), their defeat at Ain Jalut in Palestine at the hands of Egyptian forces (1260), the failure of their invasion of Japan owing to two typhoons (1274, 1281), and the difficulty of penetrating the tropical jungles of Southeast Asia. But what an empire it was! How could a Mongol confederation, with a total population of less than 1 million people and few resources beyond their livestock, assemble an imperial structure of such staggering transcontinental dimensions?

Explaining the Mongol Moment

Like the Roman Empire but far more rapidly, the Mongol realm grew of its own momentum without any grand scheme or blueprint for world conquest. Each fresh victory brought new resources for making war and new threats or insecurities that seemed to require further expansion. As the empire took shape and certainly by the end of his life, Chinggis Khan had come to see his career in terms of a universal mission. "I have accomplished a great work," he declared, "uniting the whole world in one empire."[14] Thus the Mongol Empire acquired an ideology in the course of its construction.

What made this "great work" possible? The odds seemed overwhelming, for China alone outnumbered the Mongols 100 to 1 and possessed incomparably greater resources. Nor did the Mongols enjoy any technological superiority over their many adversaries. They did, however, enjoy the luck of good timing, for China was divided, having already lost control of its northern territory to the nomadic Jurchen people, while the decrepit Abbasid caliphate, once the center of the Islamic world, had shrunk to a fraction of its earlier size. But clearly, the key to the Mongols' success lay in their army. According to one scholar, "Mongol armies were simply better led, organized, and disciplined than those of their opponents."[15] In an effort to diminish a divisive tribalism, Chinggis Khan reorganized the entire social structure of the Mongols into military units of 10, 100, 1,000, and 10,000 warriors, an arrangement that allowed for effective command and control. Conquered tribes especially were broken up and their members scattered among these new units, which enrolled virtually all nomadic men and supplied the cavalry forces of Mongol armies. A highly prestigious imperial guard, also recruited across tribal lines, marked the further decline of the old tribalism as a social revolution, imposed from above, reshaped Mongol society.

An impressive discipline and loyalty to their leaders characterized Mongol military forces, and discipline was reinforced by the provision that should any members of a unit desert in battle, all were subject to the death penalty. More positively, loyalty was cemented by the leaders' willingness to share the hardships of their men. "I eat the same food and am dressed in the same rags as my humble herdsmen," wrote Chinggis Khan. "I am always in the forefront, and in battle I am never at the rear."[16] (See Document 11.2, pp. 544–45.) Such discipline and loyalty made possible the elaborate tactics of encirclement, retreat, and deception that proved decisive in many a battle. Furthermore, the enormous flow of wealth from conquered civilizations benefited all Mongols, though not equally. Even ordinary Mongols could now dress in linens and silks rather than hides and felt, could own slaves derived from the many prisoners of war, and had far greater opportunities to improve their social position in a constantly expanding empire.

A Mongol Warrior Horseback-riding skills, honed in herding animals and adapted to military purposes, were central to Mongol conquests, as illustrated in this Ming-dynasty Chinese painting of a mounted Mongol archer. (© Victoria and Albert Museum, London)

To compensate for their own small population, the Mongols incorporated huge numbers of conquered peoples into their military forces. "People who lived in felt tents"—mostly Mongol and Turkic nomads—were conscripted en masse into the cavalry units of the Mongol army, while settled agricultural peoples supplied the infantry and artillery forces. As the Mongols penetrated major civilizations, with their walled cities and elaborate fortifications, they quickly acquired Chinese techniques and technology of siege warfare. Some 1,000 Chinese artillery crews, for example, took part in the Mongol invasion of distant Persia. Beyond military recruitment, Mongols demanded that their conquered people serve as laborers, building roads and bridges and ferrying supplies over long distances. Artisans, craftsmen, and skilled people generally were carefully identified, spared from massacre, and often sent to distant regions of the empire where their services were required. A French goldsmith, captured by Mongol forces in Hungary, wound up as a slave in the Mongol capital of Karakorum (kah-rah-KOR-um), where he constructed an elaborate silver fountain that dispensed wine and other intoxicating drinks.

A further element in the military effectiveness of Mongol forces lay in a growing reputation for a ruthless brutality and utter destructiveness. Chinggis Khan's policy was clear: "Whoever submits shall be spared, but those who resist, they shall be destroyed with their wives, children and dependents . . . so that the others who hear and see should fear and not act the same."[17] The Central Asian kingdom of Khwarizm, whose ruler had greatly offended Chinggis Khan by murdering and mutilating Mongol envoys and merchants, was among the first, but by no means the last, to feel the full effects of Mongol terror. City after city was utterly destroyed, and enemy soldiers were passed out in lots to Mongol troops for execution, while women and skilled craftsmen were enslaved. Unskilled civilians served as human shields for attacks on the next city or were used as human fill in the moats surrounding those cities.

One scholar explained such policies in this way: "Extremely conscious of their small numbers and fearful of rebellion, Chinggis often chose to annihilate a region's entire population, if it appeared too troublesome to govern."[18] These policies also served as a form of psychological warfare, a practical inducement to surrender for those who knew of the Mongol terror. Historians continue to debate the extent and uniqueness of the Mongols' brutality, but their reputation for unwavering harshness proved a military asset.

Underlying the purely military dimensions of the Mongols' success was an impressive ability to mobilize both the human and material resources of their growing empire. Elaborate census taking allowed Mongol leaders to know what was available to them and made possible the systematic taxation of conquered people. An effective system of relay stations, about a day's ride apart, provided rapid communication across the empire and fostered trade as well. Marco Polo, the Venetian trader who traveled through Mongol domains in the thirteenth century, claimed that the Mongols maintained some 10,000 such stations, together with 200,000 horses available to authorized users. The beginnings of a centralized bureaucracy with various specialized offices took shape in the new capital of Karakorum. There scribes translated official decrees into the various languages of the empire, such as Persian, Uighur, Chinese, and Tibetan.

Other policies appealed to various groups among the conquered peoples of the empire. Interested in fostering commerce, Mongol rulers often offered merchants 10 percent or more above their asking price and allowed them the free use of the relay stations for transporting their goods. In administering the conquered regions, Mongols held the highest decision-making posts, but Chinese and Muslim officials held many advisory and lower-level positions in China and Persia respectively. In religious matters, the Mongols welcomed and supported many religious traditions—Buddhist, Christian, Muslim, Daoist—as long as they did not become the focus of political opposition. This policy of religious toleration allowed Muslims to seek converts among Mongol troops and afforded Christians much greater freedom than they had enjoyed under Muslim rule.[19] Toward the end of his life and apparently feeling his approaching death, Chinggis Khan himself summoned a famous Daoist master from China and begged him to "communicate to me the means of preserving life." One of his successors, Mongke, arranged a debate among representatives of several religious faiths, after which he concluded: "Just as God gave different fingers to the hand, so has He given different ways to men."[20] Such economic, administrative, and religious policies provided some benefits and a place within the empire—albeit subordinate—for many of its conquered peoples.

SUMMING UP SO FAR

What accounts for the political and military success of the Mongols?

Encountering the Mongols: Comparing Three Cases

The Mongol moment in world history represented an enormous cultural encounter between nomadic pastoralists and the settled civilizations of Eurasia. Differences among those civilizations—Confucian China, Muslim Persia, Christian Russia—ensured considerable diversity as this encounter unfolded across a vast realm. The process of conquest, the length and nature of Mongol rule, the impact on local people, and the extent of Mongol assimilation into the cultures of the conquered—all this and more varied considerably across the Eurasian domains of the empire. The experiences of China, Persia, and Russia provide brief glimpses into several expressions of this massive clash of cultures.

China and the Mongols

Long the primary target for nomadic steppe dwellers in search of agrarian wealth, China proved the most difficult and extended of the Mongols' many conquests, lasting some seventy years, from 1209 to 1279. The invasion began in northern China, which had been ruled for several centuries by various dynasties of nomadic origin, and was characterized by destruction and plunder on a massive scale. Southern China, under the control of the native Song dynasty, was a different story, for there the Mongols were far less violent and more concerned to accommodate the local population. Landowners, for example, were guaranteed their estates in exchange for their support or at least their neutrality. By whatever methods, the outcome was the unification of a divided China, a treasured ideal among educated Chinese. This achievement persuaded some of them that the Mongols had indeed been granted the Mandate of Heaven and, despite their foreign origins, were legitimate rulers. (See Document 11.4, pp. 547–48, for a positive Chinese view of their Mongol rulers.)

Having acquired China, what were the Mongols to do with it? One possibility, apparently considered by the Great Khan Ogodei (ERG-uh-day) in the 1230s, was to exterminate everyone in northern China and turn the country into pastureland for Mongol herds. That suggestion, fortunately, was rejected in favor of extracting as much wealth as possible from the country's advanced civilization. Doing so meant some accommodation to Chinese culture and ways of governing, for the Mongols had no experience with the operation of a complex agrarian society.

That accommodation took many forms. The Mongols made use of Chinese administrative practices, techniques of taxation, and their postal system. They gave themselves a Chinese dynastic title, the Yuan, suggesting a new beginning in Chinese history. They transferred their capital from Karakorum in Mongolia to what is now Beijing, building a wholly new capital city there known as Khanbalik, the "city of the khan." Thus the Mongols were now rooting themselves solidly on the soil of a highly sophisticated civilization, well removed from their homeland on the steppes. Khubilai Khan (koo-buh-l'eye kahn), the grandson of Chinggis Khan and China's Mongol ruler from 1271 to 1294, ordered a set of Chinese-style ancestral tablets to

■ **Change**
How did Mongol rule change China? In what ways were the Mongols changed by China?

Marco Polo and Khubilai Khan
In ruling China, the Mongols employed in high positions a number of Muslims and a few Europeans, such as Marco Polo, shown here kneeling before Khubilai Khan in a painting from the fifteenth century. (Bibliothèque nationale de France, Paris, France/The Bridgeman Art Library)

honor his ancestors and posthumously awarded them Chinese names. Many of his policies evoked the values of a benevolent Chinese emperor as he improved roads, built canals, lowered some taxes, patronized scholars and artists, limited the death penalty and torture, supported peasant agriculture, and prohibited Mongols from grazing their animals on peasants' farmland. Mongol khans also made use of traditional Confucian rituals, supported the building of some Daoist temples, and were particularly attracted to a Tibetan form of Buddhism, which returned the favor with strong political support for the invaders.

Despite these accommodations, Mongol rule was still harsh, exploitative, foreign, and resented. The Mongols did not become Chinese, nor did they accommodate every aspect of Chinese culture. Deep inside the new capital, the royal family and court could continue to experience something of steppe life as their animals roamed freely in large open areas, planted with steppe grass. Many of the Mongol elite much preferred to live, eat, sleep, and give birth in the traditional tents that sprouted everywhere. In administering the country, the Mongols largely ignored the traditional Chinese examination system and relied heavily on foreigners, particularly Muslims from Central Asia and the Middle East, to serve as officials, while keeping the top decision-making posts for themselves. Few Mongols learned Chinese, and Mongol law discriminated against the Chinese, reserving for them the most severe punishments. Furthermore, the Mongols honored and supported merchants and artisans far more than Confucian bureaucrats had been inclined to do.

In social life, the Mongols forbade intermarriage and prohibited Chinese scholars from learning the Mongol script. Mongol women never adopted foot binding and scandalized the Chinese by mixing freely with men at official gatherings and riding to the hunt with their husbands. The Mongol ruler Khubilai Khan retained the Mongol tradition of relying heavily on female advisers, the chief of which was his favorite wife Chabi. Ironically, she urged him to accommodate his Chinese subjects, forcefully and successfully opposing an early plan to turn Chinese farmland into pastureland. Unlike many Mongols, biased as they were against farming, Chabi recognized the advantages of agriculture and its ability to generate tax revenue. With a vision of turning Mongol rule into a lasting dynasty that might rank with the splendor of the Tang, she urged her husband to emulate the best practices of that earlier era of Chinese history.

However one assesses Mongol rule in China, it was brief, lasting little more than a century. By the mid-fourteenth century, intense factionalism among the Mongols, rapidly rising prices, furious epidemics of the plague, and growing peasant rebellions combined to force the Mongols out of China. By 1368, rebel forces had triumphed, and thousands of Mongols returned to their homeland in the steppes. For several centuries, they remained a periodic threat to China, but during the Ming dynasty that followed, the memory of their often brutal and alien rule stimulated a renewed commitment to Confucian values and restrictive gender practices and an effort to wipe out all traces of the Mongols' impact.

Persia and the Mongols

A second great civilization conquered by the Mongols was that of an Islamic Persia. There the Mongol takeover was far more abrupt than the extended process of conquest in China. A first invasion (1219–1221), led by Chinggis Khan himself, was followed thirty years later by a second assault (1251–1258) under his grandson Hulegu (HE-luh-gee), who became the first il-khan (subordinate khan) of Persia. More destructive than the conquest of Song dynasty China, the Mongol offensive against Persia and Iraq had no precedent in their history, although Persia had been repeatedly attacked, from the invasion of Alexander the Great to that of the Arabs. The most recent incursion had featured Turkic peoples, but they had been Muslims, recently converted, small in number, and seeking only acceptance within the Islamic world. The Mongols, however, were infidels in Muslim eyes, and their stunning victory was a profound shock to people accustomed to viewing history as the progressive expansion of Islamic rule. Furthermore, Mongol military victory brought in its wake a degree of ferocity and slaughter that had no parallel in Persian experience. The Persian historian Juwayni described it in fearful terms:

■ **Comparison**

How was Mongol rule in Persia different from that in China?

Khutulun,
A Mongol Wrestler Princess[21]

Born around 1260 into the extended family network of Chinggis Khan, Khutulun was the only girl among fourteen brothers. Even among elite Mongol women, many of whom played important roles in public life, Khutulun was unique. Her father, Qaidu Khan, was the Mongol ruler of Central Asia and a bitter opponent of Khubilai Khan, the Mongol ruler of China who was trying to extend his control over Central Asia. A large and well-built young woman, Khutulun excelled in horse riding, archery, and wrestling, outperforming her brothers. Winning fame as a wrestler in public competitions, she soon joined her father on the battlefield, was awarded a medallion of office normally reserved for men alone,

A Mongol woman riding with Chinggis Khan as Khutulun rode with her father. (National Palace Museum, Taipei, Taiwan / The Bridgeman Art Library)

and gained a reputation for being blessed of the gods. According to Marco Polo, during battle Khutulun would often seize one of the enemy, "as deftly as a hawk pounces on a bird," and carry him off to her father.

It was when she became of marriageable age that trouble began. She turned down the possibility of marrying a cousin who governed Mongol Persia, for this woman of the steppes had no desire to live as a secluded urban wife. In fact she declared that she would only marry someone who could defeat her in wrestling. Many suitors tried, wagering 10, 100, or in one case 1,000 horses that they could defeat her. All of them failed, and, in the process, Khutulun accumulated a very substantial herd of horses.

Every town and every village has been several times subjected to pillage and massacre and has suffered this confusion for years so that even though there be generation and increase until the Resurrection the population will not attain to a tenth part of what it was before.[22]

The sacking of Baghdad in 1258, which put an end to the Abbasid caliphate, was accompanied by the massacre of more than 200,000 people, according to Hulegu himself.

Beyond this human catastrophe lay the damage to Persian and Iraqi agriculture and to those who tilled the soil. Heavy taxes, sometimes collected twenty or thirty times a year and often under torture or whipping, pushed large numbers of peasants off their land. Furthermore, the in-migration of nomadic Mongols, together with their immense herds of sheep and goats, turned much agricultural land into pasture and sometimes into desert. As a result, a fragile system of underground water channels that provided irrigation to the fields was neglected, and much good agricultural land was reduced to waste. Some sectors of the Persian economy gained, however. Wine production increased because the Mongols were fond of alcohol, and the Persian silk industry benefited from close contact with a Mongol-ruled China. In general, though, even more so than in China, Mongol rule in Persia represented "disaster on a grand and unparalleled scale."[23]

Khutulun's extraordinary public life and her unwilling-ness to marry provided an opening for her enemies. Rumors circulated that she refused to marry because she was engaged in an incestuous relationship with her father. To put an end to such stories, Khutulun finally agreed to wed one of her father's followers without any wrestling contest. Still, the decision was hers. As the Mongol chronicles put it: "She chose him herself for her husband."

Even after her marriage, Khutulun continued to campaign with Qaidu Khan and together they protected the steppe lands of Central Asia from incorporation into Mongol-ruled China. In 1301 her father was wounded in battle and, shortly thereafter, died. Some accounts suggest that he tried to name Khutulun as khan in his place, but the resistance of her brothers nixed that plan. "You should mind your scissors and needles," declared her rivals. "What have you to do with kingship?" Khutulun herself supported one of her brothers as khan, while she remained at the head of the army. She died in 1306, though whether in battle or as the result of an assassination remains unclear.

In her public and military life and in her fierce independence about marriage, Khutulun reflected the relative freedom and influence of Mongol women, particularly of the elite class. In her preference for the open life of the steppes and in her resistance to the intrusion of Mongol-ruled China, she aligned with those who saw themselves as "true Mongols" in opposition to those who had come under the softening influence of neighboring Chinese or Persian civilizations. To this day, when Mongolian men wrestle, they wear a vest with an open chest in honor of Khutulun, ensuring that they are wrestling with other men rather than with a woman who might throw them.

Question: What does the life of Khutulun reveal about Mongol gender relationships?

Nonetheless, the Mongols in Persia were themselves transformed far more than their counterparts in China. They made extensive use of the sophisticated Persian bureaucracy, leaving the greater part of government operations in Persian hands. During the reign of Ghazan (haz-ZAHN) (1295–1304), they made some efforts to repair the damage caused by earlier policies of ruthless exploitation by rebuilding damaged cities and repairing neglected irrigation works. Most important, the Mongols who conquered Persia became Muslims, following the lead of Ghazan, who converted to Islam in 1295. No such widespread conversion to the culture of the conquered occurred in China or in Christian Russia. Members of the court and Mongol elites learned at least some Persian, unlike most of their counterparts in China. A number of Mongols also turned to farming, abandoning their nomadic ways, while some married local people.

When the Mongol dynasty of Hulegu's descendants collapsed in the 1330s for lack of a suitable heir, the Mongols were not driven out of Persia as they had been from China. Rather they and their Turkic allies simply disappeared, assimilated into Persian society. From a Persian point of view, the barbarians had been civilized, and Persians had successfully resisted cultural influence from their uncivilized conquerors. When the great Persian historian Rashid al-Din wrote his famous history of the Mongols, he apologized for providing information about women, generally unmentioned in Islamic writing, explaining that Mongols treated their women equally and included

Mongol Rulers and Their Women
The wives of Mongol rulers exercised considerable influence at court. This fourteenth-century painting shows Chinggis Khan's fourth son Tului, the ruler of the Mongol heartland after his father's death, with his Christian wife Sorgaqtani. After her husband's early death from alcoholism, she maneuvered her children, including Khubilai Khan, into powerful positions and strongly encouraged them in the direction of religious toleration. (Bibliothèque nationale de France)

■ **Comparison**

What was distinctive about the Russian experience of Mongol rule?

them in decisions of the court.[24] Now Persian rulers could return to their more patriarchal ways.

Russia and the Mongols

When the Mongol military machine rolled over Russia between 1237 and 1240, it encountered a relatively new third-wave civilization, located on the far eastern fringe of Christendom (see Chapter 10). Whatever political unity this new civilization of Kievan Rus had earlier enjoyed was now gone, and various independent princes proved unable to unite even in the face of the Mongol onslaught. Although they had interacted extensively with nomadic people of the steppes north of the Black Sea, nothing had prepared them for the Mongols.

The devastation wrought by the Mongol assault matched or exceeded anything experienced by the Persians or the Chinese. City after city fell to Mongol forces, which were now armed with the catapults and battering rams adopted from Chinese or Muslim sources. The slaughter that sometimes followed was described in horrific terms by Russian chroniclers, although twentieth-century historians often regard such accounts as exaggerated. (See Document 11.3, pp. 545–46, for one such account.) From the survivors and the cities that surrendered early, laborers and skilled craftsmen were deported to other Mongol lands or sold into slavery. A number of Russian crafts were so depleted of their workers that they did not recover for a century or more.

If the ferocity of initial conquest bore similarities to the experiences of Persia, Russia's incorporation into the Mongol Empire was very different. To the Mongols, it was the Kipchak (KIP-chahk) Khanate, named after the Kipchak Turkic-speaking peoples north of the Caspian and Black seas, among whom the Mongols had settled. To the Russians, it was the "Khanate of the Golden Horde." By whatever name, the Mongols had conquered Russia, but they did not occupy it as they had China and Persia. Because there were no garrisoned cities, permanently stationed administrators, or Mongol settlers, the Russian experience of Mongol rule was quite different from elsewhere. From the Mongol point of view, Russia had little to offer. Its economy was far less developed than that of more established civilizations; nor was it located on major international trade routes. It was simply not worth the expense of occupying. Furthermore, the availability of extensive steppe lands for pasturing their flocks north of the Black and Caspian seas meant that the Mongols could maintain their preferred nomadic way of life, while remaining in easy reach of Russian cities when the need arose to send further military expeditions. They could dominate and exploit Russia from the steppes.

And exploit they certainly did. Russian princes received appointment from the khan and were required to send substantial tribute to the Mongol capital at Sarai, located on the lower Volga River. A variety of additional taxes created a heavy burden, especially on the peasantry, while continuing border raids sent tens of thousands of Russians into slavery. The Mongol impact was highly uneven, however. Some Russian princes benefited considerably because they were able to manipulate their role as tribute collectors to grow wealthy. The Russian Orthodox Church likewise flourished under the Mongol policy of religious toleration, for it received exemption from many taxes. Nobles who participated in Mongol raids earned a share of the loot. Some cities, such as Kiev, resisted the Mongols and were devastated, while others collaborated and were left undamaged. Moscow in particular emerged as the primary collector of tribute for the Mongols, and its princes parlayed this position into a leading role as the nucleus of a renewed Russian state when Mongol domination receded in the fifteenth century.

The absence of direct Mongol rule had implications for the Mongols themselves, for they were far less influenced by or assimilated within Russian cultures than their counterparts in China and Persia had been. The Mongols in China had turned themselves into a Chinese dynasty, with the khan as a Chinese emperor. Some learned calligraphy, and a few came to appreciate Chinese poetry. In Persia, the Mongols had converted to Islam, with some becoming farmers. Not so in Russia. There "the Mongols of the Golden Horde were still spending their days in the saddle and their nights in tents."[25] They could dominate Russia from the adjacent steppes without in any way adopting Russian culture. Even though they remained culturally separate from Christian Russians, eventually the Mongols assimilated to the culture and the Islamic faith of the Kipchak people of the steppes, and in the process they lost their distinct identity and became Kipchaks.

Despite this domination from a distance, "the impact of the Mongols on Russia was, if anything, greater than on China and Iran [Persia]," according to a leading scholar.[26]

Mongol Russia
This sixteenth-century painting depicts the Mongol burning of the Russian city of Ryazan in 1237. Similar destruction awaited many Russian towns that resisted the invaders. (Sovfoto/Eastfoto)

Russian princes, who were more or less left alone if they paid the required tribute and taxes, found it useful to adopt the Mongols' weapons, diplomatic rituals, court practices, taxation system, and military draft. Mongol policies facilitated, although not intentionally, the rise of Moscow as the core of a new Russian state, and that state made good use of the famous Mongol mounted courier service, which Marco Polo had praised so highly. Mongol policies also strengthened the hold of the Russian Orthodox Church and enabled it to penetrate the rural areas more fully than before. Some Russians, seeking to explain their country's economic backwardness and political autocracy in modern times, have held the Mongols responsible for both conditions, though most historians consider such views vastly exaggerated.

Divisions among the Mongols and the growing strength of the Russian state, centered now on the city of Moscow, enabled the Russians to break the Mongols' hold by the end of the fifteenth century. With the earlier demise of Mongol rule in China and Persia, and now in Russia, the Mongols had retreated from their brief but spectacular incursion into the civilizations of outer Eurasia. Nonetheless, they continued to periodically threaten these civilizations for several centuries, until their homelands were absorbed into the expanding Russian and Chinese empires. But the Mongol moment in world history was over.

The Mongol Empire as a Eurasian Network

During the third-wave millennium, Chinese culture and Buddhism provided a measure of integration among the peoples of East Asia; Christianity did the same for Europe, while the realm of Islam connected most of the lands in between. But it was the Mongol Empire, during the thirteenth and fourteenth centuries, that brought all of these regions into a single interacting network. It was a unique moment in world history and an important step toward the global integration of the modern era.

Toward a World Economy

■ **Connection**
What kinds of cross-cultural interactions did the Mongol Empire generate?

The Mongols themselves produced little of value for distant markets, nor were they active traders. Nonetheless, they consistently promoted international commerce, largely so that they could tax it and thus extract wealth from more developed civilizations. The Great Khan Ogodei, for example, often paid well over the asking price to attract merchants to his capital of Karakorum. The Mongols also provided financial backing for caravans, introduced standardized weights and measures, and gave tax breaks to merchants.

In providing a relatively secure environment for merchants making the long and arduous journey across Central Asia between Europe and China, the Mongol Empire brought the two ends of the Eurasian world into closer contact than ever before and launched a new phase in the history of the Silk Roads. Marco Polo was only the most famous of many European merchants, mostly from Italian cities, who made their way to China through the Mongol Empire. So many traders attempted the journey that guidebooks were published with much useful advice about the trip. Merchants returned with tales of rich lands and prosperous commercial opportunities, but what they described were long-established trading networks of which Europeans had been largely ignorant.

The Mongol trading circuit was a central element in an even larger commercial network that linked much of the Afro-Eurasian world in the thirteenth century (see Map 11.2). Mongol-ruled China was the fulcrum of this vast system, connecting the overland route through the Mongol Empire with the oceanic routes through the South China Sea and Indian Ocean.

Diplomacy on a Eurasian Scale

Not only did the Mongol Empire facilitate long-distance commerce, but it also prompted diplomatic relationships from one end of Eurasia to the other. As their invasion of Russia spilled over into Eastern Europe, Mongol armies destroyed Polish, German, and Hungarian forces in 1241–1242 and seemed poised to march on Central and Western Europe. But the death of the Great Khan Ogodei required Mongol leaders to return to Mongolia, and Western Europe lacked adequate pasture for Mongol

Map 11.2
Trade and Disease in the Fourteenth Century
The Mongol Empire played a major role in the commercial integration of the Eurasian world as well as in the spread of the plague across this vast area.

herds. Thus Western Europe was spared the trauma of conquest, but fearing the possible return of the Mongols, both the pope and European rulers dispatched delegations to the Mongol capital, mostly led by Franciscan friars. They hoped to learn something about Mongol intentions, to secure Mongol aid in the Christian crusade against Islam, and, if possible, to convert Mongols to Christianity.

These efforts were largely in vain, for no alliance or widespread conversion occurred. In fact, one of these missions came back with a letter for the pope from the Great Khan Guyuk, demanding that Europeans submit to him. "But if you should not believe our letters and the command of God nor hearken to our counsel," he warned, "then we shall know for certain that you wish to have war. After that we do not know what will happen."[27] Perhaps the most important outcome of these diplomatic probings was the useful information about lands to the east that European missions brought back. Those reports contributed to a dawning European awareness of a wider world, and they have certainly provided later historians with much useful information about the Mongols. Somewhat later, in 1287, the il-khanate of Persia sought an alliance with European powers to take Jerusalem and crush the forces of Islam, but the Persian Mongols' conversion to Islam soon put an end to any such anti-Muslim coalition.

Within the Mongol Empire itself, close relationships developed between the courts of Persia and China. They regularly exchanged ambassadors, shared intelligence information, fostered trade between their regions, and sent skilled workers back and forth. Thus political authorities all across Eurasia engaged in diplomatic relationships with one another to an unprecedented degree.

Cultural Exchange in the Mongol Realm

Accompanying these transcontinental economic and political relationships was a substantial exchange of peoples and cultures. Mongol policy forcibly transferred many thousands of skilled craftsmen and educated people from their homelands to distant parts of the empire, while the Mongols' religious tolerance and support of merchants drew missionaries and traders from afar. The Mongol capital at Karakorum was a cosmopolitan city with places of worship for Buddhists, Daoists, Muslims, and Christians. Chinggis Khan and several other Mongol rulers married Christian women. Actors and musicians from China, wrestlers from Persia, and a jester from Byzantium provided entertainment for the Mongol court. Persian and Arab doctors and administrators were sent to China, while Chinese physicians and engineers found their skills in demand in the Islamic world.

This movement of people facilitated the exchange of ideas and techniques, a process actively encouraged by Mongol authorities. A great deal of Chinese technology and artistic conventions — such as painting, printing, gunpowder weapons, compass navigation, high-temperature furnaces, and medical techniques — flowed westward. Acupuncture, for example, was poorly received in the Middle East because it required too much bodily contact for Muslim taste, but Chinese techniques for diagnosing illness by taking the pulse of patients proved quite popular, as they involved minimal body contact. Muslim astronomers brought their skills and knowledge to China because Mongol authorities wanted "second opinions on the reading of heavenly signs and portents" and assistance in constructing accurate calendars, so necessary for ritual purposes.[28] Plants and crops likewise circulated within the Mongol domain. Lemons and carrots from the Middle East found a welcome reception in China, while the Persian Il-Khan Ghazan sent envoys to India, China, and elsewhere to seek "seeds of things which are unique in that land."[29]

Europeans arguably gained more than most from these exchanges, for they had long been cut off from the fruitful interchange with Asia, and in comparison to the Islamic and Chinese worlds, they were less technologically developed. Now they could reap the benefits of much new technology, new crops, and new knowledge of a wider world. And almost alone among the peoples of Eurasia, they could do so without having suffered the devastating consequences of Mongol conquest. In these circumstances, some historians have argued, lay the roots of Europe's remarkable rise to global prominence in the centuries that followed.

The Plague: An Afro-Eurasian Pandemic

Any benefits derived from participation in Mongol networks of communication and exchange must be measured alongside the hemispheric catastrophe known as the "plague" or the "pestilence" and later called the Black Death. Originating most likely in China, the bacteria responsible for the disease, known as *Yersinia pestis*, spread across the trade routes of the vast Mongol Empire in the early fourteenth century (see Map 11.2, p. 535). Carried by rodents and transmitted by fleas to humans, the plague erupted initially in 1331 in northeastern China and had reached the Middle East and Western Europe by 1347. One lurid but quite uncertain story has the Mongols using catapults to hurl corpses infected with the plague into the Genoese city of Caffa in the Crimea. In 1409, the plague reached East Africa, probably by way of the famous Chinese maritime expeditions that encompassed the Indian Ocean basin.

The disease itself was associated with swelling of the lymph nodes, most often in the groin; terrible headaches; high fever; and internal bleeding just below the skin. Infected people generally died within a few days. In the densely populated civilizations of China, the Islamic world, and Europe as well as in the steppe lands of the nomads, the plague claimed enormous numbers of human victims, causing a sharp contraction in Eurasian population for a century or more. Chroniclers reported rates of death that ranged from 50 to 90 percent of the affected population, depending on the time and place. A recent study suggests that about half of Europe's people perished during the initial outbreak of 1348–1350.[30] A fifteenth-century Egyptian historian wrote that within a month of the plague's arrival in 1349, "Cairo had become an abandoned desert. . . . Everywhere one heard lamentations and one could not pass by any house without being overwhelmed by the howling."[31] The Middle East generally had lost perhaps one-third of its population by the early fifteenth century.[32] The intense first wave of the plague was followed by periodic visitations over the next several centuries, although India and sub-Saharan Africa were much less affected than other regions of the Eastern Hemisphere.

■ **Change**
Disease changes societies. How might this argument apply to the plague?

The Plague
This illustration depicts a European doctor visiting a patient with the plague. Notice that the doctor and others around the bedside cover their noses to prevent infection. During the Black Death, doctors were often criticized for refusing to treat dying patients, as they feared for their own lives. (The Granger Collection, New York)

But in those places where it struck, the plague left thoughtful people grasping for language with which to describe a horror of such unprecedented dimensions. One Italian man, who had buried all five of his children with his own hands, wrote in 1348 that "so many have died that everyone believes it is the end of the world."[33] Another Italian, the Renaissance scholar Francesco Petrarch, was equally stunned by the impact of the Black Death; he wrote to a friend in 1349:

> When at any time has such a thing been seen or spoken of? Has what happened in these years ever been read about: empty houses, derelict cities, ruined estates, fields strewn with cadavers, a horrible and vast solitude encompassing the whole world? Consult historians, they are silent; ask physicians, they are stupefied; seek the answers from philosophers, they shrug their shoulders, furrow their brows, and with fingers pressed against their lips, bid you be silent. Will posterity believe these things, when we who have seen it can scarcely believe it . . . ?[34]

In the Islamic world, the famous historian Ibn Khaldun, who had lost both of his parents to the plague, also wrote about it in apocalyptic terms:

> Civilization in both the East and the West was visited by a destructive plague which devastated nations and caused populations to vanish. It swallowed up many of the good things of civilization and wiped them out. . . . It was as if the voice of existence had called out for oblivion and restriction, and the world responded to its call.[35]

(See Visual Sources: The Black Death and Religion in Western Europe, pp. 550–57, for more on religious response to the plague in Europe.)

Beyond its immediate devastation, the Black Death worked longer-term changes in European society, the region where the plague's impact has been most thoroughly studied. Labor shortages following the initial outburst provoked sharp conflict between scarce workers, who sought higher wages or better conditions, and the rich, who resisted those demands. A series of peasant revolts in the fourteenth century reflected this tension, which also undermined the practice of serfdom. That labor shortage also may have fostered a greater interest in technological innovation and created, at least for a time, more employment opportunities for women. Thus a resilient European civilization survived a cataclysm that had the power to destroy it. In a strange way, that catastrophe may have actually fostered its future growth.

Whatever its impact in particular places, the plague also had larger consequences. Ironically, that human disaster, born of the Mongol network, was a primary reason for the demise of that network in the fourteenth and fifteenth centuries. Population contracted, cities declined, and the volume of trade diminished all across the Mongol world. By 1350, the Mongol Empire itself was in disarray, and within a century the Mongols had lost control of Chinese, Persian, and Russian civilizations. The Central Asian trade route, so critical to the entire Afro-Eurasian world economy, largely closed.

This disruption of the Mongol-based land routes to the east, coupled with a desire to avoid Muslim intermediaries, provided incentives for Europeans to take to the sea in their continuing efforts to reach the riches of Asia. Their naval technology gave them military advantages on the seas, much as the Mongols' skill with the bow and their mobility on horseback gave these nomads a decisive edge in land battles. As Europeans penetrated Asian and Atlantic waters in the sixteenth century, they took on, in some ways, the role of the Mongols in organizing and fostering world trade and in creating a network of communication and exchange over an even larger area. Like the Mongols, Europeans were people on the periphery of the major established civilizations; they too were economically less developed in comparison to Chinese and Islamic civilizations; both were prone to forcibly plundering the wealthier civilizations they encountered; and European empire-building in the Americas, like that of the Mongols in Eurasia, brought devastating disease and catastrophic population decline in its wake.[36] Europeans, of course, brought far more of their own culture and many more of their own people to the societies they conquered, as Christianity, European languages, settler societies, and western science and technology took root within their empires. Although their imperial presence lasted far longer and operated on a much larger scale, European actions at the beginning of their global expansion bore some resemblance to those of their Mongol predecessors. They were, as one historian put it, "the Mongols of the seas."[37]

LearningCurve
bedfordstmartins.com
/strayer/LC

Reflections: Changing Images of Pastoral Peoples

Historians frequently change their minds, and long-term consensus on most important matters has been difficult to achieve. For example, until recently, pastoral nomads generally received bad press in history books. Normally they entered the story only when they were threatening or destroying established civilizations. In presenting a largely negative image of pastoral peoples, historians were reflecting the long-held attitudes of literate elites in the civilizations of Eurasia. Fearing and usually despising such peoples, educated observers in China, the Middle East, and Europe often described them as bloodthirsty savages or barbarians, bringing only chaos and destruction in their wake. Han Kuan, a Chinese scholar of the first century B.C.E., described the Xiongnu people as "abandoned by Heaven . . . in foodless desert wastes, without proper houses, clothed in animal hides, eating their meat uncooked and drinking blood."[38] To the Christian Saint Jerome (340–420 C.E.), the nomadic Huns "filled the whole earth with slaughter and panic alike as they flitted hither and thither on their swift horses."[39] Almost a thousand years later, the famous Arab historian Ibn Khaldun described nomads in a very similar fashion: "It is their nature to plunder whatever other people possess."[40]

Because pastoral peoples generally did not have written languages, the sources available to historians came from less-than-unbiased observers in adjacent agricultural civilizations. Furthermore, in the long-running conflict across the farming/pastoral frontier, agricultural civilizations ultimately triumphed. Over the centuries, some nomadic or semi-agricultural peoples, such as the Germanic tribes of Europe and the Arabs, created new civilizations. Others, such as the Turkic and Mongol peoples, took over existing civilizations or were encompassed within established agrarian empires. By the early twentieth century, and in most places much earlier, pastoral peoples everywhere had lost their former independence and had often shed their nomadic life as well. Since "winners" usually write history, the negative views of pastoral nomads held by agrarian civilizations normally prevailed.

Reflecting more inclusive contemporary values, historians in recent decades have sought to present a more balanced picture of pastoralists' role in world history, emphasizing what they created as well as what they destroyed. These historians have highlighted the achievements of herding peoples, such as their adaptation to inhospitable environments; their technological innovations; their development of horse-, camel-, or cattle-based cultures; their role in fostering cross-cultural exchange; and their state-building efforts.

A less critical or judgmental posture toward the Mongols may also owe something to the "total wars" and genocides of the twentieth century, in which the mass slaughter of civilians became a strategy to induce enemy surrender. During the cold war, the United States and the Soviet Union were prepared, apparently, to obliterate each other's entire population with nuclear weapons in response to an attack. In light of this recent history, Mongol massacres may appear a little less unique. Historians living in the glass houses of contemporary societies are perhaps more reluctant to cast stones at the Mongols. In understanding the Mongols, as in so much else, historians are shaped by the times and circumstances of their own lives as much as by "what really happened" in the past.

Second Thoughts

LearningCurve
Check what you know.
bedfordstmartins.com /strayer/LC

Online Study Guide
bedfordstmartins.com
/highschool/strayer

What's the Significance?

Big Picture Questions

1. What accounts for the often negative attitudes of settled societies toward the pastoral peoples living on their borders?

2. Why have historians often neglected pastoral peoples' role in world history? How would you assess the perspective of this chapter toward the Mongols? Does it strike you as negative and critical of the Mongols, as bending over backward to portray them in a positive light, or as a balanced presentation?

3. In what different ways did Mongol rule affect the Islamic world, Russia, China, and Europe? In what respects did it foster Eurasian integration?

4. Why did the Mongol Empire last only a relatively short time?

5. **Looking Back:** In what ways did the Mongol Empire resemble previous empires (Arab, Roman, Chinese, or the Greek empire of Alexander, for example), and in what ways did it differ from them?

Next Steps: For Further Study

For Web sites and additional documents related to this chapter, see **Make History** at bedfordstmartins.com /highschool/strayer.

John Aberth, *The First Horseman: Disease in Human History* (2007). A global study of the history of disease, with a fine chapter on the Black Death.

Thomas Allsen, *Culture and Conquest in Mongol Eurasia* (2001). A history of cultural exchange within the Mongol realm, particularly between China and the Islamic world.

Thomas J. Barfield, *The Nomadic Alternative* (1993). An anthropological and historical survey of pastoral peoples on a global basis.

Carter Finley, *The Turks in World History* (2005). The evolution of Turkic-speaking people, from their nomadic origins to the twentieth century.

Jack Weatherford, *Genghis Khan and the Making of the Modern World* (2004). A lively, well-written, and balanced account of the world the Mongols made and the legacy they left for the future.

"The Mongols in World History," http://afe.easia.columbia.edu/mongols. A wonderful resource on the Mongols generally, with a particular focus on their impact in China.

Documents

Considering the Evidence:
Perspectives on the Mongols

How did the Mongols understand themselves and the enormous empire they had created? How did the peoples who were forcibly incorporated within that empire or threatened by it view the Mongols? In studying the Mongol phenomenon, historians use documents that reflect both the Mongols' perception of themselves and the perspectives of outsiders. The first two documents derive from Mongol sources, while the final two represent views from Russian and Chinese observers.

Sorting through these various perceptions of the Mongols raises questions about the kinds of understandings—or misunderstandings—that arise as culturally different peoples meet, especially under conditions of conquest. These documents also require reflection on the relative usefulness of sources that come from the Mongols themselves as well as those that derive from the victims of Mongol aggression.

Document 11.1

Mongol History from a Mongol Source

The major literary work to emerge from the Mongols themselves, widely known as *The Secret History of the Mongols*, was written a decade or two after the death in 1227 of Chinggis Khan. The unknown author of this work was clearly a contemporary of the Great Khan and likely a member of the royal houschold. The first selection discusses the Mongol practice of *anda*, a very close relationship between two unrelated men. The anda relationship of Temujin, the future Chinggis Khan, and his friend Jamugha was important in Temujin's rise to power, although they later broke with one another. The second selection from the *Secret History* describes the process by which Temujin was elevated to the rank of Chinggis Khan, the ruler of a united Mongol nation, while the third recounts the reflections of Ogodei, Chinggis Khan's son and successor, probably toward the end of his reign, which lasted from 1229 to 1241.

- How would you describe the *anda* relationship?

- What does the *Secret History* suggest about the nature of political authority and political relationships among the Mongols?

- What did Ogodei regard as his greatest achievements and his most notable mistakes?

- What evidence do these selections from the *Secret History* provide that the author was an insider?

The Secret History of the Mongols
ca. 1240

Anda: Temujin and Jamugha

Temujin and Jamugha pitched their tents in the Khorkonagh Valley. With their people united in one great camp, the two leaders decided they should renew their friendship, their pledge of anda. They remembered when they'd first made that pledge, and said, "We should love one another again."

That first time they'd met Temujin was eleven years old. . . . So Temujin and Jamugha said to each other: "We've heard the elders say, 'When two men become anda their lives become one, one will never desert the other and will always defend him.' This is the way we'll act from now on. We'll renew our old pledge and love each other forever."

Temujin took the golden belt he'd received in the spoils from Toghtoga's defeat and placed it around Anda Jamugha's waist. Then he led out the Merkid chief's warhorse, a light yellow mare with black mane and tail, and gave it to Anda Jamugha to ride. Jamugha took the golden belt he'd received in the spoils from Dayir Usun's defeat and placed it around the waist of Anda Temujin. Then he led out the whitish-tan warhorse of Dayir Usun and had Anda Temujin ride on it.

Before the cliffs of Khuldaghar in the Khorkhonagh Valley, beneath the Great Branching Tree of

the Mongol, they pledged their friendship and promised to love one another. They held a feast on the spot and there was great celebration. Temujin and Jamugha spent that night alone, sharing one blanket to cover them both. Temujin and Jamugha loved each other for one year, and when half of the second year had passed they agreed it was time to move camp. . . .

Temujin Becomes Chinggis Khan

Then they moved the whole camp to the shores of Blue Lake in the Gurelgu Mountains. Altan, Khuchar, and Sacha Beki conferred with each other there, and then said to Temujin: "We want you to be khan. Temujin, if you'll be our khan we'll search through the spoils for the beautiful women and virgins, for the great palace tents, . . . for the finest geldings and mares. We'll gather all these and bring them to you. When we go off to hunt for wild game, we'll go out first to drive them together for you to kill. We'll drive the wild animals of the steppe together so that their bellies are touching. We'll drive the wild game of the mountains together so that they stand leg to leg. If we disobey your command during battle, take away our possessions, our children, and wives. Leave us behind in the dust, cutting off our heads where we stand and letting them fall to the ground. If we disobey your counsel in peacetime, take away our tents and our goods, our wives, and our children. Leave us behind when you move, abandoned in the desert without a protector." Having given their word, having taken this oath, they proclaimed

Source: Paul Kahn, *The Secret History of the Mongols: The Origin of Chingis Khan* (San Francisco: North Point Press, 1984), 44–45, 48–49, 192–93.

Temujin khan of the Mongol and gave him the name Chingis Khan....

Reflections of Ogodei

Then Ogodei Khan spoke these words: "Since my father the Khan passed away and I came to sit on his great throne, what have I done? I went to war against the people of Cathay° and I destroyed them. For my second accomplishment I established a network of post stations so that my words are carried across the land with great speed. Another of my accomplishments has been to have my commanders dig wells in the desert so that there would be pasture and water for the people there. Lastly I placed spies and agents among all the people of the cities. In all directions I've brought peace to the Nation and the people....

"Since the time of my father the Khan, I added these four accomplishments to all that he did. But also since my father passed away and I came to sit on his great throne with the burden of all the numerous people on my shoulders, I allowed myself to

be conquered by wine. This was one of my mistakes. Another of my mistakes was to listen to a woman with no principles and because of her take away the daughters who belonged to my Uncle Odchigin. Even though I'm the Khan, the Lord of the Nation, I have no right to go against established principle, so this was my mistake.

"Another mistake was to secretly harm Dokholkhu. If you ask, 'Why was this wrong?' I would say that to secretly harm Dokholkhu, a man who had served his proper lord, my father the Khan, performing heroic deeds in his service, was a mistake. Now that I've done this, who'll perform heroic deeds in my service? Then my last mistake was to desire too much, to say to myself, 'I'm afraid that all the wild game born under Heaven will run off toward the land of my brothers.' So I ordered earthen walls to be built to keep the wild game from running away, but even as these walls were being built I heard my brothers speaking badly of me. I admit that I was wrong to do this. Since the time of my father the Khan I've added four accomplishments to all that he'd done and I've done four things which I admit were wrong."

°**Cathay:** China.

Document 11.2

A Letter from Chinggis Khan

Document 11.2 comes from a remarkable letter that Chinggis Khan sent to an elderly Chinese Daoist master named Changchun in 1219, requesting a personal meeting with the teacher. Changchun in fact made the arduous journey to the camp of Chinggis Khan, then located in Afghanistan, where he stayed with the Mongol ruler for almost a year, before returning to China.

- Why did Chinggis Khan seek a meeting with Changchun?

- How does Chinggis Khan define his life's work? What is his image of himself?

- How would you describe the tone of Chinggis Khan's letter to Changchun? What does the letter suggest about Mongol attitudes toward the belief systems of conquered peoples?

- How do Documents 11.1 and 11.2 help explain the success of the Mongols' empire-building efforts?

- What core Mongol values do these documents suggest?

CHINGGIS KHAN

Letter to Changchun

1219

Heaven has abandoned China owing to its haughtiness and extravagant luxury. But I, living in the northern wilderness, have not inordinate passions. I hate luxury and exercise moderation. I have only one coat and one food. I eat the same food and am dressed in the same tatters as my humble herdsmen. I consider the people my children, and take an interest in talented men as if they were my brothers. . . . At military exercises I am always in the front, and in time of battle am never behind. In the space of seven years I have succeeded in accomplishing a great work, and uniting the whole world into one empire. I have not myself distinguished qualities. But the government of the [Chinese] is inconstant, and therefore Heaven assists me to obtain the throne. . . . All together have acknowledged my supremacy. It seems to me that since the remote time . . . such an empire has not been seen. . . . Since the time I came to the throne I have always taken to heart the ruling of my people; but I could not find worthy men

to occupy [high offices]. . . . With respect to these circumstances I inquired, and heard that thou, master, hast penetrated the truth. . . . For a long time thou has lived in the caverns of the rocks, and hast retired from the world; but to thee the people who have acquired sanctity repair, like clouds on the paths of the immortals, in innumerable multitudes. . . . But what shall I do? We are separated by mountains and plains of great extent, and I cannot meet thee. I can only descend from the throne and stand by the side. I have fasted and washed. I have ordered my adjutant . . . to prepare an escort and a cart for thee. Do not be afraid of the thousand *li*.° I implore thee to move thy sainted steps. Do not think of the extent of the sandy desert. Commiserate the people in the present situation of affairs, or have pity upon me, and communicate to me the means of preserving life. I shall serve thee myself. I hope that at least thou wilt leave me a trifle of thy wisdom. Say only one word to me and I shall be happy.

Source: E. Bretschneider, *Mediaeval Researches from Eastern Asiatic Sources* Vol. I (London, 1875), 37–39.

°*li*: a great distance.

Document 11.3

A Russian View of the Mongols

The initial impression of the Mongol impact in many places was one of utter devastation, destruction, and brutality. Document 11.3 offers a Russian commentary from that perspective drawn from the *Chronicle of Novgorod*, one of the major sources for the history of early Russia.

- How did the Russian writer of the *Chronicle* account for what he saw as the disaster of the Mongol invasion?

- Can you infer from the document any additional reasons for the Mongol success?

- Beyond the conquest itself, what other aspects of Mongol rule offended the Russians?

■ To what extent was the Mongol conquest of Russia also a clash of cultures?

The Chronicle of Novgorod
1238

That same year [1238] foreigners called Tartars° came in countless numbers, like locusts, into the land of Ryazan, and on first coming they halted at the river Nukhla, and took it, and halted in camp there. And thence they sent their emissaries to the *Knyazes*° of Ryazan, a sorceress and two men with her, demanding from them one-tenth of everything: of men and *Knyazes* and horses—of everything one-tenth. And the *Knyazes* of Ryazan ... without letting them into their towns, went out to meet them to Voronazh. And the *Knyazes* said to them: "Only when none of us remain then all will be yours."... And the *Knyazes* of Ryazan sent to Yuri of Volodimir asking for help, or himself to come. But Yuri neither went himself nor listened to the request of the *Knyazes* of Ryazan, but he himself wished to make war separately. But it was too late to oppose the wrath of God.... Thus also did God before these men take from us our strength and put into us perplexity and thunder and dread and trembling for our sins. And then the pagan foreigners surrounded Ryazan and fenced it in with a stockade.... And the Tartars took the town on December 21, and they had advanced against it on the 16th of the same month. They likewise killed the *Knyaz* and *Knyaginya*, and men, women, and children, monks, nuns and priests, some by fire, some by the sword, and violated nuns, priests' wives, good women and girls in the presence of their mothers and sisters. But God saved the Bishop, for he had departed the same moment when the troops invested the town. And who, brethren, would not lament over this, among those of us left alive when they suffered this bitter and violent death? And we,

indeed, having seen it, were terrified and wept with sighing day and night over our sins, while we sigh every day and night, taking thought for our possessions and for the hatred of brothers.

...The pagan and godless Tartars, then, having taken Ryazan, went to Volodimir.... And when the lawless ones had already come near and set up battering rams, and took the town and fired it on Friday before Sexagesima Sunday, the *Knyaz* and *Knyaginya* and *Vladyka*, seeing that the town was on fire and that the people were already perishing, some by fire and others by the sword, took refuge in the Church of the Holy Mother of God and shut themselves in the Sacristy. The pagans breaking down the doors, piled up wood and set fire to the sacred church; and slew all, thus they perished, giving up their souls to God.... And Rostov and Suzhdal went each its own way. And the accursed ones having come thence took Moscow, Pereyaslavi, Yurev, Dmitrov, *Volok*, and Tver; there also they killed the son of Yaroslav. And thence the lawless ones came and invested Torzhok on the festival of the first Sunday in Lent. They fenced it all round with a fence as they had taken other towns, and here the accursed ones fought with battering rams for two weeks. And the people in the town were exhausted and from Novgorod there was no help for them; but already every man began to be in perplexity and terror. And so the pagans took the town, and slew all from the male sex even to the female, all the priests and the monks, and all stripped and reviled gave up their souls to the Lord in a bitter and a wretched death, on March 5 ...Wednesday in Easter week.

°**Tartars:** Mongols.

°***Knyazes:*** Princes.

Source: Robert Mitchell and Nevill Forbes, trans., *The Chronicle of Novgorod, 1016–1471* (New York: AMS Press, 1970; repr. from the edition of 1914, London), 81–83, 88.

Document 11.4

Chinese Perceptions of the Mongols

Chinese responses to Mongol rule varied considerably. To some, of course, the Mongols were simply foreign conquerors and therefore illegitimate as Chinese rulers. Marco Polo, who was in China at the time, reported that some Mongol officials or their Muslim intermediaries treated Chinese "just like slaves," demanding bribes for services, ordering arbitrary executions, and seizing women at will—all of which generated outrage and hostility. Document 11.4 illustrates another side to Chinese perception of the Mongols. It comes from a short biography of a Mongol official named Menggu, which was written by a well-educated Chinese scholar on the occasion of Menggu's death. Intended to be inscribed on stone and buried with the Mongol officer, it emphasizes the ways in which Menggu conformed to Chinese ways of governing. Such obituaries were an established form of Chinese historical writing, usually commissioned by the children of the deceased.

■ Why might Menggu's children have requested such a document and asked a Chinese scholar to compose it? What does this suggest about Mongol attitudes to Chinese culture?

■ What features of Menggu's governship did this Chinese author appreciate? In what ways did Menggu's actions and behavior reflect Confucian values? What might the writer have omitted from his account?

■ What might inspire a highly educated Chinese scholar to compose such a flattering public tribute to a Mongol official?

■ Why might historians be a bit skeptical about this document? Which statements might be most suspect?

Epitaph for the Honorable Menggu

1274

Emperor Taizu [Chinggis Khan] received the mandate of Heaven and subjugated all regions. When Emperor Taizong [Ogodei Khan] succeeded, he revitalized the bureaucratic system and made it more efficient and organized. At court, one minister supervised all the officials and helped the emperor rule. In the provinces, commanderies and counties

received instructions from above and saw that they got carried out. Prefects and magistrates were as a rule appointed only after submitting [to the Mongols]. Still one Mongol, called the governor, was selected to supervise them. The prefects and magistrates all had to obey his orders. . . .

In the fourth month of 1236, the court deemed Menggu capable of handling Zhangde, so promoted him . . . to be its governor. . . . Because regulations were lax, the soldiers took advantage of their victory to plunder. Even in cities and marketplaces, some

Source: Patricia Buckley Ebrey, ed. and trans., *Chinese Civilization: A Sourcebook* (New York: Free Press, 1991), 192–94.

people kept their doors closed in the daytime. As soon as Menggu arrived, he took charge. Knowing the people's grievances, he issued an order, "Those who oppress the people will be dealt with according to the law. Craftsmen, merchants, and shopkeepers, you must each go about your work with your doors open, peaceably attending to your business without fear. Farmers, you must be content with your lands and exert yourselves diligently according to the seasons. I will instruct or punish those who mistreat you." After this order was issued, the violent became obedient and no one any longer dared violate the laws. Farmers in the fields and travelers on the roads felt safe, and people began to enjoy life.

In the second month of 1238, Wang Rong, prefect of Huaizhou, rebelled. The grand preceptor and prince ordered Menggu to put down this rebellion, telling him to slaughter everyone. Menggu responded, "When the royal army suppresses rebels, those who were coerced into joining them ought to be pardoned, not to mention those who are entirely innocent." The prince approved his advice and followed it. When Wang Rong surrendered, he was executed but the region was spared. The residents, with jugs of wine and burning incense, saw Menggu off tearfully, unable to bear his leaving. Forty years later when he was put in charge of Henei, the common people were delighted with the news, saying, "We will all survive—our parents and relatives through marriage all served him before."

In 1239 locusts destroyed all the vegetation in Xiang and Wei, so the people were short of food. Menggu reported this to the great minister Quduqu,

who issued five thousand piculs of army rations to save the starving. As a consequence no one had to flee or starve. . . .

At that time [1247] the harvest failed for several years in a row, yet taxes and labor services were still exacted. Consequently, three or four of every ten houses was vacant. Menggu ordered the officials to travel around announcing that those who returned to their property would be exempt from taxes and services for three years. That year seventeen thousand households returned in response to his summons. . . .

When there was a drought in 1263, Menggu prayed for rain and it rained. That year he was given the title Brilliant and August General and made governor of Zhongshan prefecture. In 1270 he was transferred and became governor of Hezhong prefecture. In the spring of 1274 he was allowed to wear the golden tiger tablet in recognition of his long and excellent service, his incorruptibility, and the repute in which he was held where he had served. . . .

The house where Menggu lived when he governed Zhangde nearly forty years ago, and the fields from which he obtained food then, were just adequate to keep out the wind and rain and supply enough to eat. When he died there were no estates or leftover wealth to leave his sons or grandsons. Therefore they had to model themselves on him and concentrate on governing in a way that would bring peace and safety, show love for the people, and benefit all. They have no need to be ashamed even if compared to the model officials of the Han and Tang dynasties.

Using the Evidence: Perspectives on the Mongols

1. **Assessing sources:** What are the strengths and limitations of these documents for understanding the Mongols? Taking the position of their authors into account, what exaggerations, biases, or misunderstandings can you identify in these sources? What information seems credible and what should be viewed more skeptically?

2. **Characterizing the Mongols:** Based on these documents and on the text of Chapter 11, write an essay assessing the Mongol moment in

world history. How might you counteract the view of many that the Mongols were simply destructive barbarians? How do your own values affect your understanding of the Mongol moment?

3. **Considering values and practice:** How would you describe the core values of Mongol culture? (Consider their leaders' goals, attitudes toward conquered peoples, duties of rulers, views of political authority, role of women.) To what extent were these values put into practice in acquiring and ruling their huge empire? And in what ways were those values undermined or eroded as that empire took shape?

Visual Sources

Considering the Evidence: The Black Death and Religion in Western Europe

Among the most far-reaching outcomes of the Mongol moment in world history was the spread all across Eurasia and North Africa of that deadly disease known as the plague or the Black Death. While the Mongols certainly did not cause the plague, their empire facilitated the movement not only of goods and people but also of the microorganisms responsible for this pestilence (see Map 11.2, p. 535, and pp. 537–39). The impact of the Black Death was catastrophic almost everywhere it struck, but it is from Western Europe that our most detailed accounts and illustrations have survived about how people responded to that calamity.

Religion permeated the cultural world of Western Europe in the fourteenth century. The rituals of the Roman Catholic Church attended the great passages of life such as birth, marriage, and death, while the major themes of Christian teaching—sin and repentance, salvation and heaven, the comfort available through Jesus, Mary, and the saints—shaped most people's outlook on life and the world. It is hardly surprising, then, that many people would turn to religion in their efforts to understand and cope with a catastrophe of such immense proportions.

Seeking the aid of parish priests, invoking the intercession of the Virgin Mary, participating in religious processions and pilgrimages, attending mass regularly, increasing attention to private devotion—these were among the ways that beleaguered people sought to tap the resources of faith to alleviate the devastating impact of the plague. From Church leaders, the faithful heard a message of the plague as God's punishment for sins. An Italian layman reflected this understanding when he wrote *A History of the Plague* in 1348. There he pictured God witnessing the world "sinking and sliding into all kinds of wickedness." In response, "the quivering spear of the Almighty, in the form of the plague, was sent down to infect the whole human race.[41]

Accompanying such ideas were religiously based attacks on prostitutes, homosexuals, and Jews, people whose allegedly immoral behavior or alien beliefs had invited God's retribution. In Florence alone, some 17,000 men were accused of sodomy during the fifteenth century. Jews, who were sometimes held responsible for deliberately spreading the disease, were subject to terrible persecution, including the destruction of synagogues, massacres, burnings, expulsion, and seizure of property. Although several popes and kings defended them, many Jews fled to Poland, where authorities welcomed their urban and commercial skills, leading to a flourishing Jewish culture there in the several centuries that followed.

The most well-known movement reflecting an understanding of the plague as God's judgment on a sinful world was that of the flagellants, whose name derived from the Latin word *flagella*, "whips." The practice of flagellation, whipping oneself or allowing oneself to be whipped, had a long tradition within the Christian world and elsewhere as well. Flagellation served as a penance for sin and as a means of identifying with Christ, who was himself whipped prior to his crucifixion. It reemerged as a fairly widespread practice, especially in Germany, between 1348 and 1350 in response to the initial outbreak of the plague. Its adherents believed that perhaps the terrible wrath of God could be averted by performing this extraordinary act of atonement or penance. Groups of flagellants moved from city to city, where they called for repentance, confessed their sins, sang hymns, and participated in ritual dances, which climaxed in whipping themselves with knotted cords sometimes embedded with iron points. Visual Source 11.1 is a contemporary representation of the flagellants in the town of Doornik in the Netherlands in 1349. The text at the bottom reads in part:

> In [1349] it came to pass that on the day of the Assumption of the Blessed Virgin (Aug. 15) some 200 persons came here from Bruges about noon.... [I]mmediately the whole town was filled with curiosity as to why these folk had come.... Meantime the folk from Bruges prepared to perform their ceremonies which they called "penance." The inhabitants of both sexes, who had never before seen any such thing, began to imitate the actions of the strangers, to torment themselves also by the penitential exercises and to thank God for this means of penance which seemed to them most effectual.

- Flagellation was but one form of penance. What other forms of self-inflicted punishment for sin are suggested in the image?

- What is the significance of the Christ on the cross that precedes the flagellants?

- Does the procession seem spontaneous or organized? Do Church authorities appear to have instigated or approved this procession?

- How might the flagellants have understood their own actions?

- Why do you think Church authorities generally opposed the flagellant movement?

A[c]abiti anno predi[c]to q[uod] in die
A[s]umptionis virginis glo[r]i-
ose venerunt a villa b[r]ugen-
ti arater[.] .CC. homines -: quasi hora

[c]ep[er]unt com[pati] p[er]sonis er[?]
penitentie condolere et deo gra-
tias redd[e]re super tanta pesti-
lentia quam gravissimam re[?]

Visual Source 11.1 The Flagellants (Private Collection/The Bridgeman Art Library)

While many people certainly turned to religion for solace in the face of unimaginable disaster, others found traditional Christian rituals and teachings of little use or difficult to reconcile with the overwhelming realities of the disease. For some the plague prompted an orgy of hedonism, perhaps to affirm life in the face of endless death or simply to live to the full in what time remained to them. A contemporary Italian observer noted, "As they wallowed in idleness, their dissolution led them into the sin of gluttony, into banquets, taverns, delicate foods, and gambling. They rushed headlong into lust."[42] In 1394 a representative of the pope threatened excommunication for those who practiced debauchery in the graveyards.

Among the deepest traumas inflicted by the plague was its interference with proper Christian rituals surrounding death and dying, practices that were believed to assist the dead to achieve eternal rest and the living to accept their loss and find hope for reunion in heaven. Priests were scarce and sometimes refused to administer last rites, fearing contact with the dying. The sheer numbers of dead were overwhelming. City authorities at times ordered quick burials in mass graves to avoid the spread of the disease. A French observer in 1348

Visual Source 11.2 Burying the Dead (Bibliothèque Royale de Belgique, Brussels, Belgium/ The Bridgeman Art Library)

wrote, "No relatives, no friends showed concern for what might be happening. No priest came to hear the confessions of the dying, or to administer the sacraments to them."[43] The fourteenth-century Italian poet Boccaccio echoed those sentiments: "There were no tears or candles or mourners to honor the dead; in fact no more respect was accorded to dead people than would nowadays be shown toward dead goats."[44] Visual Source 11.2, published in 1352, illustrates a burial of plague victims of 1349 in the city of Tournai in what is now Belgium.

- How does this visual source support or contradict the written accounts excerpted above?

- How would you characterize the burial scene in this visual source?

- How does it differ from what an image of a proper Christian burial might contain? How might survivors of the plague have regarded such a burial?

The initial and subsequent outbreaks of the plague in Western Europe generated an understandable preoccupation with death, which was reflected in the art of the time. A stained-glass window in a church in Norwich, England, from about 1500 personified Death as a chess player contesting with a high Church official. A type of tomb called a cadaver tomb included a sculpture of the deceased as a rotting cadaver, sometimes with flesh-eating worms emerging from the body. An inscription on one such tomb in the Canterbury Cathedral in England explained the purpose of the image:

> Whoever you be who will pass by, I ask you to remember,
> You will be like me after you die,
> For all [to see]: horrible, dust, worms, vile flesh.[45]

This intense awareness of the inevitability of death and its apparently in-discriminate occurrence was also expressed in the Dance of Death, which be-gan in France in 1348 as a ritual intended to prevent the plague or to cure the afflicted. During the performance people would periodically fall to the ground, allowing others to trample on them. By 1400 such performances took place in a number of parish churches and subsequently in more secular settings. The Dance of Death also received artistic expression in a variety of poems, paint-ings, and sketches. The earliest of the paintings dates from 1425 and depicts dozens of people—from an emperor, king, pope, and bishop to a merchant, peasant, and an infant—each dancing with skeletal figures enticing them toward death. Visual Source 11.3 reproduces a portion of one of these Dance of Death paintings, originally created by the German artist Berndt Notke in 1463 and subsequently restored and reproduced many times.

In the inscriptions at the bottom of the painting, each living character ad-dresses a skeletal figure, who in turn makes a reply. Here is the exchange be-tween the empress (shown in a red dress at the far right of the image) and Death. First, the empress speaks:

> I know, Death means me! I was never terrified so greatly! I thought he was not in his right mind, after all, I am young and also an empress. I thought I had a lot of power,
> I had not thought of him or that anybody could do something against me. Oh, let me live on, this I implore you!

And then Death replies:

> Empress, highly presumptuous, I think, you have forgotten me. Fall in! It is now time.
> You thought I should let you off? No way! And were you ever so much, You must participate in this play, And you others, everybody— Hold on! Follow me, Mr Cardinal![46]

- How is the status of each of the various living figures—from left to right: the pope, the emperor, the empress—depicted?

- What does the white sheet around each of the death images represent? What do their expressions suggest about their attitude toward the living?

- Notice that the living figures face outward toward the viewer rather than toward the entreating death figures on either side of them. What might this mean?

- Does the portrayal of death pictured here reflect Christian views of death or does it challenge them?

Visual Source 11.3 A Culture of Death (St. Nicolair's Church, Tallinn, now the Niguliste Museum. Photo: Visual Connection Archive)

- How is the exchange between the empress and Death reflected in the painting?

The horrific experience of the Black Death also caused some people to question fundamental Christian teachings about the mercy and benevolence of God or even of his power to affect the outcome of the plague. A late-fourteenth-century clergyman in England expressed the dismay that many must have felt:

> For God is deaf nowadays and will not hear us
> And for our guilt, he grinds good men to dust.[47]

In a similar vein, the fourteenth-century Italian Renaissance scholar Francesco Petrarch questioned why God's vengeance had fallen so hard on the people of his own time: "While all have sinned alike, we alone bear the lash." He asked whether it was possible "that God does not care for mortal men." In the end, Petrarch dismissed that idea but still found God's judgments "inscrutable and inaccessible to human senses."[48] Thus the Black Death eroded more optimistic thirteenth-century Christian views, based on the ideas of the ancient Greek philosopher Aristotle, that human rationality could penetrate the mind of God.

Efforts to interpret Visual Source 11.4, a fifteenth-century English painting, raise similar issues to those expressed by Petrarch.

- Why is the death figure smiling?

- How does this skeletal figure differ from the ones in Visual Source 11.3?

- How are the priest and the Christ figure depicted? What possible interpretations of their gestures can you imagine?

- Notice that the death figure spears the dying person in the side, an action that evokes the biblical account of Jesus being speared in his side during

Visual Source 11.4 In the Face of Catastrophe — Questioning or Affirming the Faith (HIP/Art Resource, New York)

his crucifixion. What might the artist have sought to convey by such a reference?

■ The captions, from top to bottom, read: Christ figure: "Tho it be late ere thou mercie came: yet mercie thou shalt have." Priest figure: "Commit thy body to the grave: pray Christ thy soul to save." Death figure: "I have sought thee many a day: for to have thee to my pray." How do these captions influence your understanding of the painting?

■ Would you characterize the overall message of this painting as one of hopefulness, despair, or something else? What elements in the painting might support each of these conclusions?

Using the Evidence: The Black Death and Religion in Western Europe

1. **Assessing motives:** Do you think the artists who created these visual sources sought to reinforce traditional Christian teachings or to challenge them?

2. **Using art as evidence:** What do these visual sources tell you about the impact of and responses to the plague in fourteenth- and fifteenth-century Western Europe?

3. **Connecting past and present:** Considering the various ways that people sought to avert, cope with, or explain the plague in these visual sources, what parallels to the human responses to crises or catastrophes in more recent centuries or in our own time can you identify?

Chapter 11 Wrap Up

STEP ONE

The Word to Know: Pandemic

The *Oxford English Dictionary* defines *pandemic* as "a disease epidemic over a very large area; affecting a large proportion of a population." Write a brief paragraph explaining the ways in which the Mongols were affected negatively in the short term and the long term by the pandemic known as the Black Death.

STEP TWO

Mapping Connections across Afro-Eurasia

This exercise will help illustrate the extent to which the Mongol Empire facilitated global connections in the several centuries leading up to 1500. After creating your map, answer the questions that follow.

Using either a single outline map of Afro-Eurasia or a hand-drawn map of the Eastern Hemisphere, write labels for the following (use different colored pencils or other codes such as capital letters to show different types of labels): the four Mongol khanates; the following places on the periphery of the Mongol Empire: Vietnam, Burma, India, Arabia, Anatolia, Hungary, Siberia, and Japan; arrows showing the movement of major trade routes; arrows showing the source of the Black Death and its movement through Afro-Eurasia. For help drawing your map, consult the following maps from the book: Map 9.3, "The Growing World of Islam," p. 429; Map 9.6, "West Africa and the World of Islam," p. 432; Map 10.3, "Europe in the High Middle Ages," p. 481; Map 11.1," The Mongol Empire," p. 522; and Map 11.2, "Trade and Disease in the Fourteenth Century," p. 535.

■ Questions

1. Looking at your map, what can you conclude about the extent of the Black Death in relation to the extent of Mongol political influence?

2. On your map, look at the trade routes, the spread of the Black Death, and the spread of Islam. What conclusions can you draw about the ways in which the world was connected between 1000 and 1500?

Interpreting the Black Death through Documents and Visuals

Many people in the fourteenth-century world sought to explain the Black Death in light of their own worldviews, influenced by religion and personal experience. As you read these two quotes, consider what effect these words of respected individuals would have on their respective populations.

From Ibn Khaldun, Muqaddimah, a Muslim historian, 1337

Civilization both in the East and the West was visited by a destructive plague which devastated nations and caused populations to vanish. It swallowed up many of the good things of civilization and wiped them out. It overtook the dynasties at the time of their senility, when they had reached the limit of their duration. It lessened their power and curtailed their influence. It weakened their authority. Their situation approached the point of annihilation and dissolution. Civilization decreased with the decrease of mankind. Cities and buildings were laid waste, roads and way signs were obliterated, settlements and mansions became empty, dynasties and tribes grew weak. The entire inhabited world changed. The East, it seems, was similarly visited, though in accordance with and in proportion to [the East's more affluent] civilization. It was as if the voice of existence in the world had called out for oblivion and restriction, and the world responded to its call. God inherits the earth and whomever is upon it.

(Source: Michael W. Dols, *The Black Death in the Middle East*, Princeton University Press, 1977, p. 67.)

According to the textbook (p. 550), Boccaccio, an Italian layman, believing that the plague was a punishment sent by God for humankind's sins, wrote that the world was "sinking and sliding into all kinds of wickedness." God's response had been to send "the "quivering spear of the Almighty"— meaning, the plague.

■ Questions

1. Describe the ways in which both of the authors present the Black Death as having "human" characteristics. Why do you think the authors portrayed the Black Death in this manner?

2. In what ways do these quotes and the images in the Visual Sources section of Chapter 11 (pp. 550–57) demonstrate the fourteenth-century perceptions of the role that God (or Allah) played in plague?

3. What additional document (visual source or textual source) would help in assessing the Muslim response to the Black Death?

The Worlds of the Fifteenth Century

"Columbus was a perpetrator of genocide . . . , a slave trader, a thief, a pirate, and most certainly not a hero. To celebrate Columbus is to congratulate the process and history of the invasion."[1] This was the view Winona LaDuke, president of the Indigenous Women's Network, on the occasion in 1992 of the 500th anniversary of Columbus's arrival in the Americas. Much of the commentary surrounding the event echoed the same themes, citing the history of death, slavery, racism, and exploitation that followed in the wake Columbus's first voyage to what was for him an altogether New World. A century earlier, in 1892, the tone of celebration had been very different. A presidential proclamation cited Columbus as a brave "pioneer of progress and enlightenment" and instructed Americans to "express honor to the discoverer and their appreciation of the great achievements of four completed centuries of American life." The century that followed witnessed the erosion of Western dominance in the world and the discrediting of racism and imperialism and, with it, the reputation of Columbus.

THIS SHARP REVERSAL OF OPINION ABOUT COLUMBUS provides a reminder that the past is as unpredictable as the future. Few Americans in 1892 could have guessed that their daring hero could emerge so tarnished only a century later. And few people living in 1492 could have imagined the enormous global processes set in motion by the voyage of Columbus's three small ships—the Atlantic slave trade, the decimation of the native peoples of the Americas, the massive growth of world population, the Industrial Revolution, and the growing prominence of Europeans on the world stage. None of these developments were even remotely foreseeable in 1492.

The Meeting of Two Worlds: This famous sixteenth-century engraving by the Flemish artist Theodore de Bry shows Columbus landing in Hispaniola (Haiti), where the Taino people bring him presents, while the Europeans claim the island for God and monarch. In light of its long-range consequences, this voyage represents a major turning point in world history. (bpk, Berlin/Art Resource, NY)

Thus in historical hindsight, that voyage of Columbus was arguably the single most important event of the fifteenth century. But it was not the only significant marker of that century. A Central Asian Turkic warrior named Timur launched the last major nomadic invasion of adjacent civilizations. Russia emerged from two centuries of Mongol rule to begin a huge empire-building project across northern Asia. A new European civilization was taking shape in the Renaissance. In 1405 an enormous Chinese fleet, dwarfing that of Columbus, set out across the entire Indian Ocean basin, only to voluntarily withdraw 28 years later. The Islamic Ottoman Empire put a final end to Christian Byzantium with the conquest of Constantinople in 1453, even as Spanish Christians completed the "reconquest" of the Iberian Peninsula from the Muslims in 1492. And in the Americas, the Aztec and Inca Empires gave a final and spectacular expression to Mesoamerican and Andean civilizations before they were both swallowed up in the burst of European imperialism that followed the arrival of Columbus.

Because the fifteenth century was a hinge of major historical change on many fronts, it provides an occasion for a bird's-eye view of the world through a kind of global tour. This excursion around the world will serve to briefly review the human saga thus far and to establish a baseline from which the enormous transformations of the centuries that followed might be measured. How then might we describe the world, and the worlds, of the fifteenth century?

SEEKING THE MAIN POINT

What predictions about the future might a global traveler in the fifteenth century have reasonably made?

The Shapes of Human Communities

One way to describe the world of the fifteenth century is to identify the various types of societies that it contained. Bands of hunters and gatherers, villages of agricultural peoples, newly emerging chiefdoms or small states, nomadic/pastoral communities, established civilizations and empires—all of these social or political forms would have been apparent to a widely traveled visitor in the fifteenth century. Representing alternative ways of organizing human communities, all of them were long established by the fifteenth century, but the balance among these distinctive kinds of societies in 1500 was quite different than it had been a thousand years earlier.

Paleolithic Persistence: Australia and North America

■ **Comparison**

In what ways did the gathering and hunting people of Australia differ from those of the northwest coast of North America?

Despite millennia of agricultural advance, substantial areas of the world still hosted gathering and hunting societies, known to historians as Paleolithic (old stone age) peoples. All of Australia, much of Siberia, the arctic coastlands, and parts of Africa and the Americas fell into this category. These peoples were not simply relics of a bygone age. They too had changed over time, though more slowly than their agricultural counterparts, and they too interacted with their neighbors. In short, they had a history, although most history books largely ignore them after the age of agriculture arrived.

A Map of Time

1345–1521	Aztec Empire in Mesoamerica
1368–1644	Ming dynasty in China
1370–1406	Conquests of Timur
15th century	Spread of Islam in Southeast Asia Civil war among Japanese warlords Rise of Hindu state of Vijayanagara in southern India European renaissance Flourishing of African states of Ethiopia, Kongo, Benin, Zimbabwe
1405–1433	Chinese maritime voyages
1420	Beginning of Portuguese exploration of West African coast
1438–1533	Inca Empire along the Andes
1453	Ottoman seizure of Constantinople
1464–1591	Songhay Empire in West Africa
1492	Christian reconquest of Spain from Muslims completed; Columbus's first trans-Atlantic voyage
1497–1520s	Portuguese entry into the Indian Ocean world
1501	Founding of Safavid Empire in Persia
1526	Founding of Mughal Empire in India

Nonetheless, this most ancient way of life still had a sizable and variable presence in the world of the fifteenth century.

Consider, for example, Australia. That continent's many separate groups, some 250 of them, still practiced a gathering and hunting way of life in the fifteenth century, a pattern that continued well after Europeans arrived in the late eighteenth century. Over many thousands of years, these people had assimilated various material items or cultural practices from outsiders—outrigger canoes, fish hooks, complex netting techniques, artistic styles, rituals, and mythological ideas—but despite the presence of farmers in nearby New Guinea, no agricultural practices penetrated the Australian mainland. Was it because large areas of Australia were unsuited for the kind of agriculture practiced in New Guinea? Or did the peoples of Australia, enjoying an environment of sufficient resources, simply see no need to change their way of life?

Despite the absence of agriculture, Australia's peoples had mastered and manipulated their environment, in part through the practice of "firestick farming," a pattern of deliberately set fires, which they described as "cleaning up the country."

$\mathcal{S}$napshot   **Major Developments around the World in the Fifteenth Century**

Region	Major Developments
Central, East, and Southeast Asia	Ming dynasty China, 1368–1644
	Conquests of Timur, 1370–1406
	Zheng He's maritime voyages, 1405–1433
	Spread of Islam into Southeast Asia
	Rise of Malacca
	Civil war among competing warlords in Japan
South Asia/India	Timur's invasion of India, 1398
	Various Muslim sultanates in northern India
	Rise of Hindu state of Vijayanagar in southern India
	Founding of Mughal Empire, 1526
Middle East	Expansion of Ottoman Empire
	Ottoman seizure of Constantinople, 1453
	Founding of Safavid Empire in Persia, 1501
	Ottoman siege of Vienna, 1529
Christendom/Europe	European Renaissance
	Portuguese voyages of exploration along West African coast
	Completion of reconquest of Spain, ending Muslim control
	End of the Byzantine Empire, 1453
	End of Mongol rule in Russia; reign of Ivan the Great, 1462–1505
Africa	Songhay Empire in West Africa, 1464–1591
	Kingdom of the Kongo in West Central Africa
	Expansion of Ethiopian state in East Africa
	Kingdom of Zimbabwe/Mwene Mutapa in southern Africa
The Americas/Western Hemisphere	Aztec Empire in Mesoamerica, 1345–1521
	Inca Empire along the Andes, 1438–1533
	Iroquois confederacy (New York State)
	"Complex" Paleolithic societies along west coast of North America
Pacific Oceania	Paleolithic persistence in Australia
	Chiefdoms and stratified societies on Pacific islands
	Yap as center of oceanic trading network with Guam and Palau

These controlled burns served to clear the underbrush, thus making hunting easier and encouraging the growth of certain plant and animal species. In addition, native Australians exchanged goods among themselves over distances of hundreds of miles, created elaborate mythologies and ritual practices, and developed sophisticated traditions of sculpture and rock painting. They accomplished all of this on the basis of an economy and technology rooted in the distant Paleolithic past.

A very different kind of gathering and hunting society flourished in the fifteenth century along the northwest coast of North America among the Chinookan, Tulalip, Skagit, and other peoples. With some 300 edible animal species and an abundance of salmon and other fish, this extraordinarily bounteous environment provided the foundation for what scholars sometimes call "complex" or "affluent" gathering and hunting cultures. What distinguished the northwest coast peoples from those of Australia were permanent village settlements with large and sturdy houses, considerable economic specialization, ranked societies that sometimes included slavery, chiefdoms dominated by powerful clan leaders or "big men," and extensive storage of food.

Although these and other gathering and hunting peoples persisted still in the fifteenth century, both their numbers and the area they inhabited had contracted greatly as the Agricultural Revolution unfolded across the planet. That relentless advance of the farming frontier continued in the centuries ahead as the Russian, Chinese, and European empires encompassed the lands of the remaining Paleolithic peoples. By the early twenty-first century, what was once the only human way of life had been reduced to minuscule pockets of people whose cultures seemed doomed to a final extinction.

Agricultural Village Societies: The Igbo and the Iroquois

Far more numerous than gatherers and hunters were those many peoples who, though fully agricultural, had avoided incorporation into larger empires or civilizations and had not developed their own city- or state-based societies. Living usually in small village-based communities and organized in terms of kinship relations, such people predominated during the fifteenth century in much of North America and in parts of the Amazon River basin, Southeast Asia, and Africa south of the equator. They had created societies largely without the oppressive political authority, class inequalities, and seclusion of women that were so common in civilizations. Historians have largely relegated such societies to the periphery of world history, marginal to their overwhelming focus on states, cities, and large-scale civilizations. Viewed from within their own circles, though, these societies were at the center of things, each with its own history of migration, cultural transformation, social conflict, incorporation of new people, political rise and fall, and interaction with strangers. In short, they too changed as their histories took shape.

East of the Niger River in the heavily forested region of West Africa lay the lands of the Igbo (EE-boh) peoples. By the fifteenth century, their neighbors, the Yoruba

■ **Change**
What kinds of changes were transforming the societies of the West African Igbo and the North American Iroquois as the fifteenth century unfolded?

and Bini, had begun to develop small states and urban centers. But the Igbo, whose dense population and extensive trading networks might well have given rise to states, declined to follow suit. The deliberate Igbo preference was to reject the kingship and state-building efforts of their neighbors. They boasted on occasion that "the Igbo have no kings." Instead they relied on other institutions to maintain social cohesion beyond the level of the village: title societies in which wealthy men received a series of prestigious ranks, women's associations, hereditary ritual experts serving as mediators, a balance of power among kinship groups. It was a "stateless society," famously described in Chinua Achebe's *Things Fall Apart*, the most widely read novel to emerge from twentieth-century Africa.

But the Igbo peoples and their neighbors did not live in isolated, self-contained societies. They traded actively among themselves and with more distant peoples, such as the large African kingdom of Songhay (sahn-GEYE) far to the north. Cotton cloth, fish, copper and iron goods, decorative objects, and more drew neighboring peoples into networks of exchange. Common artistic traditions reflected a measure of cultural unity in a politically fragmented region, and all of these peoples seem to have changed from a matrilineal to a patrilineal system of tracing their descent. Little of this registered in the larger civilizations of the Afro-Eurasian world, but to the peoples of the West African forest during the fifteenth century, these processes were central to their history and their daily lives. Soon, however, all of them would be caught up in the transatlantic slave trade and would be changed substantially in the process.

Across the Atlantic in what is now central New York State, other agricultural village societies were also in the process of substantial change during the several centuries preceding their incorporation into European trading networks and empires. The Iroquois-speaking peoples of that region had only recently become fully agricultural, adopting maize- and bean-farming techniques that had originated centuries earlier in Mesoamerica. As this productive agriculture took hold by 1300 or so, the population grew, the size of settlements increased, and distinct peoples emerged. Frequent warfare also erupted among them. Some scholars have speculated that as agriculture, largely seen as women's work, became the primary economic activity, "warfare replaced successful food getting as the avenue to male prestige."[2]

Whatever caused it, this increased level of conflict among Iroquois peoples triggered a remarkable political innovation around the fifteenth century: a loose alliance or confederation among five Iroquois-speaking peoples—the Mohawk, Oneida, Onondaga, Cayuga, and Seneca. Based on an agreement known as the Great Law of Peace (see Map 12.5, p. 581), the Five Nations, as they called themselves, agreed to settle their differences peacefully through a confederation council of clan leaders, some fifty of them altogether, who had the authority to adjudicate disputes and set reparation payments. Operating by consensus, the Iroquois League of Five Nations effectively sup-

Igbo Art
Widely known for their masks, used in a variety of ritual and ceremonial occasions, the Igbo were also among the first to produce bronze castings using the "lost wax" method. This exquisite bronze pendant in the form of a human head derives from the Igbo Ukwu archeological site in eastern Nigeria and dates to the ninth century C.E. (Werner Forman/ Art Resource, NY)

pressed the blood feuds and tribal conflicts that had only recently been so widespread. It also coordinated their peoples' relationship with outsiders, including the Europeans, who arrived in growing numbers in the centuries after 1500.

The Iroquois League gave expression to values of limited government, social equality, and personal freedom, concepts that some European colonists found highly attractive. One British colonial administrator declared in 1749 that the Iroquois had "such absolute Notions of Liberty that they allow no Kind of Superiority of one over another, and banish all Servitude from their Territories."[3] Such equality extended to gender relationships, for among the Iroquois, descent was matrilineal (reckoned through the woman's line), married couples lived with the wife's family, and women controlled agriculture and property. While men were hunters, warriors, and the primary political officeholders, women selected and could depose those leaders.

Wherever they lived in 1500, over the next several centuries independent agricultural peoples such as the Iroquois and Igbo were increasingly encompassed in expanding economic networks and conquest empires based in Western Europe, Russia, China, or India. In this respect, they replicated the experience of many other village-based farming communities that had much earlier found themselves forcibly included in the powerful embrace of Egyptian, Mesopotamian, Roman, Indian, Chinese, and other civilizations.

Pastoral Peoples: Central Asia and West Africa

Nomadic pastoral peoples had long impinged more directly and dramatically on civilizations than did hunting and gathering or agricultural village societies. The Mongol incursion, along with the enormous empire to which it gave rise, was one in a long series of challenges from the steppes, but it was not quite the last. As the Mongol Empire disintegrated, a brief attempt to restore it occurred in the late fourteenth and early fifteenth centuries under the leadership of a Turkic warrior named Timur, born in what is now Uzbekistan and known in the West as Tamerlane (see Map 12.1, p. 567).

With a ferocity that matched or exceeded that of his model, Chinggis Khan, Timur's army of nomads brought immense devastation yet again to Russia, Persia, and India. Timur himself died in 1405, while preparing for an invasion of China. Conflicts among his successors prevented any lasting empire, although his descendants retained control of the area between Persia and Afghanistan for the rest of the fifteenth century. That state hosted a sophisticated elite culture, combining Turkic and Persian elements, particularly at its splendid capital of Samarkand, as its rulers patronized artists, poets, traders, and craftsmen. Timur's conquest proved to be the last great military success of nomadic peoples from Central Asia. In the centuries that followed, their homelands were swallowed up in the expanding Russian and Chinese empires, as the balance of power between steppe nomads of inner Eurasia and the civilizations of outer Eurasia turned decisively in favor of the latter.

■ **Significance**
What role did Central Asian and West African pastoralists play in their respective regions?

In Africa, pastoral peoples stayed independent of established empires several centuries longer than the nomads of Inner Asia, for not until the late nineteenth century were they incorporated into European colonial states. The experience of the Fulbe, West Africa's largest pastoral society, provides an example of an African herding people with a highly significant role in the fifteenth century and beyond. From their homeland in the western fringe of the Sahara along the upper Senegal River, the Fulbe had migrated gradually eastward in the centuries after 1000 C.E. (see Map 12.3, p. 574). Unlike the pastoral peoples of Inner Asia, they generally lived in small communities among agricultural peoples and paid various grazing fees and taxes for the privilege of pasturing their cattle. Relations with their farming hosts often were tense because the Fulbe resented their subordination to agricultural peoples, whose way of life they despised. That sense of cultural superiority became even more pronounced as the Fulbe, in the course of their eastward movement, slowly adopted Islam. Some of them in fact dropped out of a pastoral life and settled in towns, where they became highly respected religious leaders. In the eighteenth and nineteenth centuries, the Fulbe were at the center of a wave of religiously based uprisings, or jihads, which greatly expanded the practice of Islam and gave rise to a series of new states, ruled by the Fulbe themselves.

Civilizations of the Fifteenth Century: Comparing China and Europe

Beyond the foraging, farming, and pastoral societies of the fifteenth-century world were its civilizations, those city-centered and state-based societies that were far larger and more densely populated, more powerful and innovative, and much more unequal in terms of class and gender than other forms of human community. Since the First Civilizations had emerged between 3500 and 1000 B.C.E., both the geographic space they encompassed and the number of people they embraced had grown substantially. By the fifteenth century, a considerable majority of the world's population lived within one or another of these civilizations, although most of these people no doubt identified more with local communities than with a larger civilization. What might an imaginary global traveler notice about the world's major civilizations in the fifteenth century?

Ming Dynasty China

■ **Description**

How would you define the major achievements of Ming dynasty China?

Such a traveler might well begin his or her journey in China, heir to a long tradition of effective governance, Confucian and Daoist philosophy, a major Buddhist presence, sophisticated artistic achievements, and a highly productive economy. That civilization, however, had been greatly disrupted by a century of Mongol rule, and its population had been sharply reduced by the plague. During the Ming dynasty (1368–1644), however, China recovered (see Map 12.1). The early decades of that dynasty witnessed an effort to eliminate all signs of foreign rule, discouraging the use of Mon-

Map 12.1   Asia in the Fifteenth Century
The fifteenth century in Asia witnessed the massive Ming dynasty voyages into the Indian Ocean, the last major eruption of nomadic power in Timur's empire, and the flourishing of the maritime city of Malacca.

gol names and dress, while promoting Confucian learning and orthodox gender roles, based on earlier models from the Han, Tang, and Song dynasties. Emperor Yongle (YAHNG-leh) (r. 1402–1422) sponsored an enormous *Encyclopedia* of some 11,000 volumes. With contributions from more than 2,000 scholars, this work sought to summarize or compile all previous writing on history, geography, philosophy, ethics, government, and more. Yongle also relocated the capital to Beijing, ordered the building of a magnificent imperial residence known as the Forbidden City, and constructed the Temple of Heaven, where subsequent rulers performed Confucian-based rituals to ensure the well-being of Chinese society. Two empresses wrote instructions for female behavior, emphasizing traditional expectations after the disruptions of the previous century. Culturally speaking, China was looking to its past.

Politically, the Ming dynasty reestablished the civil service examination system that had been neglected under Mongol rule and went on to create a highly centralized government. Power was concentrated in the hands of the emperor himself, while a cadre of eunuchs (castrated men) personally loyal to the emperor exercised great authority, much to the dismay of the official bureaucrats. The state acted vigorously to repair the damage of the Mongol years by restoring millions of acres to cultivation;

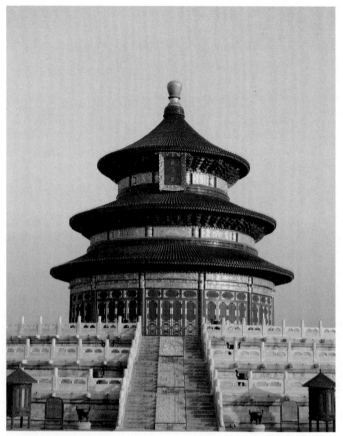

Temple of Heaven
Set in a forest of more than 650 acres, the Temple of Heaven was constructed in the early fifteenth century. In Chinese thinking it was the primary place where Heaven and Earth met. From his residence in the Forbidden City, the Chinese emperor led a procession of thousands twice a year to this sacred site, where he offered sacrifices, implored the gods for a good harvest, and performed the rituals that maintained the cosmic balance. (Imaginechina for AP Images)

rebuilding canals, reservoirs, and irrigation works; and planting, according to some estimates, a billion trees in an effort to reforest China. As a result, the economy rebounded, both international and domestic trade flourished, and the population grew. During the fifteenth century, China had recovered and was perhaps the best-governed and most prosperous of the world's major civilizations.

China also undertook the largest and most impressive maritime expeditions the world had ever seen. Since the eleventh century, Chinese sailors and traders had been a major presence in the South China Sea and in Southeast Asian port cities, with much of this activity in private hands. But now, after decades of preparation, an enormous fleet, commissioned by Emperor Yongle himself, was launched in 1405, followed over the next twenty-eight years by six more such expeditions. On board more than 300 ships of the first voyage was a crew of some 27,000, including 180 physicians, hundreds of government officials, 5 astrologers, 7 high-ranking or grand eunuchs, carpenters, tailors, accountants, merchants, translators, cooks, and thousands of soldiers and sailors. Visiting many ports in Southeast Asia, Indonesia, India, Arabia, and East Africa, these fleets, captained by the Muslim eunuch Zheng He (JUHNG-huh), sought to enroll distant peoples and states in the Chinese tribute system (see Map 12.1). Dozens of rulers accompanied the fleets back to China, where they presented tribute, performed the required rituals of submission, and received in return abundant gifts, titles, and trading opportunities. Chinese officials were amused by some of the exotic products to be found abroad — ostriches, zebras, and giraffes, for example. Officially described as "bringing order to the world," Zheng He's expeditions served to establish Chinese power and prestige in the Indian Ocean and to exert Chinese control over foreign trade in the region. The Chinese, however, did not seek to conquer new territories, establish Chinese settlements, or spread their culture, though they did intervene in a number of local disputes. (See Portrait of Zheng He, pp. 572–73.)

The most surprising feature of these voyages was how abruptly and deliberately they were ended. After 1433, Chinese authorities simply stopped such expeditions and allowed this enormous and expensive fleet to deteriorate in port. "In less than a hundred years," wrote a recent historian of these voyages, "the greatest navy the world had ever known had ordered itself into extinction."[4] Part of the reason involved the death of the emperor Yongle, who had been the chief patron of the enterprise. Many high-ranking officials had long seen the expeditions as a waste of resources because China, they believed, was the self-sufficient "middle kingdom," requiring little from the outside world. In their eyes, the real danger to China came from the north, where nomadic barbarians constantly threatened. Finally, they viewed the voyages as the project of the court eunuchs, whom these officials despised. Even as these voices of Chinese officialdom prevailed, private Chinese merchants and craftsmen continued to settle and trade in Japan, the Philippines, Taiwan, and Southeast Asia, but they did so without the support of their government. The Chinese state quite deliberately turned its back on what was surely within its reach—a large-scale maritime empire in the Indian Ocean basin.

European Comparisons: State Building and Cultural Renewal

At the other end of the Eurasian continent, similar processes of demographic recovery, political consolidation, cultural flowering, and overseas expansion were under way. Western Europe, having escaped Mongol conquest but devastated by the plague, began to regrow its population during the second half of the fifteenth century. As in China, the infrastructure of civilization proved a durable foundation for demographic and economic revival.

■ **Comparison**

What political and cultural differences stand out in the histories of fifteenth-century China and Western Europe? What similarities are apparent?

Politically too Europe joined China in continuing earlier patterns of state building. In China, however, this meant a unitary and centralized government that encompassed almost the whole of its civilization, while in Europe a decidedly fragmented system of many separate, independent, and highly competitive states made for a sharply divided Christendom (see Map 12.2). Many of these states—Spain, Portugal, France, England, the city-states of Italy (Milan, Venice, and Florence), various German principalities—learned to tax their citizens more efficiently, to create more effective administrative structures, and to raise standing armies. A small Russian state centered on the city of Moscow also emerged in the fifteenth century as Mongol rule faded away. Much of this state building was driven by the needs of war, a frequent occurrence in such a fragmented and competitive political environment. England and France, for example, fought intermittently for more than a century in the Hundred Years' War (1337–1453) over rival claims to territory in France. Nothing remotely similar disturbed the internal life of Ming dynasty China.

A renewed cultural blossoming, known in European history as the Renaissance, likewise paralleled the revival of all things Confucian in Ming dynasty China. In Europe, however, that blossoming celebrated and reclaimed a classical Greco-Roman tradition that earlier had been lost or obscured. Beginning in the vibrant commercial cities of Italy between roughly 1350 and 1500, the Renaissance reflected the belief of the wealthy male elite that they were living in a wholly new era, far removed from

Map 12.2   Europe in 1500
By the end of the fifteenth century, Christian Europe had assumed its early modern political shape as a system of competing states threatened by an expanding Muslim Ottoman Empire.

the confined religious world of feudal Europe. Educated citizens of these cities sought inspiration in the art and literature of ancient Greece and Rome; they were "returning to the sources," as they put it. Their purpose was not so much to reconcile these works with the ideas of Christianity, as the twelfth- and thirteenth-century university scholars had done, but to use them as a cultural standard to imitate and then to surpass. The elite patronized great Renaissance artists such as Leonardo da Vinci, Michelangelo, and Raphael, whose paintings and sculptures were far more naturalistic, particularly in portraying the human body, than those of their medieval counterparts. Some of these artists looked to the Islamic world for standards of excellence, sophistication, and abundance. (See Visual Sources, pp. 600–09, for the role of Islam in the European Renaissance.)

Although religious themes remained prominent, Renaissance artists now included portraits and busts of well-known contemporary figures, scenes from ancient mythology, and depictions of Islamic splendor. In the work of scholars, known as human-

The Waldseemüller Map of 1507
Just fifteen years after Columbus landed in the Western Hemisphere, this map, which was created by the German cartographer Martin Waldseemüller, reflected a dawning European awareness of the planet's global dimensions and location of the world's major landmasses. (bpk, Berlin/Staatsbibliothek zu Berlin, Stiftung Preussischer Kulturbesitz, Berlin, Germany/Ruth Schacht, Map Division/Art Resource, NY)

ists, reflections on secular topics such as grammar, history, politics, poetry, rhetoric, and ethics complemented more religious matters. For example, Niccolò Machiavelli's (1469–1527) famous work *The Prince* was a prescription for political success based on the way politics actually operated in a highly competitive Italy of rival city-states rather than on idealistic and religiously based principles. To the question of whether a prince should be feared or loved, Machiavelli replied:

> One ought to be both feared and loved, but as it is difficult for the two to go together, it is much safer to be feared than loved. . . . For it may be said of men in general that they are ungrateful, voluble, dissemblers, anxious to avoid danger, and covetous of gain. . . . Fear is maintained by dread of punishment which never fails. . . . In the actions of men, and especially of princes, from which there is no appeal, the end justifies the means.[5]

While the great majority of Renaissance writers and artists were men, among the remarkable exceptions to that rule was Christine de Pizan (1363–1430), the daughter of a Venetian official, who lived mostly in Paris. Her writings pushed against the misogyny of so many European thinkers of the time. In her *City of Ladies*, she mobilized numerous women from history, Christian and pagan alike, to demonstrate that women too could be active members of society and deserved an education equal to

PORTRAIT

Zheng He, China's Non-Chinese Admiral

At the helm of China's massive maritime expeditions in the early fifteenth century was a most unusual person named Zheng He.[6] Born in 1371 in the frontier region of Yunnan in southwestern China, his family roots were in Central Asia in what is now Uzbekistan. Both his father and grandfather were devout Muslims who had made the pilgrimage to Mecca. The family had also achieved local prominence as high officials serving the Mongol rulers of China for a century. Zheng He would surely have continued in this tradition had not a major turning point in China's history decisively altered the trajectory of his life.

Zheng He's birth, as it happened, coincided with the end of Mongol rule. His own father was killed resisting the forces of the new Ming dynasty that ousted the Mongols from Yunnan in 1382. Eleven-year-old Zheng He was taken prisoner along with hundreds of Mongols and their Muslim supporters. But young Zheng He lost more than his freedom; he also lost

Among the acquisitions of Zheng He's expeditions, none excited more interest in the Chinese court than an African giraffe. (The Philadelphia Museum of Art/Art Resource, NY)

his male sex organs, becoming a eunuch as he underwent castration. The practice had a long history in China as well as in Christian and Islamic civilizations. During the 276 years of the Ming dynasty (1368–1644), some 1 million eunuchs served the Chinese emperor and members of the elite. A small number became powerful officials, especially at the central imperial court, where their utter dependence upon and loyalty to the emperor gained them the enduring hostility of the scholar-bureaucrats of China's civil service. Strangely enough, substantial numbers of Chinese men voluntarily became eunuchs, trading their manhood for the possibility of achieving power, prestige, and wealth.

After his castration, pure chance shaped Zheng He's life as he was assigned to Zhu Di, the fourth son of the reigning emperor, who was then establishing himself in northern Chinese region around Beijing. Zheng He soon won the confidence of his master and eventually the almost seven-foot-tall

that of men. Aiding in the construction of this allegorical city is Lady Reason who offers to assist Christine in dispelling her poor opinion of her own sex. "No matter which way I looked at it," she wrote, "I could find no evidence from my own experience to bear out such a negative view of female nature and habits. Even so . . . I could scarcely find a moral work by any author which didn't devote some chapter or paragraph to attacking the female sex."[7]

Heavily influenced by classical models, Renaissance figures were more interested in capturing the unique qualities of particular individuals and in describing the world as it was than in portraying or exploring eternal religious truths. In its focus on the affairs of this world, Renaissance culture reflected the urban bustle and commercial preoccupations of Italian cities. Its secular elements challenged the other-worldliness of Christian culture, and its individualism signaled the dawning of a more capitalist economy of private entrepreneurs. A new Europe was in the making, one eunuch proved himself an effective military leader in various skirmishes against the Mongols and in the civil war that brought Zhu Di to power as the Emperor Yongle in 1402. With his master as emperor, Zheng He served first as Grand Director of Palace Servants. Now he could don the prestigious red robe, rather than the blue one assigned to lower-ranking eunuchs. But soon Zheng He found himself with a far more ambitious assignment—commander of China's huge oceangoing fleet.

The seven voyages that Zheng He led between 1405 and 1433 have defined his role in Chinese and world history. But they also revealed something of the man himself. Clearly he was not an explorer in the mold of Columbus, for he sailed in well-traveled waters and usually knew where he was going. While his journeys were largely peaceful with no effort to establish colonies or control trade, on several occasions Zheng He used force to suppress piracy or to punish those who resisted Chinese overtures. Once he personally led 2,000 Chinese soldiers against a hostile ruler in the interior of Ceylon. He also had a keen eye for the kind of exotica that the imperial court found fascinating, returning to China with ostriches, zebras, lions, elephants, and a giraffe.

The voyages also disclose Zheng He's changing religious commitments. Born and raised a Muslim, he had not lived in a primarily Islamic setting since his capture at the age of eleven. Thus, it is hardly surprising that he adopted the more eclectic posture toward religion common in China. During his third voyage in Ceylon, he erected a trilingual tablet recording lavish gifts and praise to the Buddha, to Allah, and to a local form of the Hindu deity Vishnu. He also apparently expressed some interest in a famous relic said to be a tooth of the Buddha. And Zheng He credited the success of his journeys to the Taoist goddess Tianfei, protector of sailors and seafarers.

To Zheng He the voyages surely represented the essential meaning of his own life. In an inscription erected just prior to his last voyage, Zheng He summarized his achievements: "When we arrived at the foreign countries, barbarian kings who resisted transformation [by Chinese civilization] and were not respectful we captured alive, and bandit soldiers who looted and plundered recklessly we exterminated. Because of this, the sea routes became pure and peaceful and the foreign peoples could rely upon them and pursue their occupations in safety." But after his death, Zheng He vanished from the historical record, even as his country largely withdrew from the sea and most Chinese forgot about the unusual man who had led those remarkable voyages.

Questions: How might you describe the arc of Zheng He's life? What were its major turning points? How did Zheng He's castration shape his life?

---

more different from its own recent past than Ming dynasty China was from its pre-Mongol glory.

European Comparisons: Maritime Voyaging

A global traveler during the fifteenth century might be surprised to find that Europeans, like the Chinese, were also launching outward-bound maritime expeditions. Initiated in 1415 by the small country of Portugal, those voyages sailed ever farther down the west coast of Africa, supported by the state and blessed by the pope (see Map 12.3). As the century ended, two expeditions marked major breakthroughs, although few suspected it at the time. In 1492, Christopher Columbus, funded by Spain, Portugal's neighbor and rival, made his way west across the Atlantic hoping to arrive in the East and, in one of history's most consequential mistakes, ran into the

■ Comparison

In what ways did European maritime voyaging in the fifteenth century differ from that of China? What accounts for these differences?

Map 12.3   Africa in the Fifteenth Century

By the 1400s, Africa was a virtual museum of political and cultural diversity, encompassing large empires, such as Songhay; smaller kingdoms, such as Kongo; city-states among the Yoruba, Hausa, and Swahili peoples; village-based societies without states at all, as among the Igbo; and nomadic pastoral peoples, such as the Fulbe. Both European and Chinese maritime expeditions touched on Africa during that century, even as Islam continued to find acceptance in the northern half of the continent.

Americas. Five years later, in 1497, Vasco da Gama launched a voyage that took him around the tip of South Africa, along the East African coast, and, with the help of a Muslim pilot, across the Indian Ocean to Calicut in southern India.

The differences between the Chinese and European oceangoing ventures were striking, most notably perhaps in terms of size. Columbus captained three ships and a crew of about 90, while da Gama had four ships, manned by perhaps 170 sailors.

These were minuscule fleets compared to Zheng He's hundreds of ships and a crew in the many thousands. "All the ships of Columbus and da Gama combined," according to a recent account, "could have been stored on a single deck of a single vessel in the fleet that set sail under Zheng He."[8]

Motivation as well as size differentiated the two ventures. Europeans were seeking the wealth of Africa and Asia — gold, spices, silk, and more. They also were in search of Christian converts and of possible Christian allies with whom to continue their long crusading struggle against threatening Muslim powers. China, by contrast, faced no equivalent power, needed no military allies in the Indian Ocean basin, and required little that these regions produced. Nor did China possess an impulse to convert foreigners to Chinese culture or religion as the Europeans surely did. Furthermore, the confident and overwhelmingly powerful Chinese fleet sought neither conquests nor colonies, while the Europeans soon tried to monopolize by force the commerce of the Indian Ocean and violently carved out huge empires in the Americas.

The most striking difference in these two cases lay in the sharp contrast between China's decisive ending of its voyages and the continuing, indeed escalating, European effort, which soon brought the world's oceans and growing numbers of the world's people under its control. This is why Zheng He's voyages were so long neglected in China's historical memory. They led nowhere, whereas the initial European expeditions, so much smaller and less promising, were but the first steps on a journey to world power. But why did the Europeans continue a process that the Chinese had deliberately abandoned?

In the first place, Europe had no unified political authority with the power to order an end to its maritime outreach. Its system of competing states, so unlike China's single unified empire, ensured that once begun, rivalry alone would drive the Europeans to the ends of the earth. Beyond this, much of Europe's elite had an interest in overseas expansion. Its budding merchant communities saw opportunity for profit; its competing monarchs eyed the revenue from taxing overseas trade or from seizing overseas resources; the Church foresaw the possibility of widespread conversion; impoverished nobles might imagine fame and fortune abroad. In China, by contrast, support for Zheng He's voyages was very shallow in official circles, and when the emperor Yongle passed from the scene, those opposed to the voyages prevailed within the politics of the court.

Finally, the Chinese were very much aware of their own antiquity, believed strongly in the absolute superiority of their culture, and felt with good reason that, should they desire something from abroad, others would bring it to them. Europeans too believed themselves unique, particularly in religious terms as the possessors of Christianity, the "one true religion." In material terms, though, they were seeking out the greater riches of the East, and they were highly conscious that Muslim power blocked easy access to these treasures and posed a military and religious threat to Europe itself. All of this propelled continuing European expansion in the centuries that followed.

The Chinese withdrawal from the Indian Ocean actually facilitated the European entry. It cleared the way for the Portuguese to penetrate the region, where they faced only the eventual naval power of the Ottomans. Had Vasco da Gama encountered Zheng He's massive fleet as his four small ships sailed into Asian waters in 1498, world history may well have taken quite a different turn. As it was, however, China's abandonment of oceanic voyaging and Europe's embrace of the seas marked different responses to a common problem that both civilizations shared—growing populations and land shortage. In the centuries that followed, China's rice-based agriculture was able to expand production internally by more intensive use of the land, while the country's territorial expansion was inland toward Central Asia. By contrast, Europe's agriculture, based on wheat and livestock, expanded primarily by acquiring new lands in overseas possessions, which were gained as a consequence of a commitment to oceanic expansion.

Civilizations of the Fifteenth Century: The Islamic World

■ Comparison

What differences can you identify among the four major empires in the Islamic world of the fifteenth and sixteenth centuries?

Beyond the domains of Chinese and European civilization, our fifteenth-century global traveler would surely have been impressed with the transformations of the Islamic world. Stretching across much of Afro-Eurasia, the enormous realm of Islam experienced a set of remarkable changes during the fifteenth and early sixteenth centuries, as well as the continuation of earlier patterns. The most notable change lay in the political realm, for an Islamic civilization that had been severely fragmented since at least 900 now crystallized into four major states or empires (see Map 12.4). At the same time, a long-term process of conversion to Islam continued the cultural transformation of Afro-Eurasian societies both within and beyond these new states.

In the Islamic Heartland: The Ottoman and Safavid Empires

The most impressive and enduring of the new Islamic states was the Ottoman Empire, which lasted in one form or another from the fourteenth to the early twentieth century. It was the creation of one of the many Turkic warrior groups that had earlier migrated into Anatolia. By the mid-fifteenth century, these Ottoman Turks had already carved out a state that encompassed much of the Anatolian peninsula and had pushed deep into southeastern Europe (the Balkans), acquiring in the process a substantial Christian population. In the two centuries that followed, the Ottoman Empire extended its control to much of the Middle East, coastal North Africa, the lands surrounding the Black Sea, and even farther into Eastern Europe.

The Ottoman Empire was a state of enormous significance in the world of the fifteenth century and beyond. In its huge territory, long duration, incorporation of many diverse peoples, and economic and cultural sophistication, it was one of the great empires of world history. In the fifteenth century, only Ming dynasty China and the Incas matched it in terms of wealth, power, and splendor. The empire represented the emergence of the Turks as the dominant people of the Islamic world,

Map 12.4 Empires of the Islamic World
The most prominent political features of the vast Islamic world in the fifteenth and sixteenth centuries were four large states: the Songhay, Ottoman, Safavid, and Mughal empires.

ruling now over many Arabs, who had initiated this new faith more than 800 years before. In adding "caliph" (successor to the Prophet) to their other titles, Ottoman sultans claimed the legacy of the earlier Abbasid Empire. They sought to bring a renewed unity to the Islamic world, while also serving as protector of the faith, the "strong sword of Islam."

The Ottoman Empire also represented a new phase in the long encounter between Christendom and the world of Islam. In the Crusades, Europeans had taken the aggressive initiative in that encounter, but the rise of the Ottoman Empire reversed their roles. The seizure of Constantinople in 1453 marked the final demise of Christian Byzantium and allowed Ottoman rulers to see themselves as successors to the Roman Empire. In 1529, a rapidly expanding Ottoman Empire laid siege to Vienna in the heart of Central Europe. The political and military expansion of Islam, at the expense of Christendom, seemed clearly under way. Many Europeans spoke fearfully of the "terror of the Turk."

In the neighboring Persian lands to the east of the Ottoman Empire, another Islamic state was also taking shape in the late fifteenth and early sixteenth centuries—the

Ottoman Janissaries
Originating in the fourteenth century, the Janissaries became the elite infantry force of the Ottoman Empire. Complete with uniforms, cash salaries, and marching music, they were the first standing army in the region since the days of the Roman Empire. When gunpowder technology became available, Janissary forces soon were armed with muskets, grenades, and hand-held cannon. This image dates from the seventeenth century. (Austrian National Library, picture archive, Vienna: Cod. 8626, fol. 15r)

Safavid (SAH-fah-vihd) Empire. Its leadership was also Turkic, but in this case it had emerged from a Sufi religious order founded several centuries earlier by Safi al-Din (1252–1334). The long-term significance of the Safavid Empire, which was established in the decade following 1500, was its decision to forcibly impose a Shia version of Islam as the official religion of the state. Over time, this form of Islam gained popular support and came to define the unique identity of Persian (Iranian) culture.

This Shia empire also introduced a sharp divide into the political and religious life of heartland Islam, for almost all of Persia's neighbors practiced a Sunni form of the faith. For a century (1534–1639), periodic military conflict erupted between the Ottoman and Safavid empires, reflecting both territorial rivalry and sharp religious differences. In 1514, the Ottoman sultan wrote to the Safavid ruler in the most bitter of terms:

> You have denied the sanctity of divine law ... you have deserted the path of salvation and the sacred commandments ... you have opened to Muslims the gates of tyranny and oppression ... you have raised the standard of irreligion and heresy.... [Therefore] the *ulama* and our doctors have pronounced a sentence of death against you, perjurer and blasphemer.[9]

This Sunni/Shia hostility has continued to divide the Islamic world into the twenty-first century.

On the Frontiers of Islam: The Songhay and Mughal Empires

While the Ottoman and Safavid empires brought both a new political unity and a sharp division to the heartland of Islam, two other states performed a similar role on the expanding African and Asian frontiers of the faith. In the West African savannas, the Songhay Empire rose in the second half of the fifteenth century. It was the most recent and the largest in a series of impressive states that operated at a crucial intersection of the trans-Saharan trade routes and that derived much of their revenue from taxing that commerce. Islam was a growing faith in Songhay but was limited largely to urban elites. This cultural divide within Songhay largely accounts for the religious behavior of its fifteenth-century monarch Sonni Ali (r. 1465–1492), who gave alms and fasted during Ramadan in proper Islamic style but also enjoyed a reputation as a magician and possessed a charm thought to render his soldiers invisible to their enemies. Nonetheless, Songhay had become a major center of Islamic learning and commerce by the early sixteenth century. A North African traveler known as Leo Africanus remarked on the city of Timbuktu:

> Here are great numbers of [Muslim] religious teachers, judges, scholars, and other learned persons who are bountifully maintained at the king's expense. Here too are brought various manuscripts or written books from Barbary [North Africa] which are sold for more money than any other merchandise. . . . Here are very rich merchants and to here journey continually large numbers of negroes who purchase here cloth from Barbary and Europe. . . . It is a wonder to see the quality of merchandise that is daily brought here and how costly and sumptuous everything is.[10]

Sonni Ali's successor made the pilgrimage to Mecca and asked to be given the title "Caliph of the Land of the Blacks." Songhay then represented a substantial Islamic state on the African frontier of a still-expanding Muslim world. (See the photo on p. 337 for manuscripts long preserved in Timbuktu.)

The Mughal (MOO-guhl) Empire in India bore similarities to Songhay, for both governed largely non-Muslim populations. Much as the Ottoman Empire initiated a new phase in the interaction of Islam and Christendom, so too did the Mughal Empire continue an ongoing encounter between Islamic and Hindu civilizations. Established in the early sixteenth century, the Mughal Empire was the creation of yet another Islamized Turkic group, which invaded India in 1526. Over the next century, the Mughals (a Persian term for Mongols) established unified control over most of the Indian peninsula, giving it a rare period of political unity and laying the foundation for subsequent British colonial rule. During its first 150 years, the Mughal Empire, a land of great wealth and imperial splendor, undertook a remarkable effort to blend many Hindu groups and a variety of Muslims into an effective partnership. The inclusive policies of the early Mughal emperors showed that Muslim rulers could accommodate their overwhelmingly Hindu subjects in somewhat the same fashion as Ottoman authorities provided religious autonomy for their Christian peoples. In southernmost India, however, the distinctly Hindu kingdom of Vijayanagara flourished in the fifteenth century, even as it borrowed architectural styles from the Muslim states of northern India and sometimes employed Muslim mercenaries in its military forces.

Together these four Muslim empires—Ottoman, Safavid, Songhay, and Mughal—brought to the Islamic world a greater measure of political coherence, military power, economic prosperity, and cultural brilliance than it had known since the early centuries of Islam. This new energy, sometimes called a "second flowering of Islam," impelled the continuing spread of the faith to yet new regions. The most prominent of these was oceanic Southeast Asia, which for centuries had been intimately bound up in the world of Indian Ocean commerce, while borrowing elements of both Hindu and Buddhist traditions. By the fifteenth century, that trading network was largely in Muslim hands, and the demand for Southeast Asian spices was mounting as the Eurasian world recovered from the devastation of Mongol conquest and the plague. Growing numbers of Muslim traders, many of them from India, settled in Java and Sumatra, bringing their faith with them. Eager to attract those traders to their port cities, a number of Hindu or Buddhist rulers along the Malay Peninsula and in Indonesia converted to Islam, while transforming themselves into Muslim sultans and imposing Islamic law. Thus, unlike the Middle East and India, where Islam was established in the wake of Arab or Turkic conquest, in Southeast Asia, as in West Africa, it was introduced by traveling merchants and solidified through the activities of Sufi holy men.

The rise of Malacca, strategically located on the waterway between Sumatra and Malaya, was a sign of the times (see Map 12.1, p. 567). During the fifteenth century, it was transformed from a small fishing village to a major Muslim port city. A Portuguese visitor in 1512 observed that Malacca had "no equal in the world.... Commerce between different nations for a thousand leagues on every hand must come to Malacca."[11] That city also became a springboard for the spread of Islam throughout the region. In the eclectic style of Southeast Asian religious history, the Islam of Malacca demonstrated much blending with local and Hindu/Buddhist traditions, while the city itself, like many port towns, had a reputation for "rough behavior." An Arab Muslim pilot in the 1480s commented critically: "They have no culture at all.... You do not know whether they are Muslim or not."[12] Nonetheless, Malacca, like Timbuktu on the West African frontier of an expanding Islamic world, became a center for Islamic learning, and students from elsewhere in Southeast Asia were studying there in the fifteenth century. As the more central regions of Islam were consolidating politically, the frontier of the faith continued to move steadily outward.

SUMMING UP SO FAR

In what ways do the civilizations of China, Europe, and the Islamic world in the fifteenth century seem to be moving in the same direction, and in what respects were they diverging from one another?

Civilizations of the Fifteenth Century: The Americas

■ **Comparison**
What distinguished the Aztec and Inca empires from each other?

Across the Atlantic, centers of civilization had long flourished in Mesoamerica and in the Andes. The fifteenth century witnessed new, larger, and more politically unified expressions of those civilizations, embodied in the Aztec and Inca empires. Both were the work of previously marginal peoples who had forcibly taken over and absorbed older cultures, giving them new energy, and both were decimated in the sixteenth century at the hands of Spanish conquistadores and their diseases. To conclude this global tour of world civilizations, we will send our weary traveler to the Western Hemisphere for a brief look at these American civilizations (see Map 12.5).

The Aztec Empire

The empire known to history as the Aztec state was largely the work of the Mexica (Meh-SHEEH-kah) people, a semi-nomadic group from northern Mexico who had migrated southward and by 1325 had established themselves on a small island in Lake

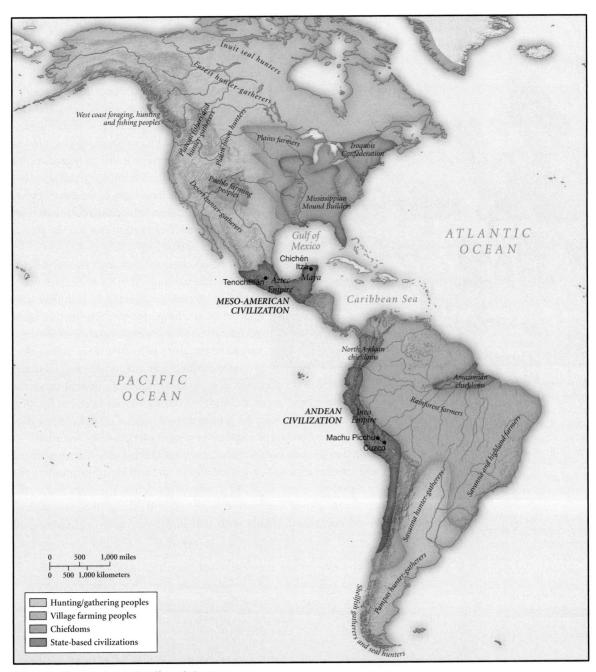

Map 12.5 The Americas in the Fifteenth Century
The Americas before Columbus represented a world almost completely separate from Afro-Eurasia. It featured similar kinds of societies, though with a different balance among them, but it completely lacked the pastoral economies that were so important in the Eastern Hemisphere.

Aztec Women
Within the home, Aztec women cooked, cleaned, spun and wove cloth, raised their children, and undertook ritual activities. Outside the home, they served as officials in palaces, priestesses in temples, traders in markets, teachers in schools, and members of craft workers' organizations. This domestic image comes from the sixteenth-century Florentine Codex, which was compiled by the Spanish but illustrated by Aztec artists. (The Art Archive at Art Resource, NY)

Texcoco. Over the next century, the Mexica developed their military capacity, served as mercenaries for more powerful people, negotiated elite marriage alliances with them, and built up their own capital city of Tenochtitlán. In 1428, a Triple Alliance between the Mexica and two other nearby city-states launched a highly aggressive program of military conquest, which in less than 100 years brought more of Mesoamerica within a single political framework than ever before. Aztec authorities, eager to shed their rather undistinguished past, now claimed descent from earlier Mesoamerican peoples such as the Toltecs and Teotihuacán.

With a core population recently estimated at 5 to 6 million people, the Aztec Empire was a loosely structured and unstable conquest state that witnessed frequent rebellions by its subject peoples. Conquered peoples and cities were required to regularly deliver to their Aztec rulers impressive quantities of textiles and clothing, military supplies, jewelry and other luxuries, various foodstuffs, animal products, building materials, rubber balls, paper, and more. The process was overseen by local imperial tribute collectors, who sent the required goods on to Tenochtitlán, a metropolis of 150,000 to 200,000 people, where they were meticulously recorded.

That city featured numerous canals, dikes, causeways, and bridges. A central walled area of palaces and temples included a pyramid almost 200 feet high. Surrounding the city were "floating gardens," artificial islands created from swamplands that supported a highly productive agriculture. Vast marketplaces reflected the commercialization of the economy. A young Spanish soldier who beheld the city in 1519 described his reaction:

> Gazing on such wonderful sights, we did not know what to say, or whether what appeared before us was real, for on one side, on the land there were great cities, and in the lake ever so many more, and the lake was crowded with canoes, and in the causeway were many bridges at intervals, and in front of us stood the great city of Mexico.[13]

Beyond tribute from conquered peoples, ordinary trade, both local and long-distance, permeated Aztec domains. The extent of empire and rapid population growth stimulated the development of markets and the production of craft goods, particularly in the fifteenth century. Virtually every settlement, from the capital city to the smallest village, had a marketplace that hummed with activity during weekly market days. The largest was that of Tlatelolco, near the capital city, which stunned the Spanish with its huge size, its good order, and the immense range of goods available. Hernán Cortés, the Spanish conquistador who defeated the Aztecs, wrote that "every kind of merchandise such as can be met with in every land is for sale there, whether of food and victuals, or ornaments of gold and silver, or lead, brass, copper, tin, precious stones, bones, shells, snails and feathers."[14] Professional merchants, known as *pochteca*, were legally commoners, but their wealth, often exceeding that of the nobility, allowed them to rise in society and become "magnates of the land." (See Document 12.1, pp. 593–96, for another Spanish view of the Aztec realm.)

Among the "goods" that the pochteca obtained were slaves, many of whom were destined for sacrifice in the bloody rituals so central to Aztec religious life. Long a part of Mesoamerican and many other world cultures, human sacrifice assumed an unusually prominent role in Aztec public life and thought during the fifteenth century. Tlacaelel (1398–1480), who was for more than half a century a prominent official of the Aztec Empire, is often credited with crystallizing the ideology of state that gave human sacrifice such great importance.

In that cyclical understanding of the world, the sun, central to all of life and identified with the Aztec patron deity Huitzilopochtli (wee-tsee-loh-pockt-lee), tended to lose its energy in a constant battle against encroaching darkness. Thus the Aztec world hovered always on the edge of catastrophe. To replenish its energy and thus postpone the descent into endless darkness, the sun required the life-giving force found in human blood. Because the gods had shed their blood ages ago in creating humankind, it was wholly proper for people to offer their own blood to nourish the gods in the present. The high calling of the Aztec state was to supply this blood, largely through its wars of expansion and from prisoners of war, who were destined for sacrifice. The victims were "those who have died for the god." The growth of the Aztec Empire therefore became the means for maintaining cosmic order and avoiding utter catastrophe. This ideology also shaped the techniques of Aztec warfare, which put a premium on capturing prisoners rather than on killing the enemy. As the empire grew, priests and rulers became mutually dependent, and "human sacrifices were carried out in the service of politics."[15] Massive sacrificial rituals, together with a display of great wealth, served to impress enemies, allies, and subjects alike with the immense power of the Aztecs and their gods.

Alongside these sacrificial rituals was a philosophical and poetic tradition of great beauty, much of which mused on the fragility and brevity of human life. Such an outlook characterized the work of Nezahualcoyotl (1402–1472), a poet and king of the city-state of Texcoco, which was part of the Aztec Empire:

> Truly do we live on Earth?
> Not forever on earth; only a little while here.
> Although it be jade, it will be broken.
> Although it be gold, it is crushed.
> Although it be a quetzal feather, it is torn asunder.
> Not forever on earth; only a little while here.[16]

■ Description

How did Aztec religious thinking support the empire?

The Inca Empire

While the Mexica were constructing an empire in Mesoamerica, a relatively small community of Quechua (KEHTCH-wah)-speaking people, known to us as the Inca, was building the Western Hemisphere's largest imperial state along the entire spine of the Andes Mountains. Much as the Aztecs drew on the traditions of the Toltecs and Teotihuacán, the Incas incorporated the lands and cultures of earlier Andean civilizations: the Chavín, Moche, Wari, and Tiwanaku. The Inca Empire, however, was much larger than the Aztec state; it stretched some 2,500 miles along the Andes and contained perhaps 10 million subjects. Although the Aztec Empire controlled only part of the Mesoamerican cultural region, the Inca state encompassed practically the whole of Andean civilization during its short life in the fifteenth and early sixteenth centuries.

Both the Aztec and Inca empires represent rags-to-riches stories in which quite modest and remotely located people very quickly created by military conquest the largest states ever witnessed in their respective regions, but the empires themselves were quite different. In the Aztec realm, the Mexica rulers largely left their conquered people alone, if the required tribute was forthcoming. No elaborate administrative system arose to integrate the conquered territories or to assimilate their people to Aztec culture.

■ Description

In what ways did Inca authorities seek to integrate their vast domains?

The Incas, on the other hand, erected a rather more bureaucratic empire. At the top reigned the emperor, an absolute ruler regarded as divine, a descendant of the creator god Viracocha and the son of the sun god Inti. In theory, the state owned all land and resources, and each of the some eighty provinces in the empire had an Inca governor. At least in the central regions of the empire, subjects were grouped into hierarchical units of 10, 50, 100, 500, 1,000, 5,000, and 10,000 people, each headed by local officials, who were appointed and supervised by an Inca governor or the emperor. A separate set of "inspectors" provided the imperial center with an independent check on provincial officials. Births, deaths, marriages, and other population data were carefully recorded on *quipus*, the knotted cords that served as an accounting device. A resettlement program moved one-quarter or more of the population to new locations, in part to disperse conquered and no doubt resentful people. Efforts at cultural integration required the leaders of conquered peoples to learn Quechua. Their sons were removed to the capital of Cuzco for instruction in Inca culture and language. Even now, millions of people from Ecuador to Chile still speak Quechua, and it is the official second language of Peru after Spanish.

But the sheer human variety of the Inca's enormous empire required great flexibility.[17] In some places Inca rulers encountered bitter resistance; in others local elites were willing to accommodate Incas and thus benefit from their inclusion in the empire. Where centralized political systems already existed, Inca overlords could delegate control to native authorities. Elsewhere they had to construct an administrative system from scratch. Everywhere they sought to incorporate local people into the lower levels of the administrative hierarchy. While the Incas required their subject peoples to acknowledge major Inca deities, these peoples were then largely free to carry on their own religious traditions. The Inca Empire was a fluid system that varied greatly from

Machu Picchu

Machu Picchu, high in the Andes Mountains, was constructed by the Incas in the 1400s on a spot long held sacred by local people. Its 200 buildings stand at some 8,000 feet above sea level, making it a "city in the sky." It was probably a royal retreat or religious center, rather than serving administrative, commercial, or military purposes. The outside world became aware of Machu Picchu only in 1911, when it was discovered by a Yale University archeologist. (fStop/Superstock)

place to place and over time. It depended as much on the posture of conquered peoples as on the Inca's demands and desires.

Like the Aztec Empire, the Inca state represented an especially dense and extended network of economic relationships within the "American web," but these relationships took shape in quite a different fashion. Inca demands on their conquered people were expressed, not so much in terms of tribute, but as labor service, known as *mita*, which was required periodically of every household.[18] What people produced at home usually stayed at home, but almost everyone also had to work for the state. Some labored on large state farms or on "sun farms," which supported temples and religious institutions; others herded, mined, served in the military, or toiled on state-directed construction projects.

Those with particular skills were put to work manufacturing textiles, metal goods, ceramics, and stonework. The most well known of these specialists were the "chosen women," who were removed from their homes as young girls, trained in Inca ideology, and set to producing corn beer and cloth at state centers. Later they were given as wives to men of distinction or sent to serve as priestesses in various temples, where they were known as "wives of the Sun." In return for such labor services, Inca ideology, expressed in terms of family relationships, required the state to provide elaborate feasts at which large quantities of food and drink were consumed. Thus the authority of the state penetrated and directed Inca society and economy far more than did that of the Aztecs. (See Document 12.2, pp. 597–99, for an early Spanish account of Inca governing practices.)

If the Inca and Aztec civilizations differed sharply in their political and economic arrangements, they resembled each other more closely in their gender systems. Both societies practiced what scholars call "gender parallelism," in which "women and men operate in two separate but equivalent spheres, each gender enjoying autonomy in its own sphere."[19]

In both Mesoamerican and Andean societies, such systems had emerged long before their incorporation into the Aztec and Inca empires. In the Andes, men reckoned their descent from their fathers and women from their mothers, while Mesoamericans had long viewed children as belonging equally to their mothers and fathers. Parallel religious cults for women and men likewise flourished in both societies. Inca men venerated the sun, while women worshipped the moon, with matching religious officials. In Aztec temples, both male and female priests presided over rituals dedicated to deities of both sexes. Particularly among the Incas, parallel hierarchies of male and female political officials governed the empire, while in Aztec society, women officials exercised local authority under a title that meant "female person in charge of people." Social roles were clearly defined and different for men and women, but the domestic concerns of women—childbirth, cooking, weaving, cleaning—were not regarded as inferior to the activities of men. Among the Aztec, for example, sweeping was a powerful and sacred act with symbolic significance as "an act of purification and a preventative against evil elements penetrating the center of the Aztec universe, the home."[20] In the Andes, men broke the ground, women sowed, and both took part in the harvest.

None of this meant gender equality. Men occupied the top positions in both political and religious life, and male infidelity was treated more lightly than was women's unfaithfulness. As the Inca and Aztec empires expanded, military life, limited to men, grew in prestige, perhaps skewing an earlier gender parallelism. In other ways, the new Aztec and Inca rulers adapted to the gender systems of the people they had conquered. Among the Aztecs, the tools of women's work, the broom and the weaving spindle, were ritualized as weapons; sweeping the home was believed to assist men at war; and childbirth for women was regarded as "our kind of war."[21] Inca rulers did not challenge the gender parallelism of their subjects but instead replicated it at a higher level, as the *sapay Inca* (the Inca ruler) and the *coya* (his female consort) governed jointly, claiming descent respectively from the sun and the moon.

Webs of Connection

■ **Connection**
In what different ways did the peoples of the fifteenth century interact with one another?

Few people in the fifteenth century lived in entirely separate and self-contained communities. Almost all were caught up, to one degree or another, in various and overlapping webs of influence, communication, and exchange.[22] Perhaps most obvious were the webs of empire, large-scale political systems that brought together a variety of culturally different people. Christians and Muslims encountered each other directly in the

Ottoman Empire, as did Hindus and Muslims in the Mughal Empire. And no empire tried more diligently to integrate its diverse peoples than the fifteenth-century Incas.

Religion too linked far-flung peoples, and divided them as well. Christianity provided a common religious culture for peoples from England to Russia, although the great divide between Roman Catholicism and Eastern Orthodoxy endured, and in the sixteenth century the Protestant Reformation would shatter permanently the Christian unity of the Latin West. Although Buddhism had largely vanished from its South Asian homeland, it remained a link among China, Korea, Tibet, Japan, and parts of Southeast Asia, even as it splintered into a variety of sects and practices. More than either of these, Islam actively brought together its many peoples. In the hajj, the pilgrimage to Mecca, Africans, Arabs, Persians, Turks, Indians, and many others joined as one people as they rehearsed together the events that gave birth to their common faith. And yet divisions and conflicts persisted within the vast realm of Islam, as the violent hostility between the Sunni Ottoman Empire and the Shia Safavid Empire so vividly illustrates.

Long-established patterns of trade among peoples occupying different environments and producing different goods were certainly much in evidence during the fifteenth century, as they had been for millennia. Hunting societies of Siberia funneled furs and other products of the forest into the Silk Road trading network traversing the civilizations of Eurasia. In the fifteenth century, some of the agricultural peoples in southern Nigeria were receiving horses brought overland from the drier regions of Africa to the north, where those animals flourished better. The Mississippi River in North America and the Orinoco and Amazon rivers in South America facilitated a canoe-borne commerce along those waterways. Coastal shipping in large seagoing canoes operated in the Caribbean and along the Pacific coast between Mexico and Peru. In the Pacific, the Micronesian island of Yap by the fifteenth century was the center of an oceanic trading network, which included the distant islands of Guam and Palau, where large stone disks served as money. Likewise the people of Tonga, Samoa, and Fiji intermarried and exchanged a range of goods, including mats and canoes.

The great long-distance trading patterns of the Afro-Eurasian world, in operation for a thousand years or more, likewise continued in the fifteenth century, although the balance among them was changing (see Map 12.6). The Silk Road overland network, which had flourished under Mongol control in the thirteenth and fourteenth centuries, contracted in the fifteenth century as the Mongol Empire broke up and the devastation of the plague reduced demand for its products. The rise of the Ottoman Empire also blocked direct commercial contact between Europe and China, but oceanic trade from Japan, Korea, and China through the islands of Southeast Asia and across the Indian Ocean picked up considerably. Larger ships made it possible to trade in bulk goods such as grain as well as luxury products, while more sophisticated partnerships and credit mechanisms greased the wheels of commerce. A common Islamic culture over much of this vast region likewise smoothed the passage of goods among very different peoples, as it also did for the trans-Saharan trade.

Map 12.6   Religion and Commerce in the Afro-Eurasian World
By the fifteenth century, the many distinct peoples and societies of the Eastern Hemisphere were linked to one another by ties of religion and commerce. Of course, most people were not directly involved in long-distance trade, and many people in areas shown as Buddhist or Islamic on the map practiced other religions. While much of India, for example, was ruled by Muslims, the majority of its people followed some form of Hinduism. And although Islam had spread to West Africa, that religion had not penetrated much beyond the urban centers of the region.

A Preview of Coming Attractions: Looking Ahead to the Modern Era, 1500–2012

While ties of empire, culture, and commerce surely linked many of the peoples in the world of the fifteenth century, none of those connections operated on a genuinely global scale. Although the densest webs of connection had been woven within the Afro-Eurasian zone of interaction, this huge region had no sustained ties with the Americas, and neither of them had meaningful contact with the peoples of Pacific

Oceania. That situation was about to change as Europeans in the sixteenth century and beyond forged a set of genuinely global relationships that generated sustained interaction among all of these regions. That huge process and the many outcomes that flowed from it marked the beginning of what world historians commonly call the modern age — the more than five centuries that followed the voyages of Columbus starting in 1492.

Over those five centuries, the previously separate worlds of Afro-Eurasia, the Americas, and Pacific Oceania became inextricably linked, with enormous consequences for everyone involved. Global empires, a global economy, global cultural exchanges, global migrations, global disease, global wars, and global environmental changes have made the past 500 years a unique phase in the human journey. Those webs of communication and exchange have progressively deepened, so much so that by the end of the twentieth century few people in the world lived beyond the cultural influences, economic ties, or political relationships of a globalized world.

Several centuries after the Columbian voyages, and clearly connected to them, a second distinctive feature of the modern era took shape: the emergence of a radically new kind of human society, first in Europe during the nineteenth century and then in various forms elsewhere in the world. The core feature of such societies was industrialization, rooted in a sustained growth of technological innovation. The human ability to create wealth made an enormous leap forward in a very short period of time, at least by world history standards. Accompanying this economic or industrial revolution was an equally distinctive and unprecedented jump in human numbers, a phenomenon that has affected not only human beings but also many other living species and the earth itself (see the Snapshot).

Moreover, these modern societies were far more urbanized and much more commercialized than ever before, as more and more people began to work for wages, to produce for the market, and to buy the requirements of daily life rather than growing or making those products for their own use. These societies gave prominence and power to holders of urban wealth — merchants, bankers, industrialists, educated professionals — at the expense of rural landowning elites, while simultaneously generating a substantial factory working class and diminishing the role of peasants and handicraft artisans.

Modern societies were generally governed by states that were more powerful and intrusive than earlier states and empires had been, and they offered more of their people an opportunity to play an active role in public and political life. Literacy in modern societies was far more widespread than ever before, while new national identities became increasingly prominent, competing with more local loyalties and with those of empire. To the mix of established religious ideas and folk traditions were now added the challenging outlook and values of modern science, with its secular emphasis on the ability of human rationality to know and manipulate the world. Modernity has usually meant a self-conscious awareness of living and thinking in new ways that deliberately departed from tradition.

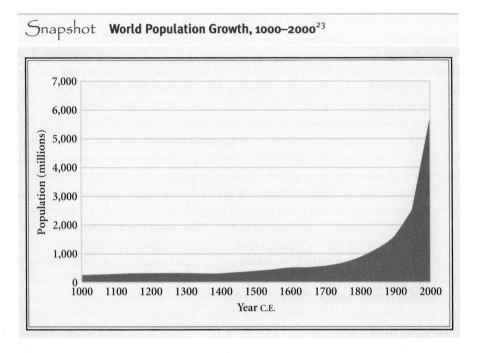

Snapshot   **World Population Growth, 1000–2000**[23]

This revolution of modernity, comparable in its pervasive consequences only to the Agricultural Revolution of some 10,000 years ago, introduced new divisions and new conflicts into the experience of humankind. The ancient tensions between rich and poor within particular societies were now paralleled by new economic inequalities among entire regions and civilizations and a much-altered global balance of power. The first societies to experience the modern transformation — those in Western Europe and North America — became both a threat and a source of envy to much of the rest of the world. As modern societies emerged and spread, they were enormously destructive of older patterns of human life, even as they gave rise to many new ways of living. Sorting out what was gained and what was lost during the modern transformation has been a persistent and highly controversial thread of human thought over the past several centuries.

A third defining feature of the last 500 years was the growing prominence of European peoples on the global stage. In ancient times, the European world, focused in the Mediterranean basin of Greek culture and the Roman Empire, was but one of several second-wave civilizations in the Eastern Hemisphere. After 500 C.E., Western Europe was something of a backwater, compared to the more prosperous and powerful civilizations of China and the Islamic world.

In the centuries following 1500, however, this western peninsula of the Eurasian continent became the most innovative, most prosperous, most powerful, most expansive, and most imitated part of the world. European empires spanned the globe. European peoples created new societies all across the Americas and as far away as Australia and New Zealand. Their languages were spoken and their Christian religion was widely practiced throughout the Americas and in parts of Asia and Africa. Their businessmen bought, sold, and produced goods around the world. It was among Europeans that the Scientific and Industrial Revolutions first took shape, with enormously powerful intellectual and economic consequences for the entire planet. The quintessentially modern ideas of liberalism, nationalism, feminism, and socialism all bore the imprint of their European origin. By the beginning of the twentieth century, Europeans or peoples of European descent exercised unprecedented influence and control over the earth's many other peoples, a wholly novel experience in human history.

For the rest of the world, growing European dominance posed a common task. Despite their many differences, the peoples of Asia, Africa, the Middle East, the Americas, and Pacific Oceania all found themselves confronted by powerful and intrusive Europeans. The impact of this intrusion and how various peoples responded to it — resistance, submission, acceptance, imitation, adaptation — represent critically important threads in the world history of the past five centuries.

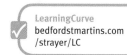

LearningCurve
bedfordstmartins.com
/strayer/LC

⊢⊣ Reflections: What If? Chance and Contingency in World History

Seeking meaning in the stories they tell, historians are inclined to look for deeply rooted or underlying causes for the events they recount. And yet, is it possible that, at least on occasion, historical change derives less from profound and long-term sources than on coincidence, chance, or the decisions of a few that might well have gone another way?

Consider, for example, the problem of explaining the rise of Europe to a position of global power in the modern era. What if the Great Khan Ogodei had not died in 1241, requiring the Mongol forces then poised for an assault on Germany to return to Mongolia? It is surely possible that Central and Western Europe might have been overrun by Mongol armies as so many other civilizations had been, a prospect that could have drastically altered the trajectory of European history. Or what if the Chinese had decided in 1433 to continue their huge maritime expeditions, creating an empire in the Indian Ocean basin and perhaps moving on to "discover" the Americas and Europe? Such a scenario suggests a wholly different future for world history than the one that in fact occurred. Or what if the forces of the Ottoman Empire had taken the besieged city of Vienna in 1529? Might they then have incorporated even larger parts of Europe into their expanding domain, requiring a halt to Europe's overseas empire-building enterprise?

None of this necessarily means that the rise of Europe was merely a fluke or an accident of history, but it does raise the issue of "contingency," the role of unforeseen or small events in the unfolding of the human story. An occasional "what if" approach to history reminds us that alternative possibilities existed in the past and that the only certainty about the future is that we will be surprised.

Second Thoughts

LearningCurve
Check what you know.
**bedfordstmartins.com
/strayer/LC**

Online Study Guide
bedfordstmartins.com
/highschool/strayer

What's the Significance?

Paleolithic persistence, 560–63
Igbo, 563–64
Iroquois, 564–65
Timur, 565
Fulbe, 566
Ming dynasty China, 566–69

European Renaissance, 569–73
Zheng He, 572–73
Ottoman Empire, 576–78
seizure of Constantinople
   (1453), 577
Safavid Empire, 577–78

Songhay Empire, 578–80
Timbuktu, 579
Mughal Empire, 579–80
Malacca, 580
Aztec Empire, 580–83
Inca Empire, 584–86

Big Picture Questions

1. Assume for the moment that the Chinese had not ended their maritime voyages in 1433. How might the subsequent development of world history have been different? What value is there in asking this kind of "what if" or counterfactual question?

2. How does this chapter distinguish among the various kinds of societies that comprised the world of the fifteenth century? What other ways of categorizing the world's peoples might work as well or better?

3. What common patterns might you notice across the world of the fifteenth century? And what variations in the historical trajectories of various regions can you identify?

4. **Looking Back:** What would surprise a knowledgeable observer from 500 or 1000 C.E., were he or she to make a global tour in the fifteenth century? What features of that earlier world might still be recognizable?

Next Steps: For Further Study

For Web sites and additional documents related to this chapter, see **Make History** at bedfordstmartins.com /highschool/strayer.

Terence N. D'Altroy, *The Incas* (2002). A history of the Inca Empire that draws on recent archeological and historical research.

Edward L. Dreyer, *Zheng He: China and the Oceans in the Early Ming Dynasty* (2006). The most recent scholarly account of the Ming dynasty voyages.

Halil Inalcik and Donald Quataert, *An Economic and Social History of the Ottoman Empire, 1300–1914* (1994). A classic study of the Ottoman Empire.

Robin Kirkpatrick, *The European Renaissance, 1400–1600* (2002). A beautifully illustrated history of Renaissance culture as well as the social and economic life of the period.

Charles Mann, *1491: New Revelations of the Americas before Columbus* (2005). A review of Western Hemisphere societies and academic debates about their pre-Columbian history.

J. R. McNeill and William H. McNeill, *The Human Web* (2003). A succinct account of the evolving webs or relationships among human societies in world history.

Michael Smith, *The Aztecs* (2003). A history of the Aztec Empire, with an emphasis on the lives of ordinary people.

"Ming Dynasty," http://www.metmuseum.org/toah/hd/ming/hd_ming.htm. A sample of Chinese art from the Ming dynasty from the collection of the Metropolitan Museum of Art.

"Renaissance Art in Italy," http://witcombe.sbc.edu/ARTHrenaissanceitaly.html. An extensive collection of painting and sculpture from the Italian Renaissance.

Documents

Considering the Evidence: The Aztecs and the Incas through Spanish Eyes

During the fifteenth century, the Western Hemisphere hosted human communities of many kinds—gathering and hunting peoples, agricultural village societies, chiefdoms, and two major state-based agrarian civilizations. Most of the population of the Americas was concentrated in those two civilizations—the Aztec and Inca empires (see Map 12.5, p. 581). Since neither had an extensive literary tradition, historians seeking to understand their history and culture have depended heavily on the records and observations of the Spanish who conquered them in the sixteenth century. This raises obvious questions about the credibility of such accounts. Can writers from a conquering power and a completely different culture accurately describe the life and history of those they have recently defeated, even if they were able to draw on the local knowledge and experience of native peoples? What follows are accounts of the Aztec and Inca empires as seen through the eyes of two remarkable Spanish observers, both of whom at least tried to understand the people of these American civilizations.

Document 12.1

Diego Durán on the Aztecs

Coming to Mexico with his family as a young boy, Diego Durán (1537–1588) subsequently became a Dominican friar, learned to speak fluently the native Nahuatl language of the Aztecs, and began a lifelong enterprise of studying their history and culture. His research often involved extensive interviewing of local people in the rural areas where he worked and resulted in three books published between 1574 and 1581. The first excerpt records a series of laws or decrees, which Durán attributes to the Aztec ruler Moctezuma I, who governed the empire between 1440 and 1469. They reveal something of the court practices and social hierarchy of the Aztec realm as the empire was establishing itself in the middle decades of the fifteenth century. The second excerpt touches on various aspects of Aztec culture—religion, human sacrifice, social mobility, commercial markets, and slavery.

■ What do Moctezuma's laws tell us about the social and moral values of the Aztecs?

■ Based on these two excerpts, how would you describe Aztec society? What distinct social groups or classes can you identify? How were they distinguished from one another? What opportunities for social mobility were available? How might people fall into slavery?

■ What impressed Durán about the markets operating within the Aztec Empire?

■ How was human sacrifice related to war, to market activity, to slavery, and to religious belief and practice?

■ Durán's accounts of Aztec life and history were written more than fifty years after the Spanish conquest of the Aztec Empire. To what extent do you think this compromises his efforts to describe preconquest Aztec society?

KING MOCTEZUMA I
Laws, Ordinances, and Regulations
ca. 1450

The following laws were decreed:

1. The king must never appear in public except when the occasion is extremely important and unavoidable.

2. Only the king may wear a golden diadem in the city, though in war all the great lords and brave captains may wear this (but on no other occasion). . . .

3. Only the king and the prime minister Tlacaelel may wear sandals within the palace. . . . [N]oblemen are the only ones to be allowed to wear sandals in the city and no one else, also under pain of death, with the exception of men who have performed some great feat in war. . . .

4. Only the king is to wear the final mantles of cotton brocaded with designs and threads of different colors and adorned with featherwork. . . .

5. The great lords, who are twelve, may wear special mantles of certain make and design, and the minor lords, according to their valor and accomplishments, may wear others.

6. The common soldiers are permitted to wear only the simplest type of mantle. They are prohibited from using any special designs that might set them off from the rest. . . .

7. The commoners will not be allowed to wear cotton clothing, under pain of death, but can use only garments of maguey fiber. . . .

8. Only the great noblemen and valiant warriors are given license to build a house with a second story; for disobeying this law a person receives the death penalty. . . .

9. Only the great lords are to wear labrets, ear plugs, and nose plugs of gold and precious stones, except for commoners who are strong men, brave captains, and soldiers, but their labrets, ear plugs, and nose plugs must be of bone, wood, or other inferior material of little value. . . .

11. In the royal palace there are to be diverse rooms where different classes of people are to be

Source: Fray Diego Durán, *The History of the Indies of New Spain*, translated by Doris Heyden (Norman: University of Oklahoma Press, 1994), 208–10.

received, and under pain of death no one is to enter that of the great lords or to mix with those men [unless of that class himself]. . . .

12. An order of judges is to be established, beginning with the judges of the supreme council. After these would come regular court judges, municipal judges, district officials, constables, and councilmen, although none of them may give the death sentence without notifying the king. Only the sovereign can sentence someone to death or pardon him. . . .

13. All the barrios will possess schools or monasteries for young men where they will learn religion and correct comportment. They are to do penance, lead hard lives, live with strict morality, practice for warfare, do physical work, fast, endure disciplinary measures, draw blood from different parts of the body, and keep watch at night. There are to be teachers and old men to correct them and chastise them and lead them in their exercises and take care that they are not idle, do not lose their time. All of these youth must observe chastity in the strictest way, under pain of death.

14. There is to be a rigorous law regarding adulterers. They are to be stoned and thrown into the rivers or to the buzzards.

15. Thieves will be sold for the price of their theft, unless the theft be grave, having been committed many times. Such thieves will be punished by death.

16. Great privileges and exemptions are to be given those who dedicate themselves to religion, to the temples and the gods. Priests will be awarded great distinction, reverence, and authority.

Diego Durán
Book of the Gods and Rites
1574–1576

I wish to tell of the way in which the natives sacrificed. . . .

So ended the ceremony of the blessing of the pieces of dough in the form of the bones and the flesh of the god. They were revered and honored in the name of Huitzilopochtli with all the respectful veneration that we ourselves hold for the Divine Sacrament of the Altar. To exalt the occasion further, the sacrificers of men were also present. . . .

Smeared with black, the six sacrificers appeared. . . . Seeing them come out with their ghastly aspect filled all the people with dread and terrible fear! The high priest carried in one hand a large stone knife, sharp and wide. Another carried a wooden yoke carved in the form of a snake. They humbled themselves before the idol and then stood in order next to a pointed stone, which stood in front of the door of the idol's chamber. . . .

All the prisoners of war who were to be sacrificed upon this feast were then brought forth. . . . They seized the victims one by one, one by one foot, another by the other, one priest by one hand, another by the other hand. The victim was thrown on his back, upon the pointed stone, where the wretch was grabbed by the fifth priest, who placed the yoke upon his throat. The high priest then opened the chest and with amazing swiftness tore out the heart, ripping it out with his own hands. Thus steaming, the heart was lifted toward the sun, and the fumes were offered up to the sun. The priest then turned toward the idol and cast the heart in its face. After the heart had been extracted, the body was allowed to roll down the steps of the pyramid. . . .

All the prisoners and captives of war brought from the towns we have mentioned were sacrificed in this manner, until none were left. After they had been slain and cast down, their owners—those who had captured them—retrieved the bodies. They were

Source: Fray Diego Durán, *Book of the Gods and Rites and the Ancient Calendar*, translated by Fernando Horcasitas and Doris Heyden (Norman: University of Oklahoma Press, 1971), 90–92, 137–38, 273–76, 279, 281–82.

carried away, distributed, and eaten, in order to celebrate the feast. There were at least forty or fifty captives, depending upon the skill which the men had shown in seizing and capturing men in war. . . .

[M]any strove, in every possible way, to lift their names on high, to obtain glory, to procure greater honors, to found lineages and titles, and [to gain] good fame for their persons. There were three established and honored ways in all the nations [for obtaining these rewards]. The first and principal path which the kings designated was soldiery—to make oneself known in war through valiant feats, to be outstanding in killing, taking prisoners, to destroy armies and squadrons, to have directed these things. These [warriors] were given great honors, rewards, weapons, and insignia which were proof of their splendid deeds and valor. . . .

The second way in which men rose was through religion, entering the priesthood. After having served in the temples in a virtuous, penitential, and cloistered way of life, in their old age they were sent out to high and honorable posts. . . . They were present when the government councils were held, their opinions and advice were listened to, and they were part of the ruling boards and juntas. Without their council and opinion kings did not dare act. . . .

The third and least glorious manner of [rising in the world] was that of becoming a merchant or trader, that of buying and selling, going forth to all the markets of the land, bartering cloth for jewels, jewels for feathers, feathers for stones, and stones for slaves, always dealing in things of importance, of renown, and of high value. These [men] strengthened their social position with their wealth. . . . They acquired wealth and obtained slaves to sacrifice to this their god [Quetzalcoatl]. And so they were considered among the magnates of the land, just as the valorious soldier brought sacrificial captives from war, gaining fame as a brave. . . .

[I]n olden times there was a god of markets and fairs. . . .

The gods of these market places threatened terrible ills and made evil omens and auguries to the neighboring villages which did not attend their market places. . . .

The markets were so inviting, pleasurable, appealing, and gratifying to these people that great crowds attended, and still attend, them, especially during the big fairs, as is well known to all. . . .

The markets in this land were all enclosed by walls and stood either in front of the temples of the gods or to one side. Market day in each town was considered a main feast in that town or city. And thus in that small shrine where the idol of the market stood were offered ears of corn, chili, tomatoes, fruit, and other vegetables, seeds, and breads—in sum, everything sold in the *tianguiz*. . . .

Furthermore, a law was established by the republic prohibiting the selling of goods outside the market place. Not only were there laws and penalties connected with this, but there was a fear of the supernatural, of misfortune, and of the ire and wrath of the god of the market. No one ventured, therefore, to trade outside [the market limits]. . . .

There were many ways of becoming a slave within the law of the Indian nations. . . .

First, he who stole the number of pieces of cloth or ears of corn, jewels, or turkeys which the laws of the republic had determined and set a penalty for was himself sold for the same amount in order to satisfy the owner of the purloined goods. . . .

Second, another way in which a native could become a slave was that of the gambler who risked all his possessions on the dice or in any other game which the natives played. . . .

Third, if the father of a family had many sons and daughters and among them was one [who was] incorrigible, disobedient, shameless, dissolute, incapable of receiving counsel or advice, the law . . . permitted [the father] to sell him in the public market place as an example and lesson to bad sons and daughters. . . .

Fourth, one became a slave if he borrowed valuable things, such as cloth, jewels, featherwork, and did not return them on the appointed date. . . .

In times of famine a man and wife could agree to a way of satisfying their needs and rise from their wretched state. They could sell one another, and thus husband sold wife and wife sold husband, or they sold one of their children.

Document 12.2

Pedro de Cieza de León on the Incas

Like Duran, Pedro de Cieza de León (1520–1554), a Spanish chronicler of the Inca Empire, came to the Americas as a boy. But unlike Duran, he came alone at the age of thirteen, and he followed a very different career. For the next seventeen years, Cieza took part as a soldier in a number of expeditions that established Spanish rule in various parts of South America. Along the way, he collected a great deal of information, especially about the Inca Empire, which he began to publish on his return to Spain in 1550. Despite a very limited education, Cieza wrote a series of works that have become a major source for historians about the workings of the Inca Empire and about the Spanish conquest of that land. The selection that follows focuses on the techniques that the Inca used to govern their huge empire.

■ How would you describe Cieza's posture toward the Inca Empire? What in particular did he seem to appreciate about it?

■ Based on this account, what difficulties did the Inca rulers face in governing their large and diverse realm?

■ What policies or practices did the Inca authorities follow in seeking to integrate their empire? How do these compare with other empires that you have studied?

■ Some modern observers have described the Inca Empire as "totalitarian" or "socialist." Do such terms seem appropriate? How else might you describe the Inca state?

PEDRO DE CIEZA DE LEÓN
Chronicles of the Incas
ca. 1550

The Incas had the seat of their empire in the city of Cuzco, where the laws were given and the captains set out to make war. . . . As soon as one of these large provinces was conquered, ten or twelve thousand of the men and their wives, or six thousand, or the number decided upon were ordered to leave and remove themselves from it. These were transferred to another town or province of the same climate and nature as that which they left. . . . And they had another device to keep the natives from hating them, and this was that they never divested the natural chieftains of their power. If it so happened that one of them committed a crime or in some way deserved to be stripped of his power, it was vested in his sons or brothers, and all were ordered to obey them. . . .

Source: *The Incas of Pedro de Cieza de León*, translated by Harriet de Onis (Norman: University of Oklahoma Press, 1959), 56–57, 158–60, 165–73, 177–78.

One of the things most to be envied these rulers is how well they knew to conquer such vast lands. . . .

[T]hey entered many lands without war, and the soldiers who accompanied the Inca were ordered to do no damage or harm, robbery or violence. If there was a shortage of food in the province, he ordered supplies brought in from other regions so that those newly won to his service would not find his rule and acquaintance irksome. . . .

In many others, where they entered by war and force of arms, they ordered that the crops and houses of the enemy be spared. . . . But in the end the Incas always came out victorious, and when they had vanquished the others, they did not do them further harm, but released those they had taken prisoner, if there were any, and restored the booty, and put them back in possession of their property and rule, exhorting them not to be foolish and try to compete with his royal majesty nor abandon his friendship, but to be his friends as their neighbors were. And saying this, he gave them a number of beautiful women and fine pieces of wool or gold. . . .

They never deprived the native chieftains of their rule. They were all ordered to worship the sun as God, but they were not prohibited from observing their own religions and customs. . . .

It is told for a fact of the rulers of this kingdom that in the days of their rule they [the Incas] had their representatives in the capitals of all the provinces. . . . They served as head of the provinces or regions, and from every so many leagues around the tributes were brought to one of these capitals. . . . This was so well organized that there was not a village that did not know where it was to send its tribute. In all these capitals the Incas had temples of the sun, mints, and many silversmiths who did nothing but work rich pieces of gold or fair vessels of silver. . . . The tribute paid by each of these districts where the capital was situated, and that turned over by the natives, whether gold, silver, clothing, arms, and all else they gave, was entered in the accounts of the [quipu-] camayocs, who kept the quipus and did everything ordered by the governor in the matter of finding the soldiers or supplying whomever the Inca ordered, or making delivery to Cuzco; but when they came from the city of Cuzco to go over the accounts, or they were ordered to go to Cuzco to give an accounting, the accountants themselves gave it by the quipus, or went to give it where there could be no fraud, but everything had to come out right. Few years went by in which an accounting of all these things was not made. . . .

When the Incas set out to visit their kingdom, it is told that they traveled with great pomp, riding in rich litters set upon smooth, long poles of the finest wood and adorned with gold and silver. . . .

So many people came to see his passing that all the hills and slopes seemed covered with them, and all called down blessings upon him. . . .

He [the Inca] traveled four leagues each day, or as much as he wished; he stopped wherever he liked to inquire into the state of his kingdom; he willingly listened to those who came to him with complaints, righting wrongs and punishing those who had committed an injustice. . . .

[T]hese rulers, as the best measure, ordered and decreed, with severe punishment for failure to obey, that all the natives of their empire should know and understand the language of Cuzco, both they and their women. . . . This was carried out so faithfully that in the space of a very few years a single tongue was known and used in an extension of more than 1,200 leagues; yet, even though this language was employed, they all spoke their own [languages], which were so numerous that if I were to list them it would not be credited. . . .

[The Inca] appointed those whose duty it was to punish wrongdoers, and to this end they were always traveling about the country. The Incas took such care to see that justice was meted out that nobody ventured to commit a felony or theft. This was to deal with thieves, ravishers of women, or conspirators against the Inca; however, there were many provinces that warred on one another, and the Incas were not wholly able to prevent this. By the river [Huatanay] that runs through Cuzco justice was executed on those who were caught or brought in as prisoners from some other place. There they had their heads cut off, or were put to death in some other manner which they chose. Mutiny and conspiracy were severely punished, and, above all, those who were thieves and known as such; even their wives and children were despised and considered to be tarred with the same brush. . . .

[I]n each of the many provinces there were many storehouses filled with supplies and other needful things; thus, in times of war, wherever the armies went they draw upon the contents of these store-houses, without ever touching the supplies of their confederates or laying a finger on what they had in their settlements. And when there was no war, all this stock of supplies and food was divided up among the poor and the widows. These poor were the aged, or the lame, crippled, or paralyzed, or those afflicted with some other diseases. . . . If there came a lean year, the storehouses were opened and the provinces were lent what they needed in the way of supplies; then, in a year of abundance, they paid back all they had received.

Using the Evidence: The Aztecs and the Incas through Spanish Eyes

1. **Assessing documents:** Both Durán and Cieza were outsiders to the societies they described, and they were part of the conquering Spanish forces. In what ways did these conditions affect their descriptions of the Aztec and Inca empires?

2. **Considering the subtext of documents:** In what ways might these authors have been using their observation of Aztec or Inca society to praise or to criticize their own European homeland?

3. **Evaluating the credibility of documents:** Which statements in these documents do you find most credible, and which ones might you be inclined to question or challenge? What criteria might you use to assess the evidence in these documents?

4. **Relating primary documents and text narrative:** How might you use the information in these documents to support the descriptions of the Aztec and Inca empires that are contained in this chapter? Are there ways the documents might challenge statements in the text?

5. **Making comparisons:** What similarities and differences between Aztec and Inca societies can you glean from these documents?

6. **Seeking more data:** What additional primary sources about the Aztec and Inca empires of the fifteenth century would you like to have? What other perspectives on those empires would be useful for historians?

Visual Sources

Considering the Evidence:
Islam and Renaissance Europe

The Renaissance era in Europe, roughly 1400 to 1600, represented the crystallization of a new civilization at the western end of Eurasia. In cultural terms, its writers and artists sought to link themselves to the legacy of the pre-Christian Greeks and Romans. But if Europeans were reaching back to their classical past, they were also reaching out—westward to the wholly new world of the Americas, southward to Africa, and eastward to Asia generally and the Islamic world in particular. The European Renaissance, in short, was shaped not only from within but also by its encounters with a wider world.

Interaction with the world of Islam was, of course, nothing new. Centuries of Muslim rule in Spain, the Crusades, and the expansion of the Ottoman Empire were markers in the long relationship of conflict, cooperation, and mutual influence between Christendom and the realm of Islam. Politically, that relationship was changing in the fifteenth century. The Christian reconquest of Spain from Muslim rule was completed by 1492. At the other end of the Mediterranean Sea, the Turkish Ottoman Empire was expanding into the previously Christian regions of the Balkans (southeastern Europe), seizing the ancient capital of the Byzantine Empire, Constantinople, in 1453, while becoming a major player in European international politics. Despite such conflicts, commerce flourished across political and religious divides. European bulk goods such as wool, timber, and glassware, along with silver and gold, were exchanged for high-value luxury goods from the Islamic world or funneled through it from farther east. These included spices, silks, carpets, tapestries, brocades, art objects, precious stones, gold, dyes, and pigments. In 1384, a Christian pilgrim from the Italian city of Florence wrote: "Really all of Christendom could be supplied for a year with the merchandise of Damascus."[24] And a fifteenth-century Italian nobleman said of Venice: "[I]t seems as if all the world flocks here, and that human beings have concentrated there all their force for trading."[25]

The acquisition of such eastern goods was important for elite Europeans as they sought to delineate and measure their emerging civilization. As that civilization began to take shape in the centuries after 1100 or so, it had drawn extensively on Arab or Muslim learning—in medicine, astronomy, philosophy, architecture, mathematics, business practices, and more. As early as the twelfth century, a Spanish priest and Latin translator of Arab texts wrote that "it befits us to imitate the Arabs, for they are as it were our teachers and the pioneers." During the Renaissance centuries as well, according to a recent account, "Europe began to define itself by purchasing and emulating the opulence and cultured sophistication of the cities, merchants, scholars, and empires of the Ottomans, Persians, and the Egyptian Mamluks." That engagement with the Islamic world found various expressions in Renaissance art, as the images that follow illustrate.

The year 1453 marked a watershed in the long relationship between Christendom and the Islamic world, for it was in that year that Ottoman Sultan Mehmed II decisively conquered the great Christian city of Constantinople, bringing the thousand-year history of Byzantium to an inglorious end. To many Europeans that event was a catastrophe, and Mehmed was the "terror of the world." On hearing the news, one Italian bishop, later to become the pope, foresaw a dismal future for both the Church and Western civilization: "Who can doubt that the Turks will vent their wrath upon the churches of God? . . . This will be a second death to Homer and a second destruction of Plato." Others, however, saw opportunity. Less than a year after that event, the northern Italian city of Venice signed a peace treaty with the Ottoman sultan, declaring "it is our intention to live in peace and friendship with the Turkish emperor." Some even expressed admiration for the conquering Muslim ruler. George of Trebizond, a Greek-speaking Renaissance scholar, described Mehmed as "a wise king and one who philosophizes about the greatest matters."

For his part, Mehmed admired both classical and contemporary European culture, even as his armies threatened European powers. This cosmopolitan emperor employed Italian scholars to read to him from ancient Greek and Roman literature, stocked his library with Western texts, and decorated the walls of his palace with Renaissance-style frescoes. Seeing himself as heir to Roman imperial authority, he now added "Caesar" to his other titles. Although Islam generally prohibited the depiction of human figures, Mehmed's long interest in caricatures and busts and his desire to celebrate his many conquests led him to commission numerous medals by European artists, bearing his image. In 1480, he also had his portrait painted by the leading artist of Venice, Gentile Bellini, who had been sent to the Ottoman court as a cultural ambassador of his city.

Visual Source 12.1 shows Bellini's portrait of the emperor sitting under a marble arch, a symbol of triumph that evokes his dramatic conquest of Constantinople. The three golden crowns on the upper left and right likely represent the lands recently acquired for the Ottoman Empire, and the inscription at the bottom describes Mehmet as "Conqueror of the World." Not long after the painting was made, Mehmed died, and shortly thereafter his son and

Visual Source 12.1 Gentile Bellini, Portrait of Mehmed II (National Gallery, London/ The Bridgeman Art Library)

successor sold it to Venetian merchants to help finance a large mosque complex. Thus the portrait returned to Venice.

- What overall impression of the sultan does this portrait convey?

- Why might this Muslim ruler want his portrait painted by a Christian artist from Venice?

- Why might Bellini and the city government of Venice be willing—even eager—to undertake the assignment, less than thirty years after the Muslim conquest of Constantinople?

- The candelabra decorating the arch were a common feature in Venetian church architecture. Why might the sultan have agreed to this element of Christian symbolism in his portrait?

- What does the episode surrounding this portrait indicate about the relationship of Venice and the Ottoman Empire in the wake of the conquest of Constantinople?

Venice had long been the primary point of commercial contact between Europe and the East and the source of the much-desired luxury goods that its merchants obtained from Alexandria in Egypt. At that time, Muslim Egypt was ruled by the Mamluks, a warrior caste of slave origins, who had checked the westward advance of the Mongols in 1260 and had driven the last of the European crusaders out of the Middle East in 1291. Venetian traders, however, were more interested in commerce than religion and by the fifteenth century enjoyed a highly profitable relationship with the Mamluk rulers of Egypt and Syria, despite the periodic opposition of the pope and threats of excommunication. Thus it is not surprising that the Renaissance artists of Venice were prominent among those who reflected the influence of the Islamic world in their work. By the late fifteenth century, something of a fad for oriental themes surfaced in Venetian pictorial art.

Visual Source 12.2, painted by an anonymous Venetian artist in 1511, expresses this intense interest in the Islamic world. The setting is Damascus in Syria, then ruled by the Egyptian Mamluk regime. The local Mamluk governor of the city, seated on a low platform with an elaborate headdress, is receiving an ambassador from Venice, shown in a red robe and standing in front of the governor. Behind him in black robes are other members of the Venetian delegation, while in the foreground various members of Damascus society—both officials and merchants—are distinguished from one another by variations in their turbans. Behind the wall lies the city of Damascus with its famous Umayyad mosque, formerly a Roman temple to Jupiter and later a Christian church, together with its three minarets. The city's lush gardens and its homes with wooden balconies and rooftop terraces complete the picture of urban Islam.

- What impressions of the city and its relationship with Venice does the artist seek to convey?

- How are the various social groups of Damascus distinguished from one another in this painting? What does the very precise visual description of these differences suggest about Venetian understanding of urban Mamluk society?

mutilated. To many Christians, Muhammad was a "false prophet," sometimes portrayed as drunk. Protestants such as Martin Luther on occasion equated their great enemy, the pope, with the Muslim "Turk," both of them leading people away from authentic religion.

The most infamous Renaissance example of hostility to Islam as a religion is displayed in Visual Source 12.5, a fresco by the Italian artist Giovanni da Modena, painted on a church wall in the northern Italian city of Bologna in 1415. It was a small part of a much larger depiction of hell, featuring a gigantic image of Satan devouring and excreting the damned, while many others endured horrific punishments. Among them was Muhammad—naked, bound to a rock, and tortured by a winged demon with long horns. It reflected common understandings of Muhammad as a religious heretic, false prophet, even the anti-Christ and therefore "hell-bound."

■ How does this fresco depict hell? What does this larger context of the fresco as a whole suggest about Modena's view of Muhammad?

■ How does this image differ from that of Visual Source 12.4, particularly in its posture toward Islam?

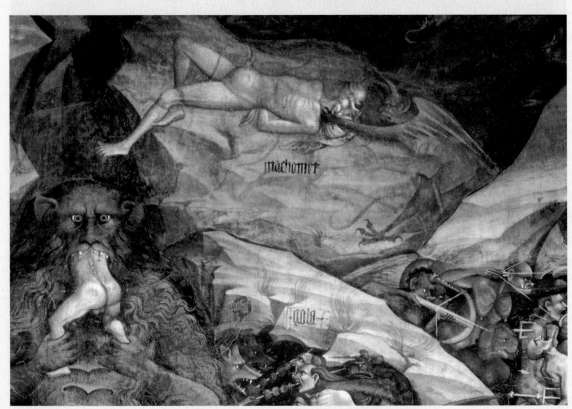

Visual Source 12.5 Giovanni da Modena, Muhammad in Hell (Scala/Art Resource, NY)

■ Italian Muslims have long objected to this image, noting that Islam portrays Jesus in a very positive light. In 2002 a radical group linked to al-Qaeda plotted to blow up the church to destroy the offending portrayal of their prophet. What particular objections do you imagine motivated Muslim opposition to this element of the fresco?

Using the Evidence: Renaissance Europe and the World of Islam

1. **Making comparisons:** What range of postures toward the Islamic world do these images convey? How might you account for the differences among them?

2. **Imagining reactions:** How might the artists who created the first four images respond to Visual Source 12.5?

3. **Examining the content of visual sources:** While all of these images deal with the Islamic world, with what different aspects of that world are they concerned?

4. **Considering art and society:** In what ways were these images shaped by the concrete political, economic, and cultural conditions of Renaissance Europe? What role did the Islamic world play in the emerging identity of European civilization?

Chapter 12 Wrap Up

LearningCurve
Check what you know.
**bedfordstmartins.com
/strayer/LC**

STEP ONE

The Word to Know: Renaissance

The *Oxford English Dictionary* defines *renaissance* as "any period of exceptional revival of the arts and intellectual culture." In a brief paragraph, explain why the fifteenth century represents a renaissance and then make an argument for or against the idea that the Renaissance was a distinctly Western European phenomenon. Provide at least three pieces of evidence from the textbook to illustrate your points.

STEP TWO

Comparing China and Europe

On the chart below, record both similarities and differences between China and Western Europe in the fourteenth through fifteenth centuries. Use different colored pencils in each row to differentiate between similarities and differences.

	China Ming dynasty (1368–1644)	Europe c. 1500
Government		
Belief systems		
Disruptions		
Domestic policy shifts		
Foreign interactions/influences		

STEP THREE

Hierarchy among the Aztecs and Incas

As seen in both the textbook narrative and the documents section in Chapter 12 (pp. 593–99), both the Incas and the Aztecs had hierarchical societies based on class and gender. Complex legal codes as well as tradition guided social practices. Review the chapter and documents and answer the questions below.

■ Questions

1. Review the image of Aztec women on p. 582. What observations can you make about women's roles in maintaining the material prosperity of a household?

2. Note three examples from Document 12.1 that illustrate how the Aztecs used material objects (fashion, housing, possessions) to demonstrate status.

3. According to Document 12.2, how were social status and material possessions demonstrated among the Incas?

4. Find an image on the Internet from the Aztec Florentine Codex or from the Inca empire that illustrates hierarchy of class or gender (or both). In what ways can you use context to get clues about social status and work?

PART FOUR

The Early Modern World

1450–1750

Contents

Debating the Character of an Era

For the sake of clarity and coherence, historians often characterize a particular period of time in a brief phrase—the age of First Civilizations, the age of empires, the era of revolutions, and so on. Though useful and even necessary, such capsule descriptions leave a lot out and vastly oversimplify what actually happened. Historical reality is always more messy, more complicated, and more uncertain than any shorthand label can convey. Such is surely the case when we examine the three centuries spanning the years from roughly 1450 to 1750.

An Early Modern Era?

Those three centuries, which are addressed in Chapters 13 through 15, are conventionally labeled as "the early modern era." In using this term, historians are suggesting that during these three centuries we can find some initial signs or markers of the modern world, such as those described at the end of Chapter 12: the beginnings of genuine globalization, elements of distinctly modern societies, and a growing European presence in world affairs.

The most obvious expression of globalization, of course, lay in the oceanic journeys of European explorers and the European conquest and colonial settlement of the Americas. The Atlantic slave trade linked Africa permanently to the Western Hemisphere, while the global silver trade allowed Europeans to use New World precious metals to buy their way into ancient Asian trade routes. The massive transfer of plants, animals, diseases, and people, known to historians as the Columbian exchange, created wholly new networks of interaction across both the Atlantic and Pacific oceans, with enormous global implications. Missionaries carried Christianity far beyond Europe, allowing it to become a genuinely world religion, with a presence in the Americas, China, Japan, the Philippines, and south-central Africa. Other threads in the emerging global web were also woven as Russians marched across Siberia to the Pacific, as China expanded deep into Inner Asia, and as the Ottoman Empire encompassed much of the Middle East, North Africa, and southeastern Europe (see Chapter 13).

Scattered signs of what later generations thought of as "modernity" appeared in various places around the world. The most obviously modern cultural development took place in Europe, where the Scientific Revolution transformed, at least for a few, their view of the world, their approach to knowledge, and their understanding of traditional Christianity. Demographically, China, Japan, India, and Europe experienced the beginnings of modern population growth as Eurasia recovered from the Black Death and Mongol wars and as the foods of the Americas—corn and potatoes, for example—provided nutrition to support larger numbers. World population more than doubled between 1400 and 1800 (from about 374 million to 968 million), even as the globalization of disease produced a demographic catastrophe in the Americas and the slave trade limited African population growth. More highly commercialized economies centered in large cities developed in various parts of Eurasia and the Americas. By the early eighteenth century, for example, Japan was one of the most urbanized societies in the world, with Edo (Tokyo) housing more than a million inhabitants and ranking as the world's largest city. In China, Southeast Asia, India, and across the Atlantic basin, more and more people found themselves, sometimes willingly and at other times involuntarily, producing for distant markets rather than for the use of their local communities.

Stronger and more cohesive states represented yet another global pattern as they incorporated various local societies into larger units while actively promoting trade, manufacturing, and a common culture within their borders. France, the Dutch Republic, Russia, Morocco, the Mughal Empire, Vietnam, Burma, Siam, and Japan all represent this kind of state.[1] Their military power likewise soared as the "gunpowder revolution" kicked in around the world. Thus large-scale empires proliferated across Asia and the Middle East, while various European powers carved out new domains in the Americas. Within these empires, human pressures on the land intensified as forests were felled, marshes drained, and the hunting grounds of foragers and the grazing lands of pastoralists were confiscated for farming or ranching.

A Late Agrarian Era?

All of these developments give some validity to the notion of an early modern era. But this is far from the whole story, and it may be misleading if it suggests that European world domination and more fully modern societies were a sure thing, an inevitable outgrowth of early modern developments. In fact, that future was far from clear in 1750.

Although Europeans ruled the Americas and controlled the world's sea routes, their political and military power in mainland Asia and Africa was very limited. Eighteenth-century China and Japan strictly controlled the European missionaries and merchants who operated in their societies, and African authorities frequently set the terms under which the slave trade was conducted. Islam, not Christianity, was the most rapidly spreading faith in much of Asia and Africa, and in 1750 Europe, India, and China were roughly comparable in their manufacturing output. In short, it was not obvious that Europeans would soon dominate the planet. Moreover, populations and economies had surged at various points in the past, only to fall back again in a cyclical pattern. Nothing guaranteed that the early modern surge would be any more lasting than the others.

Nor was there much to suggest that anything approaching modern industrial society was on the horizon. Animal and human muscles, wind, and water still provided almost all of the energy that powered human economies. Handicraft techniques of manufacturing had nowhere been displaced by factory-based production or steam power. Long-established elites, not middle-class upstarts, everywhere provided leadership and enjoyed the greatest privileges, while rural peasants, not urban workers, represented the primary social group in the lower classes. Kings and nobles, not parliaments and parties, governed. Female subordination was assumed to be natural almost everywhere. While the texture of patriarchy varied among cultures and fluctuated over time, nowhere had ideas of gender equality taken root. Modern society, with its promise of liberation from ancient inequalities and from mass poverty, hardly seemed around the corner.

Most of the world's peoples, in fact, continued to live in long-established ways, and their societies operated according to traditional principles. Kings ruled most of Europe, and male landowning aristocrats remained at the top of the social hierarchy. Another change in ruling dynasties occurred in China, while that huge country affirmed Confucian values and a social structure that privileged landowning and office-holding elites, all of them men. Most Indians practiced some form of Hinduism and owed their most fundamental loyalty to local castes, even as South Asia continued its centuries-long incorporation into the Islamic world. The realm of Islam maintained its central role in the Eastern Hemisphere as the Ottoman Empire revived the political fortunes of Islam, and the religion sustained its long-term expansion into Africa and Southeast Asia.

In short, for the majority of humankind, the three centuries between 1450 and 1750 marked less an entry into the modern era than the continuing development of older agrarian societies. It was as much a late agrarian era as an early modern age. Persistent patterns rooted in the past characterized that period, along with new departures and sprouts of modernity. Nor was change always in the direction of what we now regard as "modern." In European, Islamic, and Chinese societies alike, some people urged a return to earlier ways of living and thinking rather than embracing what was new and untried. Although Europeans were increasingly prominent on the world stage, they certainly did not hold all of the leading roles in the global drama of these three centuries.

From this mixture of what was new and what was old during the early modern era, the three chapters that follow highlight the changes. Chapter 13 turns the spotlight on the new empires of those three centuries—European, Middle Eastern, and Asian. New global patterns of long-distance trade in spices, sugar, silver, fur, and slaves represent the themes of Chapter 14. New cultural trends—both within the major religious traditions of the world and in the emergence of modern science—come together in Chapter 15. With the benefit of hindsight, we may see many of these developments as harbingers of a modern world to come, but from the viewpoint of 1700 or so, the future was open and uncertain, as it almost always is.

Mapping Part Four

North American Fur Trade
Chapter 14

Britain's thirteen colonies
Chapters 13, 15

Spain's American Empire
Chapters 13, 15

Slave trade
Chapter 14

Potosi silver mines
Chapter 14

Brazil / Portuguese Empire
Chapter 14, 15

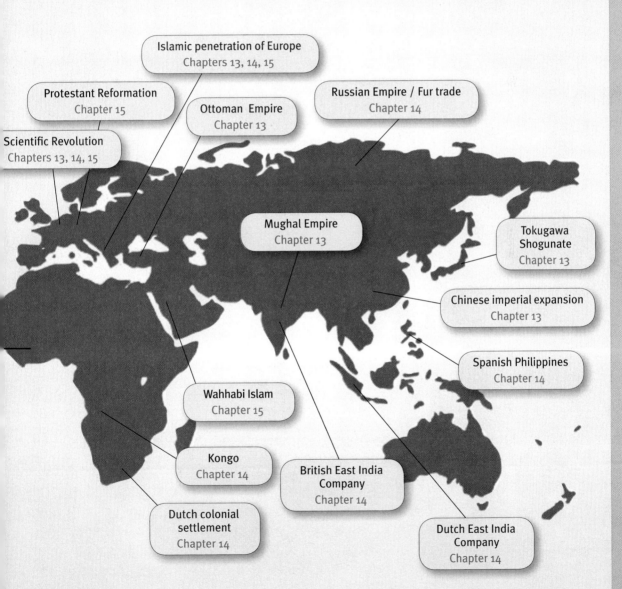

Islamic penetration of Europe
Chapters 13, 14, 15

Protestant Reformation
Chapter 15

Ottoman Empire
Chapter 13

Russian Empire / Fur trade
Chapter 14

Scientific Revolution
Chapters 13, 14, 15

Mughal Empire
Chapter 13

Tokugawa
Shogunate
Chapter 13

Chinese imperial expansion
Chapter 13

Spanish Philippines
Chapter 14

Wahhabi Islam
Chapter 15

Kongo
Chapter 14

British East India
Company
Chapter 14

Dutch colonial
settlement
Chapter 14

Dutch East India
Company
Chapter 14

Political Transformations

Empires and Encounters

1450–1750

Only a few pedestrians crossing Moscow's central square actually witnessed the death of their country, the Soviet Union—a communist giant and archrival of the United States during the cold war. It was about 7:30 p.m. on December 25, 1991, when the red flag of the Soviet Union was lowered for the last time from its perch high above the Kremlin, replaced by the tricolor flag of the new Russian republic. Soviet President Gorbachev formally resigned his office and gave a brief farewell address to the citizens of a now vanished country. Those events symbolized many endings—of the Communist Party in the land of its birth, of a state-controlled economy, of socialism as a viable ideology, of an international superpower. It also marked the end of an empire, for the Soviet Union had maintained the old Russian Empire, constructed over many centuries, bringing Ukrainians, Lithuanians, Georgians, Kazaks, and many other peoples under Russian rule. Now that empire splintered into fifteen separate and independent states. While many rejoiced in the collapse of the often brutal and economically bankrupt Soviet regime, others mourned the loss of empire and the great power status that it conveyed. In 2005, Russian President Vladimir Putin declared the Soviet collapse "the greatest geopolitical catastrophe of the twentieth century...a genuine tragedy." Many of his countrymen agreed.

THE DOWNFALL OF THE RUSSIAN EMPIRE/SOVIET UNION was but the last of a long list of empires that perished during the twentieth century: the Austro-Hungarian, German, and Ottoman empires after World

The Mughal Empire: Among the most magnificent of the early modern empires was that of the Mughals in India. In this painting by an unknown Mughal artist, the seventeenth-century emperor Shah Jahan is holding a *durbar*, or ceremonial assembly, in the audience hall of his palace. The material splendor of the setting shows the immense wealth of the court, while the halo around Shah Jahan's head indicates the special spiritual grace or enlightenment associated with emperors. (© British Library Board, Add or 385)

War I; the British, French, Belgian, Italian, and Portuguese empires in the aftermath of World War II. Elsewhere, Uighurs and Tibetans challenged Chinese rule, while Cubans, Vietnamese, Afghans, and others resisted American domination. Empire building was thoroughly discredited during the twentieth century as "imperialist" became a term of insult rather than a source of pride.

How very different were the three centuries (1450–1750) of the early modern era, when empire building was a global process! Of those empires, none were more significant than the European colonies—Spanish, Portuguese, British, French, and Dutch—constructed all across the Western Hemisphere. Within those empires, vast transformations took place: old societies were destroyed, and new societies arose as Native Americans, Europeans, and Africans came into sustained contact with one another for the first time in world history. It was a revolutionary encounter with implications that extended far beyond the Americas themselves.

But European empires in the Americas were not alone on the imperial stage of the early modern era. Across the immense expanse of Siberia, the Russians constructed what was then the world's largest territorial empire, making Russia an Asian as well as a European power. Qing (chihng) dynasty China penetrated deep into Inner Asia, doubling the size of the country while incorporating millions of non-Chinese people who practiced Islam, Buddhism, or animistic religions. On the South Asian peninsula, the Islamic Mughal Empire brought Hindus and Muslims into a closer relationship than ever before, sometimes quite peacefully and at other times with great conflict. In the Middle East, the Turkish Ottoman Empire reestablished something of the earlier political unity of heartland Islam and posed a serious military and religious threat to European Christendom.

Thus the early modern era was an age of empire. Within their borders, those empires mixed and mingled diverse peoples in a wide variety of ways. Those relationships represented a new stage in the globalization process and new arenas of cross-cultural encounter. The transformations they set in motion echo still in the twenty-first century.

SEEKING THE MAIN POINT

In what ways did European empires in the Americas resemble their Russian, Chinese, Mughal, and Ottoman counterparts, and in what respects were they different? Do you find the similarities or the differences most striking?

European Empires in the Americas

Among the early modern empires, those of Western Europe were distinctive because the conquered territories lay an ocean away from the imperial heartland, rather than adjacent to it. Following the breakthrough voyages of Columbus, the Spanish focused their empire-building efforts in the Caribbean and then, in the early sixteenth century, turned to the mainland, with stunning conquests of the powerful but fragile Aztec and Inca empires. Meanwhile the Portuguese established themselves along the coast of present-day Brazil. In the early seventeenth century, the British, French, and Dutch launched colonial settlements along the eastern coast of North America. From these beginnings, Europeans extended their empires to encompass most of the Americas, at

A Map of Time

1453	Ottoman conquest of Constantinople
1464–1591	Songhay Empire in West Africa
1480	Russia emerges from Mongol rule
1494	Treaty of Tordesillas divides the Americas between Spain and Portugal
1501	Safavid Empire established in Persia/Iran
1519–1521	Spanish conquest of Aztec Empire
1526	Mughal Empire established in India
1529	Ottoman siege of Vienna
1530s	First Portuguese plantations in Brazil
1532–1540	Spanish conquest of Inca Empire
1550	Russian expansion across Siberia begins
1565	Spanish takeover of Philippines begins
1607	Jamestown, VA: first permanent English settlement in Americas
1608	French colony established in Quebec
1680–1760	Chinese expansion into Inner Asia
1683	Second Ottoman siege of Vienna
After 1707	Fragmentation of Mughal Empire

least nominally, by the mid-eighteenth century (see Map 13.1). It was a remarkable achievement. What had made it possible?

The European Advantage

Geography provides a starting point for explaining Europe's American empires. Countries on the Atlantic rim of Europe (Portugal, Spain, Britain, and France) were simply closer to the Americas than were any potential Asian competitors. Furthermore, the fixed winds of the Atlantic blew steadily in the same direction. Once these air currents were understood and mastered, they provided a far different maritime environment than the alternating monsoon winds of the Indian Ocean, in which Asian powers had long operated. European innovations in mapmaking, navigation, sailing techniques, and ship design — building on earlier models from the Mediterranean, Indian Ocean, and Chinese regions — likewise enabled their penetration of the Atlantic Ocean. The enormously rich markets of the Indian Ocean world provided little

■ **Connection**

What enabled Europeans to carve out huge empires an ocean away from their homelands?

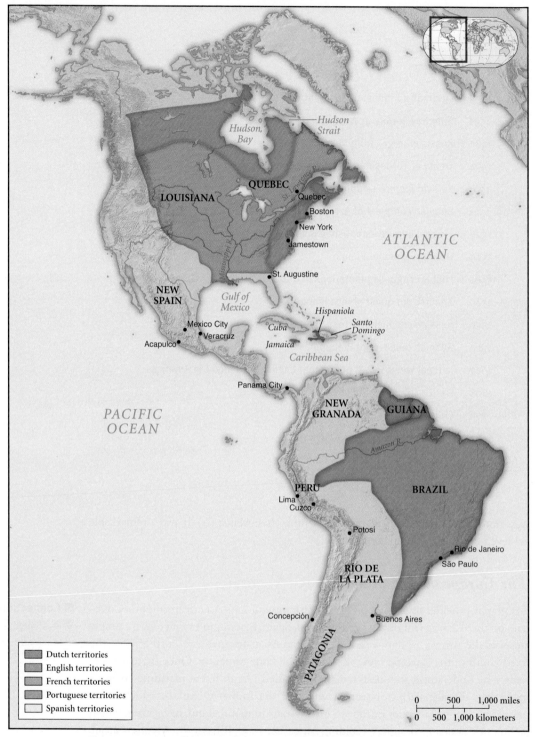

Map 13.1   European Colonial Empires in the Americas

By the beginning of the eighteenth century, European powers had laid claim to most of the Western Hemisphere. Their wars and rivalries during that century led to an expansion of Spanish and English claims, at the expense of the French.

incentive for its Chinese, Indian, or Muslim participants to venture much beyond their own waters.

Europeans, however, were powerfully motivated to do so. After 1200 or so, European elites were increasingly aware of their region's marginal position in the rich world of Eurasian commerce and were determined to gain access to that world. Furthermore, as European populations recovered from the plagues of the fourteenth century, their economies, based on wheat and livestock, could expand significantly only by adding new territory. The growing desire in Europe for grain, sugar, meat, and fish meant that "Europe needed a larger land base to support the expansion of its economy."[1] Beyond these economic or ecological motivations, rulers were driven by the enduring rivalries of competing states. The growing and relatively independent merchant class in a rapidly commercializing Europe sought direct access to Asian wealth to avoid the reliance on Muslim intermediaries that they found so distasteful. Impoverished nobles and commoners alike found opportunity for gaining wealth and status in the colonies. Missionaries and others were inspired by crusading zeal to enlarge the realm of Christendom. Persecuted minorities were in search of a new start in life. All of these compelling motives drove the relentlessly expanding imperial frontier in the Americas. Summarizing their intentions, one Spanish conquistador declared: "We came here to serve God and the King, and also to get rich."[2]

In carving out these empires, often against great odds and with great difficulty, Europeans nonetheless bore certain advantages, despite their distance from home. Their states and trading companies enabled the effective mobilization of both human and material resources. (See Document 13.4, pp. 657–58, for French state-building efforts.) Their seafaring technology, built on Chinese and Islamic precedents, allowed them to cross the Atlantic with growing ease, transporting people and supplies across great distances. Their ironworking technology, gunpowder weapons, and horses initially had no parallel in the Americas, although many peoples subsequently acquired them.

Divisions within and between local societies provided allies for the determined European invaders. Various subject peoples of the Aztec Empire, for example, resented Mexica domination and willingly joined Hernán Cortés in the Spanish assault on that empire (see Visual Sources: The Conquest of Mexico Through Aztec Eyes, pp. 660–67; the portrait of Doña Marina, pp. 622–23). Much of the Inca elite, according to a recent study, "actually welcomed the Spanish invaders as liberators and willingly settled down with them to share rule of Andean farmers and miners."[3] A violent dispute between two rival contenders for the Inca throne, the brothers Atahualpa and Huáscar, certainly helped the European invaders. Perhaps the most significant of European advantages lay in their germs and diseases, to which Native Americans had no immunities. Those diseases decimated society after society, sometimes in advance of the Europeans' actual arrival. In particular regions such as the Caribbean, Virginia, and New England, the rapid buildup of immigrant populations, coupled with the sharply diminished native numbers, allowed Europeans to actually outnumber local peoples within a few decades.

Doña Marina,
Between Two Worlds[4]

In her brief life, she was known variously as Malinal, Doña Marina, and La Malinche. By whatever name, she was a woman who experienced the encounter of the Old World and the New in particularly intimate ways, even as she became a bridge between them. Born around 1505, Malinal was the daughter of an elite and cultured family in the borderlands between the Mayan and Aztec cultures in what is now southern Mexico. Two dramatic events decisively shaped her life. The first occurred when her father died and her mother remarried, bearing a son to her new husband. To protect this boy's inheritance, Malinal's family sold her into slavery. Eventually, she came into the possession of a Maya chieftain in Tobasco on the Gulf of Mexico.

Here her second life-changing event took place in March 1519, when the Spanish conquistador Hernán Cortés landed his troops and inflicted a sharp military defeat on Tobasco. In the negotiations that followed, Tobasco authorities rendered lavish gifts to the Spanish,

Doña Marina (left) translating for Cortés. (Biblioteca Nacional Madrid/Gianni Dagli Orti/ The Art Archive/Art Resource, NY)

including twenty women, one of whom was Malinal. Described by Bernal Díaz, one of Cortés's associates, as "good-looking, intelligent, and self-assured," the teenage Malinal soon found herself in service to Cortés himself. Since Spanish men were not supposed to touch non-Christian women, these newcomers were distributed among his officers, quickly baptized, and given Christian names. Thus Malinal became Doña Marina.

With a ready ear for languages and already fluent in Maya and Nahuatl, the language of the Aztecs, Doña Marina soon picked up Spanish and quickly became indispensable to Cortés as an interpreter, cross-cultural broker, and strategist. She accompanied him on his march inland to the Aztec capital, Tenochtitlán, and on several occasions her language skills and cultural awareness allowed her to uncover spies and plots that might well have seriously impeded Cortés's defeat of the Aztec empire. Díaz reported that "Doña Marina, who understood full well what was happening, told [Cortés] what was going on." In the Aztec

The Great Dying

Whatever combination of factors explains the European acquisition of their empires in the Americas, there is no doubting their global significance. Chief among those consequences was the demographic collapse of Native American societies. Although precise figures remain the subject of much debate, scholars generally agree that the pre-Columbian population of the Western Hemisphere was substantial, perhaps 60 to 80 million. The greatest concentrations of people lived in the Mesoamerican and Andean zones, which were dominated by the Aztec and Inca empires. Long isolation from the Afro-Eurasian world and the lack of most domesticated animals meant the absence of acquired immunities to Old World diseases such as smallpox, measles, typhus, influenza, malaria, and yellow fever.

Therefore, when they came into contact with these European and African diseases, Native American peoples died in appalling numbers, in many cases up to 90 percent capital, where Cortés took the Emperor Moctezuma captive, it fell to Doña Marina to persuade him to accept this humiliating position and surrender his wealth to the Spanish. Even Cortés, who was never very gracious with his praise for her, acknowledged that "after God, we owe this conquest of New Spain to Doña Marina." Aztecs soon came to see this young woman as the voice of Cortés, referring to her as La Malinche, a Spanish approximation of her original name. So paired did Cortés and La Malinche become in Aztec thinking that Cortés himself was often called "Malinche." (See Visual Source 13.2, p. 663, for an Aztec image of La Malinche.)

More than an interpreter for Cortés, Doña Marina also became his mistress and bore him a son. But after the initial conquest of Mexico was complete and he no longer needed her skills, Cortés married Doña Marina off to another Spanish conquistador, Juan Jaramillo, with whom she lived until her death, probably around 1530. Cortés did provide her with several pieces of land, one of which, ironically, had belonged to Moctezuma. Her son, however, was taken from her and raised in Spain.

In 1523, Doña Marina performed one final service for Cortés, accompanying him on a mission to Honduras to suppress a rebellion. There her personal life seemed to come full circle, for near her hometown, she encountered her mother, who had sold her into slavery, and her half-brother.

Díaz reported that they "were very much afraid of Doña Marina," thinking that they would surely be put to death by their now powerful and well-connected offspring. But Doña Marina quickly reassured and forgave them, while granting them "many golden jewels and some clothes."

In the centuries since her death, Doña Marina has been highly controversial. For much of the colonial era, she was viewed positively as an ally of the Spanish. But after independence, some came to see her as a traitor to her own people, shunning her heritage and siding with the invaders. Still others have considered her as the mother of Mexico's mixed-race or mestizo culture. Should she be understood primarily as a victim or as a skillful survivor negotiating hard choices under difficult circumstances?

Whatever the judgments of later generations, Doña Marina herself seems to have made a clear choice to cast her lot with the Europeans. Even when Cortés had given her to another man, Doña Marina expressed no regret. According to Díaz, she declared, "Even if they were to make me mistress of all the provinces of New Spain, I would refuse the honor, for I would rather serve my husband and Cortés than anything else in the world."

Questions: How might you define the significance of Doña Marina's life? In what larger contexts might that life find a place?

---

of the population. The densely settled peoples of Caribbean islands virtually vanished within fifty years of Columbus's arrival. Central Mexico, with a population estimated at some 10 to 20 million, declined to about 1 million by 1650. A native Nahuatl (nah-watl) account depicted the social breakdown that accompanied the smallpox pandemic: "A great many died from this plague, and many others died of hunger. They could not get up to search for food, and everyone else was too sick to care for them, so they starved to death in their beds."[5]

The situation was similar in North America. A Dutch observer in New Netherland (later New York) reported in 1656 that "the Indians . . . affirm that before the arrival of the Christians, and before the small pox broke out amongst them, they were ten times as numerous as they are now, and that their population had been melted down by this disease, whereof nine-tenths of them have died."[6] To Governor Bradford of Plymouth colony (in present-day Massachusetts), such conditions represented the "good hand of God" at work, "sweeping away great multitudes of the

Disease and Death among the Aztecs
Smallpox, which accompanied the Spanish to the Americas, devastated native populations. This image, drawn by an Aztec artist and contained in the sixteenth-century *Florentine Codex*, illustrates the impact of the disease in Mesoamerica. (Private Collection / Peter Newark American Pictures/The Bridgeman Art Library)

■ **Change**
What large-scale transformations did European empires generate?

natives . . . that he might make room for us."[7] Not until the late seventeenth century did native numbers begin to recuperate somewhat from this catastrophe, and even then not everywhere.

The Columbian Exchange

In sharply diminishing the population of the Americas, the "great dying" created an acute labor shortage and certainly did make room for immigrant newcomers, both colonizing Europeans and enslaved Africans. Over the several centuries of the colonial era and beyond, various combinations of indigenous, European, and African peoples created entirely new societies in the Americas, largely replacing the many and varied cultures that had flourished before 1492. To those colonial societies, Europeans and Africans brought not only their germs and their people but also their plants and animals. Wheat, rice, sugarcane, grapes, and many garden vegetables and fruits, as well as numerous weeds, took hold in the Americas, where they transformed the landscape and made possible a recognizably European diet and way of life. Even more revolutionary were their animals—horses, pigs, cattle, goats, sheep—all of which were new to the Americas and multiplied spectacularly in an environment largely free of natural predators. These domesticated animals made possible the ranching economies and cowboy cultures of both North and South America. Horses also transformed many Native American societies, particularly in the North American West as settled farming peoples such as the Pawnee abandoned their fields to hunt bison from horseback. In the process, women lost much of their earlier role as food producers as a male-dominated hunting and warrior culture emerged. Both environmentally and socially, it was nothing less than revolutionary.

In the other direction, American food crops such as corn, potatoes, and cassava spread widely in the Eastern Hemisphere, where they provided the nutritional foundation for the immense population growth that became everywhere a hallmark of the modern era. In Europe, calories derived from corn and potatoes helped push human numbers from some 60 million in 1400 to 390 million in 1900. Those Amerindian crops later provided cheap and reasonably nutritious food for millions of industrial workers. Potatoes especially allowed Ireland's population to grow enormously and then condemned many of them to starvation or emigration when an airborne fungus, also from the Americas, destroyed the crop in the mid-nineteenth century. In China, corn, peanuts, and especially sweet potatoes supplemented the traditional rice and wheat to sustain China's modern population explosion. By the early twentieth century, food plants of American origin represented about 20 percent of total Chinese food production. In Africa, corn took hold quickly and was used as a cheap food for the human cargoes of the transatlantic trade. Scholars have speculated that corn, together with peanuts and cassava, underwrote some of Africa's population growth and partially offset the population drain of the slave trade.

Beyond food crops, American stimulants such as tobacco and chocolate were soon used around the world. By the seventeenth century, how-to manuals instructed Chinese users on smoking techniques, while tobacco became, in the words of one enamored Chinese poet, "the gentleman's companion, it warms my heart and leaves my mouth feeling like a divine furnace."[8] Tea from China and coffee from the Islamic world also spread globally, contributing to this worldwide biological exchange. Never before in human history had such a large-scale and consequential diffusion of plants and animals operated to remake the biological environment of the planet.

Furthermore, the societies that developed within the American colonies drove the processes of globalization and reshaped the world economy of the early modern era (see Chapter 14 for a more extended treatment). The silver mines of Mexico and Peru fueled both transatlantic and transpacific commerce, encouraged Spain's unsuccessful effort to dominate Europe, and enabled Europeans to buy the Chinese tea, silk, and porcelain that they valued so highly. The plantation owners of the tropical lowland regions needed workers and found them by the millions in Africa. The slave trade, which brought these workers to the colonies, and the sugar and cotton trade, which distributed the fruits of their labor abroad, created a lasting link among Africa, Europe, and the Americas, while scattering peoples of African origin throughout the Western Hemisphere.

This enormous network of communication, migration, trade, disease, and the transfer of plants and animals, all generated by European colonial empires in the Americas, has been dubbed the "Columbian exchange." It gave rise to something wholly new in world history: an interacting Atlantic world connecting four continents. Millions of years ago, the Eastern and Western hemispheres had physically drifted apart, and, ecologically speaking, they had remained largely apart. Now these two "old worlds" were joined, increasingly creating a single biological regime, a "new world" of global dimensions.

The long-term benefits of this Atlantic network were very unequally distributed. Western Europeans were clearly the dominant players in the Atlantic world, and their societies reaped the greatest rewards. Mountains of new information flooded into Europe, shaking up conventional understandings of the world and contributing to a revolutionary new way of thinking known as the Scientific Revolution. The wealth of the colonies—precious metals, natural resources, new food crops, slave labor, financial profits, colonial markets—provided one of the foundations on which Europe's Industrial Revolution was built. The colonies also provided an outlet for the rapidly growing population of European societies and represented an enormous extension of European civilization. In short, the colonial empires of the Americas greatly facili-tated a changing global balance of power, which now thrust the previously marginal Western Europeans into an increasingly central and commanding role on the world stage. "Without a New World to deliver economic balance in the Old," concluded a prominent world historian, "Europe would have remained inferior, as ever, in wealth and power, to the great civilizations of Asia."[9]

Comparing Colonial Societies in the Americas

What the Europeans had encountered across the Atlantic was another "old world," but their actions surely gave rise to a "new world" in the Americas. Their colonial empires — Spanish, Portuguese, British, and French alike — did not simply conquer and govern established societies, but rather generated wholly new societies, born of the decimation of Native American populations and the introduction of European and African peoples, cultures, plants, and animals.

Furthermore, all the European rulers of these empires viewed their realms through the lens of the prevailing economic theory known as mercantilism. This view held that European governments served their countries' economic interests best by encourag-ing exports and accumulating bullion (precious metals such as silver and gold), which were believed to be the source of national prosperity. In this scheme of things, colo-nies provided closed markets for the manufactured goods of the "mother country" and, if they were lucky, supplied great quantities of bullion as well. Mercantilist think-ing thus fueled European wars and colonial rivalries around the world in the early modern era. Particularly in Spanish America, however, it was a theory largely ignored or evaded in practice. Spain had few manufactured goods to sell, and piracy and smug-gling allowed Spanish colonists to exchange goods with Spain's rivals.

But variations across the immense colonial world of the Western Hemisphere were at least as noticeable as these similarities. Some differences grew out of the so-cieties of the colonizing power such as the contrast between a semi-feudal and Catho-lic Spain and a more rapidly changing Protestant England. The kind of economy es-tablished in particular regions — settler-dominated agriculture, slave-based plantations, ranching, or mining — likewise influenced their development. So too did the char-acter of the Native American cultures — the more densely populated and urbanized Mesoamerican and Andean civilizations versus the more sparsely populated rural villages of North America, for example.

Furthermore, women and men often experienced colonial intrusion in quite dis-tinct ways. Beyond the common burdens of violent conquest, epidemic disease, and coerced labor, both Native American and enslaved African women had to cope with the additional demands made on them as females. Conquest was often accompanied by the transfer of women to the new colonial rulers. Cortés, for example, marked his alliance with the city of Tlaxcala (tlah-SKAH-lah) against the Aztecs by an ex-change of gifts in which he received hundreds of female slaves and eight daughters of elite Tlaxcala families, whom he distributed to his soldiers. And from the Aztec ruler he demanded: "You are to deliver women with light skins, corn, chicken, eggs, and tortillas."[10]

Soon after conquest, many Spanish men married elite native women. It was a long-standing practice in Amerindian societies and was encouraged by both Spanish and indigenous male authorities as a means of cementing their new relationship. It was also advantageous for some of the women involved. One of Moctezuma's daughters, who was mistress to Cortés and eventually married several other Spaniards, wound up with the largest landed estate in the valley of Mexico. Below this elite level of interaction, however, far more women experienced sexual violence and abuse. Rape accompanied conquest in many places, and dependent or enslaved women working under the control of European men frequently found themselves required to perform sexual services. This was tragedy and humiliation for native and enslaved men as well, for they were unable to protect their women. Such variations in culture, policy, economy, and gender generated quite different colonial societies in several major regions of the Americas.

In the Lands of the Aztecs and the Incas

The Spanish conquest of the Aztec and Inca empires in the early sixteenth century gave Spain access to the most wealthy, urbanized, and densely populated regions of the Western Hemisphere. Within a century and well before the British had even begun their colonizing efforts in North America, the Spanish in Mexico and Peru had established nearly a dozen major cities; several impressive universities; hundreds of cathedrals, churches, and missions; an elaborate administrative bureaucracy; and a network of regulated international commerce.

The economic foundation for this emerging colonial society lay in commercial agriculture, much of it on large rural estates, and in silver and gold mining. In both cases, native peoples, rather than African slaves or European workers, provided most of the labor, despite their much-diminished numbers. Almost everywhere it was forced labor, often directly required by colonial authorities. In a legal system known as *encomienda*, the Spanish crown granted to particular Spanish settlers a number of local native people from whom they could require labor, gold, or agricultural produce and to whom they owed "protection" and instruction in the Christian faith. It turned into an exploitative regime not far removed from slavery and was replaced by similar system, *repartimiento*, with slightly more control by the crown and Spanish officials. By the seventeenth century the *hacienda* system had taken shape by which the owners of large estates directly employed native workers. With low wages, high taxes, and large debts to the landowners, the *peons* who worked these estates enjoyed little control over their lives or their livelihood.

On this economic base, a distinctive social order grew up, replicating something of the Spanish class and gender hierarchy while accommodating the racially and culturally different Indians and Africans as well as growing numbers of racially mixed people. At the top of this colonial society were the male Spanish settlers, who were

■ **Change**
What was the economic foundation of colonial rule in Mexico and Peru? How did it shape the kinds of societies that arose there?

politically and economically dominant and seeking to become a landed aristocracy. One Spanish official commented in 1619: "The Spaniards, from the able and rich to the humble and poor, all hold themselves to be lords and will not serve [do manual labor]."[11] Politically, they increasingly saw themselves not as colonials, but as residents of a Spanish kingdom, subject to the Spanish monarch, yet separate and distinct from Spain itself and deserving of a large measure of self-government. Therefore, they chafed under the heavy bureaucratic restrictions imposed by the Crown. "I obey but I do not enforce" was a slogan that reflected local authorities' resistance to orders from Spain.

But the Spanish minority, never more than 20 percent of the population, was itself a divided community. Descendants of the original conquistadores sought to protect their privileges against immigrant newcomers; Spaniards born in the Americas (*creoles*) resented the pretensions to superiority of those born in Spain (*peninsulares*); landowning Spaniards felt threatened by the growing wealth of commercial and mer-

Racial Mixing in Colonial Mexico

This eighteenth-century painting by the famous Zapotec artist Miguel Cabrera shows a Spanish man, a *mestiza* woman, and their child, who was labeled as *castiza*. By the twentieth century, such mixed-race people represented the majority of the population of Mexico, and cultural blending had become a central feature of the country's identity. (Scala/Art Resource, NY)

cantile groups practicing less prestigious occupations. Spanish missionaries and church authorities were often sharply critical of how these settlers treated native peoples. While Spanish women shared the racial privileges of their husbands, they were clearly subordinate in gender terms, unable to hold public office and viewed as weak and in need of male protection. But they were also regarded as the "bearers of civilization," and through their capacity to produce legitimate children, they were the essential link for transmitting male wealth, honor, and status to future generations. This required strict control of their sexuality and a continuation of the Iberian obsession with "purity of blood." In Spain, that concern had focused on potential liaisons with Jews and Muslims; in the colonies the alleged threat to female virtue derived from Native American and African men.

From a male viewpoint, the problem with Spanish women was that there were very few of them. This demographic fact led to the most distinctive feature of these new colonial societies in Mexico and Peru—the emergence of a *mestizo* (mehs-TEE-zoh), or mixed-race, population, initially the product of unions between Spanish men and Indian women. Rooted in the sexual imbalance among Spanish immigrants (seven men to one woman in early colonial Peru, for example), the emergence of a mestizo population was facilitated by the desire of many surviving Indian women for the relative security of life in a Spanish household, where they and their children would not be subject to the abuse and harsh demands made on native peoples. Over the 300 years of the colonial era, mestizo numbers grew substantially, becoming the majority of the population in Mexico sometime during the nineteenth century. Such mixed-race people were divided into dozens of separate groups known as *castas* (castes), based on their racial heritage and skin color.

Mestizos were largely Hispanic in culture, but Spaniards looked down on them during much of the colonial era, regarding them as illegitimate, for many were not born of "proper" marriages. Despite this attitude, their growing numbers and the economic usefulness of their men as artisans, clerks, supervisors of labor gangs, and lower-level officials in both church and state bureaucracies led to their recognition as a distinct social group. *Mestizas*, women of mixed racial background, worked as domestic servants or in their husbands' shops, wove cloth, manufactured candles and cigars, in addition to performing domestic duties. A few became quite wealthy. An illiterate mestiza named Mencia Perez married successively two reasonably well-to-do Spanish men and upon their deaths took over their businesses, becoming in her own right a very rich woman by the 1590s. At that point no one would have referred to her as a mestiza.[12] Particularly in Mexico, mestizo identity blurred the sense of sharp racial difference between Spanish and Indian peoples and became a major element in the identity of modern Mexico.

At the bottom of Mexican and Peruvian colonial societies were the indigenous peoples, known to Europeans as "Indians." Traumatized by "the great dying," they were subject to gross abuse and exploitation as the primary labor force for the mines and estates of the Spanish Empire and were required to render tribute payments to their Spanish overlords. Their empires dismantled by Spanish conquest, their religions attacked by Spanish missionaries, and their diminished numbers forcibly relocated into larger settlements, many Indians gravitated toward the world of their conquerors. Many learned Spanish; converted to Christianity; moved to cities to work for wages; ate the meat of cows, chickens, and pigs; used plows and draft animals rather than traditional digging sticks; and took their many grievances to Spanish courts. Indian women endured some distinctive conditions as Spanish legal codes generally defined them as minors rather than responsible adults. As those codes took hold, Indian women were increasingly excluded from the courts or represented by their menfolk. This made it more difficult to maintain female property rights. In 1804, for example, a Maya legal petition identified eight men and ten women from a particular family as owners of a piece of land, but the Spanish translation omitted the women's names altogether.[13]

But much that was native persisted. At the local level, Indian male authorities retained a measure of autonomy, and traditional markets operated regularly. Both Andean and Maya women continued to leave personal property to their female descendants. Maize, beans, and squash persisted as the major elements of Indian diets in Mexico. Christian saints in many places blended easily with specialized indigenous gods, while belief in magic, folk medicine, and communion with the dead remained strong (see pp. 728–32). Memories of the past also endured. The Tupac Amaru revolt in Peru during 1780–1781 was made in the name of the last independent Inca emperor. In that revolt, the wife of the leader, Micaela Bastidas, was referred to as La Coya, the female Inca, evoking the parallel hierarchies of male and female officials who had earlier governed the Inca Empire. (See Chapter 12, pp. 584–86.)

Thus Spaniards, mestizos, and Indians represented the major social categories in the colonial lands of what had been the Inca and Aztec empires, while African slaves and freemen were less numerous than elsewhere in the Americas. Despite the sharp divisions among these groups, some movement was possible. Indians who acquired an education, wealth, and some European culture might "pass" as mestizo. Likewise more fortunate mestizo families might be accepted as Spaniards over time. Colonial Spanish America was a vast laboratory of ethnic mixing and cultural change. It was dominated by Europeans to be sure, but with a rather more fluid and culturally blended society than in the racially rigid colonies of British North America.

Colonies of Sugar

■ Comparison

How did the plantation societies of Brazil and the Caribbean differ from those of southern colonies in British North America?

A second and quite different kind of colonial society emerged in the lowland areas of Brazil, ruled by Portugal, and in the Spanish, British, French, and Dutch colonies in the Caribbean. These regions lacked the great civilizations of Mexico and Peru. Nor did they provide much mineral wealth until the Brazilian gold rush of the 1690s and the discovery of diamonds a little later. Still, Europeans found a very profitable substitute in sugar, which was much in demand in Europe, where it was used as a medicine, a spice, a sweetener, a preservative, and in sculptured forms as a decoration that indicated high status. Although commercial agriculture in the Spanish Empire served a domestic market in its towns and mining camps, these sugar-based colonies produced almost exclusively for export, while importing their food and other necessities.

Large-scale sugar production had been pioneered by Arabs, who introduced it into the Mediterranean. Europeans learned the technique and transferred it to their Atlantic island possessions and then to the Americas. For a century (1570–1670), Portuguese planters along the northeast coast of Brazil dominated the world market for sugar. Then the British, French, and Dutch turned their Caribbean territories into highly productive sugar-producing colonies, breaking the Portuguese and Brazilian monopoly.

Sugar decisively transformed Brazil and the Caribbean. Its production, which involved both growing the sugarcane and processing it into usable sugar, was very labor intensive and could most profitably occur in a large-scale, almost industrial setting. It was perhaps the first modern industry in that it produced for an international and mass market, using capital and expertise from Europe, with production facilities located in the Americas. However, its most characteristic feature—the massive use of slave labor—was an ancient practice. In the absence of a Native American population, which had been almost totally wiped out in the Caribbean or had fled inland in Brazil, European sugarcane planters turned to Africa and the Atlantic slave trade for an alternative workforce. The vast majority of the African captives transported across the Atlantic, some 80 percent or more, ended up in Brazil and the Caribbean. (See Chapter 14 for a more extensive description of the Atlantic slave trade.)

Slaves worked on sugar-producing estates in horrendous conditions. The heat and fire from the cauldrons, which turned raw sugarcane into crystallized sugar, reminded many visitors of scenes from hell. These conditions, combined with disease, generated a high death rate, perhaps 5 to 10 percent per year, which required plantation owners to constantly import fresh slaves. A Jesuit observer in 1580 aptly summarized the situation: "The work is great and many die."[14]

Women made up about half of the field gangs that did the heavy work of planting and harvesting sugarcane. They were subject to the same brutal punishments and received the same rations as their male counterparts, though they were seldom permitted to undertake the more skilled labor inside the sugar mills. Women who worked in urban areas, mostly for white female owners, did domestic chores and were often hired out as laborers in various homes, shops, laundries, inns, and brothels. Discouraged from establishing stable families, women had to endure, often alone, the wrenching separation from their children that occurred when they were sold. Mary Prince,

Plantation Life in the Caribbean
This painting from 1823 shows the use of slave labor on a plantation in Antigua, a British-ruled island in the Caribbean. Notice the overseer with a whip supervising the tilling and planting of the field. (HIP/Art Resource, NY)

a Caribbean slave, who wrote a brief account of her life, recalled the pain of families torn apart: "The great God above alone knows the thoughts of the poor slave's heart, and the bitter pains which follow such separations as these. All that we love taken away from us—oh, it is sad, sad! and sore to be borne!"[15]

The extensive use of African slave labor gave these plantation colonies a very different ethnic and racial makeup than that of highland Spanish America, as the Snapshot indicates. Thus, after three centuries of colonial rule, a substantial majority of Brazil's population was either partially or wholly of African descent. In the French Caribbean colony of Haiti in 1790, the corresponding figure was 93 percent.

As in Spanish America, a considerable amount of racial mixing took place in Brazil. Cross-racial unions accounted for only about 10 percent of all marriages in Brazil, but the use of concubines and informal liaisons among Indians, Africans, and Portuguese produced a substantial mixed-race population. From their ranks derived much of the urban skilled workforce and supervisors in the sugar industry. *Mulattoes*, the product of Portuguese-African unions, predominated, but as many as forty separate and named groups, each indicating a different racial mixture, emerged in colonial Brazil.

The plantation complex of the Americas, based on African slavery, extended beyond the Caribbean and Brazil to encompass the southern colonies of British North America, where tobacco, cotton, rice, and indigo were major crops, but the social outcomes of these plantation colonies were quite different from those farther south. Because European women had joined the colonial migration to North America at an early date, these colonies experienced less racial mixing and certainly demonstrated less willingness to recognize the offspring of such unions and accord them a place in society. A sharply defined racial system (with black Africans, "red" Native Americans, and white Europeans) evolved in North America, whereas both Portuguese and Spanish colonies acknowledged a wide variety of mixed-race groups.

Slavery too was different, being perhaps somewhat less harsh in North America than in the sugar colonies. By 1750 or so, slaves in what became the United States proved able to reproduce themselves, and by the time of the Civil War almost all North American slaves had been born in the New World. That was never the case in Latin America, where large-scale importation of new slaves continued well into the nine-

Snapshot   Ethnic Composition of Colonial Societies in Latin America (1825)[16]

	Highland Spanish America	Portuguese America (Brazil)
Europeans	18.2 percent	23.4 percent
Mixed-race	28.3 percent	17.8 percent
Africans	11.9 percent	49.8 percent
Native Americans	41.7 percent	9.1 percent

teenth century. Nonetheless, many more slaves were voluntarily set free by their owners in Brazil than in North America, and free blacks and mulattoes in Brazil had more economic opportunities than did their counterparts in the United States. At least a few among them found positions as political leaders, scholars, musicians, writers, and artists. Some were even hired as slave catchers.

Does this mean, then, that racism was absent in colonial Brazil? Certainly not, but it was different from racism in North America. For one thing, in North America, any African ancestry, no matter how small or distant, made a person "black"; in Brazil, a person of African and non-African ancestry was considered not black, but some other mixed-race category. Racial prejudice surely persisted, for white characteristics were prized more highly than black features, and people regarded as white had enormously greater privileges and opportunities than others. Nevertheless, skin color in Brazil, and in Latin America generally, was only one criterion of class status, and the perception of color changed with the educational or economic standing of individuals. A light-skinned mulatto who had acquired some wealth or education might well pass as a white. One curious visitor to Brazil was surprised to find a darker-skinned man serving as a local official. "Isn't the governor a mulatto?" inquired the visitor. "He was, but he isn't any more," was the reply. "How can a governor be a mulatto?"[17]

Settler Colonies in North America

A third distinctive type of colonial society emerged in the northern British colonies of New England, New York, and Pennsylvania. Because the British were the last of the European powers to establish a colonial presence in the Americas, a full century after Spain, they found that "only the dregs were left."[18] The lands they acquired were widely regarded in Europe as the unpromising leftovers of the New World, lacking the obvious wealth and sophisticated cultures of the Spanish possessions. Until at least the eighteenth century, these British colonies remained far less prominent on the world stage than those of Spain or Portugal.

The British settlers came from a more rapidly changing society than did those from an ardently Catholic, semi-feudal, authoritarian Spain. When Britain launched its colonial ventures in the seventeenth century, it had already experienced considerable conflict between Catholics and Protestants, the rise of a merchant capitalist class distinct from the nobility, and the emergence of Parliament as a check on the authority of kings. Although they brought much of their English culture with them, many of the British settlers—Puritans in Massachusetts and Quakers in Pennsylvania, for example—sought to escape aspects of an old European society rather than to re-create it, as was the case for most Spanish and Portuguese colonists. The easy availability of land and the outsider status of many British settlers made it even more difficult to follow the Spanish or Portuguese colonial pattern of sharp class hierarchies, large rural estates, and dependent laborers.

Thus men in Puritan New England became independent heads of family farms, a world away from Old England, where most land was owned by nobles and gentry and

■ **Comparison**

What distinguished the British settler colonies of North America from their counterparts in Latin America?

worked by servants, tenants, and paid laborers. But if men escaped the class restrictions of the old country, women were less able to avoid its gender limitations. While Puritan Christianity extolled the family and a woman's role as wife and mother, it reinforced largely unlimited male authority. "Since he is thy Husband," declared Boston minister Rev. Benjamin Wadsworth in 1712 to the colony's women, "God has made him the Head and set him above thee."[19] Women were prosecuted for the crime of "fornication" far more often than their male companions; the inheritance of daughters was substantially less than that of sons; few girls attended school; and while women were the majority of church members, they could never become ministers.

Furthermore, British settlers were far more numerous than their Spanish counterparts, outnumbering them five to one by 1750. This disparity was the most obvious distinguishing feature of the New England and middle Atlantic colonies. By the time of the American Revolution, some 90 percent or more of these colonies' populations were Europeans. Devastating diseases and a highly aggressive military policy had largely cleared the colonies of Native Americans, and their numbers did not rebound in subsequent centuries as they did in the lands of the Aztecs and the Incas. Moreover, slaves were not needed in an agricultural economy dominated by numerous small-scale independent farmers working their own land, although elite families, especially in urban areas, sometimes employed household slaves. These were almost pure settler colonies, without the racial mixing that was so prominent in Spanish and Portuguese territories.

Other differences likewise emerged. A largely Protestant England was far less interested in spreading Christianity among the remaining native peoples than were the large and well-funded missionary societies of Catholic Spain. Although religion loomed large in the North American colonies, the church and colonial state were not so intimately connected as they were in Latin America. The Protestant emphasis on reading the Bible for oneself led to a much greater mass literacy than in Latin America, where three centuries of church education still left some 95 percent of the population illiterate at independence. By contrast, well over 75 percent of white males in British North America were literate by the 1770s, although women's literacy rates were somewhat lower. Furthermore, British settler colonies evolved traditions of local self-government more extensively than in Latin America. Preferring to rely on joint stock companies or wealthy individuals operating under a royal charter, Britain had nothing resembling the elaborate bureaucracy that governed Spanish colonies. For much of the seventeenth century, a prolonged power struggle between the English king and Parliament meant that the British government paid little attention to the internal affairs of the colonies. Therefore, elected colonial assemblies, seeing themselves as little parliaments defending "the rights of Englishmen," vigorously contested the prerogatives of royal governors sent to administer their affairs.

The grand irony of the modern history of the Americas lay in the reversal of long-established relationships between the northern and southern continents. For thousands of years, the major centers of wealth, power, commerce, and innovation lay in

Mesoamerica and the Andes. That pattern continued for much of the colonial era, as the Spanish and Portuguese colonies seemed far more prosperous and successful than their British or French counterparts in North America. In the nineteenth and twentieth centuries, however, the balance shifted. What had once been the "dregs" of the colonial world became the United States, which was more politically stable, more democratic, more economically successful, and more internationally powerful than a divided, unstable, and much less prosperous Latin America.

SUMMING UP SO FAR

In what ways might European empire building in the Americas be understood as a single phenomenon? And in what respects should it be viewed as a set of distinct and separate processes?

The Steppes and Siberia: The Making of a Russian Empire

At the same time as Western Europeans were building their empires in the Americas, the Russian Empire, which subsequently became the world's largest state, was beginning to take shape. When Columbus crossed the Atlantic, a small Russian state centered on the city of Moscow was emerging from two centuries of Mongol rule. That state soon conquered a number of neighboring Russian-speaking cities and incorporated them into its expanding territory. Located on the remote, cold, and heavily forested eastern fringe of Christendom, it was perhaps an unlikely candidate for constructing one of the great empires of the modern era. And yet, over the next three centuries, it did precisely that, extending Russian domination over the vast tundra, forests, and grasslands of northern Asia that lay to the south and east of Moscow, all the way to the Pacific Ocean. Furthermore, Russian expansion westward brought numerous Poles, Germans, Ukrainians, Belorussians, and Baltic peoples into the Russian Empire.

■ Description
What motivated Russian empire building?

Russian attention was drawn first to the grasslands south and east of the Russian heartland, an area long inhabited by various nomadic pastoral peoples, who were organized into feuding tribes and clans and adjusting to the recent disappearance of the Mongol Empire. From the viewpoint of the emerging Russian state, the problem was security because these pastoral peoples, like the Mongols before them, frequently raided their agricultural Russian neighbors and sold many into slavery. To the east across the vast expanse of Siberia, Russian motives were quite different, for the scattered peoples of its endless forests and tundra posed no threat to Russia. Numbering only some 220,000 in the seventeenth century and speaking more than 100 languages, they were mostly hunting, gathering, and herding people, living in small-scale societies and largely without access to gunpowder weapons. What drew the Russians across Siberia was opportunity—primarily the "soft gold" of fur-bearing animals, whose pelts were in great demand on the world market.

Whatever motives drove it, this enormous Russian Empire took shape in the three centuries between 1500 and 1800 (see Map 13.2). A growing line of wooden forts offered protection to frontier towns and trading centers as well as to mounting numbers of Russian farmers. Empire building was an extended process, involving the Russian

Map 13.2   The Russian Empire

From its beginnings as a small principality under Mongol control, Moscow became the center of a vast Russian Empire during the early modern era.

state and its officials as well as a variety of private interests—merchants, hunters, peasant agricultural settlers, churchmen, exiles, criminals, and adventurers. For the Russian migrants to these new eastern lands, the empire offered "economic and social improvements over what they had known at home—from more and better land to fewer lords and officials."[20] Political leaders and educated Russians generally defined the empire in grander terms: defending Russian frontiers; enhancing the power of the Russian state; and bringing Christianity, civilization, and enlightenment to savages. But what did that empire mean to those on its receiving end?

Experiencing the Russian Empire

First, of course, empire meant conquest. Although resistance was frequent, especially from nomadic peoples, in the long run Russian military might, based in modern weaponry and the organizational capacity of a state, brought both the steppes and Siberia under Russian control. Everywhere Russian authorities demanded an oath of allegiance by which native peoples swore "eternal submission to the grand tsar," the monarch of the Russian Empire. They also demanded *yasak*, or "tribute," paid in cash or in kind. In Siberia, this meant enormous quantities of furs, especially the extremely valuable sable, which Siberian peoples were compelled to produce. As in the Americas, devastating epidemics accompanied conquest, particularly in the more remote regions of Siberia, where local people had little immunity to smallpox or measles. Also accompanying conquest was an intermittent pressure to convert to Christianity. Tax breaks, exemptions from paying tribute, and the promise of land or cash provided incentives for conversion, while the destruction of many mosques and the forced resettlement of Muslims added to the pressures. Yet the Russian state did not pursue conversion with the single-minded intensity that Spanish authorities exercised in Latin America, particularly if missionary activity threatened political and social stability. The empress Catherine the Great, for example, established religious tolerance for Muslims in the late eighteenth century and created a state agency to oversee Muslim affairs.

The most profoundly transforming feature of the Russian Empire was the influx of Russian settlers, whose numbers by the end of the eighteenth century had overwhelmed native peoples, giving their lands a distinctively Russian character. By 1720, some 700,000 Russians lived in Siberia, thus reducing the native Siberians to 30 percent of the total population, a figure that dropped to 14 percent in the nineteenth century. The loss of hunting grounds and pasturelands to Russian agricultural settlers undermined long-standing economies and rendered local people dependent on Russian markets for grain, sugar, tea, tobacco, and alcohol. Pressures to encourage pastoralists to abandon their nomadic ways included the requirement to pay fees and to obtain permission to cross agricultural lands. Kazakh herders responded with outrage: "The grass and the water belong to Heaven, and why should we pay any fees?"[21] Intermarriage, prostitution, and sexual abuse resulted in some mixed-race offspring, but these were generally absorbed as Russians rather than identified as distinctive communities, as in Latin America.

Over the course of three centuries, both Siberia and the steppes were incorporated into the Russian state. Their native peoples were not driven into reservations or eradicated as in the Americas. Many of them,

■ **Change**

How did the Russian Empire transform the life of its conquered people and of the Russian homeland itself?

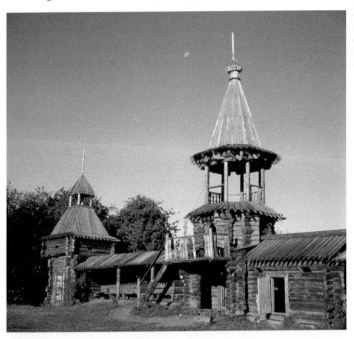

A Cossack Jail

In the vanguard of Russian expansion across Siberia were the Cossacks, bands of fiercely independent warriors consisting of peasants who had escaped serfdom as well as criminals and other adventurers. This seventeenth-century jail was part of an early Cossack settlement on the Kamchatka Peninsula at the easternmost end of Siberia. It illustrates Russian wooden architecture. (Sovfoto/Eastfoto) though, were Russified, adopting the Russian language and converting to Christianity, even as their traditional ways of life—hunting and herding—were much disrupted. The Russian Empire represented the final triumph of an agrarian civilization over the hunting societies of Siberia and over the pastoral peoples of the grasslands.

Russians and Empire

If the empire transformed the conquered peoples, it also fundamentally changed Russia itself. Within an increasingly multiethnic empire, Russians diminished as a proportion of the overall population, although they remained politically dominant. Among the growing number of non-Russians in the empire, Slavic-speaking Ukrainians and Belorussians predominated, while the vast territories of Siberia and the steppes housed numerous separate peoples, but with quite small populations.[22] The wealth of empire—rich agricultural lands, valuable furs, mineral deposits—played a major role in making Russia one of the great powers of Europe by the eighteenth century, and it has enjoyed that position ever since.

Unlike its expansion to the east, Russia's westward movement occurred in the context of military rivalries with the major powers of the region—the Ottoman Empire, Poland, Sweden, Lithuania, Prussia, and Austria. During the late seventeenth and eighteenth centuries, Russia acquired substantial territories in the Baltic region, Poland, and Ukraine. This contact with Europe also fostered an awareness of Russia's backwardness relative to Europe and prompted an extensive program of westernization, particularly under the leadership of Peter the Great (r. 1689–1725). His massive efforts included vast administrative changes, the enlargement and modernization of Russian military forces, a new educational system for the sons of noblemen, and dozens of manufacturing enterprises. Russian nobles were instructed to dress in European styles and to shave their sacred and much-revered beards. The newly created capital city of St. Petersburg was to be Russia's "window on the West." One of Peter's successors, Catherine the Great (r. 1762–1796), followed up with further efforts to Europeanize Russian cultural and intellectual life, viewing herself as part of the European Enlightenment. Thus Russians were the first of many peoples to measure themselves against the West and to mount major "catch-up" efforts.

But this European-oriented and Christian state had also become an Asian power, bumping up against China, India, Persia, and the Ottoman Empire. It was on the front lines of the encounter between Christendom and the world of Islam. This straddling of Asia and Europe was the source of a long-standing identity problem that has troubled educated Russians for 300 years. Was Russia a backward European country, destined to follow the lead of more highly developed Western European societies? Or was it different, uniquely Slavic or even Asian, shaped by its Mongol legacy and its status as an Asian power? It is a question that Russians have not completely answered even in the twenty-first century. Either way, the very size of that empire, bordering on virtually all of the great agrarian civilizations of outer Eurasia, turned Russia, like many empires before it, into a highly militarized state, "a society organized for continuous war," according to one scholar.[23] It also reinforced the highly autocratic character of the Russian Empire because such a huge state arguably required a powerful monarchy to hold its vast domains and highly diverse peoples together.

Clearly the Russians had created an empire, similar to those of Western Europe in terms of conquest, settlement, exploitation, religious conversion, and feelings of superiority. Nonetheless, the Russians had acquired their empire under different circumstances than did the Western Europeans. The Spanish and the British had conquered and colonized the New World, an ocean away and wholly unknown to them before 1492. They acquired those empires only after establishing themselves as distinct European states. The Russians, on the other hand, absorbed adjacent territories, and they did so at the same time that a modern Russian state was taking shape. "The British had an empire," wrote historian Geoffrey Hosking. "Russia *was* an empire."[24] Perhaps this helps explain the unique longevity of the Russian Empire. Whereas the Spanish, Portuguese, and British colonies in the Americas long ago achieved independence, the Russian Empire remained intact until the collapse of the Soviet Union in 1991. So thorough was Russian colonization that Siberia and much of the steppes remain still an integral part of the Russian state. But many internal administrative regions, which exercise a measure of autonomy, reflect the continuing presence of some 160 non-Russian peoples who were earlier incorporated into the Russian Empire.

Asian Empires

Even as West Europeans were building their empires in the Americas and the Russians across Siberia, other imperial projects were likewise under way. The Chinese pushed deep into central Eurasia; Turko-Mongol invaders from Central Asia created the Mughal Empire, bringing much of Hindu South Asia within a single Muslim-ruled political system; and the Ottoman Empire brought Muslim rule to a largely Christian population in southeastern Europe and Turkish rule to largely Arab populations in North Africa and the Middle East. None of these empires had the global reach or worldwide impact of Europe's American colonies; they were regional rather than global in scope. Nor did they have the same devastating and transforming impact on their conquered peoples, for those peoples were not being exposed to new diseases. Nothing remotely approaching the catastrophic population collapse of Native American peoples occurred in these Asian empires. Moreover, the process of building these empires did not transform the imperial homeland as fundamentally as did the wealth of the Americas and to a lesser extent Siberia for European imperial powers. Nonetheless, these expanding Asian empires reflected the energies and vitality of their respective civilizations in the early modern era, and they gave rise to profoundly important cross-cultural encounters, with legacies that echoed for many centuries.

Making China an Empire

In the fifteenth century, China had declined an opportunity to construct a maritime empire in the Indian Ocean, as Zheng He's massive fleet was withdrawn and left to wither away (see pp. 568–69). In the seventeenth and eighteenth centuries, however, China built another kind of empire on its northern and western frontiers that vastly enlarged the territorial size of the country and incorporated a number of non-Chinese peoples. Undertaking this enormous project of imperial expansion was China's Qing, or Manchu, dynasty (1644–1912). (See Document 13.1, pp. 651–52, for Chinese state building during the Qing dynasty.) Strangely enough, the Qing dynasty was itself of foreign and nomadic origin, hailing from Manchuria, north of the Great Wall. Having conquered China, the Qing rulers sought to maintain their ethnic distinctiveness by forbidding intermarriage between themselves and Chinese. Nonetheless, their ruling elites also mastered the Chinese language and Confucian teachings and used Chinese bureaucratic techniques to govern the empire. Perhaps because they were foreigners, Qing rulers went to great lengths to reinforce traditional Confucian gender roles, honoring men who were loyal sons, officials, and philanthropists and women who demonstrated loyalty to their spouses by resisting rape or remaining chaste as widows.

■ **Description**

What were the major features of Chinese empire building in the early modern era?

For many centuries, the Chinese had interacted with the nomadic peoples, who inhabited the dry and lightly populated regions now known as Mongolia, Xinjiang, and Tibet. Trade, tribute, and warfare ensured that these ecologically and culturally different worlds were well known to each other, quite unlike the New World "discoveries" of the Europeans. Chinese authority in the area had been intermittent and actively resisted. Then, in the early modern era, Qing dynasty China undertook an eighty-year military effort (1680–1760) that brought these huge regions solidly under Chinese control. It was largely security concerns, rather than economic need, that motivated this aggressive posture. During the late seventeenth century, the creation of a substantial state among the western Mongols, known as the Zunghars, revived Chinese memories of an earlier Mongol conquest. As in so many other cases, Chinese expansion was viewed as a defensive necessity. The eastward movement of the Russian Empire likewise appeared potentially threatening, but this danger was resolved diplomatically, rather than militarily, in the Treaty of Nerchinsk (1689), which marked the boundary between Russia and China.

Although undertaken by the non-Chinese Manchus, the Qing dynasty campaigns against the Mongols marked the evolution of China into a Central Asian empire. The Chinese, how-

Chinese Conquests in Central Asia
Painted by the Chinese artist Jin Tingbiao in the mid-eighteenth century, this image portrays Machang, a leading warrior involved in the westward extension of the Chinese empire. The painting was inscribed by the emperor himself and served to honor the bravery of Machang. (Courtesy Sotheby's)

ever, have seldom thought of themselves as an imperial power. Rather they spoke of the "unification" of the peoples of central Eurasia within a Chinese state. Nonetheless, historians have seen many similarities between Chinese expansion and other cases of early modern empire building, while noting some clear differences as well.

Clearly the Qing dynasty takeover of central Eurasia was a conquest, making use of China's more powerful military technology and greater resources. Furthermore, the area was ruled separately from the rest of China through a new office called the Court of Colonial Affairs. Like other colonial powers, the Chinese made active use of local notables — Mongol aristocrats, Muslim officials, Buddhist leaders — as they attempted to govern the region as inexpensively as possible. Sometimes these native officials abused their authority, demanding extra taxes or labor service from local people and thus earning their hostility. In places, those officials imitated Chinese ways by wearing peacock feathers, decorating their hats with gold buttons, or adopting a Manchu hairstyle that was much resented by many Chinese who were forced to wear it.

More generally, however, Chinese or Qing officials did not seek to assimilate local people into Chinese culture and showed considerable respect for the Mongolian, Tibetan, and Muslim cultures of the region. People of noble rank, Buddhist monks, and those associated with monasteries were excused from the taxes and labor service required of ordinary people. Nor was the area flooded with Chinese settlers. In parts of Mongolia, for example, Qing authorities sharply restricted the entry of Chinese merchants and other immigrants in an effort to preserve the area as a source of recruitment for the Chinese military. They feared that the "soft" and civilized Chinese ways might erode the fighting spirit of the Mongols.

The long-term significance of this new Chinese imperial state was tremendous. It greatly expanded the territory of China and added a small but important minority of non-Chinese people to the empire's vast population (see Map 13.3). The borders of contemporary China are essentially those created during the Qing dynasty. Some of those peoples, particularly those in Tibet and Xinjiang, have retained their older identities and in recent decades have actively sought greater autonomy or even independence from China.

Even more important, Chinese conquests, together with the expansion of the Russian Empire, utterly transformed Central Asia. For centuries, that region had been the cosmopolitan crossroads of Eurasia, hosting the Silk Road trading network, welcoming all of the major world religions, and generating an enduring encounter between the nomads of the steppes and the farmers of settled agricultural regions. Now under Russian or Chinese rule, it became the backward and impoverished region known to nineteenth- and twentieth-century observers. Land-based commerce across Eurasia

Map 13.3 China's Qing Dynasty Empire
After many centuries of intermittent expansion into Central Asia, the Qing dynasty brought this vast region firmly within the Chinese empire.

increasingly took a backseat to oceanic trade. Indebted Mongolian nobles lost their land to Chinese merchants, while nomads, no longer able to herd their animals freely, fled to urban areas, where many were reduced to begging. The incorporation of inner Eurasia into the Russian and Chinese empires "eliminated permanently as a major actor on the historical stage the nomadic pastoralists, who had been the strongest alternative to settled agricultural society since the second millennium B.C.E."[25] It was the end of a long era.

Muslims and Hindus in the Mughal Empire

■ **Change**

How did Mughal attitudes and policies toward Hindus change from the time of Akbar to that of Aurangzeb?

If the creation of a Chinese imperial state in the early modern era provoked a final clash of nomadic pastoralists and settled farmers, India's Mughal Empire hosted a different kind of encounter—a further phase in the long interaction of Islamic and Hindu cultures in South Asia. That empire was the product of Central Asian warriors, who were Muslims in religion and Turkic in culture and who claimed descent from Chinggis Khan and Timur (see Chapter 11). Their brutal conquests in the sixteenth century provided India with a rare period of relative political unity (1526–1707), as Mughal emperors exercised a fragile control over a diverse and fragmented subcontinent, which had long been divided into a bewildering variety of small states, principalities, tribes, castes, sects, and ethnolinguistic groups.

The central division within Mughal India was religious. The ruling dynasty and perhaps 20 percent of the population were Muslims; most of the rest practiced some form of Hinduism. Mughal India's most famous emperor, Akbar (r. 1556–1605), clearly recognized this fundamental reality and acted deliberately to accommodate the Hindu majority. After conquering the warrior-based and Hindu Rajputs of northwestern India, Akbar married several of their princesses but did not require them to convert to Islam. He incorporated a substantial number of Hindus into the political-military elite of the empire and supported the building of Hindu temples as well as mosques, palaces, and forts. (See Document 13.2, pp. 653–55, for Mughal state building under Akbar and his son Jahangir (jah-hahn-GEER). But Akbar acted to soften some Hindu restrictions on women, encouraging the remarriage of widows, discouraging child marriages and *sati* (when a widow followed her husband to death by throwing herself on his funeral pyre), and persuading merchants to set aside special market days for women so as to moderate their seclusion in the home. Nur Jahan, the twentieth and favorite wife of Emperor Jahangir (r. 1605–1627) was widely regarded as the power behind the throne of her alcohol- and opium-addicted husband, giving audiences to visiting dignitaries, consulting with ministers, and even having a coin issued in her name.

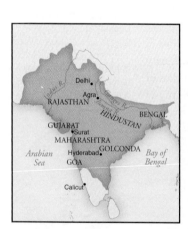

The Mughal Empire

In directly religious matters, Akbar imposed a policy of toleration, deliberately restraining the more militantly Islamic *ulama* (religious scholars) and removing the special tax (*jizya*) on non-Muslims. He constructed a special House of Worship where he presided over intellectual discussion with representatives of many religions—Muslim, Hindu, Christian, Buddhist, Jewish, Jain, and Zoroastrian. His son Jahangir wrote proudly of his father: "He associated with the good of every race and creed and persuasion. . . . The professors of various faiths had room in the broad expanse of his incomparable sway."[26] Akbar went so far as to create his own state cult, a religious faith aimed at the Mughal elite, drawing on Islam, Hinduism, and Zoroastrianism and emphasizing loyalty to the emperor himself. The overall style of the Mughal Empire was that of a blended elite culture in which both Hindus and various Muslim groups could feel comfortable. Thus Persian artists and writers were welcomed into the empire, and the Hindu epic *Ramayana* was translated into Persian, while various Persian classics appeared in Hindi and Sanskrit. In short, Akbar and his immediate successors downplayed a distinctly Islamic identity for the Mughal Empire in favor of a cosmopolitan and hybrid Indian-Persian-Turkic culture.

Such policies fostered sharp opposition among some Muslims. The philosopher Shayk Ahmad Sirhindi (1564–1624), claiming to be a "renewer" of authentic Islam in his time, strongly objected to this cultural synthesis. The worship of saints, the sacrifice of animals, and support for Hindu religious festivals all represented impure intrusions of Sufi Islam or Hinduism that needed to be rooted out. In Sirhindi's view, it was primarily women who had introduced these deviations: "Because of their utter stupidity women pray to stones and idols and ask for their help. This practice is common, especially when small pox strikes, and there is hardly a woman who is not involved in this polytheistic practice. Women participate in the holidays of Hindus and Jews. They celebrate Diwali [a major Hindu festival] and send their sisters and daughters presents similar to those exchanged by the infidels."[27] It was therefore the duty of Muslim rulers to impose the sharia (Islamic law), to enforce the jizya, and to remove non-Muslims from high office.

This strain of Muslim thinking found a champion in the emperor Aurangzeb (ow-rang-ZEHB) (r. 1658–1707), who reversed Akbar's policy of accommodation and sought to impose Islamic supremacy. While Akbar had discouraged the Hindu practice of *sati*, Aurangzeg forbade it outright. Music and dance were now banned at court, and previously tolerated vices such as gambling, drinking, prostitution, and narcotics were actively suppressed. Dancing girls were ordered to get married or leave the empire altogether. Some Hindu temples were destroyed, and the jizya was reimposed. "Censors of public morals," posted to large cities, enforced Islamic law.

Aurangzeb's religious policies, combined with intolerable demands for taxes to support his many wars of expansion, antagonized Hindus and prompted various movements of opposition to the Mughals. "Your subjects are trampled underfoot," wrote one anonymous protester. "Every province of your empire is impoverished. . . . God is the God of all mankind, not the God of Mussalmans [Muslims] alone."[28] These opposition movements, some of them self-consciously Hindu, fatally fractured the Mughal Empire, especially after Aurangzeb's death in 1707, and opened the way for a British takeover in the second half of the eighteenth century.

Thus the Mughal Empire was the site of a highly significant encounter between two of the world's great religious traditions. It began with an experiment in multicultural empire building and ended in growing antagonism between Hindus and Muslims. In the centuries that followed, both elements of the Mughal experience would be repeated.

Muslims and Christians in the Ottoman Empire

Like the Mughal state, the Ottoman Empire was also the creation of Turkic warrior groups, whose aggressive raiding of agricultural civilization was now legitimized in Islamic terms. Beginning around 1300 from a base area in northwestern Anatolia, these Ottoman Turks over the next three centuries swept over much of the Middle East, North Africa, and southeastern Europe to create the Islamic world's most significant empire (see Map 13.4). During those centuries, the Ottoman state was transformed from a small frontier principality to a prosperous, powerful, cosmopolitan empire, heir to both the Byzantine Empire and to leadership within the Islamic world. Its sultan combined the roles of a Turkic warrior prince, a Muslim caliph, and a conquering emperor, bearing the "strong sword of Islam" and serving as chief defender of the faith.

Gaining such an empire transformed Turkish social life as well. The relative independence of Central Asian pastoral women, their open association with men, and their political influence in society all diminished as the Turks adopted Islam and acquired an empire in the heartland of ancient and patriarchal Mediterranean civilizations. Now elite Turkish women found themselves secluded and often veiled; slave women from the Caucasus mountains and the Sudan grew more numerous; official imperial censuses did not count women; and orthodox Muslim reformers sought to restrict women's religious gatherings.

And yet within the new constraints of a settled Islamic empire, Turkish women retained something of the social power they had enjoyed in pastoral societies. From around 1550 to 1650, women of the royal court had such an influence in political matters that their critics referred to the "sultanate of women." Islamic law permitted women important property rights, which enabled some to become quite wealthy, endowing religious and charitable institutions. Many women actively used the Ottoman courts to protect their legal rights in matters of marriage, divorce, and inheritance, sometimes representing themselves or acting as agents for female relatives. In 1717, the wife of an English ambassador to the Ottoman Empire compared the lives of Turkish and European women, declaring "'tis very easy to see that they have more liberty than we have."[29]

■ **Significance**

In what ways was the Ottoman Empire important for Europe in the early modern era?

Within the Islamic world, the Ottoman Empire represented the growing prominence of Turkic people, for their empire now incorporated a large number of Arabs, among whom the religion had been born. The responsibility and the prestige of protecting Mecca, Medina, and Jerusalem—the holy cities of Islam—now fell to the Ottoman Empire. A century-long conflict (1534–1639) between the Ottoman Empire, espousing the Sunni version of Islam, and the Persian Safavid Empire, holding fast to the Shia form of the faith, expressed a deep and enduring division within the

Islamic world. Nonetheless, Persian culture, especially its poetry, painting, and traditions of imperial splendor, occupied a prominent position among the Ottoman elite.

The Ottoman Empire, like its Mughal counterpart, was the site of a highly significant cross-cultural encounter in the early modern era, adding yet another chapter to the long-running story of interaction between the Islamic world and Christendom. As the Ottoman Empire expanded across Anatolia, its mostly Christian population converted in large numbers to Islam as the Byzantine state visibly weakened and large numbers of Turks settled in the region. By 1500, some 90 percent of Anatolia's inhabitants were Muslims and Turkic speakers. The climax of this Turkic assault on the Christian world of Byzantium occurred in 1453, when Constantinople fell to the invaders. Renamed Istanbul, that splendid Christian city became the capital of the Ottoman Empire. Byzantium, heir to the glory of Rome and the guardian of Orthodox Christianity, was no more.

Map 13.4
The Ottoman Empire
At its high point in the mid-sixteenth century, the Ottoman Empire encompassed a vast diversity of peoples; straddled Europe, Africa, and Asia; and battled both the Austrian and Safavid empires.

In the empire's southeastern European domains, known as the Balkans, the Ottoman encounter with Christian peoples unfolded quite differently than it had in Anatolia. In the Balkans, Muslims ruled over a large Christian population, but the scarcity of Turkish settlers and the willingness of the Ottoman authorities to accommodate the region's Christian churches led to far fewer conversions. By the early sixteenth century, only about 19 percent of the area's people were Muslims, and 81 percent were Christians.

Many of these Christians had welcomed Ottoman conquest because taxes were lighter and oppression less pronounced than under their former Christian rulers. Christian communities such as the Eastern Orthodox and Armenian churches were granted considerable autonomy in regulating their internal social, religious, educational, and charitable affairs. Nonetheless, many Christian and Jewish women appealed legal cases dealing with marriage and inheritance to Muslim courts, where their property rights were greater. A substantial number of Christian men — Balkan landlords, Greek merchants, government officials, and high-ranking clergy — became part of the Ottoman elite, without converting to Islam. Jewish refugees, fleeing Christian persecution in a Spain recently "liberated" from Islamic rule, likewise found greater opportunity in the Ottoman Empire, where they became prominent in trade and banking circles. In these ways, Ottoman dealings with the Christian and Jewish populations of their empire broadly resembled Akbar's policies toward the Hindu majority of Mughal India.

In another way, however, Turkish rule bore heavily on Christians. Through a process known as the *devshirme* (dehv-SHEER-may) (the collecting or gathering), Balkan Christian communities were required to hand over a quota of young boys, who were then removed from their families, required to learn Turkish, usually converted to Islam, and trained for either civil administration or military service in elite Janissary units. Although it was a terrible blow for families who lost their children, the *devshirme* also represented a means of upward mobility within the Ottoman Empire. Nonetheless, this social gain occurred at a high price.

Even though Ottoman authorities were relatively tolerant toward Christians within their borders, the empire itself represented an enormous threat to Christendom generally. The seizure of Constantinople, the conquest of the Balkans, Ottoman naval power in the Mediterranean, and the siege of Vienna in 1529 and again in 1683 raised anew "the specter of a Muslim takeover of all of Europe."[30] (See Document 13.3, pp. 655–57.) One European ambassador reported fearfully in 1555 from the court of the Turkish ruler Suleiman:

> He tramples the soil of Hungary with 200,000 horses, he is at the very gates of Austria, threatens the rest of Germany, and brings in his train all the nations that extend from our borders to those of Persia.[31]

LearningCurve
bedfordstmartins.com
/strayer/LC

Indeed, the "terror of the Turk" inspired fear across much of Europe and placed Christendom on the defensive, even as Europeans were expanding aggressively across the Atlantic and into the Indian Ocean.

The Ottoman Siege of Vienna, 1683
In this late-seventeenth-century painting by the Flemish artist Frans Geffels, the last Ottoman incursion into the Austrian Empire was pushed back with French and Polish help, marking the end of a serious Muslim threat to Christian Europe. (Erich Lessing/Art Resource, NY)

But the Ottoman encounter with Christian Europe spawned admiration and co-operation as well as fear and trembling. Italian Renaissance artists portrayed the splendor of the Islamic world. (See Visual Sources for Chapter 12, pp. 600–09.) The sixteenth-century French philosopher Jean Bodin praised the religious tolerance of the Ottoman sultan in contrast to Christian intolerance: "The King of the Turks who rules over a great part of Europe safeguards the rites of religion as well as any prince in this world. Yet he constrains no-one, but on the contrary permits everyone to live as his conscience dictates."[32] The French government on occasion found it useful to ally with the Ottoman Empire against their common enemy of Habsburg Austria, while European merchants willingly violated a papal ban on selling firearms to the Turks. Cultural encounter involved more than conflict.

Reflections: The Centrality of Context in World History

World history is, to put it mildly, a big subject. To teachers and students alike, it can easily seem overwhelming in its detail. And yet the central task of world history is *not* the inclusion of endless facts or particular cases. It is rather to establish contexts or frameworks within which carefully selected facts and cases take on new meaning. In world history, every event, every process, every historical figure, every culture, society, or civilization gains significance from its incorporation into some larger context or framework. Contextual thinking is central to world history.

The broad outlines of European colonization in the Americas are familiar to most American and European students. And yet, when that story is set in the context of other empire-building projects of the early modern era, it takes on new and different meanings. Such a context helps to counter any remaining Eurocentrism in our thinking about the past by reminding us that Western Europe was not the only center of vitality and expansion and that the interaction of culturally different peoples, so characteristic of the modern age, derived from multiple sources. How often do we notice that a European Christendom creating empires across the Atlantic was also the victim of Ottoman imperial expansion in the Balkans?

This kind of contextualizing also allows us to see more clearly the distinctive features of European empires as we view them in the mirror of other imperial creations. The Chinese, Mughal, and Ottoman empires continued older patterns of historical development, while those of Europe represented something wholly new in human history—an interacting Atlantic world of Europe, Africa, and the Americas. Furthermore, the European empires had a far greater impact on the peoples they incorporated than did other empires. Nowhere else did empire building generate such a catastrophic population collapse as in the Americas. Nor did Asian empires foster the kind of slave-based societies and transcontinental trade in slaves that were among the chief outcomes of Europe's American colonies. Finally, Europe was enriched and transformed by its American possessions far more than China and the Ottomans were by their territorial acquisitions. Europeans gained enormous new biological resources from their empires—corn, potatoes, tomatoes, chocolate, tobacco, timber, and much more—as well as enormous wealth in the form of gold, silver, and land.

Should we need a motto for world history, consider this one: in world history, nothing stands alone; context is everything.

Second Thoughts

LearningCurve
Check what you know.
bedfordstmartins.com/strayer/LC

Online Study Guide
bedfordstmartins.com
/highschool/strayer

What's the Significance?

Big Picture Questions

1. The experience of empire for conquered peoples was broadly similar whoever their rulers were. Does the material of this chapter support or challenge this idea?

2. In thinking about the similarities and differences among the empires of the early modern era, what categories of comparison might be most useful to consider?

3. Have a look at the maps in this chapter with an eye to the areas of the world that were *not* incorporated in a major empire. Pick one or more of them and do a little research as to what was happening there in the early modern era.

4. **Looking Back:** Compared to the world of the fifteenth century, what new patterns of development are visible in the empire-building projects of the centuries that followed?

Next Steps: For Further Study

For Web sites and additional documents related to this chapter, see **Make History** at bedfordstmartins.com /highschool/strayer.

Jane Burbank and Frederick Cooper, *Empires in World History* (2010). Chapters 5–7 of this recent work describe and compare the empires of the early modern world.

Jorge Canizares-Esguerra and Erik R. Seeman, eds., *The Atlantic in Global History* (2007). A collection of essays that treats the Atlantic basin as a single interacting region.

Alfred W. Crosby, *The Columbian Voyages, the Columbian Exchange, and Their Historians* (1987). A brief and classic account of changing understandings of Columbus and his global impact.

John Kicza, *Resilient Cultures: America's Native Peoples Confront European Colonization, 1500–1800* (2003). An account of European colonization in the Americas that casts the native peoples as active agents rather than passive victims.

Charles C. Mann, *1493: Uncovering the New World Columbus Created* (2011). A global account of the Columbian Exchange that presents contemporary scholarship in a very accessible fashion.

Peter Perdue, *China Marches West: The Qing Conquest of Central Eurasia* (2005). Describes the process of China becoming an empire as it incorporated the non-Chinese people of Central Asia.

Willard Sutherland, *Taming the Wild Fields: Colonization and Empire on the Russian Steppe* (2004). An up-to-date account of Russian expansion in the steppes.

"1492: An Ongoing Voyage," http://www.ibiblio.org/expo/1492.exhibit/Intro.html. An interactive Web site based on an exhibit from the Library of Congress that provides a rich context for exploring the meaning of Columbus and his voyages.

Documents

Considering the Evidence: State Building in the Early Modern Era

The empires of the early modern era were the projects of states, though these states often made use of various private groups—missionaries, settlers, merchants, mercenaries—to achieve the goals of empire. Such imperial states— Qing dynasty China, Mughal India, the Ottoman Empire, and France, for example—were invariably headed by kings or emperors who were the source of ultimate political authority in their lands. Each of those rulers sought to govern societies divided by religion, region, ethnicity, or class.

During the three centuries between 1450 and 1750, all of these states, and a number of non-imperial states as well, moved toward greater political integration and centralization. In all of them, more effective central bureaucracies curtailed, though never eliminated, entrenched local interests; royal courts became more elaborate; and the role of monarchs grew more prominent. The growth of empire accompanied this process of political integration, and perhaps helped to cause it. However, the process of state building differed considerably across the early modern world, depending on variations in historical backgrounds, the particular problems and circumstances that each state faced, the cultural basis of political authority, and the policies that individual leaders followed.

The documents that follow allow us to examine this state-building effort in several distinct settings. Three of them were written by monarchs themselves and one represents an outsider's view. Pay attention to both the similarities and the variations in this process of state building as you study the documents. You may also want to consider how these early modern states differed from the states of later centuries. To what extent was government personal rather than institutional? In what ways was power exercised—through coercion and violence, through accommodation with established elites, through the operation of new bureaucratic structures, or by persuading people that the central authority was in fact legitimate?

Document 13.1

The "Self-Portrait" of a Chinese Emperor

Of all the early modern states, China had the longest tradition of centralized rule and political integration. By the time the Qing dynasty came to power in 1644, China could look back on many centuries of effective unity. Although interrupted periodically by peasant upheaval, external invasion, or changes in dynasties, cultural expectations nonetheless defined a unified state, headed by an emperor, as the norm. The Qing dynasty, although of Manchurian origin and proud of its military skills, generally accepted Chinese conceptions of statecraft, based on literary learning and a long-established system of civil service examinations designed to recruit scholar-officials into official positions. During the long reign of Kangxi (KAHNG-shee) (r. 1661–1722), that dynasty initiated a vast imperial project extending Chinese control deep into inner Asia. (See pp. 640–42.) Document 13.1 contains a number of Kangxi's personal reflections on the management of this huge imperial state and its bureaucracy. Drawn from his own writings, this "self-portrait" of the Chinese emperor was compiled by the highly regarded historian Jonathan Spence.

■ What major challenges to the effective exercise of state authority does Kangxi identify in this document?

■ How would you describe Kangxi's style of governance or his posture toward imperial rule?

■ Look carefully at the second paragraph of the document. Why did Kangxi impose a harsher penalty on Hu Chien-ching than the one originally given?

■ What does this document suggest about the sources of Kangxi's authority?

THE EMPEROR KANGXI

Reflections

1671–1722

Giving life to people and killing people—those are the powers that the emperor has.... He knows that sometimes people have to be persuaded into morality by the example of an execution....

Hu Chien-ching was a subdirector of the Court of Sacrificial Worship whose family terrorized their native area in Kiangsu, seizing people's lands and wives and daughters, and murdering people after falsely accusing them of being thieves. When a commoner finally managed to impeach him, the Governor was slow to hear the case and the Board of Punishment recommended that Hu be dismissed and

Source: Jonathan D. Spence, *Emperor of China* (New York: Alfred A. Knopf, 1974), 29–58.

sent into exile for three years. I ordered instead that he be executed with his family, and in his native place, so that all the local gentry might learn how I regarded such behavior. . . .

I have been merciful where possible. For the ruler must always check carefully before executions and leave room for the hope that men will get better if they are given the time. . . .

Of all the things that I find distasteful, none is more so than giving a final verdict on the death sentences that are sent to me for ratification. . . . Each year we went through the lists, sparing sixteen out of sixty-three at one session, eighteen out of fifty-seven at another. . . .

There are too many men who claim to be *ju*— pure scholars—and yet are stupid and arrogant; we'd be better off with less talk of moral principles and more practice of it. . . . This is one of the worst habits of the great officials, that if they are not recommending their teachers or their friends for high office, then they recommend their relatives. . . .

There is no way the emperor can know every official in the country, so he has to rely on the officials themselves for evaluation, or on censors to impeach the wicked. But when they are in cliques, he has to make his own inquiries as well; for no censor impeached the corrupt army officers Cho-ts'e and Hsu-sheng until I heard how they were hated by their troops and people and had them dismissed. . . .

The emperor can get extra information in audience, on tours, and in palace memorials. From the beginning of my reign, I sought ways to guarantee that discussion among the great officials be kept confidential. The palace memorials were read by me in person, and I wrote rescripts on them myself. . . . [R]egular audiences are crucial with military men, especially when they have held power for a long time. . . . And army officers on the frontiers tend to obey only their own commander, acknowledging him as the ruler. . . .

On tours I learned about the common people's grievances by talking with them, or by accepting their petitions. I asked peasants about their officials, looked at their houses and discussed their crops. I heard pleas from a woman whose husband had been wrongfully enslaved, from a traveling trader complaining about high customs dues, from a monk whose temple was falling down, and from a man who was robbed on his way to town. . . .

In 1694 I noted that we were losing talent because of the way the exams were being conducted: even in the military *chin-shih* exams, most of the successful candidates were from Cheikiang and Chiangnan, while there was only one from Honan and one from Shansi. The successful ones had often done no more than memorize old examination books, whereas the best should be selected on the basis of riding and archery. . . .

Even among the examiners, there are those who are corrupt, those who do not understand basic works, . . . those who insist entirely on memorization of the *Classics* . . . those who put candidates from their own geographical area at the top of the list. . . .

My divines have often been tempted to pass over bad auguries, but I have double-checked their calculations and warned them not to distort the truth: the Bureau of Astronomy once reported that a benevolent southeast wind was blowing, but I myself calculated the wind's direction with the palace instruments and found it to be, in fact, an inauspicious northeast wind; I told the Bureau that ours was not a dynasty that shunned bad omens; I also warned the Bureau not to guess or exaggerate in interpreting the omens that they observed, but simply to state their findings. . . . And being precise about forecasting the motions of the sun, moon, and planets, the winter and summer festivals, the eclipses of the sun and moon—all that is relevant to regulating spring planting, summer weeding, and autumn harvest. . . .

I have never tired of the *Book of Changes*, and have use it in fortune-telling and as a source of moral principles; the only thing you must not do, I told my court lecturers, is to make this book appear simple, for there are meanings here that lie beyond words.

Document 13.2

The Memoirs of Emperor Jahangir

The peoples of India, unlike those of China, had only rarely experienced a political system that encompassed most of the subcontinent. Its vast ethnic and cultural diversity and the division between its Hindu and Muslim peoples usually generated a fragmented political order of many competing states and principalities. But in the early modern era, the Mughal Empire gave to South Asia a rare period of substantial political unity. Document 13.2 offer excerpts from the memoirs of Jahangir, who ruled the Mughal state from 1605 to 1627, following the reign of his more famous father Akbar (see pp. 642–43). Written in Persian, the literary language of the eastern Islamic world, Jahangir's account of his reign followed the tradition of earlier Mughal emperors in noting major events of his lifetime, but it departed from that tradition in reflecting personally on art, politics, family life, and more.

■ Why do you think Jahangir mounted such an elaborate coronation celebration for himself?

■ In what ways did Jahangir seek to ensure the effective authority of the state he led?

■ In what ways was Jahangir a distinctly Muslim ruler? In what respects did he and his father depart from Islamic principles?

■ How would you compare the problems Jahangir faced with those of Kangxi? Notice that each of them had to adjust to a long-established cultural tradition—Kangxi to Chinese Confucianism and Jahangir to Hinduism. In what ways did they do so?

JAHANGIR

Memoirs

1605-1627

At the age of thirty-eight, I became Emperor.... As at the very instant that I seated myself on the throne, the sun rose from the horizon; I accepted this as the omen of victory, and as indicating a reign of unvarying prosperity. Hence I assumed the titles of ... the world-subduing emperor, the world-subduing king.

On this occasion I made use of the throne prepared by my father, and enriched at an expense without parallel for the celebration of the festival of the new year.... Having thus seated myself on the throne of my expectations and wishes, I caused also the imperial crown, which my father had caused to be made after the manner of that which was worn by the great kings of Persia, to be brought before

Source: *The Memoirs of the Emperor Jahangir*, translated from the Persian by Major David Price (London: Oriental Translation Committee, 1829), 1–3, 5–8, 15.

me, and then, in the presence of the whole assembled Emirs, having placed it on my brows, as an omen auspicious to the stability and happiness of my reign, kept it there for the space of a full astronomical hour. . . .

For forty days and forty nights I caused the . . . great imperial state drum, to strike up, without ceasing, the strains of joy and triumph; and . . . around my throne, the ground was spread by my directions with the most costly brocades and gold embroidered carpets. Censers° of gold and silver were disposed in different directions for the purpose of burning odoriferous drugs, and nearly three thousand camphorated wax lights . . . illuminated the scene from night till morning. Numbers of blooming youths, beautiful as young Joseph in the pavilions of Egypt, clad in dresses of the most costly materials . . . awaited my commands, rank after rank, and in attitude most respectful. And finally, the Emirs of the empire . . . covered from head to foot in gold and jewels, and shoulder to shoulder, stood round in brilliant array, also waiting for the commands of their sovereign. For forty days and forty nights did I keep open to the world these scenes of festivity and splendor, furnishing altogether an example of imperial magnificence seldom paralleled in this stage of earthly existence. . . .

I instituted . . . special regulations . . . as rules of conduct, never to be deviated from in their respective stations.

1. I remitted [canceled] altogether to my subjects three sources of revenue taxes or duties. . . .

2. I directed, when the district lay waste or destitute of inhabitants, that towns should be built. . . . I charged the Jaguir-daurs,° or feudatories of the empire, in such deserted places to erect mosques and substantial . . . stations for the accommodation of travelers, in order to render the district once more an inhabited country, and that wayfaring men might again be able to pass and repass in safety.

3. Merchants traveling through the country were not to have their bales or packages of any kind opened without their consent. But when they were perfectly willing to dispose of any article of merchandise, purchasers were permitted to deal with them, without, however, offering any species of molestation. . . .

5. No person was permitted either to make or sell either wine or any other kind of intoxicating liquor. I undertook to institute this regulation, although it is sufficiently notorious that I have myself the strongest inclination for wine, in which from the age of sixteen I have liberally indulged. . . .

6. No person [official] was permitted to take up his abode obtrusively in the dwelling of any subject of my realm. . . .

7. No person was to suffer, for any offense, the loss of a nose or ear. If the crime were theft, the offender was to be scourged with thorns, or deterred from further transgression by an attestation on the Koran.

8. [High officials] were prohibited from possessing themselves by violence of the lands of the subject, or from cultivating them on their own account. . . .

10. The governors in all the principal cities were directed to establish infirmaries or hospitals, with competent medical aid for the relief of the sick. . . .

11. During the month of my birth . . . the use of all animal food was prohibited both in town and country; and at equidistant periods throughout the year a day was set apart, on which all slaughtering of animals was strictly forbidden.

[H]aving on one occasion asked my father [Akbar] the reason why he had forbidden any one to prevent or interfere with the building of these haunts of idolatry [Hindu temples], his reply was in the following terms: "My dear child," said he, "I find myself a powerful monarch, the shadow of God upon earth. I have seen that he bestows the blessings of his gracious providence upon all his creatures without distinction. Ill should I discharge the duties of my exalted station, were I to withhold my compassion and indulgence from any of those entrusted to my charge. With all of the human race, with all of God's creatures, I am at peace: why then should I permit myself, under any consideration, to be the cause of molestation or aggression to any one? Besides, are not five parts in six of mankind either Hindus or

---

°**Censers:** containers for burning incense.

°**Jaguir-daurs:** local rulers granted a certain territory by the emperor.

aliens to the faith; and were I to be governed by motives of the kind suggested in your inquiry, what alternative can I have but to put them all to death!

I have thought it therefore my wisest plan to let these men alone. Neither is it to be forgotten, that the class of whom we are speaking . . . are usefully engaged, either in the pursuits of science or the arts, or of improvements for the benefit of mankind, and have in numerous instances arrived at the highest distinctions in the state, there being, indeed, to be found in this city men of every description, and of every religion on the face of the earth."

Document 13.3

An Outsider's View of Suleiman I

Under Suleiman I (r. 1520–1566), the Ottoman Empire reached its greatest territorial extent and perhaps its "golden age" in terms of culture and economy (see Map 13.3, p. 641). A helpful window into the life of this most powerful of Muslim states comes from the writings of Ogier Ghiselin de Busbecq, a Flemish nobleman who served as a diplomat for the Austrian Empire, which then felt under great threat from Ottoman expansion into central Europe. Busbecq's letters to a friend, excerpted in Document 13.3, present his view of the Ottoman court and his reflections on Ottoman military power.

- How do you think Busbecq's outsider status shaped his perceptions of Ottoman political and military life? To what extent does his role as a foreigner enhance or undermine the usefulness of his account for historians?

- How did he define the differences between Ottoman Empire and Austria? What do you think he hoped to accomplish by highlighting these differences?

- What sources of Ottoman political authority are apparent in Busbecq's account?

- What potential problems of the Ottoman Empire does this document imply or state?

OGIER GHISELIN DE BUSBECQ
The Turkish Letters
1555–1562

On his [Suleiman's] arrival we were admitted to an audience. . . . His air [attitude], was by no

Source: Charles Thornton Forester and F. H. Blackburne Daniell, *The Life and Letters of Ogier Ghiselin de Busbecq* (London: C. Kegan Paul, 1881), 114–15, 152–56, 219–22.

means gracious, and his face wore a stern, though dignified, expression. On entering we were separately conducted into the royal presence by the chamberlains, who grasped our arms. This has been the Turkish fashion of admitting people to the Sovereign ever since a Croat, in order to avenge the death of his master ... asked Amurath [an earlier Sultan] for an audience, and took advantage of it to slay him. After having gone through a pretense of kissing his hand, we were conducted backward to the wall opposite his seat, care being taken that we should never turn our backs on him. ...

The Sultan's hall was crowded with people, among whom were several officers of high rank. Besides these there were all the troopers of the Imperial guard and a large force of Janissaries; but there was not in all that great assembly a single man who owed his position to aught save his valor and his merit. No distinction is attached to birth among the Turks. ... In making his appointments the Sultan pays no regard to any pretensions on the score of wealth or rank, nor does he take into consideration recommendations or popularity. ... It is by merit that men rise in the service, a system which ensures that posts should only be assigned to the competent. ... Those who receive the highest offices from the Sultan are for the most part the sons of shepherds or herdsmen, and so far from being ashamed of their parentage, they actually glory in it, and consider it a matter of boasting that they owe nothing to the accident of birth. ...

Among the Turks, therefore, honors, high posts, and judgeships are the rewards of great ability and good service. If a man be dishonest, or lazy, or careless, he remains at the bottom of the ladder, an object of contempt; for such qualities there are no honors in Turkey! This is the reason that they are successful in their undertakings, that they lord it over others, and are daily extending the bounds of their empire. These are not our ideas, with us [Europeans] there is no opening left for merit; birth is the standard for everything; the prestige of birth is the sole key to advancement in the public service. ...

[T]ake your stand by my side, and look at the sea of turbaned heads, each wrapped in twisted folds of the whitest silk; look at those marvelously handsome dresses of every kind and every color; time would fail me to tell how all around is glittering with gold, with silver, with purple, with silk, and with velvet; words cannot convey an adequate idea of that strange and wondrous sight: it was the most beautiful spectacle I ever saw.

With all this luxury, great simplicity and economy are combined; every man's dress, whatever his position may be, is of the same pattern; no fringes or useless points are sewn on, as is the case with us, appendages which cost a great deal of money, and are worn out in three days. ... I was greatly struck with the silence and order that prevailed in this great crowd. There were no cries, no hum of voices, the usual accompaniments of a motley gathering, neither was there any jostling; without the slightest disturbance each man took his proper place according to his rank. ...

On leaving the assembly we had a fresh treat in the sight of the household cavalry returning to their quarters; the men were mounted on splendid horses, excellently groomed, and gorgeously accoutred. And so we left the royal presence, taking with us but little hope of a successful issue to our embassy.

The Turkish monarch going to war takes with him over 40,000 camels and nearly as many baggage mules, of which a great part, when he is invading Persia, are loaded with rice and other kinds of grain. ... The invading army carefully abstains from encroaching on its magazines° at the outset. ... The Sultan's magazines are opened, and a ration just sufficient to sustain life is daily weighed out to the Janissaries and other troops of the royal household.

From this you will see that it is the patience, self-denial, and thrift of the Turkish soldier that enable him to face the most trying circumstances. ... What a contrast to our men! Christian soldiers on a campaign refuse to put up with their ordinary food, and call for thrushes, beccaficos,° and such like dainty dishes! If these are not supplied they grow mutinous and work their own ruin; and, if they are supplied, they are ruined all the same. For each man is his own worst enemy, and has no foe more deadly than his own intemperance, which is sure to kill him, if the enemy be not quick.

It makes me shudder to think of what the result of a struggle between such different systems must be; one of us must prevail and the other be destroyed. ... On their side is the vast wealth of their empire, un-

---

°**magazines:** supplies.

°**beccafico:** a small bird.

impaired resources, experience and practice in arms, a veteran soldiery, an uninterrupted series of victories, readiness to endure hardships, union, order, discipline, thrift, and watchfulness. On ours are found an empty exchequer, luxurious habits, exhausted resources, broken spirits, a raw and insubordinate soldiery, and greedy generals; there is no regard for discipline, license runs riot, the men indulge in drunkenness and debauchery, and, worst of all, the enemy are accustomed to victory, we, to defeat. Can we doubt what the result must be? The only obstacle is Persia, whose position on his rear forces the invader to take precautions. The fear of Persia gives us a respite, but it is only for a time. When he has secured himself in that quarter, he will fall upon us with all the resources of the East. How ill prepared we are to meet such an attack it is not for me to say.

[In the following passage, Busbecq reflects on a major problem of the Ottoman state, succession to the throne.]

The sons of Turkish Sultans are in the most wretched position in the world, for, as soon as one of them succeeds his father, the rest are doomed to certain death. The Turk can endure no rival to the throne, and, indeed, the conduct of the Janissaries renders it impossible for the new Sultan to spare his brothers; for if one of them survives, the Janissaries are forever asking largesses. If these are refused, forthwith the cry is heard, "Long live the brother!" "God preserve the brother!"—a tolerably broad hint that they intend to place him on the throne. So that the Turkish Sultans are compelled to celebrate their succession by imbruing their hands in the blood of their nearest relatives.

Document 13.4

French State Building and Louis XIV

Like their counterparts in the Middle East and Asia, a number of European states in the early modern era also pursued the twin projects of imperial expansion abroad and political integration at home. But consolidating central authority was a long and difficult task. Obstacles to the ambitions of kings in Europe were many—the absence of an effective transportation and communication infrastructure; the difficulty of acquiring information about the population and resources; the entrenched interests of privileged groups such as the nobility, church, town councils, and guilds; and the division between Catholics and Protestants.

Perhaps the most well-known example of such European state-building efforts is that of France under the rule of Louis XIV (r. 1643–1715). Louis and other European monarchs, such as those in Spain and Russia, operated under a set of assumptions known as "absolutism," which held that kings ruled by "divine right" and could legitimately claim sole and uncontested authority in their realms. Louis's famous dictum *"L'etat, c'est moi"* ("I am the state") summed up the absolutist ideal. Document 13.4 illustrates at least one way in which Louis attempted to realize this ideal.

Written by Louis himself, this document focuses on the importance of "spectacle" and public display in solidifying the exalted role of the monarch. The "carousel" described here was an extravagant pageant, held in Paris in June 1662. It featured various exotic animals, slaves, princes, and nobles arrayed in fantastic costumes representing distant lands, together with much equestrian competition. Unifying this disparate assembly was King Louis himself, dressed as a Roman emperor, while on the shields of the nobles was that grand symbol of the monarchy, the sun.

■ What posture does Louis take toward his subjects in this document?

■ How does he understand the role of spectacle in general and the carousel in particular?

■ What does the choice of the sun as a royal symbol suggest about Louis's conception of his role in the French state and empire?

LOUIS XIV

Memoirs
1670

It was necessary to conserve and cultivate with care all that which, without diminishing the authority and the respect due to me, linked me by bonds of affection to my peoples and above all to the people of rank, so as to make them see by this very means that it was neither aversion for them nor affected severity, nor harshness of spirit, but simply reason and duty, that made me more reserved and more exact toward them in other matters. That sharing of pleasures, which gives people at court a respectable familiarity with us, touches them and charms them more than can be expressed. The common people, on the other hand, are delighted by shows in which, at bottom, we always have the aim of pleasing them; and all our subjects, in general, are delighted to see that we like what they like, or what they excel in. By this means we hold on to their hearts and their minds, sometimes more strongly perhaps than by recompenses and gifts; and with regard to foreigners, in a state they see flourishing and well ordered, that which is spent on expenses and which could be called superfluous, makes a very favorable impression on them, of magnificence, of power, of grandeur. . . .

The carousel, which has furnished me the subject of these reflections, had only been conceived at first as a light amusement; but little by little, we were carried away, and it became a spectacle that was fairly

grand and magnificent, both in the number of exercises, and by the novelty of the costumes and the variety of the [heraldic] devices. It was then that I began to employ the one that I have always kept since and which you see in so many places . . . it ought to represent in some way the duties of a prince, and constantly encourage me to fulfill them. For the device they chose the sun, which . . . is the most noble of all, and which, by its quality of being unique, by the brilliance that surrounds it, by the light that it communicates to the other stars which form for it a kind of court, by the just and equal share that the different climates of the world receive of this light, by the good it does in all places, ceaselessly producing as it does, in every sphere of life, joy and activity, by its unhindered movement, in which it nevertheless always appears calm, by its constant and invariable course, from which it never departs nor wavers, is the most striking and beautiful image of a great monarch.

Those who saw me governing with a good deal of ease and without being confused by anything, in all the numerous attentions that royalty demands, persuaded me to add the earth's globe, and for motto, *nec pluribus impar* (not unequal to many things): by which they meant something that flattered the aspirations of a young king, namely that, being sufficient to so many things, I would doubtless be capable of governing other empires, just as the sun was capable of lighting up other worlds if they were exposed to its rays.

Source: Robert Campbell, *Louis XIV* (London: Longmans, 1993), 117–18.

Using the Evidence: State Building in the Early Modern Era

1. **Making comparisons:** To what extent did these four early modern states face similar problems and devise similar solutions? How did they differ? In particular, how did the rulers of these states deal with subordinates? How did they use violence? What challenges to imperial authority did they face?

2. **Assessing spectacle:** In what different ways was spectacle, royal splendor, or public display evident in the documents? How would you define the purpose of such display? How effective do you think spectacle has been in consolidating state authority?

3. **Distinguishing power and authority:** Some scholars have made a distinction between "power," the ability of a state to coerce its subjects into some required behavior, and "authority," the ability of a state to persuade its subjects to do its bidding voluntarily by convincing them that it is proper, right, or natural to do so. What examples of power and authority can you find in these documents? How were they related? What are the advantages and disadvantages of each, from the viewpoint of ambitious rulers?

4. **Comparing past and present:** It is important to recognize that early modern states differed in many ways from twentieth- or twenty-first-century states. How would you define those differences? Consider, among other things, the personal role of the ruler, the use of violence, the means of establishing authority, and the extent to which the state could shape the lives of its citizens.

Visual Sources

Considering the Evidence: The Conquest of Mexico through Aztec Eyes

Among the sagas of early modern empire building, few have been more dramatic, more tragic, or better documented than the Spanish conquest of Mexico during the early sixteenth century (see Map 13.1, p. 620). In recounting this story, historians are fortunate in having considerable evidence—both documentary and visual—from the Aztec side of the encounter.

The peoples of central Mexico had long used a type of book called a codex to record their history. Codices contained primarily drawings and symbols (glyphs) painted by carefully trained high-status persons known as *tlacuilo* (artist-scribes). Although Spanish invaders destroyed most of these codices, the codex tradition continued in a modified form in the century following conquest. These new codices, often assembled under the supervision of European missionaries, were largely composed by native peoples, many of them new converts to Christianity and some of them literate in both Spanish and Latin. These codices included numerous paintings by local artists as well as written texts in a variety of Mesoamerican languages using the Roman alphabet.

The *Florentine Codex*, for example, was compiled under the leadership of Fray Bernardino de Sahagun, a Franciscan missionary who believed that an understanding of Aztec culture was essential to the task of conversion. Because Sahagun relied on Aztec informants and artists, many scholars believe that the Florentine and other codices represent indigenous understandings of the conquest. However, they require a critical reading. They date from several decades after the events they describe. Many contributors to the codices had been influenced by the Christian and European culture of their missionary mentors, and they were writing or painting in a society thoroughly dominated by Spanish colonial rule. Furthermore, the codices reflect the ethnic and regional diversity of Mesoamerica rather than a single Aztec perspective. Despite such limitations, these codices represent a unique window into Mesoamerican understandings of the conquest.

In the Aztec telling of the Spanish conquest, accounts of earlier warnings or omens of disaster abound. One of these was described as follows in the *Florentine Codex*: "Ten years before the arrival of the Spaniards an omen first appeared in the sky like a flame or tongue of fire.... For a full year it showed itself.... People were taken aback, they lamented."[33] That ominous appearance was illustrated in the *Duran Codex*, presented here in Visual Source 13.1, showing the Aztec ruler Moctezuma observing this omen of death from the rooftop of his palace. Some scholars suggest that such stories reflect a post-conquest understanding of the traumatic defeat the Aztecs suffered, for other evidence indicates that the Aztecs were not initially alarmed by the coming of the Spanish and that, instead, they viewed the Europeans as "simply another group of powerful and dangerous outsiders who needed to be controlled or accommodated."[34]

- Why might Aztec contributors to the codices have included accounts of such supernatural events preceding the arrival of the Spanish?

- Why do you think the Spanish frequently incorporated such accounts into their own descriptions of the conquest?

- Why might the artist have chosen to show Moctezuma alone rather than in the company of his supposedly fearful people?

Visual Source 13.1 Disaster Foretold (The Art Archive at Art Resource, NY)

In February 1519 Hernán Cortés, accompanied by some 350 Spanish soldiers, set off from Cuba with a fleet of eleven ships, stopping at several places along the Gulf of Mexico before proceeding to march inland toward Tenochtitlán (teh-noch-TEE-lan), the capital of the Aztec Empire. Along the way, he learned something about the fabulous wealth of this empire and about the fragility of its political structure. Through a combination of force and astute diplomacy, Cortés was able to negotiate alliances with a number of the Aztecs' restive subject peoples and with the Aztecs' many rivals or enemies, especially the Tlaxcala. With his modest forces thus greatly reinforced, Cortés arrived in Tenochtitlán on November 8, 1519, where he met with Moctezuma. Visual Source 13.2 presents an image of that epic encounter, drawn from the Lienzo de Tlaxcala, a series of paintings completed by 1560. They reflect generally the viewpoint of the Tlaxcala people.

■ How does this painting present the relationship between Cortés and Moctezuma? Are they meeting as equals, as enemies, as allies, as ruler and subject? Notice that both sit on European-style chairs, which had come to suggest authority in the decades following Spanish conquest.

■ What do the items at the bottom of the image represent?

■ Does this image support or challenge the perception that the Aztecs viewed the Spanish newcomers, at least initially, in religious terms as gods?

■ What might the painter have tried to convey by placing three attendants behind Moctezuma, while Cortés appears alone, except for his translator?

The woman standing behind Cortés in Visual Source 13.2 is Doña Marina (sometimes called La Malinche), a Nahuatl-speaking woman who had been a slave in Maya territory and was given as a gift to Cortés's forces in April 1519. She subsequently became an interpreter for the Spanish, as well as Cortés's mistress. Doña Marina appears frequently and prominently in many of the paintings of the era. (See the Portrait of Doña Marina, pp. 622–23.)

■ What impression of Doña Marina does this image suggest?

Whatever the character of their initial meeting, the relationship of the Spanish and Aztecs soon deteriorated amid mutual suspicion. Within a week, Cortés had seized Moctezuma, holding him under a kind of house arrest in his own palaces. For reasons not entirely clear, this hostile act did not immediately trigger a violent Aztec response. Perhaps Aztec authorities were concerned for the life of their ruler, or possibly their factional divisions inhibited coordinated resistance.

But in May 1520, while Cortés was temporarily away at the coast, an incident occurred that set in motion the most violent phase of the encounter. During a religious ceremony in honor of Huitzilopochtli, the Aztec patron deity of Tenochtitlán, the local Spanish commander, apparently fearing an uprising, launched a surprise attack on the unarmed participants in the celebration, killing hundreds of the leading warriors and nobles. An Aztec account from the *Florentine Codex* described the scene:

> When the dance was loveliest and when song was linked to song, the Spaniards were seized with an urge to kill the celebrants. They all ran forward, armed as if for battle. They closed the entrances and passageways . . . then [they] rushed into the Sacred Patio to slaughter the inhabitants. . . . They attacked the man who was drumming and cut

Visual Source 13.2 Moctezuma and Cortés (The Granger Collection, New York)

Visual Source 13.3 The Massacre of the Nobles (Bridgeman-Giraudon/Art Resource, NY)

off his arms. Then they cut off his head, and it rolled across the floor. They attacked all the celebrants stabbing them, spearing them, striking them with swords. . . .Others they beheaded . . . or split their heads to pieces. . . .The blood of the warriors flowed like water and gathered into pools . . . [T]hey invaded every room, hunting and killing.[35]

Visual Source 13.3 shows a vivid depiction of this "massacre of the nobles," drawn from the *Codex Duran*, first published in 1581.

- What elements of the description above are reflected in this painting?
- What image of the Spanish does this painting reflect?
- What do the drums in the center of the image represent?

The massacre of the nobles prompted a citywide uprising against the hated Spanish, who were forced to flee Tenochtitlán on June 30, 1520, across a causeway in Lake Texcoco amid ferocious fighting. Some 600 Spaniards and several thousand of their Tlaxcala allies perished in the escape, many of them laden with gold they had collected in Tenochtitlán. For the Spaniards it was La Noche Triste (the night of sorrow), while for the Aztecs it was no doubt a fitting

Visual Source 13.4 The Spanish Retreat from Tenochtitlán (The Rout of La Noche Triste [June 30, 1520], Lienzo de Tlaxcala, Pl 18. Library of Congress)

revenge and a great triumph. Visual Source 13.4, from a Tlaxcala codex, depicts the scene. Cortés and his Tlaxcala allies to the left of the image are shown on the causeway, while many others are drowning in the lake, pursued by Aztec warriors in canoes.

- Whose perspective do you think is represented in this image—that of the Spanish, their Tlaxcala allies, or the Aztecs? How might each of them have understood this retreat differently?

- In neither Visual Source 13.3 nor 13.4 are the Spanish portrayed with their firearms. How might you understand this omission?

- Notice the blending of artistic styles in this image. The water, the boats, and shields of the warriors are shown in traditional Mesoamerican fashion, while the Spanish are portrayed in European stereotypes. What does this blending suggest about the cultural processes at work in the codices?

While the Aztecs may well have thought themselves permanently rid of the Spanish, La Noche Triste offered only a temporary respite from the European invaders. Cortés and his now diminished forces found refuge among their Tlaxcala allies, where they regrouped and planned for yet another assault on

Tenochtitlán. Meanwhile, smallpox had begun to ravage the Aztec population, which lacked any immunity to this Old World disease. The *Florentine Codex* described the situation: "An epidemic broke out, a sickness of pustules. . . . [The disease] brought great desolation; a great many died of it. They could no longer walk about . . . no longer able to move or stir. . . . Starvation reigned, and no one took care of others any longer. . . . And when things were in this state, the Spaniards came."

- How does the Aztec-created image on p. 624 represent the impact of the disease?

In mid-1521, Cortés returned, strengthened with yet more Mesoamerican allies, and laid siege to the Aztec capital. Bitter fighting ensued, often in the form of house-to-house combat, ending with the surrender of the last Aztec emperor on August 13, 1521. In Tenochtitlán, all was sorrow and lamentation, as reflected in some of the poetry of the time:

> Nothing but flowers and songs of sorrow are left in Mexico and
>   Tlateloco
> where once we saw warriors and wise men. . . .
> We wander here and there in our desolate poverty.
> We are mortal men.
> We have seen bloodshed and pain where once we saw beauty and
>   valor.
> We are crushed to the ground; we lie in ruins. . . .
> Have you grown weary of your servants?
> Are you angry with your servants, O giver of Life?[36]

Using the Evidence: The Conquest of Mexico through Aztec Eyes

1. **Evaluating images as evidence:** What are the strengths and the limitations of these images as sources for understanding the colonial conquest of Mexico? How well did the native artists who created them understand the Spanish?

2. **Analyzing perspectives:** How might you define the perspective from which these visual sources approach their subjects? Keep in mind that they were drawn by native artists who had been clearly influenced by Spanish culture and religion. In what ways are they criticizing the Spanish conquest, celebrating it, or simply describing it?

3. **Portraying the Spanish:** In what ways do these visual sources portray the Spanish? How might the Spanish themselves present a different account of the conquest?

4. **Describing the conquest:** Based on the information in this section, write a brief description of the conquest from the Aztec point of view.

Chapter 13 Wrap Up

LearningCurve
Check what you know.
**bedfordstmartins.com
/strayer/LC**

STEP ONE

The Word to Know: Race

The *Oxford English Dictionary* provides three definitions for *race*: (1) "the class of humans; mankind"; (2) "a group of people, animals, or plants, connected by common descent or origin"; and (3) "a group of several tribes or peoples, regarded as forming a distinct ethnic set." Consider which definition most accurately reflects the understanding in world history that race is constructed by cultural values and local beliefs and is therefore not a meaningful way of dividing people. Then, relate this to the distinction the author makes about race and racism in North America, Brazil, and Spanish America (see pp. 627–34). Remembering that "race" does not pertain to any specific ethnic or racial group, write a brief paragraph about the function of race in these three colonial societies. In what ways did they differ? In what ways were they similar?

STEP TWO

Imperial Expansion

Compare Russian and Spanish expansion, examining the factors that led to their expansion, the processes involved, and the effects of expansion at home and abroad.

Empire	Factors promoting expansion	Process of expansion	Effects of expansion at home	Effects of expansion on conquered peoples
Russia				
Spain				

Leadership in the Early Modern World

Niccoló Machiavelli was a Renaissance thinker supported for a time by the ruling family of Florence (Italy), the Medicis, for whom he dispensed advice on how to maintain power. After reading the following excerpt from Machiavelli's seminal work *The Prince* (1513), answer the question below.

Nicoló Machiavelli, *The Prince*, 1513

"There is nothing more difficult to take in hand, more perilous to conduct, or more uncertain in its success than to take the lead in the introduction of a new order of things." "The Prince ought to have no other aim or thought, nor select anything else for his study, than war and its rules and discipline; for this is the sole art that belongs to him who rules, and it is of such force that it not only upholds those who are born princes, but it often enables men to rise from a private station to that rank. And, on the contrary, it is seen that when princes have thought more of ease than of arms they have lost their states. And the first cause of your losing it is to neglect this art; and what enables you to acquire a state is to be master of the art." "Since love and fear can hardly exist together, if we must choose between them, it is far safer to be feared than loved.... I see that one is obliged to look to the results of an action, and not to the means by which it was achieved.... The fortunate man is he who fits his plan of action to the times."

■ Question

What compliments or advice would Machiavelli give to the leaders discussed in the documents section on pp. 650–58?

Source: Niccolo Machiavelli, *The Prince*, ed. W. K. Marriott. London: J. M. Dent and Sons, 1908, pp. 117–118, 129–131

Economic Transformations

Commerce and Consequence

1450–1750

"I have come full circle back to my destiny: from Africa to America and back to Africa. I could hear the cries and wails of my ancestors. I weep with them and for them."[1] This is what an African American woman from Atlanta wrote in 2002 in the guest book of the Cape Coast Castle, one of the many ports of embarkation for slaves located along the coast of Ghana in West Africa. There she no doubt saw the whips and leg irons used to discipline the captured Africans as well as the windowless dungeons in which hundreds were crammed while waiting for the ships that would carry them across the Atlantic to the Americas. Almost certainly she also caught sight of the infamous "gate of no return," through which the captives departed to their new life as slaves.

THIS VISITOR'S EMOTIONAL ENCOUNTER WITH THE LEGACY OF THE AT-LANTIC SLAVE TRADE reminds us of the enormous significance of this commerce in human beings for the early modern world and of its continuing echoes even in the twenty-first century. The slave trade, however, was only one component of those international networks of exchange that shaped human interactions during the centuries between 1450 and 1750. Europeans now smashed their way into the ancient spice trade of the Indian Ocean, developing new relationships with Asian societies as a result. Silver, obtained from mines in Spanish America, enriched Western Europe, even as much of it made its way to China, where it allowed Europeans to participate more fully in the rich commerce of East Asia. Furs from North America and Siberia found a ready market in Europe and China, while the hunting and

---

The Atlantic Slave Trade: This eighteenth-century French painting shows the sale of slaves at Goree, a major slave trading port in what is now Dakar in Senegal. A European merchant and an African authority figure negotiate the arrangement, while the shackled victims themselves wait for their fate to be decided. (Bibliothèque des Arts Décoratifs, Paris/ Archives Charmet/The Bridgeman Art Library) trapping of those fur-bearing animals transformed both natural environments and human societies. Despite their growing prominence in long-distance exchange, Europeans were far from the only active traders. Southeast Asians, Chinese, Indians, Armenians, Arabs, and Africans likewise played major roles in the making of the world economy during the early modern era.

Thus commerce joined empire as the twin creators of a global network during these centuries. Together they gave rise to new relationships, disrupted old patterns, brought distant peoples into contact with one another, enriched some, and impoverished or enslaved others. From the various "old worlds" of the premodern era, a single "new world" emerged — slowly, amid much suffering, and accompanied by growing inequalities. What was gained and what was lost in the transformations born of global commerce have been the subject of great controversy ever since.

SEEKING THE MAIN POINT

In what different ways did global commerce transform human societies and the lives of individuals during the early modern era?

Europeans and Asian Commerce

■ **Causation**
What drove European involvement in the world of Asian commerce?

Schoolchildren everywhere know that European empires in the Western Hemisphere grew out of an accident — Columbus's unknowing encounter with the Americas — and that new colonial societies and new commercial connections across the Atlantic were the result. In Asia, it was a very different story. The voyage (1497–1499) of the Portuguese mariner Vasco da Gama, in which Europeans sailed to India for the first time, was certainly no accident. It was the outcome of a deliberate, systematic, century-long Portuguese effort to explore a sea route to the East, by creeping slowly down the West African coast, around the tip of South Africa, up the East African coast, and finally across the Indian Ocean to Calicut in southern India in 1498. There Europeans encountered an ancient and rich network of commerce that stretched from East Africa to China. They were certainly aware of the wealth of that commercial network, but largely ignorant of its workings.

The most immediate motivation for this massive effort was the desire for tropical spices — cinnamon, nutmeg, mace, cloves, and, above all, pepper — which were widely used as condiments and preservatives and were sometimes regarded as aphrodisiacs. A fifteenth-century English book declared: "Pepper [from Java] is black and has a good smack, And every man doth buy it."[2] Other products of the East, such as Chinese silk, Indian cottons, rhubarb for medicinal purposes, emeralds, rubies, and sapphires, also were in great demand.

Underlying this growing interest in Asia was the more general recovery of European civilization following the disaster of the Black Death in the early fourteenth century. During the fifteenth century, Europe's population was growing again, and its national monarchies — in Spain, Portugal, England, and France — were learning how to tax their subjects more effectively and to build substantial military forces equipped with gunpowder weapons. Its cities were growing too. Some of them — in England,

A Map of Time

Early 15th century	Beginning of Portuguese voyages along the coast of West Africa
1440s	First European export of slaves from West Africa
1492	Columbus reaches the Americas
1497	Vasco da Gama reaches India
1546	Founding of Potosi as silver mining town in Bolivia
1565	Beginning of Spanish takeover of the Philippines
1570s	Beginning of silver shipments from Mexico to Manila
17th century	Russian conquest of Siberia
1601–1602	British and Dutch East India companies established in Asia
18th century	Peak of the trans-Atlantic slave trade
1750s	British begin military conquest of India

the Netherlands, and northern Italy, for example—were becoming centers of international commerce, giving birth to economies based on market exchange, private ownership, and the accumulation of capital for further investment.

For many centuries, Eastern goods had trickled into the Mediterranean through the Middle East from the Indian Ocean commercial network. From the viewpoint of an increasingly dynamic Europe, several major problems accompanied this pattern of trade. First, of course, the source of supply for these much-desired goods lay solidly in Muslim hands. Most immediately, Muslim Egypt was the primary point of transfer into the Mediterranean basin and its European customers. The Italian commercial city of Venice largely monopolized the European trade in Eastern goods, annually sending convoys of ships to Alexandria in Egypt. Venetians resented the Muslim monopoly on Indian Ocean trade, and other European powers disliked relying on Venice as well as on Muslims. Circumventing these monopolies was yet another impetus—both religious and political—for the Portuguese to attempt a sea route to India that bypassed both Venetian and Muslim intermediaries. In addition, many Europeans of the time were persuaded that a mysterious Christian monarch, known as Prester John, ruled somewhere in Asia or Africa. Joining with his mythical kingdom to continue the Crusades and combat a common Islamic enemy was likewise a goal of the Portuguese voyages.

A further problem for Europeans lay in paying for Eastern goods. Few products of an economically less developed Europe were attractive in Eastern markets. Thus Europeans were required to pay cash—gold or silver—for Asian spices or textiles. This persistent trade deficit contributed much to the intense desire for precious metals

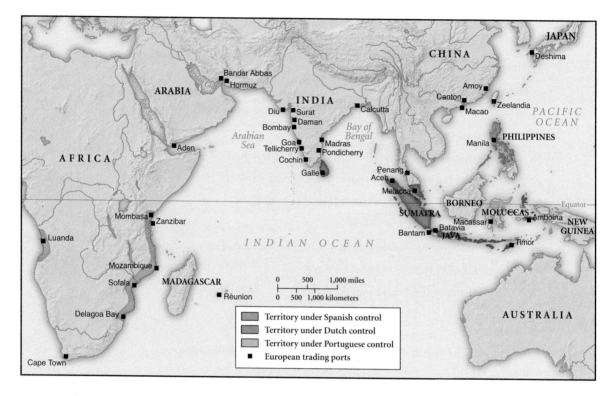

Map 14.1 Europeans in Asia in the Early Modern Era The early modern era witnessed only very limited territorial control by Europeans in Asia. Trade, rather than empire, was the chief concern of the Western newcomers, who were not, in any event, a serious military threat to major Asian states.

that attracted early modern European explorers, traders, and conquerors. Portuguese voyages along the West African coast, for example, were seeking direct access to African goldfields. The enormously rich silver deposits of Mexico and Bolivia provided at least a temporary solution to this persistent European problem.

First the Portuguese and then the Spanish, French, Dutch, and British found their way into the ancient Asian world of Indian Ocean commerce (see Map 14.1). How they behaved in that world and what they created there differed considerably among the various European countries, but collectively they contributed much to the new regime of globalized trade.

A Portuguese Empire of Commerce

■ **Connection**
To what extent did the Portuguese realize their own goals in the Indian Ocean?

The arena of Indian Ocean commerce into which Vasco da Gama and his Portuguese successors sailed was a world away from anything they had known. It was vast, both in geographic extent and in the diversity of those who participated in it. East Africans, Arabs, Persians, Indians, Malays, Chinese, and others traded freely. Most of them were Muslims, though hailing from many separate communities, but Hindus, Christians, Jews, and Chinese likewise had a role in this commercial network. Had the Portuguese sought simply to participate in peaceful trading, they certainly could have done so, but it was quickly apparent that European trade goods were crude and unattractive in Asian markets and that Europeans would be unable to compete effectively. Moreover, the Portuguese soon learned that most Indian Ocean merchant ships were not heavily armed and certainly lacked the onboard cannons that Portuguese ships carried. Since the withdrawal of the Chinese fleet from the Indian Ocean early in the fifteenth century, no major power was in a position to dominate the sea lanes, and the many smaller-scale merchants generally traded openly, although piracy was sometimes a problem.

Given these conditions, the Portuguese saw an opening, for their ships could outgun and outmaneuver competing naval forces, while their onboard cannons could devastate coastal fortifications. Although their overall economy lagged behind that of Asian producers, Europeans had more than caught up in the critical area of naval technology and naval warfare. This military advantage enabled the Portuguese to quickly establish fortified bases at several key locations within the Indian Ocean world— Mombasa in East Africa, Hormuz at the entrance to the Persian Gulf, Goa on the west coast of India, Malacca in Southeast Asia, and Macao on the south coast of China. With the exception of Macao, which had been obtained through bribery and negotiations with Chinese authorities, these Portuguese bases were obtained forcibly against small and weak states. In Mombasa, for example, the commander of a Portuguese fleet responded to local resistance in 1505 by burning and sacking the city, killing some 1,500 people, and seizing large quantities of cotton and silk textiles and carpets. The king of Mombasa wrote a warning to a neighboring city:

> This is to inform you that a great lord has passed through the town, burning it and laying it waste. He came to the town in such strength and was of such a cruelty that he spared neither man nor woman, or old nor young—nay, not even the smallest child.... Nor can I ascertain nor estimate what wealth they have taken from the town.[3]

What the Portuguese created in the Indian Ocean is commonly known as a "trading post empire," for they aimed to control commerce, not large territories or populations, and to do so by force of arms rather than by economic competition. Seeking to monopolize the spice trade, the Portuguese king grandly titled himself "Lord of the Conquest, Navigation, and Commerce of Ethiopia, Arabia, Persia, and India." Portuguese authorities in the East tried to require all merchant vessels to purchase a *cartaz*, or pass, and to pay duties of 6 to 10 percent on their cargoes. They partially blocked the traditional Red Sea route to the Mediterranean and for a century or so monopolized the highly profitable route around Africa to Europe. Even so, they never succeeded in controlling much more than half of the spice trade to Europe.[4]

Failing to dominate Indian Ocean commerce as they had hoped, the Portuguese gradually assimilated themselves to its ancient patterns. They became heavily involved in carrying Asian goods to Asian ports, selling their shipping services because they were largely unable to sell their goods. Even in their major settlements, the

The Spice Trade
For thousands of years, spices were a major trade item in the Indian Ocean commercial network, as this fifteenth-century French depiction of the gathering of pepper in southern India illustrates. In the early modern era, Europeans gained direct access to this ancient network for the first time. (Bibliothèque nationale de France)

Portuguese were outnumbered by Asian traders, and many married Asian women. Hundreds of Portuguese escaped the control of their government altogether and settled in Asian or African ports, where they learned local languages, sometimes converted to Islam, and became simply one more group in the diverse trading culture of the East.

By 1600, the Portuguese trading post empire was in steep decline. This small European country was overextended, and rising Asian states such as Japan, Burma, Mughal India, Persia, and the sultanate of Oman actively resisted Portuguese commercial control. Unwilling to accept a dominant Portuguese role in the Indian Ocean, other European countries also gradually contested Portugal's efforts to monopolize the rich spice trade to Europe.

Spain and the Philippines

■ **Comparison**

How did the Portuguese, Spanish, Dutch, and British initiatives in Asia differ from one another?

Spain was the first to challenge Portugal's position. As precious and profitable spices began to arrive in Europe on Portuguese ships in the early sixteenth century, the Spanish soon realized that they were behind in the race to gain access to the riches of the East. In an effort to catch up, they established themselves on what became the Philippine Islands, named after the Spanish king Philip II. The Spanish first encountered the region during the famous round-the-world voyage (1519–1521) of Ferdinand Magellan, a Portuguese mariner sailing on behalf of the Spanish Crown. There they found an archipelago of islands, thousands of them, occupied by culturally diverse peoples and organized in small and highly competitive chiefdoms. One of the local chiefs later told the Spanish: "There is no king and no sole authority in this land; but everyone holds his own view and opinion, and does as he prefers."[5] Some were involved in tribute trade with China, and a small number of Chinese settlers lived in the port towns. Nonetheless, the region was of little interest to the governments of China and Japan, the major powers in the area.

These conditions—proximity to China and the spice islands, small and militarily weak societies, the absence of competing claims—encouraged the Spanish to establish outright colonial rule on the islands, rather than to imitate a Portuguese-style trading post empire. Small-scale military operations, gunpowder weapons, local alliances, gifts and favors to chiefs, and the pageantry of Catholic ritual all contributed to a relatively easy and often bloodless Spanish takeover of the islands in the century or so after 1565. They remained a Spanish colonial territory until the end of the nineteenth century, when the United States assumed control following the Spanish-American War of 1898.

Accompanying Spanish rule was a major missionary effort, which turned Filipino society into the only major outpost of Christianity in Asia. That effort also opened up a new front in the long encounter of Christendom and Islam, for on the southern island of Mindanao, Islam was gaining strength and provided an ideology of resistance to Spanish encroachment for 300 years. Indeed Mindanao remains a contested part of the Philippines into the twenty-first century.

Beyond the missionary enterprise, other features of Spanish colonial practice in the Americas found expression in the Philippines. People living in scattered settlements were persuaded or forced to relocate into more concentrated Christian communities. Tribute, taxes, and unpaid labor became part of ordinary life. Large landed estates emerged, owned by Spanish settlers, Catholic religious orders, or prominent Filipinos. Women who had played major roles as ritual specialists, healers, and midwives were now displaced by male Spanish priests, and their ceremonial instruments were deliberately defiled and disgraced. Short-lived revolts and flight to interior mountains were among the Filipino responses to colonial oppression.

Yet others fled to Manila, the new capital of the colonial Philippines. By 1600, it had become a flourishing and culturally diverse city of more than 40,000 inhabitants and was home to many Spanish settlers and officials and growing numbers of Filipino migrants. Its rising prosperity also attracted some 3,000 Japanese and more than 20,000 Chinese. Serving as traders, artisans, and sailors, the Chinese in particular became an essential element in the Spanish colony's growing economic relationship with China; however, their economic prominence and their resistance to conversion earned them Spanish hostility and clearly discriminatory treatment. Periodic Chinese revolts, followed by expulsions and massacres, were the result. On one occasion in 1603, the Spanish killed about 20,000 people, nearly the entire Chinese population of the island.

The East India Companies

Far more important than the Spanish as European competitors for the spice trade were the Dutch and English, both of whom entered Indian Ocean commerce in the early seventeenth century. Together they quickly overtook and displaced the Portuguese, often by force, even as they competed vigorously with each other as well. These rising Northern European powers were both militarily and economically stronger than the Portuguese. During the sixteenth century, the Dutch had become a highly commercialized and urbanized society, and their business skills and maritime shipping operations were the envy of Europe. Around 1600, both the British and the Dutch, unlike the Portuguese, organized their Indian Ocean ventures through private trading companies, which were able to raise money and share risks among a substantial number of merchant investors. The British East India Company and the Dutch East India Company received charters from their respective governments granting them trading monopolies and the power to make war and to govern conquered peoples. Thus they established their own parallel and competing trading post empires, with the Dutch focused on the islands of Indonesia and the English on India. Somewhat later, a French company also established settlements in the Indian Ocean basin.

Operating in a region of fragmented and weak political authority, the Dutch acted to control not only the shipping but also the production of cloves, cinnamon, nutmeg, and mace. With much bloodshed, the Dutch seized control of a number of small spice-producing islands, forcing their people to sell only to the Dutch and destroying the crops of those who refused. On the Banda Islands, famous for their nutmeg, the Dutch killed, enslaved, or left to starve virtually the entire population of some 15,000 people and then replaced them with Dutch planters, using a slave labor force to produce the nutmeg crop. One Indonesian sultan asked a Dutch commander, "Do you believe that God has preserved for your trade alone islands which lie so far from your homeland?"[6] Apparently they did. And for a time in the seventeenth century, the Dutch were able to monopolize the trade in nutmeg, mace, and cloves and to sell these spices in Europe and India at fourteen to seventeen times the price they paid in Indonesia.[7] While Dutch profits soared, the local economy of the Spice Islands was shattered, and their people were impoverished.

The Dutch East India Company also established itself briefly on the large island of Taiwan, off the coast of southern China, between 1624 and 1662, hoping to produce deerskins, rice, and sugar for export.

A European View of Asian Commerce
The various East India companies (British, French, and Dutch) represented the major vehicle for European commerce in Asia during the early modern era. This wall painting, dating from 1778 and titled *The East Offering Its Riches to Britannia*, hung in the main offices of the British East India Company. (© British Library Board)

Finding the local people unwilling to take part in commercial agriculture, the Dutch opened the island to large-scale Chinese immigration. Thus under a regime of Dutch and Chinese "co-colonization," Taiwan became ethnically Chinese. Later in the century, Chinese forces expelled the Dutch, bringing Taiwan into China politically as well. And so Taiwan emerged as a place of intersection between European and Chinese expansion in the early modern era.[8]

The British East India Company operated differently than its Dutch counterpart. Less well financed and less commercially sophisticated, the British were largely excluded from the rich Spice Islands by the Dutch monopoly. Thus they fell back on India, where they established three major trading settlements during the seventeenth century: Bombay (now Mumbai), on India's west coast, and Calcutta and Madras, on the east coast. Although British naval forces soon gained control of the Arabian Sea and the Persian Gulf, largely replacing the Portuguese, on land they were no match for the powerful Mughal Empire, which ruled most of the Indian subcontinent. Therefore, the British were unable to practice "trade by warfare," as the Dutch did in Indonesia.[9] Rather they secured their trading bases with the permission of Mughal authorities or local rulers, with substantial payments and bribes as the price of admission to the Indian market. When some independent English traders plundered a Mughal ship in 1636, local authorities detained British East India Company officials for two months and forced them to pay a whopping fine. Although pepper and other spices remained important in British trade, British merchants came to focus much more heavily on Indian cotton textiles, which were becoming widely popular in England and its American colonies. Hundreds of villages in the interior of southern India became specialized producers for this British market.

Like the Portuguese before them, both the Dutch and English became heavily involved in trade within Asia. The profits from this "carrying trade" enabled them to purchase Asian goods without paying for them in gold or silver from Europe. Dutch and English traders also began to deal in bulk goods for a mass market—pepper, textiles, and later, tea and coffee—rather than just luxury goods for an elite market. In the second half of the eighteenth century, both the Dutch and British trading post empires slowly evolved into a more conventional form of colonial domination, in which the British came to rule India and the Dutch controlled Indonesia.

Asians and Asian Commerce

The attention of historians often falls disproportionately on what is new. Although European commerce in the Indian Ocean and the South China Sea certainly qualifies as "something new," the European presence was far less significant in Asia than it was in the Americas or Africa during these centuries. European political control was limited to the Philippines, parts of Java, and a few of the Spice Islands. The small Southeast Asian state of Siam was able to expel the French in 1688, outraged by their aggressive religious efforts at conversion and their plotting to extend French influence. To the great powers of Asia—Mughal India, China, and Japan—Europeans represented no real military threat and played minor roles in their large and prosperous economies. Japan provides a fascinating case study in the ability of major Asian powers to control the European intruders.

When Portuguese traders and missionaries first arrived in that island nation in the mid-sixteenth century, soon followed by Spanish, Dutch, and English merchants, Japan was plagued by endemic conflict among numerous feudal lords, known as *daimyo*, each with his own cadre of *samurai* warriors. In these circumstances, the European newcomers found a hospitable welcome, for their military technology, shipbuilding skills, geographic knowledge, commercial opportunities, and even religious ideas proved useful or attractive to various elements in Japan's fractious and competitive society. The second half of the sixteenth century, for example, witnessed the growth of a substantial Christian movement, with some 300,000 converts and a Japanese-led church.

By the early seventeenth century, however, a series of remarkable military figures had unified Japan politically, under the leadership of a supreme military commander known as the *shogun*, who hailed from the Tokugawa clan. With the end of Japan's civil wars, successive shoguns came to view Europeans as a threat to the country's newly established unity rather than an opportunity. They therefore expelled Christian missionaries and violently suppressed the practice of Christianity. This policy included the execution, often under torture, of some sixty-two missionaries and thousands of Japanese converts. Shogunate authorities also forbade Japanese from traveling abroad and banned most European traders altogether, permitting only the Dutch, who appeared less interested in spreading Christianity, to trade at a single site. Thus, for two centuries (1650–1850), Japanese authorities of the Tokugawa shogunate largely closed their country off from the emerging world of European commerce, although they maintained their trading ties to China and Korea.

Despite the European naval dominance in the Indian Ocean, Asian merchants did not disappear. Arab, Indian, Chinese, Javanese, Malay, Cham, and other traders benefited from the upsurge in seaborne commerce. Resident communities of Chinese merchants inhabited many Southeast Asian port cities and dominated the growing spice trade between that region and China. Southeast Asian merchants, many of them women, continued a long tradition of involvement in international trade. Malay proverbs from the sixteenth century, for example, encouraged "teaching daughters how to calculate and make a profit."[10] Overland trade within Asia remained wholly in Asian hands and grew considerably. Christian merchants from Armenia were particularly active in the commerce linking Europe, the Middle East, and Central Asia. Tens of thousands of Indian merchants and moneylenders, mostly Hindus representing sophisticated family firms, lived throughout Central Asia, Persia, and Russia, thus connecting this vast region to markets in India. These international Asian commercial networks, equivalent in their commercial sophistication to those of Europe, continued to operate successfully even as Europeans militarized the seaborne commerce of the Indian Ocean.

Within India, large and wealthy family firms, such as the one headed by Vijri Vora during the seventeenth century, were able to monopolize the buying and selling of particular products, such as pepper or coral, and thus dictate terms and prices to the European trading companies. "He knoweth that wee must sell," complained one English trader about Vora, "and so beats us downe till we come to his owne rates." Furthermore, Vora was often the only source of loans for the cash-strapped Europeans, forcing them to pay interest rates as high as 12 to 18 percent annually. Despite their resentments, Europeans had little choice, because "none but Virji Vora hath moneye to lend or will lend."[11]

Silver and Global Commerce

Even more than the spice trade of Eurasia, it was the silver trade that gave birth to a genuinely global network of exchange (see Map 14.2). As one historian put it, silver "went round the world and made the world go round."[12] The mid-sixteenth-century discovery of enormously rich silver deposits in Bolivia, and simultaneously in Japan, suddenly provided a vastly increased supply of that precious metal. Spanish America alone produced perhaps 85 percent of the world's silver during the early modern era. Spain's sole Asian colony, the Philippines, provided a critical link in this emerging network of global commerce. Manila, the colonial capital of the Philippines, was the destination of annual Spanish shipments of silver, which were drawn from the rich mines of Bolivia, transported initially to Acapulco in Mexico, and from

■ **Connection**

What was the world historical importance of the silver trade?

Map 14.2 The Global Silver Trade

Silver was one of the first major commodities to be exchanged on a genuinely global scale.

there shipped across the Pacific to the Philippines. This trade was the first direct and sustained link between the Americas and Asia, and it initiated a web of Pacific commerce that grew steadily over the centuries.

At the heart of that Pacific web, and of early modern global commerce generally, was China's huge economy, and especially its growing demand for silver. In the 1570s, Chinese authorities consolidated a variety of tax levies into a single tax, which its huge population was now required to pay in silver. This sudden new demand for the white metal caused its value to skyrocket. It meant that foreigners with silver could now purchase far more of China's silks and porcelains than before.

This demand set silver in motion around the world, with the bulk of the world's silver supply winding up in China and much of the rest elsewhere in Asia. The routes by which this "silver drain" operated were numerous. Chinese, Portuguese, and Dutch traders flocked to Manila to sell Chinese goods in exchange for silver. European ships carried Japanese silver to China. Much of the silver shipped across the Atlantic to Spain was spent in Europe generally and then used to pay for the Asian goods that the French, British, and Dutch so greatly desired. Silver paid for some African slaves and for spices in Southeast Asia. The standard Spanish silver coin, known as a "piece of eight," was used by merchants in North America, Europe, India, Russia, and West Africa as a medium of exchange. By 1600, it circulated widely in southern China. A Portuguese merchant in 1621 noted that silver "wanders throughout all the world . . . before flocking to China, where it remains as if at its natural center."[13]

In its global journeys, silver transformed much that it touched. At the world's largest silver mine in what is now Bolivia, the city of Potosí arose from a barren landscape high in the Andes, a ten-week mule trip away from Lima. "New people arrive by the hour, attracted by the smell of silver," commented a Spanish observer in the 1570s. With 160,000 people, Potosí became the largest city in the Americas and equivalent in size to London, Amsterdam, or Seville. Its wealthy European elite lived in luxury, with all the goods of Europe and Asia at their disposal. Meanwhile, the city's Native American miners worked in conditions so horrendous that some families held funeral services for men drafted to work the mines. One Spanish priest referred to Potosí as a "portrait of hell."[14] The environment too suffered, as highly intensive mining techniques caused severe deforestation, soil erosion, and flooding.

But the silver-fueled economy of Potosí also offered opportunity, not least to women. Spanish women might rent out buildings they owned for commercial purposes or send their slaves into the streets as small-scale traders, earning a few pesos for the household. Those less well-to-do often ran stores, pawnshops, bakeries, and taverns. Indian and *mestiza* women likewise opened businesses that provided the city with beverages, food, clothing, and credit.[15]

In Spain itself, which was the initial destination for much of Latin America's silver, the precious metal vastly enriched the Crown, making Spain the envy of its European rivals during the sixteenth century. Spanish rulers could now pursue military and political ambitions in both Europe and the Americas far beyond the country's own resource base. "New World mines," concluded several prominent historians, "sup-

Potosí

This colonial-era painting shows the enormously rich silver mines of Potosí, then a major global source of the precious metal and the largest city in the Americas. Brutally hard work and poisonous exposure to mercury, used in the refining process, led to the deaths of many thousands of workers, even as the silver itself contributed to European splendor in the early modern era. (Courtesy, The Hispanic Society of America)

ported the Spanish empire."[16] Nonetheless, this vast infusion of wealth did not fundamentally transform the Spanish economy because it generated more inflation of prices than real economic growth. A rigid economy laced with monopolies and regulations, an aristocratic class that preferred leisure to enterprise, and a crusading insistence on religious uniformity all prevented the Spanish from using their silver windfall in a productive fashion. When the value of silver dropped in the early seventeenth century, Spain lost its earlier position as the dominant Western European power. More generally, the flood of American silver that circulated in Europe drove prices higher, further impoverished many, stimulated uprisings across the continent, and contributed to what historians sometimes call a "general crisis" of upheaval and instability in the seventeenth century.

Japan, another major source of silver production in the sixteenth century, did better. Its military rulers, the Tokugawa shoguns, used silver-generated profits to defeat hundreds of rival feudal lords and unify the country. Unlike their Spanish counterparts, the shoguns allied with the country's vigorous merchant class to develop a market-based economy and to invest heavily in agricultural and industrial enterprises. Japanese state and local authorities alike acted vigorously to protect and renew Japan's dwindling forests, while millions of families in the eighteenth century took steps to have fewer children by practicing late marriages, contraception, abortion, and infanticide. The outcome was the dramatic slowing of Japan's population growth, the easing of an impending ecological crisis, and a flourishing, highly commercialized economy. These were the foundations for Japan's remarkable nineteenth-century Industrial Revolution.

In China, silver deepened the already substantial commercialization of the country's economy. To obtain the silver needed to pay their taxes, more and more people had to sell something — either their labor or their products. Communities that devoted themselves to growing mulberry trees, on which silkworms fed, had to buy their rice from other regions. Thus the Chinese economy became more regionally specialized. Particularly in southern China, this surging economic growth resulted in the loss of about half the area's forest cover as more and more land was devoted to cash crops. No Japanese-style conservation program emerged to address this growing problem. An eighteenth-century Chinese poet, Wang Dayue, gave voice to the fears that this ecological transformation wrought:

> Rarer, too, their timber grew, and rarer still and rarer
> As the hills resembled heads now shaven clean of hair.
> For the first time, too, moreover, they felt an anxious mood
> That all their daily logging might not furnish them with fuel.[17]

China's role in the silver trade is a useful reminder of Asian centrality in the world economy of the early modern era. Its large and prosperous population, increasingly operating within a silver-based economy, fueled global commerce, vastly increasing the quantity of goods exchanged and the geographic range of world trade. Despite their obvious physical presence in the Americas, Africa, and Asia, economically speaking Europeans were essentially middlemen, funneling American silver to Asia and competing with one another for a place in the rich markets of the East. The productivity of the Chinese economy was evident in Spanish America, where cheap and well-made Chinese goods easily outsold those of Spain. In 1594, the Spanish viceroy of Peru observed that "a man can clothe his wife in Chinese silks for [25 pesos], whereas he could not provide her with clothing of Spanish silks with 200 pesos."[18] Indian cotton textiles likewise outsold European woolen or linen textiles in the seventeenth century to such an extent that French laws in 1717 prohibited the wearing of Indian cotton or Chinese silk clothing as a means of protecting French industry.

The "World Hunt": Fur in Global Commerce[19]

■ Change

Describe the impact of the fur trade on North American native societies.

In the early modern era, furs joined silver, textiles, and spices as major items of global commerce. Their production had an important environmental impact as well as serious implications for the human societies that generated and consumed them. Furs, of course, had long provided warmth and conveyed status in colder regions of the world, but the integration of North America and of northern Asia (Siberia) into a larger world economy vastly increased their significance in global trade.

By 1500, European population growth and agricultural expansion had sharply diminished the supply of fur-bearing animals, such as beaver, rabbits, sable, marten, and deer. Furthermore, much of the early modern era witnessed a period of cooling temperatures and harsh winters, known as the Little Ice Age, which may well have increased the demand for furs. "The weather is bitterly cold and everyone is in furs although we are almost in July," observed a surprised visitor from Venice while in London in 1604.[20] These conditions pushed prices higher. The cost of a good-quality beaver pelt, for example, quadrupled in France between 1558 and 1611. This translated into strong economic incentives for European traders to tap the immense wealth of fur-bearing animals found in North America.

Like other aspects of imperial expansion, the fur trade was a highly competitive enterprise. The French were most prominent in the St. Lawrence valley, around the Great Lakes, and later along the Mississippi River; British traders pushed into the Hudson Bay region; and the Dutch focused their attention along the Hudson River in what is now New York. They were frequently rivals for the great prize of North American furs. In the southern colonies of British North America, deerskins by the hundreds of thousands found a ready market in England's leather industry (see Map 14.3).

Only a few Europeans directly engaged in commercial trapping or hunting. They usually waited for Indians to bring the furs or skins initially to their coastal settlements and later to their fortified trading posts in the interior of North America. European merchants paid for the furs with a variety of trade goods, including guns, blankets, metal tools, rum, and brandy, amid much ceremony, haggling over prices, and ritualized gift giving. Native Americans represented a cheap labor force in this international commercial effort, but they were not a directly coerced labor force.

Over the three centuries of the early modern era, enormous quantities of furs and deerskins found their way to Europe, where they considerably enhanced the standard of living in those cold climates. The environmental price was paid in the Americas, and it was high. A consistent demand for beaver hats led to the near extinction of that industrious animal in much of North America by the early nineteenth century. Many other fur-bearing species were seriously depleted as the trade moved inexorably westward. By the 1760s, hunters in southeastern British colonies took about 500,000 deer every year, seriously diminishing the deer population of the region.

For the Native American peoples who hunted, trapped, processed, and transported these products, the fur trade bore various benefits, particularly at the beginning. The Hurons, for example, who lived on the northern shores of Lakes Erie and Ontario in the early seventeenth century, annually exchanged some 20,000 to 30,000 pelts, mostly beaver, and in return received copper pots, metal axes, knives, cloth, firearms, and alcohol. Many of these items were of real value, which strengthened the Hurons in their relationships with neighboring peoples. These goods also enhanced

Map 14.3   The North American Fur Trade
North America, as well as Russian Siberia, funneled an apparently endless supply of furs into the circuits
of global trade during the early modern era.

the authority of Huron chiefs by providing them with gifts to distribute among their
followers. At least initially, competition among Europeans ensured that Native American leaders could negotiate reasonable prices for their goods. Furthermore, their
important role in the lucrative fur trade protected them for a time from the kind of
extermination, enslavement, or displacement that was the fate of native peoples in
Portuguese Brazil.

Nothing, however, protected them against the diseases carried by Europeans. In the 1630s and 1640s, to cite only one example of many, about half of the Hurons perished from influenza, smallpox, and other European-borne diseases. Furthermore, the fur trade generated warfare beyond anything previously known. Competition among Native American societies became more intense as the economic stakes grew higher. Catastrophic population declines owing to disease stimulated "mourning wars," designed to capture people who could be assimilated into much-diminished societies. A century of French-British rivalry for North America (1664–1763) forced Native American societies to take sides, to fight, and to die in these European imperial conflicts. Firearms, of course, made warfare far more deadly than before.

As many Native American peoples became enmeshed in commercial relationships with Europeans, they grew dependent on European trade goods. Among the Algonquians, for example, iron tools and cooking pots replaced those of stone, wood, or bone; gunpowder weapons took the place of bows and arrows; European textiles proved more attractive than traditional beaver and deerskin clothing; flint and steel were more effective for starting fires than wooden drills. A wide range of traditional crafts were thus lost, without the native peoples gaining a corresponding ability to manufacture the new items for themselves. Enthusiasm for these imported goods and continued European demands for furs and skins frequently eroded the customary restraint that characterized traditional hunting practices, resulting in the depletion of many species. One European observer wrote of the Creek Indians: "[They] wage eternal war against deer and bear . . . which is indeed carried to an unreasonable and perhaps criminal excess, since the white people have dazzled their senses with foreign superfluities."[21]

Beyond germs and guns, the most destructive of the imported goods was surely alcohol—rum and brandy, in particular. Whiskey, a locally produced grain-based alcohol, only added to the problem. With no prior experience of alcohol and little time to adjust to its easy availability, these drinks "hit Indian societies with explosive force."[22] Binge drinking, violence among young men, promiscuity, and addiction followed in many places. In 1753, Iroquois leaders complained bitterly to European authorities in Pennsylvania:"These wicked Whiskey Sellers, when they have once got the Indians in liquor, make them sell their very clothes from their backs. . . . If this practice be continued, we must be inevitably ruined."[23] In short, it was not so much the fur trade itself that decimated Native American societies, but all that accompanied it—disease, dependence, guns, alcohol, and the growing encroachment of European colonial empires.

All of this had particular implications for women. A substantial number of native women married European traders according to the "custom of the country"—with no sanction from civil or church authorities. Such marriages eased the difficulties of this cross-cultural exchange, providing traders with guides, interpreters, and negotiators. But sometimes these women were left abandoned when their husbands returned to Europe. More generally the fur trade enhanced the position of men in their societies since hunting or trapping animals was normally a male occupation.

Fur and the Russians
This colored engraving shows a sixteenth-century Russian ambassador and his contingent arriving at the court of the Holy Roman Emperor and bearing gifts of animal pelts, the richest fruit of the expanding Russian Empire. (RIA Novosti)

Among the Ojibwa, a gathering and hunting people in the northern Great Lakes region, women had traditionally acquired economic power by creating food, utensils, clothing, and decorations from the hides and flesh of the animals that their husbands caught. With the fur trade in full operation, women spent more time processing those furs for sale rather than producing household items, some of which were now available for purchase from Europeans. And so, as one scholar put it, "women lost authority and prestige." At the same time, however, women generated and controlled the trade in wild rice and maple syrup, both essential to the livelihood of European traders.[24] Thus the fur trade offered women a mix of opportunities and liabilities.

■ **Comparison**

How did the North American and Siberian fur trades differ from each other? What did they have in common?

Paralleling the North American fur trade was the one simultaneously taking shape within a rapidly expanding Russian Empire, which became a major source of furs for Western Europe, China, and the Ottoman Empire. The profitability of that trade in furs was the chief incentive for Russia's rapid expansion during the sixteenth and seventeenth centuries across Siberia, where the "soft gold" of fur-bearing animals was abundant. The international sale of furs greatly enriched the Russian state as well as many private merchants, trappers, and hunters. Here the silver trade and the fur trade intersected, as Europeans paid for Russian furs largely with American gold and silver.

The consequences for native Siberians were similar to those in North America as disease took its toll, as indigenous people became dependent on Russian goods, as the settler frontier encroached on native lands, and as many species of fur-bearing mammals were seriously depleted. In several ways, however, the Russian fur trade was unique. Whereas several European nations competed in North America and generally obtained their furs through commercial negotiations with Indian societies, no such competition accompanied Russian expansion across Siberia. Russian authorities imposed a tax or tribute, payable in furs, on every able-bodied Siberian male between eighteen and fifty years of age. To enforce the payment, they took hostages from Siberian societies, with death as a possible outcome if the required furs were not forthcoming. A further difference lay in the large-scale presence of private Russian hunters and trappers, who competed directly with their Siberian counterparts.

SUMMING UP SO FAR

What differences in the operation and impact of the spice, silver, and fur trades can you identify?

Commerce in People: The Atlantic Slave Trade

Of all the commercial ties that linked the early modern world into a global network of exchange, none had more profound or enduring human consequences than the Atlantic slave trade. Between 1500 and 1866, this trade in human beings took an estimated 12.5 million people from African societies, shipped them across the Atlantic in the infamous Middle Passage, and deposited some 10.7 million of them in the Americas, where they lived out their often brief lives as slaves. About 1.8 million (14.4 percent) died during the transatlantic crossing, while countless others perished in the process of capture and transport to the African coast.[25] (See Map 14.4 and

Map 14.4   The Atlantic Slave Trade
Stimulated by the plantation complex of the Americas, the Atlantic slave trade represented an enormous extension of the ancient practice of people owning and selling other people.

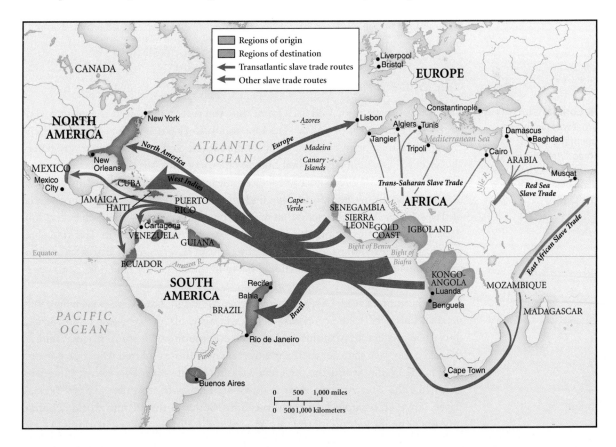

Documents: Voices from the Slave Trade, pp. 700–09, for various perspectives on the slave trade.)

Beyond the multitude of individual tragedies that it spawned—capture and sale, displacement from home cultures, forced labor, beatings and brandings, broken families—the Atlantic slave trade transformed all of its participants. Within Africa itself, that commerce thoroughly disrupted some societies, strengthened others, and corrupted many. Elites often enriched themselves, while the slaves, of course, were victimized almost beyond imagination.

In the Americas, the slave trade added a substantial African presence to the mix of European and Native American peoples. This African diaspora (the global spread of African peoples) injected into these new societies issues of race that endure still in the twenty-first century. It also introduced elements of African culture, such as religious ideas, musical and artistic traditions, and cuisine, into the making of American cultures. The profits from the slave trade and the forced labor of African slaves certainly enriched European and Euro-American societies, even as the practice of slavery contributed much to the racial stereotypes of European peoples. Finally, slavery became a metaphor for many kinds of social oppression, quite different from plantation slavery, in the centuries that followed. Workers protested the slavery of wage labor, colonized people rejected the slavery of imperial domination, and feminists sometimes defined patriarchy as a form of slavery.

The Slave Trade in Context

■ Comparison

What was distinctive about the Atlantic slave trade? What did it share with other patterns of slave owning and slave trading?

The Atlantic slave trade and slavery in the Americas represented the most recent large-scale expression of a very widespread human practice—the owning and exchange of human beings. With origins in the earliest civilizations, slavery was generally accepted as a perfectly normal human enterprise and was closely linked to warfare and capture. Before 1500, the Mediterranean and Indian Ocean basins were the major arenas of the Old World slave trade, and southern Russia was a major source of slaves. Many African societies likewise both practiced slavery themselves and sold slaves into these international commercial networks. A trans-Saharan slave trade had long funneled African captives into Mediterranean slavery, and an East African slave trade brought Africans into the Middle East and the Indian Ocean basin. Both operated largely within the Islamic world.

Furthermore, slavery came in many forms. Although slaves were everywhere vulnerable "outsiders" to their masters' societies, in many places they could be assimilated into their owners' households, lineages, or communities. In some places, children inherited the slave status of their parents; elsewhere those children were free persons. Within the Islamic world, the preference was for female slaves by a two-to-one margin, while the later Atlantic slave trade favored males by a similar margin. Not all slaves, however, occupied degraded positions. Some in the Islamic world acquired prominent military or political status. Most slaves in the premodern world worked in their owners' households, farms, or shops, with smaller numbers laboring in large-scale agricultural or industrial enterprises.

The slavery that emerged in the Americas was distinctive in several ways. One was simply the immense size of the traffic in slaves and its centrality to the economies of colonial America. Furthermore, this New World slavery was largely based on plantation agriculture and treated slaves as a form of dehumanized property, lacking any rights in the society of their owners. Slave status throughout the Americas was inherited across generations, and there was little hope of eventual freedom for the vast majority. Nowhere else, with the possible exception of ancient Greece, was widespread slavery associated with societies affirming values of human freedom and equality. Perhaps most distinctive was the racial dimension: Atlantic slavery came to be identified wholly with Africa and with "blackness." How did this exceptional form of slavery emerge?

The origins of Atlantic slavery clearly lie in the Mediterranean world and with that now common sweetener known as sugar. Until the Crusades, Europeans knew nothing of sugar and relied on honey and fruits to sweeten their bland diets. However, as they learned from the Arabs about sugarcane and the laborious techniques for producing usable sugar, Europeans established sugar-producing plantations within the Mediterranean and later on various islands off the coast of West Africa. It was a "modern" industry, perhaps the first one, in that it required huge capital investment, substantial technology, an almost factory-like discipline among workers, and a mass market of consumers. The immense difficulty and danger of the work, the limitations attached to serf labor, and the general absence of wage workers all pointed to slavery as a source of labor for sugar plantations.

Initially, Slavic-speaking peoples from the Black Sea region furnished the bulk of the slaves for Mediterranean plantations, so much so that "Slav" became the basis for the word "slave" in many European languages. In 1453, however, when the Ottoman Turks seized Constantinople, the supply of Slavic slaves was effectively cut off. At the same time, Portuguese mariners were exploring the coast of West Africa; they were looking primarily for gold, but they also found there an alternative source of slaves available for sale. Thus, when sugar, and later tobacco and cotton, plantations took hold in the Americas, Europeans had already established links to a West African source of supply. They also now had religious justification for their actions, for in 1452 the pope formally granted to the kings of Spain and Portugal "full and free permission to invade, search out, capture, and subjugate the Saracens [Muslims] and pagans and any other unbelievers . . . and to reduce their persons into perpetual slavery."[26] Largely through a process of elimination, Africa became the primary source of slave labor for the plantation economies of the Americas. Slavic peoples were no longer available; Native Americans quickly perished from European diseases; marginal Europeans were Christians and therefore supposedly exempt from slavery; and European indentured servants, who agreed to work for a fixed period in return for transportation, food, and shelter, were expensive and temporary. Africans, on the other hand, were skilled

■ **Causation**
What explains the rise of the Atlantic slave trade?

farmers; they had some immunity to both tropical and European diseases; they were not Christians; they were, relatively speaking, close at hand; and they were readily available in substantial numbers through African-operated commercial networks.

Moreover, Africans were black. The precise relationship between slavery and European racism has long been a much-debated subject. Historian David Brion Davis has suggested the controversial view that "racial stereotypes were transmitted, along with black slavery itself, from Muslims to Christians."[27] For many centuries, Muslims had drawn on sub-Saharan Africa as one source of slaves and in the process had developed a form of racism. The fourteenth-century Tunisian scholar Ibn Khaldun wrote that black people were "submissive to slavery, because Negroes have little that is essentially human and have attributes that are quite similar to those of dumb animals."[28]

Other scholars find the origins of racism within European culture itself. For the English, argues historian Audrey Smedley, the process of conquering Ireland had generated by the sixteenth century a view of the Irish as "rude, beastly, ignorant, cruel, and unruly infidels," perceptions that were then transferred to Africans enslaved on English sugar plantations of the West Indies.[29] Whether Europeans borrowed such images of Africans from their Muslim neighbors or developed them independently, slavery and racism soon went hand in hand. "Europeans were better able to tolerate their brutal exploitation of Africans," writes a prominent world historian, "by imagining that these Africans were an inferior race, or better still, not even human."[30]

The Slave Trade in Practice

■ **Connection**

What roles did Europeans and Africans play in the unfolding of the Atlantic slave trade?

The European demand for slaves was clearly the chief cause of this tragic commerce, and from the point of sale on the African coast to the massive use of slave labor on American plantations, the entire enterprise was in European hands. Within Africa itself, however, a different picture emerges, for over the four centuries of the Atlantic slave trade, European demand elicited an African supply. A few early efforts by the Portuguese at slave raiding along the West African coast convinced Europeans that such efforts were unwise and unnecessary, for African societies were quite capable of defending themselves against European intrusion, and many were willing to sell their slaves peacefully. Furthermore, Europeans died like flies when they entered the interior because they lacked immunities to common tropical diseases. Thus the slave trade quickly came to operate largely with Europeans waiting on the coast, either on their ships or in fortified settlements, to purchase slaves from African merchants and political elites. Certainly Europeans tried to exploit African rivalries to obtain slaves at the lowest possible cost, and the firearms they funneled into West Africa may well have increased the warfare from which so many slaves were derived. But from the point of initial capture to sale on the coast, the entire enterprise was normally in African hands. Almost nowhere did Europeans attempt outright military conquest; instead they generally dealt as equals with local African authorities.

An arrogant agent of the British Royal Africa Company in the 1680s learned the hard way who was in control when he spoke improperly to the king of Niumi, a small state in what is now Gambia. The company's records describe what happened next:

> [O]ne of the grandees [of the king], by name Sambalama, taught him better manners by reaching him a box on the ears, which beat off his hat, and a few thumps on the back, and seizing him . . . and several others, who together with the agent were taken and put into the king's pound and stayed there three or four days till their ransom was brought, value five hundred bars.[31]

In exchange for slaves, African sellers sought both European and Indian textiles, cowrie shells (widely used as money in West Africa), European metal goods, firearms and gunpowder, tobacco and alcohol, and various decorative items such as beads. Europeans purchased some of these items—cowrie shells and Indian textiles, for example—with silver mined in the Americas. Thus the slave trade connected with commerce in silver and textiles as it became part of an emerging worldwide network of exchange. Issues about the precise mix of goods African authorities desired, about the number and quality of slaves to be purchased, and always about the price of everything were settled in endless negotiation (see Document 14.2, pp. 703–05). Most of the time, a leading historian concluded, the slave trade took place "not unlike international trade anywhere in the world of the period."[32]

For the slaves themselves—seized in the interior, often sold several times on the harrowing journey to the coast, sometimes branded, and held in squalid slave dungeons while awaiting transportation to the New World—it was anything but a normal commercial transaction (see Document 14.1, pp. 700–03). One European engaged in the trade noted that "the negroes are so willful and loath to leave their own country, that they have often leap'd out of the canoes, boat, and ship, into the sea, and kept under water till they were drowned, to avoid being taken up and saved by our boats."[33]

Over the four centuries of the slave trade, millions of Africans underwent some such experience, but their numbers varied considerably over time. During the sixteenth century, slave exports from Africa averaged fewer than 3,000 annually. In those years, the Portuguese were at least as much interested in African gold, spices, and textiles. Furthermore, as in Asia, they became involved in transporting African goods, including slaves, from one African port

The Middle Passage
This mid-nineteenth-century painting of slaves held below deck on a Spanish slave ship illustrates the horrendous conditions of the transatlantic voyage, a journey experienced by many millions of captured Africans. (The Art Archive at Art Resource, NY)

Snapshot   **The Slave Trade in Numbers (1501–1866)**[34]

The Rise and Decline of the Slave Trade

The Destinations of Slaves

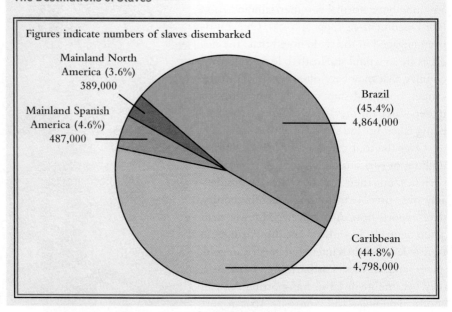

to another, thus becoming the "truck drivers" of coastal West African commerce.[35] In the seventeenth century, the pace picked up as the slave trade became highly competitive, with the British, Dutch, and French contesting the earlier Portuguese monopoly. The century and a half between 1700 and 1850 marked the high point of the slave trade as the plantation economies of the Americas boomed (see the Snapshot).

Where did these Africans come from, and where did they go? Geographically, the slave trade drew mainly on the societies of West Africa, from present-day Mauritania in the north to Angola in the south. Initially focused on the coastal regions, the slave trade progressively penetrated into the interior as the demand for slaves picked up. Socially, slaves were mostly drawn from various marginal groups in African societies—prisoners of war, criminals, debtors, people who had been "pawned" during times of difficulty. Thus Africans did not generally sell "their own people" into slavery. Divided into hundreds of separate, usually small-scale, and often rival communities—cities, kingdoms, microstates, clans, and villages—the various peoples of West Africa had no concept of an "African" identity. Those whom they captured and sold were normally outsiders, vulnerable people who lacked the protection of membership in an established community. When short-term economic or political advantage could be gained, such people were sold. In this respect, the Atlantic slave trade was little different from the experience of enslavement elsewhere in the world.

The destination of enslaved Africans, half a world away in the Americas, was very different. The vast majority wound up in Brazil or the Caribbean, where the labor demands of the plantation economy were most intense. Smaller numbers found themselves in North America, mainland Spanish America, or in Europe itself. Their journey across the Atlantic was horrendous, with the Middle Passage having an overall mortality rate of more than 14 percent (see Document 14.1, pp. 700–03). About 10 percent of the transatlantic voyages experienced a major rebellion by the desperate captives.

Consequences: The Impact of the Slave Trade in Africa

From the viewpoint of world history, the chief outcome of the slave trade lay in the new transregional linkages that it generated as Africa became a permanent part of an interacting Atlantic world. Millions of its people were now compelled to make their lives in the Americas, where they made an enormous impact both demographically and economically. Until the nineteenth century, they outnumbered European immigrants to the Americas by three or four to one, and West African societies were increasingly connected to an emerging European-centered world economy. These vast processes set in motion a chain of consequences that have transformed the lives and societies of people on both sides of the Atlantic.

Although the slave trade did not result in the kind of population collapse that occurred in the Americas, it certainly slowed Africa's growth at a time when Europe, China, and other regions were expanding demographically. Scholars have estimated

■ **Change**

In what different ways did the Atlantic slave trade transform African societies?

that sub-Saharan Africa represented about 18 percent of the world's population in 1600, but only 6 percent in 1900.[36] A portion of that difference reflects the slave trade's impact on Africa's population history.

That impact derived not only from the loss of millions of people over four centuries but also from the economic stagnation and political disruption that the slave trade generated. Economically, the slave trade stimulated little positive change in Africa because those Africans who benefited most from the traffic in people were not investing in the productive capacities of their societies. Although European imports generally did not displace traditional artisan manufacturing, no technological breakthroughs in agriculture or industry increased the wealth available to these societies. Maize and manioc (cassava), introduced from the Americas, added a new source of calories to African diets, but the international demand was for Africa's people, not its agricultural products.

Socially too the slave trade shaped African societies. It surely fostered moral corruption, particularly as judicial proceedings were manipulated to generate victims for the slave trade. A West African legend that cowrie shells, a major currency of the slave trade, grew on corpses of the slaves was a symbolic recognition of the corrupting effects of this commerce in human beings. During the seventeenth century, a movement known as the Lemba cult appeared along the lower and middle stretches of the Congo River. It brought together the mercantile elite — chiefs, traders, caravan leaders — of a region heavily involved in the slave trade. Complaining about stomach pains, breathing problems, and sterility, they sought protection against the envy of the poor and the sorcery that it provoked. Through ritual and ceremony as well as efforts to control markets, arrange elite marriages, and police a widespread trading network, Lemba officials sought to counter the disruptive impact of the slave trade and to maintain elite privileges in an area that lacked an overarching state authority.

African women felt the impact of the slave trade in various ways, beyond those who numbered among its trans-Atlantic victims. Since far more men than women were shipped to the Americas, the labor demands on those women who remained increased substantially, compounded by the growing use of cassava, a labor-intensive import from the New World. Unbalanced sex ratios also meant that far more men than before could marry multiple women. Furthermore, the use of female slaves within West African societies also grew as the export trade in male slaves expanded. Retaining female slaves for their own use allowed warriors and nobles in the Senegambia region to distinguish themselves more clearly from ordinary peasants. In the Kongo, female slaves provided a source of dependent laborers for the plantations that sustained the lifestyle of urban elites. A European merchant on the Gold Coast in the late eighteenth century observed that every free man had at least one or two slaves.

For much smaller numbers of women, the slave trade provided an opportunity to exercise power and accumulate wealth. In the Senegambia region, where women had long been involved in politics and commerce, marriage to European traders offered advantage to both partners. For European male merchants, as for fur traders in North

America, such marriages afforded access to African-operated commercial networks as well as the comforts of domestic life. Some of the women involved in these cross-cultural marriages, known as *signares*, became quite wealthy, operating their own trading empires, employing large numbers of female slaves, and acquiring elaborate houses, jewelry, and fashionable clothing.

Furthermore, the state-building enterprises that often accompanied the slave trade in West Africa offered yet other opportunities to a few women. As the Kingdom of Dahomey (deh-HOH-mee) expanded during the eighteenth century, the royal palace, housing thousands of women and presided over by a powerful Queen Mother, served to integrate the diverse regions of the state. Each lineage was required to send a daughter to the palace even as well-to-do families sent additional girls to increase their influence at court. In the Kingdom of Kongo, women held lower level administrative positions, the head wife of a nobleman exercised authority over hundreds of junior wives and slaves, and women served on the council that advised the monarch. The neighboring region of Matamba was known for its female rulers, most notably the powerful Queen Nzinga (1626–1663), who guided the state amid the complexities and intrigues of various European and African rivalries and gained a reputation for her resistance to Portuguese imperialism.

Within particular African societies, the impact of the slave trade differed considerably from place to place and over time. Many small-scale kinship-based societies, lacking the protection of a strong state, were thoroughly disrupted by raids from more powerful neighbors, and insecurity was pervasive. Oral traditions in southern Ghana, for example, reported that "there was no rest in the land," that people went about in groups rather than alone, and that mothers kept their children inside when European ships appeared.[37] Some larger kingdoms such as Kongo and Oyo slowly disintegrated as access to trading opportunities and firearms enabled outlying regions to establish their independence. (For an account of one young man's journey to slavery and back, see the Portrait of Ayuba Suleiman Diallo, pp. 696–97.)

However, African authorities also sought to take advantage of the new commercial opportunities and to manage the slave trade in their own interests. The kingdom of Benin, in the forest area of present-day Nigeria, successfully avoided a deep involvement in the trade while diversifying the exports with which it purchased European firearms and other goods. As early as 1516, its ruler began to restrict the slave trade and soon forbade the export of male slaves altogether, a ban that lasted until the early eighteenth century. By then, the ruler's authority over outlying areas had declined, and the country's major exports of pepper and cotton cloth had lost out to Asian and then European competition. In these circumstances, Benin felt compelled to resume limited participation in the slave trade. The neighboring kingdom of Dahomey, on the other hand, turned to a vigorous involvement in the slave trade in the early eighteenth century under strict royal control. The army conducted annual slave raids, and the government soon came to depend on the trade for its essential revenues. The slave trade in Dahomey became the chief business of the state and remained so until well into the nineteenth century.

LearningCurve
bedfordstmartins.com
/strayer/LC

Ayuba Suleiman Diallo, To Slavery and Back

February 1730 found Ayuba Suleiman Diallo, less than thirty years of age, living between the Gambia and Senegal rivers in West Africa among the Fulbe-speaking people.[38] Like his father, a prominent Islamic scholar and teacher, Ayuba was a Muslim, literate in Arabic, a prayer leader in the local mosque, and a *hafiz*, someone who had memorized the entire Quran. He was also husband to two wives and father to four children. Now his father sent the young man on an errand. He was to take several of their many slaves to a location some 200 miles away, where an English trading ship had anchored, and exchange them for paper and other goods. The paper was especially important, for his father's income depended on inscribing passages from the Quran on small slips of paper and selling them as protective charms.

Ayuba Suleiman Diallo. (Portrait of Ayuba Suleiman Diallo, 1733 (oil on canvas), Hoare, William, of Bath (1707-92) / Private Collection / Photo © Christie's Images / The Bridgeman Art Library)

Stephen Pike, Ayuba traveled farther south and traded his slaves for a number of cows in the land of the Mandinke people. Well beyond the safety of his own country, he was in dangerous territory. As he and his companions stopped to rest on the journey home, they were seized, their heads were shaved, and they were sold as slaves to the very same Captain Pike. Although Ayuba was able to send a message to his father asking to be ransomed in exchange for some of their slaves, the ship sailed before a reply was received. And so Ayuba, along with 168 other slaves, both men and women, headed for the British American colony of Maryland, where 150 of them arrived alive.

Sold to a local planter, Ayuba was immediately sent to the tobacco fields, but when he became

To put it mildly, things did not go as planned. Unable to reach an agreement with the English merchant Captain ill from this heavy and unaccustomed work, his owner assigned him the less arduous and more familiar task of

Reflections: Economic Globalization — Then and Now

The study of history reminds us of two quite contradictory truths. One is that our lives in the present bear remarkable similarities to those of people long ago. We are perhaps not so unique as we might think. The other is that our lives are very different from theirs and that things have changed substantially. This chapter about global commerce — long-distance trade in spices and textiles, silver and gold, beaver pelts and deerskins, slaves and sugar — provides both perspectives.

If we are accustomed to thinking about globalization as a product of the late twentieth century, early modern world history provides a corrective. Those three centuries reveal much that is familiar to people of the twenty-first century — the global circulation of goods; an international currency; production for a world market; the tending cattle. Alone with the cattle, Ayuba was able to withdraw into a nearby forest to pray, but he was spotted by a young white boy who mocked him and threw dirt in his face. Sometime later, no doubt in despair, Ayuba ran away, but he was soon captured and housed in the county jail, located in the back room of a tavern. There he became something of a local curiosity and attracted the attention of a lawyer named Thomas Bluett. When Ayuba refused wine, wrote a few lines in Arabic, and mentioned "Allah" and "Muhammad," Bluett realized that he was "no common slave." Locating an old slave who could translate for him, Bluett was fascinated by Ayuba's story, and he initiated a process that took both of them to England in 1733, where philanthropists purchased Ayuba's freedom.

Ayuba's reception in England was amazing. Now fluent in English, Ayuba was received by the English royal family and various members of the nobility, hosted by leading scholars, and entertained by wealthy merchants, eager to tap his knowledge of economic conditions in West Africa. The prominent artist William Hoare painted his portrait, complete with a small Quran hanging from his neck.

In 1734, he finally set off for home, loaded with gifts from his English friends. There he encountered, quite by chance, the same Mandinke men who had sold him only a few years before. Francis Moore, a European trader accompanying Ayuba, wrote that he "fell into a most terrible passion and was for killing them" and was restrained from doing so only with difficulty. He arrived in his hometown to find that his father had recently died. His wives and children, however, were all alive and welcomed him warmly. One of them had remarried, believing him gone forever, but her new husband readily gave way, and Ayuba resumed his place of prominence in his own community until his death in 1773.

He also resumed his life as a slave owner. Selling some of the gifts he had acquired in England, he purchased a woman slave and two horses, soon after his arrival back in West Africa. According to Moore, he "spoke always very handsomely of the English," and he continued his association with the Royal African Company, the primary English trading firm in West Africa, in their rivalry with French traders.[39] The last mention of Ayuba in the records of that company noted that he was seeking compensation for the loss of two slaves and a watch, probably the one given him by the English Queen Caroline.

Questions: What might you infer about Ayuba's own view of slavery and the slave trade? What insights or questions about the slave trade does his remarkable story suggest?

growing economic role of the West on the global stage; private enterprise, such as the British and Dutch East India companies, operating on a world scale; national governments eager to support their merchants in a highly competitive environment. By the eighteenth century, many Europeans dined from Chinese porcelain dishes called "china," wore Indian-made cotton textiles, and drank chocolate from Mexico, tea from China, and coffee from Yemen while sweetening these beverages with sugar from the Caribbean or Brazil. The millions who worked to produce these goods, whether slave or free, were operating in a world economy. Some industries were thoroughly international. New England rum producers, for example, depended on molasses imported from the Caribbean, while the West Indian sugar industry used African labor and European equipment to produce for a global market.

Nonetheless, early modern economic globalization was a far cry from that of the twentieth century. Most obvious perhaps were scale and speed. By 2000, immensely more goods circulated internationally and far more people produced for and depended on the world market than was the case even in 1750. Back-and-forth communications between England and India that took eighteen months in the eighteenth century could be accomplished in an hour by telegraph in the late nineteenth century and almost instantaneously via the Internet in the late twentieth century. Moreover, by 1900 globalization was firmly centered in the economies of Europe and North America. In the early modern era, by contrast, Asia in general and China in particular remained major engines of the world economy, despite the emerging presence of Europeans around the world. By the end of the twentieth century, the booming economies of Turkey, Brazil, India, and China suggested at least a partial return to that earlier pattern.

Early modern globalization differed in still other ways from that of the contemporary world. Economic life then was primarily preindustrial, still powered by human and animal muscles, wind, and water and lacked the enormous productive capacity that accompanied the later technological breakthrough of the steam engine and the Industrial Revolution. Finally, the dawning of a genuinely global economy in the early modern era was tied unapologetically to empire building and to slavery, both of which had been discredited by the late twentieth century. Slavery lost its legitimacy during the nineteenth century, and formal territorial empires largely disappeared in the twentieth. Most people during the early modern era would have been surprised to learn that a global economy, as it turned out, could function effectively without either of these long-standing practices.

Second Thoughts

LearningCurve
Check what you know.
bedfordstmartins.com
/strayer/LC

Online Study Guide
bedfordstmartins.com
/highschool/strayer

What's the Significance?

Indian Ocean commercial network, 672–74

trading post empire, 673

Philippines (Spanish), 674–75

British/Dutch East India companies, 676–77

Tokugawa shogunate, 678

"silver drain," 679–82

Potosí, 680

"soft gold," 686–87

African diaspora, 693–95

Benin/Dahomey, 695

Ayuba Suleiman Diallo, 696–97

Big Picture Questions

1. To what extent did Europeans transform earlier patterns of commerce, and in what ways did they assimilate into those older patterns?

2. How should we distribute the moral responsibility for the Atlantic slave trade? Is this an appropriate task for historians?

3. What lasting legacies of early modern globalization are evident in the twenty-first century? Pay particular attention to the legacies of the slave trade.

4. **Looking Back:** Asians, Africans, and Native Americans experienced early modern European expansion in quite different ways. Based on Chapters 13 and 14, how might you describe and explain those differences? In what respects were they active agents in the historical process rather than simply victims of European actions?

Next Steps: For Further Study

For Web sites and additional documents related to this chapter, see **Make History** at bedfordstmartins.com /highschool/strayer.

Glenn J. Ames, *The Globe Encompassed: The Age of European Discovery, 1500–1700* (2007). An up-to-date survey of European expansion in the early modern era.

Andre Gunder Frank, *ReOrient: Global Economy in the Asian Age* (1998). An account of the early modern world economy that highlights the centrality of Asia.

Erik Gilbert and Jonathan Reynolds, *Trading Tastes: Commodity and Cultural Exchange to 1750* (2006). A world historical perspective on transcontinental and transoceanic commerce.

David Northrup, ed., *The Atlantic Slave Trade* (2002). A fine collection of essays about the origins, practice, impact, and abolition of Atlantic slavery.

John Richards, *The Endless Frontier* (2003). Explores the ecological consequences of early modern commerce.

John Thornton, *Africa and Africans in the Making of the Atlantic World* (1998). A well-regarded but somewhat controversial account of the slave trade, with an emphasis on African authorities as active and independent players in the process.

Jerome S. Handler and Michael L. Tuite Jr., "Atlantic Slave Trade and Slave Life in the Americas: A Visual Record," http://hitchcock.itc.virginia.edu/Slavery/index.php. An immense collection of maps and images illustrating the slave trade and the life of slaves in the Americas.

Documents

Considering the Evidence:
Voices from the Slave Trade

By any measure the Atlantic slave trade was an enormous enterprise and enormously significant in modern world history: its geographical scope encompassed four continents, it endured for over four centuries, its victims numbered in the many millions, its commercial operation was complex and highly competitive, and its consequences echo still in both public and private life. The four documents that follow allow us to hear several individual voices from this vast historical process and to sample the evidence available to historians as they seek to understand this painful chapter of the human story.

Document 14.1

The Journey to Slavery

We begin with the voice of an individual victim of the slave trade — Olaudah Equiano. Born in what is now the Igbo-speaking region of Nigeria around 1745, Equiano was seized from his home at the age of eleven and sold into the Atlantic slave trade at the high point of that infamous commerce (see Map 14.4, p. 687). In service to three different owners, his experience as a slave in the Americas was quite unusual. He learned to read and write, traveled extensively as a seaman aboard one of his masters' ships, and was allowed to buy his freedom in 1766. Settling in England, he became a prominent voice in the emerging abolitionist movement of the late eighteenth century and wrote a widely read account of his life, addressed largely to European Christians: "O, ye nominal Christians! Might not an African ask you, Learned you this from your God, who says unto you, Do unto all men as you would men should do unto you?" His book was published in 1789 as abolitionism was gaining wider acceptance.

Despite some controversy about his birthplace and birth date, most historians accept Equiano's autobiography as broadly accurate. Document 14.1 presents Equiano's account of his capture, his journey to the coast, his experience on a slave ship, and his arrival in the Americas. It was a journey forcibly undertaken by millions of others as well.

- How does Equiano describe the kind of slavery he knew in Africa? How does it compare with the plantation slavery of the Americas?

- What part did Africans play in the slave trade, according to this account?

- What aspects of the shipboard experience contributed to the slaves' despair?

OLAUDAH EQUIANO

The Interesting Narrative of the Life of Olaudah Equiano
1789

As we live in a country where nature is prodigal of her favours, our wants are few and easily supplied; of course we have few manufactures. They consist for the most part of calicoes, earthen ware, ornaments, and instruments of war and husbandry. . . . We have also markets, at which I have been frequently with my mother. These are sometimes visited by stout mahogany-coloured men from the south west of us: . . . They generally bring us fire-arms, gunpowder, hats, beads, and dried fish. . . . They always carry slaves through our land; . . . Sometimes indeed we sold slaves to them, but they were only prisoners of war, or such among us as had been convicted of kidnapping or adultery, and some other crimes, which we esteemed heinous. . . .

My father, besides many slaves, had a numerous family, of which seven lived to grow up, including myself and a sister, who was the only daughter. . . . I was trained up from my earliest years in the art of war; my daily exercise was shooting and throwing javelins; and my mother adorned me with emblems, after the manner of our greatest warriors. In this way I grew up till I was turned the age of eleven, when an end was put to my happiness in the following manner. . . .

One day, when all our people were gone out to their works as usual, and only I and my dear sister were left to mind the house, two men and a woman got over our walls and in a moment seized us both, and, without giving us time to cry out, or make re-

sistance, they stopped our mouths, and ran off with us into the nearest wood. Here they tied our hands, and continued to carry us as far as they could, till night came on. . . . The next morning we left the house, and continued travelling all the day. For a long time we had kept the woods, but at last we came into a road which I believed I knew. I had now some hopes of being delivered; for we had advanced but a little way before I discovered some people at a distance, on which I began to cry out for their assistance: but my cries had no other effect than to make them tie me faster and stop my mouth, and then they put me into a large sack. . . .

The next day proved a day of greater sorrow than I had yet experienced; for my sister and I were then separated, while we lay clasped in each other's arms. It was in vain that we besought them not to part us; she was torn from me, and immediately carried away. . . .

At length, after many days traveling, during which I had often changed masters, I got into the hands of a chieftain, in a very pleasant country. This man had two wives and some children, and they all used me extremely well, and did all they could to comfort me; particularly the first wife, who was something like my mother. Although I was a great many days journey from my father's house, yet these people spoke exactly the same language with us. . . .

[After about a month], I was again sold. . . . The people I was sold to used to carry me very often, when I was tired, either on their shoulders or on their backs. I saw many convenient well-built sheds along the roads, at proper distances, to accommodate the merchants and travelers, who lay in those

Source: Olaudah Equiano, *The Interesting Narrative of the Life of Olaudah Equiano, or Gustavus Vassa, the African,* vol. 1 (London, 1789), chaps. 1, 2.

buildings along with their wives, who often accompany them; and they always go well armed.

I was again sold, and carried through a number of places, till, after traveling a considerable time, I came to a town called Tinmah, in the most beautiful country I had yet seen in Africa. . . . Their money consisted of little white shells, the size of the finger nail. I was sold here for one hundred and seventy-two of them by a merchant who lived and brought me there. I had been about two or three days at his house, when a wealthy widow, a neighbor of his, came there one evening, and brought with her an only son, a young gentleman about my own age and size. Here they saw me; and, having taken a fancy to me, I was bought of the merchant, and went home with them. . . . The next day I was washed and perfumed, and when meal-time came I was led into the presence of my mistress, and ate and drank before her with her son. This filled me with astonishment; and I could scarce help expressing my surprise that the young gentleman should suffer me, who was bound, to eat with him who was free; and not only so, but that he would not at any time either eat or drink till I had taken first, because I was the eldest, which was agreeable to our custom. Indeed everything here, and all their treatment of me, made me forget that I was a slave. The language of these people resembled ours so nearly, that we understood each other perfectly. . . . In this resemblance to my former happy state I passed about two months; and I now began to think I was to be adopted into the family, and was beginning to be reconciled to my situation, and to forget by degrees my misfortunes when all at once the delusion vanished; for, without the least previous knowledge, one morning early, while my dear master and companion was still asleep, I was wakened out of my reverie to fresh sorrow, and hurried away. . . .

Thus I continued to travel, sometimes by land, sometimes by water, through different countries and various nations, till, at the end of six or seven months after I had been kidnapped, I arrived at the sea coast. . . . The first object which saluted my eyes when I arrived on the coast was the sea, and a slave ship, which was then riding at anchor, and waiting for its cargo. These filled me with astonishment, which was soon converted into terror when I was carried on board. I was immediately handled and tossed up to see if I were sound by some of the crew; and I was now persuaded that I had gotten into a world of bad spirits, and that they were going to kill me. Their complexions too differing so much from ours, their long hair, and the language they spoke . . . united to confirm me in this belief. . . . When I looked round the ship too and saw a large furnace or copper boiling, and a multitude of black people of every description chained together, every one of their countenances expressing dejection and sorrow, I no longer doubted of my fate; and quite overpowered with horror and anguish, I fell motionless on the deck and fainted. . . .

I was soon put down under the decks, and there I received such a salutation in my nostrils as I had never experienced in my life: so that, with the loathsomeness of the stench and crying together, I became so sick and low that I was not able to eat, nor had I the least desire to taste anything. I now wished for the last friend, death, to relieve me; but soon, to my grief, two of the white men offered me eatables; and on my refusing to eat, one of them held me fast by the hands, and laid me across I think the windlass and tied my feet, while the other flogged me severely. . . .

I had never seen among any people such instances of brutal cruelty; and this not only shewn towards us blacks, but also to some of the whites themselves. One white man in particular I saw, when we were permitted to be on deck, flogged so unmercifully with a large rope near the foremast that he died in consequence of it; and they tossed him over the side as they would have done a brute. . . .

The closeness of the place, and the heat of the climate, added to the number in the ship, which was so crowded that each had scarcely room to turn himself, almost suffocated us. This produced copious perspirations, so that the air soon became unfit for respiration, from a variety of loathsome smells, and brought on a sickness among the slaves, of which many died, thus falling victims to the improvident avarice, as I may call it, of their purchasers. This wretched situation was again aggravated by the galling of the chains, now become insupportable; and the filth of the necessary tubs, into which the children often fell, and were almost suffocated. The shrieks of the women, and the groans of the dying, rendered the whole a scene of horror almost inconceivable. . . .

At last we came in sight of the island of Barbados, at which the whites on board gave a great shout, and made many signs of joy to us. . . . Many merchants and planters now came on board, though it was in the evening. They put us in separate parcels, and examined us attentively. They also made us jump, and pointed to the land, signifying we were to go there. We thought by this we should be eaten by those ugly men, as they appeared to us; . . . at last the white people got some old slaves from the land to pacify us. They told us we were not to be eaten, but to work, and were soon to go on land, where we should see many of our country people. This report eased us much; and sure enough, soon after we were landed, there came to us Africans of all languages. We were conducted immediately to the merchant's yard, where we were all pent up together like so many sheep in a fold, without regard to sex or age.

Document 14.2

The Business of the Slave Trade

For its African victims like Equiano, the slave trade was a horror beyond imagination; for kings and merchants—both European and African—it was a business. Document 14.2 shows how that business was conducted. It comes from the journal of an English merchant, Thomas Phillips, who undertook a voyage to the kingdom of Whydah in what is now the West African country of Benin in 1693–1694.

■ How would you describe the economic transactions described in the document? To what extent were they conducted between equal parties? Who, if anyone, held the upper hand in these dealings?

■ What obstacles did European merchants confront in negotiating with African authorities?

■ How might an African merchant have described the same transaction? How might Equiano describe it?

■ Notice the outcomes of Phillips's voyage to Barbados in the last two paragraphs. What does this tell you about European preferences for slaves, about the Middle Passage, and about the profitability of the enterprise?

THOMAS PHILLIPS

A Journal of a Voyage Made in the Hannibal of London
1694

As soon as the king understood of our landing, he sent two of his cappasheirs, or noblemen, to compliment us at our factory, where we design'd to continue that night, and pay our [respects] to his majesty next day . . . whereupon he sent two more of his grandees to invite us there that night, saying he waited for us, and that all former captains used to attend him the first night: whereupon being unwilling to infringe the custom, or give his majesty any of-fence, we took our hamocks, and Mr. Peirson, my-self, Capt. Clay, our surgeons, pursers, and about 12 men, arm'd for our guard, were carry'd to the king's town, which contains about 50 houses. . . .

We returned him thanks by his interpreter, and assur'd him how great affection our masters, the royal African company of England, bore to him, for his civility and fair and just dealings with their captains; and that notwithstanding there were many other places, more plenty of negro slaves that begg'd their custom, yet they had rejected all the advantageous offers made them out of their good will to him, and therefore had sent us to trade with him, to support his country with necessaries, and that we hop'd he would endeavour to continue their favour by his kind usage and fair dealing with us in our trade, that we may have our slaves with all expedition. . . . He an-swer'd that we should be fairly dealt with, and not impos'd upon; But he did not prove as good as his word . . . so after having examin'd us about our car-goe, what sort of goods we had, and what quantity of slaves we wanted, etc., we took our leaves and re-turn'd to the factory. . . .

According to promise we attended his maj-esty with samples of our goods, and made our agreement about the prices, tho' not without much difficulty; . . . next day we paid our customs to the king and cappasheirs, . . . then the bell was order'd to go about to give notice to all people to bring their slaves to the trunk to sell us. . . .

Capt. Clay and I had agreed to go to the trunk to buy the slaves by turns, each his day, that we might have no distractions or disagreement in our trade, as often happens when there are here more ships than one, and . . . their disagreements create animosities, underminings, and out-bidding each other, whereby they enhance the prices to their general loss and detriment, the blacks well knowing how to make the best use of such opportunities, and as we found make it their business, and endeavour to create and foment misunderstandings and jealousies between commanders, it turning to their great account in the disposal of their slaves.

When we were at the trunk, the king's slaves, if he had any, were the first offer'd to sale, . . . and we must not refuse them, tho' as I observ'd they were generally the worst slaves in the trunk, and we paid more for them than any others, which we could not remedy, it being one of his majesty's perogatives: then the cappasheirs each brought out his slaves ac-cording to his degree and quality, the greatest first, etc. and our surgeon examin'd them well in all kinds, to see that they were sound wind and limb, making them jump, stretch out their arms swiftly, looking in their mouths to judge of their age; for the cappa-sheirs are so cunning, that they shave them all close before we see them, so that let them be never so old we can see no grey hairs in their heads or beards; and then having liquor'd them well and sleek with palm oil, 'tis no easy matter to know an old one from a middle-age one. . . .

When we had selected from the rest such as we liked, we agreed in what goods to pay for them, the prices being already stated before the king, how much of each sort of merchandize we were to give for a man, woman, and child, which gave us much ease, and saved abundance of disputes and wranglings. . . . [T]hen we mark'd the slaves we had bought in the breast, or shoulder, with a hot iron, having the letter of the ship's name on it, the place being before anointed with a little palm oil, which caus'd but little pain, the mark being usually well in four or five days, appearing very plain and white after. . . .

After we are come to an agreement for the prices of our slaves, . . . we are oblig'd to pay our customs to the king and cappasheirs for leave to trade, pro-tection and justice; which for every ship are as fol-low, *viz.*

To the king six slaves value in cowries, or what other goods we can perswade him to take, but cow-ries are most esteem'd and desir'd; all which are measur'd in his presence, and he would wrangle with us stoutly about heaping up the measure.

To the cappasheirs in all two slaves value, as above. . . .

The best goods to purchase slaves here are cow-ries, the smaller the more esteem'd. . . .

The next in demand are brass neptunes or basons, very large, thin, and flat; for after they have bought them they cut them in pieces to make . . . bracelets, and collars for their arms legs and necks. . . .

[I]f they can discover that you have good store of cowries and brass aboard, then no other goods will serve their turn, till they have got as much as you have; and after, for the rest of the goods they will be indifferent, and make you come to their own terms, or else lie a long time for your slaves, so that those you have on board are dying while you are buying others ashore....

Having bought my compliment of 700 slaves, viz. 480 men and 220 women, and finish'd all my business at Whidaw, I took my leave of the old king, and his cappasheirs, and parted, with many affectionate expressions on both sides, being forced to promise him that I would return again the next year, with several things he desired me to bring him from England; and having sign'd bills of lading ... for the negroes aboard, I set sail the 27th of July in the morning....

I deliver'd alive at Barbadoes to the company's factors 372, which being sold, came out at about nineteen pounds per head.

_____

Source: Thomas Phillips, "A Journal of a Voyage Made in the Hannibal of London in 1694," in *Documents Illustrative of the History of the Slave Trade to America*, edited by Elizabeth Donnan (Washington DC: Carnegie Institute, 1930), 399–405, 408, 410.

Document 14.3

The Slave Trade and the Kingdom of Kongo

While African elites often eagerly facilitated the traffic in slaves and benefited from doing so, in one well-known case, quite early in the slave trade era, an African ruler sought to curtail it. This occurred in the kingdom of Kongo, in what is now Angola (see Map 14.4, p. 687). That state had welcomed Portuguese traders as early as the 1480s, for its rulers imagined that an alliance with Portugal could strengthen their regime. The royal family converted to Christianity and encouraged the importation of European guns, cattle, and horses. Several Kongolese were sent to Portugal for education, while Portuguese priests, artisans, merchants, and soldiers found a place in the kingdom. None of this worked as planned, however, and by the early sixteenth century, Kongo was in disarray and the authority of its ruler greatly undermined. This was the context in which its monarch Nzinga Mbemba, whose Christian name was Affonso I, wrote a series of letters to King Jao of Portugal in 1526, two of which are presented here.

- According to King Affonso, how had the Portuguese connection in general and the slave trade in particular transformed his state?

- How did the operation of the slave trade in Kongo differ from that of Whydah as described in Document 14.2? How did the rulers of these two states differ in their relationship to Europeans?

- To what extent did Affonso seek the end of the slave trade? What was the basis for his opposition to it? Do you think he was opposed to slavery itself?

- What did Affonso seek from Portugal? What kind of relationship did he envisage with the Portuguese?

King Affonso I

Letters to King Jao of Portugal

1526

Sir, Your Highness [of Portugal] should know how our Kingdom is being lost in so many ways that it is convenient to provide for the necessary remedy, since this is caused by the excessive freedom given by your factors and officials to the men and merchants who are allowed to come to this Kingdom to set up shops with goods and many things which have been prohibited by us, and which they spread throughout our Kingdoms and Domains in such an abundance that many of our vassals, whom we had in obedience, do not comply because they have the things in greater abundance than we ourselves; and it was with these things that we had them content and subjected under our vassalage and jurisdiction, so it is doing a great harm not only to the service of God, but to the security and peace of our Kingdoms and State as well.

And we cannot reckon how great the damage is, since the mentioned merchants are taking every day our natives, sons of the land and the sons of our noblemen and vassals and our relatives, because the thieves and men of bad conscience grab them wishing to have the things and wares of this Kingdom which they are ambitious of; they grab them and get them to be sold; and so great, Sir, is the corruption and licentiousness that our country is being completely depopulated, and Your Highness should not agree with this nor accept it as in your service. And to avoid it we need from those [your] Kingdoms no more than some priests and a few people to teach in schools, and no other goods except wine and flour for the holy sacrament. That is why we beg of Your Highness to help and assist us in this matter, commanding your factors that they should not send here either merchants or wares, because it is *our will that in these Kingdoms there should not be any trade of slaves nor outlet for them.* Concerning what is referred above, again we beg of Your Highness to agree with it,

since otherwise we cannot remedy such an obvious damage....

Moreover, Sir, in our Kingdoms there is another great inconvenience which is of little service to God, and this is that many of our people, keenly desirous as they are of the wares and things of your Kingdoms, which are brought here by your people, and in order to satisfy their voracious appetite, seize many of our people, freed and exempt men; and very often it happens that they kidnap even noblemen and the sons of noblemen, and our relatives, and take them to be sold to the white men who are in our Kingdoms; and for this purpose thay have concealed them; and others are brought during the night so that they might not be recognized.

And as soon as they are taken by the white men they are immediately ironed and branded with fire, and when they are carried to be embarked, if they are caught by our guards' men the whites allege that they have bought them but they cannot say from whom, so that it is our duty to do justice and to restore to the freemen their freedom, but it cannot be done if your subjects feel offended, as they claim to be.

And to avoid such a great evil we passed a law so that any white man living in our Kingdoms and wanting to purchase goods in any way should first inform three of our noblemen and officials of our court ... who should investigate if the mentioned goods are captives or free men, and if cleared by them there will be no further doubt nor embargo for them to be taken and embarked. But if the white men do not comply with it they will lose the aforementioned goods....

Sir, Your Highness has been kind enough to write to us saying that we should ask in our letters for anything we need, and that we shall be provided with everything, and as the peace and the health of our Kingdom depend on us, and as there are among us old folks and people who have lived for many days, it happens that we have continuously many and different diseases which put us very often in such a

Source: Basil Davidson, *The African Past* (Boston: Little, Brown, 1964), 191–94.

weakness that we reach almost the last extreme; and the same happens to our children, relatives, and natives owing to the lack in this country of physicians and surgeons who might know how to cure properly such diseases. And as we have got neither dispensaries nor drugs which might help us in this forlornness, many of those who had been already confirmed and instructed in the holy faith of Our Lord Jesus Christ perish and die; and the rest of the people in their majority cure themselves with herbs and breads and other ancient methods, so that they put all their faith in the mentioned herbs and ceremonies if they live, and believe that they are saved if they die; and this is not much in the service of God.

And to avoid such a great error and inconvenience, since it is from God in the first place and then from your Kingdoms and from Your Highness that all the goods and drugs and medicines have come to save us, we beg of you to be agreeable and kind enough to send us two physicians and two apothecaries and one surgeon, so that they may come with their drugstores and all the necessary things to stay in our kingdoms, because we are in extreme need of them all and each of them.

Document 14.4

The Slave Trade and the Kingdom of Asante

Elsewhere in Africa, the slave trade did not have such politically destabilizing effects as it did in Kongo. In the region known as the Gold Coast (now the modern state of Ghana), the kingdom of Asante (uh-SAWN-tay) arose in the eighteenth century, occupying perhaps 100,000 square miles and incorporating some 3 million people (see Map 14.4, p. 687). It was a powerful conquest state, heavily invested in the slave trade, from which much of its wealth derived. Many slaves from its wars of expansion and from the tribute of its subject people were funneled into Atlantic commerce, while still others were used as labor in the gold mines and on the plantations within Asante itself. No wonder, then, that the ruler (or Asantehene) Osei Bonsu was dismayed in the early nineteenth century when, in reaction to the expanding abolitionist movement, the British stopped buying slaves. A conversation between Osei Bonsu and a British diplomat in 1820 highlights the role of the slave trade in Asante and in the thinking of its monarch.

- How did Osei Bonsu understand the slave trade and its significance for his kingdom?

- Some scholars have argued that the slave trade increased the incidence of warfare in West Africa as various states deliberately sought captives whom they could exchange for desired goods from Europe. How might Osei Bonsu respond to that idea? What was his understanding of the relationship between war and the slave trade?

- In what ways did Osei Bonsu compare Muslim traders from the north with European merchants from the sea?

OSEI BONSU

Conversation with Joseph Dupuis

1820

Now," said the king, after a pause, "I have another palaver, and you must help me to talk it. A long time ago the great king [of England] liked plenty of trade, more than now; then many ships came, and they bought ivory, gold, and slaves; but now he will not let the ships come as before, and the people buy gold and ivory only. This is what I have in my head, so now tell me truly, like a friend, why does the king do so?" "His majesty's question," I replied, "was connected with a great palaver, which my instructions did not authorise me to discuss. I had nothing to say regarding the slave trade." "I know that too," retorted the king; "because, if my master liked that trade, you would have told me so before. I only want to hear what you think as a friend: this is not like the other palavers." I was confessedly at a loss for an argument that might pass as a satisfactory reason, and the sequel proved that my doubts were not groundless. The king did not deem it plausible, that this obnoxious traffic should have been abolished from motives of humanity alone; neither would he admit that it lessened the number either of domestic or foreign wars.

Taking up one of my observations, he remarked, "[T]he white men who go to council with your master, and pray to the great God for him, do not understand my country, or they would not say the slave trade was bad. But if they think it bad now, why did they think it good before. Is not your law an old law, the same as the Crammo° law? Do you not both serve the same God, only you have different fashions and customs? Crammos are strong people in fetische,° and they say the law is good, because the great God made the book [Quran]; so they buy slaves, and teach them good things, which they knew not before. This makes every body love the Crammos, and they go every where up and down, and the people give them food when they

want it. Then these men come all the way from the great water [Niger River], and from Manding, and Dagomba, and Killinga; they stop and trade for slaves, and then go home. If the great king would like to restore this trade, it would be good for the white men and for me too, because Ashantee is a country for war, and the people are strong; so if you talk that palaver for me properly, in the white country, if you go there, I will give you plenty of gold, and I will make you richer than all the white men."

I urged the impossibility of the king's request, promising, however, to record his sentiments faithfully. "Well then," said the king, "you must put down in my master's book all I shall say, and then he will look to it, now he is my friend. And when he sees what is true, he will surely restore that trade. I cannot make war to catch slaves in the bush, like a thief. My ancestors never did so. But if I fight a king, and kill him when he is insolent, then certainly I must have his gold, and his slaves, and the people are mine too. Do not the white kings act like this? Because I hear the old men say, that before I conquered Fantee and killed the Braffoes and the kings, that white men came in great ships, and fought and killed many people; and then they took the gold and slaves to the white country: and sometimes they fought together. That is all the same as these black countries. The great God and the fetische made war for strong men every where, because then they can pay plenty of gold and proper sacrifice. When I fought Gaman, I did not make war for slaves, but because Dinkera (the king) sent me an arrogant message and killed my people, and refused to pay me gold as his father did. Then my fetische made me strong like my ancestors, and I killed Dinkera, and took his gold, and brought more than 20,000 slaves to Coomassy. Some of these people being bad men, I washed my stool in

---

°**Crammo:** Muslim.

°**fetische:** magical powers.

Source: Joseph Dupuis, *Journal of a Residence in Ashantee* (London: Henry Colburn, 1824), 162–64.

their blood for the fetische. But then some were good people, and these I sold or gave to my captains: many, moreover, died, because this country does not grow too much corn like Sarem, and what can I do? Unless I kill or sell them, they will grow strong and kill my people. Now you must tell my master that these slaves can work for him, and if he wants 10,000 he can have them. And if he wants fine handsome girls and women to give his captains, I can send him great numbers."

Using the Evidence: Voices from the Slave Trade

1. **Highlighting differences:** What different experiences of the slave trade are reflected in these documents? How can you account for those differences?

2. **Noticing what's missing:** What perspectives are missing that might add other dimensions to our understanding of this commerce in people?

3. **Integrating documents and the text narrative:** In what ways do these documents support, illustrate, or contradict this chapter's narrative discussion of the slave trade?

4. **Assessing historical responsibility:** What light do these documents shed on the much-debated question about who should be held responsible for the tragedy of the Atlantic slave trade?

Chapter 14 Wrap Up

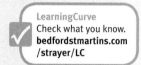

STEP ONE

The Word to Know: Commerce

The *Oxford English Dictionary* defines *commerce* as follows: "Exchange between men of the products of nature or art; buying and selling together; trading; exchange of merchandise, *esp.* as conducted on a large scale between different countries or districts; including the whole of the transactions, arrangements, etc., therein involved." One of the most profitable types of commerce in the early modern world was the slave trade, also known as human trafficking. In a paragraph, write a definition of commerce as it pertained to the Atlantic slave trade (see pp. 687–95), taking into account that this was commerce in human beings.

STEP TWO

The Fur Trade

During the early modern world, commercial connections between places increase significantly. Use either a single outline map or hand-drawn world map, show these connections as they related to the fur trade. When you are done, answer the questions that follow.

1. Using Map 14.3, "The North American Fur Trade (p. 684) as your guide, label the Hudson Bay, St Lawrence River, Gulf of Mexico, and Great Lakes. Using different colors, indicate the fur-trading regions of the France, England, and Russia. Also indicate on the map, using arrows, where furs were sent.

2. Using the text on pp. 682–687, annotate your map with at least three reasons why the fur trade was so successful, including five impacts (positive and negative) of this trade on North American society.

3. Using Map 13.2, "The Russian Empire" (p. 636) and the text on pp. 635–36 and pp. 686–687 as your guide, map the fur trade across Siberia. On the map, label Siberia and draw an arrow moving across Siberia from Moscow to Okhotsk and an arrow indicating where furs were sold. Next, label the people who moved from west to east (across Siberia). Annotate your map with a phrase describing the reasons for this movement of people and furs including five impacts (positive and negative) of this trade.

■ Question

Looking at the map you have created, compare the effects of the fur trade in Russia and North America. What are similarities in terms of where and why the trade spread? What were some of the impacts that were similar and different?

STEP THREE

Graphing Slavery

This activity will help you practice working with charts and graphs.
Using the two-part Snapshot on p. 692, answer the following questions:
The top graph shows the rise and decline of the Slave trade. Use this graph to answer questions 1–4.

1. What length of time does each column on the bar graph represent?

2. How long did it take for the slave trade to reach its height of 2 million people trafficked from Africa?

3. After the British abolition of the slave trade in 1807, how long did it take for there to be a noticeable effect and why?

4. How many people total (according to this graph) survived the Middle Passage and worked as slaves in the Western Hemisphere?

5. What does the bottom graph show? What can you conclude based on your reading of this graph?

Cultural Transformations

Religion and Science

1450–1750

Nigerian pastor Daniel Ajayi-Adeniran is a missionary to the United States, with his mission field in the Bronx. The church he represents, the Redeemed Christian Church of God, began in Nigeria in 1952. It has acquired millions of members in Nigeria and boasts a missionary network with a presence in 100 countries. According to its leader, the church was "made in heaven, assembled in Nigeria, exported to the world." And the Redeemed Church of God is not alone. As secularism and materialism born of the Scientific Revolution and modern life have eroded religious faith in the West, many believers in Asia, Africa, and Latin America have felt called to reinvigorate a declining Christianity in Europe and North America. In a remarkable reversal of an earlier pattern, they now seek to "reevangelize" the West, from which they originally received the faith. After all, more than 60 percent of the world's professing Christians now live outside Europe and North America, and, within the United States, one in six Catholic diocesan priests and one in three seminary students are foreign-born. For example, hundreds of Filipino priests, nuns, and lay workers now serve churches in the West. "We couldn't just throw up our hands and see these churches turned into nightclubs or mosques," declared Tokunboh Adeyemo, another Nigerian church leader seeking to minister to an "increasingly godless West."[1]

THE EARLY MODERN ERA OF WORLD HISTORY gave birth to two intersecting cultural trends that continue to play out in the twenty-first century. The first was the spread of Christianity to Asians, Africans, and Native Americans, some of whom now seem to be returning the

The Virgin of Guadalupe: According to Mexican tradition, a dark-skinned Virgin Mary appeared to an indigenous peasant named Juan Diego in 1531, an apparition reflected in this Mexican painting from 1720. Belief in the Virgin of Guadalupe represented the incorporation of Catholicism into the emerging culture and identity of Mexico. (The Art Archive at Art Resource, NY) favor. The second lay in the emergence of a modern scientific outlook, which sharply challenged Western Christianity even as it too acquired a global presence.

And so, alongside new empires and new patterns of commerce, the early modern centuries also witnessed novel cultural transformations that likewise connected distant peoples. Riding the currents of European empire building and commercial expansion, Christianity was established solidly in the Americas and the Philippines; far more modestly in Siberia, China, Japan, and India; and hardly at all within the vast and still growing domains of Islam. A cultural tradition largely limited to Europe in 1500 now became a genuine world religion, spawning a multitude of cultural encounters. While this ancient faith was spreading, a new understanding of the universe and a new approach to knowledge were taking shape among European thinkers of the Scientific Revolution, giving rise to another kind of cultural encounter—that between science and religion. Science was a new and competing worldview, and for some it became almost a new religion. In time, it grew into a defining feature of global modernity, achieving a worldwide acceptance that exceeded that of Christianity or any other religious tradition.

Although Europeans were central players in the globalization of Christianity and the emergence of modern science, they did not act alone in the cultural transformations of the early modern era. Asian, African, and Native American peoples largely determined how Christianity would be accepted, rejected, or transformed as it entered new cultural environments. Science emerged within an international and not simply a European context, and it met varying receptions in different parts of the world. Islam continued a long pattern of religious expansion and renewal, even as Christianity began to compete with it as a world religion. Buddhism maintained its hold in much of East Asia, as did Hinduism in South Asia and numerous smaller-scale religious traditions in Africa. And Europeans themselves were certainly affected by the many "new worlds" that they now encountered. The cultural interactions of the early modern era, in short, did not take place on a one-way street.

SEEKING THE MAIN POINT

To what extent did the cultural changes of the early modern world derive from cross-cultural interaction? And to what extent did they grow from within particular societies or civilizations?

The Globalization of Christianity

Despite its Middle Eastern origins and its earlier presence in many parts of the Afro-Asian world, Christianity was largely limited to Europe at the beginning of the early modern era. In 1500, the world of Christendom stretched from Spain and England in the west to Russia in the east, with small and beleaguered communities of various kinds in Egypt, Ethiopia, southern India, and Central Asia. Internally, Christianity was seriously divided between the Roman Catholics of Western and Central Europe and the Eastern Orthodox of Eastern Europe and Russia. Externally, it was very much on the defensive against an expansive Islam. Muslims had ousted Christian Crusaders from their toeholds in the Holy Land by 1300, and with the Ottoman seizure of Constantinople in 1453, they had captured the prestigious capital of Eastern Orthodoxy. The

A Map of Time

1453	Ottoman conquest of Constantinople
1469–1539	Life of Guru Nanak; beginning of Sikh tradition
1472–1529	Life of Wang Yangmin in China
1498–1547	Life of Mirabai, *bhakti* poet of India
1517	Luther's 95 Theses; beginning of Protestant Reformation
1543	Publication of Copernicus's master work about a sun-centered universe
1545–1563	Council of Trent
1560s	Taki Onqoy movement in Peru
1582–1610	Matteo Ricci in China
1593	Edict of Nantes proclaiming religious toleration in France
Early 1600s	European missionaries expelled from Japan
1618–1648	Thirty Years' War in Europe
1642–1727	Life of Isaac Newton; culmination of European Scientific Revolution
1700s	European Enlightenment
1721	Christian missionary preaching banned in China
1740–1818	Wahhabi movement of Islamic reform in Arabia

Ottoman siege of Vienna in 1529 marked a Muslim advance into the heart of Central Europe. Except in Spain and Sicily, which had recently been reclaimed for Christendom after centuries of Muslim rule, the future, it must have seemed, lay with Islam rather than Christianity.

Western Christendom Fragmented: The Protestant Reformation

As if these were not troubles enough, in the early sixteenth century the Protestant Reformation shattered the unity of Roman Catholic Christianity, which for the previous 1,000 years had provided the cultural and organizational foundation of Western European civilization. The Reformation began in 1517 when a German priest, Martin Luther (1483–1546), publicly invited debate about various abuses within the Roman Catholic Church by issuing a document, known as the Ninety-five Theses, allegedly nailing it to the door of a church in Wittenberg. In itself, this was nothing new, for many people were critical of the luxurious life of the popes, the corruption and immorality of some clergy, the Church's selling of indulgences (said to remove the penalties for sin), and other aspects of church life and practice.

■ **Change**

In what ways did the Protestant Reformation transform European society, culture, and politics?

The Protestant Reformation
This sixteenth-century painting by the well-known German artist Lucas Cranach the Elder shows Martin Luther and his supporters using a giant quill to write their demands for religious reform on a church door. It memorializes the posting of the Ninety-five Theses in 1517, which launched the Protestant Reformation. (Courtesy, Dr. Henning Schleifenbaum, Siegen, Germany)

What made Luther's protest potentially revolutionary, however, was its theological basis. A troubled and brooding man anxious about his relationship with God, Luther recently had come to a new understanding of salvation, which held that it came through faith alone. Neither the good works of the sinner nor the sacraments of the Church had any bearing on the eternal destiny of the soul, for faith was a free gift of God, graciously granted to his needy and undeserving people. To Luther, the source of these beliefs, and of religious authority in general, was not the teaching of the Church, but the Bible alone, interpreted according to the individual's conscience. (See Document 15.1, pp. 753–55, for more of Luther's thinking.) All of this challenged the authority of the Church and called into question the special position of the clerical hierarchy and of the pope in particular. In sixteenth-century Europe, this was the stuff of revolution.

Contrary to Luther's original intentions, his ideas provoked a massive schism within the world of Catholic Christendom, for they came to express a variety of political, economic, and social tensions as well as religious differences. Some kings and princes, many of whom had long disputed the political authority of the pope, found in these ideas a justification for their own independence and an opportunity to gain the lands and taxes previously held by the Church. In the Protestant idea that all vocations were of equal merit, middle-class urban dwellers found a new religious legitimacy for their growing role in society, since the Roman Catholic Church was associated in their eyes with the rural and feudal world of aristocratic privilege. For common people, who were offended by the corruption and luxurious living of some bishops, abbots, and popes, the new religious ideas served to express their opposition to the entire social order, particularly in a series of German peasant revolts in the 1520s. (See Visual Sources 15.1 and 15.2, pp. 764 and 765, for contrasting images of Protestant and Catholic churches.)

Although large numbers of women were attracted to Protestantism, Reformation teachings and practices did not offer them a substantially greater role in the church or society. In Protestant-dominated areas, the veneration of Mary and female saints ended, leaving the male Christ figure as the sole object of worship. Protestant opposition to celibacy and monastic life closed the convents, which had offered some women an alternative to marriage. Nor were Protestants (except the Quakers) any more willing than Catholics to offer women an official role within their churches. The importance that Protestants gave to reading the Bible for oneself stimulated education and literacy for women, but given the emphasis on women as wives and mothers subject to male supervision, they had little opportunity to use that education outside of the family.

Reformation thinking spread quickly both within and beyond Germany, thanks in large measure to the recent invention of the printing press. Luther's many pamphlets and his translation of the New Testament into German were soon widely available. "God has appointed the [printing] Press to preach, whose voice the pope is never able to stop," declared one Reformation leader.[2] As the movement spread to France, Switzerland, England, and elsewhere, it also splintered, amoeba-like, into a variety of competing Protestant churches—Lutheran, Calvinist, Anglican, Quaker, Anabaptist—many of which subsequently subdivided, producing a bewildering array of Protestant denominations. Each was distinctive, but none gave allegiance to Rome or the pope.

Thus to the divided societies and the fractured political system of Europe was now added the potent brew of religious difference, operating both within and between states (see Map 15.1). For more than thirty years (1562–1598), French society was torn by violence between Catholics and the Protestant minority known as Huguenots (HYOO-guh-naht). On a single day, August 24, 1572, Catholic mobs in Paris massacred some 3,000 Huguenots, and thousands more perished in provincial towns in the weeks that followed. Finally, a war-weary monarch, Henry IV, issued the Edict of Nantes (nahnt) (1598), which granted a substantial measure of religious toleration to French Protestants, though with the intention that they would soon return to the Catholic Church. The culmination of European religious conflict took shape in the Thirty Years' War (1618–1648), a Catholic–Protestant struggle that began in the Holy Roman Empire but eventually engulfed most of Europe. It was a horrendously destructive war, during which, scholars estimate, between 15 and 30 percent of the German population perished from violence, famine, or disease. Finally, the Peace of Westphalia (1648) brought the conflict to an end, with some reshuffling of boundaries and an agreement that each state was sovereign, authorized to control religious affairs within its own territory. Whatever religious unity Catholic Europe had once enjoyed was now permanently splintered.

The Protestant breakaway, combined with reformist tendencies within the Catholic Church itself, provoked a Catholic or Counter-Reformation. In the Council of Trent (1545–1563), Catholics clarified and reaffirmed their unique doctrines and practices, such as the authority of the pope, priestly celibacy, the veneration of saints and relics, and the importance of church tradition and good works, all of which Protestants had rejected. Moreover, they set about correcting the abuses and corruption that had stimulated the Protestant movement by placing a new emphasis on the education of priests and their supervision by bishops. A crackdown on dissidents included the censorship of books, fines, exile, penitence, and occasionally the burning of heretics. Renewed attention was given to individual spirituality and personal piety. New religious orders, such as the Society of Jesus (Jesuits), provided a dedicated brotherhood of priests committed to the renewal of the Catholic Church and its extension abroad.

Although the Reformation was profoundly religious, it encouraged a skeptical attitude toward authority and tradition, for it had, after all, successfully challenged the

Map 15.1 Reformation Europe in the Sixteenth Century

The rise of Protestantism added yet another set of religious divisions, both within and between states, to the world of Christendom, which was already sharply divided between the Roman Catholic Church and the Eastern Orthodox Church.

FINLAND

NORWAY   SWEDEN   ESTONIA

LIVONIA

SCOTLAND   *Baltic Sea*   COURLAND

North Sea   DENMARK   TEUTONIC KNIGHTS

IRELAND

Elbe R.

ENGLAND   Wittenberg•   POLAND

Canterbury•   •Cologne   *Saxony*

English Channel   •Frankfurt   *Bohemia*

Worms•   •Strasbourg   Vienna•   HUNGARY

•Paris   *Loire R.*   Zürich•   *Danube R.*

SWISS CONFED.   •Geneva   Milan•   OTTOMAN EMPIRE

FRANCE   *Po R.*

PAPAL STATES   *Adriatic Sea*

Castile   *Catalonia*   *Corsica*   Rome•   NAPLES

SPAIN   *Tyrrhenian Sea*

Sardinia

Mediterranean Sea   Sicily

☐ Protestant dominant
☐ Some Protestant influence
☐ Catholic
☐ Eastern Orthodox Christian
— Boundary of the Holy Roman Empire

0   200   400 miles
0   200   400 kilometers

immense prestige and power of the pope and the established Church. Protestant reformers fostered religious individualism as people were now encouraged to read and interpret the scriptures for themselves and to seek salvation without the mediation of the Church. In the centuries that followed, some people turned that skepticism and the habit of thinking independently against all conventional religion. Thus the Protestant Reformation opened some space for new directions in European intellectual life.

Snapshot   **Catholic/Protestant Differences in the Sixteenth Century**

	Catholic	Protestant
Religious authority	Pope and church hierarchy	The Bible, as interpreted by individual Christians
Role of the pope	Ultimate authority in faith and doctrine	Denied the authority of the pope
Ordination of clergy	Apostolic succession: direct line between original apostles and all subsequently ordained clergy	Apostolic succession denied; ordination by individual congregations or denominations
Salvation	Importance of church sacraments as channels of God's grace	By faith alone; God's grace is freely and directly granted to believers
Status of Mary	Highly prominent, ranking just below Jesus; provides constant intercession for believers	Less prominent; denied Mary's intercession on behalf of the faithful
Prayer	To God, but often through or with Mary and saints	To God alone; no role for Mary and saints
Holy Communion	Transubstantiation: bread and wine become the actual body and blood of Christ	Denied transubstantiation; bread and wine have a spiritual or symbolic significance
Role of clergy	Generally celibate; sharp distinction between priests and laypeople; mediators between God and humankind	Ministers may marry; priesthood of all believers; clergy have different functions (to preach, administer sacraments) but no distinct spiritual status
Role of Saints	Prominent spiritual exemplars and intermediaries between God and humankind	Generally disdained as a source of idolatry; saints refer to all Christians

In short, it was a more highly fragmented but also a renewed and revitalized Christianity that established itself around the world in the several centuries after 1500.

Christianity Outward Bound

Christianity motivated European political and economic expansion and also benefited from it. The resolutely Catholic Spanish and Portuguese both viewed their movement overseas as a continuation of a long crusading tradition, which only recently had completed the liberation of their countries from Muslim control. When Vasco

■ **Connection**
How was European imperial expansion related to the spread of Christianity?

Map 15.2

The Globalization of Christianity

The growing Christian presence in Asia, Africa, and especially the Americas, combined with older centers of that faith, gave the religion of Jesus a global dimension during the early modern era.

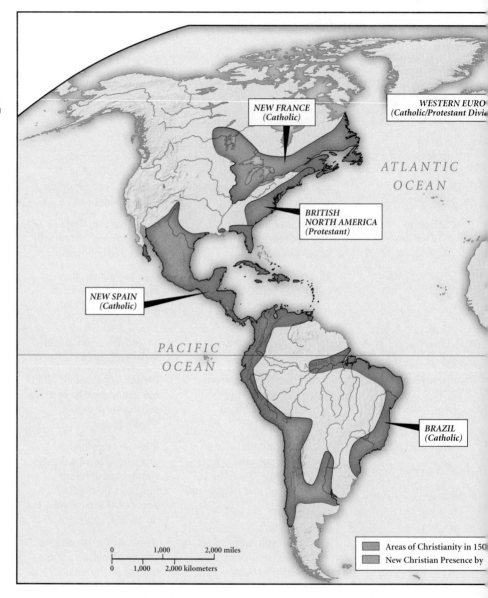

da Gama's small fleet landed in India in 1498, local authorities understandably asked, "What brought you hither?" The reply: they had come "in search of Christians and of spices."[3] Likewise, Columbus, upon arriving in the Americas, expressed the no doubt sincere hope that the people "might become Christians," even as he promised his Spanish patrons an abundant harvest of gold, spice, cotton, aloe wood, and slaves.[4] Neither man sensed any contradiction or hypocrisy in this blending of religious and material concerns.

If religion drove and justified European ventures abroad, it is difficult to imagine the globalization of Christianity (see Map 15.2) without the support of empire. Co-

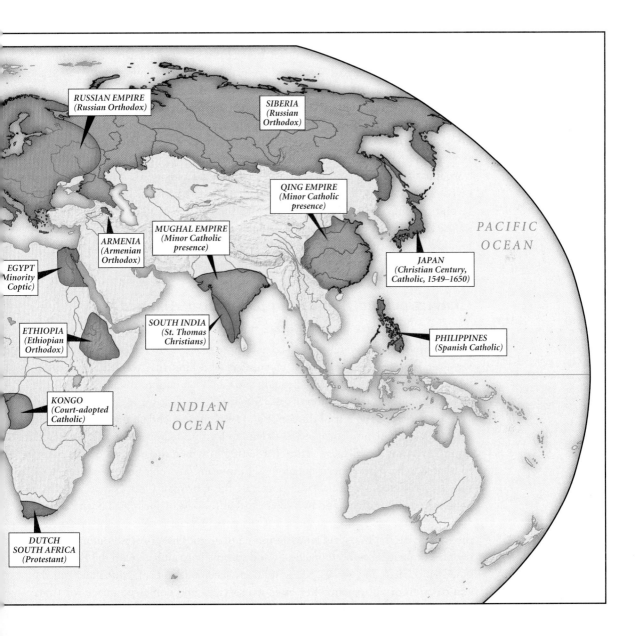

lonial settlers and traders, of course, brought their faith with them and sought to replicate it in their newly conquered homelands. New England Puritans, for example, planted a distinctive Protestant version of Christianity in North America, with an emphasis on education, moral purity, personal conversion, civic responsibility, and little tolerance for competing expressions of the faith. They did not show much interest in converting native peoples but sought rather to push them out of their ancestral territories. It was missionaries, mostly Catholic, who actively spread the Christian message beyond European communities. Organized in missionary orders such as the Dominicans, Franciscans, and Jesuits, Portuguese missionaries took the lead in Africa and

Asia, while Spanish and French missionaries were most prominent in the Americas. Missionaries of the Russian Orthodox Church likewise accompanied the expansion of the Russian Empire across Siberia, where priests and monks ministered to Russian settlers and trappers, who often donated their first sable furs to a church or monastery.

Missionaries had their greatest success in Spanish America and in the Philippines, areas that shared two critical elements beyond their colonization by Spain. Most important, perhaps, was an overwhelming European presence, experienced variously as military conquest, colonial settlement, missionary activity, forced labor, social disruption, and disease. Surely it must have seemed as if the old gods had been bested and that any possible future lay with the powerful religion of the European invaders. A second common factor was the absence of a literate world religion in these two regions. Throughout the modern era, peoples solidly rooted in Confucian, Buddhist, Hindu, or Islamic traditions proved far more resistant to the Christian message than those who practiced more localized, small-scale, orally based religions.

Conversion and Adaptation in Spanish America

■ **Connection**

In what ways was European Christianity assimilated into the Native American cultures of Spanish America?

Spanish America and China illustrate the difference between those societies in which Christianity became widely practiced and those that largely rejected it. Both cases, however, represent major cultural encounters of a kind that was becoming more frequent as European expansion brought the Christian faith to distant peoples with very different cultural traditions.

The decisive conquest of the Aztec and Inca empires and all that followed from it—disease, population collapse, loss of land to Europeans, forced labor, resettlement into more compact villages—created a setting in which the religion of the victors took hold in Spanish American colonies. Europeans saw their political and military success as a demonstration of the power of the Christian God. Native American peoples generally agreed, and by 1700 or earlier the vast majority had been baptized and saw themselves in some respects as Christians. After all, other conquerors such as the Aztecs and the Incas had always imposed their gods in some fashion on defeated peoples. It made sense, both practically and spiritually, to affiliate with the Europeans' God, saints, rites, and rituals. Many millions accepted baptism, contributed to the construction of village churches, attended services, and embraced images of saints. Despite the prominence of the Virgin Mary as a religious figure across Latin America, the cost of conversion was high, especially for women. Many women, who had long served as priests, shamans, or ritual specialists, had no corresponding role in a Catholic church, led by an all-male clergy. And, with a few exceptions, convent life, which had provided some outlet for female authority and education in Catholic Europe, was reserved largely for Spanish women in the Americas. (See the Portrait of Úrsula de Jesús, pp. 730–31, for an example of an exception.)

Earlier conquerors had made no attempt to eradicate local deities and religious practices. The flexibility and inclusiveness of Mesoamerican and Andean religions had made it possible for subject people to accommodate the gods of their new rulers while maintaining their own traditions. But Europeans were different. They claimed an exclusive religious truth and sought the utter destruction of local gods and everything associated with them. Operating within a Spanish colonial regime that actively encouraged conversion, missionaries often proceeded by persuasion and patient teaching. At times, though, their frustration with the persistence of "idolatry, superstition, and error" boiled over into violent campaigns designed to uproot old religions once and for all. In 1535, the bishop of Mexico proudly claimed that he had destroyed 500 pagan shrines and 20,000 idols. During the seventeenth and early eighteenth centuries, church authorities in the Andean region periodically launched movements of "extirpation," designed to fatally undermine native religion. They destroyed religious images and ritual objects, publicly urinated on native "idols," desecrated the remains of ancestors, flogged "idolaters," and held religious trials and "processions of shame" aimed at humiliating offenders.[5]

It is hardly surprising that such aggressive action generated resistance. Writing around 1600, the native Peruvian nobleman Guaman Poma de Ayala commented on the posture of native women toward Christianity: "They do not confess; they do not attend catechism classes . . . nor do they go to mass. . . . And resuming their ancient customs and idolatry, they do not want to serve God or the crown."[6] Occasionally, overt resistance erupted. One such example was the religious revivalist movement

Andean Christianity
In 1753 Marcos Zapata, a native Peruvian artist trained in European techniques, painted this rendering of Jesus' Last Supper with his disciples, which included a number of Andean elements. The central dish on the table was a roasted guinea pig, a traditional sacrificial animal, while a variety of colored potatoes and a local fermented corn drink called *chichi* were also part of the meal. At the bottom right, looking away from Jesus while grasping a money bag, is the figure of Judas, painted, some say, to resemble Francisco Pizarro, the Spanish conqueror of the Inca Empire. (South American Pictures)

Úrsula de Jesús, An Afro-Peruvian Slave and Christian Visionary

Úrsula de Jesús was born in the prosperous Spanish colonial city of Lima, Peru, in 1606, the daughter of slave mother. Thus she entered life at the lowest rung of Spanish colonial society. But among enslaved people, Úrsula was fortunate. Her mother's owner was a wealthy aristocratic woman, and at age eight, Úrsula was sent to live in the home of another elite woman with a reputation for piety and religious visions. Five years later, Úrsula accompanied a third woman into the Convent of Santa Clara, where she spent the rest of her life. There Úrsula found a place for herself in the world of colonial Peru and Latin American Christianity—but not easily or immediately.[7]

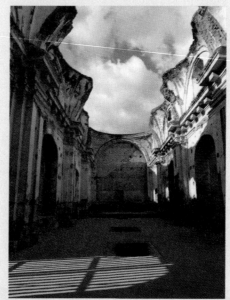

Ruins of the Convent of Santa Clara where Úrsula lived. (Nicole Melancon, photographer)

was at the bottom of the social ladder as nuns, novices, and *doñadas* (religious laywomen) all enjoyed a higher status. But the wealth of her mistress or perhaps her own day labor allowed her to dress well and to elevate herself above common slaves. She later noted that she went about "beautifully adorned from head to toe. . . . I used to wear fancy clothes and parade about the choir."

The year 1642 marked a dramatic turning point in Úrsula's life, when she almost fell into a deep well. Crediting her deliverance from certain death to the Virgin of Carmen, Úrsula turned decisively away from her earlier vain and self-centered ways and embraced an ever-deepening spiri-

For the next quarter of a century, Úrsula was one of more than a hundred slaves in the convent, where she attended to the personal needs of her mistress and participated in communal labor—cooking, cleaning, and attending the sick. In the convent, as in the larger society, Úrsula tuality. She sold her lovely clothes, devoted every spare moment to prayer, and sought out the most onerous tasks such as caring for contagious patients and washing soiled garments. She took to whipping herself twice daily, wearing a coarse and painful hair shirt, and placing a crown of

in central Peru in the 1560s, known as Taki Onqoy (dancing sickness). Possessed by the spirits of local gods, or *huacas*, traveling dancers and teachers predicted that an alliance of Andean deities would soon overcome the Christian God, inflict the intruding Europeans with the same diseases that they had brought to the Americas, and restore the world of the Andes to an imagined earlier harmony. They called on native peoples to cut off all contact with the Spanish, to reject Christian worship, and to return to traditional practices. "The world has turned about," one member declared, "and this time God and the Spaniards [will be] defeated and all the Spaniards killed and their cities drowned; and the sea will rise and overwhelm them, so that there will remain no memory of them."[8]

More common than such frontal attacks on Christianity, which colonial authorities quickly smashed, were efforts at blending two religious traditions, reinterpreting Christian practices within an Andean framework, and incorporating local elements into an emerging Andean Christianity. Even female dancers in the Taki Onqoy move-thorns beneath her hair. In Catholic religious thinking of the time, such "mortification" of the body served to enhance identification with Jesus's suffering.

Úrsula's new religious fervor incurred the displeasure of her mistress, who felt neglected by her slave. By 1645, a deeply unhappy Úrsula determined to leave the convent and find a new owner. Then one of the nuns, hoping to retain her pious services, purchased Úrsula's freedom. Nonetheless, Úrsula chose to stay in the convent as a *donada*. Doing so represented a modest elevation in her social status, an opportunity to pursue her spiritual life with fewer restrictions, and a measure of social and economic security.

Still, she continued with the same exhausting tasks she had as a slave and complained frequently about them. "I was up to my ears with cooking and other things," she confided to her diary, "desiring only to be in the mountains where there are no people." Even as she struggled with the restrictions of her position in the convent, Úrsula enhanced her reputation as a "servant of God," a woman of extraordinary devotion and humility, and as a visionary and a mystic.

In her diary, Úrsula recounted numerous direct encounters with God, Jesus, Mary, and with dead souls seeking her intervention to shorten their time in the purifying fires of purgatory. These visions frequently reflected the ten-

sions of class, race, and position within the convent and in the larger society. Several priests, suffering in purgatory for their sexual sins, luxurious living, and mistreatment of slaves, appealed to Úrsula. So too did nuns who had been lax in their spiritual practices or placed their business interests above their religious duties. Úrsula had a special concern for the female slaves and servants who asked for her intercession. One feared becoming an "orphan" in purgatory with no one to remember her. Another confessed to a lesbian love affair with a nun. Although Úrsula once questioned "whether black women went to heaven," it was later revealed to her as an abode of "great harmony," but not of social equality, for "everyone had their place . . . in accordance with their standing and the obligations of their class." By the end of her life, however, Ursula was able to affirm the spiritual equality of all. "In memory, understanding, and will," she declared, "they [blacks and whites] are all one."

When Úrsula died in 1666, a prominent nun confirmed that she had entered heaven directly, with no intervening time in purgatory. Her funeral was attended by many high officials of both state and church, and she was buried beneath the chapel of the convent she had served.

Question: To what extent did Úrsula shape her own life and in what way was it shaped by larger historical forces?

ment sometimes took the names of Christian saints, seeking to appropriate for themselves the religious power of Christian figures. Within Andean Christian communities, women might offer the blood of a llama to strengthen a village church or make a cloth covering for the Virgin Mary and a shirt for an image of a huaca with the same material. Although the state cults of the Incas faded away, missionary attacks did not succeed in eliminating the influence of local huacas. Images and holy sites might be destroyed, but the souls of the huacas remained, and their representatives gained prestige. One resilient Andean resident inquired of a Jesuit missionary: "Father, are you tired of taking our idols from us? Take away that mountain if you can, since that is the God I worship."[9] (See Visual Source 15.3, p. 767, for an illustration of the blending of Andean religious symbols and the new Christian message.)

In Mexico as well, an immigrant Christianity was assimilated into patterns of local culture. Parishes were organized largely around precolonial towns or regions. Churches built on or near the sites of old temples became the focus of community identity. *Cofradias*, church-based associations of laypeople, organized community processions and festivals and made provisions for proper funerals and burials for their members. Central to an emerging Mexican Christianity were the saints who closely paralleled the functions of precolonial gods. Saints were imagined as parents of the local community and the true owners of its land, and their images were paraded through the streets on the occasion of great feasts and were collected by individual households. Mexico's Virgin of Guadalupe (see photo, p. 718) neatly combined both Mesoamerican and Spanish notions of Divine Motherhood. Although parish priests were almost always Spanish, the *fiscal*, or leader of the church staff, was a native Christian of great local prestige, who carried on the traditions and role of earlier religious specialists.

Throughout the colonial period and beyond, many Mexican Christians also took part in rituals derived from the past, with little sense that this was incompatible with Christian practice. Incantations to various gods for good fortune in hunting, farming, or healing; sacrifices of self-bleeding; offerings to the sun; divination; the use of hallucinogenic drugs—all of these rituals provided spiritual assistance in those areas of everyday life not directly addressed by Christian rites. Conversely, these practices also showed signs of Christian influence. Wax candles, normally used in Christian services, might now appear in front of a stone image of a precolonial god. The anger of a neglected saint, rather than that of a traditional god, might explain someone's illness and require offerings, celebration, or a new covering to regain his or her favor.[10] In such ways did Christianity take root in the new cultural environments of Spanish America, but it was a distinctly Andean or Mexican Christianity, not merely a copy of the Spanish version.

An Asian Comparison: China and the Jesuits

■ **Comparison**

Why were missionary efforts to spread Christianity so much less successful in China than in Spanish America?

The Chinese encounter with Christianity was very different from that of Native Americans in Spain's New World empire. The most obvious difference was the political context. The peoples of Spanish America had been defeated, their societies thoroughly disrupted, and their cultural confidence sorely shaken. China, on the other hand, encountered European Christianity between the sixteenth and eighteenth centuries during the powerful and prosperous Ming (1368–1644) and Qing (1644–1912) dynasties. Although the transition between these two dynasties occasioned several decades of internal conflict, at no point was China's political independence or cultural integrity threatened by the handful of European missionaries and traders working there.

The reality of a strong, independent, confident China required a different missionary strategy, for Europeans needed the permission of Chinese authorities to operate in the country. Whereas Spanish missionaries working in a colonial setting sought primarily to convert the masses, the leading missionary order in China, the Jesuits, took deliberate aim at the official Chinese elite. Following the example of their most famous missionary, Matteo Ricci (in China 1582–1610), many Jesuits learned Chinese, became thoroughly acquainted with classical Confucian texts, and dressed like Chinese scholars. Initially, they downplayed their mission to convert and instead emphasized their interest in exchanging ideas and learning from China's ancient culture. As highly educated men, the Jesuits carried the recent secular knowledge of Europe — science, technology, geography, mapmaking — to an audience of curious Chinese scholars. In presenting Christian teachings, Jesuits were at pains to be respectful of Chinese culture, pointing out parallels between Confucianism and Christianity rather than portraying it as something new and foreign. They chose to define Chinese rituals honoring the emperor or venerating ancestors as secular or civil observances rather than as religious practices that had to be abandoned. Such efforts to accommodate Chinese culture contrast sharply with the frontal attacks on Native American religions in the Spanish Empire (see Visual Source 15.4, p. 769).

The religious and cultural outcomes of the missionary enterprise likewise differed greatly in the two regions. Nothing approaching mass conversion to Christianity took place in China, as it had in Latin America. During the sixteenth and seventeenth centuries, a modest number of Chinese scholars and officials did become Christians, attracted by the personal lives of the missionaries, by their interest in

Jesuits in China

In this seventeenth-century Dutch engraving, two Jesuit missionaries hold a map of China. Their mapmaking skills were among the reasons that the Jesuits were initially welcomed among the educated elite of that country. (Private Collection/The Bridgeman Art Library)

Western science, and by the moral certainty that Christianity offered. Jesuit missionaries found favor for a time at the Chinese imperial court, where their mathematical, astronomical, technological, and mapmaking skills rendered them useful. For more than a century, they were appointed to head the Chinese Bureau of Astronomy. Among ordinary people, Christianity spread very modestly amid tales of miracles attributed to the Christian God, while missionary teachings about "eternal life" sounded to some like Daoist prescriptions for immortality. At most, though, missionary efforts over the course of some 250 years (1550–1800) resulted in 200,000 to 300,000 converts, a minuscule number in a Chinese population approaching 300 million by 1800. What explains the very limited acceptance of Christianity in early modern China?

Fundamentally, the missionaries offered little that the Chinese really needed. Confucianism for the elites and Buddhism, Daoism, and a multitude of Chinese gods and spirits at the local level adequately supplied the spiritual needs of most Chinese. Furthermore, it became increasingly clear that Christianity was an all-or-nothing faith that required converts to abandon much of traditional Chinese culture. Christian monogamy, for example, seemed to require Chinese men to put away their concubines. What would happen to these deserted women?

By the early eighteenth century, the papacy and competing missionary orders came to oppose the Jesuit policy of accommodation. The pope claimed authority over Chinese Christians and declared that sacrifices to Confucius and the veneration of ancestors were "idolatry" and thus forbidden to Christians. The pope's pronouncements represented an unacceptable challenge to the authority of the emperor and an affront to Chinese culture. In 1715, an outraged Emperor Kangxi wrote:

> I ask myself how these uncultivated Westerners dare to speak of the great precepts of China. . . . [T]heir doctrine is of the same kind as the little heresies of the Buddhist and Taoist monks. . . . These are the greatest absurdities that have ever been seen. As from now I forbid the Westerners to spread their doctrine in China; that will spare us a lot of trouble.[11]

This represented a major turning point in the relationship of Christian missionaries and Chinese society. Many were subsequently expelled, and missionaries lost favor at court.

In other ways as well, missionaries played into the hands of their Chinese opponents. Their willingness to work under the Manchurian Qing dynasty, which came to power in 1644, discredited them with those Chinese scholars who viewed the Qing as uncivilized foreigners and their rule in China as disgraceful and illegitimate. Missionaries' reputation as miracle workers further damaged their standing as men of science and rationality, for elite Chinese often regarded miracles and supernatural religion as superstitions, fit only for the uneducated masses. Some viewed the Christian ritual of Holy Communion as a kind of cannibalism. Others came to see missionaries as potentially subversive, for various Christian groups met in secret, and such religious sects had often provided the basis for peasant rebellion. Nor did it escape Chinese notice that European Christians had taken over the Philippines and that their warships were active in the Indian Ocean. Perhaps the missionaries, with their great interest in maps, were spies for these aggressive foreigners. All of this contributed to the general failure of Christianity to secure a prominent presence in China.

Persistence and Change in Afro-Asian Cultural Traditions

Although Europeans were central players in the globalization of Christianity, theirs was not the only expanding or transformed culture of the early modern era. African religious ideas and practices, for example, accompanied slaves to the Americas. Common African forms of religious revelation—divination, dream interpretation, visions, spirit possession—found a place in the Africanized versions of Christianity that emerged in the New World. Europeans frequently perceived these practices as evidence of sorcery, witchcraft, or even devil worship and tried to suppress them. Nonetheless, syncretic (blended) religions such as Vodou in Haiti, Santeria in Cuba, and

Candomble and Macumba in Brazil persisted. They derived from various West African traditions and featured drumming, ritual dancing, animal sacrifice, and spirit possession. Over time, they incorporated Christian beliefs and practices such as church attendance, the search for salvation, and the use of candles and crucifixes and often identified their various spirits or deities with Catholic saints.

Expansion and Renewal in the Islamic World

The early modern era likewise witnessed the continuation of the "long march of Islam" across the Afro-Asian world. In sub-Saharan Africa, in the eastern and western wings of India, and in Central and Southeast Asia, the expansion of the Islamic frontier, a process already a thousand years in the making, extended farther still. Conversion to Islam generally did not mean a sudden abandonment of old religious practices in favor of the new. Rather it was more often a matter of "assimilating Islamic rituals, cosmologies, and literatures into . . . local religious systems."[12]

■ **Explanation**

What accounts for the continued spread of Islam in the early modern era and for the emergence of reform or renewal movements within the Islamic world?

Continued Islamization was not usually the product of conquering armies and expanding empires. It depended instead on wandering Muslim holy men or Sufis, Islamic scholars, and itinerant traders, none of whom posed a threat to local rulers. In fact, such people often were useful to those rulers and their village communities. They offered literacy in Arabic, established informal schools, provided protective charms containing passages from the Quran, served as advisers to local authorities and healers to the sick, often intermarried with local people, and generally did not insist that new converts give up their older practices. What they offered, in short, was connection to the wider, prestigious, prosperous world of Islam. Islamization extended modestly even to the Americas, where enslaved African Muslims practiced their faith in North America and particularly in Brazil, where Muslims led a number of slave revolts in the early nineteenth century. (See the Portrait of Ayuba Suleiman Diallo in Chapter 14, pp. 696–97.)

The islands of Southeast Asia illustrate the diversity of belief and practice that accompanied the spread of Islam in the early modern era. During the seventeenth century in Acheh, a Muslim sultanate on the northern tip of Sumatra, authorities sought to enforce the dietary codes and alms-giving practices of Islamic law. After four successive women ruled the area in the late 1600s, women were then forbidden from exercising political power. On Muslim Java, however, numerous women served in royal courts, and women throughout Indonesia continued their longtime role as buyers and sellers in local markets. Among ordinary Javanese, traditional animistic practices of spirit worship coexisted easily with a tolerant and accommodating Islam, while merchants often embraced a more orthodox version of the religion in line with Middle Eastern traditions.

To such orthodox Muslims, religious syncretism, which accompanied Islamization almost everywhere, became increasingly offensive, even heretical. Such sentiments played an important role in movements of religious renewal and reform that emerged throughout the vast Islamic world of the eighteenth century. The leaders of such movements sharply criticized those practices that departed from earlier patterns established by Muhammad and from the authority of the Quran. For example, in India, which was governed by the Muslim Mughal Empire, religious resistance to official policies that accommodated Hindus found concrete expression during the reign of the emperor Aurangzeb (1658–1707) (see p. 643). A series of religious wars in West Africa during the eighteenth and early nineteenth centuries took aim at corrupt Islamic practices and the rulers, Muslim and non-Muslim alike, who permitted them. In Southeast and Central Asia, tension grew between practitioners of localized and blended versions of Islam and those who sought to purify such practices in the name of a more authentic and universal faith.

The most well-known and widely visible of these Islamic renewal movements took place during the mid-eighteenth century in Arabia itself, where the religion had been born more than 1,000 years earlier. This movement originated in the teachings of the Islamic scholar Muhammad ibn Abd al-Wahhab (1703–1792). The growing difficulties of the Islamic world, such as the weakening of the Ottoman Empire, were directly related, he argued, to deviations from the pure faith of early Islam. Al-Wahhab was particularly upset by common religious practices in central Arabia that seemed to him idolatry — the widespread veneration of Sufi saints and their tombs, the adoration of natural sites, and even the respect paid to Muhammad's tomb at Mecca. All of this was a dilution of the absolute monotheism of authentic Islam.

The Wahhabi movement took a new turn in the 1740s when it received the political backing of Muhammad Ibn Saud, a local ruler who found al-Wahhab's ideas compelling. With Ibn Saud's support, the religious movement became an expansive state in central Arabia. Within that state, offending tombs were razed; "idols" were eliminated; books on logic were destroyed; the use of tobacco, hashish, and musical instruments was forbidden; and certain taxes not authorized by religious teaching were abolished.

Al-Wahhab's ideas about the role of women have attracted considerable attention in light of the highly restrictive practices of Wahhabi Islam in contemporary Saudi Arabia. He did on one occasion reluctantly authorize the stoning of a woman who persisted in an adulterous sexual relationship after numerous warnings, but more generally he emphasized the rights of women within a patriarchal Islamic framework. These included the right to consent to and stipulate conditions for a marriage, to control her dowry, to divorce, and to engage in commerce. Such rights, long embedded in Islamic law, had apparently been forgotten or ignored in eighteenth-century Arabia. Furthermore he did not insist on head to toe covering of women in public and allowed for the mixing of unrelated men and women for business or medical purposes.[13]

By the early nineteenth century, this new reformist state encompassed much of central Arabia, with Mecca itself coming under Wahhabi control in 1803 (see Map 15.3). Although an Egyptian army broke the power of the Wahhabis in 1818, the movement's influence continued to spread across the Islamic world. (See Document 15.3, pp. 758–59, for a statement of the Wahhabi outlook.) Together with the ongoing expansion of the religion, these movements of reform and renewal signaled the continuing cultural vitality of the "abode of Islam," even as the European presence on the world stage assumed larger dimensions. In the nineteenth and twentieth centuries, such movements persisted and became associated with resistance to the political, military, and cultural intrusion of the European West into the affairs of the Islamic world.

China: New Directions in an Old Tradition

Neither China nor India experienced cultural or religious change as dramatic as that of the Reformation in Europe, nor did Confucian or Hindu cultures during the early modern era spread widely, as did Christianity and Islam. Nonetheless, neither of these traditions remained static. As in Christian Europe, challenges to established orthodoxies in China and India emerged as commercial and urban life, as well as political change, fostered new thinking.

Map 15.3   The Expansion of Wahhabi Islam
From its base in central Arabia, the Wahhabi movement represented a challenge to the Ottoman Empire, while its ideas subsequently spread widely within the Islamic world.

China during the Ming and Qing dynasties continued to operate broadly within a Confucian framework, enriched now by the insights of Buddhism and Daoism to generate a system of thought called Neo-Confucianism. Chinese Ming dynasty rulers, in their aversion to the despised Mongols, embraced and actively supported this native Confucian tradition, whereas the foreign Manchu or Qing rulers did so to woo Chinese intellectuals to support the new dynasty. Within this context, a considerable amount of controversy, debate, and new thinking emerged during the early modern era.

During late Ming times, for example, the influential thinker Wang Yangming (1472–1529) argued that "intuitive moral knowledge exists in people . . . even robbers know that they should not rob."[14] Thus anyone could achieve a virtuous life by introspection and contemplation, without the extended education, study of the classical texts, and constant striving for improvement that traditional Confucianism prescribed for an elite class of "gentlemen." Such ideas figured prominently among Confucian scholars of the sixteenth century, although critics later contended that such thinking promoted an excessive individualism. They also argued that Wang Yangming's ideas had undermined the Ming dynasty and contributed to China's conquest by the foreign Manchus. Some Chinese Buddhists as well sought to make their religion more accessible to ordinary people, by suggesting that laypeople at home could undertake practices similar to those performed by monks in monasteries. Withdrawal from the

■ **Change**
What kinds of cultural changes occurred in China and India during the early modern era?

world was not necessary for enlightenment. This kind of moral or religious individualism bore some similarity to the thinking of Martin Luther, who argued that individuals could seek salvation by "faith alone," without the assistance of a priestly hierarchy.

Another new direction in Chinese elite culture took shape in a movement known as *kaozheng*, or "research based on evidence." Intended to "seek truth from facts," kaozheng was critical of the unfounded speculation of conventional Confucian philosophy and instead emphasized the importance of verification, precision, accuracy, and rigorous analysis in all fields of inquiry. During the late Ming years, this emphasis generated works dealing with agriculture, medicine, pharmacology, botany, craft techniques, and more. In the Qing era, kaozheng was associated with a recovery and critical analysis of ancient historical documents, which sometimes led to sharp criticism of Neo-Confucian orthodoxy. It was a genuinely scientific approach to knowledge, but it was applied more to the study of the past than to the natural world of astronomy, physics, or anatomy, as in the West.

While such matters occupied the intellectual elite of China, in the cities a lively popular culture emerged among the less well educated. For city-dwellers, plays, paintings, short stories, and especially novels provided diversion and entertainment that were a step up from what could be found in teahouses and wine shops. Numerous "how-to" painting manuals allowed a larger public to participate in this favorite Chinese art form. Even though Confucian scholars disdained popular fiction, a vigorous printing industry responded to the growing demand for exciting novels. The most famous was Cao Xueqin's mid-eighteenth-century novel *The Dream of the Red Chamber*, a huge book that contained 120 chapters and some 400 characters, most of them women. It explored the social life of an eighteenth-century elite family with connections to the Chinese court.

India: Bridging the Hindu/Muslim Divide

In a largely Hindu India, ruled by the Muslim Mughal Empire, several significant cultural departures took shape in the early modern era that brought Hindus and Muslims together in new forms of religious expression. One was the flourishing of a devotional form of Hinduism known as *bhakti*. Through songs, prayers, dances, poetry, and rituals, devotees sought to achieve union with one or another of India's many deities. Appealing especially to women, the bhakti movement provided an avenue for social criticism. Its practitioners often set aside caste distinctions and disregarded the detailed rituals of the Brahmin priests in favor of direct contact with the Divine. This emphasis had much in common with mystical Sufi forms of Islam and helped blur the distinction between these two traditions in India (see Document 15.4, pp. 760–61).

Among the most beloved of bhakti poets was Mirabai (1498–1547), a high-caste woman from northern India who abandoned her upper-class family and conventional Hindu practice. Upon her husband's death, tradition asserts, she declined to burn herself on his funeral pyre (a practice known as *sati*). She further offended caste restrictions by taking as her guru (religious teacher) an old untouchable shoemaker. To visit him, she apparently tied her saris together and climbed down the castle walls at night. Then she would wash his aged feet and drink the water from these ablutions. Much of her poetry deals with her yearning for union with Krishna, a Hindu deity she regarded as her husband, lover, and lord.

> What I paid was my social body, my town body, my family body, and all my inherited jewels. Mirabai says: The Dark One [Krishna] is my husband now.[15]

Yet another major cultural change that blended Islam and Hinduism emerged with the growth of Sikhism as a new and distinctive religious tradition in the Punjab region of northern India. Its founder, Guru Nanak (1469–1539), had been involved in the bhakti movement but came to believe that "there is no Hindu; there is no Muslim; only God." His teachings and those of subsequent gurus also generally ignored caste distinctions and untouchability and ended the seclusion of women, while proclaiming the "brotherhood of all mankind" as well as the essential equality of men and women. Drawing converts from Punjabi peasants and merchants, both Muslim and Hindu, the Sikhs gradually became a separate religious community. They developed their own sacred book, known as the Guru Granth (teacher book); created a central place of worship and pilgrimage in the Golden Temple of Amritsar; and prescribed certain dress requirements for men, including keeping hair and beards uncut, wearing a turban, and carrying a short sword. During the seventeenth century, Sikhs encountered hostility from both the Mughal Empire and some of their Hindu neighbors. In response, Sikhism evolved from a peaceful religious movement, blending Hindu and Muslim elements, into a militant community whose military skills were highly valued by the British when they took over India in the late eighteenth century.

Guru Nanak

In this early eighteenth-century manuscript painting, Guru Nanak, the founder of Sikhism, and his constant companion Mardana (with a musical instrument) encounter a robber (the man with a sword) along the road. According to the story accompanying the painting, that experience persuaded the robber to abandon his wicked ways and become a follower of the Sikh path. (© British Library Board)

SUMMING UP SO FAR

In what ways did religious changes in Asia and the Middle East parallel those in Europe, and in what ways were they different?

A New Way of Thinking:
The Birth of Modern Science

While some Europeans were actively attempting to spread the Christian faith to distant corners of the world, others were nurturing an understanding of the cosmos at least partially at odds with traditional Christian teaching. These were the makers of Europe's Scientific Revolution, a vast intellectual and cultural transformation that took place between the mid-sixteenth and early eighteenth centuries. These men of science would no longer rely on the external authority of the Bible, the Church, the speculations of ancient philosophers, or the received wisdom of cultural tradition. For them, knowledge would be acquired through a combination of careful observations, controlled experiments, and the formulation of general laws, expressed in mathematical terms. Those who created this revolution—Copernicus from Poland, Galileo from Italy, Descartes from France, Newton from England, and many others—saw themselves as departing radically from older ways of thinking. "The old rubbish must be thrown away," wrote a seventeenth-century English scientist. "These are the days that must lay a new Foundation of a more magnificent Philosophy."[16]

The long-term significance of the Scientific Revolution can hardly be overestimated. Within early modern Europe, it fundamentally altered ideas about the place of humankind within the cosmos and sharply challenged both the teachings and the authority of the Church. Over the past several centuries, it has substantially eroded religious belief and practice in the West, particularly among the well educated. When applied to the affairs of human society, scientific ways of thinking challenged ancient social hierarchies and political systems and played a role in the revolutionary upheavals of the modern era. But science also was used to legitimize racial and gender inequalities, giving new support to old ideas about the natural inferiority of women and enslaved people. When married to the technological innovations of the Industrial Revolution, science fostered both the marvels of modern production and the horrors of modern means of destruction. By the twentieth century, science had become so widespread that it largely lost its association with European culture and became the chief symbol of global modernity. Like Buddhism, Christianity, and Islam, modern science became a universal worldview, open to all who could accept its premises and its techniques.

The Question of Origins: Why Europe?

■ **Comparison**

Why did the Scientific Revolution occur in Europe rather than in China or the Islamic world?

Why did the breakthrough of the Scientific Revolution occur first in Europe and during the early modern era? The realm of Islam, after all, had generated the most advanced science in the world during the centuries between 800 and 1400. Arab scholars could boast of remarkable achievements in mathematics, astronomy, optics, and medicine, and their libraries far exceeded those of Europe.[17] And what of China? Its elite culture of Confucianism was both sophisticated and secular, less burdened by religious dogma than in the Christian or Islamic worlds; its technological accomplishments and economic growth were unmatched anywhere in the several centuries after 1000. In neither civilization, however, did these achievements lead to the kind of intellectual innovation that occurred in Europe.

Europe's historical development as a reinvigorated and fragmented civilization arguably gave rise to conditions uniquely favorable to the scientific enterprise. By the twelfth and thirteenth centuries, Europeans had evolved a legal system that guaranteed a measure of independence for a variety of institutions—the Church, towns and cities, guilds, professional associations, and universities. This legal revolution was based on the idea of a "corporation," a collective group of people that was treated as a unit, a legal person, with certain rights to regulate and control its own members.

Most important for the development of science in the West was the autonomy of its emerging universities. By 1215, the University of Paris was recognized as a "corporation of masters and scholars," which could admit and expel students, establish courses of instruction, and grant a "license to teach" to its faculty. Such universities—for example, in Paris, Bologna, Oxford, Cambridge, and Salamanca—became "neutral zones of intellectual autonomy" in which scholars could pursue their studies in relative freedom from the dictates of church or state authorities. Within them, the study of the natural order began to slowly separate itself from philosophy and theology and to gain a distinct identity. Their curricula featured "a basically scientific core of readings and lectures" that drew heavily on the writings of the Greek thinker Aristotle, which had only recently become available to Western Europeans. Most of the major figures in the Scientific Revolution had been trained in and were affiliated with these universities.

In the Islamic world, by contrast, science was patronized by a variety of local authorities, but it occurred largely outside the formal system of higher education. Within colleges known as madrassas, Quranic studies and religious law held the central place, whereas philosophy and natural science were viewed with great suspicion. To religious scholars, the Quran held all wisdom, and scientific thinking might well challenge it. An earlier openness to free inquiry and religious toleration was increasingly replaced by a disdain for scientific and philosophical inquiry, for it seemed to lead only to uncertainty and confusion. "May God protect us from useless knowledge" was a saying that reflected this outlook. Nor did Chinese authorities permit independent institutions of higher learning in which scholars could conduct their studies in relative freedom. Instead Chinese education focused on preparing for a rigidly defined set of civil service examinations and emphasized the humanistic and moral texts of classical Confucianism. "The pursuit of scientific subjects," one recent historian concluded, "was thereby relegated to the margins of Chinese society."[18]

Beyond its distinctive institutional development, Western Europe was in a position to draw extensively on the knowledge of other cultures, especially that of the Islamic world. Arab medical texts, astronomical research, and translations of Greek classics played a major role in the birth of European natural philosophy (as science was then called) between 1000 and 1500. Then, in the sixteenth through the eighteenth centuries, Europeans found themselves at the center of a massive new exchange of information as they became aware of lands, peoples, plants, animals, societies, and religions from around the world. This tidal wave of new knowledge, uniquely available to Europeans, shook up older ways of thinking and opened the way to new conceptions of the world. The sixteenth-century Italian doctor, mathematician, and writer Girolamo Cardano (1501–1576) clearly expressed this sense of wonderment: "The most unusual [circumstance of my life] is that I was born in this century in which the whole world became known; whereas the ancients were familiar with but a little more than a third part of it." He worried, however, that amid this explosion of knowledge, "certainties will be exchanged for uncertainties."[19] It was precisely those uncertainties—skepticism about established views—that provided such a fertile cultural ground for the emergence of modern science. The Reformation too contributed to that cultural climate in its challenge to authority, its encouragement of mass literacy, and its affirmation of secular professions.

Science as Cultural Revolution

■ **Change**

What was revolutionary about the Scientific Revolution?

Before the Scientific Revolution, educated Europeans held a view of the world that derived from Aristotle, perhaps the greatest of the ancient Greek philosophers, and from Ptolemy, a Greco-Egyptian mathematician and astronomer who lived in Alexandria during the second century C.E. To medieval European thinkers, the earth was stationary and at the center of the universe, and around it revolved the sun, moon, and stars embedded in ten spheres of transparent crystal. This understanding coincided well with the religious outlook of the Catholic Church because the attention of the entire universe was centered on the earth and its human inhabitants, among whom God's plan for salvation unfolded. It was a universe of divine purpose, with angels guiding the hierarchically arranged heavenly bodies along their way while God watched over the whole from his realm beyond the spheres. The Scientific Revolution was revolutionary because it fundamentally challenged this understanding of the universe.

The initial breakthrough in the Scientific Revolution came from the Polish mathematician and astronomer Nicolaus Copernicus, whose famous book *On the Revolutions of the Heavenly Spheres* was published in the year of his death, 1543. Its essential argument was that "at the middle of all things lies the sun" and that the earth, like the other planets, revolved around it. Thus the earth was no longer unique or at the obvious center of God's attention.

Other European scientists built on Copernicus's central insight, and some even argued that other inhabited worlds and other kinds of humans existed. Less speculatively, in the early seventeenth century Johannes Kepler, a German mathematician, showed that the planets followed elliptical orbits, undermining the ancient belief that they moved in perfect circles. The Italian Galileo (gal-uh-LAY-oh) developed an improved telescope, with which he observed sunspots, or blemishes, moving across the

Snapshot   **Major Thinkers and Achievements of the Scientific Revolution**

Thinker/Scientist	Achievements
Nicolaus Copernicus (Polish; 1473–1543)	Posited that sun is at the center of solar system, earth rotates on its axis, and earth and planets revolve around the sun
Andreas Vesalius (Flemish; 1514–1564)	"Father of anatomy"; made detailed drawings of human body based on dissection
Francis Bacon (English; 1561–1626)	Emphasized observation and experimentation as the key to modern science
Galileo Galilei (Italian; 1564–1642)	Developed an improved telescope; discovered sunspots, mountains on the moon, and Jupiter's moons; performed experimental work on the velocity of falling objects
Johannes Kepler (German; 1571–1630)	Posited that planets follow elliptical, not circular, orbits; described laws of planetary motion
William Harvey (English; 1578–1657)	Described the circulation of the blood and the function of the heart
René Descartes (French; 1596–1650)	Emphasized the importance of mathematics and logical deduction in understanding the physical world; invented analytical geometry
Isaac Newton (English; 1642–1727)	Synthesized earlier findings around the concept of universal gravitation; invented calculus; formulated concept of inertia and laws of motion

face of the sun. This called into question the traditional notion that no change or imperfection marred the heavenly bodies. His discovery of the moons of Jupiter and many new stars suggested a cosmos far larger than the finite universe of traditional astronomy. Some thinkers began to discuss the notion of an unlimited universe in which humankind occupied a mere speck of dust in an unimaginable vastness. The French mathematician and philosopher Blaise Pascal (1623–1662) perhaps spoke for many when he wrote: "The eternal silence of infinite space frightens me."[20]

The culmination of the Scientific Revolution came in the work of Sir Isaac Newton, the Englishman who formulated the modern laws of motion and mechanics, which remained unchallenged until the twentieth century. At the core of Newton's thinking was the concept of universal gravitation. "All bodies whatsoever," Newton declared, "are endowed with a principle of mutual gravitation."[21] Here was the grand unifying idea of early modern science. The radical implication of this view was that the heavens and the earth, long regarded as separate and distinct spheres, were not so

The Telescope
Johannes Hevelius, an astronomer of German Lutheran background living in what is now Poland, constructed extraordinarily long telescopes in the mid-seventeenth century with which he observed sunspots, charted the surface of the moon, and discovered several comets. Such telescopes played a central role in transforming understandings of the universe during the Scientific Revolution. (World History Archive/Alamy)

different after all, for the motion of a cannonball or the falling of an apple obeyed the same natural laws that governed the orbiting planets.

By the time Newton died, a revolutionary new understanding of the physical universe had emerged among educated Europeans. That universe was no longer propelled by supernatural forces but functioned on its own according to scientific principles that could be described mathematically. In Kepler's view, "the machine of the universe is not similar to a divine animated being but similar to a clock."[22] Furthermore, it was a machine that regulated itself, requiring neither God nor angels to account for its normal operation. Knowledge of that universe could be obtained through human reason alone—by observation, deduction, and experimentation—without the aid of ancient authorities or divine revelation. The French philosopher René Descartes (day-KAHRT) resolved "to seek no other knowledge than that which I might find within myself, or perhaps in the book of nature."[23]

Like the physical universe, the human body also lost some of its mystery. The careful dissections of cadavers and animals enabled doctors and scientists to describe the human body with much greater accuracy and to understand the circulation of the blood throughout the body. The heart was no longer the mysterious center of the body's heat and the seat of its passions; instead it was just another machine, a complex muscle that functioned as a pump.

The movers and shakers of this enormous cultural transformation were almost entirely male. European women, after all, had been largely excluded from the universities where much of the new science was discussed. A few aristocratic women, however, had the leisure and connections to participate informally in the scientific networks of their male relatives. Through her marriage to the Duke of Newcastle, Margaret Cavendish (1623–1673) joined in conversations with a circle of "natural philosophers," wrote six scientific texts, and was the only seventeenth-century English woman to attend a session of the Royal Society of London, created to foster scientific learning. In Germany, a number of women took part in astronomical work as assistants to their husbands or brothers. Maria Winkelman, for example, discovered a previously unknown comet, though her husband took credit for it. After his death, she sought to continue his work in the Berlin Academy of Sciences but was refused on the grounds that "mouths would gape" if a woman held such a position.

Much of this scientific thinking developed in the face of strenuous opposition from the Catholic Church, for both its teachings and its authority were under attack. The Italian philosopher Giordano Bruno, proclaiming an infinite universe and many worlds, was burned at the stake in 1600, and Galileo was compelled by the Church to publicly renounce his belief that the earth moved around an orbit and rotated on its axis.

But not all was conflict between the Church and an emerging science. None of the early scientists rejected Christianity. Galileo himself proclaimed the compatibility of science and faith when he wrote: "Nor is God any less excellently revealed in Nature's actions than in the sacred statements of the Bible."[24] Newton was a serious biblical scholar and saw no necessary contradiction between his ideas and belief in God. "This most beautiful system of the sun, planets, and comets," he declared, "could only proceed from the counsel and dominion of an intelligent Being."[25] The Church gradually accommodated as well as resisted the new ideas, largely by compartmentalizing them. Science might prevail in its limited sphere of describing the physical universe, but religion was still the arbiter of truth about those ultimate questions concerning human salvation, righteous behavior, and the larger purposes of life.

Science and Enlightenment

Initially limited to a small handful of scholars, the ideas of the Scientific Revolution spread to a wider European public during the eighteenth century. That process was aided by novel techniques of printing and bookmaking, by a popular press, by growing literacy, and by a host of scientific societies. Moreover, the new approach to knowledge—rooted in human reason, skeptical of authority, expressed in natural laws—was now applied to human affairs, not just to the physical universe. The Scottish professor Adam Smith (1723–1790), for example, formulated laws that accounted for the operation of the economy and that, if followed, he believed, would generate inevitably favorable results for society. Growing numbers of people believed that the long-term outcome of scientific development would be "enlightenment," a term that has come to define the eighteenth century in European history. If human reason could discover the laws that governed the universe, surely it could uncover ways in which humankind might govern itself more effectively.

"What is Enlightenment?" asked the prominent German intellectual Immanuel Kant (1724–1804). "It is man's emergence from his self-imposed . . . inability to use one's own understanding without another's guidance. . . . Dare to know! 'Have the courage to use your own understanding' is therefore the motto of the enlightenment."[26] Although they often disagreed sharply with one another, European Enlightenment thinkers shared this belief in the power of knowledge to transform human society. They also shared a satirical, critical style, a commitment to open-mindedness and inquiry, and in various degrees a hostility to established political and religious authority. Many took aim at arbitrary governments, the "divine right of kings," and the aristocratic privileges of European society. The English philosopher John Locke

■ **Change**

In what ways did the Enlightenment challenge older patterns of European thinking?

(1632–1704) offered principles for constructing a constitutional government, a contract between rulers and ruled that was created by human ingenuity rather than divinely prescribed. Much of Enlightenment thinking was directed against the superstition, ignorance, and corruption of established religion. In his *Treatise on Toleration*, the French writer Voltaire (1694–1778) reflected the outlook of the Scientific Revolution as he commented sarcastically on religious intolerance:

> This little globe, nothing more than a point, rolls in space like so many other globes; we are lost in its immensity. Man, some five feet tall, is surely a very small part of the universe. One of these imperceptible beings says to some of his neighbors in Arabia or Africa: "Listen to me, for the God of all these worlds has enlightened me; there are nine hundred million little ants like us on the earth, but only my anthill is beloved of God; He will hold all others in horror through all eternity; only mine will be blessed, the others will be eternally wretched."[27]

Voltaire's own faith, like many others among the "enlightened," was deism. Deists believed in a rather abstract and remote Deity, sometimes compared to a clockmaker, who had created the world, but not in a personal God who intervened in history or tampered with natural law. Others became *pantheists*, who believed that God and nature were identical. Here was a conception of religion shaped by the outlook of science. Sometimes called "natural religion," it was devoid of mystery, revelation, ritual, and spiritual practice, while proclaiming a God that could be "proven" by human rationality, logic, and the techniques of scientific inquiry. In this view, all else was superstition. Among the most radical of such thinkers were the several Dutchmen who wrote the *Treatise of Three Imposters*, which claimed that Moses, Jesus, and Muhammad were fraudulent impostors who based their teachings on "the ignorance of Peoples [and] resolved to keep them in it."[28]

Prominent among the debates spawned by the Enlightenment was the question of women's nature, their role in society, and the education most appropriate for them. Although well-to-do Parisian women hosted in their elegant salons many gatherings of the largely male Enlightenment figures, most of those men were anything but ardent feminists. The male editors of the famous *Encyclopedie*, a vast compendium of Enlightenment thought, included very few essays by women. One of the male authors expressed the common view that women "constitute the principal ornament of the world. . . . May they, through submissive discretion and . . . artless cleverness, spur us [men] on to virtue." In his treatise *Emile*, Jean-Jacque Rousseau described women as fundamentally different from and inferior to men and urged that "the whole education of women ought to be relative to men."

Such views were sharply contested by any number of other Enlightenment figures—men and women alike. The *Journal des Dames* (Ladies Journal), founded in Paris in 1759, aggressively defended women. "If we have not been raised up in the sciences as you have," declared Madame Beaulmer, the *Journal*'s first editor, "it is you [men] who are the guilty ones; for have you not always abused . . . the bodily strength that nature has given you?"[29] The philosopher Condorcet looked forward to the "complete destruction of those prejudices that have established an inequality

The Philosophers of the Enlightenment
This painting shows the French philosopher Voltaire with a group of intellectual luminaries at the summer palace of the Prussian King Frederick II. Such literary gatherings, sometimes called salons, were places of lively conversation among mostly male participants and came to be seen as emblematic of the European Enlightenment. (© akg-images/The Image Works)

of rights between the sexes." (See Document 15.2, pp. 756–57.) And in 1792 the British writer Mary Wollstonecraft directly confronted Rousseau's view of women and their education: "What nonsense! . . . til women are more rationally educated, the progress of human virtue and improvement in knowledge must receive continual checks." Thus was initiated a debate that echoed throughout the centuries that followed.

Though solidly rooted in Europe, Enlightenment thought was influenced by the growing global awareness of its major thinkers. Voltaire, for example, idealized China as an empire governed by an elite of secular scholars selected for their talent, which stood in sharp contrast to continental Europe, where aristocratic birth and military prowess were far more important. The example of Confucianism—supposedly secular, moral, rational, and tolerant—encouraged Enlightenment thinkers to imagine a future for European civilization without the kind of supernatural religion that they found so offensive in the Christian West. (See Visual Source 14.1, p. 711, for European fascination with things Chinese.)

The central theme of the Enlightenment—and what made it potentially revolutionary—was the idea of progress. Human society was not fixed by tradition or divine command but could be changed, and improved, by human action guided by reason. No one expressed this soaring confidence in human possibility more clearly than the French thinker the Marquis de Condorcet (1743–1794), who boldly declared that "the perfectibility of humanity is indefinite." (See Document 15.2, pp. 756–57.) Belief in progress was a sharp departure from much of premodern social thinking, and it inspired those who later made the great revolutions of the modern era in the Americas, France, Russia, China, and elsewhere. Born of the Scientific Revolution, that was the faith of the Enlightenment. For some, it was virtually a new religion.

The age of the Enlightenment, however, also witnessed a reaction against too much reliance on human reason. Jean-Jacques Rousseau (1712–1778) minimized the importance of book learning for the education of children and prescribed instead an immersion in nature, which taught self-reliance and generosity rather than the greed and envy fostered by "civilization." The Romantic movement in art and literature appealed to emotion, intuition, passion, and imagination rather than cold reason and scientific learning. Religious awakenings—complete with fiery sermons, public repentance, and intense personal experience of sin and redemption—shook Protestant Europe and North America in the eighteenth and early nineteenth centuries. The Methodist movement—with its emphasis on Bible study, confession of sins, fasting, enthusiastic preaching, and resistance to worldly pleasures—was a case in point. Science and the Enlightenment surely challenged religion, and for some they eroded religious belief and practice. Just as surely, though, religion persisted, adapted, and revived for many others.

Looking Ahead: Science in the Nineteenth Century

■ Change

How did nineteenth-century developments in the sciences challenge the faith of the Enlightenment?

The perspectives of the Enlightenment were challenged not only by romanticism and religious "enthusiasm" but also by the continued development of European science itself. This remarkable phenomenon justifies a brief look ahead at several scientific developments in the nineteenth century.

Modern science was a cumulative and self-critical enterprise, which in the nineteenth century and after was applied to new domains of human inquiry in ways that undermined some of the assumptions of the Enlightenment. In the realm of biology, for example, Charles Darwin (1809–1882) laid out a complex argument that all life was in constant change, that an endless and competitive struggle for survival over millions of years constantly generated new species of plants and animals, while casting others into extinction. Human beings were not excluded from this vast process, for they too were the work of evolution operating through natural selection. Darwin's famous books *The Origin of Species* (1859) and *The Descent of Man* (1871) were as shattering to traditional religious views as Copernicus's ideas about a sun-centered universe had been several centuries earlier.

At the same time, Karl Marx (1818–1883) articulated a view of human history that likewise emphasized change and struggle. Conflicting social classes—slave owners and slaves, nobles and peasants, capitalists and workers—successively drove the process of historical transformation. Although he was describing the evolution of human civilization, Marx saw himself as a scientist. He based his theories on extensive historical research; like Newton and Darwin, he sought to formulate general laws that would explain events in a rational way. Nor did he believe in heavenly intervention, chance, or the divinely endowed powers of kings. The coming of socialism, in this view, was not simply a good idea; it was inscribed in the laws of historical development (see Document 17.4, pp. 867–70).

Like the intellectuals of the Enlightenment, Darwin and Marx believed strongly in progress, but in their thinking, conflict and struggle rather than reason and education were the motors of progress. The Enlightenment image of the thoughtful, rational, and independent individual was fading. Individuals—plant, animal, and human alike—were now viewed as enmeshed in vast systems of biological, economic, and social conflict.

The work of the Viennese doctor Sigmund Freud (1856–1939) applied scientific techniques to the operation of the human mind and emotions and in doing so cast further doubt on Enlightenment conceptions of human rationality. At the core of each person, Freud argued, lay primal impulses toward sexuality and aggression, which were only barely held in check by the thin veneer of social conscience derived from civilization. Our neuroses arose from the ceaseless struggle between our irrational drives and the claims of conscience. This too was a far cry from the Enlightenment conception of the human condition.

European Science beyond the West

In the long run, the achievements of the Scientific Revolution spread globally, becoming the most widely sought-after product of European culture and far more desired than Christianity, democracy, socialism, or Western literature. In the early modern era, however, interest in European scientific thinking within major Asian societies was both modest and selective. The telescope provides an example. Invented in early-seventeenth-century Europe and endlessly improved in the centuries that followed, the telescope provoked enormous excitement in European scientific circles. It made possible any number of astronomical discoveries including the rugged surface of the moon, the moons of Jupiter, the rings of Saturn, and the phases of Venus. "We are here . . . on fire with these things," wrote an English astronomer in 1610.[30] Soon the telescope was available in China, Mughal India, and the Ottoman Empire. But in none of these places did it evoke much interest nor did it evolve into the kind of "discovery machine" that it was rapidly becoming in Europe.

In China, Qing dynasty emperors and scholars were most interested in European techniques, derived largely from Jesuit missionaries, for predicting eclipses, reforming the calendar, and making accurate maps of the empire. European medicine, however, was of little importance for Chinese physicians before the nineteenth century. But the reputation of the Jesuits suffered when it became apparent in the 1760s that for two centuries the missionaries had withheld information about Copernican views of a sun-centered solar system because those ideas had been condemned by the Church.

■ **Connection**
In what ways was European science received in the major civilizations of Asia in the early modern era?

Nonetheless, European science had a substantial impact on a number of Chinese scholars as it interacted with the data-based kaozheng movement, described by one participant as "an ant-like accumulation of facts."[31] European mathematics was of particular interest to kaozheng researchers who were exploring the history of Chinese mathematics. To convince their skeptical colleagues that the barbarian Europeans had something to offer in this field, some Chinese scholars argued that European mathematics had in fact grown out of much earlier Chinese ideas and could therefore be adopted with comfort.[32] In such ways, early modern Chinese thinkers selectively assimilated Western science very much on their own terms.[33]

Although Japanese authorities largely closed their country off from the West in the early seventeenth century (see Chapter 14), one window remained open. Alone among Europeans, the Dutch were permitted to trade in Japan at a single location near Nagasaki, but not until 1720 did the Japanese lift the ban on importing Western books. Then a number of European texts in medicine, astronomy, geography, mathematics, and other disciplines were translated and studied by a small group of Japanese scholars. They were especially impressed with Western anatomical studies, for in Japan dissection was work fit only for outcasts. Returning from an autopsy conducted by Dutch physicians, several Japanese observers reflected on their experience: "We remarked to each other how amazing the autopsy had been, and how inexcusable it had been for us to be ignorant of the anatomical structure of the human body."[34] Nonetheless, this small center of "Dutch learning," as it was called, remained isolated amid a pervasive Confucian-based culture. Not until the mid-nineteenth century, when Japan was forcibly opened to Western penetration, would European science assume a prominent place in Japanese culture.

Like China and Japan, the Ottoman Empire in the sixteenth and seventeenth centuries was an independent, powerful, successful society whose intellectual elites saw no need for a wholesale embrace of things European. Ottoman scholars were conscious of the rich tradition of Muslim astronomy and chose not to translate the works of major European scientists such as Copernicus, Kepler, or Newton, although they were broadly aware of European scientific achievements by 1650. Insofar as they were interested in these developments, it was for their practical usefulness in making maps and calendars rather than for their larger philosophical implications. In any event, the notion of a sun-centered solar system did not cause the kind of upset that it did in Europe.[35]

More broadly, theoretical science of any kind—Muslim or European—faced an uphill struggle in the face of a conservative Islamic educational system. In 1580, for example, a highly sophisticated astronomical observatory was dismantled under pressure from conservative religious scholars and teachers, who interpreted an outbreak of the plague as God's disapproval with those who sought to understand his secrets. As in Japan, the systematic embrace of Western science would have to await the nineteenth century, when the Ottoman Empire was under far more intense European pressure and reform seemed more necessary.

LearningCurve
bedfordstmartins.com
/strayer/LC

Reflections: Cultural Borrowing and Its Hazards

Ideas are important in human history. They shape the mental or cultural worlds that people everywhere inhabit, and they often influence behavior as well. Many of the ideas developed or introduced during the early modern era have had enormous and continuing significance in the centuries that followed. The Western Hemisphere was solidly incorporated into Christendom. A Wahhabi version of Islam remains the official faith of Saudi Arabia into the twenty-first century and has influenced many contemporary Islamic revival movements, including al-Qaeda. Modern science and the associated notions of progress have become for many people something approaching a new religion.

Accompanying the development of these ideas has been a great deal of cultural borrowing. Filipinos, Siberians, and many Native American peoples borrowed elements of Christianity from Europeans. Numerous Asian and African peoples borrowed Islam from the Arabs. North Indian Sikhs drew on both Hindu and Muslim teachings. Europeans borrowed scientific and medical ideas from the Islamic world and subsequently contributed their own rich scientific thinking to the entire planet.

In virtually every case, though, borrowing was selective rather than wholesale, even when it took place under conditions of foreign domination or colonial rule. Many peoples who appropriated Christianity or Islam certainly did not accept the rigid exclusivity and ardent monotheism of more orthodox versions of those faiths. Elite Chinese were far more interested in European mapmaking and mathematics than in Western medicine, while Japanese scholars became fascinated with the anatomical work of the Dutch. Neither, however, adopted Christianity in a widespread manner.

Borrowing was frequently the occasion for serious conflict. Some objected to much borrowing at all, particularly when it occurred under conditions of foreign domination or foreign threat. Thus members of the Taki Onqoy movement in Peru sought to wipe out Spanish influence and control, while Chinese and Japanese authorities clamped down firmly on European missionaries, even as they maintained some interest in European technological and scientific skills. Another kind of conflict derived from the efforts to control the terms of cultural borrowing. For example, European missionaries and Muslim reformers alike sought to root out "idolatry" among native converts.

To ease the tensions of cultural borrowing, efforts to "domesticate" foreign ideas and practices proliferated. Thus the Jesuits in China tried to point out similarities between Christianity and Confucianism, and Native American converts identified Christian saints with their own gods and spirits. By the late seventeenth century, some local churches in central Mexico had come to associate Catholicism less with the Spanish than with ancient pre-Aztec communities and beliefs that were now, supposedly, restored to their rightful position.

The pace of global cultural borrowing and its associated tensions stepped up even more as Europe's modern transformation unfolded in the nineteenth century and as its imperial reach extended and deepened around the world.

Second Thoughts

LearningCurve
Check what you know.
bedfordstmartins.com
/strayer/LC

Online Study Guide
bedfordstmartins.com
/highschool/strayer

What's the Significance?

Protestant Reformation, 721–25

Catholic Counter-
  Reformation, 723

Taki Onqoy, 730–31

Úrsula de Jesús, 730–31

Jesuits in China, 732–34

Wahhabi Islam, 736–37

kaozheng, 738

Mirabai, 738–39

Sikhism, 739

Copernicus, 742

Newton, 743–44

European Enlightenment,
  745–48

Voltaire, 746

Condorcet and the idea of
  progress, 746–48

Big Picture Questions

1. Why did Christianity take hold in some places more than in others?
2. In what ways was the missionary message of Christianity shaped by the cultures of Asian and American peoples?
3. In what ways did the spread of Christianity, Islam, and modern science give rise to culturally based conflicts?
4. **Looking Back:** Based on Chapters 13 through 15, how might you challenge a Eurocentric understanding of the early modern era while acknowledging the growing role of Europeans on the global stage?

For Web sites and additional documents related to this chapter, see **Make History** at bedfordstmartins.com /highschool/strayer.

Next Steps: For Further Study

Natana J. Delong-Bas, *Wahhabi Islam: From Revival and Reform to Global Jihad* (2004). A careful study of the origins of Wahhabi Islam and its subsequent development.

Patricia B. Ebrey et al., *East Asia: A Cultural, Social, and Political History* (2005). A broad survey by major scholars in the field.

Geoffrey C. Gunn, *First Globalization: The Eurasian Exchange, 1500–1800* (2003). Explores the two-way exchange of ideas between Europe and Asia in the early modern era.

Toby E. Huff, *The Rise of Early Modern Science* (2003). A fascinating and controversial explanation as to why modern science arose in the West rather than in China or the Islamic world.

Úrsula de Jesús, *The Souls of Purgatory: The Spiritual Diary of a Seventeenth-Century Afro-Peruvian Mystic* (2004). A scholarly introduction by Nancy E. van Deusen places Úrsula in a broader context.

Diarmaid MacCulloch, *Christianity: The First Three Thousand Years* (2009). A masterful exploration of global Christianity with extensive coverage of the early modern era.

Deva Sobel, *A More Perfect Heaven: How Copernicus Revolutionized the Cosmos* (2011). A fascinating account of a major breakthrough in the Scientific Revolution.

Internet Modern History Sourcebook, "The Scientific Revolution," http://www.fordham.edu/halsall/mod/modsbook09.html. A collection of primary-source documents dealing with the breakthrough to modern science in Europe.

Documents

Considering the Evidence: Renewal and Reform in the Early Modern World

Cultural and religious traditions change over time in various ways and for various reasons. Some of those changes occur as a result of internal tensions or criticisms within those traditions or in response to social and economic transformations in the larger society. The Protestant Reformation, for example, grew out of deep dissatisfaction with prevailing teachings and practices of the Roman Catholic Church and drew support from a growing middle class and a disaffected peasantry. At other times, cultural change occurred by incorporating or reacting against new ideas drawn from contact with outsiders. Chinese Confucianism took on a distinctive tone and flavor as it drew on the insights of Buddhism, and a new South Asian religion called Sikhism sought to combine elements of Hindu and Muslim belief. Whatever the stimulus for cultural change, departures from accepted ways of thinking have sometimes been expressed as a return to a purer and more authentic past, even if that past is largely imaginary. In other cases, however, change was presented as a necessary break from an outmoded past even if many elements from earlier times were retained.

All across the Eurasian world of the early modern era — in Western Europe, India, and the Middle East — significant protests against established ways of thinking were brewing. In each of the documents that follow, we are listening in on just one side of extended debates or controversies, focusing on those seeking change. To what extent were these changes moving in the same direction? How did they differ? What were the sources of these changes and how were they expressed? How might those who opposed these changes respond?

Document 15.1

Luther's Protest

Europe was home to perhaps the most substantial cultural transformations of the early modern centuries. There the Protestant Reformation sharply challenged both the doctrines and the authority of the Roman Catholic Church, ending the religious monopoly that the Church had exercised in Western

Europe for many centuries and introducing a bitter and often violent divide into the religious and political life of the region. Then the practitioners of the Scientific Revolution, and the Enlightenment that followed from it, introduced a revolutionary new understanding of both the physical world and human society while urging novel means of obtaining knowledge.

The Protestant Reformation and the Scientific Revolution/Enlightenment shared a common hostility to established authority, and they both represented a clear departure from previous patterns of thought and behavior. But they differed sharply in how they represented the changes they sought. Reformation leaders looked to the past, seeking to restore or renew what they believed was an earlier and more authentic version of Christianity. Leaders of the Scientific Revolution and the Enlightenment, on the other hand, foresaw and embraced an altogether new world in the making. They were the "moderns" combating the "ancients."

The most prominent figure in the Protestant Reformation was Martin Luther (1483–1546), a German monk, priest, and theologian (see pp. 721–23). A prolific writer, Luther composed theological treatises, translations of the Bible into German, and many hymns. The excerpts in Document 15.1, however, come from conversations with his students, friends, and colleagues, which they carefully recorded. After Luther's death, these recollections of the reformer's thoughts were collected and published under the title *Table Talk*.

- Based on this document, what issues drove the Protestant Reformation?

- What theological questions are addressed in these excerpts? How does Luther understand the concepts of law, good works, grace, and faith?

- In what ways is Luther critical of the papacy, monks, and the monastic orders of the Catholic Church?

- Why might Catholic authorities challenge Luther's singular emphasis on the Bible? In what other ways might thoughtful Catholics respond to Luther's charges? (See pp. 723–24 on the Catholic or Counter-Reformation.)

Martin Luther
Table Talk
Early Sixteenth Century

On the Bible

No greater mischief can happen to a Christian people, than to have God's Word taken from them, or falsified, so that they no longer have it pure and clear. The ungodly papists prefer the authority of the church far above God's Word; a blasphemy abominable and not to be endured; wherewith, void of all shame and piety, they spit in God's face.

Pope, cardinals, bishops, not a soul of them has read the Bible; 'tis a book unknown to them. They are a pack of guzzling, stuffing wretches, rich, wallowing in wealth and laziness, resting secure in their power, and never, for a moment, thinking of accomplishing God's will.

On Salvation

He that goes from the gospel to the law, thinking to be saved by good works, falls as uneasily as he who falls from the true service of God to idolatry; for, without Christ, all is idolatry and fictitious imaginings of God, whether of the Turkish Koran, of the pope's decrees, or Moses' law.

The Gospel preaches nothing of the merit of works; he that says the Gospel requires works for salvation, I say, flat and plain, is a liar. Nothing that is properly good proceeds out of the works of the law, unless grace be present; for what we are forced to do, goes not from the heart, nor is acceptable.

But a true Christian says: I am justified and saved only by faith in Christ, without any works or merits of my own....

Prayer in popedom is mere tongue-threshing ...; not prayer but a work of obedience.

On the Pope and the Church Hierarchy

The great prelates, the puffed-up saints, the rich usurers, the ox drovers that seek unconscionable gain, etc., these are not God's servants....

Our dealing and proceeding against the pope is altogether excommunication, which is simply the public declaration that a person is disobedient to Christ's Word. Now we affirm in public, that the pope and his retinue believe not; therefore we conclude that he shall not be saved, but be damned....

Antichrist is the pope and the Turk together; a beast full of life must have a body and soul; the spirit or soul of antichrist is the pope, his flesh or body the Turk.... Kings and princes coin money only out of metals, but the pope coins money out of every thing — indulgences, ceremonies, dispensations, pardons; 'tis all fish comes to his net....

The pope and his crew are mere worshippers of idols, and servants of the devil.... He pretends great holiness, under color of the outward service of God, for he has instituted orders with hoods, with shavings, fasting, eating of fish, saying mass, and such like.... [F]or his doctrine he gets money and wealth, honor and power, and is so great a monarch, that he can bring emperors under his girdle.

The chief cause that I fell out with the pope was this: the pope boasted that he was the head of the church, and condemned all that would not be under his power and authority....

The fasting of the friars is more easy to them than our eating to us. For one day of fasting there are three of feasting. Every friar for his supper has two quarts of beer, a quart of wine, and spice-cakes, or bread prepared with spice and salt, the better to relish their drink. Thus go on these poor fasting brethren; getting so pale and wan, they are like the fiery angels.

The state of celibacy is great hypocrisy and wickedness.... Christ with one sentence confutes all their arguments: God created them male and female.... Now eating, drinking, marrying, etc., are of God's making, therefore they are good....

A Christian's worshipping is not the external, hypocritical mask that our spiritual friars wear, when they chastise their bodies, torment and make themselves faint, with ostentatious fasting, watching, singing, wearing hair shirts, scourging themselves, etc. Such worshipping God desires not.

Source: William Hazlitt, ed. and trans., *The Table Talk of Martin Luther* (London: H. G. Bohn, 1857).

Progress and Enlightenment

If the Protestant Reformation represented a major change within the framework of the Christian faith, the Scientific Revolution and the European Enlightenment (see pp. 740–50) came to be seen by many as a challenge to all Christian understandings of the world. After all, those two movements celebrated the powers of human reason to unlock the mysteries of the universe and proclaimed the possibility of a new human society shaped by human reason. Among the most prominent spokesmen for the Enlightenment was the Marquis de Condorcet (1743–1794), a French mathematician, philosopher, and active participant in the French Revolution. In his *Sketch of the Progress of the Human Mind*, Condorcet described ten stages of human development. Document 15.2 contains excerpts from "The Ninth Epoch," whose title refers to the era in which Cordorcet was living, and the "The Tenth Epoch," referring to the age to come. Condorcet's optimism about that future was not borne out in his own life, for he fell afoul of the radicalism of the French Revolution and died in prison in 1794.

■ What is Condorcet's view of the relationship between the Scientific Revolution and the Enlightenment?

■ How, precisely, does Condorcet imagine the future of humankind?

■ How might Martin Luther respond to Condorcet's vision of the future? How do their understandings of human potential differ?

■ To what extent have Condorcet's predictions come to fruition in the two centuries since his death?

MARQUIS DE CONDORCET

Sketch of the Progress of the Human Mind
1793–1794

The Ninth Epoch: From Descartes to the Formation of the French Republic

[T]he progress of philosophy ... destroyed within the general mass of people the prejudices that have afflicted and corrupted the human race for so long a time.

Source: Marquis de Condorcet, *Sketch of the Progress of the Human Mind* (Paris: Firmin Didot Frères, 1847), Epoch IX and Epoch X.

Humanity was finally permitted to boldly proclaim the long ignored right to submit every opinion to reason, that is to utilize the only instrument given to us for grasping and recognizing the truth. Each human learned with a sort of pride that nature had never destined him to believe the word of others. The superstitions of antiquity and the abasement of reason before the madness of supernatural religion disappeared from society just as they had disappeared from philosophy. . . .

If we were to limit ourselves to showing the benefits derived from the immediate applications of the sciences, or in their applications to man-made devices for the well-being of individuals and the prosperity of nations, we would be making known only a slim part of their benefits. The most important, perhaps, is having destroyed prejudices, and reestablished human intelligence, which until then had been forced to bend down to false instructions instilled in it by absurd beliefs passed on to the children of each generation by the terrors of superstition and the fear of tyranny....

The advances of scientific knowledge are all the more deadly to these errors because they destroy them without appearing to attack them, while lavishing on those who stubbornly defend them the degrading taunt of ignorance....

Finally this progress of scientific knowledge ... results in a belief that not birth, professional status, or social standing gives anyone the right to judge something he does not understand. This unstoppable progress cannot be observed without having enlightened men search unceasingly for ways to make the other branches of learning follow the same path....

The Tenth Epoch: The Future Progress of the Human Mind

Our hopes for the future of the human species may be reduced to three important points: the destruction of inequality among nations; the progress of equality within nations themselves; and finally, the real improvement of humanity. Should not all the nations of the world approach one day the state of civilization reached by the most enlightened peoples such as the French and the Anglo-Americans? Will not the slavery of nations subjected to kings, the barbarity of African tribes, and the ignorance of savages gradually disappear? ...

If we cast an eye at the existing state of the globe, we will see right away that in Europe the principles of the French constitution are already those of all enlightened men. We will see that they are too widely disseminated and too openly professed for the efforts of tyrants and priests to prevent them from penetrating into the hovels of their slaves....

Can it be doubted that either wisdom or the senseless feuds of the European nations themselves, working with the slow but certain effects of progress in their colonies, will not soon produce the independence of the new world; and that then the European population, spreading rapidly across that immense land, must either civilize or make disappear the savage peoples that now inhabit these vast continents? ...

Thus the day will come when the sun will shine only on free men born knowing no other master but their reason; where tyrants and their slaves, priests and their ignorant, hypocritical writings will exist only in the history books and theaters.... If we consider the human creations based on scientific theories, we shall see that their progress can have no limits; ... that new tools, machines, and looms will add every day to the capabilities and skill of humans; they will improve and perfect the precision of their products while decreasing the amount of time and labor needed to produce them....

A smaller piece of land will be able to produce commodities of greater usefulness and value than before; greater benefits will be obtained with less waste; the production of the same industrial product will result in less destruction of raw materials and greater durability.... [E]ach individual will work less but more productively and will be able to better satisfy his needs....

Among the advances of the human mind we should reckon as most important for the general welfare is the complete destruction of those prejudices that have established an inequality of rights between the sexes, an inequality damaging even to the party it favors....

The most enlightened people ... will slowly come to perceive war as the deadliest plague and the most monstrous of crimes.... They will understand that they cannot become conquerors without losing their liberty; that perpetual alliances are the only way to preserve independence; and that they should seek their security, not power....

We may conclude then that the perfectibility of humanity is indefinite.

Finally, can we not also extend the same hopes to the intellectual and moral faculties? ... Is it not also probable that education, while perfecting these qualities, will also influence, modify, and improve that bodily nature itself? ...

Document 15.3

The Wahhabi Perspective on Islam

Within the Islamic world, the major cultural movements of the early modern era were those of religious renewal. Such movements sought to eliminate the "deviations" that had crept into Islamic practice over the centuries and to return to a purer version of the faith that presumably had prevailed during the foundational period of the religion. The most influential of these movements was associated with Muhammad ibn Abd al-Wahhab, whose revivalist movement spread widely in Arabia during the second half of the eighteenth century (see pp. 736–37). Document 15.3, written by the grandson of al-Wahhab shortly after the capture of Mecca in 1803, provides a window into the outlook of Wahhabi Islam.

■ What specific objections did the Wahhabis have to the prevailing practice of Islam in eighteenth-century Arabia?

■ How did Wahhabis put their ideas into practice once they had seized control of Mecca?

■ What similarities do you see between the outlook of the Wahhabis and that of Martin Luther? What differences can you identify?

■ How might you compare eighteenth-century Wahhabi Islam with movements of Islamic renewal, or "fundamentalism," in the late twentieth and early twenty-first centuries? (See Chapter 23.)

ABDULLAH WAHHAB

History and Doctrines of the Wahhabis

1803

Now I was engaged in the holy war . . . , when God, praised be He, graciously permitted us to enter Mecca. . . . Now, though we were more numerous, better armed and disciplined than the people of Mecca, yet we did not cut down their trees, neither did we hunt, nor shed any blood except the blood of victims, and of those four-footed beasts which the Lord has made lawful by his commands.

When our pilgrimage was over . . . our leader, whom the Lord saves, explained to the divines what we required of the people, . . . namely, a pure belief in the Unity of God Almighty. He pointed out to them that there was no dispute between us and them except on two points, and that one of these was a sincere belief in the Unity of God, and a knowledge of the different kinds of prayer. . . .

They then acknowledged our belief, and there was not one among them who doubted. . . . And they swore a binding oath, although we had not asked them, that their hearts had been opened and their doubts removed, and that they were convinced who-

Source: J. O'Kinealy, "Translation of an Arabic Pamphlet on the History and Doctrines of the Wahhabis," *Journal of the Asiatic Society of Bengal* 43 (1874): 68–82.

ever said, "Oh prophet of God!" or "Oh Ibn 'Abbes!" or "Oh 'Abdul Qadir!" or called on any other created being, thus entreating him to turn away evil or grant what is good (where the power belongs to God alone), such as recovery from sickness, or victory over enemies, or protection from temptation, etc.; he is a *Mushrik*, guilty of the most heinous form of shirk,° his blood shall be shed and property confiscated. . . . Again, the tombs which had been erected over the remains of the pious, had become in these times as it were idols where the people went to pray for what they required; they humbled themselves before them, and called upon those lying in them, in their distress, just as did those who were in darkness before the coming of Muhammad. . . .

We razed all the large tombs in the city which the people generally worshipped and believed in, and by which they hoped to obtain benefits or ward off evil, so that there did not remain an idol to be adored in that pure city, for which God be praised. Then the taxes and customs we abolished, all the different kinds of instruments for using tobacco we destroyed, and tobacco itself we proclaimed forbidden. Next we burned the dwellings of those selling *hashish*, and living in open wickedness, and issued a proclamation, directing the people to constantly exercise themselves in prayer. They were not to pray in separate groups . . . , but all were directed to arrange themselves at each time of prayer behind any Imam who is a follower of any of the four Imams.° . . . For in this way the Lord would be worshiped by as it were one voice, the faithful of all sects would become friendly disposed towards each other, and all dissensions would cease. . . .

[W]e do not reject anyone who follows any of the four Imams, as do the Shias. . . . We do not claim

to exercise our reason in all matters of religion, and of our faith, save that we follow our judgment where a point is clearly demonstrated to us in either the Quran or the Sunnah.° . . . We do not command the destruction of any writings except such as tend to cast people into infidelity to injure their faith, such as those on Logic, which have been prohibited by all Divines. But we are not very exacting with regard to books or documents of this nature; if they appear to assist our opponents, we destroy them. . . . We do not consider it proper to make Arabs prisoners of war, nor have we done so, neither do we fight with other nations. Finally, we do not consider it lawful to kill women or children. . . .

We consider pilgrimage is supported by legal custom, but it should not be undertaken except to a mosque, and for the purpose of praying in it. Therefore, whoever performs pilgrimage for this purpose, is not wrong, and doubtless those who spend the precious moments of their existence in invoking the Prophet, shall . . . obtain happiness in this world and the next. . . . We do not deny miraculous powers to the saints, but on the contrary allow them. . . . But whether alive or dead, they must not be made the object of any form of worship. . . .

We prohibit those forms of Bidah° that affect religion or pious works. Thus drinking coffee, reciting poetry, praising kings, do not affect religion or pious works and are not prohibited. . . .

All games are lawful. Our prophet allowed play in his mosque. So it is lawful to chide and punish persons in various ways; to train them in the use of different weapons; or to use anything which tends to encourage warriors in battle, such as a war-drum. But it must not be accompanied with musical instruments. These are forbidden, and indeed the difference between them and a war drum is clear.

°**shirk:** unbelief.

°**the four Imams:** founders of the four major schools of Islamic law.

°**Sunnah**: traditions of Muhammad's actions.

°**Bidah:** improper or erroneous behavior.

Document 15.4

The Poetry of Kabir

Early modern India was a place of much religious creativity and the interaction of various traditions. The majority of India's people practiced one or another of the many forms of Hinduism, while its Mughal rulers and perhaps 20 percent of the population were Muslims. And a new religion—Sikhism—took shape in the sixteenth century as well (see pp. 738–39). Certainly there was tension and sometimes conflict among these religious communities, but not all was hostility across religious boundaries. In the writings of Kabir (1440–1518), perhaps India's most beloved poet, the sectarian differences among these religions dissolved into a mystical and transcendent love of the Divine in all of its many forms. Born into a family of Muslim weavers, Kabir as a young man became a student of a famous Hindu ascetic, Ramananda. Kabir's own poetry was and remains revered among Hindus, Muslims, and Sikhs alike. Document 15.4 contains selections from his poetry, translated by the famous Indian writer Rabindranath Tagore in the early twentieth century.

■ In what ways was Kabir critical of conventional religious practice— both Muslim and Hindu?

■ How would you describe Kabir's religious vision?

■ How might more orthodox Hindus and Muslims respond to Kabir? How would the Wahhabis in particular take issue with Kabir's religious outlook?

KABIR

Poetry

ca. Late Fifteenth Century

O servant, where dost thou seek Me? Lo! I am beside thee.
I am neither in temple nor in mosque: I am neither in Kaaba° nor in Kailash:°
Neither am I in rites and ceremonies, nor in Yoga and renunciation.

If thou art a true seeker, thou shalt at once see Me: . . . Kabir says, "O Sadhu!° God is the breath of all breath."

It is needless to ask of a saint the caste to which he belongs;

°**Kaaba:** the central shrine of Islam in Mecca.

°**Kailash:** a mountain sacred to Hindus.

°**Sadhu:** a Hindu spiritual seeker who has abandoned ordinary life.

For the priest, the warrior, the tradesman, and all
the thirty-six castes, alike are seeking for
God....
The barber has sought God, the washerwoman,
and the carpenter—
Even Raidas° was a seeker after God.
The Rishi Swapacha was a tanner by caste [an
untouchable].
Hindus and Moslems alike have achieved that End,
where remains no mark of distinction.

Within this earthen vessel° are bowers and groves,
and within it is the Creator:
Within this vessel are the seven oceans and the
unnumbered stars.
The touchstone and the jewel-appraiser are within;
And within this vessel the Eternal soundeth, and
the spring wells up.
Kabir says: "Listen to me, my Friend! My beloved
Lord is within."

Your Lord is near: yet you are climbing the
palm-tree to seek Him.
The Brâhman priest goes from house to house
and initiates people into faith:
Alas! the true fountain of life is beside you, and
you have set up a stone to worship.
Kabir says: "I may never express how sweet my
Lord is.

°**Raidas:** a Hindu poet from a low-ranking Sudra caste.

°**earthen vessel:** the human body.

Yoga and the telling of beads, virtue and vice—
these are naught to Him."

I do not ring the temple bell:
I do not set the idol on its throne:
I do not worship the image with flowers.
It is not the austerities that mortify the flesh which
are pleasing to the Lord,
When you leave off your clothes and kill your
senses, you do not please the Lord.
The man who is kind and who practices righteousness, who remains passive amidst the affairs of
the world, who considers all creatures on earth
as his own self,
He attains the Immortal Being, the true God is
ever with him.

There is nothing but water at the holy bathing
places;
And I know that they are useless, for I have bathed
in them.
The images are all lifeless, they cannot speak; I
know, for I have cried aloud to them.
The Purana° and the Koran are mere words;
lifting up the curtain, I have seen.
Kabir gives utterance to the words of experience;
and he knows very well that all other things
are untrue.

°**Purana:** Hindu religious texts.

Source: Rabindranath Tagore, trans., *The Songs of Kabir*
(New York: Macmillan, 1915).

Using the Evidence: Renewal and Reform
in the Early Modern World

1. **Identifying the object of protest:** Each of these documents is
   protesting or criticizing something. How might you compare the ideas,
   practices, or authorities against which they are reacting? What historical
   circumstances generated these protests?

2. **Comparing views of human potential:** In what different ways might each of these authors understand human potential? What do they believe is necessary to realize or fulfill that potential?

3. **Comparing religious reformers:** Consider the religious outlook of Luther, al-Wahhab, and Kabir. What similarities and differences can you identify?

4. **Imagining a conversation:** Construct an imaginary debate or conversation between Condorcet and one or more of the religious or spiritually inclined authors of these documents.

Visual Sources

Considering the Evidence: Global Christianity in the Early Modern Era

During the early modern centuries, the world of European Christendom, long divided between its Roman Catholic and Eastern Orthodox branches, underwent two major transformations. First, the Reformation sharply divided Western Christendom into bitterly hostile Protestant and Catholic halves. And while that process was unfolding in Europe, missionaries — mostly Roman Catholic — rode the tide of European expansion to establish the faith in the Americas and parts of Africa and Asia. In those places, native converts sometimes imitated European patterns and at other times adapted the new religion to their own cultural traditions. Furthermore, smaller but ancient Christian communities persisted in Ethiopia, Armenia, Egypt, southern India, and elsewhere. Thus the Christian world of the early modern era was far more globalized and much more varied than before 1500. That variety found expression in both art and architecture, as the visual sources that follow illustrate.

Some of the differences between Protestant and Catholic Christianity become apparent in the interiors of their churches. To Martin Luther, the founder of Protestant Christianity, elaborate church interiors, with their many sculptures and paintings, represented a spiritual danger, for he feared that the wealthy few who endowed such images would come to believe that they were buying their way into heaven rather than relying on God's grace. "It would be better," he wrote, "if we gave less to the churches and altars, . . . and more to the needy."[36] John Calvin, the prominent French-born Protestant theologian, went even further, declaring that "God forbade . . . the making of any images representing him."[37]

Behind such statements lay different understandings of the church building. While Roman Catholics generally saw a church as a temple or "house of God," sacred because it is where God dwells on earth, Protestants viewed churches more as meetinghouses, gathering places for a congregation. They were not sacred in themselves as places, but only on account of the worship that occurred within them.[38] Furthermore, to Protestants, images of the saints were an invitation to idolatry. Acting on such ideas, Protestants in various places stripped older churches of the offending images, decapitated statues, and sometimes ritually burned statues and paintings at the stake. The new churches they created were often quite different from their Catholic counterparts. Visual Source 15.1, a painting by Dutch artist Pieter Saenredam from about 1645, portrays the interior of a typical Dutch Reformed (Protestant) Church.

Roman Catholic response to the Reformation took shape in the Catholic or Counter-Reformation (see pp. 723–25). That vigorous movement found expression in a style of church architecture known as Baroque, which emerged powerfully in Catholic Europe as well as in the Spanish and Portuguese colonies of Latin America during the seventeenth and eighteenth centuries. The interiors of such churches were ornately adorned with paintings, ceiling frescoes, and statues, depicting Jesus on the cross, the Virgin and child, numerous saints, and biblical stories. The exuberant art of these church interiors appealed to the senses, seeking to provoke an emotional response of mystery, awe, and grandeur while kindling the faith of the worshippers and binding them firmly to the Catholic Church in the face of Protestant competition. Visual Source 15.2 is a photograph of the interior of the Pilgrimage Church of Mariazell, located in present-day Austria. A church site since the twelfth century, the building was enlarged and refurbished in Baroque style in the seventeenth century.

Visual Source 15.1 Pieter Saenredam, Interior of a Dutch Reformed Church (Rijksmuseum, Amsterdam)

Visual Source 15.2 Catholic Baroque: Interior of Pilgrimage Church, Mariazell, Austria (Werner Forman/Art Resource)

- What obvious differences do you notice between these two church interiors? What kind of emotional responses would each of them have evoked?

- In what ways do these church interiors reflect differences between Protestant and Catholic theology? (See Snapshot, p. 725.) Why does the Protestant congregation face toward the pulpit, from which the minister presents his sermon, while the Catholic worshippers look toward the altar, where Holy Communion takes place?

■ How might Protestants and Catholics have reacted upon entering each other's churches?

■ Keep in mind that Visual Source 15.1 is a painting. Why do you think the artist showed the people disproportionately small?

Throughout Latin America, Christianity was established in the context of European conquest and colonial rule (see pp. 728–29). As the new faith took hold across the region, it incorporated much that was of European origin as the construction of many large and ornate Baroque churches illustrates. But local communities also sought to blend this European Catholic Christianity with religious symbols and concepts drawn from their own traditions in a process that historians call syncretism. In the Andes, for example, Inca religion featured a supreme creator god (Viracocha); a sun god (Inti), regarded as the creator of the Inca people; a moon goddess (Killa), who was the wife of Inti and was attended by an order of priestesses; and an earth mother goddess (Pachamama), associated with mountain peaks and fertility. Those religious figures found their way into Andean understanding of Christianity, as Visual Source 15.3 illustrates.

Painted around 1740 by an unknown artist, this striking image shows the Virgin Mary placed within the "rich mountain" of Potosí in Bolivia, from which the Spanish had extracted so much silver (see Chapter 14, p. 680). Thus, Christianity was visually expressed in an Andean tradition that viewed mountains as the embodiment of the gods. A number of smaller figures within the mountain represent the native miners whose labor had enriched their colonial rulers. A somewhat larger figure at the bottom of the mountain is an Inca ruler dressed in royal garb receiving tribute from his people. At the bottom left are the pope and a cardinal, while on the right stands the Habsburg emperor Charles V and perhaps his wife.

■ What is Mary's relationship to the heavenly beings standing above her (God the Father on the right; the dove, symbolizing the Holy Spirit in the center; and Jesus to the left) as well as to the miners at work in the mountain? What is the significance of the crown above her head and her outstretched arms?

■ The European figures at the bottom are shown in a posture of prayer or thanksgiving. What might the artist have been trying to convey? How would you interpret the relative size of the European and Andean figures?

■ Why do you think the artist placed Mary actually inside the mountain rather than on it, while depicting her dress in a mountain-like form?

■ What marks this painting and the one on p. 729 as examples of syncretism?

■ Do you read these two images from the Andes as subversive of the colonial order or as supportive of it? Do you think the artist who painted Visual Source 15.3 was a European or a Native American Christian?

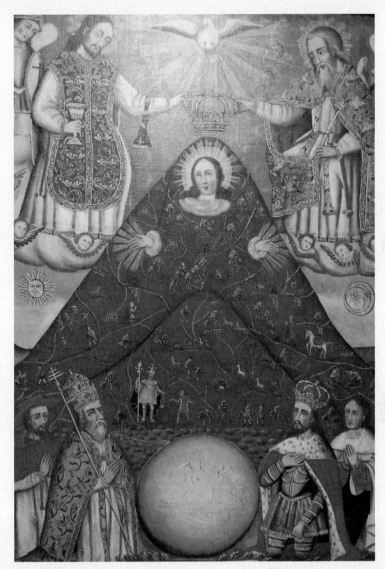

Visual Source 15.3 Cultural Blending in Andean Christianity (Nick Buxton, photographer)

In China, unlike Latin America, Christian missionaries operated in a setting wholly outside of European political control, bringing their faith to a powerful and proud civilization, long dominant in eastern Asia, where Confucianism, Daoism, and Buddhism had for many centuries mixed and mingled. The outcome of those missionary efforts was far more modest and much less successful than in the Americas. Nonetheless, in China too the tendency toward syncretism was evident. Jesuit missionaries themselves sought to present the Christian message within a Chinese cultural context to the intellectual and political elites who were their primary target audience. And Chinese Christians often transposed the new religion into more familiar cultural concepts. European critics of the Jesuit approach, however, feared that syncretism watered down the Christian message and risked losing its distinctive character.

Visual Source 15.4 provides an example of Christianity becoming Chinese.[39] In the early seventeenth century, the Jesuits published several books in the Chinese language describing the life of Christ and illustrated them with a series of woodblock prints created by Chinese artists affiliated with the Jesuits. Although they were clearly modeled on European images, those prints cast Christian figures into an altogether Chinese setting. The print in Visual Source 15.4 portrays the familiar biblical story of the annunciation, when an angel informs Mary that she will be the mother of Jesus. The house and furniture shown in the print suggest the dwelling of a wealthy Chinese scholar. The reading table in front of Mary was a common item in the homes of the literary elite of the time. The view from the window shows a seascape, mountains in the distance, a lone tree, and a "scholar's rock"—all of which were common features in Chinese landscape painting. The clouds that appear at the angel's feet and around the shaft of light shining on Mary are identical to those associated with sacred Buddhist and Daoist figures. To Chinese eyes, the angel might well appear as a Buddhist bodhisattva, while Mary may resemble a Ming dynasty noblewoman or perhaps Kuanyin, the Chinese Buddhist goddess of mercy and compassion.

- What specifically Chinese elements can you identify in this image?

- To whom might this image have been directed?

- How might educated Chinese have responded to this image?

- The European engraving on which this Chinese print was modeled included in the background the scene of Jesus' crucifixion. Why might the Chinese artist have chosen to omit that scene from his image?

- How would European critics of the Jesuits' approach to missionary work have reacted to this image? To what extent has the basic message of Catholic Christianity been retained or altered in this Chinese cultural setting?

As Chinese emperors welcomed Jesuit missionaries at court, so too did the rulers of Mughal India during the time of Akbar and Jahangir (1556–1627). But while Chinese elite circles received the Jesuits for their scientific skills, especially in astronomy, the Mughal court seemed more interested in the religious and artistic achievements of European civilization. Akbar invited the Jesuits to take part in cross-religious discussions that included Muslim, Hindu, Jain, and Zoroastrian scholars. Furthermore, the Mughal emperors eagerly embraced the art of late Renaissance Europe, which the Jesuits provided to them,

Visual Source 15.4 Making Christianity Chinese (ARSI, Jap. Sin. I 43 f. 74v)

much of it devotional and distinctly Christian. Mughal artists quickly learned to paint in the European style, and soon murals featuring Jesus, Mary, and Christian saints appeared on the walls of palaces, garden pavilions, and harems of the Mughal court, while miniature paintings adorned books, albums, and jewelry.

In religious terms, however, the Jesuit efforts were "a fantastic and extravagant failure,"[40] for these Muslim rulers of India were not in the least interested in abandoning Islam for the Christian faith, and few conversions of any kind occurred. Akbar and Jahangir, however, were cosmopolitan connoisseurs of art, which they collected, reproduced, and displayed. European religious art also had propaganda value in enhancing their status. Jesus and Mary, after all, had a prominent place within Islam. Jesus was seen both as an earlier prophet

Visual Source 15.5 Christian Art at the Mughal Court (The Holy Family (vellum)/Free Library of Philadelphia/The Bridgeman Art Library)

and as a mystical figure, similar to the Sufi masters who were so important in Indian Islam. Mughal paintings, pairing the adult Jesus and Mary side by side, were placed above the imperial throne as well as on the emperor's jewelry and his official seal, suggesting an identification of Jesus and a semi-divine emperor. That the mothers of both Akbar and Jahangir were named Mary only added to the appeal. Thus Akbar and Jahangir sought to incorporate European-style Christian art into their efforts to create a blended and tolerant religious culture for the elites of their vast and diverse realm. It was a culture that drew on Islam, Hinduism, Zoroastrianism, and Christianity.

But as Catholic devotional art was reworked by Mughal artists, it was also subtly changed. Visual Source 15.5 shows an early seventeenth-century depiction of the Holy Family painted by an Indian artist.

■ Why do you think that this Mughal painter portrayed Mary and Joseph as rather distinguished and educated persons rather than as the humble carpenter and his peasant wife, as in so many European images? Why might he have placed the family in rather palatial surroundings instead of a stable?

■ How do you imagine European missionaries responded to this representation of the Holy Family?

■ How might more orthodox Muslims have reacted to the larger project of creating a blended religion making use of elements from many traditions? Consider the possible reactions of the Wahhabis (Document 15.3, pp. 758–59) and Kabir (Document 15.4, pp. 760–61).

■ What similarities can you identify between this Indian image and the Chinese print in Visual Source 15.4? Pay attention to the setting, the clothing, and the class status of the human figures, and the scenes outside the windows.

Using the Evidence: Global Christianity in the Early Modern Era

1. **Making comparisons:** What common Christian elements can you identify in these visual sources? What differences in the expression of Christianity can you define?

2. **Considering Mary:** The Catholic Christian tradition as it developed in Latin America, China, and India as well as Europe provided a very important place for representations of the Virgin Mary. Why might this feature of the Christian message have been so widely appealing? But in what ways does the image of the Holy Mother differ in Visual Sources 15.3, 15.4, and 15.5? In what ways were those images adapted to the distinctive cultures in which they were created?

3. **Pondering syncretism:** From a missionary viewpoint, develop arguments for and against religious syncretism using these visual sources as points of reference.

4. **Considering visual sources as evidence:** What are the strengths and limitations of these visual sources, as opposed to texts, as historians seek to understand the globalization of Christianity in the early modern era? What other visual sources might be useful?

Chapter 15 Wrap Up

LearningCurve
Check what you know.
bedfordstmartins.com/strayer/LC

STEP ONE

The Word to Know: Missionary

The *Oxford English Dictionary* defines *missionary* as "a person sent on or engaged in a religious mission abroad." Think about what motivates a person to travel and spread God's word to non-believers. Then, write a paragraph from the perspective of a missionary who went to China or to Latin America. Include in your paragraph, why you went and at least two outcomes of the work that you and your colleagues did there.

STEP TWO

The Spread of Christianity in China and the Americas

Compare the conditions and process undertaken, as well as the short- and long-terms effects of the spread of Christianity to China and to Latin America.

	Conditions	Process	Short-term effects	Long-term effects
Christianity in Latin America				
Christianity in China				

STEP THREE

Protesting the Roman Catholic Church

The documents in this section provide three examples of protests against the Catholic Church. Read each document carefully, keeping in mind each author's point of view.

1. Document 15.1, Martin Luther, *Table Talk*, early sixteenth century

Begin by reading Document 15.1 on pages 753–55, an excerpt from Martin Luther's *Table Talk*, written in the early sixteenth century. Then answer the questions below.

■ Questions

a. In his critique of the Catholic Church, how does Luther describe the character of popes, cardinals, and bishops? What specific criticism does Martin Luther make of the pope?

b. What is Martin Luther's overall point of view and what did he do about it in order to redress the concerns he has with the Church?

2. Galileo Galilei, *Letter to the Grand Duchess Christina of Tuscany*, 1615

Galileo was placed on trial by the Catholic Church for writing in his scientific treatises beliefs that some felt went against what was said in the Bible. This letter was one of several responses of his to the charges. (See page 742 for a summary of Galileo's discoveries.) Read the excerpt to his patron defending his beliefs, and then answer the questions that follow.

"...I hold the sun to be situated motionless in the center of the revolution of the celestial orbs while the earth revolves about the sun.... [T]hese men ... have endeavored to spread the opinion that such propositions in general are contrary to the Bible and are consequently damnable and heretical.... But I do not feel obliged to believe that the same God who has endowed us with senses, reason, and intellect has intended us to forego their use and by some other means to give us knowledge which we can attain by them. He would not require us to deny sense and reason in physical matters which are set before our eyes and minds by direct experience or necessary demonstrations...."

Source: Stillman Drake, ed., *Discoveries and Opinions of Galileo*, (New York: Anchor-Doubleday, 1957), 173–216.

■ Questions

a. How does Galileo argue that his scientific beliefs are not heretical?

b. What is Galileo's overall point of view and what does he say in order to redress the concerns he had with the Church?

3. Emperior Kangxi, 1715

Pope Clément XI, upon learning how Christianity was being practiced in China, forbade Chinese converts to continue their own traditional practices. Read the quote from Kangxi and the surrounding text on pages 732–34. Then answer the questions below.

■ Questions

a. Why does Kangxi change his mind about tolerating Christianity?

b. What is Kangxi's overall point of view and what did he do about it in order to redress the concerns he had with the Church?

Conquest and Resistance in
Colonial Africa (p. 887)

Historically, scientists have viewed human activity as incidental to the larger processes that have shaped the physical and biological evolution of the earth. But now
they are suggesting that over the past several centuries, humankind itself has become an
active agent of change in this domain, rapidly reshaping the planet. While these changes
became more pronounced and obvious in the second half of the twentieth century,
the European moment of the long nineteenth century takes on an added significance
as the starting point of an epic transformation in the relationship of humanity to the
earth, equivalent perhaps to the early stages of the Agricultural Revolution. While human beings have long felt themselves vulnerable to nature, in recent centuries nature
has also become increasingly vulnerable to humans.

Eurocentric Geography and History

The unprecedented power that Europeans accumulated during the long nineteenth century included the ability to rewrite geography and history in ways that centered the human story on Europe and to convey those views powerfully to other people. Thus maps placed Europe at the center of the world, while dividing Asia in half. Europe was granted continental status, even though it was more accurately only the western peninsula of Asia, much as India was its southern peninsula. Other regions of the world, such as the Far East or the Near (Middle) East, were defined in terms of their distance from Europe. The entire world came to measure longitude from a line, known as the prime meridian, which passes through the Royal Astronomical Observatory in Greenwich, England.

Railroads (p. 835)

History textbooks as well often reflected a Europe-centered outlook, sometimes blatantly. In 1874, the American author William O. Swinton wrote *An Outline of the World's History*, a book intended for use in high school and college classes, in which he flatly declared that "the race to which we belong, the Aryan, has always played the leading part in the great drama of the world's progress."[1] Other peoples and civilizations, by contrast, were long believed to be static or stagnant, thus largely lacking any real history. Most Europeans assumed that these "backward" peoples and regions must either imitate the Western model or face further decline and possible extinction. Until the mid-twentieth century, such ideas went largely unchallenged in the Western world. They implied that history was a race toward the finish line of modernity. That Europeans arrived there first seemed to suggest something unique, special, or superior about them or their culture, while everyone else struggled to overcome their inadequacy and catch up.

As the discipline of world history took shape in the decades after World War II, scholars and teachers actively sought to counteract such Eurocentric understandings of the past, but they faced a special problem in dealing with recent centuries. How can we avoid an inappropriate Eurocentrism when dealing with a phase of world history in which Europeans were in fact central? The long nineteenth century, after all, was "the European moment," a time when Europeans were clearly the most powerful, most innovative, most prosperous, most expansive, and most widely imitated people on the planet.

Countering Eurocentrism

At least five answers to this dilemma are reflected in the chapters that follow. The first is simply to remind ourselves how recent and perhaps how brief the European moment in world history has been. Other peoples too had times of "cultural flowering" that granted them a period of primacy or influence—for example, the Greeks (500 B.C.E.–200 C.E.), Indians of South Asia (200–600 C.E.), Arabs (600–1000), Chinese (1000–1500), Mongols (1200–1350), Incas and Aztecs (fifteenth century)—but all of these were limited to particular regions of Afro-Eurasia or the Americas.[2] Even though the European moment operated on a genuinely global scale, Western peoples have enjoyed their worldwide primacy for at most two centuries. Some scholars have suggested that the events of the late twentieth and early twenty-first centuries—the end of colonial empires, the rise of India and especially China, and the assertion of Islam—mark the end, or at least the erosion, of the age of Europe.

Second, we need to remember that the rise of Europe occurred within an international context. It was the withdrawal of the Chinese naval fleet that allowed Europeans to enter the Indian Ocean in the sixteenth century, while Native Americans' lack of immunity to European diseases and their own divisions and conflicts greatly assisted the European takeover of the Western Hemisphere. The Industrial Revolution, explored in Chapter 17, likewise benefited from New World resources and markets and from the stimulus of superior Asian textile and pottery production. Chapters 18 and 19 make clear that European control of other regions everywhere depended on the cooperation of local elites. Such observations remind us that the remarkable—indeed revolutionary—transformations of the European moment in world history did not derive wholly from some special European genius or long-term advantage. Rather they emerged from a unique intersection of European historical development with that of other peoples, regions, and cultures. Europeans, like everyone else, were embedded in a web of relationships that shaped their own histories.

A third reminder is that the rise of Europe to a position of global dominance was not an easy or automatic process. Frequently it occurred in the face of ferocious resistance and rebellion, which often required Europeans to modify their policies and practices. The so-called Indian mutiny in mid-nineteenth-century South Asia, a massive uprising against British colonial rule, did not end British control, but it substantially transformed the character of the colonial experience. In Africa, fear of offending Muslim sensibilities persuaded the British to keep European missionaries and mission schools out of northern Nigeria during the colonial era. Even when Europeans exercised political power, they could not do so precisely as they pleased. Empire, formal and informal alike, was always in some ways a negotiated arrangement.

Fourth, peoples the world over made active use of Europeans and European ideas for their own purposes, seeking to gain advantage over local rivals or to benefit themselves in light of new conditions. In Southeast Asia, for example, a number of highland minority groups, long oppressed by the dominant lowland Vietnamese, viewed the French invaders as liberators and assisted in their takeover of Vietnam. Hindus in

India used the railroads, introduced by the British, to go on pilgrimages to holy sites more easily, while the printing press made possible the more widespread distribution of their sacred texts. During the Haitian Revolution, examined in Chapter 16, enslaved Africans made use of radical French ideas about "the rights of man" in ways that most Europeans never intended. The leaders of a massive Chinese peasant upheaval in the mid-nineteenth century adopted a unique form of Christianity to legitimate their revolutionary assault on an ancient social order. Recognizing that Asian and African peoples remained active agents, pursuing their own interests even in oppressive conditions, is another way of countering residual Eurocentrism.

Moreover, what was borrowed from Europe was always adapted to local circumstances. Thus Japanese or Russian industrial development did not wholly follow the pattern of England's Industrial Revolution. The Christianity that took root in the Americas or later in Africa evolved in culturally distinctive ways. Ideas of nationalism, born in Europe, were used to oppose European imperialism throughout Asia and Africa. Russian and Chinese socialism in the twentieth century departed in many ways from the vision of Karl Marx. The most interesting stories of modern world history are not simply those of European triumph or the imposition of Western ideas and practices but of encounters, though highly unequal, among culturally different peoples. It was from these encounters, not just from the intentions and actions of Europeans, that the dramatic global changes of the modern era arose.

A fifth and final antidote to Eurocentrism in an age of European centrality lies in the recognition that although Europeans gained an unprecedented prominence on the world stage, they were not the only game in town, nor were they the sole preoccupation of Asian, African, and Middle Eastern peoples. While China confronted Western aggression in the nineteenth century, it was also absorbing a huge population increase and experiencing massive peasant rebellions that grew out of distinctly Chinese conditions. The long relationship of Muslim and Hindu cultures in India continued to evolve under British colonial rule as it had for centuries under other political systems. West African societies in the nineteenth century experienced a wave of religious wars that created new states and extended and transformed the practice of Islam, and that faith continued its centuries-long spread on the continent even under European colonial rule. A further wave of wars and state formation in southern Africa transformed the political and ethnic landscape, even as European penetration picked up speed.

None of this diminishes the significance of the European moment in world history, but it sets that moment in a larger context of continuing patterns of historical development and of interaction and exchange with other peoples.

Mapping Part Five

U.S. westward expansion
Chapters 17, 18

Women's rights
Chapter 16

American Revolution
Chapter 16

Haitian Revolution
Chapter 16

Mexican Revolution
Chapter 17

Abolition of slavery
Chapter 16

Latin American independence and industrialization
Chapters 16, 17

Industrial
Revolution
Chapter 17

Unification of Germany
Chapter 16

French Revolution
Chapter 16

Unification of Italy
Chapter 16

Russian Revolution
Chapter 17

Russo-Japanese
War
Chapter 19

OttomanTanzimat
reforms
Chapter 19

Meiji Restoration
Chapter 19

Opium wars /
Taiping uprising
Chapter 19

British Colonial India
Chapter 18

French Colonial
Indochina
Chapter 18

Scramble for Africa
Chapter 18

Boer War
Chapter 18

British colonial Australia/
New Zealand
Chapter 18

Vive le Roi, Vive la Nation.

Isavois ben Qu'jaurions not tour.

Atlantic Revolutions, Global Echoes

1750–1914

The Haitian earthquake of January 2010 not only devastated an already impoverished country but also reawakened issues deriving from that country's revolution against slavery and French colonial rule, which finally succeeded in 1804. Twenty-one years later, the French government demanded from Haiti a payment of 150 million gold francs in compensation for the loss of its richest colony and its "property" in slaves. With French warships hovering offshore, Haitian authorities agreed. To make the heavy payments, even after they were somewhat reduced, Haiti took out major loans from French, German, and North American banks. Repaying those loans, finally accomplished only in 1947, represented a huge drain on the country's budget, costing 80 percent of the government's revenue in 1915. Now in 2010, with the country in ruins, an international petition signed by over 100 prominent people, called on the French government to repay some $17 billion, effectively returning the "independence debt" extorted from Haiti 185 years earlier. While the French government dismissed those claims, the issue provided a reminder of the continuing echoes of events from an earlier age of revolution.

THE HAITIAN REVOLUTION WAS PART OF AND LINKED to a much larger set of upheavals that shook both sides of the Atlantic world between 1775 and 1825. Haitians had drawn inspiration from the earlier North American and French revolutions, even as their successful overthrow of French rule helped shape the Latin American independence struggles that followed. These four closely related upheavals

---

Revolution and the Reversal of Class Roles: Three French female figures, representing from right to left the clergy, nobility, and commoners (Third Estate), show the reversal of class roles that the revolution generated. Now the commoner rides on the back of the noblewoman and is shown in a dominant position over the nun. (Réunion des musées nationaux/Art Resource, NY)

SEEKING THE MAIN POINT

What were the most important outcomes of the Atlantic revolutions, both immediately and in the century that followed?

reflect the new connections among Europe, Africa, North and South America, which took shape in the wake of Columbus's voyages and the European conquests that followed. Together, they launched a new chapter in the history of the Atlantic world, while the echoes of those revolutions reverberated in the larger world.

Atlantic Revolutions in a Global Context

Writing to a friend in 1772, before any of the Atlantic revolutions had occurred, the French intellectual Voltaire asked, "My dear philosopher, doesn't this appear to you to be the century of revolutions?"[1] He was certainly on target, and not only for the European/Atlantic world. From the early eighteenth century to the mid-nineteenth, many parts of the world witnessed political and social upheaval, leading some historians to think in terms of a "world crisis" or "converging revolutions." By the 1730s, the Safavid dynasty that had ruled Persia (now Iran) for several centuries had completely collapsed, even as the powerful Mughal Empire governing India also fragmented. About the same time, the Wahhabi movement in Arabia seriously threatened the Ottoman Empire, and its religious ideals informed major political upheavals in Central Asia and elsewhere (see pp. 736–37). The Russian Empire under Catherine the Great experienced a series of peasant uprisings, most notably one led by the Cossack commander Pugachev in 1773–1774, which briefly proclaimed the end of serfdom before that rebellion was crushed. China too in the late eighteenth and early nineteenth centuries hosted a number of popular though unsuccessful rebellions, a prelude perhaps to the huge Taiping revolution of 1850–1864. Beginning in the early nineteenth century, a wave of Islamic revolutions shook West Africa, while in southern Africa, a series of wars and migrations known as the *mfecane* (the breaking or crushing) involved widespread and violent disruptions as well the creation of new states and societies.

Thus the Atlantic revolutions in North America, France, Haiti, and Latin America took place within a larger global framework. Like many of the other upheavals, they too occurred in the context of expensive wars, weakening states, and destabilizing processes of commercialization. But the Atlantic revolutions were distinctive in various ways compared to upheavals elsewhere. The costly wars that strained European imperial states — Britain, France, and Spain in particular — were global rather than regional. In the so-called Seven Years' War (1754–1763), Britain and France joined battle in North America, the Caribbean, West Africa, and South Asia. The expenses of those conflicts prompted the British to levy additional taxes on their North American colonies and the French monarchy to seek new revenue from its landowners. These actions contributed to the launching of the American and French revolutions respectively.

Furthermore, the Atlantic revolutions were distinctive in that they were closely connected to one another. The American revolutionary leader Thomas Jefferson was

A Map of Time

1775–1783	American Revolution
1780s	Beginnings of antislavery movement
1789–1799	French Revolution
1791–1803	Haitian Revolution
1793–1794	Execution of Louis XVI; French terror
1799–1814	Reign of Napoleon
1807	End of slave trade in British Empire
1810–1811	Hidalgo-Morelos rebellion in Mexico
1810–1825	Latin American wars of independence
1822	Brazil gains independence from Portugal
1848	Women's Rights Convention, Seneca Falls, New York
1861	Emancipation of serfs in Russia
1861–1865	Civil War and abolition of slavery in United States
1870–1871	Unification of Germany and Italy
1886–1888	Cuba and Brazil abolish slavery
1920	Women gain the vote in United States

the U.S. ambassador to France on the eve of the French Revolution. While there, he provided advice and encouragement to French reformers and revolutionaries. Simón Bolívar, a leading figure in Spanish American struggles for independence, twice visited Haiti, where he received military aid from the first black government in the Americas.

Beyond such direct connections, the various Atlantic revolutionaries shared a set of common ideas. The Atlantic basin had become a world of intellectual and cultural exchange as well as one of commercial and biological interaction. The ideas that animated the Atlantic revolutions derived from the European Enlightenment and were shared across the ocean in newspapers, books, and pamphlets. At the heart of these ideas was the radical notion that human political and social arrangements could be engineered, and improved, by human action. Thus conventional and long-established ways of living and thinking—the divine right of kings, state control of trade, aristocratic privilege, the authority of a single church—were no longer sacrosanct and came under repeated attack. New ideas of liberty, equality, free trade, religious tolerance, republicanism, and human rationality were in the air. Politically, the core notion was "popular sovereignty," which meant that the authority to govern derived from the people rather than from God or from established tradition. As the Englishman John

■ Causation

In what ways did the ideas of the Enlightenment contribute to the Atlantic revolutions?

Locke (1632–1704) had argued, the "social contract" between ruler and ruled should last only as long as it served the people well. In short, it was both possible and desirable to start over in the construction of human communities. In the late eighteenth and early nineteenth centuries, these ideas were largely limited to the Atlantic world. While all of the Atlantic revolutions involved the elimination of monarchs, at least temporarily, across Asia and Middle East such republican political systems were virtually inconceivable until much later. There the only solution to a bad monarch was a new and better one.

In the world of the Atlantic revolutions, ideas born of the Enlightenment generated endless controversy. Were liberty and equality compatible? What kind of government—unitary and centralized or federal and decentralized—best ensured freedom? And how far should liberty be extended? Except in Haiti, the chief beneficiaries of these revolutions were propertied white men of the "middling classes." Although women, slaves, Native Americans, and men without property did not gain much from these revolutions, the ideas that accompanied those upheavals gave them ammunition for the future. Because their overall thrust was to extend political rights further than ever before, these Atlantic movements have often been referred to as "democratic revolutions."

A final distinctive feature of the Atlantic revolutions lies in their immense global impact, extending well beyond the Atlantic world. The armies of revolutionary France, for example, invaded Egypt, Germany, Poland, and Russia, carrying seeds of change. The ideals that animated these Atlantic revolutions inspired efforts in many countries to abolish slavery, to extend the right to vote, to develop constitutions, and to secure greater equality for women. Nationalism, perhaps the most potent ideology of the modern era, was nurtured in the Atlantic revolutions and shaped much of nineteenth- and twentieth-century world history. The ideas of human equality articulated in these revolutions later found expression in feminist, socialist, and communist movements. The Universal Declaration of Human Rights, adopted by the United Nations in 1948, echoed and amplified those principles while providing the basis for any number of subsequent protests against oppression, tyranny, and deprivation. In 1989, a number of Chinese students, fleeing the suppression of a democracy movement in their own country, marched at the head of a huge parade in Paris, celebrating the bicentennial of the French Revolution. And in 2011, the Middle Eastern uprisings known as the Arab Spring prompted numerous comparisons with the French Revolution. The Atlantic revolutions had a long reach.

Comparing Atlantic Revolutions

But beneath their common political vocabulary and a broadly democratic character, the Atlantic revolutions differed substantially from one another. They were triggered by different circumstances, expressed quite different social and political tensions, and varied considerably in their outcomes. Liberty, noted Simón Bolívar, "is a succulent morsel, but one difficult to digest."[2] "Digesting liberty" occurred in quite distinct ways in the various sites of the Atlantic revolutions.

The North American Revolution, 1775–1787

Every schoolchild in the United States learns early that the American Revolution was a struggle for independence from oppressive British rule. That struggle was launched with the Declaration of Independence in 1776, resulted in an unlikely military victory by 1781, and generated a federal constitution in 1787, joining thirteen formerly separate colonies into a new nation (see Map 16.1). It was the first in a series of upheavals that

■ **Change**

What was revolutionary about the American Revolution, and what was not?

Map 16.1   The United States after the American Revolution

The union of the thirteen British colonies in North America created the embryonic United States, shown here in 1788. Over the past two centuries and more of anticolonial struggles, it was the only example of separate colonies joining together after independence to form a larger and enduring nation.

rocked the Atlantic world and beyond in the century that followed. But was it a genuine revolution? What, precisely, did it change?

By effecting a break with Britain, the American Revolution marked a decisive political change, but in other ways it was, strangely enough, a conservative movement, because it originated in an effort to preserve the existing liberties of the colonies rather than to create new ones. For much of the seventeenth and eighteenth centuries, the British colonies in North America enjoyed a considerable degree of local autonomy as the British government was embroiled in its own internal conflicts and various European wars. Furthermore, Britain's West Indian colonies seemed more profitable and of greater significance than those of North America. In these circumstances, local elected assemblies in North America, dominated by the wealthier property-owning settlers, achieved something close to self-government. Colonists came to regard such autonomy as a birthright and part of their English heritage. Thus, until the mid-eighteenth century, almost no one in the colonies thought of breaking away from England because participation in the British Empire provided many advantages—protection in war, access to British markets, and confirmation of their continuing identity as "Englishmen"—and few drawbacks.

There were, however, real differences between Englishmen in England and those in the North American colonies. Within the colonies, English settlers had developed societies described by a leading historian as "the most radical in the contemporary Western world." Certainly class distinctions were real and visible, and a small class of wealthy "gentlemen"—the Adamses, Washingtons, Jeffersons, and Hancocks—wore powdered wigs, imitated the latest European styles, were prominent in political life, and were generally accorded deference by ordinary people. But the ready availability of land following the dispossession of Native Americans, the scarcity of people, and the absence of both a titled nobility and a single established church meant that social life was far more open than in Europe. No legal distinctions differentiated clergy, aristocracy, and commoners, as they did in France. All free men enjoyed the same status before the law, a situation that excluded black slaves and, in some ways, white women as well. These conditions made for less poverty, more economic opportunity, fewer social differences, and easier relationships among the classes than in Europe. The famous economist Adam Smith observed that British colonists were "republican in their manners . . . and their government" well before their independence from England.[3]

Thus the American Revolution did not grow out of social tensions within the colonies, but from a rather sudden and unexpected effort by the British government to tighten its control over the colonies and to extract more revenue from them. As Britain's global struggle with France drained its treasury and ran up its national debt, British authorities, beginning in the 1760s, looked to America to make good these losses. Abandoning its neglectful oversight of the colonies, Britain began to act like a genuine imperial power, imposing a variety of new taxes and tariffs on the colonies without their consent, for they were not represented in the British Parliament. By challenging their economic interests, their established traditions of local autonomy, and their identity as true Englishmen, such measures infuriated many of the colonists. Armed with the ideas of the Enlightenment—popular sovereignty, natural rights, the consent of the governed—they went to war, and by 1781 they had prevailed, with considerable aid from the French, who were only too pleased to harm the interests of their British rivals.

What was revolutionary about the American experience was not so much the revolution itself but the kind of society that had already emerged within the colonies. Independence from Britain was not accompanied by any wholesale social transformation. Rather the revolution accelerated the established democratic tendencies of the colonial societies. Political authority remained largely in the hands of existing elites who had led the revolution, although property requirements for voting were lowered and more white men of modest means, such as small farmers and urban artisans, were elected to state legislatures.

This widening of political participation gradually eroded the power of traditional gentlemen, but no women or people of color shared in these gains. Land was not seized from its owners, except in the case of pro-British loyalists who had fled the country. Although slavery was gradually abolished in the northern states, where it counted for little, it remained firmly entrenched in the southern states, where it counted for much. Chief Justice John Marshall later gave voice to this conservative understanding of the American Revolution: "All contracts and rights, respecting property, remained unchanged by the Revolution."[4] In the century that followed independence, the United States did become the world's most democratic country, but it was less the direct product of the revolution and more the gradual working out in a reformist fashion of earlier practices and the principles of equality announced in the Declaration of Independence.

Nonetheless, many American patriots felt passionately that they were creating "a new order for the ages." James Madison in the *Federalist Papers* made the point clearly: "We pursued a new and more noble course ... and accomplished a revolution that has no parallel in the annals of human society." Supporters abroad agreed. On the eve of the French Revolution, a Paris newspaper proclaimed that the United States was "the hope and model of the human race."[5] In both cases, they were referring primarily to the political ideas and practices of the new country. The American Revolution, after all, initiated the political dismantling of Europe's New World empires. The "right to revolution," proclaimed in the Declaration of Independence and made effective only in a great struggle, inspired revolutionaries and nationalists from Simón Bolívar in nineteenth-century Latin America to Ho Chi Minh in twentieth-century Vietnam. Moreover, the new U.S. Constitution—with its Bill of Rights, checks and balances, separation of church and state, and federalism—was one of the first sustained efforts to put the political ideas of the Enlightenment into practice. That document, and the ideas that it embraced, echoed repeatedly in the political upheavals of the century that followed.

The French Revolution, 1789–1815

Act Two in the drama of the Atlantic revolutions took place in France, beginning in 1789, although it was closely connected to Act One in North America. Thousands of French soldiers had provided assistance to the American colonists and now returned home full of republican enthusiasm. Thomas Jefferson, the U.S. ambassador in Paris,

■ **Comparison**

How did the French Revolution differ from the American Revolution?

reported that France "has been awakened by our revolution."[6] More immediately, the French government, which had generously aided the Americans in an effort to undermine its British rivals, was teetering on the brink of bankruptcy and had long sought reforms that would modernize the tax system and make it more equitable. In a desperate effort to raise taxes against the opposition of the privileged classes, the French king, Louis XVI, had called into session an ancient representative body, the Estates General. It consisted of male representatives of the three "estates," or legal orders, of prerevolutionary France: the clergy, the nobility, and the commoners. The first two estates comprised about 2 percent of the population, and the third estate included everyone else. When that body convened in 1789, representatives of the third estate soon organized themselves as the National Assembly, claiming the sole authority to make laws for the country. A few weeks later they drew up the Declaration of the Rights of Man and Citizen, which forthrightly declared that "men are born and remain free and equal in rights" (see Document 16.1, pp. 812–14). These actions, unprecedented and illegal in the *ancien régime* (the old regime), launched the French Revolution and radicalized many of the participants in the National Assembly.

That revolution was quite different from its North American predecessor. Whereas the American Revolution expressed the tensions of a colonial relationship with a distant imperial power, the French insurrection was driven by sharp conflicts within French society. Members of the titled nobility—privileged, prestigious, and wealthy—resented and resisted the monarchy's efforts to subject them to new taxes. Educated middle-class men such as doctors, lawyers, lower-level officials, and merchants were growing in numbers and sometimes in wealth and were offended by the remaining privileges of the aristocracy, from which they were excluded. Ordinary urban men and women, many of whose incomes had declined for a generation, were particularly hard-hit in the late 1780s by the rapidly rising price of bread and widespread unemployment. Peasants in the countryside, though largely free of serfdom, were subject to a variety of hated dues imposed by their landlords, taxes from the state, obligations to the Church, and the requirement to work without pay on public roads. As Enlightenment ideas penetrated French society, more and more people, mostly in the third estate but including some priests and nobles, found a language with which to articulate these grievances. The famous French writer Jean-Jacques Rousseau had told them that it was "manifestly contrary to the law of nature . . . that a handful of people should gorge themselves with superfluities while the hungry multitude goes in want of necessities."[7]

These social conflicts gave the French Revolution, especially during its first five years, a much more violent, far-reaching, and radical character than its American counterpart. It was a profound social upheaval, more comparable to the revolutions of Russia and China in the twentieth century than to the earlier American Revolution. Initial efforts to establish a constitutional monarchy and promote harmony among the classes (see Visual Source 16.1, p. 821) gave way to more radical measures, as internal resistance and foreign opposition produced a fear that the revolution might be overturned. In the process, urban crowds organized insurrections. Some peasants attacked the castles of their lords, burning the documents that recorded their dues and payments. The National Assembly decreed the end of all legal privileges and ended what remained of feudalism in France. Even slavery was abolished, albeit briefly. Church lands were sold to raise revenue, and priests were put under government authority. (See Visual Sources 16.2 and 16.3, pp. 822 and 823, for images reflecting this more radical phase of the revolution.)

In 1793, King Louis XVI and his queen, Marie Antoinette, were executed, an act of regicide that shocked traditionalists all across Europe and marked a new stage in revolutionary violence (see Visual Source 16.4, p. 824). What followed was the Terror of 1793–1794. Under the leadership of Maximilien Robespierre (ROHBS-pee-air) and his Committee of Public Safety, tens of thousands deemed enemies of the revolution lost their lives on the guillotine. Shortly thereafter, Robespierre himself was arrested and guillotined, accused of leading France into tyranny and dictatorship. "The revolution," remarked one of its victims, "was devouring its own children."

Accompanying attacks on the old order were efforts to create a wholly new society, symbolized by a new calendar with the Year 1 in 1792, marking a fresh start for France. Unlike the Americans, who sought to restore or build on earlier freedoms, French revolutionaries perceived themselves to be starting from scratch and looked to the future. For

The Execution of Robespierre
The beheading of the radical leader Robespierre, who had himself brought thousands of others to the guillotine, marked a decisive turning point in the unfolding of the French Revolution and the end of its most violent phase. (Musée de la Révolution Française, Vizille, France/ Bridgeman Art Library)

the first time in its history, the country became a republic and briefly passed universal male suffrage, although it was never implemented. The old administrative system was rationalized into eighty-three territorial departments, each with a new name. As revolutionary France prepared for war against its threatened and threatening neighbors, it created the world's largest army, with some 800,000 men, and all adult males were required to serve. Led by officers from the middle and even lower classes, this was an army of citizens representing the nation.

In terms of gender roles, the French Revolution did not create a new society, but it did raise the question of female political equality far more explicitly than the American Revolution had done. Partly this was because French women were active in the major events of the revolution. In July 1789, they took part in the famous storming of the Bastille, a large fortress, prison, and armory that had come to symbolize the oppressive old regime. In October of that year, some 7,000 Parisian women, desperate about the shortage of bread, marched on the palace at Versailles, stormed through the royal apartments searching for the despised Queen Marie Antoinette, and forced the royal family to return with them to Paris.

Backed by a few male supporters, women also made serious political demands. They signed petitions detailing their complaints: lack of education, male competition in female trades, the prevalence of prostitution, the rapidly rising price of bread and soap. One petition, reflecting the intersection of class and gender, referred to women as the "Third Estate of the Third Estate." Another demanded the right to bear arms in defense of the revolution. Over sixty women's clubs were established throughout the country. A small group called the *Cercle Social* (Social Circle) campaigned for women's rights, noting that "the laws favor men at the expense of women, because everywhere power is in your hands."[8] The French playwright and journalist Olympe de Gouges appropriated the language of the Declaration of Rights to insist that "woman is born free and lives equal to man in her rights."

But the assertion of French women in the early years of the revolution seemed wildly inappropriate and threatening to most men, uniting conservatives and revolutionaries alike in defense of male privileges. And so in late 1793, the country's all-male legislative body voted to ban all women's clubs. "Women are ill-suited for elevated thoughts and serious meditation," declared one of the male representatives. "A woman should not leave her family to meddle in affairs of government." Here was a conception of gender that defined masculinity in terms of exercising political power. Women who aspired to do so were, in the words of one revolutionary orator, "denatured *viragos*" (domineering women), in short not really women at all.[9] Thus French revolutionaries were distinctly unwilling to offer any political rights to women, even though they had eliminated class restrictions, at least in theory; granted religious freedom to Jews and Protestants; and abolished slavery. Nonetheless, according to a leading historian, "the French Revolution, more than any other event of its time, opened up the question of women's rights for consideration" and thus laid the foundations for modern feminism.[10]

If not in terms of gender, the immediate impact of the revolution was felt in many other ways. Streets got new names; monuments to the royal family were destroyed; titles vanished; people referred to one another as "citizen so-and-so." Real politics in the public sphere emerged for the first time as many people joined political clubs, took part in marches and demonstrations, served on local committees, and ran for public office. Ordinary men and women, who had identified primarily with their local communities, now began to think of themselves as belonging to a nation. The state replaced the Catholic Church as the place for registering births, marriages, and deaths, and revolutionary festivals substituted for church holidays.

More radical revolutionary leaders deliberately sought to convey a sense of new beginnings and endless possibilities. A Festival of Unity held in 1793 to mark the first anniversary of the end of monarchy burned the crowns and scepters of the royal family in a huge bonfire while releasing a cloud of 3,000 white doves. The Cathedral of Notre Dame was temporarily turned into the Temple of Reason, while the "Hymn

Map 16.2   Napoleon's European Empire
The French Revolution spawned a French empire, under Napoleon's leadership, that encompassed most of Europe and served to spread the principles of the revolution.

to Liberty" combined traditional church music with the explicit message of the Enlightenment:

> Oh Liberty, sacred Liberty
> Goddess of an enlightened people
> Rule today within these walls.
> Through you this temple is purified.
> Liberty! Before you reason chases out deception,
> Error flees, fanaticism is beaten down.
> Our gospel is nature
> And our cult is virtue.
> To love one's country and one's brothers, To serve the Sovereign People—

These are the sacred tenets
And pledge of a Republican.[11]

Elsewhere too the French Revolution evoked images of starting over. Witnessing that revolution in 1790, the young William Wordsworth, later a famous British romantic poet, imagined "human nature seeming born again." "Bliss it was in that dawn to be alive," he wrote. "But to be young was very heaven."

The French Revolution differed from the American Revolution also in the way its influence spread. At least until the United States became a world power at the end of the nineteenth century, what inspired others was primarily the example of its revolution and its constitution. French influence, by contrast, spread through conquest, largely under the leadership of Napoleon Bonaparte (r. 1799–1814). A highly successful general who seized power in 1799, Napoleon is often credited with taming the revolution in the face of growing disenchantment with its more radical features and with the social conflicts it generated. He preserved many of its more moderate elements, such as civil equality, a secular law code, religious freedom, and promotion by merit, while reconciling with the Catholic Church and suppressing the revolution's more democratic elements in a military dictatorship. In short, Napoleon kept the revolution's emphasis on social equality for men but dispensed with liberty.

Like many of the revolution's ardent supporters, Napoleon was intent on spreading its benefits far and wide. In a series of brilliant military campaigns, his forces subdued most of Europe, thus creating the continent's largest empire since the days of the Romans (see Map 16.2, p. 791). Within that empire, Napoleon imposed such revolutionary practices as ending feudalism, proclaiming equality of rights, insisting on religious toleration, codifying the laws, and rationalizing government administration. In many places, these reforms were welcomed, and seeds of further change were planted. But French domination was also resented and resisted, stimulating national consciousness throughout Europe. That too was a seed that bore fruit in the century that followed. More immediately, national resistance, particularly from Russia and Britain, brought down Napoleon and his amazing empire by 1815 and marked an end to the era of the French Revolution, though not to the potency of its ideas.

The Haitian Revolution, 1791–1804

■ Comparison

What was distinctive about the Haitian Revolution, both in world history generally and in the history of Atlantic revolutions?

Nowhere did the example of the French Revolution echo more loudly than in the French Caribbean colony of Saint Domingue, later renamed Haiti (see Map 16.3, p. 795). Widely regarded as the richest colony in the world, Saint Domingue boasted 8,000 plantations, which in the late eighteenth century produced some 40 percent of the world's sugar and perhaps half of its coffee. A slave labor force of about 500,000 people made up the vast majority of the colony's population. Whites numbered about 40,000, sharply divided between very well-to-do plantation owners, merchants, and lawyers and those known as *petits blancs* (peh-TEE blahnk), or poor whites. A third social group consisted of some 30,000 *gens de couleur libres* (free people of color), many of them of mixed-race background. Saint Domingue was a colonial society very different from the New England colonies or even the southern colonies of British North America. Given its enormous inequalities and its rampant exploitation, this Caribbean colony was primed for explosion.

In such a volatile setting, the ideas and example of the French Revolution lit several fuses and set in motion a spiral of violence that engulfed the colony for more than a decade. The principles of the revolution, however, meant different things to different people. To the *grands blancs*—the rich white landowners—it suggested greater autonomy for the colony and fewer economic restrictions on trade, but they resented the demands of the *petits blancs*, who sought equality of citizenship for all whites. Both white groups were adamantly opposed to the insistence of free people of color that the "rights of man" meant equal treatment for all free people regardless of race. To the slaves, the promise of the French Revolution was a personal freedom that challenged the entire slave labor system. In a massive revolt beginning in 1791, triggered by rumors that the French king had already declared an end to slavery, slaves burned 1,000 plantations and killed hundreds of whites as well as mixed-race people.

Soon warring factions of slaves, whites, and free people of color battled one another. Spanish and British forces, seeking to enlarge their own empires at the expense of the French, only added to the turmoil. Amid the confusion, brutality, and massacres of the 1790s, power gravitated toward the slaves, now led by the astute Toussaint Louverture, himself a former slave. He and his successor overcame internal resistance, outmaneuvered the foreign powers, and even defeated an attempt by Napoleon to reestablish French control.

When the dust settled in the early years of the nineteenth century, it was clear that something remarkable and unprecedented had taken place, a revolution unique in the Atlantic world and in world history. Socially, the last had become first. In the only completely successful slave revolt in world history, "the lowest order of the society—slaves—became equal, free, and independent citizens."[12] Politically, they had thrown off French colonial rule, becoming the second independent republic in the Americas and the first non-European state to emerge from Western colonialism. They renamed their country "Haiti," a term meaning "mountainous" or "rugged" in the language of the original Taino people. It was a symbolic break with Europe and represented

The Haitian Revolution
This early-nineteenth-century engraving, entitled *Revenge Taken by the Black Army*, shows black Haitian soldiers hanging a large number of French soldiers, thus illustrating both the violence and the racial dimension of the upheaval in Haiti. (Schomburg Center, NYPL/Art Resource, NY)

an effort to connect with the long-deceased native inhabitants of the land. Some, in fact, referred to themselves as "Incas." At the formal declaration of Haiti's independence on January 1, 1804, Jean-Jacques Dessalines, the new country's first head of state, declared: "I have given the French cannibals blood for blood; I have avenged America."[13] In defining all Haitian citizens as "black" and legally equal regardless of color or class, Haiti directly confronted elite preferences for lighter skin even as they disallowed citizenship for most whites. Economically, the country's plantation system, oriented wholly toward the export of sugar and coffee, had been largely destroyed. As whites fled or were killed, both private and state lands were redistributed among former slaves and free blacks, and Haiti became a nation of small-scale farmers producing mostly for their own needs, with a much smaller export sector.

The destructiveness of the Haitian Revolution, its bitter internal divisions of race and class, and continuing external opposition contributed much to Haiti's abiding poverty as well as to its authoritarian and unstable politics. So too did the enormous "independence debt" that the French forced on the fledgling republic in 1825, a financial burden that endured for well over a century (see p. 781). "Freedom" in Haiti came to mean primarily the end of slavery rather than the establishment of political rights for all. In the early nineteenth century, however, Haiti was a source of enormous hope and of great fear. Within weeks of the Haitian slave uprising in 1791, Jamaican slaves had composed songs in its honor, and it was not long before slave owners in the Caribbean and North America observed a new "insolence" in their slaves. Certainly its example inspired other slave rebellions, gave a boost to the dawning abolitionist movement, and has been a source of pride for people of African descent ever since.

To whites throughout the hemisphere, the cautionary saying "Remember Haiti" reflected a sense of horror at what had occurred there and a determination not to allow political change to reproduce that fearful outcome again. Particularly in Latin America, it injected a deep caution and social conservatism in the elites that led their countries to independence in the early nineteenth century. Ironically, though, the Haitian Revolution also led to a temporary expansion of slavery elsewhere. Cuban plantations and their slave workers considerably increased their production of sugar as that of Haiti declined. Moreover, Napoleon's defeat in Haiti persuaded him to sell to the United States the French territories known as the Louisiana Purchase, from which a number of "slave states" were carved out. Nor did the example of Haiti lead to successful independence struggles in the rest of the thirty or so Caribbean colonies. Unlike mainland North and South America, Caribbean decolonization had to await the twentieth century. In such contradictory ways did the echoes of the Haitian Revolution reverberate in the Atlantic world.

■ **Connection**

How were the Spanish American revolutions shaped by the American, French, and Haitian revolutions that happened earlier?

Spanish American Revolutions, 1810–1825

The final act in a half century of Atlantic revolutionary upheaval took place in the Spanish and Portuguese colonies of mainland Latin America (see Map 16.3). Their revolutions were shaped by preceding events in North America, France, and Haiti as well as by their own distinctive societies and historical experience. As in British North America, native-born elites (known as *creoles*) in the Spanish colonies were offended and insulted by the Spanish monarchy's efforts during the eighteenth century to exercise greater power over its colonies and to subject them to heavier taxes and tariffs. Creole intellectuals also had become familiar with ideas of popular sovereignty, republican government, and personal liberty derived from the European Enlightenment. But these conditions, similar to those in North America, led initially only to scattered and uncoordinated protests rather than to outrage, declarations of independence, war, and unity, as had occurred in the British colonies. Why did Spanish colonies win their independence almost 50 years later than those of British North America?

Spanish colonies had been long governed in a rather more authoritarian fashion than their British counterparts and were more sharply divided by class. In addition, whites throughout Latin America were vastly outnumbered by Native Americans, people of African ancestry, and those of mixed race. All of this

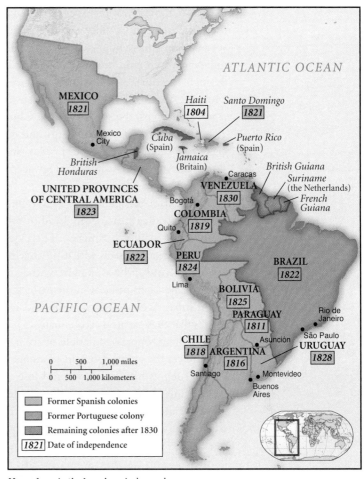

Map 16.3 Latin American Independence

With the exception of Haiti, Latin American revolutions brought independence to new states but offered little social change or political opportunity for the vast majority of people.

inhibited the growth of a movement for independence, notwithstanding the example of North America and similar provocations.

Despite their growing disenchantment with Spanish rule, creole elites did not so much generate a revolution as have one thrust upon them by events in Europe. In 1808, Napoleon invaded Spain and Portugal, deposing the Spanish king Ferdinand VII and forcing the Portuguese royal family into exile in Brazil. With legitimate royal authority now in disarray, Latin Americans were forced to take action. The outcome, ultimately, was independence for the various states of Latin America, established almost everywhere by 1826. But the way in which it occurred and the kind of societies it generated differed greatly from the experience of both North America and Haiti.

The process lasted more than twice as long as it did in North America, partly because Latin American societies were so divided by class, race, and region. In North America, violence was directed almost entirely against the British and seldom spilled over into domestic disputes, except for some bloody skirmishes with loyalists. Even then, little lasting hostility occurred, and some loyalists were able to reenter U.S. society after independence was achieved. In Mexico, by contrast, the move toward independence began in 1810 in a peasant insurrection, driven by hunger for land and by high food prices and led successively by two priests, Miguel Hidalgo and José Morelos. Alarmed by the social radicalism of the Hidalgo-Morelos rebellion, creole landowners, with the support of the Church, raised an army and crushed the insurgency. Later that alliance of clergy and creole elites brought Mexico to a more socially controlled independence in 1821. Such violent conflict among Latin Americans, along lines of race, class, and ideology, accompanied the struggle against Spain in many places.

The entire independence movement in Latin America took place under the shadow of a great fear—the dread of social rebellion from below—that had little counterpart in North America. The extensive violence of the French and Haitian revolutions was a lesson to Latin American elites that political change could easily get out of hand and was fraught with danger to themselves. An abortive rebellion of Native Americans in Peru in the early 1780s, made in the name of the last Inca emperor, Tupac Amaru, as well as the Hidalgo-Morelos rebellion in Mexico, reminded whites that they sat atop a potentially explosive society, most of whose members were exploited and oppressed people of color.

And yet the creole sponsors of independence movements, both regional military leaders such as Simón Bolívar and José de San Martín and their civilian counterparts, required the support of "the people," or at least some of them, if they were to prevail against Spanish forces. The answer to this dilemma was found in nativism, which cast all of those born in the Americas—creoles, Indians, mixed-race people, free blacks—as *Americanos*, while the enemy was defined as those born in Spain or Portugal.[14] This was no easy task, because many creole whites and mestizos saw themselves as Spanish and because great differences of race, culture, and wealth divided the Americanos. Nonetheless, nationalist leaders made efforts to mobilize people of color into the struggle with promises of freedom, the end of legal restrictions, and social advancement. Many of these leaders were genuine liberals, who had been influenced by the ideals of the Enlightenment, the French Revolution, and Spanish liberalism. In the long run, however, few of those promises were kept. Certainly the lower classes, Native Americans, and slaves benefited little from independence. "The imperial state was destroyed in Spanish America," concluded one historian, "but colonial society was preserved."[15]

Nor did women as a group gain much from the independence struggle, though they had participated in it in various ways. Upper-class or wealthy women gave and raised money for the cause and provided safe havens for revolutionary meetings. In Mexico, some women disguised themselves as men to join the struggle, while numerous working-class and peasant women served as cooks and carriers of supplies in a "women's brigade." A considerable number of women were severely punished for their disloyalty to the crown, with some forty-eight executed in Colombia. Yet, after independence, few social gains attended these efforts. Argentine General San Martín accorded national recognition to a number of women and modest improvement in educational opportunities for women appeared. But Latin American women continued to be wholly excluded from political life and remained under firm legal control of the men in their families.

A further difference in the Latin American situation lay in the apparent impossibility of uniting the various Spanish colonies, despite several failed efforts to do so. Thus no United States of Latin America emerged. Distances among the colonies and geographic obstacles to effective communication were certainly greater than in the eastern seaboard colonies of North America, and their longer colonial experience had given rise to distinct and deeply rooted regional identities. Shortly before his death in 1830, the "great liberator" Bolívar, who so admired George Washington and had so ardently hoped for greater unity, wrote in despair to a friend: "[Latin] America is ungovernable. Those who serve the revolution plough the sea."[16] (See Document 16.2, pp. 814–15, for Bolívar's views on the struggle for independence.)

The aftermath of independence in Latin America marked a reversal in the earlier relationship of the two American continents. The United States, which began its history as the leftover "dregs" of the New World, grew increasingly wealthy, industrialized, democratic, internationally influential, and generally stable, with the major exception of the Civil War. The Spanish colonies, which took shape in the wealthiest areas and among the most sophisticated cultures of the Americas, were widely regarded as the more promising region compared to the backwater reputation of England's North American territories. But in the nineteenth century, as newly independent countries in both regions launched a new phase of their histories, those in Latin America became relatively underdeveloped, impoverished, undemocratic, politically unstable, and dependent on foreign technology and investment (see Chapter 17, pp. 853–59). Begun in broadly similar circumstances, the Latin American and North American revolutions occurred in very different societies and gave rise to very different historical trajectories.

Simón Bolívar

Among the heroic figures of Spanish American independence movements, none was more significant than Simón Bolívar, shown here in a moment of triumph entering his hometown of Caracas in present-day Venezuela. But Bolívar was immensely disappointed in the outcomes of independence as his dream of a unified South America perished amid the rivalries of separate countries. (akg-images)

SUMMING UP SO FAR

Compare the North American, French, Haitian, and Spanish American revolutions. What are the most significant categories of comparisons?

Echoes of Revolution

The repercussions of the Atlantic revolutions reverberated far beyond their points of origin and persisted long after those upheavals had been concluded. Britain's loss of its North American colonies, for example, fueled its growing interest and interventions in Asia, contributing to British colonial rule in India and the Opium Wars in China. Napoleon's brief conquest of Egypt opened the way for a modernizing regime to emerge in that ancient land and stimulated westernizing reforms in the Ottoman Empire (see pp. 944–46). During the nineteenth century, the idea of a "constitution" found advocates in Poland, Latin America, Spanish-ruled Philippines, China, the Ottoman Empire, and British-governed India.

Within Europe, which was generally dominated by conservative governments following Napoleon's final defeat, smaller revolutionary eruptions occurred in 1830, more widely in 1848, and in Paris in 1870. They expressed ideas of republicanism, greater social equality, and national liberation from foreign rule. Such ideas and social pressures pushed the major states of Western Europe, the United States, and Argentina to enlarge their voting publics, generally granting universal male suffrage by 1914. An abortive attempt to establish a constitutional regime even broke out in autocratic Russia in 1825. It was led by military officers who had been influenced by ideals of the Enlightenment and the French Revolution while campaigning in Europe against Napoleon. More generally, the American and French revolutions led sympathetic elites in Central Europe and elsewhere to feel that they had fallen behind, that their countries were "sleeping." As early as 1791, a Hungarian poet gave voice to such sentiments: "O you still in the slave's collar . . . And you too! Holy consecrated kings . . . turn your eyes to Paris! Let France set out the fate of both king and shackled slave."[17]

Beyond these echoes of the Atlantic revolutions, three major movements arose to challenge continuing patterns of oppression or exclusion. Abolitionists sought the end of slavery; nationalists hoped to foster unity and independence from foreign rule; and feminists challenged male dominance. Each of these movements bore the marks of the Atlantic revolutions, and although they took root first in Europe and the Americas, each came to have a global significance in the centuries that followed.

The Abolition of Slavery

■ **Change**
What accounts for the end of Atlantic slavery during the nineteenth century?

In little more than a century, from roughly 1780 to 1890, a remarkable transformation occurred in human affairs as slavery, widely practiced and little condemned since the beginning of civilization, lost its legitimacy and was largely ended. In this amazing process, the ideas and practices of the Atlantic revolutions played an important role.

Enlightenment thinkers in eighteenth-century Europe had become increasingly critical of slavery as a violation of the natural rights of every person, and the public pronouncements of the American and French revolutions about liberty and equality likewise focused attention on this obvious breach of those principles. To this secular antislavery thinking was added an increasingly vociferous religious voice, expressed first by Quakers and then Protestant evangelicals in Britain and the United States. To them slavery was "repugnant to our religion" and a "crime in the sight of God."[18] What made these moral arguments more widely acceptable was the growing belief that, contrary to much earlier thinking, slavery was not essential for economic progress. After all, England and New England were among the most prosperous regions of the Western world in the early nineteenth century, and both were based on free labor. Slavery in this view was out of date, unnecessary in the new era of industrial technology and capitalism. Thus moral virtue and economic success were joined. It was an attractive argument. (See Document 16.3, pp. 816–17, for the views of the U.S. abolitionist Frederick Douglass.)

The actions of slaves themselves likewise hastened the end of slavery. The dramatically successful Haitian Revolution was followed by three major rebellions in the British West Indies, all of which were harshly crushed, in the early nineteenth century. They demonstrated clearly that slaves were hardly "contented," and the brutality with which the revolts were suppressed appalled British public opinion. Growing numbers of the British public came to believe that slavery was "not only morally wrong and economically inefficient, but also politically unwise."[19]

These various strands of thinking—secular, religious, economic, and political—came together in abolitionist movements, most powerfully in Britain, which brought growing pressure on governments to close down the trade in slaves and then to ban slavery itself. In the late eighteenth century, such a movement gained wide support among middle- and working-class people in Britain. Its techniques included pamphlets with heartrending descriptions of slavery, numerous petitions to Parliament, lawsuits, and boycotts of slave-produced sugar. Frequent public meetings dramatically featured the testimony of Africans who had experienced the horrors of slavery firsthand. In 1807, Britain forbade the sale of slaves within its empire and in 1834 emancipated those who remained enslaved. Over the next half century, other nations followed suit, responding to growing international pressure, particularly from Britain, then the world's leading economic and military power. British naval vessels patrolled the Atlantic, intercepted illegal slave ships, and freed their human cargoes in a small West African settlement called Freetown, in present-day Sierra Leone. Following their independence, most Latin American countries abolished slavery by the 1850s. Brazil, in 1888, was the last to do so, bringing more than four centuries of Atlantic slavery to an end. A roughly similar set of conditions—fear of rebellion, economic inefficiency, and moral concerns—persuaded the Russian tsar (zahr) to free the many serfs of that huge country in 1861, although there it occurred by fiat from above rather than from growing public pressure.

None of this happened easily. Slave economies continued to flourish well into the nineteenth century, and plantation owners

Abolitionism
This antislavery medallion was commissioned in the late eighteenth century by English Quakers, who were among the earliest participants in the abolitionist movement. Its famous motto, "Am I not a man and a brother," reflected both Enlightenment and Christian values of human equality. (The Art Archive at Art Resource, NY)

vigorously resisted the onslaught of abolitionists. So did slave traders, both European and African, who together shipped millions of additional captives, mostly to Cuba and Brazil, long after the trade had been declared illegal. Osei Bonsu, the powerful king of the West African state of Asante, was puzzled as to why the British would no longer buy his slaves. "If they think it bad now," he asked a local British representative in 1820, "why did they think it good before?"[20] (See Document 14.4, pp. 707–09.) Nowhere was the persistence of slavery more evident and resistance to abolition more intense than in the southern states of the United States. It was the only slaveholding society in which the end of slavery occurred through such a bitter, prolonged, and highly destructive civil war (1861–1865).

■ Change

How did the end of slavery affect the lives of the former slaves?

The end of Atlantic slavery during the nineteenth century surely marked a major and quite rapid turn in the world's social history and in the moral thinking of humankind. Nonetheless, the outcomes of that process were often surprising and far from the expectations of abolitionists or the newly freed slaves. In most cases, the economic lives of the former slaves did not improve dramatically. Nowhere in the Atlantic world, except Haiti, did a redistribution of land follow the end of slavery. But freedmen everywhere desperately sought economic autonomy on their own land, and in parts of the Caribbean such as Jamaica, where unoccupied land was available, independent peasant agriculture proved possible for some. Elsewhere, as in the southern United States, various forms of legally free but highly dependent labor, such as sharecropping, emerged to replace slavery and to provide low-paid and often indebted workers for planters. The understandable reluctance of former slaves to continue working in plantation agriculture created labor shortages and set in motion a huge new wave of global migration. Large numbers of indentured servants from India and China were imported into the Caribbean, Peru, South Africa, Hawaii, Malaya, and elsewhere to work in mines, on sugar plantations, and in construction projects. There they often toiled in conditions not far removed from slavery itself.

Newly freed people did not achieve anything close to political equality, except in Haiti. White planters, farmers, and mine owners retained local authority in the Caribbean. In the southern United States, a brief period of "radical reconstruction," during which newly freed blacks did enjoy full political rights and some power, was followed by harsh segregation laws, denial of voting rights, a wave of lynching, and a virulent racism that lasted well into the twentieth century. For most former slaves, emancipation usually meant "nothing but freedom."[21]

Unlike the situation in the Americas, the end of serfdom in Russia transferred to the peasants a considerable portion of the nobles' land, but the need to pay for this land with "redemption dues" and the rapid growth of Russia's rural population ensured that most peasants remained impoverished and politically volatile. In both West and East Africa, the closing of the external slave trade decreased the price of slaves and increased their use within African societies to produce the export crops that the world economy now sought. Thus, as Europeans imposed colonial rule on Africa in the late nineteenth century, one of their justifications for doing so was the need to emancipate enslaved Africans. Europeans proclaiming the need to end slavery in a continent from which they had extracted slaves for more than four centuries was surely among the more ironic outcomes of the abolitionist process.

In the Islamic world, where slavery had long been practiced and elaborately regulated, the freeing of slaves, though not required, was strongly recommended as a mark of piety. Some nineteenth-century Muslim authorities opposed slavery altogether on the grounds that it violated the Quran's ideals of freedom and equality. But unlike Europe and North America, the Islamic world generated no popular grassroots anti-slavery movements. There slavery was outlawed gradually only in the twentieth century under the pressure of international opinion.

Nations and Nationalism

In addition to contributing to the end of slavery, the Atlantic revolutions also gave new prominence to a relatively recent kind of human community—the nation. By the end of the twentieth century, the idea that humankind was divided into separate nations, each with a distinct culture and territory and deserving an independent political life, was so widespread as to seem natural and timeless. And yet for most of human experience, states did not usually coincide with the culture of a particular people, for all of the great empires and many smaller states governed culturally diverse societies. Few people considered rule by foreigners itself a terrible offense because the most important identities and loyalties were local, limited to clan, village, or region, with only modest connection to the larger state or empire that governed them. People might on occasion consider themselves part of larger religious communities (such as Christians or Muslims) or ethnolinguistic groupings such as Greek, Arab, or Mayan, but such identities rarely provided the basis for enduring states.

All of that began to change during the era of Atlantic revolutions. Independence movements in both North and South America were made in the name of new nations. The French Revolution declared that sovereignty lay with "the people," and its leaders mobilized this people to defend the "French nation" against its external enemies. In 1793, the revolutionary government of France declared a mass conscription (*levée en masse*) with a stirring call to service:

> Henceforth, until the enemies have been driven from the territory of the Republic, all the French are in permanent requisition for army service. The young men shall go to battle; the married men shall forge arms and transport provisions; the women shall make tents and clothes, and shall serve in the hospitals; the children shall turn old linen into lint; the old men shall repair to the public places, to stimulate the courage of the warriors and preach the unity of the Republic and the hatred of kings.[22]

Napoleon's conquests likewise stimulated national resistance in many parts of Europe. European states had long competed and fought with one another, but increasingly in the nineteenth century, those states were inhabited by people who felt themselves to be citizens of a nation, deeply bound to their fellows by ties of blood, culture, or

■ Explanation
What accounts for the growth of nationalism as a powerful political and personal identity in the nineteenth century?

Snapshot   **Key Moments in the Growth of Nationalism**

1776–1825	Independence of colonies in the Americas
1793	Mass conscription to defend the French Revolution
1800–1815	Wars of resistance to Napoleonic empire
1830	Greek independence from Ottoman Empire
1830, 1863	Polish insurrections against Russian rule
1842	Young Ireland movement begins
1846	First Ukrainian nationalist organization established
1848	Hungarian national uprising against Austrian Habsburg rule
1870, 1871	Unification of Italy and Germany
1880	Egyptian revolt against British and French imperialism
1885	Founding of Indian National Congress
1890s	Political Zionism emerges, seeking a homeland in Palestine for Jews

common experience, not simply common subjects of a ruling dynasty. It was a novel form of political loyalty.

Europe's modern transformation also facilitated nationalism, as older identities and loyalties eroded. Science weakened the hold of religion on some. Migration to industrial cities or abroad diminished allegiance to local communities. At the same time, printing and the publishing industry standardized a variety of dialects into a smaller number of European languages, a process that allowed a growing reading public to think of themselves as members of a common linguistic group or nation. All of this encouraged political and cultural leaders to articulate an appealing idea of their particular nations and ensured a growing circle of people receptive to such ideas. Thus the idea of the "nation" was constructed or even invented, but it was often imagined and presented as a reawakening of older linguistic or cultural identities, and it certainly drew on the songs, dances, folktales, historical experiences, and collective memories of earlier cultures (see Map 16.4).

Whatever its precise origins, nationalism proved to be an infinitely flexible and enormously powerful idea in nineteenth-century Europe and beyond. It inspired the political unification of both Germany and Italy, gathering their previously fragmented peoples into new states by 1871. It encouraged Greeks and Serbs to assert their independence from the Ottoman Empire; Czechs and Hungarians to demand more autonomy within the Austrian Empire; Poles and Ukrainians to become more aware of their oppression within the Russian Empire; and the Irish to seek "home rule" and separation from Great Britain. By the end of the nineteenth century, a small Zionist movement, seeking a homeland in Palestine, had emerged among Europe's frequently persecuted Jews. Popular nationalism made the normal rivalry among Euro-

Map 16.4   The Nations and Empires of Europe, ca. 1880

By the end of the nineteenth century, the national principle had substantially reshaped the map of Europe, especially in the unification of Germany and Italy. However, several major empires (Russian, Austro-Hungarian, and Ottoman) remained, each with numerous subject peoples who likewise sought national independence.

pean states even more acute and fueled a highly competitive drive for colonies in Asia and Africa. The immensity of the suffering and sacrifice that nationalism generated in Europe was vividly disclosed during the horrors of World War I.

Governments throughout the Western world claimed now to act on behalf of their nations and deliberately sought to instill national loyalties in their citizens through schools, public rituals, the mass media, and military service. Russian authorities, for

Nationalism in Poland

In the eighteenth century, Poland had been divided among Prussia, Austria, and Russia and disappeared as a separate and independent state. Polish nationalism found expression in the nineteenth century in a series of revolts, among which was a massive uprising in 1863, directed against Poland's Russian occupiers. This famous painting by Polish artist Jan Matejko shows a crowd of Polish prisoners awaiting transportation to imprisonment in Siberia, while Russian military officers supervise a blacksmith, who fastens fetters on a woman representing Poland. (Princes Czartoryski Foundation)

example, imposed the use of the Russian language, even in parts of the country where it was not widely spoken. They succeeded, however, only in producing a greater awareness of Ukrainian, Polish, and Finnish nationalism.

As it became more prominent in the nineteenth century, nationalism took on a variety of political ideologies. Some supporters of liberal democracy and representative government, as in France or the United States, saw nationalism, with its emphasis on "the people," as an aid to their aspirations toward wider involvement in political life. Often called "civic nationalism," such a view identified the nation with a particular territory and maintained that people of various cultural backgrounds could assimilate into the dominant culture, as in the process of "becoming American." Other versions of nationalism, in Germany for example, sometimes defined the nation in racial terms, which excluded those who did not share a common ancestry, such as

Jews. In the hands of conservatives, nationalism could be used to combat socialism and feminism, for those movements only divided the nation along class or gender lines. Thus nationalism generated endless controversy because it provided no clear answer to the questions of who belonged to the nation or who should speak for it.

Nor was nationalism limited to the Euro-American world in the nineteenth century. An "Egypt for the Egyptians" movement arose in the 1870s as British and French intervention in Egyptian affairs deepened. When Japan likewise confronted European aggression in the second half of the nineteenth century, its long sense of itself as a distinct culture was readily transformed into an assertive modern nationalism. Small groups of Western-educated men in British-ruled India began to think of their enormously diverse country as a single nation. The Indian National Congress, established in 1885, gave expression to this idea. The notion of the Ottoman Empire as a Turkish national state rather than a Muslim or dynastic empire took hold among a few people. By the end of the nineteenth century, some Chinese intellectuals began to think in terms of a Chinese nation beset both by a foreign ruling dynasty and by predatory Europeans. Along the West African coast, the idea of an "African nation" stirred among a handful of freed slaves and missionary-educated men. Although Egyptian and Japanese nationalism gained broad support, elsewhere in Asia and Africa such movements would have to wait until the twentieth century, when they exploded with enormous power on the stage of world history.

Feminist Beginnings

A third echo of the Atlantic revolutions lay in the emergence of a feminist movement. Although scattered voices had earlier challenged patriarchy, never before had an organized and substantial group of women called into question this most fundamental and accepted feature of all preindustrial civilizations—the subordination of women to men. But in the century following the French Revolution, such a challenge took shape, especially in Europe and North America. Then, in the twentieth century, feminist thinking transformed "the way in which women and men work, play, think, dress, worship, vote, reproduce, make love and make war."[23] How did this extraordinary process get launched in the nineteenth century?

Thinkers of the European Enlightenment had challenged many ancient traditions, including on occasion that of women's intrinsic inferiority (see Chapter 15, pp. 746–47). The French writer Condorcet, for example, called for "the complete destruction of those prejudices that have established an inequality of rights between the sexes." The French Revolution then raised the possibility of re-creating human societies on new foundations. Many women participated in these events, and a few insisted, unsuccessfully, that the revolutionary ideals of liberty and equality must include women. In neighboring England, the French Revolution stimulated the writer Mary Wollstonecraft to pen her famous *Vindication of the Rights of Woman*, one of the earliest expressions of a feminist consciousness. "Who made man the exclusive judge," she asked, "if woman partake with him of the gift of reason?"

■ **Significance**
What were the achievements and limitations of nineteenth-century feminism?

Within the growing middle classes of industrializing societies, more women found both educational opportunities and some freedom from household drudgery. Such women increasingly took part in temperance movements, charities, abolitionism, and missionary work, as well as socialist and pacifist organizations. Some of their working-class sisters became active trade unionists. On both sides of the Atlantic, small numbers of these women began to develop a feminist consciousness that viewed women as individuals with rights equal to those of men.[24] (See Document 16.4, pp. 818–19.) The first organized expression of this new feminism took place at a women's rights conference in Seneca Falls, New York, in 1848. At that meeting, Elizabeth Cady Stanton drafted a statement that began by paraphrasing the Declaration of Independence: "We hold these truths to be self-evident, that all men and women are created equal."

From the beginning, feminism became a transatlantic movement in which European and American women attended the same conferences, corresponded regularly, and read one another's work. Access to schools, universities, and the professions were among their major concerns as growing numbers of women sought these previously unavailable opportunities. The more radical among them refused to take their husbands' surname or wore trousers under their skirts. Elizabeth Cady Stanton published a Women's Bible, excising the parts she found offensive. As heirs to the French Revolution, feminists ardently believed in progress and insisted that it must now include a radical transformation of the position of women.

By the 1870s, feminist movements in the West were focusing primarily on the issue of suffrage and were gaining a growing constituency. Now many ordinary middle-class housewives and working-class mothers joined their better-educated sisters in the movement. By 1914, some 100,000 women took part in French feminist organizations, while the National American Woman Suffrage Association claimed 2 million members. Most operated through peaceful protest and persuasion, but the British Women's Social and Political Union organized a campaign of violence that included blowing up railroad stations, slashing works of art, and smashing department store windows. One British activist, Emily Davison, threw herself in front of the king's horse during a race in Britain in 1913 and was trampled to death. By the beginning of the twentieth century in the most highly industrialized countries of the West, the women's movement had become a mass movement.

That movement had some effect. By 1900, upper- and middle-class women had gained entrance to universities, though in small numbers, and women's literacy rates were growing steadily. In the United States, a number of states passed legislation allowing women to manage and control their own property and wages, separate from their husbands. Divorce laws were liberalized in some places. Professions such as medicine opened to a few, and teaching beckoned to many more. In Britain, Florence Nightingale professionalized nursing and attracted thousands of women into it, while Jane Addams in the United States virtually invented social work, which also became a female-dominated profession. Progress was slower in the political domain. In 1893, New Zealand became the first country to give the vote to all adult women; Finland

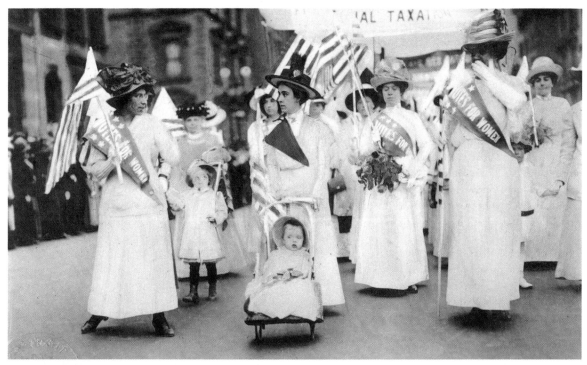

Women's Suffrage

What began as a few isolated voices of feminist protest in the early nineteenth century had become by the end of the century a mass movement in the United States and Western Europe. Here, in a photograph of an American suffrage parade in 1912, is an illustration of that movement in action. (The Granger Collection, New York)

followed in 1906. Elsewhere widespread voting rights for women in national elections were not achieved until after World War I and in France not until 1945.

Beyond these concrete accomplishments, the movement prompted an unprecedented discussion about the role of women in modern society. In Henrik Ibsen's play *A Doll's House* (1879), the heroine, Nora, finding herself in a loveless and oppressive marriage, leaves both her husband and her children. European audiences were riveted, and many were outraged. Writers, doctors, and journalists addressed previously taboo sexual topics, including homosexuality and birth control. Socialists too found themselves divided about women's issues. Did the women's movement distract from the class solidarity that Marxism proclaimed, or did it provide added energy to the workers' cause? Feminists themselves disagreed about the proper basis for women's rights. Some took their stand on the modern idea of human equality: "Whatever is right for a man is right for a woman." Others, particularly in France, based their claims more on the distinctive role of women as mothers. "It is above all this holy function of motherhood," wrote one advocate of "maternal feminism," "which requires that women watch over the futures of their children and gives women the right to intervene not only in all acts of civil life, but also in all acts of political life."[25]

PORTRAIT   Kartini, Feminism and Nationalism in Java

The ideas of the European Enlightenment and the Atlantic revolutions resonated deeply in the life of a remarkable young Javanese woman named Kartini during the late nineteenth century when her country was part of the Dutch East Indies (now Indonesia).[26] Born in 1879 into a large aristocratic Javanese family, young Kartini attended a Dutch elementary school where she learned the Dutch language and observed the relative freedom of her European classmates, in sharp contrast to the constraints and ritualized interactions of her own family. At the age of twelve, in keeping with Javanese Muslim custom, Kartini was abruptly removed from her school. For the next four years, she never left her home.

Kartini (Royal Tropical Institute)

Through her father, a high official in the Dutch colonial administration who much admired Western education, Kartini still had access to Dutch books, and later, she was tutored by several Europeans, including one woman with strong socialist and feminist leanings. She also read widely on her own and began an extensive correspondence, largely with Dutch friends in the Netherlands, which lasted until her death. By the time she was twenty, Kartini had acquired an impressive Western education and a network of relationships with prominent Europeans both in the Netherlands and in Java.

From her letters, we learn something of Kartini's thinking. In light of her exposure to Europeans and European thought, she found the absolute subordination of Javanese women completely unacceptable. The seclusion of girls, the total separation of the sexes, the absence of educational opportunities—all this drove her almost to despair. "Are fine women of no use to civilization?" she asked. But it was the prospect of a traditional high-class Javanese marriage that she found most appalling. Her husband would be "a stranger, an unknown man, whom my parents would choose for me . . . without my knowledge." During the wedding ceremony, she would be expected to prostrate herself before the bridegroom and kiss his feet as a sign of her future submission. Even then, she would be only one of several wives. "Do you understand

Not surprisingly, feminism provoked bitter opposition. Some academic and medical experts argued that the strains of education and life in the world outside the home would cause serious reproductive damage and as a consequence depopulate the nation. Thus feminists were viewed as selfish, willing to sacrifice the family or even the nation while pursuing their individual goals. Some saw suffragists, like Jews and socialists, as "a foreign body in our national life." Never before in any society had such a passionate and public debate about the position of women erupted. It was a novel feature of Western historical experience in the aftermath of the Atlantic revolutions.

Like nationalism, a concern with women's rights spread beyond Western Europe and the United States, though less widely. An overtly feminist newspaper was established in Brazil in 1852, and an independent school for girls was founded in Mexico in 1869. A handful of Japanese women and men, including the empress Haruko, now," she wrote to a Dutch confidante, "the deep aversion I have for marriage?"

Kartini was equally outraged by particular features of Dutch colonial rule, especially its racism. Conscious of her membership in a "despised brown race," she deplored the need for "creeping in the dust" before Europeans. Javanese generally were not supposed to speak Dutch with their colonial masters, as if "Dutch is too beautiful to be spoken by a brown mouth." And yet, for Kartini, it was Dutch education and its universal Enlightenment values—"freedom, equality, fraternity," as she put it, echoing the slogan of the French Revolution—that would lead to Javanese emancipation from both Dutch and Javanese oppression. "Europe will teach us to be truly free," she wrote.

Nonetheless, Kartini openly embraced much of her own culture—its art, music, and poetry; its regard for the dead; its hospitality to the poor; its spiritual depth—and she certainly did not seek to transform Javanese into "half-Europeans." But she did believe that "contact with another civilization" and modern European education in particular would enable Javanese "to develop the fine qualities that are peculiar to their race." "Emancipation is in the air," she declared in early 1901.

Kartini's fondest hope was to contribute to that emancipation by studying in the Netherlands and then opening a school for girls in Java. But these grand dreams were thwarted by opposition from her own family, from Javanese officials, and from much of the Dutch colonial bureaucracy. Java's leading newspaper denounced her intentions as "outrageous," and local gossip had it that she simply wanted to marry a European and become a Europeanized woman. A backup plan to study in the colonial capital of Batavia likewise came to naught with a sudden announcement in mid-1903 that her father had arranged for her to be married to a much older and polygamous man of her social class. Kartini was devastated. "My crown has fallen from my head. My golden illusions of purity and chastity lie shattered in the dust.... Now I am nothing more than all the rest."[27]

Despite Kartini's feeling that she was "done with all personal happiness," she determined to make her marriage a model for the future, actually meeting her husband before the wedding and extracting from him a written promise that she could continue with her plans to create a school for girls. But she soon became pregnant, and four days after the birth of her son in 1904, she died at the age of twenty-five. As her writings subsequently became known in Indonesia, Kartini came to be regarded as a pioneer of both feminist and nationalist thinking, and a number of "Kartini schools" were established in her memory.

Question: In what ways was Kartini's life shaped by living at the intersection of Javanese and European worlds?

raised issues about marriage, family planning, and especially education as the country began its modernizing process after 1868, but the state soon cracked down firmly, forbidding women from joining political parties or even attending political meetings. In Russia, the most radical feminist activists operated within socialist or anarchist circles, targeting the oppressive tsarist regime. Within the Islamic world and in China, some modernists came to believe that education and a higher status for women strengthened the nation in its struggles for development and independence and therefore deserved support. (See Portrait of Kartini, above, for an example from the Dutch East Indies.) Huda Sharawi, founder of the first feminist organization in Egypt, returned to Cairo in 1923 from an international conference in Italy and threw her veil into the sea. Many upper-class Egyptian women soon followed her example.

LearningCurve
bedfordstmartins.com
/strayer/LC

Nowhere did nineteenth-century feminism have thoroughly revolutionary consequences. But as an outgrowth of the French and Industrial revolutions, it raised issues that echoed repeatedly and more loudly in the century that followed.

Reflections: Revolutions Pro and Con

Long after the dust had settled from the Atlantic upheavals, their legacies have continued to provoke controversy. Were these revolutions necessary? Did they really promote the freedoms that they advertised? Did their benefits outweigh their costs in blood and treasure?

To the people who made these revolutions, benefited from them, or subsequently supported them, they represented an opening to new worlds of human possibility, while sweeping away old worlds of oppression, exploitation, and privilege. Modern revolutionaries acted on the basis of Enlightenment ideas, believing that the structure of human societies was not forever ordained by God or tradition and that it was both possible and necessary to reconstruct those societies. They saw themselves as correcting ancient and enduring injustices. To those who complained about the violence of revolutions, supporters pointed to the violence that maintained the status quo and the unwillingness of favored classes to accommodate changes that threatened those unjust privileges. It was persistent injustice that made revolution necessary and perhaps inevitable.

To their victims, critics, and opponents, revolutions appeared in a quite different light. Conservatives generally viewed human societies, not as machines whose parts could be easily rearranged, but as organisms that evolved slowly. Efforts at radical and sudden change only invited disaster, as the unrestrained violence of the French Revolution at its height demonstrated. The brutality and bitterness of the Haitian Revolution arguably contributed to the unhappy future of that country. Furthermore, critics charged that revolutions were largely unnecessary since societies were in fact changing. France was becoming a modern society and feudalism was largely gone well before the revolution exploded. Slavery was ended peacefully in many places, and democratic reform proceeded gradually throughout the nineteenth century. Was this not a preferable alternative to that of revolutionary upheaval?

Historians too struggle with the passions of revolution—both pro and con—as they seek to understand the origins and consequences of these momentous events. Were revolutions the product of misery, injustice, and oppression? Or did they reflect the growing weakness of established authorities, the arrival of new ideas, or the presence of small groups of radical activists able to fan the little fires of ordinary discontent into revolutionary conflagrations? The outcomes of revolutions have been as contentious as their beginnings. Did the American Revolution enable the growth of the United States as an economic and political "great power"? Did the Haitian Revolution stimulate the later end of slavery elsewhere in the Atlantic world? Did the French Revolution and the threat of subsequent revolutions encourage the democratic reforms that followed in the nineteenth century? Such questions have been central to an understanding of the Atlantic revolutions as well as to those that followed in Russia, China, and elsewhere in the twentieth century.

Second Thoughts

What's the Significance?

North American Revolution, 785–87

French Revolution, 787–91

Declaration of the Rights of Man and
   Citizen, 788

Napoleon Bonaparte, 791–92

Haitian Revolution, 792–94

Spanish American revolutions, 794–98

abolitionist movement, 798–801

nationalism, 801–05

Vindication of the Rights of Woman, 805

Elizabeth Cady Stanton, 806

maternal feminism, 807

Kartini, 808–09

LearningCurve
Check what you know.
**bedfordstmartins.com
/strayer/LC**

Online Study Guide
bedfordstmartins.com
/highschool/strayer

Big Picture Questions

1. Do revolutions originate in oppression and injustice, in the weakening of political authorities, in new ideas, or in the activities of small groups of determined activists?

2. "The influence of revolutions endured long after they ended and far beyond where they started." To what extent does this chapter support or undermine this idea?

3. Did the Atlantic Revolutions fulfill or betray the goals of those who made them? Consider this question in both short- and long-term perspectives.

4. **Looking Back:** To what extent did the Atlantic Revolutions reflect the influence of early modern historical developments (1450–1750)?

Next Steps: For Further Study

Benedict Anderson, *Imagined Communities: Reflections on the Origins and Spread of Nationalism* (1991). A now-classic though controversial examination of the process by which national identities were created.

Bonnie S. Anderson, *Joyous Greetings: The First International Women's Movement, 1830–1860* (2000). Describes the beginnings of transatlantic feminism.

David Armitage and Sanjay Subrahmanyam, eds., *The Age of Revolutions in Global Context* (2010). A recent collection of scholarly essays that seeks to explore revolutions within a global framework.

Laurent Dubois and John Garrigus, *Slave Revolution in the Caribbean, 1789–1804* (2006). A brief and up-to-date summary of the Haitian Revolution, combined with a number of documents.

Eric Hobsbawm, *The Age of Revolution, 1789–1848* (1999). A highly respected survey by a well-known British historian.

Lynn Hunt, ed., *The French Revolution and Human Rights* (1996). A collection of documents, with a fine introduction by a prominent scholar.

"Liberty, Equality, Fraternity: Exploring the French Revolution," http://chnm.gmu.edu/revolution/. A collection of cartoons, paintings, and artifacts illustrating the French Revolution.

For Web sites and additional documents related to this chapter, see **Make History** at bedfordstmartins.com /highschool/strayer.

Documents

Considering the Evidence:
Claiming Rights

In the discourse of the age of revolution, no idea had a more enduring resonance than that of "rights"—natural rights, political and civic rights, and "the rights of man" or, in a more recent expression, "human rights." However those rights were defined, they were understood as both natural and universal. They were considered inherent in the human condition rather than granted by some authority, and they were envisioned as being the same for everyone rather than depending on a person's birth, rank, or status in society. Growing out of the European Enlightenment (see pp. 745–48), this understanding of "rights" was genuinely revolutionary, challenging almost all notions of government and society prior to the late eighteenth century. But even among supporters, the idea of human rights was highly controversial. What precisely were these rights? Did they support or contradict one another? Did they really apply equally to women and slaves? How should they be established and maintained? Such questions were central to this age of revolution and have informed much of the world's political history ever since.[28]

Document 16.1

The French Revolution and the "Rights of Man"

The most prominent example of the language of rights found expression during the French Revolution in the Declaration of the Rights of Man and Citizen. It was a document hammered out in the French National Assembly early in that revolutionary upheaval and adopted at the end of August 1789 (see pp. 788–89). It has long been viewed as the philosophical core of the French Revolution.

Clearly the French document bears similarities to the language of the U.S. Declaration of Independence, for both drew on the ideas of the European Enlightenment. Furthermore, Thomas Jefferson, who largely wrote the U.S. Declaration, served as the ambassador to France at this time and was in close contact with Marquis de Lafayette, the principal author of the French Declaration. And Lafayette in turn had earlier served with the American revolutionary forces seeking independence from England.

- What purposes did the writers of the Declaration expect it to fulfill?

- What specific rights are spelled out in this document? What rights does it omit?

- What was revolutionary about the Declaration? What grievances against the old regime did the declaration reflect?

- What grounds for debate or controversy can you identify within the Declaration?

The Declaration of the Rights of Man and Citizen
1789

The representatives of the French people, constituted as a National Assembly, and considering that ignorance, neglect, or contempt of the rights of man are the sole causes of public misfortunes and governmental corruption, have resolved to set forth in a solemn declaration the natural, inalienable and sacred rights of man....

1. Men are born and remain free and equal in rights. Social distinctions may be based only on common utility.

2. The purpose of all political association is the preservation of the natural and imprescriptible rights of man. These rights are liberty, property, security, and resistance to oppression.

3. The principle of all sovereignty rests essentially in the nation. No body and no individual may exercise authority which does not emanate expressly from the nation.

4. Liberty consists in the ability to do whatever does not harm another; hence the exercise of the natural rights of each man has no other limits than those which assure to other members of society the enjoyment of the same rights. These limits can only be determined by the law.

5. The law only has the right to prohibit those actions which are injurious to society. No hindrance should be put in the way of anything not prohibited by the law, nor may any one be forced to do what the law does not require.

6. The law is the expression of the general will. All citizens have the right to take part, in person or by their representatives, in its formation. It must be the same for everyone whether it protects or penalizes. All citizens being equal in its eyes are equally admissible to all public dignities, offices, and employments, according to their ability, and with no other distinction than that of their virtues and talents.

7. No man may be indicted, arrested, or detained except in cases determined by the law and according to the forms which it has prescribed....

9. Every man being presumed innocent until judged guilty, if it is deemed indispensable to arrest him, all rigor unnecessary to securing his person should be severely repressed by the law.

10. No one should be disturbed for his opinions, even in religion, provided that their manifestation does not trouble public order as established by law.

11. The free communication of thoughts and opinions is one of the most precious of the rights of man. Every citizen may therefore speak, write, and print freely, if he accepts his own responsibility for any abuse of this liberty in the cases set by the law.

12. The safeguard of the rights of man and the citizen requires public powers. These powers are

Source: Lynn Hunt, ed., *The French Revolution and Human Rights* (Boston: Bedford/St. Martin's, 1996), 77–79.

therefore instituted for the advantage of all, and not for the private benefit of those to whom they are entrusted.

13. For maintenance of public authority and for expenses of administration, common taxation is indispensable. It should be apportioned equally among all the citizens according to their capacity to pay. . . .

17. Property being an inviolable and sacred right, no one may be deprived of it except when public necessity, certified by law, obviously requires it, and on the condition of a just compensation in advance.

Document 16.2

Rights and National Independence

The "rights of man" could be mobilized also on behalf of colonial subjects, as the American Declaration of Independence illustrated. Some thirty-five years after the outbreak of the North American revolution, Spain's American colonies also revolted. Among the most prominent political and military leaders of that struggle was Simón Bolívar (1783–1830), born in Caracas, Venezuela, and hailing from an old, wealthy, and aristocratic family. Although his struggles were successful in ending Spanish colonial rule, they manifestly failed to achieve his lifelong dream of a federation, like that of North America, among the various newly independent republics of Latin America. In a well-known letter, written in 1815, Bolívar made the case for the independence of his continent.

- What understanding of "rights" informed Bolívar's demand for independence?

- What were his chief objections to Spanish rule?

- What difficulties did Bolívar foresee in achieving the kind of stable and unified independence that he so much desired?

- What might you infer from Bolívar's statements, or his silences, about his willingness to apply human rights thinking to people of Native American, African, or mixed-race ancestry?

SIMÓN BOLÍVAR

The Jamaica Letter
1815

Success will crown our efforts because the destiny of [Latin] America is irrevocably fixed; the tie that bound her to Spain is severed. . . . The hatred we feel for the Peninsula is greater than the sea separating us from it; it would be easier to bring the two continents together than to reconcile the spirits and the minds of the two countries. The habit of obedience; a commerce of shared interests, knowledge, and religion; mutual goodwill; a tender concern for the birthland and glory of our ancestors; in brief everything that constituted our hopes came to us from Spain. . . . Today the opposite is true: death, dishonor, everything harmful threatens us and makes us fearful. That wicked stepmother is the source of all our sufferings. . . . The chains have been broken, we've been liberated, and now our enemies want to make us slaves. That is why America fights with such defiance. . . .

[W]e are moreover neither Indians nor Europeans, but a race halfway between the legitimate owners of the land and the Spanish usurpers—in short, being Americans by birth and endowed with rights from Europe—find ourselves forced to defend these rights against the natives while maintaining our position in the land against the intrusion of the invaders. Thus we find ourselves in the most extraordinary and complicated situation. . . .

The posture of those who dwell in the American hemisphere has been over the centuries purely passive. We are at a level even lower than servitude, and by that very reason hindered from elevating ourselves to the enjoyment of freedom. . . . From the beginning we were plagued by a practice that in addition to depriving us of the rights to which we were entitled left us in a kind of permanent infancy with respect to public affairs. . . .

The Americans . . . occupy no other place in society than that of servants suited for work or, at best, that of simple consumers, and even this is limited by appalling restrictions: for instance the prohibition against the cultivation of European crops or the sale of products monopolized by the king, the restriction against the construction of factories that don't even exist on the peninsula, exclusive privileges for engaging in commerce even of items that are basic necessities, the barrier between American provinces, preventing them from establishing contact, or communicating, or doing business with one another. In short, would you like to know the extent of our destiny? Fields for the cultivation of indigo, grain, coffee, sugar cane, cacao, and cotton, empty prairies for raising cattle, wilderness for hunting ferocious beasts, the bowels of the earth for excavating gold that will

never satisfy the lusts of that greedy nation. . . . Is this not an outrage and a violation of the rights of humanity?

We were . . . absent from the universe in all things relative to the science of government and the administration of the state. We were never viceroys, never governors, except in extraordinary circumstances; hardly ever bishops or archbishops; never diplomats; soldiers only in lower ranks; nobles, but without royal privileges. In short, we were never leaders, never financiers, hardly ever merchants. . . .

From the foregoing, we can deduce certain consequences: The American provinces are involved in a struggle for emancipation, which will eventually succeed. . . . The idea of merging the entire New World into a single nation with a single unifying principle to provide coherence to the parts and to the whole is both grandiose and impractical. Because it has a common origin, a common language, similar customs, and one religion, we might conclude that it should be possible for a single government to oversee a federation of different states eventually to emerge. However, this is not possible, because America is divided by remote climates, diverse geographies, conflicting interests, and dissimilar characteristics. . . . Such a corporation might conceivably emerge at some felicitous moment in our regeneration. . . .

When we are at last strong, under the auspices of a liberal nation that lends us its protection, then we will cultivate in harmony the virtues and talents that lead to glory; then we will follow the majestic path toward abundant prosperity marked out by destiny for South America; then the arts and sciences that were born in the Orient and that brought enlightenment to Europe will fly to a free Columbia, which will nourish and shelter them.

Source: David Bushnell, ed., *El Libertador: Writings of Simón Bolívar*, translated by Frederick H. Fornoff (Oxford: Oxford University Press, 2003), 13–14, 18–20, 27–28, 30.

Document 16.3

Rights and Slavery

The language of "rights" resonated not only with colonial subjects seeking independence but also with slaves demanding freedom. Clearly, the ideas and events of the French Revolution had sparked the massive slave uprising in Haiti in 1791 (see pp. 792–94). In the United States, the language of the Declaration of Independence with its affirmation that "all men are created equal" stood in glaring contrast to the brutal realities of slavery. In a famous speech, Frederick Douglass forcefully highlighted that great contradiction in the new American nation. Born a slave in 1818, Douglass had escaped from bondage to become a leading abolitionist, writer, newspaper publisher, and African American spokesperson. He was invited to address an antislavery meeting in Rochester, New York, on July 4, 1852.

- On what basis does Douglass demand the end of slavery? How do his arguments relate to the ideology of the American Revolution?

- How would you describe the rhetorical strategy of his speech?

- What does Douglass mean when he says "it is not light that is needed, but fire"?

- In what ways does he argue that slavery has poisoned American life?

- Why, in the end, can Douglass claim "I do not despair of this country"? What are the "forces in operation, which must inevitably work the downfall of slavery"?

FREDERICK DOUGLASS

What to the Slave Is the Fourth of July?
1852

Fellow-citizens, pardon me, allow me to ask, why am I called upon to speak here to-day? What have I, or those I represent, to do with your national independence? Are the great principles of political freedom and of natural justice, embodied in that Declaration of Independence, extended to us? and am I, therefore, called upon to bring our humble offering to the national altar, and to confess the benefits and express devout gratitude for the blessings resulting from your independence to us?

Would to God, both for your sakes and ours, that an affirmative answer could be truthfully returned to these questions! . . .

But, such is not the state of the case. I say it with a sad sense of the disparity between us. I am not included within the pale of this glorious anniversary! Your high independence only reveals the immeasurable distance between us. . . . This Fourth [of]

Source: Frederick Douglass, "What to the Slave Is the Fourth of July?," July 5, 1852, http://www.pbs.org/wgbh/aia/part4/4h2927t.html.

July is yours, not mine....You may rejoice, I must mourn.

I shall see, this day ... from the slave's point of view.... I do not hesitate to declare, with all my soul, that the character and conduct of this nation never looked blacker to me than on this 4th of July! ... Standing with God and the crushed and bleeding slave on this occasion, I will ... dare to call in question and to denounce, with all the emphasis I can command, everything that serves to perpetuate slavery—the great sin and shame of America!

For the present, it is enough to affirm the equal manhood of the Negro race. Is it not astonishing that ... while we are engaged in all manner of enterprises common to other men ..., we are called upon to prove that we are men!

Would you have me argue that man is entitled to liberty? that he is the rightful owner of his own body? You have already declared it. Must I argue the wrongfulness of slavery? Is that a question for Republicans? ...

At a time like this, scorching irony, not convincing argument, is needed.... For it is not light that is needed, but fire.... [T]he conscience of the nation must be roused; ... the hypocrisy of the nation must be exposed; and its crimes against God and man must be proclaimed and denounced.

What, to the American slave, is your 4th of July? I answer: a day that reveals to him, more than all other days in the year, the gross injustice and cruelty to which he is the constant victim. To him, your celebration is a sham; your boasted liberty, an unholy license; your national greatness, swelling vanity; your sounds of rejoicing are empty and heartless; your denunciations of tyrants, brass-fronted impudence; your shouts of liberty and equality, hollow mockery; your prayers and hymns, your sermons and thanksgivings, with all your religious parade, and solemnity, are, to him, mere bombast, fraud, deception, impiety, and hypocrisy—a thin veil to cover up crimes which would disgrace a nation of savages. There is not a nation on the earth guilty of practices, more shocking and bloody, than are the people of these United States, at this very hour....

Fellow-citizens! I will not enlarge further on your national inconsistencies. The existence of slavery in this country brands your republicanism as a sham, your humanity as a base pretence, and your Christianity as a lie. It destroys your moral power abroad; it corrupts your politicians at home. It saps the foundation of religion; it makes your name a hissing, and a byword to a mocking earth. It is the antagonistic force in your government, the only thing that seriously disturbs and endangers your Union. It fetters your progress; it is the enemy of improvement, the deadly foe of education; it fosters pride; it breeds insolence; it promotes vice; it shelters crime; it is a curse to the earth that supports it; and yet, you cling to it, as if it were the sheet anchor of all your hopes. Oh! be warned! be warned! a horrible reptile is coiled up in your nation's bosom; the venomous creature is nursing at the tender breast of your youthful republic; for the love of God, tear away, and fling from you the hideous monster, and let the weight of twenty millions crush and destroy it forever! ...

Allow me to say, in conclusion..., I do not despair of this country. There are forces in operation, which must inevitably work the downfall of slavery.... While drawing encouragement from the Declaration of Independence, the great principles it contains, and the genius of American Institutions, my spirit is also cheered by the obvious tendencies of the age. Nations do not now stand in the same relation to each other that they did ages ago. No nation can now shut itself up from the surrounding world, and trot round in the same old path of its fathers without interference.... But a change has now come over the affairs of mankind. Walled cities and empires have become unfashionable. The arm of commerce has borne away the gates of the strong city. Intelligence is penetrating the darkest corners of the globe. It makes its pathway over and under the sea, as well as on the earth. Wind, steam, and lightning are its chartered agents. Oceans no longer divide, but link nations together. From Boston to London is now a holiday excursion. Space is comparatively annihilated. Thoughts expressed on one side of the Atlantic are distinctly heard on the other. The far off and almost fabulous Pacific rolls in grandeur at our feet. The Celestial Empire, the mystery of ages, is being solved. The fiat of the Almighty, "Let there be Light," has not yet spent its force.

Document 16.4

The Rights of Women

But did the "rights of man" include women? During the French Revolution, the question of women's rights was sharply debated. Just two years after the famous French Declaration, the French playwright and journalist Olympe de Gouges sought to apply those rights to women when she crafted her *Declaration of the Rights of Woman and the Female Citizen.* "Woman, wake up," she wrote, "the tocsin [warning bell] of reason is being heard throughout the whole universe; discover your rights."[29] Most men, however, even ardent revolutionaries, agreed with the French lawyer Jean-Denis Lanjuinais that "the physique of women, their goal in life [marriage and motherhood], and their position distance them from the exercise of a great number of political rights and duties."[30]

Throughout the nineteenth century, such debates echoed loudly across Europe, North America, and beyond. Among the most well-known and eloquent appeals for the rights of women came from the American feminist leader Elizabeth Cady Stanton (1815–1902) in an 1892 address to a U.S. congressional committee. She was urging then, as she had for decades, an amendment to the Constitution giving women the right to vote. The success of that effort occurred only in 1920, almost two decades after Stanton died.

- What kind of rights was Stanton seeking for women? Do you think she was advocating a reform of gender relations or a more revolutionary transformation?

- How might you summarize in your own words her argument as to why women should have such rights?

- How might women and men with other points of view have argued with Stanton?

ELIZABETH CADY STANTON

The Solitude of Self
1892

The point I wish plainly to bring before you on this occasion is the individuality of each human soul. . . . In discussing the rights of woman, we are to consider, first, what belongs to her as an individual, in a world of her own. . . .

The strongest reason for giving woman all the opportunities for higher education, for the full development of her faculties . . . ; for giving her the most enlarged freedom of thought and action; a complete emancipation from all forms of bondage, of custom, dependence, superstition; from all the crippling influences of fear, is the solitude and personal responsibility of her own individual life. The

Elizabeth Cady Stanton, *Solitude of Self* (1892). http://www.wfu.edu/~zulick/340/solitude.html.

strongest reason why we ask for woman a voice in the government under which she lives; in the religion she is asked to believe; equality in social life, where she is the chief factor; a place in the trades and professions, where she may earn her bread, is because of her birthright to self-sovereignty; because, as an individual, she must rely on herself. No matter how much women prefer to lean, to be protected and supported, nor how much men desire to have them do so, they must make the voyage of life alone. . . . It matters not whether the solitary voyager is man or woman. . . . Alike amid the greatest triumphs and darkest tragedies of life we walk alone. . . .

In [old] age, when the pleasures of youth are passed, children grown up, married and gone, the hurry and hustle of life in a measure over, when the hands are weary of active service, when the old armchair and the fireside are the chosen resorts, then men and women alike must fall back on their own resources. . . .

If from a lifelong participation in public affairs a woman feels responsible for the laws regulating our system of education, the discipline of our jails and prisons, the sanitary conditions of our private homes, public buildings, and thoroughfares, an interest in commerce, finance, our foreign relations, in any or all of these questions, her solitude will at least be respectable. . . .

Seeing then that the responsibilities of life rests equally on man and woman, that their destiny is the same, they need the same preparation for time and eternity. The talk of sheltering woman from the fierce storms of life is the sheerest mockery, for they beat on her from every point of the compass, just as they do on man, and with more fatal results, for he has been trained to protect himself, to resist, to conquer. . . . Whatever the theories may be of woman's dependence on man, in the supreme moments of her life he cannot bear her burdens. . . .

[T]here is a solitude, which each and every one of us has always carried with him, more inaccessible than the ice-cold mountains, more profound than the midnight sea; the solitude of self. Our inner being, which we call ourself, no eye nor touch of man or angel has ever pierced. . . . Who, I ask you, can take, dare take, on himself the rights, the duties, the responsibilities of another human soul?

Using the Evidence: Claiming Rights

1. **Making comparisons:** In what different ways does the idea of "rights" find expression in these four documents and in the Portrait? Which documents speak more about individual rights and which focus attention on collective rights? What common understandings can you identify?

2. **Considering ideas and circumstances:** Historians frequently debate the relative importance of ideas in shaping historical events. What impact do you think the ideas about rights expressed in these documents had on the historical development of the Atlantic world and beyond? And what specific historical contexts or conditions shaped each writer's understanding of "rights"?

3. **Imagining a conversation:** How might the authors of these four documents have responded to one another? What points of agreement might they share? What differences might arise in a conversation among them?

Visual Sources

Considering the Evidence:
Representing the French Revolution

The era of the French Revolution, generally reckoned to have lasted from 1789 to 1815, unfolded as a complex and varied process. Its first several years were relatively moderate, but by 1792 it had become far more radical and violent. After 1795 a reaction set in against the chaos and upheaval that it had generated, culminating in the seizure of power in 1799 by the successful general Napoleon Bonaparte. Nor was the revolution a purely French affair. Conservative opposition in the rest of Europe prompted prolonged warfare, and French efforts under Napoleon to spread the revolution led to a huge French empire in Europe and much resistance to it (see pp. 791–92).

All of this provoked enormous controversy, which found visual expression in paintings, cartoons, drawings, and portraits. The four visual sources that follow suggest something of the changing nature of the revolution and the varied reactions it elicited.

Like all major social upheavals, the French Revolution unleashed both enormous hopes and great fears, largely depending on an individual's position in French society. Nonetheless, in the early stages of the revolution (1789–1791), many people believed that France could become a constitutional monarchy with a far more limited role for the king and that the three estates—clergy, nobility, and commoners—could live together in harmony. Visual Source 16.1, entitled "The Joyous Accord," represents this phase of the revolution as it depicts the peaceful interaction of members of the three estates. The text reads: "Then Messieur we drink to the health of our good King and the Fatherland, that we may be in agreement, at least this for life. And that virtue may be our guide and we will taste together the true pleasures of life."

- What changes during the first year of the French Revolution does this image reveal? Consider the activity portrayed in the painting and the posture of the three figures. What continuities with the past does it also suggest?

- How does it portray the ideal of national unity?

- How are the representatives of the three estates distinguished from one another?

LE JOYEUX ACCORD.

Alons Messieu buvons à la santé d'not bon Roi et de la Patrie, Soyons d'accord mais au moins qu' ce soi pour la vie. Et que la vertu soit notre guide et nous gouterons ensemble les vrais plaisirs de la vie.

Visual Source 16.1 The Early Years of the French Revolution: "The Joyous Accord" (The Bridgeman Art Library)

■ Notice the peasants hunting in the background. Keep in mind that before the revolution peasants who hunted on the estates of the nobility were subject to harsh punishment or even death. Why do you suppose the artist chose to include them in the painting?

Despite the hope for harmony, many soon came to see the revolution as a sharp reversal of class roles. Visual Source 16.2, entitled "The Awakening of the Third Estate," illustrates this stage of the revolution. In the foreground are male figures representing the three estates of old France. While a member of the Third Estate breaks his chains and takes up arms, members of the clergy and nobility recoil in horror. In the background is the Bastille, the fortress/prison and symbol of the old regime, which was seized by a crowd in July 1789 and subsequently demolished. Also displaying this reversal of class roles is the painting on page 780. Here three female figures symbolize the three estates, with the Third Estate, holding a child, now riding on the back of the nobility and in a superior position to that of the clergy. The caption reads: "I really knew we would have our turn."

■ What different impressions of the revolution are conveyed by these images as compared to that of Visual Source 16.1?

Louis XVI and Marie Antoinette, as well as the widespread violence of the Terror. Visual Source 16.4, a British political cartoon, conveys this highly critical, indeed horrified, outlook on the French Revolution. Captioned "Hell Broke Loose," it depicts the execution of Louis XVI and was printed shortly after his death in January 1793. The flying demonic figures in the image are repeating popular slogans of the revolution: "Vive la nation" ("Long live the nation") and "Ca ira" ("That will go well," or more loosely, "We will win").

- What is the significance of the demons and dragons in the cartoon? Notice how the soldiers at the bottom of the image are portrayed.

- What meaning would you attribute to the caption, "Hell Broke Loose"? What disasters might critics of the revolution have imagined coming in its wake?

- How do you understand the beam of light from heaven that falls on Louis XVI?

- Why was regicide regarded with such horror in England in the 1790s?

Visual Source 16.4 An English Response to Revolution: "Hell Broke Loose or The Murder of Louis" (Musée de la Révolution française, Vizille, France/The Bridgeman Art Library)

Using the Evidence:
Representing the French Revolution

1. **Considering political art as evidence:** Based on these four visual sources, together with those in the text itself, what are the advantages and limitations of political or satirical art in understanding a complex phenomenon such as the French Revolution?

2. **Making comparisons:** In what different ways was the French Revolution portrayed in these visual sources? How might you account for those differences? Consider issues of class, nationality, religious commitment, time period, and gender.

3. **Defining the French Revolution:** Based on these visual sources, what was revolutionary about the French Revolution? And what earlier patterns of French life persisted?

4. **Identifying opponents of the revolution:** Based on these visual sources and the text narrative, which groups of people likely opposed the revolution? Why?

Chapter 16 Wrap Up

LearningCurve
Check what you know.
**bedfordstmartins.com
/strayer/LC**

STEP ONE

The Word to Know: Revolution

The *Oxford English Dictionary* defines *revolution* as the "overthrow of an established government or social order by those previously subject to it; forcible substitution of a new form of government." Use the word "revolution" in an original paragraph to describe a revolution in the chapter and to explain why this event was a revolution rather than a rebellion, revolt, or a resistance movement.

STEP TWO

Comparing Atlantic Revolutions

Use the chart below to note the causes, short- and long-term outcomes, and the major similarities and differences among the Atlantic Revolutions discussed in Chapter 16.

	Causes	Short-term outcomes	Long-term outcomes	Similarities	Differences
The North American Revolution, 1775–1787					
The French Revolution, 1789–1815					
The Haitian Revolution, 1791–1804					
Spanish American Revolutions, 1810–1825					

Connecting the Enlightenment and the American Revolution

1. Excerpt from John Locke, *Second Treatise of Government*, 1690

Locke was one of the greatest English political theorists of the seventeenth century. He published the *Second Treatise of Government* anonymously. Read the excerpt below and answer the question that follows.

[R]evolutions happen not upon every little mismanagement in public affairs. . . . but if a long train of abuses, prevarications and artifices . . . make the design visible to the people . . . it is not to be wondered at that they should . . . endeavor to put the rule into such hands which may secure to them the ends for which government was at first erected. . . .

■ Question

According to Locke, when do people have the right of people to revolt against their government?

2. Excerpt from Jean Jacques Rousseau, *The Social Contract*, 1762

Rousseau was a Swiss philosopher of the eighteenth century. *The Social Contract* is his most famous work. Read the excerpt below and answer the question that follows.

[T]he dominant will of the prince is, or should be, nothing but the general will or the law; his force is only the public force concentrated in his hands, and, as soon as he tries to base any absolute and independent act on his own authority, the tie that binds the whole together begins to be loosened. If finally the prince should come to have a particular will more active than the will of the sovereign, and should employ the public force in his hands in obedience to this particular will, there would be, so to speak, two sovereigns . . . and the body politic would be dissolved. . . .

Source: Jean-Jacques Rousseau, *The Social Contract and Discourses*, trans. by G.D.H. Cole (London: J.M. Dent & Sons, 1913), Book 3, Chapter 1.

■ Question

According to Rousseau, what happens if the sovereign or prince does not follow the general will?

3. Excerpt from *The Declaration of Independence*, July 4, 1776

Often credited solely to Thomas Jefferson, the *Declaration* was, in fact, a team effort. On July 4, 1776, the Second Continental approved the resolution. Read the excerpt below and answer the question that follows.

. . . Governments are instituted among Men, deriving their just powers from the consent of the governed—That whenever any Form of Government becomes destructive of these ends, it is the Right of the People to alter or to abolish it, and to institute new Government, laying its foundation on such principles and organizing its powers in such form, as to them shall seem most likely to affect their Safety and Happiness.

■ Question

Using evidence from all three documents, provide an example of Locke's possible influence on the authors of *The Declaration of Independence* and an example of possible Rousseau's influence.

Revolutions of Industrialization

1750–1914

"Industrialization is, I am afraid, going to be a curse for mankind. . . . God forbid that India should ever take to industrialism after the manner of the West. The economic imperialism of a single tiny island kingdom (England) is today [1928] keeping the world in chains. If an entire nation of 300 millions took to similar economic exploitation, it would strip the world bare like locusts. . . . Industrialization on a mass scale will necessarily lead to passive or active exploitation of the villagers. . . . The machine produces much too fast."[1]

Such were the views of the famous Indian nationalist and spiritual leader Mahatma Gandhi, who subsequently led his country to independence from British colonial rule by 1947, only to be assassinated a few months later. However, few people anywhere have agreed with India's heroic figure. Since its beginning in Great Britain in the late eighteenth century, the idea of industrialization, if not always its reality, has been embraced in every kind of society, both for the wealth it generates and for the power it conveys. Even Gandhi's own country, once it achieved its independence, largely abandoned its founding father's vision of small-scale, village-based handicraft manufacturing in favor of modern industry. As the twenty-first century dawned, India was moving rapidly to develop a major high-technology industrial sector. At that time, across the river from the site in New Delhi where Gandhi was cremated in 1948, a large power plant belched black smoke.

NO ELEMENT OF EUROPE'S MODERN TRANSFORMATION HELD A GREATER SIGNIFICANCE for the history of humankind than the Industrial Revolution, which took place initially in the century and a half between 1750 and 1900. It drew on the Scientific Revolution and accompanied

Industrial Britain: The dirt, smoke, and pollution of early industrial societies are vividly conveyed in this nineteenth-century engraving of a copper foundry in Wales. (The Art Archive at Art Resource, NY)

the unfolding legacy of the French Revolution to utterly transform European society and to propel Europe into a temporary position of global dominance. Not since the breakthrough of the Agricultural Revolution some 12,000 years ago had human ways of life been so fundamentally altered. But the Industrial Revolution, unlike its agricultural predecessor, began independently in only one place, Western Europe, and more specifically Great Britain. From there, it spread much more rapidly than agriculture, though very unevenly, to achieve a worldwide presence in less than 250 years. Far more than Christianity, democracy, or capitalism, Europe's Industrial Revolution has been enthusiastically welcomed virtually everywhere.

In any long-term reckoning, the history of industrialization is very much an unfinished story. It is hard to know whether we are at the beginning of a movement leading to worldwide industrialization, stuck in the middle of a world permanently divided into rich and poor countries, or approaching the end of an environmentally unsustainable industrial era. Whatever the future holds, this chapter focuses on the early stages of an immense transformation in the global condition of humankind.

> **SEEKING THE MAIN POINT**
>
> In what ways did the Industrial Revolution mark a sharp break with the past? In what ways did it continue earlier patterns?

Explaining the Industrial Revolution

The global context for this epochal economic transformation lies in a very substantial increase in human numbers from about 375 million people in 1400 to about 1 billion in the early nineteenth century. Accompanying this growth in population was an emerging energy crisis, most pronounced in Western Europe, China, and Japan, as wood and charcoal, the major industrial fuels, became scarcer and their prices rose. In short, "global energy demands began to push against the existing local and regional ecological limits."[2] In broad terms, the Industrial Revolution marks a human response to that dilemma as nonrenewable fossil fuels such as coal, oil, and natural gas replaced the earlier reliance on the endlessly renewable energy sources of wind, water, wood, and the muscle power of people and animals. It was a breakthrough of unprecedented proportions that made available for human use, at least temporarily, immensely greater quantities of energy.

It also wrought, of course, a mounting impact on the environment. The massive extraction of nonrenewable raw materials to feed and to fuel industrial machinery—coal, iron ore, petroleum, and much more—altered the landscape in many places. Sewers and industrial waste emptied into rivers, turning them into poisonous cesspools. In 1858, the Thames River running through London smelled so bad that the British House of Commons had to suspend its session. Smoke from coal-fired industries and domestic use polluted the air in urban areas and sharply increased the incidence of respiratory illness. (See the chapter-opening image on p. 826.) Against these conditions a number of individuals and small groups raised their voices. Romantic poets such as William Blake and William Wordsworth inveighed against the "dark satanic mills" of industrial England and nostalgically urged a return to the "green and pleasant

A Map of Time

1712	Early steam engine in Britain
1780s	Beginning of British Industrial Revolution
1812	Locomotives first used to haul coal in England
1832	Reform Bill gave vote to middle-class men in England
1848	Karl Marx, *The Communist Manifesto*
1850s	Beginning of railroad building in Argentina, Cuba, Chile, Brazil
1861	Freeing of serfs in Russia
1864–1876	First International socialist organization in Europe
After 1865	Rapid growth of U.S. industrialization
After 1868	Take-off of Japanese industrialization
1869	Opening of transcontinental railroad across United States
1871	Unification of Germany
1889–1916	Second International socialist organization in Europe
1890s	Rapid growth of Russian industrialization
1891–1916	Building of trans-Siberian railroad
1905	Failed revolution in Russia
1910–1920	Mexican Revolution
1917	Russian Revolution

land" of an earlier time. Here were early and local signs of what became by the late twentieth century an issue of unprecedented and global proportions. For many historians, the Industrial Revolution marked a new era in both human history and the history of the planet that scientists increasingly call the Anthropocene, or the "age of man." Increasingly, human industrial activity left a mark not only on human society but also on the ecological, atmospheric, and geological history of the earth.

More immediately and more obviously, however, access to huge new sources of energy gave rise to an enormously increased output of goods and services. In Britain, where the Industrial Revolution began, industrial output increased some fifty-fold between 1750 and 1900. It was a wholly unprecedented and previously unimaginable jump in the capacity of human societies to produce wealth. Lying behind it was a great acceleration in the rate of technological innovation, not simply this or that invention—the spinning jenny, power loom, steam engine, or cotton gin—but a "culture of innovation," a widespread and almost obsessive belief that things could be endlessly improved.

Early signs of the technological creativity that spawned the Industrial Revolution appeared in eighteenth-century Britain, where a variety of innovations transformed cotton textile production. It was only in the nineteenth century, though, that Europeans in general and the British in particular more clearly forged ahead of the rest of the world. The great breakthrough was the coal-fired steam engine, which provided an inanimate and almost limitless source of power beyond that of wind, water, or muscle and could be used to drive any number of machines as well as locomotives and oceangoing ships. Soon the Industrial Revolution spread beyond the textile industry to iron and steel production, railroads and steamships, food processing, and construction. Later in the nineteenth century, a so-called second Industrial Revolution focused on chemicals, electricity, precision machinery, the telegraph and telephone, rubber, printing, and much more. Agriculture too was affected as mechanical reapers, chemical fertilizers, pesticides, and refrigeration transformed this most ancient of industries. Technical innovation occurred in more modest ways as well. Patents for horseshoes in the United States, for example, grew from fewer than five per year before 1840 to thirty to forty per year by the end of the century. Furthermore, industrialization soon spread beyond Britain to continental Western Europe and then, in the second half of the century, to the United States, Russia, and Japan.

In the twentieth century, the Industrial Revolution became global as a number of Asian, African, and Latin American countries developed substantial industrial sectors. Oil, natural gas, and nuclear reactions joined coal as widely available sources of energy, and new industries emerged in automobiles, airplanes, consumer durable goods, electronics, computers, and on and on. It was a cumulative process that, despite periodic ups and downs, accelerated over time. More than anything else, this continuous emergence of new techniques of production, together with the massive economic growth they made possible and the environmental impact they generated, mark the past 250 years as a distinct phase of human history.

Why Europe?

■ Change

In what respects did the roots of the Industrial Revolution lie within Europe? In what ways did that transformation have global roots?

The Industrial Revolution has long been a source of great controversy among scholars. Why did it occur first in Europe? Within Europe, why did it occur earliest in Great Britain? And why did it take place in the late eighteenth and nineteenth centuries? Some explanations have sought the answer in unique and deeply rooted features of European society, history, or culture. One recent account, for example, argued that Europeans have been distinguished for several thousand years by a restless, creative, and freedom-loving culture with its roots in the aristocratic war-like societies of early Indo-European invaders.[3] While not denying certain distinctive qualities of the West, many world historians have challenged views that seem to suggest that Europe alone was destined to lead the way to modern economic life. Such an approach, they argue, is not only Eurocentric and deterministic but also flies in the face of much recent research.

Historians now know that other areas of the world had experienced times of great technological and scientific flourishing. Between 750 and 1100 C.E., the Islamic world generated major advances in shipbuilding, the use of tides and falling water to generate power, papermaking, textile production, chemical technologies, water mills, clocks, and much more.[4] India had long been the world center of cotton textile production, the first place to turn sugarcane juice into crystallized sugar, and the source of many agricultural innovations and mathematical inventions. To the Arabs of the ninth century C.E., India was a "place of marvels."[5] More than either of these, China was clearly the world leader in technological innovation between 700 and 1400 C.E., prompting various scholars to suggest that China was on the edge of an industrial revolution by 1200 or so. For reasons much debated among historians, all of these flowerings of technological creativity had slowed down considerably or stagnated by the early modern era, when the pace of technological change in Europe began to pick up. But their earlier achievements certainly suggest that Europe was not alone in its capacity for technological innovation.

Nor did Europe enjoy any overall economic advantage as late as 1750. Over the past several decades, historians have carefully examined the economic conditions of various Eurasian societies in the eighteenth century and found "a world of surprising resemblances." Economic indicators such as life expectancies, patterns of consumption and nutrition, wage levels, general living standards, widespread free markets, and prosperous merchant communities suggest broadly similar conditions across the major civilizations of Europe and Asia.[6] Thus Europe had no obvious economic lead, even on the eve of the Industrial Revolution. Rather, according to one leading scholar, "there existed something of a global economic parity between the most advanced regions in the world economy."[7]

A final reason for doubting a unique European capacity for industrial development lies in the relatively rapid spread of industrial techniques to many parts of the world over the past 250 years, a fairly short time by world history standards. Although the process has been highly uneven, industrialization has taken root, to one degree or another, in Japan, China, India, Brazil, Mexico, Indonesia, South Africa, Saudi Arabia, Thailand, South Korea, and elsewhere. Such a pattern weakens any suggestion that European culture or society was exceptionally compatible with industrial development.

Thus, while sharp debate continues, many contemporary historians are inclined to see the Industrial Revolution erupting rather quickly and quite unexpectedly between 1750 and 1850 (see Map 17.1). Two intersecting factors help to explain why this process occurred in Europe rather than elsewhere. One lies in certain patterns of Europe's internal development that favored innovation. Its many small and highly competitive states, taking shape in the twelfth or thirteenth centuries, arguably provided an "insurance against economic and technological stagnation," which the larger Chinese, Ottoman, or Mughal empires perhaps lacked.[8] If so, then Western Europe's failure to re-create the earlier unity of the Roman Empire may have acted as a stimulus to innovation.

Furthermore, the relative newness of these European states and their monarchs' desperate need for revenue in the absence of an effective tax-collecting bureaucracy pushed European royals into an unusual alliance with their merchant classes. Small

Map 17.1 The Early Phase of Europe's Industrial Revolution

From its beginning in Great Britain, industrialization spread by 1850 across western Europe to include parts of France, Germany, Belgium, Bohemia, and Italy.

groups of merchant capitalists might be granted special privileges, monopolies, or even tax-collecting responsibilities in exchange for much-needed loans or payments to the state. It was therefore in the interest of governments to actively encourage commerce and innovation. Thus states granted charters and monopolies to private trading companies, and governments founded scientific societies and offered prizes to promote innovation. In this way, European merchants and other innovators from the fifteenth century onward gained an unusual degree of freedom from state control and in some places a higher social status than their counterparts in more established civilizations. In Venice and Holland, merchants actually controlled the state. By the eighteenth century, major Western European societies were highly commercialized and governed by states generally supportive of private commerce. In short, they were well on their way toward capitalist economies—where buying and selling on the market was a widely established practice—before they experienced industrialization. Such internally competitive economies, coupled with a highly competitive system of rival states, arguably fostered innovation in the new civilization taking shape in Western Europe.

Europe's societies, of course, were not alone in developing market-based economies by the eighteenth century. Japan, India, and especially China were likewise highly commercialized or market driven. However, in the several centuries after 1500, Western Europe was unique in another way. That region alone "found itself at the hub of the largest and most varied network of exchange in history."[9] Widespread contact with culturally different peoples was yet another factor that historically has generated extensive change and innovation. This new global network, largely the creation of Europeans themselves, greatly energized commerce and brought Europeans into direct contact with peoples around the world.

For example, Asia, home to the world's richest and most sophisticated societies, was the initial destination of European voyages of exploration. The German philosopher Gottfried Wilhelm Leibniz (1646–1716) encouraged Jesuit missionaries in China "not to worry so much about getting things European to the Chinese but rather about getting remarkable Chinese inventions to us."[10] Inexpensive and well-made Indian textiles began to flood into Europe, causing one English observer to note: "Almost everything that used to be made of wool or silk, relating either to dress of the women or the furniture of our houses, was supplied by the Indian trade."[11] The competitive stimulus of these Indian cotton textiles was certainly one factor driving innovation in the British textile industry. Likewise, the popularity of Chinese porcelain and Japanese lacquerware prompted imitation and innovation in England, France, and Holland.[12] Thus competition from desirable, high-quality, and newly available Asian goods played a role in stimulating Europe's Industrial Revolution.

In the Americas, Europeans found a windfall of silver that allowed them to operate in Asian markets. They also found timber, fish, maize, potatoes, and much else to sustain a growing population. Later, slave-produced cotton supplied an emerging textile industry with its key raw material at low prices, while sugar, similarly produced with slave labor, furnished cheap calories to European workers. "Europe's Industrial Revolution," concluded historian Peter Stearns, "stemmed in great part from Europe's ability to draw disproportionately on world resources."[13] The new societies of the Americas further offered a growing market for European machine-produced goods and generated substantial profits for European merchants and entrepreneurs. None of the other empires of the early modern era enriched their imperial heartlands so greatly or provided such a spur to technological and economic growth.

Thus the intersection of new, highly commercialized, competitive European societies with the novel global network of their own making provides a context for understanding Europe's Industrial Revolution. Commerce and cross-cultural exchange, acting in tandem, sustained the impressive technological changes of the first industrial societies.

Why Britain?

■ Comparison

What was distinctive about Britain that may help to explain its status as the breakthrough point of the Industrial Revolution?

If the Industrial Revolution was initially a Western European phenomenon generally, it clearly began in Britain in particular. The world's first Industrial Revolution unfolded spontaneously in a country that concentrated some of the more general features of European society. It was both unplanned and unexpected.

With substantial imperial possessions in the Caribbean, in North America, and, by the late eighteenth century, in India as well, Britain was the most highly commercialized of Europe's larger countries. Its landlords had long ago "enclosed" much agricultural land, pushing out the small farmers and producing for the market. A series of agricultural innovations — crop rotation, selective breeding of animals, lighter plows, higher-yielding seeds — increased agricultural output, kept food prices low, and freed up labor from the countryside. The guilds, which earlier had protected Britain's urban artisans, had largely disappeared by the eighteenth century, allowing employers to run their manufacturing enterprises as they saw fit. Coupled with a rapidly growing population, these processes ensured a ready supply of industrial workers who had few alternatives available to them. Furthermore, British aristocrats, unlike their counterparts in Europe, had long been interested in the world of business, and some took part in new mining and manufacturing enterprises. British commerce, moreover, extended around the world, its large merchant fleet protected by the Royal Navy. The wealth of empire and global commerce, however, were not themselves sufficient for spawning the Industrial Revolution, for Spain, the earliest beneficiary of American wealth, was one of the slowest industrializing European countries into the twentieth century.

British political life encouraged commercialization and economic innovation. Its policy of religious toleration, formally established in 1688, welcomed people with technical skills regardless of their faith, whereas France's persecution of its Protestant minority had chased out some of its most skilled workers. The British government favored men of business with tariffs that kept out cheap Indian textiles, with laws that made it easy to form companies and to forbid workers' unions, with roads and canals that helped create a unified internal market, and with patent laws that served to protect the interests of inventors. Checks on royal authority — trial by jury and the growing authority of Parliament, for example — provided a freer arena for private enterprise than elsewhere in Europe.

Europe's Scientific Revolution also took a distinctive form in Great Britain in ways that fostered technological innovation.[14] Whereas science on the continent was largely based on logic, deduction, and mathematical reasoning, in Britain it was much more concerned with observation, experiment, precise measurements, mechanical devices, and practical commercial applications. Discoveries about atmospheric pressure and vacuums, for example, played an important role in the invention and improvement of the steam engine. Even though most inventors were artisans or craftsmen rather than scientists, in eighteenth-century Britain they were in close contact with scientists, makers of scientific instruments, and entrepreneurs, whereas in continental

Europe these groups were largely separate. The British Royal Society, an association of "natural philosophers" (scientists) established in 1660, saw its role as one of promoting "useful knowledge." To this end, it established "mechanics' libraries," published broadsheets and pamphlets on recent scientific advances, and held frequent public lectures and demonstrations. The integration of science and technology became widespread and permanent after 1850, but for a century before, it was largely a British phenomenon.

Finally, several accidents of geography and history contributed something to Britain's Industrial Revolution. The country had a ready supply of coal and iron ore, often located close to each other and within easy reach of major industrial centers. Although Britain took part in the wars against Napoleon, the country's island location protected it from the kind of invasions that so many continental European states experienced during the era of the French Revolution. Moreover, Britain's relatively fluid society allowed for adjustments in the face of social changes without widespread revolution. By the time the dust settled from the immense disturbance of the French Revolution, Britain was well on its way to becoming the world's first industrial society.

Railroads
The popularity of railroads, long a symbol of the Industrial Revolution, is illustrated in this early-nineteenth-century watercolor, which shows a miniature train offered as a paid amusement for enthusiasts in London's Euston Square. (Science Museum, London, UK/The Bridgeman Art Library)

The First Industrial Society

Wherever it took hold, the Industrial Revolution generated, within a century or less, an economic miracle, at least in comparison with earlier technologies. The British textile industry, which used 52 million pounds of cotton in 1800, consumed 588 million pounds in 1850. Britain's output of coal soared from 5.23 million tons in 1750 to 68.4 million tons a century later.[15] Railroads crisscrossed Britain and much of Europe like a giant spider web (see Map 17.1, p. 832). Most of this dramatic increase in production occurred in mining, manufacturing, and services. Thus agriculture, for millennia the overwhelmingly dominant economic sector in every civilization, shrank in relative importance. In Britain, for example, agriculture generated only 8 percent of national income in 1891 and employed fewer than 8 percent of working Britons in 1914. Accompanying this vast economic change was an epic transformation of social life. "In two centuries," wrote one prominent historian, "daily life changed more than it had in the 7,000 years before."[16] Nowhere were the revolutionary dimensions of industrialization more apparent than in Great Britain, the world's first industrial society.

Snapshot   **Measuring the Industrial Revolution**[17]

Railroads are one useful measure of industrial development. This graph illustrates both Britain's head start and the beginning catch-up efforts of other countries.

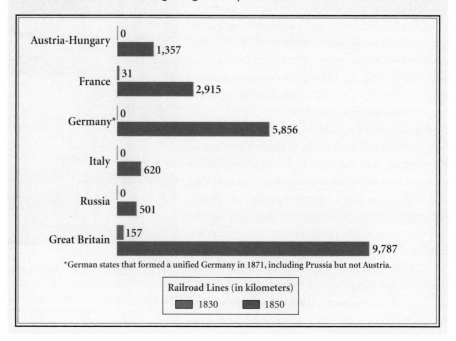

*German states that formed a unified Germany in 1871, including Prussia but not Austria.

Railroad Lines (in kilometers)
1830   1850

The social transformation of the Industrial Revolution both destroyed and created. Referring to the impact of the Industrial Revolution on British society, historian Eric Hobsbawm wrote: "In its initial stages it destroyed their old ways of living and left them free to discover or make for themselves new ones, if they could and knew how. But it rarely told them how to set about it."[18] For many people, it was an enormously painful, even traumatic process, full of social conflict, insecurity, and false starts as well as new opportunities, an eventually higher standard of living, and greater participation in public life. Scholars, politicians, journalists, and ordinary people have endlessly debated the gains and losses associated with the Industrial Revolution. Amid the controversy, however, one thing is clear: not everyone was affected in the same way. (See the Documents and Visual Sources, pp. 862–77, for both celebratory and critical perspectives on industrialization.)

The British Aristocracy

Individual landowning aristocrats, long the dominant class in Britain, suffered little in material terms from the Industrial Revolution. In the mid-nineteenth century, a few thousand families still owned more than half of the cultivated land in Britain, most of it leased to tenant farmers, who in turn employed agricultural wage laborers to work it. Rapidly growing population and urbanization sustained a demand for food products grown on that land. For most of the nineteenth century, landowners continued to dominate the British Parliament.

As a class, however, the British aristocracy declined as a result of the Industrial Revolution, as have large landowners in every industrial society. As urban wealth became more important, landed aristocrats had to make way for the up-and-coming businessmen, manufacturers, and bankers, newly enriched by the Industrial Revolution. The aristocracy's declining political clout was demonstrated in the 1840s when high tariffs on foreign agricultural imports, designed to protect the interests of British landlords, were finally abolished. By the end of the century, landownership had largely ceased to be the basis of great wealth, and businessmen, rather than aristocrats, led the major political parties. Even so, the titled nobility of dukes, earls, viscounts, and barons retained great social prestige and considerable personal wealth. Many among them found an outlet for their energies and opportunities for status and enrichment in the vast domains of the British Empire, where they went as colonial administrators or settlers. Famously described as a "system of outdoor relief for the aristocracy," the empire provided a cushion for a declining class.

■ **Change**
How did the Industrial Revolution transform British society?

The Middle Classes

Those who benefited most conspicuously from industrialization were members of that amorphous group known as the middle class. At its upper levels, this middle class contained extremely wealthy factory and mine owners, bankers, and merchants. Such rising businessmen readily assimilated into aristocratic life, buying country houses, obtaining seats in Parliament, sending their sons to Oxford or Cambridge University, and gratefully accepting titles of nobility from Queen Victoria.

Far more numerous were the smaller businessmen, doctors, lawyers, engineers, teachers, journalists, scientists, and other professionals required in any industrial society. Such people set the tone for a distinctly middle-class society with its own values and outlooks. Politically they were liberals, favoring constitutional government, private property, free trade, and social reform within limits. Their agitation resulted in the Reform Bill of 1832, which broadened the right to vote to many men of the middle class, but not to middle-class women. Ideas of thrift and hard work, a rigid morality, and cleanliness characterized middle-class culture. The central value of that culture was "respectability," a term that combined notions of social status and virtuous behavior. Nowhere were these values more effectively displayed than in the Scotsman Samuel Smiles's famous book *Self-Help*, published in 1859. Individuals are responsible for their own destiny, Smiles argued. An hour a day devoted to self-improvement "would make an ignorant man wise in a few years." According to Smiles, this enterprising spirit was what distinguished the prosperous middle class from Britain's poor. The misery of the poorer classes was "voluntary and self-imposed—the results of idleness, thriftlessness, intemperance, and misconduct."[19] (See Document 17.3, pp. 865–67, for an excerpt from Smiles's writings.)

■ **Change**
How did Britain's middle classes change during the nineteenth century?

Women in such middle-class families were increasingly cast as homemakers, wives, and mothers, charged with creating an emotional haven for their men and a refuge from a heartless and cutthroat capitalist world. They were also expected to be the moral centers of family life, the educators of "respectability," and the managers of household consumption as "shopping"—a new concept in eighteenth-century Britain—became a central activity for the middle classes. An "ideology of domesticity" defined homemaking, child rearing, charitable endeavors, and "refined" activities such as embroidery, music, and drawing as the proper sphere for women, while paid employment and public sphere of life outside the home beckoned to men.

Male elites in many civilizations had long established their status by detaching women from productive labor. The new wealth of the Industrial Revolution now allowed larger numbers of families to aspire to that kind of status. With her husband as "provider," such a woman was now a "lady." "She must not work for profit," wrote the Englishwoman Margaretta Greg in 1853, "or engage in any occupation that money can command."[20] Employing even one servant became a proud marker of such middle-class status. But the withdrawal of middle-class women from the labor force turned out to be only a temporary phenomenon. By the late nineteenth century, some middle-class women began to enter the teaching, clerical, and nursing professions, and in the second half of the twentieth century, educated middle-class women flooded into the labor force. By contrast, the withdrawal of children from productive labor into schools has proved a more enduring phenomenon as industrial economies increasingly required a more educated workforce.

The Industrial Middle Class This late-nineteenth-century painting shows a prosperous French middle-class family, attended by a servant. (Bridgeman Art Library/ SuperStock, Inc.)

As Britain's industrial economy matured, it also gave rise to a sizable lower middle class, which included people employed in the growing service sector as clerks, salespeople, bank tellers, hotel staff, secretaries, telephone operators, police officers, and the like. By the end of the nineteenth century, this growing segment of the middle class represented about 20 percent of Britain's population and provided new employment opportunities for women as well as men. In just twenty years (1881–1901), the number of female secretaries in Britain rose from 7,000 to 90,000. Almost all were single and expected to return to the home after marriage. Telephone operators had initially been boys or men, but by the end of the nineteenth century in both Britain and the United States that work had become a wholly female occupation. For both men and women, such employment represented a claim on membership in the larger middle class and a means of distinguishing themselves clearly from a working class tainted by manual labor.

The Laboring Classes

The overwhelming majority of Britain's nineteenth-century population—some 70 percent or more—were neither aristocrats nor members of the middle classes. They were manual workers in the mines, ports, factories, construction sites, workshops, and farms of an industrializing Britain. Although their conditions varied considerably and changed over time, it was the laboring classes who suffered most and benefited least from the epic transformations of the Industrial Revolution. Their efforts to accommodate, resist, protest, and change those conditions contributed much to the texture of the first industrial society.

The lives of the laboring classes were shaped primarily by the new working conditions of the industrial era. Chief among those conditions was rapid urbanization. Liverpool's population alone grew from 77,000 to 400,000 in the first half of the nineteenth century. By 1851, a majority of Britain's population lived in towns and cities, an enormous change from the overwhelmingly rural life of almost all previous civilizations. By the end of the century, London was the world's largest city, with more than 6 million inhabitants.

These cities were vastly overcrowded and smoky, with wholly inadequate sanitation, periodic epidemics, endless row houses and warehouses, few public services or open spaces, and inadequate and often polluted water supplies. This was the environment in which most urban workers lived in the first half of the nineteenth century. By 1850, the average life expectancy in England was only 39.5 years, less than it had been some three centuries earlier. Nor was there much personal contact between the rich and the poor of industrial cities. Benjamin Disraeli's novel *Sybil*, published in 1845, described these two ends of the social spectrum as "two nations between whom there is no intercourse and no sympathy; who are ignorant of each other's habits, thoughts and feelings, as if they were dwellers in different zones or inhabitants of different planets."

The industrial factories to which growing numbers of desperate people looked for employment offered a work environment far different from the artisan's shop or the tenant's farm. (See Document 17.1, pp. 862–64, for an

DEATH'S DISPENSARY.

OPEN TO THE POOR, GRATIS, BY PERMISSION OF THE PARISH.

The Urban Poor of Industrial Britain
This 1866 political cartoon shows an impoverished urban family forced to draw its drinking water from a polluted public well, while a figure of Death operates the pump. (The Granger Collection, New York)

Social Protest

For workers of the laboring classes, industrial life "was a stony desert, which they had to make habitable by their own efforts."[22] Such efforts took many forms. By 1815, about 1 million workers, mostly artisans, had created a variety of "friendly societies." With dues contributed by members, these working-class self-help groups provided insurance against sickness, a decent funeral, and an opportunity for social life in an otherwise bleak environment. Other skilled artisans, who had been displaced by machine-produced goods and forbidden to organize in legal unions, sometimes wrecked the offending machinery and burned the mills that had taken their jobs. (See Document 17.2, pp. 864–65, for the plight of unemployed artisans.) The class consciousness of working people was such that one police informer reported that "most every creature of the lower order both in town and country are on their side."[23]

Others acted within the political arena by joining movements aimed at obtaining the vote for working-class men, a goal that was gradually achieved in the second half of the nineteenth century. When trade unions were legalized in 1824, growing numbers of factory workers joined these associations in their efforts to achieve better wages and working conditions. Initially their strikes, attempts at nationwide organization, and threat of violence made them fearful indeed to the upper classes. One British newspaper in 1834 described unions as "the most dangerous institutions that were ever permitted to take root, under shelter of law, in any country,"[24] although they later became rather more "respectable" organizations.

Socialist ideas of various kinds gradually spread within the working class, challenging the assumptions of a capitalist society. Robert Owen (1771–1858), a wealthy British cotton textile manufacturer, urged the creation of small industrial communities where workers and their families would be well treated. He established one such community, with a ten-hour workday, spacious housing, decent wages, and education for children, at his mill in New Lanark in Scotland.

■ Change

How did Karl Marx understand the Industrial Revolution? In what ways did his ideas have an impact in the industrializing world of the nineteenth century?

Of more lasting significance was the socialism of Karl Marx (1818–1883). German by birth, Marx spent much of his life in England, where he witnessed the brutal conditions of Britain's Industrial Revolution and wrote voluminously about history and economics. His probing analysis led him to the conclusion that industrial capitalism was an inherently unstable system, doomed to collapse in a revolutionary upheaval that would give birth to a classless socialist society, thus ending forever the ancient conflict between rich and poor. (See Document 17.4, pp. 867–70, for Marx's own understanding of industrial-era capitalism.)

In his writings, the combined impact of Europe's industrial, political, and scientific revolutions found expression. Industrialization created both the social conditions against which Marx protested so bitterly and the enormous wealth he felt would make socialism possible. The French Revolution, still a living memory in Marx's youth, provided evidence that grand upheavals, giving rise to new societies, had in fact taken place and could do so again. Moreover, Marx regarded himself as a scientist, discovering the laws of social development in much the same fashion as Newton discovered the laws of motion. His was therefore a "scientific socialism," embedded in these laws of historical change; revolution was a certainty and the socialist future inevitable.

It was a grand, compelling, prophetic, utopian vision of human freedom and community—and it inspired socialist movements of workers and intellectuals amid the grim harshness of Europe's industrialization in the second half of the nineteenth century. Socialists established political parties in most European states and linked them together in international organizations as well. These parties recruited members, contested elections as they gained the right to vote, agitated for reforms, and in some cases plotted revolution.

In the later decades of the nineteenth century, such ideas echoed among more radical trade unionists and some middle-class intellectuals in Britain, and even more so in a rapidly industrializing Germany and elsewhere. By then, however, the British working-class movement was not overtly revolutionary. When a working-class political party, the Labour Party, was established in the 1890s, it advocated a reformist program and a peaceful democratic transition to socialism, largely rejecting the class struggle and revolutionary emphasis of classical Marxism. Generally known as "social democracy," this approach to socialism was especially prominent in Germany during the late nineteenth century and spread more widely in the twentieth century when it came into conflict with the more violent and revolutionary movements calling themselves "communist."

Improving material conditions during the second half of the nineteenth century helped to move the working-class movement in Britain, Germany, and elsewhere away from a revolutionary posture. Marx had expected industrial capitalist societies to polarize into a small wealthy class and a huge and increasingly impoverished proletariat. However, standing between "the captains of industry" and the workers was a sizable middle and lower middle class, constituting perhaps 30 percent of the population, most of whom were not really wealthy but were immensely proud that they were not manual laborers. Marx had not foreseen the development of this intermediate social group, nor had he imagined that workers could better their standard of living within a capitalist framework. But they did. Wages rose under pressure from unions; cheap imported food improved working-class diets; infant mortality rates fell; and shops and chain stores catering to working-class

The Socialist Outlook

This 1911 poster was first published in the newspaper of the Industrial Workers of the World, a radical American trade union organization. It illustrates a socialist perspective on capitalist societies. At the bottom of the pyramid, supporting the entire social edifice, are the workers, while above them are arrayed the various oppressive layers of the social hierarchy: the bourgeoisie, the police and militias, religious figures, and state officials. (From *Pyramid of Capitalist System*, issued by Nedelkovich, Brashick and Kuharich, Cleveland (International Publishing Co., 1911)/Library of Congress) families multiplied. As English male workers gradually obtained the right to vote, politicians had an incentive to legislate in their favor, by abolishing child labor, regulating factory conditions, and even, in 1911, inaugurating a system of relief for the unemployed. Sanitary reform considerably cleaned up the "filth and stink" of early nineteenth-century cities, and urban parks made a modest appearance. Contrary to Marx's expectations, capitalist societies demonstrated some capacity for reform.

Further eroding working-class radicalism was a growing sense of nationalism, which bound workers in particular countries to their middle-class employers and compatriots, offsetting to some extent the economic and social antagonism between them. When World War I broke out, the "workers of the world," far from uniting against their bourgeois enemies as Marx had urged them, instead set off to slaughter one another in enormous numbers on the battlefields of Europe. National loyalty had trumped class loyalty.

Nonetheless, as the twentieth century dawned, industrial Britain was hardly a stable or contented society. Immense inequalities still separated the classes. Some 40 percent of the working class continued to live in conditions then described as "poverty." A mounting wave of strikes from 1910 to 1913 testified to the intensity of class conflict. The Labour Party was becoming a major force in Parliament. Some socialists and some feminists were becoming radicalized. "Wisps of violence hung in the English air," wrote Eric Hobsbawm, "symptoms of a crisis in economy and society, which the [country's] self-confident opulence . . . could not quite conceal."[25] The world's first industrial society remained dissatisfied and conflicted.

It was also a society in economic decline relative to industrial newcomers such as Germany and the United States. Britain paid a price for its early lead, for its businessmen became committed to machinery that became obsolete as the century progressed. Latecomers invested in more modern equipment and in various ways had surpassed the British by the early twentieth century.

Europeans in Motion

Europe's industrial revolution prompted a massive migratory process that uprooted many millions, setting them in motion both internally and around the globe. Within Europe itself, the movement of men, women, and families from the countryside to the cities involved half or more of the region's people by the mid-nineteenth century. More significant for world history was the exodus between 1815 and 1939 of fully 20 percent of Europe's population, some 50 to 55 million people, who left home for the Americas, Australia, New Zealand, South Africa, and elsewhere (see Map 17.2). They were pushed by a rapidly growing population, poverty, and the displacement of peasant farming and artisan manufacturing. And they were pulled abroad by the enormous demand for labor overseas, the ready availability of land in some places, and the relatively cheap transportation of railroads and steamships. But not all found a satisfactory life in their new homes, and perhaps 7 million returned to Europe.[26]

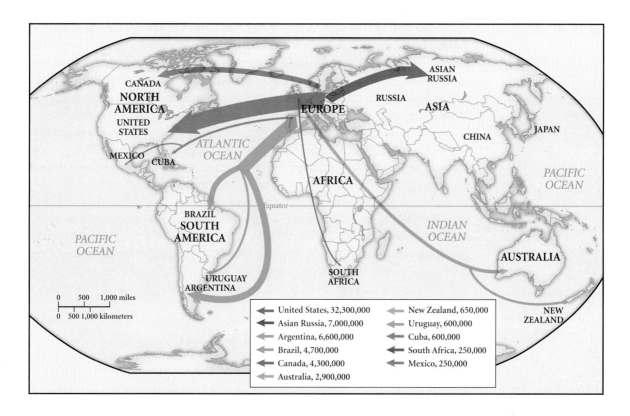

Map 17.2
European Migration in the Industrial Age
The Industrial Revolution not only transformed European society, but it also scattered millions of Europeans to the far corners of the world.

This huge process had a transformative global impact, temporarily increasing Europe's share of the world's population and scattering Europeans around the world. In 1800, less than 1 percent of the total world population consisted of overseas Europeans and their descendants; by 1930, they represented 11 percent.[27] In particular regions, the impact was profound. Australia and New Zealand became settler colonies, outposts of European civilization in the South Pacific that overwhelmed their native populations. Smaller numbers found their way to South Africa, Kenya, Rhodesia, Algeria, and elsewhere, where they injected a sharp racial divide into those colonized territories.

But it was the Americas that felt the brunt of this huge movement of people. Latin America received about 20 percent of the European migratory stream, mostly from Italy, Spain, and Portugal, with Argentina and Brazil accounting for some 80 percent of those immigrants. Considered "white," they enhanced the social weight of the European element in those countries and thus enjoyed economic advantages over the mixed-race, Indian, and African populations.

In several ways the immigrant experience in the United States was distinctive. It was far larger and more diverse than elsewhere, with some 30 million newcomers arriving from all over Europe between 1820 and 1930. Furthermore, the United States offered affordable land to many and industrial jobs to many more, neither of which was widely available in Latin America. And the United States was unique in turning the immigrant experience into a national myth—that of the melting pot. Despite this ideology of assimilation, the earlier immigrants, mostly Protestants from Britain and Germany, were anything but welcoming to those who arrived later as Catholics and Jews from Southern and Eastern Europe. The newcomers were seen as distinctly inferior, even "un-American," and blamed for crime, labor unrest, and socialist ideas.

In the vast domains of the Russian Empire, a parallel process of European migration likewise unfolded. After the freeing of the serfs in 1861, some 10 million or more Russians and Ukrainians migrated to Siberia where they soon overwhelmed the native population of the region. By the end of the century, native Siberians totaled only 10 percent of the population. The availability of land, the prospect of greater freedom from tsarist restrictions and from the exploitation of aristocratic landowners, and the construction of the trans-Siberian railroad—all of this facilitated the continued Europeanization of Siberia. As in the United States, the Russian government encouraged and aided this process, hoping to forestall Chinese pressures in the region and relieve growing population pressures in the more densely settled western lands of the empire.

Variations on a Theme: Industrialization in the United States and Russia

Not for long was the Industrial Revolution confined to Britain. It soon spread to continental Western Europe, and by the end of the nineteenth century, it was well under way in the United States, Russia, and Japan. The globalization of industrialization had begun. Everywhere it took hold, industrialization bore a range of broadly similar outcomes. New technologies and sources of energy generated vast increases in production and spawned an unprecedented urbanization as well. Class structures changed as aristocrats, artisans, and peasants declined as classes, while the middle classes and a factory working class grew in numbers and social prominence. Middle-class women generally withdrew from paid labor altogether, and their working-class counterparts sought to do so after marriage. Working women usually received lower wages than their male counterparts, had difficulty joining unions, and were accused of taking jobs from men. Working-class frustration and anger gave rise to trade unions and socialist movements, injecting a new element of social conflict into industrial societies.

Nevertheless, different histories, cultures, and societies ensured that the Industrial Revolution unfolded variously in the diverse countries in which it became established. Differences in the pace and timing of industrialization, the size and shape of major industries, the role of the state, the political expression of social conflict, and many other factors have made this process rich in comparative possibilities. French industrialization, for example, occurred more slowly and perhaps less disruptively than did that of Britain. Germany focused initially on heavy industry—iron, steel, and coal—rather than on the textile industry with which Britain had begun. Moreover, German industrialization was far more highly concentrated in huge companies called cartels, and it generated a rather more militant and Marxist-oriented labor movement than in Britain.

Nowhere were the variations in the industrializing process more apparent than in those two vast countries that lay on the periphery of Europe. To the west across the Atlantic Ocean was the United States, a young, vigorous, democratic, expanding country, populated largely by people of European descent, along with a substantial number of slaves of African origin. To the east was Russia, with its Eastern Orthodox Christianity, an autocratic tsar, a huge population of serfs, and an empire stretching across all of northern Asia. In the 1830s, the French observer Alexis de Tocqueville famously commented on these two emerging giants in his book *Democracy in America*:

> The Anglo-American relies upon personal interest to accomplish his ends and gives free scope to the unguided strength and common sense of the people; the Russian centers all the authority of society in a single arm. . . . Their starting-point is different and their courses are not the same; yet each of them seems marked out by the will of Heaven to sway the destinies of half the globe.

By the early twentieth century, his prediction seemed to be coming true. Industrialization had turned the United States into a major global power and in Russia had spawned an enormous revolutionary upheaval that made that country the first outpost of global communism.

The United States: Industrialization without Socialism

American industrialization began in the textile factories of New England during the 1820s but grew explosively in the half century following the Civil War (1861–1865) (see Map 17.3). The country's huge size, the ready availability of natural resources, its expanding domestic market, and its relative political stability combined to make the United States the world's leading industrial power by 1914. At that time, it produced 36 percent of the world's manufactured goods, compared to 16 percent for Germany, 14 percent for Great Britain, and 6 percent for France. Furthermore, U.S. industrialization was closely linked to that of Europe. About one-third of the capital investment that financed its remarkable growth came from British, French, and German capitalists. But unlike Latin America, which also received much foreign investment, the United States was able to use those funds to generate an independent Industrial Revolution of its own.

As in other second-wave industrializing countries, the U.S. government played an important role, though less directly than in Germany or Japan. Tax breaks, huge grants of public land to the railroad companies, laws enabling the easy formation of corporations, and the absence of much overt regulation of industry all fostered the rise of very large business enterprises. The U.S. Steel Corporation, for example, by 1901 had an annual budget three times the size of the federal government. In this respect, the United States followed the pattern of Germany but differed from that of France and Britain, where family businesses still predominated.

■ **Comparison**

What were the differences between industrialization in the United States and that in Russia?

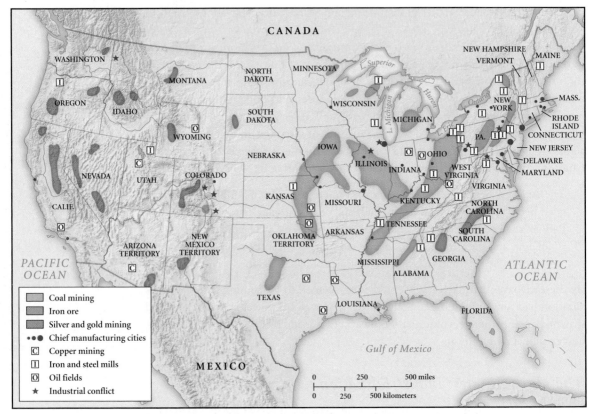

Map 17.3   The Industrial United States in 1900

By the early twentieth century, manufacturing industries were largely in the Northeast and Midwest, whereas mining operations were more widely scattered across the country.

■ **Explanation**

Why did Marxist socialism not take root in the United States?

The United States also pioneered techniques of mass production, using interchangeable parts, the assembly line, and "scientific management" to produce for a mass market. The nation's advertising agencies, Sears Roebuck's and Montgomery Ward's mail-order catalogs, and urban department stores generated a middle-class "culture of consumption." When the industrialist Henry Ford in the early twentieth century began producing the Model T at a price that many ordinary people could afford, he famously declared: "I am going to democratize the automobile." More so than in Europe, with its aristocratic traditions, self-made American industrialists of fabulous wealth such as Henry Ford, Andrew Carnegie, and John D. Rockefeller became cultural heroes, widely admired as models of what anyone could achieve with daring and hard work in a land of endless opportunity.

Nevertheless, well before the first Model T rolled off the assembly line, serious social divisions of a kind common to European industrial societies mounted. Preindustrial America had boasted of a relative social equality, quite unlike that of Europe, but by the end of the nineteenth century, a widening gap separated the classes. In

Carnegie's Homestead steel plant near Pittsburgh, employees worked every day except Christmas and the Fourth of July, often for twelve hours a day. In Manhattan, where millions of European immigrants disembarked, many lived in five- or six-story buildings with four families and two toilets on each floor. In every large city, such conditions prevailed close by the mansions of elite neighborhoods. To some, the contrast was a betrayal of American ideals, while others saw it as a natural outcome of competition and "the survival of the fittest."

As elsewhere, such conditions generated much labor protest, the formation of unions, and strikes, sometimes leading to violence. In 1877, when the eastern railroads announced a 10 percent wage cut for their workers, strikers disrupted rail service across the eastern half of the country, smashed equipment, and rioted. Both state militias and federal troops were called out to put down the movement. Class consciousness and class conflict were intense in the industrial America of the late nineteenth and early twentieth centuries.

Unlike many European countries, however, no major political party emerged in the United States to represent the interests of the working class. Nor did the ideas of socialism, and especially Marxism, appeal to American workers nearly as much as they did to European laborers. At its high point, the Socialist Party of America garnered just 6 percent of the vote for its presidential candidate in the 1912 election, whereas socialists at the time held more seats in Germany's Parliament than any other party. Even in the depths of the Great Depression of the 1930s, no major socialist movement emerged to champion American workers. How might we explain this distinctive feature of American industrial development?

One answer lies in the relative conservatism of major American union organizations, especially the American Federation of Labor. Its focus on skilled workers excluded the more radical unskilled laborers, and its refusal to align with any party limited its influence in the political arena. Furthermore, massive immigration from Europe, beginning in the 1840s, created a very diverse industrial labor force on top of the country's sharp racial divide. This diversity contrasted sharply with the more homogeneous populations of many European countries. Catholics and Protestants; whites and blacks; English, Irish, Germans, Slavs, Jews, and Italians—such differences undermined the class solidarity of American workers, making it far more difficult to sustain class-oriented political parties and a socialist labor movement. Moreover, the country's remarkable economic growth generated on average a higher standard of living for American workers than their European counterparts experienced. Land was cheaper, and home ownership was more available. Workers with property generally found socialism less attractive than those without. By 1910, a particularly large group of white-collar workers in sales, services, and offices outnumbered factory laborers. Their middle-class aspirations further diluted impulses toward radicalism.

But political challenges to the abuses of capitalist industrialization did arise. In the 1890s, among small farmers in the U.S. South, West, and Midwest, "populists" railed against banks, industrialists, monopolies, the existing money system, and both major political parties, all of which they thought were dominated by the corporate interests of the eastern elites. More successful, especially in the early twentieth century, were the Progressives, who pushed for specific reforms, such as wages-and-hours legislation, better sanitation standards, antitrust laws, and greater governmental intervention in the economy. Socialism, however, came to be defined as fundamentally "un-American" in a country that so valued individualism and so feared "big government." It was a distinctive feature of the American response to industrialization.

Russia: Industrialization and Revolution

As a setting for the Industrial Revolution, it would be hard to imagine two more different environments than the United States and Russia. If the United States was the Western world's most exuberant democracy during the nineteenth century, Russia remained the sole outpost of absolute monarchy, in which the state exercised far greater control over individuals and society than anywhere in the Western world.

At the beginning of the twentieth century, Russia still had no national parliament, no legal political parties, and no nationwide elections. The tsar, answerable to God alone, ruled unchecked. Furthermore, Russian society was dominated by a titled nobility of various ranks. Its upper levels included great landowners, who furnished the state with military officers and leading government officials. Until 1861, most Russians were peasant serfs, bound to the estates of their masters, subject to sale, greatly exploited, and largely at the mercy of their owners. A vast cultural gulf separated these two classes. Many nobles were highly Westernized, some speaking French better than Russian, whereas their serfs were steeped in a backwoods Orthodox Christianity that incorporated pre-Christian spirits, spells, curses, and magic.

■ **Change**

What factors contributed to the making of a revolutionary situation in Russia by the beginning of the twentieth century?

A further difference between Russia and the United States lay in the source of social and economic change. In the United States, such change bubbled up from society as free farmers, workers, and businessmen sought new opportunities and operated in a political system that gave them varying degrees of expression. In autocratic Russia, change was far more often initiated by the state itself, in its continuing efforts to catch up with the more powerful and innovative states of Europe. This kind of "transformation from above" found an early expression in the reign of Peter the Great (r. 1689–1725). (See Chapter 13, p. 638.) Such state-directed change continued in the nineteenth century with the freeing of the serfs in 1861, an action stimulated by military defeat at the hands of British and French forces in the Crimean War (1854–1856). To many thoughtful Russians, serfdom seemed incompatible with modern civilization and held back the country's overall development, as did its economic and industrial backwardness. Thus, beginning in the 1860s, Russia began a program of industrial development, which was more heavily directed by the state than was the case in Western Europe or the United States.

By the 1890s, Russia's Industrial Revolution was launched and growing rapidly. It focused particularly on railroads and heavy industry and was fueled by a substantial amount of foreign investment. By 1900, Russia ranked fourth in the world in steel production and had major industries in coal, textiles, and oil. Its industrial enterprises, still modest in comparison to those of Europe, were concentrated in a few major cities—Moscow, St. Petersburg, and Kiev, for example—and took place in factories far larger than in most of Western Europe.

All of this contributed to the explosive social outcomes of Russian industrialization. A growing middle class of businessmen and professionals increasingly took shape. As modern and educated people, many in the middle class objected strongly to the deep conservatism of tsarist Russia and sought a greater role in political life,

Russian Serfdom
This nineteenth-century cartoon by the French artist Gustave Doré shows Russian noblemen gambling with tied bundles of stiff serfs. Serfdom was not finally abolished in Russia until 1861. (The Granger Collection, New York)

but they were also dependent on the state for contracts and jobs and for suppressing the growing radicalism of the workers, which they greatly feared. Although factory workers constituted only about 5 percent of Russia's total population, they quickly developed a radical class consciousness, based on harsh conditions and the absence of any legal outlet for their grievances. As in Western Europe, millions flocked to the new centers of industrial development. By 1897, over 70 percent of the population in Moscow and St. Petersburg were recent migrants from the rural areas. Their conditions of life resembled those of industrial migrants in New York or Berlin. One observer wrote that "people live in impossible condition: filth, stench, suffocating heat. They lie down together barely a few feet apart; there is no division between the sexes and adults sleep with children."[28] Until 1897, a thirteen-hour working day was common, while ruthless discipline and overt disrespect from supervisors created resentment. In the absence of legal unions or political parties, these grievances often erupted in the form of large-scale strikes.

In these conditions, a small but growing number of educated Russians found in Marxist socialism a way of understanding the changes they witnessed daily as well as hope for the future in a revolutionary upheaval of workers. In 1898, they created an illegal Russian Social-Democratic Labor Party and quickly became involved in workers' education, union organizing, and, eventually, revolutionary action. By the early twentieth century, the strains of rapid change and the state's continued intransigence had reached the bursting point, and in 1905, following its defeat in a naval war with Japan, Russia erupted in spontaneous insurrection. (See Map 17.4) Workers in Moscow and St. Petersburg went on strike and created their own representative councils, called soviets. Peasant uprisings, student demonstrations, revolts of non-Russian nationalities, and mutinies in the military all contributed to the upheaval. Recently formed political parties, representing intellectuals of various persuasions, came out into the open.

Map 17.4   Industrialization and Revolution in Russia
Only in Russia did industrialization lead to violent revolutionary upheavals, both in 1905 and more successfully in 1917.

The 1905 revolution, though brutally suppressed, forced the tsar's regime to make more substantial reforms than it had ever contemplated. It granted a constitution, legalized both trade unions and political parties, and permitted the election of a national assembly, called the Duma. Censorship was eased, and plans were under way for universal primary education. Industrial development likewise continued at a rapid rate, so that by 1914 Russia stood fifth in the world in terms of overall output. But in the first half of that year, some 1,250,000 workers, representing about 40 percent of the entire industrial workforce, went out on strike.

Thus the tsar's limited political reforms, which had been granted with great reluctance and were often reversed in practice, failed to tame working-class radicalism or to bring social stability to Russia. In Russian political life, the people generally, and even the middle class, had only a very limited voice. Representatives of even the privileged classes had become so alienated by the government's intransigence that many felt revolution was inevitable. Various revolutionary groups, many of them socialist, published pamphlets and newspapers, organized trade unions, and spread their messages among workers and peasants. Particularly in the cities, these revolutionary parties had an impact. They provided a language through which workers could express their grievances; they created links among workers from different factories; and they furnished leaders who were able to act when the revolutionary moment arrived.

World War I provided that moment. The enormous hardships of that war, coupled with the immense social tensions of industrialization within a still autocratic political system, sparked the Russian Revolution of 1917 (see Chapter 21). That massive upheaval quickly brought to power the most radical of the socialist groups operating in the country—the Bolsheviks, led by the charismatic Vladimir Ilyich Ulyanov, better known as Lenin. Only in Russia was industrialization associated with violent social revolution. This was the most distinctive feature of Russia's modern historical development. And only in Russia was a socialist political party, inspired by the teachings of Karl Marx, able to seize power, thus launching the modern world's first socialist society, with enormous implications for the twentieth century.

SUMMING UP SO FAR

What was common to industrialization everywhere, and in what ways did it vary from place to place?

The Industrial Revolution and Latin America in the Nineteenth Century

Beyond the world of Europe and North America, only Japan underwent a major industrial transformation during the nineteenth century, part of that country's overall response to the threat of European aggression. (See Chapter 19, pp. 952–53, for a more detailed examination of Japan's industrialization.) Elsewhere—in colonial India, Egypt, the Ottoman Empire, China, and Latin America—very modest experiments in modern industry were undertaken, but nowhere did they drive the kind of major social transformation that had taken place in Britain, Europe, North America, and Japan. However, even in societies that did not experience their own Industrial Revolution, the profound impact of European and North American industrialization was hard to avoid. Such was the case in Latin America during the nineteenth century.

After Independence in Latin America

The struggle for independence in Latin America had lasted far longer and proved far more destructive than in North America. Decimated populations, diminished herds of livestock, flooded or closed silver mines, abandoned farms, shrinking international trade and investment capital, and empty national treasuries—these were among the conditions under which Latin American countries greeted independence. Furthermore, the four major administrative units (vice-royalties) of Spanish America ultimately dissolved into eighteen separate countries, and regional revolts wracked Brazil in the early decades of its independent life. A number of international wars in the post-independence century likewise shook these new nations. Peru and Bolivia briefly united and then broke apart in a bitter conflict (1836–1839); Mexico lost huge territories to the United States (1846–1848); and an alliance of Argentina, Brazil, and Uruguay went to war with Paraguay (1864–1870) in a conflict that devastated Paraguay's small population.

Within these new countries, political life was turbulent and unstable. Conservatives favored centralized authority and sought to maintain the social status quo of the colonial era in alliance with the Catholic Church, which at independence owned perhaps half of all productive land. Their often bitter opponents were liberals, who attacked the Church in the name of Enlightenment values, sought at least modest social reforms, and preferred federalism. In many countries, conflicts between these factions, often violent, enabled military strongmen known as *caudillos* (kaw-DEE-yos) to achieve power as defenders of order and property, although they too succeeded one another with great frequency. One of them, Antonio López de Santa Anna of Mexico, was president of his country at least nine separate times between 1833 and 1855. Constitutions too replaced one another with bewildering speed. Bolivia had ten constitutions during the nineteenth century, while Ecuador and Peru each had eight.

Social life did not change fundamentally in the aftermath of independence. As in Europe and North America, women remained disenfranchised and wholly outside of formal political life. Slavery, it is true, was abolished in most of Latin America by midcentury, although it persisted in both Brazil and Cuba until the late 1880s. Most of the legal distinctions among various racial categories also disappeared, and all free people were considered, at least officially, equal citizens. Nevertheless, productive economic resources such as businesses, ranches, and plantations remained overwhelmingly in the hands of creole white men, who were culturally oriented toward Europe. The military provided an avenue of mobility for a few skilled and ambitious mestizo men, some of whom subsequently became caudillos. Other mixed-race men and women found a place in a small middle class as teachers, shopkeepers, or artisans. The vast majority — blacks, Indians, and many mixed-race people of both sexes — remained impoverished, working small subsistence farms or laboring in the mines or on the *haciendas* (ah-see-EHN-duhz) (plantations) of the well-to-do. Only rarely did the poor and dispossessed actively rebel against their social betters. One such case was the Caste War of Yucatán (1847–1901), a prolonged struggle of the Maya people of Mexico, aimed at cleansing their land of European and mestizo intruders.

Facing the World Economy

■ **Connection**

In what ways and with what impact was Latin America linked to the global economy of the nineteenth century?

During the second half of the nineteenth century, a measure of political consolidation took hold in Latin America, and countries such as Mexico, Peru, and Argentina entered periods of greater stability. At the same time, Latin America as a whole became more closely integrated into a world economy driven by the industrialization of Western Europe and North America. The new technology of the steamship cut the sailing time between Britain and Argentina almost in half, while the underwater telegraph instantly brought the latest news and fashions of Europe to Latin America.

The most significant economic outcome of this growing integration was a rapid growth of Latin American exports to the industrializing countries, which now needed the food products, raw materials, and markets of these new nations. Latin American landowners, businessmen, and governments proved eager to supply those needs, and in the sixty years or so after 1850, an export boom increased the value of Latin American goods sold abroad by a factor of ten.

Mexico continued to produce large amounts of silver, supplying more than half the world's new supply until 1860. Now added to the list of raw materials flowing out of Latin America were copper from Chile, a metal that the growing electrical industry required; tin from Bolivia, which met the mounting demand for tin cans; and nitrates from Chile and guano (bird droppings) from Peru, both of which were used for fertilizer. Wild rubber from the Amazon rain forest was in great demand for bicycle and automobile tires, as was sisal from Mexico, used to make binder twine for the proliferating mechanical harvesters of North America. Bananas from Central America, beef from Argentina, cacao from Ecuador, coffee from Brazil and Guatemala, and sugar from Cuba also found eager markets in the rapidly growing and increasingly prosperous world of industrializing countries. In return for these primary products, Latin Americans imported the textiles, machinery, tools, weapons, and luxury goods of Europe and the United States (see Map 17.5).

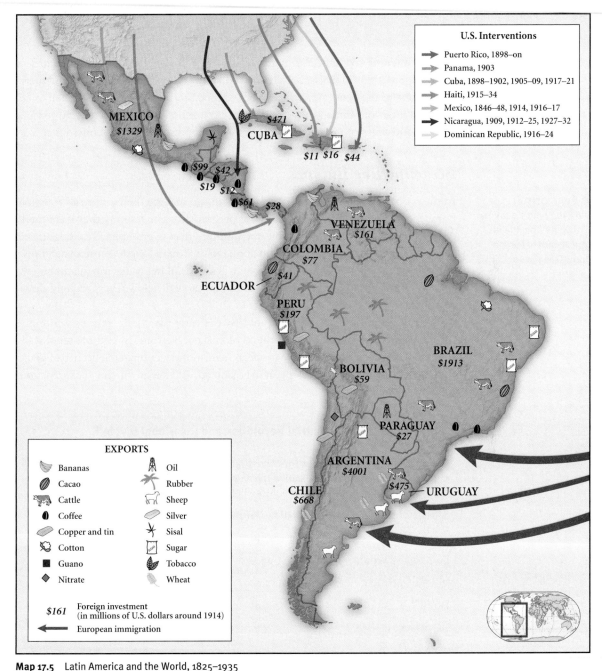

Map 17.5 Latin America and the World, 1825–1935

During the nineteenth and early twentieth centuries, Latin American countries interacted with the industrializing world via investment, trade, immigration, and military intervention from the United States.

Accompanying this burgeoning commerce was large-scale investment of European capital in Latin America, $10 billion alone between 1870 and 1919. Most of this capital came from Great Britain, which invested more in Argentina in the late nineteenth century than in its colony of India, although France, Germany, Italy, and the United States also contributed to this substantial financial transfer. By 1910, U.S.

business interests controlled 40 percent of Mexican property and produced half of its oil. Much of this capital was used to build railroads, largely to funnel Latin American exports to the coast, where they were shipped to overseas markets. Mexico had only 390 miles of railroad in 1876; it had 15,000 miles in 1910. By 1915, Argentina, with 22,000 miles of railroad, had more track per person than the United States.

Becoming like Europe?

■ **Comparison**
Did Latin America follow or diverge from the historical path of Europe during the nineteenth century?

To the economic elites of Latin America, intent on making their countries resemble Europe or the United States, all of this was progress. In some respects, they were surely right. Economies were growing, producing more than ever before. The population also was burgeoning; it increased from about 30 million in 1850 to more than 77 million in 1912 as public health measures (such as safe drinking water, inoculations, sewers, and campaigns to eliminate mosquitoes that carried yellow fever) brought down death rates.

Urbanization also proceeded rapidly. By the early twentieth century, wrote one scholar, "Latin American cities lost their colonial cobblestones, white-plastered walls, and red-tiled roofs. They became modern metropolises, comparable to urban giants anywhere. Streetcars swayed, telephones jangled, and silent movies flickered from

Snapshot   **The Industrial Revolution and the Global Divide**[29]

During the nineteenth century, the Industrial Revolution generated an enormous and unprecedented economic division in the world, as measured by the share of manufacturing output. What patterns can you see in this table?

SHARE OF TOTAL WORLD MANUFACTURING OUTPUT (PERCENT)

	1750	1800	1860	1880	1900
Europe as a Whole	23.2	28.1	53.2	61.3	62.0
UNITED KINGDOM	1.9	4.3	19.9	22.9	18.5
FRANCE	4.0	4.2	7.9	7.8	6.8
GERMANY	2.9	3.5	4.9	8.5	13.2
RUSSIA	5.0	5.6	7.0	7.6	8.8
United States	0.1	0.8	7.2	14.7	23.6
Japan	3.8	3.5	2.6	2.4	2.4
The Rest of the World	73.0	67.7	36.6	20.9	11.0
CHINA	32.8	33.3	19.7	12.5	6.2
SOUTH ASIA (INDIA/PAKISTAN)	24.5	19.7	8.6	2.8	1.7

Montevideo and Santiago to Mexico City and Havana."[30] Buenos Aires, Argentina's metropolitan center, boasted 750,000 people in 1900 and billed itself the "Paris of South America." There the educated elite, just like the English, drank tea in the afternoon, while discussing European literature, philosophy, and fashion, usually in French.

To become more like Europe, Latin America sought to attract more Europeans. Because civilization, progress, and modernity apparently derived from Europe, many Latin American countries actively sought to increase their "white" populations by deliberately recruiting impoverished Europeans with the promise, mostly unfulfilled, of a new and prosperous life in the New World. Argentina received the largest wave of European immigrants (some 2.5 million between 1870 and 1915), mostly from Spain and Italy. Brazil and Uruguay likewise attracted substantial numbers of European newcomers.

Only a quite modest segment of Latin American society saw any great benefits from the export boom and all that followed from it. Upper-class landowners certainly gained as exports flourished and their property values soared. Middle-class urban dwellers—merchants, office workers, lawyers, and other professionals—also grew in numbers and prosperity as their skills proved valuable in a modernizing society. As a percentage of the total population, however, these were narrow elites. In Mexico in the mid-1890s, for example, the landowning upper class made up no more than 1 percent and the middle classes perhaps 8 percent of the population. Everyone else was lower-class, and most of them were impoverished.[31]

A new but quite small segment of this vast lower class emerged among urban workers who labored in the railroads, ports, mines, and a few factories. They organized themselves initially in a variety of mutual aid societies, but by the end of the nineteenth century, they were creating unions and engaging in strikes. To authoritarian governments interested in stability and progress, such activity was highly provocative and threatening, and they acted harshly to crush or repress unions and strikes. In 1906, the Mexican dictator Porfirio Díaz invited the Arizona Rangers to suppress a strike at Cananea near the U.S. border, an action that resulted in dozens of deaths. The following year in the Chilean city of Iquique, more than 1,000 men, women, and children were slaughtered by police when nitrate miners protested their wages and working conditions.

The vast majority of the lower class lived in rural areas, where they suffered the most and benefited the least from the export boom. Government attacks on communal landholding and peasant indebtedness to wealthy landowners combined to push many farmers off their land or into remote and poor areas where they could barely make a living. Many wound up as dependent laborers or peons on the haciendas of the wealthy, where their wages were often too meager to support a family. Thus women and children, who had earlier remained at home to tend the family plot, were required to join their menfolk as field laborers. Many immigrant Italian farmworkers in Argentina and Brazil were unable to acquire their own farms, as they had expected, and so drifted into the growing cities or returned to Italy.

Although local protests and violence were frequent, only in Mexico did these vast inequalities erupt into a nationwide revolution. There, in the early twentieth century, middle-class reformers joined with workers and peasants to overthrow the long dictatorship of Porfirio Díaz (1876–1911). What followed was a decade of bloody conflict (1910–1920) that cost Mexico some 1 million lives, or roughly 10 percent of the population. Huge peasant armies under charismatic leaders such as Pancho Villa and Emiliano Zapata helped oust Díaz. Intent on seizing land and redistributing it to the peasants, they then went on to attack many of Mexico's large haciendas. But unlike the later Russian and Chinese revolutions, in which the most radical elements seized state power, Villa and Zapata proved unable to do so on a long-term basis, in part because they were hobbled by factionalism and focused on local or regional issues. Despite this limitation and its own internal conflicts, the Mexican Revolution transformed the country. When the dust settled, Mexico had a new constitution (1917) that proclaimed universal male suffrage; provided for the redistribution of land; stripped the Catholic Church of any role in public education and forbade it to own land; announced unheard-of rights for workers, such as a minimum wage and an eight-hour workday; and placed restrictions on foreign ownership of property. Much of Mexico's history in the twentieth century involved working out the implications of these nationalist and reformist changes. The revolution's direct influence, however, was largely limited to Mexico itself and a few places in Central America and the Andes, but without the wider international impact of the Russian and Chinese upheavals.

The Mexican Revolution
Women were active participants in the Mexican Revolution. They prepared food, nursed the wounded, washed clothes, and at times served as soldiers on the battlefield, as illustrated in this cover image from a French magazine in 1913. (© Archivo Iconografico, S.A./Corbis)

Perhaps the most significant outcome of the export boom lay in what did *not* happen, for nowhere in Latin America did it jump-start a thorough Industrial Revolution, despite a few factories that processed foods or manufactured textiles, clothing, and building materials. The reasons are many. A social structure that relegated some 90 percent of its population to an impoverished lower class generated only a very small market for manufactured goods. Moreover, economically powerful groups such as landowners and cattlemen benefited greatly from exporting agricultural products and had little incentive to invest in manufacturing. Domestic manufacturing enterprises could only have competed with cheaper and higher-quality foreign goods if they had been protected for a time by high tariffs. But Latin American political leaders had thoroughly embraced the popular European doctrine of prosperity through free trade, and many governments depended on taxing imports to fill their treasuries.

Instead of its own Industrial Revolution, Latin Americans developed a form of economic growth that was largely financed by capital from abroad and dependent on European and North American prosperity and decisions. Brazil experienced this kind of dependence when its booming rubber industry suddenly collapsed in 1910–1911, after seeds from the wild rubber tree had been illegally exported to Britain and were used to start competing and cheaper rubber plantations in Malaysia.

Later critics saw this "dependent development" as a new form of colonialism, expressed in the power exercised by foreign investors. The influence of the U.S.-owned United Fruit Company in Central America was a case in point. Allied with large land-owners and compliant politicians, the company pressured the governments of these "banana republics" to maintain conditions favorable to U.S. business. This indirect or behind-the-scenes imperialism was supplemented by repeated U.S. military intervention in support of American corporate interests in Cuba, Haiti, the Dominican Republic, Nicaragua, and Mexico. The United States also controlled the Panama Canal and acquired Puerto Rico as a territory in the aftermath of the Spanish-American War (see Map 17.5, p. 855).

Thus, despite Latin America's domination by people of European descent and its close ties to the industrializing countries of the Atlantic world, that region's historical trajectory in the nineteenth century diverged considerably from that of Europe and North America.

LearningCurve
bedfordstmartins.com
/strayer/LC

Reflections: History and Horse Races

Historians and students of history seem endlessly fascinated by "firsts"—the first breakthrough to agriculture, the first domestication of horses, the first civilization, the first use of gunpowder, the first printing press, and so on. Each of these firsts presents a problem of explanation: why did it occur in some particular time and place rather than somewhere else or at some other time? Such questions have assumed historical significance because "first achievements" represent something new in the human journey and because many of them conveyed unusual power, wealth, status, or influence on their creators.

Nonetheless, the focus on firsts can be misleading as well. Those who accomplished something first may see themselves as generally superior to those who embraced that innovation later. Historians too can sometimes adopt a winners-and-losers mentality, inviting a view of history as a horse race toward some finish line of accomplishment. Most first achievements in history, however, were not the result of intentional efforts but rather were the unexpected outcome of converging circumstances.

The Industrial Revolution is a case in point. Understanding the European beginnings of this immense breakthrough is certainly justified by its pervasive global consequences and its global spread over the past several centuries. In terms of human ability to dominate the natural environment and to extract wealth from it, the Industrial Revolution marks a decisive turning point in the history of our species. But Europeans' attempts to explain their Industrial Revolution have at times stated or implied their own unique genius. In the nineteenth century, many Europeans saw their technological mastery as a sure sign of their cultural and racial superiority as they came to use "machines as the measure of men."[32] In pondering the "why Europe?" question, historians too have sometimes sought an answer in some distinct or even superior feature of European civilization.

In emphasizing the unexpectedness of the first Industrial Revolution, and the global context within which it occurred, world historians have attempted to avoid a "history as horse race" outlook. Clearly the first industrial breakthrough in Britain was not a self-conscious effort to win a race; it was the surprising outcome of countless decisions by many people to further their own interests. Subsequently, however, other societies and their governments quite deliberately tried to catch up, seeking the wealth and power that the Industrial Revolution promised.

The rapid spread of industrialization across the planet, though highly uneven, may diminish the importance of the "why Europe?" issue. Just as no one views agriculture as a Middle Eastern phenomenon, even though it occurred first in that region, it seems likely that industrialization will be seen increasingly as a global process rather than one uniquely associated with Europe. If industrial society proves to be a sustainable future for humankind—and this is presently an open question—historians of the future may well be more interested in the pattern of its global spread and in efforts to cope with its social and environmental consequences than with its origins in Western Europe.

Second Thoughts

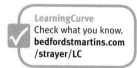

LearningCurve
Check what you know.
**bedfordstmartins.com
/strayer/LC**

Online Study Guide
bedfordstmartins.com
/highschool/strayer

What's the Significance?

steam engine, 830
Indian cotton textiles, 831
middle-class values, 837–38
lower middle class, 838
Ellen Johnston, 840–41
Karl Marx, 842–44

Labour Party, 844
socialism in the United
    States, 849–50
Progressives, 850
Russian Revolution of
    1905, 851–52

caudillos, 853
Latin American export
    boom, 854–56
Mexican Revolution, 858
dependent development, 859

Big Picture Questions

1. What did humankind gain from the Industrial Revolution, and what did it lose?

2. In what ways might the Industrial Revolution be understood as a global rather than simply a European phenomenon?

3. How might you situate the Industrial Revolution in the long history of humankind? How do you think the material covered in this chapter will be viewed 50, 100, or 200 years into the future?

4. **Looking Back:** How did the Industrial Revolution interact with the Scientific Revolution and the French Revolution to generate Europe's modern transformation?

Next Steps: For Further Study

John Charles Chasteen, *Born in Blood and Fire* (2006). A lively and well-written account of Latin America's turbulent history since the sixteenth century.

Jack Gladstone, *Why Europe? The Rise of the West in World History, 1500–1850* (2009). An original synthesis of recent research provided by a leading world historian.

David S. Landes, *The Wealth and Poverty of Nations* (1998). An argument that culture largely shapes the possibilities for industrialization and economic growth.

Robert B. Marks, *The Origins of the Modern World* (2007). An effective summary of new thinking about the origins of European industrialization.

Peter Stearns, *The Industrial Revolution in World History* (1998). A global and comparative perspective on the Industrial Revolution.

Peter Waldron, *The End of Imperial Russia, 1855–1917* (1997). A brief account of Russian history during its early industrialization.

Bridging World History, Units 18 and 19, http://www.learner.org/channel/courses/worldhistory. An innovative world history Web site that provides pictures, video, and text dealing with "Rethinking the Rise of the West" and "Global Industrialization."

For Web sites and additional documents related to this chapter, see **Make History** at bedfordstmartins.com /highschool/strayer.

Documents

Considering the Evidence:
Experiencing Industrialization

The immense economic and social transformations of the Industrial Revolution left almost no one untouched in those societies that experienced it most fully. Its impact unfolded gradually and varied greatly across social classes; among men, women, and children; and over time. In seeking to understand how individuals experienced and responded to this unprecedented transformation, historians have at their disposal a wealth of evidence, both documentary and visual. Each of the documents in this section evokes a particular experience or understanding of industrialization in its early stages. In the Visual Sources feature that follows, the images also offer a range of perceptions, while the Portrait of Ellen Johnston (see pp. 840–41) provides yet another perspective. Taken together, these sources offer rich material for reflecting on this decisive turning point in the human journey.

Document 17.1

The Experience of an English Factory Worker

The early Industrial Revolution represented not only a technological breakthrough of epic proportions but also a transformation in the organization of work, expressed most fully in the factory. Unlike the artisan's workshop, which it largely replaced, the factory concentrated human labor in a single place and separated workers from the final product by assigning them highly specialized and repetitive tasks. In the name of efficiency and productivity, owners and managers imposed strict discipline in their factories and regulated workers' lives according to clock time. Finally, workers were wage earners, dependent on a modest and uncertain income for their economic survival. One such worker was Elizabeth Bentley, a twenty-three-year-old woman, who testified in 1831 before a British parliamentary committee investigating conditions in textile mills. A subsequent inquiry elicited testimony from William Harter, a mill owner. As a result of these investigations, legislation in 1833 limited the hours of employment for women and children.

■ Child labor was nothing new, for children had long worked in the fields and workshops of pre-industrial Europe. What was different about the conditions under which children worked in early industrial factories?

■ Why do you think the investigator queried Elizabeth specifically about the treatment of girls?

■ Compare this description of factory work with the images contained in Visual Sources 17.2 and 17.3 on pp. 873–74. How might Elizabeth Bentley have responded to these images?

■ How does William Harter's testimony explain the willingness of factory owners to impose these conditions on their workers? How might he respond to Elizabeth Bentley's testimony?

Elizabeth Bentley, Factory Worker

Testimony
1831

What age are you?—Twenty-three.

Where do you live?—At Leeds.

What time did you begin to work at a factory?—When I was six years old.

What kind of mill is it?—Flax-mill.

What was your business in that mill?—I was a little doffer [cleaner of the machines].

What were your hours of labour in that mill?—From 5 in the morning till 9 at night, when they were thronged [busy].

For how long a time together have you worked that excessive length of time?—For about half a year.

What were your usual hours when you were not so thronged?—From 6 in the morning till 7 at night.

What time was allowed for your meals?—Forty minutes at noon.

Had you any time to get your breakfast or drinking?—No, we got it as we could.

Explain what it is you had to do?—When the frames are full, they have to stop the frames, and take the flyers off, and take the full bobbins off, and carry them to the roller; and then put empty ones on, and set the frame going again.

Does that keep you constantly on your feet?—Yes, there are so many frames, and they run so quick.

Suppose you flagged a little, or were too late, what would they do?—Strap us.

Are they in the habit of strapping those who are last in doffing?—Yes.

Constantly?—Yes.

Girls as well as boys?—Yes.

Have you ever been strapped?—Yes.

Severely?—Yes.

Were the girls struck so as to leave marks upon their skin?—Yes, they have had black marks many times, and their parents dare not come to him about it, they were afraid of losing their work.

Could you eat your food well in that factory?—No, indeed I had not much to eat, and the little I had I could not eat it, my appetite was so poor, and being covered with dust; and it was no use to take it home, I could not eat it, and the overlooker took it, and gave it to the pigs.

How far had you to go for dinner?—We could not go home to dinner.

Where did you dine?—In the mill.

Source: *British Sessional Papers*, Vol. 15 (London, 1832), 195196; Vol. 21, pt. D-3 (London, 1833), 2628.

Did you live far from the mill?—Yes, two miles.

Supposing you had not been in time enough in the morning at these mills, what would have been the consequence?—We should have been quartered. If we were a quarter of an hour too late, they would take off half an hour; we only got a penny an hour, and they would take a halfpenny more.

Were you also beaten for being too late?—No, I was never beaten myself, I have seen the boys beaten for being too late.

Were you generally there in time?—Yes; my mother had been up at 4 o'clock in the morning, and at 2 o'clock in the morning; the colliers used to go to their work about 3 or 4 o'clock, and when she heard them stirring she has got up out of her warm bed, and gone out and asked them the time; and I have sometimes been at Hunslet Car at 2 o'clock in the morning, when it was streaming down with rain, and we have had to stay until the mill was opened.

WILLIAM HARTER, MILL OWNER
Testimony
1832

What effect would it have on your manufacture to reduce the hours of labor to ten?—It would instantly much reduce the value of my mill and machinery, and consequently far prejudice my manufacture. . . . To produce the same quantity of work under a ten-hours bill will require an additional outlay of 3,000 or 4,000 pounds; therefore a ten-hours bill would impose upon me the necessity of this additional outlay in such perishable property as buildings and machinery, or I must be content to relinquish one-sixth portion of my business.

Document 17.2
A Weaver's Lament

As industrialization generated new work in the factories, it also destroyed older means of livelihood, particularly that of skilled artisans. By the early 1860s, the silk weavers of Coventry, England, a long-established and previously thriving group of artisans, were in desperate straits, owing in part to a decline in the fashion of wearing silk ribbons. Many individual weavers had to sell their looms to the larger manufacturers who were organizing more efficient production in factories. The song that follows was sung by unemployed weavers as they paraded through the streets of Coventry on their way to relief work, often in stone quarries. It reflects the costs of the Industrial Revolution for a body of proud and skilled artisans and their distress at an economic system that seemed to cast them adrift.

- Who or what does the song blame for the plight of the weavers?

- What does the song mean by mentioning the "commercial plan" and "political economy"? And how do you understand the line "He's only a weaver that no one owns"?

- What does the song imply about the contrast between the former life of these weavers and their present circumstances?

- How might you compare the life of an unemployed weaver with that of a factory worker like Elizabeth Bentley?

Only a Weaver
1860s

Who is that man coming up the street
With weary manner and shuffling feet;
With a face that tells of care and grief
And in hope that seems to have lost belief.
For wickedness past he now atones
He's only a weaver that no one owns.

He's coming no doubt from breaking stones
With saddened heart and aching bones.
But why should he grumble, he gets good pay
A loaf and six pence every day.
He thought if he worked both night and day

He ought to receive equivalent pay;
But he's just an inconsistent man
Who doesn't understand the commercial plan.

Political economy now must sway
And say when a man shall work or play.
If he's wanted his wages may be high
If he isn't, why then, he may starve and die.

If you employ him, don't mend the price
He's starving, you know and has no choice—
And give him to weave the worst of silk
For it's only a weaver's time you bilk . . .
Yet take no heed of his sighs and groans
His careworn face, his agonized moans;
For wickedness past he now atones
He's only a weaver that no one owns.

Source: Joseph Gutteridge, *Light and Shadows in the Life of an Artisan* (1893), 153, abridged and adapted in *Poverty Knock*, edited by Roy Palmer (New York: Cambridge University Press, 1974), 24.

Document 17.3

A Middle-Class Understanding of the Industrial Poor

If Elizabeth Bentley and the unemployed weavers of Coventry might be forgiven for not appreciating the wonders of industrialization, many in the growing middle classes of nineteenth-century Europe certainly did. Perhaps the most prominent expression of middle-class values and aspirations came from Samuel Smiles (1812–1904), a Scottish writer and businessman, whose bestselling book *Self-Help* extolled individual effort, discipline, morality, and hard work as a guaranteed path to personal success. In a subsequent work titled *Thrift*, he sought to explain the paradox of industrial wealth and widespread poverty.

- What is Smiles's explanation for poverty amid plenty?

- What hope does he hold out for improving the condition of the industrial poor?

- How might Elizabeth Bentley and the weavers of Coventry respond to Smiles's analysis?

- Why might middle-class men and women appreciate Smiles's point of view? In what ways might they find it offensive?

SAMUEL SMILES

Thrift

1875

England is one of the richest countries in the world. Our merchants are enterprising, our manufacturers are industrious, our labourers are hard-working. There is an accumulation of wealth in the country to which past times can offer no parallel. The Bank is gorged with gold. There never was more food in the empire; there never was more money. There is no end to our manufacturing productions, for the steam-engine never tires. And yet notwithstanding all this wealth, there is an enormous mass of poverty. Close alongside the Wealth of Nations [a famous book by Adam Smith in 1776], there gloomily stalks the Misery of Nations,—luxurious ease resting upon a dark background of wretchedness.

Parliamentary reports have again and again revealed to us the miseries endured by certain portions of our working population. They have described the people employed in factories, workshops, mines, and brickfields, as well as in the pursuits of country life. We have tried to grapple with the evils of their condition by legislation, but it seems to mock us. . . . Thus the Haves and the Have-nots, the opulent and the indigent, stand at the two extremes of the social scale, and a wide gulf is fixed between them.

Much of the existing misery is caused by selfishness—by the greed to accumulate wealth on the one hand, and by improvidence on the other. . . . High profits are regarded as the *summum bonum*

[highest good]—no matter how obtained, or at what sacrifice. Money is our god. . . . With respect to the poorer classes,—what has become of them in the midst of our so-called civilization? An immense proportion of them remain entirely uncivilized. Though living in a Christian country, Christianity has never reached them. . . . They work, eat, drink, and sleep: that constitutes their life. They think nothing of providing for to-morrow, or for next week, or for next year. . . . In these respects, they resemble the savage tribes, who know no better, and do no worse. Like the North American Indians, they debase themselves by the vices which accompany civilization, but make no use whatever of its benefits and advantages.

Hence, the skilled workman, unless trained in good habits, may exhibit no higher a life than that of the mere animal; and the earning of increased wages will only furnish him with increased means for indulging in the gratification of his grosser appetites. . . . This habitual improvidence—though of course there are many admirable exceptions—is the real cause of the social degradation of the artisan. . . . But the misery is entirely the result of human ignorance and self-indulgence. . . . Misery is the result of moral causes, most commonly of individual vice and improvidence. . . . Everything that is wrong in Society results from that which is wrong in the Individual. When men are bad, society is bad. . . . [I]t is perfectly clear that people who live from day to day without plan, without rule, without forethought—who spend all their earnings, without saving anything for the future—are preparing beforehand for inevitable

Source: Samuel Smiles, *Thrift* (London: John Murray, 1875; Project Gutenberg, 2004), chap. 3, http://www .gutenberg.org/ebooks/14418.

distress....What hope can there be for a people whose only maxim seems to be, "Let us eat and drink, for to-morrow we die"?

All this may seem very hopeless; yet it is not entirely so. The large earnings of the working classes is an important point to start with. The gradual diffusion of education will help them to use, and not abuse, their means of comfortable living. The more extended knowledge of the uses of economy, frugality, and thrift will help them to spend their lives more soberly, virtuously, and religiously....Surely it ought not to be so difficult to put an end to the Satanic influences of thriftlessness, drunkenness, and improvidence!

Document 17.4

Socialism According to Marx

If Samuel Smiles reflected a middle-class response to the Industrial Revolution, the most prominent advocate for the new factory working class was Karl Marx (1818–1883). No worker himself, Marx was born to a wealthy middle-class family in what is now Germany and became a radical intellectual and journalist. Chased out of Germany and later France for his political ideas and activities, Marx found a refuge in London in 1849, where he lived until his death. In his new home, Marx pursued both a political life devoted to organizing workers for revolution and, more importantly for world history, an intellectual life studying the evolution of capitalism during the industrial age. One of the most influential thinkers of the modern era, Marx provided the ideas that informed much of European socialism in the nineteenth century and world communism in the twentieth.

Marx's life coincided with the harshest phase of capitalist industrialization in Europe. At that time an encompassing market economy was rudely shattering older institutions and traditions, but the benefits of this new and highly productive system were not yet widely shared. In this brutal process, Marx discerned the inevitable approach of a new world order. Document 17.4 presents excerpts from the most famous of Marx's writings, the *Communist Manifesto*, first published in 1848. In this effort and throughout much of his life, Marx was assisted by another German thinker, Friedrich Engels (1820–1895), the son of a successful textile manufacturer who had become radicalized as he witnessed the devastating social results of capitalist industrialization.

Marx and Engels's *Manifesto* begins by placing the modern industrial era into a larger world historical framework. Much of the document then analyzes what the authors call the "bourgeoisie" or the "bourgeois epoch," terms that refer to the age of industrial capitalism.

- How do Marx and Engels understand the motor of change in human history? How do they view the role of class?

- Notice that Marx and Engels have much that is positive to say about capitalism. What do they see as its major achievements? And why then do they believe that the capitalist system is doomed?

■ Which of Marx and Engels's descriptions and predictions ring true even now? In what respects was their analysis disproved by later developments?

■ By what process do Marx and Engels think that capitalism will collapse and socialism emerge? How do they describe that postcapitalist socialist society?

Karl Marx and Friedrich Engels
The Communist Manifesto
1848

The history of all hitherto existing society is the history of class struggles. Freeman and slave, patrician and plebeian, lord and serf, guild-master and journeyman, in a word, oppressor and oppressed, stood in constant opposition to one another, carried on an uninterrupted, now hidden, now open fight, a fight that each time ended, either in a revolutionary reconstitution of society at large, or in the common ruin of the contending classes. . . .

Our epoch, the epoch of the bourgeoisie, possesses, however, this distinct feature: it has simplified class antagonisms. Society as a whole is more and more splitting up into two great hostile camps, into two great classes directly facing each other — bourgeoisie and proletariat. . . .

Modern industry has established the world market, for which the discovery of America paved the way. This market has given an immense development to commerce, to navigation, to communication by land. . . .

[T]he bourgeoisie has at last, since the establishment of Modern Industry and of the world market, conquered for itself, in the modern representative state, exclusive political sway. The executive of the modern state is but a committee for managing the common affairs of the whole bourgeoisie.

The bourgeoisie, historically, has played a most revolutionary part.

The bourgeoisie, wherever it has got the upper hand, has put an end to all feudal, patriarchal, idyllic relations. It has pitilessly torn asunder the motley feudal ties that bound man to his "natural superiors," and has left no other nexus between people than naked self-interest, than callous "cash payment." It has drowned out the most heavenly ecstasies of religious fervor, of chivalrous enthusiasm, of philistine sentimentalism, in the icy water of egotistical calculation. It has resolved personal worth into exchange value, and in place of the numberless indefeasible chartered freedoms, has set up that single, unconscionable freedom — Free Trade. In one word, for exploitation, veiled by religious and political illusions, it has substituted naked, shameless, direct, brutal exploitation.

The bourgeoisie has stripped of its halo every occupation hitherto honored and looked up to with reverent awe. It has converted the physician, the lawyer, the priest, the poet, the man of science, into its paid wage laborers.

The bourgeoisie has torn away from the family its sentimental veil, and has reduced the family relation into a mere money relation. . . .

It has been the first to show what man's activity can bring about. It has accomplished wonders far surpassing Egyptian pyramids, Roman aqueducts, and Gothic cathedrals. . . .

The need of a constantly expanding market for its products chases the bourgeoisie over the entire surface of the globe. It must nestle everywhere, settle everywhere, establish connections everywhere. . . .

All old-established national industries have been destroyed or are daily being destroyed. They are

Source: John E. Toews, ed., *The Communist Manifesto by Karl Marx and Frederick Engels with Related Documents* (Boston: Bedford/St. Martin's, 1999), 63–96.

dislodged by new industries, whose introduction becomes a life and death question for all civilized nations . . . , In place of the old wants, satisfied by the production of the country, we find new wants, requiring for their satisfaction the products of distant lands and climes. In place of the old local and national seclusion and self-sufficiency, we have intercourse in every direction, universal interdependence of nations. . . .

The bourgeoisie, by the rapid improvement of all instruments of production, by the immensely facilitated means of communication, draws all, even the most barbarian, nations into civilization. The bourgeoisie has subjected the country to the rule of the towns. It has created enormous cities, has greatly increased the urban population as compared with the rural, and has thus rescued a considerable part of the population from the idiocy of rural life. Just as it has made the country dependent on the towns, so it has made barbarian and semi-barbarian countries dependent on the civilized ones, nations of peasants on nations of bourgeois, the East on the West. . . .

The bourgeoisie, during its rule of scarce one hundred years, has created more massive and more colossal productive forces than have all preceding generations together. Subjection of nature's forces to man, machinery, application of chemistry to industry and agriculture, steam navigation, railways, electric telegraphs, clearing of whole continents for cultivation, canalization or rivers, whole populations conjured out of the ground. . . .

It is enough to mention the commercial crises that, by their periodical return, put the existence of the entire bourgeois society on its trial, each time more threateningly. . . . In these crises, there breaks out an epidemic that, in all earlier epochs, would have seemed an absurdity — the epidemic of over-production. . . .

But not only has the bourgeoisie forged the weapons that bring death to itself; it has also called into existence the men who are to wield those weapons — the modern working class — the proletarians. . . .

These laborers, who must sell themselves piecemeal, are a commodity, like every other article of commerce, and are consequently exposed to all the vicissitudes of competition, to all the fluctuations of the market.

Owing to the extensive use of machinery, and to the division of labor, the work of the proletarians has lost all individual character, and, consequently, all charm for the workman. He becomes an appendage of the machine, and it is only the most simple, most monotonous, and most easily acquired knack, that is required of him. . . .

Masses of laborers, crowded into the factory, are organized like soldiers. As privates of the industrial army, they are placed under the command of a perfect hierarchy of officers and sergeants. Not only are they slaves of the bourgeois class, and of the bourgeois state; they are daily and hourly enslaved by the machine, by the overlooker, and, above all, by the individual bourgeois manufacturer himself. . . .

The lower strata of the middle class — the small tradespeople, shopkeepers, and retired tradesmen generally, the handicraftsmen and peasants — all these sink gradually into the proletariat. . . . Thus, the proletariat is recruited from all classes of the population. . . .

This organization of the proletarians into a class, and, consequently, into a political party, is continually being upset again by the competition between the workers themselves. But it ever rises up again, stronger, firmer, mightier. . . .

Finally, in times when the class struggle nears the decisive hour, . . . a small section of the ruling class cuts itself adrift, and joins the revolutionary class, the class that holds the future in its hands. . . . What the bourgeoisie therefore produces, above all, are its own grave-diggers. Its fall and the victory of the proletariat are equally inevitable. . . .

We have seen above that the first step in the revolution by the working class is to raise the proletariat to the position of ruling class, to win the battle of democracy.

The proletariat will use its political supremacy to wrest, by degree, all capital from the bourgeoisie, to centralize all instruments of production in the hands of the state, i.e., of the proletariat organized as the ruling class; and to increase the total productive forces as rapidly as possible.

Of course, in the beginning, this cannot be effected except by means of despotic inroads on the rights of property....

These measures will, of course, be different in different countries.

Nevertheless, in most advanced countries, the following will be pretty generally applicable.

1. Abolition of property in land and application of all rents of land to public purposes.
2. A heavy progressive or graduated income tax.
3. Abolition of all rights of inheritance.
4. Confiscation of the property of all emigrants and rebels.
5. Centralization of credit in the banks of the state, by means of a national bank with state capital and an exclusive monopoly.
6. Centralization of the means of communication and transport in the hands of the state.
7. Extension of factories and instruments of production owned by the state; the bringing into cultivation of waste lands, and the improvement of the soil generally in accordance with a common plan.
8. Equal obligation of all to work. Establishment of industrial armies, especially for agriculture.
9. Combination of agriculture with manufacturing industries; gradual abolition of all the distinction between town and country by a more equable distribution of the populace over the country.
10. Free education for all children in public schools. Abolition of children's factory labor in its present form. Combination of education with industrial production, etc.

When, in the course of development, class distinctions have disappeared, and all production has been concentrated in the hands of a vast association of the whole nation, the public power will lose its political character.... In place of the old bourgeois society, with its classes and class antagonisms, we shall have an association in which the free development of each is the condition for the free development of all....

The Communists disdain to conceal their views and aims. They openly declare that their ends can be attained only by the forcible overthrow of all existing social conditions. Let the ruling classes tremble at a communist revolution. The proletarians have nothing to lose but their chains. They have a world to win.

Using the Evidence:
Experiencing Industrialization

1. **Comparing Marx and Smiles:** How might Marx and Smiles criticize each other's views? What common ground might they find?

2. **Considering the appeal of Marxism:** Why might ordinary working-class men and women, such as Elizabeth Bentley and Ellen Johnston, be attracted to the ideas of a middle-class intellectual like Karl Marx? Do you think that artisans, such as the silk weavers of Coventry, would find his ideas equally appealing?

3. **Understanding class:** How do these documents, coupled with the Portrait of Ellen Johnston (pp. 840–41), help you to understand the experience of "class" during the early industrial era?

Visual Sources

Considering the Evidence:
Art and the Industrial Revolution

Variations in attitudes toward industrialization registered not only in politics, literature, and song, but also in the work of visual artists. Through their eyes and in their images we can find the full range of perceptions and reactions—from celebratory to devastatingly critical—which this epic upheaval generated. From the endless visual representations of the Industrial Revolution that are available to historians, the five images that follow derive mostly from Great Britain, where it all began.

By the mid-nineteenth century, the Industrial Revolution and a growing global empire had generated for many people in Great Britain feelings of enormous pride, achievement, and superiority. Nowhere did that sensibility register more clearly than in the Crystal Palace Exhibition of 1851. Held in London, the exhibition was housed in a huge modernistic structure made of cast iron and glass and constructed in only nine months. It attracted more than 6 million visitors and contained some 14,000 exhibits from all around the world, allowing Britain to contrast its own achievements with those of "lesser" peoples. Visual Source 17.1, an engraving from the exhibition's "machinery department" first published in a London newspaper, illustrates the growing tendency of Europeans to view "technology as the main measure of human achievement."[33]

- What overall impression of Britain's industrial technology was this engraving intended to convey? Notice the building itself as well as the machinery.

- How are the visitors to this exhibit portrayed? What segment of British society do you think they represent? What does their inclusion suggest about the beneficiaries of the Industrial Revolution?

- Why did technological development become such a prominent "measure of human achievement" in industrial age Europe? To what extent was this a new phenomenon?

The most prominent symbol of the Industrial Revolution was the railroad (see the painting on p. 835). To industrial-age enthusiasts, it was a thing of wonder, power, and speed. Samuel Smiles, the nineteenth-century British advocate

Visual Source 17.1 The Machinery Department of the Crystal Palace (Mary Evans Picture Library/The Image Works)

of self-help, thrift, and individualism, wrote rhapsodically of the railroad's beneficent effects:

> The iron rail proved a magicians' road. The locomotive gave a new
> celerity to time. It virtually reduced England to a sixth of its size. It
> brought the country nearer to the town and the town to the country. . . .
> It energized punctuality, discipline, and attention; and proved a moral
> teacher by the influence of example.[34]

Visual Source 17.2, dating from the 1870s, shows a family in a railroad compartment, returning home from a vacation.

- What attitude toward the railroad in particular and the industrial age in
  general does this image suggest?

- Notice the view out the window. What do the telegraph lines and St.
  Paul's Cathedral, a famous feature of the London landscape, contribute
  to the artist's message?

- What marks this family as middle class? How would you compare this
  image with the painting of middle-class life on page 838? Do the two

families derive from the same segments of the middle class? Do you think they could mix socially?

■ What does the poem at the top of the image suggest about the place of "home" in industrial Britain? How does the image itself present the railway car as a home away from home?

And Papa and Mamma took them
home the same day,—
They were glad to go home, and yet
wanted to stay;
But the train went quite fast, and it
seemed a nice change
To be back in their own home, where
nothing was strange:

And always they reckon'd that
seeing these sights
Was a thing to remember—a week of
delights;
And, though they may see them all
many times more,
They'll never enjoy them so much, I
am sure.

Visual Source 17.2 The Railroad as a Symbol of the Industrial Era (Mary Evans Picture Library/The Image Works)

For many men and women, the modern factory represented their primary experience of the Industrial Revolution. Certainly, the human impact of factory labor was a central feature in the debate about this massive transformation of economic life. Visual Source 17.3, an 1874 painting by English artist Eyre Crowe, shows a number of young women factory workers during their dinner hour outside the cotton textile mill in the industrial town of Wigan.

- How do you respond to Crowe's painting? Do you think it was an honest portrayal of factory life for women? What might be missing?

- Why do you think Crowe set this scene outside the factory rather than within it?

- Notice the details of the painting—the young women's relationship to one another, the hairnets on their heads, their clothing, their activities during this break from work. What marks them as working-class women? What impression of factory life did Crowe seek to convey? Was he trying to highlight or minimize the class differences of industrial Britain?

Visual Source 17.3 Outside the Factory: Eyre Crowe, *The Dinner Hour, Wigan* (© Manchester Art Gallery, UK/The Bridgeman Art Library)

■ Notice the small male figure in a dark coat and carrying a cane, perhaps the owner of the mill. If so, how would you imagine his relationship to the young women?

Visual Source 17.4 presents a sharply contrasting image of factory life in this colorized photograph of women and children at work in a vegetable cannery in Baltimore in 1912. It was taken by Lewis W. Hine (1874–1940), a prominent American photographer who spent much of his professional life documenting child labor and factory working life. Often Hine briefly interviewed the children he photographed. When he asked one young girl her age, she replied: "I don't remember. I'm not old enough to work, but do just the same." A twelve-year-old illiterate boy told Hine: "Yes I want to learn, but can't when I work all the time."[35] Hine's photographs played a role in the passage of child labor laws in the United States.

■ What impressions of factory life does Hine seek to convey in this photograph?

Visual Source 17.4 Inside the Factory: Lewis Hine, *Child Labor, 1912* (Oil over photograph, 1912, by Lewis W. Hine. The Granger Collection, New York)

- How do the women and children in this image compare with those in Visual Source 17.3?

- How would you imagine a conversation between Hine and Crowe discussing these two images?

- Notice the male figure smoking a pipe. What do you think his role in the factory might be?

- Is a photograph necessarily a more truthful image than a painting? Consider the advantages and disadvantages of each as a source of information for historians.

Visual Source 17.5, an image by British artist John Leech, moves beyond the impact of industrial life on individuals to a larger social critique. Published in 1843 in *Punch*, a magazine of humor and social satire, it reflects a common theme in the artistic and literary representations of industrial Britain.

- How precisely would you define that theme?

CAPITAL AND LABOUR.

Visual Source 17.5 John Leech, *Capital and Labour* (The Granger Collection, New York)

- How are the sharp class differences of industrial Britain represented in this visual source?

- How does this visual source connect the Industrial Revolution with Britain's colonial empire? Notice the figure in the upper right reclining in exotic splendor, perhaps in India.

- To what extent does the image correspond to Karl Marx and Friedrich Engels's description of industrial society in Document 17.4 (pp. 867–70)? How does it compare with the poster on p. 843?

- How might you understand the figure of the woman and small angel behind a door at the left?

Using the Evidence:
Art and the Industrial Revolution

1. **Deciphering class:** In what different ways is social class treated in these visual sources?

2. **Celebrating industrialization:** Based on these visual sources, the documents, and the text of Chapter 17, construct an argument in celebration of the Industrial Revolution.

3. **Criticizing industrialization:** Construct another argument based on the evidence in the chapter criticizing the Industrial Revolution.

4. **Considering images as evidence:** What are the strengths and limitations of visual sources, as compared to documents, in helping historians understand the Industrial Revolution?

5. **Distinguishing capitalism and industrialization:** To what extent are these visual and documentary sources actually dealing with the Industrial Revolution itself and in what ways are they addressing the economic system known as capitalism? How useful is this distinction for understanding reactions to the industrial age?

Chapter 17 Wrap Up

STEP ONE

The Word to Know: Anthropocene

Collins English Dictionary defines *anthropocene* as a term, proposed by scientist Paul Crutzen (and not yet in the *Oxford English Dictionary*, nor accepted by the American Geological Society), "for the present geological epoch (from the time of the Industrial Revolution onwards), during which humanity has begun to have a significant impact on the environment." From the evidence found in Chapter 17, write a paragraph justifying the term "anthropocene" to describe the modern age.

STEP TWO

Reading Tables

Review the Snapshot on p. 856 and answer the questions that follow.

■ Questions

1. What patterns can you identify from this table?
2. What conclusions can you draw about the Industrial Revolution and its global impact from 1750 to 1900?

STEP THREE

Evaluating Point of View in Reponses to Industrialization

This exercise explores point of view in both textual and visual sources. In textual documents, consider tone, language, the intended audience, and whether the actual document communicates a particular agenda. In visual sources, think about color, style, what is and is not included, and setting. The guiding questions after each source will assist in helping you with the final answer.

1. Document 17.1, Elizabeth Bentley, Factory Worker, *Testimony*, 1831

Read through Document 17.1, pp. 863–64, and note passages that indicate Elizabeth Bentley's point of view. Then answer the question below.

■ **Question**

What factors evidence in her testimony shape Bentley's point of view?

2. Ellen Johnston, *An Address to Napier's Dockyard*, c. 1867

Review the Portrait of Ellen Johnston, on pp. 840–41 and then read the excerpt below from one of her poems. Then, answer the question that follows.

A thousand times I'd be a Factory Girl!
To live near thee, and thy anvils clink,
And with thy sons that hard-won pleasure drink.
That joy that springs from wealth of daily toil,
Than be a queen sprung forth from royal soil."

_____

Source: *Poems and Songs of Ellen Johnston, The Factory Girl.* Glasgow: William Love, 1867. 9–12.

■ **Question**

How does Johnston's point of view differ from Bentley's? What might account for this difference? What hints do you get that Johnston shared some of Bentley's perspective?

3. "Death's Dispensary" Political Cartoon, 1866

Examine the political cartoon, Death's Dispensary, on p. 839, taking note of the caption and the specific detail within the image. Then answer the question below.

■ **Question**

What is the artist's point of view about the conditions of the urban poor? What, if anything, can you conclude about the artist and the intended audience for this cartoon? What do you think he would argue should be done?

4. Visual Source 17.3, Eyre Crowe, *The Dinner Hour, Wigan*, 1874

Examine Visual Source 17.3, on p. 874 and then answer the question below.

■ **Question**

What hints does this painting provide about Crowe's background that might have influenced this point of view? The painting was produced in late Victorian England during the height of the Industrial Age—how might this context influence his point of view?

CHAPTER EIGHTEEN

Colonial Encounters in Asia and Africa

1750–1950

In mid-1967, I was on summer break from a teaching assignment with the Peace Corps in Ethiopia and was traveling with some friends in neighboring Kenya, just four years after that country had gained its independence from British colonial rule. The bus we were riding on broke down, and I found myself hitchhiking across Kenya, heading for Uganda. Soon I was picked up by a friendly Englishman, one of Kenya's many European settlers who had stayed on after independence. At one point, he pulled off the road to show me a lovely view of Kenya's famous Rift Valley, and we were approached by a group of boys selling baskets and other tourist items. They spoke to us in good English, but my British companion replied to them in Swahili. He later explained that Europeans generally did not speak English with the "natives." I was puzzled, but reluctant to inquire further.

Several years later, while conducting research about British missionaries in Kenya in the early twentieth century, I found a clue about the origins of this man's reluctance to speak his own language with Kenyans. It came in a letter from a missionary in which the writer argued against the teaching of English to Africans. Among his reasons were "the danger in which such a course would place our white women and girls" and "the danger of organizing against the government and Europeans."[1] Here, clearly displayed, was the European colonial insistence on maintaining distance and distinction between whites and blacks, for both sexual and political reasons. Such monitoring of racial boundaries was a central feature of many nineteenth- and early twentieth-century colonial societies and, in the case of my

The Imperial Durbar of 1903: To mark the coronation of British monarch Edward VII and his installation as the Emperor of India, colonial authorities in India mounted an elaborate assembly, or durbar. The durbar was intended to showcase the splendor of the British Empire, and its pageantry included sporting events; a state ball; a huge display of Indian arts, crafts, and jewels; and an enormous parade in which a long line of British officials and Indian princes passed by on bejeweled elephants. (© Topham/The Image Works) new British acquaintance, a practice that persisted even after the colonial era had ended.

FOR MANY MILLIONS OF AFRICANS AND ASIANS, COLONIAL RULE—by the British, French, Germans, Italians, Belgians, Portuguese, Russians, or Americans—was the major new element in their historical experience during the long nineteenth century (1750–1914). Of course, no single colonial experience characterized this vast region. Much depended on the cultures and prior history of various colonized people. Policies of the colonial powers sometimes differed sharply and changed over time. Men and women experienced the colonial era differently, as did traditional elites, Western-educated groups, artisans, peasant farmers, and migrant laborers. Furthermore, the varied actions and reactions of such people, despite their oppression and exploitation, shaped the colonial experience, perhaps as much as the policies, practices, and intentions of their temporary European rulers. All of them—colonizers and colonized alike—were caught up in the flood of change that accompanied this new burst of European imperialism.

SEEKING THE MAIN POINT

In what ways did colonial rule transform the societies that it encompassed?

Industry and Empire

■ **Change**

In what ways did the Industrial Revolution shape the character of nineteenth-century European imperialism?

Behind much of Europe's nineteenth-century expansion lay the massive fact of its Industrial Revolution, a process that gave rise to new economic needs, many of which found solutions abroad. The enormous productivity of industrial technology and Europe's growing affluence now created the need for extensive raw materials and agricultural products: wheat from the American Midwest and southern Russia, meat from Argentina, bananas from Central America, rubber from Brazil, cocoa and palm oil from West Africa, tea from Ceylon, gold and diamonds from South Africa. This demand radically changed patterns of economic and social life in the countries of their origin.

Furthermore, Europe needed to sell its own products. One of the peculiarities of industrial capitalism was that it periodically produced more manufactured goods than its own people could afford to buy. By 1840, for example, Britain was exporting 60 percent of its cotton-cloth production, annually sending 200 million yards to Europe, 300 million yards to Latin America, and 145 million yards to India. This last figure is particularly significant because for centuries Europe had offered little that Asian societies were willing to buy. Part of European and American fascination with China during the nineteenth and twentieth centuries lay in the enormous market potential represented by its huge population.

Much the same could be said for capital, for European investors often found it more profitable to invest their money abroad than at home. Between 1910 and 1913, Britain was sending about half of its savings overseas as foreign investment. In 1914, it had some 3.7 billion pounds sterling invested abroad, about equally divided between

A Map of Time

1750s	Beginnings of British takeover of India
1788	Initial British settlement of Australia
1798	Napoleon's invasion of Egypt
1830	French invasion of Algeria
1840s	Beginning of major British settlement in New Zealand
1857–1858	Indian Mutiny and rebellion
1858–1893	French conquest of Indochina
1869	Opening of Suez Canal
1875–1914	Scramble for Africa
1898	United States acquires the Philippines from Spain and annexes Hawaii
1899–1902	Boer War in South Africa
1901–1910	Completion of Dutch conquest of Indonesia
1904–1905	Maji Maji rebellion in East Africa
1910	Japan annexes Korea
Twentieth century	Spread of Christianity in non-Muslim Africa
1920s–1947	Gandhi's leadership of Indian National Congress

Europe, North America, and Australia on the one hand and Asia, Africa, and Latin America on the other.

Wealthy Europeans also saw social benefits to foreign markets, which served to keep Europe's factories humming and its workers employed. The English imperialist Cecil Rhodes confided his fears to a friend:

> Yesterday I attended a meeting of the unemployed in London and having listened to the wild speeches which were nothing more than a scream for bread, I returned home convinced more than ever of the importance of imperialism. . . . In order to save the 40 million inhabitants of the United Kingdom from a murderous civil war, the colonial politicians must open up new areas to absorb the excess population and create new markets for the products of the mines and factories. . . . The British Empire is a matter of bread and butter. If you wish to avoid civil war, then you must become an imperialist.[2]

Thus imperialism promised to solve the class conflicts of an industrializing society while avoiding revolution or the serious redistribution of wealth.

THE DEVILFISH IN EGYPTIAN WATERS.

An American View of British Imperialism
In this American cartoon dating to 1882, the British Empire is portrayed as an octopus whose tentacles are already attached to many countries, while one tentacle is about to grasp yet another colony, Egypt. (The Granger Collection, New York)

But what made imperialism so broadly popular in Europe, especially in the last quarter of the nineteenth century, was the growth of mass nationalism. By 1871, the unification of Italy and Germany made Europe's already competitive international relations even more so, and much of this rivalry spilled over into the struggle for colonies or economic concessions in Asia and Africa. Colonies and spheres of influence abroad became symbols of "Great Power" status for a nation, and their acquisition was a matter of urgency, even if they possessed little immediate economic value. After 1875, it seemed to matter, even to ordinary people, whether some remote corner of Africa or some obscure Pacific island was in British, French, or German hands. Imperialism, in short, appealed on economic and social grounds to the wealthy or ambitious, seemed politically and strategically necessary in the game of international power politics, and was emotionally satisfying to almost everyone. This was a potent mix indeed.

If the industrial era made overseas expansion more desirable or even urgent, it also provided new means for achieving those goals. Steam-driven ships, moving through the new Suez Canal, completed in 1869, allowed Europeans to reach distant Asian and African ports more quickly and predictably and to penetrate interior rivers as well. The underwater telegraph made possible almost instant communication with far-flung outposts of empire. The discovery of quinine to prevent malaria greatly reduced European death rates in the tropics. Breech-loading rifles and machine guns vastly widened the military gap between Europeans and everyone else.

■ **Change**
What contributed to changing European views of Asians and Africans in the nineteenth century?

Industrialization also occasioned a marked change in the way Europeans perceived themselves and others. In earlier centuries, Europeans had defined others largely in religious terms. "They" were heathen; "we" were Christian. Even as they held onto this sense of religious superiority, Europeans nonetheless adopted many of the ideas and techniques of more advanced societies. They held many aspects of Chinese and Indian civilization in high regard; they freely mixed and mingled with Asian and African elites and often married their women; some even saw more technologically simple peoples as "noble savages."

With the advent of the industrial age, however, Europeans developed a secular arrogance that fused with or in some cases replaced their notions of religious superiority. They had, after all, unlocked the secrets of nature, created a society of unprecedented wealth, and used both to produce unsurpassed military power. These became the criteria by which Europeans judged both themselves and the rest of the world.

By such standards, it is not surprising that their opinions of other cultures dropped sharply. The Chinese, who had been highly praised in the eighteenth century, were reduced in the nineteenth century to the image of "John Chinaman"—weak, cunning, obstinately conservative, and, in large numbers, a distinct threat, represented by the "yellow peril" in late-nineteenth-century European thinking. African societies, which had been regarded even in the slave-trade era as nations and their leaders as kings, were demoted in nineteenth-century European eyes to the status of tribes led by chiefs as a means of emphasizing their "primitive" qualities.

Increasingly, Europeans viewed the culture and achievements of Asian and African peoples through the prism of a new kind of racism, expressed now in terms of modern science. Although physical differences had often been a basis of fear or dislike, in the nineteenth century, Europeans increasingly used the prestige and apparatus of science to support their racial preferences and prejudices. Phrenologists, craniologists, and sometimes physicians used allegedly scientific methods and numerous instruments to classify the size and shape of human skulls and concluded, not surprisingly, that those of whites were larger and therefore more advanced. Nineteenth-century biologists, who classified the varieties of plants and animals, applied these notions of rank to varieties of human beings as well. The result was a hierarchy of races, with the whites on top and the less developed "child races" beneath them.

European Racial Images This nineteenth-century chart, depicting the "Progressive Development of Man" from apes to modern Europeans, reflected the racial categories that were so prominent at the time. It also highlights the influence of Darwin's evolutionary ideas as they were applied to varieties of human beings. (The Granger Collection, New York)

Race, in this view, determined human intelligence, moral development, and destiny. "Race is everything," declared the British anatomist Robert Knox in 1850. "Civilization depends on it."[3] Furthermore, as the germ theory of disease took hold in nineteenth-century Europe, it was accompanied by fears that contact with "inferiors" threatened the health and even the biological future of more advanced or "superior" peoples.

These ideas influenced how Europeans viewed their own global expansion. Almost everyone saw it as inevitable, a natural outgrowth of a superior civilization. For many, though, this viewpoint was tempered with a genuine, if condescending,

PROGRESSIVE DEVELOPMENT OF MAN.—(a) EVOLUTION ILLUSTRATED WITH THE SIX CORRESPONDING LIVING FORMS.

sense of responsibility to the "weaker races" that Europe was fated to dominate. "Superior races have a right, because they have a duty," declared the French politician Jules Ferry in 1883. "They have the duty to civilize the inferior races."[4] That "civilizing mission" included bringing Christianity to the heathen, good government to disordered lands, work discipline and production for the market to "lazy natives," a measure of education to the ignorant and illiterate, clothing to the naked, and health care to the sick, all while suppressing "native customs" that ran counter to Western ways of living. In European thinking, this was "progress" and "civilization."

A harsher side to the ideology of imperialism derived from an effort to apply, or perhaps misapply, the evolutionary thinking of Charles Darwin to an understanding of human societies. The key concept of this "social Darwinism," though not necessarily shared by Darwin himself, was "the survival of the fittest," suggesting that European dominance inevitably involved the displacement or destruction of backward peoples or "unfit" races. Referring to native peoples of Australia, a European bishop declared:

> Everyone who knows a little about aboriginal races is aware that those races which are of a low type mentally and who are at the same time weak in constitution rapidly die out when their country comes to be occupied by a different race much more rigorous, robust, and pushing than themselves.[5]

Such views made imperialism, war, and aggression seem both natural and progressive, for they were predicated on the notion that weeding out "weaker" peoples of the world would allow the "stronger" to flourish. These were some of the ideas with which industrializing and increasingly powerful Europeans confronted the peoples of Asia and Africa in the nineteenth century.

A Second Wave of European Conquests

■ **Comparison**

In what different ways was colonial rule established in various parts of Africa and Asia?

If the sixteenth- and seventeenth-century takeover of the Americas represented the first phase of European colonial conquests, the century and a half between 1750 and 1914 was a second and quite distinct round of that larger process. Now it was focused in Asia and Africa rather than in the Western Hemisphere. And it featured a number of new players — Germany, Italy, Belgium, the United States, and Japan — who were not at all involved in the earlier phase, while the Spanish and Portuguese now had only minor roles. In general, Europeans preferred informal control, which operated through economic penetration and occasional military intervention but without a wholesale colonial takeover. Such a course was cheaper and less likely to provoke wars. But where rivalry with other European states made it impossible or where local governments were unable or unwilling to cooperate, Europeans proved more than willing to undertake the expense and risk of conquest and outright colonial rule.

The construction of these new European empires in the Afro-Asian world, like empires everywhere, involved military force or the threat of it. Initially, the European military advantage lay in organization, drill and practice, and command structure. Increasingly in the nineteenth century, the Europeans also possessed overwhelming advantages in firepower, deriving from the recently invented repeating rifles and machine guns. A much-quoted jingle by the English writer Hilaire Belloc summed up the situation:

> Whatever happens we have got
> The Maxim gun [an automatic machine gun] and they have not.

Nonetheless, Europeans had to fight, often long and hard, to create their new empires, as countless wars of conquest attest. In the end, though, they prevailed almost everywhere, largely against adversaries who did not have Maxim guns or in some cases any guns at all. Thus were African and Asian peoples of all kinds incorporated within one or another of the European empires. Gathering and hunting bands in Australia, agricultural village societies or chiefdoms on Pacific islands and in parts of Africa, pastoralists of the Sahara and Central Asia, residents of states large and small, and virtually everyone in the large and complex civilizations of India and Southeast Asia—all of them alike lost the political sovereignty and freedom of action they had previously exercised. For some, such as Hindus governed by the Muslim Mughal Empire, it was an exchange of one set of foreign rulers for another. But now all were subjects of a European colonial state.

The passage to colonial status occurred in various ways. For the peoples of India and Indonesia, colonial conquest grew out of earlier interaction with European trading firms. Particularly in India, the British East India Company, rather than the British government directly, played the leading role in the colonial takeover of South Asia. The fragmentation of the Mughal Empire and the absence of any overall sense of cultural or political unity both invited and facilitated European penetration. A similar situation of many small and rival states assisted the Dutch acquisition of Indonesia. However, neither the British nor the Dutch had a clear-cut plan for conquest. Rather it evolved slowly as local authorities and European traders made and unmade a variety of alliances over roughly a century in India (1750–1850). In Indonesia, a few areas held out until the early twentieth century (see Map 18.1).

For most of Africa, mainland Southeast Asia, and the Pacific islands, colonial conquest came later, in the second half of the nineteenth century, and rather more abruptly and deliberately than in India or Indonesia. The "scramble for Africa," for example, pitted half a dozen European powers against one another as they partitioned the entire continent among themselves in only about twenty-five years (1875–1900). (See Visual Sources: The Scramble for Africa, pp. 922–29, for various perspectives on the "scramble.") European leaders themselves were surprised by the intensity of their rivalries and the speed with which they acquired huge territories, about which they knew very little (see Map 18.2, p. 887).

That process involved endless but peaceful negotiations among the competing Great Powers about "who got what" and extensive and bloody military action, sometimes lasting decades, to make their control effective on the ground. It took the French

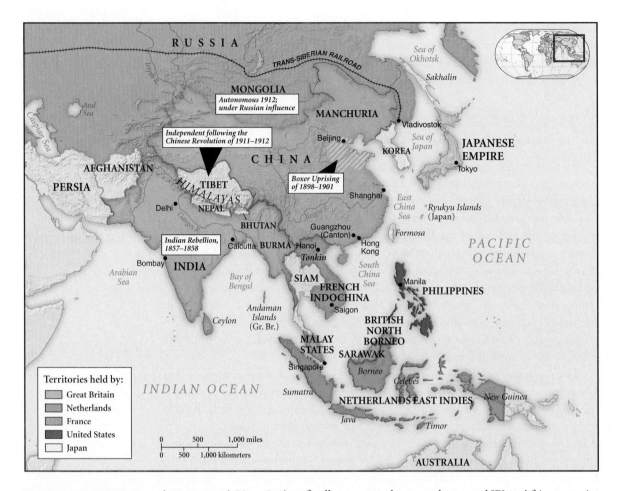

Map 18.1   Colonial Asia in the Early Twentieth Century
By the early 1900s, several of the great population centers of Asia had come under the colonial control of Britain, the Netherlands, France, the United States, or Japan.

sixteen years (1882–1898) to finally conquer the recently created West African empire led by Samori Toure. Among the most difficult to subdue were those decentralized societies without any formal state structure. In such cases, Europeans confronted no central authority with which they could negotiate or that they might decisively defeat. It was a matter of village-by-village conquest against extended resistance. As late as 1925, one British official commented on the process as it operated in central Nigeria: "I shall of course go on walloping them until they surrender. It's a rather piteous sight watching a village being knocked to pieces and I wish there was some other way, but unfortunately there isn't."[6] Another very difficult situation for the British lay in South Africa, where they were initially defeated by a Zulu army in 1879 at the Battle of Ishandlwana. And twenty years later in what became known as the Boer War (1899–1902), the Boers, white descendants of the earlier Dutch settlers in South Africa, fought bitterly for three years before succumbing to British forces. Perhaps the great disparity in military forces made the final outcome of European victory inevitable, but the conquest of Africa was intensely contested.

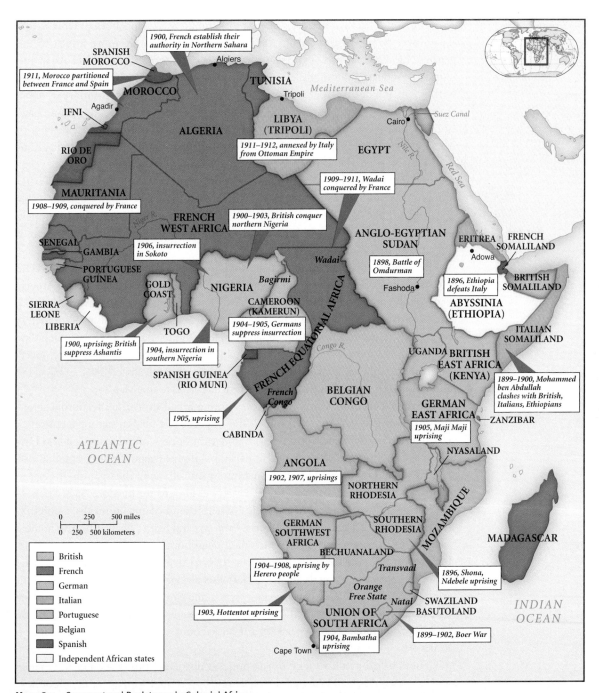

Map 18.2   Conquest and Resistance in Colonial Africa

By the early twentieth century, the map of Africa reflected the outcome of the "scramble for Africa," a conquest that was heavily resisted in many places. The boundaries established during that process still provide the political framework for Africa's independent states.

The South Pacific territories of Australia and New Zealand, both of which were taken over by the British during the nineteenth century, were more similar to the earlier colonization of North America than to contemporary patterns of Asian and African conquest. In both places, conquest was accompanied by large-scale European settlement and diseases that reduced native numbers by 75 percent or more by 1900. Like Canada and the United States, these became settler colonies, "neo-European" societies in the Pacific. Aboriginal Australians constituted only about 2.4 percent of their country's population in the early twenty-first century, and the indigenous Maori comprised a minority of about 15 percent in New Zealand. With the exception of Hawaii, nowhere else in the nineteenth-century colonial world were existing populations so decimated and overwhelmed as they were in Australia and New Zealand. Unlike these remote areas, most of Africa and Asia shared with Europe a broadly similar disease environment and so were less susceptible to the pathogens of the conquerors.

Elsewhere other variations on the theme of imperial conquest unfolded. The westward expansion of the United States, for example, overwhelmed Native American populations and involved the country in an imperialist war with Mexico. Seeking territory for white settlement, the United States practiced a policy of removing, sometimes almost exterminating, Indian peoples. On the "reservations" to which they were confined and in boarding schools to which many of their children were removed, reformers sought to "civilize" the remaining Native Americans, eradicating tribal life and culture, under the slogan, "Kill the Indian and Save the Man."

Japan's takeover of Taiwan and Korea bore marked similarities to European actions, as that East Asian nation joined the imperialist club. Russian penetration of Central Asia brought additional millions under European control as the Russian Empire continued its earlier territorial expansion. Filipinos acquired new colonial rulers when the United States took over from Spain following the Spanish-American War of 1898. Some 13,000 freed U.S. slaves, seeking greater freedom than was possible at home, migrated to West Africa, where they became, ironically, a colonizing elite in the land they named Liberia. Ethiopia and Siam (Thailand) were notable for avoiding the colonization to which their neighbors succumbed. Those countries' military and diplomatic skills, their willingness to make modest concessions to the Europeans, and the rivalries of the imperialists all contributed to these exceptions to the rule of colonial takeover in East Africa and Southeast Asia. Ethiopia, in fact, considerably expanded its own empire, even as it defeated Italy at the famous Battle of Adowa in 1896. (See pp. 928–29 for an account of Ethiopia's defeat of Italian forces.)

These broad patterns of colonial conquest dissolved into thousands of separate encounters as Asian and African societies were confronted with decisions about how to respond to encroaching European power in the context of their local circumstances. Many initially sought to enlist Europeans in their own internal struggles for power or in their external rivalries with neighboring states or peoples. As pressures mounted and European demands escalated, some tried to play off imperial powers against one another, while others resorted to military action. Many societies were sharply divided between those who wanted to fight and those who believed that resistance was futile. After extended resistance against French aggression, the nineteenth-century Vietnamese emperor Tu Duc argued with those who wanted the struggle to go on:

> Do you really wish to confront such a power with a pack of [our] cowardly soldiers? It would be like mounting an elephant's head or caressing a tiger's tail.... With what you presently have, do you really expect to dissolve the enemy's rifles into air or chase his battleships into hell?[7]

Still others negotiated, attempting to preserve as much independence and power as possible. The rulers of the East African kingdom of Buganda, for example, saw opportunity in the British presence and negotiated an arrangement that substantially enlarged their state and personally benefited the kingdom's elite class.

Under European Rule

In many places and for many people, incorporation into European colonial empires was a traumatic experience. Especially for small-scale societies, the loss of life, homes, cattle, crops, and land was devastating. In 1902, a British soldier in East Africa described what happened in a single village: "Every soul was either shot or bayoneted.... We burned all the huts and razed the banana plantations to the ground."[8]

For the Vietnamese elite, schooled for centuries in Chinese-style Confucian thinking, conquest meant that the natural harmonies of life had been badly disrupted; it was a time when "water flowed uphill." Nguyen Khuyen (1835–1909), a senior Vietnamese official, retired to his ancestral village to farm and write poetry after the French conquest. In his poems he expressed his anguish at the passing of the world he had known:

> Fine wine but no good friends,
> So I buy none though I have the money.
> A poem comes to mind, but I choose not to write it down.
> If it were written, to whom would I give it?
> The spare bed hangs upon the wall in cold indifference.
> I pluck the lute, but it just doesn't sound right.[9]

Many others also withdrew into private life, feigning illness when asked to serve in public office under the French.

Cooperation and Rebellion

Although violence was a prominent feature of colonial life both during conquest and after, various groups and many individuals willingly cooperated with colonial authorities to their own advantage. Many men found employment, status, and security

■ **Explanation**

Why might subject people choose to cooperate with the colonial regime? What might prompt them to violent rebellion or resistance?

in European-led armed forces. The shortage and expense of European administrators and the difficulties of communicating across cultural boundaries made it necessary for colonial rulers to rely heavily on a range of local intermediaries. Thus Indian princes, Muslim emirs, and African rulers, often from elite or governing families, found it possible to retain much of their earlier status and privileges while gaining considerable wealth by exercising authority, legally and otherwise, at the local level. For example, in French West Africa, an area eight times the size of France and with a population of about 15 million in the late 1930s, the colonial state consisted of just 385 French administrators and more than 50,000 African "chiefs." Thus colonial rule rested on and reinforced the most conservative segments of Asian and African societies.

Both colonial governments and private missionary organizations had an interest in promoting a measure of European education. From this process arose a small Western-educated class, whose members served the colonial state, European businesses, and Christian missions as teachers, clerks, translators, and lower-level administrators. A few received higher education abroad and returned home as lawyers, doctors, engineers, or journalists. As colonial governments and business enterprises became more sophisticated, Europeans increasingly depended on the Western-educated class at the expense of the more traditional elites.

If colonial rule enlisted the willing cooperation of some, it provoked the bitter opposition of many others. Thus periodic rebellions, both large and small, erupted in colonial regimes everywhere. The most famous among them was the Indian Rebellion of 1857–1858, which was triggered by the introduction into the colony's military forces of a new cartridge smeared with animal fat from cows and pigs. Because Hindus venerated cows and Muslims regarded pigs as unclean, both groups viewed the innovation as a plot to render them defiled and to convert them to Christianity. Behind this incident were many groups of people with a whole series of grievances generated by the British colonial presence: local rulers who had lost power, landlords deprived of their estates or their rent, peasants overtaxed and exploited by urban moneylenders and landlords alike, unemployed weavers displaced by machine-manufactured textiles, and religious leaders outraged by missionary preaching. A mutiny among Indian troops in Bengal triggered the rebellion, which soon spread to other regions of the colony and other social groups. Soon much of India was aflame. Some rebel leaders presented their cause as an effort to revive an almost-vanished Mughal Empire and thereby attracted support from those with strong resentments against the British (see Document 18.2, pp. 915–16). Although it was crushed in 1858, the rebellion greatly widened the racial divide in colonial India and eroded British tolerance for those they viewed as "nigger natives" who had betrayed their trust. It made the British more conservative and cautious about deliberately trying to change Indian society for fear of provoking another rebellion. Moreover, it convinced the British government to assume direct control over India, ending the era of British East India Company rule in the subcontinent.

Colonial Empires with a Difference

At one level, European colonial empires were but the latest in a very long line of imperial creations, all of which had enlisted cooperation and experienced resistance from their subject peoples, but the nineteenth-century European version of empire was distinctive in several remarkable ways. One was the prominence of race in distinguishing rulers and ruled, as the high tide of "scientific racism" in Europe coincided with the acquisition of Asian and African colonies. In East Africa, for example, white men expected to be addressed as *bwana* (Swahili for "master"), whereas Europeans regularly called African men "boy." Education for colonial subjects was both limited and skewed toward practical subjects rather than scientific and literary studies, which were widely regarded as inappropriate for the "primitive mind" of "natives." Particularly affected by European racism were those whose Western education and aspirations most clearly threatened the racial divide. Europeans were exceedingly reluctant to allow even the most highly educated Asians and Africans to enter the higher ranks of the colonial civil service. A proposal in 1883 to allow Indian judges to hear cases involving whites provoked outrage and massive demonstrations among European inhabitants of India.

In those colonies that had a large European settler population, the pattern of racial separation was much more pronounced than in places such as Nigeria, which had few permanently settled whites. The most extreme case was South Africa, where a large European population and the widespread use of African labor in mines and industries brought blacks and whites into closer and more prolonged contact than elsewhere. The racial fears that were aroused resulted in extraordinary efforts to establish race as a legal, not just a customary, feature of South African society. This racial system provided for separate "homelands," educational systems, residential areas, public facilities, and much more. In what was eventually known as apartheid, South African whites attempted the impossible task of creating an industrializing economy based on cheap African labor, while limiting African social and political integration in every conceivable fashion.

A further distinctive feature of nineteenth-century European empires lay in the extent to which colonial states were able to penetrate the societies they governed. Centralized tax-collecting bureaucracies, new means of communication and transportation, imposed changes in landholding patterns, integration of colonial economies into a global network of exchange, public health and sanitation measures, and the activities of missionaries—all this touched the daily lives of many people far more deeply than in earlier empires. Not only were Europeans foreign rulers, but they also bore the seeds of a very different way of life, which grew out of their own modern transformation.

Nineteenth-century European colonizers were extraordinary as well in their penchant for counting and classifying their subject people. With the assistance of anthropologists and missionaries, colonial governments collected a vast amount of

■ **Comparison**
What was distinctive about European colonial empires of the nineteenth century?

information, sought to organize it "scientifically," and used it to manage the unfa-miliar, complex, varied, and fluctuating societies that they governed. In India, the British found in classical texts and Brahmin ideology an idealized description of the caste system, based on the notion of four ranked and unchanging varnas, which made it possible to bring order out of the immense complexity and variety of caste as it actually operated. Thus the British invented or appropriated a Brahmin version of "traditional India" that they favored and sought to preserve, while scorning as "non-Indian" the new elite educated in European schools and enthusiastic about Western ways of life (see Document 18.1, pp. 913–15). This view of India reflected the great influence of Brahmins on British thinking and clearly served the interests of this Indian upper class.

Likewise within African colonies, Europeans identified, and sometimes invented, distinct tribes, each with its own clearly defined territory, language, customs, and chief. The notion of a "tribal Africa" expressed the Western view that African societies were primitive or backward, representing an earlier stage of human development. It was also a convenient idea, for it reduced the enormous complexity and fluidity of Afri-can societies to a more manageable state and thus made colonial administration easier.

Gender too entered into European efforts to define both themselves and their newly acquired subject peoples. European colonizers—mostly male—took pride in their "active masculinity" while defining the "conquered races" as soft, passive, and feminine. Indian Bengali men, wrote a British official in 1892, "are disqualified for political enfranchisement by the possession of essentially feminine characteristics."[10] By linking the inferiority of women with that of people of color, gender ideology and race prejudice were joined in support of colonial rule. But the intersection of race, gender, and empire was complex and varied. European men in the colonies often viewed their own women as the bearers and emblems of civilization, "upholding the moral dignity of the white community" amid the darkness of inferior peoples.[11] As such they had to be above reproach in sexual matters, protected against the alleged lust of native men by their separation from local African or Asian societies. Further-more, certain colonized people, such as the Sikhs and Gurkhas in India, the Kamba in Kenya, and the Hausa in Nigeria, were gendered as masculine or "martial races" and targeted for recruitment into British military or police forces.

Finally, European colonial policies contradicted their own core values and their practices at home to an unusual degree. While nineteenth-century Britain and France were becoming more democratic, their colonies were essentially dictatorships, offer-ing perhaps order and stability, but certainly not democratic government, because few colonial subjects were participating citizens. Empire of course was wholly at odds with European notions of national independence, and ranked racial classifications went against the grain of both Christian and Enlightenment ideas of human equality. Fur-thermore, many Europeans were distinctly reluctant to encourage within their colo-nies the kind of modernization—urban growth, industrialization, individual values, religious skepticism—that was sweeping their own societies. They feared that this kind of social change, often vilified as "detribalization," would encourage unrest and challenge colonial rule. As a model for social development, they much preferred "traditional" rural society, with its established authorities and social hierarchies, though shorn of abuses such as slavery and *sati* (widow burning). Such contradictions between what Europeans preached at home and what they practiced in the colonies became increasingly apparent to many Asians and Africans and played a major role in undermining the foundations of colonial rule in the twentieth century.

Ways of Working: Comparing Colonial Economies

Colonial rule affected the lives of its subject people in many ways, but the most pronounced change was in their ways of working. The colonial state—with its power to tax, to seize land for European enterprises, to compel labor, and to build railroads, ports, and roads—played an important role in these transformations. Even more powerful was the growing integration of Asian and African societies into a world economy that increasingly demanded their gold, diamonds, copper, tin, rubber, coffee, cotton, sugar, cocoa, and many other products. But the economic transformations born of these twin pressures were far from uniform. Various groups—migrant workers and cash-crop farmers, plantation laborers and domestic servants, urban elites and day laborers, men and women—experienced the colonial era differently as their daily working lives underwent profound changes.

To various degrees, old ways of working were eroded almost everywhere in the colonial world. Subsistence farming, in which peasant families produced largely for their own needs, diminished as growing numbers directed at least some of their energies to working for wages or selling what they produced for a cash income. That money was both necessary to pay taxes and school fees and useful for buying the various products—such as machine-produced textiles, bicycles, and kerosene—that the industrial economies of Europe sent their way. As in Europe, artisans suffered greatly when cheaper machine-manufactured merchandise displaced their own hand-made goods. A flood of inexpensive textiles from Britain's new factories ruined the livelihood of tens of thousands of India's handloom weavers. Iron smelting largely disappeared in Africa, and occupations such as blacksmithing and tanning lost ground. Furthermore, Asian and African merchants, who had earlier handled the trade between their countries and the wider world, were squeezed out by well-financed European commercial firms.

Economies of Coercion: Forced Labor and the Power of the State

Many of the new ways of working that emerged during the colonial era derived directly from the demands of the colonial state. The most obvious was required and unpaid labor on public projects, such as building railroads, constructing government buildings, and transporting goods. In French Africa, all "natives" were legally obligated for "statute labor" of ten to twelve days a year, a practice that lasted through 1946. It

■ **Connection**

How did the policies of colonial states change the economic lives of their subjects?

the Irrawaddy Delta boomed, migrants from Upper Burma and India poured into the region, and rice exports soared. Local small farmers benefited considerably because they were now able to own their own land, build substantial houses, and buy imported goods. For several decades in the late nineteenth century, standards of living improved sharply, and huge increases in rice production fed millions of people in other parts of Asia and elsewhere. It was a very different situation from that of peasants forced to grow crops that seriously interfered with their food production.

But that kind of colonial development, practiced also in the Mekong River delta of French-ruled Vietnam, had important environmental consequences. It involved the destruction of mangrove forests and swamplands along with the fish and shell-fish that supplemented local diets. New dikes and irrigation channels inhibited the depositing of silt from upstream and thus depleted soils in the deltas of these major river systems. And, unknown to anyone at the time, this kind of agriculture generates large amounts of methane gas, a major contributor to global warming.[17]

Profitable cash-crop farming also developed in the southern Gold Coast (present-day Ghana), a British territory in West Africa. Unlike Burma, it was African farmers themselves who took the initiative to develop export agriculture. Planting cacao trees in huge quantities, they became the world's leading supplier of cocoa, used to make chocolate, by 1911. Cacao was an attractive crop because, unlike cotton, it was compatible with the continued production of foods and did not require so much labor time. In the early twentieth century, it brought a new prosperity to many local farmers. "A hybrid society was taking shape," wrote one scholar, "partly peasant, in that most members farmed their own land with family labor . . . and partly capitalist, in that a minority employed wage laborers, produced chiefly for the market, and re-invested profits."[18]

That success brought new problems in its wake. A shortage of labor fostered the employment of former slaves as dependent and exploited workers and also generated tensions between the sexes when some men married women for their labor power but refused to support them adequately. Moreover, the labor shortage brought a huge influx of migrants from the drier interior parts of West Africa, generating ethnic and class tensions. Furthermore, many colonies came to specialize in one or two cash crops, creating an unhealthy dependence when world market prices dropped. Thus African and Asian farmers were increasingly subject to the uncertain rhythms of the international marketplace as well as to those of the seasons and the weather.

Economies of Wage Labor: Migration for Work

Yet another new way of working in colonial societies involved wage labor in some European enterprise. Driven by the need for money, by the loss of land adequate to support their families, or sometimes by the orders of colonial authorities, millions of colonial subjects across Asia and Africa sought employment in European-owned plantations, mines, construction projects, and homes. Often this required migration to distant work sites, many of them overseas. In this process, colonized migrants were joined by millions of Chinese, Japanese, and others, who lived in more independent states. Together they generated vast streams of migration that paralleled and at least equaled in numbers the huge movement of Europeans during the nineteenth and early twentieth centuries (see Chapter 17, pp. 844–46). For Europeans, Asians, and Africans alike, the globalizing world of the colonial era was one of people in motion.

The African segment of this migratory stream moved in several directions. For much of the nineteenth century, the Atlantic slave trade continued, funneling well over 3 million additional people to the Americas, mostly to Brazil. As the slave trade diminished and colonial rule took shape in Africa, internal migration mounted within or among particular colonies. More than in Asia, Africans migrated to European farms or plantations because they had lost their own land. In the settler colonies of Africa—Algeria, Kenya, Southern Rhodesia (Zimbabwe), and South Africa, for example—permanent European communities, with the help of colonial governments, obtained huge tracts of land, much of which had previously been home to African societies. A 1913 law in South Africa legally defined 88 percent of the land as belonging to whites, who were then about 20 percent of the population. Much of highland Kenya, an enormously rich agricultural region that was home to the Gikuyu and Kamba peoples, was taken over by some 4,000 white farmers. In such places, some Africans stayed on as "squatters," working for the new landowners as the price of remaining on what had been their own land. Others were displaced to "native reserves," limited areas that could not support their growing populations, thus forcing many to work for wages on European farms. Most notably in South Africa, such reserved areas, known as Bantustans, became greatly overcrowded: soil fertility declined, hillsides were cleared, forests shrank, and erosion scarred the land. This kind of ecological degradation was among the environmental consequences of African wage labor on European farms and estates.

The gold and diamond mines of South Africa likewise set in motion a huge pattern of labor migration that encompassed all of Africa south of the Belgian Congo. With skilled and highly paid work reserved for white miners, Africans worked largely as unskilled laborers at a fraction of the wages paid to whites. Furthermore, they were recruited on short-term contracts, lived in all-male prison-like barracks that were often surrounded by barbed wire, and were forced to return home periodically to prevent them from establishing a permanent family life near the mines.

Asians too were in motion and in large numbers. Some 29 million Indians and 19 million Chinese migrated to Southeast Asia, the South Pacific, or the lands around the Indian Ocean basin.[19] All across Southeast Asia in the later nineteenth and early twentieth centuries, huge plantations sprouted, which were financed from Europe and which grew sugarcane, rubber, tea, tobacco, sisal (used for making rope), and more. Impoverished workers by the hundreds of thousands came from great distances (India, China, Java) to these plantations, where they were subject to strict control, often housed in barracks, and paid poorly, with women receiving 50 to 75 percent of a man's wage. Disease was common, and death rates were at least double that of the colony as a whole. In 1927 in southern Vietnam alone, one in twenty plantation workers died. British colonial authorities in India facilitated the migration of millions of Indians to work sites elsewhere in the British Empire—Trinidad, Jamaica,

■ **Change**
What kinds of wage labor were available in the colonies? Why might people take part in it? How did doing so change their lives?

Economic Change in the Colonial World

These workers on a Ceylon tea plantation in the early twentieth century are moving sacks of tea into a drying house in preparation for export. The Lipton label on the bags is a reminder of the role of large-scale foreign investment in the economic transformations of the colonial era. (© Hulton-Deutsch Collection/Corbis)

Fiji, Malaysia, Ceylon, South Africa, Kenya, and Uganda, for example—with some working as indentured laborers, receiving free passage and enough money to survive in return for five to seven years of heavy labor. Others operated as independent merchants. Particularly in the Caribbean region, Indian migration rose as the end of slavery created a need for additional labor. Since the vast majority of these Asian migrants were male, it altered gender ratios in the islands and in their countries of origin, where women faced increased workloads.

Mines were another source of wage labor for many Asians. In the British-ruled Malay States (Malaysia), tin mining accelerated greatly in the late nineteenth century, and by 1895 that colony produced some 55 percent of the world's tin. Operated initially by Chinese and later by European entrepreneurs, Malaysian tin mines drew many millions of impoverished Chinese workers on strictly controlled three-year contracts. Appalling living conditions, disease, and accidents generated extraordinarily high death rates.

Beyond Southeast Asia, Chinese migrants moved north to Manchuria in substantial numbers, encouraged by a Chinese government eager to prevent Russian encroachment in the area. The gold rushes of Australia, Peru, and California also attracted hundreds of thousands of Chinese, who often found themselves subject to sharp discrimination from local people, including recently arrived European migrants. For example, Dennis Kearney, who led a California anti-immigrant labor organization with the slogan "The Chinese must go," was himself an Irish-born immigrant. Canada, Australia, New Zealand and the United States all enacted measures to restrict or end Chinese immigration in the late nineteenth century.

Snapshot   **Long-Distance Migration in an Age of Empire, 1846–1940**[20]

The age of empire was also an age of global migration. Beyond the three major patterns of long-distance migration shown here, shorter migrations within particular regions or colonies set millions more into motion.

Origins	Destination	Numbers
Europe	Americas	55–58 million
India, southern China	Southeast Asia, Indian Ocean rim, South Pacific	48–52 million
Northeast Asia, Russia	Manchuria, Siberia, Central Asia, Japan	46–51 million

A further destination of African and Asian migrants lay in the rapidly swelling cities of the colonial world—Lagos, Nairobi, Cairo, Calcutta, Rangoon, Batavia, Singapore, Saigon. Racially segregated, often unsanitary, and greatly overcrowded, these cities nonetheless were seen as meccas of opportunity for people all across the social spectrum. Traditional elites, absentee landlords, and wealthy Chinese businessmen occupied the top rungs of Southeast Asian cities. Western-educated people everywhere found opportunities as teachers, doctors, and professional specialists, but more often as clerks in European business offices and government bureaucracies. Skilled workers on the railways or in the ports represented a working-class elite, while a few labored in the factories that processed agricultural goods or manufactured basic products such as beer, cigarettes, cement, and furniture. Far more numerous were the construction workers, rickshaw drivers, food sellers, domestic servants, prostitutes, and others who made up the urban poor of colonial cities. In 1955, a British investigating commission described life in Nairobi, the capital of Kenya, one of Britain's richest colonies:

> The wages of the majority of African workers are too low to enable them to obtain accommodation which is adequate to any standard. The high cost of housing relative to wages is in itself a cause of overcrowding, because housing is shared to lighten the cost. This, with the high cost of food in towns, makes family life impossible for the majority.[21]

Thus, after more than half a century of colonial rule, British authorities themselves acknowledged that normal family life in the colony's major urban center proved out of reach for the vast majority. It was quite an admission.

Women and the Colonial Economy: Examples from Africa

If economic life in European empires varied greatly from place to place, even within the same colony, it also offered a different combination of opportunities and hardships to women than it did to men, as the experience of colonial Africa shows.[22] In precolonial Africa, women were almost everywhere active farmers, with responsibility

■ **Change**
How were the lives of African women altered by colonial economies?

for planting, weeding, and harvesting in addition to food preparation and child care. Men cleared the land, built houses, herded the cattle, and in some cases assisted with field work. Within this division of labor, women were expected to feed their own families and were usually allocated their own fields for that purpose. Many also were involved in local trading activity. Though clearly subordinate to men, African women nevertheless had a measure of economic autonomy.

As the demands of the colonial economy grew, women's lives increasingly diverged from those of men. In colonies where cash-crop agriculture was dominant, men often withdrew from subsistence production in favor of more lucrative export crops. Among the Ewe people of southern Ghana, men almost completely dominated the highly profitable cacao farming, whereas women assumed near total responsibility for domestic food production. In neighboring Ivory Coast, women had traditionally grown cotton for their families' clothing; but when that crop acquired a cash value, men insisted that cotton grown for export be produced on their own personal fields. Thus men acted to control the most profitable aspects of cash-crop agriculture and in doing so greatly increased the subsistence workload of women. One study from Cameroon estimated that women's working hours increased from forty-six per week in precolonial times to more than seventy by 1934.

Further increasing women's workload and differentiating their lives from those of men was labor migration. As growing numbers of men sought employment in the cities, on settler farms, or in the mines, their wives were left to manage the domestic economy almost alone. In many cases, women also had to supply food to men in the cities to compensate for very low urban wages. They often took over such traditionally male tasks as breaking the ground for planting, milking the cows, and supervising the herds, in addition to their normal responsibilities. In South Africa, where the demands of the European economy were particularly heavy, some 40 to 50 percent of able-bodied adult men were absent from the rural areas, and women headed 60 percent of households. In Botswana, which supplied much male labor to South Africa, married couples by the 1930s rarely lived together for more than two months at a time. Increasingly, men and women lived in different worlds with one focused on the cities and working for wages and the other on village life and subsistence agriculture.

Women coped with these difficult circumstances in a number of ways. Many sought closer relations with their families of birth rather than with their absent husbands' families, as would otherwise have been expected. Among the Luo of Kenya, women introduced labor-saving crops, adopted new farm implements, and earned some money as traders. In the cities, they established a variety of self-help associations, including those for prostitutes and for brewers of beer.

The colonial economy sometimes provided a measure of opportunity for enterprising women, particularly in small-scale trade and marketing. In some parts of West Africa, women came to dominate this sector of the economy by selling foodstuffs, cloth, and inexpensive imported goods, while men or foreign firms controlled the more profitable wholesale and import-export trade. Such opportunities sometimes gave women considerable economic autonomy. By the 1930s, for example, Nupe women in northern Nigeria had gained sufficient wealth as itinerant traders that they were contributing more to the family income than their husbands and frequently lent money to them. Among some Igbo groups in southern Nigeria, men were responsible for growing the prestigious yams, but women's crops—especially cassava—came to have a cash value during the colonial era, and women were entitled to keep the profits from selling it. "What is man? I have my own money" expressed the growing economic independence of such women.[23]

At the other end of the social scale, women of impoverished rural families, by necessity, often became virtually independent heads of household in the absence of their husbands. Others took advantage of new opportunities in mission schools, towns, and mines to flee the restrictions of rural patriarchy. Such challenges to patriarchal values elicited various responses from men, including increased accusations of witchcraft against women and fears of impotence. Among the Shona in Southern Rhodesia, and no doubt elsewhere, senior African men repeatedly petitioned the colonial authorities for laws and regulations that would criminalize adultery and restrict women's ability to leave their rural villages.[24] The control of women's sexuality and mobility was a common interest of European and African men.

Assessing Colonial Development

Beyond the many and varied changes that transformed the working lives of millions in the colonial world lies the difficult and highly controversial question of the overall economic impact of colonial rule on Asian and African societies. Defenders, both then and now, praise it for jump-starting modern economic growth, but numerous critics cite a record of exploitation and highlight the limitations and unevenness of that growth.

Amid the continuing debates, three things seem reasonably clear. First, colonial rule served, for better or worse, to further the integration of Asian and African economies into a global network of exchange, now centered in Europe. In many places, that process was well under way before conquest imposed foreign rule, and elsewhere it occurred without formal colonial control. Nonetheless, it is apparent that within the colonial world far more land and labor were devoted to production for the global market at the end of the colonial era than at its beginning. Many colonized groups and individuals benefited from their new access to global markets—Burmese rice farmers and West African cocoa farmers, for example. Others were devastated. In India, large-scale wheat exports to Britain continued unchecked—or even increased—despite a major drought and famine that claimed between 6 and 10 million lives in the late 1870s. A colonial government committed to free market principles declined to interfere with those exports or to provide much by way of relief. One senior official declared it "a mistake to spend so much money to save a lot of black fellows."[25]

Second, Europeans could hardly avoid conveying to the colonies some elements of their own modernizing process. It was in their interests to do so, and many felt

■ **Change**
Did colonial rule bring "economic progress" in its wake?

duty bound to "improve" the societies they briefly governed. Modern administrative and bureaucratic structures facilitated colonial control; communication and transportation infrastructure (railroads, motorways, ports, telegraphs, postal services) moved products to the world market; schools trained the army of intermediaries on which colonial rule depended; and modest health care provisions fulfilled some of the "civilizing mission" to which many Europeans felt committed. These elements of modernization made an appearance, however inadequately, during the colonial era.

Third, nowhere in the colonial world did a major breakthrough to modern industrial society occur. When India became independent after two centuries of colonial rule by the world's first industrial society, it was still one of the poorest of the world's developing countries. The British may not have created Indian poverty, but neither did they overcome it to any substantial degree. Scholars continue to debate the reasons for that failure: was it the result of deliberate British policies, or was it due to the conditions of Indian society? The nationalist movements that surged across Asia and Africa in the twentieth century had their own answer. To their many millions of participants, colonial rule, whatever its earlier promise, had become an economic dead end, whereas independence represented a grand opening to new and more hopeful possibilities. Paraphrasing a famous teaching of Jesus, Kwame Nkrumah, the first prime minister of an independent Ghana, declared, "Seek ye first the political kingdom, and all these other things [schools, factories, hospitals, for example] will be added unto you."

SUMMING UP SO FAR

In what different ways did the colonial experience reshape the economic lives of Asian and African societies?

Believing and Belonging: Identity and Cultural Change in the Colonial Era

The experience of colonial rule—its racism, its exposure to European culture, its social and economic upheavals—contributed much to cultural change within Asian and African societies. Coping with these enormous disruptions induced many colonized peoples to alter the ways they thought about themselves and their communities. Cultural identities, of course, are never static, but the transformations of the colonial era catalyzed substantial and quite rapid changes in what people believed and in how they defined the societies to which they belonged. Those transformed identities continued to echo long after European rule had ended.

Education

■ **Change**
What impact did Western education have on colonial societies?

For an important minority, it was the acquisition of Western education, obtained through missionary or government schools, that generated a new identity. To many European colonizers, education was a means of "uplifting native races," a paternalistic obligation of the superior to the inferior. To previously illiterate people, the knowledge of reading and writing of any kind often suggested an almost magical power. Within the colonial setting, it could mean an escape from some of the most onerous

The Educated Elite
Throughout the Afro-Asian world of the nineteenth century, the European presence generated a small group of people who enthusiastically embraced the culture and lifestyle of Europe. Here King Chulalongkorn of Siam poses with the crown prince and other young students, all of them impeccably garbed in European clothing. (© Hulton-Deutsch Collection/Corbis)

obligations of living under European control, such as forced labor. More positively, it meant access to better-paying positions in government bureaucracies, mission organizations, or business firms and to the exciting imported goods that their salaries could buy. Moreover, education often provided social mobility and elite status within their own communities and an opportunity to achieve, or at least approach, equality with whites in racially defined societies. An African man from colonial Kenya described an encounter he had as a boy in 1938 with a relative who was a teacher in a mission school:

> Aged about 25, he seems to me like a young god with his smart clothes and shoes, his watch, and a beautiful bicycle. I worshipped in particular his bicycle that day and decided that I must somehow get myself one. As he talked with us, it seemed to me that the secret of his riches came from his education, his knowledge of reading and writing, and that it was essential for me to obtain this power.[26]

Many such people ardently embraced European culture, dressing in European clothes, speaking French or English, building European-style houses, getting married in long white dresses, and otherwise emulating European ways. Some of the early Western-educated Bengalis from northeastern India boasted about dreaming in English and deliberately ate beef, to the consternation of their elders. In a well-known poem entitled "A Prayer for Peace," Léopold Senghor, a highly educated West African writer and political leader, enumerated the many crimes of colonialism and yet confessed, "I have a great weakness for France." Asian and African colonial societies now had a new cultural divide: between the small number who had mastered to varying degrees the ways of their rulers and the vast majority who had not. Literate Christians in the East African kingdom of Buganda referred with contempt to their "pagan" neighbors as "those who do not read."

Many among the Western-educated elite saw themselves as a modernizing vanguard, leading the regeneration of their societies in association with colonial authorities. For them, at least initially, the colonial enterprise was full of promise for a better future. The Vietnamese teacher and nationalist Nguyen Thai Hoc, while awaiting execution in 1930 by the French for his revolutionary activities, wrote about his earlier hopes: "At the beginning, I had thought to cooperate with the French in Indochina in order to serve my compatriots, my country, and my people, particularly in the areas of cultural and economic development."[27] Senghor too wrote wistfully about an earlier time when "we could have lived in harmony [with Europeans]."

In nineteenth-century India, Western-educated men organized a variety of reform societies, which drew inspiration from the classic texts of Hinduism while seeking a renewed Indian culture that was free of idolatry, caste restrictions, and other "errors" that had entered Indian life over the centuries. Much of this reform effort centered on improving the status of women. Thus reformers campaigned against *sati*, the ban on remarriage of widows, female infanticide, and child marriages, while advocating women's education and property rights. For a time, some of these Indian reformers saw themselves working in tandem with British colonial authorities. One of them, Keshub Chunder Sen (1838–1884), spoke to his fellow Indians in 1877: "You are bound to be loyal to the British government that came to your rescue, as God's ambassador, when your country was sunk in ignorance and superstition. . . . India in her present fallen condition seems destined to sit at the feet of England for many long years, to learn western art and science."[28] (See Document 18.1, pp. 913–15, for another such view.)

Such fond hopes for the modernization or renewal of Asian and African societies within a colonial framework would be bitterly disappointed. Europeans generally declined to treat their Asian and African subjects—even those with a Western education—as equal partners in the enterprise of renewal. The frequent denigration of their cultures as primitive, backward, uncivilized, or savage certainly rankled, particularly among the well-educated. "My people of Africa," wrote the West African intellectual James Aggrey in the 1920s, "we were created in the image of God, but men have made us think that we are chickens, and we still think we are; but we are eagles. Stretch forth your wings and fly."[29] In the long run, the educated classes in colonial societies everywhere found European rule far more of an obstacle to their countries' development than a means of achieving it. Turning decisively against a now-despised foreign imperialism, they led the many struggles for independence that came to fruition in the second half of the twentieth century.

Religion

Religion too provided the basis for new or transformed identities during the colonial era. Most dramatic were those places where widespread conversion to Christianity took place, such as New Zealand, the Pacific islands, and especially non-Muslim Africa. Some 10,000 missionaries had descended on Africa by 1910; by the 1960s, about 50 million Africans, roughly half of the non-Muslim population, claimed a Christian identity. The attractions of the new faith were many. As in the Americas centuries earlier, military defeat shook confidence in the old gods and local practices, fostering openness to new sources of supernatural power that could operate in the wider world now impinging on their societies. Furthermore, Christianity was widely associated with modern education, and, especially in Africa, mission schools were the primary providers of Western education. The young, the poor, and many women—all of them oppressed groups in many African societies—found new opportunities and greater freedom in some association with missions. Moreover, the spread of the Christian message was less the work of European missionaries than of those many thousands of African teachers, catechists, and pastors who brought the new faith to remote villages as well as the local communities that begged for a teacher and supplied the labor and materials to build a small church or school.

But missionary teaching and practice also generated conflict and opposition, particularly when they touched on gender roles. A wide range of issues focusing on the lives of women proved challenging for missionaries and spawned opposition from

African converts or potential converts. Female nudity offended Western notions of modesty. Polygyny contradicted Christian monogamy, though such prescriptions sat uneasily beside Old Testament practices, and the question of what male converts should do with their additional wives was always difficult. Bride wealth made marriage seem "a mere mercantile transaction." Marriages between Christians and non-Christians remained problematic. African sexual activity outside of monogamous marriage often resulted in disciplinary action or expulsion from the church. Missionaries' efforts to enforce Western gender norms were in part responsible for considerable turnover in the ranks of African church members.

Among the more explosive issues that agitated nascent Christian communities in colonial Kenya was that of "female circumcision," the excision of a pubescent girl's

■ Change

What were the attractions of Christianity within some colonial societies?

The Missionary Factor
Among the major change agents of the colonial era were the thousands of Christian missionaries who brought not only a new religion but also elements of European medicine, education, gender roles, and culture. Here is an assembly at a mission school for girls in New Guinea in the early twentieth century. (Rue des Archives/The Granger Collection, New York)

Wanjiku of Kenya: An Ordinary Woman in Extraordinary Times

Born in 1910 among the Gikuyu people of East Africa, Wanjiku witnessed almost the entire twentieth century.[30] Her life encompassed the dramatic intrusion of British colonialism, the coming of Christianity, the Mau Mau rebellion against European rule, the achievement of independence for Kenya in 1963, and the challenges of modernization in the decades that followed.

And yet, the first 30 years or more of Wanjiku's life were shaped far more by the customary patterns of rural Gikuyu culture than by the transformations of colonial rule. She grew up in her father's compound where her mother, three other wives, and more than a dozen children also lived. As a child, she began contributing to the household—fetching water, firewood, and vegetables—even as she learned the stories, riddles, and proverbs of Gikuyu folklore. At age fourteen, she had her ears pierced, thus achieving a "new stage of maturity."

Far more important, however, was her "circumcision," a procedure that involved the cutting of her genitals and the excision of the clitoris. For Wanjiku, as for virtually

A Gikuyu woman, such as Wanjiku, being instructed by a Home Guard official during the Mau Mau rebellion. (© Bettmann/Corbis)

all Gikuyu girls, this procedure was a prerequisite for becoming "a grown-up person" and eligible for marriage. Described as "buying maturity with pain," the operation was, as Wanjiku later recalled, "like being slaughtered." Circumcision also marked Wanjiku's entry into an age-set, a group of girls who had undergone this initiation into womanhood together. As adults they worked together in the fields, provided help and gifts at the birth of children, and protected one another from sexual abuse by men.

Now Wanjiku was also able to attend the evening dances where young men and women mingled. There she met her first husband, Wamai, who initiated the long process of negotiation between families and the payment of numerous goats and cows to the bride's father. Marriage, she found, "was a big change—learning about sex and my husband's habits." Tragedy struck, however, when both her husband and her first child died. A few years later, Wanjiku married Kamau, the younger brother of her first husband, with whom she had three sons. Her second marriage, unlike the first, was accompanied by a

clitoris and adjacent genital tissue as a part of initiation rites marking her coming-of-age.[31] To the Gikuyu people, among whom it was widely practiced, it was a prerequisite for adult status and marriage. To missionaries, it was physically damaging to girls and brought "unnecessary attention . . . to the non-spiritual aspects of sex." When missionaries in 1929 sought to enforce a ban on the practice among their African converts, outrage ensued. Thousands abandoned mission schools and churches, but they did not abandon Christianity or modern education. Rather they created a series of independent schools and churches in which they could practice their new faith and pursue their educational goals without missionary intrusion. Some recalled that the New Testament itself had declared that "circumcision is nothing and uncircumchurch service and a wedding ring, signs of encroaching Western culture. Both marriages were apparently relatively satisfying, and she reported with pride that neither man mistreated or beat her.

During the 1940s and 1950s, the new realities of colonial life began to touch Wanjiku more personally than before. She and Kamau became Christians around 1940, and in 1948, Wanjiku "became saved." "The saved ones," she declared, "do not take tobacco nor drink. And they don't abuse anybody." She then joined a church-based "Mother's Union," vowing "never again to carry out old Gikuyu customs." For Wanjiku, this group became a major source of social support that operated outside of traditional Gikuyu culture.

In 1952, Wanjiku found herself caught up in the Gikuyu-based Mau Mau rebellion against colonial rule. To separate the general population from the Mau Mau "freedom fighters" in the surrounding forests, the colonial government forced most Gikuyu to relocate into compact villages closely and brutally supervised by the Home Guard, local African police appointed by European authorities. Wanjiku and many others were required to dig a large trench around the village to keep the rebels out. "We were like prisoners," Wanjiku reported. "If we started to drag behind working, we were beaten." Caught between the opposing forces of the Home Guard and the Mau Mau fighters, Wanjiku lived in fear. "If you made a mistake with the Home Guard, you would die. If you made a mistake with the Mau Mau, you would die too."

The British crushed the Mau Mau rebellion by 1956, but, by 1963 Kenya, like dozens of other African countries, had achieved its independence. Wanjiku remembered the day with exhilaration. "We spent the whole night singing and dancing. We were so happy because we would never be ruled by foreigners again. It also meant the end of the beatings." It was perhaps the high point of Wanjiku's consciousness as a public person and a participant in a new nation.

In the decades following independence, Wanjiku experienced still further changes. She and her husband began to grow tea as a cash crop, something limited to European farmers for much of the colonial era. Kenya's new government tried to forbid female circumcision, and, as young people were increasingly drawn to the larger cities, older rural social patterns broke down. Boys and girls of different age-sets mingled far more freely than before. Educated young people felt superior and sometimes behaved disrespectfully to illiterate elders such as Wanjiku.

By the 1990s, Wanjiku was an old woman afflicted with arthritis and much diminished vision. She saw herself less as a Kenyan than as a Gikuyu. No longer able to farm, she counseled her children, looked after her grandchildren, and enjoyed recounting her life story to a visiting anthropologist.

Question: How does Wanjiku's life reflect both the continuities and changes of the twentieth century in African history?

cision is nothing." And so, wrote one angry convert to a local missionary, "Has God spoken to you this time and informed you that those who circumcise will not enter in to God's place? It is better for a European like you to leave off speaking about such things because you can make the Gospel to be evil spoken of." (See the Portrait above for the experience of Wanjiku, a Gikuyu woman.)

As elsewhere, Christianity in Africa soon became Africanized. Within mission-based churches, many converts continued using protective charms and medicines and consulting local medicine men, all of which caused their missionary mentors to speak frequently of "backsliding." Other converts continued to believe in their old gods and spirits but now deemed them evil and sought their destruction. Furthermore,

■ Change

How and why did Hinduism emerge as a distinct religious tradition during the colonial era in India?

thousands of separatist movements established a wide array of independent churches, which were thoroughly Christian but under African rather than missionary control and which in many cases incorporated African cultural practices and modes of worship. It was a twentieth-century "African Reformation."

In India, where Christianity made only very modest inroads, leading intellectuals and reformers began to define their region's endlessly varied beliefs, practices, sects, rituals, and philosophies as a more distinct, unified, and separate religion now known as Hinduism. It was in part an effort to provide for India a religion wholly equivalent to Christianity, "an accessible tradition and a feeling of historical worth when faced with the humiliation of colonial rule."[32] To Swami Vivekananda (1863–1902), one of nineteenth-century India's most influential religious figures, a revived Hinduism, shorn of its distortions, offered a means of uplifting the country's village communities, which were the heart of Indian civilization. Moreover, it could offer spiritual support to a Western world mired in materialism and militarism, a message that he took to the First World Parliament of Religions held in 1893 in Chicago. Here was India speaking back to Europe:

Let the foreigners come and flood the land with their armies, never mind. Up, India and conquer the world with your spirituality. . . . The whole of the Western world is a volcano which may burst tomorrow. . . . Now is the time to work so that India's spiritual ideas may penetrate deep into the West.[33]

This new notion of Hinduism provided a cultural foundation for emerging ideas of India as a nation, but it also contributed to a clearer sense of Muslims as a distinct community in India. Before the British takeover, little sense of commonality united the many diverse communities who practiced Islam—urban and rural dwellers; nomads and farmers; artisans, merchants, and state officials. But the British had created separate inheritance laws for all Muslims and others for all Hindus; in their census taking, they counted the numbers of people within these now sharply distinguished groups; and they allotted seats in local councils according to these artificial categories. As some anti-British patriots began to cast India in Hindu terms, the idea of Muslims as a separate community, which was perhaps threatened by the much larger number of Hindus, began to make sense to some who practiced Islam. In the early twentieth century, a young Hindu Bengali schoolboy noticed that "our Muslim school-fellows were beginning to air the fact of their being Muslims rather more consciously than before and with a touch

Hinduism in the West
The cultural interactions of the colonial era brought Asian traditions such as Hinduism to the attention of small groups in Europe and the United States. The visit of India's Swami Vivekananda, shown here, to the First World Parliament of Religions in Chicago in 1893 was part of that process. (Archiv Peter Ruhe/akg-images)

of assertiveness."[34] Here were the beginnings of what became in the twentieth century a profound religious and political division within the South Asian peninsula.

"Race" and "Tribe"

In Africa as well, intellectuals and ordinary people alike forged new ways of belonging as they confronted the upheavals of colonial life. Central to these new identities were notions of race and ethnicity. By the end of the nineteenth century, a number of African thinkers, familiar with Western culture, began to define the idea of an "African identity." Previously, few if any people on the continent had regarded themselves as Africans. Rather they were members of particular local communities, usually defined by language; some were also Muslims; and still others inhabited some state or empire. Now, however, influenced by the common experience of colonial oppression and by a highly derogatory European racism, well-educated Africans began to think in broader terms, similar to Indian reformers who were developing the notion of Hinduism. It was an effort to revive the cultural self-confidence of their people by articulating a larger, common, and respected "African tradition," equivalent to that of Western culture.

> **■ Change**
> In what way were "race" and "tribe" new identities in colonial Africa?

This effort took various shapes. One line of argument held that African culture and history in fact possessed the very characteristics that Europeans exalted. Knowing that Europeans valued large empires and complex political systems, African intellectuals pointed with pride to the ancient kingdoms of Ethiopia, Mali, Songhay, and others. C. A. Diop, a French-educated scholar from Senegal, insisted that Egyptian civilization was in fact the work of black Africans. Reversing European assumptions, Diop argued that Western civilization owed much to Egyptian influence and was therefore derived from Africa. Black people, in short, had a history of achievement fully comparable to that of Europe and therefore deserved just as much respect and admiration.

An alternative approach to defining an African identity lay in praising the differences between African and European cultures. The most influential proponent of such views was Edward Blyden (1832–1912), a West African born in the West Indies and educated in the United States who later became a prominent scholar and political official in Liberia. Blyden accepted the assumption that the world's various races were different but argued that each had its own distinctive contribution to make to world civilization. The uniqueness of African culture, Blyden wrote, lay in its communal, cooperative, and egalitarian societies, which contrasted sharply with Europe's highly individualistic, competitive, and class-ridden societies; in its harmonious relationship with nature as opposed to Europe's efforts to dominate and exploit the natural order; and particularly in its profound religious sensibility, which Europeans had lost in centuries of attention to material gain. Like Vivekananda in India, Blyden argued that Africa had a global mission "to be the spiritual conservatory of the world."[35]

In the twentieth century, such ideas resonated with a broader public. Hundreds of thousands of Africans took part in World War I, during which they encountered other Africans as well as Europeans. Some were able to travel widely. Contact with American black leaders such as Booker T. Washington, W. E. B. DuBois, Marcus Garvey, and various West Indian intellectuals further stimulated among a few a sense of belonging to an even larger pan-African world. Such notions underlay the growing nationalist movements that contested colonial rule as the twentieth century unfolded.

For the vast majority, however, the most important new sense of belonging that evolved from the colonial experience was not the notion of "Africa"; rather, it was the idea of "tribe" or, in the language of contemporary scholars, that of ethnic identity. African peoples, of course, had long recognized differences among themselves based on language, kinship, clan, village, or state, but these were seldom sharp or clearly defined. Boundaries fluctuated and were hazy; local communities often incorporated a variety of culturally different peoples. The idea of an Africa sharply divided into separate and distinct "tribes" was in fact a European notion that facilitated colonial administration and reflected Europeans' belief in African primitiveness. For example, when the British began to rule the peoples living along the northern side of Lake Tanganyika, in present-day Tanzania, they found a series of communities that were similar to one another in language and customs but that governed themselves separately and certainly had not regarded themselves as a distinct "tribe." It was British attempts to rule them as a single people, first through a "paramount chief" and later through a council of chiefs and elders, that resulted in their being called, collectively, the Nyakyusa. A tribe had been born. By requiring people to identify their tribe on applications for jobs, schools, and identity cards, colonial governments spread the idea of tribe widely within their colonies.

New ethnic identities were not simply imposed by Europeans; Africans increasingly found ethnic or tribal labels useful. This was especially true in rapidly growing urban areas. Surrounded by a bewildering variety of people and in a setting where competition for jobs, housing, and education was very intense, migrants to the city found it helpful to categorize themselves and others in larger ethnic terms. Thus, in many colonial cities, people who spoke similar languages, shared a common culture, or came from the same general part of the country began to think of themselves as a single people—a new tribe. They organized a rich variety of ethnic or tribal associations to provide mutual assistance while in the cities and to send money back home to build schools or clinics. Migrant workers, far from home and concerned to protect their rights to land and to their wives and families, found a sense of security in being part of a recognized tribe, with its chiefs, courts, and established authority.

The Igbo people of southeastern Nigeria represent a case in point. Prior to the twentieth century, they were organized in a series of independently governed village groups. Although they spoke related languages, they had no unifying political system and no myth of common ancestry. Occupying a region of unusually dense population, many of these people eagerly seized on Western education and moved in large numbers to the cities and towns of colonial Nigeria. There they gradually discovered what they had in common and how they differed from the other peoples of Nigeria.

By the 1940s, they were organizing on a national level and calling on Igbos every-where to "sink all differences" to achieve "tribal unity, cooperation, and progress of all the Igbos." Fifty years earlier, however, no one had regarded himself or herself as an Igbo. One historian summed up the process of creating African ethnic identities in this way: "Europeans believed Africans belonged to tribes; Africans built tribes to belong to."[36]

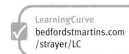

LearningCurve
bedfordstmartins.com
/strayer/LC

Reflections: Who Makes History?

Winners may write history, but they do not make history, at least not alone. Domi-nant groups everywhere — slave owners, upper classes, men generally, and certainly colonial rulers — have found their actions constrained and their choices limited by the sheer presence of subordinated people and the ability of those people to act. Euro-peans who sought to make their countries self-sufficient in cotton by requiring colo-nized Africans to grow it generally found themselves unable to achieve that goal. Missionaries who tried to impose their own understanding of Christianity in the colonies found their converts often unwilling to accept missionary authority or the cultural framework in which the new religion was presented. In the twentieth century, colonial rulers all across Asia and Africa found that their most highly educated sub-jects became the leaders of those movements seeking to end colonial rule. Clearly this was not what they had intended.

In recent decades, historians have been at pains to uncover the ways in which subordinated people — slaves, workers, peasants, women, the colonized — have been able to act in their own interests, even within the most oppressive conditions. This kind of "history from below" found expression in a famous book about American slavery that was subtitled *The World the Slaves Made*. Historians of women's lives have sought to show women not only as victims of patriarchy but also as historical actors in their own right.

Likewise, colonized people in any number of ways actively shaped the history of the colonial era. On occasion, they resisted and rebelled; in various times and places, they embraced, rejected, and transformed a transplanted Christianity; many eagerly sought Western education but later turned it against the colonizers; women both suffered from and creatively coped with the difficulties of colonial life; and every-where people created new ways of belonging. None of this diminishes the hardships, the enormous inequalities of power, or the exploitation and oppression of the colo-nial experience. Rather it suggests that history is often made through the struggle of unequal groups and that the outcome corresponds to no one's intentions.

Perhaps we might let Karl Marx have the last word on this endlessly fascinating topic: "Men make their own history," he wrote, "but they do not make it as they please nor under conditions of their own choosing." In the colonial experience of the nine-teenth and early twentieth centuries, both the colonizers and the colonized "made history," but neither was able to do so as they pleased.

Second Thoughts

What's the Significance?

European racism, 883–84

scramble for Africa, 885–86

Indian Rebellion, 1857–1858, 890

Congo Free State/Leopold II, 894

cultivation system, 895–96

cash-crop agriculture, 895–96

Western-educated elite, 902–04

Wanjiku, 906–07

Africanization of Christianity, 907–08

Swami Vivekananda, 908

Edward Blyden, 909

Big Picture Questions

1. In what ways did colonial rule rest on violence and coercion, and in what ways did it elicit voluntary cooperation or generate benefits for some people?

2. In what respects were colonized people more than victims of colonial conquest and rule? To what extent could they act in their own interests within the colonial situation?

3. Was colonial rule a transforming, even a revolutionary, experience, or did it serve to freeze or preserve existing social and economic patterns? What evidence can you find to support both sides of this argument?

4. **Looking Back:** How would you compare the colonial experience of Asian and African peoples during the long nineteenth century to the earlier colonial experience in the Americas?

Next Steps: For Further Study

For Web sites and additional documents related to this chapter, see **Make History** at bedfordstmartins.com /highschool/strayer.

A. Adu Boahen, *African Perspectives on Colonialism* (1987). An examination of the colonial experience by a prominent African scholar.

Alice Conklin and Ian Fletcher, *European Imperialism, 1830–1930* (1999). A collection of both classical reflections on empire and examples of modern scholarship.

Scott B. Cook, *Colonial Encounters in the Age of High Imperialism* (1996). Seven case studies of the late nineteenth-century colonial experience.

Adam Hochschild, *King Leopold's Ghost* (1999). A journalist's evocative account of the horrors of early colonial rule in the Congo.

Douglas Peers, *India under Colonial Rule* (2006). A concise and up-to-date exploration of colonial India.

Bonnie Smith, ed., *Imperialism* (2000). A fine collection of documents, pictures, and commentary on nineteenth- and twentieth-century empires.

Margaret Strobel, *Gender, Sex, and Empire* (1994). A brief account of late twentieth- century historical thinking about colonial life and gender.

"History of Imperialism," http://members.aol.com/TeacherNet/World.html. A Web site with dozens of links to documents, essays, maps, cartoons, and pictures dealing with modern empires.

Documents

Considering the Evidence:
Indian Responses to Empire

The European empires of the nineteenth and early twentieth centuries elicited a variety of responses from their colonial subjects—acceptance and even gratitude, disappointment with unfulfilled promises, active resistance, and sharp criticism. The documents that follow present a range of Indian commentary on British rule during this time.

India was Britain's "jewel in the crown," the centerpiece of its expanding empire in Asia and Africa (see Map 18.1, p. 886). Until the late 1850s, Britain's growing involvement with South Asia was organized and led by the British East India Company, a private trading firm that had acquired a charter from the Crown allowing it to exercise military, political, and administrative functions in India as well as its own commercial operations (see pp. 676–77). But after the explosive upheaval of the Indian Rebellion of 1857–1858, the British government itself assumed control of the region. Throughout the colonial era, the British relied heavily on an alliance with traditional elite groups in Indian society—landowners; the "princes" who governed large parts of the region; and the Brahmins, the highest-ranking segment of India's caste-based society.

Document 18.1

Seeking Western Education

Ram Mohan Roy (1772–1833), born and highly educated within a Brahmin Hindu family, subsequently studied both Arabic and Persian, learned English, came into contact with British Christian missionaries, and found employment with the British East India Company. He emerged in the early nineteenth century as a leading advocate for religious and social reform within India, with a particular interest in ending *sati*, the practice in which widows burned themselves on their husbands' funeral pyres. In 1823, he learned about a British plan to establish a school in Calcutta that was to focus on Sanskrit texts and traditional Hindu learning. Document 18.1 records his response to that school, and to British colonial rule, in a letter to the British governor-general of India.

■ Why was Roy opposed to the creation of this school?

■ What does this letter reveal about Roy's attitude toward Indian and European cultures?

■ What future did Roy imagine for India?

■ How would you describe Roy's attitude toward British colonial rule in India?

RAM MOHAN ROY
Letter to Lord Amherst
1823

The establishment of a new Sanskrit School in Calcutta evinces the laudable desire of Government to improve the natives of India by education, a blessing for which they must ever be grateful.... When this seminary of learning was proposed ... we were filled with sanguine hopes that [it would employ] European gentlemen of talent and education to instruct the natives of India in Mathematics, Natural Philosophy, Chemistry, Anatomy, and other useful sciences, which the natives of Europe have carried to a degree of perfection that has raised them above the inhabitants of other parts of the world.... Our hearts were filled with mingled feelings of delight and gratitude; we already offered up thanks to Providence for inspiring the most generous and enlightened nations of the West with the glorious ambition of planting in Asia the arts and sciences of Modern Europe.

We find [however] that the Government are establishing a Sanskrit school under Hindu Pandits° to impart such knowledge as is already current in India. This seminary can only be expected to load the minds of youth with grammatical niceties and metaphysical distinctions of little or no practical use to the possessors or to society. The pupils will there acquire what was known two thousand years ago

with the addition of vain and empty subtleties since then produced by speculative men, such as is already commonly taught in all parts of India.…

Neither can much improvement arise from such speculations as the following which are the themes suggested by the Vedanta:° in what manner is the soul absorbed in the Deity? What relation does it bear to the Divine Essence? Nor will youths be fitted to be better members of society by the Vedantic doctrines which teach them to believe that all visible things have no real existence, that as father, brother, etc., have no actual entity, they consequently deserve no real affection, and therefore the sooner we escape from them and leave the world the better.…

[T]he Sanskrit system of education would be the best calculated to keep this country in darkness, if such had been the policy of the British legislature. But as the improvement of the native population is the object of the Government, it will consequently promote a more liberal and enlightened system of instruction, embracing Mathematics, Natural Philosophy, Chemistry, Anatomy, with other useful sciences, which may be accomplished with the sums proposed by employing a few gentlemen of talent and learning educated in Europe and providing a College furnished with necessary books, instruments, and other apparatus. In presenting this subject to your Lordship, I conceive myself discharging a solemn duty which I owe to my countrymen, and

°**Pandits:** learned teachers.

Source: Rammohun Roy, *The English Works of Raja Rammohun Roy* (Allahabad, India: Panini Office, 1906), 471–74.

°**Vedanta:** a branch of Hindu philosophy.

also to that enlightened sovereign and legislature which have extended their benevolent care to this distant land, actuated by a desire to improve the in-habitants, and therefore humbly trust you will ex-cuse the liberty I have taken in thus expressing my sentiments to your Lordship.

Document 18.2

The Indian Rebellion

In 1857–1858, British-ruled India erupted in violent rebellion (see p. 890). Some among the rebels imagined that the Mughal Empire might be restored to its former power and glory. Such was the hope that animated the Azamgarh Proc-lamation, issued in the summer of 1857, allegedly by the grandson of the last and largely powerless Mughal emperor, Bahadur Shah.

■ What grievances against British rule does this document disclose?

■ How does the proclamation imagine the future of India, should the rebellion succeed? How does this compare to Ram Mohan Roy's vision of India's future in Document 18.1?

■ To what groups or classes of people was the proclamation directed? What classes were left out in the call to rebellion? Why might they have been omitted?

■ Does the proclamation represent the strength and authority of the Mughal Empire or its weakness and irrelevance?

Prince Feroze Shah

The Azamgarh Proclamation
1857

It is well known to all that in this age the people of Hindustan,° both Hindus and Muslims, are being ruined under the tyranny and oppression of the infidel and the treacherous English. It is there-fore the bounden duty of all the wealthy people of India, especially of those who have any sort of con-nection with any of the Muslim royal families and are considered the pastors and masters of their people, to stake their lives and property for the well-being of the public. . . . I, who am the grandson of Bahadur Shah, have . . . come here to extirpate the infidels re-siding in the eastern part of the country, and to liber-ate and protect the poor helpless people now groan-ing under their iron rule. . . .

Section I: Regarding Zamindars°
It is evident the British government, in making [land] settlements, have imposed exorbitant jummas,° and have disgraced and ruined several zamindars, by

°**Hindustan:** northern India.

Source: "The Azamgarh Proclamation," *Delhi Gazette,* September 29, 1857.

°**Zamindars:** large landowners.

°**jummas:** taxes.

putting up their estates to public auction for arrears of rent, insomuch, that on the institution of a suit by a common ryot° yet, a maidservant, or a slave, the respectable zamindars are summoned into court arrested, put in gaol, and disgraced. . . . Besides this, the coffers of the zamindars are annually taxed with subscriptions for schools, hospitals, roads, etc. Such extortions will have no manner of existence in the Badshahi government;° but, on the contrary, the jummas will be light, the dignity and honour of the zamindars safe, and every zamindar will have absolute rule in his own zamindary.

Section II: Regarding Merchants

It is plain that the infidel and treacherous British government have monopolized the trade of all the fine and valuable merchandise such as indigo, cloth, and other articles of shipping, leaving only the trade of trifles to the people, and even in this they are not without their share of the profits, which they secure by means of customs and stamp fees, etc., in money suits, so that the people have merely a trade in name. Besides this, the profits of the traders are taxed with postages, tolls, and subscriptions for schools. Notwithstanding all these concessions, the merchants are liable to imprisonment and disgrace at the instance or complaint of a worthless man. When the Badshahi government is established, all these aforesaid fraudulent practices shall be dispensed with, and the trade of every article, without exception both by land and water, shall be open to the native merchants of India, who will have the benefit of the government steam-vessels and steam carriages for the conveyance of their merchandise gratis. . . .

Section III: Regarding Public Servants

It is not a secret thing, that under the British government, natives employed in the civil and military services have little respect, low pay, and no manner of influence; and all the posts of dignity and emolument in both the departments are exclusively bestowed upon Englishmen. . . . But under the Badshahi government, [these] posts . . . will be given to the natives. . . . Natives, whether Hindus or Muslims, who fall fighting against the English, are sure to go to heaven; and those killed fighting for the English, will, doubtless, go to hell; therefore, all the natives in the British service ought to be alive to their religion and interest, and, abjuring their loyalty to the English, side with the Badshahi government and obtain salaries of 200 or 300 rupees per month for the present, and be entitled to high posts in future.

Section IV: Regarding Artisans

It is evident that the Europeans, by the introduction of English articles into India, have thrown the weavers, the cotton-dressers, the carpenters, the blacksmiths, and the shoemakers, etc., out of employ, and have engrossed their occupations, so that every description of native artisan has been reduced to beggary. But under the Badshahi government the native artisan will exclusively be employed in the services of the kings, the rajahs, and the rich; and this will no doubt insure their prosperity.

Section V: Regarding Pundits,° Fakirs,° and Other Learned Persons

The pundits and fakirs being the guardians of the Hindu and Muslim religions, respectively, and the European being the enemies of both the religions, and as at present a war is raging against the English on account of religion, the pundits and fakirs are bound to present themselves to me and take their share in the holy war, otherwise they will stand condemned . . . but if they come, they will, when the Badshahi government is well established, receive rent-free lands.

Lastly, be it known to all, that whoever out of the above-named classes, shall . . . still cling to the British government, all his estates shall be confiscated, and his property plundered, and he himself, with his whole family, shall be imprisoned, and ultimately put to death.

°**ryot:** peasant farmer.

°**Badshahi government:** restored imperial government.

°**Pundits:** scholars.

°**Fakirs:** religious mystics.

Document 18.3

The Credits and Debits of British Rule in India

Dadabhai Naoroji (1825–1917) was a well-educated Indian intellectual, a cotton trader in London, and a founding member of the Indian National Congress, an elite organization established in 1885 to press for a wider range of opportunities for educated Indians within the colonial system. He was also the first Indian to serve in the British Parliament. In 1871, while addressing an English audience in London, he was asked about the impact of British rule in India. Representing a "moderate" view within Indian political circles at the time, he organized his response in terms of "credits" and "debits."

■ According to Naoroji, what are the chief advantages and drawbacks of British rule?

■ What is Naoroji seeking from Britain?

■ How does Naoroji's posture toward British rule compare to that of Ram Mohan Roy in Document 18.1 or the Azamgarh Proclamation in Document 18.2?

DADABHAI NAOROJI

Speech to a London Audience

1871

Credit

In the Cause of Humanity: Abolition of *suttee*° and infanticide. Destruction of *Dacoits, Thugs, Pindarees*° and other such pests of Indian society. Allowing remarriage of Hindu widows, and charitable aid in time of famine. Glorious work all this, of which any nation may well be proud. . . .

In the Cause of Civilization: Education, both male and female. Though yet only partial, an inestimable

blessing as far as it has gone, and leading gradually to the destruction of superstition, and many moral and social evils. Resuscitation of India's own noble literature, modified and refined by the enlightenment of the West.

Politically: Peace and order. Freedom of speech and liberty of the press. Higher political knowledge and aspirations. Improvement of government in the native states. Security of life and property. Freedom from oppression caused by the caprice or greed of despotic rulers, and from devastation by war. Equal justice between man and man (sometimes vitiated by partiality to Europeans). Services of highly educated administrators, who have achieved the above-mentioned results.

Materially: Loans for railways and irrigation. Development of a few valuable products, such as

---

°*suttee:* variant spelling of *sati*, the practice of widows burning themselves on their husbands' funeral pyres.

°*Dacoits, Thugs, Pindarees:* thieves, murderers, bands of robbers.

Source: Dadabhai Naoroji, *Essays, Speeches, Addresses and Writings* (Bombay: Caxton Printing Works, 1887), 131–36.

indigo, tea, coffee, silk, etc. Increase of exports. Telegraphs.

Generally: A slowly growing desire of late to treat India equitably, and as a country held in trust. Good intentions. No nation on the face of the earth has ever had the opportunity of achieving such a glorious work as this. . . . I appreciate, and so do my countrymen, what England has done for India, and I know that it is only in British hands that her regeneration can be accomplished. Now for the debit side.

Debit

In the Cause of Humanity: Nothing. Everything, therefore, is in your favor under this heading.

In the Cause of Civilization: As I have said already, there has been a failure to do as much as might have been done, but I put nothing to the debit. Much has been done, though.

Politically: Repeated breach of pledges to give the natives a fair and reasonable share in the higher administration of their own country, which has much shaken confidence in the good faith of the British word. Political aspirations and the legitimate claim to have a reasonable voice in the legislation and the imposition and disbursement of taxes, met to a very slight degree, thus treating the natives of India not as British subjects, in whom representation is a birthright. Consequent on the above, an utter disregard of the feelings and views of the natives. . . .

Financially: All attention is engrossed in devising new modes of taxation, without any adequate effort to increase the means of the people to pay; and the consequent vexation and oppressiveness of the taxes imposed, imperial and local. Inequitable financial relations between England and India, i.e., the political debt of £100,000,000 clapped on India's shoulders, and all home charges also, though the British Exchequer contributes nearly £3,000,000 to the expense of the colonies.

Materially: The political drain, up to this time, from India to England, of above £500,000,000, at the lowest computation, in principal alone, which with interest would be some thousands of millions. The further continuation of this drain at the rate, at present, of above £12,000,000 per annum, with a tendency to increase. The consequent continuous impoverishment and exhaustion of the country, except so far as it has been very partially relieved and replenished by the railway and irrigation loans, and the windfall of the consequences of the American war, since 1850. Even with this relief, the material condition of India is such that the great mass of the poor have hardly tuppence a day and a few rags, or a scanty subsistence. The famines that were in their power to prevent, if they had done their duty, as a good and intelligent government. The policy adopted during the last fifteen years of building railways, irrigation works, etc., is hopeful, has already resulted in much good to your credit, and if persevered in, gratitude and contentment will follow. An increase of exports without adequate compensation; loss of manufacturing industry and skill. Here I end the debit side.

Summary:

To sum up the whole, the British rule has been: morally, a great blessing; politically, peace and order on one hand, blunders on the other; materially, impoverishment, relieved as far as the railway and other loans go. The natives call the British system "Sakar ki Churi," the knife of sugar. That is to say, there is no oppression, it is all smooth and sweet, but it is the knife, notwithstanding. I mention this that you should know these feelings. Our great misfortune is that you do not know our wants. When you will know our real wishes, I have not the least doubt that you would do justice. The genius and spirit of the British people is fair play and justice.

Document 18.4

Gandhi on Modern Civilization

Mahatma Gandhi (1869–1948), clearly modern India's most beloved leader, is best known for his theories of *satyagraha*. This was an aggressive but nonviolent approach to political action that directly challenged and disobeyed unjust laws, while seeking to change the hearts of their British oppressors (see pp. 1094–96 in Chapter 22). But Gandhi's thinking was distinctive in another way as well, for he objected not only to the foreign and exploitative character of British rule but also more fundamentally to the modern civilization that it carried. In 1908, he spelled out that critique in a pamphlet titled *Hind Swaraj* ("Indian Home Rule"). There Gandhi assumes the role of an "editor," responding to questions from a "reader."

■ What is Gandhi's most fundamental criticism of British rule in India?

■ What is the difference between his concept of "civilization" and that which he ascribes to the British?

■ How does Gandhi reconcile the idea of India as a single nation with the obvious religious division between Hindus and Muslims?

■ What kind of future does Gandhi seek for his country?

■ What criticisms do you imagine that Gandhi met as he sought to introduce his ideas into India's increasingly nationalist political life?

MAHATMA GANDHI

Indian Home Rule
1909

READER: Now you will have to explain what you mean by civilization.

EDITOR: Let us first consider what state of things is described by the word "civilization." . . . The people of Europe today live in better-built houses than they did a hundred years ago. This is considered an emblem of civilization. . . . If people of a certain country, who have hitherto not been in the habit of wearing much clothing, boots, etc., adopt European clothing, they are supposed to have become civilized out of savagery. Formerly, in Europe, people ploughed their lands mainly by manual labor. Now, one man can plough a vast tract by means of steam engines and can thus amass great wealth. This is called a sign of civilization. Formerly, only a few men wrote valuable books. Now, anybody writes and prints anything he likes and poisons people's minds. Formerly, men traveled in wagons. Now, they fly through the air in trains at the rate of four hundred and more miles per day. This is considered the height of civilization. It has been stated that, as men progress, they shall be able to travel in airship

Source: Mohandas Gandhi, *Indian Home Rule* (Madras: Ganesh, 1922), pts. 6, 8, 9, 10, 13.

and reach any part of the world in a few hours.... Everything will be done by machinery. Formerly, when people wanted to fight with one another, they measured between them their bodily strength; now it is possible to take away thousands of lives by one man working behind a gun from a hill. This is civilization.... Formerly, men were made slaves under physical compulsion. Now they are enslaved by temptation of money and of the luxuries that money can buy.... This civilization takes note neither of morality nor of religion. Its votaries calmly state that their business is not to teach religion. Some even consider it to be a superstitious growth.... This civilization is irreligion, and it has taken such a hold on the people in Europe that those who are in it appear to be half mad. They lack real physical strength or courage. They keep up their energy by intoxication. They can hardly be happy in solitude. Women, who should be the queens of households, wander in the streets or they slave away in factories. For the sake of a pittance, half a million women in England alone are laboring under trying circumstances in factories or similar institutions.

This civilization is such that one has only to be patient and it will be self-destroyed.... I cannot give you an adequate conception of it. It is eating into the vitals of the English nation. It must be shunned.... Civilization is not an incurable disease, but it should never be forgotten that the English are at present afflicted by it.

READER: I now understand why the English hold India. I should like to know your views about the condition of our country.

EDITOR: It is a sad condition.... It is my deliberate opinion that India is being ground down, not under the English heel, but under that of modern civilization. It is groaning under the monster's terrible weight. [M]y first complaint is that India is becoming irreligious.... We are turning away from God.... [W]e should set a limit to our worldly ambition.... [O]ur religious ambition should be illimitable....

EDITOR: Railways, lawyers, and doctors have impoverished the country so much so that, if we do not wake up in time, we shall be ruined.

READER: I do now, indeed, fear that we are not likely to agree at all. You are attacking the very

institutions which we have hitherto considered to be good.

EDITOR: It must be manifest to you that, but for the railways, the English could not have such a hold on India as they have. The railways, too, have spread the bubonic plague. Without them the masses could not move from place to place. They are the carriers of plague germs. Formerly we had natural segregation. Railways have also increased the frequency of famines because, owing to facility of means of locomotion, people sell out their grain and it is sent to the dearest markets. People become careless and so the pressure of famine increases. Railways accentuate the evil nature of man. Bad men fulfill their evil designs with greater rapidity....

READER: You have denounced railways, lawyers, and doctors. I can see that you will discard all machinery. What, then, is civilization?

EDITOR: The answer to that question is not difficult. I believe that the civilization India has evolved is not to be beaten in the world.... India is still, somehow or other, sound at the foundation.... India remains immovable and that is her glory. It is a charge against India that her people are so uncivilized, ignorant, and stolid that it is not possible to induce them to adopt any changes. It is a charge really against our merit. What we have tested and found true on the anvil of experience, we dare not change. Many thrust their advice upon India, and she remains steady. This is her beauty: it is the sheet-anchor of our hope.

Civilization is that mode of conduct which points out to man the path of duty. Performance of duty and observance of morality are convertible terms. To observe morality is to attain mastery over our mind and our passions. So doing, we know ourselves.... If this definition be correct, then India ... has nothing to learn from anybody else.... Our ancestors, therefore, set a limit to our indulgences. [They] dissuaded us from luxuries and pleasures. We have managed with the same kind of plough as existed thousands of years ago. We have retained the same kind of cottages that we had in former times and our indigenous education remains the same as before. We have had no system of life-corroding competition. Each followed his own occupation or trade and charged a regulation wage.

It was not that we did not know how to invent machinery, but our forefathers knew that, if we set our hearts after such things, we would become slaves and lose our moral fiber. . . . They were, therefore, satisfied with small villages. . . . A nation with a constitution like this is fitter to teach others than to learn from others. . . .

The tendency of the Indian civilization is to elevate the moral being; that of the Western civilization is to propagate immorality. The latter is godless; the former is based on a belief in God. So understanding and so believing, it behooves every lover of India to cling to the Indian civilization even as a child clings to the mother's breast.

Using the Evidence:
Indian Responses to Empire

1. **Noticing differences and changes:** What different understandings of British colonial rule are reflected in these documents? In what ways did those understandings change over time? How might you account for those differences and changes?

2. **Describing alternative futures:** What can you infer about the kind of future for India that the authors of these documents anticipate?

3. **Noticing what's missing:** What Indian voices are not represented in these documents? How might such people have articulated a different understanding of the colonial experience?

4. **Responding to Gandhi:** How might each of the other authors have responded to Gandhi's analysis of British colonial rule and his understanding of "civilization"? To what extent do you find Gandhi's views relevant to the conditions of the early twenty-first century?

Visual Sources

Considering the Evidence:
The Scramble for Africa

The centerpiece of Europe's global expansion during the nineteenth century occurred in the so-called scramble for Africa, during which a half dozen or so European countries divided up almost the entire continent into colonial territories (see Map 18.2, p. 887). The "scramble" took place very quickly (between roughly 1875 and 1900), surprising even the European leaders who initiated it, as well as the many African societies that suddenly found themselves confronting highly aggressive and well-armed foreign forces. Each of the rival powers—Britain, France, Germany, Belgium, Portugal, Spain, and Italy—sought to get a piece of a continent that many believed held the promise of great wealth. Given Europe's wars over colonial possessions in the early modern era, it is remarkable that the entire partition of Africa took place without any direct military conflict between the competing imperial countries. But in establishing their control on the ground, Europeans faced widespread African resistance, making the scramble an extremely bloody process of military conquest. The images that follow illustrate some of the distinctive features of the scramble for Africa as well as the differing ways in which it was perceived and represented.

As the Atlantic slave trade diminished over the course of the nineteenth century, Europeans began to look at Africa in new ways—as a source of raw materials, as an opportunity for investment, as a market for industrial products, as a field for exploration, and as an opportunity to spread Christianity. But it was not until the last quarter of the nineteenth century that Europeans showed much interest in actually acquiring territory and ruling large populations in Africa. Visual Source 18.1, from a late-nineteenth-century French board game, illustrates the widespread interest in the growing missionary enterprise in Africa as well as in the celebrated adventures of the intrepid explorers who penetrated the dangerous interior of the continent. It enabled ordinary Europeans to participate in exciting events in distant lands. This game featured the travels of David Livingstone and Henry Stanley. Livingstone (1813–1873) was a British missionary and explorer of central Africa whose work in exposing the horrors of the Arab slave trade gave him an almost mythic status among Eu-

Visual Source 18.1 Prelude to the Scramble (Private Collection/Archives Charmet/The Bridgeman Art Library)

ropeans. Stanley (1841–1904), a British journalist and explorer, gained lasting fame by finding Livingstone, long out of touch with his homeland, deep in the African interior.

- What images of Africa are suggested by this board game? Notice carefully the landscape, the animals, and the activities in which people are engaged.

- How does the game depict European activities in Africa?

- What might be the meaning of the large sun arising at the top of the image?

- What nineteenth-century realities are missing from this portrayal of Africa?

As the scramble for Africa got under way in earnest in the 1880s and 1890s, it became a highly competitive process. French designs on Africa, for example, focused on obtaining an uninterrupted East–West link from the Atlantic Ocean to the Red Sea. But the British, entrenched in Egypt and in control of the Suez Canal, were determined that no major European power should be allowed to control the headwaters of the Nile on which Egypt depended. Those conflicting goals came to a head in 1898, when British forces moving south from Egypt met a French expedition moving northeast from the Atlantic coast of what is now Gabon. That encounter took place along the Nile River at Fashoda in present-day Sudan, threatening war between France and Great Britain. In the end, negotiations persuaded the French to withdraw.

Visual Source 18.2, the cover of a French publication, shows the commander of the French expedition, Jean-Baptiste Marchand, who gained heroic stature in leading his troops on an epic journey across much of Africa for more than eighteen months.

- How did the artist portray Marchand? How might a British artist have portrayed him?

- What does this visual source suggest about the role of violence in the scramble for Africa?

- Notice the large number of African troops among Marchand's forces. What does that suggest about the process of colonial conquest? Why might Africans have agreed to fight on behalf of a European colonial power?

- How do you understand the fallen soldier lying between Marchand's legs?

Nowhere did the vaulting ambition of European colonial powers in Africa emerge more clearly than in the British vision of a North–South corridor of British territories along the eastern side of the continent stretching from South Africa to Egypt, or in the more popular phrase of the time, "from the Cape to Cairo." A part of this vision was an unbroken railroad line running the entire length of the African continent. That grand idea was popularized by Cecil Rhodes, a British-born businessman and politician who made a fortune in South African diamonds and became an enthusiastic advocate of British imperialism. Visual Source 18.3, an 1892 cartoon published in the popular British magazine of satire and humor named *Punch*, shows Rhodes bestriding the continent with one foot in Egypt and the other in South Africa.

- Is this famous image criticizing or celebrating Rhodes's Cape-to-Cairo dream? Explain your reasoning.

- What does this visual source suggest about the purpose of the Cape-to-Cairo scheme and the means to achieve it? Notice the telegraph wire in Rhodes's hands and the rifle on his shoulder.

- How did the artist portray the African continent? What does the absence of African people suggest? How does this image compare to Visual Source 18.1?

Visual Source 18.2 Conquest and Competition (Alinari/Art Resource, NY)

THE RHODES COLOSSUS
STRIDING FROM CAPE TOWN TO CAIRO.

Visual Source 18.3 From the Cape to Cairo (The Granger Collection, NY)

■ Scholars have sometimes argued that the scramble for Africa was driven less by concrete economic interests than by emotional, even romantic, notions of national grandeur and personal adventure. In what ways do Visual Sources 18.2 and 18.3 support or challenge this interpretation?

In North Africa the primary European rivalries for territory involved Great Britain, which occupied Egypt in 1881; France, which came to control Tunisia, Algeria, and Morocco; and Italy, which seized Libya in 1912. Visual Source 18.4 portrays two of these rivals — Britain, on the right, and France on the left — toasting one another while standing on piles of skeletons. This image appeared in the Cairo *Punch*, a British-owned magazine in Egypt published in Arabic, probably around 1910.

Visual Source 18.4 refers specifically to two incidents. On the British side, the cartoon evokes a 1906 quarrel between British soldiers hunting pigeons and local villagers of Denshway that resulted in the death of one of the soldiers. In response, outraged British authorities hung several people and flogged dozens of others. The following year in Morocco, French civilians building a small railway near the harbor of Casablanca dug up parts of a Muslim cemetery "churning up piles of bones." When attacks against European laborers followed, killing eight, the French bombarded the Arab quarter of the city, with many casualties—European and Arab alike—in the fighting that ensued. Both incidents stimulated nationalist feelings in these two North African countries.

- What references to these incidents can you find in Visual Source 18.4?

- The British and French generally saw themselves as rivals in the scramble for Africa. How are they portrayed here?

- What criticisms of colonial rule does this image contain? While the artist remains unknown, do you think it more likely to have been an Egyptian or a European?

Visual Source 18.4 British and French in North Africa (History Pictures/Instructional Resources Corporation)

One exception to the general European takeover of Africa during the scramble was the kingdom of Ethiopia. Located in the mountainous highlands of northeastern Africa, Ethiopia boasted an ancient pedigree, a long-established Christian culture, a literate elite, and rich agricultural resources. During the scramble for Africa, that country also had an astute monarch in Menelik II (r. 1889–1913). Playing various European powers against one another, he acquired from them a considerable arsenal of modern weapons and gained substantial territory for his kingdom, in effect taking part in the scramble. In the famous Battle of Adowa in 1896, Menelik's forces decisively defeated the Italians, who were seeking to add Ethiopia to their country's African empire. By this victory, Ethiopia preserved its independence and became a continental symbol of African bravery and resistance in the face of European imperialism.

In Visual Source 18.5, an unknown Ethiopian artist, working during the 1940s, celebrated the victory at Adowa at a time when Ethiopia had just fought off yet another Italian effort at conquest, this time led by Mussolini during World War II. The painting itself replicated in both style and content many earlier artistic celebrations of the victory at Adowa. In the upper left corner, Emperor Menelik is shown wearing a crown and seated under a royal umbrella. His queen, Empress Taytu, is visible in the lower left on horseback and holding a revolver. The commander of the Ethiopian forces sits on a brown horse, while leading his troops. At the top of the painting, St. George, the patron saint of Ethiopia, presides over the battle scene within a halo of red, yellow, and green, the colors of the Ethiopian flag adopted shortly after the battle.[37]

Visual Source 18.5 The Ethiopian Exception (© Trustees of the British Museum)

- How does this painting represent the Ethiopian triumph at Adowa?

- What features of the painting might help explain that improbable victory, at least to Ethiopian observers? How does the artist portray the resources available to each side?

- How did the Ethiopian painter depict the Italian enemy? Keep in mind that Ethiopian artists generally portrayed the forces of good in full face, while the wicked or evil were shown in profile.

- How do you imagine the news of the Battle of Adowa was received elsewhere in Africa and among peoples of African descent in the Americas? What might this painting have meant to Ethiopians in the wake of Mussolini's invasion of their country during the 1930s?

Using the Evidence:
The Scramble for Africa

1. **Distinguishing viewpoints:** From what different perspectives do these visual sources represent the scramble for Africa? What criticisms of the scramble can you read in them?

2. **Portraying Africans and Europeans:** Both Africans and Europeans are portrayed variously in these visual sources. What differences can you identify?

3. **Using images . . . selectively:** In what ways might visual sources such as these be most useful to historians seeking to understand the scramble for Africa? For what kinds of questions about the scramble might they have little to offer?

4. **Considering moral visions:** How do these visual sources deal with issues of morality or visions of right and wrong?

Chapter 18 Wrap Up

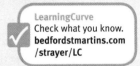

LearningCurve
Check what you know.
**bedfordstmartins.com
/strayer/LC**

STEP ONE

The Word to Know: Indentured

The *Oxford English Dictionary* defines *indentured* as "bound by indentures, esp. as an apprentice or servant." This form of forced labor expanded following the abolition of slavery and the advance of industrialization in the nineteenth century (see pp. 986–99). Based on your understanding of the Communist Manifesto (pp. 867–70), and the ideas of Karl Marx (842–44), write a Marxist "definition" of "indentured" labor.

STEP TWO

Economic Consequences of Imperialism

In this exercise, take notes based on your reading of the chapter on the short- and long-term consequences of European colonial economic policies. In the last column, provide one case study (society of country) that best demonstrates the consequences of these policies.

	Short-term results	Long-term results	Case study
Power to tax			
Power to compel labor (forced labor)			
Integration into global economy			
Loss of land by locals due to European seizure			

Responses to Empire

Consider the following documents as commentary on the civilizing mission as perceived by Europeans, Indians, and Africans. What messages do you see within the documents and within the visuals about how the authors or artists think individuals should be treated?

1. Document 18.2, Prince Fereze Shah, The Azambgarh Proclamation, 1857

Read Document 18.2 (pp. 915–916) and answer the question below.

■ **Question**

In what ways does Prince Fereze believe that Hindus and Muslims are being denied their human rights under British rule?

2. Document 18.3, Dadabhai Naoroji, *Speech to a London Audience*, 1871

Review Document 18.3, pp. 917–18 and answer the question below.

■ **Question**

Using specific evidence from the document, explain why Naoroji believes British rule to be a "knife of sugar." How does this point to the injustices of British rule as they relate to the human condition?

3. Visual Source 18.2, Conquest and Competition

Examine Visual Source 18.2 on page 925 and then answer the question below.

■ **Question**

It is clear from the stance of the French commander that there is a callous disregard of the dead. Why would a French publication use this image as its cover? What impression do you think that this cover gave to the publication's audience?

4. Visual Source 18.4, British and French in North Africa

Next, examine the political cartoon on page 927 and answer the question below.

■ **Question**

Using specific evidence from this cartoon, explain what the artist is saying about European colonial rule in Africa, specifically as it connects to the treatment of local people in Morocco and Egypt. What evidence is missing from this depiction?

5. Summary Question

Synthesize your evidence about how colonial rulers show respect (or not) to local peoples and cultural traditions.

Empires in Collision

Europe, the Middle East, and East Asia

1800–1914

"In the 170-plus years since the Opium War of 1840, our great country has weathered untold hardships. . . . Following the Opium War, China gradually became a semi-colonial . . . society, and foreign powers stepped up their aggression against China."[1] Speaking in 2011, Chinese President Hu Jintao thus reminded his listeners of Britain's violent intrusion into China's history in order to sell highly addictive opium to China's people. This conflict marked the beginning of what Chinese still describe as a "century of humiliation." In Hu Jintao's view it was only the victory of the Chinese Communist Party that enabled his country to finally escape from that shameful past. Memories of the Opium War remain a central element of China's "patriotic education" for the young, serve as a warning against uncritical admiration of the West, and provide a rejoinder to any Western criticism of China. Some 170 years after that clash between the Chinese and British empires, the Opium War retains an emotional resonance for many Chinese and offers a politically useful tool for the country's government.

CHINA WAS AMONG THE COUNTRIES THAT CONFRONTED an aggressive and industrializing West while maintaining its formal independence, unlike the colonized areas discussed in Chapter 18. So too did Japan, the Ottoman Empire, Persia (now Iran), Ethiopia, and Siam (now Thailand). Latin America also falls in this category (see pp. 853–61 in Chapter 17). The governments of these regions avoided outright incorporation into European colonial empires, retaining some ability to resist European aggression and to reform or transform their own

Carving Up the Pie of China: In this French cartoon from the late 1890s, the Great Powers of the day (from left to right: Great Britain's Queen Victoria, Germany's Kaiser Wilhelm, Russia's Tsar Nicholas II, a female figure representing France, and the Meiji emperor of Japan) participate in dividing China, while a Chinese figure behind them tries helplessly to stop the partition of his country. (The Art Archive at Art Resource, NY) societies. But they shared with their colonized counterparts the need to deal with four dimensions of the European moment in world history. First, they faced the immense military might and political ambitions of rival European states. Second, they became enmeshed in networks of trade, investment, and sometimes migration that arose from an industrializing and capitalist Europe to generate a new world economy. Third, they were touched by various aspects of traditional European culture, as some among them learned the French, English, or German language; converted to Christianity; or studied European literature and philosophy. Finally, they too engaged with the culture of modernity—its scientific rationalism; its technological achievements; its belief in a better future; and its ideas of nationalism, socialism, feminism, and individualism. In those epic encounters, they sometimes resisted, at other times accommodated, and almost always adapted what came from the West. They were active participants in the global drama of nineteenth-century world history, not simply its passive victims or beneficiaries.

Dealing with Europe, however, was not the only item on their agendas. Population growth and peasant rebellion wracked China; internal social and economic changes eroded the stability of Japanese public life; the great empires of the Islamic world shrank or disappeared; rivalry among competing elites troubled Latin American societies; Ethiopia launched its own empire-building process even as it resisted European intrusions. Encounters with an expansive Europe were conditioned everywhere by particular local circumstances. Among those societies that remained independent, albeit sometimes precariously, while coping simultaneously with their internal crises and the threat from the West, this chapter focuses primarily on China, the Ottoman Empire, and Japan. Together with Latin America, they provide a range of experiences, responses, and outcomes and many opportunities for comparison.

> ### SEEKING THE MAIN POINT
>
> What differences can you identify in how China, the Ottoman Empire, and Japan experienced Western imperialism and responded to it? How might you account for those differences?

Reversal of Fortune: China's Century of Crisis

In 1793, just a decade after British King George III lost his North American colonies, he received yet another rebuff, this time from China. In a famous letter to the British monarch, the Chinese emperor Qianlong (chyan-loong) sharply rejected British requests for a less restricted trading relationship with his country. "Our Celestial Empire possesses all things in prolific abundance," he declared. "There was therefore no need to import the manufactures of outside barbarians." Qianlong's snub simply continued the pattern of the previous several centuries, during which Chinese authorities had strictly controlled and limited the activities of European missionaries and merchants. But by 1912, little more than a century later, China's long-established imperial state had collapsed, and the country had been transformed from a central presence in the global economy to a weak and dependent participant in a European-dominated world system in which Great Britain was the major economic and political

A Map of Time

1793	Chinese reject British requests for open trade
1798	Napoleon invades Egypt
1830s	Famine and rebellions in Japan
1838–1842	First Opium War in China
1838–1876	Tanzimat Reforms in the Ottoman Empire
1850–1864	Taiping Uprising in China
1856–1858	Second Opium War in China
1853	Admiral Perry arrives in Japan
1868	Meiji Restoration in Japan
1894–1895	Sino-Japanese War
1896	Ethiopian defeat of Italy preserves Ethiopia's independence
1899–1901	Boxer Rebellion in China
1904–1905	Russo-Japanese War
1908	Young Turk takeover in Ottoman Empire
1910	Japan annexes Korea
1911	Chinese revolution; end of Qing dynasty

player. It was a stunning reversal of fortune for a country that in Chinese eyes was the civilized center of the entire world—in their terms, the Middle Kingdom.

The Crisis Within

In many ways, China was the victim of its own earlier success. Its robust economy and American food crops had enabled substantial population growth, from about 100 million people in 1685 to some 430 million in 1853. Unlike Europe, though, where a similar population spurt took place, no Industrial Revolution accompanied this vast increase in the number of people, nor was agricultural production able to keep up. Neither did China's internal expansion to the west and south generated anything like the wealth and resources that derived from Europe's overseas empires. The result was growing pressure on the land, smaller farms for China's huge peasant population, and, in all too many cases, unemployment, impoverishment, misery, and starvation.

Furthermore, China's famed centralized and bureaucratic state did not enlarge itself to keep pace with the growing population. Thus the state was increasingly unable to effectively perform its many functions, such as tax collection, flood control, social

■ **Causation**
What accounts for the massive peasant rebellions of nineteenth-century China?

welfare, and public security. Gradually the central state lost power to provincial officials and local gentry. Among such officials, corruption was endemic, and harsh treatment of peasants was common. According to an official report issued in 1852, "Day and night soldiers are sent out to harass taxpayers. Sometimes corporal punishments are imposed upon tax delinquents; some of them are so badly beaten to exact the last penny that blood and flesh fly in all directions."[2] Finally, European military pressure and economic penetration during the first half of the nineteenth century (see pp. 936–38) disrupted internal trade routes, created substantial unemployment, and raised peasant taxes.

This combination of circumstances, traditionally associated with a declining dynasty, gave rise to growing numbers of bandit gangs roaming the countryside and, even more dangerous, to outright peasant rebellion. Beginning in the late eighteenth century, such rebellions drew on a variety of peasant grievances and found leadership in charismatic figures proclaiming a millenarian religious message. Increasingly they also expressed opposition to the Qing dynasty because of its foreign Manchu origins. "We wait only for the northern region to be returned to a Han emperor," declared one rebel group in the early nineteenth century.[3]

The culmination of China's internal crisis lay in the Taiping Uprising, which set much of the country aflame between 1850 and 1864. This was a different kind of peasant upheaval. Its leaders largely rejected Confucianism, Daoism, and Buddhism alike, finding their primary ideology in a unique form of Christianity. Its leading figure, Hong Xiuquan (1814–1864), proclaimed himself the younger brother of Jesus, sent to cleanse the world of demons and to establish a "heavenly kingdom of great peace." Nor were these leaders content to restore an idealized Chinese society; instead they insisted on genuinely revolutionary change. They called for the abolition of private property, a radical redistribution of land, the end of prostitution and opium smoking, and the organization of society into sexually segregated military camps of men and women. Hong fiercely denounced the Qing dynasty as foreigners who had "poisoned China" and "defiled the emperor's throne." His cousin, Hong Rengan, developed plans for transforming China into an industrial nation, complete with railroads, health insurance for all, newspapers, and widespread public education.

Among the most revolutionary dimensions of the Taiping Uprising was

Taiping Rebellion
The Taiping rebels captured the city of Nanjing in 1853, making it their capital. Eleven years later, in 1864, imperial forces retook the city as illustrated in this Chinese print, effectively ending the Taiping Uprising. (The Art Archive at Art Resource, NY.)

its posture toward women and gender roles. This outlook reflected its origins among the minority Hakka people of southern China where women were notably less restricted than Confucian orthodoxy prescribed. During the uprising, Hakka women, whose feet had never been bound, fought as soldiers in their own regiments; in liberated regions, Taiping officials ordered that the feet of other women be unbound. Their land reform program promised women and men equal shares of land. Women were now permitted to sit for civil service examinations and were appointed to supervisory positions, though usually where they exercised authority over other women rather than men. Mutual attraction rather than family interests was promoted as a basis for marriage.

None of this was consistently implemented during the short period of Taiping power, and the movement's leadership demonstrated considerable ambivalence about equality for women. Hong himself reflected a much more traditional understanding of elite women's role when he assembled a large personal harem and declared: "The duty of the palace women is to attend to the needs of their husbands; and it is arranged by Heaven that they are not to learn of the affairs outside."[4] Nonetheless, the Taiping posture toward women represented a sharp challenge to long-established gender roles and contributed to the hostility that the movement generated among many other Chinese, including women.

With a rapidly swelling number of followers, Taiping forces swept out of southern China and established their capital in Nanjing in 1853. For a time, the days of the Qing dynasty appeared to be over. But divisions and indecisiveness within the Taiping leadership and their inability to link up with several other rebel groups also operating separately in China provided an opening for Qing dynasty loyalists to rally and by 1864 to crush this most unusual of peasant rebellions. Western military support for pro-Qing forces likewise contributed to their victory. It was not, however, the imperial military forces of the central government that defeated the rebels. Instead provincial military leaders, fearing the radicalism of the Taiping program, mobilized their own armies, which in the end crushed the rebel forces.

Thus the Qing dynasty was saved, but it was also weakened as the provincial gentry consolidated their power at the expense of the central state. The intense conservatism of both imperial authorities and their gentry supporters postponed any resolution of China's peasant problem, delayed any real change for China's women, and deferred vigorous efforts at modernization until the communists came to power in the mid-twentieth century. More immediately, the devastation and destruction occasioned by this massive civil war seriously disrupted and weakened China's economy. Estimates of the number of lives lost range from 20 to 30 million. In human terms, it was the most costly conflict in the world during the nineteenth century, and it took China more than a decade to recover from its devastation. China's internal crisis in general and the Taiping Uprising in particular also provided a highly unfavorable setting for the country's encounter with a Europe newly invigorated by the Industrial Revolution.

Western Pressures

■ **Connection**
How did Western pressures stimulate change in China during the nineteenth century?

Nowhere was the shifting balance of global power in the nineteenth century more evident than in China's changing relationship with Europe, a transformation that registered most dramatically in the famous Opium Wars. Derived from Arab traders in the eighth century or earlier, opium had long been used on a small scale as a drinkable medicine, regarded as a magical cure for dysentery and described by one poet as "fit for Buddha."[5] It did not become a serious problem until the late eighteenth century, when the British began to use opium, grown and processed in India, to cover their persistent trade imbalance with China. By the 1830s, British, American, and other Western merchants had found an enormous, growing, and very profitable market for this highly addictive drug. From 1,000 chests (each weighing roughly 150 pounds) in 1773, China's opium imports exploded to more than 23,000 chests in 1832 (see Snapshot).

By then, Chinese authorities recognized a mounting problem on many levels. Because opium importation was illegal, it had to be smuggled into China, thus flouting Chinese law. Bribed to turn a blind eye to the illegal trade, many officials were

Snapshot   **Chinese/British Trade at Canton, 1835–1836[6]**

What do these figures suggest about the role of opium in British trade with China? Calculate opium exports as a percentage of British exports to China, Britain's trade deficit without opium, and its trade surplus with opium. What did this pattern mean for China?

	Item	Value (in Spanish dollars)
British Exports to Canton	Opium	17,904,248
	Cotton	8,357,394
	All other items (sandalwood, lead, iron, tin, cotton yarn and piece goods, tin plates, watches, clocks)	6,164,981
	Total	32,426,623
British Imports from Canton	Tea (black and green)	13,412,243
	Raw silk	3,764,115
	Vermilion	705,000
	All other goods (sugar products, camphor, silver, gold, copper, musk)	5,971,541
	Total	23,852,899

corrupted. Furthermore, a massive outflow of silver to pay for the opium reversed China's centuries-long ability to attract much of the world's silver supply, and this imbalance caused serious economic problems. Finally, China found itself with many millions of addicts—men and women, court officials, students preparing for exams, soldiers going into combat, and common laborers seeking to overcome the pain and drudgery of their work. Following an extended debate at court in 1836—whether to legalize the drug or to crack down on its use—the emperor decided on suppression. An upright official, Commissioner Lin Zexu (lin zuh-SHOO), led the campaign against opium use as a kind of "drug czar." (See the Portrait of Lin Zexu, pp. 940–41.) The British, offended by the seizure of their property in opium and emboldened by

Addiction to Opium
Throughout the nineteenth century, opium imports created a massive addiction problem in China, as this photograph of an opium den from around 1900 suggests. Not until the early twentieth century did the British prove willing to curtail the opium trade from their Indian colony. (© Hulton-Deutsch Collection/ Corbis)

their new military power, sent a large naval expedition to China, determined to end the restrictive conditions under which they had long traded with that country. In the process, they would teach the Chinese a lesson about the virtues of free trade and the "proper" way to conduct relations among countries. Thus began the first Opium War, in which Britain's industrialized military might proved decisive. The Treaty of Nanjing, which ended the war in 1842, largely on British terms, imposed numerous restrictions on Chinese sovereignty and opened five ports to European traders. Its provisions reflected the changed balance of global power that had emerged with Britain's Industrial Revolution. To the Chinese, that agreement represented the first of the "unequal treaties" that seriously eroded China's independence by the end of the century.

But it was not the last of those treaties. Britain's victory in a second Opium War (1856–1858) was accompanied by the brutal vandalizing of the emperor's exquisite Summer Palace outside Beijing and resulted in further humiliations. Still more ports were opened to foreign traders. Now those foreigners were allowed to travel freely and buy land in China, to preach Christianity under the protection of Chinese authorities, and to patrol some of China's rivers. Furthermore, the Chinese were forbidden to use the character for "barbarians" to refer to the British in official documents. Following military defeats at the hands of the French (1885) and Japanese (1895), China lost control of Vietnam, Korea, and Taiwan. By the end of the century, the Western nations plus Japan and Russia all had carved out spheres of influence within China, granting themselves special privileges to establish military bases, extract raw materials, and build railroads. Many Chinese believed that their country was being "carved up like a melon" (see Map 19.1 and the chapter-opening photo on p. 930).

Coupled with its internal crisis, China's encounter with European imperialism had reduced the proud Middle Kingdom to dependency on the Western powers as it

Map 19.1   China and the World in the Nineteenth Century
As China was reeling from massive internal upheavals during the nineteenth century, it also faced external assaults from Russia, Japan, and various European powers. By the end of the century, large parts of China were divided into spheres of influence, each affiliated with one of the major industrial powers of the day.

became part of a European-based "informal empire." China was no longer the center of civilization to which barbarians paid homage and tribute, but just one weak and dependent nation among many others. The Qing dynasty remained in power, but in a weakened condition, which served European interests well and Chinese interests poorly. Restrictions imposed by the unequal treaties clearly inhibited China's industrialization, as foreign goods and foreign investment flooded the country largely unrestricted. Chinese businessmen mostly served foreign firms, rather than developing as an independent capitalist class capable of leading China's own Industrial Revolution.

The Failure of Conservative Modernization

Chinese authorities were not passive in the face of their country's mounting crises, both internal and external. Known as "self-strengthening," their policies during the 1860s and 1870s sought to reinvigorate a traditional China while borrowing cautiously from the West. An overhauled examination system, designed to recruit qualified candidates for official positions, sought the "good men" who could cope with the massive reconstruction that China faced in the wake of the Taiping rebellion. Support for landlords and the repair of dikes and irrigation helped restore rural social and economic order. A few industrial factories producing textiles and steel were established, coal mines were expanded, and a telegraph system was initiated. One Chinese general in 1863 confessed his humiliation that "Chinese weapons are far inferior to those of foreign countries."[7] A number of modern arsenals, shipyards, and foreign-language schools sought to remedy this deficiency.

Self-strengthening as an overall program for China's modernization was inhibited by the fears of conservative leaders that urban, industrial, or commercial development would erode the power and privileges of the landlord class. Furthermore, the new industries remained largely dependent on foreigners for machinery, materials, and expertise. And they served to strengthen local authorities, who largely controlled those industries, rather than the central Chinese state.

The general failure of "self-strengthening" became apparent at the end of the century, when an anti-foreign movement known as the Boxer Uprising (1898–1901) erupted in northern China. Led by militia organizations calling themselves the Society of Righteous and Harmonious Fists, the "Boxers" killed numerous Europeans and Chinese Christians and laid siege to the foreign embassies in Beijing. When Western powers and Japan occupied Beijing to crush the rebellion and imposed a huge payment on China as a punishment, it was clear that China remained a dependent country, substantially under foreign control.

No wonder, then, that growing numbers of educated Chinese, including many in official elite positions, became highly disillusioned with the Qing dynasty, which was both foreign and ineffective in protecting China. By the late 1890s, such people were organizing a variety of clubs, study groups, and newspapers to examine China's desperate situation and to explore alternative paths. The names of these organizations reflect their outlook—the National Rejuvenation Study Society, Society to Protect the Nation, and Understand the National Shame Society. They admired not only Western science and technology but also Western political practices that limited the authority of the ruler and permitted wider circles of people to take part in public life. They believed that only a truly unified nation in which rulers and ruled were closely related could save China from dismemberment at the hands of foreign imperialists. Among the small number of women who took part in these discussions, traditional gender roles became yet another focus of opposition. Qiu Jin (1875–1907), the rebellious daughter of a gentry family, left a husband and two children to study in Japan. Upon her return to China, she started a women's journal, arguing that liberated

■ **Connection**
What strategies did China adopt to confront its various problems? In what ways did these strategies reflect China's own history and culture as well as the new global order?

Lin Zexu,
Confronting The Opium Trade[8]

When the Chinese emperor decided in 1838 on firm measures to suppress the opium trade, he selected Lin Zexu to enforce that policy. Born in 1785, Lin was the son of a rather poor but scholarly father, who had never achieved an official position. Lin, however, excelled academically, passing the highest level examinations in 1811 after two failed attempts, and then rising rapidly in the ranks of China's bureaucracy. In the process, he gained a reputation as a strict and honest official, immune to bribery, genuinely concerned with the welfare of the peasantry, and unafraid to confront the corruption and decadence of rich and poor alike.

And so in December of 1838, after some nineteen personal audiences with the emperor, Lin found himself in Canton, the center of the opium trade and the only Chinese city legally open to foreign merchants. He was facing the greatest challenge of his professional life. Undertaken with the best of inten-

Commissioner Lin Zexu. (From Alexander Murray, Doings in China: Being the personal narrative of an officer engaged in the late Chinese Expedition, from the Recapture of Chusan in 1841, to the Peace of Nankin in 1842, *(London: Richard Bentley, New Burlington Street, Publisher in Ordinary to Her Majesty, 1843), pl. ii.)*

tions, his actions propelled the country into a century of humiliating subservience to an industrializing Europe and forced growing numbers of Chinese to question their vaunted civilization.

In established Confucian fashion, Lin undertook his enormous task with a combination of moral appeals, reasoned argument, political pressure, and coercion, while hoping to avoid outright armed conflict. It was an approach that focused on both the demand and supply sides of the problem. In dealing with Chinese opium users, Lin emphasized the health hazards of the drug and demanded that everyone turn in their supplies of opium and the pipes used to smoke it. By mid-1839, he had confiscated some 50,000 pounds of the drug together with over 70,000 pipes and arrested some 1,700 dealers. Hundreds of local students were summoned to an assembly where they were invited to identify opium distributors and to suggest ways of dealing with the problem. Opium-using officials

women were essential for a strong Chinese nation. Recruiting students into the anti-Qing movement, she often dressed in male clothing. "My aim is to dress like a man," she declared. "In China, men are strong and women are oppressed because they are supposed to be weak."[9] (See Document 19.3, pp. 962–63.) Thus was born the immensely powerful force of Chinese nationalism, directed alike against Western imperialists, the foreign Qing dynasty, and aspects of China's traditional culture.

The Qing dynasty response to these new pressures proved inadequate. A flurry of progressive imperial edicts in 1898, known as the Hundred Days of Reform, was soon squelched by conservative forces. More extensive reform in the early twentieth century, including the end of the old examination system and the promise of a national parliament, was a classic case of too little too late. In 1911, the ancient imperial became the target of investigations, and five-person teams were established to enforce the ban on opium smoking on one another.

Lin applied a similar mix of methods to the foreign suppliers of opium. A moralistic appeal to Queen Victoria argued that the articles the English imported from China—silk, tea, and rhubarb—were all beneficial. "By what right," he asked, "do [the barbarians] use this poisonous drug to injure Chinese people?" He pointedly reminded Europeans that new regulations, applying to Chinese and foreigners alike, fixed the penalty for dealing in opium at "decapitation or strangling." Then he demanded that foreign traders hand over their opium, and without compensation. When the merchants hesitated, Lin tightened the screws, ordering all Chinese employed by foreigners to leave their jobs and blockading the Europeans in their factories. After six weeks of negotiations, the Europeans capitulated, turning over some 3 million pounds of raw opium to Lin Zexu.

Disposing of the drug was an enormous task. Workers, stripped and searched daily to prevent looting, dug three huge trenches into which they placed the opium mixed with water, salt, and lime and then flushed the concoction into the sea. Lin offered a sacrifice to the Sea Spirit, apologizing for introducing this poison into its domain and "advising the Spirit to tell the creatures of the water to move away for a time." He informed the emperor that throngs of local people flocked to witness the destruction of the opium. And foreigners too came to observe the

spectacle. According to Lin, they "do not dare to show any disrespect, and indeed I should judge from their attitudes that they have the decency to feel heartily ashamed."

Had Lin been correct in his appraisal, history would have taken a very different turn. But neither Lin nor his superiors anticipated the response that these actions provoked from the British government. They were also largely unaware of the European industrial and military advances, which had decisively shifted the balance of power between China and the West. Arriving in 1840, a British military expedition quickly demonstrated its superiority and initiated the devastating Opium War that marked Lin's policies in Canton as a failure.

As a punishment for his unsatisfactory performance, the emperor sent Lin to a remote post in western China. Although his career rebounded somewhat after 1845, he died in 1850 while on the way to an appointment aimed at suppressing the Taiping Rebellion. While his reputation suffered in the nineteenth century, it recovered in the twentieth as an intensely nationalist China recalled his principled stand against Western imperialism.

Questions: How might Lin Zexu have handled his task differently or more successfully? Or had he been given an impossible mission?

order that had governed China for two millennia collapsed, with only a modest nudge from organized revolutionaries. It was the end of a long era in China and the beginning of an immense struggle over the country's future.

The Ottoman Empire and the West in the Nineteenth Century

Like China, the Islamic world represented a highly successful civilization that felt little need to learn from the "infidels" or "barbarians" of the West until it collided with an expanding and aggressive Europe in the nineteenth century. Unlike China, though, Islamic civilization had been a near neighbor to Europe for 1,000 years. Its most prominent state, the Ottoman Empire, had long governed substantial parts of the Balkans and posed a clear military and religious threat to Europe in the sixteenth and seventeenth centuries. But if its encounter with the West was less abrupt than that of China, it was no less consequential. Neither the Ottoman Empire nor China fell under direct colonial rule, but both were much diminished as the changing balance of global power took hold; both launched efforts at "defensive modernization" aimed at strengthening their states and preserving their independence; and in both societies, some people held tightly to old identities and values, even as others embraced new loyalties associated with nationalism and modernity.

"The Sick Man of Europe"

In 1750, the Ottoman Empire was still the central political fixture of a widespread Islamic world. From its Turkish heartland in Anatolia, it ruled over much of the Arab world, from which Islam had come. It protected pilgrims on their way to Mecca, governed Egypt and coastal North Africa, and incorporated millions of Christians in the Balkans. Its ruler, the sultan, claimed the role of caliph, successor to the Prophet Muhammad, and was widely viewed as the leader, defender, and primary representative of the Islamic world. But by the middle, and certainly by the end, of the nineteenth century, the Ottoman Empire was no longer able to deal with Europe from a position of equality, let alone superiority. Among the Great Powers of the West, it was now known as "the sick man of Europe." Within the Muslim world, the Ottoman Empire, once viewed as "the strong sword of Islam," was unable to prevent region after region — India, Indonesia, West Africa, Central Asia — from falling under the control of Christian powers.

■ Change

What lay behind the decline of the Ottoman Empire in the nineteenth century?

The Ottoman Empire's own domains shrank considerably at the hands of Russian, British, Austrian, and French aggression (see Map 19.2). In 1798, Napoleon's invasion of Egypt, which had long been a province of the Ottoman Empire, was a particularly stunning blow. A contemporary observer, Abd al-Rahman al-Jabarti, described the French entry into Cairo:

> [T]he French entered the city like a torrent rushing through the alleys and streets without anything to stop them, like demons of the Devil's army....And the French trod in the Mosque of al-Azhar with their shoes, carrying swords and rifles....They plundered whatever they found in the mosque....They treated the books and Quranic volumes as trash.... Furthermore, they soiled the mosque, blowing their spit in it, pissing and defecating in it. They guzzled wine and smashed bottles in the central court.[10]

When the French left, a virtually independent Egypt pursued a modernizing and empire-building program of its own and on one occasion came close to toppling the Ottoman Empire itself.

Beyond territorial losses to stronger European powers, other parts of the empire, such as Greece, Serbia, Bulgaria, and Romania, achieved independence based on their

Map 19.2 The Contraction of the Ottoman Empire Foreign aggression and nationalist movements substantially diminished the Ottoman Empire during the nineteenth century, but they also stimulated a variety of efforts to revive and reform Ottoman society. (Credit line TK.)

own surging nationalism and support from the British or the Russians. The continued independence of the core region of the Ottoman Empire owed much to the inability of Europe's Great Powers to agree on how to divide it up among themselves.

Behind the contraction of the Ottoman Empire lay other problems. As in China, the central Ottoman state had weakened, particularly in its ability to raise necessary revenue, as provincial authorities and local warlords gained greater power. Moreover, the Janissaries, once the effective and innovative elite infantry units of Ottoman military forces, lost their military edge, becoming a highly conservative force within the empire. The technological and military gap with the West was clearly growing.

Economically, the earlier centrality of the Ottoman and Arab lands in Afro-Eurasian commerce diminished as Europeans achieved direct oceanic access to the treasures of Asia. Competition from cheap European manufactured goods hit Ottoman artisans hard and led to urban riots protesting foreign imports. Furthermore, a series of agreements, known as capitulations, between European countries and the Ottoman Empire granted Westerners various exemptions from Ottoman law and taxation. Like the unequal treaties with China, these agreements facilitated European penetration of the Ottoman economy and became widely resented. Such measures eroded Ottoman sovereignty and reflected the changing position of that empire relative to Europe. So too did the growing indebtedness of the Ottoman Empire, which came to rely on foreign loans to finance its efforts at economic development. By 1882, its inability to pay the interest on those debts led to foreign control of much of its revenue-generating system, while a similar situation in Egypt led to its outright occupation by the British. Like China, the Ottoman Empire had fallen into a position of considerable dependency on Europe.

Reform and Its Opponents

■ **Change**
In what different ways did the Ottoman state respond to its various problems?

The leadership of the Ottoman Empire recognized many of its problems and during the nineteenth century mounted increasingly ambitious programs of "defensive modernization" that were earlier, more sustained, and far more vigorous than the timid and half-hearted measures of self-strengthening in China. One reason perhaps lay in the absence of any internal upheaval, such as the Taiping Uprising in China, which threatened the very existence of the ruling dynasty. Nationalist revolts on the empire's periphery, rather than Chinese-style peasant rebellion at the center, represented the primary internal crisis of nineteenth-century Ottoman history. Nor did the Middle East in general experience the explosive population growth that contributed so much to China's nineteenth-century crisis. Furthermore, the long-established Ottoman leadership was Turkic and Muslim, culturally similar to its core population, whereas China's Qing dynasty rulers were widely regarded as foreigners from Manchuria.

Ottoman reforms began in the late eighteenth century when Sultan Selim III sought to reorganize and update the army and to draw on European advisers and techniques. Even these modest innovations stirred the hostility of powerful factions among both the *ulama* (religious scholars) and the elite military corps of Janissaries, who saw them in conflict with both Islam and their own institutional interests. Opposition to his measures was so strong that Selim was overthrown in 1807 and then murdered. Subsequent sultans, however, crushed the Janissaries and brought the ulama more thoroughly under state control than elsewhere in the Islamic world.

Then, in the several decades after 1839, more far-reaching reformist measures, known as Tanzimat (TAHNZ-ee-MAT) (reorganization), took shape as the Ottoman leadership sought to provide the economic, social, and legal underpinnings for a strong and newly recentralized state. Factories producing cloth, paper, and armaments; modern mining operations; reclamation and resettlement of agricultural land; telegraphs, steamships, railroads, and a modern postal service; Western-style law codes and courts; new elementary and secondary schools—all of these new departures began a long process of modernization and Westernization in the Ottoman Empire.

Even more revolutionary, at least in principle, were changes in the legal status of the empire's diverse communities, which now gave non-Muslims equal rights under the law. An imperial proclamation of 1839 declared:

> Every distinction or designation tending to make any class whatever of the subjects of my Empire inferior to another class, on account of their religion, language or race shall be forever effaced. . . . No subject of my Empire shall be hindered in the

exercise of the religion that he professes. . . . All the subjects of my Empire, without distinction of nationality, shall be admissible to public employment.

This declaration represented a dramatic change that challenged the fundamentally Islamic character of the state. Mixed tribunals with representatives from various religious groups were established to hear cases involving non-Muslims. More Christians were appointed to high office. A mounting tide of secular legislation and secular schools, drawing heavily on European models, now competed with traditional Islamic institutions.

Although Tanzimat-era reforms did not directly address gender issues, they did stimulate modest educational openings for women, mostly in Istanbul, with a training program for midwives in 1842, a girls' secondary school in 1858, and a teacher training college for women in 1870. Furthermore, the reform-minded class that emerged from the Tanzimat era generally favored greater opportunities for women as a means of strengthening the state, and a number of upper- and middle-class women were involved in these discussions. During the 1870s and 1880s, the prominent female poet Sair Nigar Hanim held weekly "salons" in which reformist intellectuals of both sexes participated.

The reform process raised profound and highly contested questions. What was the Ottoman Empire, and who were its people? To those who supported the reforms, the Ottoman Empire was a secular state whose people were loyal to the dynasty that ruled it, rather than a primarily Muslim state based on religious principles. This was the outlook of a new class spawned by the reform process itself—lower-level officials, military officers, writers, poets, and journalists, many of whom had a modern Western-style education. Dubbed the Young Ottomans, they were active during the middle decades of the nineteenth century, as they sought major changes in the Ottoman political system itself. They favored a more European-style democratic, constitutional regime that could curtail the absolute power of the emperor. Only such a political system, they felt, could mobilize the energies of the country to overcome backwardness and preserve the state against European aggression. Known as Islamic modernism, such ideas found expression in many parts of the Muslim world in the second half of the century. Muslim societies, they argued, needed to embrace Western technical and scientific knowledge, while rejecting its materialism. Islam in their view could accommodate a full modernity without sacrificing its essential religious character. After all, the Islamic world had earlier hosted impressive scientific achievements and had incorporated elements of Greek philosophical thinking.

In 1876, the Young Ottomans experienced a short-lived victory when the Sultan Abd al-Hamid II (r. 1876–1909) accepted a constitution and an elected parliament, but not for long. Under the pressure of war with Russia, the Sultan soon suspended the reforms and reverted to an older style of despotic rule for the next thirty years, even renewing the claim that he was the caliph, successor to the Prophet, and the protector of Muslims everywhere.

■ **Comparison**

In what different ways did various groups define the Ottoman Empire during the nineteenth century?

The First Ottoman Constitution
This Ottoman era postcard celebrates the short-lived constitutional era of 1876–1878 and the brief political victory of the Young Ottoman reformers. The country is represented by an unveiled woman being released from her chains, while an angel carries a banner inscribed with the slogan of the French Revolution: liberty, equality, fraternity. ("The Ottoman Constitution, December 1895," color postcard. Artist unknown)

Opposition to this revived despotism soon surfaced among both military and civilian elites known as the Young Turks. Largely abandoning any reference to Islam, they advocated a militantly secular public life, were committed to thoroughgoing modernization along European lines, and increasingly thought about the Ottoman Empire as a Turkish national state. "There is only one civilization, and that is European civilization," declared Abdullah Cevdet, a prominent figure in the Young Turk movement. "Therefore we must borrow western civilization with both its rose and its thorn."[11]

A military coup in 1908 finally allowed the Young Turks to exercise real power. They pushed for a radical secularization of schools, courts, and law codes; permitted elections and competing parties; established a single Law of Family Rights for all regardless of religion; and encouraged Turkish as the official language of the empire. They also opened modern schools for women, including access to Istanbul University; allowed them to wear Western clothing; restricted polygamy; and permitted women to obtain divorces in some situations. Women established a number of publications and organizations, some of them linked to British suffrage groups. In the western cities of the empire, some women abandoned their veils.

But the nationalist Turkish conception of Ottoman identity antagonized non-Turkic peoples and helped stimulate Arab and other nationalisms in response. For some, a secular nationality was becoming the most important public loyalty, with Islam relegated to private life. Nationalist sentiments contributed to the complete disintegration of the Ottoman Empire following World War I, but the secularizing and Westernizing principles of the Young Turks informed the policies of the Turkish republic that replaced it.

Outcomes: Comparing China and the Ottoman Empire

By the beginning of the twentieth century, both China and the Ottoman Empire, recently centers of proud and vibrant civilizations, had experienced the consequences of a rapidly shifting balance of global power. Now they were "semi-colonies" within the "informal empires" of Europe, although they retained sufficient independence for their governments to launch catch-up efforts of defensive modernization. But neither was able to create the industrial economies or strong states required to fend off European intrusion and restore their former status in the world. Despite their diminished power, however, both China and the Ottoman Empire gave rise to new nationalist conceptions of society, which were initially small and limited in appeal but of great significance for the future.

In the early twentieth century, that future witnessed the end of both the Chinese and Ottoman empires. In China, the collapse of the imperial system in 1911 was followed by a vast revolutionary upheaval that by 1949 led to a communist regime within largely the same territorial space as the old empire. By contrast, the collapse of the Ottoman Empire following World War I led to the creation of the new but much smaller nation-state of Turkey in the Anatolian heartland of the old empire, which lost its vast Arab and European provinces.

China's twentieth-century revolutionaries rejected traditional Confucian culture far more thoroughly than the secularizing leaders of modern Turkey rejected Islam. Almost everywhere in the Islamic world, traditional religion retained its hold on the private loyalties of most people and later in the twentieth century became a basis for social renewal in many places. Islamic civilization, unlike its Chinese counterpart, had many independent centers and was never so closely associated with a single state. Furthermore, it was embedded in a deeply religious tradition that was personally meaningful to millions of adherents, in contrast to the more elitist and secular outlook of Confucianism. Many rural Chinese, however, retained traditional Confucian values such as filial piety, and Confucianism has made something of a comeback in China over the past several decades. Nonetheless, Islam retained a hold on its civilization in the twentieth century rather more firmly than Confucianism did in China.

SUMMING UP SO FAR

In what ways were the histories of China and the Ottoman Empire similar during the nineteenth century? And how did they differ?

The Japanese Difference: The Rise of a New East Asian Power

Like China and the Ottoman Empire, the island country of Japan confronted the aggressive power of the West during the nineteenth century, most notably in the form of U.S. commodore Matthew Perry's "black ships," which steamed into Tokyo Bay in 1853 and forcefully demanded that this reclusive nation open up to more "normal" relations with the world. However, the outcome of that encounter differed sharply from the others. In the second half of the nineteenth century, Japan undertook a radical transformation of its society—a "revolution from above," according to some historians—turning it into a powerful, modern, united, industrialized nation. It was an achievement that neither China nor the Ottoman Empire was able to duplicate. Far from succumbing to Western domination, Japan joined the club of imperialist countries by creating its own East Asian empire, at the expense of China and Korea. In building a society that was both modern and distinctly Japanese, Japan demonstrated that modernity was not a uniquely European phenomenon. This "Japanese miracle," as some have called it, was both promising and ominous for the rest of Asia. How had it occurred?

The Tokugawa Background

For 250 years prior to Perry's arrival, Japan had been governed by a shogun (a military ruler) from the Tokugawa family who acted in the name of a revered but powerless emperor, who lived in Kyoto, 300 miles away from the seat of power in Edo (Tokyo). The chief task of this Tokugawa shogunate was to prevent the return of civil war among some 260 rival feudal lords, known as daimyo, each of whom had a cadre of armed retainers, the famed samurai warriors of Japanese tradition.

Based on their own military power and political skills, successive shoguns gave Japan more than two centuries of internal peace (1600–1850). To control the restive daimyo, they required these local authorities to create second homes in Edo, the country's capital, where they had to live during alternate years. When they left for their rural residences, families stayed behind, almost as hostages. Nonetheless, the daimyo, especially the more powerful ones, retained substantial autonomy in their own domains and behaved in some ways like independent states with separate military forces, law codes, tax systems, and currencies. With no national army, no uniform currency, and little central authority at the local level, Tokugawa Japan was "pacified . . . but not really unified."[12] To further stabilize the country, the Tokugawa regime issued highly detailed rules governing occupation, residence, dress, hairstyles, and behavior of the four hierarchically ranked status groups into which Japanese society was divided—samurai at the top, then peasants, artisans, and, at the bottom, merchants.

■ **Change**

In what ways was Japan changing during the Tokugawa era?

Much was changing within Japan during these 250 years of peace in ways that belied the control and orderliness of Tokugawa regulations. For one thing, the samurai, in the absence of wars to fight, evolved into a salaried bureaucratic or administrative class amounting to 5 to 6 percent of the total population, but they were still fiercely devoted to their daimyo lords and to their warrior code of loyalty, honor, and self-sacrifice.

More generally, centuries of peace contributed to a remarkable burst of economic growth, commercialization, and urban development. Entrepreneurial peasants, using fertilizers and other agricultural innovations, grew more rice than ever before and engaged in a variety of rural manufacturing enterprises as well. By 1750, Japan had become perhaps the world's most urbanized country, with about 10 percent of its population living in sizable towns or cities. Edo, with perhaps a million residents, was among the world's largest cities. Well-functioning markets linked urban and rural areas, marking Japan as an emerging capitalist economy. The influence of Confucianism encouraged education and generated a remarkably literate population, with about 40 percent of men and 15 percent of women able to read and write. Although no one was aware of it at the time, these changes during the Tokugawa era provided a solid foundation for Japan's remarkable industrial growth in the late nineteenth century.

Such changes also undermined the shogunate's efforts to freeze Japanese society in the interests of stability. Some samurai found the lowly but profitable path of commerce too much to resist. "No more shall we have to live by the sword," declared one of them in 1616 while renouncing his samurai status. "I have seen that great profit can be made honorably. I shall brew *sake* and soy sauce, and we shall prosper."[13] Many merchants, though hailing from the lowest-ranking status group, prospered in the new commercial environment and supported a vibrant urban culture, while not a few daimyo found it necessary, if humiliating, to seek loans from these social inferiors. Thus merchants had money, but little status, whereas samurai enjoyed high status but were often indebted to inferior merchants. Both resented their positions.

Despite prohibitions to the contrary, many peasants moved to the cities, becoming artisans or merchants and imitating the ways of their social betters. A decree of 1788 noted that peasants "have become accustomed to luxury and forgetful of their status." They wore inappropriate clothing, used umbrellas rather than straw hats in the rain, and even left the villages for the city. "Henceforth," declared the shogun, "all luxuries should be avoided by the peasants. They are to live simply and devote themselves to farming."[14] This decree, like many others before it, was widely ignored.

More than social change undermined the Tokugawa regime. Corruption was widespread, to the disgust of many. The shogunate's failure to deal successfully with a severe famine in the 1830s eroded confidence in its effectiveness. At the same time, a mounting wave of local peasant uprisings and urban riots expressed the many grievances of the poor. The most striking of these outbursts left the city of Osaka in flames in 1837. Its leader, Oshio Heihachiro, no doubt spoke for many ordinary people when he wrote:

> We must first punish the officials who torment the people so cruelly; then we must execute the haughty and rich Osaka merchants. Then we must distribute the gold, silver, and copper stored in their cellars, and bands of rice hidden in their storehouses.[15]

From the 1830s on, one historian concluded, "there was a growing feeling that the *shogunate* was losing control."[16]

American Intrusion and the Meiji Restoration

It was foreign intervention that brought matters to a head. Since the expulsion of European missionaries and the harsh suppression of Christianity in the early seventeenth century (see p. 678), Japan had deliberately limited its contact with the West to a single port, where only the Dutch were allowed to trade. By the early nineteenth century, however, various European countries and the United States were knocking at the door. All were turned away, and even shipwrecked sailors or whalers were expelled, jailed, or executed. As it happened, it was the United States that forced the issue, sending Commodore Perry in 1853 to demand humane treatment for castaways, the right of American vessels to refuel and buy provisions, and the opening of ports for trade. Authorized to use force if necessary, Perry presented his reluctant hosts, among other gifts, with a white flag for surrender should hostilities follow. (For a Japanese perception of Perry and his ships, see Visual Sources: Japanese Perceptions of the West, pp. 966–71.)

Viewing the Americans
This print shows a Japanese view of Admiral Perry (on the right) and his second-in-command (on the left) not long after the Americans' unwelcome arrival in Japan. (Courtesy, Ryosenji Treasure Museum)

In the end, the Japanese avoided war. Aware of what had happened to China in resisting European demands, Japan agreed to a series of unequal treaties with various Western powers. That humiliating capitulation to the demands of the "foreign devils" further eroded support for the shogunate, triggered a brief civil war, and by 1868 led to a political takeover by a group of young samurai from southern Japan. This decisive turning point in Japan's history was known as the Meiji (MAY-jee) restoration, for the country's new rulers claimed that they were restoring to power the young emperor, then a fifteen-year-old boy whose throne name was Meiji, or Enlightened Rule. Despite his youth, he was regarded as the most recent link in a chain of descent that traced the origins of the imperial family back to the sun goddess Amaterasu. Having eliminated the shogunate, the patriotic young men who led the takeover soon made their goals clear—to save Japan from foreign domination not by futile resistance, but by a thorough transformation of Japanese society drawing on all that the modern West had to offer. "Knowledge shall be sought throughout the world," they declared, "so as to strengthen the foundations of imperial rule."

Japan now had a government committed to a decisive break with the past, and it had acquired that government without massive violence or destruction. By contrast, the defeat of the Taiping Uprising had deprived China of any such opportunity for a fresh start, while saddling it with enormous devastation and massive loss of life. Furthermore, Japan was of less interest to Western powers than either China, with its huge potential market and reputation for riches, or the Ottoman Empire, with its strategic location at the crossroads of Asia, Africa, and Europe. The American Civil War and its aftermath likewise deflected U.S. ambitions in the Pacific for a time, further reducing the Western pressure on Japan.

Modernization Japanese Style

■ **Change**
In what respects was Japan's nineteenth-century transformation revolutionary?

These circumstances gave Japan some breathing space, and its new rulers moved quickly to take advantage of that unique window of opportunity. Thus they launched a cascading wave of dramatic changes that rolled over the country in the last three decades of the nineteenth century. Like the more modest reforms of China and the Ottoman Empire, Japanese modernizing efforts were defensive, based on fears that Japanese independence was in grave danger. Those reforms, however, were revolutionary in their cumulative effect, transforming Japan far more thoroughly than even the most radical of the Ottoman efforts, let alone the limited "self-strengthening" policies of the Chinese.

The first task was genuine national unity, which required an attack on the power and privileges of both the daimyo and the samurai. In a major break with the past, the new regime soon ended the semi-independent domains of the daimyo, replacing them with governors appointed by and responsible to the national government. The central state, not the local authorities, now collected the nation's taxes and raised a national army based on conscription from all social classes.

Thus the samurai relinquished their ancient role as the country's warrior class and with it their cherished right to carry swords. The old Confucian-based social order with its special privileges for various classes was largely dismantled, and almost all Japanese became legally equal as commoners and as subjects of the emperor. Limitations on travel and trade likewise fell as a nationwide economy came to parallel the centralized state. Although there was some opposition to these measures, including a brief rebellion of resentful samurai in 1877, it was on the whole a remarkably peaceful process in which a segment of the old ruling class abolished its own privileges. Many, but not all, of these displaced elites found a soft landing in the army, bureaucracy, or business enterprises of the new regime, thus easing a painful transition.

Accompanying these social and political changes was a widespread and eager fascination with almost everything Western (see Visual Sources 19.2 and 19.3, pp. 968–69). Knowledge about the West—its science and technology; its various political and constitutional arrangements; its legal and educational systems; its dances, clothing, and hairstyles—was enthusiastically sought out by official missions to Europe and the United States, by hundreds of students sent to study abroad, and by many ordinary Japanese at home. Western writers were translated into Japanese; for example, Samuel Smiles's *Self-Help*, which focused on "achieving success and rising in the world," sold a million copies. "Civilization and Enlightenment" was the slogan of the time, and both were to be found in the West. The most prominent popularizer of Western knowledge, Fukuzawa Yukichi, summed up the chief lesson of his studies in the mid-1870s—Japan was backward and needed to learn from the West: "If we compare the knowledge of the Japanese and Westerners, in letters, in technique, in commerce, or in industry, from the largest to the smallest matter, there is not one thing in which we excel. . . . In Japan's present condition there is nothing in which we may take pride vis-à-vis the West."[17]

After this initial wave of uncritical enthusiasm for everything Western receded, Japan proceeded to borrow more selectively and to combine foreign and Japanese elements in distinctive ways (see Visual Source 19.3, p. 969). For example, the Constitution of 1889, drawing heavily on German experience, introduced an elected parliament, political parties, and democratic ideals, but that constitution was presented as a gift from a sacred emperor descended from the Sun Goddess. The parliament could advise, but ultimate power, and particularly control of the military, lay theoretically with the emperor and in practice with an oligarchy of prominent reformers acting in his name. Likewise, a modern educational system, which achieved universal primary schooling by the early twentieth century, was also laced with Confucian-based moral instruction and exhortations of loyalty to the emperor. Christianity made little headway in Meiji Japan, but Shinto, an ancient religious tradition featuring ancestors and nature spirits, was elevated to the status of an official state cult. Japan's earlier experience in borrowing massively but selectively from Chinese culture perhaps served it better in these new circumstances than either the Chinese disdain for foreign cultures or the reluctance of many Muslims to see much of value in the infidel West.

Like their counterparts in China and the Ottoman Empire, some reformers in Japan—male and female alike—argued that the oppression of women was an obstacle to the country's modernization and that family reform was essential to gaining the respect of the West. The widely read commentator Fukuzawa Yukichi urged an end to concubinage and prostitution, advocated more education for girls, and called for gender equality in matters of marriage, divorce, and property rights. But most male reformers understood women largely in the context of family life, seeing them as "good wife, wise mother." By the 1880s, however, a small feminist movement arose, demanding—and modeling—a more public role for women. Some even sought the right to vote at a time when only a small fraction of men could do so. A leading feminist, Kishida Toshiko, not yet twenty years old, astonished the country in 1882 when she undertook a two-month speaking tour, where she addressed huge audiences. Only "equality and equal rights," she argued, would allow Japan "to build a new society." Japan must rid itself of the ancient habit of "respecting men and despising women."

While the new Japanese government included girls in their plans for universal education, it was with a gender-specific curriculum and in schools segregated by sex. Any thought of women playing a role in public life was harshly suppressed. A Peace Preservation Law of 1887, in effect until 1922, forbade women from joining political parties and even from attending meetings where political matters were discussed. The Constitution of 1889 made no mention of any political rights for women. The Civil Code of 1898 accorded absolute authority to the male head of the family, while grouping all wives with "cripples and disabled persons" as those who "cannot undertake any legal action." To the authorities of Meiji Japan, a serious transformation of gender roles was more of a threat than an opportunity.

At the core of Japan's effort at defensive modernization lay its state-guided industrialization program. More than in Europe or the United States, the government itself established a number of enterprises, later selling many of them to private investors. It also acted to create a modern infrastructure by building railroads, creating a postal system, and establishing a national currency and banking system. By the early twentieth century, Japan's industrialization, organized around a number of large firms called *zaibatsu*, was well under way. The country became a major exporter of textiles and was able to produce its own munitions and industrial goods as well. Its major cities enjoyed mass-circulation newspapers, movie theaters, and electric lights. All of this was accomplished through its own resources and without the massive foreign debt that

Japan's Modernization
In Japan, as in Europe, railroads quickly became a popular symbol of the country's modernization, as this woodblock print from the 1870s illustrates. (The Art Gallery Collection/Alamy)

so afflicted Egypt and the Ottoman Empire. No other country outside of Europe and North America had been able to launch its own Industrial Revolution in the nineteenth century. It was a distinctive feature of Japan's modern transformation.

Less distinctive, however, were the social results of that process. Taxed heavily to pay for Japan's ambitious modernization program, many peasant families slid into poverty. Their sometimes violent protests peaked in 1883–1884 as the Japanese countryside witnessed infanticide, the sale of daughters, and starvation.

If state authorities rigidly excluded women from political life and denied them adult legal status, they badly needed female labor in the country's textile industry, which was central to Japan's economic growth. Accordingly, the majority of Japan's textile workers were young women from poor families in the countryside. Recruiters toured rural villages contracting with parents for their daughters' labor in return for a payment which the girls had to repay from their wages. That pay was low and their working conditions terrible. Most lived in factory-provided dormitories and worked twelve or more hours per day. While some committed suicide or ran away and many left after earning enough to pay off their contracts, others organized strikes and joined the anarchist or socialist movements that were emerging among a few intellectuals. One such woman, Kanno Suga, was hanged in 1911 for participating in a plot to assassinate the emperor. Efforts to create unions and organize strikes, both illegal in Japan at the time, were met with harsh repression even as corporate and state authorities sought to depict the company as a family unit to which workers should give their loyalty, all under the beneficent gaze of the divine emperor.

Japan and the World

■ **Connection**

How did Japan's relationship to the larger world change during its modernization process?

Japan's modern transformation soon registered internationally. By the early twentieth century, its economic growth, openness to trade, and embrace of "civilization and enlightenment" from the West persuaded the Western powers to revise the unequal treaties in Japan's favor. This had long been a primary goal of the Meiji regime, and the Anglo-Japanese Treaty of 1902 now acknowledged Japan as an equal player among the Great Powers of the world.

Not only did Japan escape from its semi-colonial entanglements with the West, but it also launched its own empire-building enterprise, even as European powers and the United States were carving up much of Asia and Africa into colonies or spheres of influence. It was what industrializing Great Powers did in the late nineteenth century, and Japan followed suit. Successful wars against China (1894–1895) and Russia (1904–1905) established Japan as a formidable military competitor in East Asia and the first Asian state to defeat a major European power. Through those victories, Japan also gained colonial control of Taiwan and Korea and a territorial foothold in Manchuria. (See Visual Source 19.4, p. 970, for an image of Japan's new relationship with China and the West.)

Japan's entry onto the broader global stage was felt in many places (see Map 19.3). It added yet one more imperialist power to those already burdening a beleaguered China. Defeat at the hands of Japanese upstarts shocked Russia and triggered the 1905 revolution in that country. To Europeans and Americans, Japan was now an economic, political, and military competitor in Asia.

In the world of subject peoples, the rise of Japan and its defeat of Russia generated widespread admiration among those who saw Japan as a model for their own modern development and perhaps as an ally in the struggle against imperialism. Some Poles, Finns, and Jews viewed the Russian defeat in 1905 as an opening for their own liberation from the Russian Empire and were grateful to Japan for the opportunity. Despite Japan's aggression against their country, many Chinese reformers and nationalists found in the Japanese experience valuable lessons for themselves. Thousands flocked to Japan to study its achievements. Newspapers throughout the Islamic world celebrated Japan's victory over Russia as an "awakening of the East," which might herald Muslims' own liberation. Some Turkish women gave their children Japanese names. Indonesian Muslims from Aceh wrote to the Meiji emperor asking for help in their struggle against the Dutch, and Muslim poets wrote odes in his honor. The Egyptian nationalist Mustafa Kamil spoke for many when he declared: "We are amazed by Japan because it is the first Eastern government to utilize Western civilization to resist the shield of European imperialism in Asia."[18]

Those who directly experienced Japanese imperialism in Taiwan or Korea no doubt had a less positive view, for its colonial policies matched or exceeded the brutality of European practices. In the twentieth century, China and much of Southeast Asia suffered bitterly under Japanese imperial aggression. Nonetheless, both the idea of Japan as a liberator of Asia from the European yoke and the reality of Japan as an

LearningCurve
bedfordstmartins.com
/strayer/LC ✓

Map 19.3

The Rise of Japan

As Japan modernized after the Meiji restoration, it launched an empire-building program that provided a foundation for further expansion in the 1930s and during World War II.

oppressive imperial power in its own right derived from the country's remarkable modern transformation and its distinctive response to the provocation of Western intrusion.

Reflections: Success and Failure in History

Beyond describing what happened in the past and explaining why, historians often find themselves evaluating the events they study. When they make judgments about the past, notions of success and failure frequently come into play. Should Europe's Industrial Revolution and its rise to global power be regarded as a success? If so, does that imply that others were failures? Should we consider Japan more successful than China or the Ottoman Empire during the nineteenth century? Three considerations suggest that we should be very careful in applying these ideas to the complexities of the historical record.

First, and most obviously, is the question of criteria. If the measure of success is national wealth and power, then the Industrial Revolution surely counts as a great accomplishment. But if preservation of the environment, spiritual growth, and the face-to-face relationships of village life are more highly valued, then industrialization, as Gandhi argued, might be more reasonably considered a disaster.

Second, there is the issue of "success for whom?" British artisans who lost their livelihood to industrial machines as well as those Japanese women textile workers who suffered through the early stages of industrialization might be forgiven for not appreciating the "success" of their countries' transformation, even if their middle-class counterparts and subsequent generations benefited. In such cases, issues of both social and generational justice complicate any easy assessment of the past.

Finally, success is frequently associated with good judgment and wise choices, yet actors in the historical drama are never completely free in making their decisions, and none, of course, have the benefit of hindsight, which historians enjoy. Did the leaders of China and the Ottoman Empire fail to push industrial development more strongly, or were they not in a position to do so? Were Japanese leaders wiser and more astute than their counterparts elsewhere, or did their knowledge of China's earlier experience and their unique national history simply provide them with circumstances more conducive to modern development? Such questions regarding the possibilities and limitations of human action have no clear-cut answers, but they might caution us about any easy assessment of success and failure.

Second Thoughts

What's the Significance?

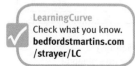

LearningCurve
Check what you know.
**bedfordstmartins.com
/strayer/LC**

Online Study Guide
bedfordstmartins.com
/highschool/strayer

Taiping Uprising, 933–35
Opium Wars, 936–37
unequal treaties, 937
self-strengthening movement, 939
Boxer Uprising, 939
Commissioner Lin, 940–41
Chinese Revolution of 1911, 940–41
"the sick man of Europe," 942–44

Tanzimat, 944–46
Young Ottomans, 945
Sultan Abd al-Hamid II, 945
Young Turks, 946
informal empires, 946–47
Tokugawa Japan, 948–49
Meiji restoration, 949–50
Russo-Japanese War, 1904–1905, 954

Big Picture Questions

1. "The response of each society to European imperialism grew out of its larger historical development and its internal problems." What evidence might support this statement?

2. "Deliberate government policies were more important than historical circumstances policies in shaping the history of China, the Ottoman Empire, and Japan during the nineteenth century." How might you argue for and against this statement?

3. What kinds of debates, controversies, and conflicts were generated by European intrusion within each of the societies examined in this chapter?

4. **Looking Back:** How did the experiences of China, the Ottoman Empire, Japan, and Latin America, which retained their independence despite much European pressure, differ from that of Africa, India, and Southeast Asia, which fell under formal colonial rule?

Next Steps: For Further Study

For Web sites and additional documents related to this chapter, see **Make History** at bedfordstmartins.com /highschool/strayer.

William Bowman et al., *Imperialism in the Modern World* (2007). A collection of short readings illustrating the various forms and faces of European expansion over the past several centuries.

Carter V. Finley, *The Turks in World History* (2004). A study placing the role of Turkish-speaking peoples in general and the Ottoman Empire in particular in a global context.

Maurice Jansen, *The Making of Modern Japan* (2000). A well-regarded account of Japan since 1600 by a leading scholar.

Jonathan Spence, *The Search for Modern China* (1999). Probably the best single-volume account of Chinese history from about 1600 through the twentieth century.

E. Patricia Tsurumi, *Factory Girls: Women in the Thread Mills of Meiji Japan* (1990). An examination of the lives of women in Japan's nineteenth-century textile factories.

Arthur Waley, *The Opium War through Chinese Eyes* (1968). An older classic that views the Opium War from various Chinese points of view.

MIT, "Visualizing Cultures: Image Driven Scholarship," 2002. http://ocw.mit.edu/ans7870/21f/ 21f.027/home/index.html A collection of thoughtful essays and stunning images dealing with China and Japan during the nineteenth century.

Documents

Considering the Evidence:
Changing China

By the end of the nineteenth century, growing numbers of thoughtful Chinese recognized that their country was in crisis. Repeated European military interventions since the first Opium War in 1839 had humiliated the once proud Middle Kingdom, reducing it to a semicolonial dependent of various European powers. A decisive military defeat in a war with Japan in 1894–1895 represented a further humiliation at the hands of a small country long under the cultural influence of China. China also continued to face the enormous problem of widespread poverty among its peasant population, a dilemma reflected in repeated upheavals in the countryside. Both of these issues—foreign imperialism and peasant rebellion—found expression in the Boxer Uprising of 1898–1901 (see p. 939). This upheaval demonstrated—once again—the ability of China's vast peasant population to make its presence felt in the political life of the country as it had in the Taiping Uprising of the 1850s and '60s (see pp. 934–35). The Boxer Rebellion's virulent anti-foreign and anti-Christian outlook disclosed the depth of feeling against imperialism even among rural dwellers. The outcome of that rebellion—foreign occupation of Beijing and large reparation payments from China's government—revealed China's continuing weakness relative to European and Japanese powers.

In this context, many plans for changing China emerged. Some of them were reformist and aimed at preserving the Qing dynasty regime; others were more revolutionary and sought to replace dynastic China with a new society and political system altogether. During a brief three-month period in 1898, known as the Hundred Days of Reform, and then again in the decade following the Boxer Uprising, some of these reform proposals began to be implemented, including the end of the traditional civil service examination system and creation of elected provincial assemblies. But more substantial change in China had to await the collapse of the Qing dynasty and the end of the monarchy in 1912, and the most dramatic changes occurred after the communists came to power in 1949. Nonetheless, the proposals of the late nineteenth and early twentieth centuries were significant, for they reveal both the mounting pressures for a new path and the obstacles that confronted those who advocated such changes.

Document 19.1

Toward a Constitutional Monarchy

Among the leading advocates of reform in the aftermath of China's defeat by Japan was Kang Youwei (1858–1927), a brilliant Confucian scholar, whose views informed the Hundred Days of Reform in 1898. Understanding Confucius as a reformer, Kang Youwei argued that the Chinese emperor could be an active agent for China's transformation while operating in a parliamentary and constitutional setting. With its emphasis on human goodness, self-improvement, and the moral example of superiors, Confucianism could provide a framework for real change even as it protected China from "moral degeneration" and an indiscriminate embrace of Western culture. In a memorial to the emperor in early 1898, Kang Youwei spelled out his understanding of what China needed.

- In what ways does Kang Youwei reflect a Confucian outlook, and in what respects does he show an awareness of a larger world?

- What obstacles to reform does Kang Youwei identify?

- Why does he advocate the Russia of Peter the Great and the Japan of the Meiji reforms as models for China?

Kang Youwei
Memorial to Emperor Guangxu
1898

A survey of all states in the world will show that those states which undertook reforms became stronger while those states which clung to the past perished. . . . If Your Majesty, with your discerning brilliance, observes the trends in other countries, you will see that if we can change, we can preserve ourselves; but if we cannot change, we will perish.

It is a principle of things that the new is strong but the old is weak. . . . [T]here are no institutions that should remain unchanged for a hundred years. Moreover our present institutions are but unworthy vestiges of the Han, Tang, Yuan, and Ming dynasties. . . . [T]hey are the products of fancy writing and corrupt dealing of the petty officials rather than the original ideas of the ancestors. To say that they are ancestral institutions is an insult to the ancestors. Furthermore institutions are for the purpose of preserving one's territories. Now that the ancestral territory cannot be preserved, what good is it to maintain the ancestral institutions?

Nowadays the court has been undertaking some reforms, but the action of the emperor is obstructed by the ministers, and the recommendations of the able scholars are attacked by old-fashioned bureaucrats. If the charge is not "using barbarian ways to change China," then it is "upsetting ancestral institutions." Rumors and scandal are rampant, and people fight each other like fire and water. A reform in this way is as effective as attempting a forward march by walking backward. . . . I beg Your Majesty to make up your mind and to decide on the national policy.

Source: J. Mason Gentzler, *Changing China* (New York: Praegar, 1977), 86–87.

After studying ancient and modern institutions, Chinese and foreign, I have found that the institutions of the sage-kings and the Three Dynasties [Xia, Shang, and Zhou dynasties of very ancient times] were excellent, but ancient times were different from today. I hope that Your Majesty will daily read Mencius [a famous Confucian writer] and follow his example of loving the people. The development of the Han, Tang, Song and Ming dynasties may be learned, but it should be remembered that the [present] age of universal unification is different from that of sovereign nations. . . . As to the republican governments of the United States and France and the constitutional governments of Britain and Germany, these countries are far away and their customs are different from ours. . . . Consequently I beg Your Majesty to adopt the purpose of Peter the Great of Russia as our purpose and to take the Meiji Reform of Japan as the model of our reform. The time and place of Japan's reforms are not remote and her religion and customs are somewhat similar to ours. Her success is manifest; her example can be followed.

Document 19.2

Education and Examination

At the heart of Chinese culture and government lay the country's fabled examination system and the Confucian-based educational system on which it rested. Those examinations had long been used to select the officials who governed China. The classical texts and rhetorical style that the examinations tested were widely regarded as essential to preserving the essence of Chinese culture while creating common values among the elite. But for those seeking fundamental change in China, the examination system represented everything that was conservative, backward, and out of date, preventing the country from effectively modernizing. In 1905, that ancient examination system was formally and permanently abolished. The two brief selections that follow make the case for educational reform. The first comes from an anonymous editorial in a Chinese newspaper in 1898, while the second was part of an edict from the reforming Emperor Guangxu during the Hundred Days of Reform, also in 1898.

- What criticisms of the old examination system do these excerpts make?

- What kind of education do they advocate?

- How might conservatives respond to these documents?

ANONYMOUS

Editorial on China's Examination System
1898

The dynasty's examination system is extremely annoying and cumbersome.... Students go through innumerable hardships before they can obtain the right to wear the robes designating them as officially authorized students. Hence year after year they persist in their studies until their hair turns white. One half of each year is taken up with examinations, and the other half is burdened with wife, children, home, and family. Any spare time is spent trying to master the eight-legged essay. And yet it is very difficult to attain satisfactory competence in the eight-legged style, even though it is considered so vital. What then, if in addition, one wants to read useful books and study useful subjects? ...

For the court to use poetry, rhyme-prose, and fine script as the criteria for passing or failing the examinations for men of ability is truly vulgar and ridiculous.... [T]he multitude of problems on the coast [a reference to European penetration] has steadily weakened the nation. Poetry and rhyme-prose are not adequate to cope with this changing situation, and fine script is not adequate to withstand the enemy. How are we to devise a policy to bring peace and to emulate the wealth and power [of the Western nations]? Every meaningless and extravagant custom should be reformed.... Only then will officials of the court ... be able to devote themselves to useful studies. Their ambitions will no longer be diverted by eight-legged essays, poetry, rhyme-prose and fine script, nor will their minds be disturbed by all the various examinations.

Sources: J. Mason Gentzler, *Changing China* (New York: Praegar, 1977), 88–89; Isaac Taylor Headland, *Court Life in China* (New York: F. H. Revell, 1909).

EMPEROR GUANGXU

Edict on Education
1898

Our scholars are now without solid and practical education; our artisans are without scientific instructors; when compared with other countries. We soon see how weak we are. Does anyone think that our troops are as well drilled or as well led as those of the foreign armies? Or that we can successfully stand against them? Changes must be made to accord with the necessities of the times.... Keeping in mind the morals of the sages and wise men, we must make them the basis on which to build newer and better structures. We must substitute modern arms and western organization for our old regime; we must select our military officers according to western methods of military education; we must establish elementary and high schools, colleges and universities, in accordance with those of foreign countries; we must abolish the Wen-chang (literary essay) and obtain a knowledge of ancient and modern world-history, a right conception of the present-day state of affairs, with special reference to the governments and institutions of the countries of the five great continents; and we must understand their arts and sciences.

Document 19.3

Gender, Reform, and Revolution

Among those seeking to change China, the question of women's roles in society frequently arose. Kang Youwei (see Document 19.1), for example, looked forward to the end of traditional marriage, hoping it would be replaced by a series of one-year contracts between a man and woman, which he thought would ensure gender equality. But the most well-known advocate for women was Qiu Jin (1875–1907). Born into a well-to-do family with liberal inclinations, she received a fine literary education, developing a passion for reading as well as for swordplay, horseback riding, and fighting with boys. Married to a much older man at age 18, she was distinctly unsatisfied in such a conventional life. In 1903, she did something almost unthinkable for a Chinese woman when she left her husband and children to pursue an education in Japan. Returning in 1906, she started a women's magazine and became active in revolutionary circles. For her role in an abortive plot to overthrow the Qing dynasty, she was arrested and beheaded in 1907. The selection that follows comes from her most famous appeal for the rights of women.

- What are the "injustices" that Qiu Jin identifies?

- How does she account for the sad conditions which Chinese women faced?

- What does she advocate as a remedy for the problems she identifies?

- How might you compare Qiu Jin's address with that of Elizabeth Cady Stanton in Document 16.4, pp. 818–19?

QIU JIN

An Address to Two Hundred Million Fellow Countrywomen

1904

Alas! The greatest injustice in this world must be the injustice suffered by our female population of two hundred million. If a girl is lucky enough to have a good father, then her childhood is at least tolerable. But if by chance her father is an ill-tempered and unreasonable man, he may curse her birth: "What rotten luck: another useless thing." Some men go as far as killing baby girls while most hold the opinion that "girls are eventually someone else's property" and treat them with coldness and disdain. In a few years, without thinking about whether it is right or wrong, he forcibly binds his daughter's soft, white feet with white cloth so that even in her sleep she cannot find comfort and relief until the flesh becomes rotten and the bones broken. What is

Source: Patricia Buckley Ebrey, *Chinese Civilization: A Sourcebook*, trans. Nancy Gibbs (New York: Free Press, 1993), 343–344 (excerpts).

all this misery for? Is it just so that on the girl's wedding day friends and neighbors will compliment him, saying, "Your daughter's feet are really small"? Is that what the pain is for?

But that is not the worst of it. When the time for marriage comes, a girl's future is placed in the hands of shameless matchmakers and a family seeking rich and powerful in-laws.... [T]he girl ... is not allowed to breathe one word about her future. After her marriage, if the man doesn't do her any harm, she is told that she should thank Heaven for her good fortune. But if the man is bad or he illtreats her, she is told that her marriage is retribution for some sin committed in her previous existence.... When Heaven created people it never intended such injustice because if the world is without women, how can men be born? Why is there no justice for women?

Dear sisters, you must know that you'll get nothing if you rely upon others. You must go out and get things for yourselves.... It seems clear now that it was we women who abandoned our responsibilities to ourselves and felt content to let men do everything for us. As long as we could live in comfort and leisure, we let men make all the decisions for us.... At the same time we were insecure in our good fortune and our physical comfort, so we did everything to please men. When we heard that men like small feet, we immediately bound them just to please them, just to keep our free meal tickets....

Let us put aside our former selves and be resurrected as complete human beings.... If your husbands want to open schools, don't stop them; if your good sons want to study abroad, don't hold them back.... After your sons are born, send them to schools. You must do the same for your daughters and, whatever you do, don't bind their feet. As for you young girls among us, go to school if you can. If not, read and study at home.... You must know that when a country is near destruction, women cannot rely on the men anymore because they aren't even able to protect themselves. If we don't take heart now and shape up, it will be too late when China is destroyed.

Document 19.4

Prescriptions for a Revolutionary China

While some advocates for changing China pressed for various reforms within the framework of Qing dynasty China, others felt that the millennia-old monarchy itself had to be overthrown if China was to modernize and prosper as a nation. The leading figure among China's late-nineteenth century revolutionaries was Sun Yat-sen (1866–1925), a convert to Christianity, a trained medical doctor, and by the 1890s an ardent revolutionary. From exile in Europe, the United States, and Japan, Sun plotted various uprisings against the Qing dynasty and in 1905 created the Revolutionary Alliance in an effort to bring together the various groups seeking to end the ancient imperial system. But what kind of society and political structure did Sun envisage for his country? In 1906 Sun spelled out an early formulation of his "three people's principles"—nationalism, democracy, and people's livelihood—that articulated his vision for China's future.

- Why does Sun Yat-sen believe that China requires a revolution rather than reform?

- In his view, who are the enemies of the Chinese nation?

■ What elements of Sun's prescriptions for China's future derive from traditional Chinese practice and which reflect Western influence?

■ Is Sun Yat-sen advocating a socialist future for China?

■ How might Kang Youwei in Document 19.1 respond to Sun Yat-sen's prescriptions for the future?

SUN YAT-SEN

The Three People's Principles and the Future of the Chinese People

1906

Nationalism . . . has to do with human nature and applies to everyone. Today, more than 260 years have passed since the Manchus entered China proper, yet even as children we Han [ethnic Chinese] would certainly not mistake them for fellow Han. This is the root of nationalism. . . . It simply means not allowing such people [the Manchu rulers of the Qing dynasty] to seize our political power, for only when we Han are in control politically do we have a nation. . . .

Actually we are already a people without a nation. . . . Our nation is the most populous, most ancient, and most civilized in the world, yet today we are a lost nation. . . . We Han are now swiftly being caught up in a tidal wave of nationalist revolution, yet the Manchus continue to discriminate against the Han. They boast that their forefathers conquered the Han because of their superior unity and that they intend . . . to dominate the Han forever. . . . Certainly once we Han unite, our power will be thousands of times greater than theirs and the success of our nationalist revolution will be assured.

As for the Principle of Democracy, it is the foundation of the political revolution. . . . For several thousand years China has been a monarchial autocracy, a type of political system intolerable to those living in freedom and equality. A nationalist revolution is not itself sufficient to get rid of such a

system . . . a political revolution is an absolute necessity. The aim of the political revolution is to create a constitutional democratic political system. . . . [Such a] revolution would be necessary even if the monarch were a Han.

As for the Principle of the People's Livelihood . . . , we must try to improve the economic structures of society so as to preclude a social revolution in the future. . . . As civilization advanced, people relied less on physical labor and more on natural forces, since electricity and steam could accomplish things a thousand times faster than physical strength. . . . [N]ow with the development of natural forces that human labor cannot match, agriculture and industry have fallen completely into the hands of capitalists. Unable to compete, the poor have naturally been reduced to destitution. . . . [E]very informed person knows that a social revolution is inevitable in Europe and America.

Indeed this constitutes a lesson for China. . . . Civilization [advanced industrial capitalist countries] yields both good and bad fruits, and we should embrace the good and reject the bad. In Europe and America the rich monopolize the good fruits of civilization, while the poor suffer from its evil fruits. . . .

With respect to a solution . . . the procedure I most favor is land valuation. For example, if a landlord has land worth 1000 dollars, its price can be set at 1000 or even 2000 dollars. Perhaps in the future, after communications have been developed, the value of his land will rise to 10,000 dollars; the owner should receive 2000, which entails a profit and no

Julie Lee Wei et al., *Prescriptions for Saving China: Selected Writings of Sun Yat-sen* (Stanford, CA: Hoover Institution Press, 1994), 41–50.

loss, and the 8000 increment will go to the state. Such an arrangement will greatly benefit both the state and the people's livelihood. Naturally it will also eliminate the shortcomings that have permitted a few people to monopolize wealth....

As to the future constitution I propose that we introduce a new principle, that of the "five separate powers." Under this system there will be two other powers in addition to the [executive, legislative, and judicial]. One is the examination power.... American official are either elected or appointed. Formerly there were no civil service examinations, which led to serious shortcomings.... With respect to elections, those endowed with eloquence ingratiated themselves with the public and won elections, while those who had learning and ideals but lacked eloquence were ignored. Consequently members of America's House of Representatives have often been foolish and ignorant people who have made its history quite ridiculous.... Therefore the future constitution of the Republic of China must provide for an independent branch expressly responsible for civil service examinations. Furthermore all officials, however high their rank, must undergo examinations in order to determine their qualifications.

The other power is the supervisory power, responsible for monitoring matters involving impeachment.... Since ancient times, China had a supervisory organization, the Censorate, to monitor the traditional social order.

Using The Evidence: Changing China

1. **Defining obstacles to change:** What hindrances to China's effective transformation are stated or implied in these documents? Do their authors perceive any positive qualities in Chinese civilization that might facilitate the country's transformation?

2. **Assessing goals:** "China as a culture and a political system must be destroyed in order to preserve China as nation." To what extent would the authors of these documents have agreed or disagreed with this statement?

3. **Identifying differences:** Imagine a conversation among the authors of these documents. What points of agreement might they find? What conflicts among them would likely arise?

4. **Considering "Westernization" and "modernization":** To what extent do these proposals represent plans to "Westernize" China? Or might they rather be considered "modernizing" efforts? What is the difference between the two concepts?

Visual Sources

Considering the Evidence:
Japanese Perceptions of the West

The second half of the nineteenth century witnessed a profound transformation of Japanese life (see pp. 947–53). The Tokugawa shogunate, which had governed the country for over two centuries, came to an inglorious end in the Meiji restoration of 1868, and the country then embarked on a massive process of modernization and industrialization. Accompanying these upheavals, Japan's political and military relationship to the West changed dramatically, as its government and its people found themselves required to confront both Western power and Western culture, a common feature of nineteenth-century world history in many places. Accordingly, Japanese understanding of the West, and what they had to fear or gain from it, also changed. Those evolving perceptions of the West found artistic expression, especially in Japanese woodblock printing, an art form that reached its high point in the late nineteenth century. Such images provide for historians a window into Japanese thinking about their own society and the larger world impinging on them during this critical half century.

The initial occasion for serious Japanese reflection on the West occurred in 1853–1854, in the context of American commodore Matthew Perry's efforts to "open" Japan to regular commercial relationships with the United States. His nine coal-fired steamships, belching black smoke and carrying a crew of some 1,800 men and more than 100 mounted cannons, became known in Japan as the "black ships." Visual Source 19.1, created around 1854, represents perhaps the best known of many such Japanese depictions of the American warships.

- What general impression of the American intrusion did the artist seek to convey?

- What specific features of the image help the artist make his case?

- Why might the artist have chosen to depict the gunfire coming from the American ship as streams of light?

Beyond portraying the American warships, Japanese artists sought to depict their inhabitants, especially Commodore Perry and his top aides. Some Japanese men rowed their small boats out to the black ships, hoping to catch a glimpse of Perry himself. But the commodore remained largely inaccessible, and the Japanese called his secluded on-board cabin "The Abode of His High and Mighty Mysteriousness." The image on page 950 depicts one of many portrayals of Perry (on the right), together with his second-in-command. They are shown here as a particular kind of goblin, known as *tengu*, that have long noses and are viewed as dangerous, demonic, and warlike. His creased and hairy face likewise conveys a sense of otherness compared to the smooth and hairless faces of respected Japanese figures.

By the 1880s, Japan was in the midst of an amazing transformation, in part the outcome of Perry's forced "opening" of the country. By then Japan had a new government committed to the country's rapid modernization. Particularly among the young, there was an acute awareness of the need to create a new culture that could support a revived Japan. "We have no history," declared one of these students; "our history begins today."[19] In this context, much that was Western was enthusiastically embraced. The technological side of this borrowing was illustrated in the woodblock print on page 953.

But borrowing extended as well to more purely cultural matters. Eating beef became popular, despite Buddhist objections. Many men adopted Western

Visual Source 19.1 The Black Ships (Courtesy, Ryosenji Treasure Museum)

Visual Source 19.2 Women and Westernization (Hashimoto Chikanobu, Japanese, 1838–1912. Publisher: Ōmori Kakutarō, Japanese. Singing by the Plum Garden (Baien shōka zu). Japanese, Meiji era, 1887 (Meiji 20), December. Woodblock print (nishiki-e); ink and color on paper. Vertical ōban triptych; 35.4 x 71.6 cm (13 15/16 x 28 3/16 in.). Museum of Fine Arts, Boston. Gift of L. Aaron Lebowich. RES.53.82-4. Photograph © 2014 Museum of Fine Arts, Boston.)

hairstyles and grew beards, even though the facial hair of Westerners had earlier been portrayed as ugly. In 1872, Western dress was ordered for all official ceremonies. Women in elite circles likewise adopted Western ways, as illustrated in Visual Source 19.2, an 1887 woodblock print titled *Illustration of Singing by the Plum Garden*. At the same time, the dress of the woman in the middle seems to reflect earlier Japanese court traditions that encouraged women to wear many layers of kimonos.

- What elements of Western culture can you identify in this visual source?

- In what ways does this print reflect the continuing appeal of Japanese culture? Pay attention to the scenery, the tree, and the flowers.

- Why were so many Japanese so enamored of Western culture during this time? And why did the Japanese government so actively encourage their interest?

Not everyone in Japan was so enthusiastic about the adoption of Western culture, and by the late 1870s and into the next decade numerous essays and images satirized the apparently indiscriminate fascination with all things European. Visual Source 19.3, drawn by Japanese cartoonist Kobayashi Kiyochika in 1879, represents one of those images. Its full English-language caption read as follows: "Mr. Morse [an American zoologist who introduced Darwin's theory of evolution to Japan in 1877] explains that all human beings were monkeys in the beginning. In the beginning—but even now aren't we still monkeys?

Monkey-show. 猿芝居の楽屋

All the monkeys dressed in European style, and in every respect trying to ape Foreigners.

Visual Source 19.3 Kobayashi Kiyochika's Critique of Wholesale Westernization (Library of Congress)

When it comes to Western things we think the red beards are the most skillful at everything."[20]

- What specific aspects of Japan's efforts at Westernization is the artist mocking?

- Why might the artist have used a Western scientific theory (Darwinian evolution) to criticize excessive Westernization in Japan?

- Why do you think a reaction set in against the cultural imitation of Europe?

Behind Japan's modernization and Westernization was the recognition that Western imperialism was surging in Asia and that China was a prime example of what happened to countries unable to defend themselves against it. Accordingly, achieving political and military equality with the Great Powers of Europe and the United States became a central aim of Japan's modernization program.

Strengthening Japan against Western aggression increasingly meant "throwing off Asia," a phrase that implied rejecting many of Japan's own cultural traditions and its habit of imitating China as well as creating an Asian empire of its own. Fukuzawa Yukichi, a popular advocate of Western knowledge, declared:

We must not wait for neighboring countries to become civilized so that we can together promote Asia's revival. Rather we should leave their ranks and join forces with the civilized countries of the West. We don't have to give China and Korea any special treatment just because they are neighboring countries. We should deal with them as Western people do. Those who have bad friends cannot avoid having a bad reputation. I reject the idea that we must continue to associate with bad friends in East Asia.[21]

Historically the Japanese had borrowed a great deal from China — Buddhism, Confucianism, court rituals, city-planning ideas, administrative traditions, and elements of the Chinese script. But Japan's victory in a war with China in 1894–1895 showed clearly that it had thrown off the country in whose cultural shadow it had lived for centuries. Furthermore, Japan had begun to acquire an East Asian empire in Korea and Taiwan. And its triumph over Russia in another war ten years later illustrated its ability to stand up to a major European power. The significance of these twin victories is expressed in Visual Source 19.4, a Japanese image created during the Russo-Japanese War and titled *The Japanese Navy Uses China as Bait to Trap the Greedy Russian.*

Visual Source 19.4 Japan, China, and Europe: A Reversal of Roles (Artist Unknown, Japanese. Publisher: Manzai kan. The Avarice and A Trap of Wisdom from the series Laughing Stock. Japanese, late Meiji era, about 1904–05. Color lithograph; ink on card stock. Overall: 8.8 x 13.8 cm (3 7/16 x 5 7/16 in.). Museum of Fine Arts, Boston. Leonard A. Lauder Collection of Japanese Postcards. 2002.3504. Photograph © 2014 Museum of Fine Arts, Boston.)

- What overall message did the artist seek to convey in this print?

- What is the significance of the Chinese figure with a chicken in hand, lying as "bait" at the bottom of the image?

- How is the Russia character portrayed?

- What had changed in Japanese thinking about China and Europe during the nineteenth century?

Using the Evidence:
Japanese Perceptions of the West

1. **Explaining change:** How and why had Japanese perceptions of themselves and their relationship to the West changed in the half century since the Meiji restoration? What elements of continuity in Japanese traditions are evident in these visual sources?

2. **Making comparisons:** Based on these visual sources and the documents about "Changing China," how might you compare Japanese and Chinese perceptions of the West by the end of the nineteenth century? What accounts for both the similarities and differences?

3. **Distinguishing modernization and Westernization:** Based on a careful reading of Chapter 19, including the documents and images, do you think that technological borrowing (modernization) requires cultural borrowing (Westernization) as well? Was it possible during the nineteenth century to modernize while avoiding the incorporation of Western culture at the same time? What do the examples of China, the Ottoman Empire, and Japan suggest about this question?

Chapter 19 Wrap Up

LearningCurve
Check what you know.
**bedfordstmartins.com
/strayer/LC**

STEP ONE

The Word to Know: Reform

The *Oxford English Dictionary* defines *reform* as "the action or process of making changes in an institution, organization, or aspect of social or political life, so as to remove errors, abuses, or other hindrances to proper performance." Sometimes, a nation's subjects will demand reforms if they feel that their government is not addressing their needs. Write a brief paragraph explaining how the Ottoman Empire responded to calls for reform in the nineteenth century.

STEP TWO

Timeline of the Ottoman Empire

The Ottoman Empire spans a period of over 600 years and had a major impact on the history of Eurasia in general and the Middle East specifically. Review the relevant pages in the book (Chapter 9, p. 413 and pp. 430–32; Chapter 10, p. 465 and pp. 470–71; Chapter 12, p. 561 and pp. 576–78; Chapter 13, p. 619 and pp. 644–47; and Chapter 19, p. 933 and pp. 942–47) and create a timeline of Ottoman history using at least 10 relevant events. Afterward, write a paragraph explaining why you included what you did and analyze how these events reflects changes and/or continuities in the history of the Ottoman Empire.

Defensive Modernization in Siam and Ethiopia: A Web Search

There is a wealth of material available on the Web for doing historical research. Review the following Web sites looking for evidence of modernization efforts by Menelik II in Ethiopia and either Mongkut Rama IV, or his son King Chulalongkorn of Siam. As you review the sites, use the chart below to think about how both Ethiopia and Siam escaped becoming European colonies in the nineteenth century.

Ethiopia

britishmuseum.org/explore/highlights/highlight_objects/aoa/e/emperor_menelik_ii,
_painting.aspx

angelfire.com/ny/ethiocrown/menelikII.html

Siam

heliograph.com/trmgs/trmgs4/siam1.shtml

guidetothailand.com/thailand-history/new-siam.php

chiangmai-chiangrai.com/the-great-visionary-king-chulalongkorn.html

	Ethiopia	Siam
Economic		
Political/Military		
Cultural Technological		

Globalization in Action: Trade and Investment in the Early Twenty-first Century (p. 1141)

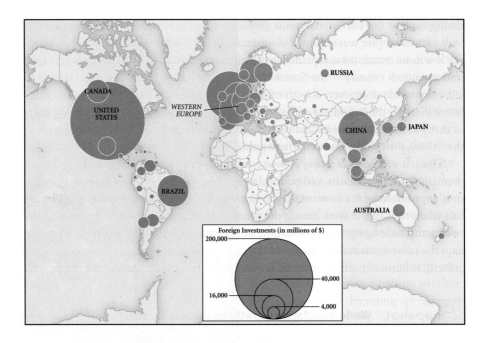

about 7 billion people by 2011. This was an absolutely unprecedented rate of growth that conditioned practically every other feature of the century's history. Still, this new element of twentieth-century world history built on earlier achievements, most notably the increased food supply deriving from the global spread of American crops such as corn and potatoes. Improvements in medicine and sanitation, which grew out of the earlier Scientific and Industrial Revolutions, likewise drove down death rates and thus spurred population growth.

While global population increased fourfold in the twentieth century, industrial output grew fortyfold. Despite large variations over time and place, this unprecedented economic growth was associated with a cascading rate of scientific and technological innovation as well as with the extension of industrial production to many regions of the world. This too was a wholly novel feature of twentieth-century world history and, combined with population growth, resulted in an extraordinary and mounting human impact on the environment. Historian J. R. McNeill wrote that "this is the first time in human history that we have altered ecosystems with such intensity, on such a scale, and with such speed. . . . The human race, without intending anything of the sort, has undertaken a gigantic uncontrolled experiment on the earth."[1] By the late twentieth century, that experiment had taken humankind well into what many scientists have been calling the Anthropocene era, the age of man, in which human activity is leaving an enduring and global mark on the geological, atmospheric, and biological history of the planet itself. From a longer-term perspective, of course, these developments represent a continued unfolding of the Scientific and Industrial Revolutions. Both began in Europe, but in the twentieth century they largely lost their unique association with the West as they took hold in many cultures. Furthermore, the human impact on the earth and other living creatures has a history dating back to the extinction of some large mammals at the hands of Paleolithic hunters, although the scope and extent of that impact during the past century is without precedent.

Much the same might be said about that other grand process of contemporary world history—globalization, which is the focus of Chapter 23. It too has a genealogy reaching deep into the past, reflected in the Silk Road trading network; Indian Ocean and trans-Saharan commerce; the spread of Buddhism, Christianity, and Islam; and the Columbian exchange. But the most recent century deepened and extended the connections among the distinct peoples, nations, and regions of the world in ways unparalleled in earlier times. A few strokes on a keyboard can send money racing around the planet; radio, television, and the Internet link the world in an unprecedented network of communication; far more people than ever before produce for and depend on the world market; and global inequalities increasingly surface as sources of international conflict. For good or ill, we live—all of us—in a new phase of an ancient process.

The four chapters of Part Six explore these global themes that have so decisively shaped the history of the past century. Perhaps there is enough that is new about that century to treat it, tentatively, as a distinct era in human history, but only what happens next will determine how this period will be understood by later generations. Will it be regarded as the beginning of the end of the modern age, as human demands on the earth prove unsustainable? Or will it be seen as the midpoint of an ongoing process that extends a full modernity to the entire planet? Will recognition of our common fate as human beings generate shared values, a culture of tolerance, and an easing of international tensions? Or will global inequalities and rivalry over diminishing resources foster even greater and more dangerous conflicts? Like all of our ancestors, every one of them, we too live in a fog when contemplating our futures and see more clearly only in retrospect. In this strange way, our future will shape the telling of the past, even as the past shapes the living of the future.

Mapping Part Six

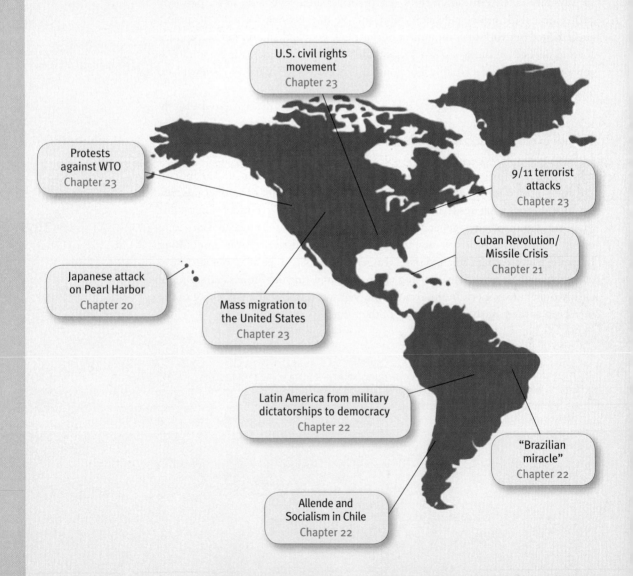

U.S. civil rights movement
Chapter 23

Protests against WTO
Chapter 23

9/11 terrorist attacks
Chapter 23

Cuban Revolution/ Missile Crisis
Chapter 21

Japanese attack on Pearl Harbor
Chapter 20

Mass migration to the United States
Chapter 23

Latin America from military dictatorships to democracy
Chapter 22

"Brazilian miracle"
Chapter 22

Allende and Socialism in Chile
Chapter 22

World Wars in Europe
Chapter 20

Rise and fall of Communism in Russia and Eastern Eurpope
Chapters 21 and 23

European Union
Chapter 23

Iranian Revolution
Chapter 22

Communist Revolution in China
Chapter 21

Korean War
Chapter 21

Atomic bombs on Hiroshima and Nagasaki
Chapter 20

Arab uprising
Chapter 23

Israel established
Chapter 22

Vietnam War
Chapter 23

India and Pakistan independence
Chapter 22

End of Apartheid
Chapter 22

African independence from colonialism
Chapter 22

Indonesian independence
Chapter 22

1778   1943

AMERICANS
will <u>always</u> fight for liberty

Collapse at the Center

World War, Depression, and the Rebalancing of Global Power

1914–1970S

"I was told that I was fighting a war that would end all wars, but that wasn't the case." Spoken a few years before his death, these were the thoughts of Alfred Anderson, a World War I veteran who died in Scotland in November 2005, at the age of 109. He was apparently the last survivor of the famous Christmas truce of 1914, when British and German soldiers, enemies on the battlefield of that war, briefly mingled, exchanged gifts, and played football in the no-man's land that lay between their entrenchments in Belgium. He had been especially dismayed when in 2003 his own unit, the famous Black Watch regiment, was ordered into Iraq along with other British forces.[1] Despite his disappointment at the many conflicts that followed World War I, Anderson's own lifetime had witnessed the fulfillment of the promise of the Christmas truce. By the time he died, the major European nations had put aside their centuries-long hostilities, and war between Britain and Germany, which had erupted twice in the twentieth century, seemed unthinkable.

THE "GREAT WAR," WHICH CAME TO BE CALLED THE FIRST WORLD WAR OR WORLD WAR I (1914–1918), effectively launched the twentieth century, considered as a new phase of world history. That bitter conflict—essentially a European civil war with a global reach—provoked the Russian Revolution and the beginnings of world communism. It was followed by the economic meltdown of the Great Depression, by the rise of Nazi Germany and the horror of the Holocaust, and by an even bloodier and more destructive World

---

The United States and World War II: The Second World War and its aftermath marked the decisive emergence of the United States as a global superpower. In this official 1943 poster, U.S. soldiers march forward to "fight for liberty" against fascism while casting a sideways glance for inspiration at the ragged colonial militiamen of their Revolutionary War. (Library of Congress, LC-USZC4-2119)

War II, a struggle that encompassed much of the world. During those three decades, Western Europe—for more than a century the dominant and dominating center of the modern "world system"—largely self-destructed, in a process with profound and long-term implications far beyond Europe itself. By 1945, an outside observer might well have thought that Western civilization, which for several centuries was in the ascendancy on the global stage, had damaged itself beyond repair. Certainly the subsequent emergence of the United States and the Soviet Union as rival super-powers marked a very different balance of global power.

In the second half of the century, however, European civilization proved resilient. Western Europe recovered remarkably from the devastation of war, rebuilt its indus-trial economy, and set aside its war-prone nationalist passions in a loose European

SEEKING THE MAIN POINT

In what ways were the world wars and the Great Depression motors of global change in the history of the twentieth century?

Union. But as Europe revived after 1945, it lost both its overseas colonial possessions and its position as the political, economic, and military core of Western civilization. That role now passed across the Atlantic to the United States, marking a major change in the historical development of the West. The offspring now overshadowed its parent.

The First World War: European Civilization in Crisis, 1914–1918

Since 1500, Europe had assumed an increasingly prominent position on the global stage, driven by its growing military capacity and the marvels of its Scientific and In-dustrial Revolutions. By 1900, Europeans, or people with a European ancestry, largely controlled the world's other peoples through their formal empires, their informal influence, or the weight of their numbers (see Map 20.1). That unique situation pro-vided the foundation for Europeans' pride, self-confidence, and sense of superiority. Few could have imagined that this "proud tower" of European dominance would lie shattered less than a half century later. The starting point in that unraveling was the First World War.

An Accident Waiting to Happen

Europe's modern transformation and its global ascendancy were certainly not accom-panied by a growing unity or stability among its own peoples—quite the opposite. The most obvious division was among its competing states, a long-standing feature of European political life. Those historical rivalries further sharpened as both Italy and Germany joined their fragmented territories into two major new powers around 1870. The arrival on the international scene of a powerful and rapidly industrializing Germany, seeking its "place in the sun," was a disruptive new element in European political life, especially for the more established powers, such as Britain, France, and Russia. Since the defeat of Napoleon in 1815, a fragile and fluctuating balance of power had generally maintained the peace among Europe's major countries. By the

A Map of Time

1914–1918	World War I
1917	Bolshevik Revolution in Russia; United States enters World War I
1919	Treaty of Versailles ending World War I; founding of Nazi Party
1920	Treaty of Sevres, dissolving the Ottoman Empire
1922	Mussolini comes to power in Italy
1929	Beginning of Great Depression
1933	Hitler assumes power in Germany
1937–1938	Japan invades China, beginning World War II in Asia; Rape of Nanjing
1939	Germany invades Poland, beginning World War II in Europe
1939–1945	World War II; the Holocaust
1941	Japanese attack on Pearl Harbor
1945	Atomic bombing of Hiroshima and Nagasaki; United Nations created
1945–1952	U.S. occupation of Japan
1947–1991	Cold war
1948–1952	Marshall Plan for Europe
1957	European Economic Community established
1994	European Union established
2002	Introduction of the euro

early twentieth century, that balance of power was expressed in two rival alliances, the Triple Alliance of Germany, Italy, and the Austro-Hungarian Empire and the Triple Entente of Russia, France, and Britain. Those commitments, undertaken in the interests of national security, transformed a relatively minor incident in the Balkans into a conflagration that consumed almost all of Europe.

That incident occurred on June 28, 1914, when a Serbian nationalist assassinated the heir to the Austro-Hungarian throne, Archduke Franz Ferdinand. To the rulers of Austria-Hungary, the surging nationalism of Serbian Slavs was a mortal threat to the cohesion of their fragile multinational empire, which included other Slavic peoples as well. Thus, they determined to crush it. But behind Austria-Hungary lay its far more powerful ally, Germany; and behind tiny Serbia lay Russia, with its self-proclaimed mission of protecting other Slavic peoples. Allied to Russia were the French and the British. Thus a system of alliances intended to keep the peace created obligations that drew the Great Powers of Europe into a general war by early August 1914 (see Map 20.2, p. 986).

■ Explanation
What aspects of Europe's nineteenth-century history contributed to the First World War?

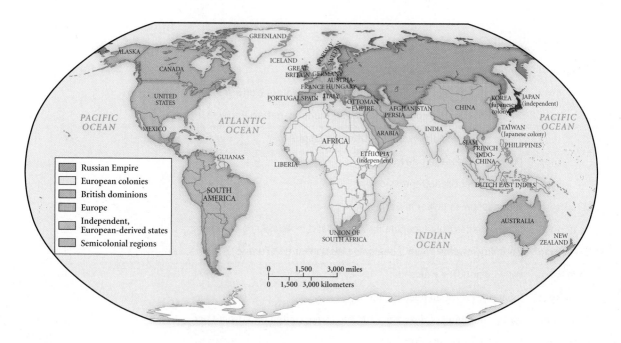

Russian Empire
European colonies
British dominions
Europe
Independent, European-derived states
Semicolonial regions

Map 20.1
The World in 1914
A map of the world in 1914 shows an unprecedented situation in which one people — Europeans or those of European descent — exercised enormous control and influence over virtually the entire planet.

The outbreak of that war was something of an accident, in that none of the major states planned or predicted the archduke's assassination or deliberately sought a prolonged conflict, but the system of rigid alliances made Europe vulnerable to that kind of accident. Moreover, behind those alliances lay other factors that contributed to the eruption of war and shaped its character. One of them was a mounting popular nationalism (see pp. 882–84). Slavic nationalism and Austro-Hungarian opposition to it certainly lay at the heart of the war's beginning. More importantly, the rulers of the major countries of Europe saw the world as an arena of conflict and competition among rival nation-states. The Great Powers of Europe competed intensely for colonies, spheres of influence, and superiority in armaments. Schools, mass media, and military service had convinced millions of ordinary Europeans that their national identities were profoundly and personally meaningful. The public pressure of these competing nationalisms allowed statesmen little room for compromise and ensured widespread popular support, at least initially, for the decision to go to war. Many men rushed to recruiting offices, fearing that the war might end before they could enlist. Celebratory parades sent them off to the front. British women were encouraged to present a white feather, a symbol of cowardice, to men not in uniform, thus affirming a warrior understanding of masculinity. For conservative governments, the prospect of war was a welcome occasion for national unity in the face of the mounting class- and gender-based conflicts in European societies.

Also contributing to the war was an industrialized militarism. Europe's armed rivalries had long ensured that military men enjoyed great social prestige, and most heads of state wore uniforms in public. All of the Great Powers had substantial standing armies and, except for Britain, relied on conscription (compulsory military service) to staff them. One expression of the quickening rivalry among these states was a mounting arms race in naval warships, particularly between Germany and Britain. Furthermore, each of the major states had developed elaborate "war plans" that spelled out in great detail the movement of men and materials that should occur immediately upon the outbreak of war. Such plans created a hair-trigger mentality since each country had an incentive to strike first so that its particular strategy could be implemented on schedule and without interruption or surprise. The rapid industrialization of warfare had generated an array of novel weapons, including submarines, tanks, airplanes, poison gas, machine guns, and barbed wire. This new military technology contributed to the staggering casualties of the war, including some 10 million deaths, the vast majority male; perhaps twice that number were wounded, crippled, or disfigured. For countless women, as a result, there would be no husbands or children.

Europe's imperial reach around the world likewise shaped the scope and conduct of the war. It funneled colonial troops and laborers by the hundreds of thousands into the war effort, with men from Africa, India, China, Southeast Asia, Australia, New Zealand, Canada, and South Africa taking part in the conflict (see Visual Source 20.3, p. 1029). Battles raged in Africa and the South Pacific as British and French forces sought to seize German colonies abroad. Japan, allied with Britain, took various German possessions in China and the Pacific and made heavy demands on China itself. The Ottoman Empire, which entered the conflict on the side of Germany, became the site of intense military actions and witnessed an Arab revolt against Ottoman control. Finally, the United States, after initially seeking to avoid involvement in European quarrels, joined the war in 1917 when German submarines threatened American shipping. Some 2 million Americans took part in the first U.S. military action on European soil and helped turn the tide in favor of the British and French. Thus the war, though centered in Europe, had global dimensions and certainly merited its title as a "world war."

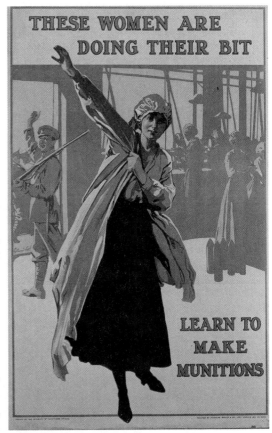

Women and the Great War
World War I temporarily brought a halt to the women's suffrage movement as well as to women's activities on behalf of international peace. Most women on both sides actively supported their countries' war efforts, as suggested by this British wartime poster, inviting women to work in the munitions industry. (The Art Archive at Art Resource, NY)

Legacies of the Great War

The Great War shattered almost every expectation. Most Europeans believed in the late summer of 1914 that "the boys will be home by Christmas," but instead the war ground relentlessly on for more than four years before ending in a German defeat

Map 20.2   Europe on the Eve of World War I
Despite many elements of common culture, Europe in 1914 was a powder keg, with its major states armed to the teeth and divided into two rival alliances. In the early stages of the war, Italy changed sides to join the French, British, and Russians.

■ **Change**

In what ways did World War I mark new departures in the history of the twentieth century?

in November 1918. (See Visual Sources: Propaganda and Critique in World War I, pp. 1025–33, for various representations of the war.) At the beginning, most military experts expected a war of movement and attack, but it soon bogged down on the western front into a war of attrition, in which trench warfare resulted in enormous casualties while gaining or losing only a few yards of muddy, blood-soaked ground. Extended battles lasting months—such as those at Verdun and the Somme in France—

Map 20.3 Europe and the Middle East after World War I

The Great War brought into existence a number of new states that were carved out of the old German, Austro-Hungarian, Russian, and Ottoman empires. Turkey and the new states in Europe were independent, but those in the Middle East—Syria, Palestine, Iraq, and Transjordan—were administered by Britain or France as mandates of the League of Nations.

generated casualties of a million or more each, as the destructive potential of industrialized warfare made itself tragically felt. Moreover, everywhere it became a "total war," requiring the mobilization of each country's entire population. Thus the authority of governments expanded greatly. The German state, for example, assumed such control over the economy that its policies became known as "war socialism." Vast propaganda campaigns sought to arouse citizens by depicting a cruel and inhuman enemy who killed innocent children and violated women. Labor unions agreed to suspend strikes and accept sacrifices for the common good, while women, replacing the men who had left the factories for the battlefront, temporarily abandoned the struggle for the vote.

No less surprising were the longer-term outcomes of the war. In the European cockpit of that conflict, unprecedented casualties, particularly among elite and well-educated groups, and physical destruction, especially in France, led to a widespread disillusionment among intellectuals with their own civilization (see Visual Source 20.5, p. 1032). The war seemed to mock the Enlightenment values of progress, tolerance, and rationality. Who could believe any longer that the West was superior or that its vaunted science and technology were unquestionably good things? In the most famous novel to emerge from the war, the German veteran Erich Remarque's *All Quiet on the Western Front*, one soldier expressed what many no doubt felt: "It must all be lies and of no account when the culture of a thousand years could not prevent this stream of blood being poured out."

The aftermath of war also brought substantial social and cultural changes to ordinary Europeans and Americans. Integrating millions of returning veterans into civilian life was no easy task, for they had experienced horrors almost beyond imagination. Governments sought to accommodate them, in Britain for example, with housing programs called "homes for heroes" emphasizing traditional family values. Women were urged to leave factory work and return to their homes where they would not compete for "men's jobs." French authorities proclaimed Mother's Day as a new holiday designed to encourage childbearing and thus replace the millions lost in the war.

Nonetheless, the war had loosened the hold of tradition in various ways. Enormous casualties promoted social mobility, allowing the less exalted to move into positions previously dominated by the upper classes. As the war ended, suffrage movements revived and women received the right to vote in a number of countries—Britain, the United States, Germany, the Soviet Union, Hungary, and Poland—in part perhaps because of the sacrifices they had made during the conflict. Young middle-class women, sometimes known as "flappers," began to flout convention by appearing at nightclubs, smoking, dancing, drinking hard liquor, cutting their hair short, wearing revealing clothing, and generally expressing a more open sexuality. A new consumerism encouraged those who could to acquire cars, washing machines, vacuum cleaners, electric irons, gas ovens, and other newly available products. Radio and the movies now became vehicles of popular culture, transmitting American jazz to Europe and turning Hollywood stars into international celebrities.

The war also transformed international political life. From the collapse of the German, Russian, and Austro-Hungarian empires emerged a new map of Central Europe with an independent Poland, Czechoslovakia, Yugoslavia, and other nations (see Map 20.3, p. 987). Such new states were based on the principle of "national self-determination," a concept championed by U.S. president Woodrow Wilson, but each of them also contained dissatisfied ethnic minorities, who claimed the same principle. In Russia, the strains of war triggered a vast revolutionary upheaval that brought the radical Bolsheviks to power in 1917 and took Russia out of the war. Thus was launched world communism, which was to play such a prominent role in the history of the twentieth century (see Chapter 21).

The Treaty of Versailles, which formally concluded the war in 1919, proved in retrospect to have established conditions that contributed to a second world war only twenty years later. In that treaty, Germany lost its colonial empire and 15 percent of its European territory, was required to pay heavy reparations to the winners, had its military forces severely restricted, and had to accept sole responsibility for the outbreak of the war. All of this created immense resentment in Germany. One of the country's many demobilized and disillusioned soldiers declared in 1922: "It cannot be that two million Germans should have fallen in vain.... No, we do not pardon, we demand—vengeance."[2] His name was Adolf Hitler, and within two decades he had begun to exact that vengeance.

The Great War generated profound changes in the world beyond Europe as well. During the conflict, Ottoman authorities, suspecting that some of their Armenian subjects were collaborating with the Russian enemy, massacred or deported an estimated 1 million Armenians. Although the term "genocide" had not yet been invented, some historians have applied it to those atrocities, arguing that they established a precedent on which the Nazis later built. The war also brought a final end to a declining Ottoman Empire, creating the modern map of the Middle East, with the new states of Turkey, Syria, Iraq, Jordan, and Palestine. Thus Arabs emerged from Turkish rule, but many of them were governed for a time by the British or French, as "mandates" of the League of Nations (see Map 20.3, p. 987). Conflicting British promises to both Arabs and Jews regarding Palestine set the stage for an enduring struggle over that ancient and holy land. Although Latin American countries remained bystanders in the war, many of them benefited from the growing demand for their primary products such as Chilean nitrates, used in explosives. But the sharp drop in nitrate exports after the war ended brought to Chile mass unemployment, urban riots, bloody strikes, and some appeal for the newly established Chilean Communist Party.

In the world of European colonies, the war echoed loudly. Millions of Asian and African men had watched Europeans butcher one another without mercy, had gained new military skills and political awareness, and returned home with less respect for their rulers and with expectations for better treatment as a reward for their service. To gain Indian support for the war, the British had publicly promised to put that colony on the road to self-government, an announcement that set the stage for the independence struggle that followed. In East Asia, Japan emerged strengthened from the war, with European support for its claim to take over German territory and privileges in China. That news enraged Chinese nationalists and among a few sparked an interest in Soviet-style communism, for only the new communist rulers of Russia seemed willing to end the imperialist penetration of China.

Finally, the First World War brought the United States to center stage as a global power. Its manpower had contributed much to the defeat of Germany, and its financial resources turned the United States from a debtor nation into Europe's creditor.

When the American president Woodrow Wilson arrived in Paris for the peace conference in 1919, he was greeted with an almost religious enthusiasm. His famous Fourteen Points seemed to herald a new kind of international life, one based on moral principles rather than secret deals and imperialist machinations. Particularly appealing to many was his idea for the League of Nations, a new international peacekeeping organization committed to the principle of "collective security" and intended to avoid any repetition of the horrors that had just ended. Wilson's idealistic vision largely failed, however. Germany was treated more harshly than he had wished. And in his own country, the U.S. Senate refused to join the League, on which Wilson had pinned his hopes for a lasting peace. Its opponents feared that Americans would be forced to bow to "the will of other nations." That refusal seriously weakened the League of Nations as a vehicle for a new international order.

Capitalism Unraveling: The Great Depression

■ **Connection**

In what ways was the Great Depression a global phenomenon?

Far and away the most influential change of the postwar decades lay in the Great Depression. If World War I represented the political collapse of Europe, this catastrophic downturn suggested that Western capitalism was likewise failing. During the nineteenth century, that economic system had spurred the most substantial economic growth in world history and had raised the living standards of millions, but to many people it was a troubling system. Its very success generated an individualistic materialism that seemed to conflict with older values of community and spiritual life. To socialists and many others, its immense social inequalities were unacceptable. Furthermore, its evident instability—with cycles of boom and bust, expansion and recession—generated profound anxiety and threatened the livelihood of both industrial workers and those who had gained a modest toehold in the middle class.

Never had the flaws of capitalism been so evident or so devastating as during the decade that followed the outbreak of the Great Depression in 1929. All across the Euro-American heartland of the capitalist world, this vaunted economic system seemed to unravel. For the rich, it meant contracting stock prices that wiped out paper fortunes almost overnight. On the day that the American stock market initially crashed (October 24, 1929), eleven Wall Street financiers committed suicide, some by jumping out of skyscrapers. Banks closed, and many people lost their life savings. Investment dried up, world trade dropped by 62 percent within a few years, and businesses contracted when they were unable to sell their products. For ordinary people, the worst feature of the Great Depression was the loss of work. Unemployment soared everywhere, and in both Germany and the United States it reached 30 percent or more by 1932 (see the Snapshot on p. 993). Vacant factories, soup kitchens, bread lines, shantytowns, and beggars came to symbolize the human reality of this economic disaster.

Explaining its onset, its spread from America to Europe and beyond, and its continuation for a decade has been a complicated task for historians. Part of the story lies in the United States' booming economy during the 1920s. In a country physically untouched by the Great War, wartime demand had greatly stimulated agricultural and industrial capacity. By the end of the 1920s, its farms and factories were producing more goods than could be sold because a highly unequal distribution of income meant that many people could not afford to buy the products that American factories were churning out. Nor were major European countries able to purchase those goods. Germany and Austria had to make huge reparation payments and were able to do so only with extensive U.S. loans. Britain and France, which were much indebted to the United States, depended on those reparations to repay their loans. Furthermore, Europeans generally had recovered enough to begin producing some of their own goods, and their expanding production further reduced the demand for American products. Meanwhile, a speculative stock market frenzy had driven up stock prices to an unsustainable level. When that bubble burst in late 1929, this intricately connected and fragile economic network across the Atlantic collapsed like a house of cards.

Much as Europe's worldwide empires had globalized the Great War, so too its economic linkages globalized the Great Depression. Countries or colonies tied to exporting one or two products were especially hard-hit. Colonial Southeast Asia, the world's major rubber-producing region, saw the demand for its primary export

Contrasts of the Great Depression
This 1937 *Life* magazine image by famed photographer Margaret Bourke-White shows black victims of a flood in Louisville, Kentucky, standing in a breadline during the Depression while behind them rises a billboard of a happy and prosperous white family. (Margaret Bourke-White/Time & Life Pictures/Getty Images)

drop dramatically as automobile sales in Europe and the United States were cut in half. In Britain's West African colony of the Gold Coast (present-day Ghana), farmers who had staked their economic lives on producing cocoa for the world market were badly hurt by the collapse of commodity prices. Latin American countries, whose economies were based on the export of agricultural products and raw materials, were also vulnerable to major fluctuations in the world market. The region as a whole saw the value of its exports cut by half during the Great Depression. In an effort to maintain the price of coffee, Brazil destroyed enough of its crop to have supplied the world for a year. Such conditions led to widespread unemployment and social tensions.

Those tensions of the Depression era often found political expression in Latin America in the form of a military takeover of the state. Such governments sought to steer their countries away from an earlier dependence on exports toward a policy of generating their own industries. Known as import substitution industrialization, such policies hoped to achieve greater economic independence by manufacturing for the domestic market goods that had previously been imported. These efforts were accompanied by more authoritarian and intrusive governments that played a greater role in the economy by enacting tariffs, setting up state-run industries, and favoring local businesses. They often adopted a highly nationalist and populist posture as they sought to extricate themselves from economic domination by the United States and Europe and to respond to the growing urban classes of workers and entrepreneurs.

In Brazil, for example, the Depression discredited the established export elites such as coffee growers and led to the dictatorship of Getulio Vargas (1930–1945). Supported by the military, his government took steps to modernize the urban industrial sector of the economy including a state enterprise to manufacture trucks and airplane engines and regulations that gave the state considerable power over both unions and employers. But little was done to alleviate rural poverty. In Mexico, the Depression opened the way to a revival of the principles of the Mexican Revolution under the leadership of Lazaro Cardenas (1934–1940). He pushed land reform, favored Mexican workers against foreign interests, and nationalized an oil industry dominated by American capital.

These were but two cases of the many political and economic changes stimulated in Latin America by the Great Depression. Many of those changes—the growing role of the army in politics; authoritarian, populist, and interventionist governments; import substitution industrialization; and the assumption that governments should improve economic life—persisted in the decades that followed.

The Great Depression also sharply challenged the governments of industrialized capitalist countries, which generally had believed that the economy would regulate itself through the market. The market's apparent failure to self-correct led many people to look twice at the Soviet Union, the communist state that grew out of the Russian Revolution and encompassed much of the territory of the old Russian Empire (see pp. 635–39). There, the dispossession of the propertied classes and a state-controlled economy had generated an impressive economic growth with almost no

Snapshot   **Comparing the Impact of the Depression**[3]

As industrial production dropped during the Depression, unemployment soared. Yet the larger Western capitalist countries differed considerably in the duration and extent of this unemployment. Note especially the differences between Germany and the United States. How might you account for this difference?

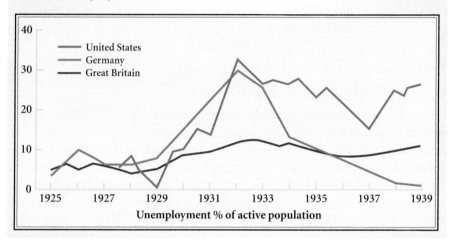

unemployment in the 1930s, even as the capitalist world was reeling. No Western country opted for the dictatorial and draconian socialism of the Soviet Union, but in Britain, France, and Scandinavia, the Depression energized a "democratic socialism" that sought greater regulation of the economy and a more equal distribution of wealth through peaceful means and electoral politics.

The United States' response to the Great Depression came in the form of President Franklin Roosevelt's New Deal (1933–1942), an experimental combination of reforms seeking to restart economic growth and to prevent similar calamities in the future. These measures reflected the thinking of John Maynard Keynes, a prominent British economist who argued that government actions and spending programs could moderate the recessions and depressions to which capitalist economies were prone. Although this represented a departure from standard economic thinking, none of it was really "socialist," even if some of the New Deal's opponents labeled it as such.

Nonetheless, Roosevelt's efforts permanently altered the relationship among government, the private economy, and individual citizens. Through immediate programs of public spending (for dams, highways, bridges, and parks), the New Deal sought to prime the pump of the economy and thus reduce unemployment. The New Deal's longer-term reforms, such as the Social Security system, the minimum wage, and various relief and welfare programs, attempted to create a modest economic safety net to sustain the poor, the unemployed, and the elderly. By supporting labor unions, the New Deal strengthened workers in their struggles with business owners or managers. Subsidies for farmers gave rise to a permanent agribusiness that encouraged continued production even as prices fell. Finally, a mounting number of government agencies marked a new degree of federal regulation and supervision of the economy.

Ultimately, none of the New Deal's programs worked very well to end the Great Depression. Not until the massive government spending required by World War II kicked in did that economic disaster abate in the United States. The most successful efforts to cope with the Depression came from unlikely places—Nazi Germany and an increasingly militaristic Japan.

Democracy Denied: Comparing Italy, Germany, and Japan

Despite the victory of the democratic powers in World War I—Britain, France, and the United States—their democratic political ideals and their cultural values celebrating individual freedom came under sharp attack in the aftermath of that bloody conflict. One challenge derived from communism, which was initiated in the Russian Revolution of 1917 and expressed most fully in the cold war during the second half of the twentieth century (see Chapter 21). In the 1920s and 1930s, however, the more immediate challenge to the victors in the Great War came from highly authoritarian, intensely nationalistic, territorially aggressive, and ferociously anticommunist regimes, particularly those that took shape in Italy, Germany, and Japan. (See Documents: Ideologies of the Axis Powers, pp. 1018–24, for the ideas underlying these regimes.) Such common features of these three countries drew them together by 1936–1937 in a political alliance directed against the Soviet Union and international communism. In 1940, they solidified their relationship in a formal military alliance, creating the so-called Axis powers. Within this alliance, Germany and Japan clearly stand out, though in quite different ways, in terms of their impact on the larger patterns of world history, for it was their efforts to "establish and maintain a new order of things," as the Axis Pact put it, that generated the Second World War both in East Asia and in Europe.

The Fascist Alternative in Europe

■ **Change**

In what ways did fascism challenge the ideas and practices of European liberalism and democracy?

Between 1919 and 1945, a new political ideology, known as fascism, found expression across much of Europe. At the level of ideas, fascism was intensely nationalistic, seeking to revitalize and purify the nation and to mobilize its people for some grand task. Its spokesmen praised violence against enemies as a renewing force in society, celebrated action rather than reflection, and placed their faith in a charismatic leader. Fascists also bitterly condemned individualism, liberalism, feminism, parliamentary democracy, and communism, all of which, they argued, divided and weakened the nation. In their determination to overthrow existing regimes, they were revolutionary; in their embrace of traditional values and their opposition to much of modern life, however, they were conservative or reactionary.

Such ideas appealed to aggrieved people all across the social spectrum. In the devastation that followed the First World War, the numbers of such people grew substantially. In the aftermath of the Russian Revolution of 1917, some among the middle and upper classes felt the rise of socialism and communism as a dire threat; small-scale merchants, artisans, and farmers feared the loss of their independence to either big business or socialist revolution; demobilized soldiers had few prospects and nursed many resentments; and intellectuals were appalled by the materialism and artificiality of modern life. Such people had lost faith in the capacity of liberal democracy and capitalism to create a good society and to protect their interests. Some among them proved a receptive audience for the message of fascism.

Small fascist movements appeared in many Western European countries, including France, Great Britain, and the Netherlands, but they had little political impact. More substantial movements took shape in Austria, Hungary, and Romania. In Spain, the rise of a fascist movement led to a bitter civil war (1936–1939) and a dictatorial regime that lasted into the 1970s. Conservative and authoritarian regimes or social movements in Latin America sometimes adopted the trappings of fascism—one-man rule, state-controlled parties, youth organizations or militias, a rhetoric of national renewal, anti-Semitic measures, though without implementing its more revolutionary features. But in Italy and Germany, such movements achieved prolonged power in major states, with devastating consequences for Europe and the world.

The fascist alternative took shape first in Italy. That nation had become a unified state only in 1870 and had not yet developed a modern and thoroughly democratic culture. In the early twentieth century, conservative landlords still dominated much of the countryside. Northern Italy, however, had begun to industrialize in the late nineteenth century, generating the characteristic tension between an industrial working class and a substantial middle class. The First World War gave rise to resentful veterans, many of them unemployed, and to patriots who believed that Italy had not gained the territory it deserved from the Treaty of Versailles. During the serious economic downturn after World War I, trade unions, peasant movements, and various communist and socialist parties threatened the established social order with a wave of strikes and land seizures.

Into this setting stepped a charismatic orator and a former journalist with a socialist background, Benito Mussolini (1883–1945). With the help of a private army of disillusioned veterans and jobless men known as the Black Shirts, Mussolini swept to power in 1922, promising an alternative to both communism and ineffective democratic rule. Considerable violence accompanied Mussolini's rise to power as bands of Black Shirts destroyed the offices of socialist newspapers and attacked striking workers. Fearful of communism, big business threw its support to Mussolini, who promised order in the streets, an end to bickering party-based politics, and the maintenance of the traditional social order. That Mussolini's government allegedly made the trains run on time became evidence that these promises might be fulfilled. The symbol of this movement was the *fasces*, a bundle of birch rods bound together around an axe, which represented power and strength in unity and derived from ancient Rome. Thus fascism was born.

The Faces of European Fascism
Benito Mussolini (left) and Adolf Hitler came to symbolize fascism in Europe in the several decades between the two world wars. In this photograph from September 1937, they are reviewing German troops in Munich during Mussolini's visit to Germany, a trip that deepened the growing relationship between their two countries. (Luce/Keystone/Getty Images)

In Mussolini's thinking, fascism was resolutely anticommunist, "the complete opposite . . . of Marxist socialism" and equally antidemocratic. "Fascism combats the whole complex system of democratic ideology, and repudiates it," he wrote. At the core of Mussolini's fascism was his conception of the state. "Fascism conceives of the State as an absolute, in comparison with which all individuals and groups are relative, only to be conceived of in their relation to the State." To Mussolini, the State was a conscious entity with "a will and a personality," which represents the "spirit of the nation." Its expansion in war and empire building was "an essential manifestation of vitality."[4]

Mussolini promised his mass following major social reforms, though in practice he concentrated on consolidating the power of the central state. His government suspended democracy and imprisoned, deported, or sometimes executed opponents. Italy's fascist regime also disbanded independent labor unions and peasant groups as well as all opposing political parties. In economic life, a "corporate state" took shape, at least in theory, in which workers, employers, and various professional groups were organized into "corporations" that were supposed to settle their disagreements and determine economic policy under the supervision of the state.

Culturally, fascists invoked various aspects of traditional Italian life. Though personally an atheist, Mussolini embraced the Catholic culture of Italy in a series of agreements with the Church, known as the Lateran Accords of 1929, which made the Vatican a sovereign state and Catholicism Italy's national religion. In fascist propaganda, women were portrayed in highly traditional domestic terms, particularly as mothers creating new citizens for the fascist state, with no hint of equality or liberation. Nationalists were delighted when Italy invaded Ethiopia in 1935, avenging the embarrassing defeat that Italians suffered at the hands of Ethiopians in 1896. In the eyes of Mussolini and fascist believers, all of this was the beginning of a "new Roman Empire" that would revitalize Italian society and give it a global mission.

Hitler and the Nazis

Far more important in the long run was the German expression of European fascism, which took shape as the Nazi Party under the leadership of Adolf Hitler (1889–1945). In many respects, it was similar to its Italian counterpart. Both espoused an extreme nationalism, openly advocated the use of violence as a political tool, generated a single-party dictatorship, were led by charismatic figures, despised parliamentary democracy, hated communism, and viewed war as a positive and ennobling experience.[5] The circumstances that gave rise to the Nazi movement were likewise broadly similar to those of Italian fascism, although the Nazis did not achieve national power until 1933.

The end of World War I witnessed the collapse of the German imperial government, itself less than a half century old. It was left to the democratic politicians of a new government—known as the Weimar Republic—to negotiate a peace settlement with the victorious allies. Traditional elites, who had withdrawn from public life in disgrace, never explicitly took responsibility for Germany's defeat; instead they attacked the democratic politicians who had the unenviable task of signing the Treaty of Versailles and enforcing it. In this setting, some began to argue that German military forces had not really lost the war but that civilian socialists, communists, and Jews had betrayed the nation, "stabbing it in the back."

As in postwar Italy, liberal or democratic political leaders during the 1920s faced considerable hostility. Paramilitary groups of veterans known as the Freikorps assassinated hundreds of supporters of the Weimar regime. Gradually, some among the middle classes as well as conservative landowners joined in opposition to the Weimar regime, both groups threatened by the ruinous inflation of 1923 and then the Great Depression. The German economy largely ground to a halt in the early 1930s amid massive unemployment among workers and the middle class alike. Everyone demanded decisive action from the state. Many industrial workers looked to socialists and communists for solutions; others turned to fascism. Large numbers of middle-class people deserted moderate political parties in favor of conservative and radical right-wing movements.

This was the context in which Adolf Hitler's National Socialist, or Nazi, Party gained growing public support. Founded shortly after the end of World War I, that Party under Hitler's leadership proclaimed a message of intense German nationalism cast in terms of racial superiority, bitter hatred for Jews as an alien presence, passionate opposition to communism, a determination to rescue Germany from the humiliating requirements of the Treaty of Versailles, and a willingness to decisively tackle the country's economic problems. Throughout the 1920s, the Nazis were a minor presence in German politics, gaining only 2.6 percent of the vote in the national elections of 1928. Just four years later, however, in the wake of the Depression's terrible impact and the Weimar government's inability to respond effectively, the Nazis attracted 37 percent of the vote. In 1933, Hitler was legally installed as the chancellor of the German government. Thus did the Weimar Republic, a democratic regime that never gained broad support, give way to the Third Reich.

Once in power, Hitler moved quickly to consolidate Nazi control of Germany. All other political parties were outlawed; independent labor unions were ended; thousands of opponents were arrested; and the press and radio came under state control. Far more thoroughly than Mussolini in Italy, Hitler and the Nazis established their control over German society.[6]

■ **Comparison**

What was distinctive about the German expression of fascism? What was the basis of popular support for the Nazis?

By the late 1930s, Hitler apparently had the support of a considerable majority of the population, in large measure because his policies successfully brought Germany out of the Depression. The government invested heavily in projects such as super-highways, bridges, canals, and public buildings and, after 1935, in rebuilding and rearming the country's diminished military forces. These policies drove down the number of unemployed Germans from 6.2 million in 1932 to fewer than 500,000 in 1937. Two years later Germany had a labor shortage. Erna Kranz, a teenager in the 1930s, later remembered the early years of Nazi rule as "a glimmer of hope . . . not just for the unemployed but for everybody because we all knew that we were downtrodden. . . . It was a good time . . . there was order and discipline."[7] Millions agreed with her.

Other factors as well contributed to Nazi popularity. Like Italian fascists, Hitler too appealed to rural and traditional values that many Germans feared losing as their country modernized. In Hitler's thinking and in Nazi propaganda, Jews became the symbol of the urban, capitalist, and foreign influences that were undermining traditional German culture. Thus the Nazis reflected and reinforced a broader and long-established current of anti-Semitism that had deep roots in much of Europe. In his book *Mein Kampf* (*My Struggle*), Hitler outlined his case against the Jews and his call for the racial purification of Germany in vitriolic terms. (See Document 20.1, pp. 1018–21, for a statement of Hitler's thinking.)

Far more than elsewhere, this insistence on a racial revolution was a central feature of the Nazi program and differed from the racial attitudes in Italy, where Jews were a tiny minority of the population and deeply assimilated into Italian culture. Early on, Mussolini had ridiculed Nazi racism, but as Germany and Italy drew closer together, Italy too began a program of overt anti-Semitism, though nothing approaching the extremes that characterized Nazi Germany.

Upon coming to power, Hitler implemented policies that increasingly restricted Jewish life. Soon Jews were excluded from universities, professional organizations, and civil employment. In 1935, the Nuremberg Laws ended German citizenship for Jews and forbade marriage or sexual relations between Jews and Germans. On the night of November 9, 1938, known as Kristallnacht, persecution gave way to terror, when Nazis smashed and looted Jewish shops. Such actions made clear the Nazis' determination to rid Germany of its Jewish population, thus putting into effect the most radical element of Hitler's program. Still, it was not yet apparent that this "racial revolution" would mean the

Nazi Hatred of the Jews
This picture served as the cover of a highly anti-Semitic book of photographs entitled *The Eternal Jew*, published by the Nazis in 1937. It effectively summed up many of the themes of the Nazi case against the Jews, showing them as ugly and subhuman, as the instigators of communism (the hammer and sickle on a map of Russia), as greedy capitalists (coins in one hand), and as seeking to dominate the world (the whip). (akg-images)

mass killing of Europe's Jews. That horrendous development emerged only in the context of World War II.

Beyond race, gender too figured prominently in Nazi thought and policies. Deeply antifeminist and resentful of the liberating changes that modern life had brought to European women, Nazis wanted to limit women largely to the home, removing them from the paid workforce. To Hitler, the state was the natural domain of men, while the home was the realm of women. "Woman in the workplace is an oppressed and tormented being," declared a Nazi publication.[8] Concerned about declining birth-rates, Italy and Germany alike promoted a cult of motherhood, glorifying and reward-ing women who produced children for the state. Accordingly, fascist regimes in both countries generally opposed abortion, contraception, family planning, and sex edu-cation, all of which were associated with feminist thinking.

Yet such an outlook did not necessarily coincide with conservative or puritani-cal sexual attitudes. In Germany, a state-sponsored system of brothels was initiated in the mid-1930s, for it was assumed that virile men would be promiscuous and that sol-diers required a sexual outlet, if they were to contribute to the nation's military strength. Because of this "need," Nazi policy exempted condoms from the ban on birth con-trol. Heinrich Himmler, a leading Nazi official, also openly encouraged illegitimate births among Aryans to augment the nation's numbers. Thus, Nazi rhetoric about the chaste Aryan family was trumped—or supplemented—by a concern to use sexu-ality to advance the cause of the nation.

Also sustaining Nazi rule were massive torch-light ceremonies celebrating the superiority of the German race and its folk culture. In these settings, Hitler was the mystical leader, the Führer, a mesmerizing orator who would lead Germany to na-tional greatness and individual Germans to personal fulfillment.

If World War I and the Great Depression brought about the political and eco-nomic collapse of Europe, the Nazi phenomenon represented a moral collapse within the West, deriving from a highly selective incorporation of earlier strands of European culture. On the one hand, the Nazis actively rejected some of the values—rationalism, tolerance, democracy, human equality—that for many people had defined the core of Western civilization since the Enlightenment. On the other hand, they claimed the legacy of modern science, particularly in their concern to classify and rank various hu-man groups. Thus they drew heavily on the "scientific racism" of the late nineteenth century and its expression in phrenology, which linked the size and shape of the skull to human behavior and personality (see pp. 891–92). Moreover, in their effort to pu-rify German society, the Nazis reflected the Enlightenment confidence in the per-fectibility of humankind and in the social engineering necessary to achieve it.

Japanese Authoritarianism

In various ways, the modern history of Japan paralleled that of Italy and Germany. All three were newcomers to great power status, with Japan joining the club of in-dustrializing and empire-building states only in the late nineteenth century as its sole

■ Comparison

How did Japan's experience during the 1920s and 1930s resemble that of Germany, and how did it differ?

Asian member (see pp. 950–53). Like Italy and Germany, Japan had a rather limited experience with democratic politics, for its elected parliament was constrained by a very small electorate (only 1.5 million men in 1917) and by the exalted position of a semidivine emperor and his small coterie of elite advisers. During the 1930s, Japan too moved toward authoritarian government and a denial of democracy at home, even as it launched an aggressive program of territorial expansion in East Asia.

Despite these broad similarities, Japan's history in the first half of the twentieth century was clearly distinctive. In sharp contrast to Italy and Germany, Japan's participation in World War I was minimal, and its economy grew considerably as other industrialized countries were consumed by the European conflict. At the peace conference ending that war, Japan was seated as an equal participant, allied with the winning side of democratic countries such as Britain, France, and the United States.

During the 1920s, Japan seemed to be moving toward more democratic politics and Western cultural values. Universal male suffrage was achieved in 1925; cabinets led by leaders of the major parties, rather than bureaucrats or imperial favorites, governed the country; and a two-party system began to emerge. Supporters of these developments generally embraced the dignity of the individual, free expression of ideas, and greater gender equality. Education expanded; an urban consumer society developed; middle-class women entered new professions; young women known as *moga* (modern girls) sported short hair and short skirts, while dancing with *mobo* (modern boys) at jazz clubs and cabarets. To such people, the Japanese were becoming world citizens and their country was becoming "a province of the world" as they participated increasingly in a cosmopolitan and international culture.

In this environment, the accumulated tensions of Japan's modernizing and industrializing processes found expression. "Rice riots" in 1918 brought more than a million people into the streets of urban Japan to protest the rising price of that essential staple. Union membership tripled in the 1920s as some factory workers began to think in terms of entitlements and workers' rights rather than the benevolence of their employers. In rural areas, tenant unions multiplied, and disputes with landowners increased amid demands for a reduction in rents. A mounting women's movement advocated a variety of feminist issues, including suffrage and the end of legalized prostitution. "All the sleeping women are now awake and moving," declared Yosano Akiko, a well-known poet, feminist, and social critic. Within the political arena, a number of "proletarian parties"—the Labor-Farmer Party, the Socialist People's Party, and a small Japan Communist Party—promised in various ways to "bring about the political, economic and social emancipation of the proletarian class."[9]

For many people in established elite circles—bureaucrats, landowners, industrialists, military officials—all of this was both appalling and alarming, suggesting echoes of the Russian Revolution of 1917. A number of political activists were arrested, and a few were killed. A Peace Preservation Law, enacted in 1925, promised long prison sentences, or even the death penalty, to anyone who organized against the existing imperial system of government or private property.

As in Germany, however, it was the impact of the Great Depression that paved the way for harsher and more authoritarian action. That worldwide economic catastrophe hit Japan hard. Shrinking world demand for silk impoverished millions of rural dwellers who raised silk-worms. Japan's exports fell by half between 1929 and 1931, leaving a million or more urban workers unemployed. Many young workers returned to their rural villages only to find food scarce, families forced to sell their daughters to urban brothels, and neighbors unable to offer the customary money for the funerals of their friends. In these desperate circumstances, many began to doubt the ability of parliamentary democracy and capitalism to address Japan's "national emergency." Politicians and business leaders alike were widely regarded as privileged, self-centered, and heedless of the larger interests of the nation.

Such conditions energized a growing movement in Japanese political life known as Radical Nationalism or the Revolutionary Right. Expressed in dozens of small groups, it was especially appealing to younger army officers. The movement's many separate organizations shared an extreme nationalism, hostility to parliamentary democracy, a commitment to elite leadership focused around an exalted emperor, and dedication to foreign expansion. The manifesto of one of those organizations, the Cherry Blossom Society, expressed these sentiments clearly in 1930:

Japan's Modern Girl
This photo from the 1920s shows a young Japanese woman curling her hair in the bobbed style popular among "flappers" in the West. Its easy-to-care-for style suggested modernity and liberation from ancient tradition. (DUITS, Tokyo, Japan)

> As we observe recent social trends, top leaders engage in immoral conduct, political parties are corrupt, capitalists and aristocrats have no understanding of the masses, farming villages are devastated, unemployment and depression are serious. . . . The rulers neglect the long term interests of the nation, strive to win only the pleasure of foreign powers and possess no enthusiasm for external expansion. . . . The people are with us in craving the appearance of a vigorous and clean government that is truly based upon the masses, and is genuinely centered around the Emperor.[10]

Members of such organizations managed to assassinate a number of public officials and prominent individuals, in the hope of provoking a return to direct rule by the emperor, and in 1936 a group of junior officers attempted a military takeover of the government, which was quickly suppressed. In sharp contrast to developments in Italy and Germany, however, no right-wing party gained wide popular support, nor was any such party able to seize power in Japan. Although individuals and small groups sometimes espoused ideas similar to those of European fascists, no major fascist party emerged. Nor did Japan produce any charismatic leader on the order of Mussolini or Hitler. People arrested for political offenses were neither criminalized nor exterminated, as in Germany, but instead were subjected to a process of "resocialization" that brought the vast majority of them to renounce their "errors" and return to the "Japanese way." Japan's established institutions of government were sufficiently strong, and traditional notions of the nation as a family headed by the emperor were suffi-ciently intact, to prevent the development of a widespread fascist movement able to take control of the country.[11]

In the 1930s, though, Japanese public life clearly changed in ways that reflected the growth of right-wing nationalist thinking. Parties and the parliament continued to operate, and elections were held, but major cabinet positions now went to prominent bureaucratic or military figures rather than to party leaders. The military in particular came to exercise a more dominant role in Japanese political life, although military men had to negotiate with business and bureaucratic elites as well as party leaders. Censorship limited the possibilities of free expression, and a single news agency was granted the right to distribute all national and most international news to the country's newspapers and radio stations. An Industrial Patriotic Federation replaced independent trade unions with factory-based "discussion councils" to resolve local disputes between workers and managers.

Established authorities also adopted many of the ideological themes of the Radi-cal Right. In 1937, the Ministry of Education issued a new textbook, *Cardinal Principles of the National Entity of Japan*, for use in all Japanese schools (see Document 20.2, pp. 1021–23). That document proclaimed the Japanese to be "intrinsically quite dif-ferent from the so-called citizens of Occidental [Western] countries." Those nations were "conglomerations of separate individuals" with "no deep foundation between ruler and citizen to unite them." In Japan, by contrast, an emperor of divine origin related to his subjects as a father to his children. It was a natural, not a contractual, relationship, expressed most fully in the "sacrifice of the life of a subject for the Em-peror." In addition to studying this text, students were now required to engage in more physical training, in which Japanese martial arts replaced baseball in the physi-cal education curriculum.

The erosion of democracy and the rise of the military in Japanese political life reflected long-standing Japanese respect for the military values of its ancient samurai warrior class as well as the relatively independent position of the military in Japan's Meiji constitution. The state's success in quickly bringing the country out of the De-pression likewise fostered popular support. As in Nazi Germany, state-financed credit, large-scale spending on armaments, and public works projects enabled Japan to emerge from the Depression more rapidly and more fully than major Western countries. "By the end of 1937," noted one Japanese laborer, "everybody in the country was work-ing."[12] By the mid-1930s, the government increasingly assumed a supervisory or man-agerial role in economic affairs that included subsidies to strategic industries; profit ceilings on major corporations; caps on wages, prices, and rents; and a measure of cen-tral planning. Private property, however, was retained, and the huge industrial enter-prises called *zaibatsu* continued to dominate the economic landscape.

Although Japan during the 1930s shared some common features with fascist Italy and Nazi Germany, it remained, at least internally, a less repressive and more plural-istic society than either of those European states. Japanese intellectuals and writers had to contend with government censorship, but they retained some influence in the country. Generals and admirals exercised great political authority as the role of an elected parliament declined, but they did not govern alone. Political prisoners were few and were not subjected to execution or deportation as in European fascist states. Japanese conceptions of their racial purity and uniqueness were directed largely against foreigners rather than an internal minority. Nevertheless, like Germany and Italy, Japan developed extensive imperial ambitions. Those projects of conquest and empire building collided with the interests of established world powers such as the United States and Britain, launching a second, and even more terrible, global war.

A Second World War

World War II, even more than the Great War, was a genuinely global conflict with independent origins in both Asia and Europe. Their common feature lay in dissatisfied states in both continents that sought to fundamentally alter the international arrangements that had emerged from World War I. Many Japanese, like their counterparts in Italy and Germany, felt stymied by Britain and the United States as they sought empires that they regarded as essential for their national greatness and economic well-being.

The Road to War in Asia

World War II began in Asia before it occurred in Europe. In the late 1920s and the 1930s, Japanese imperial ambitions mounted as the military became more powerful in Japan's political life and as an earlier cultural cosmopolitanism gave way to more nationalist sentiments. An initial problem was the rise of Chinese nationalism, which seemed to threaten Japan's sphere of influence in Manchuria, acquired after the Russo-Japanese War of 1904–1905. Acting independently of civilian authorities in Tokyo, units of the Japanese military seized control of Manchuria in 1931 and established a puppet state called Manchukuo. This action infuriated Western powers, prompting Japan to withdraw from the League of Nations, to break politically with its Western allies, and in 1936 to align more closely with Germany and Italy. By that time, relations with an increasingly nationalist China had deteriorated further, leading to a full-scale attack on heartland China in 1937 and escalating a bitter conflict that would last another eight years. World War II in Asia had begun (see Map 20.4).

As Japan's war against China unfolded, the view of the world held by Japanese authorities and many ordinary people hardened. Increasingly, they felt isolated, surrounded, and threatened. A series of international agreements in the early 1920s that had granted Japan a less robust naval force than Britain or the United States as well as anti-Japanese immigration policies in the United States convinced some Japanese that racism prevented the West from acknowledging Japan as an equal power. Furthermore, Japan was quite dependent on foreign and especially American sources of strategic goods. By the late 1930s, some 73 percent of Japan's scrap iron, 60 percent of its imported machine tools, 80 percent of its oil, and about half of its copper came from the United States, which was becoming increasingly hostile to Japanese ambitions in Asia. Moreover, Western imperialist powers—the British, French, and Dutch—controlled resource-rich colonies in Southeast Asia. Finally, the Soviet Union, proclaiming an

■ **Comparison**

In what ways were the origins of World War II in Asia and in Europe similar to each other? How were they different?

Map 20.4   World War II in Asia and the Pacific
Japanese aggression temporarily dislodged the British, French, Dutch, and Americans from their colonial possessions in Asia, while inflicting vast devastation on China. Much of the American counterattack involved "island hopping" across the Pacific until the dropping of the atomic bombs on Hiroshima and Nagasaki finally prompted the Japanese surrender in August 1945.

alien communist ideology, loomed large in northern Asia. To growing numbers of Japanese, their national survival was at stake.

Thus in 1940–1941, Japan extended its military operations to the French, British, Dutch, and American colonies of Indochina, Malaya, Burma, Indonesia, and the Philippines in an effort to acquire those resources that would free it from dependence on the West. In carving out this Pacific empire, the Japanese presented themselves as liberators and modernizers, creating an "Asia for Asians" and freeing their continent from European dominance. Experience soon showed that Japan's concern was far more for Asia's resources than for its liberation and that Japanese rule exceeded in brutality even that of the Europeans.

A decisive step in the development of World War II in Asia lay in the Japanese attack on the United States at Pearl Harbor in Hawaii in December 1941. Japanese authorities undertook that attack with reluctance and only after negotiations to end American hostility to Japan's empire-building enterprise proved fruitless and an American oil embargo was imposed on Japan in July 1941. American opinion in the 1930s increasingly saw Japan as aggressive, oppressive, and a threat to U.S. economic interests in Asia. In the face of this hostility, Japan's leaders felt that the alternatives for their country boiled down to either an acceptance of American terms, which they feared would reduce Japan to a second- or third-rank power, or a war with an uncertain outcome. Given those choices, the decision for war was made more with foreboding than with enthusiasm. A leading Japanese admiral made the case for war in this way in late 1941: "The government has decided that if there were no war the fate of the nation is sealed. Even if there is a war, the country may be ruined. Nevertheless a nation that does not fight in this plight has lost its spirit and is doomed."[13]

As a consequence of the attack on Pearl Harbor, the United States entered the war in the Pacific, beginning a long and bloody struggle that ended only with the use of atomic bombs against Hiroshima and Nagasaki in 1945. The Pearl Harbor action also joined the Asian theater of the war and the ongoing conflict in Europe into

Hiroshima
The dropping of atomic bombs on Hiroshima (August 6, 1945) and a few days later on Nagasaki marked the end of World War II in the Pacific and the opening of a nuclear arms race that has cast an enormous shadow on the world ever since. In this photograph from an utterly devastated Hiroshima, a group of survivors waits for help in the southern part of the city a few hours after the bomb was dropped. (AP Photo)

a single global struggle that pitted Germany, Italy, and Japan (the Axis powers) against the United States, Britain, and the Soviet Union (the Allies).

The Road to War in Europe

If Japan was the dissatisfied power in Asia, Nazi Germany clearly occupied that role in Europe. As a consequence of their defeat in World War I and the harsh terms of the Treaty of Versailles, many Germans harbored deep resentments about their country's position in the international arena. Taking advantage of those resentments, the Nazis pledged to rectify the treaty's perceived injustices. Thus, to most historians, the origins of World War II in Europe lie squarely in German aggression, although with many twists and turns and encouraged by the initial unwillingness of Britain, France, or the Soviet Union to confront that aggression forcefully. If World War I was accidental and unintended, World War II was deliberate and planned—perhaps even desired—by the German leadership and by Hitler in particular.

War was central to the Nazi agenda in several ways. Nazism was born out of World War I, the hated treaty that ended it, and the disillusioned ex-soldiers who emerged from it. Furthermore, the celebration of war as a means of ennobling humanity and enabling the rise of superior peoples was at the core of Nazi ideology. "Whoever would live must fight," Hitler declared. "Only in force lies the right of possession." He consistently stressed the importance for Germany of gaining *lebensraum* (living space) in the east, in the lands of Slavic Poland and Russia. Inevitably, this required war (see Document 20.1, pp. 1018–21).

Slowly at first and then more aggressively, Hitler prepared the country for war as he also pursued territorial expansion. A major rearmament program began in 1935. The next year, German forces entered the Rhineland, which the Treaty of Versailles had ordered demilitarized. In 1938, Germany annexed Austria and the German-speaking parts of Czechoslovakia. At a famous conference in Munich in that year, the British and the French gave these actions their reluctant blessing, hoping that this "appeasement" of Hitler could satisfy his demands and avoid all-out war. But it did not. On September 1, 1939, Germany unleashed a devastating attack on Poland, triggering the Second World War in Europe, as Britain and France declared war on Germany. Quickly defeating France, the Germans launched a destructive air war against Britain and in 1941 turned their war machine loose on the Soviet Union. By then, most of Europe was under Nazi control (see Map 20.5).

Although Germany was central to both world wars, the second one was quite different from the first. It was not welcomed with the kind of mass enthusiasm across Europe that had accompanied the opening of World War I in 1914. The bitter experience of the Great War suggested to most people that only suffering lay ahead. The conduct of the two wars likewise differed. The first war had quickly bogged down in trench warfare that emphasized defense, whereas in the second war the German tactic of *blitzkrieg* (lightning war) coordinated the rapid movement of infantry, tanks, and airpower over very large areas.

Map 20.5 World War II in Europe and Africa

For a brief moment during World War II, Nazi Germany came close to bringing all of Europe and North Africa under its rule. Then in late 1942 the allies began a series of counterattacks that led to German surrender in May 1945.

Such military tactics were initially successful and allowed German forces, aided by their Italian allies, to sweep over Europe, the western Soviet Union, and North Africa. The tide began to turn in 1942 when the Soviet Union absorbed the German onslaught and then began to counterattack, slowly and painfully moving westward toward the German heartland. The United States, with its enormous material and human resources, fully joined the struggle against Germany in 1942. Three more years of bitter fighting ensued before the German defeat in May 1945.

The Outcomes of Global Conflict

■ **Comparison**

How did World War II
differ from World War I?

The Second World War was the most destructive conflict in world history, with total deaths estimated at around 60 million, some six times that of World War I. More than half of those casualties were civilians. Partly responsible for this horrendous toll were the new technologies of warfare—heavy bombers, jet fighters, missiles, and atomic weapons. Equally significant, though, was the almost complete blurring of the traditional line between civilian and military targets, as entire cities and whole populations came to be defined as the enemy.

Nowhere was that blurring more complete than in the Soviet Union, which accounted for more than 40 percent of the total deaths in the war—probably around 25 million, with an equal number made homeless and thousands of towns, villages, and industrial enterprises destroyed. German actions fulfilled Hitler's instructions to his leading generals: "The war against Russia will be such that it cannot be conducted in a knightly fashion; the struggle is one of ideologies and racial differences and will have to be conducted with unprecedented, unmerciful, and unrelenting harshness. . . . German soldiers guilty of breaking international law . . . will be excused."[14]

In China as well, perhaps 15 million deaths and uncounted refugees grew out of prolonged Chinese resistance and the shattering Japanese response, including the killing of every person and every animal in many villages. Within a few months, during the infamous Rape of Nanjing in 1937–1938, some 200,000 to 300,000 Chinese civilians were killed and often mutilated, and countless women were sexually assaulted. Indiscriminate German bombing of British cities and the Allied firebombing of Japanese and German cities likewise reflected the new morality of total war, as did the dropping of atomic bombs on Hiroshima and Nagasaki, which in a single instant vaporized tens of thousands of people. This was total war with a scale, intensity, and indiscriminate brutality that exceeded even the horrors of World War I.

A further dimension of total war lay in governments' efforts to mobilize their economies, their people, and their propaganda machines even more extensively than before. Colonial resources were harnessed once again. The British in particular made extensive use of colonial troops and laborers from India and Africa. Japan compelled several hundred thousand women from Korea, China, and elsewhere to serve the sexual needs of Japanese troops as so-called comfort women, who often accommodated twenty to thirty men a day.

As in World War I, though on a much larger scale, the needs of the war drew huge numbers of women into both industry and the military. In the United States, "Rosie the Riveter" represented those women who now took on heavy industrial jobs, which previously had been reserved for men. In the Soviet Union, women constituted more than half of the industrial workforce by 1945 and almost completely dominated agricultural production. Soviet women also participated actively in combat with some 100,000 of them winning military honors. A much smaller percentage of German and Japanese women were mobilized for factory work, but a Greater Japan Women's Society enrolled some 19 million members, who did volunteer work and promised to lay aside their gold jewelry and abandon extravagant weddings. As always, war heightened the prestige of masculinity, and given the immense sacrifices that men had made, few women were inclined to directly challenge the practices of patriarchy immediately following the war.

But, while women had largely escaped death and injury in the First World War, neither women nor children were able to do so amid the indiscriminate slaughter of World War II. Urban bombing, blockades, mass murder, starvation, concentration camps—all of this affected men, women, and children alike. But women were almost exclusively the victims of the widespread rape that accompanied World War II— Japanese soldiers against Chinese women, Soviet troops against German women, among others. A prominent American observer commenting on the pervasive vic-timization of European women in 1945 commented: "Europe is now a place where woman has lost her perennial fight for decency because the indecent alone live."[15]

Among the most haunting outcomes of the war was the Holocaust. The out-break of that war closed off certain possibilities, such as forced emigration, for imple-menting the Nazi dream of ridding Germany of its Jewish population. It also brought millions of additional Jews in Poland and the Soviet Union under German control and triggered among Hitler's enthusiastic subordinates various schemes for a "final solution" to the Jewish question. From this emerged the death camps that included Auschwitz, Dachau, and Bergen-Belsen. Altogether, some 6 million Jews perished in a technologically sophisticated form of mass murder that set a new standard for human depravity. Millions more whom the Nazis deemed inferior, undesirable, or dangerous—Russians, Poles, and other Slavs; Gypsies, or the Roma; mentally or physically handicapped people; homosexuals; communists; and Jehovah's Witnesses— likewise perished in Germany's efforts at racial purification. (For the personal story of a Holocaust victim, see the Portrait of Etty Hillesum, pp. 1010–11.)

Although the Holocaust was concentrated in Germany, its significance in twentieth-century world history has been huge. It has haunted postwar Germany in particular and the Western world in general. How could such a thing have occurred in a Europe bearing the legacy of both Christianity and the Enlightenment? More specifically, it sent many of Europe's remaining Jews fleeing to Israel and gave urgency to the establishment of a modern Jewish nation in the ancient Jewish homeland. That action outraged many Arabs, some of whom were displaced by the arrival of the Jews, and has fostered an enduring conflict in the Middle East. Furthermore, the Holocaust defined a new category of crimes against humanity—genocide, the at-tempted elimination of entire peoples. Universal condemnation of the Holocaust, however, did not end the practice, as cases of mass slaughter in Cambodia, Rwanda, Bosnia, and the Sudan have demonstrated.

On an even larger scale than World War I, this second global conflict rearranged the architecture of world politics. As the war ended, Europe was impoverished, its industrial infrastructure shattered, many of its great cities in ruins, and millions of its people homeless or displaced. Within a few years, this much-weakened Europe was effectively divided, with its western half operating under an American security

Etty Hillesum, Witness to the Holocaust

Not often can historians penetrate the inner worlds of the people they study. But in the letters and diary of Etty Hillesum, a young Dutch Jewish woman caught up in the Nazi occupation of her country during the early 1940s, we can catch a glimpse of her expanding interior life even as her external circumstances contracted sharply amid the unfolding of the Holocaust.[16]

Born in 1914, Etty was the daughter of a Dutch academic father and a Russian-born mother. She attended university, tutored students in the Russian language, and hoped to become a writer. The Nazi invasion of the Netherlands in May 1940 found Etty living in Amsterdam with five other people. There she experienced and described Nazi rule and its mounting impact on Jews. "More arrests, more terror, concentration camps; the arbitrary dragging off of fathers, sisters, brothers," she wrote in June 1941. Soon Amsterdam's Jews were required to wear identifying yellow stars and were forbidden from walking on certain streets, riding the tram, visiting particular shops,

Etty Hillesum. (Collection Jewish Historical Museum, Amsterdam)

or eating in cafes. Signs reading "no admittance to Jews" sprang up across the city.

Etty initially reacted to these events with hatred and depression. She felt "beside myself with anger, cursing and swearing at the Germans," and was even upset with a German woman living in her house who had no connections whatever with the Nazis. "They are out to destroy us completely," she wrote on July 3, 1942. "Today I am filled with despair." Over time, however, her perspective changed. "I really see no other solution than to turn inward and to root out all the rottenness there." One day, with the "sound of fire, shooting, bombs" raging outside, Etty listened to a Bach recording and wrote: "I know and share the many sorrows a human being can experience, but I do not cling to them; they pass through me, like life itself, as a broad eternal stream ... and life continues.... If you have given sorrow the space that its gentle origins demand, then you may say that life is beautiful and so rich ... that it makes you want to believe in God."

umbrella and the eastern half subject to Soviet control. It was clear that Europe's dominance in world affairs was finished.

Over the next two decades, Europe's greatly diminished role in the world registered internationally as its Asian and African colonies achieved independence. Not only had the war weakened both the will and the ability of European powers to hold onto their colonies, but it had also emboldened nationalist and anticolonial movements everywhere (see Chapter 22). Japanese victories in Southeast Asia had certainly damaged European prestige, for British, Dutch, and American military forces fell to Japanese conquerors, sometimes in a matter of weeks. Japanese authorities staged long and brutal marches of Western prisoners of war, partly to drive home to local people that the era of Western domination was over. Furthermore, tens of thousands of Africans had fought for the British or the French, had seen white people die, had enjoyed the company of white women, and had returned home with very different

Meanwhile Etty had fallen deeply in love with her fifty-five-year-old German Jewish therapist, Julius Spier. She worried that she was becoming overly dependent on a man, particularly since she was already sleeping with another man in whose house she lived. Yet, Spier had become her spiritual companion and mentor as well as her lover. When he died in September 1942, she was devastated but determined to go on. "You were the mediator between God and me," she wrote of Spier, "and now you have gone and my path leads straight to God."

Eventually, Etty found herself in Westerbork, a transit camp for Dutch Jews awaiting transport to the east and almost certain death. Friends had offered to hide her, but Etty insisted on voluntarily entering the camp, where she operated as an unofficial social worker and sought to become the "thinking heart of the barracks." In the camp, panic erupted regularly as new waves of Jews were transported east. Babies screamed as they were awakened to board the trains. "The misery here is really indescribable," she wrote in mid-1943. "People live in those big barracks like so many rats in a sewer."

Even there, however, Etty's emerging inner life found expression. "Late at night . . . ," she wrote, "I often walk with a spring in my step along the barbed wire. And then time and again, it soars straight from my heart . . . the feeling that life is glorious and magnificent and that one day we shall be building a whole new world. Against every new outrage and every fresh horror, we shall put up one more piece of love and goodness, drawing strength from within ourselves. We may suffer, but we must not succumb."

Etty's transport came on September 7, 1943, when she, her parents, and a brother boarded a train for Auschwitz. Her parents were gassed immediately upon arrival, and Etty followed on November 30. Her last known writing was a postcard tossed from the train as it departed Westerbork. It read in part: "I am sitting on my rucksack in the middle of full freight car. Father, mother, and Mischa [her brother] are a few cars behind. . . . We left the camp singing."

Etty Hillesum's public life, like that of most people, left little outward mark on the world she briefly inhabited, except for the small circle of her friends and family. But the record of her inner life, miraculously preserved, remains among the greatest spiritual testaments to emerge from the horrors of the Nazi era, a tribute to the possibilities of human transformation, even amid the most horrendous of circumstances.

Questions: In what ways did Etty experience the Nazi phenomenon? How might you assess Etty's interior response to the Nazis? Was it a "triumph of the human spirit" or an evasion of the responsibility to resist evil more directly?

---

ideas about white superiority and the permanence of colonial rule. Colonial subjects everywhere were very much aware that U.S. President Franklin Roosevelt and British Prime Minister Winston Churchill had solemnly declared in 1941 that "we respect the right of all peoples to choose the form of government under which they will live." Many asked whether those principles should not apply to people in the colonial world as well as to Europeans.

A further outcome of World War II lay in the consolidation and extension of the communist world. The Soviet victory over the Nazis, though bought at an unimaginable cost in blood and treasure, gave immense credibility to that communist regime and to its leader, Joseph Stalin. In the decades that followed, Soviet authorities nurtured a virtual cult of the war: memorials were everywhere; wedding parties made pilgrimages to them, and brides left their bouquets behind; May 9, Victory Day, saw elaborately orchestrated celebrations; veterans were honored and granted modest privileges. Furthermore, communist parties, largely dominated by the Soviet Union and supported by its armed forces, took power all across Eastern Europe, pushing the communist frontier deep into the European heartland. Even more important was a communist takeover in China in 1949. The Second World War allowed the Chinese Communist Party to gain support and credibility by leading the struggle against Japan. By 1950, the communist world seemed to many in the West very much on the offensive (see Chapter 21).

The horrors of two world wars within a single generation prompted a renewed interest in international efforts to maintain the peace in a world of competing and sovereign states. The chief outcome was the United Nations (UN), established in 1945 as a successor to the moribund League of Nations. As a political body dependent on agreement among its most powerful members, the UN proved more effective as a forum for international opinion than as a means of resolving the major conflicts of the postwar world, particularly the Soviet/American hostility during the cold war decades. Further evidence for a growing internationalism lay in the creation in late 1945 of the World Bank and International Monetary Fund, whose purpose was to regulate the global economy, prevent another depression, and stimulate economic growth, especially in the poorer nations.

What these initiatives shared was the dominant presence of the United States. Unlike the aftermath of World War I, when an isolationist United States substantially withdrew from world affairs, the half century following the end of World War II witnessed the emergence of the United States as a global superpower. This was one of the major outcomes of the Second World War and a chief reason for the remarkable recovery of a badly damaged and discredited Western civilization.

SUMMING UP SO FAR

Is it more useful to view the two world wars as separate and distinct conflicts or as a single briefly interrupted phenomenon?

The Recovery of Europe

■ **Change**

How was Europe able to recover from the devastation of war?

The tragedies that afflicted Europe in the first half of the twentieth century — fratricidal war, economic collapse, the Holocaust — were wholly self-inflicted, and yet despite the sorry and desperate state of heartland Europe in 1945, that civilization had not permanently collapsed. In the twentieth century's second half, Europeans rebuilt their industrial economies and revived their democratic political systems, while the United States, a European offshoot, assumed a dominant and often dominating role both within Western civilization and in the world at large.

Three factors help to explain this astonishing recovery. One is the apparent resiliency of an industrial society, once it has been established. The knowledge, skills, and habits of mind that enabled industrial societies to operate effectively remained intact, even if the physical infrastructure had been substantially destroyed. Thus even the most terribly damaged countries — Germany, the Soviet Union, and Japan — had largely recovered, both economically and demographically, within a quarter of a century. A second factor lay in the ability of the major Western European countries to integrate their recovering economies. After centuries of military conflict climaxed by the horrors of the two world wars, the major Western European powers were at last willing to put aside some of their prickly nationalism in return for enduring peace and common prosperity.

Equally important, Europe had long ago spawned an overseas extension of its own civilization in what became the United States. In the twentieth century, that country served as a reservoir of military manpower, economic resources, and political leadership for the West as a whole. By 1945, the center of gravity within Western civilization had shifted decisively, relocated now across the Atlantic. With Europe diminished, divided, and on the defensive against the communist threat, leadership of the Western world passed, almost by default, to the United States. It was the only major country physically untouched by the war. Its economy had demonstrated enormous productivity during that struggle and by 1945 was generating fully 50 percent of total world production. Its overall military strength was unmatched, and it was briefly in sole possession of the atomic bomb, the most powerful weapon ever constructed. Thus the United States became the new heartland of the West as well as a global superpower. In 1941, the publisher Henry Luce had proclaimed the twentieth century as "the American century." As the Second World War ended, that prediction seemed to be coming true.

An early indication of the United States' intention to exercise global leadership took shape in its efforts to rebuild and reshape shattered European economies. Known as the Marshall Plan, that effort funneled into Europe some $12 billion, at the time a very large amount, together with numerous advisers and technicians. It was motivated by some combination of genuine humanitarian concern, a desire to prevent a new depression by creating overseas customers for American industrial goods, and an interest in undermining the growing appeal of European communist parties. This economic recovery plan was successful beyond anyone's expectations. Between 1948 and the early 1970s, Western European economies grew rapidly, generating a widespread prosperity and improving living standards. At the same time, Western Europe became both a major customer for American goods and a major competitor in global markets.

The Marshall Plan also required its European recipients to cooperate with one another. After decades of conflict and destruction almost beyond description, many Europeans were eager to do so. That process began in 1951 when Italy, France, West Germany, Belgium, the Netherlands, and Luxembourg created the European Coal and Steel Community to jointly manage the production of these critical items. In 1957, these six countries deepened their level of cooperation by establishing the European Economic Community (EEC), more widely known as the Common Market, whose members reduced their tariffs and developed common trade policies. Over the next half century, the EEC expanded its membership to include almost all of Europe, including many former communist states. In 1994, the EEC was renamed the European Union, and in 2002 twelve of its members, later increased to seventeen, adopted a common currency, the euro (see Map 20.6). All of this sustained Europe's remarkable economic recovery and expressed a larger European identity, although it

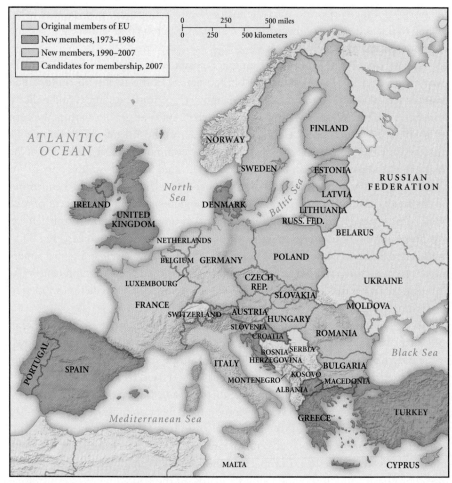

Map 20.6　The Growth of European Integration

Gradually during the second half of the twentieth century, Europeans put aside their bitter rivalries and entered into various forms of economic cooperation with one another, although these efforts fell short of complete political union. This map illustrates the growth of what is now called the European Union (EU). Notice the eastward expansion of the EU following the collapse of communism in Eastern Europe and the Soviet Union.

certainly did not erase deeply rooted national loyalties or lead, as some had hoped, to a political union, a United States of Europe. Nor did it generate persistent economic stability as the European financial crisis beginning in 2010 called into question the viability of the euro zone and perhaps the European Union.

Beyond economic assistance, the American commitment to Europe soon came to include political and military security against the distant possibility of renewed German aggression and the more immediate communist threat from the Soviet Union. Without that security, economic recovery was unlikely to continue. Thus was born the military and political alliance known as the North Atlantic Treaty Organization (NATO) in 1949. It committed the United States and its nuclear arsenal to the defense of Europe against the Soviet Union, and it firmly anchored West Germany within the Western alliance. Thus, as Western Europe revived economically, it did so under the umbrella of U.S. political and military leadership, which Europeans generally welcomed. It was perhaps an imperial relationship, but to historian John Gaddis, it was "an empire by invitation" rather than by imposition.[17]

A parallel process in Japan, which was under American occupation between 1945 and 1952, likewise revived that country's devastated but already industrialized economy. In the two decades following the occupation, Japan's economy grew at the remarkable rate of 10 percent a year, and the nation became an economic giant on the world stage. This "economic miracle" received a substantial boost from some $2 billion in American aid during the occupation and even more from U.S. military purchases in Japan during the Korean War (1950–1953). Furthermore, the democratic constitution imposed on Japan by American occupation authorities required that "land, sea, and air forces, as well as other war potential, will never be maintained." This meant that Japan, even more so than Europe, depended on the United States for its military security. Because it spent only about 1 percent of its gross national product on defense, more was available for productive investment.

The world had changed dramatically during the first seventy years of the twentieth century. That century began with a Europe of rival nations as clearly the dominant imperial center of a global network. But European civilization substantially self-destructed in the first half of the century, though it revived during the second half in a changed form—without its Afro-Asian colonies and with new leadership in the United States. Accompanying this process and intersecting with it was another major theme of twentieth-century world history—the rise and fall of world communism, which is the focus of the next chapter.

LearningCurve
bedfordstmartins.com
/strayer/LC

Reflections: War and Remembrance: Learning from History

When asked about the value of studying history, most students respond with some version of the Spanish-born philosopher George Santayana's famous dictum: "Those who cannot remember the past are condemned to repeat it." At one level, this notion of learning from the "lessons of history" has much to recommend it, for there is, after all, little else except the past on which we can base our actions in the present. And yet historians in general are notably cautious about drawing particular lessons from the past and applying them to present circumstances.

For one thing, the historical record, like the Bible or any other sacred text, is sufficiently rich and complex to allow many people to draw quite different lessons from it. The world wars of the twentieth century represent a case in point, as writer Adam Gopnik has pointed out:

The First World War teaches that territorial compromise is better than full-scale war, that an "honor-bound" allegiance of the great powers to small nations is a recipe for mass killing, and that it is crazy to let the blind mechanism of armies and alliances trump common sense. The Second teaches that searching for an accommodation with tyranny by selling out small nations only encourages the tyrant, that refusing to fight now leads to a worse fight later on....The First teaches us never to rush into a fight, the Second never to back down from a bully.[18]

Did the lessons of the First World War lead Americans to ignore the rise of fascism until the country was directly threatened by Japanese attack? Did the lessons of World War II contribute to unnecessary wars in Vietnam and more recently in Iraq? There are no easy answers to such questions, for the lessons of history are many, varied, and changing.

Behind any such lesson is the common assumption that history repeats itself. This too is a notion to which historians bring considerable skepticism. They are generally more impressed with the complexity and particularity of major events such as wars rather than with their common features. Here is a further basis for caution in easily drawing lessons from the past.

But the wars of the past century perhaps share one broad similarity: all of them led to unexpected consequences. Few people expected the duration and carnage of World War I. The Holocaust was literally unimaginable when Hitler took power in 1933 or even at the outbreak of the Second World War in 1939. Who would have expected an American defeat at the hands of the Vietnamese? And the invasion of Iraq in 2003 generated a long list of surprises for the United States, including the absence of weapons of mass destruction and a prolonged insurgency. History repeats itself most certainly only in its unexpectedness.

Second Thoughts

What's the Significance?

LearningCurve
Check what you know.
bedfordstmartins.com /strayer/LC

Online Study Guide
bedfordstmartins.com
/highschool/strayer

World War I, 982–88
Treaty of Versailles, 989
Woodrow Wilson/Fourteen Points, 990
Great Depression, 990–94
New Deal, 993–94
fascism, 994–99
Mussolini, 995–96
Nazi Germany, 996–99
Hitler, 996–98

Revolutionary Right (Japan), 1001–03
World War II in Asia, 1003–06
World War II in Europe, 1006–07
total war, 1008
Holocaust, 1009
Etty Hillesum, 1010–11
European Economic Community, 1013
Marshall Plan, 1013–14
NATO, 1014–15

Big Picture Questions

1. What explains the disasters that befell Europe in the first half of the twentieth century?
2. To what extent did the two world wars settle the issues that caused them? What legacies to the future did they leave?
3. In what ways did Europe's internal conflicts between 1914 and 1945 have global implications?
4. **Looking Back:** In what ways were the major phenomena of the first half of the twentieth century — world wars, the Great Depression, fascism, the Holocaust, the emergence of the United States as a global power — rooted in earlier times?

Next Steps: For Further Study

For Web sites and additional documents related to this chapter, see **Make History** at bedfordstmartins.com /highschool/strayer.

Michael Burleigh, *The Third Reich: A New History* (2001). A fresh and thorough look at the Nazi era in Germany's history.

John Keegan, *The Second World War* (2005). A comprehensive account by a well-known scholar.

Bernd Martin, *Japan and Germany in the Modern World* (1995). A comparative study of these two countries' modern history and the relationship between them.

Mark Mazower, *Dark Continent* (2000). A history of Europe in the twentieth century that views the era as a struggle among liberal democracy, fascism, and communism.

Michael S. Nieberg, *Fighting the Great War: A Global History* (2006). An exploration of the origins and conduct of World War I.

Dietman Rothermund, *The Global Impact of the Great Depression, 1929–1939* (1996). An examination of the origins of the Depression in America and Europe and its impact in Asia, Africa, and Latin America.

First World War.com, http://www.firstworldwar.com. A Web site rich with articles, documents, photos, diaries, and more that illustrate the history of World War I.

"The Holocaust," http://www.jewishvirtuallibrary.org/jsource/holo.html. A wealth of essays, maps, photographs, and timelines that explores the Holocaust and the context in which it arose.

Documents

Considering the Evidence:
Ideologies of the Axis Powers

Even more than the Great War of 1914–1918, the Second World War was a conflict of ideas and ideologies as well as a struggle of nations and armies. The ideas of the losing side in that war, repellant as they were to their enemies, had for a time attracted considerable support. Described variously as fascist, authoritarian, right-wing, or radically nationalist, the ideologies of the Axis powers differed in tone and emphasis. But they shared a repudiation of mainstream Western liberalism and democracy, as well as an intense hatred of Marxist communism. The documents that follow provide a taste of this thinking as it took shape in Germany and Japan.

Document 20.1

Hitler on Nazism

Adolph Hitler published his political views well before he came to power. Born in Austria, Hitler absorbed a radical form of German nationalism, which he retained as a profoundly disillusioned veteran of World War I. In 1919, he joined a very small extremist group called the German Workers Party, where he rose quickly to a dominant role based on his powerful oratorical abilities. Inspired by Mussolini's recent victory in Italy, Hitler launched in 1923 an unsuccessful armed uprising in Munich for which he was arrested and imprisoned. During his brief stay in prison (less than a year), he wrote *Mein Kampf* (*My Struggle*), part autobiography and part an exposition of his political and social philosophy. Armed with these ideas, Hitler assumed the leadership of Germany in 1933 (see pp. 996–99).

- What larger patterns in European thinking do Hitler's ideas reflect and what elements of European thought does he reject? Consider in particular his use of social Darwinism, then an idea with wide popularity in Europe.

- How does Hitler distinguish between Aryans and Jews? How does he understand the role of race in human affairs?

- What kind of political system does Hitler advocate?

- What goals for Germany—both domestic and foreign—did Hitler set forth in *Mein Kampf*?

- What aspects of Hitler's thinking might have had wide appeal in Germany during the 1930s?

ADOLPH HITLER

Mein Kampf (My Struggle)
1925–1926

Nation and Race

There are some truths which are so obvious that for this very reason they are not seen or at least not recognized by ordinary people. . . . Every animal mates only with a member of the same species. . . . Any crossing of two beings not at exactly the same level produces a medium between the level of the two parents. . . . Such mating is contrary to the will of Nature for a higher breeding of all life. . . . The stronger must dominate and not blend with the weaker, thus sacrificing his own greatness. Only the born weakling can view this as cruel . . . , for if this law did not prevail, any conceivable higher development of organic living beings would be unthinkable.

In the struggle for daily bread all those who are weak and sickly or less determined succumb, while the struggle of the males for the female grants the right or opportunity to propagate only to the healthiest. . . . No more than Nature desires the mating of weaker with stronger individuals, even less does she desire the blending of a higher with a lower race, since, if she did, her whole work of higher breeding, over perhaps hundreds of thousands of years, might be ruined with one blow. . . . All great cultures of the past perished only because the originally creative race died out from blood poisoning.

Those who want to live, let them fight, and those who do not want to fight in this world of eternal struggle do not deserve to live. . . .

All the human culture, all the results of art, science, and technology that we see before us today, are almost exclusively the creative product of the Aryan. . . . [H]e alone was the founder of all higher humanity, therefore representing the prototype of all that we understand by the word "man." He is the Prometheus of mankind from whose bright forehead the divine spark of genius has sprung at all times. . . .

All who are not of good race in this world are chaff.

The mightiest counterpart to the Aryan is represented by the Jew. . . . Since the Jew . . . was never in possession of a culture of his own, the foundations of his intellectual work were always provided by others. His intellect at all times developed through the cultural world surrounding him. . . .

He lacks completely the most essential requirement for a cultured people, the idealistic attitude. In the Jewish people the will to self-sacrifice does not go beyond the individual's naked instinct of self-preservation. Their apparently great sense of solidarity is based on the very primitive herd instinct that is seen in many other living creatures in this world. . . . [T]he Jew is led by nothing but the naked egoism of the individual.

With satanic joy in his face, the black-haired Jewish youth lurks in wait for the unsuspecting girl whom he defiles with his blood, thus stealing her from her people. With every means he tries to destroy the racial foundations of the people he has set out to subjugate. . . . And so he tries systematically to lower the racial level by a continuous poisoning

Source: Adolph Hitler, *Mein Kampf* (originally published 1925–26).

of individuals. And in politics he begins to replace the idea of democracy by the dictatorship of the proletariat. In the organized mass of Marxism he has found the weapon which lets him ... subjugate and govern the peoples with a dictatorial and brutal fist.

In economics he undermines the states until the social enterprises which have become unprofitable are taken from the state and subjected to his financial control.

In the political field he refuses the state the means for its self-preservation, destroys the foundations of all national self-maintenance and defense, destroys faith in the leadership, scoffs at its history and past, and drags everything that is truly great into the gutter.

Culturally he contaminates art, literature, the theater, makes a mockery of natural feeling, overthrows all concepts of beauty and sublimity, of the noble and the good, and instead drags men down into the sphere of his own base nature. Religion is ridiculed, ethics and morality represented as outmoded, until the last props of a nation in its struggle for existence in this world have fallen.

If we pass all the causes of the German collapse [defeat in World War I] in review, the ultimate and most decisive remains the failure to recognize the racial problem and especially the Jewish menace.... The lost purity of the blood alone destroys inner happiness forever, plunges man into the abyss for all time, and the consequences can never more be eliminated from body and spirit.... All really significant symptoms of decay of the pre-War period can in the last analysis be reduced to racial causes.

The State

The State is only a means to an end.... Above all, it must preserve the existence of the race.... We, as Aryans, can consider the State only as the living organism of a people, an organism which does not merely maintain the existence of a people, but functions in such a way as to lead its people to a position of supreme liberty by the progressive development of the intellectual and cultural faculties.

We National Socialists know that in holding these views we take up a revolutionary stand in the world of today and that we are branded as revolutionaries....

As a State the German Reich shall include all Germans. Its task is not only to gather in and foster the most valuable sections of our people but to lead them slowly and surely to a dominant position in the world.... It will be the task of the People's State to make the race the centre of the life of the community. It must make sure that the purity of the racial strain will be preserved.... Those who are physically and mentally unhealthy and unfit must not perpetuate their own suffering in the bodies of their children....

One thing is certain: our world is facing a great revolution. The only question is whether the outcome will be propitious for the Aryan portion of mankind or whether the everlasting Jew will profit by it. By educating the young generation along the right lines, the People's State will have to see to it that a generation of mankind is formed which will be adequate to this supreme combat that will decide the destinies of the world....

[T]he People's State must mercilessly expurgate ... the parliamentarian principle, according to which decisive power through the majority vote is invested in the multitude. Personal responsibility must be substituted in its stead.... The best constitution and the best form of government is that which makes it quite natural for the best brains to reach a position of dominant importance and influence in the community.... Genius of an extraordinary stamp is not to be judged by normal standards whereby we judge other men.

There are no decisions made by the majority vote, but only by responsible persons. And the word "council" is once more restored to its original meaning. Every man in a position of responsibility will have councilors at his side, but the decision is made by that individual person alone....

[T]he principle of parliamentarian democracy, whereby decisions are enacted through the majority vote, has not always ruled the world. On the contrary, we find it prevalent only during short periods of history, and those have always been periods of decline in nations and States. . . .

Eastern Orientation or Eastern Policy

[W]e National Socialists must hold unflinchingly to our aim in foreign policy, namely, to secure for the German people the land and soil to which they are entitled on this earth. . . . If we speak of soil in Europe today, we can primarily have in mind only Russia and her vassal border states. . . .

The National Socialist movement must strive to eliminate the disproportion between our population and our area—viewing this latter as a source of food as well as a basis for power politics—between our historical past and the hopelessness of our present impotence. And in this it must remain aware that we, as guardians of the highest humanity on this earth, are bound by the highest obligation, and the more it strives to bring the German people to racial awareness . . . , the more it will be able to meet this obligation. . . .

State boundaries are made by man and changed by man. . . . And in this case, right lies in this strength alone. . . . Just as our ancestors did not receive the soil on which we live today as a gift from Heaven, but had to fight for it at the risk of their lives, in the future no folkish grace will win soil for us . . . but only the might of a victorious sword. . . .

Never forget that the most sacred right on this earth is a man's right to have earth to till with his own hands, and the most sacred sacrifice the blood that a man sheds for this earth.

Document 20.2

The Japanese Way

In the Japanese language the word *kokutai* is an evocative term that refers to the national essence or the fundamental character of the Japanese nation and people. Drawing both on long-established understandings and on recently developed nationalist ideas, the Ministry of Education in 1937 published a small volume, widely distributed in schools and homes throughout the country, entitled the *Kokutai No Hongi* (*Cardinal Principles of the National Entity of Japan*). That text, excerpted in Document 20.2, defined the uniqueness of Japan and articulated the philosophical foundation of its authoritarian regime. (See pp. 999–1002 for the background to this document.) When the Americans occupied a defeated and devastated Japan in 1945, they forbade the further distribution of the book.

- According to *Cardinal Principles*, what was *kokutai*? How did the document define the national essence of Japan? How did its authors compare Japan to the West?

- What was the ideal role of the individual in Japanese society?

- To whom might these ideas have been attractive? Why?

- How might this document have been used to justify Japan's military and territorial expansion?

- Why do you think the American occupation authorities banned the document?

Cardinal Principles of the National Entity of Japan

1937

The various ideological and social evils of present-day Japan are the result of ignoring the fundamental and running after the trivial, of lack of judgment, and a failure to digest things thoroughly; and this is due to the fact that since the days of *Meiji* so many aspects of European and American culture, systems, and learning, have been imported, and that, too rapidly. As a matter of fact, the foreign ideologies imported into our country are in the main ideologies of the [European] Enlightenment that have come down from the eighteenth century, or extensions of them. The views of the world and of life that form the basis of these ideologies . . . lay the highest value on, and assert the liberty and equality of, individuals. . . .

We have already witnessed the boundless Imperial virtues. Wherever this Imperial virtue of compassion radiates, the Way for the subjects naturally becomes clear. The Way of the subjects exists where the entire nation serves the Emperor united in mind. . . . That is, we by nature serve the Emperor and walk the Way of the Empire. . . .

We subjects are intrinsically quite different from the so-called citizens of the Occidental countries. . . .

When citizens who are conglomerations of separate individuals independent of each other give support to a ruler, . . . there exists no deep foundation between ruler and citizen to unite them. However, the relationship between the Emperor and his subjects arises from the same fountainhead, and has prospered ever since the founding of the nation as one in essence. . . .

Our country is established with the Emperor. . . . For this reason, to serve the Emperor and to receive the Emperor's great august Will as one's own is the rationale of making our historical "life" live in the present. . . .

Loyalty means to reverence the Emperor as [our] pivot and to follow him implicitly. . . . Hence, offering our lives for the sake of the Emperor does not mean so-called self-sacrifice, but the casting aside of our little selves to live under his august grace and the enhancing of the genuine life of the people of a State. . . . An individual is an existence belonging to the State and her history, which forms the basis of his origin, and is fundamentally one body with it. . . .

We must sweep aside the corruption of the spirit and the clouding of knowledge that arises from setting up one's "self" and from being taken up with one's "self" and return to a pure and clear state of mind that belongs intrinsically to us as subjects, and thereby fathom the great principle loyalty. . . .

Indeed, loyalty is our fundamental Way as subject, and is the basis of our national morality. Through loyalty are we become Japanese subjects; in loyalty do we obtain life and herein do we find the source of all morality. . . .

In our country filial piety is a Way of the highest importance. Filial piety originates with one's family as its basis, and in its larger sense has the nation for its foundation. . . .

Our country is a great family nation, and the Imperial Household is the head family of the subjects and the nucleus of national life. The subjects revere the Imperial Household, which is the head family, with the tender esteem they have for their ancestors; and the Emperor loves his subjects as his very own. . . .

When we trace the marks of the facts of the founding of our country and the progress of our history, what we always find there is the spirit of harmony. . . . The spirit of harmony is built upon the concord of all things. When people determinedly count themselves as masters and assert their egos, there is nothing but contradictions and the setting of one against the other; and harmony is not begotten. . . . That is, a society of individualism is one of the clashes between [masses of]

Source: J. O. Gauntlett, trans., and R. K. Hall, ed., *Kokutai No Hongi: Cardinal Principles of the National Entity of Japan* (Cambridge, MA: Harvard University Press, 1949), 52, 79, 80, 81, 82, 83, 87, 89–90, 93, 94, 144–145, 178, 181–182.

people . . . and all history may be looked upon as one of class wars. . . .

And this, this harmony is clearly seen in our nation's martial spirit. Our nation is one that holds bushido° in high regard, and there are shrines deifying warlike spirits. . . . Bushido may be cited as showing an outstanding characteristic of our national morality. . . . That is to say, though a sense of obligation binds master and servant, this has developed in a spirit of self-effacement and meeting death with a perfect calmness. In this, it was not that death was made light of so much as that man tempered himself to death and in a true sense regarded it with esteem. In effect, man tried to fulfill true life by the way of death. . . .

To put it in a nutshell, while the strong points of Occidental learning and concepts lie in their analytical and intellectual qualities, the characteristics of Oriental learning and concepts lie in their intuitive and aesthetic qualities. These are natural tendencies that arise through racial and historical differences; and when we compare them with our national spir-

its, concepts, or mode of living, we cannot help recognizing further great and fundamental differences. Our nation has in the past imported, assimilated, and sublimated Chinese and Indian ideologies, and has therewith supported the Imperial Way, making possible the establishment of an original culture based on her national polity. . . .

Since the *Meiji* restoration our nation has adapted the good elements of the advanced education seen among European and American nations, and has exerted efforts to set up an educational system and materials for teaching. The nation has also assimilated on a wide scale the scholarship of the West, not only in the fields of natural science, but of the mental sciences, and has thus striven to see progress made in our scholastic pursuits and to make education more popular. . . .

However, at the same time, through the infiltration of individualistic concepts, both scholastic pursuits and education have tended to be taken up with a world in which the intellect alone mattered. . . .

In order to correct these tendencies, the only course open to us is to clarify the true nature of our national polity, which is at the very source of our education, and to strive to clear up individualistic and abstract ideas.

———————————

°**bushido:** the way of the warrior.

Using the Evidence: Ideologies of the Axis Powers

1. **Making comparisons:** What aspects of the Japanese document might Hitler have viewed with sympathy, and what parts of it might he have found distasteful or offensive?

2. **Criticizing the West:** In what ways did Hitler and the authors of *Cardinal Principles* find fault with mainstream Western societies and their political and social values?

3. **Considering ideas and circumstances:** From what sources did the ideas expressed in these documents arise? What kinds of people would have found them attractive and why?

4. **Considering ideas and action:** To what extent did the ideas articulated in these documents find expression in particular actions or policies of political authorities?

5. **Noticing continuity and change:** To what extent were the ideas in these documents new and revolutionary? In what respects did they draw on long-standing traditions in their societies? In what ways did they embrace modern life and what aspects of it did they reject? Have these ideas been completely discredited or do they retain some resonance in contemporary political discourse?

Visual Sources

Considering the Evidence:
Propaganda and Critique in World War I

As an overwhelmingly intense human experience, war has long caught the attention of artists. World War I was no exception. Among the most pervasive uses of art and artists during the Great War was the prolific creation, under government auspices, of posters designed to generate public support for the struggle. But independent artists, those not beholden to state authorities and often highly critical of the war, portrayed a very different face of those hostilities and their aftermath. The visual sources that follow illustrate both of these perspectives on the First World War.

Among the chief uses of wartime propaganda posters was to portray the enemy in the most despicable terms. German posters, for example, often depicted the country's enemies as animals or misbehaving children, suggesting that they were something less than fully human. They usually showed Russians as alcoholics. Visual Source 20.1 is a French poster from around 1915. It pictures Germany as Thor, an ancient pagan Germanic god of thunder, who had been turned into a demonic figure as Christianity took hold in Europe. The caption at the top of the image reads: "The god Thor—the most barbaric of the barbarian divinities of old Germany."

■ What does the poster convey by presenting Germany as Thor?

■ Note the Prussian imperial eagle standing on a bomb. What impression of German goals does that convey?

■ How do you understand the religious imagery of this French print? Notice Thor preparing to destroy a church with his hammer as well as the broken cross between his feet at the bottom.

■ To whom do you think such images were directed and for what purpose?

The "total" character of World War I ensured that women would be mobilized for the struggle in many ways (see pp. 984–88). American women, for example, were strongly encouraged to save food, especially wheat, to support the war effort. Posters also gave the great struggle a feminine face, as illustrated in Visual Source 20.2. A 1917 U.S. poster, it sought to encourage people

Visual Source 20.1 Defining the Enemy (The Art Archive at Art Resource, NY)

Visual Source 20.2 Women and the War (Library of Congress, LC-USZCA-9462)

to buy Liberty Bonds, which raised money for the war effort and demonstrated the buyer's patriotism.

■ How would you describe the posture of the woman in this poster? What image of a woman does it seek to convey?

- What message does the backdrop of the poster communicate? Notice the church and city in flames.

- In appealing for sacrifice or public support in time of war, why might a feminine image be more effective than a masculine image?

- Compare this poster with the British one shown on page 985 in this chapter. What different message about the role of women does this image convey? To what kind of audience did each of these posters appeal?

A distinctive feature of World War I was the extensive use of troops drawn from the colonies of the contending powers. Many thousands of African and Asian men took part in that struggle, both in their homelands and in Europe. The French, for example, were initially reluctant to employ colonial troops, fearing to arm black men and perhaps uncertain of their loyalty. But the desperate need for manpower finally overcame these reservations, and France recruited large numbers of men from its North and West African colonies as well as from Southeast Asia. Some 71,000 French colonial soldiers died in the war. Visual Source 20.3 shows a French wartime poster with a caption that reads "Day of the African Army and Colonial Troops."

- What image of African soldiers does the poster suggest? How might this image be at variance with that of earlier European stereotypes of their African subjects?

- What is conveyed by the juxtaposition of an African soldier and his French counterpart fighting together?

- Why might the French have set aside a special day to honor colonial troops?

- How might the experience of fighting in Europe have affected the outlook of a West African soldier?

The destructiveness of the Great War was almost beyond the imagination of contemporary Europeans. Among its most notable and horrific features was the long period of trench warfare, in which lines of entrenched men, often not far apart, periodically went "over the top," only to gain a few yards of bloody ground before being thrown back with enormous casualties. Visual Source 20.4 shows a particular instance of this process by the British painter John Nash (1893–1977), who was an official war artist.

Nash was also part of an eighty-man British unit that was sent over the top in late 1917 and one of only twelve survivors of that attack. Three months later he painted this haunting picture from his memory of that experience.

- What posture toward the war does this image convey? How do you think Nash's military superiors reacted to the painting?

- How does the painting portray the attitude of the soldiers?

Visual Source 20.3 War and the Colonies (Private collection/Barbara Singer/The Bridgeman Art Library)

Visual Source 20.4 The Battlefield (Imperial War Museum, London/The Bridgeman Art Library)

- What does war do to human beings? What answer to this question does this image suggest?

- How might you imagine the response of those who created the earlier images to John Nash and this portrayal of trench warfare?

Among the many outcomes of the Great War was the presence in every European country of disillusioned, maimed, and disfigured veterans, many of them literally "men without faces." For some intellectuals and artists, they represented the fundamentally flawed civilization that had given rise to such carnage. Often neglected or overlooked, such men were reminders of a terrible past that others wanted to forget. The German artist Otto Dix (1891–1969), who served in his country's military forces throughout the war and was seriously wounded, portrayed this situation in a 1920 painting called *Prague Street*, shown here as Visual Source 20.5. In 1924, he joined with other artists to mount an exhibition entitled "No More War." His antiwar activism later earned Dix the enmity of the Hitler regime, which fired him from his academic position and destroyed some of his paintings. Artistically, Dix worked in a style known as the new objectivity, which focused heavily on the horrendous outcomes of the war. It deliberately included subject matter that was upsetting and even ugly, and it made little attempt to create a unified image, preferring to present disconnected "particles of experience."

- How does the painting describe the situation of the veterans?

- On the left, the arm of a wealthy man drops a coin into the outstretched hand of a maimed veteran, while on the right, a well-dressed woman in a pink dress and high heels walks by with her dog. What do these features add to the portrayal of the plight of the veterans?

- Notice the leaflet on the skateboard of the legless cripple at the bottom. It reads *"Juden raus"* (Jews out). What does this suggest about the political views of these veterans? Keep in mind that Hitler, although not maimed, was a disillusioned veteran of World War I, as were many of his early followers.

- What do the images in the store windows suggest?

- What commentary does this painting make on German society after the country's defeat in World War I? How does it foreshadow what was to come?

Visual Source 20.5 The Aftermath of War (Kunstmuseum Stuttgart © 2014 Artists Rights Society (ARS), New York/ VC Bild-Kunst, Bonn)

Using the Evidence:
Propaganda and Critique in World War I

1. **Describing the war:** Based on these visual sources, how would you define the novel or distinctive features of World War I compared to earlier European conflicts?

2. **Considering war and progress:** How do you think Otto Dix and John Nash might have responded to the ideas of Condorcet contained in Document 15.2, pages 756–57?

3. **Images as propaganda and criticism:** This selection of visual sources contains a mix of those that express essentially government-sponsored messages and those that convey the outlook of individual artists. What ideas about the war did governments seek to inculcate in their citizens? How do the paintings of John Nash and Otto Dix respond to those ideas?

4. **Seeking further evidence:** What other kinds of visual sources would be useful in constructing a visual history of World War I?

Chapter 20 Wrap Up

LearningCurve
Check what you know.
**bedfordstmartins.com
/strayer/LC**

STEP ONE

The Word to Know: Nationalism

The *Oxford English Dictionary* defines *nationalism* as "advocacy of or support for the interests of one's own nation, esp. to the exclusion or detriment of the interests of other nations." Using evidence from Chapter 20, as well as Chapter 16 (pp. 801–05), Chapter 18 (pp. 882–84 and 888–902), and Chapter 19 (pp. 937–44), write an essay about the development of nationalism from the late eighteenth century through the post-World War II era.

STEP TWO

Comparing the Legacies of the Two World Wars

In the chart below, compare the legacies of World War I and World War II. Then complete the exercise that follows.

	World War I	World War II
Nature of warfare		
Psychological effects		
Social and cultural changes		
International politics		
Internationalism		

Reading the Evidence of Nationalism

As you read the following excerpts and examine the visuals again, consider the ways that nationalism was a unifying force for Germany, Japan, and France.

1. Excerpt from Document 20.1, Adolf Hitler, *Mein Kampf*

Review the following excerpt from Document 20.1 and answer the question that follows. To read a longer excerpt, see pp. 1019–21.

"As a State the German Reich shall include all Germans. Its task is not only to gather in and foster the most valuable sections of our people but to lead them slowly and surely to a dominant position in the world. . . . It will be the task of the People's State to make the race the centre of the life of the community. It must make sure that the purity of the racial strain will be preserved. . . ."

■ Question

Describe Hitler's vision of German nationalism. Who is included and who is excluded from this vision?

2. Visual Source 20.1, Defining the Enemy

Examine Visual Source 20.1 on p. 1026, a French poster from 1915, and then answer the question below.

■ Question

How does this poster illustrate French nationalism?

3. Excerpt from Document 20.2, The Japanese Way

Read the excerpt from Document 20.2 and answer the question that follows. To read a longer excerpt, see pp. 1022–23.

"Our nation has in the past imported, assimilated, and sublimated Chinese and Indian ideologies, and has therewith supported the Imperial Way, making possible the establishment of an original culture based on her national polity. . . ."

■ Question

How do the Japanese seek to unite their people around a common culture, while simultaneously addressing the argument that there is much in the outside world that has benefitted their nation?

4. Visual Source 20.3, War and the Colonies

Examine Visual Source 20.3 on p. 1029, a French poster from the World War I era. Then, answer the question below.

■ Question

In what ways does this poster encourage French nationalism in its colonies?

to power almost everywhere in the tumultuous wake of war, revolution, or both. Once established, those regimes set about a thorough and revolutionary transformation of their societies—"building socialism," as they so often put it. Internationally, world communism posed a profound military and political/ideological threat to the Western world of capitalism and democracy, particularly during the decades of the cold war (1946–1991). That struggle divided continents, countries, and cities into communist and noncommunist halves. It also prompted a global rivalry between the United States and the Soviet Union (USSR) for influence in the Global South. Most hauntingly, it spawned an arms race in horrendously destructive nuclear weapons that sent schoolchildren scrambling under their desks during air raid drills, while sober scientists speculated about the possible extinction of human life, and perhaps all life, in the event of a major war.

Then, to the amazement of everyone, it was over, more with a whimper than a bang. The last two decades of the twentieth century witnessed the collapse of communist regimes or the abandonment of communist principles practically everywhere. The great global struggle of capitalism and communism, embodied in the United States and the Soviet Union, was resolved in favor of the former far more quickly and much more peacefully than anyone had imagined possible.

SEEKING THE MAIN POINT

What was the appeal of communism, both in terms of its promises and its achievements? To what extent did promise match achievements?

Global Communism

■ **Description**

When and where did communism exercise influence during the twentieth century?

Modern communism found its political and philosophical roots in nineteenth-century European socialism, inspired by the teachings of Karl Marx. (See p. 852 and Document 17.4, pp. 867–70.) Although most European socialists came to believe that they could achieve their goals peacefully and through the democratic process, those who defined themselves as communists in the twentieth century disdained such reformism and advocated uncompromising revolution as the only possible route to a socialist future. Russia, later called the Soviet Union, was the first country to experience such a revolution. Other movements that later identified or allied with the Soviet Union likewise defined themselves as communist. In Marxist theory, communism also referred to a final stage of historical development when social equality and collective living would be most fully developed, largely without private property. Socialism was an intermediate stage along the way to that final goal.

By the 1970s, almost one-third of the world's population lived in societies governed by communist regimes. By far the most significant were the Soviet Union, the world's largest country in size, and China, the world's largest country in population. But communism also came to Eastern Europe in the wake of World War II and the extension of the Soviet military presence there. In Asia, Mongolia came under a communist regime in 1924 as a spillover of the Russian Revolution. Following Japan's defeat in World War II, its Korean colony was partitioned, with the northern half coming under Soviet and therefore communist control. In Vietnam, a much more

A Map of Time

1917	Russian Revolution
1921	Founding of Chinese Communist Party
1929–1953	Stalin in power in Soviet Union
1934–1935	Long March in China
1945–1950	Imposition of communist regimes in Eastern Europe
1949	Communist triumph in China
1950–1953	Korean War
1958–1961	China's Great Leap Forward and massive famine
1959	Cuban revolution
1962	Cuban missile crisis
1965–1973	U.S.–Vietnam war
1966–1976	China's Cultural Revolution
1968	Prague Spring: communist reform movement in Czechoslovakia
1976–early 1990s	Deng Xiaoping and beginnings of communist reforms in China
1979	Soviet invasion of Afghanistan
1985–1991	Gorbachev reforms in USSR
1989	Collapse of communist regimes in Eastern Europe
1991	Disintegration of Soviet Union

locally based communist movement, under the leadership of Ho Chi Minh, embodied both a socialist vision and Vietnamese nationalism as it battled Japanese, French, and later American invaders and established communist control first in the northern half of the country and after 1975 throughout the whole country. The victory of the Vietnamese communists spilled over into neighboring Laos and Cambodia, where communist parties took power in the mid-1970s. In Latin America, Fidel Castro led a revolutionary nationalist movement against a repressive, American-backed government in Cuba. On coming to power in 1959, Castro moved toward communism and an alliance with the Soviet Union. Finally, a shaky communist regime took power in Afghanistan in 1979, propped up briefly by massive Soviet military support. None of these countries had achieved the kind of advanced industrial capitalism that Karl Marx had viewed as a prerequisite for revolution and socialism. Indeed, in one of history's strange twists, the communist revolutions of the twentieth century took place in largely agrarian societies. (See Map 21.3, p. 1055, for a global view of the communist world in the 1970s, the period of its greatest extent.)

In addition to those countries where communist governments controlled state power, communist movements took root in still other places, where they exercised various degrees of influence. In the aftermath of World War II, communist parties played important political roles in Greece, France, and Italy. In the 1950s, a small communist party in the United States became the focus of an intense wave of fear and political repression known as McCarthyism. Revolutionary communist movements threatened established governments in the Philippines, Malaysia, Indonesia, Bolivia, Peru, and elsewhere, sometimes provoking brutal crackdowns by those governments. A number of African states in the 1970s proclaimed themselves Marxist for a time and aligned with the Soviet Union in international affairs. All of this was likewise part of global communism.

These differing expressions of communism were linked to one another in various ways. They shared a common ideology derived from European Marxism, although it was substantially modified in many places. That ideology minimized the claims of national loyalty and looked forward to an international revolutionary movement of the lower classes and a worldwide socialist federation. The Russian Revolution of 1917 served as an inspiration and an example to aspiring revolutionaries elsewhere, and the new Soviet Communist Party and government provided them aid and advice. Through an organization called Comintern (Communist International), Soviet authorities also sought to control their policies and actions.

During the cold war decades, the Warsaw Pact brought the Soviet Union and Eastern European communist states together in a military alliance designed to counter the threat from the Western capitalist countries of the NATO alliance. A parallel organization called the Council on Mutual Economic Assistance tied Eastern European economies tightly to the economy of the Soviet Union. A Treaty of Friendship between the Soviet Union and China in 1950 joined the two communist giants in an alliance that caused many in the West to view communism as a unified international movement aimed at their destruction. Nevertheless, rivalry, outright hostility, and on occasion military conflict marked the communist world as much or more than solidarity and cooperation. Eastern European resentment of their Soviet overlords boiled over in periodic rebellions, even as the Soviet Union and China came close to war in the late 1960s.

Although the globalization of communism found expression primarily in the second half of the twentieth century, that process began with two quite distinct and different revolutionary upheavals—one in Russia and the other in China—in the first half of the century.

Revolutions as a Path to Communism

■ **Comparison**

Identify the major differences between the Russian and Chinese revolutions.

Communist movements of the twentieth century quite self-consciously drew on the mystique of the earlier French Revolution, which suggested that new and better worlds could be constructed by human actions. Like their French predecessors, communist revolutionaries ousted old ruling classes and dispossessed landed aristocracies. Those twentieth-century upheavals also involved vast peasant upheavals in the countryside and an educated leadership with roots in the cities. All three revolutions—French, Russian, and Chinese—found their vision of the good society in a modernizing future, not in some nostalgic vision of the past. Communists also worried lest their revolutions end up in a military dictatorship like that of Napoleon following the French Revolution.

But the communist revolutions were distinctive as well. They were made by highly organized parties guided by a Marxist ideology, were committed to an industrial future, pursued economic as well as political equality, and sought the abolition of private property. In doing so, they mobilized, celebrated, and claimed to act on behalf of society's lower classes—exploited urban workers and impoverished rural peasants. The middle classes, who were the chief beneficiaries of the French Revolution, numbered among the many victims of the communist upheavals. And unlike the French or American revolutions, communists also carried an explicit message of gender equality. The Russian and Chinese revolutions shared these general features, but in other respects they differed sharply from each other.

Russia: Revolution in a Single Year

In Russia, communists came to power on the back of a revolutionary upheaval that took place within a single year, 1917. The immense pressures of World War I, which was going very badly for the Russians, represented the catalyst for that revolution as the accumulated tensions of Russian society exploded. Much exploited and suffering from wartime shortages, workers—men and women alike—took to the streets to express their outrage at the incompetence and privileges of the elites. In St. Petersburg, some 100,000 wives of soldiers demonstrated for bread and peace. Activists from various parties, many of them socialist, recruited members, organized demonstrations, published newspapers, and plotted revolution. By February 1917, Tsar Nicholas II had lost almost all support and was forced to abdicate the throne, thus ending the Romanov dynasty, which had ruled Russia for more than three centuries.

That historic event opened the door for a massive social upheaval. Ordinary soldiers, seeking an end to a terrible war and despising their upper-class officers, deserted in substantial numbers. In major industrial centers such as St. Petersburg and Moscow, new trade unions arose to defend workers' interests, and some workers seized control of their factories. Grassroots organizations of workers and soldiers, known as soviets, emerged to speak for ordinary people. Peasants, many of whom had been serfs only a generation or two earlier, seized landlords' estates, burned their manor houses, and redistributed the land among themselves. Non-Russian nationalists in Ukraine, Poland, Muslim Central Asia, and the Baltic region demanded greater autonomy or even independence (see Map 21.1, p. 1040).

This was social revolution, and it quickly demonstrated the inadequacy of the Provisional Government, which had come to power after the tsar abdicated. Consisting of middle-class politicians and some moderate socialist leaders, that government was divided and ineffectual, unable or unwilling to meet the demands of Russia's

■ **Change**

Why were the Bolsheviks able to ride the Russian Revolution to power?

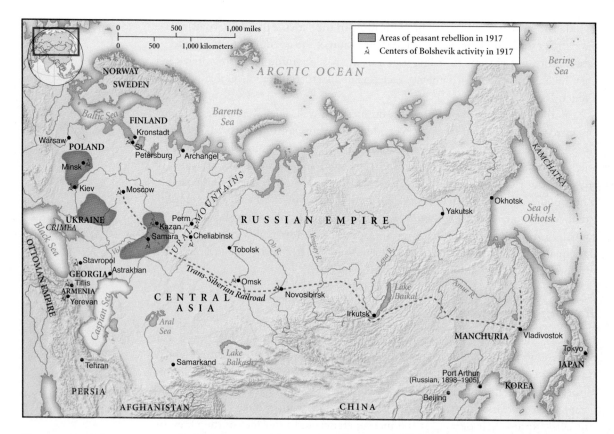

Map 21.1   Russia in 1917
In 1917 during the First World War, the world's largest state, bridging both Europe and Asia, exploded in revolution. The Russian Revolution brought to power the twentieth century's first communist government and launched an international communist movement that eventually incorporated about one-third of the world's people.

revolutionary masses. Nor was it willing to take Russia out of the war, as many were now demanding. Impatience and outrage against the Provisional Government provided an opening for more radical groups. The most effective were the Bolsheviks (BOHL-shih-vehks), a small socialist party with a determined and charismatic leader, Vladimir Ilyich Ulyanov, more commonly known as Lenin. He had long believed that Russia, despite its industrial backwardness, was nonetheless ready for a socialist revolution that would, he expected, spark further revolutions in the more developed countries of Europe. Thus backward Russia would be a catalyst for a more general socialist breakthrough. It was a striking revision of Marxist thinking to accommodate the conditions of a largely agrarian Russian society.

In the desperate circumstances of 1917, his party's message—an end to the war, land for the peasants, workers' control of factories, self-determination for non-Russian nationalities—resonated with an increasingly rebellious public mood, particularly in the major cities. On the basis of this program, the Bolsheviks—claiming to act on behalf of the highly popular soviets—seized power in late October during an overnight coup in the capital city of St. Petersburg.

Taking or claiming power was one thing; holding on to it was another. A three-year civil war followed in which the Bolsheviks, now officially calling their party "communist," battled an assortment of enemies—tsarist officials, landlords, disaffected socialists, and regional nationalist forces, as well as troops from the United States, Britain, France, and Japan, all of which were eager to crush the fledgling communist regime. Remarkably, the Bolsheviks held on and by 1921 had staggered to victory over their divided and uncoordinated opponents. That remarkable victory was assisted by the Bolsheviks' willingness to sign a separate peace treaty with Germany, thus taking Russia out of World War I in early 1918, but at a great, though temporary, loss of Russian territory.

During the civil war (1918–1921), the Bolsheviks harshly regimented the economy, seized grain from angry peasants, suppressed nationalist rebellions, and perpetrated bloody atrocities, as did their enemies as well. But they also integrated many lower-class men into the Red Army, as Bolshevik military forces were

The Russian Civil War through Bolshevik Eyes
This Bolshevik poster from 1921, entitled "Electrification and Counter-Revolution," presents a communist view of the civil war that followed the Russian Revolution. It shows a worker bringing electricity and more generally the light of modernity and progress to a backward country, while depicting their opponents, which include a priest, a general, and a businessman, as seeking to extinguish that light. (The New York Public Library/Art Resource, NY)

known, and into new local governments, providing them a fresh avenue of social mobility. By battling foreign troops, the Bolsheviks claimed to be defending Russia from imperialists and protecting the downtrodden masses from their exploiters. The civil war exaggerated even further the Bolsheviks' authoritarian tendencies and their inclination to use force. Shortly after that war ended, they renamed their country the Union of Soviet Socialist Republics (USSR or Soviet Union) and set about its transformation.

For the next twenty-five years, the Soviet Union remained a communist island in a capitalist sea. The next major extension of communist control occurred in Eastern Europe in the aftermath of World War II, but it took place quite differently than in Russia. That war ended with Soviet military forces occupying much of Eastern Europe. Stalin, the USSR's longtime leader, determined that Soviet security required "friendly" governments in the region to permanently end the threat of invasion from the West. When the Marshall Plan seemed to suggest American efforts to incorporate Eastern Europe into a Western economic network, Stalin acted to install fully communist governments, loyal to himself, in Poland, East Germany, Czechoslovakia, Hungary, Romania, and Bulgaria. Backed by the pressure and presence of the Soviet army, communism was largely imposed on Eastern Europe from outside rather than growing out of a domestic revolution, as had happened in Russia itself.

Local communist parties, however, had some domestic support, deriving from their role in the resistance against the Nazis and their policies of land reform. In Hungary and Poland, for example, communist pressures led to the redistribution of much land to poor or landless peasants, and in free elections in Czechoslovakia in 1946, communists received 38 percent of the vote. The situation in Yugoslavia differed sharply from the rest of Eastern Europe. There a genuinely popular communist movement had played a leading role in the struggle against Nazi occupation and came to power on its own with little Soviet help. Its leader, Josef Broz, known as Tito, openly defied Soviet efforts to control Yugoslav communism, claiming that "our goal is that everyone should be master in his own house."[1]

China: A Prolonged Revolutionary Struggle

■ Change

What was the appeal of communism in China before 1949?

Communism triumphed in the ancient land of China in 1949, about thirty years after the Russian Revolution, likewise on the heels of war and domestic upheaval. But that revolution, which was a struggle of decades rather than a single year, was far different from its earlier Russian counterpart. The Chinese imperial system had collapsed in 1911, under the pressure of foreign imperialism, its own inadequacies, and mounting internal opposition (see pp. 932–41). Unlike Russia, where intellectuals had been discussing socialism for half a century or more before the revolution, the ideas of Karl Marx were barely known in China in the early twentieth century. Not until 1921 was a small Chinese Communist Party (CCP) founded, aimed initially at organizing the country's minuscule urban working class.

Over the next twenty-eight years, that small party, with an initial membership of only sixty people, grew enormously, transformed its strategy, found a charismatic leader in Mao Zedong, engaged in an epic struggle with its opponents, fought the Japanese heroically, and in 1949 emerged victorious as the rulers of China. That victory was all the more surprising because the CCP faced a far more formidable foe than the weak Provisional Government over which the Bolsheviks had triumphed in Russia. That opponent was the Guomindang (GWOH-mihn-dahng) (Nationalist Party), which governed China after 1928. Led by a military officer, Chiang Kai-shek, that party promoted a measure of modern development (railroads, light industry, banking, airline services) in the decade that followed. However, the impact of these achievements was limited largely to the cities, leaving the rural areas, where most people lived, still impoverished. The Guomindang's base of support was also narrow, deriving from urban elites, rural landlords, and Western powers.

Chased out of China's cities in a wave of Guomindang-inspired anticommunist terror in 1927, the CCP groped its way toward a new revolutionary strategy, quite at odds with both classical Marxism and Russian practice. Whereas the Bolsheviks had found their primary audience among workers in Russia's major cities, Chinese communists increasingly looked to the country's peasant villages for support. Thus European Marxism was adapted once again, this time to fit the situation of a mostly peasant China. Still, it was no easy sell. Chinese peasants did not rise up spontaneously against their landlords, as Russian peasants had. However, years of guerrilla warfare, experiments with land reform in areas under communist control, and the creation of a communist military force to protect liberated areas slowly gained for the CCP a growing measure of respect and support among China's peasants. In the process, Mao Zedong, the son of a prosperous Chinese peasant family and a professional revolutionary since the early 1920s, emerged as the party's leader.

To recruit women for the revolution, communists drew on a theoretical commitment to their liberation and in the areas under their control established a Marriage Law that outlawed arranged or "purchased" marriages, made divorce easier, and gave women the right to vote and own property. Early experiments with land reform offered equal shares to men and women alike. Women's associations enrolled hundreds of thousands of women and promoted literacy, fostered discussions of women's issues, and en-

Mao Zedong and the Long March
An early member of China's then minuscule Communist Party, Mao rose to a position of dominant leadership during the Long March of 1934–1935, when beleaguered communists from southeastern China trekked to a new base area in the north. This photograph shows Mao on his horse during that epic journey of some 6,000 miles. (Collection J.A. Fox/Magnum Photos)

couraged handicraft production such as making clothing, blankets, and shoes, so essential for the revolutionary forces. But resistance to such radical measures from more traditional rural villagers, especially the male peasants and soldiers on whom the communists depended, persuaded them to modify these measures. Women were not permitted to seek divorce from men on active military duty. Women's land deeds were often given to male family heads and were regarded as family property. Female party members found themselves limited to work with women or children.

It was Japan's brutal invasion of China that gave the CCP a decisive opening, for that attack destroyed Guomindang control over much of the country and forced it to retreat to the interior, where it became even more dependent on conservative landlords. The CCP, by contrast, grew from just 40,000 members in 1937 to more than 1.2 million in 1945, while the communist-led People's Liberation Army mushroomed to 900,000 men, supported by an additional 2 million militia troops (see Map 21.2). Much of this growing support derived from the vigor with which the CCP waged war against the Japanese invaders. Using guerrilla warfare techniques learned in the struggle against the Guomindang, communist forces established themselves behind enemy lines and, despite periodic setbacks, offered a measure of security to many Chinese faced with Japanese atrocities. The Guomindang, by contrast, sometimes seemed to be more interested in eliminating the communists than in actively fighting the Japanese. Furthermore, in the areas it controlled, the CCP reduced rents, taxes, and interest payments for peasants; taught literacy to adults; and mobilized women for the

Map 21.2 The Rise of Communism in China
Communism arose in China at the same time as the country was engaged in a terrible war with Japan and in the context of a civil war with Guomindang forces.

struggle. As the war drew to a close, more radical action followed. Teams of activists encouraged poor peasants to "speak bitterness" in public meetings, to "struggle" with landlords, and to "settle accounts" with them.

Thus the CCP frontally addressed both of China's major problems—foreign imperialism and peasant exploitation. It expressed Chinese nationalism as well as a demand for radical social change. It gained a reputation for honesty that contrasted sharply with the massive corruption of Guomindang officials. It put down deep roots among the peasantry in a way that the Bolsheviks never did. And whereas the Bolsheviks gained support by urging Russian withdrawal from the highly unpopular First

World War, the CCP won support by aggressively pursuing the struggle against Japanese invaders during World War II. In 1949, four years after the war's end, the Chinese communists swept to victory over the Guomindang, many of whose followers fled to Taiwan. Mao Zedong announced triumphantly in Beijing's Tiananmen Square that "the Chinese people have stood up."

Building Socialism

Once they came to power, communist parties everywhere set about the construction of socialist societies. In the Soviet Union, this massive undertaking occurred under the leadership of Joseph Stalin in the 1920s and 1930s. The corresponding Chinese effort took place during the 1950s and 1960s with Mao Zedong at the helm.

To communist regimes, building socialism meant first of all the modernization and industrialization of their backward societies. They sought, however, a distinctly socialist modernity. This involved a frontal attack on long-standing inequalities of class and gender, an effort to prevent the making of new inequalities as the process of modern development unfolded, and the promotion of cultural values of selflessness and collectivism that could support a socialist society.

Those imperatives generated a political system thoroughly dominated by the Communist Party. Top-ranking party members enjoyed various privileges but were expected to be exemplars of socialism in the making by being disciplined, selfless, and utterly loyal to their country's Marxist ideology. The party itself penetrated society in ways that Western scholars called "totalitarian," for other parties were forbidden, the state controlled almost the entire economy, and political authorities ensured that the arts, education, and the media conformed to approved ways of thinking. Mass organizations for women, workers, students, and various professional groups operated under party control, with none of the independence that characterized civil society in the West.

In undertaking these tasks, the Soviet Union and China started from different places, most notably their international positions. In 1917 Russian Bolsheviks faced a hostile capitalist world alone, while Chinese communists, coming to power over thirty years later, had an established Soviet Union as a friendly northern neighbor and ally. Furthermore, Chinese revolutionaries had actually governed parts of their huge country for decades, gaining experience that the new Soviet rulers had altogether lacked, since they had come to power so quickly. And the Chinese communists were firmly rooted in the rural areas and among the country's vast peasant population, while their Russian counterparts had found their support mainly in the cities.

If these comparisons generally favored China in its efforts to "build socialism," in economic terms that country faced even more daunting prospects than did the Soviet Union. Its population was far greater, its industrial base far smaller, and the availability of new agricultural land far more limited than in the Soviet Union. China's literacy and modern education as well as its transportation network were likewise much less developed. Even more than the Soviets, Chinese communists had to build a modern society from the ground up.

Communist Feminism

■ **Change**
What changes did communist regimes bring to the lives of women?

Among the earliest and most revolutionary actions of these new communist regimes were efforts at liberating and mobilizing women. Communist countries in fact pioneered forms of women's liberation that only later were adopted in the West. This communist feminism was largely state-directed, with the initiative coming from the top rather than bubbling up from grassroots movements as in the West. In the Soviet Union, where a small women's movement had taken shape in pre–World War I Russia, the new communist government almost immediately issued a series of laws and decrees regarding women. These measures declared full legal and political equality for women; marriage became a civil procedure among freely consenting adults; divorce was legalized and made easier, as was abortion; illegitimacy was abolished; women no longer had to take their husbands' surnames; pregnancy leave for employed women was mandated; and women were actively mobilized as workers in the country's drive to industrialization. Addressing a Congress of Women Workers and Peasants, Lenin declared: "Root out old habits. Every cook must learn to rule the state."[2]

In 1919, the party set up a special organization called Zhenotdel (zhen-ut-DEL) (Women's Department), whose radical leaders, all women, pushed a decidedly feminist agenda during the 1920s. They organized numerous conferences for women, trained women to run day-care centers and medical clinics, published newspapers and magazines aimed at a female audience, provided literacy and prenatal classes, and encouraged Muslim women to take off their veils. Alexandra Rodionova, a former streetcar conductor who had played an active role in the revolution, recalled the impact of participation in Zhenotdel: "This former illiterate working girl had been transformed into a person, powerful with the knowledge of her own rights, a consciousness of responsibility for everything happening in the country."[3] Much of this encountered opposition from male communist officials and from ordinary people as well, and Stalin abolished Zhenotdel in 1930. While it lasted, though, it was a remarkable experiment in

Mobilizing Women for Communism
As the Soviet Union mobilized for rapid economic development in the 1930s, women entered the workforce in great numbers. Here two young women are mastering the skills of driving a tractor on one of the large collective farms that replaced the country's private agriculture. (Sovfoto/Eastfoto)

women's liberation by means of state action, animated by an almost utopian sense of new possibilities set loose by the revolution.

Similar policies took shape in communist China. The Marriage Law of 1950 was a direct attack on patriarchal and Confucian traditions. It decreed free choice in marriage, relatively easy divorce, the end of concubinage and child marriage, permission for widows to remarry, and equal property rights for women. A short but intense campaign by the CCP in the early 1950s sought to implement these changes, often against strenuous opposition. The party also launched a Women's Federation, a mass organization that enrolled millions of women. Its leadership, however, was far less radical than that of the Bolshevik feminists who led Zhenotdel in the 1920s. In China, there was little talk of "free love" or the "withering away of the family," as there had been in the USSR. Nevertheless, like their Soviet counterparts, Chinese women became much more actively involved in production outside the home. By 1978, 50 percent of agricultural workers and 38 percent of nonagricultural laborers were female. "Women can do anything" became a famous party slogan in the 1960s (see Visual Source 21.3, p. 1083).

Still, communist-style women's liberation had definite limits. Fearing that the "woman question" would detract from his emphasis on industrial production, Stalin declared it "solved" in 1930. Little direct discussion of women's issues was permitted in the several decades that followed. In neither the Soviet Union nor China did the Communist Party undertake a direct attack on male domination within the family. Thus the double burden of housework and child care plus paid employment continued to afflict most women. Moreover, women appeared only very rarely in the top political leadership of either country.

Socialism in the Countryside

In their efforts to build socialism, both the Soviet Union and China first expropriated landlords' estates and redistributed that land on a much more equitable basis to the peasantry. Such actions, although clearly revolutionary, were not socialist, for peasants initially received their land as private property. In Russia, the peasants had spontaneously redistributed the land among themselves, and the victorious Bolsheviks merely ratified their actions. In China after 1949, land reform was a more prolonged and difficult process. Hastily trained teams were dispatched to the newly liberated areas, where they mobilized the poorer peasants in thousands of separate villages to confront and humiliate the landlords or the more wealthy peasants. Their land, animals, tools, houses, and money were then redistributed to the poorer members of the village. In these villages, land reform teams encountered the age-old deference that peasants traditionally had rendered to their social superiors. One young woman activist described the confrontational meetings intended to break this ancient pattern:

> "Speak bitterness meetings," as they were called, would help [the peasants] to understand how things really had been in the old days, to realize that their lives

■ **Comparison**

How did the collectivization of agriculture differ between the USSR and China?

were not blindly ordained by fate . . . and that far from owing anything to the feudal landlords, it was the feudal landlords who owed them a debt of suffering beyond all reckoning.[4]

It was, as Mao Zedong put it, "not a dinner party." Approximately 1 to 2 million landlords were killed in the process, which was largely over by 1952.

A second and more distinctly socialist stage of rural reform sought to end private property in land by collectivizing agriculture. In China, despite brief resistance from richer peasants, collectivization during the 1950s was a generally peaceful process, owing much to the close relationship between the Chinese Communist Party and the peasantry, which had been established during three decades of struggle. This contrasted markedly with the earlier experience of the Soviet Union from 1928 to 1933, when peasants were forced into collective farms and violence was extensive. Russian peasants slaughtered and consumed hundreds of thousands of animals rather than surrender them to the collectives. Stalin singled out the richer peasants, known as *kulaks* (koo-LAHKS), for exclusion from the new collective farms. Some were killed, and many others were deported to remote areas of the country. With little support or experience in the countryside, Soviet communists, who came mostly from the cities, were viewed as intrusive outsiders in Russian peasant villages. A terrible famine ensued, with some 5 million deaths from starvation or malnutrition. (See Document 21.2, pp. 1071–73, for a firsthand account of the collectivization process.)

China, however, pushed collectivization even further than the Soviet Union did, particularly in huge "people's communes" during the Great Leap Forward in the late 1950s. It was an effort to mobilize China's enormous population for rapid development and at the same time to move toward a more fully communist society with an even greater degree of social equality and collective living. (See Visual Source 21.2, p. 1082, for more on communes.) Administrative chaos, disruption of marketing networks, and bad weather combined to produce a massive famine that killed an amazing 20 million people or more between 1959 and 1962, dwarfing even the earlier Soviet famine.

Communism and Industrial Development

■ Change

What were the achievements of communist efforts at industrialization? What problems did these achievements generate?

Both the Soviet Union and China defined industrialization as a fundamental task of their regimes. That process was necessary to end humiliating backwardness and poverty, to provide the economic basis for socialism, and to create the military strength that would enable their revolutions to survive in a hostile world. Though strongly anticapitalist, communists everywhere were ardent modernizers.

When the Chinese communists began their active industrialization efforts in the early 1950s, they largely followed the model pioneered by the Soviet Union in the late 1920s and the 1930s. That model involved state ownership of property, centralized planning embodied in successive five-year plans, priority to heavy industry, massive mobilization of the nation's human and material resources, and intrusive Communist

Party control of the entire process. (See Document 21.1, pp. 1069–71, and Document 21.3, pp. 1073–75, for more on Soviet industrialization.) Both countries experienced major—indeed unprecedented—economic growth. The Soviet Union constructed the foundations of an industrial society in the 1930s that proved itself in the victory over Nazi Germany in World War II and that by the 1960s and 1970s generated substantially improved standards of living. China also quickly expanded its output (see the Snapshot). In addition, both countries achieved massive improvements

Snapshot   **China under Mao, 1949–1976**

The following table reveals some of the achievements, limitations, and tragedies of China's communist experience during the era of Mao Zedong.[5]

Steel production	from 1.3 million to 23 million tons
Coal production	from 66 million to 448 million tons
Electric power generation	from 7 million to 133 billion kilowatt-hours
Fertilizer production	from 0.2 million to 28 million tons
Cement production	from 3 million to 49 million tons
Industrial workers	from 3 million to 50 million
Scientists and technicians	from 50,000 to 5 million
"Barefoot doctors" posted to countryside	1 million
Annual growth rate of industrial output	11 percent
Annual growth rate of agricultural output	2.3 percent
Total population	from 542 million to 1 billion
Average population growth rate per year	2 percent
Per capita consumption of rural dwellers	from 62 to 124 yuan annually
Per capita consumption of urban dwellers	from 148 to 324 yuan
Overall life expectancy	from 35 to 65 years
Counterrevolutionaries killed (1949–1952)	between 1 million and 3 million
People labeled "rightists" in 1957	550,000
Deaths from famine during Great Leap Forward	20 million or more
Deaths during Cultural Revolution	500,000
Officials sent down to rural labor camps during Cultural Revolution	3 million or more
Urban youth sent down to countryside (1967–1976)	17 million

in their literacy rates and educational opportunities, allowing far greater social mobility for millions of people than ever before. In both countries, industrialization fostered a similar set of social outcomes: rapid urbanization, exploitation of the countryside to provide resources for modern industry in the cities, and the growth of a privileged bureaucratic and technological elite intent on pursuing their own careers and passing on their new status to their children.

Perhaps the chief difference in the industrial histories of the Soviet Union and China lies in the leadership's response to these social outcomes. In the Soviet Union under Stalin and his successors, they were largely accepted. Industrialization was centered in large urban areas, which pulled from the countryside the most ambitious and talented people. A highly privileged group of state and party leaders emerged in the Stalin era and largely remained the unchallenged ruling class of the country until the 1980s. Even in the 1930s, the outlines of a conservative society, which had discarded much of its revolutionary legacy, were apparent. Stalin himself endorsed Russian patriotism, traditional family values, individual competition, and substantial differences in wages to stimulate production, as an earlier commitment to egalitarianism was substantially abandoned. Increasingly the invocation of revolutionary values was devoid of real content, and by the 1970s the perception of official hypocrisy was widespread.

The Great Leap Forward
This Chinese poster from 1960 celebrates both the agricultural and industrial efforts of the Great Leap Forward. The caption reads: "Start the movement to increase production and practice thrift, with foodstuffs and steel at the center, with great force!" The great famine that accompanied this "great leap" belied the optimistic outlook of the poster. (IISH/Stefan R. Landsberger collections http:chineseposters.net)

The unique feature of Chinese history under Mao Zedong's leadership was a recurrent effort to combat these perhaps inevitable tendencies of any industrializing process and to revive and preserve the revolutionary spirit, which had animated the Communist Party during its long struggle for power. By the mid-1950s, Mao and some of his followers had become persuaded that the Soviet model of industrialization was leading China away from socialism and toward new forms of inequality, toward individualistic and careerist values, and toward an urban bias that privileged the cities at the expense of the countryside. The Great Leap Forward of 1958–1960 marked Mao's first response to these distortions of Chinese socialism. It promoted small-scale industrialization in the rural areas rather than focusing wholly on large enterprises in the cities; it tried to foster widespread and practical technological education for all rather than relying on a small elite of highly trained technical experts; and it envisaged an immediate transition to full communism in the "people's communes" rather than waiting for industrial development to provide the material basis for that transition. The massive famine that followed temporarily discredited Mao's radicalism.

Nonetheless in the mid-1960s, Mao launched yet another campaign—the Great Proletarian Cultural Revolution—to combat the capitalist tendencies that he believed had penetrated even the highest ranks of the Communist Party itself. The Cultural Revolution also involved new policies to bring health care and education to the countryside and to reinvigorate earlier efforts at rural industrialization under local rather than central control. In these ways, Mao struggled, though without great success, to overcome the inequalities associated with China's modern development and to create a model of socialist modernity quite distinct from that of the Soviet Union.

The Cultural Revolution also rejected feminism, any specific concern with women's issues, and much that was feminine. A popular slogan stated: "The times have changed; men and women are the same." Yet the supposedly gender-neutral model seemed strikingly masculine. Women cut their hair short, wore army clothes, and learned to curse; they were depicted in propaganda posters as "iron girls," strong, muscular, and performing heavy traditionally male work (see Visual Source 21.3, p. 1083). Art, literature, ballet, and opera cast them as militant revolutionary participants. And yet, factory managers continued to prefer women workers because of their alleged patience and manual dexterity. Young women sent to the countryside to work with peasants found themselves subject to sexual abuse by male officials.[6] Thus strenuous Maoist efforts to eliminate differences between classes, between urban and rural life, and between men and women largely failed.

A final commonality among communist industrializers lay in their great confidence in human rationality and centralized planning embodied in huge projects— enormous factories, large collective farms, gigantic dams. Soviet officials saw the environment as an enemy, spoke about "the struggle against nature," and looked forward to "a profound rearrangement of the entire living world."[7] This attitude, no less than capitalist assumptions, led to immense environmental devastation and a very difficult legacy for postcommunist regimes. In the Soviet Union, for example, huge industrial complexes such as Magnitogorsk concentrated air and water pollution. A scheme to bring millions of acres of semi-arid land under cultivation in Central Asia depleted and eroded the fragile soil. Diverting the waters of several rivers feeding the Aral Sea for irrigating cotton fields reduced the size of that huge inland sea by 90 percent. By the late 1980s, such environmental heedlessness meant that about half of the cultivated land in the country was endangered by erosion, salinization, or swamping; some 30 percent of food products were contaminated by pesticides or herbicides; 75 percent of the surface water was severely polluted; and 70 million people lived in cities with air pollution five times or more the acceptable level.[8]

The Search for Enemies

Despite their totalitarian tendencies, the communist societies of the Soviet Union and China were laced with conflict. Under both Stalin and Mao, those conflicts erupted in a search for enemies that disfigured both societies. An elastic concept of "enemy" came to include not only surviving remnants from the prerevolutionary elites but also, and more surprisingly, high-ranking members and longtime supporters of the

■ **Explanation**

Why did communist regimes generate terror and violence on such a massive scale?

Anna Dubova, A Russian Peasant Girl and Urban Woman

Born into a large peasant family near Smolensk in western Russia in 1916, Anna Dubova lived through the entire communist experience of her country.[9] Hers was a life that illustrates the complexities that ordinary individuals faced as they sought to navigate the communist system.

Anna was one of fourteen children, of whom seven survived. Her family was dominated by a strict, hard-working, and highly religious father, who was choirmaster of the local church. Anna's father was suspicious of the communists when they came to power the year after Anna's birth, but her grandmother was more forthright. "We have a new tsar," she declared. "The forces of the Antichrist have triumphed." Nonetheless, her father accepted an appointment in 1922 as chairman of the village soviet, the new communist organ of local government. During the 1920s, the village and Anna's family flourished under Lenin's New Economic Policy, which briefly permitted a considerable measure of private enterprise and profit making. Her father even opened a

A 1941 image of a woman factory worker in Moscow. (Library of Congress, LC-USW33-024241-C)

small shop in the village where he sold goods purchased in the city.

By 1928, however, everything changed as the Soviet regime, now under Joseph Stalin's leadership, abruptly moved to collectivize agriculture and root out *kulaks*, supposedly wealthy peasants who were thought to bear the germ of a hated capitalism. Because of her father's shop, the family was labeled as *kulak*, their property confiscated. "I remember so well how Mama sat and cried when they took away the cow," Anna recalled years later. The family forestalled their expected deportation to the far north of the Soviet Union only by promising Anna, then just thirteen, in marriage to the local Communist Party secretary. The marriage never took place, however, and the family was forced to leave. Later, Anna was permitted to join her older sister in Moscow, but approval for that much-coveted move came at a very high price. "I had to write out an official statement that I renounced my parents, that I no longer had any ties with them."

Communist Party who allegedly had been corrupted by bourgeois ideas. Refracted through the lens of Marxist thinking, these people became class enemies who had betrayed the revolution and were engaged in a vast conspiracy, often linked to foreign imperialists, to subvert the socialist enterprise and restore capitalism. In the rhetoric of the leadership, the class struggle continued and even intensified as the triumph of socialism drew closer.

In the Soviet Union, that process culminated in the Terror, or the Great Purges, of the late 1930s, which enveloped tens of thousands of prominent communists, including virtually all of Lenin's top associates, and millions of more ordinary people. (See Document 21.4, pp. 1075–78, and the Portrait of Anna Dubova, above, for individual experiences of the Terror.) Based on suspicious associations in the past, denunciations by colleagues, connections to foreign countries, or simply bad luck,

Thus Anna, a rural teenager, joined millions of other peasants who flocked to the city to pursue new opportunities that became available as the Soviet Union launched its industrialization drive. In Moscow, she gained a basic education, a vocation in cake decorating, which she enjoyed, and a brief stint as a mechanic and chauffeur, which she detested. All the while the shadow of her *kulak* label followed her. Had it been discovered, she could have lost her job and her permission to live in Moscow. And so she married a party activist from a poor peasant family, "just so I could cover up my background." Her husband drank heavily, leaving her with a daughter when he went off to war in 1941.

In the Soviet Union, the late 1930s witnessed the Terror when millions of alleged "enemies of the people" were arrested and hauled off to execution or labor camps. Anna recalled what it was like: "You'd come home and they'd say, Yesterday they took away Uncle Lesha....You'd go to see a girlfriend, they'd say, We have an empty room now; they've exiled Andreitsev." Like most people not directly involved, Anna believed in the guilt of these people. And she feared that she herself might be mistakenly accused, for those with a *kukak* label were particular targets of the search for enemies. "I was only afraid," she remembered, "that I would be raped in prison."

Beyond her *kulak* background, Anna also felt compelled to hide a deep religious sensibility derived from her childhood. She remembered the disappearance of the village priest, the looting of the churches, and the destruction of icons. And so she never entered a church or prayed in front of others. But she wore a cross under her clothing. "I never stopped [believing]," she recalled. "But I concealed it. Deep down . . . I believed." Nor did she ever seek to join the Communist Party, though it may well have advanced her career prospects and standard of living. Perhaps she feared that the investigations accompanying party membership would have disclosed her compromising social and religious background.

In the decades following World War II and especially after Stalin's death in 1953, Anna's life seemed to stabilize. She entered into a thirty-year relationship with a man and found satisfying work in a construction design office, though the lack of higher education and party connections prevented her from moving into higher-paid jobs. Looking back on her life, she regretted the communist intrusion, particularly in its Stalinist phase, into what she remembered as a happy childhood. She had come to value, perhaps nostalgically, the life of a peasant, where "I would have lived on the fruits of my labor," over that of an urban worker, where, she felt, "I've lived someone else's life."

Question: In what ways did communism shape Anna's life, and in what respects was she able to construct her own life within that system?

such people were arrested, usually in the dead of night, and then tried and sentenced either to death or to long years in harsh and remote labor camps known as the gulag. A series of show trials publicized the menace that these "enemies of the people" allegedly posed to the country and its revolution. Close to 1 million people were executed between 1936 and 1941. Perhaps an additional 4 or 5 million were sent to the gulag, where they were forced to work in horrendous conditions and died in appalling numbers. Victimizers too were numerous: the Terror consumed the energies of a huge corps of officials, investigators, interrogators, informers, guards, and executioners, many of whom themselves were arrested, exiled, or executed in the course of the purges.

In the Soviet Union, the search for enemies occurred under the clear control of the state. In China, however, it became a much more public process, escaping the control of the leadership, particularly during the Cultural Revolution of 1966–1969. Mao had become convinced that many within the Communist Party had been seduced by capitalist values of self-seeking and materialism and were no longer animated by the idealistic revolutionary vision of earlier times. Therefore, he called for rebellion, against the Communist Party itself. Millions of young people responded, and, organized as Red Guards, they set out to rid China of those who were "taking the capitalist road." Following gigantic and ecstatic rallies in Beijing, they fanned out across the country and attacked local party and government officials, teachers, intellectuals, factory managers, and others they defined as enemies. (See Visual Sources 21.1 and 21.4, pp. 1080 and 1084.) Rival revolutionary groups soon began fighting with one another, violence erupted throughout the country, and civil war threatened China. Mao was forced to call in the military to restore order and Communist Party control. Both the Soviet Terror and the Chinese Cultural Revolution badly discredited the very idea of socialism and contributed to the ultimate collapse of the communist experiment at the end of the century.

■ SUMMING UP SO FAR

How did the Soviet Union and China differ in terms of the revolutions that brought communists to power and in the construction of socialist societies? What commonalities are also apparent?

East versus West: A Global Divide and a Cold War

Not only did communist regimes bring revolutionary changes to the societies they governed, but their very existence launched a global conflict that restructured international life and touched the lives of almost everyone, particularly in the twentieth century's second half. That rift began soon after the Russian Revolution when the new communist government became the source of fear and loathing to many in the Western capitalist world. The common threat of Nazi Germany temporarily made unlikely allies of the Soviet Union, Britain, and the United States, but a few years after World War II ended, that division erupted again in what became known as the cold war. Underlying that conflict were the geopolitical and ideological realities of the postwar world. The Soviet Union and the United States were now the major political/military powers, replacing the shattered and diminished states of Western Europe, but they represented sharply opposed views of history, society, politics, and international relations. Conflict, in retrospect, seemed almost inevitable.

Military Conflict and the Cold War

■ Connection

In what different ways was the cold war expressed?

The initial arena of the cold war was Europe, where Soviet insistence on security and control in Eastern Europe clashed with American and British desires for open and democratic societies with ties to the capitalist world economy. What resulted were rival military alliances (NATO and the Warsaw Pact), a largely voluntary American sphere of influence in Western Europe, and an imposed Soviet sphere in Eastern Europe. The heavily fortified border between Eastern and Western Europe came to be known as the Iron Curtain. Thus Europe was bitterly divided. But although tensions flared across this dividing line, particularly in Berlin, no shooting war occurred between the two sides (see Map 21.3).

By contrast, the extension of communism into Asia—China, Korea, and Vietnam—globalized the cold war and occasioned its most destructive and prolonged "hot wars." A North Korean invasion of South Korea in 1950 led to both Chinese and American involvement in a bitter three-year war (1950–1953), which ended in an essential standoff that left the Korean peninsula still divided in the early twenty-first century. Likewise in Vietnam, military efforts by South Vietnamese communists and the already communist North Vietnamese government to unify their country prompted massive American intervention in the 1960s. To American authorities, a communist victory opened the door to further communist expansion in Asia and beyond. Armed and supported by the Soviets and Chinese and willing to endure enormous losses, the Vietnamese communists bested the Americans, who were hobbled by growing protest at home. The Vietnamese united their country under communist control by 1975.

Map 21.3   The Global Cold War

The cold war witnessed a sharp division between the communist world and the Western democratic world. It also divided the continent of Europe; the countries of China, Korea, Vietnam, and Germany; and the city of Berlin. In many places, it also sparked crises that brought the nuclear-armed superpowers of the United States and the USSR to the brink of war, although in every case they managed to avoid direct military conflict between themselves.

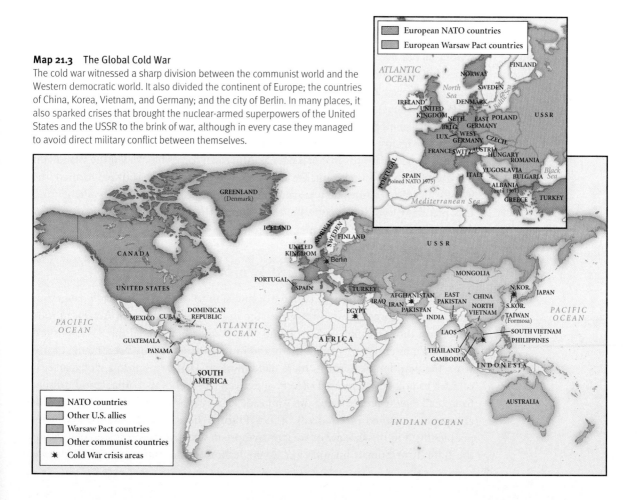

A third major military conflict of the cold war era occurred in Afghanistan, where a Marxist party had taken power in 1978. Soviet leaders were delighted at this extension of communism on their southern border, but radical land reforms and efforts to liberate Afghan women soon alienated much of this conservative Muslim country and led to a mounting opposition movement. Fearing the overthrow of a new communist state and its replacement by Islamic radicals, Soviet forces intervened militarily and were soon bogged down in a war they could not win. For a full decade (1979–1989), that war was a "bleeding wound," sustained in part by U.S. aid to Afghan guerrillas. Under widespread international pressure, Soviet forces finally withdrew in 1989, and the Afghan communist regime soon collapsed. In Vietnam and Afghanistan, both superpowers painfully experienced the limits of their power.

The most haunting battle of the cold war era was one that never happened. The setting was Cuba. When the revolutionary Fidel Castro came to power in 1959, his nationalization of American assets provoked great U.S. hostility and efforts to overthrow his regime. Such pressure only pushed this revolutionary nationalist closer to the Soviet Union, and gradually he began to think of himself and his revolution as Marxist. Soviet authorities were elated. "You Americans must realize what Cuba means to us old Bolsheviks," declared one high-ranking Soviet official. "We have been waiting all our lives for a country to go communist without the Red Army. It has happened in Cuba, and it makes us feel like boys again."[10] Fearing the loss of their newfound Caribbean ally to American aggression, the Soviet leader Nikita Khrushchev (KROOSH-chef), who had risen to power after Stalin's death in 1953, secretly deployed nuclear-tipped Soviet missiles to Cuba, believing that this would deter further U.S. action against Castro. When the missiles were discovered in October 1962, the world held its breath for thirteen days as American forces blockaded the island and prepared for an invasion. A nuclear exchange between the superpowers seemed imminent, but that catastrophe was averted by a compromise between Khrushchev and U.S. president John F. Kennedy. Under its terms, the Soviets removed their missiles from Cuba in return for an American promise not to invade the island.

Nuclear Standoff and Third World Rivalry

The Cuban missile crisis gave concrete expression to the most novel and dangerous dimension of the cold war—the arms race in nuclear weapons. An American monopoly on those weapons when World War II ended prompted the Soviet Union to redouble its efforts to acquire them, and in 1949 it succeeded. Over the next forty years, the world moved from a mere handful of nuclear weapons to a global arsenal of close to 60,000 warheads. Delivery systems included bomber aircraft and missiles that could rapidly propel numerous warheads across whole continents and oceans with accuracies measured in hundreds of feet. During those decades, the world's many peoples lived in the shadow of weapons whose destructive power is scarcely within the bounds of human imagination. A single bomb in a single instant could have obliterated any major city in the world. The detonation of even a small fraction of the weapons then in the arsenals of the Soviet Union and the United States could have reduced the target countries to radioactive rubble and social chaos. Responsible scientists seriously discussed the possible extinction of the human species under such conditions.

Awareness of this possibility is surely the primary reason that no shooting war of any kind occurred between the two superpowers. In the two world wars, the participants had been greatly surprised by the destructiveness of modern weapons. During the cold war, however, the leaders of the two superpowers knew beyond any doubt that a nuclear war would produce only losers and utter catastrophe. Already in 1949, Stalin had observed that

The Hydrogen Bomb

During the 1950s and early 1960s, tests in the atmosphere of ever larger and more sophisticated hydrogen bombs made images of enormous fireballs and mushroom-shaped clouds the universal symbol of these weapons, which were immensely more powerful than the atomic bombs dropped on Japan. The American test pictured here took place in 1957. (Image courtesy The Nuclear Weapon Archive)

"atomic weapons can hardly be used without spelling the end of the world."[11] Particularly after the frightening Cuban missile crisis of 1962, both sides carefully avoided further nuclear provocation, even while continuing the buildup of their respective arsenals. Moreover, because they feared that a conventional war would escalate to the nuclear level, they implicitly agreed to sidestep any direct military confrontation at all.

Still, opportunities for conflict abounded as the U.S.–Soviet rivalry spanned the globe. Using military and economic aid, educational opportunities, political pressure, and covert action, both sides courted countries emerging from colonial rule. Cold war fears of communist penetration prompted U.S. intervention, sometimes openly and often secretly, in Iran, the Philippines, Guatemala, El Salvador, Chile, the Congo, and elsewhere. In the process the United States frequently supported anticommunist but corrupt and authoritarian regimes. However, neither superpower was able to completely dominate its supposed allies, many of whom resisted the role of pawns in superpower rivalries. Some countries, such as India, took a posture of nonalignment in the cold war, while others tried to play off the superpowers against each other. Indonesia received large amounts of Soviet and Eastern European aid, but that did not prevent it from destroying the Indonesian Communist Party in 1965, killing half a million suspected communists in the process. When the Americans refused to assist Egypt in building the Aswan Dam in the mid-1950s, that country developed a close relationship with the Soviet Union. Later, in 1972, Egypt expelled 21,000 Soviet advisers and again aligned more clearly with the United States.

The Cold War and the Superpowers

■ **Connection**

In what ways did the United States play a global role after World War II?

World War II and the cold war provided the context for the emergence of the United States as a global superpower, playing a role that has often been compared to that of Great Britain in the nineteenth century. Much of that effort was driven by the perceived demands of the cold war, during which the United States spearheaded the Western effort to contain a worldwide communist movement that seemed to be advancing. By 1970, one writer observed, "the United States had more than 1,000,000 soldiers in 30 countries, was a member of four regional defense alliances and an active participant in a fifth, had mutual defense treaties with 42 nations, was a member of 53 international organizations, and was furnishing military or economic aid to nearly 100 nations across the face of the globe."[12]

The need for quick and often secret decision making gave rise in the United States to a strong or "imperial" presidency and a "national security state," in which defense and intelligence agencies acquired great power within the government and were often unaccountable to Congress. This served to strengthen the influence of what U.S. president Dwight Eisenhower (1953–1961) called the "military-industrial complex," a coalition of the armed services, military research laboratories, and private defense industries that both stimulated and benefited from increased military spending and cold war tensions.

Sustaining this immense military effort was a flourishing U.S. economy and an increasingly middle-class society. The United States was the only major industrial country to escape the physical devastation of war on its own soil. As World War II ended with Europe, the Soviet Union, and Japan in ruins, the United States was clearly the world's most productive economy. "The whole world is hungry for American goods," wrote one American economist in 1945.[13] Beyond their goods, Americans sent their capital abroad in growing amounts—from $19 billion in 1950 to $81 billion in 1965. Huge American firms such as General Motors, Ford, Mobil, Sears, General Electric, and Westinghouse established factories, offices, and subsidiaries in many countries and sold their goods locally. The U.S. dollar replaced the British pound as the most trusted international currency.

Accompanying the United States' political and economic penetration of the world was its popular culture. In musical terms, first jazz, then rock-and-roll, and most recently rap have found receptive audiences abroad, particularly among the young. By the 1990s, American movies took about 70 percent of the market in Europe, and in 2012 some 33,000 McDonald's restaurants in 119 countries served 68 million customers every day. Various American brand names—Kleenex, Coca-Cola, Jeep, Spam, Nike, Kodak—became common points of reference around the world. English became a global language, while American slang terms—"groovy," "crazy," "cool"— were integrated into many of the world's languages.

On the communist side, the cold war was accompanied by considerable turmoil both within and among the various communist states. Joseph Stalin, Soviet dictator and acknowledged leader of the communist world in general, died in 1953 as that

global conflict was mounting. His successor, Nikita Khrushchev, stunned his country and communists everywhere with a lengthy speech delivered to a party congress
in 1956 in which he presented a devastating account of Stalin's crimes, particularly
those against party members. These revelations shocked many of the party faithful,
for Stalin had been viewed as the "genius of all time." Now he was presented as a
criminal.

In the Soviet Union, the superpower of the communist world, the cold war justified a continuing emphasis on military and defense industries after World War II
and gave rise to a Soviet version of the military-industrial complex. Soviet citizens,
even more than Americans, were subject to incessant government propaganda that
glorified their system and vilified that of their American opponents.

As the communist world expanded, so too did divisions and conflicts among its
various countries. Many in the West had initially viewed world communism as a
monolithic force whose disciplined members meekly followed Soviet dictates in cold
war solidarity against the West. And Marxists everywhere contended that revolutionary socialism would erode national loyalties as the "workers of the world" united
in common opposition to global capitalism. Nonetheless, the communist world experienced far more bitter and divisive conflict than did the Western alliance, which
was composed of supposedly warlike, greedy, and highly competitive nations.

In Eastern Europe, Yugoslav leaders early on had rejected Soviet domination of
their internal affairs and charted their own independent road to socialism. Fearing that
reform might lead to contagious defections from the communist bloc, Soviet forces
actually invaded their supposed allies in Hungary (1956–1957) and Czechoslovakia
(1968) to crush such movements. In the early 1980s, Poland was seriously threatened
with a similar action. The brutal suppression of these reform movements gave credibility to Western perceptions of the cold war as a struggle between tyranny and freedom and badly tarnished the image of Soviet communism as a reasonable alternative
to capitalism.

Even more startling, the two communist giants, the Soviet Union and China, found
themselves sharply opposed, owing to territorial disputes, ideological differences, and
rivalry for communist leadership. The Chinese bitterly criticized Khrushchev for
backing down in the Cuban missile crisis, while to the Soviet leadership, Mao was
insanely indifferent to the possible consequences of a nuclear war. In 1960, the Soviet
Union backed away from an earlier promise to provide China with the prototype
of an atomic bomb and abruptly withdrew all Soviet advisers and technicians, who
had been assisting Chinese development. By the late 1960s, China on its own had developed a modest nuclear capability, and the two countries were at the brink of war,
with the Soviet Union hinting at a possible nuclear strike on Chinese military targets.
Their enmity certainly benefited the United States, which in the 1970s was able to
pursue a "triangular diplomacy," easing tensions and simultaneously signing arms control agreements with the USSR and opening a formal relationship with China. Beyond this central conflict, a communist China in fact went to war against a communist Vietnam in 1979, while Vietnam invaded a communist Cambodia in the late 1970s.

■ **Description**

What were the strengths
and weaknesses of the
communist world by the
1970s?

China: Abandoning Communism and Maintaining the Party

As the dust settled from the political shakeout following Mao's death in 1976, Deng Xiaoping (dung shee-yao-ping) emerged as China's "paramount leader," committed to ending the periodic upheavals of the Maoist era while fostering political stability and economic growth. Soon previously banned plays, operas, films, and translations of Western classics reappeared, and a "literature of the wounded" exposed the sufferings of the Cultural Revolution. Some 100,000 political prisoners, many of them high-ranking communists, were released and restored to important positions. A party evaluation of Mao severely criticized his mistakes during the Great Leap Forward and the Cultural Revolution, while praising his role as a revolutionary leader.

After Communism in China
Although the Communist Party still governed China in the early twenty-first century, communist values of selflessness, community, and simplicity had been substantially replaced for many by Western-style consumerism. This New Year's Good Luck poster from 1993 illustrates the new interest in material wealth in the form of American dollars and the return of older Chinese cultural patterns represented by the traditional gods of wealth, happiness, and longevity. The caption reads: "The gods of wealth enter the home from everywhere." (IISH/Stefan R. Landsberger collections http:chineseposters.net)

Even more dramatic were Deng's economic reforms. In the rural areas, these reforms included a rapid dismantling of the country's system of collectivized farming and a return to something close to small-scale private agriculture. Impoverished Chinese peasants eagerly embraced these new opportunities and pushed them even further than the government had intended. Industrial reform proceeded more gradually. Managers of state enterprises were given greater authority and encouraged to act like private owners, making many of their own decisions and seeking profits. China opened itself to the world economy and welcomed foreign investment in special enterprise zones along the coast, where foreign capitalists received tax breaks and other inducements. Local governments and private entrepreneurs joined forces in thousands of flourishing "township and village enterprises" that produced food, clothing, building materials, and much more.

The outcome of these reforms was stunning economic growth and a new prosperity for millions. Better diets, lower mortality rates, declining poverty, massive urban construction, and surging exports—all of this accompanied China's rejoining of the world economy and contributed to a much-improved material life for millions of its citizens. To many observers, China was the emerging economic giant of the twenty-first century. On the other hand, the country's burgeoning economy also generated massive corruption among Chinese officials, sharp inequalities between the coast and the interior, a huge problem of urban overcrowding, terrible pollution in major cities, and periodic inflation as the state loosened its controls over the economy. Urban vices such as street crime, prostitution, gambling, drug addiction, and a criminal underworld, which had been largely eliminated after 1949, surfaced again in China's booming cities. Nonetheless, something remarkable had occurred in China: an essentially capitalist economy had been restored, and by none other than the Communist Party itself. Mao's worst fears had been realized, as China "took the capitalist road."

Although the party was willing to largely abandon communist economic policies, it was adamantly unwilling to relinquish its political monopoly or to promote democracy at the national level. "Talk about democracy in the abstract," Deng Xiaoping declared, "will inevitably lead to the unchecked spread of ultra-democracy and anarchism, to the complete disruption of political stability, and to the total failure of our modernization program. . . . China will once again be plunged into chaos, division, retrogression, and darkness."[14] Such attitudes associated democracy with the chaos and uncontrolled mass action of the Cultural Revolution. Thus, when a democracy movement spearheaded by university and secondary school students surfaced in the late 1980s, Deng ordered the brutal crushing of its brazen demonstration in Beijing's Tiananmen Square before the television cameras of the world.

China entered the new millennium as a rapidly growing economic power with an essentially capitalist economy presided over by an intact and powerful Communist Party. Culturally, some combination of nationalism, consumerism, and a renewed respect for ancient traditions had replaced the collectivist and socialist values of the Maoist era. It was a strange and troubled hybrid.

The Soviet Union: The Collapse of Communism and Country

By the mid-1980s, the reformist wing of the Soviet Communist Party, long squelched by an aging conservative establishment, had won the top position in the party as Mikhail Gorbachev assumed the role of general secretary. Like Deng Xiaoping in China, Gorbachev was committed to aggressively tackling the country's many problems—economic stagnation, a flourishing black market, public apathy, and cynicism about the party. His economic program, launched in 1987 and known as *perestroika* (per-uh-STROI-kuh) (restructuring), paralleled aspects of the Chinese approach by freeing state enterprises from the heavy hand of government regulation, permitting small-scale private businesses called cooperatives, offering opportunities for private farming, and cautiously welcoming foreign investment in joint enterprises.

But in cultural and political affairs, Gorbachev moved far beyond Chinese reforms. His policy of *glasnost* (GLAHS-nohst) (openness), now permitted an unprecedented range of cultural and intellectual freedoms. In the late 1980s, glasnost hit the Soviet Union like a bomb. Newspapers and TV exposed social pathologies—crime, prostitution, child abuse, suicide, corruption, and homelessness—that previously had been presented solely as the product of capitalism. Films broke the ban on nudity and explicit sex. TV reporters climbed the wall of a secluded villa to film the luxurious

■ **Comparison**

How did the end of communism in the Soviet Union differ from communism's demise in China?

homes of the party elite. Soviet history was also reexamined as revelations of Stalin's crimes poured out of the media. The Bible and the Quran became more widely available, atheistic propaganda largely ceased, and thousands of churches and mosques were returned to believers and opened for worship. Plays, poems, films, and novels that had long been buried "in the drawer" were now released to a public that virtually devoured them. "Like an excited boy reads a note from his girl," wrote one poet, "that's how we read the papers today."[15] And beyond glasnost lay democratization and a new parliament with real powers, chosen in competitive elections. When those elections occurred in 1989, dozens of leading communists were rejected at the polls. In foreign affairs, Gorbachev moved to end the cold war by making unilateral cuts in Soviet military forces, engaging in arms control negotiations with the United States, and refusing to intervene as communist governments in Eastern Europe were overthrown.

But almost nothing worked out as Gorbachev had anticipated. Far from strengthening socialism and reviving a stagnant Soviet Union, the reforms led to its further weakening and collapse. In a dramatic contrast with China's booming economy, the Soviet Union spun into a sharp decline as its planned economy was dismantled before a functioning market-based system could emerge. Inflation mounted; consumer goods were in short supply, and ration coupons reappeared; many feared the loss of their jobs. Unlike Chinese peasants, few Soviet farmers were willing to risk the jump into private farming, and few foreign investors found the Soviet Union a tempting place to do business.

Furthermore, the new freedoms provoked demands that went far beyond what Gorbachev had intended. A democracy movement of unofficial groups and parties now sprang to life, many of them seeking a full multiparty democracy and a market-based economy. They were joined by independent labor unions, which actually went on strike, something unheard of in the "workers' state." Most corrosively, a multitude of nationalist movements used the new freedoms to insist on greater autonomy, or even independence, from the Soviet Union. In the face of these mounting demands, Gorbachev resolutely refused to use force to crush the protesters, another sharp contrast with the Chinese experience.

Events in Eastern Europe now intersected with those in the Soviet Union. Gorbachev's reforms had lit a fuse in these Soviet satellites, where communism had been imposed and maintained from outside. If the USSR could practice glasnost and hold competitive elections, why not Eastern Europe as well? This was the background for the "miracle year" of 1989. Massive demonstrations, last-minute efforts at reforms, the breaching of the Berlin Wall, the surfacing of new political groups—all of this and more quickly overwhelmed the highly unpopular communist regimes of Poland, Hungary, East Germany, Bulgaria, Czechoslovakia, and Romania, which were quickly swept away. This success then emboldened nationalists and democrats in the Soviet Union. If communism had been overthrown in Eastern Europe, perhaps it could be overthrown in the USSR as well. Soviet conservatives and patriots, however, were outraged. To them, Gorbachev had stood idly by while the political gains of World War II, for which the Soviet Union had paid in rivers of blood, vanished before their eyes. It was nothing less than treason.

A brief and unsuccessful attempt to restore the old order through a military coup in August 1991 triggered the end of the Soviet Union and its communist regime. From the wreckage there emerged fifteen new and independent states, following the internal political divisions of the USSR (see Map 21.4).

The Soviet collapse represented a unique phenomenon in the world of the late twentieth century. Simultaneously, the world's largest state and its last territorial empire vanished; the world's first Communist Party disintegrated; a powerful command economy broke down; an official socialist ideology was repudiated; and a forty-five-year global struggle between the East and the West ended. In Europe, Germany was reunited, and a number of former communist states joined NATO and the European Union, ending the division of the continent. At least for the moment, capitalism and democracy seemed to triumph over socialism and authoritarian governments. In many places, the end of communism allowed simmering ethnic tensions to explode into open conflict. Beyond the disintegration of the Soviet Union, both Yugoslavia and Czechoslovakia fragmented, the former amid terrible violence and the latter peacefully. Chechens in Russia, Abkhazians in Georgia, Russians in the Baltic states

Map 21.4 The Collapse of the Soviet Empire
Soviet control over its Eastern European dependencies vanished as those countries threw off their communist governments in 1989. Then, in 1991, the Soviet Union itself disintegrated into fifteen separate states, none of them governed by communist parties.

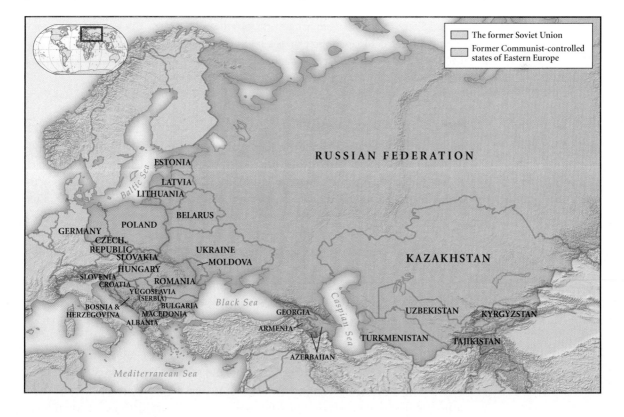

and Ukraine, Tibetans and Uighurs in China—all of these minorities found themselves in opposition to the states in which they lived.

As the twenty-first century dawned, the communist world had shrunk considerably from its high point just three decades earlier. In the Soviet Union and Eastern Europe, communism had disappeared entirely as the governing authority and dominant ideology. China had largely abandoned its communist economic policies as a market economy took shape. Like China, Vietnam and Laos remained officially communist, even while they pursued Chinese-style reforms, though more cautiously. Even Cuba, which was beset by economic crisis in the 1990s after massive Soviet subsidies ended, allowed small businesses, private food markets, and tourism to grow, while harshly suppressing opposition political groups. By 2011 a growing cultural openness allowed films highly critical of Cuban society to be produced and shown publically, including one, "Juan of the Dead," that portrayed Cuba as a country of dazed zombies. Cubans were increasingly engaged in private enterprise, able to buy and sell cars and houses, and enthusiastically embracing mobile phones and computers. An impoverished North Korea remained the most unreformed and repressive of the remaining communist countries.

International tensions born of communism remained only in East Asia and the Caribbean. North Korea's threat to develop nuclear weapons posed a serious international issue. Continuing tension between China and Taiwan as well as between the United States and Cuba were hangovers from the cold war era. But either as a primary source of international conflict or as a compelling path to modernity and social justice, communism was effectively dead. The brief communist era in world history had ended.

LearningCurve
bedfordstmartins.com
/strayer/LC

⊥⊥ Reflections: To Judge or Not to Judge

Should historians or students of history make moral judgments about the people and events they study? On the one hand, some would argue, scholars do well to act as detached and objective observers of the human experience. The task is to describe what happened and to explain why things turned out as they did. Whether we approve or condemn the outcomes of the historical process is, in this view, beside the point. On the other hand, all of us, scholars and students alike, stand somewhere. We are members of particular cultures; we have values and outlooks on the world that inevitably affect the way we think about the past. Perhaps it is better to recognize and acknowledge these limitations than to pretend to some unattainable objectivity that places us above it all. Furthermore, making judgments is a way of caring about the past, of affirming our continuing relationship with those who have gone before us.

The question of making judgments arises strongly in any examination of the communist phenomenon. In a United States lacking a major socialist tradition, sometimes saying anything positive about communism or even noting its appeal to millions of people has brought charges of whitewashing its crimes. Within the communist world, even modest criticism was usually regarded as counterrevolutionary and was largely forbidden and harshly punished. Certainly few observers were neutral in their assessment of the communist experiment.

Were the Russian and Chinese revolutions a blow for human freedom and a cry for justice on the part of oppressed people, or did they simply replace one tyranny with another? Was Stalinism a successful effort to industrialize a backward country or a ferocious assault on its moral and social fabric? Did Chinese reforms of the late twentieth century represent a return to sensible policies of modernization, a continued denial of basic democratic rights, or an opening to capitalist inequalities, corruption, and acquisitiveness? Passionate debate continues on all of these questions.

Communism, like many human projects, has been an ambiguous enterprise. On the one hand, communism brought hope to millions by addressing the manifest injustices of the past; by providing new opportunities for women, workers, and peasants; by promoting rapid industrial development; and by ending Western domination. On the other hand, communism was responsible for mountains of crimes—millions killed and wrongly imprisoned; massive famines partly caused by radical policies; human rights violated on an enormous scale; lives uprooted and distorted by efforts to achieve the impossible.

Studying communism challenges our inclination to want definitive answers and clear moral judgments. Can we hold contradictory elements in some kind of tension? Can we affirm our own values while acknowledging the ambiguities of life, both past and present? Doing so is arguably among the essential tasks of growing up and achieving a measure of intellectual maturity. In that undertaking, history can be helpful.

Second Thoughts

What's the Significance?

Russian Revolution (1917), 1039–42
Bolsheviks/Lenin, 1040–41
Guomindang, 1042
Mao Zedong, 1042–43
Chinese Revolution, 1043–45
Stalin, 1045; 1047–50
building socialism, 1045–51
Zhenotdel, 1046–47
collectivization, 1048

Cultural Revolution, 1051
Great Purges/Terror, 1052–53
Anna Dubova, 1052–53
Cuban missile crisis, 1056
Nikita Khrushchev, 1056–59
Deng Xiaoping, 1062–63
perestroika/glasnost, 1063
Mikhail Gorbachev, 1063–65

LearningCurve
Check what you know.
bedfordstmartins.com
/strayer/LC

Online Study Guide
bedfordstmartins.com
/highschool/strayer

Big Picture Questions

1. Why did the communist experiment, which was committed to equality, abundance, and a humane socialism, generate such oppressive, brutal, and totalitarian regimes and failed economies?

2. In what ways did communism have a global impact beyond those countries that were governed by communist parties?
3. What was the global significance of the cold war?
4. "The end of communism was as revolutionary as its beginning." Do you agree with this statement?
5. **Looking Back:** What was distinctive about twentieth-century communist industrialization and modernization compared to the same processes in the West a century earlier?

For Web sites and additional documents related to this chapter, see **Make History** at bedfordstmartins.com /highschool/strayer.

Next Steps: For Further Study

Archie Brown, *The Rise and Fall of Communism* (2009). A global overview of the communist phenomenon in the twentieth century by a respected scholar.

Jung Chang, *Wild Swans* (2004). A compelling view of twentieth-century Chinese history through the eyes of three generations of women in a single family.

Timothy Check, *Mao Zedong and China's Revolutions* (2002). A collection of documents about the Chinese Revolution and a fine introduction to the life of Mao.

John L. Gaddis, *The Cold War: A New History* (2005). An overview by one of the most highly regarded historians of the cold war.

Peter Kenez, *A History of the Soviet Union from the Beginning to the End* (1999). A thoughtful overview of the entire Soviet experience.

Robert Strayer, *The Communist Experiment* (2007). A comparative study of Soviet and Chinese communism.

"Mao Zedong Reference Archive," http://www.marxists.org/reference/archive/mao. A Web site offering the translated writings of Mao, including poetry and some images.

"Soviet Archives Exhibit," http://www.ibiblio.org/expo/soviet.exhibit/entrance.html. A rich Web site from the Library of Congress, focusing on the operation of the Soviet system and relations with the United States.

Documents

Considering the Evidence:
Experiencing Stalinism

For the Soviet Union, the formative period in establishing communism encompassed the years of Joseph Stalin's rule (1929–1953). Born in Georgia in 1878, rather than in Russia itself, the young Stalin grew up with a brutal and abusive father, trained for the priesthood as a young man, but slowly gravitated toward the emerging revolutionary movement of the time. He subsequently joined the Bolsheviks, led by Lenin, though he played only a modest role in the Russian Revolution of 1917. After Lenin's death in 1924, Stalin rose to the dominant position in the Communist Party amid a long and bitter struggle among the Bolsheviks. By 1929 he had consolidated his authority and exercised enormous personal power until his death in 1953.

To Stalin and the Soviet leadership, the 1930s was a time of "building socialism." Undertaking that gigantic task meant upheaval on an enormous scale, offering undreamed of opportunities for some and disruption and trauma beyond imagination for others. The documents that follow allow us to see something of the Stalinist vision for the country as well as to gain some insight into the lives of ordinary people — peasants, workers, women, ethnic minorities, the young, and the upwardly mobile — as they experienced what historians have come to call simply "Stalinism."

Document 21.1

Stalin on Stalinism

In January 1933, Stalin appeared before a group of high-ranking party officials to give a report on the achievements of the country's first five-year plan for overall development. The years encompassed by that plan, roughly 1928–1932, coincided with Stalin's rise to the position of supreme leader within the governing Communist Party of the Soviet Union.

- What larger goals for the country underlay Stalin's report? Why did he believe those goals had to be achieved so rapidly?

- To what indications of success did Stalin point? Which of these claims do you find most and least credible?

- What criticisms of Stalin's policies can you infer from the document?

- What do you think Stalin meant when he referred to the "world-wide historic significance" of the Soviet Union's achievement? Keep in mind what was happening in the capitalist world at the time.

JOSEPH STALIN

The Results of the First Five-Year Plan

1933

The fundamental task of the five-year plan was to convert the U.S.S.R. . . . into an industrial and powerful country, fully self-reliant and independent of the caprices of world capitalism, . . . to completely oust the capitalist elements, to widen the front of socialist forms of economy, and to create the economic basis for the abolition of classes in the U.S.S.R., for the building of a socialist society. . . .

Let us pass now to the results of the fulfillment of the five-year plan. . . .

We did not have an iron and steel industry, the basis for the industrialization of the country. Now we have one.

[Stalin follows with a long list of new industries developed during the first five-year plan: tractors, automobiles, machine tools, chemicals, agricultural machinery, electric power, oil and coal, metals.]

And we have not only created these new great industries, but have created them on a scale and in dimensions that eclipse . . . European industry.

And as a result of all this the capitalist elements have been completely and irrevocably ousted from industry, and socialist industry has become the sole form of industry in the U.S.S.R. . . .

Finally, as a result of all this the Soviet Union has been converted from a weak country, unprepared for defense, into a country mighty in defense . . . ,

a country capable of producing on a mass scale all modern means of defense and of equipping its army with them in the event of an attack from abroad.

We are told: This is all very well; many new factories have been built, and the foundations for industrialization have been laid; but it would have been far better . . . to produce more cotton fabrics, shoes, clothing, and other goods for mass consumption. . . . Then we would now have more cotton fabrics, shoes, and clothing. But we would not have a tractor industry or an automobile industry; we would not have anything like a big iron and steel industry; we would not have metal for the manufacture of machinery—and we would remain unarmed while encircled by capitalist countries armed with modern technique. . . .

It was necessary to urge forward a country which was a hundred years behindhand and which was faced with mortal danger because of its backwardness. . . .

The five-year plan in the sphere of agriculture was a five-year plan of collectivization. . . . [I]t was necessary in addition to industrialization, to pass from small, individual peasant farming to . . . large collective farms, equipped with all the modern implements of highly developed agriculture, and to cover unoccupied land with model state farms. . . .

The Party has succeeded in routing the kulaks° as a class, although they have not yet been dealt the

---

Source: Joseph Stalin, "The Results of the First Five-Year Plan," *Pravda*, January 10, 1933.

°**kulaks:** relatively rich peasants.

final blow; the laboring peasants have been emancipated from kulak bondage and exploitation, and the Soviet regime has been given a firm economic basis in the countryside, the basis of collective farming.

In our country, the workers have long forgotten unemployment. . . . Look at the capitalist countries: what horrors result there from unemployment! There are now no less than 30–40 million unemployed in those countries. . . .

The same thing must be said of the peasants. . . . It has brought them into the collective farms and

placed them in a secure position. It has thus eliminated the possibility of the differentiation of the peasantry into exploiters—kulaks—and exploited—poor peasants—and abolished destitution in the countryside. . . . Now the peasant is in a position of security, a member of a collective farm which has at its disposal tractors, agricultural machinery, seed funds, reserve funds. . . .

[W]e have achieved such important successes as to evoke admiration among the working class all over the world; we have achieved a victory that is truly of world-wide historic significance.

Document 21.2

Living through Collectivization

For Russian peasants, and those of other nationalities as well, the chief experience of Stalinism was collectivization—the enforced bringing together of many small-scale family farms into much larger collective farms called *kolhozy*. Thus private ownership of land was largely ended, except for some small plots, which peasants could till individually. That process generally began with the arrival of outside "agitators" or Community Party officials who sought to persuade, or if necessary to force, the villagers to enter the *kolhoz*. They divided peasants (*muzhiks*) into class categories: rich peasants (*kulaks*) were to be excluded from the collective farms as incipient capitalists; poor (*bedniak*) and middle (*seredniak*) peasants were expected to join.

One witness to this process was Maurice Hindus, a Russian-born American writer who returned to his country of origin in 1929, when Soviet collectivization was beginning in earnest. There he roamed on foot around the countryside, recording conversations with those he met. The extract that follows begins with a letter he received from "Nadya," a young activist who was among many sent to the rural areas to initiate collectivization. Then Hindus records a discussion between peasants objecting to collectivization and an "agitator," like Nadya, seeking to convince them of its benefits.

■ How do Nadya and the "agitator" understand collectivization and their role in this process? Why do they believe that it was so critical to building socialism?

■ How do village peasants view collectivization? On what grounds do they object to it? How might they view the role of the agitators?

■ How did the peasants understand themselves and their village community? How did they respond to the communists' insistence on defining them in rigid class terms? Why do you think they finally entered the collective farms?

■ Why were Stalin and the Communist Party so insistent on destroying the *kulaks*?

MAURICE HINDUS

Red Bread

1931

Nadya Speaks

I am off in villages with a group of other brigadiers organizing *kolhozy*. It is a tremendous job, but we are making amazing progress. It would do you worlds of good to be with us and watch us draw the stubborn peasant into collectivization. Contrary to all your affirmations and prophecies, our *muzhik* is yielding to persuasion. He is joining the *kolhozy*, and I am confident that in time not a peasant will remain on his own land. We shall yet smash the last vestiges of capitalism and forever rid ourselves of exploitation. . . . The very air here is afire with a new spirit and a new energy.

The Peasants Speak

"There was a time,". . . began Lukyan, who had been a blacksmith, . . . "when we were just neighbors in this village. We quarreled, we fooled, sometimes we cheated one another. But we were neighbors. Now we are *bedniaks, seredniaks, koolacks.*° I am a *seredniak,* Boris here is a *bedniak,* and Nisko is a *koolack,* and we are supposed to have a class war—pull each other's hair or tickle each other on the toes, eh? One against the other, you understand? . . .

"But it is other things that worry us," continued the flat-faced *muzhik* . . . , "it is the *kolhoz.* That, citizen, is a serious matter—the most serious we have ever encountered. Who ever heard of such a thing— to give up our land and our cows and our horses

and our tools and our farm buildings, to work all the time and divide everything with others? Nowadays members of the same family get in each other's way and quarrel and fight, and here we, strangers, are supposed to be like one family. . . .

"We won't even be sure," someone else continued the lament, "of having enough bread to eat. Now, however poor we may be, we have our own rye and our own potatoes and our own cucumbers and our own milk. We know we won't starve. But in the *kolhoz,* no more potatoes of our own, no more anything of our own. Everything will be rationed out by orders; we shall be like mere *batraks*° on the landlord's estates in the old days. Serfdom—that is what it is—and who wants to be a serf?" . . .

"Dark-minded beasts we may be," wailed another *muzhik.* . . . "We are not learned; we are not wise. But a little self-respect we have, and we like the feeling of independence. Today we feel like working, and we work; tomorrow we feel like lying down, and we lie down; the next day we feel like going to town, and we go to town. We do as we please. But in the *kolhoz,* brother, it is do-as-you-are-told, like a horse—go this way and that, and don't dare turn off the road or you get it hard, a stroke or two of the whip on bare flesh. . . . We'll just wither away on the socialist farm, like grass torn out by the roots." . . .

The Communist Party Official Speaks

At this point a new visitor arrived, a tall youth, in boots, in a black blouse and with a shaved head. . . .

°**koolacks:** variant spelling of *kulaks.*

Source: Maurice Hindus, *Red Bread: Collectivization in a Russian Village* (Bloomington: Indiana University Press, 1988), 1, 22–34.

°**batraks:** hired help.

A stranger in the village, he was the organizer of the *kolhoz*, therefore a person of stern importance. . . .

"Everything is possible, grandfather, if we all pool our resources and our powers together," replied the visitor.

More laughter and more derisive comment. . . .

"Tell me, you wretched people, what hope is there for you if you remain on individual pieces of land? Think, and don't interrupt. . . . From year to year as you increase in population you divide and subdivide your strips of land. You cannot even use machinery on your land because no machine man ever made could stand the rough ridges that the strip system creates. You will have to work in your own old way and stew in your old misery. Don't you see that under your present system there is nothing ahead of you but ruin and starvation? . . . You do not think of a future, often, twenty, a hundred years from now, and we do. That's the difference between you and us. The coming generations mean nothing to you. Else you would see a real deliverance in the *kolhoz*, where you will work with machinery in a modern organized way, with the best seeds obtainable and under the direction of experts. . . . Isn't it about time you stopped thinking each one for him-self, for his own piggish hide? You *koolacks* of course will never become reconciled to a new order. You love to fatten on other people's blood. But we know how to deal with you. We'll wipe you off the face of the earth, even as we have the capitalists in the city. Make no mistake about our intentions and our powers. We shan't allow you to profit from the weakness of the *bedniak*. And we shan't allow you to poison his mind, either! Enough. But the others here— you *bedniaks* and you *seredniaks*—what have you gained from this stiff-necked individualism of yours? What? Look at yourselves, at your homes— mud, squalor, fleas, bedbugs, cockroaches, *lapti*.° Are you sorry to let these go? Oh, we know you *muzhiks*—too well. . . . You can whine eloquently and pitifully. . . . But we know you—you cannot fool us. We have grown hardened to your wails. Remember that. Cry all you want to, curse all you want to. You won't hurt us, and I warn you that we shan't desist. We shall continue our campaign for the *kolhozy* until we have won our goal and made you free citizens in a free land."

———————

°**lapti:** cheap wooden shoes.

Document 21.3

Living through Industrialization

Another major feature of the Stalinist era was rapid state-controlled industrialization. "We are fifty to a hundred years behind the advanced countries," declared Stalin. "We must make good this distance in ten years. Either we shall do it or we shall go under." During the 1930s, that enormous process brought huge numbers of peasants from the countryside to the cities. Many found their way to new and distant industrial sites such as Magnitogorsk—a huge new iron and steel enterprise, and millions entered recently established technical institutes where they learned new skills and nurtured new ambitions. The brief excerpts in Document 21.3 disclose the voices of some of these workers as they celebrated the new possibilities and lamented the disappointments and injustices of Stalinist industrialization. These sources come from letters written to newspapers or to high government officials, from private letters and diaries, or from reports filed by party officials based on what they had heard in the factories.

- In what respects did Soviet workers benefit from Stalinist industrialization?

- What criticisms were voiced in these extracts? Do they represent fundamental opposition to the idea of socialism or disappointments in how it was implemented?

- Which of these selections do you find most credible?

- Through its control of education and the media, the Stalinist regime sought to instill a single view of the world in its citizens. Based on these selections, to what extent had they succeeded or failed?

Personal Accounts of Soviet Industrialization
1930s

Letter in a Newspaper from a Tatar Electrician

I am a Tatar.° . . . [I]n old tsarist Russia, we weren't even considered people. We couldn't even dream about education, or getting a job in a state enterprise. And now I'm a citizen of the USSR. Like all citizens, I have the right to a job, to education, to leisure. I can elect and be elected to the soviet [legislative council]. Is this not an indication of the supreme achievements of our country? . . .

Two years ago I worked as the chairman of a village soviet in the Tatar republic. I was the first person there to enter the kolhoz and then I led the collectivization campaign. Collective farming is flourishing with each year in the Tatar republic.

In 1931 I came to Magnitogorsk. From a common laborer I have turned into a skilled worker. I was elected a member of the city soviet. As a deputy, every day I receive workers who have questions or need help. I listen to each one like to my own brother, and try to do what is necessary to make each one satisfied.

°**Tatar:** a Turkic ethnic group.

Source: First and second selections: Stephen Kotkin, *Magnetic Mountain* (Berkeley: University of California Press, 1995), 221–22, 349–50; third through seventh selections: Sarah Davies, *Popular Opinion in Stalin's Russia* (New York: Cambridge University Press, 1997), 39, 72, 134–35, 139, 173–74.

I live in a country where one feels like living and learning. And if the enemy should attack this country, I will sacrifice my life in order to destroy the enemy and save my country.

Newspaper Commentary by an Engineer, 1938

Soon it will be seven years that I'm working in Magnitogorsk. With my own eyes I've seen the pulsating, creative life of the builders of the Magnitogorsk giant. I myself have taken an active part in this construction with great enthusiasm. Our joy was great when we obtained the first Magnitogorsk steel from the wonderful open-hearth ovens. At the time there was no greater happiness for me than working in the open-hearth shop. . . . Here I enriched my theoretical knowledge and picked up practical habits . . . of work. Here as well I grew politically, acquired good experience in public-political work. I came to Magnitogorsk nonparty. The party organization . . . accepted me into a group of sympathizers. Not long ago I entered the ranks of the Leninist-Stalinist [communist] party. . . . I love my hometown Magnitka with all my heart. I consider my work at the Magnitogorsk factory to be a special honor and high trust shown to me, a Soviet engineer, by the country.

Letter to a Soviet Official from a Worker, 1938

In fact, there's been twenty years of our [Soviet] power. Fifteen to sixteen of these have been peaceful construction. . . . The people struggled with zeal, overcame difficulties. Socialism has been built in the main. As we embark on the third five-year plan we shout at meetings, congresses, and in newspapers "Hurray, we have reached a happy, joyful life!" However, incidentally, if one is to be honest, those shouts are mechanical, made from habit, pumped by social organizations. The ordinary person makes such speeches like a street newspaper-seller. In fact, in his heart, when he comes home, this bawler, eulogist, will agree with his family, his wife who reproaches him that today she has been torturing herself in queues and did not get anything—there are no suits, no coats, no meat, no butter.

Letter from a Student to His Teacher, No Date

I worked at a factory for five years. Now I'll have to leave my studies at the institute. Who will study? Very talented Lomonosovs° and the sons of Soviet rulers, since they have the highest posts and are the best paid. In this way education will be available only to the highest strata (a sort of nobility), while for the lowest strata, the laboring people, the doors will be closed.

Two Comments from Factory Workers Found in Soviet Archives, 1930s

What is there to say about the successes of Soviet power? It's lies. The newspapers cover up the real state of things. I am a worker, wear torn clothes, my four children go to school half-starving, in rags. I, an

---

°**Lomonosovs:** i.e., brilliant students (Mikhal Lomonosov, 1711–1765, was a Russian scientist and writer).

honest worker, am a visible example of what Soviet power has given the workers in the last twenty years.

How can we liquidate classes, if new classes have developed here, with the only difference being that they are not called classes? Now there are the same parasites who live at the expense of others. The worker produces and at the same time works for many people who live off him. From the example of our factory it is clear that there is a huge apparat of factory administrators, where idlers sit. There are many administrative workers who travel about in cars and get three to four times more than the worker. These people live in the best conditions and live at the expense of the labor of the working class.

Entry from a Worker's Diary, 1936

[T]he portraits of party leaders are now displayed the same way icons used to be: a round portrait framed and attached to a pole. Very convenient, hoist it onto your shoulder and you're on your way. And all these preparations are just like what people used to do before church holidays....They had their own activists then, we have ours now. Different paths, the same old folderol.

Comment from an Anonymous Communist in Soviet Archives, 1938

Do you not think that comrade Stalin's name has begun to be very much abused? ....Everything is Stalin, Stalin, Stalin. You only have to listen to a radio program about our achievements, and every fifth or tenth word will be the name of comrade Stalin. In the end this sacred and beloved name—Stalin—may make so much noise in people's heads that it is very possible that it will have the opposite effect.

Document 21.4

Living through the Terror

More than anything else, it was the Terror—sometimes called the Great Purges—that came to define Stalinism as a distinctive phenomenon in the history of Soviet communism (see p. 1052). Millions of people were caught up in this vast process of identifying and eliminating so-called enemies of the people, many of them loyal communist citizens. The three selections that follow, all from women, provide a small taste of what it meant to experience arrest and interrogation, life in the camps of the Gulag, and the agony of those left behind waiting for loved ones who had vanished into the Terror.

- What might you infer from these selections about the purposes of the Terror, the means by which it was implemented, and its likely outcomes, whether intended or not?

- Many innocent people who were arrested believed that others were guilty as charged, while in their own case a mistake had been made. How might you account for this widespread response to the Terror?

- In what different ways did people experience the Stalinist Terror? What do you think motivated each of these women who wrote about it?

- The extent of the Terror did not become widely known until well after Stalin's death in 1953. How do you imagine that knowledge was used by critics of communism? What impact might it have had on those who had ardently believed in the possibilities of a socialist future?

- How might you compare the Soviet Terror and the Nazi Holocaust?

Personal Accounts of the Terror
1930s

[The first excerpt is from the memoirs of Irina Kakhovskaya, an ardent revolutionary, though not a party member, who was arrested in 1937 and spent seventeen years either in prison or in a labor camp. Here she describes her arrest and interrogation.]

Early on the morning of February 8, 1937, a large group of men appeared at the door of our quiet apartment in Ufa. We were shown a search warrant and warrants for our arrest. The search was carried out in violent, pogrom-like fashion and lasted all day. Books went pouring down from the shelves; letters and papers, out of boxes. They tapped the walls

Source: First selection: Irina Kakhovskaya, "Our Fate" in *An End to Silence*, translated by George Saunders and edited by Stephen Cohen (New York: Norton, 1982), 81–90; second selection: Eugenia Semyonovna Ginzburg, *Journey into the Whirlwind* (New York: Harcourt, Brace Jovanovich, 1967), 366–67; third selection: Anna Akhmatova, *Poems*, selected and translated by Lyn Coffin (New York: Norton, 1983), 82, 85.

and, when they encountered hollow spots, removed the bricks. Everything was covered with dust and pieces of brick....

At the prison everything was aimed at breaking prisoners' spirits immediately, intimidating and stupefying them, making them feel that they were no longer human, but "enemies of the people," against whom everything was permitted. All elementary human needs were disregarded (light, air, food, rest, medical care, warmth, toilet facilities)....

In the tiny, damp, cold, half-lit cell were a bunk and a half bunk. The bunk was for the prisoner under investigation and on the half bunk, their legs drawn up, the voluntary victims, the informers from among the common criminals, huddled together. Their duty was never to let their neighbor out of their sight, never to let the politicals communicate with one another ... and above all to prevent the politicals from committing suicide....The air was fouled by the huge wooden latrine bucket....

The interrogation began on the very first night.... Using threats, endearments, promises and enigmatic hints, they tried to confuse, wear down, frighten, and break the will of each individual, who was kept totally isolated from his or her comrades. . . . Later stools were removed and the victim had to simply stand for hours on end. . . .

At first it seemed that the whole thing was a tremendous and terrible misunderstanding, that it was our duty to clear it up. . . . But it soon became apparent that what was involved was deliberate ill will and the most cynical possible approach to the truth. . . .

In the interrogation sessions, I now had several investigators in a row, and the "conveyor belt" questioning would go on for six days and nights on end. . . . Exhaustion reached the ultimate limit. The brain, inadequately supplied with blood, began to misfunction. . . . "Sign! We won't bother you anymore. We'll give you a quiet cell and a pillow and you can sleep. . . ." That was how the investigator would try to bribe a person who was completely debilitated and stupefied from lack of sleep.

Each of us fought alone to keep an honest name and save the honor of our friends, although it would have been far easier to die than to endure this hell month after month. Nevertheless the accused remained strong in spirit and, apart from the unfortunate Mayorov, not one real revolutionary did they manage to break.

[The second selection comes from the memoirs of Eugenia Ginsberg, a woman who survived many years in perhaps the most notorious of the gulag camps — Kolyma in the frigid northeastern corner of the Soviet Union. In this selection, Ginsberg recounts an ordinary day in the camps.]

The work to which I was assigned . . . went by the imposing name of "land improvement." We set out before dawn and marched in ranks of five for about three miles, to the accompaniment of shouts from the guards and bad language from the common criminals who were included in our party as a punishment for some misdeed or other. In time we reached a bleak, open field where our leader, another common criminal called Senka — a disgusting type who preyed on the other prisoners and made no bones about offering a pair of warm breeches in return for an hour's "fun and games" — handed out picks and iron spades with which we attacked the frozen soil of Kolyma until one in the afternoon. I cannot remember, and perhaps I never knew, the rational purpose this "improvement" was supposed to serve. I only remember the ferocious wind, the forty-degree frost, the appalling weight of the pick, and the wild, irregular thumping of one's heart. At one o'clock we were marched back for dinner. More stumbling in and out of snowdrifts, more shouts and threats from the guards whenever we fell out of line. Back in the camp we received our longed-for piece of bread and soup and were allowed half an hour in which to huddle around the stove in the hope of absorbing enough warmth to last us halfway back to the field. After we had toiled again with our picks and spades till late in the evening, Senka would come and survey what we had done and abuse us for not doing more. How could the assignment ever be completed if we spoiled women fulfilled only thirty percent of the norm? . . . Finally a night's rest, full of nightmares, and the dreaded banging of a hammer on an iron rail which was the signal for a new day to begin.

[The third selection is from the poetry of Anna Akhmatova, probably Russia's most famous modern poet. In this poem, "Requiem," Akhmatova writes passionately about endlessly standing in line, either seeking information about her imprisoned son or trying to send him parcels, an experience that paralleled that of countless other mothers and wives during the Terror.]

In the awful years of Yezhovian horror,° I spent seventeen months standing in line in front of various prisons in Leningrad. One day someone "recognized" me. Then a woman with blue lips, who was standing behind me, and who, of course, had never heard my name, came out of the stupor which typified all of us, and whispered into my ear (everyone there spoke only in whispers):

— Can you describe this?

°**Yezhovian horror:** i.e., the Terror (Nikolay Yezhov, 1895–1939, a communist official, administered the most severe stage of the purges).

And I said:
—I can.
Then something like a fleeting smile passed over
what once had been her face.

For months I've filled the air with pleas,
Trying to call you back.
I've thrown myself at the hangman's knees,
You are my son and my rack. . . .
I've seen how a face can fall like a leaf,
How, from under the lids, terror peeks,

I've seen how suffering and grief
Etches hieroglyphs on cheeks,
How ash-blonde hair, from roots to tips,
Turns black and silver overnight.
How smiles wither on submissive lips,
And in a half-smile quivers fright.
Not only for myself do I pray,
But for those who stood in front and
    behind me,
In the bitter cold, on a hot July day
Under the red wall that stared blindly.

Using the Evidence:
Experiencing Stalinism

1. **Defending Stalinism:** Develop an argument that the fundamental goals of Stalinism (building socialism) were largely achieved during the 1930s.

2. **Criticizing Stalinism:** Develop an argument that genuine socialism was essentially betrayed or perverted by the developments of the Stalin era.

3. **Assessing change:** In what ways did the Stalin era represent a revolutionary transformation of Soviet society? In what ways did it continue older patterns of Russian history?

4. **Considering moral judgments:** Why do you think that historians have found it so difficult to write about the Stalin era without passing judgment on it? Does this represent a serious problem for scholars? Should students of the past seek to avoid moral judgments or is it an inevitable, perhaps even useful, part of the historian's craft?

Visual Sources

Considering the Evidence: Poster Art in Mao's China

" I wanted to be the girl in the poster when I was growing up. Every day I dressed up like that girl in a white cotton shirt with a red scarf around my neck, and I braided my hair in the same way. I liked the fact that she was surrounded by revolutionary martyrs whom I was taught to worship since kindergarten."[16] As things turned out, this young girl, Anchee Min, did become the subject of one of the many thousands of propaganda posters with which the Chinese communist government flooded the country during the thirty years or so following the Chinese Revolution of 1949.

In China, as in other communist countries, art served the state and the Communist Party. Nowhere was this more apparent than in these propaganda posters, which were found in homes, schools, workplaces, railway stations, and elsewhere. The artists who created these images were under the strict control of Communist Party officials and were expected to use their skills to depict the party's leaders and achievements favorably, even grandly. They were among the "engineers of the human soul" who were reshaping the consciousness of individuals and remaking their entire society. One young man, born in 1951, testified to the effectiveness of these posters: "They . . . were my signposts through life. They made sure we did not make mistakes. . . . [M]y life is reflected in them."[17]

The posters that follow illustrate the kind of society and people that the communist leadership sought to create during the years that Mao Zedong ruled the country (1949–1976). The realities behind these images, of course, were often far different.

Coming to power in 1949, Chinese Communist Party leaders recognized that their enemies were by no means totally defeated. A persistent theme throughout the years of Mao's rule was an effort to eliminate those enemies or convert them to the communist cause. Spies, imperialist sympathizers, those infected with "bourgeois values" such as materialism and individualism, landowners or capitalists yearning for the old life—all of these had to be identified and confronted. So too were many "enemies" within the Communist Party itself, people who were suspected of opposition to the radical policies of Mao.

Some of these alleged enemies were killed, others imprisoned, and still others—
millions of them—were subjected to endless self-criticism sessions or sent
down to remote rural areas to "learn from the peasants." This need to demolish
the old society and old values is reflected in Visual Source 21.1, a poster from
1967, the height of the Cultural Revolution (see pp. 1050–51). Its caption reads:
"Destroy the Old World; Establish the New World."

■ Notice the various items beneath this young revolutionary's feet. What
  do they represent to the ardent revolutionaries seeking to "destroy the

Visual Source 21.1 Smashing the Old Society (Courtesy, University of
Westminster Poster Collection, London)

old world"? What groups of people were most likely to be affected by such efforts?

- What elements of a new order are being constructed in this image?

- How does the artist distinguish visually between the old and the new? Note the use of colors and the size of various figures and objects in the poster.

The centerpiece of Mao's plans for the vast Chinese countryside lay in the "people's communes." Established during the Great Leap Forward in the late 1950s, these were huge political and economic units intended to work the land more efficiently and collectively, to undertake large-scale projects such as building dams and irrigation systems, to create small-scale industries in the rural areas, and to promote local self-reliance. They also sought to move China more rapidly toward genuine communism by eliminating virtually every form of private property and emphasizing social equality and shared living. Commune members ate together in large dining halls, and children were cared for during the day in collective nurseries rather than by their own families. Visual Source 21.2, a poster created in 1958 under the title "The People's Communes Are Good," shows a highly idealized image of one such commune. See also the celebratory poster on page 1050.

- What appealing features of commune life and a communist future are illustrated in these posters? Notice the communal facilities for eating and washing clothes as well as the drill practice of a "people's militia" unit at the bottom of the picture.

- One of Mao's chief goals was to overcome the sharp division between industrial cities and the agricultural countryside. How is this effort illustrated in these posters?

The actual outcomes of the commune movement departed radically from their idealistic goals. Economic disruption occasioned by the creation of communes contributed a great deal to the enormous famines of the late 1950s, in which many millions perished. Furthermore, efforts to involve the peasants in iron and steel production through the creation of much-heralded "backyard furnaces," illustrated in this image, proved a failure. Most of the metal produced in these primitive facilities was of poor quality and essentially unusable. Such efforts further impoverished the rural areas as peasants were encouraged to contribute their pots, pans, and anything made of iron to the smelting furnaces.

Among the core values of Maoist communism were human mastery over the natural order, rapid industrialization, and the liberation of women from ancient limitations and oppressions in order to mobilize them for the task of building socialism. Visual Source 21.3, a 1975 poster, illustrates these values. Its caption reads: "Women Can Hold Up Half the Sky; Surely the Face of Nature Can Be Transformed."

我們心中最紅最紅的紅太陽毛主席和我們在一起

Visual Source 21.4 The Cult of Mao (IISH/Stefan R. Landsberger collections http:chineseposters.net) to almost all problems, both public and private. Many families erected "tablets of loyalty" to Mao, much like those previously devoted to ancestors. People made pilgrimages to "sacred shrines" associated with key events in his life. Schoolchildren began the day by chanting, "May Chairman Mao live ten thousand times ten thousand years."

And Mao was the centerpiece of endless posters. Visual Source 21.4, a poster created in 1968, portrays a familiar scene from the Cultural Revolution. Millions of young people, organized as Red Guards and committed to revolutionary action, flocked to Beijing, where enormous and ecstatic rallies allowed them to catch a glimpse of their beloved leader and to unite with him in the grand task of creating communism in China. The poster's caption reads: "The reddest, reddest, red sun in our heart, Chairman Mao, and us together."

■   What relationship between Mao and his young followers does the poster suggest? Why might some scholars have seen a quasi-religious dimension to that relationship?

■   How do you understand the significance of the "Red Treasured Book" of quotations from Mao, which the young people are waving?

■   How might you account for the unbridled enthusiasm expressed by the Red Guards? In this case, the poster portrays the realities of these rallies with considerable accuracy. Can you think of other comparable cases of such mass enthusiasm?

Using the Evidence: Poster Art in Mao's China

1. **Reading communist intentions:** Based on these visual sources, how would you describe the kind of society that the Chinese Communist Party sought to create in China during Mao's lifetime?

2. **Distinguishing image and reality:** Based on the narrative of this chapter and especially on what happened after Mao's death, assess the realities that lay behind these visual sources. To what extent do the posters accurately represent the successes of Maoist communism? What insights do they shed on its failures?

3. **Defining audience and appeal:** To whom do you think these posters were directed? What appeal might they have for the intended audience?

4. **Noticing change:** How could you use these posters to define the dramatic changes that transformed China since 1949? How might a traditional Chinese official from the nineteenth century respond to them?

5. **Assessing posters as evidence:** What are the strengths and limitations of poster art for understanding Chinese communism under Mao?

Chapter 21 Wrap Up

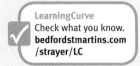

LearningCurve
Check what you know.
bedfordstmartins.com/strayer/LC

STEP ONE

The Word to Know: Ideology

The *Oxford English Dictionary* defines *ideology* as "a systematic scheme of ideas, usually relating to politics, economics, or society and forming the basis of action or policy; a set of beliefs governing conduct." Write a paragraph that assesses the impact of communism on the history of the twentieth century, including at least five events or processes that were shaped by global communism.

STEP TWO

The Rise and Fall of the Soviet Union

What were the economic, military, political, and cultural events that led to the rise and fall of communism in Russia/Soviet Union? Fill in the chart below to illustrate these changes, taking note as well of what did not change.

Revolution	Impetus for change	Effects of change	What stayed the same
February Revolution			
Bolshevik Revolution			
Collapse of the Soviet Union			

STEP THREE

Historical Interpretations of Stalin

Use the two documents that follow to show how the historical interpretation of Stalin changed over time.

1. Excerpt from Nikita Khrushchev, Speech before the Twentieth Party Congress of the Communist Party, 1956

Nikita Khrushchev, successor to Stalin and leader of the Soviet Union from 1955 to 1964), gave a speech to a secret session of the Community Party Congress in 1956. Read the excerpt and answer the question that follows.

"Fearing the future fate of the party and of the Soviet nation, V. I. Lenin made a completely correct characterization of Stalin, pointing out that it was necessary to consider the question of transferring Stalin from the position of Secretary General because of the fact that Stalin is excessively rude, that he does not have a proper attitude toward his comrades, that he is capricious, and abuses his power. . . .

"When we analyze the practice of Stalin in regard to the direction of the party and of the country, when we pause to consider everything which Stalin perpetrated, we must be convinced that Lenin's fears were justified. The negative characteristics of Stalin, which, in Lenin's time, were only incipient, transformed themselves during the last years into a grave abuse of power by Stalin, which caused untold harm to our party . . . Stalin acted not through persuasion, explanation, and patient cooperation with people, but by imposing his concepts and demanding absolute submission to his opinion. Whoever opposed this concept or tried to prove his viewpoint, and the correctness of his position — was doomed to removal from the leading collective and to subsequent moral and physical annihilation."

Source: *Congressional Record: Proceedings and Debates of the 84th Congress, 2nd Session* (May 22, 1956–June 11, 1956).

■ Question

How and why does Khrushchev question the legitimacy of Stalin's rule?

2. Excerpt from Mikhail Gorbachev, Speech to the Kremlin, 1987

Mikhail Gorbachev was the last leader of the Soviet Union, coming to power in 1985 and forced from his position with the dissolution of the Soviet Union in 1991. Gorbachev is most famous for his policies that led to an opening of freedoms for Soviet peoples.

"To remain faithful to historical truth, we have to see both Stalin's incontestable contribution to the struggle for socialism and the gross political errors and the abuses committed by him and those around him. Contrary to the assertions of our ideological opponents, the Stalin personality cult was certainly not inevitable. The process of restoring justice was not seen through to the end and was actually suspended in the middle of the 1960s. . . . The guilt of Stalin and his entourage before the party and the people for the wholesale repressive measures and acts of lawlessness is enormous and unforgiveable. This is a lesson for all generations."

Source: Philip Taubman, "Gorbachev Assails Crimes of Stalin, Lauds Khrushchev," *New York Times*, November 3, 1987.

■ Question

How does Gorbachev portray Stalin? What additional source would you want to help assess the changing historical interpretation of Stalin?

CHAPTER TWENTY-TWO

The End of Empire

The Global South on the Global Stage

1914–PRESENT

"During my lifetime I have dedicated myself to this struggle of the African people. I have fought against white domination, and I have fought against black domination. I have cherished the ideal of a democratic and free society in which all persons live together in harmony and with equal opportunity. It is an ideal which I hope to live for and to achieve. But, if need be, it is an ideal for which I am prepared to die."[1]

Nelson Mandela, South Africa's nationalist leader, first uttered these words in 1964 at his trial for treason, sabotage, and conspiracy to overthrow the apartheid government of his country. Convicted of those charges, he spent the next twenty-seven years in prison, sometimes working at hard labor in a stone quarry. Often the floor was his bed, and a bucket was his toilet. For many years, he was allowed one visitor a year for thirty minutes and permitted to write and receive one letter every six months. When he was finally released from prison in 1990 under growing domestic and international pressure, he concluded his first speech as a free person with the words originally spoken at his trial. Four years later, in 1994, South Africa held its first election in which blacks and whites alike were able to vote. The outcome of that election made Mandela the country's first black African president, and it linked South Africa to dozens of other countries all across Africa and Asia that had thrown off European rule or the control of white settlers during the second half of the twentieth century.

VARIOUSLY CALLED THE STRUGGLE FOR INDEPENDENCE OR DECOLONIZATION, that process carried an immense significance for the history

---

Independence and Development: In the eyes of most Asians and Africans, the struggle for national independence from European colonial rule was but a prelude to and prerequisite for the even greater struggle for modern development, symbolized here by some students in a computer lab of a small technical college. (© Anna Kari/In Pictures/Corbis) of the twentieth century. It marked a dramatic change in the world's political architecture, as nation-states triumphed over the empires that had structured much of the world's political life in the nineteenth and early twentieth centuries. It mobilized millions of people, thrusting them into political activity and sometimes into violence and warfare. Decolonization signaled the declining legitimacy of both empire and race as a credible basis for political or social life. It promised not only national freedom but also personal dignity, abundance, and opportunity.

What followed in the decades after independence was equally significant. Political, economic, and cultural experiments proliferated across these newly independent nations, which faced enormous challenges: the legacies of empire; their own deep divisions of language, ethnicity, religion, and class; their rapidly growing numbers; the competing demands of the capitalist West and the communist East; the difficult tasks of simultaneously building modern economies, stable politics, and coherent nations; and all of this in a world still shaped by the powerful economies and armies of the wealthy, already industrialized nations. The emergence of these new nations onto the world stage as independent and assertive actors has been a distinguishing feature of world history in this most recent century.

SEEKING THE MAIN POINT

In what ways did the experience of the "global south" during the past century register on the larger stage of world history?

Toward Freedom: Struggles for Independence

In 1900, European colonial empires in Africa and Asia appeared as permanent features of the world's political landscape. Well before the end of the twentieth century, they were gone. The first major breakthroughs occurred in Asia and the Middle East in the late 1940s, when the Philippines, India, Pakistan, Burma, Indonesia, Syria, Iraq, Jordan, and Israel achieved independence. The period from the mid-1950s through the mid-1970s was the age of African independence as colony after colony, more than fifty in total, emerged into what was then seen as the bright light of freedom.

The End of Empire in World History

■ **Comparison**

What was distinctive about the end of Europe's African and Asian empires compared to other cases of imperial disintegration?

At one level, this vast process was but the latest case of imperial dissolution, a fate that had overtaken earlier empires, including those of the Assyrians, Romans, Arabs, and Mongols. But never before had the end of empire been so associated with the mobilization of the masses around a nationalist ideology; nor had these earlier cases generated a plethora of nation-states, each claiming an equal place in a world of nation-states. More comparable perhaps was that first decolonization, in which the European colonies in the Americas threw off British, French, Spanish, or Portuguese rule during the late eighteenth and early nineteenth centuries (see Chapter 16). Like their earlier counterparts, the new nations of the twentieth century claimed an international status equivalent to that of their former rulers. In the Americas, however, many of the colonized people were themselves of European origin, sharing much of their culture with their colonial rulers. In that respect, the African and Asian struggles of the twentieth century were very different, for they not only asserted political independence but also

A Map of Time

1915	Gandhi returns to India from South Africa
1923–1938	Turkey's secular modernization initiated under Kemal Ataturk
1928	Muslim Brotherhood established in Egypt
1947	Independence of India/Pakistan
1948	Establishment of state of Israel; apartheid formally established in South Africa
1949	Independence of Indonesia; communist victory in China
1955	Bandung Conference of nonaligned nations
1957–1975	Independence of African countries
1959	Cuban revolution
1960–1970s	Wave of military coups in Africa and Latin America
1967	Six-day Arab/Israeli war
1973	OPEC oil embargo
1979	Revolution in Iran
1980s–1990s	Growth of democratic movements and governments in Africa and Latin America
1994	End of apartheid in South Africa; genocide in Rwanda
2011	Arab Spring in the Middle East

affirmed the vitality of their cultures, which had been submerged and denigrated during the colonial era.

The twentieth century witnessed the demise of many empires. The Austrian and Ottoman empires collapsed following World War I, giving rise to a number of new states in Europe and the Middle East. The Russian Empire also unraveled, although it was soon reassembled under the auspices of the Soviet Union. World War II ended the German and Japanese empires. African and Asian movements for independence shared with these other end-of-empire stories the ideal of national self-determination. This novel idea—that humankind was naturally divided into distinct peoples or nations, each of which deserved an independent state of its own—was loudly proclaimed by the winning side of both world wars. It gained an Afro-Asian following in the twentieth century and rendered empire illegitimate in the eyes of growing numbers of people.

Empires without territory, such as the powerful influence that the United States exercised in Latin America, likewise came under attack from highly nationalist governments. An intrusive U.S. presence was certainly one factor stimulating the Mexican Revolution, which began in 1910. One of the outcomes of that upheaval was

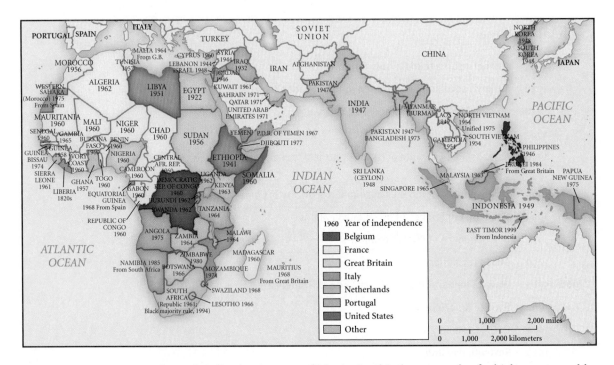

Map 22.1 The End of Empire in Africa and Asia
In the second half of the twentieth century, under pressure from nationalist movements, Europe's Asian and African empires dissolved into dozens of new independent states.

the nationalization in 1937 of Mexico's oil industry, much of which was owned by American and British investors. Similar actions accompanied Cuba's revolution of 1959–1960 and also occurred in other places throughout Latin America and elsewhere. National self-determination and freedom from Soviet control likewise lay behind the eastern European revolutions of 1989 as well. The disintegration of the Soviet Union itself in 1991 brought to an inglorious end the last of the major territorial empires of the twentieth century and the birth of fifteen new national states. Although the winning of political independence for Europe's African and Asian colonies was perhaps the most spectacular challenge to empire in the twentieth century, that process was part of a larger pattern in modern world history (see Map 22.1).

Explaining African and Asian Independence

As the twentieth century closed, the end of European empires seemed an almost inevitable phenomenon, for colonial rule had lost any credibility as a form of political order. What could be more natural than for people to seek to rule themselves? Yet at the beginning of the century, few observers were predicting the collapse of these empires, and the idea that "the only legitimate government is national self-government" was not nearly so widespread as it subsequently became. This situation has presented historians with a problem of explanation — how to account for the fall of European colonial empires and the emergence of dozens of new nation-states.

One approach to explaining the end of colonial empires focuses attention on fundamental contradictions in the entire colonial enterprise. The rhetoric of Christianity,

Enlightenment thought, and material progress sat awkwardly with the realities of colonial racism, exploitation, and poverty. The increasingly democratic values of European states ran counter to the essential dictatorship of colonial rule. The ideal of national self-determination was profoundly at odds with the possession of colonies that
were denied any opportunity to express their own national character. The enormously
powerful force of nationalism, having earlier driven the process of European empire
building, now played a major role in its disintegration. Colonial rule, in this argument,
dug its own grave.

But why did this "fatal flaw" of European colonial rule lead to independence in
the post–World War II decades rather than earlier or later? In explaining the timing of
the end of empire, historians frequently use the notion of "conjuncture," the coming
together of several separate developments at a particular time. At the international
level, the world wars had weakened Europe, while discrediting any sense of European
moral superiority. Both the United States and the Soviet Union, the new global superpowers, generally opposed the older European colonial empires, even as they created
empire-like international relationships of their own. Meanwhile, the United Nations
provided a prestigious platform from which to conduct anticolonial agitation. All of
this contributed to the global illegitimacy of empire, a novel and stunning transformation of social values that was enormously encouraging to Africans and Asians seeking
political independence.

At the same time, social and economic circumstances within the colonies themselves generated the human raw material for anticolonial movements. By the early
twentieth century in Asia and the mid-twentieth century in Africa, a second or third
generation of Western-educated elites, largely male, had arisen throughout the colonial world. These young men were thoroughly familiar with European culture; they
were deeply aware of the gap between its values and its practices; they no longer
viewed colonial rule as a vehicle for their peoples' progress as their fathers had; and
they increasingly insisted on immediate independence. Moreover, growing numbers
of ordinary people — women and men alike — were receptive to this message. Veterans of the world wars; young people with some education but no jobs commensurate
with their expectations; a small class of urban workers who were increasingly aware of
their exploitation; small-scale female traders resentful of European privileges; rural
dwellers who had lost land or suffered from forced labor; impoverished and insecure
newcomers to the cities — all of these groups had reason to believe that independence
held great promise.

Such pressures increasingly placed colonial rulers on the defensive. As the twentieth century wore on, these colonial rulers began to plan — tentatively at first — for a
new political relationship with their Asian and African subjects. The colonies had been
integrated into a global economic network and local elites were largely committed to
maintaining those links. In these circumstances, Europeans could imagine retaining
profitable economic interests in Asia and Africa without the expense and trouble of
formal colonial governments. Deliberate planning for decolonization included gradual
political reforms; investments in railroads, ports, and telegraph lines; the holding of

■ **Change**

What international cir-
cumstances and social
changes contributed
to the end of colonial
empires?

elections; and the writing of constitutions. To some observers, it seemed as if independence was granted by colonial rulers rather than gained or seized by nationalist movements.

■ Description
What obstacles confronted the leaders of movements for independence?

But these reforms, and independence itself, occurred only under considerable pressure from mounting nationalist movements. Creating such movements was no easy task. Leaders, drawn everywhere from the ranks of the educated few and almost always male, organized political parties, recruited members, plotted strategy, developed an ideology, and negotiated with one another and with the colonial state. The most prominent among them became the "fathers" of their new countries as independence dawned — Gandhi and Nehru in India, Sukarno in Indonesia, Ho Chi Minh in Vietnam, Nkrumah in Ghana, and Mandela in South Africa. In places where colonial rule was particularly intransigent — settler-dominated colonies and Portuguese territories, for example — leaders also directed military operations and administered liberated areas. While such movements drew on memories of earlier, more localized forms of resistance, nationalist leaders did not seek to restore a vanished past. Rather they looked forward to joining the world of independent nation-states, to membership in the United Nations, and to the wealth and power that modern technology promised.

A further common task of the nationalist leadership was to recruit a mass following, and to varying degrees, they did. Millions of ordinary men and women joined Gandhi's nonviolent campaigns in India; tens of thousands of freedom fighters waged guerrilla warfare in Algeria, Kenya, Mozambique, and Zimbabwe; in West Africa workers went on strike and market women joined political parties, as did students, farmers, and the unemployed. The relationship between nationalist leaders and their followers was frequently fraught with tension. One such Indonesian leader, educated in Holland, spoke of his difficulty in relating to the common people: "Why am I vexed by the things that fill their lives, and to which they are so attached? Why are the things that contain beauty for them . . . only senseless and displeasing for me? We intellectuals here are much closer to Europe or America than we are to the primitive Islamic culture of Java and Sumatra."[2]

Thus struggles for independence were rarely if ever cohesive movements of uniformly oppressed people. More often, they were fragile alliances representing different classes, ethnic groups, religions, or regions. Beneath the common goal of independence, they struggled with one another over questions of leadership, power, strategy, ideology, and the distribution of material benefits, even as they fought and negotiated with their colonial rulers. The very notion of "national self-government" posed obvious but often contentious questions: What group of people constituted the "nation" that deserved to rule itself? And who should speak for it?

Comparing Freedom Struggles

Beyond these common features of most nationalist movements lay many variations. In some places, that struggle, once begun, produced independence within a few years, four in the case of the Belgian Congo. Elsewhere it was measured in decades.

Nationalism surfaced in Vietnam in the early 1900s, but the country achieved full political independence only in the mid-1970s, having fought French colonial rulers, Japanese invaders during World War II, and U.S. military forces in the 1960s and 1970s as well as Chinese forces during a brief war in 1979. Tactics too varied considerably. In many places, West Africa for example, nationalists relied on peaceful political pressure—demonstrations, strikes, mass mobilization, and negotiations—to achieve independence. Elsewhere armed struggle was required. Eight years of bitter guerrilla warfare preceded Algerian independence from France in 1962.

While all nationalist movements sought political independence for modern states, their ideologies and outlooks also differed. Many in India and the Islamic world viewed their new nations through the prism of religion, while elsewhere more secular outlooks prevailed. In Indonesia an early nationalist organization, the Islamic Union, appealed on the basis of religion, while later groups espoused Marxism. Indonesia's primary nationalist leader, Sukarno, sought to embrace and reconcile these various outlooks. "What is Sukarno?" he asked. "A nationalist? An Islamist? A Marxist? ... Sukarno is a mixture of all these isms."[3] Nationalist movements led by communist parties, such as those in Vietnam and China, sought major social transformations as well as freedom from foreign rule, while those in most of Africa focused on ending racial discrimination and achieving political independence with little concern about emerging patterns of domestic class inequality.

Two of the most extended freedom struggles—in India and South Africa—illustrate both the variations and the complexity of this process, which was so central to twentieth-century world history. India was among the first colonies to achieve independence and provided both a model and an inspiration to others, whereas South Africa, though not formally a colony, was among the last to throw off political domination by whites.

The Case of India: Ending British Rule

Surrounded by the Himalayas and the Indian Ocean, the South Asian peninsula, commonly known as India, enjoyed a certain geographic unity. But before the twentieth century few of its people thought of themselves as "Indians." Cultural identities were primarily local and infinitely varied, rooted in differences of family, caste, village, language, region, tribe, and religious practice. In earlier centuries—during the Mauryan, Gupta, and Mughal empires, for example—large areas of the subcontinent had been temporarily enclosed within a single political system, but always these were imperial overlays, constructed on top of enormously diverse Indian societies.

So too was British colonial rule, but the British differed from earlier invaders in ways that promoted a growing sense of Indian identity. Unlike previous foreign rulers, the British never assimilated into Indian society because their acute sense of racial and cultural distinctiveness kept them apart. This served to intensify Indians' awareness of their collective difference from their alien rulers. Furthermore, British railroads, telegraph lines, postal services, administrative networks, newspapers, and

■ **Change**

How did India's nationalist movement change over time?

schools as well as the English language bound India's many regions and peoples together more firmly than ever before and facilitated communication, especially among those with a modern education. Early nineteenth-century cultural nationalists, seeking to renew and reform Hinduism, registered this sense of India as a cultural unit.

The most important political expression of an all-Indian identity took shape in the Indian National Congress (INC), often called the Congress Party, which was established in 1885. This was an association of English-educated Indians—lawyers, journalists, teachers, businessmen—drawn overwhelmingly from regionally prominent high-caste Hindu families. It represented the beginning of a new kind of political protest, quite different from the rebellions, banditry, and refusal to pay taxes that had periodically erupted in the rural areas of colonial India. The INC was largely an urban phenomenon and quite moderate in its demands. Initially, its well-educated members did not seek to overthrow British rule; rather they hoped to gain greater inclusion within the political, military, and business life of British India. From such positions of influence, they argued, they could better protect the interests of India than could their foreign-born rulers. The British mocked their claim to speak for ordinary Indians, referring to them as "babus," a derogatory term that implied a semi-literate "native" with only a thin veneer of modern culture.

As an elite organization, the INC had difficulty gaining a mass following among India's vast peasant population. That began to change in the aftermath of World War I. To attract Indian support for the war effort, the British in 1917 had promised "the gradual development of self-governing institutions," a commitment that energized nationalist politicians to demand more rapid political change. Furthermore, British attacks on the Islamic Ottoman Empire antagonized India's Muslims. The end of the war was followed by a massive influenza epidemic, which cost the lives of millions of Indians. Finally, a series of violent repressive British actions antagonized many. This was the context in which Mohandas Gandhi (1869–1948) arrived on the Indian political scene and soon transformed it.

Gandhi was born in the province of Gujarat in western India to a pious Hindu family of the Vaisya, or business, caste. He was married at the age of thirteen, had only a mediocre record as a student, and eagerly embraced an opportunity to study law in England when he was eighteen. He returned as a shy and not very successful lawyer, and in 1893

Mahatma Gandhi
The most widely recognized and admired figure in the global struggle against colonial rule was India's Mahatma Gandhi. In this famous photograph, he is sitting cross-legged on the floor, clothed in a traditional Indian garment called a dhoti, while nearby stands a spinning wheel, symbolizing the independent and non-industrial India that Gandhi sought. (Margaret Bourke-White/ Time Life Pictures/Getty Images)

he accepted a job with an Indian firm in South Africa, where a substantial number of Indians had migrated as indentured laborers during the nineteenth century. While in South Africa, Gandhi personally experienced overt racism for the first time and as a result soon became involved in organizing Indians, mostly Muslims, to protest that country's policies of racial segregation. He also developed a concept of India that included Hindus and Muslims alike and pioneered strategies of resistance that he would later apply in India itself. His emerging political philosophy, known as *satyagraha* (truth force), was a confrontational, though nonviolent, approach to political action. As Gandhi argued,

> Non-violence means conscious suffering. It does not mean meek submission to the will of the evil-doer, but it means the pitting of one's whole soul against the will of the tyrant. . . . [I]t is possible for a single individual to defy the whole might of an unjust empire to save his honour, his religion, his soul.[4]

Returning to India in 1915, Gandhi quickly rose within the leadership ranks of the INC. During the 1920s and 1930s, he applied his approach in periodic mass campaigns that drew support from an extraordinarily wide spectrum of Indians—peasants and the urban poor, intellectuals and artisans, capitalists and socialists, Hindus and Muslims. The British responded with periodic repression as well as concessions that allowed a greater Indian role in political life. Gandhi's conduct and actions—his simple and unpretentious lifestyle, his support of Muslims, his frequent reference to Hindu religious themes—appealed widely in India and transformed the INC into a mass organization. To many ordinary people, Gandhi possessed magical powers and produced miraculous events. He was the Mahatma, the Great Soul.

His was a radicalism of a different kind. He did not call for social revolution but sought the moral transformation of individuals. He worked to raise the status of India's untouchables, the lowest and most ritually polluting groups within the caste hierarchy, but he launched no attack on caste in general and accepted support from businessmen and their socialist critics alike. His critique of India's situation went far beyond colonial rule. "India is being ground down," he argued, "not under the English heel, but under that of modern civilization"—its competitiveness, its materialism, its warlike tendencies, its abandonment of religion.[5] Almost alone among nationalist leaders in India or elsewhere, Gandhi opposed a modern industrial future for his country, seeking instead a society of harmonious self-sufficient villages drawing on ancient Indian principles of duty and morality. (See Document 18.4, pp. 919–21, for a more extended statement of Gandhi's thinking.)

Gandhi also embraced efforts to mobilize women for the struggle against Britain and to elevate their standing in marriage and society. While asserting the spiritual and mental equality of women and men, he regarded women as uniquely endowed with a capacity for virtue, self-sacrifice, and endurance and thus particularly well suited for nonviolent protest. They could also contribute by spinning and weaving their families' clothing, while boycotting British textiles. But Gandhi never completely

■ Change

What was the role of Gandhi in India's struggle for independence?

broke with older Indian conceptions of gender roles. "The duty of motherhood . . . ," he wrote, "requires qualities which man need not possess. She is passive; he is active. She is essentially mistress of the house. He is the bread-winner."[6] Hundreds of thousands of women responded to Gandhi's call for participation in the independence struggle, marching, demonstrating, boycotting, and spinning. The moral and religious context in which he cast his appeal allowed them to do so without directly challenging traditional gender roles.

■ **Description**

What conflicts and differences divided India's nationalist movement?

Gandhi and the INC leadership had to contend with a wide range of movements, parties, and approaches whose very diversity tore at the national unity that they so ardently sought. Whereas Gandhi rejected modern industrialization, his own chief lieutenant, Jawaharlal Nehru, thoroughly embraced science, technology, and industry as essential to India's future. Nor did everyone accept Gandhi's nonviolence or his inclusive definition of India. A militant Hindu organization preached hatred of Muslims and viewed India as an essentially Hindu nation. Some in the Congress Party believed that efforts to improve the position of women or untouchables were a distraction from the chief task of gaining independence. Whether to participate in British-sponsored legislative bodies without complete independence also became a divisive issue. Furthermore, a number of smaller parties advocated on behalf of particular regions or castes. India's nationalist movement, in short, was beset by division and controversy.

By far the most serious threat to a unified movement derived from the growing divide between the country's Hindu and Muslim populations. As early as 1906, the formation of an All-India Muslim League contradicted the Congress Party's claim to speak for all Indians. As the British allowed more elected Indian representatives on local councils, the League demanded separate electorates, with a fixed number of seats for Muslims. As a distinct minority within India, some Muslims feared that their voice could be swamped by a numerically dominant Hindu population, despite Gandhi's inclusive philosophy. Some Hindu politicians confirmed those fears when they cast the nationalist struggle in Hindu religious terms, hailing their country, for example, as a goddess, Bande Mataram (Mother India). When the 1937 elections gave the Congress Party control of many provincial governments, some of those governments began to enforce the teaching of Hindi in schools, rather than Urdu, which is written in a Persian script and favored by Muslims. This policy, as well as Hindu efforts to protect cows from slaughter, antagonized Muslims.

As the movement for independence gained ground, the Muslim League and its leader, Muhammad Ali Jinnah (JIN-uh), argued that those parts of India that had a Muslim majority should have a separate political status. They called it Pakistan, the land of the pure. In this view, India was not a single nation, as Gandhi had long argued. Jinnah put his case succinctly:

> The Muslims and Hindus belong to two different religious philosophies, social customs, and literatures. They neither intermarry nor interdine [eat] together and, indeed, they belong to two different civilizations.[7]

With great reluctance and amid mounting violence, Gandhi and the Congress Party finally agreed to partition as the British declared their intention to leave India after World War II (see Map 22.2).

Thus colonial India became independent in 1947 as two countries—a Muslim Pakistan, itself divided into two wings 1,000 miles apart, and a mostly Hindu India governed by a secular state. Dividing colonial India in this fashion was horrendously painful. A million people or more died in the communal violence that accompanied partition, and some 12 million refugees moved from one country to the other to join their religious compatriots. Gandhi himself, desperately trying to stem the mounting tide of violence in India's villages, refused to attend the independence celebrations. Only a year after independence, he was assassinated by a Hindu extremist. The great triumph of independence, secured from the powerful British Empire, was overshadowed by the great tragedy of the violence of partition. (See the portrait of Abdul Ghaffar Khan, a Muslim pacifist who admired the work of Gandhi, pp. 1098–99.)

Map 22.2   The Partition of British South Asia
The independence of British India witnessed the violent partition of the subcontinent into a largely Hindu India and a Muslim Pakistan. Later in 1975, East Pakistan established itself as the separate state of Bangladesh.

The Case of South Africa: Ending Apartheid

The setting for South Africa's freedom struggle was very different from that of India. In the twentieth century, that struggle was not waged against an occupying European colonial power, for South Africa had in fact been independent of Great Britain since 1910. Independence, however, had been granted to a government wholly controlled by a white settler minority, which represented less than 20 percent of the total population. The country's black African majority had no political rights whatsoever within the central state. Black South Africans' struggle therefore was against this internal opponent rather than against a distant colonial authority, as in India. Economically, the most prominent whites were of British descent. They or their forebears had come to South Africa during the nineteenth century, when Great Britain was the ruling colonial power. But the politically dominant section of the white community, known as Boers or Afrikaners, was descended from the early Dutch settlers, who had arrived in the mid-seventeenth century. The term "Afrikaner" reflected their image of themselves as "white Africans," permanent residents of the continent rather than

■ Comparison

Why was African rule in South Africa delayed until 1994, when it had occurred decades earlier elsewhere in the colonial world?

"native reserves," or Bantustans, served as ethnic homelands that kept Africans divided along tribal lines. Even though racism was present in colonial India, nothing of this magnitude developed there.

■ Change

How did South Africa's struggle against white domination change over time?

As in India, various forms of opposition—resistance to conquest, rural rebellions, urban strikes, and independent churches—arose to contest the manifest injustices of South African life. There too an elite-led political party provided an organizational umbrella for many of the South African resistance efforts in the twentieth century. Established in 1912, the African National Congress (ANC), like its Indian predecessor, was led by male, educated, professional, and middle-class Africans who sought not to overthrow the existing order, but to be accepted as "civilized men" within it. They appealed to the liberal, humane, and Christian values that white society claimed. For four decades, its leaders pursued peaceful and moderate protest—petitions, multiracial conferences, delegations appealing to the authorities—even as racially based segregationist policies were implemented one after another. Women were denied full membership in the ANC until 1943 and were restricted to providing catering and entertainment services for the men. But they took action in other arenas. In 1913, they organized a successful protest against carrying passes, an issue that endured through much of the twentieth century. Rural women in the 1920s used church-based networks to organize boycotts of local shops and schools. Women were likewise prominent in trade union protests, including wage demands for domestic servants and washerwomen. By 1948, when the Afrikaner-led National Party came to power on a platform of apartheid, it was clear that peaceful protest, whether organized by men or women, had produced no meaningful movement toward racial equality.

During the 1950s, a new and younger generation of the ANC leadership, which now included Nelson Mandela, broadened its base of support and launched nonviolent civil disobedience—boycotts, strikes, demonstrations, and the burning of the hated passes that all Africans were required to carry. All of these actions were similar to and

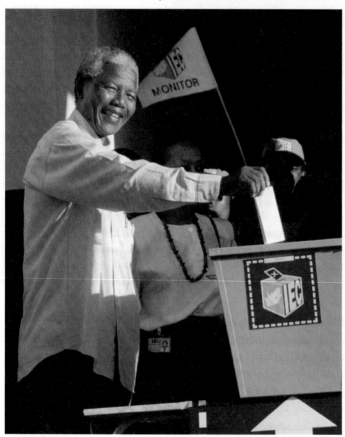

Nelson Mandela

In April 1994, the long struggle against apartheid and white domination in South Africa came to an end in the country's first democratic and nonracial election. The symbol of that triumph was Nelson Mandela, long a political prisoner, head of the African National Congress, and the country's first black African president. He is shown here voting in that historic election. (© Peter Turnley/Corbis) inspired by the tactics that Gandhi had pioneered in South Africa and used in India twenty to thirty years earlier. The government of South Africa responded with tremendous repression, including the shooting of sixty-nine unarmed demonstrators at Sharpville in 1960, the banning of the ANC, and the imprisonment of its leadership, including Nelson Mandela.

At this point, the freedom struggle in South Africa took a different direction than it had in India. Its major political parties were now illegal. Underground nationalist leaders turned to armed struggle, authorizing selected acts of sabotage and assassination, while preparing for guerrilla warfare in camps outside the country. Active opposition within South Africa was now primarily expressed by student groups that were part of the Black Consciousness movement, an effort to foster pride, unity, and political awareness among the country's African majority, with a particular emphasis on mobilizing women for the struggle. Such young people were at the center of an explosion of protest in 1976 in a sprawling, segregated, impoverished black neighborhood called Soweto, outside Johannesburg, in which hundreds were killed. The initial trigger for the uprising was the government's decision to enforce education for Africans in the hated language of the white Afrikaners rather than English. However, the momentum of the Soweto rebellion persisted, and by the mid-1980s, spreading urban violence and the radicalization of urban young people had forced the government to declare a state of emergency. Furthermore, South Africa's black labor movement, legalized only in 1979, became increasingly active and political. In June 1986, to commemorate the tenth anniversary of the Soweto uprising, the Congress of South African Trade Unions orchestrated a general strike involving some 2 million workers.

Beyond this growing internal pressure, South Africa faced mounting international demands to end apartheid as well. Exclusion from most international sporting events, including the Olympics; the refusal of many artists and entertainers to perform in South Africa; economic boycotts; the withdrawal of private investment funds—all of this isolated South Africa from a Western world in which its white rulers claimed membership. None of this had any parallel in India.

The combination of these internal and external pressures persuaded many white South Africans by the late 1980s that discussion with African nationalist leaders was the only alternative to a massive, bloody, and futile struggle to preserve white privileges. The outcome was the abandonment of key apartheid policies, the release of Nelson Mandela from prison, the legalization of the ANC, and a prolonged process of negotiations that in 1994 resulted in national elections, which brought the ANC to power. To the surprise of almost everyone, the long nightmare of South African apartheid came to an end without a racial bloodbath (see Map 22.3, p. 1102).

As in India, the South African nationalist movement was divided and conflicted. Unlike India, though, these divisions did not occur along religious lines. Rather it was race, ethnicity, and ideology that generated dissension and sometimes violence. Whereas the ANC generally favored a broad alliance of everyone opposed to apartheid

Map 22.3   South Africa after Apartheid

Under apartheid, all black Africans were officially desig-nated as residents of small, scattered, impoverished Bantustans, shown on the inset map. Many of these people, of course, actually lived in white South Africa, where they worked. The main map shows the new internal organization of the country as it emerged after 1994, with the Bantustans abolished and the country divided into nine provinces. Lesotho and Swaziland had been British protectorates during the colonial era and subsequently became separate indepen-dent countries, although surrounded by South African territory.

(black Africans, Indians, "coloreds" or mixed-race people, and sympathetic whites), a smaller group known as the Pan Africanist Congress rejected cooperation with other racial groups and limited its membership to black Africans. During the urban upris-ings of the 1970s and 1980s, young people supporting the Black Consciousness move-ments and those following Mandela and the ANC waged war against each other in the townships of South African cities. Perhaps most threatening to the unity of the nationalist struggle were the separatist tendencies of the Zulu-based Inkatha Freedom Party. Its leader, Gatsha Buthelezi, had cooperated with the apartheid state and even received funding from it. As negotiations for a transition to African rule un-folded in the early 1990s, considerable violence between Inkatha followers, mostly Zulu migrant workers, and ANC supporters broke out in a num-ber of cities. None of this, however, approached the massive killing of Hin-dus and Muslims that accompanied the partition of India. South Africa, un-like India, acquired its political freedom as an intact and unified state.

SUMMING UP SO FAR

How and why did the anticolonial struggles in India and South Africa differ?

Experiments with Freedom

Africa's first modern nationalist hero, Kwame Nkrumah (KWAH-may ehn-KROO-mah) of Ghana, paraphrased a biblical quotation when he urged his followers, "Seek ye first the political kingdom and all these other things will be added unto you." But would winning the political kingdom of independence or freedom from European rule really produce "all these other things"—release from oppression, industrial growth, economic development, reasonably unified nations, and a better life for all? That was the central question confronting the new nations emerging from colonial rule. They were joined in that quest by already independent but nonindustrialized countries and regions such as China, Thailand, Ethiopia, Iran, Turkey, and Central and South America. Together they formed the bloc of nations known variously as the third world, the developing countries, or the Global South. Those countries accounted for about 90 percent of the fourfold increase in human numbers that the world experienced during the twentieth century. Between 1950 and 2000, the populations of Asia and Africa alone grew from 64 percent of the world's total to 70 percent with an estimated increase to 79 percent by 2050 (see Snapshot, p. 1104). That immense surge in global population, at one level a great triumph for the human species, also underlay many of the difficulties these nations faced as they conducted their various experiments with freedom.

Almost everywhere, the moment of independence generated something close to euphoria. Having emerged from the long night of colonial rule, free peoples had the opportunity to build anew. The developing countries would be laboratories for fresh approaches to creating modern states, nations, cultures, and economies. In the decades that followed, experiments with freedom multiplied, but the early optimism was soon tempered by the difficulties and disappointments of those tasks.

Experiments in Political Order: Party, Army, and the Fate of Democracy

All across the developing world, efforts to create political order had to contend with a set of common conditions. Populations were exploding, and expectations for independence ran very high, often exceeding the available resources. Many developing countries were culturally very diverse, with little loyalty to the central state. Nonetheless, public employment mushroomed as the state assumed greater responsibility for economic development. In conditions of widespread poverty and weak private economies, groups and individuals sought to capture the state, or parts of it, both for the salaries and status it offered and for the opportunities for private enrichment that public office provided.

This was the formidable setting in which developing countries had to hammer out new political systems. The range of that effort was immense: Communist Party control in China, Vietnam, and Cuba; multiparty democracy in India and South Africa; one-party democracy in Mexico, Tanzania, and Senegal; military regimes for a

$\mathcal{S}$napshot   **World Population Growth, 1950–2011**[12]

The great bulk of the world's population growth in the second half of the twentieth century occurred in the developing countries of Asia, Africa, the Middle East, and Latin America.

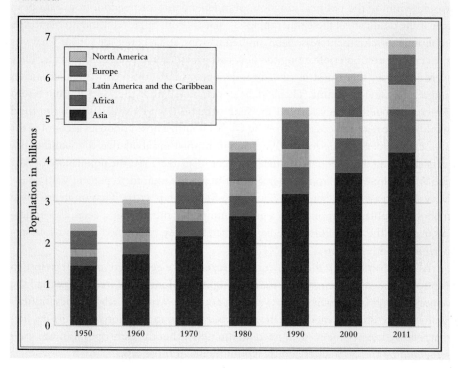

time in much of Latin America, Africa, and the Middle East; personal dictatorships in Uganda and the Philippines. In many places, one kind of political system followed another in kaleidoscopic succession.

As colonial rule drew to a close, European authorities in many places attempted to transplant democratic institutions to colonies they had long governed with such a heavy and authoritarian hand. They established legislatures, permitted elections, allowed political parties to operate, and in general anticipated the development of constitutional, parliamentary, multiparty democracies similar to their own.

It was in India that such a political system established its deepest roots. There Western-style democracy, including regular elections, multiple parties, civil liberties, and peaceful changes in government, has been practiced almost continuously since independence. What made this remarkable democratic continuity possible?

The struggle for independence in India had been a prolonged affair, thus providing time for an Indian political leadership to sort itself out. Furthermore, the British began to hand over power in a gradual way well before complete independence was granted in 1947. Thus a far larger number of Indians had useful administrative or technical skills than was the case elsewhere. In sharp contrast to most African countries, for example, the nationalist movement in India was embodied in a single national party (the Congress Party), which encompassed a wide variety of other parties and interest groups. Its leaders, Gandhi and Nehru in particular, were genuinely committed to democratic practice, which, some have argued, allowed elites from the many and varied groups of Indian society to find a place in the political system. Even the tragic and painful partition of colonial India into two countries eliminated a major source of internal discord as independent India was born. Moreover, Indian statehood could be built on common cultural and political traditions that were far more deeply rooted than in many former colonies.

Elsewhere in the colonial world, democracy proved a far more fragile transplant. Among the new states of Africa, for example, few retained their democratic institutions beyond the initial post-independence decade. Many of the apparently popular political parties that had led the struggle for independence lost mass support and were swept away by military coups. When the army took power in Ghana in 1966, no one lifted a finger to defend the party that had led the country to independence only nine years earlier. Other states evolved into one-party systems, and still others degenerated into personal tyrannies or dictatorships. Freedom from colonial rule certainly did not automatically generate the internal political freedoms associated with democracy.

Africans sometimes suggested that their traditional cultures, based on communal rather than individualistic values and concerned to achieve consensus rather than majority rule, were not compatible with the competitiveness of party politics. Others argued that Western-style democracy was simply inadequate for the tasks of development confronting the new states. Creating national unity was surely more difficult when competing political parties identified primarily with particular ethnic or "tribal" groups, as was frequently the case in Africa. Certainly Europe did not begin its modernizing process with such a system. Why, many Africans asked, should they be expected to do so?

The economic disappointments of independence also contributed to the erosion of support for democracy. By almost any measure, African economic performance since independence has been the poorest in the developing world. As a result, college and high school graduates were unable to find the white-collar careers they expected; urban migrants had little opportunity for work; farmers received low prices for their cash crops; consumers resented shortages and inflation; and millions of impoverished and malnourished peasants lived on the brink of starvation. These were people for whom independence was unable to fulfill even the most minimal of expectations, let alone the grandiose visions of a better life that so many had embraced in the early 1960s. Since modern governments everywhere staked their legitimacy on economic performance, it is little wonder that many Africans became disaffected and withdrew their support from governments they had enthusiastically endorsed only a few years earlier. Further resentments arose from the privileges of the relatively well-educated elite who had found high-paying jobs in the growing bureaucracies of the newly independent states. Such grievances often found expression in ethnic conflict,

■ Change

What led to the erosion of democracy and the establishment of military government in much of Africa and Latin America?

as Africa's immense cultural diversity became intensely politicized. An ethnically based civil war in Nigeria during the late 1960s cost the lives of millions, while in the mid-1990s ethnic hatred led Rwanda into the realm of genocide.

These economic disappointments, class resentments, and ethnic conflicts provided the context for numerous military takeovers. By the early 1980s, the military had intervened in at least thirty of Africa's forty-six independent states and actively governed more than half of them. In doing so they swept aside the old political parties and constitutions and vowed to begin anew, while promising to return power to civilians and restore democracy at some point in the future.

A similar wave of military interventions swept over Latin America during the 1960s and 1970s, leaving Brazil, Argentina, Peru, Chile, Uruguay, Bolivia, the Dominican Republic, and other countries governed at times by their armed forces (see Map 22.4). However, the circumstances in Latin America were quite different from

Map 22.4 Authoritarian Regimes in Latin America
For much of the twentieth century, many Latin American countries experienced authoritarian governments headed by military men, dictators, or single parties. Much of that was swept away during a wave of democratization in the last two decades of the century.

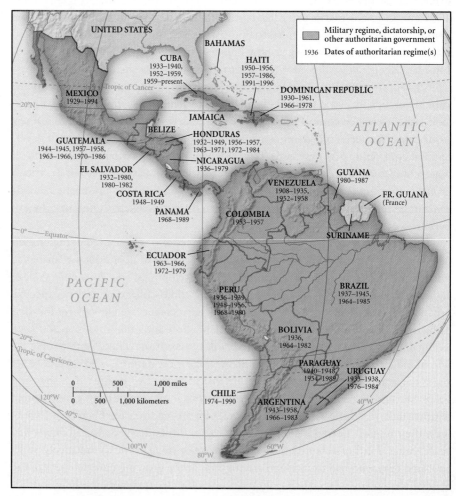

Legend:
Military regime, dictatorship, or other authoritarian government
1936 Dates of authoritarian regime(s)

UNITED STATES

BAHAMAS

CUBA
1933–1940,
1952–1959,
1959–present

HAITI
1950–1956,
1957–1986,
1991–1996

MEXICO
1929–1994

DOMINICAN REPUBLIC
1930–1961,
1966–1978

JAMAICA

BELIZE

HONDURAS
1932–1949, 1956–1957,
1963–1971, 1972–1984

GUATEMALA
1944–1945, 1957–1958,
1963–1966, 1970–1986

NICARAGUA
1936–1979

EL SALVADOR
1932–1980,
1980–1982

COSTA RICA
1948–1949

PANAMA
1968–1989

VENEZUELA
1908–1935,
1952–1958

GUYANA
1980–1987

FR. GUIANA
(France)

COLOMBIA
1953–1957

SURINAME

ATLANTIC OCEAN

ECUADOR
1963–1966,
1972–1979

PACIFIC OCEAN

PERU
1936–1939,
1948–1956,
1968–1980

BRAZIL
1937–1945,
1964–1985

BOLIVIA
1936,
1964–1982

PARAGUAY
1940–1948,
1954–1989

URUGUAY
1933–1938,
1976–1984

CHILE
1974–1990

ARGENTINA
1943–1958,
1966–1983

0   500   1,000 miles
0 500 1,000 kilometers

those in Africa. While military rule was something new and unexpected in Africa, Latin American armed forces had long intervened in political life. The region had also largely escaped the bitter ethnic conflicts that afflicted so many African states, though its class antagonisms were more clearly defined and expressed. Furthermore, Latin American societies in general were far more modernized and urbanized than those of Africa. And while newly independent African states remained linked to their former European rulers, long independent Latin American states lived in shadow of a dominant United States. "Poor Mexico," bemoaned Porfirio Díaz, that country's dictator before the Mexican revolution, "so far from God and so close to the United States."

Rapid population growth, chronic inflation, sharp class conflict, rural poverty, mass migration to city slums—such conditions combined in postwar Latin America to provoke a series of challenges to the privileges of the rich and powerful. These included guerrilla warfare in Bolivia and Colombia, short-lived left-wing governments in Guatemala, Brazil, and Chile, reformist programs elsewhere, and increasingly assertive movements of urban social protest. Perhaps most threatening was the Cuban revolution of 1959, which brought Fidel Castro to power, establishing in Latin America a communist outpost intent on spreading its revolutionary message. This was the backdrop to the wave of military coups that erupted in the 1960s and after. Intent on containing and counteracting such threats to the established order, they were backed by threatened local elites and often by the United States, equally fearful of growing radicalism.

Chile provides a fascinating case study. With a long tradition of electoral politics and rival parties, in 1970 Chileans narrowly elected to the presidency a Marxist politician, Salvador Allende, whose Popular United Party brought together the country's socialists and communists. Despite his modest victory at the polls, Allende soon launched an ambitious program to achieve a peaceful transition to socialism. In an effort to redistribute wealth, he ordered prices frozen and wages raised. Nationalization of major industries followed—including copper, coal, steel, and many banks—without compensation to their former owners, many of whom were foreign corporations. In the rural areas, land reform programs soon seized the large estates, redistributing them to small farmers. And Allende warmly welcomed Fidel Castro for a month-long visit in 1971. It was an audacious effort to achieve genuinely revolutionary change by legal and peaceful means.

But it failed. How much of this failure was a product of divisions within the

Castro and Allende
The socialist intentions of Salvador Allende's government in Chile were demonstrated by his embrace of the Cuban communist leader Fidel Castro, shown here on a visit to Chile in 1971. (AP Photo)

ruling party and mistakes by Allende's government remains a matter of controversy. But internal opposition mounted—from the bureaucracy, military officers, church hierarchy, wealthy business and landlord elites as well as various small business and middle-class elements, climaxing in a huge strike in late 1972. Furthermore, the U.S. government, which had long armed, funded, and trained military forces throughout Latin America, actively opposed the Allende regime as did U.S. corporations. A CIA document declared that "it is firm and continuing policy that Allende be overthrown by a coup." And in September 1973, he was.

What followed was an extraordinarily repressive and long-lasting military regime, headed by General Augusto Pinochet. Political parties were outlawed and the constitution suspended. Thousands were killed, tortured, or made to disappear. Free market economic policies attracted the foreign investors who had fled the country during Allende's regime. By the end of the 1970s, economic growth had reached an impressive 7 percent per year even as rural landlessness increased, workers' wages declined, and social services shrank.

Despite the democratic setbacks of the 1960s and 1970s, beginning in the early 1980s, a remarkable political reversal brought popular movements, multiparty elections, and new constitutions to a number of developing countries. It was part of an even broader late twentieth-century globalization of democracy. This worldwide trend included the end of military and autocratic rule in Spain, Portugal, and Greece as well as the stunning rise of democratic movements, parties, and institutions amid the collapse of communism in the Soviet Union and Eastern Europe. But the most extensive expression of this global reemergence of democracy lay in the developing countries. By 2000, almost all Latin American countries had abandoned their military-controlled regimes and returned to some form of democratic governance. So too did most African states previously ruled by soldiers, dictators, or single parties. In Asia, authoritarian regimes, some long established, gave way to more pluralistic and participatory political systems in South Korea, Taiwan, Thailand, the Philippines, Iraq, and Indonesia. And in 2011, mass movements in various Arab countries—Tunisia, Egypt, Libya, Syria, Bahrain, Yemen—had challenged or ended the hold of entrenched, corrupt, and autocratic rulers, while proclaiming their commitment to democracy, human dignity, and honest government. What might explain this global pattern and its expression in the Global South in particular?

One factor surely was the untethering of the ideas of democracy and human rights from their Western origins. By the final quarter of the twentieth century, democracy increasingly was viewed as a universal political principle to which all could aspire rather than an alien and imposed system deriving from the West. Democracy, like communism, feminism, modern science, and Christianity, was a Western import that took root and substantially lost its association with the West. It was therefore increasingly available as a vehicle for social protest in the rest of the world.

Perhaps the most important internal factor favoring a revival of democracy lay in the apparent failure of authoritarian governments to remedy disastrous economic situations, to raise standards of living, to provide jobs for the young, and to curb pervasive corruption. The oppressive and sometimes brutal behavior of repressive governments humiliated and outraged many. Furthermore, the growth of civil society with its numerous voluntary groups provided a social foundation, independent of the state, for demanding change. Disaffected students, professionals, urban workers, religious organizations, women's groups, and more joined in a variety of grassroots movements to insist on democratic change as a means to a better life. Such movements found encouragement in the demands for democracy that accompanied the South African struggle against apartheid and the collapse of Soviet and Eastern European communism. And the end of the cold war reduced the willingness of the major industrial powers to underwrite their authoritarian client states.

The consolidation of democratic practice in newly democratic states was a highly variable process. Some elected leaders, such as Hugo Chavez in Venezuela and Vladimir Putin in Russia, turned authoritarian once in office. Even where parliaments existed, they were often quite circumscribed in their powers. Outright electoral fraud tainted democratic institutions in many places, while established elites and oligarchies found it possible to exercise considerable influence even in formal democracies. Chinese authorities brutally crushed a democratic movement in 1989. The Algerian military sponsored elections in 1992 and then abruptly cancelled them when an Islamic party seemed poised to win. And the political future of the Arab Spring remains highly uncertain. Nonetheless, the worldwide revival of democracy represented the globalization of what had been a Western idea and the continuation of the political experiments that had begun with independence.

Experiments in Economic Development: Changing Priorities, Varying Outcomes

At the top of the agenda everywhere in the Global South was economic development, a process that meant growth or increasing production as well as distributing the fruits of that growth to raise living standards. This quest for development, now operating all across the planet, represented the universal acceptance of beliefs unheard of not many centuries earlier — that poverty was no longer inevitable and that it was possible to deliberately improve the material conditions of life for everyone. Economic development was a central promise of all independence struggles, and it was increasingly the standard by which people measured and granted legitimacy to their governments.

Achieving economic development, however, was no easy or automatic task. It took place in societies sharply divided by class, religion, ethnic group, and gender and in the face of explosive population growth. In many places, colonial rule had provided only the most slender foundations for modern development, for new nations often came to independence with low rates of literacy, few people with managerial experience, a weak private economy, and transportation systems oriented to export rather than national integration. Furthermore, the entire effort occurred in a world split by rival superpowers and economically dominated by the powerful capitalist economies

■ **Change**
What obstacles impeded the economic development of third-world countries?

of the West. Despite their political independence, most developing countries had little leverage in negotiations with the wealthy nations of the Global North and their immense transnational corporations. It was hardly an auspicious environment in which to seek a fundamental economic transformation.

Beyond these difficulties lay the question of what strategies to pursue. The academic field of "development economics" was new; its experts disagreed and often changed their minds; and conflicting political pressures, both internal and international, only added to the confusion. All of this resulted in considerable controversy, changing policies, and much experimentation.

■ **Change**

How and why did thinking about strategies for economic development change over time?

One fundamental issue lay in the role of the state. All across the developing world and particularly in newly independent nations, most people expected that state authorities would take major responsibility for spurring the economic development of their countries. After all, the private economy was weakly developed; few entrepreneurs had substantial funds to invest; the example of rapid Soviet industrialization under state direction was hopeful; and state control held the promise of protecting vulnerable economies from the ravages of international capitalism. Some state-directed economies had real successes. China launched a major industrialization effort and massive land reform under the leadership of the Communist Party. A communist Cuba, even while remaining dependent on its sugar production, wiped out illiteracy and provided basic health care to its entire population, raising life expectancy to seventy-six years by 1992, equivalent to that of the United States. Elsewhere as well—in Turkey, India, South Korea, and much of Africa—the state provided tariffs, licenses, loans, subsidies, and overall planning, while most productive property was owned privately.

Yet in the last three decades of the twentieth century, an earlier consensus in favor of state direction largely collapsed, replaced by a growing dependence on the market to generate economic development. This was most apparent in the abandonment of much communist planning in China and the return to private farming (see p. 1062). India and many Latin American and African states privatized their state-run industries and substantially reduced the role of the state in economic affairs. In part, this sharp change in economic policies reflected the failure, mismanagement, and corruption of many state-run enterprises, but it also was influenced by the collapse in the Soviet Union of the world's first state-dominated economy. Western pressures, exercised through international organizations such as the World Bank, likewise pushed developing countries in a capitalist direction. In China and India, the new approach generated rapid economic growth, but also growing inequalities and social conflict. But as the new millennium dawned, a number of developing countries once again asserted a more prominent role for the state in their quests for economic development and social justice. In China, Russia, Brazil, Saudi Arabia, Mexico, India, and elsewhere, state-owned companies buy and sell shares on the stock market, seeking profits in an economic system that has been called "state capitalism." Thus the search for an appropriate balance between state action and market forces in the management of modern economies continues.

A related issue involved the most appropriate posture for developing countries to adopt toward the world market as they sought to industrialize. Should they try to shield themselves from the influences of international capitalism, or were they better off vigorously engaging with the global economy? In the aftermath of the Great Depression of the 1930s, many Latin American countries followed the first path. Their traditional reliance on exporting agricultural products and raw materials had largely collapsed as the world economy sharply contracted (see p. 992). The alternative, known as import substitution industrialization, sought to reduce their dependence on the uncertain global marketplace by processing their own raw materials and manufacturing their own consumer goods behind high tariff barriers if necessary.

Brazil, for example, largely followed such policies from the 1930s through the late 1970s with some success. Between 1968 and 1974, the country experienced rapid industrial growth, dubbed the "Brazilian miracle." By the early 1980s, the country produced about 90 percent of its own consumer goods. But Brazil's industrialization was also accompanied by massive investment by foreign corporations, by the accumulation of a huge national debt to foreign lenders, by periodic bouts of inflation, and by very high levels of social inequality and poverty. Brazil's military president famously remarked in 1971: "The economy is doing fine but the people are doing badly."

The classic contrast to Latin American approaches to industrial development lay in East Asia where South Korea, Taiwan, Hong Kong, and Singapore chose a different strategy. Rather than focusing on industrial production for domestic consumption, they chose to specialize in particular products for an export market — textiles, electronic goods, and automobiles, for example. Many of these industries were labor intensive, drawing large numbers of women into the workforce, though at very low wages. Initiated in the 1960s, this export-driven development strategy generated rapid economic growth, propelling these countries into the ranks of the industrialized world by the end of the century. In the 1980s and 1990s, Brazil too entered the world market more vigorously, developing export industries in automobiles, steel, aircraft, computers, and more.

Other issues as well inspired debate. In many places, an early emphasis on city-based industrial development, stirred by visions of a rapid transition to modernity, led to a neglect or exploitation of rural areas and agriculture. This "urban bias" subsequently came in for much criticism and some adjustment in spending priorities. A growing recognition of the role of women in agriculture led to charges of "male bias" in development planning and to mounting efforts to assist women farmers directly. Women also were central to many governments' increased interest in curtailing population growth. Women's access to birth control, education, and employment, it turned out, provided powerful incentives to limit family size. Another debate pitted the advocates of capital- and technology-driven projects (dams and factories, for example) against those who favored investment in "human capital," such as education, technical training, health care, and nutrition. The benefits and drawbacks of foreign aid, investment, and trade have likewise been contentious issues.

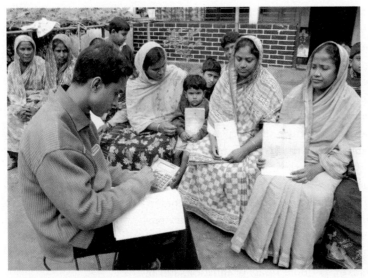

Microloans
Bangladesh's Grameen Bank pioneered an innovative approach to economic development by offering modest loans to poor people, enabling them to start small businesses. Here a group of women who received such loans meet in early 2004 to make an installment payment to an officer of the bank. (© Rafiqur Rahman/Reuters/Corbis)

Economic development was never simply a matter of technical expertise or deciding among competing theories. Every decision was political, involving winners and losers in terms of power, advantage, and wealth. Where to locate schools, roads, factories, and clinics, for example, provoked endless controversies, some of them expressed in terms of regional or ethnic rivalries. It was an experimental process, and the stakes were high.

The results of those experiments have varied considerably. (See Snapshot in Chapter 23, p. 1145, for global variations in economic development.) East Asian countries in general have had the strongest record of economic growth. South Korea, Taiwan, Singapore, and Hong Kong were dubbed "newly industrialized countries," and China boasted the most rapid economic growth in the world by the end of the twentieth century, replacing Japan as the world's second-largest economy. In the 1990s, Asia's other giant, India, opened itself more fully to the world market and launched rapid economic growth with a powerful high-tech sector and an expanding middle class. Oil-producing countries reaped a bonanza when they were able to demand much higher prices for that essential commodity in the 1970s and after. By 2008 Brazil ranked as the eighth-largest economy in the world with a rapidly growing industrial sector, while Turkey and Indonesia numbered in the top twenty. Limited principally to Europe, North America, and Japan in the nineteenth century, industrialization had become a global phenomenon by the early twenty-first.

Elsewhere, the story was very different. In most of Africa, much of the Arab world, and parts of Asia—regions representing about one-third of the world's population—there was little sign of catching up and frequent examples of declining standards of living since the end of the 1960s. Between 1980 and 2000, the average income in forty-three of Africa's poorest countries dropped by 25 percent, pushing living standards for many below what they had been at independence. But in the first decade of the twenty-first century, a number of African countries began to experience more encouraging economic growth.

Scholars and politicians alike argue about the reasons for such sharp differences in economic performance. Variables such as geography and natural resources, differing colonial experiences, variations in regional cultures, the degree of political stability and social equality, state economic policies, population growth rates, and varying forms of involvement with the world economy—all of these have been invoked to explain the widely diverging trajectories among developing countries.

Experiments with Culture: The Role of Islam in Turkey and Iran

The quest for economic development represented the embrace of an emerging global culture of modernity with its scientific outlook, its technological achievements, and its focus on material values. Developing countries were also exposed to the changing culture of the West, including feminism, rock and rap, sexual permissiveness, consumerism, and democracy. But the peoples of the Global South had inherited cultural patterns from the more distant past as well. A common issue all across the developing world involved the uneasy relationship between these older traditions and the more recent outlooks associated with modernity and the West. How should traditional African "medicine men" relate to modern hospitals? What happens to Confucian-based family values when confronted with the urban and commercial growth of recent Chinese history? Such tensions provided the raw material for a series of cultural experiments in the twentieth century, and nowhere were they more consequential than in the Islamic world. No single answer emerged to the question of how Islam and modernity should relate to each other, but the experience of Turkey and Iran illustrate two quite different approaches to this fundamental issue (see Map 22.5). (See Documents: Contending for Islam, pp. 1120–28, for more on this topic.)

In the aftermath of World War I, modern Turkey emerged from the ashes of the Ottoman Empire, led by an energetic general, Mustafa Kemal Atatürk (AT-tuh-terk) (1881–1938), who fought off British, French, Italian, and Greek efforts to dismember what was left of the old empire. Often compared to Peter the Great in Russia (see p. 638), Atatürk then sought to transform his country into a modern, secular, and national state. Such ambitions were not entirely new, for they built upon the efforts of nineteenth-century Ottoman reformers, who, like Atatürk, greatly admired European Enlightenment thinking and sought to bring its benefits to their country.

To Atatürk and his followers, to become modern meant "to enter European civilization completely." They believed that this required the total removal of Islam from public life, relegating it to the personal and private realm. Atatürk argued that "Islam will be elevated, if it will cease to be a political instrument." In fact, he sought to broaden access to the religion by translating the Quran into Turkish and issuing the call to prayer in Turkish rather than Arabic.

Atatürk largely ended, however, the direct political role of Islam. The old sultan or ruler of the Ottoman Empire, whose position had long been sanctified by Islamic tradition, was deposed as Turkey became a

■ Comparison

In what ways did cultural revolutions in Turkey and Iran reflect different understandings of the role of Islam in modern societies?

Map 22.5 Iran, Turkey, and the Middle East
Among the great contrasts of a very diverse Middle East has been between Turkey, the most secular and Western-oriented country of the region, and Iran, home to the most sustained Islamic revolution in the area.

Westernization in Turkey
Mustafa Kemal Atatürk, the founder of modern Turkey, often appeared in public in elegant European dress, symbolizing for his people a sharp break with traditional Islamic ways of living. Here he is dancing with his adopted daughter at her high-society wedding in 1929. (Hulton Archive/Getty Images)

republic. Furthermore the caliphate, by which Ottoman sultans had claimed leadership of the entire Islamic world, was abolished. Various Sufi organizations, sacred tombs, and religious schools were closed and a number of religious titles abolished. Islamic courts were likewise dissolved, while secular law codes, modeled on those of Europe, replaced the *sharia*. In history textbooks, pre-Islamic Turkish culture was celebrated as the foundation for all ancient civilizations. The Arabic script in which the Turkish language had long been written was exchanged for a new Western-style alphabet that made literacy much easier but rendered centuries of Ottoman culture inaccessible to these newly literate people. (See Document 22.1, pp. 1120–21, for an example of Atatürk's thinking.)

The most visible symbols of Atatürk's revolutionary program occurred in the realm of dress. Turkish men were ordered to abandon the traditional headdress known as the fez and to wear brimmed hats. According to Atatürk,

> A civilized, international dress is worthy and appropriate for our nation, and we will wear it. Boots or shoes on our feet, trousers on our legs, shirt and tie, jacket and waistcoat— and of course, to complete these, a cover with a brim on our heads.[13]

Although women were not forbidden to wear the veil, many elite women abandoned it and set the tone for feminine fashion in Turkey.

In Atatürk's view, the emancipation of women was a cornerstone of the new Turkey. In a much-quoted speech, he declared:

> If henceforward the women do not share in the social life of the nation, we shall never attain to our full development. We shall remain irremediably backward, incapable of treating on equal terms with the civilizations of the West.[14]

Thus polygamy was abolished; women were granted equal rights in divorce, inheritance, and child custody; and in 1934 Turkish women gained the right to vote and hold public office, a full decade before French women gained that right. Public beaches were now opened to women as well.

These reforms represented a "cultural revolution" unique in the Islamic world of the time, and they were imposed against considerable opposition. After Atatürk's death in 1938, some of them were diluted or rescinded. The call to prayer returned to the traditional Arabic in 1950, and various political groups urged a greater role for Islam in the public arena. Since 2002, a moderate Islamic party has governed the country, while the political role of the military, long the chief defender of Turkish secularism, diminished. By 2010 an earlier prohibition on women wearing headscarves in universities had largely ended. Nevertheless, the essential secularism of the Turkish state remained an enduring legacy of the Atatürk revolution. But elsewhere in the Islamic world, other solutions to the question of Islam and modernity took shape.

A very different answer emerged in Iran in the final quarter of the twentieth century. That country seemed an unlikely place for an Islamic revolution. Under the government of Shah Mohammad Reza Pahlavi (r. 1941–1979), Iran had undertaken what many saw as a quite successful and largely secular modernization effort. The country had great wealth in oil, a powerful military, a well-educated elite, and a solid alliance with the United States. Furthermore, the shah's so-called White Revolution, intended to promote the country's modernization, had redistributed land to many of the Iran's impoverished peasantry, granted women the right to vote, invested substantially in rural health care and education, initiated a number of industrial projects, and offered workers a share in the profits of those industries. But beneath the surface of apparent success, discontent and resentment were brewing. Traditional small-scale merchants felt threatened by an explosion of imported Western goods and by competition from large businesses. Religious leaders, the *ulama*, were offended by secular education programs that bypassed Islamic schools and by state control of religious institutions. Educated professionals found Iran's reliance on the West disturbing. Rural migrants to the country's growing cities, especially Tehran, faced rising costs and uncertain employment.

A repressive and often brutal government allowed little outlet for such grievances. Thus, opposition to the shah's regime came to center on the country's many mosques, where Iran's Shi'ite religious leaders invoked memories of earlier persecution and martyrdom as they mobilized that opposition and called for the shah's removal. The emerging leader of that movement was the high-ranking Shia cleric Ayatollah Ruholla Khomeini (ko-MAY-nee) (1902–1989), who in 1979 returned from long exile in Paris to great acclaim. By then, massive urban demonstrations, strikes, and defections from the military had eroded support for the shah, who abdicated the throne and left the country.

What followed was also a cultural revolution, but one that moved in precisely the opposite direction from that of Atatürk's Turkey — toward, rather than away from, the Islamization of public life. The new government defined itself as an Islamic republic, with an elected parliament and a constitution, but in practice conservative Islamic clerics, headed by Khomeini, exercised dominant power. A Council of Guardians, composed of leading legal scholars, was empowered to interpret the

Women and the Iranian Revolution
One of the goals of Iran's Islamic revolution was to enforce a more modest and traditional dress code for the country's women. In this photo from 2004, a woman clad in hijab and talking on her cell phone walks past a poster of the Ayatollah Khomeini, who led that revolution in 1979. (AP Images)

constitution, to supervise elections, and to review legislation—all designed to ensure compatibility with a particular vision of Islam. Opposition to the new regime was harshly crushed, with some 1,800 executions in 1981 alone for those regarded as "waging war against God."[15]

Khomeini believed that the purpose of government was to apply the law of Allah as expressed in the sharia (see Document 22.2). Thus all judges now had to be competent in Islamic law, and those lacking that qualification were dismissed. The secular law codes under which the shah's government had operated were discarded in favor of those based solely on Islamic precedents. Islamization likewise profoundly affected the domain of education and culture. In June 1980, the new government closed some 200 universities and colleges for two years while textbooks, curricula, and faculty were "purified" of un-Islamic influences. Elementary and secondary schools, largely secular under the shah, now gave priority to religious instruction and the teaching of Arabic, even as about 40,000 teachers lost their jobs for lack of sufficient Islamic piety. Pre-Islamic Persian literature and history were now out of favor, while the history of Islam and Iran's revolution predominated in schools and the mass media. Western loan words were purged from the Farsi language, replaced by their Arabic equivalents.

As in Turkey, the role of women became a touchstone of this Islamic cultural revolution. By 1983, all women were required to wear the modest head-to-toe covering known as hijab, a regulation enforced by roving groups of militants or "revolutionary guards." Those found with "bad hijab" were subject to harassment and sometimes lashings or imprisonment. Sexual segregation was imposed in schools, parks, beaches, and public transportation. The legal age of marriage for girls, set at eighteen under the shah, was reduced to nine with parental consent and thirteen, later raised to fifteen, without it. Married women could no longer file for divorce or attend school. Yet, despite such restrictions, many women supported the revolution and over the next several decades found far greater opportunities for employment and higher education than before. By the early twenty-first century, almost 60 percent of university students were women. And women's right to vote remained intact.

While Atatürk's cultural revolution of Westernization and secularism was largely an internal affair that freed Turkey from the wider responsibilities of the caliphate, Khomeini clearly sought to export Iran's Islamic revolution. He openly called for the replacement of insufficiently Islamic regimes in the Middle East and offered training and support for their opponents. In Lebanon, Syria, Bahrain, Saudi Arabia, Iraq, and elsewhere, Khomeini appealed to Shi'ite minorities and other disaffected people, and Iran became a model to which many Islamic radicals looked. An eight-year war with Saddam Hussein's highly secularized Iraq (1980–1988) was one of the outcomes and generated enormous casualties. That conflict reflected the differences between Arabs and Persians, between Sunni and Shia versions of Islam, and between a secular Iraqi regime and Khomeini's revolutionary Islamic government.

After Khomeini's death in 1989, some elements of this revolution eased a bit. For a time, enforcement of women's dress code was not so stringent, and a more moderate government came to power in 1997, raising hopes for a loosening of strict Islamic regulations. By 2005, however, more conservative elements were back in control and a new crackdown on women's clothing soon surfaced. A heavily disputed election in 2009 revealed substantial opposition to the country's rigid Islamic regime. Iran's ongoing Islamic revolution, however, did not mean the abandonment of economic modernity. The country's oil revenues continued to fund its development, and by the early twenty-first century, Iran was actively pursuing nuclear power and perhaps nuclear weapons, in defiance of Western opposition to these policies.

LearningCurve
bedfordstmartins.com
/strayer/LC

⎯⊢ Reflections: History in the Middle of the Stream

Historians are usually more at ease telling stories that have clear endings, such as those that describe ancient Egyptian civilization, Chinese maritime voyages, the collapse of the Aztec Empire, or the French Revolution. There is a finality to these stories and a distance from them that makes it easier for historians to assume the posture of detached observers, even if their understandings of those events change over time. Finality, distance, and detachment are harder to come by when historians are describing the events of the past century, for many of its processes are clearly not over. The United States' role as a global superpower and its wars in Iraq and Afghanistan, the fate of democracy in Latin America and the Arab world, the rise of China and India as economic giants, the position of Islam in Turkey and Iran—all of these are unfinished stories, their outcomes unknown and unknowable. In dealing with such matters, historians write from the middle of the stream, often uncomfortably, rather than from the banks, where they might feel more at ease.

In part, that discomfort arises from questions about the future that such issues inevitably raise. Can the spread of nuclear weapons be halted? Will democracy flourish globally? Are Islamic and Christian civilizations headed for a global clash? Can African countries replicate the economic growth experience of India and China? Historians in particular are uneasy about responding to such questions because they are so aware of the unexpectedness and surprising quality of the historical process. Yet those questions about the future are legitimate and important, for as the nineteenth-century Danish philosopher Søren Kierkegaard remarked: "Life can only be understood backward, but it is lived forward." History, after all, is the only guide we have to the possible shape of that future. So, like everyone before us, we stumble on, both individually and collectively, largely in the dark, using analogies from the past as we make our way ahead.

These vast uncertainties about the future provide a useful reminder that although we know the outcomes of earlier human stories—the Asian and African struggles for independence, for example—those who lived that history did not. Such awareness can perhaps engender in us a measure of humility and greater sympathy with those whose lives we study. However we may differ from our ancestors across time and place, we share with them an immense ignorance about what the future holds.

Second Thoughts

LearningCurve
Check what you know.
**bedfordstmartins.com
/strayer/LC**

Online Study Guide
bedfordstmartins.com
/highschool/strayer

What's the Significance?

decolonization, 1088–92
Indian National Congress, 1094
Mahatma Gandhi/satyagraha, 1094–97
Muslim League, 1096
Muhammad Ali Jinnah, 1096
Abdul Ghaffar Khan, 1098–99
African National Congress, 1100–02
Nelson Mandela, 1100–02

Black Consciousness/Soweto, 1101
military government, 1105–08
globalization of democracy, 1108–09
import substitution and export-led industrialization, 1111
Mustafa Kemal Atatürk, 1113–15
Ayatollah Ruholla Khomeini, 1115–17

Big Picture Questions

1. In what ways did the colonial experience and the struggle for independence shape the agenda of developing countries in the second half of the twentieth century?

2. How would you compare the historical experiences of India and China in the twentieth century?

3. From the viewpoint of the early twenty-first century, to what extent had the goals of nationalist or independence movements been achieved?

4. **Looking Back:** To what extent did the struggle for independence and the postcolonial experience of African and Asian peoples in the twentieth century parallel or diverge from that of the earlier "new nations" in the Americas in the eighteenth and nineteenth centuries?

Next Steps: For Further Study

Chinua Achebe, *Anthills of the Savannah* (1989). A brilliant fictional account of post-independence Nigeria by that country's foremost novelist.

Frederick Cooper, *Africa since 1940* (2002). A readable overview of the coming of independence and efforts at development by a leading historian of Africa.

Ramachandra Guha, *India after Gandhi: The History of the World's Largest Democracy* (2007). A thoughtful account of India's first six decades of independence.

John Isbister, *Promises Not Kept* (2006). A well-regarded consideration of the obstacles to and struggles for development in the Global South.

Nelson Mandela, *Long Walk to Freedom: The Autobiography of Nelson Mandela* (1995). Mandela's account of his own amazing life as nationalist leader and South African statesman.

W. David McIntyre, *British Decolonization, 1946–1997* (1998). A global history of the demise of the British Empire.

Complete Site on Mahatma Gandhi, http://www.mkgandhi.org. A wealth of resources for exploring the life of Gandhi.

For Web sites and additional documents related to this chapter, see **Make History** at bedfordstmartins.com /highschool/strayer.

Documents

Considering the Evidence: Contending for Islam

Over the past century, the growing intrusion of the West and of modern secular culture into the Islamic world has prompted acute and highly visible debate among Muslims. Which ideas and influences flowing from the West could Muslims safely utilize and which should they decisively reject? Are women's rights and democracy compatible with Islam? To what extent should Islam find expression in public life as well as in private religious practice? The documents that follow show something of these controversies while illustrating sharp variations in the understanding of Islam.

Document 22.1

A Secular State for an Islamic Society

Modern Turkey emerged from the ashes of the Ottoman Empire after World War I and adopted a distinctive path of modernization, Westernization, and secularism under the leadership of Mustafa Kemal Atatürk (see pp. 1113–15). Such policies sought to remove Islam from any significant role in public life, restricting it to the realm of personal devotion, and included abolition of the caliphate, by which Ottoman rulers had claimed leadership of the entire Islamic world. In a speech delivered in 1927, Atatürk explained and justified these policies, which went against the grain of much Islamic thinking.

■ On what grounds did Atatürk justify the abolition of the caliphate?

■ What additional actions did he take to remove Islam from a public or political role in the new Turkish state?

■ What can you infer about Atatürk's view of Islam?

■ How did Atatürk's conception of a Turkish state differ from that of Ottoman authorities? In what ways did he build upon Ottoman reforms of the nineteenth century? (See pp. 944–46 in Chapter 19.)

Mustafa Kemal Atatürk

Speech to the General Congress of the Republican Party

1927

[Our Ottoman rulers] hoped to unite the entire Islamic world in one body, to lead it and to govern it. For this purpose, [they] assumed the title of Caliph.° . . . It is an unrealizable aim to attempt to unite in one tribe the various races existing on the earth, thereby abolishing all boundaries. . . .

If the Caliph and the Caliphate were to be invested with a dignity embracing the whole of Islam . . . , a crushing burden would be imposed on Turkey. . . . [Furthermore], will Persia or Afghanistan, which are [Muslim] states, recognize the authority of the Caliph in a single matter? No, and this is quite justifiable, because it would be in contradiction to the independence of the state, to the sovereignty of the people.

[The current constitution] laid down as the first duty of the Grand National Assembly that "the prescriptions of the Shari'a° should be put into force. . . ." [But] if a state, having among its subjects elements professing different religions and being compelled to act justly and impartially toward all of them . . . , it is obliged to respect freedom of opinion and conscience. . . . The Muslim religion includes freedom of religious opinion. . . . Will not every grownup person in the new Turkish state be free to select his own religion? . . . When the first favorable opportunity arises, the nation must act to eliminate these superfluities [the enforcement of sharia] from our Constitution. . . .

Under the mask of respect for religious ideas and dogmas, the new Party [in opposition to Atatürk's reformist plans] addressed itself to the people in the following words: "We want the re-establishment of the Caliphate; we are satisfied with the religious law; we shall protect the Medressas,° the Tekkes,° the pious institutions, the Softahs,° the Sheikhs,° and their disciples. . . . The party of Mustapha Kemal, having abolished the Caliphate, is breaking Islam into ruins; they will make you into unbelievers . . . they will make you wear hats." Can anyone pretend that the style of propaganda used by the Party was not full of these reactionary appeals? . . .

Gentlemen, it was necessary to abolish the fez,° which sat on our heads as a sign of ignorance, of fanaticism, of hatred to progress and civilization, and to adopt in its place the hat, the customary headdress of the whole civilized world, thus showing that no difference existed in the manner of thought between the Turkish nation and the whole family of civilized mankind. . . . [Thus] there took place the closing of the Tekkes, of the convents, and of the mausoleums, as well as the abolition of all sects and all kinds of [religious] titles. . . .

Could a civilized nation tolerate a mass of people who let themselves be led by the nose by a herd of Sheikhs, Dedes, Seids, Tschelebis, Babas, and Emirs°. . . . Would not one therewith have committed the greatest, most irreparable error to the cause of progress and awakening?

°**Caliph:** successor to the prophet Muhammad.

°**Shari'a:** Islamic law.

Source: *A Speech Delivered by Ghazi Mustapha Kemal, October 1927* (Leipzig: K. F. Koehler, 1929), 377–79, 591–93, 595–98, 717, 721–22.

°**Medressas:** Islamic schools.

°**Tekkes:** places for Sufi worship.

°**Softahs:** students in religious schools.

°**Sheikhs:** Sufi masters.

°**fez:** a distinctive Turkish hat with no brim.

°**Sheikhs . . . Emirs:** various religious titles.

Document 22.2

Political Islam

In sharp contrast to Turkey, an Islamic revolution in Iran brought to power in 1979 a government committed to the thorough Islamization of public life (see pp. 1115–17). That revolution had been inspired and led by the Ayatollah Khomeini (1902–1989), an Iranian religious scholar, who became the rallying point for those opposed to the regime of the Shah of Iran, which was strongly backed by the United States. Document 22.2 provides a sample of Khomeini's thinking about imperialism and Islamic government, written well before the revolution actually occurred. As the Supreme Leader of Iran during the 1980s, he was in a position to put many of those ideas into practice.

■ How does Khomeini define the obstacles to achieving a proper government and society in Iran?

■ How would you summarize his case against European imperialism and the Shah's government?

■ In what ways does Khomeini seek to apply Islamic principles in the public life of Iran? What is his view of Iranian popular culture?

■ What kind of government does Khomeini foresee for Iran?

■ To whom might Khomeini's views be most appealing? What kinds of people might oppose them?

AYATOLLAH KHOMEINI
Writings and Declarations
1941, 1970

From the very beginning, the historical movement of Islam has had to contend with the Jews, for it was they who first established anti-Islamic propaganda ... Later they were joined by other groups ... These new groups [Europeans] began their imperialist penetration of the Muslim countries about three hundred years ago, and they regarded it as necessary to work for the extirpation of Islam ...

Islam is the religion of militant individuals who are committed to truth and justice. It is the religion of those who desire freedom and independence. It is the school of those who struggle against imperialism. ...

Islam does not recognize monarchy and hereditary succession ... Islam has laid down no laws for the practice of usury [lending money at high interest rates], for banking with usury, for the consumption of alcohol, or for the cultivation of sexual vices, having radically prohibited all of these ...

The agents of imperialism sometimes write ... that the legal provisions of Islam are too harsh ... They [imperialists] kill people for possessing ten gram of heroin ... When Islam, however, stipulates that the drinker of alcohol should receive eighty lashes, they consider it "too harsh." ... They are not aware that these penal provisions of Islam are in-

Source: Hamid Algar, trans., *Islam and Revolution: Writings and Declarations of Imam Khomeini (1940-1980)* (Berkeley, CA: Mizan Press, 1981), 27–28, 31, 33–34, 37–38, 41, 43–44, 48–51, 54, 171–173.

tended to keep great nations from being destroyed by corruption. Sexual vice has now reached such proportions that it is destroying entire generations, corrupting our youth and causing them to neglect all forms of work . . .

Their plan is to keep us backward, to keep us in our present miserable state, so that they can exploit our riches, our underground wealth, our lands, and our human resources . . . Instead of surrendering to the injunctions of Islam, which provide a solution to the problem of poverty, they and their agents wish to go on living in huge palaces and enjoying lives of abominable luxury.

In the time of the Prophet, laws were not merely expounded . . . ; they were also implemented. The Messenger of God . . . implemented the penal provisions of Islam: he cut off the hand of the thief and administered lashings and stonings. The successor to the Prophet must do the same . . . *Know that it is your duty to establish an Islamic government.*

This slogan of the separation of religion and politics and the demand that Islamic scholars not intervene in social and political affairs have been formulated and propagated by the imperialists; it is only the irreligious who repeat them.

According to one of the noble verses of the Quran, the ordinances of Islam are . . . permanent and must be enacted until the end of time.

The laws of the *sharia* embrace a diverse body of laws and regulations, which amounts to a complete social system. In this system of laws, all the needs of man have been met: his dealings with neighbors, fellow citizens, and clans as well as children and relatives; the concerns of private and marital life; regulations concerning war and peace and intercourse with other nations; penal and commercial law; regulations pertaining to trade and agriculture. Islamic law contains provisions relating to the preliminaries of marriage and the form in which it should be contracted, and others relating to the development of the embryo in the womb and what food parents should eat at the time of conception. It further stipulates the duties that are incumbent upon them while the infant is being suckled and specifies how the child should be reared and how the husband and wife should relate to each other and to their children. Islam provides laws and instruction for all of these matters, aiming . . . to produce

integrated and virtuous human beings who are walking embodiments of the law . . .

We see, too, that together, the imperialists and the tyrannical self-seeking rulers have divided the Islamic homeland. They have separated the various segments of the Islamic umma from each other and artificially created separate nations. There once existed the great Ottoman state, and that, too, the imperialists divided . . .

[T]he imperialists have also imposed on us an unjust economic order, and thereby divided our people into two groups: oppressors and oppressed. Hundreds of millions of Muslims are hungry and deprived of all form of health care and education, while minorities comprised of the wealth and powerful live a life of indulgence, licentiousness, and corruption. . . . It is the duty of Islamic scholars and all Muslims to put an end to this system of oppression and for the sake of the well-being of hundreds of millions of human beings to overthrow these oppressive governments and form an Islamic government.

The influence and sovereignty of Islam in society have declined; the nation of Islam has fallen victim to division and weakness; the laws of Islam have remained in abeyance and have been subjected to change and modification; and the imperialist have propagated foreign laws and alien culture . . . , causing people to be infatuated with the West . . . We need proper and righteous organs of government; that much is self-evident.

We know that all of this [Islamic government] is unpalatable to those who have grown up with lechery, treachery, music, and dancing, and a thousand other varieties of corruption. Of course they regard the civilization and advancement of the country as dependent upon women's going naked in the streets or . . . turning half the population into workers by unveiling them . . . They will not agree to the country's being administered rationally and in accordance with God's law. We have nothing to say to those whose powers of perception are so limited that they regard the wearing of European hats . . . as a sign of national progress. . . . With a European hat on your head, you would parade around the streets enjoying the naked girls, taking pride in this "achievement" totally heedless of the fact that meanwhile, the historic patrimony of the country was being plundered from one end to the other, all its sources of wealth were being carried off . . .

[T]hese idiotic and treacherous rulers, these officials—high and low—these reprobates and smugglers must change in order for the country to change. Otherwise you will experience worse times than these, times so bad that the present will seem like paradise by comparison.

Document 22.3

Progressive Islam

In the early twenty-first century, the international face of an assertive Islamic radicalism was that of Osama bin Laden, whose al-Qaeda organization launched the attacks on the United States on September 11, 2001, and called for the overthrow of compromised governments in Saudi Arabia and elsewhere in the Islamic world (see pp. 1157–60). Substantial numbers of Muslims no doubt shared bin Laden's outrage at the sorry state of many Muslim societies as well as his opposition to heavy U.S. backing for the state of Israel and to American military interventions in Iraq and Afghanistan.

But bin Laden and his followers were certainly not the only voices laying claim to Islam in the aftermath of 9/11. All across the Islamic world, others argued that Muslims could retain their distinctive religious sensibility while embracing democracy, women's rights, technological progress, freedom of thought, and religious pluralism. Such thinkers were following in the tradition of nineteenth-century Islamic modernism (see p. 945), even as they recalled earlier centuries of Islamic intellectual and scientific achievement and religious tolerance. That viewpoint was expressed in a pamphlet composed by a leading American Muslim scholar, translator, and Sufi teacher, Sheikh Kabir Helminski, in 2009. It is also reflected in Document 23.4, pp. 1178–79, which argues for women's rights within an Islamic framework.

- Against what charges does Sheikh Kabir seek to defend Islam? How does this document reflect the experience of 9/11?

- In what ways are Sheikh Kabir's views critical of radical or "fundamentalist" ideas and practices?

- How does this document, together with Document 23.4, articulate the major features of a more progressive or liberal Islam? What kinds of arguments are employed to make their case?

- To whom might these arguments appeal? What obstacles do they face in being heard within the Islamic world?

- How might the Ayatollah Khomeini (Document 22.2) or Osama bin Laden have responded to the arguments in this document? In what ways does this vision of a "liberal" or "moderate" Islam differ from those of Kemal Atatürk (Document 22.1)?

KABIR HELMINSKI
"Islam and Human Values"
2009

If the word "Islam" gives rise to fear or mistrust today, it is urgent that American Muslims clarify what we believe Islam stands for in order to dispel the idea that there is a fundamental conflict between the best values of Western civilization and the essential values of Islam. . . .

Islamic civilization, which developed out of the revelation of the Qur'an in the seventh century, affirms the truth of previous revelations, affirms religious pluralism, cultural diversity, and human rights, and recognizes the value of reason and individual conscience. . . .

[One issue] is the problem of violence. . . . Thousands of Muslim institutions and leaders, the great majority of the world's billion or more Muslims, have unequivocally condemned the hateful and violent ideologies that kill innocents and violate the dignity of all humanity. . . .

Islamic civilizations have a long history of encouraging religious tolerance and guaranteeing the rights of religious minorities. The reason for this is that the Qur'an explicitly acknowledges that the diversity of religions is part of the Divine Plan and no religion has a monopoly on truth or virtue. . . .

Jerusalem, under almost continuous Islamic rule for nearly fourteen centuries, has been a place where Christians and Jews have lived side by side with Muslims, their holy sites and religious freedom preserved. Medieval Spain also created a high level of civilization as a multi-cultural society under Islamic rule for several centuries. The Ottoman Empire, the longest lived in history, for the more than six centuries of its existence encouraged ethnic and religious minorities to participate in and contribute to society. It was the Ottoman sultan who gave sanctuary to the Jews expelled from Catholic Spain. India was governed for centuries by Muslims, even while the majority of its people practiced Hinduism. . . .

[T]he acceptance of Islam must be an act of free will. Conversion by any kind of coercion was universally condemned by Islamic scholars. . . .

There are many verses in the Qur'an that affirm the actuality and even the necessity of diversity in ways of life and religious belief: [For example,] *O mankind, truly We [God] have created you male and female, and have made you nations and tribes that ye may know one another.* [Surah 49:13] . . .

In general, war is forbidden in Islam, except in cases of self-defense in response to explicit aggression. If there is a situation where injustice is being perpetrated or if the community is being invaded, then on a temporary basis permission is given to defend oneself. This principle is explained in the following verses: *And fight in God's cause against those who war against you, but do not commit aggression—for, verily, God does not love aggressors.* [Surah 2:190]

[I]n recent decades . . . an intolerant ideology has been unleashed. A small minority of the world's one and a half billion Muslims has misconstrued the teachings of Islam to justify their misguided and immoral actions. It is most critical at this time for Muslims to condemn such extreme ideologies and their manifestations. It is equally important that non-Muslims understand that this ideology violates the fundamental moral principles of Islam and is repugnant to the vast majority of Muslims in the world. . . . So-called "suicide-bombers" did not appear until the mid-1990s. Such strategies have no precedent in Islamic history. The Qur'an says quite explicitly: *Do not kill yourselves.* [4:29] . . .

Muslims living in pluralistic societies have no religious reasons to oppose the laws of their own societies as long as they are just, but rather are encouraged to uphold the duly constituted laws of their own societies. . . . Islam and democracy are compatible and can coexist because Islam organizes humanity on the basis of the rule of law and human dignity.

The first four successors to the Prophet Muhammad were chosen by the community through

Source: Selections from Kabir Helminski, "Islam and Human Values," unpublished pamphlet, 2009.

consultation, i.e., a representative democracy. The only principle of political governance expressed in the Qur'an is the principle of Consultation (Shura), which holds that communities will *"rule themselves by means of mutual consultation."* [Surah 42:38]

Following the principles of the Qur'an, Muslims are encouraged to cooperate for the well-being of all. The Qur'an emphasizes three qualities above all others: peace, compassion, and mercy. The standard greeting in Islam is "As-Salam alaykum (Peace be with you)."

An American Muslim scholar, Abdul Aziz Sachedina, expresses it this way: "Islam does not en-courage turning God into a political statement since humans cannot possess God. . . ."

[T]here is nothing in the Qur'an that essentially contradicts reason or science. . . . Repeatedly the Qur'an urges human beings to "reflect" and "use their intelligence."

Islam is not an alien religion. It does not claim a monopoly on virtue or truth. It follows in the way of previous spiritual traditions that recognized One Spirit operating within nature and human life. It continues on the Way of the great Prophets and Messengers of all sacred traditions.

Document 22.4

Abandoning Islam

Far different from the experience of most Muslims has been the evolution of Ayaan Hirsi Ali, a Somali immigrant to the Netherlands and later to the United States, who repudiated much of her Somali culture and Islamic faith. Born in 1969, Hirsi Ali was the daughter of a prominent political opponent of the Somali government. Fleeing the country with her family, Hirsi Ali spent much of her childhood in Saudi Arabia, Ethiopia, and Kenya, where she was attracted for a time to a strict form of Islam. As a teenager, she willingly wore a *hijab*, the traditional covering often prescribed for Muslim women.

But in 1992, Hirsi Ali fled an arranged marriage to a man she regarded as a "bigot" and an "idiot" and found political asylum in the Netherlands. For this act of disobedience and rebellion, she was disowned by her father. In the Netherlands, Hirsi Ali flourished, moving from work as a cleaner to that of a translator in a refugee center and obtaining a master's degree in the process. Her encounter with Western individualism and Enlightenment thought produced a growing disenchantment with Islam, and she came to see herself as an atheist. She also lived with a man for five years, got involved in politics, was elected to the Dutch parliament, and participated in the making of a film highly critical of Muslim treatment of women, for which she received numerous death threats. In 2006 she relocated to the United States, "in search of an opportunity to build a life and livelihood in freedom" as she put it. She has been working at the American Enterprise Institute, a conservative think tank. By now a prominent public figure both in Europe and North America, Hirsi Ali spelled out her remarkable—and very rare—personal transformation in a number of books, articles, and interviews.

- What aspects of her own culture does Hirsi Ali explicitly reject?

- What are the major points of conflict between Islam and Western values in her view?

- What criticisms of her views can you imagine? How might other Muslims respond to her? How might American advocates of multicultural tolerance react to her denunciation of Islam?

- How would you assess her views of Western society? Do you find them accurate or romanticized?

AYAAN HIRSI ALI

From Islam to America

2010

For a long time, I teetered between the clear ideals of the Enlightenment that I learned about at university [in Holland] and my submission to the equally clear dictates of Allah that I feared to disobey. Working my way through university as a Dutch-Somali translator for the Dutch social services, I met many Muslims in difficult circumstances, in homes for battered women, prisons, special education classes.... I could not see the connection between their religion and the oppression of women and the lack of free individual choice.

It was, ironically, Osama bin Laden who freed me of those blinkers. After 9/11 I found it impossible to ignore his claims that the murderous destruction of innocent (if infidel) lives is consistent with the Quran. I looked in the Quran and found it to be so. To me this meant I could no longer be a Muslim ...

I see three main problems to this process of integration [of Muslims into Western culture]....The first is Islam's treatment of women. The will of little girls is stifled by Islam. By the time they menstruate, they are rendered voiceless. They are reared to become submissive robots, who serve in the house as cleaners and cooks. They are required to comply

with their father's choice of a mate, and after the wedding their lives are devoted to the sexual pleasure of their husbands and to a life of childbearing. Their education is often cut short....

All Muslims are reared to believe that Muhammad, the founder of their religion, was perfectly virtuous and that the moral strictures he left behind should never be questioned. The Quran, as "revealed" to Mohammad, is considered infallible ... and all its commands must be obeyed without question....

Personally, I felt a sense of intense relief when I accepted the possibility that there is no life after death, no hell, no punishment, no burning, no sin.... I too still sometimes feel this pain of separation from my family and from the simplicity of Islam....

The adults in my life (my mother and grandmother, other relatives and teachers) had systematically rejected and punished inquisitive behavior as insolence toward authority. In Holland I was permitted to question authority and was entitled to an answer....

I strongly believe that the Muslim mind can be opened. But when I have criticized the teachings of the Quran, as Enlightenment thinkers once challenged the revealed truths of the Bible, I have been accused of blasphemy. Muhammad says my husband can beat me and that I am worth half as much as a man. Is it I who am being disrespectful of

Source: Ayaan Hirsi Ali, *Nomad: From Islam to America* (New York: Free Press, 2010), xii, xiii, xvi–xvii, 85, 86, 88–90, 207, 210, 214, 273–74.

Muhammad in criticizing his legacy, or is it he who is disrespectful to me?

From a Letter to My Grandmother: I do not wail for your passing, but I am filled with a sense of guilt. I wish I too had been there for you. . . . When I was in pain . . . , you called in the help of your forefathers on my behalf. . . . [Y]ou took me to the witch doctor, who took your money and your sheep, and burned wounds in my chest with a long blacksmith's nail. . . .

I am sorry Grandmother that I was not there in your old age. . . . I would have summoned the spirits of my new world. Here they have salves to cleanse and sooth the itch in folded skin; they have hearing aids; they have walking sticks on wheels. . . .

I have lived with the infidels for almost two decades. I have come to learn, appreciate, and adopt their way of life. I know this would make you sad. . . .

Gone with you are the rigid rules of custom. . . . Gone with you is that bloodline [clan or tribal loyalties], for better or worse, and gone is the idiot tradition that meant you cherished mares and she-camels more than your daughters and granddaughters. . . . When we heard news of the birth of a girl in the family, you clicked and pouted and sometimes sulked for days. . . .

The secret of the Dutchman's success is his ability to adapt, to invent. . . . We bow to a God who says we must not change a thing; it is he who has chosen it.

The infidel does not see life as a test, a passage to the hereafter, but as an end and a joy in itself. . . . He may take care of his parents, but has no use for a memory filled with an endless chain of ancestors. All the seeds of his toil are spent on his own offspring, not those of his brothers or uncles.

Because the infidel trusts and studies new ideas, there is abundance in the infidel lands . . . the birth of a girl is just fine. . . . The little girl sits right next to the little boy in school . . . she gets to eat as much as he does . . . and when she matures, she gets the same opportunity to seek and find a mate as he does. . . .

Grandmother, I no longer believe in the old ways. . . . I love you, and I love some of my memories of Somalia, though not all. But I will not serve the bloodline or Allah any longer. . . . I will even strive to persuade my fellow nomads to take on the ways of the infidel. . . .

Using the Evidence: Contending for Islam

1. **Understanding the uses of history:** How does each of these authors use history to make his or her arguments? To what different historical contexts do they appeal?

2. **Comparing Islamic modernists:** How do you think Kemal Atatürk would respond to later Islamic modernists such as Sheikh Kabir? Consider also his reaction to Benazir Bhutto in Document 23.4, pp. 1178–79.

3. **Imagining a conversation:** What issue might arise in a conversation among the four authors represented here? Can you identify any areas of agreement? On which points would they probably never agree?

4. **Explaining variations:** What historical circumstances might help to account for the very different understandings of Islam that are reflected in these documents?

Visual Sources

Considering the Evidence: Representing Independence

For millions of people in Africa and Asia, the achievement of political independence from foreign domination marked a singular moment in their personal and collective histories. That moment represented a triumph against great odds and an awakening to the possibility of building new lives and new societies. As India's Nehru put it, independence was a "tryst with destiny." Both during the struggle and after, the various meanings attributed to independence found expression in a proliferation of poster art, as illustrated in the visual sources that follow. Such images served to inspire and mobilize large numbers of people for the tasks ahead, to articulate a vision of the future, and sometimes to celebrate success. Those grand hopes became a baseline from which future generations measured the realities of the post-independence period.

The decades-long march to freedom in South Africa, led by the African National Congress (ANC), finally achieved success in 1994 (see pp. 1100–02). Visual Source 22.1, an undated ANC poster, shows the organization's flag and various symbols of its long struggle. The colors of the flag depict South Africa's resources: black for the vast majority of its population, green for its rich land, and yellow for the gold that had long provided a basis for the country's wealth.

- Does the poster reflect the ANC's earlier, more peaceful and elite-based politics or its later, more aggressive posture? On what do you base your conclusion?

- How might you understand the wheel, the fist, the spear, and the shield shown on the poster? Why do you think the poster used these traditional weapons rather than modern rifles?

- Notice the mass march that provides the background to the poster's primary images. What message does this convey?

- Pay attention to the several red flags, representing the South African Communist Party, among the crowd. What posture toward communism is suggested by these flags? Keep in mind that the South African Communist Party was a longtime ally of the ANC.

- How might white, Indian, and mixed-race ("colored") supporters of the ANC react to this poster? How might white advocates of apartheid respond to it?

Visual Source 22.1 African National Congress (Special Collections, Senate House Library, University of London)

Following decades of opposition to French colonial rule and Japanese aggression, Vietnam found itself in a long struggle against American military intervention during the 1960s and 1970s. That struggle took shape as an effort by North Vietnam and communist supporters in the south to reunify their country and to drive out the American military forces, which numbered over a half million by the mid-1960s. By 1975, the North Vietnamese had succeeded. It was a stunning reversal for the American superpower and an equally stunning triumph for the small Southeast Asian country. While the reasons for this surprising turn of events have been debated ever since, it was clearly of enormous significance for Vietnamese understandings of their national independence. Visual Source 22.2 presents a Vietnamese poster, dating from somewhere between 1965 and 1975, that celebrates one aspect of that unlikely achievement. The caption reads: "Bravo for Hanoi's Tremendous Victory When 23 B-52s Were Shot Down!"

■ How does this poster present the struggle against the United States?

■ In what way does it anticipate or celebrate the victory over the United States? What meaning does it attach to that victory? How might you

Visual Source 22.2 Vietnamese Independence and Victory over the United States (Courtesy Track 16 / Smart Art Press, Culver City, California)

understand the flowers that the soldier is holding and the small pagoda in the upper left?

■ What other perspectives on this victory for national independence can you imagine? Consider various viewpoints within the United States as well as those of the anticommunist elements in Vietnamese society.

The establishment of the independent state of Israel in 1948 marked an enormous victory for Jewish people that took on rich meaning for them in many contexts. The most historically significant context no doubt lay in the return of widely scattered Jewish people to the ancient biblical homeland from which so many Jews had fled or been expelled by various foreign rulers — Babylonian, Assyrian, Roman, Byzantine, and Crusader European. Since the first century C.E., the majority of the world's Jews had lived in diaspora in the Middle East, North Africa, or Europe, with smaller numbers retaining a Jewish presence in what was then called Palestine. For those whose families had long lived in exile, the opportunity to return to an authentically Jewish state in the area comprising the ancient Land of Israel must have seemed miraculous.

A more immediate context for the establishment of Israel was that of the Zionist movement, formally initiated in Europe in 1897 with the goal of creating a "home for the Jewish people in Palestine." It was a response to the racism and anti-Semitism of European culture, and it drew on currents of nationalist thinking then surging across Europe. A major expression of Zionism lay in growing Jewish emigration to their ancient homeland, especially during the 1920s and 1930s and even more so in the several years following World War II and the Holocaust. Many among those who survived sought refuge and security in a land of their own.

Two major obstacles confronted these Jewish emigrants. One was British control of Palestine, granted to Great Britain as a mandate of the League of Nations following World War I. While the British favored the eventual creation of a Jewish state, they also feared antagonizing their Arab allies by allowing unfettered Jewish immigration. The second obstacle was opposition from the Arab majority of Palestine, who feared not only the loss of their land as Jewish settlers bought up growing amounts of it but also the loss of their cultural identity as Muslims in what they feared would become a Jewish land. The creation of Israel in 1948, with support from the United Nations, marked the triumph of Zionism and a victory over both British imperialism and Arab resistance.

Visual Source 22.3 shows a Zionist poster created around 1940 and intended to encourage emigration to the Land of Israel and to persuade donors to contribute money for the purchase of land in Palestine. It was titled "Redeem the Land," a reference to the Zionist goal of using up-to-date farming techniques to provide the agricultural basis for a modern society.[16]

- What features of the poster contributed to the Zionists' message?

- Why do you think the land is shown without any people?

- How do you understand the contrast between the richly plowed land and the adjacent barren areas? What image of the new Israel does this poster project?

- The fruits on the left side of the poster reflect the biblical description of "promised land" as recorded in Deuteronomy 8:7–10. What is their function in the poster?

If the establishment of Israel as an independent state was a great triumph for Jewish nationalism, it was a disaster for Arabs in general and Palestinian Arabs in particular. In the decades that followed, Israel and various Arab states (Egypt, Jordan, and Syria, for example) went to war repeatedly. The so-called Six Day War of 1967 brought under Israeli control additional Palestinian land, including the West Bank, the Gaza Strip, and East Jerusalem, areas now known as the Palestinian Territories.

At the same time, the Arabs of Palestine, both within Israel and in the adjacent territories, were developing a distinct national identity of their own.

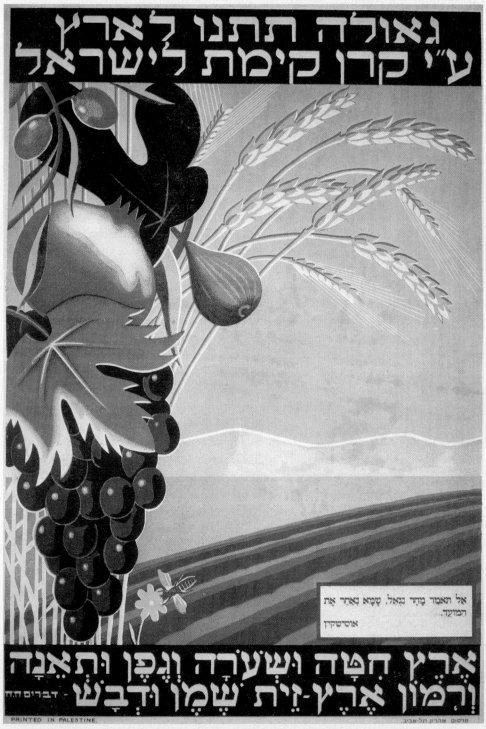

Visual Source 22.3 Winning a Jewish National State (The Central Zionist Archives, Jerusalem)

Many of them had lost their land and had lived for several generations as refugees in overcrowded camps in neighboring countries or territories where they were dependent on services provided by the United Nations. Almost all Palestinians felt oppressed, constrained, or discriminated against by Israeli authorities. Their emerging national identity found expression in the Palestinian Liberation Organization (PLO), founded in 1964. Initially the PLO called for the complete liberation of Palestine from Zionist colonialism, but by the late 1980s the organization had implicitly recognized the right of Israel to exist and sought a "two-state solution" with an independent Palestine and Israel living side by side.

Achieving even a limited Palestinian state, however, has proved extraordinarily difficult. In pursuit of their national goals, Palestinians have conducted raids, suicide bombing missions, and rocket attacks on Israel from camps in neighboring territories and on several occasions have organized large-scale violent resistance movements known as *intifada*. For its part, Israel has launched highly destructive large-scale military actions in the Palestinian territories, imposed economic blockades that have brought immense suffering to Palestinians, built walls and fences that have disrupted the normal movement of Palestinians, and continued to enlarge the Jewish settlements, especially in the West Bank. Both sides have presented their actions as largely defensive and reactive to the provocations of the other. They have also engaged in periodic negotiations with each other, but those efforts have thus far foundered on unbridgeable differences as to the size and nature of a future Palestinian state, the status of Jerusalem, and the right of Palestinian refugees to return to their lands in Israel. Divisions among Palestinians have also hampered their movement, particularly the recent rivalry between the PLO and Hamas, an Islamic organization with both welfare and political/military functions.

Like other peoples seeking an independent state, Palestinians have represented their struggles in posters such as Visual Source 22.4, created by the Palestinian artist Abdel Rahman Al Muzain in 1984. Featuring a Palestinian farmer, it was undertaken to commemorate Land Day, an annual observance of the occasion in 1976 when six Palestinians were killed in demonstrations against Israeli confiscation of their land.[17]

- How might you read this poster as a response to the Israeli poster in Visual Source 22.3?

- What significance would you attach to the posture and the traditional clothing of the farmer? Why do you think the artist depicted him with a pickax rather than a rifle?

- What message is conveyed by the rows of traditional houses on the hillside behind the farmer?

- What expectations for the future does the poster imply? Consider the meaning of the doves between the feet and on the shoulder of the farmer as well as the sun's swirling rays that seem to link the earth and sky.

Visual Source 22.4
A Palestinian Nation in the Making (Palestine Poster Project/ Visual Connection Archive)

Using the Evidence: Representing Independence

1. **Making comparisons:** Movements of national independence can be defined by the conditions they were opposing as well as the kind of future they were seeking. With these two criteria in mind, what similarities and what differences can you identify among these visual sources and the movements they represented?

2. **Defining points of view:** How would you identify the point of view that each of these visual sources conveys? Can you imagine a visual source with an alternative point of view for each of them?

3. **Seeking meaning in visual sources:** How do visual sources such as these help to illuminate the meaning of national independence? In what ways are they limited as sources of evidence for historians?

Chapter 22 Wrap Up

STEP ONE

The Word to Know: Decolonization

The *Oxford English Dictionary* defines *decolonization* as "the withdrawal from its former colonies of a colonial power; the acquisition of political or economic independence by such colonies." Review A Map of Time on page 1089, as well as Chapter 22. Then write a paragraph to explain how at least three of the events on the timeline relate to the process of global decolonization in the twentieth century.

STEP TWO

Mapping the End of Empires

This exercise asks you to examine three of the maps from Chapter 22 and analyze in conjunction with evidence from the chapter's narrative to better understand decolonization and the challenges that newly independent nations in the Global South faced.

1. Begin by examining Map 22.1, "The End of Empire in Africa and Asia" (p. 1090), then answer the questions below.

   a. Identify three similarities in decolonization and three unique events.

   b. Ask at least three good questions that the map raises.

2. Next examine Map 22.2, "The Partition of British South Asia" (p. 1097), and then identify three potentially problematic issues that arise with South Asian independence.

3. Finally, consider Map 22.3, "South Africa after Apartheid" (p. 1102), as well as the inset map, South Africa under Apartheid.

   a. Describe the map of South Africa under apartheid.

   b. Predict a challenge that might come from the redrawing of the map after the end of apartheid.

STEP THREE

Debating Development in Africa

The African nations that gained independence from colonial rule from the 1950s through the 1970s faced a number of development challenges. Read the documents below and the relevant pages from Chapter 22 (pp. 1109–1112 in particular) and then answer the question that follows.

1. Excerpt from A. Adu Boahen, *African Perspectives on Colonialism*, 1987

A. Adu Boahen was a prominent historian and scholar in Ghana who acknowledged some positive aspects of colonialism but who, on the whole, was negative in his assessment of the legacy of colonialism.

"It is this loss of sovereignty and the consequent isolation from the outside world that one finds one of the most pernicious impacts of colonialism on Africa and one of the fundamental causes of its present underdevelopment and technological backwardness."

Source: A. Adu Boahen, *African Perspectives on Colonialism* (Baltimore: The Johns Hopkins University Press, 1987), p. 99

2. Excerpt from Mildred Malineo Tau, "Women: Critical to African Development," 1981

Post-independence planning for African economic development focused almost exclusive on men. In 1981, Mildred Malineo Tau wrote an essay on the importance of women for Africa's economic development.

"Recognition of the role of women in development is critical.... The issue of women's access to wage work and other sources of cash income in the African continent is more than one of equity. It goes beyond the question of equal rights for women to become one of economic survival for them and their children."

Source: Mildred Malineo Tau, "Women: Critical To African Development," *Africa Report* (March/April, 1981): 4–6.

3. Excerpt from George B.N. Ayittey, *Africa Betrayed*, 1992

George Ayittey is a prominent Ghanaian economist and scholar. His writings have focused on the internal problems that have hampered African development.

"It is easy for African leaders to put the blame somewhere else ... on Western aid donors or on an allegedly hostile international economic environment, ... but in my view the internal factors ... have played far greater roles than the external ones ... [I]n Africa, government officials do not serve the people. The African state has been reduced to a mafia-like bazaar, where anyone with an official designation can pillage at will."

Source: George B. N. Ayittey, *Africa Betrayed* (New York: St. Martin's Press, 1992), 100, 335–36.

■ Question

Now that you have read the documents and reviewed the textbook chapter, write an essay that answers the following question: What are the development challenges that African nations faced with decolonization? What were the reasons and some of the possible solutions for these challenges?

CHAPTER TWENTY-THREE

Capitalism and Culture

A New Phase of Global Interaction

SINCE 1945

"I think every Barbie doll is more harmful than an American missile," declared Iranian toy seller Masoumeh Rahimi in 2002. To Rahimi, Barbie's revealing clothing, her shapely appearance, and her close association with Ken, her longtime unmarried companion, were "foreign to Iran's culture." Thus Rahimi warmly welcomed the arrival of Sara and Dara, two Iranian Muslim dolls meant to counteract the negative influence of Barbie and Ken, who had long dominated Iran's toy market. Sara and her brother, Dara, represented eight-year-old twins. Sara came complete with a headscarf to cover her hair in modest Muslim fashion and a full-length white chador enveloping her from head to toe. They were described as helping each other solve problems, while looking to their loving parents for guidance, hardly the message that Barbie and Ken conveyed.[1]

The widespread availability of Barbie in Muslim Iran provides one small example of the power of global commerce in the world of the early twenty-first century. The creation of Sara and Dara illustrates resistance to the cultural values associated with this American product. Still, Sara and Barbie had something in common: both were manufactured in China. This triangular relationship of the United States, Iran, and China neatly symbolized the growing integration of world economies and cultures as well as the divergences and conflicts that this process generated. Those linked but contrasting patterns are the twin themes of this final chapter.

DURING THE TWENTIETH CENTURY, AN INCREASINGLY DENSE WEB OF PO-LITICAL RELATIONSHIPS, economic transactions, and cultural influences

One World: This NASA photograph, showing both the earth and the moon, reveals none of the national, ethnic, religious, or linguistic boundaries that have long divided humankind. Such pictures have both reflected and helped create a new planetary consciousness among growing numbers of people. (Image created by Reto Stockli, Nazmi El Saleous, and Marit Jentoft-Nilsen, NASA GSFC) cut across the world's many peoples, countries, and regions, binding them together more tightly, but also more contentiously. By the 1990s, this process of accelerating engagement among distant peoples was widely known as globalization.

Although the term was relatively new, the process was not. From the viewpoint of world history, the genealogy of globalization reached far into the past. The Arab, Mongol, Russian, Chinese, and Ottoman empires; the Silk Road, Indian Ocean, and trans-Saharan trade routes; the spread of Buddhism, Christianity, and especially Islam— all of these connections had long linked the societies of the Eastern Hemisphere, bringing new rulers, religions, products, diseases, and technologies to many of its peoples. Later, in the centuries after 1500, European maritime voyages and colonizing efforts launched the Columbian exchange, incorporating the Western Hemisphere and inner Africa firmly and permanently into a genuinely global network of communication, exchange, and often exploitation. During the nineteenth century, as the Industrial Revolution took hold and Western nations began a new round of empire building in Asia and Africa, that global network tightened further, and its role as generator of social and cultural change only increased.

These were the foundations on which twentieth-century globalization was built. A number of prominent developments of the past century, explored in the previous three chapters, operated on a global scale: the world wars, the Great Depression, communism, the cold war, the end of empire, and the growing prominence of developing countries. But global interaction quickened its pace and deepened its impact after World War II, an acceleration illustrated by four major processes: the transformation of the world economy, the emergence of global feminism, the confrontation of world religions with modernity, and the growing awareness of humankind's enormous impact on the environment.

SEEKING THE MAIN POINT

To what extent has globalization fostered converging values and common interests among the world's peoples? In what ways has it generated new conflicts among them?

The Transformation of the World Economy

■ **Change**
What factors contributed to economic globalization in the second half of the twentieth century?

When most people speak of globalization, they are referring to the immense acceleration in international economic transactions that took place in the second half of the twentieth century and continued into the twenty-first. Many have come to see this process as almost natural, certainly inevitable, and practically unstoppable. Yet the first half of the twentieth century, particularly the decades between the two world wars, witnessed a deep contraction of global economic linkages as the aftermath of World War I and then the Great Depression wreaked havoc on the world economy. International trade, investment, and labor migration dropped sharply as major states turned inward, favoring high tariffs and economic autonomy in the face of a global economic collapse.

The aftermath of World War II was very different. The capitalist victors in that conflict, led by the United States, were determined to avoid any return to such Depression-era conditions. At a conference in Bretton Woods, New Hampshire, in 1944, they forged a set of agreements and institutions (the World Bank and the In-

A Map of Time

1919–1946	League of Nations
1945	United Nations, World Bank, and International Monetary Fund established
1960	Organization of Petroleum Exporting Countries founded
1962	Rachel Carson publishes *Silent Spring*
1963	Betty Friedan publishes *Feminine Mystique*
1970	Greenpeace established
1979	Convention on the Elimination of All Forms of Discrimination against Women adopted by UN
1979	Iranian revolution
1982	Law of the Sea Convention introduced
1994	NAFTA enacted
1995	World Trade Organization created
1997	Kyoto Protocol on global warming introduced
2001	Sept. 11 attacks on World Trade Center and Pentagon
2008	Global economic crisis begins
2011	Osama bin Laden killed

ternational Monetary Fund [IMF]) that laid the foundation for postwar globalization. This "Bretton Woods system" negotiated the rules for commercial and financial dealings among the major capitalist countries, while promoting relatively free trade, stable currency values linked to the U.S. dollar, and high levels of capital investment.

Technology also contributed to the acceleration of economic globalization. Containerized shipping, huge oil tankers, and air express services dramatically lowered transportation costs, while fiber-optic cables and later the Internet provided the communication infrastructure for global economic interaction. In the developing countries, population growth, especially when tied to growing economies and modernizing societies, further fueled globalization as dozens of new nations entered the world economy.

The kind of economic globalization taking shape in the 1970s and after was widely known as neoliberalism. Major capitalist countries such as the United States and Great Britain abandoned many earlier political controls on economic activity as their leaders and businesspeople increasingly viewed the entire world as a single market. This approach to the world economy favored the reduction of tariffs, the free global movement of capital, a mobile and temporary workforce, the privatization of many state-run enterprises, the curtailing of government efforts to regulate the economy, and both tax and spending cuts. Powerful international lending agencies such as the World Bank and the IMF imposed such free market and pro-business conditions on many poor countries if they were to qualify for much-needed loans. The collapse of the state-controlled economies of the communist world only furthered such unrestricted global capitalism. In this view, the market, operating both globally and within nations, was the most effective means of generating the holy grail of economic growth. As communism collapsed by the end of the twentieth century, "capitalism was global and the globe was capitalist."[2]

Reglobalization

■ Connection

In what ways has economic globalization more closely linked the world's peoples?

These conditions provided the foundations for a dramatic quickening of global economic transactions after World War II, a "reglobalization" of the world economy following the contractions of the 1930s. This immensely significant process was expressed in the accelerating circulation of goods, capital, and people.

World trade, for example, skyrocketed from a value of some $57 billion in 1947 to about $16 trillion in 2009. Department stores and supermarkets around the world stocked their shelves with goods from every part of the globe. Twinings of London marketed its 120 blends of tea in more than 100 countries, and the Australian-based Kiwi shoe polish was sold in 180 countries. In 2005, about 70 percent of Walmart products reportedly included components from China. And the following year, Toyota replaced General Motors as the world's largest automaker with manufacturing facilities in at least eighteen countries.

Money as well as goods achieved an amazing global mobility in three ways. The first was "foreign direct investment," whereby a firm in, say, the United States opens a factory in China or Mexico (see Map 23.1 and Visual Source 23.1, p. 1183). Such investment exploded after 1960 as companies in rich countries sought to take advantage of cheap labor, tax breaks, and looser environmental regulations in developing countries. A second form of money in motion has been the short-term movement of capital, in which investors annually spent trillions of dollars purchasing foreign currencies or stocks likely to increase in value and often sold them quickly thereafter, with unsettling consequences. A third form of money movement involved the personal funds of individuals. By the end of the twentieth century, international credit cards had taken hold almost everywhere, allowing for easy transfer of

A World Economy
Indian-based call centers that serve North American or European companies and customers have become a common experience of globalization for many. Here employees in one such call center in Patna, a major city in northeastern India, undergo voice training in order to communicate more effectively with their English-speaking callers. (Indiapicture/Alamy)

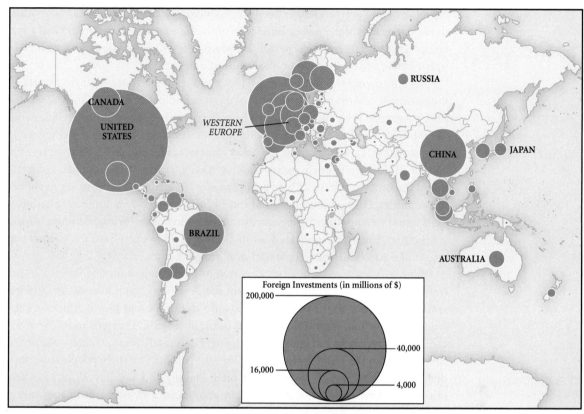

Map 23.1 Globalization in Action: Foreign Direct Investment in the Late Twentieth Century
Investment across national borders has been a major expression of globalization. This map shows the global distribution of investment inflows as of 1998. Notice which countries or regions were receiving the most investment from abroad and which received the least. How might you account for this pattern? Keep in mind that some regions, such as the United States, Western Europe, and Japan, were major sources of such investment as well as recipients of it.

money across national borders. In 2012, MasterCard was accepted at some 33 million businesses in 220 countries or territories.

Central to the acceleration of economic globalization have been huge global businesses known as transnational corporations (TNCs), which produce goods or deliver services simultaneously in many countries. For example, Mattel Corporation produced Barbie, that quintessentially American doll, in factories located in Indonesia, Malaysia, and China, using molds from the United States, plastic and hair from Taiwan and Japan, and cotton cloth from China. From distribution centers in Hong Kong, more than a billion Barbies were sold in 150 countries by 1999. Burgeoning in number since the 1960s, those TNCs, such as Royal Dutch Shell, Sony, and General Motors, often were of such an enormous size and had such economic clout that their assets and power dwarfed that of many countries. By 2000, 51 of the world's 100 largest economic units were in fact TNCs, not countries. In the permissive economic climate of recent decades, such firms have been able to move their facilities quickly from place to place in search of the lowest labor costs or the least restrictive environmental regulations. During one five-year period, for example, Nike closed twenty factories and opened thirty-five others, often thousands of miles apart.

Accompanying the movement of goods and capital in the globalizing world of the twentieth century were new patterns of human migration, driven by war, revolution, poverty, and the end of empire. The collapse of the Ottoman Empire following World War I witnessed the "repatriation" of over a million Greeks from Turkey, while some 400,000 Turks moved in the other direction. Fleeing anti-Semitism, fascism, and the Holocaust, Jews emigrated to what is now Israel in large numbers, generating in the process a flow of Palestinian refugees to squalid settlements in neighboring countries. Political repression and forced labor in the Soviet Union pushed millions into the camps of gulag, primarily in Siberia. In South Africa, an industrializing economy and apartheid policies drew millions of male workers from the countryside into mines and factories, often under horrific conditions.

But perhaps the most significant pattern of global migration since the 1960s has featured a vast movement of people from the developing countries of Asia, Africa, and Latin America to the industrialized world of Europe and North America. Pakistanis, Indians, and West Indians moved to Great Britain; Algerians and West Africans to France; Turks and Kurds to Germany; Filipinos, Koreans, Cubans, Mexicans, and Haitians to the United States. A considerable majority of these people have been dubbed "labor migrants." Most moved, often illegally and with few skills, to escape poverty in their own lands, drawn by an awareness of Western prosperity and a belief that a better future awaited them in the developed countries. By 2003, some 4 million Filipino domestic workers were employed in 130 countries. Young women by the hundreds of thousands from poor countries have been recruited as sex workers in wealthier nations, sometimes in conditions approaching slavery. Smaller numbers of highly skilled and university-trained people, such as doctors and computer scientists, came in search of professional opportunities less available in their own countries. All of this represented a kind of reverse "development aid"—either as cheap labor or intellectual resources—from poor countries to rich. Still other peoples moved as refugees, fleeing violence or political oppression in places such as Vietnam, Cambodia, Sudan, Uganda, Cuba, and Haiti.

Many of those people in motion were headed for the United States, drawn by its reputation for wealth and opportunity. In the forty years between 1971 and 2010, almost 20 million immigrants arrived in the United States legally, and millions more entered illegally, the vast majority of both from the Latin American/Caribbean region and from Asia. Mexicans have been by far the largest group of immigrants to the United States, and many have arrived without legal documentation, an estimated 6.65 million during the first decade of the twenty-first century alone. Often their journeys north have been dangerous as they confronted long treks through burning deserts, sought to evade American immigration authorities, and had to depend on expensive and sometimes unreliable "coyotes" who facilitate the smuggling of people across the border. Once in the United States, many of these immigrants provided inexpensive manual labor in fields, factories, and homes of the well-to-do, even as the money they sent back to their families in Mexico represented that nation's largest source of foreign exchange. The presence of migrants from the Global South has prompted considerable cultural and political conflict in both the United States and Europe, illustrated by a prolonged controversy about the wearing of headscarves by Muslim girls in French public schools.

Growth, Instability, and Inequality

The impact of these tightening economic links has prompted enormous debate and controversy. Amid the swirl of contending opinion, one thing seemed reasonably clear: economic globalization accompanied, and arguably helped generate, the most remarkable spurt of economic growth in world history. On a global level, total world output grew from a value of $7 trillion in 1950 to $73 trillion in 2009 and on a per capita basis from $2,652 to $10,728.[3] This represents an immense, rapid, and unprecedented creation of wealth with a demonstrable impact on human welfare. Life expectancies expanded almost everywhere, infant mortality declined, and literacy increased. The UN Human Development Report in 1997 concluded that "in the past 50 years, poverty has fallen more than in the previous 500."[4]

■ **Connection**
What new or sharper divisions has economic globalization generated?

Far more problematic have been the instability of this emerging world economy and the distribution of the wealth it has generated. Amid overall economic growth, periodic crises and setbacks have shaped recent world history. Soaring oil prices contributed to a severe stock market crash in 1973–1974 and great hardship for many developing countries. Inability to repay mounting debts triggered a major financial crisis in Latin America during the 1980s and resulted in a "lost decade" in terms of economic development. Another financial crisis in Asia during the late 1990s resulted in the collapse of many businesses, widespread unemployment, and political upheaval in Indonesia and Thailand.

But nothing since the Great Depression more clearly illustrated the unsettling consequences of global connectedness in the absence of global regulation than the worldwide economic contraction that began in 2008. An inflated housing market—or "bubble"—in the United States collapsed, triggering millions of home foreclosures, growing unemployment, the tightening of credit, and declining consumer spending. Soon this crisis rippled around the world. Iceland's rapidly growing economy collapsed almost overnight as three major banks failed, the country's stock market dropped by 80 percent, and its currency lost more than 70 percent of its value—all in a single week. In Africa, reduced demand for exports threatened to halt a promising decade of economic progress. In Sierra Leone, for example, some 90 percent of the country's diamond-mine workers lost their jobs. The slowing of China's booming economy led to unemployment for one in seven of the country's urban migrants, forcing them to return to already overcrowded rural areas. Impoverished Central American and Caribbean families, dependent on money sent home by family members working abroad, suffered further as those remittances dropped sharply. Contracting economies contributed to debt crises in Greece, Italy, and Spain and threatened to unravel European economic integration. Calls for both protectionism and greater regulation suggested that the wide-open capitalist world economy of recent decades was perhaps not as inevitable as some had thought. Whatever the overall benefits of the modern global system, economic stability and steady progress were not among them.

Nor was equality. Since Europe's Industrial Revolution took hold in the early nineteenth century, a wholly new division appeared within the human community—between the rich industrialized countries, primarily in Europe and North America, and everyone else. In 1820, the ratio between the income of the top and bottom 20 percent of the world's population was three to one. By 1991, it was eighty-six to one.[5] The accelerated economic globalization of the twentieth century did not create this global rift, but it arguably has worsened the North/South gap and certainly has not greatly diminished it. Even the well-known capitalist financier and investor George Soros, a billionaire many times over, acknowledged this reality in 2000: "The global capitalist system has produced a very uneven playing field. The gap between the rich and the poor is getting wider."[6] That gap has been evident, often tragically, in great disparities in incomes, medical care, availability of clean drinking water, educational and employment opportunities, access to the Internet, and dozens of other ways. It has shaped the life chances of practically everyone (see Snapshot).

These disparities were the foundations for a new kind of global conflict. As the East/West division of capitalism and communism faded, differences between the rich nations of the Global North and the developing countries of the Global South assumed greater prominence in world affairs. Highly contentious issues have included the rules for world trade, availability of and terms for foreign aid, representation in international economic organizations, the mounting problem of indebtedness, and environmental and labor standards. Such matters surfaced repeatedly in international negotiations during the second half of the twentieth century and into the twenty-first. In the 1970s, for example, a large group of developing countries joined together to demand a "new international economic order" that was more favorable to the poor countries. Not much success attended this effort. More recently, developing countries have contested protectionist restrictions on their agricultural exports imposed by the rich countries seeking to protect their own politically powerful farmers.

Beyond active resistance by the rich nations, a further obstacle to reforming the world economy in favor of the poor lay in growing disparities among the developing countries themselves. The oil-rich economies of the Middle East had little in common with the banana-producing countries of Central America. The rapidly industrializing states of China, India, and South Korea had quite different economic agendas than impoverished African countries. These disparities made common action difficult to achieve.

Economic globalization has contributed to inequalities not only at the global level and among developing countries but also within individual nations, rich and poor

Snapshot   **Global Development and Inequality, 2011**[7]

This table shows twelve commonly used indicators of "development" and their variations in 2011 across four major groups of countries defined by average level of per capita income. In which areas has the Global South most nearly caught up with the Global North?

Gross National Income per capita with sample countries	Low Income $995 or less (Congo, Kenya, Ethiopia, Afghanistan, Myanmar)	Lower Middle $996–3945 (India, China, Egypt, Algeria, Indonesia, Nigeria)	Upper Middle $3946–12,195 (Mexico, Brazil, Turkey, Russia, Iran)	Upper $12,196 or more (USA, Western Europe, Japan, South Korea, Australia)
Life Expectancy M/F in years	58/60	66/70	68/75	77/83
Deaths under age 5 per 1000 live births	120	60	24	7
Deaths from infectious disease: %	36	14	11	7
Access to toilets: %	35	50	84	99
Years of education	7.9	10.3	13.8	14.5
Literacy rate: %	66	80	93	99
Population growth: % annual	2.27	1.27	.96	.39
Urban population: %	27	41	74	78
Cell phones per 100 people	22	47	92	106
Internet users per 100 people	2.3	13.7	29.9	68.3
Personal computers per 100 people	1.2	4.3	11.9	60.4
Cars per 1,000 people	5.8	20.3	125.2	435.1
Carbon dioxide emissions: metric tons per capita	1	3	5	13

alike. In the United States, for example, a shifting global division of labor required the American economy to shed millions of manufacturing jobs. With recent U.S. factory wages far higher than those of China, many companies moved their manufacturing operations offshore to Asia or Latin America. This left many relatively unskilled American workers in the lurch, forcing them to work in the low-wage service sector, even as other Americans were growing prosperous in emerging high-tech industries. Even some highly skilled work, such as computer programming, was outsourced to lower-wage sites in India, Ireland, Russia, and elsewhere. By 2012, mounting income inequality and the erosion of the country's middle class had become major issues in American political debate.

Globalization divided Mexico as well. The northern part of the country, with close business and manufacturing ties to the United States, grew much more prosperous than the south, which was a largely rural agricultural area and had a far more slowly growing economy. Beginning in 1994, southern resentment boiled over in the Chiapas rebellion, which featured a strong anti-globalization platform. Its leader, known as Subcomandante Marcos, referred to globalization as a "process to eliminate that multitude of people who are not useful to the powerful."[8] (See Document 23.5, pp. 1180–81.) China's rapid economic growth likewise fostered mounting inequality between its rural households and those in its burgeoning cities, where income by 2000 was three times that of the countryside. Economic globalization may have brought people together as never before, but it also divided them sharply.

The hardships and grievances of those left behind or threatened by the march toward economic integration have fueled a growing popular movement aimed at criticizing and counteracting globalization. Known variously as an anti-globalization, alternative globalization, or global justice movement, it emerged in the 1990s as an international coalition of political activists, concerned scholars and students, trade unions, women's and religious organizations, environmental groups, and others, hailing from rich and poor countries alike. Thus opposition to neoliberal globalization was itself global in scope. Though reflecting a variety of viewpoints, that opposition largely agreed that free trade, market-driven corporate globalization had lowered labor standards, fostered ecological degradation, prevented poor countries from protecting themselves against financial speculators, ignored local cultures, disregarded human rights, and enhanced global inequality, while favoring the interests of large corporations and the rich countries.

This movement appeared dramatically on the world's radar screen in late 1999 in Seattle at a meeting of the World Trade Organization (WTO) (see Visual Source 23.3, p. 1186). An international body representing 149 nations and charged with negotiating the rules for global commerce and promoting free trade, the WTO had become a major target of globalization critics. "The central idea of the WTO," argued one such critic, "is that *free trade*—actually the values and interests of global corporations—should supersede all other values."[9] Tens of thousands of protesters—academics, activists, farmers, labor union leaders from all over the world—descended on Seattle in what became a violent, chaotic, and much-publicized protest. At the city's harbor, protest organizers created a Seattle Tea Party around the slogan "No globalization without representation," echoing the Boston Tea Party of 1773. Subsequent meetings of the WTO and other high-level international economic gatherings were likewise greeted with large-scale protest and a heavy police presence. In 2001, alternative globalization activists created the World Social Forum, an annual gathering to co-ordinate strategy, exchange ideas, and share experiences, under the slogan "Another world is possible." It was an effort to demonstrate that neoliberal globalization was not inevitable and that the processes of a globalized economy could and should be regulated and subjected to public accountability.

Globalization and an American Empire

For many people, opposition to this kind of globalization also expressed resistance to mounting American power and influence in the world. An "American Empire," some have argued, is the face of globalization (see Map 23.2), but scholars, commentators, and politicians have disagreed about how best to describe the United States' role in the postwar world. Certainly it has not been a colonial territorial empire such as that of the British or the French in the nineteenth century. Americans generally, seeking to distinguish themselves from Europeans, have vigorously denied that they have an empire at all.

In some ways, the U.S. global presence might be seen as an "informal empire," similar to the ones that Europeans exercised in China and the Middle East during the nineteenth century. In both cases, economic penetration, political pressure, and periodic military action sought to create societies and governments compatible with the values and interests of the dominant power, but without directly governing large populations for long periods. In its economic dimension, American dominance has been termed an "empire of production," which uses its immense wealth to entice or intimidate potential collaborators.[10] Some scholars have emphasized the United States' frequent use of force around the world, while others have focused attention on the "soft power" of its cultural attractiveness, its political and cultural freedoms, the economic benefits of cooperation, and the general willingness of many to follow the American lead voluntarily.

With the collapse of the Soviet Union and the end of the cold war by the early 1990s, U.S. military dominance was unchecked by any equivalent power. When the United States was attacked by Islamic militants on September 11, 2001, that power was unleashed first against Afghanistan (2001), which had sheltered the al-Qaeda instigators of that attack, and then against Iraq (2003), where Saddam Hussein allegedly had been developing weapons of mass destruction. In the absence of the Soviet Union, the United States could act unilaterally without fear of triggering a conflict with another major power. Although the Afghan and Iraqi regimes were quickly defeated, establishing a lasting peace and rebuilding badly damaged Muslim countries have proved difficult tasks. Thus, within a decade of the Soviet collapse, the United States found itself in yet another global struggle, an effort to contain or eliminate Islamic "terrorism."

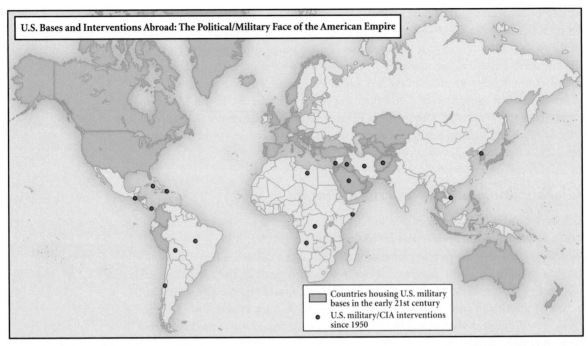

U.S. Bases and Interventions Abroad: The Political/Military Face of the American Empire

Countries housing U.S. military bases in the early 21st century

U.S. military/CIA interventions since 1950

Global McDonald's: The Economic/Cultural Face of the American Empire

Global McDonald's Restaurants by Country, 2003

1–19
20–99
100–499
500–999
1,000–1,999
2,000–9,999
10,000 +

Map 23.2 Two Faces of an "American Empire"
Those who argue that the United States constructed an empire in the second half of the twentieth century point both to its political/military alliances and interventions around the world and to U.S. economic and cultural penetration of many countries. The distribution of U.S. military bases, a partial indication of its open and covert interventions, and the location of McDonald's restaurants indicates something of the scope of America's global presence in the early twenty-first century.

Since the 1980s, as its relative military strength peaked, the United States faced growing international economic competition. The recovery of Europe and Japan and the emergent industrialization of South Korea, Taiwan, China, and India substantially reduced the United States' share of overall world production from about 50 percent in 1945 to 20 percent in the 1980s. By 2008 the United States accounted for just 8.1 percent of world merchandise exports. Accompanying this relative decline was a sharp reversal of the country's trade balance as U.S. imports greatly exceeded its exports. China was on track to overtake the United States as the world's largest economy by the 2020s even as it held much of the mounting American national debt.

However it might be defined, the exercise of American power, like that of many empires, was resisted abroad and contested at home. In Korea, Vietnam, Cuba, Iraq, Afghanistan, and elsewhere, armed struggle against U.S. intervention was both costly and painful. During the cold war, the governments of India, Egypt, and Ethiopia sought to diminish American influence in their affairs by turning to the Soviet Union or playing off the two superpowers against each other. Even France, resenting U.S. domination, withdrew from the military structure of NATO in 1967 and expelled all foreign-controlled troops from the country. Many intellectuals, fearing the erosion of their own cultures in the face of well-financed American media around the world, have decried American "cultural imperialism." By the early twenty-first century, the United States' international policies—such as its refusal to accept the jurisdiction of the International Criminal Court; its refusal to ratify the Kyoto protocol on global warming; its doctrine of preemptive war, which was exercised in Iraq; and its apparent use of torture—had generated widespread opposition.

Within the United States as well, the global exercise of American power generated controversy. The Vietnam War, for example, divided the United States more sharply than at any time since the Civil War. It split families and friendships, churches and political parties. The war provided a platform for a growing number of critics, both at home and abroad, who had come to resent American cultural and economic dominance in the post–1945 world. It stimulated a new sense of activism among students in the nation's colleges and universities. Many of them came to see America itself as an imperialist power. A similar set of issues, protests, and controversies followed the American invasion of Iraq in 2003.

The Globalization of Liberation: Focus on Feminism

More than goods, money, and people traversed the planet during the most recent century. So too did ideas, and none was more powerful than that of liberation. Communism promised workers and peasants liberation from capitalist oppression. Nationalism offered subject peoples liberation from imperialism. Advocates of democracy sought liberation from authoritarian governments.

The 1960s in particular witnessed an unusual convergence of protest movements around the world, suggesting the emergence of a global culture of liberation. Within the United States, the civil rights demands of African Americans and Hispanic Americans; the youthful counterculture of rock music, sex, and drugs; the prolonged and highly divisive protests against the war in Vietnam—all of this gave the 1960s a distinctive place in the country's recent history. Across the Atlantic, swelling protests against unresponsive bureaucracy, consumerism, and middle-class values likewise erupted, most notably in France in 1968. There a student-led movement protesting conditions in universities attracted the support of many middle-class people, who were horrified at the brutality of the police, and stimulated an enormous strike among some 9 million workers. France seemed on the edge of another revolution. Related but smaller-scale movements took place in Germany, Italy, Japan, Mexico, Argentina, and elsewhere.

The communist world too was rocked by protest. In 1968, a new Communist Party leadership in Czechoslovakia, led by Alexander Dubcek, initiated a sweeping series of reforms aimed at creating "socialism with a human face." Censorship ended, generating an explosion of free expression in what had been a highly repressive regime; unofficial political clubs emerged publicly; victims of earlier repression were rehabilitated; secret ballots for party elections were put in place. To the conservative leaders of the Soviet Union, this "Prague Spring" seemed to challenge communist rule itself, and they sent troops and tanks to crush it. Across the world in communist China, another kind of protest was taking shape in that country's Cultural Revolution (see Chapter 21, p. 1051).

In the developing countries, a substantial number of political leaders, activists, scholars, and students developed the notion of a "third world." Their countries, many only recently free from colonial rule, would offer an alternative to both a decrepit Western capitalism and a repressive Soviet communism. They claimed to pioneer new forms of economic development, of grassroots democracy, and of cultural renewal. By the late 1960s, the icon of this third-world ideology was Che Guevara, the Argentine-born revolutionary who had embraced the Cuban revolution and subsequently attempted to replicate its experience of liberation through guerrilla warfare in parts of Africa and Latin America. Various aspects of his life story—his fervent anti-imperialism, cast as a global struggle; his self-sacrificing lifestyle; his death in 1967 at the hands of the Bolivian military, trained and backed by the American CIA—made him a heroic figure to third world revolutionaries. He was popular as well among Western radicals, who were disgusted with the complacency and materialism of their own societies.

No expression of this global culture of liberation held a more profound potential for change than feminism, for it represented a rethinking of the most fundamental and personal of all human relationships—that between women and men. Feminism had begun in the West in the nineteenth century with a primary focus on suffrage and in several countries had achieved the status of a mass movement by the outbreak of World War I (see

Che Guevara

In life, Che was an uncompromising but failed revolutionary, while in death he became an inspiration to third-world liberation movements and a symbol of radicalism to many in the West. His image appeared widely on T-shirts and posters, and in Cuba itself a government-sponsored cult featured schoolchildren chanting each morning "We will be like Che." This billboard image of Che was erected in Havana in 1988. (© Tim Page/Corbis)

pp. 805–10). The twentieth century, however, witnessed the globalization of feminism as organized efforts to address the concerns of women took shape across the world. Communist governments—in the Soviet Union, China, and Cuba, for example—mounted vigorous efforts to gain the support of women and to bring them into the workforce by attacking major elements of older patriarchies (see pp. 1046–47 and Document 23.1, pp. 1173–75). But feminism took hold in many cultural and political settings, where women confronted different issues, adopted different strategies, and experienced a range of outcomes.

Feminism in the West

In the West, organized feminism had lost momentum by the end of the 1920s, when most countries had achieved universal suffrage. When it revived in the 1960s in both Western Europe and the United States, it did so with a quite different agenda. In France, for example, the writer and philosopher Simone de Beauvoir in 1949 had published *The Second Sex*, a book arguing that women had historically been defined as "other," or deviant from the "normal" male sex. The book soon became a central statement of a reviving women's movement. French feminists staged a counter–Mother's Day parade under the slogan "Celebrated one day; exploited all year." To highlight their demand to control their own bodies, some 343 women signed a published manifesto stating that they had undergone an abortion, which was then illegal in France.

> **■ Comparison**
> What distinguished feminism in the industrialized countries from that in the Global South?

Across the Atlantic, millions of American women responded to Betty Friedan's book *The Feminine Mystique* (1963), which disclosed the identity crisis of educated women, unfulfilled by marriage and motherhood. Some adherents of this second-wave feminism took up the equal rights agenda of their nineteenth-century predecessors, but with an emphasis now on employment and education rather than voting rights. A more radical expression of American feminism, widely known as "women's liberation," took broader aim at patriarchy as a system of domination, similar to those of race and class. (See Document 23.2, pp. 1175–76.) One manifesto from 1969 declared:

> We are exploited as sex objects, breeders, domestic servants, and cheap labor. We are considered inferior beings, whose only purpose is to enhance men's lives.... Because we live so intimately with our oppressors, we have been kept from seeing our personal suffering as a political condition.[11]

Thus liberation for women meant becoming aware of their own oppression, a process that took place in thousands of consciousness-raising groups across the country. Many such women preferred direct action rather than the political lobbying favored by equal rights feminists. They challenged the Miss America contest of 1968 by tossing stink bombs in the hall, crowning a live sheep as their Miss America, and disposing of girdles, bras, high-heeled shoes, tweezers, and other "instruments of oppression" in a Freedom Trashcan. They also brought into open discussion issues involving sexuality, insisting that free love, lesbianism, and celibacy should be accorded the same respect as heterosexual marriage.

Yet another strand of Western feminism emerged from women of color. For many of them, the concerns of white, usually middle-class, feminists were hardly relevant to their oppression. Black women had always worked outside the home and so felt little need to be liberated from the chains of homemaking. Whereas white women might find the family oppressive, African American women viewed it as a secure base from which to resist racism. Solidarity with black men, rather than separation from them, was essential in confronting a racist America. Viewing mainstream feminism as "a family quarrel between White women and White men," many women of African descent in the United States and Britain established their own organizations, with a focus on racism and poverty.[12] (See Document 23.3, pp. 1176–78.)

Feminism in the Global South

As women mobilized outside of the Western world during the twentieth century, they faced very different situations than did white women in the United States and Europe. For much of Asia, Africa, and Latin America, the predominant issues — colonialism, racism, the struggle for independence, poverty, development, political oppression, and sometimes revolution — were not directly related to gender. (See Document 23.5, pp. 1180–81.) Women were affected by and engaged with all of these efforts and were welcomed by nationalist and communist leaders, mostly men, who needed their support. But once independence or the revolution was achieved, the women who had joined those movements often were relegated to marginal positions.

The different conditions within developing countries sometimes generated sharp criticism of Western feminism. To many African feminists in the 1970s and beyond, the concerns of their American or European sisters were too individualistic, too focused on sexuality, and insufficiently concerned with issues of motherhood, marriage, and poverty to be of much use. Furthermore, they resented Western feminists' insistent interest in cultural matters such as female genital mutilation and polygamy, which sometimes echoed the concerns of colonial-era missionaries and administrators. Western feminism could easily be seen as a new form of cultural imperialism. Moreover, many African governments and many African men defined feminism of any kind as "un-African" and associated with a hated colonialism.

Women's movements in the Global South took shape around a wide range of issues, not all of which were explicitly gender based. In the East African country of Kenya, a major form of mobilization was the women's group movement. Some 27,000 small associations of women, an outgrowth of traditional self-help groups, had a combined membership of more than a million by the late 1980s. They provided support for one another during times of need, such as weddings, births, and funerals; they took on community projects, such as building water cisterns, schools, and dispensaries; in one province, they focused on providing permanent iron roofing for their homes. Some became revolving loan societies or bought land or businesses. One woman testified to the sense of empowerment she derived from membership in her group:

I am a free woman. I bought this piece of land through my group. I can lie on it, work on it, keep goats or cows. What more do I want? My husband cannot sell it. It is mine.[13]

Elsewhere, other issues and approaches predominated. In the North African Islamic kingdom of Morocco, a more centrally directed and nationally focused feminist movement targeted the country's Family Law Code, which still defined women as minors. In 2004, a long campaign by Morocco's feminist movement, often with the help of supportive men and a liberal king, resulted in a new Family Law Code, which recognized women as equals to their husbands and allowed them to initiate divorce and to claim child custody, all of which had previously been denied. (See Document 23.4, pp. 1178–79, for an Islamic-based feminist argument.)

In Chile, a women's movement emerged as part of a national struggle against the military dictatorship of General Augusto Pinochet, who ruled the country from 1973 to 1990. Because they were largely regarded as "invisible" in the public sphere, women were able to organize extensively, despite the repression of the Pinochet regime. From this explosion of organizing activity emerged a women's movement that crossed class lines and party affiliations. Human rights activists, most of them women, called attention to the widespread use of torture and to the "disappearance" of thousands of opponents of the regime, while demanding the restoration of democracy. Poor urban women by the tens of thousands organized soup kitchens, craft workshops, and shopping collectives, all aimed at the economic survival of their families. Smaller numbers of middle-class women brought more distinctly feminist perspectives to the movement and argued pointedly for "democracy in the country and in the home." This diverse women's movement was an important part of the larger national protest that returned Chile to democratic government in 1990.

International Feminism

Perhaps the most impressive achievement of feminism in the twentieth century was its ability to project the "woman question" as a global issue and to gain international recognition for the view that "women's rights are human rights."[14] Like slavery and empire before it, patriarchy lost at least some of its legitimacy during this most recent century, although clearly it has not been vanquished.

Feminism registered as a global issue when the United Nations (UN), under pressure from women activists, declared 1975 as International Women's Year and the next ten years as the Decade for Women. The UN also sponsored a series of World Conferences on Women over the next twenty years. By 2006, 183 nations, though not the United States, had ratified a UN Convention on the Elimination of All Forms of Discrimination against Women, which committed them to promote women's legal equality, to end discrimination, to actively encourage women's development, and to protect women's human rights. Clearly this international attention to women's

An Aspect of Brazilian Feminism
Protesting macho culture and violence against women, this demonstration in Sao Paulo, Brazil in mid-2011 sought to counter the assumption that female victims of rape were responsible for those attacks because of how they dressed. And so they marched as "sluts," wearing sexually provocative clothing, while urging the "transformation of the world by feminism." The yellow sign declares: "It's my body." (Australfoto)

issues was encouraging to feminists operating in their own countries and in many places stimulated both research and action.

This growing international spotlight on women's issues also revealed sharp divisions within global feminism. One issue was determining who had the right to speak on behalf of women at international gatherings—the official delegates of male-dominated governments or the often more radical unofficial participants representing various nongovernmental organizations. North/South conflicts also surfaced at these international conferences. In preparing for the Mexico City gathering in 1975, the United States attempted to limit the agenda to matters of political and civil rights for women, whereas delegates from third world and communist countries wanted to include issues of economic justice, decolonization, and disarmament. Feminists from the South resented the dominance and contested the ideas of their Northern sisters. One African group highlighted the differences:

> While patriarchal views and structures oppress women all over the world, women are also members of classes and countries that dominate others and enjoy privileges in terms of access to resources. Hence, contrary to the best intentions of "sisterhood," not all women share identical interests.[15]

Nor did all third world groups have identical views. Some Muslim delegates at the Beijing Conference in 1995 opposed a call for equal inheritance for women because Islamic law required that sons receive twice the amount that daughters inherit. In contrast, Africans, especially in non-Muslim countries, were aware of how many children had been orphaned by AIDS and felt that girls' chances for survival depended on equal inheritance.

Finally, beyond such divisions within international feminism lay a global backlash among those who felt that its radical agenda had undermined family life, the proper relationship of men and women, and civilization generally. To Phyllis Schlafly, a prominent American opponent of the Equal Rights Amendment, feminism was a "disease" that brought in its wake "fear, sickness, pain, anger, hatred, danger, violence, and all manner of ugliness."[16] In the Islamic world, Western-style feminism, with its claims of gender equality and open sexuality, was highly offensive to many and fueled movements of religious revivalism that invited or compelled women to wear the veil and sometimes to lead highly restricted lives. The Vatican, some Catholic and Muslim countries, and at times the U.S. government took strong exception to aspects of global feminism, particularly its emphasis on reproductive rights, including access to abortion and birth control. Thus feminism was global as the twenty-first century dawned, but it was very diverse and much contested.

Religion and Global Modernity

Beyond liberation and feminism, a further dimension of cultural globalization took shape in the challenge that modernity presented to the world's religions. To the most "advanced" thinkers of the past several hundred years—Enlightenment writers in the eighteenth century, Karl Marx in the nineteenth, many academics and secular-minded intellectuals in the twentieth—religion was headed for extinction in the face of modernity, science, communism, or globalization. In some places—Britain, France, the Netherlands, and the Soviet Union, for example—religious belief and practice had declined sharply. Moreover, the spread of a scientific culture around the world persuaded small minorities everywhere, often among the most highly educated, that the only realities worth considering were those that could be measured with the techniques of science. To such people, all else was superstition, born of ignorance. Nevertheless, the far more prominent trends of the last century have been those that involved the further spread of major world religions, their resurgence in new forms, their opposition to elements of a secular and global modernity, and their political role as a source of community identity and conflict. Contrary to earlier expectations, religion has played an unexpectedly powerful role in this most recent century.

Buddhism, Christianity, and Islam had long functioned as transregional cultures, spreading far beyond their places of origin. That process continued in the twentieth century. Buddhist ideas and practices such as meditation found a warm reception in the West, as did yoga, originally a mind-body practice of Indian origin. Christianity of various kinds spread widely in non-Muslim Africa and South Korea and less extensively in parts of India. By the end of the twentieth century, it was growing even in China, where perhaps 7 to 8 percent of China's population—some 84 to 96 million people—claimed allegiance to the faith. No longer a primarily European or North American religion, Christianity by the early twenty-first century found some 62 percent of its adherents in Asia, Africa, and Latin America. In some instances missionaries from those regions have set about the "re-evangelization" of Europe and North America. Moreover, millions of migrants from the Islamic world planted their religion solidly in the West. In the United States, for example, a substantial number of African Americans and smaller numbers of European Americans engaged in Islamic practice. For several decades the writings of the thirteenth-century Islamic

Sufi poet Rumi have been bestsellers in the United States. Religious exchange, in short, has been a two-way street, not simply a transmission of Western ideas to the rest of the world. More than ever before, religious pluralism characterized many of the world's societies, confronting people with the need to make choices in a domain of life previously regarded as given and fixed.

Fundamentalism on a Global Scale

■ Change
In what respect did the various religious fundamentalisms of the twentieth century express hostility to global modernity?

Religious vitality in the twentieth century was expressed not only in the spread of particular traditions to new areas but also in the vigorous response of those traditions to the modernizing and globalizing world in which they found themselves. One such response has been widely called "fundamentalism," a militant piety—defensive, assertive, and exclusive—that took shape to some extent in every major religious tradition. Many features of the modern world, after all, appeared threatening to established religion. The scientific and secular focus of global modernity challenged the core beliefs of religion, with its focus on an unseen realm of reality. Furthermore, the social upheavals connected with capitalism, industrialization, and globalization thoroughly upset customary class, family, and gender relationships that had long been sanctified by religious tradition. Nation-states, often associated with particular religions, were likewise undermined by the operation of a global economy and challenged by the spread of alien cultures. In much of the world, these disruptions came at the hands of foreigners, usually Westerners, in the form of military defeat, colonial rule, economic dependency, and cultural intrusion.

To such threats, fundamentalism represented a religious response, characterized by one scholar as "embattled forms of spirituality . . . experienced as a cosmic war between the forces of good and evil."[17] Although fundamentalisms everywhere have looked to the past for ideals and models, their rejection of modernity was selective, not wholesale. What they sought was an alternative modernity, infused with particular religious values. Most, in fact, made active use of modern technology to communicate their message and certainly sought the potential prosperity associated with modern life. Extensive educational and propaganda efforts, political mobilization of their followers, social welfare programs, and sometimes violence ("terrorism" to their opponents) were among the means that fundamentalists employed.

The term "fundamentalism" derived from the United States, where religious conservatives in the early twentieth century were outraged by critical and "scientific" approaches to the Bible, by Darwinian evolution, and by liberal versions of Christianity that accommodated these heresies. They called for a return to the "fundamentals" of the faith, which included the literal truthfulness of the scriptures, the virgin birth and physical resurrection of Jesus, and a belief in miracles. After World War II, American Protestant fundamentalism came to oppose political liberalism and "big government," the sexual revolution of the 1960s, homosexuality and abortion rights, and secular humanism generally. Many fundamentalists saw the United States on the edge of an abyss. For one major spokesman, Francis Schaeffer (1912–1984), the West was about to enter

> an electronic dark age, in which the new pagan hordes, with all the power of technology at their command, are on the verge of obliterating the last strongholds of civilized humanity. A vision of darkness lies before us. As we leave the shores of Christian Western man behind, only a dark and turbulent sea of despair stretches endlessly ahead ... unless we fight.[18]

And fight they did! At first, fundamentalists sought to separate themselves from the secular world in their own churches and schools, but from the 1970s on, they entered the political arena as the "religious right," determined to return America to a "godly path." "We have enough votes to run this country," declared Pat Robertson, a major fundamentalist evangelist and broadcaster who ran for president in 1988. Conservative Christians, no longer willing to restrict their attention to personal salvation, had emerged as a significant force in American political life well before the end of the century.

In the very different setting of independent India, another fundamentalist movement—known as Hindutva (Hindu nationalism)—took shape during the 1980s. Like American fundamentalism, it represented a politicization of religion within a democratic context. To its advocates, India was, and always had been, an essentially Hindu land, even though it had been overwhelmed in recent centuries by Muslim invaders, then by the Christian British, and most recently by the secular state of the post-independence decades. The leaders of modern India, they argued, and particularly its first prime minister, Jawaharlal Nehru, were "the self-proclaimed secularists who ... seek to remake India in the Western image," while repudiating its basically Hindu religious character. The Hindutva movement took political shape in an increasingly popular party called the Bharatiya Janata Party (BJP), with much of its support coming from urban middle-class or upper-caste people who resented the state's efforts to cater to the interests of Muslims, Sikhs, and the lower castes. Muslims in particular were defined as outsiders, potentially more loyal to a Muslim Pakistan than to India. The BJP became a major political force in India during the 1980s and 1990s, winning a number of elections at both the state and national levels and promoting a distinctly Hindu identity in education, culture, and religion.

Creating Islamic Societies: Resistance and Renewal in the World of Islam

The most prominent of the late twentieth-century fundamentalisms was surely that of Islam. Expressed in many and various ways, it was an effort among growing numbers of Muslims to renew and reform the practice of Islam and to create a new religious/political order centered on a particular understanding of their faith. Earlier renewal movements, such as the eighteenth-century Wahhabis (see pp. 736–37), focused

■ **Change**
From what sources did Islamic renewal movements derive?

largely on the internal problems of Muslim societies, while those of the twentieth century responded as well to the external pressures of colonial rule, Western imperialism, and secular modernity.

Emerging strongly in the last quarter of the century, Islamic renewal movements gained strength from the enormous disappointments that had accumulated in the Muslim world by the 1970s. Conquest and colonial rule; awareness of the huge technological and economic gap between Islamic and European civilizations; the disappearance of the Ottoman Empire, long the chief Islamic state; elite enchantment with Western culture; the retreat of Islam for many to the realm of private life—all of this had sapped the cultural self-confidence of many Muslims by the mid-twentieth century. Political independence for former colonies certainly represented a victory for Islamic societies, but it had given rise to major states—Egypt, Pakistan, Indonesia, Iraq, Algeria, and others—that pursued essentially Western and secular policies of nationalism, socialism, and economic development, often with only lip service to an Islamic identity.

Even worse, these policies were not very successful. A number of endemic problems—vastly overcrowded cities with few services, widespread unemployment, pervasive corruption, slow economic growth, a mounting gap between the rich and poor—flew in the face of the great expectations that had accompanied the struggle against European domination. Despite formal independence, foreign intrusion still persisted. Israel, widely regarded as an outpost of the West, had been reestablished as a Jewish state in the very center of the Islamic world in 1948. In 1967, Israel inflicted a devastating defeat on Arab forces in the Six-Day War and seized various Arab territories, including the holy city of Jerusalem. Furthermore, broader signs of Western cultural penetration persisted—secular schools, alcohol, Barbie dolls, European and American movies, scantily clad women. The largely secular leader of independent Tunisia, Habib Bourguiba, argued against the veil for women as well as polygamy for men and discouraged his people from fasting during Ramadan. In 1960 he was shown on television drinking orange juice during the sacred month to the outrage of many traditional Muslims.

This was the context in which the idea of an Islamic alternative to Western models of modernity began to take hold. The intellectual and political foundations of this Islamic renewal had been established earlier in the century. Its leading figures, such as the Indian Mawlana Mawdudi and the Egyptian Sayyid Qutb, insisted that the Quran and the *sharia* (Islamic law) provided a guide for all of life—political, economic, and spiritual—and a blueprint for a distinctly Islamic modernity not dependent on Western ideas. It was the departure from Islamic principles, they argued, that had led the Islamic world into decline and subordination to the West, and only a return to the "straight path of Islam" would ensure a revival of Muslim societies. That effort to return to Islamic principles was labeled *jihad*, an ancient and evocative religious term that refers to "struggle" or "striving" to please God. In its twentieth-century political expression, jihad included the defense of an authentic Islam against Western aggression and vigorous efforts to achieve the Islamization of social and political life within

Muslim countries. It was a posture that would enable Muslims to resist the seductive but poisonous culture of the West. Sayyid Qutb had witnessed that culture during a visit to the United States in the late 1940s and was appalled by what he saw:

> Look at this capitalism with its monopolies, its usury . . . at this individual freedom, devoid of human sympathy and responsibility for relatives except under force of law; at this materialistic attitude which deadens the spirit; at this behavior like animals which you call "free mixing of the sexes"; at this vulgarity which you call "emancipation of women"; at this evil and fanatical racial discrimination.[19]

The earliest mass movement to espouse such ideas was Egypt's Muslim Brotherhood, founded in 1928 by an impoverished schoolteacher Hassan al-Banna (1906–1949). Advocating "government that will act in conformity to the law and Islamic principles," the Brotherhood soon attracted a substantial following, including many poor urban residents recently arrived from the countryside. Still a major presence in Egyptian political life, the Brotherhood has frequently come into conflict with state authorities.

By the 1970s, such ideas and organizations echoed widely across the Islamic world and found expression in many ways. At the level of personal life, many people became more religiously observant, attending mosque, praying regularly, and fasting. Substantial numbers of women, many of them young, urban, and well educated, adopted modest Islamic dress and the veil quite voluntarily. Participation in Sufi mystical practices increased in some places. Furthermore, many governments sought to anchor themselves in Islamic rhetoric and practice. During the 1970s, President Anwar Sadat of Egypt claimed the title of "Believer-President," referred frequently to the Quran, and proudly displayed his "prayer mark," a callus on his forehead caused by touching his head to the ground in prayer. Under pressure from Islamic activists, the government of Sudan in the 1980s adopted Quranic punishments for various crimes (such as amputating the hand of a thief) and announced a total ban on alcohol, dramatically dumping thousands of bottles of beer and wine into the Nile.

All over the Muslim world, from North Africa to Indonesia (see Map 23.3, p. 1160), Islamic renewal movements spawned organizations that operated legally to provide social services — schools, clinics, youth centers, legal-aid societies, financial institutions, publishing houses — that the state offered inadequately or not at all. Islamic activists took leadership roles in unions and professional organizations of teachers, journalists, engineers, doctors, and lawyers. Such people embraced modern science and technology but sought to embed these elements of modernity within a distinctly Islamic culture. Some served in official government positions or entered political life and contested elections where it was possible to do so. The Algerian Islamic Salvation Front was poised to win elections in 1992, when a frightened military government intervened to cancel the elections, an action that plunged the country into a decade of bitter civil war.

Another face of religious renewal, however, sought the overthrow of what they saw as compromised regimes in the Islamic world, most successfully in Iran in 1979

■ **Comparison**

In what different ways did Islamic renewal express itself?

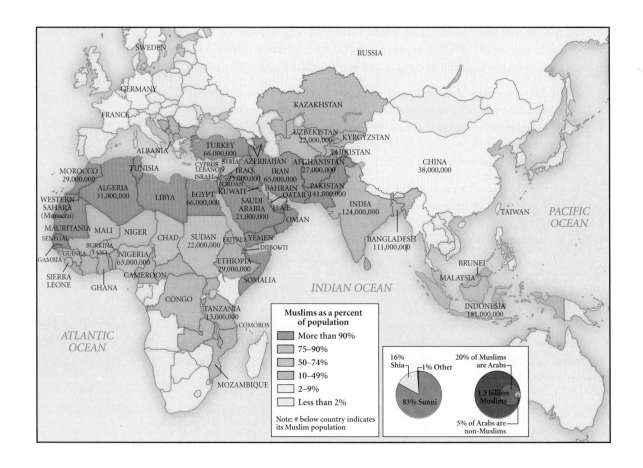

Map 23.3 The Islamic World in the Early Twenty-first Century

An Islamic world of well over a billion people incorporated much of the Afro-Asian landmass but was divided among many nations and along linguistic and ethnic lines as well. The long-term split between the majority Sunnis and the minority Shias also sharpened in the new millennium.

(see pp. 1115–17), but also in Afghanistan (1996) and parts of northern Nigeria (2000). Here Islamic movements succeeded in coming to power and began to implement a program of Islamization based on the sharia. Elsewhere military governments in Pakistan and Sudan likewise introduced elements of sharia-based law. Hoping to spark an Islamic revolution, the Egyptian Islamic Jihad organization assassinated President Sadat in 1981, following Sadat's brutal crackdown on both Islamic and secular opposition groups. One of the leaders of Islamic Jihad explained:

> We have to establish the Rule of God's Religion in our own country first, and to make the Word of God supreme. . . . There is no doubt that the first battlefield for jihad is the extermination of these infidel leaders and to replace them by a complete Islamic Order.[20]

Islamic revolutionaries also took aim at hostile foreign powers. Hamas in Palestine and Hezbollah in Lebanon, supported by the Islamic regime in Iran, targeted Israel with popular uprisings, suicide bombings, and rocket attacks in response to the Israeli occupation of Arab lands. For some, Israel's very existence was illegitimate. The Soviet invasion of Afghanistan in 1979 prompted widespread opposition aimed at lib-

Hamas in Action

The Palestinian militant organization Hamas, founded in 1987 as an offshoot of Egypt's Muslim Brotherhood, illustrates two dimensions of Islamic radicalism. On the one hand, Hamas repeatedly sent suicide bombers to target Israeli civilians and sought the elimination of the Israeli state. A group of would-be suicide bombers are shown here in white robes during the funeral of colleagues killed by Israeli security forces in late 2003. On the other hand, Hamas ran a network of social services, providing schools, clinics, orphanages, summer camps, soup kitchens, and libraries for Palestinians. The classroom pictured here was part of a school founded by Hamas. (© Andrea Comas/Reuters/Corbis)

erating that country from atheistic communism and creating an Islamic state. Sympathetic Arabs from the Middle East flocked to the aid of their Afghan compatriots.

Among them was the young Osama bin Laden, a wealthy Saudi Arab, who created an organization, al-Qaeda (meaning "the base" in Arabic), to funnel fighters and funds to the Afghan resistance. At the time, bin Laden and the Americans were on the same side, both opposing Soviet expansion into Afghanistan, but they soon parted ways. Returning to his home in Saudi Arabia, bin Laden became disillusioned and radicalized when the government of his country allowed the stationing of "infidel" U.S. troops in Islam's holy land during and after the first American war against Iraq in 1991. By the mid-1990s, he had found a safe haven in Taliban-ruled Afghanistan, from which he and other leaders of al-Qaeda planned their attack on the World Trade Center and other targets in the United States on September 11, 2001. Although they had no standing as Muslim clerics, in 1998 they had issued a *fatwa* (religious edict) declaring war on America:

> [F]or over seven years the United States has been occupying the lands of Islam in the holiest of places, the Arabian Peninsula, plundering its riches, dictating to its rulers, humiliating its people, terrorizing its neighbors, and turning its bases in the Peninsula into a spearhead through which to fight the neighboring Muslim peoples. . . . [T]he ruling to kill the Americans and their allies—civilians and military—is an individual duty for every Muslim who can do it in any country in which it is possible to do it, in order to liberate the al-Aqsa Mosque in Jerusalem

and the holy mosque (in Mecca) from their grip, and in order for their armies to move out of all the lands of Islam, defeated and unable to threaten any Muslim.[21]

Elsewhere as well—in East Africa, Indonesia, Great Britain, Spain, Saudi Arabia, and Yemen—al-Qaeda or groups associated with it launched scattered attacks on Western interests. At the international level, the great enemy was not Christianity itself or even Western civilization, but irreligious Western-style modernity, U.S. imperialism, and an American-led economic globalization so aptly symbolized by the World Trade Center. Ironically, al-Qaeda itself was a modern and global organization, many of whose members were highly educated professionals from a variety of countries.

Despite this focus on the West, the violent struggles undertaken by politicized Islamic activists were as much within the Islamic world as they were with the external enemy. Their understanding of Islam, heavily influenced by Wahhabi ideas, was in various ways quite novel and at odds with classical Islamic practice. It was highly literal and dogmatic in its understanding of the Quran, legalistic in its effort to regulate the minute details of daily life, deeply opposed to any "innovation" in religious practice, inclined to define those who disagreed with them as "non-Muslims," and drawn to violent jihad as a legitimate part of Islamic life. It was also deeply skeptical about the interior spiritual emphasis of Sufism, which had informed so much of earlier Islamic culture. The spread of this version of Islam, often known as Salafism, owed much to massive financial backing from oil-rich Saudi Arabia, which funded Wahhabi/Salafi mosques and schools across the Islamic world and in the West as well.

Religious Alternatives to Fundamentalism

Militant revolutionary fundamentalism has certainly not been the only religious response to modernity and globalization within the Islamic world. Many who shared a concern to embed Islamic values more centrally in their societies have acted peacefully and within established political structures. In Turkey, Egypt, Jordan, Iraq, Palestine, Morocco, Tunisia, and Lebanon, Islamic parties with various agendas made impressive electoral showings in the 1990s and the early twenty-first century. Considerable debate among Muslims has raised questions about the proper role of the state, the difference between the eternal law of God (sharia) and the human interpretations of it, the rights of women, the possibility of democracy, and many other issues. (See Document 22.3, pp. 1124–26, and Document 23.4, pp. 1178–79.) Some Muslim intellectuals and political leaders have called for a dialogue between civilizations; others have argued that traditions can change in the face of modern realities without losing their distinctive Islamic character. In 1996, Anwar Ibrahim, a major political and intellectual figure in Malaysia, insisted that

> [Southeast Asian Muslims] would rather strive to improve the welfare of the women and children in their midst than spend their days elaborately defining the nature and institutions of the ideal Islamic state. They do not believe it makes one less of a Muslim to promote economic growth, to master the information revolution, and to demand justice for women.[22]

In Turkey, a movement inspired by the teachings of Fethullah Gulen, a Turkish Muslim scholar and preacher, has sought to apply the principles of Islamic spirituality and Sufi piety to the problems of modern society. Gaining a mass following in the 1990s and after, the Gulen movement has advocated interfaith and cross-cultural dialogue, multiparty democracy, nonviolence, and modern scientifically based education for girls and boys alike. Operating through schools, universities, conferences, newspapers, radio and TV stations, and various charities, it has a presence in more than 100 countries around the world. Claiming to be "faith-based but not faith limited," the movement rejects the "fundamentalist" label even as it has challenged a wholly secular outlook on public life. And in 2004–2005, a gathering in Jordan of scholars from all major schools of Islamic thought issued the "Amman Message," which called for Islamic unity, condemned terrorism, forbade Muslims from declaring one another as "apostate" or nonbelievers, and emphasized the commonalities shared by Muslims, Christians, and Jews.

Within other religious traditions as well, believers found various ways of responding to global modernity. More liberal or mainstream Christian groups spoke to the ethical issues arising from economic globalization. Many Christian organizations, for example, were active in agitating for debt relief for poor countries. Pope John Paul II was openly concerned about "the growing distance between rich and poor, unfair competition which puts the poor nations in a situation of ever-increasing inferiority." "Liberation theology," particularly in Latin America, sought a Christian basis for action in the areas of social justice, poverty, and human rights, while viewing Jesus as liberator as well as savior. In Asia, a growing movement known as "socially engaged Buddhism" addressed the needs of the poor through social reform, educational programs, health services, and peacemaking action during times of conflict and war. The Dalai Lama has famously advocated a peaceful resolution of Tibet's troubled relationship with China. Growing interest in communication and exchange among the world's religions was expressed in a UN resolution designating the first week of February 2011 as World Interfaith Harmony Week. In short, religious responses to global modernity were articulated in many voices.

SUMMING UP SO FAR

How might you compare feminism and fundamentalism as global movements? In what ways did they challenge earlier values and expectations? To what extent were they in conflict with one another?

Experiencing the Anthropocene Era: Environment and Environmentalism

Even as world religions, fundamentalist and otherwise, challenged global modernity on cultural or spiritual grounds, burgeoning environmental movements in the 1960s and after also did so with an eye to the human impact on the earth and its many living creatures, including ourselves. Among the distinctive features of the twentieth century, none has been more pronounced than humankind's growing ability to alter the natural order and the mounting awareness of this phenomenon. When the wars, revolutions, and empires of this most recent century have faded from memory, environmental transformation and environmental consciousness may well seem to future generations the decisive feature of that century. Already, many scientists have begun to refer to the current era, since at least the advent of the Industrial Revolution, as the Anthropocene or the Age of Man. That informal term has called attention to the lasting impact of human activity on the planet, even measured on a geological scale.[23]

The Global Environment Transformed

■ **Change**
How can we explain the dramatic increase in the human impact on the environment in the twentieth century?

Underlying the environmental changes of the twentieth century were three factors that vastly magnified the human impact on earth's ecological systems far beyond anything previously known.[24] One was the explosion of human numbers, an unprecedented quadrupling of the world's population in a single century, leaving the world of 2012 with over 7 billion people compared to about 1.6 billion in 1900. It was a demographic revolution born of medical and sanitation advances that dramatically lowered death rates and Green Revolution technologies such as genetically modified seeds and fertilizers that substantially increased world food supplies. A second cause of environmental stress lay in the amazing new ability of humankind to tap the energy potential of fossil fuels—coal in the nineteenth century and oil in the twentieth. Hydroelectricity, natural gas, and nuclear power added to the energy resources available to our species. These new sources of energy made possible a third contribution to environmental transformation—phenomenal economic growth—as modern science and technology immensely increased the production of goods and services. Between the 1890s and the 1990s, global industrial output grew by a factor of 40, although very unevenly across the planet. An average North American in the 1990s, for example, used 50 to 100 times more energy than an average Bangladeshi (see Map 23.4). But almost everywhere—in capitalist, communist, and developing countries alike—the idea of economic growth or "development" as something possible and desirable took hold as a novel element of global culture.

These three factors were the foundations for the immense environmental transformations of the twentieth century. Human activity had always altered the natural order, usually on a local basis, but now the scale of that impact assumed global and perhaps even geological proportions. The growing numbers of the poor and the growing consumption of the rich led to the doubling of cropland, a corresponding contraction of the world's forests and grasslands, and dramatic increases in the rate of erosion. Huge urban complexes have transformed the landscape in many places. With diminished habitats, numerous species of plants and animals either disappeared or were threatened with extinction at a rate many times greater than the background level. Certainly massive species extinctions have occurred much earlier in the history of the planet (the dinosaurs, for example), but this wave of extinctions is happening at the hands of humankind. The human remaking of the ecosystem has also greatly increased the presence of plants and animals that have benefited from human activity—cattle, pigs, chickens, rats, wheat, corn, and dandelions. By some estimates, 90 percent of all plant activity now occurs in environments shaped by human action.

The global spread of modern industry, heavily dependent on fossil fuels, created a pall of air pollution in many major cities. By the 1970s, traffic police in Tokyo fre-

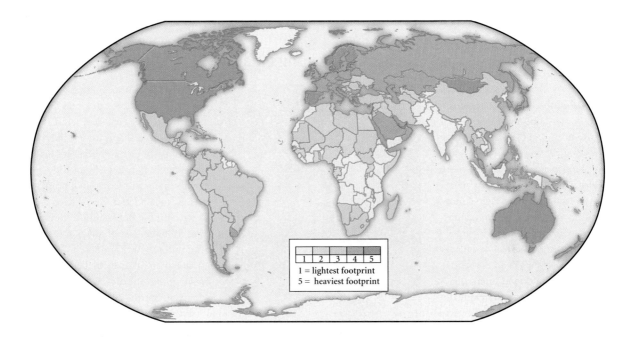

quently wore face masks. In Mexico City, officials estimated in 2002 that air pollution killed 35,000 people every year. Industrial pollution in the Soviet Union rendered about half of the country's rivers severely polluted by the late 1980s, while fully 20 percent of its population lived in regions defined as "ecological disasters." The release of chemicals known as chlorofluorocarbons thinned the ozone layer, which protects the earth from excessive ultraviolet radiation.

The most critical and intractable environmental transformation was global warming. By the end of the twentieth century, a worldwide scientific consensus had emerged that the vastly increased burning of fossil fuels, which emit heat-trapping greenhouse gases such as carbon dioxide, as well as the loss of trees that would otherwise remove it from the air, had begun to warm the atmosphere significantly. By 2010, carbon dioxide concentration in the atmosphere was about one-third higher than preindustrial levels. Although considerable disagreement existed about the rate and likely consequences of this process, indications of melting glaciers and polar ice caps, rising sea levels, thawing permafrost, extreme hurricanes, further species extinctions, and other ecological threats have punctuated global discussion of this issue. It was clearly a global phenomenon and, for many people, it demanded global action.

Green and Global

Environmentalism began in the nineteenth century as Romantic poets such as William Blake and William Wordsworth denounced the industrial era's "dark satanic mills," which threatened the "green and pleasant land" of an earlier England. The "scientific management" of nature, both in industrializing countries and in European colonies, represented another element of emerging environmental awareness among a few. So

Map 23.4
Ecological Footprints[25]
According to a recent study, the overall human footprint on the planet since the 1970s has exceeded the earth's capacity to replace natural resource consumption and to absorb carbon dioxide waste. By 2007, that "overshoot" was about 50 percent. This map shows regional differences in generating that increasingly heavy human footprint on the earth.

Rachel Carson,
Pioneer of Environmentalism

Rachel Carson
(© Post-Gazette/ZUMA Press/Corbis)

"Over increasingly large areas of the United States, spring now comes unheralded by the return of the birds, and the early mornings are strangely silent."[26] This was the appalling vision that inspired *Silent Spring*, a book that effectively launched the American environmental movement in 1962 with its devastating critique of unregulated pesticide use. Its author, Rachel Carson, was born in 1907 on a farm near Pittsburgh. Her childhood interest in nature led to college and graduate studies in biology and then a career as a marine biologist with the U.S. Department of Fisheries, only the second woman hired for such a position. She was also finding her voice as a writer, penning three well-received books on the ecology of the sea.

Through this work, Carson gained an acute awareness of the intricate and interdependent web of life, but she assumed that "much of nature was forever beyond the tampering hand of man." However, the advent of the atomic age, with the dramatic bombings of Hiroshima and Nagasaki in 1945, shook her confidence that nature was immune to human action, and she began to question the widely held assumption that science always held positive outcomes for human welfare. That skepticism gradually took shape around the issue of pesticides and other toxins deliberately introduced into the environment in the name of progress. In 1958 a letter from a friend describing the death of birds in her yard following aerial spraying for mosquito control prompted Carson to take on a project that became *Silent Spring*. Initially she called it "man against the earth."

From government agencies, independent scientists, public health specialists, and her own network of contacts, Carson began to assemble data about the impact of pesticides on natural ecosystems and human health. While she never called for their complete elimination, she argued for much greater care and sensitivity to the environment in employing chemical pesticides. She further urged natural biotic agents as a preferable alternative for pest control. The book also criticized the government regulatory agencies for their negligent oversight and scientific specialists for their "fanatical zeal" to create "a chemically sterile insect-

did the "wilderness idea," which aimed to preserve untouched areas from human disruption, as, for example, in the U.S. national parks.[27] None of these strands of environmentalism attracted a mass following or provoked a global response. Not until the second half of the twentieth century, and then quite rapidly, did environmentalism achieve a worldwide dimension, although it was expressed in many quite different ways.

■ **Comparison**

What differences emerged between environmentalism in the Global North and that in the Global South?

This second-wave environmentalism began in the West with the publication in 1962 of Rachel Carson's *Silent Spring*, exposing the chemical contamination of the environment. (See the Portrait of Rachel Carson, above.) Here, as virtually everywhere else, the impetus for action came from the grass roots and citizen protest. By the early 1990s, some 14 million Americans—one in seven adults—had joined one of the many environmental organizations. In Europe, the Club of Rome, a global free world." Chemical companies, she wrote, gave out only "little tranquilizing pills of half-truth" when confronted with evidence of their products' harmful results. While she worked hard to ensure the book's scientific credentials, it was a passionate work, fueled by Carson's "anger at the senseless brutish things that were being done." It was also a book written under growing personal difficulties. Her mother, for whom she had long been a caretaker, died in 1958, while Carson's own health too deteriorated as cancer and other ailments took their toll.

When *Silent Spring* finally published in 1962, the book provoked a firestorm of criticism. Velsicol, a major chemical company, threatened a lawsuit to prevent its publication. Critics declared that following her prescriptions would mean "the end of all human progress," even a "return to the Dark Ages [when] insects and diseases and vermin would once again inherit the earth." Some of the attacks were more personal. Rachel Carson had never married, and Ezra Taft Benson, a former secretary of agriculture, wondered "why a spinster with no children was so concerned about genetics," while opining that she was "probably a communist." It was the height of the cold war era, and challenges to government agencies and corporate capitalism were often deemed "un-American" and "sinister."

Carson evoked such a backlash because she had called into question the whole idea of science as progress, so central to Western culture since the Enlightenment. Humankind had acquired the power to "alter the very nature of

the [earth's] life," she declared. The book ended with a dire warning: "It is our alarming misfortune that so primitive a science has armed itself with the most modern and terrible weapons, and that in turning them against the insects, it has also turned them against the earth."

But Carson also had a growing number of enthusiastic supporters. Before she died in 1964, she witnessed the vindication of much of her work. Honors and awards poured in; she more than held her own against her critics in a CBS News program devoted to her book; and a presidential Science Advisory Committee cited Carson's work while recommending the "orderly reduction of persistent pesticides." Following her death, a range of policy changes reflected her work including the creation of the Environmental Protection Agency in 1970 and the banning of the insecticide DDT in 1973. *Silent Spring* also motivated many to join the growing array of environmentalist groups.

Approaching her death, Carson applied her ecological understanding of the world to herself as well. In a letter to her best friend not long before she died, she recalled seeing some monarch butterflies leaving on a journey from which they would not return. And then she added: "When the intangible cycle has run its course, it is a natural and not unhappy thing that a life comes to an end."

Question: In what larger contexts might we understand Rachel Carson and the book that gained her such attention?

think tank, issued a report in 1972 called *Limits to Growth*, which warned of resource exhaustion and the collapse of industrial society in the face of unrelenting economic growth. The German environmental movement was distinctive in that its activists directly entered the political arena as the Green Party, with a focus on opposition to nuclear energy. Beyond addressing environmental pollution, Western activists focused much attention on wilderness issues, opposing logging, road building, and other development efforts in remaining unspoiled areas.

Quite quickly, during the 1970s and 1980s, environmentalism took root in the developing countries as well. There it often assumed a different character: it was more locally based and had fewer large national organizations than in the West; it involved poor people rather than affluent members of the middle class; it was less engaged in political lobbying and corporate strategies; it was more concerned with issues of food security, health, and basic survival than with the rights of nature or wilderness protection; and it was more closely connected to movements for social justice.[28] Thus, whereas Western environmentalists defended forests where few people lived, the Chikpo, or "tree-hugging," movement in India sought to protect the livelihood of farmers, artisans, and herders living in areas subject to extensive deforestation. A massive movement to prevent or limit the damming of India's Narmada River derived from the displacement of local people; similar anti-dam protests in the American Northwest were more concerned with protecting salmon runs.

Western environmentalists often called on individuals to change their values by turning away from materialism toward an appreciation of the intricate and fragile web of life that sustains us all. In the Philippines, by contrast, environmental activists confronting the operation of foreign mining companies have sought fundamental changes in the political and social structure of their country. There, environmental protest has overlapped with other movements seeking to challenge established power structures and social hierarchies. Coalitions of numerous local groups—representing various religious, women's, human rights, indigenous peoples', peasant, and political organizations—frequently mobilized large-scale grassroots movements against the companies rather than seeking to negotiate with them. Occasionally these movements have included violent actions by "green armies." Such mass mobilization contributed to the decision of the Australian-based Western Mining Corporation in 2000 to abandon its plans for developing a huge copper mine in Mindanao.

By the late twentieth century, environmentalism had become a matter of global concern. That awareness motivated legislation aimed at pollution control in many countries; it pushed many businesses in a "green" direction; it fostered research on alternative and renewable sources of energy; it stimulated UN conferences on global warming; it persuaded millions of people to alter their way of life; and it generated a number of international agreements addressing matters such as whaling, ozone depletion, and global warming.

The globalization of environmentalism also disclosed sharp conflicts, particularly between the Global North and South. Both activists and governments in the developing countries have often felt that Northern initiatives to address atmospheric pollution and global warming would curtail their industrial development, leaving the North/South gap intact. "The threat to the atmospheric commons has been building over centuries," argued Indian environmentalist Vandana Shiva, "mainly because of industrial activity in the North. Yet . . . the North refuses to assume extra responsibility for cleaning up the atmosphere. No wonder the Third World cries foul when it is asked to share the costs." A Malaysian official put the dispute succinctly: "The developed countries don't want to give up their extravagant lifestyles, but plan to curtail our development."[29] Western governments argued that newly industrializing countries such as China and India must also agree to specific limits on their growing emissions if further global warming is to be prevented. Such deep disagreements between industrialized and developing countries have long contributed to the failure of global efforts to substantially reduce greenhouse gas emissions. But in late 2011, at an international conference in Durban, South Africa, delegates from 194 countries agreed to move toward a climate change treaty that would be legally binding on all parties.

Beyond these and other conflicts, global environmentalism, more than any other widespread movement, came to symbolize "one-world" thinking, a focus on the common plight of humankind across the artificial boundaries of nation-states. It also marked a challenge to modernity itself, particularly its consuming commitment to endless growth. The ideas of sustainability and restraint, certainly not prominent in any list of modern values, entered global discourse and marked the beginnings of a new environmental ethic. This change in thinking was perhaps the most significant achievement of global environmentalism.

Environmentalism in Action
These South Korean environmental activists are wearing death masks and holding crosses representing various countries during an anti-nuclear protest in Seoul in 1996, exactly ten years after a large-scale nuclear accident at Chernobyl in the Soviet Union. The lead protester holds a placard reading "Don't forget Chernobyl!" (AP Photo/Yun Jai-hyoung)

Reflections: Pondering the Past

Everyone who studies world history has been witness to something of the broad contours of the human journey, or at least a part of it. That remarkable field of study involves selectively describing major changes, making frequent comparisons, noticing connections among distant peoples, and explaining, as best we can and amid much controversy, why things turned out as they did. But world history provides endless raw material for yet another kind of inquiry, that of pondering or musing, turning over in our minds again and again, those fundamentally human and personal questions for which definitive answers are elusive.

Consider, for example, the issue of suffering and compassion. History is, among other things, a veritable catalog of the varieties of human suffering. It provides ample evidence, should we need it, that suffering is a common and bedrock human experience . . . and none of us is exempt. But it also highlights the extent to which that suffering has derived from our own actions in the shape of war, racism, patriarchy, exploitation, inequality, oppression, and neglect. Is it possible that some exposure to the staggering sum of human suffering revealed in the historical record can soften our hearts, fostering compassion for our own suffering and for that of others? Might the study of history generate kindness, expressed at the level of day-to-day personal interactions and at the wider level of acting to repair the brokenness of the world?

A related issue is that of hope, so important for our posture toward both the world and our individual lives. Does history offer a basis for a hopeful outlook? Based on the recent past, it would not be difficult to make a case for despair. The deterioration of environment and the availability of immensely destructive nuclear weapons suggest at least the possibility of a sorry outcome for the human experiment on this planet. The difficulty of achieving agreement about effective remedies for major issues, both within and among nations, only adds to the prospect of an unhappy future.

And yet, individuals and societies have often hovered on the knife-edge of possibility and disaster. But we have survived and even flourished as a species, and civilization has proven resilient in the face of catastrophes such as the Black Death and world wars. Furthermore, things have changed, sometimes for the better, and frequently people have changed things. Abolitionists contributed to the ending of slavery. Colonized peoples broke free of empire. Women secured the vote and defied patriarchy. Socialists and communists challenged the inequities of capitalism, while popular protest brought repressive communist regimes to their knees in the Soviet Union and Eastern Europe. The wonders of modern science and technology have demonstrably improved the lives of billions of people. Thus the historical record offers a wealth of material for pondering the issue of hope.

Yet another question deals with our response to "otherness." We are, most of us, inclined to be insular, to regard our own ways as the norm, to be fearful of difference. Nor is this tendency largely our own fault. We all have limited experience. Few of us have had much personal encounter with cultures beyond our own, and none of us, of course, knows personally what life was like before we were born. But we do know that a rich and mature life involves opening up to a wider world, and we can be assured that the twenty-first century will demand that we do so. If we base our understanding of life only on what we personally experience, we render ourselves both impoverished and ineffective.

In this task of opening up, history in general and world history in particular have much to offer. They provide a marvelous window into the unfamiliar. They confront us with the whole panorama of human achievement, tragedy, and sensibility. They give context and perspective to our own limited experience. They allow us some modest entry into the lives of people far removed from us in time and place. And they offer us company for the journey of our own lives. Pondering the global past with a receptive heart and an open mind can assist us in enlarging and deepening our sense of self. In exposing us to the wider experience of "all under heaven," as the Chinese put it, world history can aid us in becoming wiser and more mature persons. That is among the many gifts, sometimes painful but always enriching, that the study of history offers to us all.

Second Thoughts

What's the Significance?

neoliberalism, 1139–40

reglobalization, 1140–43

transnational corporations, 1141–42

North/South gap, 1144

anti-globalization, 1146–47

Prague Spring, 1150

Che Guevara, 1150

second-wave feminism, 1151–52

fundamentalism, 1156–57

Hindutva, 1157

Islamic renewal, 1157–62

Osama bin Laden/al-Qaeda, 1161–62

global warming, 1165

environmentalism, 1165–70

Rachel Carson, 1166–67

LearningCurve
Check what you know.
**bedfordstmartins.com
/strayer/LC**

Online Study Guide
bedfordstmartins.com
/highschool/strayer

Big Picture Questions

1. In what ways did the Global North/South divide find expression in the past century?

2. What have been the benefits and drawbacks of globalization since 1945?

3. Do the years since 1914 confirm or undermine Enlightenment predictions about the future of humankind?

4. "The most recent century marks the end of the era of Western dominance in world history." What evidence might support this statement? What evidence might contradict it?

5. To what extent did the various liberation movements of the past century — communism, nationalism, democracy, feminism, internationalism — achieve their goals?

6. **Looking Back:** To what extent did the processes discussed in this chapter (globalization, feminism, fundamentalism, environmentalism) have roots in the more distant past? In what respects did they represent something new in the past century?

Next Steps: For Further Study

Karen Armstrong, *The Battle for God* (2000). A comparison of Christian, Jewish, and Islamic fundamentalism in historical perspective.

Nayan Chanda, *Bound Together: How Traders, Preachers, Adventurers, and Warriors Shaped Globalization* (2007). An engaging, sometimes humorous, long-term view of the globalization process.

For Web sites and additional documents related to this chapter, see **Make History** at bedfordstmartins.com /highschool/strayer.

Jeffrey Frieden, *Global Capitalism: Its Fall and Rise in the Twentieth Century* (2006). A thorough, thoughtful, and balanced history of economic globalization.

Michael Hunt, *The World Transformed* (2004). A thoughtful global history of the second half of the twentieth century.

J. R. McNeill, *Something New under the Sun: An Environmental History of the Twentieth Century World* (2001). A much-acclaimed global account of the rapidly mounting human impact on the environment during the most recent century.

Bonnie Smith, ed., *Global Feminisms since 1945* (2000). A series of essays about feminist movements around the world.

"No Job for a Woman," http://www.iwm.org.uk/upload/package/30/women/index.htm. A Web site illustrating the impact of war on the lives of women in the twentieth century.

Documents

Considering the Evidence:
Voices of Global Feminism

With its focus on equal rights and opportunities for women, modern feminism has challenged the most ancient and perhaps deeply rooted of human inequalities—that of patriarchy or the dominance of men over women. Beginning in Western Europe and the United States during the nineteenth century, it was born in the context of democratic gains for men from which women were excluded. Like science, industrialism, socialism, and electoral democracy, feminism was a Western cultural innovation that acquired a global reach during the most recent century.

In doing so, feminism has found expression in many voices, giving rise to much controversy and many questions within feminist circles. How relevant has mainstream Western feminism been to women of color in the West and in the developing countries? What is it precisely that oppresses women—the family, capitalism, cultural assumptions about male superiority, women's acquiescence to patriarchy? To what extent do all women share common interests? In what ways do differences of class, race, nation, religion, sexual orientation, and economic condition generate quite distinct feminist agendas? How important is sexual freedom to the feminist cause? What tactics are most effective in realizing the varying goals of feminists? The documents that follow provide a sample of the divergent voices in which global feminism has been articulated during the past century.

Document 23.1

Communist Feminism

Following the Russian revolution of 1917, the communist Soviet Union was the site of a remarkable experiment in state-directed feminism during the 1920s. (See Chapter 21, pp. 1046–47.) Among the most prominent leaders of that movement was Alexandra Kollontai (1872–1952), who was born to a privileged, gentry family and became involved in socialist politics and revolution with a focus on women's issues. For several years, Kollontai was the head of Zhenotdel, the communist organization dedicated to female emancipation. Her outspokenness on women's issues and her opposition to an emerging Soviet dictatorship soon diminished her influence within Soviet leadership circles. By the 1960s, however, her ideas resonated among some participants in a reviving feminist movement in the West. Her essay on "Communism and the Family," written in 1920, gives expression to a distinctly communist feminism.

- Why does Kollontai believe that the individual family is both oppressive and doomed?

- How does she imagine the future of marriage and family life under communism?

- To whom might such a vision appeal and who might be deeply offended by it?

- What useful elements might later Western feminists have seen in Kollontai's ideas?

ALEXANDRA KOLLONTAI

"Communism and the Family"

1920

Will the family continue to exist under communism? ... [One] fact that invites attention is that divorce has been made easier in Soviet Russia. ... A working woman will not have to petition for months or even for years to secure the right to live separately from a husband who beats her and makes her life a misery with his drunkenness and uncouth behaviour. Divorce by mutual agreement now takes no more than a week or two to obtain. ...

[T]he old family in which the man was everything and the woman nothing ... is changing before our very eyes. ... It is the universal spread of female labour that has contributed most of all to the radical change in family life. ... Capitalism has placed a crushing burden on woman's shoulders: it has made her a wage-worker without having reduced her cares as housekeeper or mother. Woman staggers beneath the weight of this triple load. ...

The circumstances that held the family together no longer exist. The family is ceasing *to be necessary either to its members or to the nation as a whole.* ...

All that was formerly produced in the bosom of the family is now being manufactured on a mass scale in workshops and factories. ... The family no longer produces; it only consumes. ... The individual household is dying. It is giving way in our society to collective housekeeping. Instead of the working woman cleaning her flat, the communist society can arrange for men and women whose job it is to go round in the morning cleaning rooms. ... Instead of the working woman having to struggle with the cooking and spend her last free hours in the kitchen preparing dinner and supper, communist society will organise public restaurants and communal kitchens. ... The working woman will not have to slave over the washtub any longer, ... she will simply take these things to the central laundries each week and collect the washed and ironed garments later. ...

Just as housework withers away, so the obligations of parents to their children wither away gradually until finally society assumes the full responsibility. ... Communist society will come to the aid of the parents. In Soviet Russia ... we already have homes for very small babies, creches, kinder-

Source: Alexandra Kollontai, "Communism and the Family," *The Worker*, 1920.

gartens, children's colonies and homes, hospitals and health resorts for sick children, restaurants, free lunches at school and free distribution of text books, warm clothing and shoes to schoolchildren. All this goes to show that the responsibility for the child is passing from the family to the collective....

In place of the old relationship between men and women, a new one is developing: a union of affection and comradeship, a union of two equal members of communist society, both of them free, both of them independent, and both of them workers. No more domestic bondage for women. No more inequality within the family. No need for women to fear being left without support and with children to bring up. The woman in communist society no longer depends upon her husband but on her work.... She need have no anxiety about her

children. The workers' state will assume responsibility for them. Marriage will lose all the elements of material calculation which cripple family life. Marriage will be a union of two persons who love and trust each other.... [T]here is no more room for the old proprietary attitude which says: "These are my children...." [T]here are only our children, the children of Russia's communist workers....

In place of the individual and egoistic family, a great universal family of workers will develop, in which all the workers, men and women, will above all be comrades. This is what relations between men and women in the communist society will be like. These new relations will ensure for humanity all the joys of a love unknown in the commercial society, of a love that is free and based on the true social equality of the partners.

Document 23.2

Western Feminism

In the West, where modern feminism had begun in the nineteenth century, a new phase of that movement took shape during the 1960s and after. Moving well beyond the earlier focus on suffrage and property rights, "second-wave" feminists gave voice to a wide range of new issues. Some continued Elizabeth Cady Stanton's emphasis on "equal rights" with a focus now on the home and housework, discrimination in the workplace, access to education, and political involvement. "Socialist feminists" looked to the workings of capitalist economies and their class inequalities as the basis of women's oppression. Still others turned the spotlight on cultural issues—media portrayal of women, sexuality and the family, reproductive rights, lesbianism, violence against women, pornography, and prostitution. Among the spokespersons for this cultural critique of patriarchy was the American writer Andrea Dworkin (1946–2005). In a speech at the University of Toronto in 1995, she spelled out her understanding of the achievements and continuing tasks of modern feminism.

- How does Dworkin's feminist agenda compare with that of Kollontai?

- How does it compare with the ideas of Elizabeth Cady Stanton in Document 16.4, pp. 818–19?

- Why do you think that issues of sexuality and violence against women have been so prominent in recent Western feminism?

ANDREA DWORKIN

"Remember, Resist, Do Not Comply"

1995

I want us to think about far we have come politically.

We have named force as such when it is used against us. . . . It used to be a legal right, for instance, that men had in marriage. They could force their wives to have intercourse and it was not called force or rape; it was called desire or love. We have challenged the old ideology of sexual conquest as a natural game in which women are targets and men are conquering heroes. . . . We have identified rape; we have identified incest; we have identified battery; we have identified prostitution; we have identified pornography—as crimes against women, as means of exploiting women, as ways of hurting women that are systematic and supported by the practices of the societies in which we live. We have identified sexual exploitation as abuse. We have identified objectification and turning women into commodities for sale as dehumanizing, deeply dehumanizing. . . . We have identified patterns of violence that take place in intimate relationships. We know now that most rape is not committed by the dangerous and predatory stranger but by the dangerous and predatory boyfriend, lover, friend, husband, neighbor, the man we are closest to, not the man who is farthest away.

What remains to be done? . . . We need to end rape . . . , incest . . . , battery . . . , prostitution, and . . . pornography. That means that we need to refuse to

Source: Andrea Dworkin, *Life and Death* (New York: Free Press, 1997), 169–78.

accept that these are natural phenomena that just happen because some guy is having a bad day. . . .

In my view, we need to concentrate on the perpetrators of crimes against women instead of asking ourselves over and over and over again, why did that happen to her? . . . There is no women's movement if it does not include the women who are being hurt and the women who have the least. The women's movement has to take on the family systems in our countries. . . .

We have to take on prostitution as an issue. . . . Most prostituted women in the West are incest victims who ran away from home, who have been raped, who are pimped when they are still children—raped, homeless, poor, abandoned children. We have to take on poverty: not in the liberal sense of heartfelt concern but in the concrete sense, in the real world. We have to take on what it means to stand up for women who have nothing because when women have nothing, it's real nothing: no homes, no food, no shelter, often no ability to read.

Now, I know, in this room, some of you are the women I have been talking about. . . . I am going to ask you to use every single thing you can remember about what was done to you—how it was done, where, by whom, when, and, if you know, why—to begin to tear male dominance to pieces, to pull it apart, to vandalize it, to destabilize it. . . . I have to ask you to resist, not to comply, to destroy the power men have over women, to refuse to accept it, to abhor it, and to do whatever is necessary, despite its cost to you, to change it.

Document 23.3

Black American Feminism

Within North American feminism, a distinctive voice arose among women of color—especially blacks and Hispanics. Many among them resented the claims of white, middle-class feminists to speak for all women and objected to the exclusive prominence given to gender issues. Capitalism, race, class, and compulsory heterosexuality, they insisted, combined with patriarchy to generate an interlocking system of oppression, unique to women of color. Such a perspective is reflected in the 1977 statement of the Combahee River Collective, a black feminist organization.

■ What differences in perspective can you identify between this document and that of Andrea Dworkin in Document 23.2?

■ What issues divide black and white feminists in the United States?

■ What difficulties have black American feminists experienced in gaining support for their movement?

■ On what basis might this statement generate opposition and controversy?

COMBAHEE RIVER COLLECTIVE
A Black Feminist Statement
1977

We are a collective of Black feminists who have been meeting together since 1974.... [W]e are actively committed to struggling against racial, sexual, heterosexual, and class oppression ... based upon the fact that the major systems of oppression are interlocking....

[W]e find our origins in the historical reality of Afro-American women's continuous life-and-death struggle for survival and liberation.... Black women have always embodied an adversary stance to white male rule.... Black feminist politics also have an obvious connection to movements for Black liberation, particularly those of the 1960s and 1970s.... It was our experience and disillusionment within these liberation movements, as well as experience on the periphery of the white male left, that led to the need to develop a politics that was anti-racist, unlike those of white women, and anti-sexist, unlike those of Black and white men.... [A]s we developed politically we [also] addressed ourselves to heterosexism and economic oppression under capitalism....

Although we are feminists and Lesbians, we feel solidarity with progressive Black men and do not advocate the fractionalization that white women who are separatists demand.... We struggle together with Black men against racism, while we also struggle with Black men about sexism.... We are socialists because we believe that work must be organized for the collective benefit of those who do the work and create the products, and not for the profit of the bosses.... We need to articulate the real class situation of persons ... for whom racial and sexual oppression are significant determinants in their working/economic lives.... No one before has ever examined the multilayered texture of Black women's lives.... "Smart-ugly" crystallized the way in which most of us had been forced to develop our intellects at great cost to our "social" lives.... We have a great deal of criticism and loathing for what men have been socialized to be in this society ... [b]ut we do not have the misguided notion that it is their maleness, per se—i.e., their biological maleness—that makes them what they are.

The major source of difficulty in our political work is that we are ... trying ... to address a whole range of oppressions.... We do not have racial, sexual, heterosexual, or class privilege to rely upon....The psychological toll of being a Black woman and the difficulties this presents in reaching political consciousness and doing political work can never be

Source: Zillah R. Eisenstein, ed., *Capitalist Patriarchy and the Case for Socialist Feminism* (New York: Monthly Review Press, 1979), 362–72.

underestimated. . . . As an early group member once said, "We are all damaged people merely by virtue of being Black women."... The material conditions of most Black women would hardly lead them to upset both economic and sexual arrangements that seem to represent some stability in their lives. . . . Accusations that Black feminism divides the Black struggle are powerful deterrents to the growth of an autonomous Black women's movement.

The inclusiveness of our politics makes us concerned with any situation that impinges upon the lives of women, Third World and working people. . . . One issue that is of major concern to us and that we have begun to publicly address is racism in the white women's movement. . . . Eliminating racism in the white women's movement is by definition work for white women to do, but we will continue to speak to and demand accountability on this issue. . . .

Document 23.4

Islamic Feminism

Beyond the Western world and the communist world, modern feminism has also found expression in the developing countries (see pp. 1152–53). Nowhere has this provoked greater controversy than in the Islamic world. For a few women, exposure to Western gender norms and liberal thought has occasioned the abandonment of Islam altogether. (See Document 22.4, pp. 1126–28.) Far more common have been efforts to root gender equality in both personal and public life within the traditions of Islam. Such was the argument of Benazir Bhutto, several times the prime minister of Pakistan, in a speech delivered in 1985.

- On what basis does Bhutto argue that "Islam provides justice and equality for women"?

- How does she account for the manifest inequality of women in so many Muslim societies?

- How do you think Kemal Atatürk (Document 22.1, p. 1120), the Ayatollah Khomeini (Document 22.2, p. 1122), and Ayaan Hirsi Ali (Document 22.4, p. 1126) might respond to Bhutto's ideas?

- How might you compare Bhutto's case for feminism with those of the communist and American writers in the preceding documents?

BENAZIR BHUTTO
Politics and the Muslim Woman
1985

[O]ne of the first things that we must appreciate about the religion of Islam is that there is no one interpretation to it. . . .

I would describe Islam in two main categories: reactionary Islam and progressive Islam. We can

have a reactionary interpretation of Islam which tries to uphold the status quo, or we can have a progressive interpretation of Islam which tries to move with a changing world, which believes in human dignity, which believes in consensus, and which believes in giving women their due right. . . .

I believe that Islam within it provides justice and equality for women, and I think that those aspects of Islam which have been highlighted by the *mullas* [religious scholars] do not do a service to our religion. . . . But . . . as more and more people in Muslim countries, both men and women, achieve education and begin to examine the Qur'an in the light of their education, they are beginning not to agree with the *mullas* on their orthodox or reactionary version of Islam.

Let us start with the story of the Fall. Unlike Christianity, it is not Eve who tempts Adam into tasting the apple and being responsible for original sin. According to Islam — and I mention this because I believe that Islam is an egalitarian religion — both Adam and Eve are tempted, both are warned, both do not heed the warning, and therefore the Fall occurs.

As far as opportunity is concerned, in Islam there is equal opportunity for both men and women. I refer to the Sura *Ya Sin* [Quran 36, 34–35], which says: "We produce orchids and date gardens and vines, and we cause springs to gush forth, that they may enjoy the fruits of it." God does not give fruits, orchids, or the fruit of the soil just for men to enjoy or men to plow; he gives it for both men and women. . . . Sura *an-Nisa* [Quran 4, 32]: "To men is allotted what they earn, and to women what they earn." . . .

The references [in the Quran] are to men and women. . . . The attributes are the same. Both are the creatures of God. Both have certain rights. Both have certain duties. . . . [T]hey have to give alms to the needy, they have to help orphans — the behavior is applicable to both men and women. It is not re-

ligion which makes the difference. The difference comes from man-made law. It comes from the fact that soon after the Prophet died, it was not the Islam of the Prophet that remained. What took place was the emergence or the reassertiveness of the patriarchal society, and religion was taken over to justify the norms of the tribal society. . . .

[About] the right of divorce and polygamy. It is often said that Islam provides for four wives for a man. But in my interpretation of this, and in the interpretation of many other Muslims, that is simply not true.

What the Qur'an does say, and I quote: "Marry as many women as you wish, wives two or three or four. If you fear not to treat them equally, marry only one. . . . I doubt you will be able to be just between your wives, even if you try" [Quran 4:3, 129]. So if God Himself and His message says that He doubts that you can be equal, I don't know how any man can turn around and say that "God has given me this right to get married more than once."

I would like to say that within Islamic history there are very strong roles for women. For instance, the Prophet's wife, Bibi Khadija, was a woman of independent means. She had her own business, she traded, she dealt with society at large, she employed the Prophet Muhammad, peace be upon him, when he was a young boy, and subsequently, Bibi Khadija herself sent a proposal [of marriage] to the Prophet. So she is the very image of somebody who is independent, assertive, and does not conform to the passive description of women in Muslim societies that we have grown accustomed to hearing about. . . .

So when we have such powerful role models of women . . . then one must ask, why is it that today in Muslim countries, one does not see that much of women? . . . Why is it that women are secluded? Why is it that women are subject to social control? Why is it that women are not given their due share of property? . . . It has got nothing to do with the religion, but it has got very much to do with material or man-made considerations. . . . It is not Islam which is averse to women rulers, I think — it is men.

Source: Benazir Bhutto, "Politics and the Muslim Woman," transcript of audio recording, April 11, 1985, in *Liberal Islam: A Sourcebook*, ed. Charles Kurzman (New York: Oxford University Press, 1998), 107–11.

Document 23.5

Mexican Zapatista Feminists

Mexican feminists, like those in much of Latin America, have operated in societies shaped by widespread poverty, sharp class inequalities, racial and ethnic conflict, and frequently authoritarian or corrupt governments. Thus feminists have often sought to address the ways in which multiple sources of oppression, not only gender relations, affect both women and men. Such was the case in the Zapatista rebellion that erupted in 1994 among the Maya people in the Chiapas region of southern Mexico. It was a protest against a long history of injustice and impoverishment for indigenous peoples. Women activists within this largely peasant movement had to confront the sexist attitudes of their male comrades as well as an oppressive Mexican government that marginalized its Maya citizens. Although they usually rejected the "feminist" label, these women articulated their demands in an Indigenous Women's Petition and succeeded in embedding their concerns in a Women's Revolutionary Law, both of which are reproduced here.

- How would you describe the issues that these documents articulate? How do they reflect class, ethnic, and gender realities of Mexican life?

- Should these documents be regarded as feminist? Why or why not? Why might Zapatista women be reluctant to call themselves feminists?

- Which of these demands might provoke the strongest male resistance? Why?

- With which of the previous feminist statements might Zapatista women be most sympathetic?

Indigenous Women's Petition
March 1, 1994

We the indigenous *campesina* women ask for the immediate solution to our urgent needs, which the government has never met.

Sources: "The Zapatista Women: The Movement from Within," app. II, "Indigenous Women's Petition," Zapatista Women, accessed March 20, 2012, http://www.actlab.utexas.edu/~geneve/zapwomen/goetze/thesis.html (first excerpt); *Zapatistas! Documents of the New Mexican Revolution* (Brooklyn: Autonomedia, 1994) (second excerpt).

1. Child birth clinics with gynecologists....
2. Day care centers....
3. Enough food for the children ... such as milk, corn starch, rice, corn, soy, oil, beans, cheese, eggs, sugar, soup, oatmeal.
4. Kitchens and dining halls, with all the necessary equipment, for the children in the communities.
5. Corn mills and tortilla-makers ... according to the number of families in each area.
6. [M]aterials necessary to raise chickens, rabbits, sheep, pigs, etc., including technical advice and veterinary services.

7. [O]vens and necessary materials to build bakeries.
8. [C]raft workshops . . . including machinery and materials.
9. [A] market where crafts can be sold at a fair price.
10. Schools . . . where women can receive technical training.
11. [P]re-schools and day-care centers in rural communities.
12. [S]ufficient transportation to move from one place to another and to transport the products of our various projects.

The Women's Revolutionary Law
January 1, 1994

[T]aking into account the situation of the woman worker in Mexico, the revolution supports their just demands for equality and justice in the following Women's Revolutionary Law.

First: Women, regardless of their race, creed, color or political affiliation, have the right to participate in the revolutionary struggle in a way determined by their desire and capacity.

Second: Women have the right to work and receive a just salary.

Third: Women have the right to decide the number of children they will have and care for.

Fourth: Women have the right to participate in the affairs of the community and hold positions of authority if they are freely and democratically elected.

Fifth: Women and their children have the right to primary attention in matters of health and nutrition.

Sixth: Women have the right to an education.

Seventh: Women have the right to choose their partner, and are not to be forced into marriage.

Eighth: Women shall not be beaten or physically mistreated by their family members or by strangers. Rape and attempted rape will be severely punished.

Ninth: Women will be able to occupy positions of leadership in the organization and hold military ranks in the revolutionary armed forces.

Using the Evidence: Voices of Global Feminism

1. **Identifying similarities:** What common concerns animate these documents?

2. **Defining differences:** What variations or conflicting feminist perspectives can you identify in these sources? What accounts for those differences?

3. **Considering change over time:** How do you think Elizabeth Cady Stanton (see Document 16.4, p. 818) and nineteenth-century Western feminists in general would have responded to each of these twentieth-century statements?

4. **Evaluating global feminism:** What aspects of global feminism were most revolutionary, liberating, or threatening to established authorities and ways of living? To what extent do you think the goals of these varying feminist efforts have been realized?

Visual Sources

Considering the Evidence:
Experiencing Globalization

Not many people in the world of the early twenty-first century remain untouched by globalization. For most of humankind, the pervasive processes of interaction among distant peoples has shaped the clothing we wear, the foods we eat, the products we consume, the ways we work, the music we listen to, the religions we practice, and the identities we assume. Globalization has bound the various peoples of the planet more tightly together and in some respects has made us more alike. Almost all of us, for example, live in nation-states and seek the health, wealth, and prosperity that modern science and technology promise. And yet in other ways we are very different, divided, and conflicted. The enormous gap in wealth between the rich countries of the Global North and the poorer nations of the Global South represents a sharp and quite recent rift in the human community. The visual sources that follow illustrate just a few of the ways in which the world's peoples have experienced globalization in recent decades and have responded to it.

Among the common experiences of globalization for some people living in Asia, Africa, or Latin America has been that of working in foreign-owned production facilities. Companies in wealthier countries have often found it advantageous to build such facilities in places where labor is less expensive or environmental regulations are less restrictive. China, Vietnam, Indonesia, Bangladesh, the Philippines, Mexico, Brazil, and various African states are among the countries that have hosted foreign-owned manufacturing operations. The worst of them—in terms of child labor, low pay, few benefits, and dangerous working conditions—have been called "sweatshops." Such abuses have generated an international movement challenging those conditions. Visual Source 23.1 illustrates an interesting twist on this common feature of a globalized world economy—a Chinese-owned company producing Western-style blue jeans in Lesotho, a small country in southern Africa.

■ Why might China, itself the site of many foreign-owned factories, place such a factory in Africa? What does this suggest about the changing

Visual Source 23.1 Globalization and Work (brianafrica/Alamy)

position of China in the world economy? What is the significance of the blue jeans for an understanding of contemporary globalization?

■ Does this photograph conform to your image of a sweatshop? Why might many developing countries accept foreign-owned production facilities, despite the criticisms of the working conditions in them?

■ Why do you think most of the workers in this photo are women? How might you imagine their motivations for seeking this kind of work? Keep in mind that the unemployment rate in Lesotho in the early twenty-first century was 45 percent.

■ What differences can you observe between the workers in this assembly factory and those in the Indian call center shown on page 1140? What similarities might you identify?

If globalization offered employment opportunities — albeit in often wretched conditions — to some people in the developing countries, it also promoted a worldwide culture of consumerism. That culture placed the accumulation of material goods, many of them of Western origin, above older values of spiritual attainment or social responsibility. Nowhere has this culture of consumerism been more prominent than in China, where the fading of Maoist communism, the country's massive economic growth, and its new openness to the wider world combined to generate an unabashed materialism in the late twentieth and early twenty-first centuries. A popular slogan suggested that life in modern China required the "eight bigs": color TV, refrigerator, stereo, camera, motorcycle, a suite of furniture, washing machine, and an electric fan. Visual Source 23.2 illustrates this culture of consumerism as well as one of the "eight bigs" in a poster from the post-Mao era. The poster on page 1062 in Chapter 21 provides further illustration of Chinese consumerism.

- In what ways might these images be used to illustrate Westernization, modernization, globalization, and consumerism?

- How might the young people on the motorcycle understand their own behavior? Do you think they are conscious of behaving in Western ways or have these ways become Chinese? What is the significance of a Chinese couple riding a Suzuki motorcycle, a Japanese product probably manufactured in China under a license agreement?

- Beyond consumerism, how does this poster reflect changes in relationships between men and women in China after Mao? Is this yet another face of globalization or does it remain a distinctly Western phenomenon?

- How might these images be read as a celebration of Chinese success? How might they be used to criticize contemporary Chinese society?

During the last several decades of the twentieth century, the process of economic globalization spawned various movements of resistance and criticism (see pp. 1165–69). In dozens of developing countries, protesters demonstrated or rioted against government policies that removed subsidies, raised prices on essential products, froze salaries, or cut back on social services. Because such policies were often required by the World Bank or the International Monetary Fund as a condition for receiving much-needed loans, protesters often directed their anger at these international financial institutions. In the wealthier countries of the world as well, activists have mounted large-scale protests against what they see as the abuses of unregulated corporate power operating in the world economy. Visual Source 23.3 shows a display of this anger that occurred during the protests in Seattle that coincided with the 1999 gathering of the World Trade Organization.

- How does this image reflect the concerns of globalization's many critics? What political message does it convey?

- Why have these criticisms come to focus so heavily on the activities of the World Trade Organization?

- To what groups of people might such images be most compelling? How might advocates of corporate globalization respond to these protesters?

入 勤 春 早

Visual Source 23.2 Globalization and Consumerism (IISH/Stefan R. Landsberger collections
http:chineseposters.net)

Visual Source 23.3
Globalization and
Protest (Michael
McGuerty)

Visual Source 23.4, a composite satellite photograph of the world at night taken in late 2000, reflects three aspects of the globalization process. The first is the growing consciousness of the earth as a single place, the common home of humankind. Such thinking has been fostered by and expressed in those many remarkable images of the earth taken from space or from the moon (see the photo on p. 1136). In such photographs no artificial boundaries of state or nation are visible, just a solitary planet cast against the immeasurable vastness of space. Second, this photograph shows the globalization of electricity, a central feature of modern life, which has taken place since the late nineteenth century. Finally, this image discloses sharp variations in modern development across the planet as the twenty-first century dawned.

- To what extent has your thinking about the earth and its inhabitants been shaped by images such as this?

- Based on the electrification evident in this photo, what does this image show about the economic divisions of the world in the early twenty-first century?

- Does this image support or contradict the Snapshot on page 1145? What features of this image might you find surprising?

Visual Source 23.4 Globalization: One World or Many? (NASA/GSFC Digital Archive)

Using the Evidence: Experiencing Globalization

1. **Defining differences:** Based on these visual sources and the text of Chapter 23, in what different ways have various groups of people experienced globalization since the end of World War II?

2. **Noticing change:** Based on these visual sources and those in the text of Chapter 23 as well, in what respects does contemporary globalization differ from that of earlier times? What continuities might you observe? Consider in particular the question of who is influencing who. Does recent globalization represent largely the impact of the West on the rest of the world or is it more of a two-way street?

3. **Making assessments:** Opinions about contemporary globalization depend heavily on the position of observers—their class, gender, or national locations. How might you illustrate this statement from the visual sources in this chapter?

4. **Seeking further evidence:** What additional images might add to this effort to illustrate visually the various dimensions of globalization? What visual sources do you think might be added to it fifty or a hundred years from now?

Chapter 23 Wrap Up

LearningCurve
Check what you know.
bedfordstmartins.com
/strayer/LC

STEP ONE

The Words to Know: Transnational/supranational

International organizations, as well as corporations, can be both transnational and supranational. The *Oxford English Dictionary* defines *transnational* as "extending or having interests extending beyond national bounds or frontiers; multinational." The *Oxford English Dictionary* defines *supranational* as "having power or influence that overrides or transcends national boundaries, governments, or institutions." Using evidence from the text, write an essay about the roles that transnational and supranational organizations play in confronting one of the following global challenges: the environment, the economy, gender equity, or religious understanding. In your essay, you might also consider the limitations of these kinds of organizations in meeting these challenges.

STEP TWO

The Development of Global Environmentalism

Using the text as well as the timelines on pages 1089 and 1139, Map 23.4 on p. 1165, and the Snapshots on pages 1104 and 1145, consider the rise of environmentalism over the past 50 years and how environmentalism fits fit into the larger story of world history by answering the questions below.

■ Questions

1. What environmental issues is the world currently facing?

2. How has the growth of population contributed to the environmental challenges we face today?

3. How has globalization helped to both aggravate environmental problems as well as help to find global solutions to these contemporary challenges?

4. What events on the timeline on p. 1139 can be linked together to show why there was a new wave of ecological consciousness after 1960?

5. Based on your understanding of Chapter 23, what more do you need to know to explain fully the global historical context of environmentalism?

STEP THREE

Environmentalism, Sustainability, and Consumerism

Consider the relationship among globalization, sustainable development, consumerism, and climate change, taking into account the impact that they have on the Global South. First examine the Snapshot on page 1145, the narrative on pp. 1163–69, and the visual sources section on pp. 1182–87. Then write an essay addressing the problems and possible solutions involved in one of the following issues that global development raises: climate change or sustainability or consumerism.

Notes

Prologue

1. Adapted from Carl Sagan, *The Dragons of Eden* (New York: Random House, 1977), 13–17.

2. See David Christian, *Maps of Time* (Berkeley: University of California Press, 2004).

3. Voltaire, *Treatise on Toleration*, chap. 22.

4. See David Christian, "World History in Context," *Journal of World History* 14, no. 4 (December 2003), 437–58.

Chapter 1

1. Richard Rainsford, "What Chance, the Survival Prospects of East Africa's Last Hunting and Gathering Tribe the Hadzabe, in a Gameless Environment?," Information about Northern Tanzania, March 1997, http://www.ntz.info/gen/n00757.html.

2. What follows comes from Sally McBreatry and Alison S. Brooks, "The Revolution That Wasn't: A New Interpretation of the Origin of Modern Human Behavior," *Journal of Human Evolution* 39 (2000): 453–563.

3. John Mulvaney and Johan Kaminga, *Prehistory of Australia* (Washington, DC: Smithsonian Institution Press, 1999), 93–102.

4. For a recent summary of this debate, see Charles C. Mann, *1491: New Revelations of the Americas before Columbus* (New York: Alfred Knopf, 2005), chap. 5.

5. Brian M. Fagan, *Ancient North America* (London: Thames and Hudson, 1995), 77–87.

6. Ben Finney, "The Other One-Third of the Globe," *Journal of World History* 5, no. 2 (1994): 273–85.

7. Fred Spier, *Big History and the Future of Humanity* (West Sussex: Wiley-Blackwell, 2011), 132; David Christian, *Maps of Time* (Berkeley: University of California Press, 2004), 143.

8. Richard B. Lee, *The Dobe Ju/'hoansi* (New York: Harcourt Brace, 1993), 58.

9. J. C. Beaglehole, *The Journals of Captain James Cook* (Cambridge: Hakluyt Society, 1968), 1:399.

10. Inga Clendinnen, *Dancing with Strangers* (Cambridge: Cambridge University Press, 2005), 159–67.

11. Steven Pinker, *The Better Angels of Our Nature* (New York: Viking, 2011), 47–52.

12. Marshall Sahlins, *Stone Age Economics* (London: Tavistock, 1972), 1–39.

13. Christopher Ehret, *The Civilizations of Africa* (Charlottesville: University of Virginia Press, 2002), chap. 2.

14. Marija Gimbutas, *The Language of the Goddess* (San Francisco: HarperCollins, 1989), 316–18.

15. D. Bruce Dickson, *The Dawn of Belief* (Tucson: University of Arizona Press, 1990), 210.

16. Derived from Christian, *Maps of Time*, 208.

17. Brian Fagan, *People of the Earth* (New York: HarperCollins, 1992), 200–201.

18. Charles C. Mann, "The Birth of Religion," *National Geographic*, June 2011, 35–59.

19. Bruce Smith, *The Emergence of Agriculture* (New York: Scientific American Library, 1995), 206–14.

20. Jared Diamond, *Guns, Germs, and Steel* (New York: Vintage, 1997), 132, 157–75.

21. Peter Bellwood, *First Farmers: The Origins of Agricultural Societies* (Malden, MA: Blackwell, 2005), 54–55.

22. Neil Roberts, *The Holocene: An Environmental History* (Oxford: Blackwell, 1998), 116.

23. Nina V. Federoff, "Prehistoric GM Corn," *Science* 302 (November 2003): 1158.

24. Theodora Kroeber, *Ishi in Two Worlds* (Berkeley: University of California Press, 1961), 229. See also Karl Kroeber and Clifton Kroeber, *Ishi in Three Centuries* (Lincoln: University of Nebraska Press, 2003).

25. Clive Ponting, *A Green History of the World* (New York: St. Martin's Press, 1991), 69.

26. Elizabeth Wayland Barber, *Women's Work: The First 20,000 Years* (New York: W. W. Norton, 1994), chap. 3.

27. Andrew Sherrat, "The Secondary Exploitation of Animals in the Old World," *World Archeology* 15, no. 1 (1983): 90–104.

28. Tom Standage, *A History of the World in Six Glasses* (New York: Walker and Company, 2005), chaps. 1, 2; Li Zhengping, *Chinese Wine* (Cambridge: Cambridge University Press, 2011), 1–3.

29. Anatoly M. Khazanov, *Nomads and the Outside World* (Madison: University of Wisconsin Press, 1994), 15.

30. Ian Hodder, "Women and Men at Catalhoyuk," *Scientific American* 15, no. 1 (2005): 35–41.

31. Marija Gimbutas, *The Language of the Goddess* (New York: Harper and Row, 1989), xix.

32. Allen W. Johnson and Timothy Earle, *The Evolution of Human Societies* (Stanford, CA: Stanford University Press, 2000), 281–94.

33. Elaine Godden and Jutta Malnic, *Rock Paintings of Aboriginal Australia* (London: New Holland, 2001), preface.

34. Gregory Curtin, *The Cave Painters* (New York: Random House, 2006), 96.

35. Ian Hodder, "Discussions with the Goddess Community," Çatalhöyük: Excavations of a Neolithic Anatolian Höyük, accessed January 23, 2012, http://www.catalhoyuk.com/library/goddess.html.

36. Jack Linthicum,, "A Journey to 9,000 Years Ago," January 17, 2008, http://sci.tech-archive.net/Archive/sci.archaeology/2008-01/msg00519.html.

37. Robin Melrose, *The Druids and King Arthur* (Jefferson, NC: McFarland, 2011), 94.

38. Reuters, "Stonehedge May Have Been Pilgrimage Site for the Sick," September 23, 2008, http://uk.reuters.com/article/2008/09/23/us-britain-stonehenge-idUKTRE48M0R320080923.

Chapter 2

1. Personal Development for Smart People Forum: Fun and Recreation, "Escaping Civilization," May 30, 2007, http://www.stevepavlina.com/forums/fun-recreation/7504-escaping-civilization.html.

2. Charles C. Mann, *1491: New Revelations of the Americas before Columbus* (New York: Alfred A. Knopf, 2005), 174–91; Proyecto Arqueológico Norte Chico, "Project Description," Field Museum, 2005, http://archive.fieldmuseum.org/research_collections/anthropology/anthro_sites/PANC/proj_desc.htm.

3. Jonathan Mark Kenoyer, *Ancient Cities of the Indus Valley Civilization* (Oxford: Oxford University Press, 1998), 83–84.

4. David Christian, *A History of Russia, Central Asia and Mongolia* (Oxford: Blackwell, 1998), 114.

5. For a summary of many theories, see Stephen K. Sanderson, *Social Transformations* (Oxford: Blackwell, 1995), chap. 3.

6. Robert Carneiro, "A Theory of the Origin of the State," *Science* 169 (1970): 733–38.

7. Susan Pollock, *Ancient Mesopotamia* (Cambridge: Cambridge University Press, 1999), 48.

8. *The Epic of Gilgamesh*, translated and edited by Benjamin R. Foster (New York: W. W. Norton, 2001), 10, tablet 1: 226–32.

9. Samuel Noah Kramer, *History Begins at Sumer* (Philadelphia: University of Pennsylvania Press, 1981), 3–4.

10. James Legge, trans., *The Chinese Classics* (London: Henry Frowde, 1893), 4:171–72.

11. Margaret Ehrenberg, *Women in Prehistory* (London: British Museum, 1989), 107.

12. Sherry Ortner, "Is Female to Male as Nature Is to Culture?" in *Women, Culture, and Society*, edited by Michelle Rosaldo and Louise Lamphere (Stanford, CA: Stanford University Press, 1974), 67–88.

13. Gerda Lerner, *The Creation of Patriarchy* (New York: Oxford University Press, 1986), 70.

14. Marian Lichtheim, *Ancient Egyptian Literature* (Berkeley: University of California Press, 1975), 2:168–75.

15. Steven Pinker, *The Better Angels of our Nature* (New York: Viking, 2011), chaps. 2, 3.

16. Prologue to *The Code of Hammurabi*, http://www.thenagain.info/Classes/Sources/Hammurabi-Prologue.

17. Adolf Erman, *The Literature of the Ancient Egyptians*, translated by Aylward M. Blackman (London: Methuen, 1927), 136–37.

18. Henri Frankfort et al., *Before Philosophy: The Intellectual Adventure of Ancient Man* (Baltimore: Penguin Books, 1963), 39, 138.

19. Quoted in Peter Stearns et al., *World Civilizations* (New York: Longman, 1996), 1:30.

20. See Clive Ponting, *A Green History of the World* (New York: St. Martin's Press, 1991), chap. 5.

21. K. J. W. Oosthoek, "The Role of Wood in World History," Environmental History Resources, 1998, http://www.eh-resources.org/wood.html#_ednref1.

22. Pascal Vernus, *Affairs and Scandals in Ancient Egypt* (Ithaca, NY: Cornell University Press, 2003), 70–86; Toby Wilkinson, *Lives of the Ancient Egyptians* (London: Thames and Hudson, 2007), 259–61.

23. Cyril Aldred, *The Egyptians* (London: Thames and Hudson, 1998), 138.

24. For a summary of a long debate about the relationship of Egypt and Africa, see David O'Connor and Andrew Reid, eds., *Ancient Egypt in Africa* (London: UCL Press, 2003).

25. James B. Pritchard, ed., *Ancient Near Eastern Texts Relating to the Old Testament* (Princeton, NJ: Princeton University Press, 1969), 647–48.

26. Lichtheim, *Ancient Egyptian Literature*, 1:25–27.

27. M. J. Rowlands et al., eds., *Center and Periphery in the Ancient World* (Cambridge: Cambridge University Press, 1987), 59.

28. Marvin Harris, ed., *Cannibals and Kings* (New York: Vintage, 1978), 102.

29. Lichtheim, *Ancient Egyptian Literature*, 2:177.

30. Jonathan M. Kenoyer, *Ancient Cities of the Indus Valley Civilization* (Karachi: Oxford University Press, 1998), 84.

31. Ibid., 100.

32. Gregory L. Possehl, *The Indus Civilization: A Contemporary Perspective* (Walnut Creek, CA: AltaMira Press, 2002), 114.

Part 2

1. Stephen K. Sanderson, *Social Transformation* (Oxford: Blackwell, 1995), chap. 4.
2. From ibid., 103.
3. Colin Ronan and Joseph Needham, *The Shorter Science and Civilization in China* (Cambridge: Cambridge University Press, 1978), 58.
4. William H. McNeill, *Plagues and Peoples* (New York: Doubleday, 1977), 94.

Chapter 3

1. Cullen Murphy, *Are We Rome? The Fall of an Empire and the Fate of America* (Boston: Houghton Mifflin, 2007).
2. J. M. Cook, *The Persian Empire* (London: J. M. Dent & Sons, 1983), 76.
3. George Rawlinson, trans., *The Histories of Herodotus* (London: Dent, 1910), 1:131–40.
4. Erich F. Schmidt, *Persepolis I: Structures, Reliefs, Inscriptions*, OIP 68 (Chicago: University of Chicago Press, 1953), 63.
5. Quoted in Anthony N. Penna, *The Human Footprint* (Oxford: Wiley-Blackwell, 2010), 151.
6. Quoted in Thomas R. Martin, *Ancient Greece from Prehistoric to Hellenistic Times* (New Haven, CT: Yale University Press, 1996), 86.
7. Christian Meier, *Athens* (New York: Metropolitan Books, 1993), 93.
8. Arrian, *The Campaigns of Alexander*, translated by Aubrey de Selincourt, revised by J. R. Hamilton (London: Penguin, 1971), 395–96.
9. Stanley Burstein, *The Hellenistic Period in World History* (Washington, DC: American Historical Association, 1996), 12.
10. Norman F. Cantor, *Antiquity* (New York: HarperCollins, 2003), 25.
11. Paul Halsall, "Early Western Civilization Under the Sign of Gender," in *A Companion to Gender History*, edited by Teresa A. Meade and Merry E. Wiesner-Hanks (London: Blackwell, 2004), 293–94.
12. Keith W. Taylor, *The Birth of Vietnam* (Berkeley: University of California Press, 1983), 334.
13. S. A. M. Adshead, *China in World History* (London: McMillan Press, 1988), 4–21.
14. See Padma Manian, "Harappans and Aryans: Old and New Perspectives on Ancient Indian History," *History Teacher* 32, no. 1 (1998): 17–32.
15. Roger Boesche, *The First Great Political Realist: Kautilya and His Arthashastra* (Lanham, MD: Lexington Books, 2002), 17.
16. Stanley Wolpert, *A New History of India* (New York: Oxford University Press, 1993), 90.

17. Zhengyuan Fu, *Autocratic Tradition and Chinese Politics* (New York: Cambridge University Press, 1993), 188.
18. *The Sculptures and Inscription of Darius the Great on the Rock of Behistûn in Persia* (London, 1907), 71–72.
19. Jane Portal, ed., *The First Emperor: China's Terracotta Army* (London: British Museum Press, 2007), 110.
20. Quoted in Anders Blixt, "Qin Shi Huang Di, 'The Tiger Emperor': The First Emperor of China," accessed February 1, 2012, http://biphome.spray.se/coif/history/qin/shie09.html.
21. Paul Zanker, *The Power of Images in the Age of Augustus* (Ann Arbor: University of Michigan Press, 1988), 187.

Chapter 4

1. "Birthday of Confucius . . . ," China View, September 28, 2009. [http://news.xinhuanet.com/english/2009-09/28/content_12123115.html]
2. S. N. Eisenstadt, ed., *The Origins and Diversity of Axial Age Civilizations* (Albany: SUNY Press, 1986), 1–4; Karen Armstrong, *The Great Transformation* (New York: Alfred A. Knopf, 2006).
3. Quoted in Arthur Waley, *Three Ways of Thought in Ancient China* (Garden City, NY: Doubleday, 1956), 159–60.
4. Nancy Lee Swann, trans., *Pan Chao: Foremost Woman Scholar of China* (New York: Century, 1932), 111–14.
5. Kam Louie and Morris Low, *Asian Masculinities* (London: Rutledge, 2003), 3–6.
6. Quoted in Huston Smith, *The Illustrated World's Religions* (San Francisco: HarperCollins, 1994), 123.
7. Lao Tsu, *Tao Te Ching*, translated by Gia-Fu Feng and Jane English (New York: Vintage Books, 1972), 80.
8. Catherine Clay et al., *Envisioning Women in World History* (New York: McGraw-Hill, 2009), 1:67–77.
9. Quoted in Karen Andrews, "Women in Theravada Buddhism," Institute of Buddhist Studies, accessed February 19, 2012, http://www.enabling.org/ia/vipassana/Archive/A/Andrews/womenTheraBudAndrews.html.
10. A. L. Basham, *The Wonder That Was India* (London: Sidgwick and Jackson, 1967), 309.
11. S. A. Nigosian, *The Zoroastrian Faith: Tradition and Modern Research* (Montreal: McGill–Queen's University Press, 1993), 95–97.
12. Isaiah 1:11–17.
13. Plato, *Apologia*, translated by Benjamin Jowett (1891).
14. Hippocrates, *On the Sacred Disease*, translated by Francis Adams, Internet Classics Archive, accessed February 2, 2012, http://classics.mit.edu/Hippocrates/sacred.html.
15. Thanissaro Bhikkhu, trans., "Karaniya Metta Sutta: Good Will," 2004, http://www.accesstoinsight.org/tipitaka/kn/snp/snp.1.08.than.html.

16. Matthew 5:43–44.

17. See Marcus Borg, ed., *Jesus and Buddha: The Parallel Sayings* (Berkeley, CA: Ulysses Press, 1997).

18. For a popular summary of the voluminous scholarship on Jesus, see Stephen Patterson et al., *The Search for Jesus: Modern Scholarship Looks at the Gospels* (Washington, DC: Biblical Archeological Society, 1994).

19. Galatians 3:28.

20. Cynthia Bourgeault, *The Meaning of Mary Magdalene* (Boston: Shambala, 2010).

21. Ephesians 5:22–23; 1 Corinthians 14:35.

22. Ekkehard W. Stegemann and Wolfgang Stegemann, *The Jesus Movement: A History of Its First Century* (Minneapolis: Fortress Press, 1999), 291–96.

23. Peter Brown, *The Rise of Western Christendom* (London: Blackwell, 2003), 69–71.

24. Robert Sider, "Early Christians in North Africa," *Coptic Church Review* 19, no. 3 (1998): 2.

25. "The Martyrdom of Saints Perpetua and Felicitas," *Frontline*, "From Jesus to Christ," PBS, April 1998, http://www.pbs.org/wgbh/pages/frontline/shows/religion/maps/primary/perpetua.html.

26. Mary Ann Rossi, "Priesthood, Precedent, and Prejudice: On Recovering the Women Priests of Early Christianity," *Journal of Feminist Studies* 7, no. 1 (1991): 73–94.

27. Chai-Shin Yu, *Early Buddhism and Christianity* (Delhi: Motilal Banarsidass, 1981), 211.

28. "Footprints of the Buddha," Internet Sacred Text Archive, accessed February 2, 2012, http://www.sacred-texts.com/shi/igj/igj09.htm.

Chapter 5

1. Lydia Polgreen, "Business Class Rises in Ashes of Caste System," *New York Times*, September 10, 2010.

2. Po Chu-I, "After Passing the Examination," in *More Translations from the Chinese*, by Arthur Waley (New York: Alfred A. Knopf, 1919), 37.

3. Quoted in Michael Lowe, *Everyday Life in Early Imperial China* (New York: Dorset, 1968), 38.

4. "Ge Hong's Autobiography," in *Chinese Civilization*, 2nd ed., edited by Patricia B. Ebrey (New York: Free Press, 1993), 91–96; Keith Knapp, "Ge Hong," *Internet Encyclopedia of Philosophy*, 2005, http://www.iep.utm.edu/gehong/.

5. Selected Poems from T'ang Dynasty, Li Shen, "Old Style," http://xinshi.org/xlib/lingshidao/hanshi/tang1.htm, accessed February 21, 2012.

6. Robert Ford Campany, *To Live as Long as Heaven and Earth* (Berkeley: University of California Press, 2002), 91–96.

7. Karl Jacoby, "Slaves by Nature: Animals and Human Slaves," *Slavery and Abolition* 15 (1994): 89–97.

8. Orlando Patterson, *Slavery and Social Death* (Cambridge, MA: Harvard University Press, 1982).

9. A. L. Basham, *The Wonder That Was India* (London: Sidgwick and Jackson, 1967), 152.

10. Sarah Pomeroy et al., *Ancient Greece* (New York: Oxford University Press, 1999), 63, 239.

11. R. Zelnick-Abramovitz, *Not Wholly Free* (Leiden: Brill, 2005), 337, 343.

12. Keith Bradley, *Slavery and Society at Rome* (Cambridge: Cambridge University Press, 1994), 30.

13. 1 Peter 2:18.

14. Milton Meltzer, *Slavery: A World History* (New York: Da Capo Press, 1993), 189.

15. Judith Bennett, *History Matters: Patriarchy and the Challenge of Feminism* (Philadelphia: University of Pennsylvania Press, 2006), chap. 4.

16. Quoted in Bret Hinsch, *Women in Early Imperial China* (Oxford: Rowman and Littlefield, 2002), 155.

17. Nancy Lee Swann, trans., *Pan Chao: Foremost Woman Scholar of China* (New York: Century, 1932), 111–14.

18. Lisa Raphals, *Sharing the Light: Representations of Women and Virtue in Early China* (Albany: SUNY Press, 1998).

19. Valerie Hansen, *The Open Empire* (New York: Norton, 2000), 183–84; Thomas Barfield, *The Perilous Frontier* (Cambridge: Blackwell, 1989), 140.

20. Vivian-Lee Nyitray, "Confucian Complexities," in *A Companion to Gender History*, edited by Teresa A. Meade and Merry E. Weisner-Hanks (Oxford: Blackwell, 2004), 278.

21. Aristotle, *Politica*, translated by H. Rackham, Loeb Classical Library No. 264 (Cambridge, MA: Harvard University Press, 1932), 1254b10–14.

22. Quoted in Pomeroy et al., *Ancient Greece*, 146.

23. "The Destruction of Pompeii, 79 AD," EyeWitness to History, 1999, www.eyewitnesstohistory.com/pompeii.htm.

24. August Mau, *Pompeii: Its Life and Art* (New Rochelle: Caratzas Bros., 1982), 16.

25. "Graffiti from Pompeii," Pompeiana.org, accessed February 2, 2012, http://www.pompeiana.org/Resources/Ancient/Graffiti%20from%20Pompeii.htm.

Chapter 6

1. "Morales Becomes Head of a Pluri-national State Blessed by Aymara Gods," *MercoPress*, January 22, 2010, http://en.mercopress.com/2010/01/22/morales-becomes-head-of-a-pluri-national-state-blessed-by-aymara-gods.

2. Population figures are taken from Paul Adams et al., *Experiencing World History* (New York: New York University Press, 2000), 334.

3. "The Stela of Piye," accessed February 3, 2012, http://wysinger.homestead.com/piyevictorystela.html.

4. Toby Wilkinson, *Lives of the Ancient Egyptians* (London: Thames and Hudson, 2007), 287.

5. Stanley Burstein, "State Formation in Ancient Northeast Africa and the Indian Ocean Trade," History Cooperative, 2001, http://www.historycooperative.org/proceedings/interactions/burstein.html.

6. Roderick J. McIntosh, *Ancient Middle Niger* (Cambridge: Cambridge University Press, 2005), 10.

7. Roderick J. McIntosh, *The Peoples of the Middle Niger* (Oxford: Blackwell, 1998), 1776.

8. Richard E. W. Adams, *Prehistoric Mesoamerica* (Norman: University of Oklahoma Press, 2005), 16.

9. Richard E. W. Adams, *Ancient Civilizations of the New World* (Boulder, CO: Westview Press, 1997), 53–56; T. Patrick Culbert, "The New Maya," *Archeology* 51, no. 5 (1998): 47–51.

10. William Haviland, "State and Power in Classic Maya Society," *American Anthropologist* 94, no. 4 (1992): 937.

11. Jared Diamond, *Collapse: How Societies Choose to Fail or Succeed* (New York: Viking, 2005), chap. 5.

12. Esther Pasztory, *Teotihuacán: An Experiment in Living* (Norman: University of Oklahoma Press, 1997), 193.

13. George L. Cowgill, "The Central Mexican Highlands . . . ," in *The Cambridge History of the Native Peoples of the Americas*, vol. 2, pt. 1, "Mesoamerica," edited by Richard E. W. Adams and Murdo J. MacLeod (Cambridge: Cambridge University Press, 2000), 289.

14. Karen Olsen Bruhns, *Ancient South America* (Cambridge: Cambridge University Press, 1994), 126–41; Sylvia R. Kembel and John W. Rick, "Building Authority at Chavín de Huántar," in *Andean Archeology*, edited by Helaine Silverman (Oxford: Blackwell, 2004), 59–76.

15. Garth Bawden, *The Moche* (Oxford: Blackwell, 1996), chaps. 9, 10.

16. Gordon F. McEwan, *The Inca: New Perspectives* (New York: W. W. Norton, 2008), 39–41.

17. Charles C. Mann, *1491* (New York: Alfred A. Knopf, 2005), 234.

18. Kairn A. Klieman, *"The Pygmies Were Our Compass": Bantu and Batwa in the History of West Central Africa, Early Times to c. 1900 C.E.* (Portsmouth, NH: Heinemann, 2003), chaps. 4, 5.

19. Christopher Ehret, *The Civilizations of Africa* (Charlottesville: University of Virginia Press, 2002), 175.

20. David Schoenbrun, "Gendered Themes in Early African History" in *A Companion to Gender History*, edited by Teresa Meade and Merry Wiesner-Hanks (Oxford: Blackwell, 2004), 253–56.

21. See Jan Vansina, *Paths in the Rainforest* (Madison: University of Wisconsin Press, 1990), 95–99.

22. John E. Kicza, *The Peoples and Civilizations of the Americas before Contact* (Washington, DC: American Historical Association, 1998), 43–44.

23. Much of this section draws on Brian M. Fagan, *Ancient North America* (London: Thames and Hudson, 2005), chaps. 14, 15. The quote is on page 345.

24. George R. Milner, *The Moundbuilders: Ancient Peoples of Eastern North America* (London: Thames and Hudson, 2004).

25. David Hurst Thomas, *Exploring Ancient Native America* (New York: Routledge, 1999), 137–42.

26. Stephen H. Lekson and Peter N. Peregrine, "A Continental Perspective for North American Archeology," *SAA Archeological Record* 4, no. 1 (2004): 15–19.

27. Fagan, *Ancient North America*, 475.

28. Quoted in Lynda Norene Shaffer, *Native Americans before 1492* (Armonk, NY: M. E. Sharpe, 1992), 70.

29. See Stanley Burstein, *Ancient African Civilizations: Kush and Axum* (Princeton, NJ: Markus Weiner, 1998), 14–20. I am grateful to Professor Burstein and this book for references to many of the documents in this section.

30. Mary Ellen Miller, *Maya Art and Architecture* (London: Thames and Hudson, 1999), 8–11.

31. Linda Schele and Mary Ellen Miller, *The Blood of Kings* (London: Thames and Hudson, 1992), 176.

32. Mary Miller and Simon Martin, *Courtly Art of the Ancient Maya* (New York: Thames and Hudson, 2004), 63.

Part Three

1. Marshall G. S. Hodgson, *The Venture of Islam* (Chicago: University of Chicago Press, 1974), 1:71.

Chapter 7

1. Nayan Chanda, *Bound Together* (New Haven, CT: Yale University Press, 2007), 35–36.

2. William J. Bernstein, *A Splendid Exchange* (New York: Grove Press, 2008), 58–66; Proverbs 7:17–18.

3. Patricia B. Ebrey, *The Inner Quarters* (Berkeley: University of California Press, 1993), 150.

4. Seneca the Younger, *Declamations*, vol. 1.

5. Liu Xinru, "Silks and Religion in Eurasia, A.D. 600–1200," *Journal of World History* 6, no. 1 (1995): 25–48.

6. Jerry Bentley, "Hemispheric Integration, 500–1500 C.E.," *Journal of World History* 9, no. 2 (1998): 241–44.

7. See Jerry Bentley, *Old World Encounters* (New York: Oxford University Press, 1993), 42–53, 69–84.

8. Liu Xinru, *The Silk Road* (Washington, DC: American Historical Association, 1998), 10.

9. See William H. McNeill, *Plagues and Peoples* (New York: Doubleday, 1977), chaps. 3, 4.

10. Boccaccio, *The Decameron*, translated by M. Rigg (London: David Campbell, 1921), 1:5–11.

11. Kenneth McPherson, *The Indian Ocean* (Oxford: Oxford University Press, 1993), 15.

12. Janet L. Abu-Lughod, *Before European Hegemony* (Oxford: Oxford University Press, 1989), 269.

13. Stanley Burstein, "State Formation in Ancient Northeast Africa and the Indian Ocean Trade" (paper presented at Interactions: Regional Studies, Global Processes, and Historical Analysis, Library of Congress, Washington, DC, February 28–March 3, 2001), http://www.historycooperative.org/proceedings/interactions/burstein.html.

14. Nigel D. Furlonge, "Revisiting the Zanj and Revisioning Revolt," *Negro History Bulletin* 62 (December 1999), 7–14.

15. Patricia Risso, *Merchants and Faith: Muslim Commerce and Culture in the Indian Ocean* (Boulder, CO: Westview, 1995), 54.

16. McPherson, *Indian Ocean*, 97.

17. This section draws heavily on Craig A. Lockard, *Southeast Asia in World History* (Oxford: Oxford University Press, 2009), chaps. 2, 3. See also Victor Lieberman, *Strange Parallels* (Cambridge: Cambridge University Press, 2009), chaps. 1, 7.

18. Kenneth R. Hall, *Maritime Trade and State Development in Early Southeast Asia* (Honolulu: University of Hawaii Press, 1985), 101.

19. M. C. Horton and T. R. Burton, "Indian Metalwork in East Africa: The Bronze Lion Statuette from Shanga," *Antiquities* 62 (1988): 22.

20. Ross Dunn, *The Adventures of Ibn Battuta* (Berkeley: University of California Press, 1986), 124.

21. Christopher Ehret, *The Civilizations of Africa* (Charlottesville: University of Virginia Press, 2002), 255.

22. Ibid., 227–32.

23. Nehemia Levtzion and Jay Spaulding, eds., *Medieval West Africa: Views from Arab Scholars and Merchants* (Princeton, NJ: Marcus Wiener, 2003), 5.

24. David Schoenbrun, "Gendered Themes in Early African History" in *A Companion to Gender History*, edited by Teresa Meade and Merry Wiesner-Hanks (Oxford: Blackwell, 2004), 263.

25. Quoted in John Iliffe, *Africans: The History of a Continent* (Cambridge: Cambridge University Press, 1995), 75–76.

26. "The Saga of Eric the Red" and "The Saga of Thorsfinn Karlsefni" in *The Norse Discovery of America*, translated by Arthur Reeves et al. (London: Norroena Society, 1906), http://www.sacred-texts.com/neu/nda/index.htm.

27. J. R. McNeill and William McNeill, *The Human Web* (New York: W. W. Norton, 2003), 160.

28. Lauren Ristvet, *In the Beginning* (New York: McGraw-Hill, 2007), 165.

29. Maria Rostworowski de Diez Canseco, *History of the Inca Realm* (Cambridge: Cambridge University Press, 1999), 209–12.

30. Michael Haederle, "Mystery of Ancient Pueblo Jars Is Solved," *New York Times*, February 4, 2009.

31. Anthony Andrews, "America's Ancient Mariners," *Natural History*, October 1991, 72–75.

32. Richard Blanton and Gary Feinman, "The Mesoamerican World System," *American Anthropologist* 86, no. 3 (1984): 677.

33. Li Rongxi, trans., *A Biography of the Tripitaka Master* (Berkeley: Numata Center for Buddhist Translation, 1995), 31.

34. For a brief account of Xuanzang's life and travels, see Stephen S. Gosch and Peter N. Stearns, *Premodern Travel in World History* (New York: Routledge, 2008), 75–101.

35. Susan Whitfield, *Life Along the Silk Road* (Berkeley: University of California Press, 1999), 2–6.

36. Jonathan Tucker, *The Silk Road: Art and History* (London: Philip Wilson, 2003), 128.

37. Craig Benjamin, "The Kushans in World History," *World History Bulletin* 25, no. 1 (2009): 30.

38. Carter Findley, *The Turks in World History* (Oxford: Oxford University Press, 2005), 61–64.

39. Bahodir Sidikov, "Sufism and Shamanism" in *Shamanism*, edited by Eva Fridman and Mariko Walter (Santa Barbara, CA: ABC-Clio, 2004), 241.

Chapter 8

1. *Guardian*, June 15, 2006.

2. John K. Fairbank, ed., *The Chinese World Order* (Cambridge, MA: Harvard University Press, 1968).

3. Quoted in Mark Elvin, *The Retreat of the Elephants* (New Haven, CT: Yale University Press, 2004), chap. 1. The quote is on page 19.

4. Mark Elvin, *The Pattern of the Chinese Past* (London: Eyre Methuen, 1973), 55.

5. Samuel Adshead, *Tang China: The Rise of the East in World History* (New York: Palgrave, 2004), 30.

6. Elvin, *Pattern of the Chinese Past*, pt. 2; William McNeill, *The Pursuit of Power* (Chicago: University of Chicago Press, 1984), 50.

7. See "The Attractions of the Capital," in *Chinese Civilization: A Sourcebook*, edited by Patricia B. Ebrey (New York: Free Press, 1993), 178–85.

8. Marco Polo, *The Travels of Marco Polo* (Toronto: General, 1993), 2:185.

9. John K. Fairbank, *China: A New History* (Cambridge, MA: Harvard University Press, 1992), 89.

10. J. R. McNeill and William H. McNeill, *The Human Web* (New York: W. W. Norton, 2003), 123.

11. Francesca Bray, *Technology and Gender: Fabrics of Power in Late Imperial China* (Berkeley: University of California Press, 1997), 116.

12. Patricia Ebrey, *The Inner Quarters* (Berkeley: University of California Press, 1993), 207.

13. Ibid., 37–43.

14. Ibid., 6.

15. See Nicolas DiCosmo, *Ancient China and Its Enemies* (Cambridge: Cambridge University Press, 2002), chap. 6.

16. Ibid., 94.

17. Quoted in Thomas J. Barfield, "Steppe Empires, China, and the Silk Route," in *Nomads in the Sedentary World*, edited by Anatoly M. Khazanov and Andre Wink (Richmond: Kurzon Press, 2001), 237.

18. Quoted in Edward H. Shafer, *The Golden Peaches of Samarkand* (Berkeley: University of California Press, 1963), 28.

19. Susan Mann, "Women in East Asia," in *Women's History in Global Perspective*, edited by Bonnie Smith (Urbana: University of Illinois Press, 2005), 2:53–56.

20. Joseph Buttinger, *A Dragon Defiant: A Short History of Vietnam* (New York: Praeger, 1972), 32–34; Jerry Bentley, *Old World Encounters* (New York: Oxford University Press, 1993), 85–86.

21. Liam C. Kelley, *Beyond the Bronze Pillars: Envoy Poetry and the Sino-Vietnamese Relationship* (Honolulu: University of Hawai'i Press, 2005).

22. Teresa Meade and Merry Wiesner-Hanks (eds.), *A Companion to Gender History* (Oxford: Blackwell, 2004), 188, 281–82, 332–33.

23. H. Paul Varley, "Japan, 550–838," in *Asia in Western and World History*, edited by Ainslee T. Embrey and Carol Gluck (Armonk, NY: M. E. Sharpe, 1997), 353.

24. Quoted in McNeill, *Pursuit of Power*, 40.

25. John K. Fairbank et al., *East Asia: Tradition and Transformation* (Boston: Houghton Mifflin, 1978), 353.

26. Quoted in Jane Hirshfield, trans., *The Ink Dark Moon* (New York: Vintage Books, 1990), xiii.

27. Edwin A. Cranston, trans., *The Izumi Shikibu Diary* (Cambridge, MA: Harvard University Press, 1969), 11.

28. Hirshfield, *Ink Dark Moon*, 94, 148.

29. Quoted in Earl Miner, *Japanese Poetic Diaries* (Berkeley: University of California Press, 1969), 33.

30. Cranston, *Izumi Shikibu Diary*, 18, 206.

31. Hirshfield, *Ink Dark Moon*, 49, 65, 96, 139.

32. Chieko Irie Mulhern, ed., *Japanese Women Writers* (Westport, CT: Greenwood Press, 1994), 155.

33. Compiled from Joseph Needham, *Science and Civilization in China* (Cambridge: Cambridge University Press, 1965),

1:242; and Robert Temple, *The Genius of China* (New York: Simon and Schuster, 1986).

34. Arnold Pacey, *Technology in World Civilization* (Cambridge, MA: MIT Press, 1991), 50–53.

35. McNeill, *Pursuit of Power*, 24–25.

36. Hugh Clark, "Muslims and Hindus in the Culture and Morphology of Quanzhou from the Tenth to the Thirteenth Century," *Journal of World History* 6, no. 1 (1995): 49–74.

37. Quoted in Arthur F. Wright, *Studies in Chinese Buddhism* (New Haven, CT: Yale University Press, 1990), 16.

38. Arthur F. Wright, *Buddhism in Chinese History* (Stanford, CA: Stanford University Press, 1959), 36–39.

39. Quoted in Wright, *Buddhism in Chinese History*, 67.

40. Quoted in Eric Zurcher, *The Buddhist Conquest of China* (Leiden: E. J. Brill, 1959), 1:262.

41. Jacquet Gernet, *A History of Chinese Civilization* (Cambridge: Cambridge University Press, 1996), 291–96.

42. Edwin O. Reischauer, *Ennin's Travels in Tang China* (New York: Ronald Press, 1955), 221–24.

43. William Theodore de Bary et al., *Sources of Japanese Tradition* (New York: Columbia University Press, 2001), 1:42.

44. Donald Keene, *Seeds in the Heart* (New York: Henry Holt, 1993), 477–78.

45. Quoted in "Jake Holman's Selection of Favourite Chinese Poems," China History Forum, accessed February 7, 2012, http://www.chinahistoryforum.com/index.php?showtopic=17789&st=30&start=30.

46. I Lo-fen, "Dialogue Between the 'Fatuous Emperor' and the 'Treacherous Minister': Song Hui Zong's 'Literary Gathering' Painting (Wen-Hui Tu) and Its Poetic Inscriptions," *Literature and Philosophy* 8 (June 2006): 253–78.

Chapter 9

1. Letter from Malcolm X, April 1964. http://www.malcolm-x.org/docs/let_mecca.htm.

2. Reza Aslan, *No God but God* (New York: Random House, 2005), 14.

3. Quoted in Karen Armstrong, *A History of God* (New York: Ballantine Books, 1993), 146.

4. Quran 1:5 and 41:53.

5. Ibid., 3:110.

6. Ibid., 9:71.

7. "Prophet Muhammad's Farewell Sermon," http://www.islamicity.com/articles/Articles.asp?ref=ic0107-322.

8. Fred M. Donner, *Muhammad and the Believers* (Cambridge. MA: Harvard University Press, 2010), 114. The preceding section draws on chapter 3.

9. Richard Bulliet, *Conversion to Islam in the Medieval Period* (Cambridge, MA: Harvard University Press, 1979), 33.

10. Nehemiah Levtzion, ed., *Conversion to Islam* (New York: Holmes and Meier, 1979), chap. 1.

11. Bertold Spuler. *The Muslim World*, vol. 1, *The Age of the Caliph* (Leiden: E. J. Brill, 1960), 29.

12. Bernard Lewis, *Islam and the West* (New York: Oxford University Press, 1993), 157.

13. Quoted in Patricia Crone, "The Rise of Islam in the World," in *Cambridge Illustrated History of the Islamic World*, edited by Francis Robinson (Cambridge: Cambridge University Press, 1996), 14.

14. Aslan, *No God but God*, 201.

15. Quran 33:35.

16. Ibid., 4:34.

17. Quoted in Judith Tucker, "Gender and Islamic History," in *Islamic and European Expansion*, edited by Michael Adas (Philadelphia: Temple University Press, 1993), 46.

18. Nikki R. Keddie, "Women in the Middle East since the Rise of Islam," in *Women's History in Global Perspective*, edited by Bonnie G. Smith (Urbana: University of Illinois Press, 2005), 74–75.

19. Ria Kloppenborg and Wouter Hanegraaf, eds., *Female Stereotypes in Religious Traditions* (Leiden: E. J. Brill, 1995), 111.

20. Quoted in William T. de Bary, ed., *Sources of Indian Tradition* (New York: Columbia University Press, 1958), 2:355–57.

21. V. L. Menage, "The Islamization of Anatolia," in Levtzion, *Conversion to Islam*, chap. 4.

22. Ira M. Lapidus, *A History of Islamic Societies* (Cambridge: Cambridge University Press, 1988), 304–6.

23. Quoted in Keddie, "Women in the Middle East," 81.

24. Ross Dunn, *The Adventures of Ibn Battuta* (Berkeley: University of California Press, 1986), 300.

25. Al-Umari, "The Kingdoms of the Muslim Sudan," in *Medieval West Africa*, edited by Nehemia Levtzion and Jay Spaulding (Princeton, NJ: Markus Weiner, 2003), 60.

26. Marq de Villiers and Sheila Hirtle, *Timbuktu* (New York: Walker, 2007), 77.

27. Al-Umari, "Kingdoms of the Muslim Sudan," 59.

28. Ibid.

29. Jane I. Smith, "Islam and Christendom," in *The Oxford History of Islam*, edited by John L. Esposito (Oxford: Oxford University Press, 1999), 317–21.

30. Richard Eaton, "Islamic History as Global History," in Adas, *Islamic and European Expansion*, 12.

31. Francis Robinson, "Knowledge, Its Transmission and the Making of Muslim Societies," in Robinson, *Cambridge Illustrated History of the Islamic World*, 230.

32. Janet L. Abu-Lughod, *Before European Hegemony* (Oxford: Oxford University Press, 1989), 216–24.

33. Andrew Watson, *Agricultural Innovation in the Early Islamic World* (Cambridge: Cambridge University Press, 1983);

Michael Decker, "Plants and Progress: Rethinking the Islamic Agricultural Revolution," *Journal of World History* 20, no. 2 (2009): 187–206.

34. Arnold Pacey, *Technology in World History* (Cambridge, MA: MIT Press, 1991), 8, 74.

35. Robinson, "Knowledge, Its Transmission," 215.

36. Ahmad Dallal, "Science, Medicine, and Technology: The Making of a Scientific Culture," in Esposito, *Oxford History of Islam*, chap. 4.

37. David W. Tschanz, "The Arab Roots of European Medicine," *Aramco World*, May–June 1997, 20–31.

38. Lohoucine Ouzgan, ed., *Islamic Masculinities* (London: Zed Books, 2006), 57–59.

39. Oleg Grabar, *Mostly Miniatures: An Introduction to Persian Painting* (Princeton, NJ: Princeton University Press, 2000), 2.

40. Biographical details about the life of Muhammad derive largely from Karen Armstrong, *Muhammad: A Biography of the Prophet* (New York: HarperCollins, 1992).

Chapter 10

1. Louisa Lim, "In The Land of Mao, a Rising Tide of Christianity," *All Things Considered*, NPR, July 19, 2010, http://www.npr.org/templates/story/story.php?storyId=128546334.

2. This section relies heavily on Diarmaid MacCulloch, *Christianity: The First Three Thousand Years* (New York, Viking, 2010), chap. 8.

3. Oleg Grabar, "The Umayyad Dome of the Rock in Jerusalem," in *Late Antique and Medieval Art of the Mediterranean World*, edited by Eva R. Hoffman (London: John Wiley and Sons, 2007), 166.

4. Quoted in Roger Boase, ed., *Islam and Global Dialogue* (Burlington, VT: Ashgate, 2005), 95.

5. Martin Palmer, *The Jesus Sutras* (New York: Random House, 2001).

6. Jack Weatherford, *Genghis Khan and the Making of the Modern World* (New York: Crown, 2004), 29.

7. Leonora Neville, *Authority in Byzantine Provincial Society*, 950–1100 (Cambridge: Cambridge University Press, 2004), 2.

8. Quoted in Deno John Geanakoplos, *Byzantium: Church, Society, and Civilization Seen through Contemporary Eyes* (Chicago: University of Chicago Press, 1984), 389.

9. Quoted in ibid., 143.

10. Quoted in A. A. Vasiliev, *History of the Byzantine Empire* (Madison: University of Wisconsin Press, 1978), 79–80.

11. Quoted in Geanakoplos, *Byzantium*, 362.

12. Quoted in ibid., 369.

13. Rowena Loverance, *Byzantium* (Cambridge, MA: Harvard University Press, 2004), 43.

14. Daniel H. Kaiser and Gary Marker, *Reinterpreting Russian History* (Oxford: Oxford University Press, 1994), 63–67.

15. Quoted in Patrick J. Geary, *Before France and Germany* (New York: Oxford University Press, 1988), 79.

16. Quoted in Stephen Williams, *Diocletian and the Roman Recovery* (London: Routledge, 1996), 218.

17. Peter Brown, *The Rise of Western Christendom* (London: Blackwell, 1996), 305.

18. Quoted in John M. Hobson, *The Eastern Origins of Western Civilization* (New York: Cambridge University Press, 2004), 113.

19. Clive Ponting, *A Green History of the World* (New York: St. Martin's, 1991), 121–23.

20. Judith M. Bennett, *A Medieval Life* (Boston: McGraw-Hill, 1998).

21. Bonnie Anderson and Judith Zinsser, *A History of Their Own* (Oxford: Oxford University Press, 2000), 1:210.

22. Anderson and Zinsser, *History of Their Own*, 393–94.

23. Christopher Tyerman, *Fighting for Christendom: Holy Wars and the Crusades* (Oxford: Oxford University Press, 2004), 16.

24. Elizabeth Hallam, *Chronicles of the Crusades* (New York: Welcome Rain, 2000), 127.

25. Edward Peters, "The Firanj Are Coming — Again," *Orbis* 48, no. 1 (2004): 3–17.

26. Quoted in Peter Watson, *Ideas* (New York: Harper, 2006), 319.

27. Quoted in Jean Gimple, *The Medieval Machine* (New York: Holt, 1976), 178.

28. Quoted in Stuart B. Schwartz, ed., *Victors and Vanquished* (Boston: Bedford/St. Martin's, 2000), 147.

29. Quoted in Carlo Cipolla, *Before the Industrial Revolution* (New York: Norton, 1976), 207.

30. Quoted in S. Lilley, *Men, Machines, and History* (New York: International, 1965), 62.

31. See Toby Huff, *The Rise of Early Modern Science* (Cambridge: Cambridge University Press, 1993).

32. Quoted in Edward Grant, *Science and Religion from Aristotle to Copernicus* (Westport, CT: Greenwood Press, 2004), 158.

33. Quoted in L. Thorndike, *A History of Magic and Experimental Science* (New York: Columbia University Press, 1923), 2:58.

34. Quoted in Edward Grant, *God and Reason in the Middle Ages* (Cambridge: Cambridge University Press, 2001), 70.

35. Grant, *Science and Religion*, 228–29.

36. Marcia L. Colish, *Medieval Foundations of the Western Intellectual Tradition* (New Haven, CT: Yale University Press, 1997), 128.

37. Charles G. Herbermann, ed., *The Catholic Encyclopedia* (New York: Encyclopedia Press, 1913), 7:668.

38. Simon Morsink, *The Power of Icons* (Ghent: Snoek, 2006), 12; Robin Cormack, *Icons* (London: British Museum Press, 2007), 29.

Chapter 11

1. Jack Weatherford, *Genghis Khan and the Making of the Modern World* (New York: Crown, 2004), xv.

2. Giovanni Carpini, *The Story of the Mongols*, translated by Erik Hildinger (Boston: Braden, 1996), 54.

3. Data derived from Thomas J. Barfield, "Pastoral Nomadic Societies," in *Berkshire Encyclopedia of World History* (Great Barrington, MA: Berkshire, 2005), 4:1432–37.

4. Quoted in Peter B. Golden, "Nomads and Sedentary Societies in Eurasia," in *Agricultural and Pastoral Societies in Ancient and Classical History*, edited by Michael Adas (Philadelphia: Temple University Press, 2001), 73.

5. Thomas J. Barfield, *The Nomadic Alternative* (Englewood Cliffs, NJ: Prentice Hall, 1993), 12.

6. Anatoly Khazanov, "The Spread of World Religions in Medieval Nomadic Societies of the Eurasian Steppes," in *Nomadic Diplomacy, Destruction and Religion from the Pacific to the Adriatic*, edited by Michael Gervers and Wayne Schlepp (Toronto: Joint Center for Asia Pacific Studies, 1994), 11.

7. Quoted in J. Otto Maenchen-Helfer, *The World of the Huns* (Berkeley: University of California Press, 1973), 14.

8. Carter Finley, *The Turks in World History* (Oxford: Oxford University Press, 2005), 28–37.

9. Ibid., 40.

10. David Christian, *A History of Russia, Central Asia, and Mongolia* (London: Blackwell, 1998), 1:385.

11. Quoted in ibid., 389.

12. David Morgan, *The Mongols* (Oxford: Blackwell, 1986), 63–67.

13. Weatherford, *Genghis Khan*, 86.

14. Chinggis Khan, "Letter to Changchun" in E. Bretschneider, *Mediaeval Researches from Eastern Asiatic Sources*, Vol. I (London: Kegan, Paul, Trench, Trübner, 1875), 37–39.

15. Thomas T. Allsen, *Mongol Imperialism* (Berkeley: University of California Press, 1987), 6.

16. Chinggis Khan, "Letter to Changchun," 38.

17. Quoted in Weatherford, *Genghis Khan*, 111.

18. Barfield, *Nomadic Alternative*, 166.

19. Peter Jackson, "The Mongols and the Faith of the Conquered," in *Mongols, Turks, and Others*, edited by Reuven Amitai and Michael Biran (Leiden: Brill, 2005), 262.

20. Quoted in Christian, *History of Russia*, 425.

21. This portrait is based on Jack Weatherford, *The Secret History of the Mongol Queens* (New York: Random House, 2010), 116–26, 274.

22. Quoted in David Morgan, *Medieval Persia* (London: Longman, 1988), 79.

23. Morgan, *Medieval Persia*, 82.

24. Guity Nashat, "Women in the Middle East" in *A Companion to Gender History*, edited by Teresa A. Meade and Merry E. Wiesner-Hanks (London: Blackwell, 2004), 243.

25. Charles J. Halperin, *Russia and the Golden Horde* (Bloomington: Indiana University Press, 1985), 126.

26. Charles H. Halperin, "Russia in the Mongol Empire in Comparative Perspective," *Harvard Journal of Asiatic Studies* 43, no. 1 (1983): 261.

27. Quoted in Christopher Dawson, *Mission to Asia* (New York: Harper and Row, 1966), 83–84.

28. Thomas Allsen, *Culture and Conquest in Mongol Eurasia* (Cambridge: Cambridge University Press, 2001), 211.

29. Quoted in ibid., 121.

30. John Aberth, *From the Brink of the Apocalypse* (New York: Routledge, 2000), 122–31.

31. Quoted in John Aberth, *The Black Death: The Great Mortality of 1348–1350* (Boston: Bedford/St. Martin's, 2005), 84–85.

32. Michael Dols, *The Black Death in the Middle East* (Princeton, NJ: Princeton University Press, 1977), 212, 223.

33. Quoted in John Aberth, *A Knight at the Movies: Medieval History on Film* (New York: Routledge, 2003), 225.

34. Aberth, *Black Death*, 72.

35. Quoted in Dols, *Black Death in the Middle East*, 67.

36. Andre Gunder Frank, *ReOrient: Global Economy in the Asian Age* (Berkeley: University of California Press, 1998), 256.

37. Arnold Pacey, *Technology in World Civilization* (Cambridge, MA: MIT Press, 1990), 62.

38. Quoted in Golden, "Nomads and Sedentary Societies," 72–73.

39. Quoted in Gregory Guzman, "Were the Barbarians a Negative or Positive Factor in Ancient and Medieval History?" *Historian* 50 (August 1988): 558–72.

40. Quoted in Barfield, *Nomadic Alternative*, 3.

41. Quoted in John Aberth, *The Black Death: The Great Mortality of 1348–1350: A Brief History with Documents* (Boston: Bedford/St. Martin's, 2005), 99.

42. Quoted in David Herlihy, *The Black Death and the Transformation of the West* (Cambridge, MA: Harvard University Press, 1997), 65.

43. Quoted in ibid., 62.

44. Quoted in Aberth, *Black Death*, 79.

45. Quoted in ibid., 174.

46. "Lübeck's Dance of Death," accessed February 10, 2012, http://www.dodedans.com/Etext2.htm.

47. Quoted in Norman Cantor, *In the Wake of the Plague* (New York: Free Press, 2001), 6.

48. Quoted in Aberth, *Black Death*, 73–74.

Chapter 12

1. Winona LaDuke, "We Are Still Here: The 500 Year Celebration," *Sojourners*, October 1991.

2. Brian Fagan, *Ancient North America* (London: Thames and Hudson, 2005), 503.

3. Quoted in Charles C. Mann, *1491: New Revelations of the Americas before Columbus* (New York: Alfred A. Knopf, 2005), 334.

4. Louise Levanthes, *When China Ruled the Seas* (New York: Simon and Schuster, 1994), 175.

5. Niccolò Machiavelli, *The Prince* (New York: New American Library, 1952), 90, 94.

6. Edward Dreyer, *Zheng He* (New York: Pearson Longman, 2007).

7. Christine de Pisan, *The Book of the City of Ladies*, translated by Rosalind Brown-Grant (New York: Penguin Books, 1999), pt. 1, p. 1.

8. Frank Viviano, "China's Great Armada," *National Geographic*, July 2005, 34.

9. Quoted in John J. Saunders, ed., *The Muslim World on the Eve of Europe's Expansion* (Englewood Cliffs, NJ: Prentice Hall, 1966), 41–43.

10. Leo Africanus, *History and Description of Africa* (London: Hakluyt Society, 1896), 824–25.

11. Quoted in Craig A. Lockhard, *Southeast Asia in World History* (Oxford: Oxford University Press, 2009), 67.

12. Quoted in Patricia Risso, *Merchants and Faith* (Boulder, CO: Westview Press, 1995), 49.

13. Quoted in Stuart B. Schwartz, ed., *Victors and Vanquished* (Boston: Bedford/St. Martin's, 2000), 8.

14. Quoted in Michael E. Smith, *The Aztecs* (London: Blackwell, 2003), 108.

15. Smith, *Aztecs*, 220.

16. Miguel Leon-Portilla, *Aztec Thought and Culture*, translated from the Spanish by Jack Emory Davis (Norman: University of Oklahoma Press, 1963), 7.

17. For this perspective, see Michael E. Malpass and Sonia Alconini, *Distant Provinces in the Inca Empire* (Iowa City: University of Iowa Press, 2010).

18. Terence N. D'Altroy, *The Incas* (London: Blackwell, 2002), chaps. 11, 12.

19. For a summary of this practice among the Aztecs and Incas, see Karen Vieira Powers, *Women in the Crucible of Conquest* (Albuquerque: University of New Mexico Press, 2005), chap. 1.

20. Ibid., 25.

21. Louise Burkhart, "Mexica Women on the Home Front," in *Indian Women of Early Mexico*, edited by Susan Schroeder et al. (Norman: University of Oklahoma Press, 1997), 25–54.

22. The "web" metaphor is derived from J. R. McNeill and William H. McNeill, *The Human Web* (New York: W. W. Norton, 2003).

23. Graph from David Christian, *Map of Time* (Berkeley: University of California Press, 2004), 343.

24. Rosamund E. Mack, *Bazaar to Piazza* (Berkeley: University of California Press, 2002), 1.

25. This and all subsequent quotes come from Jerry Brotton, *The Renaissance Bazaar* (Oxford: Oxford University Press, 2002).

Part Four

1. Victor Lieberman, *Strange Parallels*, vol. 2 (Cambridge: Cambridge University Press, 2009).

Chapter 13

1. Immanuel Wallerstein, *The Modern World System* (New York: Academic Press, 1974), 51.

2. Quoted in Thomas E. Skidmore and Peter H. Smith, *Modern Latin America* (New York: Oxford University Press, 2001), 15.

3. George Raudzens, ed., *Technology, Disease, and Colonial Conquest* (Boston: Brill Academic, 2003), xiv.

4. A major source for the life of Doña Marina is Bernal Díaz, *The Conquest of New Spain*, translated by J. M. Cohen (Baltimore: Penguin Books, 1963).

5. Quoted in Noble David Cook, *Born to Die: Disease and the New World Conquest* (Cambridge: Cambridge University Press, 1998), 202.

6. Quoted in ibid., 206.

7. Quoted in Charles C. Mann, *1491* (New York: Alfred A. Knopf, 2005), 56.

8. Quoted in Charles Mann, *1493* (New York: Alfred A. Knopf, 2011), 165.

9. Felipe Fernandez-Armesto, "Empires in Their Global Context," in *The Atlantic in Global History*, edited by Jorge Canizares-Esguerra and Erik R. Seeman (Upper Saddle River, NJ: Prentice-Hall, 2007), 105.

10. Quoted in Alejandro Lugo, *Fragmented Lives; Assembled Parts* (Austin: University of Texas Press, 2008), 53.

11. Quoted in Anthony Padgen, "Identity Formation in Spanish America," in *Colonial Identity in the Atlantic World, 1500–1800*, edited by Nicholas Canny and Anthony Padgen (Princeton, NJ: Princeton University Press, 1987), 56.

12. Colin M. MacLachlan and Jaime E. Rodriguez, *The Forging of the Cosmic Race* (Berkeley: University of California Press, 1990), 244–45.

13. Ann Twinam, "Women and Gender in Colonial Latin America," in *Women's History in Global Perspective*, edited by Bonnie G. Smith (Urbana: University of Illinois Press, 2005), 2:195.

14. Quoted in James Lockhart and Stuart B. Schwartz, *Early Latin America* (Cambridge: Cambridge University Press, 1983), 206.

15. Mary Prince, *The History of Mary Prince* (1831; Project Gutenberg, 2006), http://www.gutenberg.org/ebooks/17851.

16. Derived from Skidmore and Smith, *Modern Latin America*, 25.

17. Kevin Reilly et al., eds., *Racism: A Global Reader* (Armonk, NY: M. E. Sharpe, 2003), 136–37.

18. Felipe Fernandez-Armesto, *The Americas: A Hemispheric History* (New York: Modern Library, 2003), 58–59.

19. Benjamin Wadsworth, *The Well-Ordered Family* (1712), 39.

20. Willard Sutherland, *Taming the Wild Fields: Colonization and Empire on the Russian Steppe* (Ithaca, NY: Cornell University Press, 2004), 223–24.

21. Quoted in Michael Khodarkovsky, *Russia's Steppe Frontier* (Bloomington: Indiana University Press, 2002), 216.

22. Andreas Kappeler, *The Russian Empire* (New York: Longman, 2001), 115–17, 397–99.

23. Khodarkovsky, *Russia's Steppe Frontier*, 222.

24. Geoffrey Hosking, "The Freudian Frontier," *Times Literary Supplement*, March 10, 1995, 27.

25. Peter Perdue, *China Marches West: The Qing Conquest of Central Eurasia* (Cambridge, MA: Harvard University Press, 2005), 10–11.

26. Quoted in Stephen F. Dale, "The Islamic World in the Age of European Expansion," in *The Cambridge Illustrated History of the Islamic World*, edited by Francis Robinson (Cambridge: Cambridge University Press, 1996), 80.

27. Quoted in P. Lewis, *Pirs, Shrines, and Pakistani Islam* (Rawalpindi, Pakistan: Christian Study Centre, 1985), 84.

28. Quoted in Stanley Wolpert, *A New History of India* (New York: Oxford University Press, 1993), 160.

29. Lewis Melville, *Lady Mary Wortley Montagu: Her Life and Letters* (Whitefish, MT: Kessinger, 2004), 88.

30. Jane I. Smith, "Islam and Christendom," in *The Oxford History of Islam*, edited by John Esposito (Oxford: Oxford University Press, 1999), 342.

31. Charles Thornton Forester and F. H. Blackburne Daniell, *The Life and Letters of Ogier Ghiselin de Busbecq* (London: C. Kegan Paul, 1881), 1:405–6.

32. Jean Bodin, "The Rise and Fall of Commonwealths," chap. 7, Constitution Society, accessed Feb. 21, 2012, http://www.constitution.org/bodin/bodin_4.htm.

33. Quoted in Stuart B. Schwartz, ed., *Victors and Vanquished* (Boston: Bedford/St. Martin's, 2000), 31.

34. Schwartz, *Victors and Vanquished*, 29.

35. Quoted in ibid., 164.

36. Miguel Leon-Portilla, *The Broken Spears* (Boston: Beacon Press, 1992), 80–81.

Chapter 14

1. Jacob Wheeler, "From Slave Post to Museum," *Christian Science Monitor*, December 31, 2002.

2. M. N. Pearson, ed., *Spices in the Indian Ocean World* (Aldershot: Valorium, 1996), xv.

3. Quoted in Paul Lunde, "The Coming of the Portuguese," *Saudi Aramco World*, July–August 2005, 56.

4. Philip Curtin, *Cross Cultural Trade in World History* (Cambridge: Cambridge University Press, 1984), 144.

5. Quoted in Patricio N. Abinales and Donna J. Amoroso, *State and Society in the Philippines* (Lanham, MD: Rowman and Littlefield, 2005), 50.

6. Quoted in Craig A. Lockard, *Southeast Asia in World History* (Oxford: Oxford University Press, 2009), 85.

7. Anthony Reid, *Southeast Asia in the Age of Commerce, 1450–1680* (New Haven, CT: Yale University Press, 1993), 2:274, 290.

8. Tonio Andrade, *How Taiwan Became Chinese* (New York: Columbia University Press, 2008).

9. Anthony Reid, *Charting the Shape of Early Modern Southeast Asia* (Chiang Mai: Silkworm Books, 1999), 227.

10. Kenneth Pomeranz and Steven Topic, *The World That Trade Created* (Armonk, NY: M. E. Sharpe, 2006), 28.

11. Makrand Mehta, *Indian Merchants and Entrepreneurs in Historical Perspective* (Delhi: Academic Foundation, 1991), chap. 4.

12. Andre Gunder Frank, *ReOrient: Global Economy in the Asian Age* (Berkeley: University of California Press, 1998), 131.

13. Quoted in Richard von Glahn, "Myth and Reality of China's Seventeenth Century Monetary Crisis," *Journal of Economic History* 56, no. 2 (June 1996): 132.

14. Pomeranz and Topik, *The World That Trade Created*, 151–54.

15. Jane E. Mangan, *Trading Roles* (Durham, NC: Duke University Press, 2005), 181–83.

16. Dennis O. Flynn and Arturo Giraldez, "Born with a 'Silver Spoon,'" *Journal of World History* 6, no. 2 (1995): 210.

17. Quoted in Mark Elvin, *The Retreat of the Elephant* (New Haven, CT: Yale University Press, 2004), 37.

18. Quoted in Robert Marks, *The Origins of the Modern World* (Lanham, MD: Rowman and Littlefield, 2002), 81.

19. See John Richards, *The Endless Frontier* (Berkeley: University of California Press, 2003), pt. 4. Much of this section is drawn from this source.

20. Elspeth M. Veale, *The English Fur Trade in the Later Middle Ages* (Oxford: Clarendon Press, 1966), 141.

21. Quoted in Richards, *Endless Frontier*, 499.

22. Richards, *Endless Frontier*, 504.

23. Quoted from "Fur Trader," The Iroquois Confederacy, Portland State University Graduate School of Education, October 1, 2001, http://www.iroquoisdemocracy.pdx.edu/html/furtrader.htm.

24. Pamela McVay, *Envisioning Women in World History* (New York: McGraw Hill, 2009), 86. See also Bruce M. White, "The Woman Who Married a Beaver: Trade Patterns and Gender Roles in the Ojibwa Fur Trade," in *In the Days of Our Grandmothers*, edited by Mary-Ellen Kelm and Lorn Townsend (Toronto: University of Toronto Press, 2006), chap. 3.

25. These figures derive from the Trans-Atlantic Slave Trade Database, accessed February 22, 2012, http://www.slavevoyages.org/tast/assessment/estimates.faces.

26. Charles E. Curran, *Change in Official Catholic Moral Teaching* (Mahwah, NJ: Paulist Press, 2003), 67.

27. David Brion Davis, *Challenging the Boundaries of Slavery* (Cambridge, MA: Harvard University Press, 2003), 13.

28. Quoted in Bernard Lewis, *Race and Slavery in the Middle East* (New York: Oxford University Press, 1990), 52–53.

29. Audrey Smedley, *Race in North America* (Boulder, CO: Westview Press, 1993).

30. Kevin Reilly et al., eds., *Racism: A Global Reader* (Armonk, NY: M. E. Sharpe, 2003), 131.

31. Quoted in Donald R. Wright, *The World and a Very Small Place in Africa* (Armonk, NY: M. E. Sharpe, 1997), 109–10.

32. John Thornton, *Africa and Africans in the Making of the Atlantic World* (Cambridge: Cambridge University Press, 1998), 72.

33. Thomas Phillips, "A Journal of a Voyage Made in the Hannibal of London in 1694," in *Documents Illustrative of the History of the Slave Trade to America*, edited by Elizabeth Donnan (Washington, DC: Carnegie Institute, 1930), 399–410.

34. Trans-Atlantic Slave Trade Database, accessed February 22, 2012, http://www.slavevoyages.org/tast/assessment/estimates.faces.

35. Erik Gilbert and Jonathan T. Reynolds, *Africa in World History* (Upper Saddle River, NJ: Pearson Educational, 2004), 160.

36. Paul Adams et al., *Experiencing World History* (New York: New York University Press, 2000), 334.

37. Anne Bailey, *African Voices in the Atlantic Slave Trade* (Boston: Beacon Press, 2005), 153–54.

38. This account is based largely on Thomas Bluett, *Some Memoirs of the Life of Job . . .* (London, 1734), http://docsouth.unc.edu/neh/bluett/bluett.html/; and James T. Campbell, *Middle Passages* (New York: Penguin Books, 2007), 1–14.

39. Francis Moore, *Travels into the Inland Parts of Africa* (London, 1755), 146–47.

40. Erik Gilbert and Jonathan Reynolds, *Trading Tastes: Commodity and Cultural Exchange to 1750* (Upper Saddle River, NJ: Pearson/Prentice Hall, 2006), 9.

41. Alex Szogyi, ed., *Chocolate: Food of the Gods* (Santa Barbara, CA: Greenwood Press, 1997), 166.

42. James Grehan, "Smoking and 'Early Modern' Sociability: The Great Tobacco Debate in the Ottoman Middle East (Seventeenth to Eighteenth Centuries)," *American*

Historical Review 111, no. 5 (2006): 1352–77, http://www.historycooperative.org/journals/ahr/111.5/grehan.html.

43. Uzi Baram and Lynda Carroll, eds., *A Historical Archeology of the Ottoman Empire* (New York: Springer, 2000), 172–74.

Chapter 15

1. Andrew Rice, "Mission from Africa," *New York Times Magazine*, April 8, 2009; "African Missionaries Take Religion to the West," *Church Shift*, August 7, 2006, http://www.churchshift.org.

2. Dr. Peter Hammond, "The Reformation," Frontline Fellowship, accessed February 22, 2012, http://www.frontline.org.za/articles/thereformation_lectures.htm.

3. Glenn J. Ames, *Vasco da Gama: Renaissance Crusader* (New York: Pearson/Longman, 2005), 50.

4. Cecil Jane, ed. and trans., *Selected Documents Illustrating the Four Voyages of Columbus* (London: Hakluyt Society, 1930–1933), 2:2–18.

5. Kenneth Mills, *Idolatry and Its Enemies* (Princeton, NJ: Princeton University Press, 1997), chap. 9.

6. Marysa Navarro et al., *Women in Latin America and the Caribbean* (Bloomington: Indiana University Press, 1999), 37.

7. Nancy E. van Deusen, "Úrsula de Jesús" in *The Human Tradition in Colonial Latin America*, edited by Kenneth J. Andrien (Wilmington, DE: Scholarly Resources, 2002), 88–103; Úrsula de Jesús, *The Souls of Purgatory: The Spiritual Diary of a Seventeenth-Century Afro-Peruvian Mystic*, edited and with a scholarly introduction by Nancy E. van Deusen (Albuquerque: University of New Mexico Press, 2004).

8. Quoted in James Rinehart, *Apocalyptic Faith and Political Violence* (New York: Palgrave Macmillan, 2006), 42.

9. Quoted in Nicolas Griffiths, *The Cross and the Serpent* (Norman: University of Oklahoma Press, 1996), 263.

10. See James Lockhart, *The Nahuas after Conquest* (Stanford, CA: Stanford University Press, 1992), chap. 6.

11. Quoted in Joanna Waley-Cohen, *The Sextants of Beijing* (New York: W. W. Norton, 1999), 76–77.

12. Richard M. Eaton, "Islamic History as Global History," in *Islamic and European Expansion*, edited by Michael Adas (Philadelphia: Temple University Press, 1993), 25.

13. Natana J. DeLong-Bas, *Wahhabi Islam* (Oxford: Oxford University Press, 2004), 123–91.

14. Patricia Buckley Ebrey, ed and trans., *Chinese Civilization: A Sourcebook* (New York: Free Press, 1993), 257.

15. Robert Bly and Jane Hirshfield, trans., *Mirabai: Ecstatic Poems* (Boston: Beacon Press, 2004), ix–xi.

16. Quoted in Steven Shapin, *The Scientific Revolution* (Chicago: University of Chicago Press, 1996), 66.

17. This section draws heavily on Toby E. Huff, *The Rise of Early Modern Science* (Cambridge: Cambridge University Press, 2003), 48, 52, 76.

18. Ibid., 87, 288.

19. Jerome Cardano, *The Book of My Life*, translated by Jean Stoner (London: J. M. Dent, 1931), 189.

20. Quoted in Shapin, *Scientific Revolution*, 28.

21. Quoted in ibid., 61.

22. Quoted in ibid., 33.

23. Quoted in ibid., 68.

24. Stillman Drake, trans., *Discoveries and Opinions of Galileo* (Garden City, NY: Doubleday, 1957), 183.

25. H. S. Thayer, ed., *Newton's Philosophy of Nature: Selections from His Writings* (New York: Hafner Library of Classics, 1953), 42.

26. Immanuel Kant, "What Is Enlightenment?," translated by Peter Gay, in *Introduction to Contemporary Civilization in the West* (New York: Columbia University Press, 1954), 1071.

27. Voltaire, *A Treatise on Toleration* (1763), chap. 22, http://www.constitution.org/volt/tolerance.htm.

28. Quoted in Margaret C. Jacob, *The Enlightenment* (Boston: Bedford/St. Martin's, 2001), 103.

29. Quoted in Karen Offen, *European Feminisms, 1700–1950* (Stanford, CA: Stanford University Press, 2000), 39.

30. Toby E. Huff, *Intellectual Curiosity and the Scientific Revolution* (Cambridge: Cambridge University Press, 2010), 48

31. Quoted in Jonathan Spence, *The Search for Modern China* (New York: W. W. Norton, 1999), 104.

32. Waley-Cohen, *Sextants of Beijing*, 105–14.

33. Benjamin A. Elman, *On Their Own Terms: Science in China, 1550–1900* (Cambridge, MA: Harvard University Press, 2005).

34. Quoted in David R. Ringrose, *Expansion and Global Interaction, 1200–1700* (New York: Longman, 2001), 188.

35. Ekmeleddin Ihsanoglu, *Science, Technology, and Learning in the Ottoman Empire* (Burlington, VT: Ashgate, 2004).

36. Quoted in Sergiusz Michalski, *The Reformation and the Visual Arts* (New York: Routledge, 1993), 7.

37. Quoted in Angela Vanhalaen, "Iconoclasm and the Creation of Images in Emanuel de Witte's Old Church in Amsterdam," *Art Bulletin*, June 2005, 5.

38. David Brett, *The Plain Style* (Cambridge: Letterworth Press, 2004), 61–62.

39. Gauvin Alexander Bailey, *Art on the Jesuit Missions in Asia and Latin America* (Toronto: University of Toronto Press, 1999), 102–4.

40. John W. O'Malley et al., *The Jesuits* (Toronto: University of Toronto Press, 1999), 381.

Part Five

1. Quoted in Ross Dunn, *The New World History* (Boston: Bedford/St. Martin's, 2000), 17.
2. William H. McNeill, "*The Rise of the West* after 25 Years," *Journal of World History* 1, no. 1 (1990): 7.

Chapter 16

1. Quoted in Keith M. Baker, "A World Transformed," *Wilson Quarterly* (Summer 1989): 37.
2. Quoted in Thomas Benjamin et al., *The Atlantic World in the Age of Empire* (Boston: Houghton Mifflin, 2001), 205.
3. Jack P. Greene, "The American Revolution," *American Historical Review* 105, no. 1 (2000): 96–97.
4. Quoted in ibid., 102.
5. Quoted in Susan Dunn, *Sister Revolutions* (New York: Faber and Faber, 1999), 11, 12.
6. Quoted in ibid., 9.
7. Quoted in Lynn Hunt et al., *The Making of the West* (Boston: Bedford/St. Martin's, 2003), 625.
8. Lynn Hunt, ed., *The French Revolution and Human Rights* (Boston: Bedford, 1996), 123.
9. Bonnie S. Anderson and Judith P. Zinsser, *A History of Their Own* (New York: Harper and Row, 1988), 283.
10. Hunt, *French Revolution*, 29.
11. From James Leith, "Music for Mass Persuasion during the Terror," copyright James A. Leith, Queen's University Kingston.
12. Franklin W. Knight, "The Haitian Revolution," *American Historical Review* 105, no. 1 (2000): 103.
13. Quoted in David P. Geggus, *Haitian Revolutionary Studies* (Bloomington: Indiana University Press, 2002), 27.
14. John C. Chasteen, *Born in Blood and Fire* (New York: W. W. Norton, 2006), 103.
15. Peter Winn, *Americas: The Changing Face of Latin America and the Caribbean* (Berkeley: University of California Press, 2006), 83.
16. Quoted in Thomas E. Skidmore and Peter H. Smith, *Modern Latin America* (New York: Oxford University Press, 2001), 33.
17. Quoted in David Armitage and Sanjay Subrahmanyam, *The Age of Revolutions in Global Context* (New York: Palgrave Macmillan, 2010), xxiii.
18. James Walvin, "The Public Campaign in England against Slavery," in *The Abolition of the Atlantic Slave Trade*, edited by David Eltis and James Walvin (Madison: University of Wisconsin Press, 1981), 76.
19. Michael Craton, "Slave Revolts and the End of Slavery," in *The Atlantic Slave Trade*, edited by David Northrup (Boston: Houghton Mifflin, 2002), 200.
20. Joseph Dupuis, *Journal of a Residence in Ashantee* (London: Henry Colburn, 1824), 162–64.
21. Eric Foner, *Nothing but Freedom* (Baton Rouge: Louisiana State University Press, 1983).
22. Quoted in Daniel Moran and Arthur Waldron, eds., *The People in Arms: Military Myth and National Mobilization since the French Revolution* (Cambridge: Cambridge University Press, 2003), 14.
23. Barbara Winslow, "Feminist Movements: Gender and Sexual Equality," in *A Companion to Gender History*, edited by Teresa A. Meade and Merry E. Weisner-Hanks (London: Blackwell, 2004), 186.
24. Bonnie S. Anderson, *Joyous Greetings: The First International Women's Movement, 1830–1860* (Oxford: Oxford University Press, 2000).
25. Quoted in Claire G. Moses, *French Feminism in the Nineteenth Century* (Albany: SUNY Press, 1984), 135.
26. Raden Adjeng Kartini, *Letters of a Javanese Princess* (New York: W. W. Norton, 1964). Unless otherwise noted, all quotes come from this source.
27. Jooste Cote, "Raden Ajeng Kartini" in *Gender, Colonialism and Education*, edited by Joyce Goodman and Jayne Martin (London: Woburn Press, 2002), 204.
28. See Hunt, *French Revolution*, 1–31.
29. Quoted in Olympe de Gouges, "The Rights of Women," 1791, http://www.pinn.net/~sunshine/book-sum/gouges.html.
30. Jean-Denis Lanjuinais, "Discussion of Citizenship under the Proposed New Constitution" in *The French Revolution and Human Rights*, edited by Lynn Hunt (Boston: Bedford, 1996), 133.

Chapter 17

1. "Mahatma Gandhi on Industrialization," Tiny Tech Plants, accessed February 24, 2012, http://www.tinytechindia.com/gandhi3.htm#1.
2. Edmund Burke III and Kenneth Pomeranz, eds., *The Environment and World History* (Berkeley: University of California Press, 2009), 41.
3. Ricardo Duchesne, *The Uniqueness of Western Civilization* (Leiden: Brill, 2011).
4. Joel Mokyr, *The Lever of Riches* (New York: Oxford University Press, 1990), 40–44.
5. Lynda Shaffer, "Southernization," *Journal of World History* 5, no. 1 (1994): 1–21.
6. Kenneth Pomeranz, *The Great Divergence* (Princeton, NJ: Princeton University Press, 2000). See also Jack Goldstone, *Why Europe? The Rise of the West in World History* (Boston: McGraw-Hill, 2009).

7. Pier Vries, "Are Coal and Colonies Really Crucial?" *Journal of World History* 12, no. 2 (2001): 411.

8. E. L. Jones, *The European Miracle* (Cambridge: Cambridge University Press, 1981), 119.

9. David Christian, *Maps of Time* (Berkeley: University of California Press, 2004), 390.

10. Quoted in Mokyr, *Lever of Riches*, 188.

11. Quoted in Prasannan Parthansaranthi, "Rethinking Wages and Competitiveness in the Eighteenth Century," *Past and Present* 158 (February 1998): 79.

12. Maxine Berg, *Luxury and Pleasure in Eighteenth-Century Britain* (Oxford: Oxford University Press, 2005), 79–84.

13. Peter Stearns, *The Industrial Revolution in World History* (Boulder, CO: Westview Press, 1998), 36.

14. Goldstone, *Why Europe?,* chap. 8.

15. Eric Hopkins, *Industrialization and Society* (London: Routledge, 2000), 2.

16. Mokyr, *Lever of Riches*, 81.

17. Lynn Hunt et al., *The Making of the West* (Boston: Bedford/ St. Martin's, 2009), 656.

18. Eric Hobsbawm, *Industry and Empire* (New York: New Press, 1999), 58. This section draws heavily on Hobsbawm's celebrated account of British industrialization.

19. Samuel Smiles, *Thrift* (London: John Murray, 1875), 30–40.

20. Bonnie S. Anderson and Judith P. Zinsser, *A History of Their Own* (New York: Harper and Row, 1988), 2:131.

21. Ellen Johnston, *Autobiography, Poems, and Songs* (Glascow: William Love, 1867), http://books.google.com/.

22. Hobsbawm, *Industry and Empire*, 65.

23. Peter Stearns and John H. Hinshaw, *Companion to the Industrial Revolution* (Santa Barbara, CA: ABC-CLIO, 1996), 150.

24. Quoted in Herbert Vere Evatt, *The Tolpuddle Martyrs* (Sydney: Sydney University Press, 2009), 49.

25. Hobsbawm, *Industry and Empire*, 171.

26. Dirk Hoeder, *Cultures in Contact* (Durham, NC: Duke University Press, 2002), 331–32.

27. Carl Guarneri, *America in the World* (Boston: McGraw-Hill, 2007), 180.

28. Quoted in Hoeder, *Cultures in Contact*, 318.

29. Derived from Paul Kennedy, *The Rise and Fall of the Great Powers* (New York: Random House, 1987), 149.

30. John Charles Chasteen, *Born in Blood and Fire* (New York: W. W. Norton, 2006), 181.

31. Peter Bakewell, *A History of Latin America* (Oxford: Blackwell, 1997), 425.

32. Michael Adas, *Machines as the Measure of Men* (Ithaca, NY: Cornell University Press, 1990).

33. Ibid., 133.

34. Quoted in Francis D. Klingender, *Art and the Industrial Revolution* (New York: Augustus M. Kelley, 1968), 139.

35. "Child Labor in America: Photographs of Lewis W. Hine, 1908–1912," The History Place, accessed February 24, 2012, http://www.historyplace.com/unitedstates/childlabor/.

Chapter 18

1. Quoted in Robert Strayer, *The Making of Mission Communities in East Africa* (London: Heinemann, 1978), 89.

2. Quoted in Heinz Gollwitzer, *Europe in the Age of Imperialism* (London: Thames and Hudson, 1969), 136.

3. Robert Knox, *Races of Man* (Philadelphia: Lea and Blanchard, 1850), v.

4. Quoted in Ralph Austen, ed., *Modern Imperialism* (Lexington, MA: D. C. Heath, 1969), 70–73.

5. Quoted in Julian Burger, "Echoes of History," *New Internationalist*, August 1988, http://www.newint.org/ issue186/echoes.htm.

6. Quoted in John Iliffe, *Africans: The History of a Continent* (Cambridge: Cambridge University Press, 1995), 191.

7. Quoted in Nicholas Tarling, "The Establishment of Colonial Regimes," in *The Cambridge History of Southeast Asia*, edited by Nicholas Tarling (Cambridge: Cambridge University Press, 1992), 2:76.

8. R. Meinertzhagen, *Kenya Diary* (London: Oliver and Boyd, 1957), 51–52.

9. Quoted in Neil Jamieson, *Understanding Vietnam* (Berkeley: University of California Press, 1993), 49–57.

10. Mrinalini Sinha, *Colonial Masculinity* (Manchester: Manchester University Press, 1995), 35; Jane Burbank and Frederick Cooper, *Empires in World History* (Princeton, NJ: Princeton University Press, 2010), 308–9.

11. Nupur Chaudhuri, "Clash of Cultures" in *A Companion to Gender History*, edited by Teresa A. Meade and Merry E. Wiesner-Hanks (London: Blackwell, 2004), 437.

12. Quoted in Donald R. Wright, *The World and a Very Small Place in Africa* (Armonk, NY: M. E. Sharpe, 2004), 170.

13. Quoted in Scott B. Cook, *Colonial Encounters in the Age of High Imperialism* (New York: HarperCollins, 1996), 53.

14. Craig Timberg and Daniel Halperin, *Tinderbox* (New York: Penguin Press, 2012), 52.

15. D. R. SarDesai, *Southeast Asia: Past and Present* (Boulder, CO: Westview Press, 1997), 95–98.

16. Quoted in G. C. K. Gwassa and John Iliffe, *Records of the Maji Maji Rising* (Nairobi: East African, 1967), 1:4–5.

17. Michael Adas, "Continuity and Transformation: Colonial Rice Frontiers and Their Environmental Impact . . . ," in *The Environment and World History*, edited by Edmund Burke III and Kenneth Pomeranz (Berkeley: University of California Press, 2009), 191–207.

18. Iliffe, *Africans*, 216.

19. Adam McKeown, "Global Migration, 1846–1940" *Journal of World History* 15, no. 2 (2004): 157.

20. Derived from ibid., 156.

21. Quoted in Basil Davidson, *Modern Africa* (London: Longmans, 1983), 79, 81.

22. This section draws heavily on Margaret Jean Hay and Sharon Stichter, eds., *African Women South of the Sahara* (London: Longman, 1984), especially chaps. 1–5.

23. Quoted in Robert A. Levine, "Sex Roles and Economic Change in Africa," in *Black Africa*, edited by John Middleton (London: Macmillan, 1970), 178.

24. Elizabeth Schmidt, *Peasants, Traders, and Wives: Shona Women in the History of Zimbabwe, 1870–1939* (Portsmouth, NH: Heinemann, 1992), chap. 4.

25. Mike Davis, *Late Victorian Holocausts* (London: Verso, 2001), 37.

26. Josiah Kariuki, *Mau Mau Detainee* (London: Oxford University Press, 1963), 5.

27. Quoted in Harry Benda and John Larkin, *The World of Southeast Asia* (New York: Harper and Row, 1967), 182–85.

28. William Theodore de Bary, *Sources of Indian Tradition* (New York: Columbia University Press, 1958), 619.

29. Quoted in Edward W. Smith, *Aggrey of Africa* (London: SCM Press, 1929).

30. Jean Davison, *Voices from Mutira* (Boulder, CO: Lynne Reinner, 1996), 51–74.

31. Strayer, *Making of Mission Communities*, 78–82, 136–39.

32. C. A. Bayly, *The Birth of the Modern World* (Oxford: Blackwell, 2004), 343.

33. de Bary, *Sources of Indian Tradition*, 652.

34. Nirad Chaudhuri, *Autobiography of an Unknown Indian* (London: John Farquharson, 1968), 229.

35. Edward Blyden, *Christianity, Islam, and the Negro Race* (Edinburgh: Edinburgh University Press, 1967), 124.

36. John Iliffe, *A Modern History of Tanganyika* (Cambridge: Cambridge University Press, 1979), 324.

37. British Museum, http://www.britishmuseum.org/explore/highlights/highlight_objects/aoa/b/the_battle_of_adwa,_painting.aspx.

Chapter 19

1. "Full Text of Hu Jintao's Speech," July 1, 2011. http://english.gov.cn/2011-07/01/content_1897641.htm

2. Dun J. Li, ed., *China in Transition, 1517–1911* (New York: Van Nostrand Reinhold, 1969), 112.

3. Quoted in Jonathan D. Spence, *The Search for Modern China* (New York: W. W. Norton, 1999), 169.

4. Vincent Shih, *The Taiping Ideology: Its Sources, Interpretations, and Influences* (Seattle: University of Washington Press, 1967), 73.

5. Barbara Hodgson, *Opium: A Portrait of the Heavenly Demon* (San Francisco: Chronicle Books, 1999), 32.

6. Hsin-Pao Chang, ed., *Commissioner Lin and the Opium War* (New York: W. W. Norton, 1970), 226–27.

7. Quoted in Teng Ssu and John K. Fairbanks, eds. and trans., *China's Response to the West* (New York: Atheneum, 1963), 69.

8. This account of Lin Zexu draws from Jonathan D. Spence, *The Search for Modern China* (New York: W. W. Norton, 1990), and Arthur Waley, *The Opium War Through Chinese Eyes* (London: George Allen and Unwin), 1958.

9. Kazuko Ono, *Chinese Women in a Century of Revolution* (Stanford, CA: Stanford University Press, 1989), 60.

10. Quoted in Magali Morsy, *North Africa: 1800–1900* (London: Longman, 1984), 79.

11. Quoted in M. Sukru Hanioglu, *The Young Turks in Opposition* (New York: Oxford University Press, 1995), 17.

12. Marius B. Jansen, *The Making of Modern Japan* (Cambridge, MA: Harvard University Press, 2002), 33.

13. Quoted in Carol Gluck, "Themes in Japanese History," in *Asia in Western and World History*, ed. Ainslie T. Embree and Carol Gluck (Armonk, NY: M. E. Sharpe, 1997), 754.

14. Quoted in S. Hanley and K. Yamamura, *Economic and Demographic Change in Pre-Industrial Japan* (Princeton, NJ: Princeton University Press, 1977), 88–90.

15. Quoted in Harold Bolitho, "The Tempo Crisis," in *The Cambridge History of Japan*, vol. 5, *The Nineteenth Century*, ed. Maurice B. Jansen (Cambridge: Cambridge University Press, 1989), 230.

16. Kenneth Henshall, *A History of Japan* (New York: Palgrave, 2004), 67.

17. Quoted in James L. McClain, *Japan: A Modern History* (New York: W. W. Norton, 2002), 177.

18. Selcuk Esenbel, "Japan's Global Claim to Asia and the World of Islam," *American Historical Review* 109, no. 4 (2004), pars. 1, 9, http://www.historycooperative.org/journals/ahr/109.4/esenbel.html.

19. Quoted in Marius B. Jansen, *The Making of Modern Japan* (Cambridge, MA: Harvard University Press, 2000), 460.

20. Quoted in Julia Meech-Pekarik, *The World of the Meiji Print: Impressions of a New Civilization* (New York: Weatherhill, 1986), 182.

21. Quoted in Oka Yoshitake, Prologue to Marlene Mayo, ed., *The Emergence of Imperial Japan* (Lexington, MA: D. C. Heath, 1970).

Part Six

1. J. R. McNeill, *Something New under the Sun* (New York: W. W. Norton, 2000), 3–4.

Chapter 20

1. John Innes, "Scotland's Oldest Man Turns 107," *Scotsman*, June 25, 2003, http://www.aftermathww1.com/oldestscot

.asp; "One of Last British WWI Veterans Dies at 109," MSNBC.com, November 21, 2005, http://www.msnbc.msn.com/id/10138446/.

2. Quoted in John Keegan, *The First World War* (New York: Vintage Books, 1998), 3.

3. Adapted from Lynn Hunt et al., *The Making of the West: Peoples and Cultures* (Boston: Bedford/St. Martin's, 2001), 1024.

4. Benito Mussolini, *The Political and Social Doctrine of Fascism*, trans. Jane Soames (London: Leonard and Virginia Woolf at the Hogarth Press, 1933).

5. Stanley Payne, *History of Fascism, 1914–1945* (Madison: University of Wisconsin Press, 1995), 208.

6. Richard Bessel, ed., *Fascist Italy and Nazi Germany: Comparisons and Contrasts* (Cambridge: Cambridge University Press, 1996), 8.

7. Quoted in Laurence Rees, *The Nazis: A Warning from History* (New York: New Press, 1997), 62.

8. Quoted in Claudia Koonz, *Mothers in the Fatherland* (New York: St. Martin's Press, 1987), 75.

9. James L. McClain, *Japan: A Modern History* (New York: W. W. Norton, 2002), 378.

10. Quoted in ibid., 414.

11. Bernd Martin, *Japan and Germany in the Modern World* (Providence, RI: Berghahn Books, 1995), 155–81.

12. Quoted in Marius B. Jansen, *The Making of Modern Japan* (Cambridge, MA: Harvard University Press, 2000), 607.

13. Quoted in ibid., 639.

14. Quoted in John Keegan, *The Second World War* (New York: Viking Penguin, 1989), 186.

15. Quoted in Ralph F. Keeling, *Gruesome Harvest* (Chicago: Institute of American Economics, 1947), 60.

16. Klaas A. D. Smelik, ed., *Etty: The Letters and Diaries of Etty Hillesum* (Grand Rapids: Erdmans, 2002).

17. John Lewis Gaddis, *We Now Know: Rethinking Cold War History* (Oxford: Oxford University Press, 1997), 52.

18. Adam Gopnik, "The Big One: Historians Rethink the War to End All Wars," *New Yorker*, August 23, 2004, 78.

Chapter 21

1. Quoted in Ronald Suny, *The Soviet Experiment* (Oxford: Oxford University Press, 1998), 357.

2. Bonnie S. Anderson and Judith P. Zinsser, *A History of Their Own* (New York: Harper and Row, 1988), 2:299.

3. William M. Mandel, *Soviet Women* (Garden City, NJ: Doubleday, 1975), 44.

4. Yuan-tsung Chen, *The Dragon's Village* (New York: Penguin Books, 1980), 85.

5. Such figures are often highly controversial. See Maurice Meisner, *Mao's China and After* (New York: Free Press, 1999),

413–25; Roderick MacFarquhar, ed., *The Politics of China* (Cambridge: Cambridge University Press, 1997), 243–45.

6. Emily Honig, "Maoist Mappings of Gender," in *Chinese Femininities/Chinese Masculinities*, ed. Susan Brownell and Jeffrey N. Wasserstrom (Berkeley: University of California Press, 2002), 255–56.

7. Douglas Weiner, "The Predatory Tribute-Taking State" in *The Environment and World History*, ed. Edmund Burke III and Kenneth Pomeranz (Berkeley: University of California Press, 2009), 284–90.

8. Richard F. Kaufman and John P. Hardt, eds., *The Former Soviet Union in Transition* (Armonk, NY: M. E. Sharpe, 1993), 580–83.

9. Barbara Engel and Anastasia Posadskaya-Vanderbeck, eds., *A Revolution of Their Own* (Boulder, CO: Westview Press, 1998), 17–46.

10. Quoted in Richard Rusk, *As I Saw It* (New York: Norton, 1990), 245.

11. Quoted in John L. Gaddis, *The Cold War: A New History* (New York: Penguin Press, 2005), 57.

12. Ronald Steel, *Pax Americana* (New York: Viking Press, 1970), 254.

13. Quoted in Donald W. White, *The American Century* (New Haven, CT: Yale University Press, 1996), 164.

14. Deng Xiaoping, "The Necessity of Upholding the Four Cardinal Principles in the Drive for the Four Modernizations," in *Major Documents of the People's Republic of China* (Beijing: Foreign Language Press, 1991), 54.

15. Quoted in Abraham Brumberg, *Chronicle of a Revolution* (New York: Pantheon Books, 1990), 225–26.

16. Quoted in Anchee Min et.al., *Chinese Propaganda Posters* (Koln: Taschen, 2003), 5.

17. Quoted in ibid., 10.

Chapter 22

1. Nelson Mandela, "Statement from the Dock ... in the Rivonia trial," April 20, 1964, http://www.anc.org.za/show.php?id=3430&t=Famous Speeches.

2. Quoted in Craig A. Lockard, *Southeast Asia in World History* (Oxford: Oxford University Press, 2009), 138–39.

3. Quoted in J. D. Legge, *Sukarno: A Political Biography* (New York: Praeger, 1972), 341.

4. Quoted in Jim Masselos, *Nationalism on the Indian Subcontinent* (Melbourne: Nelson, 1972), 122.

5. Mohandas Gandhi, *Hind Swaraj*, 1909, http://www.mkgandhi-sarvodaya.org/hindswaraj.htm.

6. Bidyut Chakrabarty, *Social and Political Thought of Mahatma Gandhi* (New York: Routledge, 2006), 139.

7. Quoted in Stanley Wolpert, *A New History of India* (Oxford: Oxford University Press, 1993), 331.

8. Badshah Khan, *My Life and Struggle* (Delhi: Hind Pocket Books, 1969), 96–97.

9. Jawaharlal Nehru, *The Discovery of India* (New York: John Day Co., 1946), 486.

10. M. S. Korejo, *The Frontier Gandhi* (New York: Oxford University Press, 1993), 25.

11. Khan, *My Life*, 209–10.

12. Adapted and updated from Lynn Hunt et al., *The Making of the West: Peoples and Cultures* (Boston: Bedford/St. Martin's, 2009), 968; Population Reference Bureau, *World Population Data Sheet, 2011*, http://www.prb.org/pdf11/2011population-data-sheet_eng.pdf.

13. Quoted in Bernard Lewis, *The Emergence of Modern Turkey* (London: Oxford University Press, 1968), 268–69.

14. Quoted in Patrick B. Kinross, *Ataturk: A Biography of Mustafa Kemal* (New York: Morrow, 1965), 390.

15. Sandra Mackey, *The Iranians* (New York: Penguin, 1998), 306.

16. Liberation Graphics, "Palestine Poster Project," accessed March 19, 2012, http://www.liberationgraphics.com/ppp/Redeem_the_Land.html.

17. Ibid., http://www.liberationgraphics.com/ppp/landday.html.

Chapter 23

1. "Muslim Dolls Tackle 'Wanton' Barbie," BBC News, March 5, 2002, http://news.bbc.co.uk/2/hi/middle_east/1856558.stm.

2. Jeffrey Frieden, *Global Capitalism* (New York: W. W. Norton, 2006), 476.

3. "Gross World Product, 1950–2009" in *World on the Edge*, by Lester R. Brown (New York: W. W. Norton, 2011), http://www.earth-policy.org/books/wote/wote_data.

4. United Nations, *Human Development Report 1997*, 2, http://hdr.undp.org/reports/global/1997/en.

5. Michael Hunt, *The World Transformed* (Boston: Bedford/St. Martin's, 2004), 442.

6. Quoted in Frieden, *Global Capitalism*, 408.

7. "Map Supplement," *National Geographic* (Washington, DC: National Geographic Society, March 2011).

8. Quoted in Manfred B. Steger, *Globalization: A Very Short Introduction* (Oxford: Oxford University Press, 2003), 122.

9. Quoted in Frieden, *Global Capitalism*, 459.

10. Charles S. Maier, *Among Empires: American Ascendancy and Its Predecessors* (Cambridge, MA: Harvard University Press, 2006), chap. 5.

11. Quoted in Sarah Shaver Hughes and Brady Hughes, *Women in World History* (Armonk, NY: M. E. Sharpe, 1997), 2:268.

12. Susan Kent, "Worlds of Feminism," in *Women's History in Global Perspective*, ed. Bonnie G. Smith (Urbana: University of Illinois Press, 2004), 1:305–6.

13. Quoted in Wilhelmina Oduol and Wanjiku Mukabi Kabira, "The Mother of Warriors and Her Daughters: The Women's Movement in Kenya," in *Global Feminisms since 1945*, ed. Bonnie Smith (London: Routledge, 2000), 111.

14. Elisabeth Jay Friedman, "Gendering the Agenda," *Women's Studies International Forum* 26, no. 4 (2003): 313–31.

15. Quoted in Mary E. Hawkesworth, *Globalization and Feminist Activism* (New York: Rowman and Littlefield, 2006), 124.

16. Phyllis Schlafly, *The Power of the Christian Woman* (Cincinnati: Standard, 1981), 117.

17. Karen Armstrong, *The Battle for God* (New York: Alfred A. Knopf, 2000), xi.

18. Quoted in ibid., 273.

19. Quoted in John Esposito, *Unholy War* (Oxford: Oxford University Press, 2002), 57.

20. Quoted in ibid., 63.

21. "Al Qaeda's Fatwah," http://www.pbs.org/newshour/terrorism/international/fatwa_1998.html.

22. Anwar Ibrahim, "The Ardent Moderates," *Time*, September 23, 1996, 24.

23. Jan Zalasiewicz et al., "The New World of the Anthropocene," *Environmental Science and Technology* 44, no. 7 (2010): 2228–31.

24. See J. R. McNeill, *Something New under the Sun: An Environmental History of the Twentieth Century World* (New York: W. W. Norton, 2001).

25. *Living Planet Report, 2010* (Oakland: Global Footprint Network, 2010), 33–34.

26. Rachel Carson, *Silent Spring* (Boston: Houghton Mifflin, 1962), 103. In addition to Carson's book, this account of her life draws on Mark H. Lytle, *Gentle Subversive* (New York: Oxford University Press, 2007), and Arlene R. Quaratiello, *Rachel Carson: A Biography* (Westport, CT: Greenwood Press, 2004).

27. Ramachandra Guha, *Environmentalism: A Global History* (New York: Longman, 2000), pt. 1.

28. Timothy Doyle, *Environmental Movements in Minority and Majority Worlds: A Global Perspective* (New Brunswick, NJ: Rutgers University Press, 2005).

29. Quoted in Shiraz Sidhva, "Saving the Planet: Imperialism in a Green Garb," *UNESCO Courier*, April 2001, 41–43.

Acknowledgments

Chapter 1

Document 1.1: Marjorie Shostak. Reprinted by permission of the publisher from *Nisa: The Life and Words of a !Kung Woman* by Marjorie Shostak, pp. 37, 63, 79, 80, 138–139, 140, 149, 189, 190, 203–204, 243, 267, 268, 269, 283, 284, Cambridge, Mass.: Harvard University Press, Copyright © 1981 by Marjorie Shostak.

Chapter 2

Benjamin R. Foster. From *The Epic of Gilgamesh*, translated by Benjamin R. Foster. Copyright © 2001 by W. W. Norton & Company. Used by permission of W. W. Norton & Company, Inc. This selection may not be reproduced, stored in a retrieval system, or transmitted in any form of by any means without the prior written permission of the publisher.

Miriam Lichtheim. *Ancient Egyptian Literature, Volume II: The New Kingdom* by Miriam Lichtheim, © 2006 by the Regents of the University of California. Published by the University of California Press. Used by permission.

Adolf Erman. "He has come unto us . . ." from *The Literature of the Ancient Egyptians*, translated by Aylward M. Blackman. Copyright © 1927 Methuen. Reproduced by permission of Taylor & Francis Books UK.

Pritchard, James B. (ed.). *Ancient Near Eastern Texts Relating to the Old Testament—Third Edition with Supplement.* © 1950, 1955, 1969, renewed 1978 by Princeton University Press. Reprinted by permission of Princeton University Press.

Document 2.1: N. K. Sanders. Excerpts from *The Epic of Gilgamesh*, translated with an introduction by N. K. Sandars (Penguin Classics 1960, Third Edition, 1972). Copyright © N. K. Sandars, 1960, 1964, 1972. Reproduced by permission of Penguin Books, Ltd.

Document 2.3: Miriam Lichtheim. "The Afterlife of a Pharaoh: A Pyramid Text." From *Ancient Egyptian Literature, Volume 1: The Old and Middle Kingdoms*, by Miriam Lichtheim. © 2006 by the Regents of the University of California. Published by the University of California Press. Used by permission.

Document 2.5: Miriam Lichtheim. "The Occupations of Old Egypt: Be a Scribe." Excerpt from *Ancient Egyptian Literature, Volume II: The Middle Kingdom*, by Miriam Lichtheim. © 2006 by the Regents of the University of California. Published by the University of California Press. Used by permission.

Chapter 3

Document 3.2: Aelius Aristides. "In praise of the Roman Empire: Aelius Aristides, The Roman Oration." Excerpt from *Aelius Aristides: The Complete Works*, Volume II, translated by C.A. Behr, copyright © 1986. Reprinted by permission of the Koninklijke Brill NV.

Document 3.3: Han Fei. "The writings of Master Han Fei." From *Basic Writings of Mo Tzu, Hsun Tzu and Han Fei Tzu*, translated by Burton Watson. Copyright © 1967 Columbia University Press. Reprinted by permission of the publisher.

Document 3.4: Ashoka. "Governing an Indian Empire." Excerpt from *The Edicts of King Asoka: An English Rendering* by Ven S. Dhammika. Copyright © 1993. Reprinted by permission of the Buddhist Publication Society.

Chapter Wrap Up From *The Sui Dynasty: The Unification of China, A.D. 581–617*, by Arthur F. Wright, copyright © 1978 by The Estate of Arthur F. Wright. Used by permission of Alfred A. Knopf, a division of Random House, Inc. Any third party use of this material, outside of this publication, is prohibited. Interested parties must apply directly to Random House, Inc. for permission.

Chapter 4

Lao Tsu. "Verse Eighty" from *Tao Te Ching*, by Gia-fu Feng, translation copyright © 1972 by Gia-fu Feng and Jane English, copyright renewed 2000 by Carol Wilson and Jane English. Used by permission of Alfred A. Knopf, an imprint of the Knopf Doubleday Publishing Group, division of Random House, LLC. All rights reserved. Any third party use of this material, outside of this publication, is prohibited. Interested parties must apply directly to Random House, LLC for permission.

Chapter 5

Document 5.1: Pan Chao. "A Chinese Woman's Instructions to Her Daughters: Ban Zhou," "Lessons for Women."

Excerpt from *Pan Chao: Foremost Woman Scholar of China*, translated by Nancy Lee Swann. Copyright © 1932. (New York: Century Co., 1932), 82–90. Reprinted with permission.

Document 5.3: Livy. "Roman Women in Protest: Livy, History of Rome." Translated by Maureen B. Fant. Excerpt as it appears in Lefkowitz, Mary R., and Maureen B. Fant. *Women's Life in Greece and Rome*. pp. 143–147. © 1982 by M. B. Fant and M. R. Lefkowitz. Reprinted with permission of The Johns Hopkins Press.

Chapter 6

Document 6.3: Rufinus. "The Coming of Christianity to Axum: On the Evangelization of Abyssinia." Excerpt as appears in *A History of Abyssinia* by Arnold H.M. Jones & Elizabeth Monroe (1935): c. 695 words (pp. 26–27). By permission of Oxford University Press.

Chapter 7

Document 7.3: Ibn Battuta. *A Moroccan Muslim in West Africa: Ibn Battuta, Travels in Asia and Africa 1325–1354*, translated and edited by H. A. R. Gibb (London: Broadway House, 1929), 319–334. Copyright © 1929. Used by permission of The Hakluyt Society.

Chapter 8

Edward H. Shafer. *The Golden Peaches of Samarkand: A Study of T'ang*, (University of California Press, 1963). © 1985 by the Regents of the University of California. Published by the University of California Press. Used by permission of the University of California Press and the Estate of Edward H. Shafer.

Document 8.2: Kitabatake Chikafusa. "The Uniqueness of Japan." Excerpt from The Chronicle of the Direct Descent of Gods and Sovereigns; from *Sources of Japanese Tradition*, by William Theodore de Bary et al. Copyright © 2001 Columbia University Press. Reprinted with permission of the publisher.

Document 8.3: Sei Shōnagon. "Social Life at Court." Excerpt from *The Pillow Book of Sei Shonagon*, translated and edited by Ivan Morris. c. 1025 words (pp. 25–26, 39, 44–45, 47, 49–50, 53, 254–255) Copyright © 1991 by Columbia University Press. Reprinted with permission of Columbia University Press and Oxford University Press.

Document 8.4a: Thomas Cleary. From *Training the Samurai Mind*, edited and translated by Thomas Cleary, © 2008 by Thomas Cleary. Reprinted by arrangement with Shambhala Publications Inc., Boston, MA. www.shambhala.com.

Document 8.4b: Frin Carl Steenstrup. "The Imagawa Letter." From *Monumenta Nipponica* Vol. 28, No. 3 (Autumn 1973), 295–316. Copyright © 1973 by Sophia University. Reproduced with permission of Sophia University.

Chapter 9

Document 9.1: Muhammad Asad. "The Voice of Allah: The Quran." Extracts from Surah 1, 2, 4, 5 in *The Message of the Quran*, published by The Book Foundation, 2003. Reprinted by permission of Kabir Edmund Helminski.

Document 9.2: Arthur Jeffery. *The Voice of the Prophet Muhammad: The Hadith: A Reader on Islam*. Copyright © 1962. (The Hague: Mouton & Company, 1962.) Used by permission of Walter de Gruyter GmbH & Co.

Document 9.3: John Alden Williams. "The Voice of the Law: The Sharia." Excerpt from *The Word of Islam*, edited by John Alden Williams. Copyright © 1994. By permission of the University of Texas Press.

Document 9.4a: The Voice of the Sufis. First Selection, Inscription on Rumi's Tomb. Second Selection, Rumi. Excerpt from *A History of Muslim Philosophy*, Volume II. "Drowned in God." From *The Pocket Rumi Reader*. Copyright © 2001 by Kabir Edmund Helminski. Reprinted with permission of the author and Shambhala Publication Inc., Boston, MA. www.shambhala.com.

Document 9.4b: M. M. Sharif. *A History of Muslim Philosophy*, Volume II, copyright © 1966. Used by permission of OTTO HARRASSOWITZ GmbH & Co. KG.

Document 9.4c: From *Jewels of Remembrance*, by Rumi, selected and translated by Camille and Kabir Helminski, © 1996 by Camille and Kabir Helminski. Reprinted by arrangement with Shambhala Publications Inc., Boston, MA. www.shambhala.com.

Chapter 10

Document 10.5: Karen Louise Jolly. "The Leechbook." From *Popular Religion in Saxon England: Elf Charms in Context*, by Karen Louise Jolly. Copyright © 1996 by the University of North Carolina Press. Used by permission of the publisher. www.uncpress.unc.edu.

Chapter 11

Document 11.1: Paul Kahn. "Mongol History from a Mongol." Excerpt from *The Secret History of the Mongols: The Origins of Chingis Khan*. An adaption by Paul Kahn. (San Francisco: North Point Press, 1984). Copyright © 1984 by Paul Kahn. Reprinted by permission of the author.

Document 11.4: Patricia Buckley Ebrey. Reprinted and edited with the permission of Free Press, a Division of Simon & Schuster, Inc. From *Chinese Civilization: A Sourcebook*, by Patricia Buckley Ebrey. Copyright © 1993

Chapter 21

Chapter 22

Chapter 23

Index

blitzkrieg (lightning war), 1006
in earliest civilizations, 72(i), 74, 83
guerrilla, 1043, 1150
industrialization of, 984–85
innovations and technology for. *See*
    military innovations
Mongol tactics, 525–26, 530, 532, 533(i)
preemptive and U.S., 1149
relationship to patriarchy, 74
siege warfare, 525
total war, 987–88, 1008
trench warfare, 986, 1006, 1028(v),
    1030(v)
war plans, 985
Wari civilization (Peru), 278(m), 281–82
precursor to, 66
time frame of, 263(t)
warring states era (China), 133–34,
    150, 169
warrior societies
Cossacks, 637(i)
Germanic peoples, 477
Kshatriya caste, 129, 203, 225–27
Moche, 279–80
Mongols, 524–26, 530–31
nomadic pastoralists, 477, 517
Roman, 132
samurai, 194, 382, 382(i), 401–3(d),
    678, 948–49
Sikhs, 739
Sparta, 239
wars. *See also* revolts, rebellions, resistance;
    revolutions; *specific wars*
Atlantic Revolutions (1750–1914),
    781–825
Boer (1899–1902), 886, 1098
cold war, 1054–60
of colonial conquest (1750–1914),
    884–89
Crimean, 850
Greco-Persian, 125–26
Hundred Years', 569
Iran-Iraq (1980–1988), 1117
Iraq (2003), 1147, 1149
Korean (1950–1953), 1055
Mayan, 301
Opium, 936–37, 941
Peloponnesian, 126
Punic, 130–32
of religion. *See* religious wars
Russo-Japanese (1904–1905), 954, 1003

Six-Day (1967), 1132, 1158
Spanish-American (1898), 675,
    859, 888
Vietnam, 1055, 1130–31(v)
World War I, 982–90
World War II, 1003–15
Warsaw Pact, 1038, 1055(m)
war socialism, 987
Washington, Booker T., 910
water drilling, 439
water pollution, Soviet Union, 1051, 1165
waterways, man-made. *See also* canals
Chinese system, 366–67, 369
wealth
American industrialists, 848–49
Aztec empire, 489, 582–83
British empire, 834
Buddhists, 322–23, 390
European colonial empires, 625–26
gap, and economic globalization,
    1144–46
maritime voyages in search of, 575,
    621, 670–72
of merchants, 224, 316, 321, 327–28,
    438–39, 483, 583
Mongol empire, 525
Mughal empire, 616(i), 617
Roman Catholic Church, 479
and social class. *See* elites; nobility
weapons
development of. *See* military
    innovations
and Native Americans, 603
weaving. *See also* textile industry
in Agricultural Revolution, 38
industrialization, impact on, 864–65(d)
and women, 38, 41, 72, 236(i), 320,
    372, 483
Weimar Republic, 997
Wen (Chinese emperor), 519
Wendi (Chinese emperor,
    r. 581–604 C.E.)
Buddhist monasteries construction,
    390
reunification of China, 137
wen/wu (ideal men), 171
West Africa. *See also specific countries and
    people*
agricultural village societies, 563–64
civilizations, second-wave, 307
crops of, 32

environmental variations within, 334
European colonies in, 886,
    887(m), 890
exchange networks, 334–35
free slaves migration to, 888
Fulbe pastoral society, 566
Ghana, kingdom of, 336(m)
Igbo people, 563–64
independence tactics, 1093
Islam, spread to, 337, 351, 432(m),
    432–33, 566
Islam/native religion, 433–34, 735–36
Mali, kingdom of, 335–37, 336(m)
nationalism, 805
Niger Valley civilizations, 270–72
Sand Roads trade, impact on, 334–37
slave labor in, 336–37, 694
slave trade, 337, 689–93
Songhay civilization, 335, 564–65,
    578–79
trans-Saharan trade routes, 336(m)
women in authority, 336, 695, 900–901
West Bank, 1132, 1134
Western Christendom
agricultural expansion, 480, 490(t), 491
Black Death (plague), 537–38, 538(i)
Charlemagne's empire, 477–78, 478(m)
Christian connection. *See* Roman
    Catholic Church
cities, growth of, 482, 493
comparative backwardness of, 489,
    537, 590
Crusades, 486–88
environmental strengths of, 476
feudalism, 478–79, 482
in fifteenth century, 562(t), 569–76,
    570(m)
Germanic kingdoms of, 477–78,
    478(m)
global dominance, emergence of,
    590–91
guilds, 482, 483
High Middle Ages, expansion/
    innovation during, 480–84, 481(m),
    491, 491(i)
Holy Roman Empire, 478
industrialization during, 491, 491(i)
intellectual thought, 493–96, 569–71
invasions upon, 477, 480, 481(m),
    485–86
modern era. *See* Europe

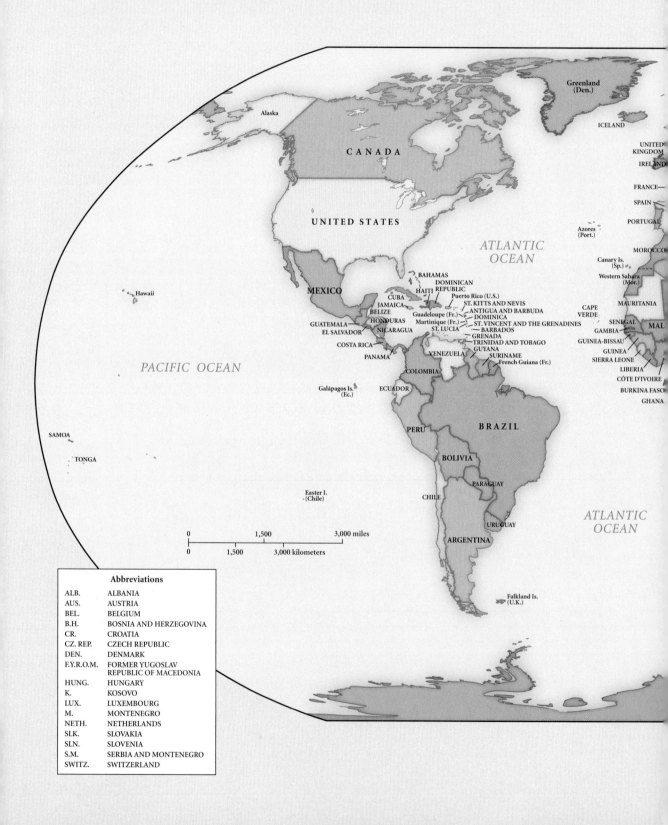

Greenland
(Den.)

ICELAND

Alaska

UNITED
KINGDOM

IRELAND

CANADA

FRANCE—

SPAIN

UNITED STATES

PORTUGAL

ATLANTIC
OCEAN

Azores
(Port.)

MOROCCO

Canary Is.
(Sp.)

Western Sahara
(Mor.)

BAHAMAS

DOMINICAN
REPUBLIC

Hawaii

MEXICO

CUBA

HAITI

Puerto Rico (U.S.)

ST. KITTS AND NEVIS

MAURITANIA

JAMAICA

ANTIGUA AND BARBUDA

CAPE
VERDE

BELIZE

Guadeloupe (Fr.)

DOMINICA

SENEGAL

MAL

HONDURAS

Martinique (Fr.)

ST. VINCENT AND THE GRENADINES

GAMBIA

GUATEMALA

ST. LUCIA

BARBADOS

GUINEA-BISSAU

EL SALVADOR

NICARAGUA

GRENADA

GUINEA

TRINIDAD AND TOBAGO

SIERRA LEONE

COSTA RICA

VENEZUELA

GUYANA

SURINAME

LIBERIA

PANAMA

French Guiana (Fr.)

CÔTE D'IVOIRE

COLOMBIA

BURKINA FASO

PACIFIC OCEAN

Galápagos Is.
(Ec.)

ECUADOR

GHANA

PERU

BRAZIL

SAMOA

BOLIVIA

TONGA

PARAGUAY

Easter I.
(Chile)

CHILE

ATLANTIC
OCEAN

URUGUAY

ARGENTINA

| 0 | | 1,500 | | 3,000 miles |
| 0 | 1,500 | | 3,000 kilometers | |

Falkland Is.
(U.K.)

Abbreviations

ALB.	ALBANIA
AUS.	AUSTRIA
BEL.	BELGIUM
B.H.	BOSNIA AND HERZEGOVINA
CR.	CROATIA
CZ. REP.	CZECH REPUBLIC
DEN.	DENMARK
F.Y.R.O.M.	FORMER YUGOSLAV REPUBLIC OF MACEDONIA
HUNG.	HUNGARY
K.	KOSOVO
LUX.	LUXEMBOURG
M.	MONTENEGRO
NETH.	NETHERLANDS
SLK.	SLOVAKIA
SLN.	SLOVENIA
S.M.	SERBIA AND MONTENEGRO
SWITZ.	SWITZERLAND

ARCTIC   OCEAN

RUSSIAN FEDERATION

NORWAY
SWEDEN
FINLAND
DEN.
NETH.
GERMANY
LUX. CZ. REP.
AUS. HUNG.
SWITZ.
ITALY
ALB.
GREECE
MALTA
TUNISIA

ESTONIA
LATVIA
LITHUANIA
POLAND BELARUS
UKRAINE
SLK.
MOLDOVA
CRO.
ROMANIA
B.H.
BULGARIA
M. F.Y.R.O.M.

KAZAKHSTAN

MONGOLIA

GEORGIA
ARMENIA
AZERBAIJAN
TURKEY
CYPRUS
SYRIA
LEBANON
ISRAEL
IRAQ
West Bank
Gaza Strip
JORDAN
KUWAIT
SAUDI ARABIA
QATAR
UNITED ARAB
EMIRATES
YEMEN

UZBEKISTAN
TURKMENISTAN
KYRGYZSTAN
TAJIKISTAN

AFGHANISTAN

IRAN

BAHRAIN

OMAN

PAKISTAN

CHINA

N. KOREA
S. KOREA
JAPAN

TAIWAN

BHUTAN
NEPAL
BANGLADESH
INDIA
MYANMAR
(BURMA)
LAOS
THAILAND
VIETNAM
CAMBODIA

PACIFIC OCEAN

Mariana Is.
(U.S.)
Guam
(U.S.)
MARSHALL
IS.

PHILIPPINES

NIGERIA
LIBYA
EGYPT

NIGER
CHAD
SUDAN

ERITREA
DJIBOUTI

NIGERIA
BENIN
TOGO
CENTRAL
AFRICAN REP.
SOUTH
SUDAN
ETHIOPIA

CAMEROON
EQ.
GUINEA
GABON
CONGO
SÃO
TOMÉ
& PRÍNCIPE

RWANDA
DEM. REP. OF
THE CONGO
BURUNDI

UGANDA
KENYA
TANZANIA

SOMALIA

MALDIVES

SRI
LANKA

BRUNEI

PALAU

MALAYSIA

SINGAPORE

FEDERATED STATES
OF MICRONESIA

NAURU

KIRIBATI

TUVALU

INDONESIA

PAPUA
NEW
GUINEA

SOLOMON
IS.

COMOROS
SEYCHELLES

INDIAN OCEAN

ANGOLA

ZAMBIA
MALAWI

NAMIBIA
BOTSWANA
ZIMBABWE
MADAGASCAR

MAURITIUS

EAST
TIMOR

VANUATU

FIJI

New Caledonia
(Fr.)

AUSTRALIA

MOZAMBIQUE
SOUTH
AFRICA
SWAZILAND
LESOTHO

NEW
ZEALAND

Tasmania
(Aust.)

ANTARCTICA

ROCKY MTS.

APPALACHIAN MTS.

Mississippi R.

ATLANTIC
OCEAN

Gulf of
Mexico

Tropic of Cancer

PACIFIC OCEAN

Equator

Amazon R.

ANDES MTS.

Tropic of Capricorn

ATLANTIC
OCEAN

URAL MTS.

Volga R.

Ob R.

ALPS

Mediterranean Sea

SYRIAN
DESERT

GOBI

Yellow R.

HIMALAYA MTS.

Yangzi R.

Tropic of Cancer

PACIFIC OCEAN

H A R A

Nile R.

Arabian
Sea

Bay of
Bengal

South
China
Sea

Congo R.

Equator

INDIAN OCEAN

Zambezi R.

Tropic of Capricorn

KALAHARI
DESERT

Vegetation Zones

Tundra
Northern forest
Temperate forest
Temperate grassland
Desert and dry shrub
Mediterranean shrub
Mountain grassland
Tropical grassland and savanna
Tropical forest
Permanent ice cover